PERSONAL FINANCE
Turning Money into Wealth

PERSONAL FINANCE
Turning Money into Wealth

Arthur J. Keown

Virginia Polytechnic Institute and State University
R.B. Pamplin Professor of Finance

Prentice Hall

Upper Saddle River, New Jersey 07458

Acquisitions Editor: Paul Donnelly
Development Editor: David Cohen
Assistant Editor: Gladys Soto
Editorial Assistant: MaryBeth Sanok
Editorial Director: James Boyd
Director of Development: Steve Deitmer
Marketing Manager: Patrick Lynch
Production Editor: Louise Rothman
Production Coordinator: Carol Samet
Associate Managing Editor: David Salierno
Managing Editor: Dee Josephson
Manufacturing Supervisor: Arnold Vila
Manufacturing Manager: Vincent Scelta
Design Director: Patricia Smythe
Interior Design: Geri Davis
Cover Design: Cheryl Asherman
Composition: TSI Graphics
Cover Art: © Douglas Bowles/SIS

Photo Credits: Cover photo: © Douglas Bowles/SIS; Chapter 1: Globe Photos, Inc.,
page 3; Chapter 2: Fred Jewell, AP/Wide World Photos, page 33; Chapter 3: The Historical Society of Pennsylvania, page 67; Doug Mills, AP/Wide World Photos, page 72;
Uniphoto Picture Agency, page 70; Chapter 4: Paul S. Howell, Gamma-Liaison, Inc.,
page 97; Chapter 5: Photofest, page 143; Chapter 6: Michael Newman, PhotoEdit,
page 173; Chapter 7: Globe Photos, Inc., page 203; Chapter 8: Suzanne Tenner,
Photofest, page 233, copyright Touchstone Pictures. All rights reserved; Chapter 9:
Rangefinders, Globe Photos, Inc., page 283, copyright 1995 Metro-Goldwyn-Mayer,
Inc. All rights reserved; Chapter 10: Eric Draper, AP/Wide World Photos, page 319;
Chapter 11: Lois D. Bernstein, AP/Wide World Photos, page 349; Chapter 12: Mark
Lyons, AP/Wide World Photos, page 379; Chapter 13: David Young-Wolf, PhotoEdit,
page 413; Adam Nadel, AP/Wide World Photos, page 418; Chapter 14: AP/Wide World
Photos, page 445; Chapter 15: Photofest, page 475; Chapter 16: Jamed D. Wilson,
Gamma-Liaison, Inc., page 507; Chapter 17: Frank Augstein, AP/Wide World Photos,
page 543; Chapter 18: Photofest, page 575; Just Do It! boxes: Marcy Furney; In the
News boxes: Photo Researchers, Inc.

© 1998 by Prentice-Hall, Inc.
A Simon & Schuster Company
Upper Saddle River, New Jersey 07458

Library of Congress Cataloging-in-Publication Data
Keown, Arthur J.
     Personal Finance: Turning Money into Wealth/Arthur J. Keown.
       p.   cm.
     Includes index.
     ISBN 0-13-616442-0
     1. Finance.   Personal.   2. Investments.   I. Title.
     HG179.K47   1998
     332.024—dc21   97-40198
                                                  CIP

Prentice-Hall International (UK) Limited, London
Prentice-Hall of Australia Pty. Limited, Sydney
Prentice-Hall Canada, Inc., Toronto
Prentice-Hall Hispanoamericana, S.A., Mexico
Prentice-Hall of India Private Limited, New Delhi
Prentice-Hall of Japan, Inc., Tokyo
Simon & Schuster Asia Pte. Ltd., Singapore
Editora Prentice-Hall do Brasil, Ltda., Rio de Janeiro

Printed in the United States of America

10 9 8 7 6 5 4 3 2 1

To Barb, my partner and my love—
for showing me happiness that money can't buy.

About the
AUTHOR

Arthur J. Keown is the R. B. Pamplin Professor of Finance at Virginia Polytechnic Institute and State University. He received his bachelor's degree from Ohio Wesleyan University, his M.B.A. from the University of Michigan, and his doctorate from Indiana University. An award-winning teacher, he is a member of the Academy of Teaching Excellence at Virginia Tech, has received five Certificates of Teaching Excellence, the W. E. Wine Award for Teaching Excellence, and the Alumni Teaching Excellence Award. Professor Keown is widely published in academic journals. His work has appeared in *The Journal of Finance*, the *Journal of Financial Economics*, the *Journal of Financial and Quantitative Analysis*, *The Journal of Financial Research*, the *Journal of Banking and Finance*, *Financial Management*, the *Journal of Portfolio Management*, and many others. Two of his books are widely used in college finance classes all over the country—*Basic Financial Management* and *Foundations of Finance: The Logic and Practice of Financial Management*. Professor Keown is a Fellow of the Decision Sciences Institute and former head of the finance department. In addition, he was recently appointed co-editor of the Financial Management Association's Survey and Synthesis Series. He is also the co-editor of *The Journal of Financial Research*. He lives with his wife and two children in Blacksburg, Virginia, where he collects original art from *Mad Magazine*.

Brief CONTENTS

CONTENTS

Chapter 2
Financial Planning: Measuring Your Financial Health and Establishing a Plan 32

Part 2   Managing Your Money

Chapter 5
Cash or Liquid Asset Management   *142*

Chapter 6
Using Credit Cards: The Role of Open Credit in Personal Financial Management   *172*

Part 3	Protecting Yourself with Insurance

Chapter 9
The Role of Life Insurance   282

Part 4 Managing Your Investments

Part 5   Retirement and Estate Planning

Chapter 17
Retirement Planning   *542*

PREFACE

Personal Finance: Turning Money into Wealth introduces the student to the concepts, tools, and applications of personal finance and investments. It's written as an introduction, assuming little or no prior knowledge of the subject matter, thereby allowing the student to take the first steps toward understanding the process of financial planning and the logic that drives it. In so doing, this text will provide coverage of the planning process itself, as well as insurance, investments, and estate planning.

For many students this course is their initial and only exposure to personal finance, and as such, the material must be presented in a way that leaves a lasting understanding. Tools, techniques, and equations are easily forgotten, but the logic and underlying fundamentals that drive their use, if stressed and presented in an intuitive way, will stay. Moreover, once the student understands the underlying principles, learning the techniques and tools is much easier. In effect, if the student knows *why* something is being done, it makes much more sense. For this reason the text centers around 15 fundamental axioms of personal finance that are introduced in an intuitive manner in chapter 1 and then reappear in every chapter. By first presenting the student with the principles that drive the techniques, the student is afforded the opportunity to see the "big picture," or distinguish the "forest from the trees," as you will. As we all know, after an introductory course is over, there's a rush to forget. Unfortunately, this is many times the case with personal finance—"I don't have any money now, so this isn't important." However, although it's relatively easy to forget tools and techniques, it's much more difficult to forget underlying principles. Once the principles are known, they become a part of the student's "financial personality" and are applied unknowingly. The end result is that in the future, when the student is far removed from this course, an understanding of these fundamental principles of personal finance will allow the student to effectively deal with the ever-changing financial world.

Tying the topics of personal finance together through the use of basic principles or axioms is a radical change from the presentation provided in alternative personal finance texts. The present generation of these texts tend to be descriptive in nature, emphasizing listings and procedures. The chapters appear to be unrelated to each other—bound together only by the book's binding. The purpose of this text is to educate the student in the discipline of personal finance. It is only through an understanding of the principles that students can adapt to the changing world that they'll face.

FEATURES

Axioms. Fifteen axioms are introduced in an intuitive manner in chapter 1 and appear throughout the text, tying the topics together.

In the News.   Boxes with excerpts from such periodicals as *Smart Money*, *Money*, *The Wall Street Journal*, and the *Washington Post* are provided with annotated commentary, tying the boxes to the chapter material. The excerpts appear as clippings torn out of the paper marked with magic marker to note the comments.

Accessible Writing Style.   Attempts were made to keep the writing style as accessible to the student as possible, keeping it as interesting, fluid, and loose as possible while making sure that no assumptions were made with respect to terminology—terms were not used before they were introduced. A book is no good unless the student is willing to read it.

Complete and Integrated Coverage of the Taxpayer Relief Act of 1997. The Taxpayer Relief Act of 1997 had a dramatic effect on personal finance, making IRAs more attractive for millions of Americans, changing the capital gains tax rate, and affecting estate and retirement planning. These changes are fully integrated within the text.

Chapter Vignettes Featuring Famous People.   Again, to keep the book as interesting as possible, opening vignettes feature the likes of Elvis, Dennis Rodman, Willie Nelson, Meatloaf, Jerry Garcia, Tina Turner, Carol Hathaway (the nurse from *ER*), Christopher Reeve, and Johnny Depp.

Learning Objectives at the Beginning of Each Chapter.   Each chapter opens with a set of action-oriented learning objectives. As these learning objectives are covered in the text, an icon identifying the objective appears in the margin. In addition, all the end-of-chapter problems and questions are linked back to the learning objectives.

Margin Glossary.   Key terms are defined in the margin as they first appear, allowing students to read through the chapter without becoming stumped by technical terms.

Stop and Think.   These short boxes provide the student with insights as to what the material actually means—implications and the big picture.

The Facts of Life.   These short boxes present interesting "real-life" facts related to the material being presented.

Take It to the Net.   This feature, which appears in the margins at the end of each chapter, provides interesting Internet sites related to the material in the chapter.

Just Do It!   At the end of each chapter, there is a box written by Marcy Furney ("From the Desk of Marcy Furney, CFP"), which provides a checklist of things you should do—in effect, free advice from a certified financial planner.

Decision-Making Worksheets.   Worksheets that allow for a step-by-step analysis of many personal finance decisions are provided at the end of the text.

Mini-Cases.   Each chapter closes with a set of mini-cases that provide students with a real life setting that ties together the topics in the chapter and allows for a practical financial decision.

The Continuing Case—Don and Maria Chang.   At the end of each section in the book, the continuing case of Don and Maria Chang appears, providing the student with the opportunity to synthesize and integrate the many different financial planning concepts presented in this book. It gives the student a chance to construct financial statements, analyze a changing financial situation, calculate taxes, measure risk exposure, and develop a financial plan.

PERSONAL WEALTH NAVIGATOR Web Site (http://www.prenhall.com/ persfin). Developed specifically for this text is the much acclaimed *PERSONAL WEALTH NAVIGATOR* Web site. This activity-based site guides you to the most current financial information possible. As a companion site to the text, the activities and source data have been organized to follow the chapter sequence identical to the text with separate listings of links to other sites, articles, and exercises, all aimed at getting you financially organized. These listings are continuously monitored to ensure that they are both current and accurate. Click onto Internet sites and articles of interest to help you plan your college finance requirements, make a lease-versus-purchase decision on that new car, get job-hunting and investment information, understand tax changes, find out where to get the best loan deal, and much more. In addition to enlivening material in the text, *PERSONAL WEALTH NAVIGATOR* has been designed for your personal use and for in-class activities your instructor may wish to assign.

SUPPLEMENTARY MATERIALS

The following supplements are available with *Personal Finance: Turning Money into Wealth:*

- *Instructor's Manual.* The Instructor's Manual was written by Ruth Lytton at Virginia Tech, John Grable at Texas Tech University, and Derek Klock at Virginia Tech and provides chapter summaries along with solutions to the questions, problems, and cases that appear in each chapter.
- *Student Study Guide.* The student study guide was prepared by Ruth Lytton at Virginia Tech, John Grable at Texas Tech University, and Derek Klock at Virginia Tech and includes chapter summaries, highlights, key terms, and practice test questions.
- *Test Item File.* The test item file was prepared by David W. Murphy at Madisonville Community College. These questions vary in type and degree of difficulty, covering all topics.
- *PowerPoint Lectures.* A set of PowerPoint Lectures developed by Derek Klock of Virginia Tech with lectures corresponding to all chapters is available to adopters.

ACKNOWLEDGMENTS

I gratefully acknowledge the assistance, support, and encouragement of those individuals who have contributed to *Personal Finance: Turning Money into Wealth.* Specifically, I wish to recognize the very helpful insights provided by many of my colleagues. For their careful comments and helpful reviews of the text, I am indebted to:

Lynda S. Clark, Maple Woods Community College
Bobbie D. Corbett, Northern Virginia Community College
Charles P. Corcoran, University of Wisconsin–River Falls
Kathy J. Daruty, Los Angeles Pierce College
Richard A. Deus, Sacramento City College
Marilynn E. Hood, Texas A&M University
Edward Krohn, Miami-Dade Community College
Dianne R. Morrison, University of Wisconsin–LaCrosse
David W. Murphy, Madisonville Community College
Irving E. Richards, Cuyahoga Community College
Daniel L. Schneid, Central Michigan University
Martha A. Zenns, Jamestown Community College

I would also like to thank a wonderful group of people at Prentice Hall. In a perfect world, Paul Donnelly would be every author's editor. He is creative and insightful, always with an eye toward delivering the student the finest possible textbook and supplementary package possible. Even more important, he is a wonderful person and a true friend. Also in a perfect world, David Cohen would be every author's developmental editor. If he were, there wouldn't be any more boring textbooks. His efforts go well beyond—both in magnitude and quality—what an author might ever expect of a developmental editor. Never one to hold back on criticism, he is responsible for making the book as student-friendly as it is. He was truly a collaborator on this book. I would also like to extend thanks to Gladys Soto for her administrative deftness. She offered insights and direction, often serving as a sounding board to new ideas—I cannot say enough good things about Gladys. Jodi Hirsch also deserves thanks for providing superb coordinating skills. To Louise Rothman, my production editor, I express a very special thank-you. Her skills in coordinating this book through a very complex production process and keeping it all on schedule while maintaining the highest quality was well "beyond the call of duty." For his marketing prowess in locating potential adopters, I owe Patrick Lynch, the Marketing Manager, a debt of gratitude—he was great! I also am in debt to Janet Ferrugia, the Marketing Communications Director, for the amazing job she did in alerting the market—another of the "gifted ones." My appreciation to the people at Prentice Hall would be incomplete without the mention of the highly professional Prentice Hall field sales staff and their managers. In my opinion they are the best in the business and I am honored to work with them. In particular I must single out Bill Beville, the regional acquistions editor. To say the least, he is one of the most dogged and delightful people I have ever met. Bill relentlessly pursued me until I agreed to Paul's proposal to do this book. I will always owe Bill a debt of gratitude for this. Bill, I'm glad you're on my side. Thanks also go to Ruth Lytton, John Grable, Derek Klock, and Barbara O'Neil for their outstanding work on the cases and end-of-chapter material. They're always the professionals and the perfectionists, and their efforts have resulted in a pedagogy that works. Their comments and suggestions on earlier drafts of the book also added greatly to its value. Ruth, who is the consummate teacher, was also the perfectionist in reviewing chapters and writing problems and cases that teach—which is the ultimate goal of this text. Likewise, John wrote outstanding problems and cases, and contributed well more than I had ever anticipated. Indeed, Texas Tech is extremely lucky to have John joining them—my congratulations to Texas Tech. A salute goes also to Marcy Furney for her exceptional work on the "Just Do It!" boxes. She also read and reviewed the book, providing insightful comments that materially improved the book. I must also thank Glenn Furney at Texas Instruments for his help in bringing to life the use of calculators in the teaching of personal finance. Given the contributions of Marcy, Ruth, John, and Derek, I think it is only fitting that I provide a short biography of each. I thank you all.

Marcy Furney, Certified Financial Planner, is a Registered Representative of Allmerica Investments, Inc. She resides in Dallas, Texas, where she has been affiliated with Gekiere and Associates since 1990. With 12 years in the financial services industry, she has worked extensively in insurance, executive deferred compensation plans, retirement programs, small business benefits, and personal financial needs. Marcy graduated Summa Cum Laude with a Bachelor of Arts degree from Texas Tech University and attended graduate school at the University of Texas.

Ruth Lytton is an Associate Professor of Resource Management at Virginia Polytechnic Institute and State University where she works with the family financial management program, a Certified Financial Planner Board of Standards, Inc. registered program. Her personal finance course is a popular elective for students throughout the campus. Dr. Lytton received the 1994–95 College of Human Resources Certificate of Teaching Excellence and in 1995 was recognized by the Association for Financial Counseling and Planning Education (AFCPE) as the Mary

Ellen Edmondson Educator of the Year. Honorary memberships include Phi Upsilon Omicron, Phi Sigma Society, Kappa Omicron Nu, Phi Kappa Phi, and Golden Key National Honor Society.

John Grable, CFP, is an Assistant Professor of Family Financial Planning at Texas Tech University. He received his Ph.D. in Family Financial Management from Virginia Polytechnic Institute and State University, a Master's degree in Business Administration from Clarkson University, and a B.S. degree in business and economics from the University of Nevada. Dr. Grable received his Certified Financial Planner (CFP) designation in 1992, and in 1997 was awarded a research grant from the Certified Financial Planner Board of Standards, Inc.

Derek Klock completed a B.S. degree from Virginia Polytechnic Institute and State University in the family financial management program and is a personal banker with First American Savings Bank. Building on a 15-year history of tracking and analyzing investments, work on this project gave him the opportunity to share his enthusiasm for financial management and influence the materials used for instructing others.

As a final word, I express my sincere thanks to those using *Personal Finance: Turning Money into Wealth* in the classroom. I thank you for making me a part of your team.

Chapter 1

FINANCIAL PLANNING:
The Ties That Bind

When he graduated from high school in June 1953, he took a job at the Precision Tool Company and later drove a truck for Crown Electric. His career goal at that time was to become a truck driver, but all that changed when he met Sam Phillips, who owned Sun Records. From there it didn't take long for Elvis Presley to make his name as a rock 'n' roll star. For the rest of his life he continued to be a musical force to be reckoned with, and over his lifetime he made millions and millions of dollars. Yet, toward the end of his life he faced financial ruin. How did this happen? The answer is that he ignored the financial planning side of his life. He used his father, a former truck driver who had once served an 8-month prison sentence for passing bad checks, as his business advisor, he naively allowed his business manager to earn almost 50-percent commission as opposed to the industry standard of 10 percent, he opposed tax shelters on principle, and he impulsively gave away cash and expensive gifts. Moreover, it took over half a million dollars a year just to maintain Graceland (Elvis's estate).

Being financially secure involves more than just making money—it involves balancing what you make with what you spend. Basically, you must live within your means, regardless of what you make. Elvis certainly made plenty of money, but he managed to spend even more. After Elvis died in 1977, Priscilla Presley took over the management of the estate, which was valued at only $5 million. What happened? With the help of some serious personal financial planning,

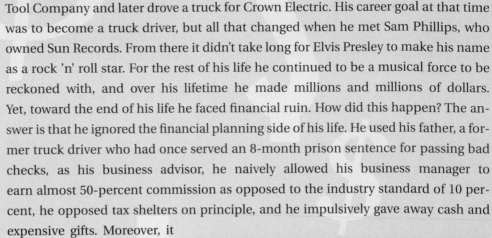

Learning Objectives

After reading this chapter you should be able to:

1. Explain the role of personal financial planning.
2. Describe the five basic steps of personal financial planning.
3. Set your financial goals.
4. Describe the different stages of the financial life cycle.
5. Explain why education is the key factor in determining your income level.
6. Explain the 15 axioms that form the foundations of personal financial planning.

part one
FINANCIAL PLANNING

Priscilla was able to turn the Presley financial affairs around, and today the estate is worth over $100 million. What's the point? Life works better with a bit of personal financial planning.

It's easier to spend than to save—that's true for everyone. It was true for Elvis, and it's no doubt true for you. If that weren't the case, there wouldn't be much need for this or the hundreds of other personal finance books that litter the shelves of bookstores. Unfortunately, financial planning is not something that comes naturally to most people, and as a result many people work themselves into a financial corner that is much easier to avoid than it is to get out of. This text will provide you with the needed know-how to avoid the financial pitfalls that are lurking in your future and to achieve all your financial goals. In fact, with good financial planning, you can get that car you've always wanted or that vacation home by the beach, or you could retire early. This text not only provides you with the necessary tools and techniques for managing your personal finances, but also explains the basic *logic* behind them. That way you can understand why the tools and techniques work and how to apply them outside of this textbook. To make life a little easier, we've sorted the underlying logic behind all of financial planning into 15 axioms, or basic principles, that we use to guide you through this book. If you can understand these axioms, you're well on your way to successful financial planning. And you'll be doing even better than Elvis.

THE ROLE OF PERSONAL FINANCIAL PLANNING

How big are the financial challenges and goals that face you? They're very big indeed. You are no doubt gaining an appreciation for the incredible cost of college. At many small private schools a college education can cost $1,000 a week. Once you've got the diploma, there's a good chance you've also got a student loan. Paying off your loan may be one of your first financial challenges. You know how expensive it is. College tuition at a private school averages around $12,500 per year, and nearly $3,000 at a public school. Add to this housing costs of $3,000 per year, $2,000 for food, a computer and printer for $1,600, and the essentials: a minirefrigerator, a parking permit, lots of change for the laundry, a bit more cash to cover library fines, and late-night pizza money. How do most students finance it? The answer is, by borrowing.

Today, the average student graduates with $11,000 in debts, and many students are far more in debt than that. Take, for example, Sheri Springs-Phillips, who was recently written up in *The Wall Street Journal*. She's a second-year neurology resident at Loyola University Medical Center. On her 11-year journey from the South Side of Chicago to becoming a doctor, she piled up $102,000 in debt. Although her friends think she's got it made being a doctor, she worries about the $2,500 monthly loan payments that'll begin when she finishes her residency. Fortunately, Sheri is an exception, but even the average level of $11,000 in debt is daunting. However, it is an unsolvable problem only in the absence of financial planning.

Why do people *need* to make a financial plan? Because it's always easier to spend than to save. Certainly that was the case for Elvis. For example, a recent CNN/USA Today/Gallup poll survey about retirement showed that most people are worried they won't be able to save enough to retire comfortably (see Table 1.1). Why not? Because there always seems to be something better to spend your money on instead of saving it. Remember, though, that without a financial plan for saving, you might not be able to afford to retire!

Why should people *want* to make a financial plan? Because it can help you achieve all your financial goals. "Achieving financial goals" may seem a little abstract to you, so let's put it in context. Say you really want to be able to buy a Jeep with a stereo loud enough to wake the neighbors (and the dead) when you graduate.

TABLE 1.1

Retirement Planning Survey

	Strongly Agree (%)	Somewhat Agree (%)	No Opinion (%)	Somewhat Disagree (%)	Strongly Disagree (%)
You don't earn enough money right now to be able to save for retirement.	34	25	2	22	17
There always seems to be something else to spend your money on rather than save it for the future.	51	30	1	11	7
You are worried you will not have enough money to live comfortably when you retire.	36	38	1	15	10

SOURCE: CNN/USA Today/Gallop poll, April 1995.

That's a financial goal, and a good financial plan will help you achieve it. A good plan may also help you get to Europe someday, or have your own place instead of having a roommate. Financial planning may not help you earn more, but it can help you use the money you do earn to achieve the goals you really want to achieve. In the real world, either you control your finances, or they control you—it's your choice.

Managing your finances isn't a skill you're born with. In fact, there really aren't too many skills that you're born with. Most people have to be taught the skills they are to use in life. For example, if you're planning on becoming a teacher, you've probably taken a course or two on teaching; if your career choice is engineering, you've no doubt taken a number of courses in engineering. Unfortunately, personal finance courses aren't the norm in high school, and in many families money is not something to talk about—only to disagree on. In fact, financial problems and disagreements can be a major cause of marital problems. Family disagreements and fights about money can instill a "fear of finance" in kids at an early age, and a lack of financial education just makes matters worse. As a result, most people feel very uncomfortable about finance in general.

Unfortunately, the particulars of finance itself don't serve to soothe anybody's fears. At first glance, personal finance seems to offer an almost unending number of investment, insurance, and estate planning choices. In addition, poor advice and un-ethical characters abound in the land of personal finance. Even more confusing is the fact that investments and personal finance have a language of their own. How can you make decisions among the choices when you don't speak the language? Well, you can't. That's why you're reading this text and taking this course—to allow you to navigate in the world of money. The bottom line is that personal financial planning works—it certainly worked for Priscilla Presley—and ignoring personal financial planning can have painful results, regardless of how much you make—that's the lesson of Elvis.

Specifically, we hope that this text and this course will allow you to accomplish the following:

- **Manage the Unplanned.**   It may seem odd to plan to deal with the unexpected or unplanned. Hey, stuff happens. Unfortunately, no matter how well you plan, much of life is unexpected. A sound financial plan will allow you to bounce back from a few hard knocks, instead of going down for the count.

- **Accumulate Wealth for Special Expenses.**   College for your children, a summer home, travel—these are all special expenses that will probably be impossible if you don't plan ahead for them. Financial planning helps you to map out a strategy to pay for that house by the beach.

- **Realistically Save for Retirement.**   You may not think much about it now, but you don't want to be penniless when you're 65. A strong financial plan will help you to realistically look at the costs of retirement and develop a plan that allows you to live a life of retirement ease.

- **"Cover Your Assets."**   A financial plan is no good if it doesn't protect what you've got. A complete financial plan will include adequate insurance at as low a cost as possible.

- **Invest Intelligently.**   When it comes to investing savings, the uninformed don't do it very well. Quite frankly, there are too many shady investment advisors and dirty deals out there to enter the investments arena unarmed. Before making a financial plan, arm yourself with an understanding of the basic principles of investment.

- **Minimize Your Payments to Uncle Sam.**   Why earn money for the government when you can instead earn it for yourself? Part of financial planning is to help you legally reduce the amount of tax you have to pay on your earnings.

THE PERSONAL FINANCIAL PLANNING PROCESS: BUDGETING WITHIN THE PLANNING CYCLE

The benefits of a solid financial plan certainly seem to be valuable. The question now is how to put them in place. Financial planning is an ongoing process that changes as your financial situation and position in life change. However, there are five basic steps to personal financial planning that need to be examined before moving on.

Step 1: Evaluate Your Financial Health

A financial plan begins with an examination of your current financial situation. How wealthy are you? How much money do you make? How much are you spending, and what are you spending it on? To survive financially, you have to step back and see your whole financial picture. Of course, seeing your whole financial picture and evaluating your current situation are going to require a lot of careful record keeping, especially when it comes to spending. Keeping track of what you spend may simply be a matter of taking a few minutes each evening to enter all of the day's expenses into a little budget book. Is this record keeping dull and tedious? Sure, but it will also be revealing, and it's a first step to taking control of your financial well-being.

The Facts of Life
A recent survey showed that typical Americans feel they need $1.5 million in order to feel rich. Unfortunately, that's a goal that few reach. In fact, 59 percent of those over 65 have saved less that $100,000. Even worse, almost 45 percent of Americans over 65 have annual incomes of less than $15,000, and only 30 percent have annual incomes over $25,000—and this includes Social Security benefits! That's one reason why financial planning is so important. As Carl Sandburg once wrote, "Nothing happens unless first a dream."

Step 2: Define Your Financial Goals

You can't get what you want if you don't know what you want. Thus, the second step of the financial planning process involves defining your goals. These goals may include accumulating wealth for retirement, providing funds for your child's college education, or buying a new pickup truck. In a later section we'll look in detail at possible goals and financial concerns that you might want to provide for in your financial plan. You'll notice that, as you age, your goals will change. Keep in mind, though, that your goals aren't elusive and ever-changing. Rather, as events pass and goals are achieved, they give way to other goals in turn. Goals, then, are like stepping-stones, and without the solid footing of a sound financial plan, it's easy to lose your step.

Step 3: Develop a Plan of Action

The third step of the financial planning process involves developing a plan of action to achieve your goals. Although everyone's plan is a bit different (owing to the wide range of goals that we all have), there are some common concerns that should guide all financial plans. These are: flexibility, liquidity, protection, and minimization of taxes.

Flexibility.   Remember when we mentioned planning for the unplanned? That's what flexibility is all about. Your financial plan must be flexible enough to respond to changes in your life and unexpected events (like wrapping your Honda around a telephone

FOR BABY BOOMERS, Retirement Years May Be a Bust

Beverly Duncan, 45, born early in the baby boom years, has a condo, a Ford Explorer and a Lincoln Continental, and a business that she operates with her husband, Richard, for a combined family income of "$50,000 to $75,000 a year, depending on how good business is."

But like many others in the huge generation born between 1946 and 1964, the Fort Lauderdale, Fla., woman does not have a juicy retirement plan for the golden years.

"We have no pensions, only small IRAs—a few thousand each—and we're just starting a profit sharing plan, but we haven't put anything in yet," said Duncan, whose business, Franklin Duncan, Inc., sells electronic and other educational learning tools and games to school systems.

After years of using all the couple's spare money to build up the business, pay for their health insurance and help support and educate her husband's children by a previous marriage, "I most likely will be high and dry in retirement, with almost nothing but Social Security," she said.

Duncan's case illustrates one scenario in a raging public debate on whether baby boomers, who will reach age 65 from 2011 to 2030, are saving enough and earning enough pension credits to live well in retirement. It is a 21st century problem with very immediate political consequences. Both the Republican Congress and the Democratic Clinton administration have proposed broad cuts in the growth of Medicare, the health insurance program for the elderly, to keep it from going bust. A further budget crisis looms over the Social Security system, which faces potential bankruptcy when the baby boom generation joins the rolls.

If the boomers are not saving for their old age and the federal government reduces benefits to the elderly, then many experts believe the nation will confront an extremely painful choice in the next century: "dramatically reduced living standards for baby boomer retirees" as they leave jobs and drop to much lower incomes when they retire, as the Committee for Economic Development (CED) puts it, "or intolerable tax burdens on working Americans" to help support the disproportionately large retired population represented by the boomers.

Source: Spencer Rich, "For Baby Boomers, Retirement Years May Be a Bust," *The Washington Post*, June 27, 1995, p. A1. © 1995 *The Washington Post.* Reprinted with permission.

(A)

(B)

(C)

Analysis and Implications …

A. It's awfully easy to postpone personal financial planning. Unfortunately, the consequences of putting it off are grave. Fortunately, it is never too late to begin. Think of it as being akin to preventive maintenance on your car—the longer you put it off, the more expensive it becomes.

B. As Congress and the president deal with the budget deficit, it becomes pretty clear that the government probably won't be much of a help when you retire. You've got to do it yourself, and the earlier you start, the better. It may seem like retirement is a long way off, but now is the time to start thinking about it. If you plan for retirement when you're only a few years away from it, your only decision may be which poorhouse, as it were, to live in.

C. Let's face it, when it comes to personal finance, you're the one who benefits from good decisions and suffers from bad ones. The buck literally stops with you. The only good decision is to take full responsibility for yourself and your family.

pole). For example, an investment plan that doesn't give you any access to your money whatsoever until you retire doesn't do you much good when you suddenly get fired for using your office computer to play Doom.

Liquidity.   Dealing with the unplanned requires more than just flexibility. Sometimes it requires cold, hard cash, and it requires it immediately. **Liquidity** involves having access to your money when you need it. No one likes to think about things like illnesses, losing a job, or even wrecking your car. But if they happen, you want to make sure you have access to enough money to make it through.

Protection.   What happens if the unexpected turns out to be catastrophic? Liquidity will get you through the repair bill for an unexpected fender bender, but what happens if the accident is a lot worse and you wind up seriously injured? What if the cost of an unexpected event is a lot more than you've got? Liquidity allows you to carry on during an unexpected event, but insurance shields you from those events that might threaten your financial security. Insurance offers you protection against the worst, and costliest, unexpected events, such as flood, fire, major illness, and death. However, insurance isn't free. A good financial plan includes enough insurance to prevent financial ruin, either from catastrophe or from paying too much for your insurance.

Minimization of Taxes.   Finally, your financial plan should take taxes into account. Keep in mind that a chunk of your earnings goes to the government, so if you need to earn $1,000 from an investment, make sure it yields $1,000 *after taxes*. It's always good to pay as little in taxes as possible, but it's even better to understand in advance that taxes will lessen your earnings and to plan accordingly. In effect, your goal is not necessarily to minimize taxes, but to maximize the cash that is available to you after taxes have been paid.

Besides considering these four factors, a plan of action should take into account all your goals. For example, it should involve creating an informed and controlled budget; determining your investment strategy; planning for big-ticket items, such as a house or a car; debt planning; insurance planning; funding for raising children or sending them to college; planning for retirement; and providing for your loved ones after you pass on. At this point, developing a game plan for your financial future may seem overwhelming at best, so you may be tempted to turn to investment advisors or professional financial planners for help. Before you do so, you should develop an understanding of personal finance for your own financial protection. Planners and advisors can help you; in fact, for many individuals they are their financial salvation, but in the end, you're still the one who must decide on your own plan.

Step 4: Implement Your Plan

Although it's important to carefully and thoughtfully develop your financial plan, it is even more important to implement and actually stick to that plan. For most people, sticking to the plan also means using common sense and moderation—you don't want to become a slave to your financial plan. If you force yourself to write down every penny spent and track every expenditure, your efforts will probably wilt in no time. Keep in mind that your financial plan is not the goal; it is the tool you use to achieve your goals. In effect, think of your financial plan not as punishment, but as a financial road map to guide you through life. Your destination may change, and you may get lost or even go down a few dead ends, but if your road map is good enough, you'll always find your way again. Remember to add in new roads as they are built, and be prepared to pave a few yourself to get to where you want to go. Always keep your goals in mind and keep driving toward them.

Liquidity
The relative ease and quickness with which you can convert noncash assets into cash. In effect, it involves having access to your money when you need it.

FIGURE 1.1

The Budgeting and Planning Process

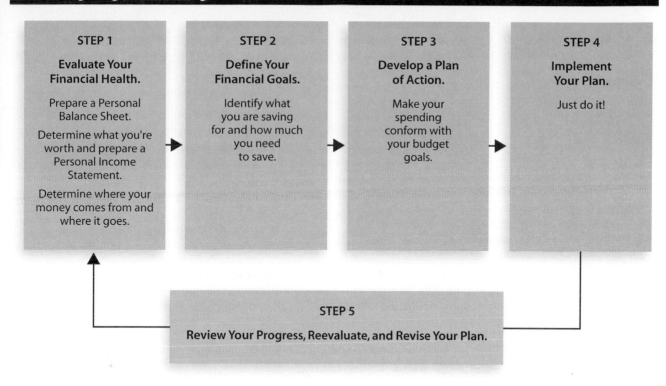

STEP 1

Evaluate Your Financial Health.

Prepare a Personal Balance Sheet.

Determine what you're worth and prepare a Personal Income Statement.

Determine where your money comes from and where it goes.

STEP 2

Define Your Financial Goals.

Identify what you are saving for and how much you need to save.

STEP 3

Develop a Plan of Action.

Make your spending conform with your budget goals.

STEP 4

Implement Your Plan.

Just do it!

STEP 5

Review Your Progress, Reevaluate, and Revise Your Plan.

Step 5: Review Your Progress, Reevaluate, and Revise Your Plan

What happens if you want to go to Seattle but all you have is a road map of Philadelphia? Time to get a new road map! Periodically you must review your financial progress and reexamine your financial plan. If necessary, you must be prepared to start all over again and formulate a different plan. In other words, the last step in financial planning often returns to the first. No plan is fixed for life. Still, this doesn't in any way detract from the importance of setting up a personal financial plan and using it. Goals are mere fantasy without a plan.

Figure 1.1 summarizes these five basic steps to financial planning.

DEFINING YOUR GOALS

You've already seen that the second step of the financial planning process is setting goals. Defining your goals involves writing down or formalizing your financial goals, attaching costs to them, and determining when the money to accomplish those goals will be needed. Unfortunately, establishing personal financial goals is something most people never actually do. Although not a difficult task, it's an easy one to put off, but if you never set goals, you'll never reach them either. Actually, goal setting is nothing new to most people. You may have a target grade point average you're shooting for at graduation, or perhaps you have a goal of getting an A in this course. Goals are second nature to most people. However, in the financial arena, many people don't set goals because they feel financially illiterate—they have absolutely no idea how to go about achieving them. That's what this course and this text are all about—giving you the tools and understanding to make your goals a reality.

LEARNING OBJECTIVE #3

Set your financial goals.

Financial goals cover three time horizons: (1) short-term, (2) intermediate-term, and (3) long-term. Short-term goals are any financial goals that can be accomplished within a 1-year period, such as buying a television or taking a vacation. An intermediate-term goal is one that would take between 1 year and 10 years to accomplish. Examples might include paying for college for an older child or accumulating enough money for a down payment on a new house. A long-term goal is one for which it takes more than 10 years to accumulate the money. Retirement is a common example of a long-term financial goal.

Figure 1.2 provides a worksheet listing a number of possible short-, intermediate-, and long-term goals. The purpose of this worksheet isn't to present an all-inclusive listing of possible goals, but rather to provide you with a handy tool for determining your own specific goals. In defining your goals it is important that you be as specific as possible. Rather than list "saving money" as a goal, state the purpose of your saving efforts, such as buying a car, and exactly how much you want saved by what time. Also, it's important to be realistic. That is, your goals should reflect your financial and life situation. It's a bit unrealistic to plan for a million-dollar home on an income of $15,000 a year.

Once you've set up a list of goals, you need to prioritize them. At this point you may need to reevaluate and refine your goals. You may realize that your goals are simply unrealistic. However, once you have set your finalized goals in place, they will become the cornerstone of your personal financial plan, serving as a guide to action and a benchmark for evaluating the effectiveness of the plan. As you will see in the following section, the process of setting goals and determining an appropriate personal financial plan is ongoing. Looking back at the Presley estate after Elvis died, without goals, a realistic financial plan, and discipline, we see that Priscilla would have lost everything. Instead, today she has over 100 million reasons for believing in personal financial planning.

THE LIFE CYCLE OF FINANCIAL PLANNING

As we said earlier, people's goals change throughout their lives. Although many of these changes are due to unexpected events, the majority are based on a general financial life cycle pattern that applies to most people, even you. Figure 1.3 illustrates the financial life cycle of a typical individual. What's the significance of this financial life cycle? Well, it allows you to better understand the timing and areas of financial concern that you'll probably experience. It thereby allows you to focus on those concerns earlier and to plan ahead to avoid future financial problems.

LEARNING OBJECTIVE #4

Describe the different stages of the financial life cycle.

FIGURE 1.2

Personal Financial Goals Worksheet

Make sure your goals are realistic and stated in specific, measurable terms. In addition, prioritize your goals and identify a specific time frame within which you would like to accomplish them. The listing below is not meant to be all-inclusive, but merely to provide a framework within which goals can be formalized.

SHORT-TERM GOALS (less than 1 year)

Goal	Priority Level	Desired Achievement Date	Anticipated Cost
Accumulate Emergency Funds Equal to Three Months' Living Expenses			
Pay Off Outstanding Bills			
Pay Off Outstanding Credit Cards			
Purchase Adequate Property, Health, Disability, and Liability Insurance			
Purchase a Major Item			
Finance a Vacation or Some Other Entertainment Item			
Other Short-Term Goals (Specify)			

INTERMEDIATE-TERM GOALS (1 to 10 years)

Goal	Priority Level	Desired Achievement Date	Anticipated Cost
Save Funds for College for an Older Child			
Save for a Major Home Improvement			
Save for a Down Payment on a House			
Pay Off Outstanding Major Debt			
Finance Very Large Items (Weddings)			
Purchase a Vacation Home or Time-Share Unit			
Finance a Major Vacation (Overseas)			
Other Intermediate-Term Goals (Specify)			

LONG-TERM GOALS (greater than 10 years)

Goal	Priority Level	Desired Achievement Date	Anticipated Cost
Save Funds for College for a Young Child			
Purchase a Second Home for Retirement			
Create a Retirement Fund Large Enough to Supplement Your Pension so that You Can Live at Your Current Standard			
Take Care of Your Parents After They Retire			
Start Your Own Business			
Other Long-Term Goals (Specify)			

FIGURE 1.3

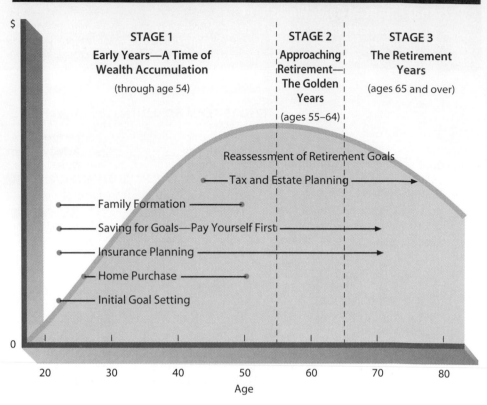

A Typical Individual's Financial Life Cycle

STAGE 1
Early Years—A Time of Wealth Accumulation
(through age 54)

STAGE 2
Approaching Retirement— The Golden Years
(ages 55–64)

STAGE 3
The Retirement Years
(ages 65 and over)

Reassessment of Retirement Goals

Tax and Estate Planning

Family Formation

Saving for Goals—Pay Yourself First

Insurance Planning

Home Purchase

Initial Goal Setting

Age — 20 30 40 50 60 70 80

Complicating Influences
- Marital Status—single, married, divorced, widowed
- Employment Status—employed, unemployed, facing downsizing uncertainty
- Economic Outlook—interest rates, employment level
- Age
- Number of Dependents—children, parents
- Family Money—inheritance

Stop and Think

Examining the financial life cycle makes it easier to figure out what your goals are. Look at retirement. If you're a typical student, retirement is probably the furthest thing from your mind—in fact, you probably don't even have a job now. However, if you understand the financial life cycle, you'll realize that you'll need to make retirement funding one of your first goals.

The first 18 to 20 years of an individual's life tend to involve negative income (and you thought it was only you). You can think of this as the "prenatal" stage of your financial life cycle. During this period most people are in school and still depend on their parents to pay the bills. However, once your education is completed, your financial life cycle should begin in earnest. The first stage of the financial life cycle involves a long period that centers on the accumulation of wealth. For most people that period continues through their mid-50s. During this time, goal setting, insurance, home buying, and family formation get the spotlight in terms of financial planning. The second stage of the life cycle involves a shorter period approaching retirement. Financial goals shift to the preservation and continued growth of the wealth that you have already accumulated. This second stage is generally the period during which most people begin the process of **estate planning**, that is, planning for the passage of their wealth to their heirs. Then, for most people, the third and final stage, retirement, begins in their mid-60s. During retirement you are no longer saving; you are spending. However, you must still allow for some growth in your savings simply to keep **inflation** from eating it away, with safety, income, and estate planning taking on increased importance.

You can probably best understand the general financial life cycle if you look at it in terms of a family life cycle. Many people marry in their 20s and 30s, have kids shortly thereafter, spend the next 18 or 50 years raising the kids, putting the kids through college, and settling down as a couple again when and if the kids move out to form their own families. Obviously, a typical individual's experiences don't fit everyone perfectly. Today, with more single-parent families and more young people postponing marriage, it simply isn't reasonable to refer to any family experience as typical. However, regardless of how unusual your life is, you'll be surprised at how much it has in common with a typical financial life cycle. Although your experiences with respect to your insurance needs, planning for retirement, or planning for your children's college education may not match precisely what we outline here, the life cycle approach will provide you with a starting point, one that can be modified to fit your own experiences.

The financial life cycle has also typically been seen as a career life cycle. Today though, career changes are becoming more the norm. As a result, it becomes more difficult to generalize about what a typical career experience actually is. However, for most people retirement occurs at approximately the same time, which gives you a target date for having your financial state in order. Again, while experiences may vary, the life cycle approach should provide you with a framework you can modify to fit your goals and career cycle.

We now examine the three stages of the financial life cycle in a little more detail.

Stage 1: The Early Years—A Time of Wealth Accumulation

In general, the biggest investment of your lifetime, purchasing a home, occurs during these early years. With a house comes a long-term borrowing commitment and your introduction to debt planning. Although this event may seem to dominate your financial life during this period, you can't lose track of the rest of your financial plan.

During this period you must develop a regular pattern of saving. The importance of making saving a habit cannot be overstressed. Once you make a commitment to save, the question then becomes, How much can be saved, is that enough, and where should those savings dollars be invested? Your savings will hopefully go beyond merely helping to fund the down payment on your home, with some of the savings being directed toward your children's education, the establishment of an emergency fund, and your retirement. You'll also wind up funding the government, so don't forget to keep an eye on the tax implications of your savings.

To say the least, the early years aren't the same for everyone. Decisions that may not seem financial will have a major impact on your financial situation. Take, for example, something as routine as raising a child. Although having children isn't considered a financial decision, it certainly has enormous financial implications, as Table 1.2 illustrates. As you can see, kids cost a lot. In fact, for a middle-income family, the total cost of raising a child from birth to age 18 is $132,660. As you might expect, the more you make, the more you spend on raising children. Those with annual incomes of more than $54,000 spend about twice that of those with annual incomes less than $32,000. The major differences occur in housing, child care, and education. As you look at these figures, keep in mind that they cover only the costs of a child from birth to age 18—they don't include the costs of college. Considering the $5,000 to $10,000 a

---

Estate Planning
Planning for your eventual death and the passage of your wealth to your inheritants.

Inflation
An economic condition in which rising prices reduce the purchasing power of money.

TABLE 1.2

The Cost of Raising a Child

These calculations are for the second child in a two-child family. For families with only one child, the costs of raising that child are more and can be determined by multiplying the totals by 1.26. For families with two or more children, the costs of an additional child can be determined by multiplying the totals by 0.78.

Annual Income	Annual Spending First 3 Years	Total Spent Over 18 Years For							
		All Expenses	Housing	Food	Transportation	Clothing	Health Care	Child Care and Education	Other[a]
Less than $32,000	$ 4,960	$ 97,710	$30,540	$19,650	$16,530	$ 9,330	$ 6,840	$ 5,790	$ 9,030
$32,000–$54,100	6,870	132,660	43,020	23,700	23,070	10,860	8,460	9,840	13,710
More than $54,100	10,210	192,780	69,780	30,270	27,750	14,370	10,050	16,590	23,970

[a]Other expenses include personal-care items, entertainment, and reading material.

SOURCE: U.S. Department of Agriculture, Agricultural Research Service.

year it costs to raise a child, saving to finance your child's college education may seem like a real challenge. Without a sound financial plan developed early on, you might not be up to that challenge.

You must also begin using insurance to protect your assets during this period. Initially you may require only medical, disability, and liability insurance, but as your family grows, the needs of your dependents draw into play, and you will need to provide for them in the event of a tragedy. For example, for those families with young children, adequate life insurance is essential. Similarly, you may need home, auto, and property insurance to protect your family.

The Facts of Life

People say you can't put a price tag on the happiness a child brings you. Well, yes, you can. Here are some things you might be expected to pay for over the next 21 years or so; and what you might have bought for yourself with that money if you decided to forgo the undeniable pleasures of parenthood. —*Clifton Leaf*

What You'll Spend on Your Child			What You Could Have Bought for Yourself	
0+:	Birth: average cost	$4,700*	Artesian home spa	$5,000
1:	Live-in nanny	16,900	Gold Rolex	15,850
3:	Preschool (3 days/week)	4,220	14 nights at Venice's Gritti Palace	4,200
5:	Summer day camp (4 weeks)	1,000	Long ski weekend for two at Snowbird (Park City, Utah)	922
6:	Sneakers (one pair/3 months)	300	Dozen Cohiba Cuban cigars	300
7:	Clothing at Gap Kids	2,000	Armani suit	2,000

8:	Music lessons (once a week)	1,800	Personal training sessions (an hour a week)		1,820
10:	Sleep-away camp (summer)	6,000	Country club annual dues		6,000
11:	Child psychologist (the kid suddenly won't talk)	3,900	Facelift		4,120
12:	Braces	3,500	A week at Canyon Ranch		3,500
13:	Bat mitzvah	15,000	1964 Pontiac GTO 2-door convertible		15,000
14:	Clearasil and pimple-fighting face pads	150	Avocet altimeter barometric watch		150
15:	Boy Scouts	500	Night-vision binoculars		495
17:	Princeton Review course/fees for SAT	720	Shearling coat		795
18:	Harvard tuition, fees, room and board (first of 4 years)	30,900	Chaparral 23-foot powerboat		31,000
21:	. . . And until graduation	100,315	A 1997 Mercedes E420W plus a Denon Home Theater and a Tiffany bezel-set diamond bracelet		100,200
	TOTAL	$191,905	TOTAL		$191,352

*All prices are an annual basis, unless otherwise noted.

Source: Clifton Leaf, "Pricing That Bundle of Joy," *Smart Money*, September 1996, p. 105. Used by permission.

Just as you begin your retirement planning early on, you should also begin your estate planning. If you have children, the first task becomes preparing a will. Your will should not only oversee the disposition of your estate, but also preselect a guardian for your children in the event that both you and your spouse die.

In short, this first stage sees many of your financial goals accomplished and sets the stage for the rest of them. After all, this is the building stage on which everything else rests. During this stage, short-term goals such as buying a car and getting insurance are met, intermediate-term goals such as buying a house and saving for college for your eldest are begun and met, and long-term goals such as retirement saving are started.

Stop and Think

It's important to start planning for your financial future. Just because many people avoid saving for their future doesn't make that an acceptable approach. Forty-five percent of those aged 65 are dependent on relatives, and another 30 percent live on charity. If you're like most young people, fresh out of college, you probably will have an urge to spend all that cash that you may be seeing for the first time in your life, but you need to be reminded to set aside enough to pay off your student loan and to accumulate some savings. Feel free to spend, as long as you manage to save for your goals, and *make sure you begin planning for your financial future now.*

Stage 2: Approaching Retirement—The Golden Years

Stage 2 involves a transition from your earning years, when you will earn more than you spend, to your retirement years, when you will spend more than you earn. Much of this stage involves fine-tuning, with your retirement goal becoming the center of your attention. During this stage, goals such as buying a home and putting your children through college are generally accomplished. As you approach retirement, you must continuously review your financial decisions, including your insurance protection and estate planning. In fact, very few financial decisions are not modified over time. Moreover, unplanned events, such as being a victim of corporate downsizing, a divorce, or the death of a spouse, may have dramatic effects on your goals. The point is that personal financial planning is an extremely dynamic process—one that must be attended to on a regular basis.

Stage 3: The Retirement Years

During your retirement years, you'll be living off your savings. Certainly, the decision of when to retire will reflect how well you have saved for retirement. Once you retire, much of your financial focus deals with ensuring your continued wealth, despite not having an income.

Once again, the management of savings and assets must be continuously reviewed and monitored. Your investment strategy will probably become less risky as your attention moves toward preserving rather than creating wealth. In addition, your insurance planning must be continuously reviewed. For example, now your insurance concerns may include protection against the costs of an extended nursing home stay.

Finally, estate planning decisions become paramount. You should move to trim estate tax bills at this time. In addition, wills, living wills, power of attorney, and record keeping should all be in place to help protect your assets for your heirs.

The fact that financial planning is a continuous, ongoing process can't be overemphasized. In addition, how well you live during retirement will depend upon how well you planned and saved during your early years. The key is to start the personal financial planning process early on in life, and make saving a habitual part of your life.

YOUR INCOME: WHAT DETERMINES IT

As we said before, your financial plan needs to be realistic, and to be realistic, it needs to be based on your income level. What you earn does not determine how happy you are, but it does determine the standard of living you can afford. Although there is great variation in what different people earn at the same job with different companies, Table 1.3 provides a listing of typical salaries at the entry level, average,

LEARNING OBJECTIVE #5

Explain why education is the key factor in determining your income level.

TABLE 1.3

Average Salary Ranges			
Profession	**Initial Pay**	**Industry Average**	**Typical Top Pay**
Accounting and Finance			
Public Accountant			
Big Six firm	$ 30,125	$ 38,625	$ 69,750
Small firm	24,750	36,500	63,000
			(continued)

TABLE 1.3
(continued)

Profession	Initial Pay	Industry Average	Typical Top Pay
Advertising			
Advertising copywriter	30,000	50,000	90,000
Account executive	28,000	62,500	375,000
Education			
University professor	39,050	49,490	63,450
Elementary teacher	25,693	36,357	50,600
Secondary teacher	26,077	37,764	53,300
Financial services			
Financial planner	27,000	50,000	200,000
Portfolio manager	40,000	100,000	150,000
Actuary	25,382	36,914	58,432
Life insurance underwriter	23,500	37,564	52,563
Health care			
Family practice physician			
Private	86,300	123,700	169,400
HMO	96,700	123,300	170,000
Neurosurgeon	158,500	263,300	450,400
Registered nurse	34,600	39,800	45,700
Law			
Private practice			
Associate	58,942	74,318	103,562
Partner	114,213	183,364	301,611
Public prosecutor	23,000	30,000	38,000
Corporate lawyer	61,932	79,297	111,708
Manufacturing			
Foreman	32,240	40,300	48,360
Purchasing agent	42,240	52,800	63,360
Marketing			
Marketing assistant	18,900	24,000	30,000
Marketing research manager	45,770	57,000	103,000
Media			
Newspaper reporter	21,856	24,127	37,113
Book editor	21,000	44,090	72,990
TV news reporter	16,560	30,400	92,688
TV news anchor	25,453	65,824	248,183
Movie producer	400,000	1,000,000	5,000,000
Sales			
Sales trainee	19,800	30,700	35,400
Sales representative	38,900	48,400	59,900
Sales manager	55,800	65,300	80,300
Wall Street			
Investment banker			
Generalist	95,000	440,000	1,250,000
Trader			
General instruments	60,000	290,000	1,000,000
Foreign exchange or			
derivatives specialist	60,000	360,000	2,000,000
Retail stockbrokers	50,000	150,000	620,000

SOURCE: Justin Martin, "How Does Your Pay Really Stack Up?" *FORTUNE*, June 26, 1995, pp. 79–86.
© 1995 Time, Inc. All rights reserved.

and high end for a number of different jobs. One thing that sticks out in these salary averages is that the more special skills and training a job requires, the higher paying it tends to be.

As Table 1.4 shows, the key factor in determining your income level is how well educated you are. Whereas only 29 percent of the middle-class householders finished college, 70 percent of the wealthy householders finished college. Moreover, the percentage of wealthy householders with a postgraduate degree was almost four times that of the middle class. Right now, you may be making the best single investment you will ever make—your education.

TABLE 1.4

The Financial Profiles of a Middle-Class and a Wealthy Household

We define a middle-class household as one with annual income between $25,000 and $100,000. A wealthy household is one with annual income greater than $100,000.

Profile of the Middle Class: Making $25,000 to $100,000

Population	Families	Education[a]	Financial Security	Possessions
• 52 million households • 54% of all households • 31% of all children • 8% of all people over 65	• Headed by married couple: 70% • Headed by single mother: 8% • Headed by single father: 3%	• Finished high school: 87% • Finished college: 29% • Finished postgraduate degree: 10%	• Workers with full-time jobs: 97% • Own stocks: 31%[b] • Average tax rate[c]: 33%	• Own home: 78%[d] • Own at least one vehicle: 97%[b] • Median net worth: $139,600[b]

Profile of the Rich[e]: Making $100,000 and Up

Population	Families	Education[f]	Financial Security	Possessions
• 6 million households • 6% of all households • 3% of all children • Less than 1% of all people over 65	• Headed by married couple: 85% • Headed by single mother: 3% • Headed by single father: 2%	• Finished high school: 97% • Finished college: 70% • Finished postgraduate degree: 38%	• Workers with full-time jobs: 97% • Own stocks: 49% • Average tax rate[g]: 39%	• Own home: 92%[h] • Own at least one vehicle: 97% • Median net worth: $569,000

[a]Of householders 25 and older
[b]Of households with income from $50,000 through $99,999
[c]Includes all income, FCIA, sales, excise, and property taxes for taxpayers with income from $60,000 through $75,000
[d]Estimate: assumes family income from $30,000 through $99,999
[e]Rich refers to households with income of $100,000 or more
[f]Of householders 25 and older
[g]Includes all income, FICA, sales excise, and property taxes for taxpayers with income from $150,000 through $300,000
[h]Estimate
SOURCES: Department of Housing and Urban Development, *Federal Reserve Bulletin,* Tax Foundation, U.S. Census Bureau, the Urban Institute. Reprinted from the May 1995 issue of *MONEY* by special permission; copyright 1995, Time, Inc.

THE 15 AXIOMS THAT FORM THE FOUNDATIONS OF PERSONAL FINANCE

To the first-time student of personal finance, this text may seem like a collection of tools and techniques held together solely by the binding on the book. Not so! In fact, the techniques and tools are all based on some very straightforward logic, which we've summed up in 15 simple axioms. *Although it's not necessary to understand personal finance in order to understand these axioms, it's necessary to understand these axioms in order to understand personal finance.* These axioms will be used throughout the text to unify and relate the topics being presented. They'll also allow you to focus on the conceptual underpinnings of personal finance and thereby not lose sight of the concepts as you are introduced to the techniques. Let's face it, your situation and the personal finance challenges you'll face won't fall into a simple textbook-setting formula. You have to understand the logic behind the material in the book in order to apply it to your life. Here, then, are the 15 axioms that form the foundations of personal finance. Keep in mind that although these axioms may at first appear simple or even trivial, they will provide the driving force behind the rest of the book. If all you can remember from this course are these axioms, you'll still have an excellent grasp of personal finance and thus a better chance of attaining wealth and achieving your financial goals.

Axiom 1: The Risk-Return Trade-Off—Investors Don't Take on Additional Risk Unless They Expect to Be Compensated with Additional Return

At some point just about everyone has saved up some money. Why? The answer is simple: to buy goods or services in the future—in economic terms, to delay consumption. You generally invest your savings to make it earn interest and grow, so you can buy even more in the future. You are able to earn a return on your savings dollars because some individuals, businesses, and governments are willing to pay you for the use of your money. In effect, you are lending them your savings and earning a fee for doing so. Assuming there are a lot of different borrowers out there that would like to have use of your savings, what determines how much return you get on your money?

Actually, the answer is quite simple, and it provides the logic behind much of what is done in finance. Investors demand a minimum return for delaying consumption. This return must be greater than the anticipated level of inflation. Why? If the return isn't enough to cover the loss of purchasing power due to inflation, then the investor has, in effect, lost money, and there's no sense in making an investment that loses money.

Now that you know what the minimum return is, how do you decide among all the various investment alternatives? Obviously, some of these investments are safer

LEARNING OBJECTIVE #6

Explain the 15 axioms that form the foundations of personal financial planning.

than others. Why should investors put their money in a risky investment when there are safer investment alternatives? Basically, investors won't unless they are compensated for taking that additional risk. In other words, investors demand additional expected return for taking on added risk. Notice that we refer to "expected" return rather than "actual" return. You may have expectations and even assurances of what the returns from investing will be, but because risk exists, you never know what those returns are actually going to be. If investors could see into the future, no one would have invested money in the drug maker Liposme on July 23, 1997, the day before its stock dropped 61.5 percent. Until after the fact, you are never sure what the return on an investment will be. That's why Apple Computer bonds pay more interest than do U.S. Treasury bonds of the same **maturity date**—because the government will be around to pay off its borrowing, but Apple may not be. It's that added incentive of additional interest that convinces some investors to take on the added risk of an Apple Computer bond rather than a U.S. Treasury bond. The more risk an investment has, the higher its expected return should be. This relationship between risk and expected return is shown graphically in Figure 1.4.

Needless to say, Figure 1.4 shows a simple relationship that makes a good deal of sense: Investors demand a return for delaying consumption and an additional return for taking on added risk. We'll get into risk measurement later in this course when we discuss valuing such investments as stocks and bonds.

Axiom 2: The Time Value of Money—A Dollar Received Today Is Worth More Than a Dollar Received in the Future

Perhaps the most important concept in personal finance is that money has a time value associated with it. Simply stated, because you can earn interest on any money you receive, money received today is worth more than money received in, say, a year. Although this idea is not a major surprise to most people, they simply don't grasp its importance. The importance of the concept of the time value of money is twofold. First, it allows us to understand how investments grow over time. Second, it allows us to compare dollar amounts that occur in different time periods.

In this text, we focus on the creation and preservation of wealth. To create wealth, we invest savings and allow it to grow over time. This growth is an illustration of the time value of money. In fact, much of personal finance involves efforts to move money through time. Early in your financial life cycle you may borrow money to buy a house.

FIGURE 1.4

The Risk-Return Trade-Off

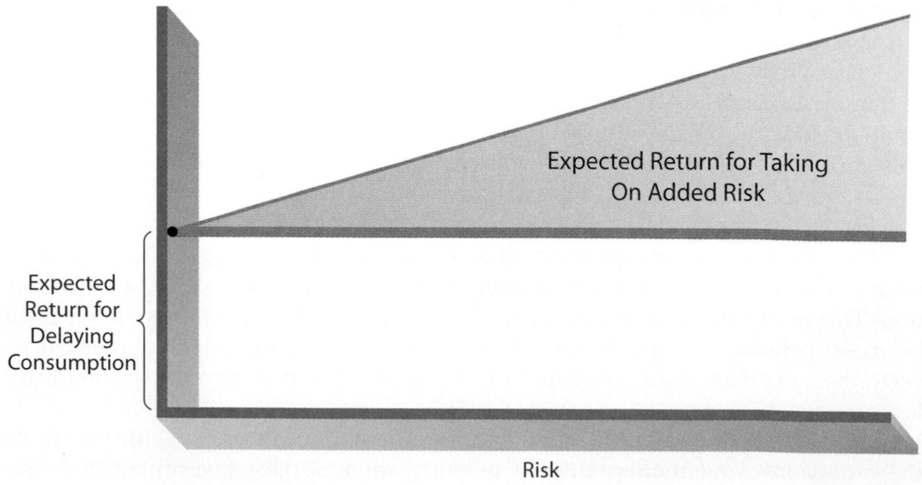

Expected Return for Taking On Added Risk

Expected Return for Delaying Consumption

Risk

EDUCATION MARKS a Widening Income Divide

ROCKFORD, ILLINOIS At a community-college welding class here, 29-year-old Rich Morrison works for a certificate to burnish his résumé, which stops with a high-school diploma, and, more to the point, to help him earn as much as $2 an hour more from his employer.

"I'm falling behind," he says. "As a general laborer, your income isn't good."

Mr. Morrison's sense of frustration contrasts with the satisfaction that college grads generally voice, both here in the heartland city and elsewhere in the nation, according to a new Wall Street Journal poll. Dave Tyska, a 40-year-old insurance-company employee here with two preteen sons, says he will vote for Bill Clinton this year simply "because I am content with my own personal situation."

(A) It's hardly news that college grads generally enjoy a higher standard of living than high-school grads. What's new is that the income gap is widening, and largely because less-educated workers—particularly men—are losing ground. For all the talk of Americans' economic insecurity, it's this growing economic inequality between the less and more educated that is more precisely the problem.

(B) Between 1980 and 1995, the average weekly earnings of a male high-school grad fell to just under 60% of a male college grad's pay, down from

77%. Similarly, among women, the average earnings of high-school grads is down to 55% of a college grad's salary, from nearly 70% in 1980. Economist Frank Levy of the Massachusetts Institute of Technology, exploring the paradox of the public's wide-spread pessimism amid a pretty good economy, writes in a new study for the Competitiveness Policy Council, a federal advisory committee, that one of the most important developments of recent years is "the growth in the high school/college earnings gap."

The latest poll for the Journal and NBC News, conducted by Peter Hart and Bob Teeter, suggests how that gap translates into differences in attitude between the two groups. Significantly, six out of 10 respondents with a high school education or less say they aren't keeping up with the cost of living, while just a third of college grads say that. In responses to a number of questions devised as an "economic satisfaction index," only a quarter of those without a college education registered as satisfied with their standard of living while almost half of college grads did.

Source: Jackie Calmes, "Education Marks a Widening Income Divide," *The Wall Street Journal*, June 28, 1996, p. R7. Reprinted by permission of *The Wall Street Journal*, © 1996 Dow Jones & Company, Inc. All Rights Reserved Worldwide

Analysis and Implications …

A. One reason an education pays off is that it gives you skills that most people don't possess. In fact, earning a college degree puts you in a minority—only 21 percent of those 18 and older have one. In fact, according to the 1995 Census data covering the educational level for those over 18, 19 percent do not have a high school diploma, 34 percent have a high school diploma only, 27 percent have some college, and 21 percent have a bachelor's or higher degree.

B. There is no question that a high level of education translates into more dollars over the course of a worker's lifetime. The lifetime earnings for someone who did not graduate from high school average $609,000. They climb to $821,000 for a high school graduate, $1,421,000 for those with a bachelor's degree, and $3,013,000 for those with a professional degree (for example, a doctor or a lawyer).

In taking out that home mortgage, you are really spending money today and paying later. In saving for your retirement, you are saving money today with the intention of spending it later. In each case money is moved through time. You either spend in today's dollars and pay back in tomorrow's dollars, or save in today's dollars and later spend in tomorrow's dollars. Without recognizing the existence of the time value of money, it is impossible to understand the concept of **compound interest**—which allows investments to grow over time.

Axiom 3: Diversification Reduces Risk

Axiom 1 introduced us to risk. The concept of **diversification** enters the picture by allowing you to reduce or "diversify away" some of your risk without affecting your expected return. The concept of diversification is one that you are probably already familiar with. There is an old saying that goes, "Don't put all your eggs in one basket." When you diversify you are spreading your money around several investments instead of putting all your money in one investment. Then, when one of those investments goes bust, another goes boom to make up for the loss. In effect, diversification allows you to iron out the ups and downs of investing. You don't experience the great returns, but you don't experience great losses either—instead you receive the average return.

Because of its importance, you must understand the process of diversification. Perhaps the easiest way to understand it is to look at it graphically. Consider what happens when you combine two stocks, as is depicted in Figure 1.5. In this case, the returns from these stocks move in opposite directions, and when they are combined, their highs and lows cancel each other out. You'll notice that the average return has not changed—both stocks and their combined returns average 10 percent. As you'll see, for most investments, some risk, but not all, can be eliminated through random diversification, while some risk cannot.

Axiom 4: Diversification and Risk—All Risk Is Not Equal, Because Some Risk Can Be Diversified Away and Some Cannot

As you saw in Axiom 3, the process of diversification allows for much of an investment's risk or variability to be eliminated or "diversified away." The degree to which the total risk is reduced is a function of how the two investments' returns move together. For example, if two stocks move in an exactly opposite manner, combining them can result in the elimination of all variability for the combination. However, because most stocks move together—climbing during market upswings and declining during market

Compound Interest
Interest paid on interest. This occurs when interest paid on an investment is reinvested and added to the principal, thus allowing you to earn interest on the interest, as well as on the principal.

Diversification
Acquisition of a variety of different investments instead of just one to reduce risk.

FIGURE 1.5

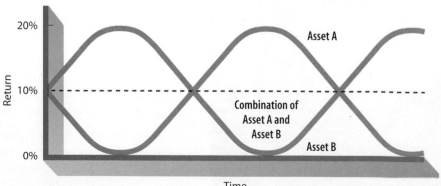

Reducing Risk Through Diversification

downswings—not all of their variability can be diversified away when they are combined. *The bottom line here is that all risk is not equal, and we are going to be very concerned with risk that we cannot remove through diversification.*

Axiom 5: The Curse of Competitive Investment Markets—Why It's Hard to Find Exceptionally Profitable Investments

Your goal as an investor is to create wealth for yourself. Therefore, you need to understand what different investments, such as stocks, bonds, and real estate, are really worth. As you will see, it's very difficult finding investments that are exceptionally profitable, that is, ones that outperform other similar investments. To understand why, it is necessary to have an understanding of the concept of **efficient markets**.

In an efficient market, information such as new earnings figures or the announcement of a new product is reflected in investment prices with such speed that there are no opportunities for investors to earn higher than expected profits from publicly available information. In other words, all investments return what Axiom 1 says they should return—the more risk they have, the higher their expected return. This situation comes about because in an efficient market there are a large number of profit-driven investors who act independently of one another—each looking for investments with whopping returns. In effect, investors buy investments they feel are underpriced—pushing them upwards—and sell investments they feel are overpriced—pushing them downward until equilibrium is reached. In short, investors' hunger for profits ensures that different investments earn what Axiom 1 says they should.

What are the implications of the concept of efficient markets for us? It means that, in general, it is very difficult to "beat the market," that is, to find that investment with a whoppingly high return. It means that you should look carefully at "hot tips" and most recommendations before acting upon them. The point is that, in competitive investment markets, investment "bargains" don't remain as "bargains" for very long.

Axiom 6: Taxes Bias Personal Finance Decisions

Because they help determine the realized return of an investment, taxes play an important role in personal finance. In fact, hardly a decision can be made without considering the impact of taxes. All you should be concerned with is the results of your investment or planning strategy *after taxes.* Your goal will not necessarily be to minimize taxes, but to maximize the after-tax income available to you. Thus, you must look at all your investment alternatives on an after-tax basis. Taxes aren't the same on all investments, so you will find that effective personal financial planning requires you to have an understanding of the tax laws and how they impact investment decisions.

Axiom 7: Stuff Happens, or the Importance of Liquidity

Although much of the focus of personal financial planning is on long-term investing with lifetime goals in mind, you must also plan for the unexpected. If liquid funds are not available, an unexpected need, such as job loss or injury, may force you to liquidate a longer-term investment. The unexpected forces us to act immediately, which might entail selling real estate when prices are low or selling common stock and, as a result, taking on an unwanted tax liability. Such actions might ruin your best-laid plans and cause you to miss opportunities. For example, if an emergency forced you to sell immediately a rental house you owned, you might receive only a fraction of what you could have sold the property for if you had had 2 or 3 months to sell it. What if you don't have something to sell? The answer is that you'll have to borrow some money fast. That kind of borrowing will probably bring along with it a high interest rate and payments you aren't ready for. Unfortunately, once you take on unplanned borrowing, it's generally pretty tough to pay it off. We can't emphasize enough the importance of having adequate liquid funds available.

Efficient Market
A situation in which investment prices instantly reflect all publicly available information and, as a result, the price of any investment accurately reflects the best estimate of its value.

Axiom 8: Nothing Happens Without a Plan—Even (or Especially) a Simple Plan

Most people spend more time planning their summer vacation than they do planning their financial future. It's incredibly easy to avoid thinking about retirement, to avoid just thinking about how you're going to pay for your children's education, and to avoid thinking—at least when it comes to unpleasantries such as tightening your financial belt and saving money. We began this book with the statement that it is easier to spend than to save. We can go beyond even that and say it is easier to think about how you're going to spend your money than it is to think about how you're going to save your money. However, if you're like most people, you can probably spend money without thinking about it, but you can't save money without thinking about it. That's the problem. Saving isn't a natural event. It must be planned. Unfortunately, by the same token, planning isn't natural either. For that reason, although an elaborate, complicated plan might be ideal, in general it never comes to fruition. Start off with a modest, uncomplicated financial plan. Once the discipline of saving becomes second nature, or at least accepted behavior, modify and expand your plan. The bottom line is that a financial plan cannot be postponed. The longer you put it off, the more difficult accomplishing goals becomes. As a result, when goals look insurmountable, they may not be attempted.

Axiom 9: The Best Protection Is Knowledge

In your personal finance affairs, the easiest cop-out is to rely on someone else for guidance and advice. Although a professional financial planner can many times do wonders in helping set up and establish a lifetime financial plan, you simply must take responsibility for your own affairs. Knowledge is your best friend for four major reasons. First, without an understanding of personal financial planning, you are a prime target for the unethical and incompetent. Unfortunately, the personal finance arena has attracted its share of incompetent and unscrupulous characters. Any time the primary resource that is being dealt with is money, an entire cast of dubious characters will most certainly be lurking around, waiting to take more than their share. Second, an appreciation of personal finance and valuation will provide you with an understanding of the importance of planning for your future. Third, without an understanding of personal finance, and valuation in particular, you will not have the ability to take advantage of changes in the economy and interest rates that spontaneously occur. Finally, because financial problems in real life seldom perfectly reflect textbook problems and solutions, you must be able to abstract from what you learn in order to apply it. The only way you can effectively abstract something is to understand it. To invest intelligently in finance, you must understand the process of valuation and the risk-return relationship from Axiom 1. As with most else in life, it's much easier to do it right if you understand what you're doing.

Axiom 10: Protect Yourself Against Major Catastrophes— The Case for Insurance

The worst time to find out that you don't have the right amount or right kind of insurance is just after a tragedy occurs. With terminology like "double indemnity rider" and "accelerated death benefits rider," it almost appears as if the insurance industry has created an incomprehensible language of its own. Fortunately, this is not the case. However, as witnessed by the devastating losses associated with recent hurricanes in the Southeast, floods in the Midwest, and earthquakes in California, not everyone has adequate levels of catastrophe insurance.

As you 'll see, insurance is an unusual item to purchase. In fact, most people don't "buy" insurance, they're "sold" insurance. It's generally the insurance salesperson who initiates the sale and leads the client through the process of determining what to purchase. What makes this process a problem is that it is extremely difficult to compare policies, because of the many subtle differences they contain. Moreover, most individuals have insurance, but have never read their insurance policies because insurance is dull. However, to avoid the consequences of a major tragedy, you need to buy the kind of insurance that's right for you and to know what your insurance policy really says.

The focus of insurance should be on major catastrophes—those events that, although remote, can be financially devastating. These are the events that you can't afford, and these are the events that insurance should provide you protection against.

Axiom 11: The Time Dimension of Risk, or Why Investments Become Less Risky When You Plan to Hold Them Longer

In general, the longer you hold an investment, the less risky it becomes. Take stocks, for example—although the same principle holds for all investments. Over the past 71 years, large-company stock prices have risen at an average rate of 10.71 percent per year. However, to say the least, it has not been a smooth ride. The problem with stocks is that "on average" may not be what you actually get. You may, for whatever reason, put your money in the stock market during the wrong period. As a result, if you need your money for your child's college education, which begins next year, the stock market is not the right place to invest it. You do not want to stake your child's college education on the hope that this will be a good year, or, more importantly, that this will not be a bad year. However, if you are in your 20s and saving for your retirement, investing in the stock market isn't nearly so risky. Although you can almost guarantee that there will be some down times, there will also be some up times canceling them out. As a result, by investing for a longer period, the exceptionally good and exceptionally bad times cancel each other out, giving your investment less risk.

Axiom 12: The Agency Problem in Personal Finance— Differentiating Between Advice and a Sales Pitch

Whereas your goal may be to accumulate and protect your wealth, the agency problem may interfere with the implementation of this goal. The **agency problem** in personal finance is the result of the fact that those who act as your agents—insurance salespeople, personal financial advisors, and stockbrokers—may actually be acting in *their own* interests rather than in *your* best interest. For example, an insurance salesperson, motivated by the commission, may try to sell you insurance that you don't need. Similarly, a personal financial advisor may try to sell you financial products, such as insurance policies or mutual funds, that are more expensive than similar products that are available because a hefty commission is received on them. The agency problem doesn't mean you should avoid insurance salespeople or financial planners, but that you should choose them carefully. Just as you pick a competent and trustworthy doctor, so should you pick a financial planner. If you trust your doctor—or financial planner—you have to believe that your best interests are at heart. Just keep your eyes open.

Of course, you must be aware of ulterior motives in making financial decisions. This brings us back to **Axiom 9: The Best Protection Is Knowledge**, for without an understanding of the world of investments, you may be forced to rely on agents who are less concerned with your financial well-being and more concerned with taking your money. If you need professional help, we suggest that you look very carefully before you choose an advisor, and never choose at random. Try to find an advisor who fits your needs and has a proven record of ethical and effective assistance to clients.

Agency Problem
A condition in which those who act as your agents—insurance salespeople, personal financial advisors, and stockbrokers—may actually be acting in their own interests rather than your best interest.

Axiom 13: Pay Yourself First—Making Your Financial Well-Being the Top Priority

It's much easier to save than to spend, right? No, just checking—you know the opposite is true. For most people, savings are a residual. That means that you spend what you like and save what is left, and the amount that you save is simply what you earn minus what you spend. When you pay yourself first, what you spend becomes the residual. That is, you first set aside your savings, and what is left becomes the amount you can spend.

By paying yourself first, you acknowledge the fact that your long-term goals are of paramount importance. "Buying into" these goals is the first expenditure you make, which ensures the fact that these goals actually get funded. In short, this axiom dictates a behavioral pattern in which saving for long-term goals becomes automatic, and excuses for why this month's savings can be passed up no longer work.

Axiom 14: Money Isn't Everything

The purpose of personal financial planning is to allow you to extend your financial planning beyond the present—to allow you to achieve goals that are well off in the future. In effect, personal financial planning allows you to be realistic about your finances—to act your wage. Unfortunately, for some the financial goals become all consuming. As a result, some people see nothing but dollar signs and lose a healthy perspective on what is actually important in life. In the movie *Arthur* there is an exchange between Dudley Moore and Liza Minelli in which Moore, who plays Arthur Bach, says, "Money has screwed me up my whole life. I've always been rich, and I've never been happy." To this Minelli, who plays Linda Marolla (Arthur's girlfriend), replies, "Well, I've always been poor, and I've usually been happy." Arthur's mother then steps in and responds, "I've always been rich, and I've always been happy!" Money doesn't necessarily bring on happiness; however, facing college expenses or retirement without the necessary funding certainly brings on anxiety.

Axiom 15: Just Do It!

Making the commitment to actually get started may be the most difficult step in the entire personal financial planning process. However, the positive reinforcement associated with making financial progress toward your goals and taking control of your financial affairs generally means that, once you take your first steps, the following steps become much easier.

One of your investment allies is stronger now than it ever will be. That investment ally is time. Because of **Axiom 2: The Time Value of Money—A Dollar Received Today Is Worth More Than a Dollar Received in the Future**, taking investment action now—just doing it—becomes even more critical. If you are 20 right now and you are saving your money at 12 percent for retirement at age 67, a dollar saved today is worth about $11 saved at age 40, and is worth about the same as $40 saved at age 50. Table 1.5 provides a listing of the level of monthly saving necessary to accumulate $1 million by age 67. As you can see, it's a lot easier if you start early. The bottom line is that with investing and financial planning, there simply is no good reason to postpone them. Just do it!

A Final Note on the Axioms

Hopefully, these axioms are as much statements of common sense as they are theoretical statements. They provide the logic behind what is to follow, and we will build on them and attempt to draw out their implications for financial decision making. As we continue, try to keep in mind that, although the topics being treated may change from chapter to chapter, the logic driving our treatment of them is constant and finds its roots in these 15 axioms.

TABLE 1.5

Importance of Starting Early—Just Do It!—to Accumulate $1 Million at Age 67 Investing Your Money at 12%	
Making Your Last Payment on Your 67th Birthday and Your First When You Turn	**Your Monthly Payment Would Have to Be**
20	$ 33
21	37
22	42
23	47
24	53
25	60
26	67
27	76
28	85
29	96
30	109
31	123
32	138
33	156
34	176
35	199
40	366
50	1,319
60	6,253

SUMMARY

Personal financial planning will allow you to accomplish the following:

- *Manage the Unplanned.* A sound financial plan will allow you to withstand minor financial setbacks along the way.
- *Accumulate Wealth for Special Expenses.* Financial planning helps you to map out a strategy to pay for such expenses as college for your children, a summer home, and travel—all expenses that will probably be impossible if you don't plan ahead for them.
- *Realistically Save for Retirement.* A strong financial plan will let you realistically look at the costs of retirement and develop a plan that allows you to live a life of retirement ease.
- *"Cover Your Assets."* A complete financial plan will include adequate insurance at as low a cost as possible.
- *Invest Intelligently.* Before making a financial plan, arm yourself with an understanding of the basic principles of investments.
- *Minimize Your Payments to Uncle Sam.* Part of financial planning is to help you legally reduce the amount of tax you have to pay on your earnings.

There are five basic steps to personal financial planning:

Step 1:   Evaluate Your Financial Health.

Step 2:   Define Your Financial Goals.

Step 3:   Develop a Plan of Action.

Step 4: Implement Your Plan.

Step 5: Review Your Progress, Reevaluate, and Revise Your Plan.

In fact, the last step in financial planning is often the first. No plan is fixed for life. Still, this fact does not in any way take away from the importance of setting up a personal financial plan and using it.

To reach your financial goals you must first set them. This process involves writing down your financial goals and attaching costs to them, along with when the money to accomplish those goals will be needed. Your goals should reflect your financial and life situation, and once you have set your finalized goals in place, they will become the cornerstone of your personal financial plan, serving as a guide to action and a benchmark for evaluation of the effectiveness of the plan.

For most people, their goals change throughout their lives. Many of these changes are due to unexpected events, and many changes are based on a general financial life cycle pattern that applies to most people, even you. There are three stages in the financial life cycle:

Stage 1: The Early Years—A Time of Wealth Accumulation. It's during this period that you must develop a regular pattern of saving. It's also a time of wealth accumulation when you'll be saving more than you spend.

Stage 2: Approaching Retirement—The Golden Years. Stage 2 involves a transition from your earning years, when you will earn more than you spend, to your retirement years, when you will spend more than you earn. Much of what is done involves fine-tuning.

Stage 3: The Retirement Years. During your retirement years, you'll be living off your savings and, perhaps, supplementing this with some part-time work. Once you retire, much of the focus of the final phase of your financial life cycle deals with ensuring continued financial security during retirement.

In general, the more educated you are, the more you will earn. This is because the more special skills and training needed for the job, the higher the pay tends to be.

This chapter closes with an examination of the 15 axioms on which personal financial planning is built and that motivate the techniques and tools introduced in this text.

Axiom 1: The Risk-Return Trade-Off—Investors Don't Take on Additional Risk Unless They Expect to Be Compensated with Additional Return

Axiom 2: The Time Value of Money—A Dollar Received Today Is Worth More Than a Dollar Received in the Future

Axiom 3: Diversification Reduces Risk

Axiom 4: Diversification and Risk—All Risk Is Not Equal, Because Some Risk Can Be Diversified Away and Some Cannot

Axiom 5: The Curse of Competitive Investment Markets — Why It's Hard to Find Exceptionally Profitable Investments

Axiom 6: Taxes Bias Personal Finance Decisions

Axiom 7: Stuff Happens, or the Importance of Liquidity

Axiom 8: Nothing Happens Without a Plan—Even (or Especially) a Simple Plan

Axiom 9: The Best Protection Is Knowledge

Axiom 10: Protect Yourself Against Major Catastrophes—The Case for Insurance

Axiom 11: The Time Dimension of Risk, or Why Investments Become Less Risky When You Plan to Hold Them Longer

Axiom 12: The Agency Problem in Personal Finance—Differentiating Between Advice and a Sales Pitch

The ABC's of Finding an Advisor

☑ **Analyze your needs.** Are you a "do-it-yourselfer" who needs just a basic plan to follow, or do you need assistance in implementing any recommendations? Are you just starting out, or do you have a family and estate planning needs? Perhaps you have both personal and business concerns, such as a professional practice or your own firm.

☑ **Decide what type of advisor you want.** Are you set on a "fee only" planner? Do you like the idea of a general practitioner, or does your situation dictate the need for a highly specialized individual, such as an estate attorney? Once you've figured out what type of advisor you want, attend seminars, or better yet, ask for referrals from friends and family.

☑ **Visit with one or more advisors before you make a decision.** Most offer a complementary initial consultation. *Caution:* Don't feel you have to keep shopping if you're fortunate to find the right person on the first try.

☑ **Investigate your candidates.** Ask for an explanation of services or a sample plan. Check for complaints and resolutions through the Better Business Bureau or regulatory bodies such as the CFP Board of Standards. Find out how long the firm has been in business (will they be there when you need them?). How is the advisor compensated?

☑ **Set a deadline for selecting your advisor and stick to it.** I have met people who admit to spending 5+ years searching for the "perfect planner."

☑ **Open your mind!** Gray hair and wrinkles don't always mean wisdom, and peach fuzz is not synonymous with fresh ideas. If the candidates are relatively new in practice, make sure they have, or are pursuing, a professional designation and that they have associates who can take over for them if they don't continue in the practice.

☑ **Rely on your knowledge and instincts.** If you're not comfortable enough with the person to reveal *all* your financial details, run, don't walk, away. Annoying "faults" and suspicions become major roadblocks with time. Select someone you like, trust, and respect—someone you think could be your lifetime financial advisor. As Mom always said, "Don't date 'em, if you wouldn't marry 'em."

Axiom 13: Pay Yourself First—Making Your Financial Well-Being the Top Priority

Axiom 14: Money Isn't Everything

Axiom 15: Just Do It!

Review Questions [and Related Learning Objectives (LO)]

1. Why do people need to plan their finances? Why should they want to? (LO 1)
2. Explain why it is difficult to manage your finances. (LO 1)
3. What are the five steps that make up the financial planning process? (LO 2)
4. Procrastination, or postponing the development and implementation of a financial plan, is a common problem. Why? (LO 1, 2, 6)
5. List and explain the four common concerns that should guide all financial plans. (LO 2)
6. What fundamental financial goals should everyone consider as a foundation for developing a financial plan of action? (LO 2, 3)

7. Compare and contrast short-term, intermediate-term, and long-term goals. Give an example of each. (LO 3)
8. Why are financial goals the cornerstone of your financial plan? (LO 3)
9. List and characterize the stages of the life cycle. (LO 4)
10. What is the relationship among income/earnings potential, education, and standard of living or lifestyle? (LO 5)
11. For what two reasons do investors demand that they be compensated when making an investment? (LO 6)
12. Define the terms "maturity date," "diversification," and "liquidity." Give an example to illustrate each concept. (LO 6)
13. Time is a central concept in Axioms 2, 11, 13, and 15. Explain the importance of time in the context of each.

Problems and Activities

1. As a result of studying personal financial planning, what changes can you hope to accomplish in your financial situation? What financial problems might you avoid? (LO 1)
2. List the five steps in the financial planning process. For each, list an activity, or financial task, that you should be accomplishing. (LO 1)
3. Financial goals should be specific, realistic, prioritized, and anchored in time. Using these characteristics, identify five financial goals for yourself. (LO 3)
4. As the cornerstone of your financial plan, goals should reflect your lifestyle, serve as a guide to action, and act as a benchmark for evaluating the effectiveness of your plan. For one of the goals identified in problem 3, explain this statement. (LO 3)
5. The goal of financing the cost of education is obviously important in your present stage of the financial life cycle. Could this goal continue to be important in future stages? How? Why? Explain your answer. (LO 3,4)
6. Explain how **Axiom 7: Stuff Happens, or the Importance of Liquidity** and **Axiom 10: Protect Yourself Against Major Catastrophes—The Case for Insurance** may be related. What are you currently doing to protect yourself, and your financial future, from "stuff" and other major catastrophes?

Suggested Projects

1. Interview three people in charge of managing their household's finances, each from a different stage of the life cycle. Inquire about their financial planning process and their strategies to save for retirement. Share your findings with the class. Was procrastination a problem? (LO 1,3,5)
2. A financial plan can be thought of as a "financial road map to guide you through life." Develop a visual display that illustrates this principle and the five steps of the financial planning process. Try to incorporate examples that illustrate how the "new roads" on the map may change over the life cycle. (LO 2,3,4)
3. Identify two professionals in your community who could assist you in accomplishing your financial goals. Rate each professional using Axiom 12. (LO 2,6)
4. Talk with your academic advisor and a professional employed in a career field that interests you. What educational requirements are necessary for entry in the field? Is continuing education required for advancement? What salary increases result from additional education? (LO 5)
5. As a group project, have each member of your group visit a financial professional (for example, benefits officer, stockbroker, insurance salesperson, loan officer, banker, financial planner, and so on). Present the list of 15 axioms that form the foundations of personal finance. Ask the professional to pick the three to five axioms that are considered most important to personal financial success. Share the results in your group and compare your findings. Which axioms appear to be *most* important? (LO 6)

Discussion Case 1

Fred, a machinist, and Daphne, a graduate student, are newlyweds who've just returned from their honeymoon in the Bahamas. Now that they're settling down, they've been encouraged by their parents to establish some personal and financial goals for their future. However, they don't know how to set or achieve these goals because neither one took a personal finance class. They know that they'd like to own their home and have children, but those are the only goals they've considered. Fred knows of a financial advisor who might be able to help them with their predicament, but they don't think that they can afford professional help. Daphne's father thinks that Fred should return to school instead of continuing as a machinist, but Fred doesn't like the idea of giving up his job.

Questions

1. If you were serving as the couple's financial advisor, how would you explain the five steps in financial planning and their importance to financial success? (LO 2)

2. In what stage of the financial life cycle are Fred and Daphne? (LO 4)

3. What financial goals (short-, intermediate-, and long-term) would you determine to be the most important or least important to Daphne and Fred, considering their current life cycle stage? Support your answer. *Hint:* See Figure 1.2. (LO 3)

4. Why might Daphne's father think that Fred should return to school? Do you think returning to school for an advanced degree has any financial benefits? (LO 5)

5. Do you think a course in personal finance would have better prepared them to handle their finances? *Hint:* Consider Axioms 8, 9, 14, and 15. (LO 6)

6. In your own words, explain to Fred and Daphne why personal financial planning is crucial to their future. (LO 1)

Discussion Case 2

Doug and Marita Jones from Rochester, New York, are the proud but surprised new parents of twin baby girls. They weren't prepared for twins, and the extra baby has left their financial plans in ruins. They'd been planning to pay for education costs for their two-year old, Derek, and one new baby, but now they're unsure whether they'll be able to send three children to college at the same time. The Joneses want to start over with new objectives and reestablish a long-term plan that takes all three of their children into account. Marita has told Doug that she wants to attend a personal finance seminar given at a local conference center, but Doug doesn't think they can afford the cost. After all, he points out, they have a pile of medical bills to deal with and their day care costs are tripling. Marita feels that their new tight finances are the main reason they need to go to the seminar. Marita's not sure how they can arrange their finances to meet their goals without some kind of help.

Questions

1. Using the information in Table 1.2, estimate the cost of raising the twins from birth to age 18 if the Joneses' current annual income is approximately $75,000 and both parents plan to continue working full-time.

2. With three children to consider, how might Axioms 7, 10, and 11 affect the Joneses? (LO 6)

3. Why should Doug and Marita establish a financial plan as soon as possible? How would a plan help them ensure their financial future?

4. Now that the Joneses have an idea about what they want to do with their money in the future, what's the first thing they need to do to establish a plan of action?

5. How could attending the seminar help the Joneses establish a smart financial plan? What information do you think the seminar would need to convey to be worthwhile?

Chapter 2

FINANCIAL PLANNING:
Measuring Your Financial Health and Establishing a Plan

Dennis Rodman didn't play basketball in high school. In fact, when he graduated he stood only 5 foot 11. It wasn't until age 20, when he was working the graveyard shift at the Dallas–Fort Worth Airport and had grown 8 inches, that he decided to pursue basketball. With this goal in mind, he entered Cooke County Junior College in Texas and later transferred to Southeastern Oklahoma State. Although he had a strong college career, he was still relatively obscure when the Detroit Pistons drafted him in the second round of the 1986 NBA draft. He played in Detroit for seven seasons and was a major part of the Pistons "Bad Boys" teams that won two NBA championships. Then, prior to the 1994–1995 season, the Pistons traded Rodman to San Antonio. Finally, in 1995, he was sent to Chicago, where he helped the Bulls to several NBA championships. When basketball's Bad (as he wants to be) Boy got to Chicago, he had a lot of recognition, notoriety, and even infamy to his name, but not much money. Rodman had managed to go

through a relationship with Madonna, countless hair dyes and tattoos—and millions of dollars. Despite all the money he had made during his pro career, Rodman arrived in Chicago broke—in fact, about $1 million in debt, and that after making $2.5 million a year. After a year in Chicago, though, his personal finances completely turned around. How did he do it? With the help of a professional financial advisor, he established a financial plan and then lived by it.

What's involved in establishing such a plan and

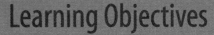

Learning Objectives

After reading this chapter you should be able to:

1. Calculate your level of net worth or wealth using a balance sheet.

2. Analyze where your money comes from and where it goes using an income statement.

3. Use ratios to identify your financial strengths and weaknesses.

4. Set up a sound record-keeping system to track your income and expenditures.

5. Implement a financial plan or budget that will provide for the level of savings needed to achieve your goals.

6. Decide what role, if any, a professional financial planner will play in your financial affairs.

taking control of your financial life? The first step to financial control is determining where you stand. Once you know where you stand, you need to figure out where you want to go, set budget goals, and allocate the necessary resources. For Dennis Rodman, this process involved a great deal of restraint—he set financial goals and did what it took to achieve them. This involved being put on a $1,000 per week "budget." Today he is living what he calls a "debt free life," and has even set up a trust for Alexis, his daughter from his first marriage. In Rodman's words, "It was stupid not to plan ahead. Now the bottom line is, if I save and stay conservative, five years down the road I'll be set for life."

It's incredibly easy to avoid thinking about your financial future. For most people their present financial situation is difficult enough. However, don't forget **Axiom 8: Nothing Happens Without a Plan—Even (or Especially) a Simple Plan**. If you're like most people, you can probably spend money without thinking about it, but you can't save money without thinking about it. For Dennis Rodman, that certainly was the case, and, as he saw, the consequences can be grave. Saving isn't a natural event. It must be planned.

Planning and budgeting require control, they don't come naturally. For Rodman, financial planning involved looking into the future, facing financial reality and the sacrifices that it brings on, and taking action, something that no doubt was not fun to face. However, without the ability to measure his financial health and develop a plan and budget to achieve his goals, Rodman's goals would simply never be achieved. Showing financial restraint isn't as much fun as spending with reckless abandon, but it's a lot more fun than winding up broke. Making and sticking to a plan isn't necessarily easy, and it often involves what some people would consider sacrifices, such as not buying tickets to Lollapalooza if you can't really afford them. The fact is, though, that the rewards of taking financial control are worth any small sacrifices and more. Just ask Dennis Rodman. He went from being the man with no money to being the man with a plan.

AXIOM #8

Nothing Happens Without a Plan—Even (or Especially) a Simple Plan

Personal Balance Sheet

A statement of your financial position on a given date. It includes the assets you own, the debt or liabilities you have incurred, and your level of wealth, which is referred to as net worth.

Assets

What you own.

Liabilities

Something that is owed or the borrowing of money.

Net Worth or Equity

A measure of the level of your wealth. It is determined by subtracting the level of your debt or borrowing from the value of your assets.

FIGURE 2.1

USING YOUR BALANCE SHEET TO MEASURE YOUR WEALTH

Before you can decide how much you need to save to reach your financial goals, you first have to measure your financial condition—what you own and what you owe. Corporations use a balance sheet for this purpose and so can you. A **personal balance sheet** is a statement of your financial position on a given date—a snapshot of your financial status at a particular point in time. It lists the **assets** you own, the debt or **liabilities** you've incurred, and your general level of wealth, which is your **net worth** or **equity**. Assets represent what you own, whereas liabilities represent your debt or what you owe. To determine your level of wealth or net worth, you merely need to subtract your level of debt or borrowing from the value of your assets.

Figure 2.1 shows the relationship of these three main balance sheet elements. As you can see, a balance sheet gets its name from the fact that the two sides of a balance sheet have to balance, or be equal. The first major section of your balance sheet represents all your assets—the things you own. All your possessions are considered assets regardless of whether or not you still owe money on them. From the value of your assets, you subtract the amount of debt you owe. This total, your assets minus your borrowing, equals your net worth. This means that your net worth or wealth is actually how much you own after all borrowing has been paid off. We now examine everything that goes into putting together a personal balance sheet. Figure 2.2 provides a sample balance sheet worksheet.

Your Assets: What You Own

To create a balance sheet you must first estimate the value of all your assets, and when you do this, list your assets using their **fair market value**, not what they cost or what they will be worth a year from now. The fair market value can be more or less than the price you paid for a given asset, depending on what others are willing to pay for that asset now. Remember, a balance sheet is a snapshot in time, so all values must be current.

As Figure 2.2 shows, there are a number of different types of assets. A monetary asset is basically a liquid asset—one that is either cash or can easily be turned into cash with little or no loss in value. Monetary assets include the cash you hold, your checking and savings account balances, and your money market funds. These are your cash and cash equivalents that you use for everyday life. They also provide the necessary liquidity in case of an emergency.

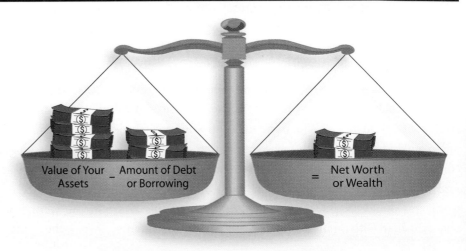

Net Worth

Value of Your Assets − Amount of Debt or Borrowing = Net Worth or Wealth

Assets (What You Own)

A.	Monetary Assets (bank account, etc.)	_____
B.	Investments	+ _____
C.	Retirement Plans	+ _____
D.	Housing (market value)	+ _____
E.	Automobiles	+ _____
F.	Personal Property	+ _____
G.	Other Assets	+ _____
H.	Your Total Assets (add lines A–G)	= _____

Liabilities or Debt (What You Owe)

Current Debt

I.	Current Bills	_____
J.	Credit Card Debt	+ _____

Long-Term Debt

K.	Housing	_____
L.	Automobile Loans	+ _____
M.	Other Debt	+ _____
N.	Your Total Debt (add lines I–M)	= _____

Your Net Worth

H.	Total Assets	_____
N.	Less: Total Debt	– _____
O.	Equals: Your Net Worth	= _____

The second major category of assets, investments, involves such financial assets as common stocks, mutual funds, or bonds. In general, the purpose of these assets is to accumulate wealth to satisfy a goal like buying a house or having sufficient savings for college or retirement. You can usually determine the value of your investments by reading the financial quotes in *The Wall Street Journal*. Your insurance policy may also be an investment asset. Many insurance policies have a savings element that accumulates over time. This type of insurance policy would be an investment asset because its purpose is to generate wealth to satisfy the goal of providing for your loved ones in the case of your death. For example, with permanent or cash value life insurance, which accounts for more than half of all life insurance policies sold in the United States, the policy can be terminated prior to the insured's death, at which time the policyholder will receive the cash value of the policy. If you have an insurance policy with a cash surrender value (the dollar amount that you would receive if you cashed in the policy today), then the cash surrender value of this policy should be included as part of your investment assets. If you have an annuity—a contract written by an insurance company that provides the contract holder with a constant income, generally for the remainder of the holder's life—the cash value of this annuity should also be included as one of your investment

Fair Market Value
What an asset could be sold for rather than what it cost or what it will be worth sometime in the future.

assets. Finally, any real estate that you've purchased for investment purposes should also appear as an asset. The common thread among all these investment assets is that they're not assets that you use, as you would use a car or a house. Instead, investments are assets that have been purchased for the purpose of generating wealth.

The next category of assets is retirement plans. These include investments made by you or your employer aimed directly at achieving your goal of saving for retirement. Retirement plans are usually in the form of IRAs, 401(k) or 403(b) plans, Keogh plans, SEP-IRA plans, and company pension plans. IRAs are individual retirement accounts to which individuals, depending upon their income level, can make a tax-deductible contribution of up to $2,000 per year. The 401(k) and 403(b) plans allow employees to place a portion of their salary into a tax-deferred investment account, and Keogh and SEP-IRA plans are tax-deductible retirement plans for self-employed individuals. The current value of your stake in your company's pension plan should also be included as a retirement plan asset. If you work for a company that offers a pension plan, the easiest way to value your stake in the plan is to call up your benefits office and ask them how much it's worth.

Your house comprises another asset category. Although a house is an asset that you use—a **tangible asset**—it usually holds the majority of your savings. The value of your house recorded on the balance sheet should be its fair market value, even though at that price it may take several months for it to sell. You might consult with a real estate agent for help in valuing your home. Keep in mind, though, that even if you owe money on your home, it's still yours. For example, you may have a large home mortgage, but you still own your home—you just borrowed a lot of money to buy it.

Your car, truck, motorcycle, or other vehicle also gets its own asset category. Like your home, your vehicle is a tangible asset—one you probably use on a daily basis. However, unlike your home, your vehicle is likely to be worth less than you paid for it. The fair market value for vehicles almost always goes down, often starting right after you take it home from the showroom. You can find the fair market value for most vehicles in an automotive **Blue Book**. Note that you shouldn't include any cars you lease as assets. If the car is leased, you don't hold title to it and thus don't actually own it. In effect, you are just renting it for an extended period. Likewise, a company car that you get to use but don't own wouldn't count as an asset.

Personal property is another category of assets. All personal property consists of tangible assets. Basically, personal property is all your possessions—furniture, appliances, jewelry, TVs, and so forth. In general, although you may have spent a good deal of money on these items, their fair market value will be only a fraction of their original amount.

Finally, the "other" category includes anything that has not yet been accounted for. For example, you might have an ownership share in a business, you might own a massive collection of semivaluable (or so you think) Pez dispensers, or you might be owed money by your deadbeat friend. All of these count as assets and must appear at their fair market value on your balance sheet. Of course, if your friend is a deadbeat, the amount owed shouldn't appear as an asset—you'll never see it!

Summed up, these asset categories represent the total value of everything you own. You might be surprised to find out you are worth much more than you originally thought.

Tangible Asset

A physical asset, such as a house or a car, as opposed to an investment.

Blue Book

A listing of used-car prices, giving the average price a particular year and model sells for and what you might expect to receive for it as a trade-in. Blue Books are generally available at public libraries and banks.

The Facts of Life

Do you hope to make a million dollars at your job? Well, you probably will. Over the course of your life you'll work for an average of 85,000 hours. Assuming you make an average of $12 per hour (roughly $25,000 per year), you'll have earned $1.02 million by the time you retire. If you could save it all, you'd be set!

Liabilities: What You Owe

A liability is anything you owe. It may refer to such debts as your unpaid credit card balance or your unpaid student loan. In any case, it's a debt that you have taken on and that you must repay in the future. Most financial planners classify liabilities as either current or long-term. Current liabilities are those that must be paid off within the next year, and long-term liabilities come due beyond a year's time. In listing your liabilities, be sure to include only the unpaid balances on those liabilities. Remember, you owe only the unpaid portion of any loan.

In general, your unpaid bills and credit card debt will be the only sources of current liabilities. Unpaid utility bills, past due rent, cable TV bills, insurance premiums that you owe, and so forth all involve money you currently owe and as such should be included as liabilities. In fact, even if you have not yet received a bill for a purchase you made on credit, the amount you owe on this purchase should be included as a liability. Similarly, the unpaid balance on your credit cards represents a current liability because it's a debt that you should pay off within a year.

Long-term debt tends to consist of debt on larger assets, such as your home or car, although your biggest source of long-term debt right now is probably your student loan. Because of the nature of the assets it finances, long-term debt almost always involves larger amounts owed than does current debt. If you think about it, the very reason long-term debt covers the long term is that it involves sums too large for the average individual to be able to pay off within one year. The largest debt you ever take on, and thus the longest-term debt you ever take on, will probably be the mortgage on your home.

Car loans are another major category of long-term debt. Just as a leased car is not considered an asset, the remaining lease obligation should not be considered a liability, or something that you owe. In effect, you are "renting" your car when you lease it. Actually, it's a very fine line between a debt obligation and a lease contract—some leases simply can't be broken so they may be considered debt. However, the point to keep in mind is that things such as future lease payments, future insurance payments, and future rent payments are something you may owe in the future, but they are not something you owe right now.

Finally, any other loans that you have outstanding should be included. For example, student loans, loans on your life insurance policy, bank loans, and installment loans are liabilities. Together, long-term debt and current liabilities represent what you owe.

Stop and Think

If you ever saw the movie *Willie Wonka and the Chocolate Factory,* or read the book *Charlie and the Chocolate Factory,* on which the movie is based, you'll remember a little girl named Veruca Salt. She was a nasty piece of work. She constantly demanded material things, screaming out, **"I WANT IT NOW!"** Her desires and the way she acted were clearly out of control. She didn't make it through the story—but if she had, with that attitude her financial future would not have been very bright. There's no easier way to foil a financial plan than with a lack of control and impulse buying. Control is crucial.

Your Net Worth: A Measure of Your Wealth

Your net worth represents the level of wealth that you or your family have accumulated. To calculate your net worth, simply subtract your liabilities from the value of your assets. If your liabilities are greater than the value of your assets, then your net worth has a negative value, and you're considered **insolvent**. Insolvency results from consuming more than you take in financially, and in some instances it can lead to bankruptcy.

What, then, is a "good" level of net worth? That depends upon your goals and your place in the financial life cycle. You would expect a 25-year-old to have a considerably lower net worth than would a 45-year-old. Likewise, a 45-year-old who has saved for college for three children may have a higher net worth than a 45-year-old with no children. Which one is in better financial shape? The answer doesn't necessarily rest on who has the larger net worth, but on who has done a better job of achieving financial goals. Just to give you an idea of where most people stand, Table 2.1 presents Americans' average net worth in 1993, as well as a listing of the average value of most Americans.

Your goal in financial planning is to manage your net worth or wealth in such a way that your goals are met in a timely fashion. You use the balance sheet to measure your progress toward these goals, to monitor your financial well-being. You will use the balance sheet to detect changes in your financial well-being that might otherwise go unnoticed and correct them early on. In effect, you will use the balance sheet to monitor your financial health in the same way a doctor would use a medical instrument to monitor your physical health. It provides you with an understanding of how "healthy" you are in addition to alerting you to when you have taken a turn in the wrong direction.

An Example Balance Sheet for Lou and Mary Grant

To illustrate the construction and use of a balance sheet, we have a sample from Lou and Mary Grant in Figure 2.3. Remember, a balance sheet provides a snapshot of an

Insolvent

The condition in which you owe more money than your assets are worth.

TABLE 2.1

What We're Worth (percent of U.S. households with selected assets ranked by median value for households that own them, 1993)

The biggest egg in most people's nests is the nest itself—their homes and the ones they rent to others.

	Percent of Households Owning	Median Value[a]
Total net worth	—	$37,587
Equity in own home	64.3%	$46,669
Rental property	8.4	29,300
Other financial investments	5.2	21,001
Other real estate	9.3	19,415
Other interest-earning assets	8.6	12,998
IRA/Keogh accounts	23.1	12,985
Business or profession	10.8	7,000
Stocks and mutual fund shares	20.9	6,960
Vehicles	85.7	5,140
Interest-earning bank accounts	71.1	2,999
U.S. savings bonds	18.5	775
Checking accounts	45.9	499

[a]Notes: Sum of assets adds to more than total net worth because not all households own all assets.
SOURCE: "Who's Holding Onto Wealth?" *American Demographics*, March 1996, p. 22. Used by permission.

individual's or family's financial worth at a given point in time. As investment values fluctuate on a daily basis with the movements in the stock market, so does net worth. The balance sheet in Figure 2.3 was constructed on December 31, 1997, and reflects the value of the Grants' assets, liabilities, and net worth on that specific date.

FIGURE 2.3

A Balance Sheet for Mary and Lou Grant
December 31, 1997

Assets (What You Own)

	Cash		340
	Checking	+	250
	Savings/CDs	+	1,500
	Money Market Funds	+	1,500
A.	**Monetary Assets**	A. =	**3,590**
	Mutual Funds		5,600
	Stocks	+	8,500
	Bonds	+	1,000
	Life Insurance (cash value)	+	0
	Cash Value of Annuities	+	0
	Investment Real Estate (REITs, partnerships)	+	0
B.	**Investments**	B. =	**15,100**
	401(k) and 403(b)		0
	Company Pension	+	8,000
	Keogh	+	2,500
	IRA	+	8,000
C.	**Retirement Plans**	C. =	**18,500**
	Primary Residence		170,000
	2nd Home	+	0
	Time-Shares/Condominiums	+	70,000
D.	**Housing (market value)**	D. =	**240,000**
	Automobile #1		9,000
	Automobile #2	+	3,000
E.	**Automobiles**	E. =	**12,000**
	Collectibles		3,000
	Boats	+	0
	Furniture	+	8,000
F.	**Personal Property**	F. =	**11,000**
	Money Owed You		0
	Market Value of Your Business	+	0
	Other	+	0
G.	**Other Assets**	G. =	**0**
H.	**Total Assets (add lines A–G)**	H. =	**$300,190**

(continued)

FIGURE 2.3

(continued)

Liabilities or Debt (What You Owe)

I.	Current Bills (unpaid balance)	I. =	350
	Visa		1,150
	MasterCard	+	0
	Other Credit Cards	+	0
J.	Credit Card Debt	J. =	1,150
	First Mortgage		105,000
	2nd Home Mortgage	+	52,000
	Home Equity Loan	+	9,000
K.	Housing	K. =	166,000
	Automobile #1		3,000
	Automobile #2	+	0
L.	Automobile Loans	L. =	3,000
	College Loans		4,000
	Loans on Life Insurance Policies	+	0
	Bank Loans	+	0
	Installment Loans	+	1,000
	Other	+	0
M.	Other Debt	M. =	5,000
N.	Total Debt (add lines I–M)	N. =	$175,500

Your Net Worth

H.	Total Assets	H. +	$300,190
N.	Less: Total Debt	N. −	$175,500
O.	Equals: Net Worth	O. =	$124,690

To gain an understanding of what their balance sheet means, let's look at the Grants' background. The Grants are both 35 years old, have been married for 10 years, and have two children, 4 and 2 years old. Lou is a production supervisor for a large home builder in the Denver, Colorado, area. He's been working there for 13 years, ever since his graduation from college with a degree in building construction. Over that time he has progressed steadily in his job, moving up the corporate ladder to a position where he now has over 200 employees working for him. For Lou, the future looks bright. After college, Mary worked for 9 years as a laboratory technician in a blood bank. When the children arrived, she quit her job and took a part-time job as a medical supplies salesperson, which allowed her to spend most of her time at home raising her children. The Grants live just outside Boulder in an older house they purchased 7 years ago. Since that time they have put an addition on the house as well as remodeled the kitchen and bathrooms. Living in Colorado, they love skiing and hiking in the mountains and have already started taking their kids along. In fact, 6 years ago they purchased a condominium in Vail, and they try to visit it at least twice a month. On the financial front, they don't seem to have serious concerns regarding the future; however, they have begun to save for their children's college education.

Calculating What the Grants Own: Their Total Assets

The Grants' primary investments are in their home and their vacation condominium in Vail, which have market values of $170,000 and $70,000, respectively. They have total monetary assets of $3,590 spread among cash, checking and savings accounts, certificates of deposit, and money market mutual funds. These assets are aimed at both paying off bills and debts that are coming due and providing the Grants with a cash buffer to guard against any unexpected emergencies. Their long-term savings, aimed at providing college funds for their children and building a retirement nest egg for themselves, total $15,100 and are primarily invested in common stock and mutual funds. They also have $18,500 in retirement plans. Their final assets are two cars valued at $12,000, personal property of $8,000, which is mostly furniture, and collectibles valued at $3,000 which include Lou's collection of Three Stooges memorabilia, the highlight of which is a set of letters between Moe and his mother. Thus, the Grants own, or have total assets of, $300,190.

Calculating What the Grants Owe: Their Total Liabilities

Just as the Grants' homes make up their primary assets, their mortgages on these homes make up their primary liabilities. Their mortgage loans total $166,000, which includes a home equity loan of $9,000 taken out 2 years ago to remodel the bathrooms and kitchen area of their primary residence. The Grants have a relatively low level of current liabilities, with only $350 in unpaid bills and an unpaid credit card balance of $1,150. Their other liabilities include an outstanding car loan of $3,000, an education loan of $4,000, and an installment loan of $1,000, associated with the purchase of a big-screen television earlier this year. Thus, the Grants' total liabilities, or what they owe, equals $175,500.

Calculating the Grants' Wealth: Their Net Worth

By subtracting the Grants' total liabilities from their total assets, you can determine the Grants' net worth to be $124,690. This sum represents the amount of wealth the Grants have accumulated as of December 31, 1997. This wealth could have resulted either from the Grants saving money (spending less than they earn) or from the appreciation in value of some of their assets, such as stocks, mutual funds, or their homes. In effect, if the Grants sold all their assets and paid off all their debts, they would have $124,690 in cash. Because the Grants won't be selling off their assets in the near future, what does this net worth figure really mean? Actually, it's a measure by which the Grants will gauge their financial progress. If in future balance sheets their net worth figure is higher, the Grants will know that they're accumulating more wealth for meeting their financial goals. If their net worth goes down, they'll know that they need to be more careful protecting the wealth they have. Still, the balance sheet alone does not give a complete picture of your financial status. You also need a personal income statement.

Income Statement

A statement that tells you where your money has come from and where it has gone over some *period of time*. Although it is generally called an income statement, it is really an income and expenditure statement, because it looks at both what is taken in and what goes out.

USING AN INCOME STATEMENT TO TRACE YOUR MONEY

A balance sheet is like a financial snapshot in that it tells you how much wealth you have accumulated as of a *certain date*. An **income statement** is more like a financial motion picture in that it tells you where your money has come from and where it has gone over some *period of time*, perhaps a month, 6 months, or a year. Actually, although it's generally called an income statement, it's really an income and expenditure, or net income statement, because it looks at both what you take in and what you spend. An income statement can help you stay solvent by telling you whether or not you're earning more than you spend. If you're spending too much, your income statement shows exactly where your money is going so that you can spot problem areas quickly. Of course, if you don't have a spending problem, your income statement tells you how much of your income is available for savings and for meeting your financial goals. With a good income statement, you'll never end another month wondering where all of your money went—you'll already know.

Personal income statements are prepared on a cash basis, meaning they're based entirely on actual cash flows. You record income only when you actually receive money, and you record expenditures only when you actually pay money out. For example, giving someone an IOU wouldn't appear on an income statement, but receiving a paycheck would. Similarly, buying a stereo on credit wouldn't appear on your income statement, but making a payment to the credit card company would. As a result, a personal income statement truly reflects the pattern of cash flows that the individual or family experiences. To construct an income statement, you need only record your income for the given time period and subtract from it the expenses you incurred during that period, which tells you your contribution to savings.

Net Income or Contribution to Savings	=	Income on a Cash Basis	−	Taxes on a Cash Basis	−	Living Expenses on a Cash Basis

Figure 2.4 shows a general outline for an income statement.

Your Income: Where Your Money Comes From

In preparing your income statement, income, or cash inflows, will include such items as wages, salary, bonuses, tips, royalties, and commissions, in addition to any other sources of income you may have. Additional sources of income might include family income, payments from the government (for example, veterans' benefits or welfare income), retirement income, investment income, and those yearly checks you get from Ed McMahon for winning the Publishers' Clearinghouse Sweepstakes. In short, any funds that you actually receive would be considered income. Some of your income may not ever reach your pocketbook. Instead, it may be automatically invested in a voluntary retirement plan, pay for insurance you buy through work, or sent to the government to cover taxes. For example, if your total earnings are $50,000 and you automatically have $10,000 deducted for taxes, then your income would be $50,000 even though your take-home pay is only $40,000. Thus, you must make sure to record the full amount of what you earned—your full earnings and taxes paid, not just the dollar value of your paycheck. The key point here is that any money that you receive, even if you automatically spend it (even for taxes), is considered income at the point in time when it is received.

FIGURE 2.4

A Simplified Income Statement

Your Take-Home Pay

A.	Total Income	A. _____
B.	Total Income Taxes	− B. _____
C.	After-Tax Income Available for Living Expenditures or Take-Home Pay (line A minus line B)	= C. _____

Your Living Expenses

D.	Total Housing Expenditures	D. _____
E.	Total Food Expenditures	+ E. _____
F.	Total Clothing and Personal Care Expenditures	+ F. _____
G.	Total Transportation Expenditures	+ G. _____
H.	Total Recreation Expenditures	+ H. _____
I.	Total Medical Expenditures	+ I. _____
J.	Total Insurance Expenditures	+ J. _____
K.	Total Other Expenditures	+ K. _____
L.	Total Living Expenditures (add lines D–K)	= L. _____
M.	Income Available for Savings and Investment (line C minus line L)	= M. _____

Your Expenditures: Where Your Money Goes

Although your income is usually very easy to calculate, your expenditures usually are not. Why? Because many expenditures are cash transactions and as such do not leave a paper trail. Also, it's harder to keep track of all the little things you spend your money on. If you don't keep careful track of your expenses, though, you'll never figure out where your money goes. One way to make tracking expenditures a bit less formidable is to categorize them as in Figure 2.4. The two general categories that you will use are income taxes and living expenses. Income taxes include both federal and state income taxes in addition to Social Security taxes. This is income that is taken out of your paycheck before you receive it. If you take your total income and subtract from that your total income taxes, you'll arrive at your after-tax income available for living expenditures, or take-home pay. This amount gives you an understanding of what level of cash flow you have for living expenditures. Once living expenses have been subtracted out, the remainder contributes to savings and investments, as shown in Figure 2.4.

Some financial planners also classify living expenses as being either **variable** or **fixed expenditures**, depending upon whether you have control over the expenditure. These classifications are appealing, but not all expenses fit neatly into them. For example, it's difficult to categorize car or home repairs as being either variable (you have a choice in spending this money) or fixed (you have no choice in spending this money). They may be somewhat postponable, but probably not for too long.

Variable Expenditure

An expenditure over which you have control. That is, you are not obligated to make that expenditure, and as such it may vary from month to month.

Fixed Expenditure

An expenditure over which you have no control. You are obligated to make this expenditure, and it is generally at a constant level each month.

What does the average American household spend its money on? That depends upon how much it earns. The more it earns, the more it spends on such things as education and entertainment. Figure 2.5 provides a breakdown of spending for the average U.S. household measured as a fraction of each 8-hour workday. Interestingly, in 1997 the average American worked 2 hours 49 minutes each workday laboring to pay for taxes—more time than it takes to pay for food, housing, and clothing combined. Most of this time, 1 hour 53 minutes will be spent to pay off the federal tax bill. The remainder, 56 minutes, will be spent working to pay state and local taxes. After taxes, the big expenses are food, housing, and medical care. You should keep in mind that the amounts in Figure 2.5 are spending averages, and they tend to vary across the country. For example, people living in San Francisco spend quite a bit more on food because they tend to eat out much more often than those who live elsewhere (better restaurants, I guess).

Preparing an Income Statement: Mary and Lou Grant

To get a better understanding of the preparation of an income statement, take a look at the one for Mary and Lou Grant in Figure 2.6. Last year Lou earned $57,500 at his management job in building construction, and Mary earned $12,000 at her part-time sales job. In addition, they received $720 in interest and dividends. Approximately 19.5 percent of their income went toward income taxes. As a result, for every dollar the Grants

FIGURE 2.5

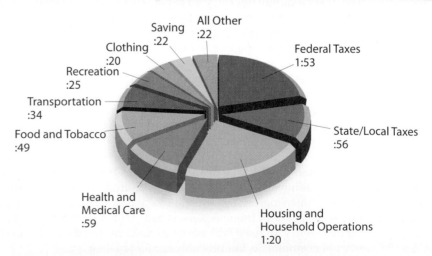

How Americans Spend Their Money, Measured as Minutes of Each Eight-Hour Workday, 1997

Saving :22
All Other :22
Clothing :20
Recreation :25
Transportation :34
Food and Tobacco :49
Health and Medical Care :59
Housing and Household Operations 1:20
State/Local Taxes :56
Federal Taxes 1:53

Source: "Tax Freedom Day 1997 Is May 9! Average American's Tax Bite Grows" (Washington, DC: The Tax Foundation, 1997).

TO GET AHEAD, You've Really Got to Know Where You're Starting From

Where does money go?

That's the question many people ask at the end of each month. And it's a critical question from anyone who is trying to get a better handle on his or her personal finances.

A central part of managing one's money is figuring out whether current resources and additional dollars being set aside will be enough to pay for important life goals. You obviously can't answer that question if you don't know where you stand today.

If you're like many people, a surprisingly large sum of money disappears in "miscellaneous" spending. Consider carrying around a small notebook for one month and jotting down each and every expenditure.

Alarm bells should go off, of course, if you're spending more money than you take in. "One of the biggest problems I see," says Karen Schaeffer, a Silver Spring, Maryland, financial planner, "is people refusing to live within their means." Some people dig themselves into a hole by running up big credit-card debt to pay for a lifestyle they really can't afford.

For people who are saving, the big question is how much is enough. If you are within several years of retirement, for instance, it's time for a careful analysis of whether your net worth and current savings will suffice to finance the lifestyle

you envision. You may want to hire a financial planner for a few hours' consultation or use a computer program to assist with some of the math.

Many other people should simply focus on saving something on a regular basis. "The hardest thing for people is to commit themselves to find some dollars to save," says Karen W. Spero, a Cleveland financial planner. "I am talking about wealthy people as well as not wealthy people. It's difficult for everyone."

Reviewing one's financial picture can also be a valuable opportunity to rethink broader goals and values. For instance, too many people get caught up in the idea of making more and saving more "for more's sake," says James D. Schwartz, an Englewood, Colorado, planner.

Mr. Schwartz urges his mostly affluent clients to define what is enough money for them and to focus more on their nonfinancial goals. For a business owner who is a seven-day-a-week "slave" to the enterprise, he says, that might mean cutting back to spend more time with family or other interests.

Source: "To Get Ahead, You've Really Got to Know Where You're Starting From," *The Wall Street Journal,* June 4, 1993, p. C16. Reprinted by permission of *The Wall Street Journal,* © 1993 Dow Jones & Company, Inc. All Rights Reserved Worldwide.

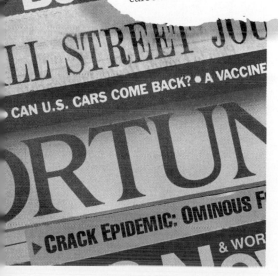

Analysis and Implications ...

A. One of the main reasons for examining your personal income statement is to force yourself to recognize exactly what your financial means are. Today, with all the credit cards available, it's simply too easy and tempting to live beyond your financial means or spend more than you earn. Unfortunately, overspending always catches up with you. As the song says, "it ain't no joke to be stone broke," but it's even worse to be stone broke and up to your eyeballs in debt.

B. The key to financial control is commitment. That all goes back to **Axiom 15: Just Do It!** And the balance sheet and income statement are the perfect tools to begin with if you want control.

C. While financial goals are extremely important, they are not everything. In other words, keep **Axiom 14: Money Isn't Everything** in mind.

FIGURE 2.6

Mary and Lou Grant's Personal Income Statement

Income

Wages and Salaries		
Wage Earner 1	$57,500	
+ Wage Earner 2	12,000	
= Total Wages and Salaries		69,500
+ Interest and Dividends		720
+ Royalties, Commissions, and Rents		0
+ Other Income		0
= A. **Total Income**		**$70,220**

Taxes

Federal Income and Social Security	11,830
+ State Income	1,880
= B. **Total Income Taxes**	**$ 13,710**
C. **After-Tax Income Available for Living Expenditures or Take-Home Pay (line A minus line B)**	**$56,510**

Living Expenses

Housing

Rent	0
+ Mortgage Payments	19,656
+ Utilities	3,420
+ Maintenance	1,200
+ Real Estate and Property Taxes	4,800
+ Fixed Assets—furniture, appliances, televisions, etc.	1,700
+ Other Living Expenses _____	0
= D. **Total Housing Expenditures**	**$30,776**

Food

Food and Supplies	5,800
+ Restaurant Expenses	1,400
= E. **Total Food Expenditures**	**$ 7,200**

Clothing and Personal Care

New Clothes	2,100
+ Cleaning	190
+ Tailoring	0
+ Personal Care—hair care	200
+ Other Clothing and Personal Care Expenses _____	0
= F. **Total Clothing and Personal Care Expenditures**	**$2,490**

(continued)

FIGURE 2.6
(continued)

Transportation

Automobile Purchase		0
+ Payments		2,588
+ Gas, Tolls, Parking		840
+ Automobile Registration/Tags/Stickers		110
+ Repairs		600
+ Other Transportation Expenses _____		0
= G.	Total Transportation Expenditures	$ 4,138

Recreation

Movies, Theater, Sporting Events		670
+ Club Memberships		240
+ Vacations		2,000
+ Hobbies		150
+ Sporting Goods		100
+ Gifts		80
+ Reading Materials (books, newspapers, magazines)		30
+ Other Recreation Expenses (big screen TV payments)		230
= H.	Total Recreation Expenditures	$ 3,500

Medical Expenditures

Doctor		180
+ Dental		70
+ Prescription Drugs and Medicines		160
= I.	Total Medical Expenditures	$ 410

Insurance Expenditures

Health		0
+ Life		420
+ Automobile		1260
+ Disability		260
+ Liability		0
+ Other Insurance Expenses _____		0
= J.	Total Insurance Expenditures	$ 1,940

Other Expenditures

Educational Expenditures (college loan payments)		1,600
+ Child Care		180
+ Other Expenses _____		0
= K.	Total Other Expenditures	$ 1,780
L.	Total Living Expenditures (add lines D–K)	$52,234
M.	Income Available for Savings and Investment (line C minus line L)	$ 4,276

earned, only about 79.5¢ was available after taxes for living expenses. The largest item in their living expenses was housing, which totaled $30,776, or approximately 44 percent of the Grants' income. The Grants' housing expenditures are this large because they own both a house and a vacation condominium. Other expenditures are given in Figure 2.6.

Once their total living expenditures (line L) have been subtracted from the after-tax income available for living expenditures (line C), the Grants arrive at their cash flow, or income available for savings and investment. As you can see, the Grants have $4,276 they can use to either pay off debt or to invest in new assets. Note that this $4,276 increases the Grants' net worth. Thus, if they were to prepare a balance sheet at the beginning and end of the period covered by the income statement in Figure 2.6, the amount of their net worth would increase by exactly $4,276.

The income statement and balance sheet, then, can and should be used in conjunction. The balance sheet lets you judge your financial standing by showing you your net worth, and the income statement tells you exactly how your spending and saving habits affect that net worth. If your balance sheet shows you that you're not building your net worth as much as or as quickly as you'd like, or if you're overspending and actually decreasing your net worth, your income statement can help. By reviewing all of your expenses and your spending patterns, you can set specific spending goals to cut back on your purchases and increase your savings. This process of setting spending goals for the upcoming month or year is referred to as setting a **budget**. As you will see later in this chapter, a smart budget includes estimates of all of your future expenses and helps you manage your money to meet your specific financial goals.

Before you can design and implement a budget plan, you first need to analyze your balance sheet and income statement using ratios to better understand any financial shortcomings or deficiencies you may have.

Budget

A plan for controlling cash inflows and cash outflows. Based upon your goals and financial obligations, a budget is developed that limits spending in different categories (such as food, entertainment, travel, and so on).

LEARNING OBJECTIVE #3

Use ratios to identify your financial strengths and weaknesses.

USING A FINANCIAL THERMOMETER—RATIOS

By themselves the numbers in your balance sheet and income statement are helpful and informative, but they don't tell you everything you need to know about your financial well-being. Instead, you need a tool to help you pick out all the meaning you can from these numbers. That tool is ratios. Financial ratios allow you to analyze the raw data in your balance sheet and income statement and to compare it with either a preset target or your own previous performance. In general, your purpose in using ratios is to gain a better understanding of how you're managing your financial resources. Specifically, you'll try to answer the following questions:

1. Do I have adequate liquidity to meet emergencies?
2. Do I have the ability to meet my debt obligations?
3. Am I saving as much as I think I am?

We will now look at these questions in turn.

Question 1: Do I Have Adequate Liquidity to Meet Emergencies?

If your TV died in the middle of the playoffs or that miniseries you've been watching, would you have enough cash on hand to buy another one immediately? To judge your liquidity, you need to compare the amount of your cash and other liquid assets with the amount of debt you have currently coming due. In other words, you need to look at your balance sheet and divide your monetary assets by your current liabilities. The resultant measure of your liquidity is called the current ratio:

$$\text{current ratio} = \frac{\text{monetary assets}}{\text{current liabilities}}$$

Returning to our example of Lou and Mary Grant, we can see from their balance sheet that their monetary assets total $3,590 and their current liabilities (current bills and credit card debt) total $1,500. Thus, the Grants' current ratio is:

$$\text{current ratio} = \frac{\$3,590}{\$1,500} = 2.39$$

Although there's no set rule for how large the current ratio should be, it certainly should be greater than 1.0, and most financial advisors look for a current ratio above 2.0. More important than the level of the current ratio is its trend—is it going up, or more important, is it going down? If it is going down, you have to try to find the cause. To do this you would have to look at the numbers and see what changes have caused the ratio to decrease.

One problem with the current ratio is that people generally have a number of monthly expenses that are not considered current liabilities. For example, an individual usually has long-term debt payments such as mortgage payments, auto loan payments, and so forth that may not be considered current liabilities but still must be paid on a monthly basis. Therefore, it's also helpful to calculate the ratio of monetary assets to monthly living expenses, called the months living expenses covered ratio.

$$\text{months living expenses covered ratio} = \frac{\text{monetary assets}}{\text{annual living expenditures}/12}$$

As the name suggests, this ratio tells you how many months of living expenditures you can cover with your present level of monetary assets. Again, the numerator is the level of monetary assets, and the denominator is the annual living expenditures (as on line L of the income statement in Figure 2.6) divided by 12 to determine the living expenses per month. For the Grants this ratio would be:

$$\text{months living expenses covered ratio} = \frac{\$3,590}{\$52,234/12} = \frac{\$3,590}{\$4,353} = 0.825 \text{ months}$$

This ratio means that the Grants currently have enough cash and liquid assets on hand to cover 0.825 months of expenditures.

The traditional rule of thumb in personal finance is that an individual or family should have enough liquid assets to cover 3 to 6 months of expenditures. The Grants fall well short of this amount. However, as with all rules of thumb, you must use some caution in applying them. This is one of those rules that was set up long before the deluge of credit cards and home equity lines of credit. The logic behind it is that you need money set aside in case of the untimely death of a television, a major car repair, or some other unexpected event. When you have emergency funds, you don't need to tap into money set aside for long-term goals. If you have sufficient credit from your credit cards or a home equity line of credit to cover emergency expenses, you also won't have to disturb this money. Of course, you may have to pay high interest on any credit you use, but the return you get from lowering the amount of your emergency funds may be enough to compensate. You see, most emergency funds earn very little return, because as you gain liquidity you give up expected return. That all comes from **Axiom 1: The Risk-Return Trade-Off**—liquid investments are low risk because the money is always safe and readily available. As a result, their return is lower than with riskier alternative investments. For example, you expect a higher return on an investment in a stock fund, but what if you need your money for an emergency during a bear market? The bottom line is that the Grants, and most people, may be better off investing most of their emergency funds in higher yielding, less liquid investments rather than in lower-paying, but more liquid accounts. For example, if the Grants invest their emergency funds in a money market fund paying 5 percent, those funds will grow 63 percent over the next 10 years, whereas if they invested them in a stock fund

AXIOM #1

The Risk-Return Trade-Off

that grew at an annual rate of 9 percent, their investment would have grown 137 percent over that same period. Thus, given enough credit and insurance protection to provide income in the face of an emergency, you can safely reduce the number of months of living expenses you keep in your emergency fund to three or below. Regardless of what you do with your emergency funds, the months living expenses covered ratio still provides a good, easy-to-understand indication of the relative level of cash a family has on hand. As such, it's a better personal liquidity measure than the current ratio. In particular, you would want to track it over time to make sure that it does not drop unexpectedly.

Question 2: Do I Have the Ability to Meet My Debt Obligations?

A second question you can answer using ratios is, Have you taken on too much debt, or do you have the ability to meet your debt obligations? In other words, you saw it, you borrowed money and bought it, now can you pay for it? To answer this question you need to look at the debt ratio and the debt coverage ratio. The debt ratio answers the question dealing with what percentage of your assets has been financed by borrowing. This ratio can be expressed as follows:

$$\text{debt ratio} = \frac{\text{total debt or liabilities}}{\text{total assets}}$$

Looking at the Grants' balance sheet, we see that the level of their total debt or liabilities is $175,500, while their total assets or what they own is $300,190. Thus, their debt ratio becomes $175,500/$300,190 = 0.5846. This ratio figure means that just over half of their assets are financed with borrowing. This ratio should go down as you get older.

The long-term debt coverage ratio relates the amount of funds available for debt repayment to the size of the debt payments. In effect, this ratio is the number of times you could make your debt payments with your current income. It focuses on long-term obligations such as home mortgage payments, auto loan payments, and any other long-term credit obligations. For example, if credit card debt has gotten large enough, it, too, represents a long-term obligation. The denominator of this ratio represents your total outstanding long-term debt payments (excluding short-term borrowing such as credit cards and bills coming due), and the numerator represents the funds available to make these payments.

$$\frac{\text{long-term}}{\text{debt coverage ratio}} = \frac{\text{total income available for living expenses}}{\text{total long-term debt payments}}$$

For the Grants, total income available for living expenses is found on line C of their income statement and is $56,510. The only long-term debt obligations they have are their mortgage payments of $19,656, their automobile loan payments of $2,588, college loan payments of $1,600, and an installment loan on a TV of $230. Thus, their debt coverage ratio is [$56,510/($19,656 + $2,588 + $1,600 + $230)] = 2.35 times. In general, a debt coverage ratio of less than approximately 2.5 should raise a caution flag. You should also keep track of your long-term debt coverage ratio looking for trends and making sure it does not creep downward. The Grants, then, are at their limit in terms of the level of debt that they can manage comfortably. Such a low debt coverage ratio, though, is not surprising, because most of their assets are tied up in housing, with housing accounting for almost 80 percent of their assets.

Another way of looking at the debt coverage ratio is to take its inverse; that is, divide the total debt payments by the total income available for living expenses. In this case, the inverse of the Grants' debt coverage ratio is 0.43, or 43 percent, indicating that 43 percent of the Grants' total income available for living expenses goes to cover debt payments.

Question 3: Am I Saving as Much as I Think I Am?

The final question you can answer using ratios is, How much of your income are you really saving? In effect, are you really saving as much as you think you are? To answer this question you need to look at the savings ratio, which is simply the ratio of income available for savings and investment (line M of Figure 2.6) to income available for living expenses (line C of Figure 2.6). This ratio tells you what proportion of your after-tax income is being saved.

$$\text{savings ratio} = \frac{\text{income available for savings and investment}}{\text{income available for living expenses}}$$

For the Grants, this ratio is ($4,276/$56,510) = .076 or 7.6 percent. This figure is in range with what is typically saved in this country. Actually, for families saving for their first house it tends to be higher, and for families that have just purchased their first house and now, for the first time, are experiencing large mortgage payments, it tends to be lower. Again, as with the other ratios, this ratio should be compared with past savings ratios and target savings ratios to determine whether or not the Grants' savings efforts are as desired.

Because it's unlikely you'll win the lottery, you have to plan for your financial future. If you're not presently saving, then you're living above your means. The only effective way to make saving work is to put to work **Axiom 13: Pay Yourself First—Making Your Financial Well-Being the Top Priority**. That is, you first set aside your savings, and what is left becomes the amount you can spend. As a result, saving for long-term goals becomes automatic. By paying yourself first, you acknowledge the fact that your long-term goals are of paramount importance.

RECORD KEEPING

Most people keep records of the important things in their lives. They keep them stuffed in a drawer, or in a file folder, or somewhere in the house, and say, "If you'll just give me a day or two, I'm sure I'll find them." One of the keys to good personal financial planning is organizing and maintaining these records. Keeping accurate, detailed records is important for three main reasons. First, without adequate records it's extremely difficult to prepare taxes. Second, a strong record-keeping system allows you to track expenses and know exactly how much you're spending and where you're spending it. In short, if you don't know where and how much you're spending, you don't have control of your finances. Third, organized record keeping makes it easier for someone else to step in during an emergency and understand your complete financial situation. Record keeping really involves two steps: tracking your personal financial dealings, and filing and storing your financial records in such a way that they are readily accessible. Very simply, if you don't know where financial records are, you won't feel in control of your financial affairs. Also record keeping should involve the safekeeping of documents and records such as birth certificates and passports, which might be needed in the event of an emergency.

In determining how best to track your personal financial dealings, you must keep in mind that the best system is one that you will use. This may sound silly, but because of the tedious nature of record keeping, anything too complex just won't be used. Do yourself a favor and keep your system simple and easy to use.

In general, credit card and check expenditures are easy to track because they leave an obvious paper trail. However, it's the cash expenditures that cause the most concern. Cash expenditures must be tracked as they occur; if not, they will be lost and forgotten. The simplest way to keep track of all cash expenditures is by recording them in a notebook or your checkbook register as they occur and then using

AXIOM #13

Pay Yourself First—Making Your Financial Well-Being the Top Priority

LEARNING OBJECTIVE #4

Set up a sound record-keeping system to track your income and expenditures.

these records, in addition to check and credit card transactions, to generate a monthly income statement. You would then compare this monthly income statement with your annual and target income statements to determine whether or not you have any problems. Sure, this process of tracking expenditures may be tedious, but it's necessary. Remember, no matter how annoying it may seem, your budget is your best friend, because the key to controlling expenditures is to keep track of them.

Stop and Think

If you don't have the self-control to track all of your expenditures, start out by keeping spending records for just 2 weeks. You'll be surprised to find where your money goes. Once you try this 2-week experiment and see how easy the process is, you may be willing to extend the experiment. Remember, keeping track of expenditures is the first step to controlling them.

Once you've tracked your expenditures, you need to record them in an organized way. How should you do this? Your record keeping can be either simple or sophisticated. A relatively easy way is to set up a budget book similar to the income statement shown in Figure 2.4 and manually enter your expenditures. Alternatively, there are a number of personal finance computer programs that track your monthly and yearly expenses and your financial position once you've entered your daily expenditures. This approach is ideal. However, for those without a PC, the money for such a software program, or the time to set up such a system, the manual approach works just as well. The most popular of the personal financial management programs for the PC is Intuit's Quicken, which has about 10 million users. Other excellent programs include Managing Your Money by MECA Software, Simply Money by Computer Associates, and Microsoft's Money. If you shop carefully, some of these programs can be purchased for less than $20.

When recording your transactions, you should have a section in your **ledger** for each month broken down by the major types of expenditures. In addition, each month should be broken down by day. The more detailed your records are, the easier it is to track your money. For example, when you spend $200 on new clothes, you should enter the expense in the new clothes subsection of the clothes and personal care section of the proper month on the day on which the expenditure occurred (it sounds more complicated than it is). At the end of the month you should add up your expenditures and compile your monthly income statement.

After you've been keeping records for a while, you'll notice that they really start to pile up. How long do you have to hang on to these records? This, of course, depends upon the item. In general, items dealing with taxes must be kept for at least 6 years after the transaction takes place; some items should be kept for life. Table 2.2 provides a summary of where and for how long financial records should be kept.

PUTTING IT ALL TOGETHER: BUDGETING WITHIN THE PLANNING CYCLE

Chapter 1 introduced the planning cycle as a five-step process (see Figure 1.1 on p. 9). Now that you have a better understanding of the tools involved in that process, how about a little review? Let's see how the balance sheet and income statement fit

Ledger
A book or notebook set aside to record your expenditures in.

LEARNING OBJECTIVE #5

Implement a financial plan or budget that will provide for the level of savings needed to achieve your goals.

TABLE 2.2

Storing Financial Files

If you're stuck on what to store and where, consider buying a kit to help you. Two such products are Homefile (800-695-3453) and FileSolutions (972-488-0100).

Long-Term or Permanent Storage (keep at home in a file cabinet or safe spot):

Tax Records (may be discarded after 6 years)

Tax returns
Paychecks
W-2 forms
1099 forms
Charitable contributions
Alimony payments
Medical bills
Property taxes
Any other documentation

Investment Records

Bank records and nontax-related checks less than a year old
Safety deposit box information
Stock, bond, and mutual fund transactions
Brokerage statements
Dividend records
Any additional investment documentation

Retirement and Estate Planning

Copy of will
Pension plan documentation
IRA documentation
Keogh plan transactions
Social Security information
Any additional retirement documentation

Personal Planning

Personal balance sheet
Personal income statement
Personal budget
Insurance policies and documentation
Warranties
Receipts for major purchases
Credit card information (account numbers and telephone numbers)
Birth certificates
Rental agreement if renting a dwelling
Automobile registration
Powers of attorney
Any additional personal planning documentation

Safety Deposit Box Storage

Investment Records

Certificates of deposit
Listing of bank accounts
Stock and bond certificates
Collectibles

(continued)

TABLE 2.2

(continued)

Retirement and Estate Planning

Copy of will
Nondeductible IRA records

Personal Planning

Copy of will
Deed for home
Mortgage
Title insurance policy
Personal papers (birth and death certificates, alimony, adoption/custody,
          divorce, military, immigration, etc.)
Documentation of valuables (videotape or photos)
Home repair/improvement receipts
Auto title
Listing of insurance policies
Credit card information (account numbers and telephone numbers)

Throw Out

Nontax-related checks over a year old
Records from cars and boats you no longer own
Expired insurance polices on which there will be no future claims
Expired warranties
Non tax-related credit card slips over a year old

into the planning process. The planning process starts off by evaluating your financial health, which is exactly what the balance sheet and income statement are all about. Your balance sheet sums up everything you own or owe and lets you know your net worth, the most basic element of your financial health. Your income statement furthers your understanding of your financial standing by showing you where your money comes from, where it goes, and your spending patterns. Once you understand how much you have coming in and how you tend to spend your money, you can figure out how much you can realistically afford to save. If you don't know how much you can actually save, you can't come up with realistic financial goals, the second step of the planning process.

By providing you with information on how far you need to go to achieve a certain level of wealth and how you might realistically balance your spending and saving to get there, your balance sheet and income statement not only help you set goals, they also help you achieve them. Developing a plan of action to achieve your goals is the third step in the planning process, and your income statement is the key to doing so. Your income statement helps you set up a cash budget (which we'll examine in more detail in the next section), which allows you to manage your saving toward achieving your goals while considering flexibility, liquidity, protection, and minimization of taxes. Once your plan is in place, you'll need to monitor your progress, the final step in the planning cycle. Because this last step is really the same as the first, you're right back to using your balance sheet and income statement again. As you can see, without your balance sheet and income statement, the planning process isn't nearly as effective.

REALITY BITES: A Spending Plan for the Young

Anne and James Phillips Jr. of Olathe, Kansas, had come a long way since their newlywed days.

James, now 32 years old, a salesman for a medical-device company, and Anne, 30, a part-time clothing manufacturer's representative, had seen their income triple by last year, from the time of their marriage in 1987. Yet the former college sweethearts found they had no money to put away at the end of the month.

(A) "We figured we were making enough that we should have money left over," says Anne. "It just seemed like we were spending everything we were making."

You may feel you're making economic progress. Meanwhile, though, you're not saving a dime. And although you may feel a vague uneasiness about that, the thought of getting on a budget makes you want to bury yourself in a double espresso at the nearest bookstore-cafe.

For many young people, a budget "is like a diet," says Lewis Altfest, a certified public accountant and financial planner in New York. "They don't want to deny themselves."

(B) But a sensible spending plan—some financial-planning pros won't even use the "B" word—doesn't have to be as painful as you may fear. It takes neither an oppressive amount of work nor a Spartan's self-discipline to gain control over your spending, stash away money for the future, and still treat yourself—*sometimes.*

When the Phillipses started tracking their expenses last year, they were surprised to find they were spending $500 a month eating out and another $500 a month on gifts. Since then, they've cut back on dinners out from three times a week to once. To avoid buying budget-busting presents, they give friends and relatives $25 gift certificates. Such steps have saved them about $400 a month.

(C) To get a handle on your spending, track it for a few months like Mr. and Mrs. Phillips did.

Once folks put some numbers on their spending, they're often shocked into making changes. "Just having the numbers in front of your eyes is more than half the battle," says Savvas Giannakopoulos, a financial planner with Cambridge Associates in Franklin, Michigan.

Source: Nancy Ann Jeffrey, "Reality Bites: A Spending Plan for the Young," *The Wall Street Journal,* June 2, 1995, p. C1. Reprinted by permission of *The Wall Street Journal,* © 1995 Dow Jones & Company, Inc. All Rights Reserved Worldwide.

Analysis and Implications ...

A. Unfortunately, for many successful people in their late 20s and 30s, this story is depressingly familiar. In spite of the fact that they may no longer be cash-strapped students (as you probably are), their saving level hasn't climbed.

B. You can easily track your expenditures using pencil and paper. If you have a personal computer, there are a number of programs that will make the whole process simpler.

C. ATMs are a real threat to many young people because they're so easy to use and hard to track. It's too easy to get cash from an ATM and end up spending a tidy sum without knowing where it's gone.

Developing a Cash Budget

A budget is really nothing more than a plan for controlling cash inflows and cash outflows. The purpose of the cash budget is to keep income in line with expenditures plus savings for goals. Your cash budget should allocate certain dollar amounts for different spending categories, based on your goals and financial obligations.

To prepare a cash budget, you begin with your most recent annual personal income statement. First, examine last year's total income, making any adjustments to it you expect for the coming year. Perhaps you have received a raise, taken a second job, or anticipate an increase in royalty payments. Based upon your income level, you then estimate what your taxes will be. This figure then provides you with an estimate of your anticipated after-tax income available for living expenditures, which is commonly called take-home pay.

Just as your estimate of anticipated take-home pay flows from your most recent annual personal income statement, so does your estimate of living expenses. Looking at last year's personal income statement, you first identify expenditures over which you have no discretion—your fixed expenditures. Once you've determined your fixed expenses, you then must determine your variable expenses. Again, these are the expenses over which you have complete control, and you can increase or decrease them as you see fit. This is the category in which you have to start looking for ways to reduce your spending and increase your saving. For example, you can generate savings just by reducing the amount you spend on food—substitute bean dip for those exotic fresh fruits as your evening snack (of course, any savings there will probably be offset in an increase in exercise equipment this year). You must also keep in mind that when you buy on credit, you obligate yourself to future expenditures to pay off your debt. Remember, when you borrow you are spending your future income, which limits your ability to save.

Finally, you subtract your anticipated living expenditures from your anticipated take-home pay to determine your income available for savings and investment. You then compare your anticipated monthly savings with your target savings level, which is, as we mentioned earlier, based upon a quantification of your goals. If it doesn't look as if you'll be able to fund all your goals, then you must either earn more, spend less, or downsize your goals. The choice is, of course, personal; however, you should keep in mind that regardless of what your level of income is, there are an awful lot of people who are living on less than what you're earning.

How do Mary and Lou Grant develop a cash budget? First, assume that the only change in income they expect for the coming year is a $5,000 increase in wages and salaries from $69,500 to $74,500. Last year, the Grants paid approximately 20 percent in federal and state income taxes. If they pay the same percentage this year, their $5,000 raise will result in an increase in take-home pay of $4,000, with 20 percent of the raise, or $1,000, going to pay increased taxes.

An examination of the Grants' personal income statement is given in Figure 2.6. They're planning minor changes in several of their expenditure categories from last year. Interestingly, some of the anticipated expenditure changes involve increases in planned spending from the prior year. A cash budget, then, does not necessarily curb spending in all areas. Instead it allows you to decide ahead of time how much to spend where, so that you have greater control over your expenses.

Assume that the Grants' target level of savings for the entire year is $6,400. Thus, if the Grants stick to this cash budget, they will exceed their target level of savings. Were this not the case, they would have been forced to adjust their budget so that it covered their target savings. To make your annual cash budget easier to control, you should break it down into monthly budgets by simply dividing by 12.

A key point to remember when budgeting is that no budget is set in stone. As **Axiom 7** says, **Stuff Happens**. A TV, a car, a washer—unexpected expenditures seem to appear out of nowhere. Conversely, you may be pleasantly surprised that you wound up spending far less than you planned to. Then again, you may change your goals— you don't want that house, your apartment's fine for the moment, but you do want to be able to buy a yak farm in Peru. Basically, the budgeting process is a dynamic process: You must continuously monitor the financial impact of change upon your spending and saving habits.

Implementing the Cash Budget

Now that you have your plan, how do you make it work? Essentially, you just put it in place and try to make a go of it for a month. At the end of the month, compare your actual expenditures in each category with your budgeted amounts. If you spent more than you budgeted, you may want to pay closer attention to expenditures in that category or you may want to change the budgeted amount. If you do need to increase one budgeted amount, you might try to reduce spending in another area to compensate. Keep in mind that responsibility for sticking to the budget remains with you, but by examining deviations from desired spending patterns on a monthly basis, you can focus on where you need to exert additional self-control.

If sticking to a desired budget remains a problem, one possible control method is using what's generally called the envelope system. Under this system, at the beginning of each month the dollar amount of each major expenditure category is put into a separate envelope. To spend money in that area, simply take it out of the envelope, and when the envelope is empty, you're done spending in that area. Alternatively, if you are having trouble controlling spending only in certain areas, envelope systems could be instituted just for those areas. For example, if you budgeted $120 per month for restaurant expenditures, you'd put $120 in an envelope each month and use it for spending at restaurants. When it is exhausted, trips to the restaurant would be over for the month. This includes pizza home delivery, so no cheating!

MANAGING YOUR OWN AFFAIRS VERSUS HIRING A PROFESSIONAL

The goal of this course and text is to give you the understanding, tools, and motivation to manage your own personal financial affairs. Sometimes, though, good management involves knowing when to ask for help. Fortunately, when it comes to personal financial management, there's good help to be found. Actually, you have four options available regarding financial planning and working with professionals: Go it alone, make your own plan and have it checked by a professional, work with a professional to come up with a plan, or leave it all in the hands of a pro (though preferably not one with a bad toupee, leisure suit, and a beat-up Ford Pinto). Although this is a question that

should not be answered until you have finished this course and have a better grasp of the process and alternatives available to you and of your ability to set your own plan of action, take a moment to look further at the options.

For relatively simple personal financial matters, computerized financial planning programs are now available that provide basic budgeting tools and advice. However, as with most standardized advice, they simply may not fit your particular financial situation. The more unique your situation, the greater the need for professional help.

A professional financial planner might be used to validate the financial plan you've developed yourself. For example, if you design your own home, it would be a good idea to pass the plans by an architect before building, just to make sure there are no flaws in the design. Moreover, the architect may provide suggestions for improving the plans based upon the family's needs and interests. Similarly, you might hire a professional financial planner to look over your financial plan and point out any flaws, in addition to suggesting improvements that might be made, based upon your goals, values, and interests.

Alternatively, you can also work directly with a professional financial planner to develop your plan, with the planner helping out on complex tax and legal issues. This option offers the most logical use of financial planners—using them as a reference tool and letting their expertise supplement your understanding of personal finance. However, for this approach to work, you must have a solid understanding of personal finance, the logic that drives it, and time and willingness to give it the attention required.

Finally, you could hire a professional financial planner to put your entire plan together for you, from start to finish. In this case, you'll provide the planner with information on your goals, values, and lifestyle, and the planner will craft a plan that addresses your desires. Depending upon your net worth or income, the planner's reputation, and whether or not the planner also collects commissions on investments you make in addition to his fee, this service could cost between $500 and $10,000. A downside to this approach is that without enough knowledge to thoroughly understand the planner's proposal, you can't judge its merits. This makes it extremely important that you find a competent and trustworthy financial planner. However, if something goes wrong, you bear the consequences. For that reason, you must understand the basics of personal financial planning in order to monitor your financial game plan. Thus, using a financial planner to put together the entire plan is reasonable only if you realize that you are merely receiving advice and that you bear the ultimate responsibility for the effectiveness of the plan.

Hopefully, if you decide you need the help of a financial planner, this relationship will be a win-win situation. Although the overwhelming majority of financial planners are dedicated, responsible, and competent, that doesn't guarantee that you won't pick one of the incompetent or unethical ones. Although there are regulations in place that are meant to protect consumers, these regulations don't mean that all planners are equally qualified. Unfortunately, many unethical people call themselves "planners" simply because it is one of the industry buzzwords. In dealing with financial planners keep in mind that they may actually be acting in their own interests rather than in your best interest. Remember **Axiom 12: The Agency Problem in Personal Finance—Differentiating Between Advice and a Sales Pitch**. For example, financial planners may try to sell you financial products that are more expensive because they receive a commission on them. To avoid this problem, you need to take care in selecting a financial planner. Be wary of those who promise you quick riches, and walk away from anyone with high-pressure tactics. Building wealth takes time and constant attention. Take your time in selecting the financial planner who's right for you. Still, your best protection is knowledge, bringing you back to **Axiom 9: The Best Protection Is Knowledge**. Without an understanding of the world of investments, you

AXIOM #12

The Agency Problem in Personal Finance— Differentiating Between Advice and a Sales Pitch

AXIOM #9

The Best Protection Is Knowledge

can't determine whether the planner's recommendations make sense for you, and you may end up relying on someone who may, in turn, be working in his or her best interests rather than in yours.

Paying Your Financial Planner: Commission-Based Versus Fee-Only Planners

Financial planners or advisors come in all shapes and sizes. One way of differentiating them is by the services they offer. For example, some are full-service advisors, and some specialize in such areas as estate planning or investments. Another way of differentiating them is how they're compensated for their services. These classifications can have a big effect on how much advice will cost you, so let's take a look at different compensation plans.

Fee-only planners earn income only through the fees they charge and thus may charge more for a plan than the person just starting out may want to pay. There are fewer of this type of planner than any other, and they tend to work with bigger, more involved and specialized planning situations. The plus of using this kind of planner is that you personally will have total control of the products that are purchased to complete your plan, and therefore you can control commission costs. However, you then have to sort through a sometimes overwhelming array of options and deal with several different vendors. Whether the planner charges an hourly rate, operates with a schedule of services and prices, or has some other pricing structure, make sure you sign a fee agreement before you begin.

Some planners who charge fees also collect commissions on products they recommend to implement a plan. The upside of this configuration is that fees may be smaller if you do choose to use some of their commissioned products. The downside is that if you're dealing with a less than ethical person, you could be directed toward higher-commission products. The key to making a decision on this type of advisor is, again, to be aware of what you're paying for.

Finally, there are commission-based advisors. As in any category, there are good and bad ones, but this segment is by far the most available type of advisor. They can provide an analysis of your personal financial situation, offer solutions to problems, and assist you in implementing the plan. Except for some noncommission investments, most financial products pay a commission to someone. Some commission-based planners represent only one or two companies, while others work with a wide range of companies. You want to make sure your planner has a wide range of choices available to you.

Choosing a Professional Planner

Once you decide to solicit help from a professional planner, you must then locate one who's competent and with whom you're comfortable. There are an awful lot of excellent financial planners out there, but unfortunately, there are enough bad ones that you should use care in picking someone to help. One approach is to limit your search to those who have received accreditation from a professional organization. For example, a personal financial specialist (PFS) is a certified public accountant. To receive this designation, an individual must pass certification tests in personal financial planning administered by the American Institute of Certified Public Accountants, in addition to having 3 years of personal financial planning experience. Another certification, certified financial planner (CFP), requires the satisfactory completion of a 10 hour, 2-day exam and a minimum of 3 years of experience in the field. There are also chartered financial consultants, or ChFCs. The requirements for a ChFC designation, which is administered by the American College, includes coursework and 10 exams. Regardless of the credentials of the planner, you should be concerned with the planner's experience. In addition, you should feel comfortable that the advice you're receiving is a function of your specific financial circumstance rather than preprogrammed or canned advice. You should also look to referrals—do you have friends or relatives who have had good experiences with financial planners in the past?

In choosing an advisor, beware of those who try to sell you something on the first visit. At that point they probably don't know enough about your situation to make a good recommendation. In effect, it may be the commission that's motivating them. Also, be wary of high-pressure tactics or promises of high returns. Remember, it's your money and financial future at stake, and it's OK to say no.

Make sure you interview several financial planners thoroughly before you decide to use their services or sign any agreements. Keep in mind that the title "financial planner" is not legally defined—it just means that the individual offers comprehensive financial planning services and says nothing about competence. You should ask the following about financial planners' background:

- How long have they been a financial planner?
- What are their credentials and professional designations?
- Do they actively participate in continuing education to keep apace with changes in financial planning?
- How do they keep up with the latest financial changes?
- Would they provide you with references?
- Could you see a copy of a financial plan that they made up for someone with a somewhat similar financial situation to you, with, of course, names removed to preserve confidentiality?
- Who will work with you on a regular basis, and will the creation of the plan be done by a junior staffer or using a computer program?
- How many companies do they represent?
- How will they be paid—fee or commission? What will it be, and how will that fee be calculated?
- Would they provide you with a written estimate of the services you can expect and the cost of those services?

If you have trouble getting recommendations, try calling the Institute of Certified Financial Planners at 800-282-7526 or the CFP Board of Standards at 303-830-7543 for help. Remember, there are a lot of good financial planners out there, but there are some bad ones, too. You bear all the consequences of bad decisions, and, as such, you must take responsibility for doing it right.

SUMMARY

A personal balance sheet represents a statement of your financial position on a given date. It includes the assets you own, the debt, or liabilities, you have incurred, and your level of wealth, which is referred to as net worth or equity. The difference between the value of your assets (what you own) and your liabilities (what you owe) is your net worth. Your net worth represents the level of wealth that you or your family have accumulated. What is viewed as a "good" level of net worth depends upon how good a job you have done in achieving your financial goals.

Whereas a balance sheet tells you how much wealth you have accumulated as of a *certain date*, an income statement tells you where your money has come from and where it has gone over some *period of time*— perhaps a month, 6 months, or a year. Actually, an income statement is really an income and expenditure or net income statement, because it looks at both cash inflows and cash outflows. From an income statement you can construct a budget. Once you have an understanding of where your money comes from and where it goes, you'll be able to determine whether you're saving enough to meet your goals and how you might change your expenditure patterns to meet your goals. Then you'll be able to construct a budget.

Financial ratios are used to help you in identifying your financial standing. These ratios are analyzed over time to determine any trends and are also compared with standards or target ratios. The purpose in using ratios is to gain a better understanding of how you are managing your financial resources. Specifically, ratios are used to answer the following questions:

1. Do I have adequate liquidity to meet emergencies?
2. Do I have the ability to meet my debt obligations?
3. Am I saving as much as I think I am?

To keep track of your income and expenditures and to calculate your net worth, you need a sound system of record keeping. Such a system not only helps with tax preparation, but also allows you to accurately track expenses—identifying how much you are spending and where you are spending it.

Developing a plan of action involves setting up a cash budget that allows for enough in the way of savings to achieve your goals. The starting point for the cash budget, which is the center point of the plan of action, flows directly from the personal income statement. By comparing the income available for savings and investments with the level of savings needed to achieve your goals, you can determine whether your current spending patterns need to be altered and by how much. Once you have established a plan, it's your responsibility to stick to your budget. To help you stick to it, you can examine deviations from desired spending patterns on a monthly basis, which should identify areas in which you need to exert additional self-control.

If you need help in financial planning, there are professional planners out there who can provide such help. These professional financial planners can be used simply to validate the financial plan you have developed, or, alternatively, they can be hired to put the entire plan, from start to finish, together.

Review Questions

1. What's the purpose of a balance sheet, and how is it used to measure financial health? (LO 1)
2. What's a current liability? How do current liabilities differ from long-term liabilities? (LO 1)
3. Define and give examples of the seven different categories of assets. (LO 2)
4. What's the primary use of the income statement? (LO 2)
5. What information needs to be gathered to calculate an accurate income statement? (LO 2)
6. Why are financial ratios important to someone trying to determine financial well-being? (LO 3)
7. If Mary and Lou Grant were trying to determine how long they would be able to continue paying their bills if they both lost their jobs, which financial ratio would be most useful. (LO 3)
8. What are the three most important reasons for keeping accurate financial records? Failing to keep accurate financial records can result in what kind of problems? (LO 4)
9. Think about the last time you visited the ATM machine. Can you remember where you spent your money? How could you benefit from setting up a cash budget? (LO 5)
10. Summarize the steps in the process of establishing a cash budget. (LO 5)
11. How could **Axiom 13: Pay Yourself First** make budgeting easier? (LO 5)
12. What is the major difference between a fee-only planner and a commission-based planner? Which one would you recommend using? Why? (LO 6)
13. Explain why hiring a certified financial planner may or may not be the best thing to do in all situations. (LO 6)

Problems and Activities

1. Bruce and Mary Jane have a yearly income of $55,000 and own a house worth $80,000, two cars worth a total of $12,000, and furniture worth $10,000. The house has a mortgage of $50,000, and the cars have outstanding loans of $2,000 each. Prepare a balance sheet and determine their net worth. (LO 1)

2. Using the information in problem 1, calculate the debt ratio for Bruce and Mary Jane. (LO 3)

3. Hank and Gracie get paid $2,250 after taxes every month and spend $500 on housing, $400 on transportation, $300 on food, and $500 on clothing and other expenses. What is their savings ratio? *Hint:* Prepare an income statement and then compute the ratio. (LO 2, 3)

4. Barry and Karen have the following assets and liabilities:

Checking account	$2,000
Savings account	4,000
Stocks	8,000
Utility bills	500
Credit card bills	1,000
Auto loan	2,600

What is their current ratio? *Hint:* Set up a balance sheet. (LO 1, 3)

5. A recent college graduate has assets totaling $18,000 and liabilities totaling $19,000. Determine her net worth. Is she solvent? (LO 1, 3)

6. Harry Doyle is a 28-year-old college graduate who didn't take a personal finance class. Now his finances are in a mess. Given the following information, prepare an income statement and balance sheet. Calculate and interpret the current ratio, savings ratio, monthly living expenses covered ratio, and debt ratio. (LO 1, 2, 3)

VISA bill (Average monthly payment)	$ 355
Stocks	5,500
Money Market Account	2,700
MasterCard bill (Average monthly payment)	445
Monthly paycheck, net	2,400
Mortgage payment, monthly	530
Phone bill	85
Cable bill	42
Templeton mutual fund	1,800
Retirement account	2,500
Car payment, monthly	235
Electric bill	60
Natural gas bill	70
Water and sewer bill	50
Savings account	2,100
Checking account	825
Auto insurance, quarterly	450 (Due this month)
Residence	65,000
Food, monthly	225
Auto	9,000
Furnishings	2,000
Baseball card collection	500
Mortgage outstanding	52,000
Auto loan outstanding	4,225
Other personal property	1,800
Other expenses, monthly	150

7. Hannibal Lechter tried to establish a budget. Unfortunately, he has no idea how to budget. Explain to Hannibal why he should establish a budget and how to go about establishing one. (LO 5)

8. If J. J. Garcia spends $29,000 annually on all living expenses and long-term debt, calculate how much he would need to have an emergency fund should he lose his job as a musician.

WWW.
Take It to the Net

We invite you to visit the Keown Personal Finance page on the Prentice Hall Web site at:

http://www.prenhall.com/ persfin

for this chapter's World Wide Web exercise.

You might also want to visit the following Web sites:

Free software from Oakland University's Software Repository: http://mars.acs.oakland.edu/oak/

Information on Funding your college education: http://www.signet.com/collegemoney

College Solutions (more on choosing the right college and funding it): http://college-solutions.com

North Dakota State University's Extension on Family Finances: http://ndsuext.nodak.edu/extpubs/yf/fammgmt/he258w.htm

CNNfn The Financial Network: http://www.cnnfn.com/

Suggested Projects

1. Talk to your parents about their finances. Determine their monthly bills as well as their long-term debt. Prepare an income statement for them and categorize all liabilities as either fixed or variable. Taxes need not be calculated. However, include as much information as possible. Finally, calculate your parents' savings ratio and discuss with them if they're saving this amount. (LO 2, 3, 4)

2. Prepare a 2-week spending chart for yourself and compile an accurate income and expense statement. (LO 2, 4)

3. Keep accurate spending records for 2 weeks. At the end of that time prepare a spending analysis and determine where you spent too much. Prepare a budget based on the modified spending analysis. See how long you can follow the budget. Should you consider an envelope system? (LO 4, 5)

4. Determine an item that you want to purchase (over $200) and instead of buying it on credit, save a little each month. Determine when the item can be purchased and how much you need to save each month to reach your goal. (LO 5)

5. Call a certified financial planner (CFP) and tell him or her that you're a student doing research for a class. Ask the CFP to explain why someone would benefit from his or her service. Keep the phone call brief, but get as much information as possible. Summarize your findings in a written report. (LO 6)

6. Interview five people who use a computer or computer software to track their finances or do budgeting. List the different types of software they use and the capabilities of each. Which one of these software programs would best suit your needs? Why?

7. Find as many of your financial records as you can, including bank and credit card statements. Now calculate how much money you spent in the past 12 months. Was this amount more or less than you anticipated? List and explain five ways that you could spend less in the coming 12 months. (LO 4, 5)

8. Write a one-page essay explaining at least four reasons why you believe that people don't budget. *Hint:* Consider each of the six chapter objectives in your response.

Discussion Case 1

Brenda and Eddie, both 25 years old, want to buy their first home. Their current combined net income is $36,000, and they have loans totaling $15,000. They have $10,000 in checking and savings accounts, but $7,000 is for the purchase of the home. They have total assets worth $21,000. Both of them have very secure jobs and anticipate generous salary increases in the near future. Eddie has always been cautious about spending large amounts of money, but Brenda really likes the idea of owning their own home. They don't have a budget, but they do keep track of their expenses, which amounted to $31,000 last year. They pay off all credit card bills on a monthly basis and don't have any other debt or loans outstanding. Unfortunately, they don't spend a great deal of time tracking their finances.

Questions

1. What financial statements should Brenda and Eddie prepare?

2. Calculate their net worth and income surplus.

3. Calculate and interpret their months living expenses covered ratio and debt ratios.

4. What records should they keep in the future? Why? Be specific.

5. How would you suggest to Brenda and Eddie that they start a budget?

6. Would you suggest that they see a financial planner? What might the planner tell them to do?

Discussion Case 2

Homer and Marge Scott are preparing for retirement. Homer has worked for the electric company his entire life and has participated in all of the retirement savings opportunities that the company offers. As a result, the Scotts have a very large retirement portfolio that's currently being handled by an investment broker. Marge has scrimped and saved every penny for 40 years and would like to live "the good life" for a while but is concerned about overspending their resources. Homer, however, figures "I earned it, I'll spend it." However, Homer and Marge agree on two things. First, they want to be able to leave money to help pay for their grandchildren's education. Second, they are committed to taking control of their financial life.

Questions

1. The Scotts just received a statement from their broker outlining the total value of their investment portfolio. How can they use this information?

2. Why might it be important for the Scotts to establish the market value of their investments?

3. How might an expense statement ensure that they will have the desired amount to leave for their grandchildren?

4. If both their income and expenses change, how would you suggest to them that they not "go overboard in living the good life" during retirement?

5. Should they try to manage the funds themselves, or should they leave them in the care of the financial advisor? Why?

6. Do the Scotts need to track their expenses more or less closely now that Homer has retired? Why?

UNDERSTANDING THE TIME VALUE OF MONEY

Born in Boston in 1706, Ben was the fifteenth of 17 children born to Josiah Franklin, a poor soap and candle maker. With fewer than 2 years of formal education, Ben went to work at an early age, and at age 17 he arrived in Philadelphia looking for work with only $1 in his pocket. Printing became his first love, and in 1732 he published *Poor Richard's Almanack*. It was there that his familiar sayings, such as "A penny saved is a penny earned" and "In this world nothing can be said to be certain, except death and taxes," first appeared.

From there Ben went on to become an American statesman and defender of American rights, a scientist, and a writer. Along the way, his famous kite experiment, in which he flew a kite with a wire attached to a key in a thunderstorm, proved lightning was a form of electricity. He also founded an academy that later became the University of Pennsylvania, established a hospital and an insurance company, invented hand paddles to help you swim faster, and helped draft the Declaration of Independence. For all this, he now looks out at us from the front of a $100 bill. Not bad for someone starting off with only $1 in his pocket.

Benjamin Franklin also was one of this nation's first philanthropists. In this regard, when he died in 1790, he left £1,000 (that was equivalent to about $4,444 in those days) each to his hometown of Boston and to Philadelphia, where he made it rich. With the gift, he left instructions that the cities were to lend the money, charging the going interest rate, to help young married tradesmen start their own businesses.

Learning Objectives

After reading this chapter you should be able to:

1. Explain the mechanics of compounding.

2. Use a financial calculator to determine the time value of money.

3. Understand the power of time in compounding.

4. Explain the importance of the interest rate in determining how an investment grows.

5. Calculate the present value of money to be received in the future.

6. Define an annuity and calculate its compound or future value.

Then, after the money had been invested in this way for 100 years, the cities were to divide it up, using approximately three-fourths for public works and maintaining the rest as a loan fund for tradesmen. Two hundred years later Franklin's Boston gift has helped countless medical students—tradesmen proved hard to find in the last 50 years—with very low cost loans. Today, there's still $4.6 million left in the account. There's no question that Ben Franklin knew how his gift would grow. After all, one of the sayings from *Poor Richard's Almanack* was, "Money makes money. And the money that money makes, makes money." That's the 1700s version of the time value of money.

As we saw in **Axiom 2: The Time Value of Money**, a dollar received today is worth more than a dollar received in the future. Obviously, a dollar received and invested today starts earning interest sooner than a dollar received and invested some time in the future. However, the time value of money means more to personal finance than the ability to generate additional interest. It means that we can't compare amounts of money from two different periods without adjusting for the time value. It means that money you invest today will grow to fund your goals tomorrow. In short, it means that if you want a firm grasp on personal finance, you'd better understand the time value of money.

So just how powerful is the time value of money? Well, if we were to invest $1,000 at only 8 percent interest for 400 years, we'd end up with $23 quadrillion—approximately $5 million per person on earth. Of course, your investments won't span 400 years, but they will rely on the time value of money. If you manage properly, as Boston did with Ben Franklin's gift, time can be the ace up your investment sleeve—the one that lets you rake in more than you would have otherwise imagined possible. Remember that in personal finance, the time value of money is just as widespread as it is powerful. We're always comparing money from different periods—for example, buying a bond today and receiving interest payments in the future, borrowing money to buy a house today and paying it back over the next 30 years, or determining exactly how much to save annually to achieve a certain goal. In fact, there's very little in personal finance that doesn't have some thread of the time value of money woven through it.

AXIOM #2

The Time Value of Money

Time Value of Money
The concept that a dollar received today is worth more than a dollar received in the future, and therefore comparisons between sums in different time periods cannot be made without adjustments to their values.

LEARNING OBJECTIVE #1

Explain the mechanics of compounding.

Compound Interest
The effect of earning interest on interest, resulting from the reinvestment of interest paid on an investment's principal.

Future Value (FV)
The value of an investment at some future point in time.

Present Value (PV)
The current value, that is, the value in today's dollars of a future sum of money.

Reinvesting
Taking money that you have earned on an investment and plowing it back into that investment.

COMPOUND INTEREST AND FUTURE VALUES

So how does the time value of money turn small sums of money into extremely large sums of money? Through compound interest. **Compound interest** is basically interest paid on interest. If you take the interest you earn on an investment and reinvest it, you then start earning interest on the principal and the reinvested interest. In this way, the amount of interest you earn grows, or compounds. Anyone who has ever had a savings account has received compound interest. For example, suppose you place $100 in a savings account that pays 6 percent interest annually. How will your savings grow? At the end of the first year you'll have earned 6 percent, or $6 on your initial deposit of $100, giving you a total of $106 in your savings account. That $106 is the **future value** or **FV** of your investment, that is, the value of your investment at some future point in time. The mathematical formula illustrating the payment of interest is

$$FV_1 = PV(1 + i) \qquad (3.1)$$

where

FV_1 = the future value of the investment at the end of 1 year

i = the annual interest rate

PV = the **present value**, or the current value, that is the value in today's dollars of a sum of money

In our example

$$FV_1 = PV(1 + i) \qquad (3.1)$$
$$= \$100(1 + 0.06)$$
$$= \$100(1.06)$$
$$= \$106$$

Assuming you leave your $6 interest payment in your savings account, known as **reinvesting**, what will your savings look like at the end of the second year? The future value of $106 at the end of the first year, FV_1, becomes the present value at the beginning of the second year. Adding this number into equation (3.1), we get

$$FV_2 = FV_1(1 + i) \qquad (3.2)$$

which, for the example, gives

$$FV_2 = \$106(1.06)$$
$$= \$112.36$$

What will your savings look like at the end of three years? Five years? Ten years? Figure 3.1 illustrates how your investment of $100 would continue to grow for the first 10 years at a compound interest rate of 6 percent. Notice how the amount of interest earned annually increases each year because of compounding.

Why do you earn more interest during the second year than you did during the first? Simply because you now earn interest on the sum of the original principal, or present value, *and* the interest you earned in the first year. In effect, you are now earning interest on interest, which is the concept of compound interest.

How did we determine all the future values of your investment in Figure 3.1? We started with equations (3.1) and (3.2). Because those two equations share a common element, FV_1, we combine them to get

$$FV_2 = PV(1 + i)(1 + i) \qquad (3.3)$$
$$FV_2 = PV(1 + i)^2$$

FIGURE 3.1

Compound Interest at 6% Over Time

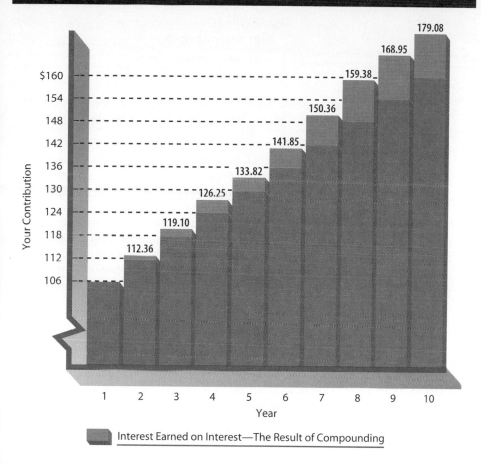

Interest Earned on Interest—The Result of Compounding

We can generalize equation (3.3) to illustrate the value of your investment for any number of years by using the following equation:

$$FV_n = PV(1 + i)^n \qquad (3.4)$$

where

FV_n = the future value of the investment at the end of n years

n = the number of years during which the compounding occurs

i = the annual interest rate

PV = the present value, or the current value; that is, the value in today's dollars of a sum of money

Equation (3.4) *is* the time value of money formula, and it will work for any investment that pays a fixed amount of interest, i, for the life of the investment. As we work through this chapter, sometimes we will solve for i and other times we will solve for PV or n. Regardless, equation (3.4) will be the basis for almost all of our time value calculations.

Example. You receive a $1,000 academic award this year for being the best student in your personal finance course, and you place it in a savings account paying 5 percent annual interest **compounded annually**. How much will your account be

Compounded Annually
With annual compounding the interest is received at the end of each year and then reinvested back into the investment. Then, at the end of the second year, interest is earned on this new sum.

worth in 10 years? Substituting $PV = \$1000$, $i = 5$ percent, and $n = 10$ years into equation (3.4), you get

$$FV_n = PV(1 + i)^n \qquad (3.4)$$
$$= \$1,000(1 + 0.05)^{10}$$
$$= \$1,000(1.62889)$$
$$= \$1,628.89$$

Thus, at the end of 10 years you will have \$1,628.89 in your savings account. Unless, of course, you decide to add in or take out money along the way.

Future-Value Interest Factor (FVIF$_{i,n}$)

The value of $(1 + i)^n$ used as a multiplier to calculate an amount's future value.

Calculating future values by hand can be a serious chore. Luckily, you can use a calculator. Also, there are tables for the $(1 + i)^n$ part of the equation which will now be called the **future-value interest factor** for i and n (**FVIF$_{i,n}$**). These tables simplify your future value calculations by giving you the various values for combinations of i and n. Table 3.1 provides one such table (a more comprehensive version of this table appears in Appendix B at the back of this book). Note that the amounts given in this table represent the value of \$1 compounded at rate i at the end of the nth year. Thus, to calculate the future value of an initial investment, you need only determine the $FVIF_{i,n}$ using a calculator or a table and multiply this amount by the initial investment. In effect, you can rewrite equation (3.4) as follows:

$$\text{future value} = \text{present value} \times \text{future-value interest factor}$$

or $$FV_n = PV(FVIF_{i,n}) \qquad (3.4a)$$

Let's look back at the previous example of investing \$1,000 at 5 percent compounded annually for 10 years. Looking in Table 3.1 at the intersection of the $n = 10$ row and the 5% column, we find a value for $FVIF_{5\%,\,10\,yr} = 1.629$. Thus,

$$FV_{10} = \$1,000 \, (1.629)$$
$$= \$1,629$$

This is the same answer we got before. You can also use this equation to solve for n and i.

TABLE 3.1

FVIF$_{i,n}$, or the Compound Sum of $1

n	1%	2%	3%	4%	5%	6%	7%	8%	9%	10%
1	1.010	1.020	1.030	1.040	1.050	1.060	1.070	1.080	1.090	1.100
2	1.020	1.040	1.061	1.082	1.102	1.124	1.145	1.166	1.188	1.210
3	1.030	1.061	1.093	1.125	1.158	1.191	1.225	1.260	1.295	1.331
4	1.041	1.082	1.126	1.170	1.216	1.262	1.311	1.360	1.412	1.464
5	1.051	1.104	1.159	1.217	1.276	1.338	1.403	1.469	1.539	1.611
6	1.062	1.126	1.194	1.265	1.340	1.419	1.501	1.587	1.677	1.772
7	1.072	1.149	1.230	1.316	1.407	1.504	1.606	1.714	1.828	1.949
8	1.083	1.172	1.267	1.369	1.477	1.594	1.718	1.851	1.993	2.144
9	1.094	1.195	1.305	1.423	1.551	1.689	1.838	1.999	2.172	2.358
10	1.105	1.219	1.344	1.480	1.629	1.791	1.967	2.159	2.367	2.594
11	1.116	1.243	1.384	1.539	1.710	1.898	2.105	2.332	2.580	2.853
12	1.127	1.268	1.426	1.601	1.796	2.012	2.252	2.518	2.813	3.138
13	1.138	1.294	1.469	1.665	1.886	2.133	2.410	2.720	3.066	3.452
14	1.149	1.319	1.513	1.732	1.980	2.261	2.579	2.937	3.342	3.797
15	1.161	1.346	1.558	1.801	2.079	2.397	2.759	3.172	3.642	4.177

Now let's assume that the Chrysler Corporation has guaranteed that the price of a new Jeep will always be $20,000, and you'd like to buy one, but currently you have only $7,752. How many years will it take for your initial investment of $7,752 to grow to $20,000 if it is invested at 9 percent compounded annually? We can use equation (3.4a) to solve for this problem as well. Substituting the known values in equation (3.4a), you find

$$FV_n = PV(FVIF_{i,\,n}) \qquad\qquad (3.4a)$$

$$\$20{,}000 = \$7{,}752(FVIF_{9\%,\,n\,\mathrm{yr}})$$

$$\frac{\$20{,}000}{\$7{,}752} = \frac{\$7{,}752(FVIF_{9\%,\,n\,\mathrm{yr}})}{\$7{,}752}$$

$$2.58 = FVIF_{9\%,\,n\,\mathrm{yr}}$$

Thus, you're looking for a value of 2.58 in the $FVIF_{i,\,n}$ tables, and you know it must be in the 9% column. To finish solving the problem, look down the 9 percent column for the value closest to 2.58. You'll find that it occurs in the $n = 11$ row. Thus, it will take 11 years for an initial investment of $7,752 to grow to $20,000 if it is invested at 9 percent compounded annually.

Now let's solve for the compound annual growth rate, and let's go back to that Jeep that always costs $20,000. In 10 years you'd really like to have $20,000 to buy a new Jeep, but you have only $11,167. At what rate must your $11,167 be compounded annually for it to grow to $20,000 in 10 years? Substituting the known variables into equation (3.4a), you get

$$FV_n = PV(FVIF_{i,\,n}) \qquad\qquad (3.4a)$$

$$\$20{,}000 = \$11{,}167(FVIF_{i,\,10\,\mathrm{yr}})$$

$$\frac{\$20{,}000}{\$11{,}167} = \frac{\$11{,}167(FVIF_{i,\,10\,\mathrm{yr}})}{\$11{,}167}$$

$$1.791 = FVIF_{i,\,10\,\mathrm{yr}}$$

You know you are looking in the $n = 10$ row of the $FVIF_{i,\,n}$ tables for a value of 1.791, and you find this in the $i = 6\%$ column. Thus, if you want your initial investment of $11,167 to grow to $20,000 in 10 years, you must invest it at 6 percent.

The Rule of 72

Now you know how to determine the future value of any investment. What if all you want to know is how long will it take to double your money in that investment? One simple way to approximate how long it will take for a given sum to double in value is called the **Rule of 72**. This "rule" states that you can determine how many years it will take for a given sum to double by dividing the investment's annual growth rate into 72. For example, if an investment grows at an annual rate of 9 percent per year, according to the Rule of 72 it should take $^{72}\!/_9 = 8$ years for that sum to double. Keep in mind that this is not a hard and fast rule, just an approximation, but it's a pretty good approximation at that. For example, the future-value interest factor from Table 3.1 for 8 years at 9 percent is 1.993, which is pretty close to the Rule of 72's approximation of 2.0.

Rule of 72
A helpful investment rule that states that you can determine how many years it will take for a sum to double by dividing the annual growth rate into 72.

Example. Using the "Rule of 72," how long will it take to double your money if you invest it at 12 percent compounded annually?

$$\text{number of years to double} = \frac{72}{\text{annual compound growth rate}}$$

$$= \frac{72}{12}$$

$$= 6 \text{ years}$$

TABLE 3.2

The Value of $100 Compounded at Various Intervals

For 10 Years at *i* Percent	*i* =	2%	5%	10%	15%
Compounded annually		$121.90	$162.89	$259.37	$404.56
Compounded semiannually		122.02	163.86	265.33	424.79
Compounded quarterly		122.08	164.36	268.51	436.04
Compounded monthly		122.12	164.70	270.70	444.02
Compounded weekly (52)		122.14	164.83	271.57	447.20
Compounded daily (365)		122.14	164.87	271.79	448.03

Compound Interest with Nonannual Periods

Until now we've assumed that the compounding period is always annual. Sometimes, though, financial institutions compound interest on a quarterly, daily, or even continuous basis. What happens to your investment when your compounding period is nonannual? You earn more money faster. The sooner your interest is paid, the sooner you start earning interest on it, and the sooner you experience the benefits of compound interest.

The bottom line here is that your money grows faster as the compounding period becomes shorter—for example, from annual compounding to monthly compounding. Thus, because interest is earned on interest more frequently as the length of the compounding period declines, there is an inverse relationship between the length of the compounding period and the **effective annual interest rate**. This effective annual interest rate is often defined as

$$\text{effective annual interest rate} = \frac{\text{the amount of annual interest earned (or paid)}}{\text{amount of money invested (or borrowed)}}$$

In effect, as compounding happens more frequently than annually, annual interest rates are actually misstated because the frequent compounding increases them. Table 3.2 illustrates the importance of nonannual compounding.

Effective Annual Interest Rate
What the interest rate actually is, after adjusting for nonannual compounding, that is, the amount of interest earned (or paid) over the amount of money invested (or borrowed).

TIME VALUE CALCULATIONS WITH A FINANCIAL CALCULATOR

Time value of money calculations can be made simple with the aid of a financial calculator. Before you try to whoop it up solving time value of money problems on your financial calculator, you might want to take note of a few keys that will prove helpful (necessary, actually).

Menu Key Description

N Stores (or calculates) the total number of payments or compounding periods.

I/Y Stores (or calculates) the interest or discount rate.

PV Stores (or calculates) the present value.

FV Stores (or calculates) the future value.

PMT Stores (or calculates) the dollar amount of each annuity payment. (We will talk about these later in the chapter, but an annuity is a series of equal dollar payments for a specified number of time periods, for example, years).

LEARNING OBJECTIVE #2

Use a financial calculator to determine the time value of money.

CPT This is the compute key on the Texas Instruments BAII Plus calculator, the calculator we will use in examples in this text. For example, if you want to compute the present value, you enter the known variables and press CPT PV.

Something to keep in mind when using a financial calculator is that each problem will have two cash flows, and one will be a positive number and one a negative number. The idea is that you deposit money in the bank at some point in time (a negative number, because it "leaves your hands"), and at some other point in time you take money out of the bank (a positive number, because it "returns to your hands"). Also, every calculator operates a bit differently with respect to entering variables. Needless to say, it is a good idea to familiarize yourself with exactly how your calculator functions. To solve a time value of money problem using a financial calculator, all you need to do is enter the appropriate numbers for three of the four variables and then press the key of the final variable to calculate its value.

Now let's solve the previous example using a financial calculator. We were trying to find at what rate $11,167 must be compounded annually for it to grow to $20,000 in 10 years. The solution using a financial calculator would be as follows:

Step 1: Input Values of Known Variables

Data Input	Function Key	Description
10	N	Stores $N = 10$ years
–11,167	PV	Stores $PV = -\$11,167$
20,000	FV	Stores $FV = \$20,000$
0	PMT	Clears PMT to $= 0$, since that variable is not included in this problem

Step 2: Calculate the Value of the Unknown Variable

Function Key	Answer	Description
CPT I/Y	6.00%	Calculates $I/Y = 6.00\%$

Any of the problems in this chapter can easily be solved using a financial calculator. If you are using the TI BAII Plus, make sure that you have selected both the "one payment per year" ($P/Y = 1$) and "END MODE." This sets the payment conditions to a maximum of one payment per period occurring at the end of the period. One final point: You will notice that solutions using the present value tables versus solutions using a calculator may vary slightly. Don't worry—this discrepancy is just a result of rounding errors in the tables.

For further explanation of financial calculators see Appendix A at the end of the book.

COMPOUNDING AND THE POWER OF TIME

Manhattan Island was purchased by Peter Minuit from Native Americans in 1624 for $24 in "knickknacks" and jewelry. If at the end of 1624 the Native Americans had invested their $24 at 8 percent compounded annually, it would be worth over $70.3 trillion today (by the end of 1997, 373 years later). That's certainly enough to buy back all of Manhattan. In fact, with $70 trillion in the bank, the $50 billion to $60 billion you'd

have to pay to buy back all of Manhattan would seem like only pocket change. This story illustrates the incredible power of time in compounding. There simply is no substitute for it.

Why should you care about compounding? Well, the sooner you start saving for retirement and other long-term goals, the less painful the process of saving will be. Consider the tale of twin sisters who work at the Springfield DMV—Selma and Patty Bouvier, who decide to save for retirement, which is 35 years away. They'll both receive an 8 percent annual return on their investment over the next 35 years. Selma invests $2,000 per year at the end of each year *only* for the first 10 years of the 35-year period—for a total of $20,000 saved. Patty doesn't start saving for 10 years and then saves $2,000 per year at the end of each year for the remaining 25 years—for a total of $50,000 saved. When they retire, Selma will have accumulated just under $200,000, while Patty will have accumulated just under $150,000, despite the fact that Selma saved for only 10 years while Patty saved for 25 years. Figure 3.2 presents their results and illustrates the power of time in compounding.

Let's look at another example to see what this really means to you. The compound growth rate on the stock market over the period 1926–1996 was approximately 10.71 percent.[1] Although the rate of return on stocks has been far from

[1]See Ibbotson Associates, *Stocks, Bonds, Bills, & Inflation 1997 Yearbook*™ (Chicago, 1997).

FIGURE 3.2

The Power of Time in Compounding

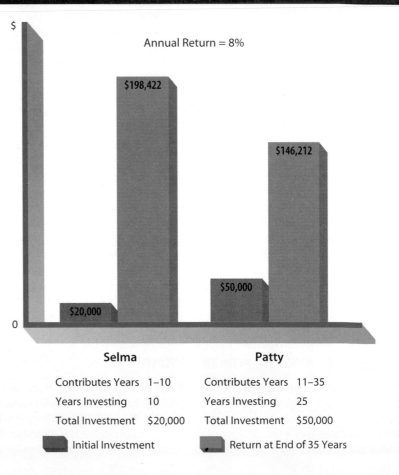

	Selma	Patty
Contributes Years	1–10	11–35
Years Investing	10	25
Total Investment	$20,000	$50,000

Initial Investment | Return at End of 35 Years

constant over this period, assume for the moment that you could earn a constant annual return of 10.71 percent compounded annually on an investment in stocks. If you invested $500 in stocks at the beginning of 1926 and earned 10.71 percent compounded annually, your investment would have grown to $759,317 by the end of 1997 (72 years). That would make you one wealthy senior citizen. The power of compounding is truly amazing. Say you're 22 and intend to retire at age 65—43 years from now. If you place $12,588 in stocks and they earn 10.71 percent compounded annually over those 43 years, you'd have accumulated $1 million by retirement—all in just 15,695 days! Of course, by then you might have become a strict Buddhist and renounced money, but what the hey.

One final example illustrates the danger in just looking at the bottom-line numbers without considering the time value of money. One of today's "hot" collectibles is the Schwinn Deluxe Tornado boys' bicycle, which sold for $49.95 in 1959. In 1997, 38 years later, a Schwinn Tornado in mint condition sells for $600, which is about 12 times its original cost. On first glance you might view this as a 1,200-percent return—but you'd be ignoring the time value of money. At what rate did this investment really compound? The answer is 6.76 percent per year—which ignores any storage costs that might have been incurred. The Schwinn may provide a great ride, but, given what you just saw common stocks doing over the same period, it doesn't provide a very good return.

THE IMPORTANCE OF THE INTEREST RATE IN COMPOUNDING

It's not just time that makes money grow in value, it's also the interest rate. Most people understand that a higher interest rate earns you more money—that's why some people are willing to buy a risky bond issued by MGM Grand that pays 11 percent rather than a very safe bond issued by the government that pays only 6.5 percent—but most people don't understand just how dramatic a difference the interest rate can really make. This brings us back to **Axiom 9: The Best Protection Is Knowledge**. Without an understanding of investment concepts such as the time value of money, you're a prime target for bozos offering bad advice. You're also at a real disadvantage because you might not be able to take advantage of good deals and even basic financial principles, such as those that apply to interest rates. The bottom line here is that it's much easier to do things correctly if you understand what you're doing, so let's take a closer look at interest rates.

Obviously, the choice of the interest rate plays a critical role in how much an investment grows, but do small changes in the interest rate have much of an impact on future values? To answer this question, let's look back to Peter Minuit's purchase of Manhattan. If the Native Americans had invested their $24 at 10 percent rather than 8 percent compounded annually at the end of 1624, they would have over $66 quadrillion by the end of 1997 (373 years). That's 66 followed by 15 zeros, or $66,000,000,000,000,000. Actually, that's enough to buy back not only Manhattan Island, but the entire world and still have plenty left over! Now let's assume a lower interest rate, say 6 percent. In that case the $24 would have only grown to a mere $66.0 billion—about one thousandth of what it grew to at 8 percent, and only one millionth of what it would have grown to at 10 percent. With today's real estate prices, you could probably buy Manhattan, but you probably couldn't pay your taxes! To say the least, the interest rate is extremely important in investing.

Now let's take another look at some historical returns and see what you might have earned from 1926 through 1996. Recall that the compound growth rate on stocks over that period was approximately 10.71 percent. The average return on long-term corporate bonds over that same period was only 5.64 percent compounded annually. If you'd invested $500 in bonds rather than stocks at the

TABLE 3.3

The Daily Double	
Day	**"Daily double": 1¢ at 100% Compounded Daily Would Become**
Day 1	$ .01
Day 2	.02
Day 3	.04
Day 4	.08
Day 5	.16
Day 6	.32
Day 7	.64
Day 8	1.28
Day 15	163.84
Day 20	5,242.88
Day 25	167,772.16
Day 30	5,368,709.12
Day 31	10,737,418.24

beginning of 1926 and earned 5.64 percent compounded annually, your investment would have grown to $25,979 by the end of 1997 (72 years). This amount is well below the $759,317 you would have ended up with if your money had been invested in the stock market, which grew at 10.71 percent.

To illustrate the power of a high interest rate in compounding, let's look at a "daily double." A "daily double" simply means that your money doubles each day. In effect, it assumes an interest rate of 100 percent compounded on a daily basis. Let's see what can happen to a mere penny over a month's worth of daily doubles, assuming that the month has 31 days in it. The first day begins with 1¢, the second day it compounds to 2¢, the third day it becomes 4¢, the fourth day 8¢, the fifth day 16¢, and so forth. As shown in Table 3.3, by the day 20 it would have grown to $5,242.88, and by the day 31 it would have grown to over $10 million. Going from 1¢ to $10 million in 31 days is a lot more of a rush than going from 0 to 60 mph in 6 seconds!

These examples explain why Albert Einstein once marveled that "Compound interest is the eighth wonder of the world."

> ### The Facts of Life
> If you receive an inheritance of $25,000 and invest it at 6 percent (ignoring taxes) for 40 years, it will accumulate to $257,125. If you invest it at 12 percent (again ignoring taxes) over this same period, it would accumulate to $2,326,225! Almost 10 times more!

LEARNING OBJECTIVE #5

Calculate the present value of money to be received in the future.

PRESENT VALUE

Up until this point we've been moving money forward in time; that is, we know how much we have to begin with and are trying to determine how much that sum will grow in a certain number of years when compounded at a specific rate. We're now going to look at the reverse question: What's the value in today's dollars of a sum of money to be received in the future? That is, what's the present value? Why is present value important to us? It'll let us strip away the effects of inflation and see what future cash flows are worth in today's dollars. Also, it let's us compare dollar values from different periods. In later chapters we'll use the present value to determine how much to pay for stocks and bonds.

In finding the present value of a future sum, we're moving future money back to the present. What we're doing is, in fact, nothing other than inverse compounding. In compounding we talked about the compound interest rate and the initial investment; in determining the present value we will talk about the **discount rate** and present value. When we use the term discount rate, we mean the interest rate used to bring future money back to present, that is, the interest rate used to "discount" that future money back to present. Other than that, the technique and the terminology remain the same, and the mathematics are simply reversed. Let's return to equation (3.4), the time value of money equation. We now want to solve for present value instead of future value, so we divide both sides of the equation by $(1 + i)^n$ to get

$$FV_n = PV(1 + i)^n \qquad\qquad (3.4)$$

$$\frac{FV_n}{(1 + i)^n} = \frac{PV(1 + i)^n}{(1 + i)^n}$$

$$FV_n\left(\frac{1}{(1 + i)^n}\right) = PV$$

$$\text{or} \qquad PV = FV_n\left(\frac{1}{(1 + i)^n}\right) \qquad\qquad (3.5)$$

where

FV_n = the future value of the investment at the end of n years

n = the number of years until the payment will be received

i – the annual discount (or interest) rate

PV = the present value of the future sum of money

Because the mathematical procedure for determining the present value is exactly the inverse of determining the future value, we find that the relationships among n, i, and PV are just the opposite of those we observed in future value. The present value of a future sum of money is inversely related to both the number of years until the payment will be received and the discount rate. Figure 3.3 shows this relationship graphically.

Discount Rate
The interest rate used to bring future dollars back to the present.

FIGURE 3.3

The Present Value of $100

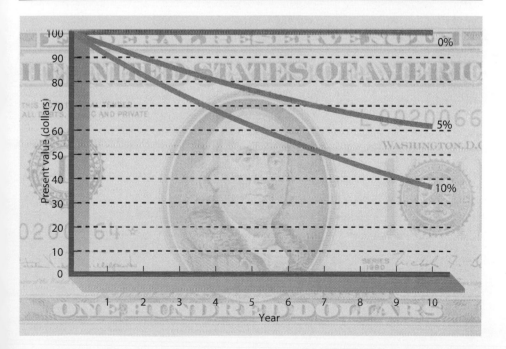

CHAPTER 3 · Understanding the Time Value of Money

Present-Value Interest Factor (PVIF$_{i, n}$)

The value $[1/(1+i)^n]$ used as a multiplier to calculate an amount's present value.

To aid in the computation of present values, we once again have some handy tables. This time they calculate the $[1/(1 + i)^n]$ part of the equation, which we call the **present-value interest factor** for i and n, or **PVIF$_{i, n}$**. These tables simplify the math involved by giving us the various values for combinations of i and n defined as $[1/(1 + i)^n]$. Appendix C at the back of this book presents fairly complete versions of these tables, and an abbreviated version of these tables appears in Table 3.4. A close examination of Table 3.4 shows that the values in these tables are merely the inverse of the tables found in Appendix B and Table 3.1. Of course, this inversion makes sense because the values in Appendix B are $(1 + i)^n$ and those in Appendix C are $[1/(1 + i)^n]$. Now, to determine the present value of a sum of money to be received at some future date, you need only determine the value of the appropriate PVIF$_{i, n}$, either by using a calculator or consulting the tables, and multiply it by the future value. In effect, you can use the new notation and rewrite equation (3.5) as follows:

$$present\ value = future\ value \times present\text{-}value\ interest\ factor$$

or

$$PV = FV_n(PVIF_{i,n}) \qquad (3.5a)$$

Example. You're on vacation in a rather remote part of Florida and see an advertisement stating that if you take a sales tour of some condominiums that "you will be given $100 just for taking the tour." However, the $100 that you get is in the form of a savings bond that will not pay you the $100 for 10 years. What is the present value of $100 to be received 10 years from today if your discount rate is 6 percent? By looking at the $n = 10$ row and $i = 6\%$ column of Table 3.4, you find the $PVIF_{6\%, 10\ yr}$ is 0.558. Substituting $FV_{10} = \$100$ and $PVIF_{6\%, 10\ yr} = 0.558$ into equation (3.5a), you find

$$PV = \$100(PVIF_{6\%, 10\ yr}]$$
$$= \$100(0.558)$$
$$= \$55.80$$

Thus, the value in today's dollars of that $100 savings bond is only $55.80. Still, that's not a bad take for touring some condominiums, but it's not $100.

TABLE 3.4

PVIF$_{i, n}$, or the Present Value of $1

n	1%	2%	3%	4%	5%	6%	7%	8%	9%	10%
1	.990	.980	.971	.962	.952	.943	.935	.926	.917	.909
2	.980	.961	.943	.925	.907	.890	.873	.857	.842	.826
3	.971	.942	.915	.889	.864	.840	.816	.794	.772	.751
4	.961	.924	.888	.855	.823	.792	.763	.735	.708	.683
5	.951	.906	.863	.822	.784	.747	.713	.681	.650	.621
6	.942	.888	.837	.790	.746	.705	.666	.630	.596	.564
7	.933	.871	.813	.760	.711	.655	.623	.583	.547	.513
8	.923	.853	.789	.731	.677	.627	.582	.540	.502	.467
9	.914	.837	.766	.703	.645	.592	.544	.500	.460	.424
10	.905	.820	.744	.676	.614	.558	.508	.463	.422	.386
11	.896	.804	.722	.650	.585	.527	.475	.429	.388	.350
12	.887	.789	.701	.625	.557	.497	.444	.397	.356	.319
13	.879	.773	.681	.601	.530	.469	.415	.368	.326	.290
14	.870	.758	.661	.577	.505	.442	.388	.340	.299	.263
15	.861	.743	.642	.555	.481	.417	.362	.315	.275	.239

Example. You own a $1,000 savings bond that will mature at the end of 10 years. Because of an economic report that you just heard, you assume that between now and then, inflation will be at an annual rate of 5 percent. You've been doing a little financial planning, and want to know how helpful your savings bond will be in achieving your future goals. The only problem is that all of your best estimates are based on today's dollars, not the inflated dollars of 10 years from now. To help your financial planning, you need to adjust the value of your savings bond for inflation. What is the value of this $1,000 to be received 10 years from now in today's dollars? By looking at the $n = 10$ row and $i = 5\%$ column of Table 3.4, you find the $PVIF_{5\%,\ 10\ yr}$ is 0.614. Substituting this value into equation (3.5a), you find

$$PV = \$1000(0.614)$$
$$= \$614.00$$

Thus, the present value of this $1,000 payment is $614.00. That means that if the inflation rate is 5 percent over the next 10 years, the purchasing power of the $1,000 that you receive at that time will be only $614.00 in today's dollars. It looks like it's best not to plan on using that bond to buy anything that currently costs more than $614.

Stop and Think

Why should you be interested in stripping away the effects of inflation from money that you receive in the future? Because the dollar value of future money is not as important as that money's purchasing power. For example, you might be excited if you were told that you were going to receive $1 million in 20 years. However, if you then found out that in 20 years a new car will cost $800,000, your average monthly food bill would be $15,000, and a typical month's rent on your apartment would be $30,000, you would have a different view of the $1 million. Dollar amounts aren't important, but purchasing power is, and using the time value of money to strip away the effects of inflation allows you to calculate the value of a future amount in the purchasing power of today's dollars.

Keep in mind that there is really only one present value–future value equation. That is, equations (3.4) and (3.5) are actually identical, they simply solve for different variables. The logic behind both equations is the same: To adjust for the time value of money, we must compare dollar values, present and future, in the same time period. Because all present values are comparable (they are all measured in dollars of the same time period), you can add and subtract the present value of inflows and outflows to determine the present value of an investment.

Example. What is the present value of an investment that yields both $500 to be received in 5 years and $1,000 to be received in 10 years if the discount rate is

4 percent? Substituting the values of $n = 5$, $i = 4\%$, and $FV_5 = \$500$; and $n = 10$, $i = 4\%$, and $FV_{10} = \$1,000$ into equation (3.5a) and adding these values together, we find

$$PV = \$500(PVIF_{4\%,\ 5\ yr}) + \$1,000(PVIF_{4\%,\ 10\ yr})$$
$$= \$500(0.822) + \$1,000(0.676)$$
$$= \$411 + \$676$$
$$= \$1,087$$

Again, present values are comparable and can be added together because they are measured in the same time period's dollars.

ANNUITIES

To this point, we've been examining single deposits—moving them back and forth in time. Now we're going to examine annuities. An **annuity** is a series of equal dollar payments coming at the end of each time period for a specified number of time periods (years, months, etc.). Because annuities occur frequently in finance—for example, as bond interest payments and mortgage payments—they are treated specially. Although compounding and determining the present value of an annuity can be done using equations (3.4) and (3.5), these calculations can be time-consuming, especially for larger annuities. Thus, we have modified the formulas to deal directly with annuities.

Compound Annuities

A **compound annuity** involves depositing or investing an equal sum of money at the end of each year (or time period) for a certain number of years (or time periods, for example, months) and allowing it to grow. Perhaps you are saving money for education, a new car, or a vacation home. In each case you'll want to know how much your savings will have grown by some point in the future.

Actually, you can find the answer by using equation (3.4) and compounding each of the individual deposits to its future value. For example, if to provide for a college education you are going to deposit $500 at the end of each year for the next 5 years in a bank where it will earn 6 percent interest, how much will you have at the end of 5 years? Compounding each of these values using equation (3.4), you find that you will have $2,818.50 at the end of 5 years.

$$FV_5 = \$500(1 + 0.06)^4 + \$500(1 + 0.06)^3 + \$500(1 + 0.06)^2 + \$500(1 + 0.06) + \$500$$
$$= \$500(1.262) + \$500(1.191) + \$500(1.124) + \$500(1.060) + \$500$$
$$= \$631.00 + \$595.50 + \$562.00 + \$530.00 + \$500.00$$
$$= \$2,818.50$$

As Table 3.5 shows, all we're really doing in the preceding calculation is summing up a number of consecutive future-value interest factors. To simplify this process once again, there are tables providing the **future-value interest factor for an annuity** for i and n (**FVIFA$_{i,\ n}$**). Appendix D provides a fairly complete version of these tables, and Table 3.6 presents an abbreviated version. Using this new factor, we can calculate the future value of an annuity as follows:

$$\text{future value of an annuity} = \text{annual payment} \times \text{future value interest factor of an annuity}$$

or

$$FV_n = PMT(FVIFA_{i,\ n}) \tag{3.6}$$

LEARNING OBJECTIVE #6

Define an annuity and calculate its compound or future value.

Annuity
A series of equal dollar payments coming at the end of each time period for a specified number of time periods.

Compound Annuity
An investment that involves depositing an equal sum of money at the end of each year for a certain number of years and allowing it to grow.

Future-Value Interest Factor for an Annuity (FVIFA$_{i,\ n}$)
A multiplier used to determine the future value of an annuity. The future-value interest factors are found in Appendix D in the back of the book.

TABLE 3.5

Illustration of a 5-Year $500 Annuity Compounded at 6%

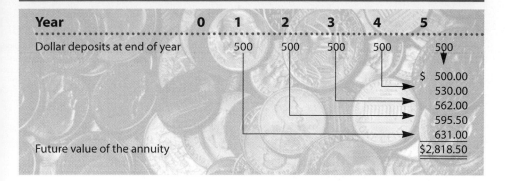

Year	0	1	2	3	4	5
Dollar deposits at end of year		500	500	500	500	500

$ 500.00
530.00
562.00
595.50
631.00

Future value of the annuity $2,818.50

where

FV_n = the future value of the annuity at the end of the nth year

PMT = the annuity payment deposited or received at the end of each year

i = the annual interest (or discount) rate

n = the number of years for which the annuity will last

Using the future-value interest factor for an annuity ($FVIFA$) to solve our previous example involving 5 years of deposits of $500, invested at 6 percent interest, we would look in the $i = 6\%$ column and $n = 5$ row and find the value of the $FVIFA_{6\%, 5\ yr}$ to be 5.637. Substituting this value into equation (3.6), we get

$$FV_5 = \$500(FVIFA_{6\%, 5\ yr})$$
$$FV_5 = \$500(5.637)$$
$$= \$2,818.50$$

This is the same answer we obtained earlier. (If it weren't, I'd need to get a new job!) Rather than ask how much you'll accumulate if you deposit an equal sum in a savings

TABLE 3.6

$FVIFA_{i, n}$, or the Sum of an Annuity of $1 for n Years

n	1%	2%	3%	4%	5%	6%	7%	8%	9%	10%
1	1.000	1.000	1.000	1.000	1.000	1.000	1.000	1.000	1.000	1.000
2	2.010	2.020	2.030	2.040	2.050	2.060	2.070	2.080	2.090	2.100
3	3.030	3.060	3.091	3.122	3.152	3.184	3.215	3.246	3.278	3.310
4	4.060	4.122	4.184	4.246	4.310	4.375	4.440	4.506	4.573	4.641
5	5.101	5.204	5.309	5.416	5.526	5.637	5.751	5.867	5.985	6.105
6	6.152	6.308	6.468	6.633	6.802	6.975	7.153	7.336	7.523	7.716
7	7.214	7.434	7.662	7.898	8.142	8.394	8.654	8.923	9.200	9.487
8	8.286	8.583	8.892	9.214	9.549	9.897	10.260	10.637	11.028	11.436
9	9.368	9.755	10.159	10.583	11.027	11.491	11.978	12.488	13.021	13.579
10	10.462	10.950	11.464	12.006	12.578	13.181	13.816	14.487	15.193	15.937
11	11.567	12.169	12.808	13.486	14.207	14.972	15.784	16.645	17.560	18.531
12	12.682	13.412	14.192	15.026	15.917	16.870	17.888	18.977	20.141	21.384
13	13.809	14.680	15.618	16.627	17.713	18.882	20.141	21.495	22.953	24.523
14	14.947	15.974	17.086	18.292	19.598	21.015	22.550	24.215	26.019	27.975
15	16.097	17.293	18.599	20.023	21.578	23.276	25.129	27.152	29.361	31.772

account each year, a more common question is, How much must you deposit each year to accumulate a certain amount of savings? This question often arises when saving for large expenditures, such as retirement or a down payment on a home.

For example, you may know that you'll need $10,000 for education in 8 years. How much must you put away at the end of each year at 6-percent interest to have the college money ready? In this case, you know the values of n, i, and FV_n in equation (3.6), but you don't know the value of *PMT*. Substituting these example values in equation (3.6), you find

$$\$10,000 = PMT(FVIFA_{6\%,\ 8\ yr})$$

$$\$10,000 = PMT(9.897)$$

$$\frac{\$10,000}{9.897} = PMT$$

$$PMT = \$1,010.41$$

Thus, you must invest $1,010.41 at the end of each year at 6-percent interest to accumulate $10,000 at the end of 8 years.

For a moment let's use the future value of an annuity and think back to the discussion of the power of time. There's no question of the power of time. One way to illustrate this power is to look at how much you'd have to save each month to reach some far-off goal. For example, you'd like to save up $50,000 by the time you turn 60 to use to go see a Rolling Stones concert (there's a good chance they'll still be on tour and that concert tickets will cost that much). If you can invest your money at 12 percent and start saving when you turn 21, making your last payment on your sixtieth birthday, you'll need to put aside only $4.25 per month. If you started at age 31, that figure would be $14.31 per month. However, if you waited until age 51, it would rise up to $217.35 per month. There's no question, when it comes to compounding, time is on your side.

> ### *The Facts of Life*
> If a couple goes out to dinner and a movie four times a month at $75 an outing and cuts this down to two times per month, they will save $1,800 per year. If they take this saved money and invest it at the end of each year, earning 10 percent compounded annually (ignoring taxes), in 30 years they would accumulate $296,089!

Example.   You'd like to take a world cruise in 10 years and you know that the cost of the cruise at that time will be $5,000. How much must you deposit in an 8-percent savings account at the end of each year to accumulate $5,000 at the end of 10 years? Substituting the values $FV_{10} = \$5,000$, $n = 10$, and $i = 8\%$ into equation (3.6), we find

$$\$5,000 = PMT(FVIFA_{8\%,\ 10\ yr})$$

$$\$5,000 = PMT(14.487)$$

$$\frac{\$5,000}{14.487} = PMT$$

$$PMT = \$345.14$$

Thus, you must deposit $345.14 per year for 10 years at 8 percent to accumulate $5,000.

LOSING MONEY AS YOU SLEEP:
Inflation's Constant Erosion

To Americans who lived through the 1970s, today's inflation rate seems mild, almost negligible.

Public pronouncements reinforce that sense. The challenge is "keeping the lid on" inflation, or "preventing a resurgence" of inflation—as if inflation is under control and the only problem is keeping it there.

But inflation is not gone. Nor is it merely sleeping. Even at the current rate of just under 3 percent, it is hard at work like some insidious weevil eating away at Americans' savings and investment returns.

"The biggest problem investors and retirees have is dealing with inflation," said H. Lynn Hopewell of the Monitor Group, a Fairfax money management and advisory firm. "People who think [inflation] is gone don't deal with real money."

Think about it, said Hopewell: "If inflation is just 4 percent, your buying power [on the same amount of income] is cut in half in just 16 years. In 30 years, you're down to a quarter of the purchasing power" you originally had.

For the tens of millions of Americans who are being forced to assume personal responsibility for their long-term financial well-being, the effects of inflation offer more threat than benefit. Labor contracts with inflation protections are becoming rare, in contrast to the 1970s, and there also is the well-known shift of pension and retirement saving away from company-managed plans to those that depend on the individual's own investment decisions.

The tax treatment of these retirement savings plans eases the tax bite, but it doesn't shelter them from inflation. Invest $10,000 at 6 percent for 30 years and it will grow to more than $57,000. But that amount will have the buying power of only about $23,000 of today's dollars if inflation remains at 3 percent. If you get 10.5 percent on your $10,000 for 30 years, it will grow to just under $200,000. But at 3 percent inflation, that's the equivalent of only about $80,000 in today's dollars.

Source: Albert B. Crenshaw, "Losing Money as You Sleep: Inflation's Constant Erosion," *The Washington Post,* June 9, 1996, p. H1. © 1996, *The Washington Post.* Reprinted with permission.

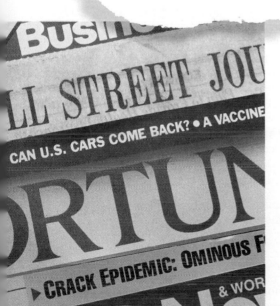

Analysis and Implications ...

A. Although inflation may not look like much at 3 or 4 percent, it remains painful because it's a continuous effect. Moreover, it erodes both the value of your income and your assets. With taxes, you get hit only once—not so with inflation.

B. We should note that some people benefit from inflation: those who've borrowed money and are now able to repay their debt with "cheaper" dollars, that is, dollars with reduced purchasing power.

C. Obviously, earning 10.5-percent interest during a period of 3-percent inflation is quite good (you're effectively earning 7.5-percent interest), but you must also consider taxes when you talk about how much you are earning. Moreover, if you're saving up for something such as your children's college education—something that's rising in cost much faster than inflation—the situation is a bit more grave, especially when you consider the effect of taxes. The bottom line here is that even a 3-percent level of inflation is painful.

Example. Let's take one more look at the power of compounding. Assume you empty the change out of your pocket each day—averaging a dollar a day—and set it aside. Then, at the end of each year, invest it at 12 percent. If you began doing this at age 18, 50 years later you would have accumulated $876,007. If you waited until you were 33 to begin your pocket-emptying ritual, you'd accumulate only $157,557. Keep in mind that between the time you were 18 and when you turned 33 you invested only a total of $5,475. The point here goes back to **Axiom 15: Just Do It**. There is no substitute for time in the world of investing.

The Facts of Life

If you take one vacation instead of two per year, saving $2,000 annually for 30 years in an account earning 11 percent compounded annually (ignoring taxes), your savings would grow to $398,042! That's enough for one whole lot of vacations during your retirement.

Present Value of an Annuity

Most people deal with a great number of annuities. Pension funds, insurance obligations, and interest received from bonds all involve annuities. In planning your finances, you'll need to examine the relative value of all your annuities. To compare them, you need to know the present value of each. Although you can find the present value of an annuity by using the present value table in Appendix C, this process can be tedious, particularly when the annuity lasts for several years. For example, if you wish to know what $500 received at the end of the next 5 years is worth to you given the appropriate discount rate of 6 percent, you can simply substitute the appropriate values into equation (3.6), such that

$$PV = \$500(PVIF_{6\%, \, 1 \, yr}) + \$500(PVIF_{6\%, \, 2 \, yr}) + \$500(PVIF_{6\%, \, 3 \, yr}) +$$
$$\$500(PVIF_{6\%, \, 4 \, yr}) + \$500(PVIF_{6\%, \, 5 \, yr})$$
$$= \$500(0.943) + \$500(0.890) + \$500(0.840) + \$500(0.792) + \$500(0.747)$$
$$= \$2,106$$

Thus, the present value of this annuity is $2,106.00. As Table 3.7 shows, all we're really doing in the preceding calculation is simply adding up *PVIF*s. Because annuities occur so frequently in personal finance, the process of determining the present value of an annuity has been simplified by defining the **present-value interest factor for an annuity** for i and n (**$PVIFA_{i, \, n}$**). The $PVIFA_{i, \, n}$ is simply the sum of the *PVIF*s for years 1 to n. Tables for values of $PVIFA_{i, \, n}$ have once again been compiled for various combinations of i and n. Appendix E provides a fairly complete version of these tables, and Table 3.8 provides an abbreviated version.

Using this new factor we can determine the present value of an annuity as follows:

$$\frac{\text{present value}}{\text{of an annuity}} = \frac{\text{annual}}{\text{payment}} \times \frac{\text{present-value interest}}{\text{factor of an annuity}}$$

or

$$PV = PMT(PVIFA_{i, \, n}) \tag{3.7}$$

Using the present-value interest factor for an annuity (*PVIFA*) to solve our previous example involving $500 received annually and discounted back to the present at 6 percent,

---

Present-Value Interest Factor for an Annuity ($PVIFA_{i, \, n}$)

A multiplier used to determine the present value of an annuity. The present-value interest factors are found in Appendix E in the back of the book.

In the News ...

The Wall Street Journal, April 22, 1994

MAKE A CHILD A MILLIONAIRE, Just Take Your Time

Thanks a million.

Even if you haven't got a lot of money, you can easily give $1 million or more to your children, grandchildren or favorite charity. All it takes is a small initial investment and a lot of time.

Suppose your 16-year-old daughter plans to take a summer job, which will pay her at least $2,000. Because she has earned income, she can open an individual retirement account. If you would like to help fund her retirement, Kenneth Klegon, a financial planner in Lansing, Mich., suggests giving her $2,000 to set up the IRA. He then advises doing the same in each of the next five years, so that your daughter stashes away a total of $12,000.

(A) Result? If the money is invested in stocks, and stocks deliver their historical average annual return of 10%, your daughter will have more than $1 million by the time she turns 65.

(B) Because of the corrosive effect of inflation, that $1 million will only buy a quarter of what $1 million buys today, presuming the cost of living rises at 3% a year. Nonetheless, your $12,000 gift will go a long way toward paying your daughter's retirement. The huge gain is possible because of the way stock market compounding works, with money earned each year not only on your initial investment, but also on the gains accumulated from earlier years.

Source: Jonathan Clements, "Make a Child a Millionaire," *The Wall Street Journal*, April 22, 1994, page C1. Reprinted by permission of *The Wall Street Journal*, © 1994 Dow Jones & Company, Inc. All Rights Reserved Worldwide.

Analysis and Implications ...

A. Using the principles and techniques set out in this chapter, we can easily see how big this IRA investment will grow. We can first take the $2,000 six-year annuity and determine its future value, that is, its value when your daughter is 21 and the last payment takes place, as follows:

$$FV = PMT(FVIFA_{10\%,\ 6\ yr})$$
$$= \$2,000(FVIFA_{10\%,\ 6\ yr})$$
$$= \$15,431.22$$

We could take this amount that your daughter has when she is 21 and compound it out 44 years to when she is 65 as follows:

$$FV = PV(FVIF_{10\%,\ 44\ yr})$$
$$= \$15,431.22(FVIF_{10\%,\ 44\ yr})$$
$$= \$1,022,535.54$$

Thus, your daughter's IRA would have accumulated to $1,022,535.54 by age 65 if it grew at 10 percent compounded annually.

B. To determine how much this amount is worth in today's dollars, we calculate the present value of $1,022,535.54 to be received in 49 years given a discount rate of 3 percent:

$$PV = FV(PVIF_{3\%,\ 49\ yr})$$
$$= \$1,022,235.54(PVIF_{3\%,\ 49\ yr})$$
$$= \$240,245.02$$

You can change the growth and inflation rates and come up with all kinds of numbers, but one thing holds—there is incredible power in compounding!

TABLE 3.7

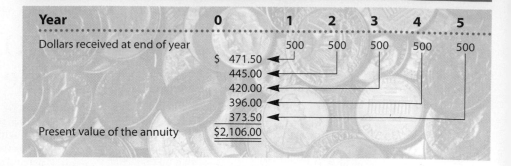

Illustration of a 5-Year $500 Annuity Discounted Back to the Present at 6%

Year		0	1	2	3	4	5
Dollars received at end of year			500	500	500	500	500
	$ 471.50						
	445.00						
	420.00						
	396.00						
	373.50						
Present value of the annuity	$2,106.00						

we would look in the $i = 6\%$ column and the $n = 5$ row and find the $PVIFA_{6\%,\ 5\ yr}$ to be 4.212. Substituting the appropriate values into equation (3.7), we find

$$PV = PMT(PVIFA_{i,\ n})$$
$$PV = \$500(PVIFA_{6\%,\ 5\ yr})$$
$$= \$500(4.212)$$
$$= \$2,106$$

Again, we get the same answer we previously did. (We're on a roll now!) We didn't get the same answer just because we're smart. Actually, we got the same answer both times because the *PVIFA* tables are calculated by adding up the values in the *PVIF* table. That is, the *PVIFA* table value found in Table 3.8 for an n-year annuity for any discount rate i is merely the sum of the first n *PVIF* values in Table 3.4. You can see this by comparing the value in the *PVIFA* table (Table 3.8) for $i = 8\%$ and $n = 6$ years, which is 4.623, with the sum of the values in the $i = 8\%$ column and $n = 1, \ldots,$

TABLE 3.8

$PVIFA_{i,\ n}$, or the Present Value of an Annuity of $1

n	1%	2%	3%	4%	5%	6%	7%	8%	9%	10%
1	0.990	0.980	0.971	0.962	0.952	0.943	0.935	0.926	0.917	0.909
2	1.970	1.942	1.913	1.886	1.859	1.833	1.808	1.783	1.759	1.736
3	2.941	2.884	2.829	2.775	2.723	2.673	2.624	2.577	2.531	2.487
4	3.902	3.808	3.717	3.630	3.546	3.465	3.387	3.312	3.240	3.170
5	4.853	4.713	4.580	4.452	4.329	4.212	4.100	3.993	3.890	3.791
6	5.795	5.601	5.417	5.242	5.076	4.917	4.767	4.623	4.486	4.355
7	6.728	6.472	6.230	6.002	5.786	5.582	5.389	5.206	5.033	4.868
8	7.652	7.326	7.020	6.733	6.463	6.210	5.971	5.747	5.535	5.335
9	8.566	8.162	7.786	7.435	7.108	6.802	6.515	6.247	5.995	5.759
10	9.471	8.983	8.530	8.111	7.722	7.360	7.024	6.710	6.418	6.145
11	10.368	9.787	9.253	8.760	8.306	7.887	7.499	7.139	6.805	6.495
12	11.255	10.575	9.954	9.385	8.863	8.384	7.943	7.536	7.161	6.814
13	12.134	11.348	10.635	9.986	9.3942	8.853	8.358	7.904	7.487	7.103
14	13.004	12.106	11.296	10.563	9.899	9.295	8.746	8.244	7.786	7.367
15	13.865	12.849	11.938	11.118	10.380	9.712	9.108	8.560	8.061	7.606

TABLE 3.9

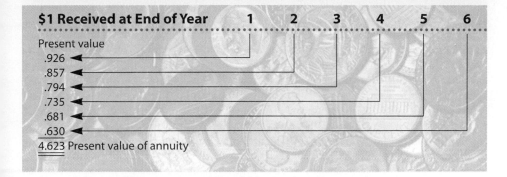

**Present Value of a 6-Year Annuity Discounted at 8%
(the present value of each $1 is taken from Table 3.4)**

$1 Received at End of Year	1	2	3	4	5	6

Present value
.926
.857
.794
.735
.681
.630
4.623 Present value of annuity

6 rows of the present value table (Table 3.4), which is equal to 4.623, as shown in Table 3.9.

Example. What is the present value of a 10-year $1,000 annuity discounted back to the present at 5%? Substituting $n = 10$ years, $i = 5\%$, and $PMT = \$1,000$ into equation (3.7), you find

$$PV = \$1,000(PVIFA_{5\%,\ 10\ yr})$$

Determining the value for the $PVIFA_{5\%,10\ yr}$ from Table 3.8, row $n - 10$, column $i = 5\%$, and substituting it into our equation, we get

$$PV = \$1,000(7.722)$$
$$PV = \$7,722$$

Thus, the present value of this annuity is $7,722.

As with the other problems involving compounding and present value tables, given any three of the four unknowns in equation (3.7), we can solve for the fourth. In the case of the $PVIFA$ table, we may be interested in solving for PMT, if we know i, n, and PV. The financial interpretation of this action would be: How much can be withdrawn, perhaps as a pension or to make loan payments, from an account that earns i percent compounded annually for each of the next n years if you wish to have nothing left at the end of n years? For example, say you have saved $1 million in an account earning 8-percent interest for your retirement. The day you turn 60 years old and retire, how large an annuity can you draw out at the end of each year if you want nothing left at the end of 40 years? (You plan on living to be 100—after all, George Burns made it to 100 and he smoked an average of 5,475 cigars per year.) In this case the present value, PV, of the annuity is $1,000,000, $n = 40$ years, $i = 8\%$, and PMT is unknown. Substituting this into equation (3.7), you find

$$PV = PMT(PVIFA_{8\%,\ 40\ yr})$$
$$\$1,000,000 = PMT(11.925)$$
$$\frac{\$1,000,000}{11.925} = \frac{PMT(11.925)}{11.925}$$
$$\$83,857.44 = PMT$$

Thus, this account will fall to zero at the end of 40 years if you withdraw $83,857.44 at the end of each year. On that kind of money you could go for Cuban cigars.

Amortized Loans

Don't think that you're always on the receiving end of an annuity. More often, your annuity will involve payments associated with paying off a loan in equal installments over time. Loans that are paid off this way, in equal periodic payments, are called **amortized loans**. Examples of amortized loans include car loans and mortgages. For example, suppose you borrowed $6,000 at 15-percent interest to buy a car and wish to repay it in four equal payments at the end of each of the next 4 years. We can use equation (3.7) to determine what the annual payments associated with the repayment of this car loan will be and solve for the value of *PMT*, the annual annuity. Again, you know three of the four values in that equation, *PV, i,* and *n. PV*, the present value of the future annuity, is $6,000; *i*, the annual interest rate, is 15 percent; and *n*, the number of years for which the annuity will last, is 4 years. *PMT*, the annuity payment received (by the lender and paid by you) at the end of each year, is unknown. Substituting these values into equation (3.7) you find

$$PV = PMT(PVIFA_{i\%,\ n\,yr})$$
$$\$6,000 = PMT(PVIFA_{15\%,\ 4\,yr})$$
$$\$6,000 = PMT(2.855)$$
$$\frac{\$6,000}{2.855} = \frac{PMT(2.855)}{2.855}$$
$$\$2,101.58 = PMT$$

To repay the principal and interest on the outstanding loan in 4 years, the annual payments would be $2,101.58. The breakdown of interest and principal payments is given in the loan amortization schedule in Figure 3.4. As you can see, the interest payment declines each year as the loan outstanding declines.

Amortized Loan

A loan paid off in equal installments.

FIGURE 3.4

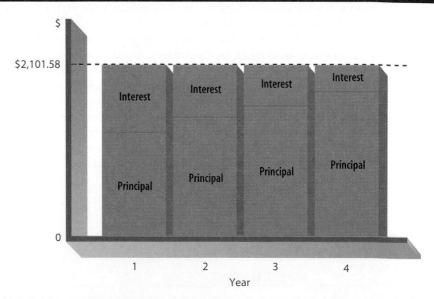

Loan Amortization Schedule Involving a $6,000 Loan at 15% to Be Repaid in 4 Years

Total Principal Paid = $6,000.00
Total Interest Paid = $2,436.32

Example.   The Virginia State Lottery runs like most other state lotteries: You must select 6 out of 44 numbers correctly in order to win the jackpot. If you come close there are some significantly lesser prizes—we will ignore them for now. For each million dollars in the lottery jackpot, you receive $50,000 per year for 20 years, and your chance of winning is 1 in 7.1 million. One of the recent advertisements for the Virginia State Lottery went as follows: "Okay, you got two kinds of people. You've got the kind who play Lotto all the time, and the kind who play Lotto some of the time. You know, like only on a Saturday when they stop in at the store on the corner for some peanut butter cups and diet soda and the jackpot happens to be really big. I mean, my friend Ned? He's like, 'Hey, it's only two million dollars this week.' Well, hellloooo, anybody home? I mean, I don't know about you, but I wouldn't mind having a measly two mill coming *my* way. . . ." What is the present value of these payments? The answer to this question depends upon what assumption you make as to the time value of money—in this case, let's assume that your required rate of return on an investment with this level of risk is 10 percent. Keeping in mind that the Lotto is an annuity—that is, on a $2 million lottery you would get $100,000 per year for 20 years.[1] Thus, the present value of this 20-year annuity discounted back to present at 10 percent becomes

$$PV = PMT(PVIFA_{i\%, \, n \, \text{yr}})$$
$$= \$100,000(PVIFA_{10\%, \, 20 \, \text{yr}})$$
$$= \$100,000(8.514)$$
$$= \$851,400.$$

Thus, the present value of the $2 million Lotto jackpot is less than $1 million if 10 percent is the appropriate discount rate. Moreover, because the chance of winning is only 1 in 7.1 million, the expected value of each dollar "invested" in the lottery is only (1/7.1 million) × ($851,400) = 11.99¢. That is, for every dollar you spend on the lottery when the jackpot is $2 million, you should expect to get, *on average*, about 12¢ back—not a particularly good deal. While this ignores the minor prizes for coming close, it also ignores taxes and the prize splitting that takes place if more than one person guesses all six numbers correctly. In this case, it looks like "my friend Ned" is doing the right thing by staying clear of the lottery. Obviously, the main value of the lottery is entertainment—unfortunately, without an understanding of the time value of money, it can sound like a good investment.

Perpetuities

A **perpetuity** is an annuity that continues forever. That is, every year from its establishment, this investment pays the same dollar amount and never stops paying. Determining the present value of a perpetuity is delightfully simple: You merely need to divide the payment amount by the discount rate. For example, the present value of a perpetuity that pays a constant dividend of $10 per share forever if the appropriate

Perpetuity
An annuity that continues forever.

---

[1]Actually, we've simplified things a bit here. With the Virginia State Lottery you get your first $100,000 immediately and then at the end of each of the next 19 years you get another $100,000. Remember, we assume that cash flows occur at the end of each year with annuities. We've also ignored taxes.

discount rate is 5 percent is $^{\$1}\%_{.05} = \$200$. Thus, the equation representing the present value of a perpetuity is

$$PV = PP/i \qquad (3.8)$$

where

$PV =$ the present value of the perpetuity

$PP =$ the annual dollar amount provided by the perpetuity

$i =$ the annual interest (or discount) rate

SUMMARY

Almost every decision in personal finance involves the techniques of compounding and time value of money—putting aside money now to achieve some future goal. The cornerstone of the time value of money is the concept of compound interest, which is interest paid on interest. With the time value of money you can determine how much an investment will grow over time using the following formula:

$$FV_n = PV(1 + i)^n \qquad (3.4)$$

where

$FV_n =$ the future value of the investment at the end of n years

$n =$ the number of years during which the compounding occurs

$i =$ the annual interest (or discount) rate

$PV =$ the present value, or the current value; that is, the value in today's dollars of a sum of money

To simplify these calculations, there are tables for the $(1 + i)^n$ part of the equation (the future-value interest factor for i and n, or $FVIF_{i,n}$). In effect, you can rewrite equation (3.4) as follows:

$$\text{future value} = \text{present value} \times \text{future-value interest factor}$$

or

$$FV_n = PV(FVIF_{i,n}) \qquad (3.4a)$$

It is also important to understand the role of the interest rate in determining how large an investment grows. Together, time and the interest rate determine how much you will need to save in order to achieve your goals.

We can also use the Rule of 72 to determine how long it will take to double your invested money. This "rule" is only an approximation, and says

$$\text{number of years to double} = 72 / \text{annual compound growth rate}$$

Many times we will also want to solve for present value instead of future value. We will use the following formula to do this:

$$PV = FV_n[1/(1 + i)^n] \qquad (3.5)$$

where

FV_n = the future value of the investment at the end of n years

n = the number of years until the payment will be received

i = the annual discount (or interest) rate

PV = the present value of the future sum of money

An annuity is a series of equal annual dollar payments coming at the end of each year for a specified number of years. Because annuities occur frequently in finance—for example, as bond interest payments and mortgage payments—they are treated specially. A compound annuity involves depositing or investing an equal sum of money at the end of each year for a certain number of years and allowing it to grow.

$$\text{future value} \atop \text{of an annuity} = {\text{annual} \atop \text{payment}} \times {\text{future-value interest} \atop \text{factor of an annuity}}$$

or

$$FV_n = PMT(FVIFA_{i,\,n}) \qquad\qquad (3.6)$$

where

FV_n = the future value of the annuity at the end of the nth year

PMT = the annuity payment deposited or received at the end of each year

i = the annual interest (or discount) rate

n = the number of years for which the annuity will last

Many times annuities involve paying off a loan in equal installments over time. Loans that are paid off this way, in equal periodic payments, are called amortized loans. Examples of amortized loans include car loans and mortgages.

Review Questions

1. Define the time value of money. Why is it an important concept in financial planning? (LO 3)
2. What is compound interest? How is compound interest related to the time value of money? (LO 1)
3. What two factors affect how much people need to save to achieve their financial goals? (LO 3, 4)
4. Describe how the Rule of 72 can be used to make financial planning decisions. (LO 4)
5. What is effective annual interest? How is it affected by compounding? (LO 4)
6. Why do you think that Albert Einstein once called compound interest the "eighth wonder of the world"? (LO 4)
7. What is "present value" and why is it important to calculate? (LO 5)
8. What is the discount rate in a time value of money calculation? Why is it called "inverse compounding"? (LO 5)
9. What is an annuity? Name at least five examples of annuities (payments or receipt of income) in personal finance. (LO 6)
10. Define an amortized loan and give two common examples. (LO 6)
11. What four variables are needed to solve a time value of money problem with a compound interest table or financial calculator? (LO 2)
12. What is the relationship between present- and future-value interest factors and present- and future-value interest factors for annuities? (LO 6)

Problems and Activities

1. Linda Baer has saved $5,000 for a "new used" car. She needs $7,500. Ignoring taxes and assuming her savings is earning 5 percent in a CD, how long will it take to buy the car? *Hint:* the answer is between 6 and 10 years. (LO 2)
2. Paul Ramos just graduated from college and landed his first "real" job, which pays $23,000 a year. In 15 years, what will he need to earn to maintain the same purchasing power if inflation averages 4 percent? (LO 2)
3. John and Wendy Eby just got married and received $30,000 in cash gifts for their wedding. If they place half of this money in a growth mutual fund earning 10 percent, how much will they have on their tenth, twenty-fifth and fiftieth anniversaries? (LO 2)

4. Your rich uncle is giving you a $20,000 inheritance. The only "catch" is that you can't get the money until your thirty-fifth birthday. You just turned 27. What is the value of your gift today if your trust earns 7-percent interest? What is the present value if you must wait until age 35 to receive the money? (LO 5)

5. Sue Jones just turned 22 and wants to have $10,000 saved by her thirtieth birthday. Assuming no additional deposits, if she currently has $6,000 in a money market account earning 5 percent will she reach her goal? (LO 5)

6. Your employer guarantees you a $40,000 a year defined benefit pension if you work until age 67. For the current year how much must your company set aside in today's dollars for your pension? Assume you're 27 and your employer invested pension plan contributions earn 7-percent interest annually. (LO 5)

7. Joe Eiss, 22, just started working full-time and plans to deposit $2,000 annually into an IRA earning 9-percent interest. How much would he have in 20 years? In 30 years? In 40 years? If he increased his investment return to 12 percent, how much would he have after these same three time periods? Comment on the differences over time. (LO 6)

8. Four years ago, you began contributing to an employer 401(k) plan, which now contains $5,000. If you deposit $3,000 a year for the next 15 years, how much will the account be worth assuming a 10-percent average annual return? (LO 2,6)

9. Your mother just won $500,000 for splitting a Nobel Prize with a coworker. If she invests her prize money in a diversified portfolio earning 9-percent interest, approximately how long will it take her to become a millionaire? (LO 1)

10. You and 11 coworkers just won $12 million from the state lottery. Assuming you each receive your share over 20 years and that the state lottery earns an 8 percent return on its funds, what is the present value of your prize before taxes? (LO 5)

11. Joe Gorman is 65 years old and about to retire. He has $500,000 saved to supplement his pension and Social Security and would like to withdraw it in equal annual dollars amounts so that nothing is left after 15 years. How much does he have to withdraw each year if he earns 9 percent on his money? (LO 5)

Suggested Projects

1. Develop and solve a future value, a present value, a future value of an annuity, and a present value of an annuity problem. Describe the three known variables in each problem and solve for the fourth. Explain the results. (LO 2)

2. Research the cost of five products or services that were advertised in newspapers or magazines published more than 20 years ago. Then find the current cost of these items. Calculate the rate of inflation in prices between the two time periods. (LO 4)

3. Study advertisements for bank products (for example, savings accounts, CDs) that compound interest more frequently than once a year. Explain the difference between the annual interest rate and the effective annual interest rate. (LO 3)

4. Ask older friends and relatives about the cost of specific items (such as a gallon of gas, a cup of coffee, and so on) during their youth. Also inquire about average wages in the past. Compare these figures to current expenses and incomes. Discuss your findings using time value of money concepts. (LO 1)

5. Calculate what an Individual Retirement Account (IRA) would be worth if you begin contributing $2,000 annually following graduation. Define your own retirement age and make any other assumptions as needed. Explain the key factors that will influence the amount of money saved at retirement. (LO 1)

WWW.
Take It to the Net

We invite you to visit the Keown Personal Finance page on the Prentice Hall Web site at:

http://www.prenhall.com/ persfin

for this chapter's World Wide Web exercise.

You might also want to visit the following Web sites:

The Legg Mason Financial Planning Calculator: http:// www.leggmason.com/ Invest/fincalc.html

Financial calculators from the Money Advisor: http:// www.moneyadvisor.com/calc/

Kiplinger Online—They have a calculator built into this one: http://www.kiplinger.com/

Investor's Guide to Financial Aid (a link to financial calculators): http://www.investorguide.com/ FinAid.htm#calculators

Online Money Calculators: http://pathfinder.com/ @@icj1BgYAUpdyy@XE/money/ websites/calc.html

Financial Goals Calculator: http://tqd.advanced.org/ 3096/3calcin.htm

Hugh's Mortgage and Financial Calculators: http:// alfredo.wustl.edu/mort_links.html

6. Develop an example of an amortized loan with specific figures for the amount borrowed, the interest rate, and the term of the loan. Calculate the annual payment required by the lender. (LO 5)

7. Assume you can save $4,000 a year (about $80 per week) after graduation. Set a financial goal for yourself. Specify the time frame and future dollar cost, and assume that you've saved nothing to date. Calculate the interest rate required to achieve the goal. Is it possible, with moderate risk, in today's financial market? If not, describe changes that could be made to bring the goal closer to reality. (LO 6)

8. Pretend that "the Prize Patrol" has just visited your house, promising to send you and your sister each a check for $10,000 a year for the next 5 years. Assume that both of you decide to invest your windfall, but you select different investment products. Compare recent rates of return on two different types of investments and calculate an expected value for the two accounts at the end of 5 years. Explain your results. (LO 6)

9. Investigate a specific financial planning issue or decision that involves the use of time value of money concepts. Describe why it is necessary to make a time value of money calculation. (LO 1)
   Examples: determining how much retirement income to withdraw per year over expected life, calculation of loan payments, calculating present pension plan contributions needed to find future benefits, calculating future value of an IRA or 401(k) or calculating present value (purchasing power) of money to be received in the future.

Discussion Case 1

Jenny Smith, 26, just received a promotion at work. Her salary has increased to $30,000, and she is now eligible to participate in her employer's 401(k) plan. The employer matches half of workers' contributions up to 6 percent of their salary. Jenny wants to buy a new car in 2 years. The model she wants to buy currently costs $18,000. She wants to save enough to make a $5,000 down payment and plans to finance the balance. At age 30, Jenny will be eligible to receive a $50,000 inheritance left by her late uncle. Her trust fund is invested in bonds that pay 8-percent interest. Also in her plans is a wedding. Jenny and her boyfriend, Paul, have set a wedding date 2 years in the future, after he finishes graduate school. Paul will have $40,000 of student loans to repay after graduation. Both Jenny and Paul want to buy a home of their own as soon as possible.

Questions

1. Justify Jenny's participation in her employer's 401(k) plan using time value of money concepts.

2. Calculate the amount that Jenny needs to save each year for the down payment on a new car, assuming she can earn 6 percent on her savings.

3. What will be the value of Jenny's trust fund at age 60, assuming she takes possession of the money at age 30, uses half for a house down payment, and leaves half of the money untouched where it is currently invested?

4. If Paul wants to repay his student loans in full within 5 years and pays an 8 percent interest rate, what will be his annual payment?

5. List at least three actions that Jenny and Paul could take to make the time value of money work in their favor.

Discussion Case 2

Jay Bronson, 70, is about to retire. A widower, he worked after "normal" retirement age to keep busy and avoid thinking about his late wife. Jay will receive a $300,000 lump-sum distribution from his employer. He also has $50,000 saved in an IRA and received $50,000 from his late wife's insurance policy. The latter is currently sitting in a 5-percent money market fund until he can decide what do with it. Jay has requested help deciding how much money he should withdraw each year and where he should invest his retirement nest egg. He is afraid of outliving his assets. Jay's monthly expenses are $2,500, and he expects to receive $600 a month in Social Security. He says he is willing to assume some risk to increase the return on his investment portfolio.

Questions

1. Assume that Jay already has money set aside for emergencies. How much of his other assets should he withdraw each year to supplement Social Security, assuming his investments currently average a 5-percent return and he assumes a life expectancy of 15 years?

2. Is this amount sufficient to pay Jay's monthly living expenses? Explain.

3. How could Jay extend his retirement nest egg to age 90 or 100?

4. If inflation averages 4 percent during Jay's retirement, calculate approximately how long it will take for prices to double.

Chapter 4

TAX PLANNING AND STRATEGIES

To say the least, country singer Willie Nelson's life has been wild. Nelson was raised by his grandparents, worked in the cotton fields until he was 10, was a Baylor University dropout, sold Bibles door-to-door, and, eventually, won six Grammy Awards. Along the way he made millions of dollars, spent millions of dollars, and for quite some time ignored his finances—including his taxes—entirely. This lack of attention to his taxes finally caught up with him in 1990, when the IRS sent him a bill for $16.7 million. How did Nelson manage to run up such a tax bill? On bad advice, he got involved in a number of tax shelters (investments aimed at lowering your taxes) that were disallowed by the IRS because they were such blatant tax-avoidance schemes. They included a cattle-feeding tax shelter and one involving exotic trades in government securities. Eventually Nelson and the IRS settled on a $9-million payment, and Willie sued the accounting firm of Price Waterhouse, claiming they had mismanaged his finances by recommending the disallowed tax shelters to him.

The end result of his lack of attention to financial and tax planning was that Nelson had to auction off nearly all of his possessions—leaving him with his long hair and beard, headband, worn blue jeans, guitar, and little else, and prompting a headline seen in supermarkets across the country in the *National Enquirer:* WILLIE NELSON HOMELESS AND BROKE. To help pay the bill, he came out with an album that year sold through an 800 number, titled "Who'll Buy My Memories? (The IRS Tapes)," filled with dark night songs such as "What Can You Do to Me

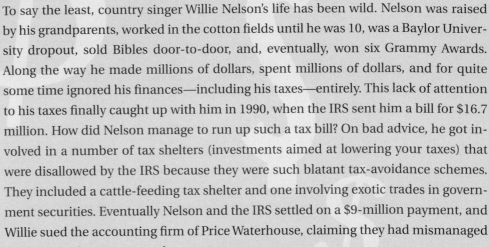

Learning Objectives

After reading this chapter you should be able to:

1. Describe how the present U.S. income tax system came into being.
2. Identify and understand the major tax features that affect all taxpayers.
3. Explain how your taxes are collected.
4. Understand what is taxable income and how taxes are determined.
5. Choose the tax form that's right for you.
6. Calculate your income taxes.
7. Explain the procedure for filing late and amended returns.
8. Know what to do if you are selected for an audit.
9. Explain what tax help alternatives are and how to get help in preparing your taxes if you need it.
10. Use the tools of tax planning.
11. Describe other, nonincome-based taxes that you must pay.

Now?" Unfortunately, Nelson didn't realize the importance of knowledge—remember **Axiom 9: The Best Protection Is Knowledge**, and that using a tax advisor is reasonable only if you realize that you are merely receiving advice and that you bear the ultimate responsibility for the effectiveness of the plan.

Ben Franklin once said that the only sure things in life were death and taxes, and these days, some people prefer death to taxes. Most people cringe at the thought of tax planning and the mention of the IRS because taxes are unavoidable, too high, and determined by a tax code that is close to incomprehensible. People just don't like taxes—everyone knows that. However, like them or not, taxes are a fact of life, and they have a dramatic impact on many aspects of your finances, in particular your investment choices. In fact, most of the decisions that you make are affected in one way or another by taxes—that's **Axiom 6: Taxes Bias Personal Finance Decisions**. Given that an average American pays about $8,000 annually in taxes, tax planning and limiting Uncle Sam's cut of your income is important. Remember, what you pay in April each year is based on income, expenses, and tax-planning decisions from the previous year, and if you don't understand the tax system, you're probably paying more than you have to. The purpose of this chapter is not to teach you all the ins and outs of filing your own return, but rather to help you understand how taxes are imposed, what strategies can be used to reduce them, and the role of tax planning in personal financial planning. With proper tax planning you will be able to avoid wasting money in tax payments and, instead, invest those funds to achieve your financial goals.

AXIOM #9

The Best Protection Is Knowledge

AXIOM #6

Taxes Bias Personal Finance Decisions

AN OVERVIEW OF THE TAX SYSTEM—HOW IT ALL BEGAN

Before examining strategies for tax planning, it's a good idea to look briefly at how the present U.S. tax system came into being.

A Little Background

Our present income tax system first appeared in 1913, when the Sixteenth Amendment gave Congress authorization to impose such a tax. That was the year zippers were invented, Cracker Jacks first put toys in their boxes, and Americans first paid income taxes. Back then the rate was only 1 percent on income greater than $3,000 for an individual, or $4,000 for a married couple. Although a break on the first $3,000 to $4,000 may not sound like much now, back in 1913 it was quite a bit. In fact, only about 1 percent of the population had to pay income taxes. The first tax was also progressive, or graduated, meaning that the tax rose as income rose above $20,000. The tax rose from an additional 1 percent on income between $20,000 and $50,000 all the way to an additional 6 percent on income greater than $300,000. It was also a simple, easy-to-understand code with a conspicuous lack of loopholes to avoid paying taxes.

Since that time, continuous tinkering to fund the government, influence the economy, promote socially desirable actions, and simply satisfy powerful special interest groups has produced a 2,000-page tax code with countless forms. These changes have generally been made in a piecemeal fashion—changing one aspect of the tax code one year and another aspect another year. The end result is that the logic of the tax code has been overpowered by its complexity, and in the minds of many, fairness has fallen through the countless loopholes.

The Importance of Tax Planning

The current U.S. tax system dictates the single largest annual expenditure for most families —your taxes. Thus, regardless of what you think of the system, it's one that you have no choice but to face. The initial reaction of many is that tax planning is for the wealthy. Yes, wealthy people probably have the most to gain from effective tax planning. As a result, the wealthy, in general, do a good job of tax planning. Unfortunately, those of you who don't fall into the wealthy range—that is, those who need the tax savings the most—don't do a very good job of tax planning. In fact, most people view tax planning as a problem, not an aid. Well, what's more of a problem, doing a few hours' worth of planning, or paying Uncle Sam a few thousand dollars more than you really need to?

Everyone works too hard to earn money to pay more than is necessary in the way of taxes. In fact, the Tax Foundation, a private research group, each year determines the Tax Freedom Day as a means of showing how hard everyone works to pay taxes each year. The Tax Freedom Day is the day by which the average American has earned enough to pay total federal, state, and local taxes for the year. As shown in Table 4.1, back in 1950 the average American had earned enough to pay the annual tax bill by April 3; in 1997, the Tax Freedom Day had crept all the way to May 9. In other words, all the money the average American earns before May 9 will have to go to paying taxes. Given the fact that the average American spends over a third of each year earning money just to pay taxes, it's important to make sure that you don't actually overpay. Remember, the longer you work to pay taxes, the less time you can work to pay yourself.

INCOME TAX STRUCTURE

The starting point for tax planning is in understanding what the tax rates actually are. Because the U.S. tax code is so complicated, we must learn a bit about the overall structure of the income tax before we examine actual tax rates. Our present tax

TABLE 4.1

Tax Freedom Day
The day the average American has earned enough
to pay for federal, state, and local taxes.

Year	Day
1950	April 3
1955	April 9
1960	April 17[a]
1965	April 15
1970	April 28
1975	April 28
1980	May 1[a]
1985	April 30
1990	May 3
1995	May 7
1996	May 7[a]
1997	May 9

[a]Due to leap year, Tax Freedom Day came a day later.
SOURCE: Tax Foundation, Washington, DC, 1997.

The Facts of Life

It was the Massachusetts Bay Colony that first imposed income taxes in the new world in 1643. They've been around forever, but that doesn't mean you pay more than your fair amount. In fact, in 1934 Judge Learned Hand of the U.S. Court of Appeals said, "Anyone may so arrange his affairs that his taxes shall be as low as possible; he is not bound to choose that pattern which will best pay the treasury; there is not even a patriotic duty to increase one's taxes."

structure is a **progressive** or **graduated tax**, meaning that increased income is taxed at increasing rates. This system is based upon the idea that those who earn more can afford to have a higher percentage of their income taken away in taxes.

However, just knowing the **tax brackets** is not enough, because not all income is taxed. Some income is tax-free because of **personal exemptions**, and other income is shielded either by **itemized** or **standard deductions**. In effect, your **taxable income** is a function of two numbers—your income and your deductions. From there, the tax rates take over to determine how much of the difference between income and deductions will be taken away in taxes. Table 4.2 provides the 1996 federal income tax rates for four different classifications of taxpayers.

To better understand what the rates in Table 4.2 actually mean, check out what you might pay in taxes in 1996 if you were married with three children, had a combined income of $70,000, and were filing a joint return. As you can see from Table 4.2, $70,000 falls between $40,101 and $96,900, which puts you into the 28-percent tax bracket. Remember, however, that your total income of $70,000 isn't taxed; *only the difference between your income and your deductions is taxed*. To determine how much you would pay in taxes, you must first subtract out your deductions. To begin with, you receive one exemption for each family member you claim on your tax return—one for you and your spouse and

Progressive or **Graduated Tax**
A tax system in which tax rates increase for higher incomes.

Tax Brackets
Income ranges in which the same marginal tax rates apply. For example, an individual might fall into the 15-percent or 28-percent marginal tax bracket.

Personal Exemptions
An IRS-allowed reduction in your income before you compute your taxes. You are given one exemption for yourself, one for your spouse, and one for each dependent.

Deductions
Expenses that reduce your taxable income.

Itemized Deductions
Deductions calculated using Schedule A. The allowable deductions are added up and then subtracted from taxable income.

Standard Deduction
An alternative to itemizing deductions, in which taxpayers take a set deduction allowed by the IRS regardless of what their expenses actually were.

Taxable Income
Income that is subject to taxes.

TABLE 4.2

1996 Tax Rates

Taxable Income	Tax
Single	
Up to $24,000	15% of taxable income
$24,001 to $58,150	$3,600 plus 28% of amount over $24,000
$58,151 to $121,300	$13,162 plus 31% of amount over $58,150
$121,301 to $263,750	$32,738.50 plus 36% of amount over $121,300
Over $263,750	$84,020.50 plus 39.6% of amount over $263,750
Married Filing Jointly and Surviving Spouses	
Up to $40,100	15% of taxable income
$40,101 to $96,900	$6,015 plus 28% of amount over $40,100
$96,901 to $147,700	$21,919 plus 31% of amount over $96,900
$147,701 to $263,750	$37,667 plus 36% of amount over $147,700
Over $263,750	$79,445 plus 39.6% of amount over $263,750
Heads of Household	
Up to $32,150	15% of taxable income
$32,151 to $83,050	$4,822.50 plus 28% of amount over $32,150
$83,051 to $134,500	$19,074.50 plus 31% of amount over $83,050
$134,501 to $263,750	$35,024 plus 36% of amount over $134,500
Over $263,750	$81,554 plus 39.6% of amount over $263,750
Married Filing Separately	
Up to $20,050	15% of taxable income
$20,051 to $48,450	$3,007.50 plus 28% of amount over $20,050
$48,451 to $73,850	$10,959.50 plus 31% of amount over $48,450
$73,851 to $131,875	$18,833.50 plus 36% of amount over $73,850
Over $131,875	$39,722.50 plus 39.6% of amount over $131,875

each of your three children. Each exemption allows you to deduct or subtract $2,550 from your income, resulting in a total deduction of $12,750. Next, you need to subtract your deduction, either standard or itemized. For simplicity's sake, let's assume you use the standard deduction because it's higher than your itemized deduction would be. By the 1996 tax year rates (the most recent year for which tax forms were available at the time this is being written), that would give you a deduction of $6,700. Thus, the minimum level of deductions that you will have will be $12,750 + $6,700 = $19,450. Subtracting these deductions from your income of $70,000 leaves taxable income of $50,550.

Even after your deductions, you're still in the 28-percent tax bracket. Do you then have to pay 28 percent of your taxable income of $50,550 in taxes? No. It means that the last dollars that you earned will be taxed at 28 percent. As Table 4.2 shows, the first $40,100 of taxable income is taxed at 15 percent; then the next $10,450 of your taxable income, that is, your income from $40,101 to $50,550, is taxed at 28 percent, resulting in a total tax bill of $8,941.[1]

[1]This drops even more for the 1998 tax year when the child tax credit provision of the Taxpayer Relief Act of 1997 takes effect. This law provides qualifying families with a tax credit for each child under age 17 as of the close of each year. The credit amount will be $400 in 1998 and $500 thereafter. This tax credit offsets taxes owed on a dollar-for-dollar basis.

Taxable Income		$\times$	Tax Rate	=	Taxes Paid
$0 to $40,100	($40,100)	$\times$	15%	=	$6,015
$40,101 to $50,550	($10,450)	$\times$	28%	=	$2,926
			Total Taxes	=	$8,941

Marginal versus Average Rates

Let's take a different look at the amount of taxes you paid in the previous example. You paid taxes of $8,941 on taxable income of $50,550, so your average tax rate on *taxable income* was $8,941/$50,550, or 18 percent. Your average tax rate on your *overall* income of $70,000 was $8,941/$70,000, or about 13 percent. The term average tax rate refers to this latter figure—the average amount of your total income taken away in taxes. Although your goal is to keep your average tax rate as low as possible, you'll need to focus more on your marginal tax rate. Your **marginal tax rate** or **marginal tax bracket** refers to the percentage of the last dollar you made that will go to taxes. In effect, it is the tax bracket that your taxable income falls into. If your taxable income is $50,550, and $50,550 falls in the 28-percent tax bracket, then 28 percent is your marginal tax rate. Thus, if you get a $5,000 raise, it is your marginal tax rate that will determine how much of that raise you have left to spend after you pay taxes on it. In addition, if you are in the 28-percent marginal tax bracket and have a choice of investing in either tax-free bonds that earn 7 percent or taxable bonds that earn 9 percent, your marginal tax rate can help you determine which is the better investment. Even though your average tax rate may be only 13 percent, this additional income is taxed at your marginal tax rate—which in this example is 28 percent. To make a fair comparison you must look at your after-tax returns. The tax-free bond would still return 7 percent after taxes, but the 9 percent bond would have 28 percent of its returns confiscated for taxes, resulting in a return of $9\% \times (1 - 0.28) = 6.48\%$.

Your marginal tax rate also becomes important when you're considering investing in a **tax-deferred** retirement plan. The government many times allows tax deductions for any funds you contribute into the retirement plan. So, if you are in the 28-percent marginal tax bracket and you contribute $1,000 to a tax-deferred retirement plan, you would lower your taxes by $280 ($0.28 \times $1,000$). This reduction allows you to invest the entire $1,000 rather than only $720, that is, $1,000 less $280 in taxes.

As you can see from Table 4.2, once you earn enough to pay taxes—rising beyond the personal exemption and standard deduction levels—there are five different marginal tax rates: 15 percent, 28 percent, 31 percent, 36 percent, and 39.6 percent. Although these are the present marginal tax rates, they are far from set in stone. Whenever Congress wishes, it can change the tax rates and the tax code. In fact, in 1964 the top marginal rate was 91 percent, and in 1981 it was still at 70 percent. Needless to say, changes in the marginal tax rates have a major impact on investment strategies, and as such, you should keep a close eye on tax law changes.[2]

Effective Marginal Tax Rate

Although most people think Federal income taxes are far more than enough, these are not the only income-based taxes that you pay. Many states impose state income taxes, there are also Social Security taxes, and in some cases there are also city income taxes.

Marginal Tax Rate or **Marginal Tax Bracket**
The percentage of the last dollar you earn that will go toward taxes.

Tax-Deferred
Income on which the payment of taxes is postponed until some future date.

[2]Actually, although the listed rates seem to be quite straightforward, the IRS also phases out deductions and exemptions for those in the higher income brackets. For example, for the tax year 1996 for those filing as single, the phaseout for deductions and exemptions only affects those with adjusted gross income greater than $117,950. This phaseout level is adjusted annually for inflation. As a result, the marginal tax bracket for those in the highest brackets can actually be 1 to 5 percent higher than it appears, depending on income level and how many exemptions you have. That's because as you earn more, you lose deductions and exemptions.

For example, New York City imposes such a tax. As a result of all these taxes, your effective marginal tax rate is greater than the marginal tax rate on your federal income taxes. To determine your effective marginal tax rate, you need merely add up the rates of the different taxes you pay on your income. Let's assume you have a marginal federal tax rate of 28 percent, a state income tax rate of 4.75 percent, and a city income tax rate of 2 percent. The tax on Social Security is 7.65 percent, so your total effective marginal tax rate would be 42.40 percent (28% + 4.75% + 2% +7.65%).

> ## Stop and Think
>
> You really should know what your marginal tax rate is. It's important because it not only tells you how much more you'll have to pay in taxes on any additional income (the bad news), but also tells you how any additional deductions will save you in the way of reducing your taxes (the good news).

Capital Gains Taxes and the Taxpayer Relief Act of 1997

The income you make on your investments is taxed somewhat differently than is your other income. Almost any asset you own, except for certain business assets, including stocks and bonds, is called a **capital asset**. A **capital gain** is what you make if you sell a capital asset for a profit, and a **capital loss** is what you lose when you sell a capital asset for a loss. Capital losses can be used to offset capital gains and if the losses exceed the gains, you may deduct the excess from up to $3,000 of other income. For example, if you purchase 100 shares of GM stock for $50 per share and sell them 2 years later for $70 per share, your capital gain would be 100 shares times ($70 − $50) = $2,000. The tax you pay on your capital gains is called, appropriately, the **capital gains tax**. Exactly how much you will pay in capital gains taxes is dependent upon how long you've held your investments.

The Taxpayer Relief Act of 1997 both redefined what is a long-term capital gain and cut the long-term capital gains tax rate. Effective July 29, 1997, an asset must be held for 18 months, up from 12 months, to qualify as long-term. The maximum tax rate paid on net long-term capital gains on any trades made on or after May 7, 1997, dropped from 28 to 20 percent. For those in the 15-percent tax bracket, the net long-term capital gains tax rate dropped to 10 percent. Then, beginning in the year 2001, a new top rate of 18 percent on long-term capital gains on assets purchased in or after the year 2001 and held for at least 5 years goes into effect. As a result, no one will benefit from this 18-percent rate until 2006. For investors in the 15-percent tax bracket who sell assets held for at least 5 years, the rate drops to 8 percent. In addition to all this, there is a "mid-term gains" rate for those who held assets more than 12 months but less than 18 months; the maximum tax bracket for "mid-term" gains is 28 percent.

While the new long-term capital gains tax applies to profits from the sale of stocks, bonds, and most other investments, it doesn't apply to gains from the sale of collectibles. In addition, real estate investments don't necessarily receive full benefit of the cut.

How much do capital gains save you? That depends upon what tax bracket you're in. If you're in the 39.6-percent tax bracket and have long-term capital gains income of $50,000, you would only pay $10,000 in taxes, and, eventually, when the 18-percent tax bracket comes into place, only $9,000. If this $50,000 of income had been from wages or dividends, you would have paid $19,800, about twice what you would have paid on long-term capital gains.

Just as valuable as the tax break on capital gains income is the fact that you do not have to claim it—and therefore pay taxes on it—until you sell the asset. That is, you can time when you want to claim your capital gains. For example, at the end of 1994 you

Capital Asset
An asset you own, except for certain business assets, including stocks, bonds, real estate, or collectibles.

Capital Gain/Capital Loss
The amount by which the selling price of a capital asset differs from its purchase price. If the selling price is higher than the purchase price, a capital gain results; if the purchase price is higher than the selling price, a capital loss results.

Capital Gains Tax
The tax you pay on your capital gains.

may have invested $20,000 in Berkshire Hathaway stock, only to see it grow in value, reaching $47,500 by mid-1997. Although you've "made" $27,500 on your investment, you don't have to pay any taxes on this gain. You pay taxes only when you sell your stock and realize the gain. In effect, you can postpone your capital gains taxes. As long as you can earn interest on money you don't pay out in taxes, it's better to postpone paying taxes for as long as possible—that's what we learned in **Axiom 2: The Time Value of Money**. Because the maximum tax rate on long-term capital gains is lower than the ordinary tax rate and you have the ability to postpone its tax liability, capital gains income is preferable to ordinary income.

AXIOM #2

The Time Value of Money

What does this mean to you?   The effect of the cut in the long-term capital gains tax rate that came with the Taxpayer Relief Act of 1997 is that it's even more important to avoid frequent trading. That means buying and holding on to your investment—holding it for at least 18 months before selling, and at least five years after 2001. If you invest in mutual funds, you should look for mutual funds that do a minimum of trading—that is, tax-managed mutual funds. This capital gains tax cut also puts a premium on stocks that pay small dividends or none at all. That's because dividends are taxed as ordinary income while capital gains are taxed at lower rates. Given all this, your strategy should be to:

- **Head for low-turnover, "tax managed" mutual funds.**   The typical mutual fund has a turnover ratio of about 90 percent, meaning, on average, any stock in that fund is only held for about 13 months. To benefit from the new capital gains law, you need to put your money in a mutual fund that is tax-managed, that is, it trades in such a way that your profits are taxed at the capital gains rate rather than the ordinary rate. Unfortunately, there aren't too many of these funds around, although it's likely that the new tax laws will inspire quite a few new entries. Most indexed funds work much like tax-managed funds since they have very little trading; however, they generally have more income from dividends than do tax-managed funds.

- **Buy individual stocks and make your own mutual fund.**   One way to make sure that all trading profits qualify as long-term capital gains is to put your money into stocks rather than mutual funds so you can control the trades and can focus on stocks that pay little in dividends. The only problem here is that you need enough money to diversify sufficiently, while making sure you invest enough in each individual stock position to avoid excessive brokerage costs. This probably means that you'd need to invest at least $100,000 with about $5,000 put in each of 20 stocks. This would allow you sufficient diversification, in addition to letting you buy 100 shares of each stock to help keep brokerage fees down. Unfortunately, $100,000 is more than most people have to invest, so investing in tax managed mutual funds should work almost as well.

Long-Term Capital Gains on Homes and the Taxpayer Relief Act of 1997.
For most homeowners, the Taxpayer Relief Act of 1997 effectively eliminates capital gains taxes on the sale of their homes. It does this by exempting from taxation gains of up to $500,000 for couples filing jointly or $250,000 for those filing single on the sale of a principal residence. To be eligible for the complete exemption, the home must be your principal residence and you must have occupied it for at least two years during the five years prior to the sale. This is not a one-time exemption. In fact, you are eligible for this exemption once every two years. Under the old law, you paid no tax on profits from the sale of your house if the gain was "rolled over" by buying another home worth at least as much as the one that you sold.

Filing Status

Table 4.2 shows that your filing status plays a major role in determining what you pay in the way of taxes. Although it plays an important role in determining how much you'll pay in taxes, you may not have much of a choice in deciding your filing status. Filing status is somewhat akin to marital status, but, as is always the case with taxes, it's not that simple. Let's look at what the different filing status classifications are.

Single Status.   If you are single at the end of the year and do not have any dependent children, you fall into the single status.

Married Filing Jointly and Surviving Spouses.   This status allows you to file a joint return with your spouse, combining your incomes and deductions into a single return. If your spouse dies and you have a child living with you, you can still qualify for this filing status for up to 2 years after the year in which your spouse died. To qualify as a surviving spouse, you must have a dependent child living with you, you must pay more than half the cost of keeping up your home, and you must not be remarried. Of course, if you remarry, you can file a joint return with your new spouse.

Married Filing Separately.   If you're married you also have the choice of filing separately. For most married couples this filing status makes little financial sense—in effect, the rates are set up to encourage you to file a joint return if you're married. In some rare cases though, filing separately may be financially advantageous. However, this status is actually most often used when a couple is separated or in the process of getting a divorce. They wind up paying more than they would if they filed a joint return, but given the strained relationship, filing separately may be the only choice.

Head of Household.   Head of household status applies to someone who is unmarried and has at least one child or relative living with him or her. The advantage of this filing status is that your tax rate will be lower than it would be if you had filed with single status. You also receive a higher standard deduction than if you file using single status. To qualify for the head of household filing status, you must be unmarried on the last day of the tax year, have paid more than half the cost of keeping up your home, and had a child or dependent live with you for at least half of the year.

Cost of Living Increases in Tax Brackets, Exemptions, and Deductions

Since 1985, tax brackets have changed annually to reflect increases in the cost of living (inflation). For example, if the 28-percent tax bracket presently begins at $40,100 and the cost of living rises by 4.74 percent, this tax bracket would shift upward by 4.74 percent and begin at $40,100 × 1.0474 = $42,000. In addition, the standard deductions and personal exemptions are also increased to reflect the increased cost of living. The purpose of these adjustments is to make sure that your tax payments don't go up as your wages increase to keep pace with inflation. In the past, taxpayers' incomes rose during periods of high inflation, but their purchasing power didn't. As a result, the rising incomes that only kept pace with inflation resulted in nudging taxpayers into higher tax brackets. In effect, taxpayers would pay more taxes while the real value of their wages remained constant. This tax increase caused by inflation is referred to as **bracket creep**. For those whose earnings remain the same each year, this inflation adjustment of tax brackets actually results in lower taxes. Of course, if your earnings don't increase to keep pace with inflation, you're worse off with each passing year and probably deserve a reduced tax bill!

What actually happened in 1996? The cost of living rose by about 2.75 percent and as a result the 28-percent married filing jointly bracket shifted upward from $40,100 to $41,200. In fact all the tax brackets shifted upward by 2.75 percent, as did the personal exemptions and the standard deductions. A few examples of this cost of living shift from tax year 1996 to tax year 1997 include:

Bracket Creep

The movement into higher tax brackets as a result of inflation increasing wages.

- 28% Bracket Taxable Income Minimum for Single rose from $24,000 to $24,650
- 31% Bracket Taxable Income Minimum for Single rose from $58,150 to $59,750
- 28% Bracket Taxable Income Minimum for Married Filing Jointly rose from $40,100 to $41,200
- 31% Bracket Taxable Income Minimum for Married Filing Jointly rose from $96,900 to $99,600

Personal exemption cost of living shift from tax year 1996 to tax year 1997:

- $2,550 to $2,650

Standard deduction cost of living shift from tax year 1996 to tax year 1997:

- Single (under age 65): $4,000 to $4,150
- Married Filing Jointly (under age 65): $6,700 to $6,900

Social Security or FICA

Social Security is really a mandatory insurance program administered by the government, which provides for you and your family in the event of death, disability, health problems, or retirement. To pay for these benefits, both you and your employer pay into the system—each paying 7.65 percent of your gross salary. This deduction appears on your pay slip as "FICA," which stands for the Federal Insurance Contributions Act. These funds actually go to both Social Security and **Medicare**, which is a government health care insurance program. The FICA tax is deducted from your salary at a rate of 7.65 percent (6.20 percent for Social Security and 1.45 percent for Medicare) until your salary reaches a certain cap ($62,700 in 1996 and $65,400 for 1997), at which point your remaining salary is no longer taxed. Medicare, however, keeps on taxing after the Social Security cap has been reached—taking an additional 1.45 percent of your total salary from both you and your employer. Thus, if your salary is $70,000 in 1996, your FICA contribution would be [$62,700 × 7.65% + (70,000 − $62,700) × 1.45%] = ($4,796.55 + $105.85) = $4,902.40. If you are self-employed, you have to pay both the employer and employee portion of FICA for a total rate of 15.3 percent, up to the 1996 limit of $62,700, paying a total of ($62,700 × 15.3%) = $9,593.10. However, if you're self-employed, half of your contribution is tax-deductible. Also, if you're self-employed and you earned more than $62,700 in 1996, you'd continue to pay both the employer (1.45%) and employee (1.45%) portions of the Medicare tax—a total of 2.9 percent—on any income above $62,700, again with half of this contribution being tax-deductible.

Social Security
A federal program that provides disability and retirement benefits based upon years worked, amount paid into the plan, and retirement age.

Medicare
The federal government's insurance program to provide medical benefits to those over 65.

Stop and Think

"Isn't this exciting! I earned this. I wiped tables for it, I steamed milk for it, and it's—[*opening her pay check*]—not worth it! Who's FICA? Why is he getting my money?" The words of Rachel Green on the TV show *Friends,* seeing her first Central Perk paycheck on the episode "The One with George Stephanopoulos." Your first paycheck will be a real shock. Federal, state, and local taxes, in addition to FICA, your contribution to your firm's hospitalization plan, retirement savings—all these payments take a real bite out of your paycheck. It all makes financial planning more important.

Unfortunately, the Social Security system is feeling financial strains. As a result, it's impossible to forecast what will happen to the level of Social Security taxes over the next 20 years. As you'll see, the problem facing Social Security is that there are more people receiving Social Security benefits than ever before. Forty years ago there were 16 workers contributing for every Social Security recipient. Today, the ratio is down to 3 workers for every recipient, and in another 40 years it will be down to a 2 to 1 ratio. As a result, the system can't continue in its present form.

State and Local Income Taxes

As mentioned earlier, in addition to Social Security and federal income taxes, most individuals also face state and, in some cases, even local income taxes. The level of state income taxes tends to vary greatly from state to state, with some states, for example, Texas, not even imposing income taxes. However, most states impose some type of income tax. Local income taxes are relatively uncommon and are generally confined to large cities; for example, New York City imposes an income tax.

The Facts of Life

Most European countries impose a value added tax, or VAT, which is a form of national sales tax. Under such a system, a tax is added to the price of the product as it is produced as well as at the time of purchase by the consumer. Periodically, such a tax is called for here in the United States, with advocates claiming that it would be an efficient way of raising funds and lowering income taxes. With the VAT you don't feel like you're paying a tax, because it's built into the price of whatever is being purchased, but you're still paying it. In effect, this type of tax shows up in the form of an increased sales price.

LEARNING OBJECTIVE #3

Explain how your taxes are collected.

PAYING YOUR INCOME TAXES

Taxes are collected on a pay-as-you-go basis through withholdings or by sending in estimated tax payments as you earn money. Although there are a number of ways taxes can be collected, the majority of taxes are withheld from wages. In fact, generally about 70 percent of individual income taxes are collected through withholdings. The idea behind withholding is to collect taxes gradually so that when your taxes are due in the spring, you won't feel the pain of paying taxes in one lump sum. Also, without withholding, too many people would spend the money they should be saving for their taxes. These withholdings also cover your Social Security, state, and local taxes. Other ways in which taxes are collected include quarterly estimated taxes sent to the IRS, payments with your tax return, and withholdings from stock dividends, retirement funds, and prizes or gambling winnings.

Actually, you do have some control over how much is deducted for taxes from your wages. Your withholdings are determined by your income level and by the information you provide on your W-4 form. The W-4 form provides information on your marital status, the number of exemptions you wish to claim, and any additional withholding you would like. Most people fill out their W-4 when they begin employment and never think about it or change it again. However, if your tax level doesn't match your withholdings, revising your W-4 form to make any appropriate adjustments might not be a bad idea.

CALCULATING YOUR TAXES

As we mentioned earlier, once you've determined your income and your deductions, calculating your taxes is mainly just a matter of using the U.S. tax rates. Although this sounds quite simple, the IRS has a way of complicating things. To begin with, not all income is the same. For tax purposes, the IRS defines three different types of income—**active income** (from wages or a business), **portfolio** or **investment income** (from securities), and **passive income** (from activities in which the taxpayer does not actively participate)—and with some minor exceptions limits the deductions from each of these sources to the amount of income derived from that source of income. That is, your passive income deductions are limited to the level of passive income you received, your active income deductions are limited to the level of active income received, and so on. Think this classification is complicated? Just wait—tax calculations got worse.

Who Has to File an Income Tax Return?

The first step to take even before calculating your taxes is determining whether you need to file a tax return. If you don't think you need to file a tax return, you still might want to calculate your taxes, because if you don't file, you won't get a refund. According to 1996 regulations, if your income is more than $13,400, you need to file a return. If it's less than this amount, you may not need to file, depending upon your filing status, age, and whether you can be claimed as a **dependent** on someone else's tax return. Figure 4.1 lists the rules for who must file a return. The only exception to these rules deals with dependents. The income threshold for filing a tax return is generally lower for anyone who may be claimed as a dependent than for nondependents. Dependents with income generally include children who have a job or earn investment income, or elderly parents who have some investment income. If you are considered a dependent on someone else's tax return, you'll want to check carefully to make sure that you don't have to file a return even if your income is below the levels in Figure 4.1. For example, if you're a dependent child and have income in 1996 from a job of more than $4,000, you must file a return. If your income is "unearned," that is, from investments, an income level of only $650 will trigger the need to file a return.

Determining Gross or Total Income

If you do need to fill out an income tax return, the first step in calculating your taxes is determining your total income. **Total income** is simply the sum of all your taxable income from all sources. It includes wages, salaries, and tips, in addition to any taxable interest income and dividends. Generally, your wages will be reported to you on a W-2 form, while interest and dividends will be reported on a Form 1099. It also includes alimony, business income, capital gains, taxable IRA distributions, pensions and annuities, rental income, royalties, farm income, unemployment compensation, taxable Social Security benefits, and any other income. In short, whatever you receive in taxable income is summed to make up your total income:

> Gross Income = Sum of Income from All Sources

Although this calculation sounds simple and relatively straightforward, it's harder than it looks due to the IRS and its lovely little rules.

Remember that not all income is taxable, and as such, not all income is included in total income. The main source of tax-exempt income is interest on state and local debt. Other sources listed in Table 4.3 include gifts, inheritances, earnings on your IRA, and federal income tax refunds.

Understand what is taxable income and how taxes are determined.

Active Income
Income that comes from wages or a business.

Portfolio or **Investment Income**
Income that comes from securities.

Passive Income
Income that comes from activities in which the taxpayer does not actively participate.

Dependent
Person you take financial care of.

Total Income
The sum of all your taxable income from all sources.

FIGURE 4.1

Who Has to File an Income Tax Return*
If your gross income is equal to or greater than the amount listed below, you must, in general, file a return.

What if you're a dependent? If another taxpayer can claim you as a dependent on his or her tax return, the filing thresholds are usually much lower. If you are single and under 65 (and you are not blind), have any unearned income (such as interest or dividends), and have total gross income of over $650 (both earned and unearned, or unearned only), you must file a tax return. If you have no unearned income, you don't need to file unless your gross income exceeds your standard deduction (earned income up to $4,000).

FILING STATUS

Age	Gross Income†
SINGLE	
● Under 65	$ 6,550
● 65 or older	$ 7,550
MARRIED FILING JOINTLY	
● Both under 65	$11,800
● One 65 or older	$12,600
● Both 65 or older	$13,400
MARRIED FILING SEPARATELY	
● Under 65	$ 2,550
● 65 or older	$ 2,550
HEAD OF HOUSEHOLD	
● Under 65	$ 8,450
● 65 or older	$ 9,450
SURVIVING SPOUSE	
● Under 65	$ 9,250
● 65 or older	$10,050

Gross Income is your total income before exclusions and deductions. Gross income includes such common forms of income as wages, interest, dividends, and business income.

*Based on tax year 1996 laws.
†Gross income does not include tax-exempt income.

TABLE 4.3

Common Sources of Tax-Free Income

Interest on municipal bonds
Tax-free money market funds—mutual funds that invest in tax-exempt municipal notes
Gifts
Inheritances
Earnings on your IRA
Interest earned inside a life insurance policy—on which no taxes are paid until you cash the policy
Social Security benefits—with the amount that is tax-free dependent upon total income
Child support payments
Federal income tax refunds
Veterans' benefits
Workers' compensation benefits
Welfare benefits

IRS PROBLEMS? Try Calling the IRS—Really

The long weekend leading up to the Fourth of July, that most patriotic of American holidays, seems like an appropriate time to say something nice about the Internal Revenue Service.

Granted, it may have credited your tax payments to someone else's account. It may have lost your refund. Or it may be threatening to garnish your paycheck if you don't reply to notices that you answered by certified mail six months ago.

Believe it or not, though, IRS officials share your frustration. And they have a little-known rescue operation for taxpayers plagued by red tape and bureaucratic ignorance, indifference or just plain obstinacy.

The agency's 17-year-old Problem Resolution Program has snatched hundreds of thousands of taxpayers from the jaws of bureaucratic bunglers. In fiscal 1994, ended Sept. 30, problem resolution officers in IRS districts and service centers answered about 420,000 cries for help.

These people cannot change the amount of tax you owe or fight your legal battles. They don't intercede in audits, because there is an IRS appeals process for that.

But program officers can restart the system after it grinds to a halt through no fault of yours. They take care of stalled refunds, erroneous penalties, muddled records, wrongheaded notices and violations of your rights. The officers also can block an IRS seizure of your pay or property that threatens you with a severe handicap.

"PRP can take a case that the system can't deal with and get it resolved quickly, correctly and completely," declares Linda Martin, a former program staff director who is now a senior technical adviser at the accounting firm Deloitte & Touche.

The program even wins praise from such sometime IRS adversaries as the American Institute of Certified Public Accountants and the National Association of enrolled Agents, an organization of tax specialists.

Source: Scott R. Schmedel, "IRS Problems? Try Calling the IRS—Really," *The Wall Street Journal*, June 30, 1995, p. C1. Reprinted by permission of *The Wall Street Journal*, © 1995 Dow Jones & Company, Inc. All Rights Reserved Worldwide.

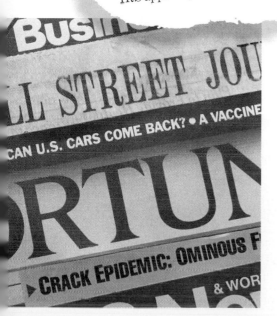

Analysis and Implications ...

A. In most areas, you can reach Internal Revenue Service problem resolution officers by telephoning 800-829-1040. For voice-recorded information about the program, you can call IRS Tele-Tax; in most areas, the number is 800-829-4477.

B. If you need additional help, or just want to know how the program works, you can call 800-829-3676 and ask for IRS Publication 1546, "How to Use the Problem Resolution Program," and Publication 1, "Your Rights as a Taxpayer."

Adjusted Gross Income (AGI)

Total income less allowable deductions.

Adjusted gross income (AGI) is simply total income less allowable deductions. Adjustments to total income center on payments set aside for retirement, and also include moving and alimony payments. In effect, the IRS allows you to reduce your taxable income when you either incur specific expenses or when you contribute to certain retirement plans. The advantage of these deductions is that they lower your taxes, allowing you to invest or spend (hopefully, invest) money that you would otherwise send to Uncle Sam.

For example, if neither you nor your spouse is covered by a retirement plan at work, you can annually deduct a contribution up to $2,000 on a tax deferred basis to your IRA. Since 1997 a married couple with only one spouse working outside the home may contribute a total of $4,000 to an IRA, provided the "working spouse" has at least $4,000 in earned income. If you are covered by a pension plan at work there are limits on the size of your deductible contribution. The Taxpayers Relief Act of 1997 expands the ability of individuals to make tax deductible contributions to **Individual Retirement Accounts** or **IRAs**—increasing the income limits for those who can make contributions. Table 4.4 provides a listing of the deduction limits for individuals who are active participants in employer-sponsored retirement plans. The bill also permits deductible contributions for nonworking spouses of individuals who are in an employer-sponsored retirement plan. The deduction is phased out for taxpayers with adjusted gross incomes between $150,000 and $160,000. In addition, the Taxpayer Relief Act of 1997 created new tax-favored accounts, called Roth IRAs, to which after-tax dollars are contributed and are allowed to grow tax free and be withdrawn for retirement without taxes after a reasonable holding period.

IRA

An individual retirement account, which is a tax-deferred retirement savings account allowed by the government.

The Facts of Life

There's no minimum age for having an IRA. So, if your 14-year-old earns $2,000 baby-sitting and mowing lawns, he or she can put that $2,000 into an IRA. If that single $2,000 contribution grows at 12 percent compounded annually, it will grow to $1,140,878 by the time your child turns 70!

Other adjustments to income include moving expenses associated with taking a job at a new location that is at least 50 miles farther from your home than was your previous job. In addition, self-employed tax filers are allowed to deduct half of the Social Security and Medicare taxes that they pay as well as 30 percent of the cost of their family's health insurance. Alimony payments, provided certain requirements are met, are also deductible, because the person receiving the payments must pay taxes on them. Because adjustments to income reduce your taxes, it's important both to understand these adjustments and take advantage of them. After adding up all your adjustments to income, you subtract this amount from your total income to arrive at adjusted gross income (AGI):

Gross Income = Sum of Income from All Sources

Less

Adjustments to Gross Income: Tax-Deductible Expenses and Retirement Contributions (traditional IRA, Keogh contributions, moving expenses, and so on)

Equals

Adjusted Gross Income (AGI)

TABLE 4.4

The Effect of the Taxpayer Relief Act of 1997—Adjusted Gross Income (AGI) and the Deductibility of IRA Contributions for Those Who Participate in a Retirement Plan at Work			
Tax Year 1998: **Filing Status**	**You Can Take a Full IRA Deduction if Your AGI Is Less Than**	**You Can Take a Partial IRA Deduction if Your AGI Is Between**	**You Cannot Take Any IRA Deduction if Your AGI Is Greater Than**
Single	$30,000	$30,000 to $40,000	$40,000
Married Filing Jointly	$50,000	$50,000 to $60,000	$60,000
Tax Year 2004: **Filing Status**	**You Can Take a Full IRA Deduction if Your AGI Is Less Than**	**You Can Take a Partial IRA Deduction if Your AGI Is Between**	**You Cannot Take Any IRA Deduction if Your AGI Is Greater Than**
Single	$50,000	$50,000 to $60,000	$60,000
Married Filing Jointly	$80,000	$80,000 to $100,000	$100,000

Subtracting Out Deductions

Once you know your AGI, the next step in calculating taxable income is to subtract out your deductions. You have your choice of taking either the standard deduction or itemizing your deductions, whichever one is larger and benefits you the most. Obviously, taking the largest possible deduction is important. In fact, if you're in the 31 percent marginal tax bracket and you're able to take an additional $5,000 in deductions, you've actually reduced your tax bill by $5,000 × 0.31 = $1,550. That's $1,550 that you can spend on Domino's pizza or invest for your retirement—whichever seems more important.

What's the difference between standardized and itemized deductions? On the simplest level, one's calculated for you and the other you have to calculate yourself. Of course, the answer's really more complicated than that. Let's start by taking a look at the deduction you have to calculate yourself—the itemized deduction.

IRS Limits on Itemized Deductions.　We should note that taxpayers in higher income brackets don't get credit for all their itemized deductions. These limits don't affect many taxpayers—only those in the highest income brackets. The limits don't come into play unless your AGI is greater than $117,950 for those filing as single, joint, or head of household status.[3]

Itemizing Your Deductions.　The IRS has decided that you shouldn't be taxed on income that's used to pay for certain expenses. These are considered deductible expenses. Itemizing is simply the listing of all the deductions you're allowed to take. Of course, it's your responsibility to determine and document your deductible expenses. Which expenses count as deductible? Let's take a look at the most common ones.

[3]According to tax year 1996 laws. This phaseout is inflation adjusted and as a result the phaseout begins at $121,200 for the tax year 1997.

- **Medical and Dental Expenses.** Although medical and dental expenses are deductible, they're deductible only to the extent that they exceed 7.5 percent of your AGI. For an individual with an AGI of $60,000, only those medical and dental expenses in excess of $4,500 would be deductible. If that individual had total medical and dental expenses of $4,750, only $250 would be deductible. The definition of what's considered a medical or dental expense is quite broad and includes medical treatment, hospital care, prescription drugs, and health insurance.

- **Tax Expenses.** Some, but not all, tax expenses are deductible. Although the biggest chunk of taxes you pay—your federal, Social Security, and all sales taxes—are not tax-deductible, your state and local income taxes, along with your real estate taxes, are deductible. Most taxpayers have to pay state income taxes. These are deductible in the year in which they are paid. In addition, if you paid any county or city income taxes, these, too, would be tax-deductible. Some states also impose a personal property tax—generally a tax on automobiles—which is also tax-deductible.

- **Home Mortgage and Investment Interest Payments.** Several types of interest are tax-deductible. Interest that you pay on your home mortgage is deductible. Interest on the amount of a mortgage over $1 million isn't deductible, but few taxpayers are really affected by this limitation. Interest you pay on **home equity loans** is also deductible on home equity debt up to $100,000. The last type of tax-deductible interest is investment interest, or interest on money that you borrowed to invest. The maximum deduction that you can take on investment interest is limited to the amount of investment income that you earn. Why does the IRS let you deduct these interest payments? Because it wants to make it easier for you to buy a house and make investments to help the overall economy. By making home interest payments tax-deductible, the government is in effect subsidizing your purchase of a home. In other words, the government allows these tax deductions to encourage you to buy a house and to make investments.

> ### The Facts of Life
> Once you buy a home, you're generally better off itemizing deductions because of the home mortgage interest payments. Your home mortgage interest payments act to push you over the threshold where you have enough deductible expenses to make itemizing worthwhile. As a result, expenses that previously had no value, such as personal property taxes, charitable contributions, and the cost of your safety deposit box, may now be deductible and, thus, result in tax savings.

- **Gifts to Charity.** Charitable gifts to qualified organizations are tax-deductible. If you're in the 28-percent tax bracket and you give $1,000 to a charitable organization, it really only costs you $720, because you've given away $1,000 and as a result lowered your taxes by $280 (0.28 × $1,000). In effect, Congress is encouraging you, through the use of a tax break, to make charitable gifts. The only requirement for this deduction is that the gift go to a qualified organization and that if you make a single gift of more than $250, you show a receipt for that gift (a canceled check won't do). Of course, regardless of the size of the gift, you must make sure that you maintain good records. If you can't keep track of your donations, how can you deduct them?

- **Casualty and Theft Loss.** Although you're able to deduct casualty and theft losses, this deduction is rather limited and is of value only to those who suffer huge losses or have very low earnings. The reason for its limited usefulness is that (1) for tax purposes, the first $100 of losses is excluded and (2) you can deduct losses only to the extent that the remaining losses exceed 10 percent of your AGI. For example, if

Home Equity Loan

A loan that uses your home as collateral, that is, a loan that is secured by your home. If you default, the lender can take possession of your home to recapture money lost on the loan.

your AGI were $50,000 and you suffered a loss of $5,200, your deductible loss would be calculated by first subtracting $100 from your losses, leaving you with a $5,100 loss. Then you could deduct that loss only to the extent that it exceeded 10 percent of your AGI of $50,000, which is $5,000. Thus, you could only deduct $100 out of this $5,200 loss. Also, the deductible level of your loss would be further reduced by any reimbursement that you receive from insurance.

- **Miscellaneous Deductibles.**   These deductions include unreimbursed job-related expenses, tax preparation expenses, and investment-related expenses. The problem with these expenses is that they are only deductible to the extent that they are in excess of 2 percent of your AGI. In general, this percentage is a tough hurdle to pass, and, as a result, most taxpayers are not able to benefit from miscellaneous deductions.

Earlier we mentioned that once your income gets above a certain level, you begin losing a percentage of your itemized deductions. For those filing as married filing separately, the threshold is $58,975 in 1996. These threshold values are indexed for inflation and will rise in the future accordingly. In fact, this threshold rose to $60,600 for the 1997 tax year. This erosion of the value of itemized deductions is relatively complicated and doesn't affect all deductions equally. As a result, we won't explore its specifics. However, if your AGI is greater than this threshold level, you should have a clear understanding of how the reduction in deductions affects you.

The Standard Deduction.   The alternative to itemizing deductions is to take the standard deduction. Basically, the standard deduction is the government's best estimate of what the average person would be able to deduct by itemizing. In other words, with the standard deduction you needn't itemize—the government has done it for you already. You don't need to figure out your expenses and provide receipts or justification. You just need to sit back and take an automatic deduction. Unlike itemized deductions, which are limited for higher AGI levels, the standard deduction remains the same regardless of your income level. In fact, the level of the standard deduction increases every year to keep up with inflation. Figure 4.2 provides the standard deductions for both 1996 and 1997. Note that additional standard deductions are given to the elderly and the blind.

FIGURE 4.2

Standard Deduction Amounts

Filing Status	1996	1997
Single	$4,000	$4,150
Married Filing Jointly or Surviving Spouse	$6,700	$6,900
Head of Household	$5,900	$6,100
Married Filing Separately	$3,350	$3,450

Additional Standard Deductions for Elderly and Blind: For a taxpayer (and spouse) who is elderly (age 65 or over) or blind, the following applies:
- *Unmarried Taxpayer:* An additional $1,000 standard deduction amount is allowed ($2,000 for a taxpayer who is both elderly and blind).
- *Married Taxpayer:* An additional $800 standard deduction is allowed ($1,600 for a taxpayer who is both elderly and blind).

The Choice: Itemizing or Taking the Standard Deduction. The decision between taking the standard deduction or itemizing may not be particularly difficult if one provides a greater deduction than the other. The choice becomes much more difficult, and also more interesting, when they are close in value. In that case, it may be best to bunch your deductions and alternate each year between taking the standard deduction and itemizing. This year you may speed up your payment of deductible expenses, for example, make your January mortgage payment on December 31. That way you have more deductible expenses in the present year at the expense of the following year's deductible expenses. As a result, this year your itemized deduction will fall well above the standard deduction level, and you'll be better off itemizing. The following year, you'll have fewer itemized deductions, and you'll be better off taking the standard deduction. In effect, you try to avoid incurring deductible expenses in years that you don't itemize. Instead, if possible, you postpone them to years when you do itemize and therefore get credit for them. There's no question that taking the standard deduction is easier than itemizing, but don't choose to take the standard deduction just because it's simpler—you don't want laziness to cost you money.

A Deduction for (Almost) Everyone: Interest on Student Loans. With the passage of the Taxpayer Relief Act of 1997, you can now deduct interest on student loans regardless of whether you itemize—provided you aren't making "too much money." Under this legislation individuals can deduct interest payments on student loans of up to $1,000 per year starting in 1998 and increasing by $500 a year to $2,500 by 2001. This deduction begins phasing out at $60,000 for those filing as couples and is completely eliminated for couples with modified adjusted gross incomes above $75,000. Singles making less than $40,000 receive the full deduction, while those making between $40,000 and $55,000 receive a partial deduction. In addition, this deduction is limited to the first five years of the loan. For existing loans, interest payments can be deducted provided the loan isn't more than 5 years old. Remember, this deduction is even available to those who don't itemize. It also extends, for three years, a provision that allows (undergraduate) students to deduct up to $5,250 in tuition costs paid by their employers.

Claiming Your Exemptions

Once you've subtracted your deductions from your AGI, you're ready to now subtract your exemptions. An exemption is a deduction that you can make on your return for each person that's supported by the income on your tax return. The government provides these exemptions so that everyone will have a little bit of untaxed money to spend on necessities. In effect, each exemption allows you to lower your taxable income by $2,550 for the 1996 tax year and $2,650 for 1997.[4] Thus, if you're in the 31 percent marginal tax bracket, each exemption you take in 1996 will lower your taxes by $790.50. You can claim anyone as an exemption, even if you're not related to them, if you provide more than half of their support. However, if you claim someone as a dependent on your return, that individual can't appear as an exemption on anyone else's return—even the dependent's own.

There are two types of exemptions—personal and dependency. You receive a personal exemption for yourself regardless of your filing status, or yourself and your spouse if filing a joint return, no questions asked. However, qualifying for a dependency exemption is more difficult. First, dependents must pass a relationship or household member test. If they're related to you as children, grandchildren, stepchildren, siblings, parents, grandparents, stepparents, uncles, aunts, nieces, nephews, in-laws, and so forth, they're considered to have a qualifying relationship. In fact, almost any relationship short of being a cousin qualifies under the IRS. If they're not related to you, then they must have lived with you over the entire tax year. Second, the individual

[4]Exemptions, like standard deductions, are raised each year to match inflation rates.

being claimed as a dependent generally can't earn more than the exemption amount. However, this income test does not apply to your children under the age of 19 or to children under the age of 24 who are full-time students. Third, you must provide more than half of the dependent's support. In addition, the dependent must also be a U.S. citizen, resident or national, or a resident of either Mexico or Canada.

Just as with itemized deductions, once your AGI reaches a certain level, the value of your exemptions is reduced. For example, for those filing joint returns, once their AGI reaches the threshold level of $176,950, all exemption amounts claimed on the return are reduced by 2 percent for each $2,500 of AGI in excess of the threshold amount.[5] Naturally, the higher your AGI, the lower your exemption until your exemption is phased out altogether. Table 4.5 presents the thresholds where phaseouts begin and the points where the phaseout of exemptions is completed. These threshold points are adjusted annually for inflation. Essentially, if your AGI is above the threshold point, your marginal tax rate is effectively increased because as you earn more, you lose a percentage of your exemptions. The more exemptions you have, the more important this phaseout becomes. For example, if, in 1996, you had 12 exemptions and an AGI level above the phaseout threshold, for each additional $2,500 of AGI you received, your exemptions would be reduced by $612, which is 2 percent of the value of your total exemptions (12 exemptions × $2,550 × 0.02 = $612).

TABLE 4.5

Phaseout of Exemptions

Exemption claims are reduced by 2% for each $2,500 of AGI in excess of the appropriate threshold amount, with the threshold amounts annually adjusted for inflation.

1996

Filing Status	Phaseout Begins When AGI Exceeds	Phaseout Completed When AGI Exceeds
Single	$117,950	$240,450
Married Filing Jointly or Surviving Spouse	176,950	299,450
Head of Household	147,450	269,950
Married Filing Separately	88,475	149,725

1997

Filing Status	Phaseout Begins When AGI Exceeds	Phaseout Completed When AGI Exceeds
Single	$121,200	$243,700
Married Filing Jointly or Surviving Spouse	181,800	304,300
Head of Household	151,500	274,000
Married Filing Separately	90,900	152,150

[5]Based on tax year 1996 laws. This threshold level is raised each year to match inflation. In 1997 this threshold rose to $181,800.

Calculating Your Base Income Tax

Now that you've subtracted your deductions and your exemptions from your AGI, you know your taxable income, which is the amount that your taxes are based upon. Figure 4.3 shows these calculations. For most taxpayers, once you've determined your taxable income, your income tax can be determined directly using the tax tables found in the middle of your federal income tax instructions booklet. The intersection of your taxable income and your filing status determines your taxes due, as shown in Figure 4.4.

If your taxable income is greater than $100,000, you must determine your taxes using the rate schedules because the tax tables don't go that high. The tax rate schedules are found at the end of your federal income tax instructions booklet and were provided earlier in Table 4.2.

There's also an alternative minimum tax that's aimed at preventing the very wealthy from using tax breaks to the extent that they pay little or nothing. For most people this tax isn't a concern, but for the very wealthy, it's got to be dealt with. It applies different rules in calculating taxable income and then applies a 26 percent and a 28-percent tax rate to all income. It's really Congress's method of ensuring that everyone pays taxes.

Determining Your Credits

Tax credits offset your taxes in a direct dollar-for-dollar manner. That is, they don't merely reduce your taxable income, they offset taxes. With the passage of Taxpayer Relief Act of 1997 several new credits appeared.

FIGURE 4.3

Calculation of Taxable Income

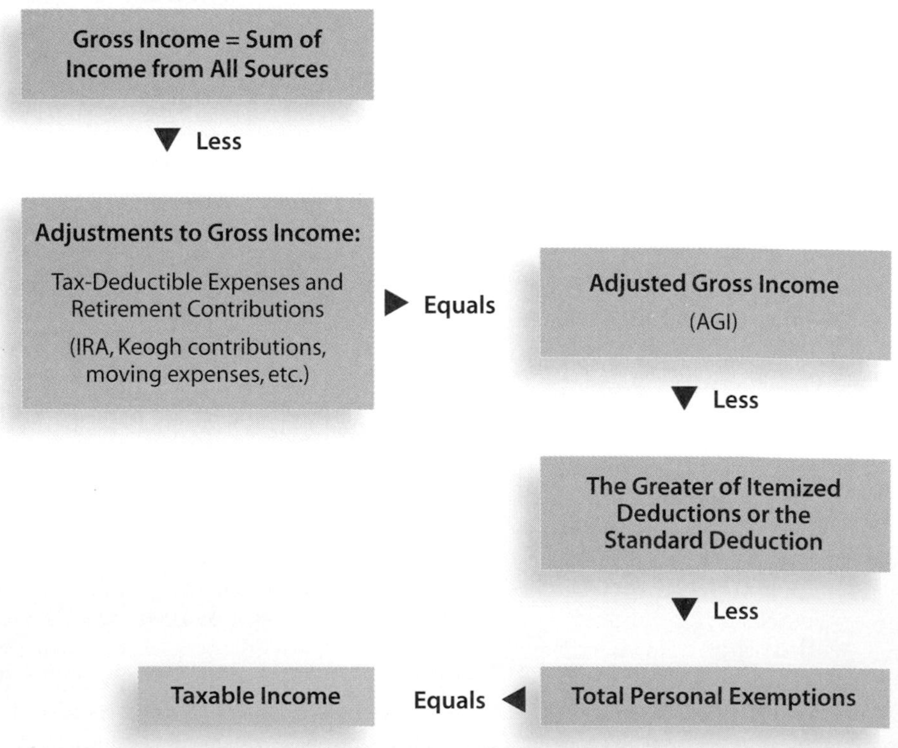

Gross Income = Sum of Income from All Sources

▼ Less

Adjustments to Gross Income:

Tax-Deductible Expenses and Retirement Contributions

(IRA, Keogh contributions, moving expenses, etc.)

▶ Equals

Adjusted Gross Income (AGI)

▼ Less

The Greater of Itemized Deductions or the Standard Deduction

▼ Less

Total Personal Exemptions

Equals ◀

Taxable Income

FIGURE 4.4

Determining Your Taxes Using the 1996 Tax Tables
Assuming you are married filing jointly with taxable income of $38,701, your taxes would be $5,809.

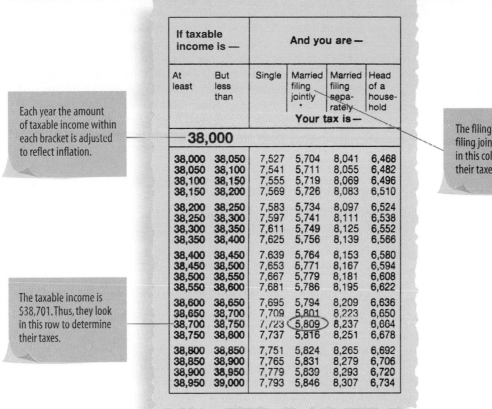

Each year the amount of taxable income within each bracket is adjusted to reflect inflation.

The filing status is married filing jointly. Thus, they look in this column to calculate their taxes.

The taxable income is $38,701. Thus, they look in this row to determine their taxes.

If taxable income is —		And you are —			
At least	But less than	Single	Married filing jointly	Married filing separately	Head of a household
			Your tax is—		
38,000					
38,000	38,050	7,527	5,704	8,041	6,468
38,050	38,100	7,541	5,711	8,055	6,482
38,100	38,150	7,555	5,719	8,069	6,496
38,150	38,200	7,569	5,726	8,083	6,510
38,200	38,250	7,583	5,734	8,097	6,524
38,250	38,300	7,597	5,741	8,111	6,538
38,300	38,350	7,611	5,749	8,125	6,552
38,350	38,400	7,625	5,756	8,139	6,566
38,400	38,450	7,639	5,764	8,153	6,580
38,450	38,500	7,653	5,771	8,167	6,594
38,500	38,550	7,667	5,779	8,181	6,608
38,550	38,600	7,681	5,786	8,195	6,622
38,600	38,650	7,695	5,794	8,209	6,636
38,650	38,700	7,709	5,801	8,223	6,650
38,700	38,750	7,723	5,809	8,237	6,664
38,750	38,800	7,737	5,816	8,251	6,678
38,800	38,850	7,751	5,824	8,265	6,692
38,850	38,900	7,765	5,831	8,279	6,706
38,900	38,950	7,779	5,839	8,293	6,720
38,950	39,000	7,793	5,846	8,307	6,734

Child Credit and the Taxpayer Relief Act of 1997. Beginning in 1998, there will be a $400 child tax credit for each child under 17, with the size of this child tax credit rising to $500 per child in 1999. This child tax credit comes on top of the personal exemption for each child. Again, this is a tax credit, which means it cuts your tax bill dollar for dollar. Thus, a family with three children under 17 would save $1,200 in taxes in 1998 and $1,500 in 1999. This tax credit can even come in the form of a tax refund for low-income families who don't pay any taxes. At the high end of the income scale, this child tax credit begins being phased out after a single parent's income reaches $75,000 or a couple's income reaches $110,000 regardless of the number of children they have. Once the phaseout begins, the credit is reduced by $25 for every $1,000 that the couple earns over $110,000.

The Hope Scholarship Tax Credit and the Lifetime Learning Credit. For most parents, thinking about how much they need to save for their children's education results in paralyzing horror and guilt. As a result, the Taxpayer Relief Act of 1997 tried to make college funding at bit easier (not painless, just easier). Under this legislation, parents get a 100-percent tax credit for the first $1,000 of college expenses during each of the first two years of college. On top of that they also get a 50-percent tax

Hope Scholarship Tax Credit

A tax credit of up to $1,500 per year for the first two years of college.

credit on the next $1,000 of expenses for a total tax credit of up to $1,500 a year for the first two years of college. This tax credit is called the **Hope Scholarship tax credit**. Qualifying expenses include tuition and books, but not room and board. To qualify, the student must be enrolled on at least a part-time basis in an accredited vocational school, college, or university.

There are, of course, a number of restrictions that the IRS imposes on the use of Hope Scholarship tax credit. First, to qualify, you must both pay the student's tuition and list the student as a dependent on your tax return. In addition, parents who are taking distributions from an education IRA can't claim a Hope Scholarship tax credit in the same year. The size of the tax credit you receive can also be affected by the amount of financial aid and scholarship funds that are received. As with most other tax breaks, the Hope Scholarship tax credit gets phased out for single individuals with incomes greater than $40,000 and for families filing joint returns with incomes greater than $80,000, and is totally eliminated for single filers with modified adjusted gross incomes above $50,000 and for joint filers above $100,000.

> ### Stop and Think
>
> The Hope Scholarship is set up to help everyone get at least a two-year degree at a community college. In fact, the $1,500 credit is about $300 above the 1997 national average community college tuition rate. That means that a community college education is "tuition-free" for all those who qualify, which is about two-thirds of all community college students.

Lifetime Learning Tax Credit

A tax credit for third and fourth year of college or graduate students. It also applies to working adults taking classes to improve their work skills.

During the third and fourth year, or for graduate students, the **Lifetime Learning tax credit** applies. It also applies to working adults taking classes to improve their work skills. This tax credit amounts to 20 percent of the first $5,000 through 2002, rising to 20 percent of the first $10,000 in 2003. Just as with the Hope Scholarship, the Lifetime Learning tax credit gets phased out for those in the higher income bracket. This tax credit is fully available for those filing single returns with incomes less than $40,000 and for families filing joint returns with incomes less than $80,000. Partial credits are available for single filers with modified adjusted gross incomes between $40,000 and $50,000 and for joint filers with modified adjusted gross incomes between $80,000 and $100,000. Again, as with the Hope scholarship, if you're taking money out of an education IRA to pay expenses, you can't claim the Lifetime Learning credit. In addition, parents must be paying their child's tuition and claiming the child as a dependent in order to qualify for the Lifetime Learning tax credit. This tax credit had an effective date of June 30, 1998.

Child and Dependent Care Credit

A tax credit that offsets your taxes in a direct dollar-for-dollar manner for child and dependent care expenses.

Other Tax Credits.   Another common tax credit is the **child and dependent care credit**. The logic behind the child care credit is that child care is an expense of having a job; that is, you have to spend money on child care to earn a living, and, as such, you should get income tax credit for your expenditures. With the increased number of single-parent and dual-income families, the child and dependent care credit is used quite often. As the name implies, the credit applies both to dependent children under the age of 13 and to disabled dependents or a disabled spouse, regardless of age. In addition, to qualify, you must have earned income—that is, noninvestment income—and if you file a joint return, both spouses must have earned income. The maximum amount of child and dependent care expenses that qualified for the credit in 1996 was $2,400 for one child/dependent and $4,800 for two or more, and you receive only a percentage of that amount as a tax credit. The size of the tax credit that you actually receive then depends upon how much you spent on child/dependent care and your AGI. For example, those with AGI of less than $10,000 receive 30 percent of their child/dependent care expenses up to $2,400 or $4,800 as a tax credit; however, those earning over $28,000 only receive 20 percent of their child/dependent care expenses up to $2,400 or $4,800 as a tax credit. Thus, if your AGI was $35,000 and you had two children in child care at a total cost of $5,000, your child care credit would be $960. Why? Because only the first $4,800 of your child care expenses qualifies for the credit, and because your AGI is over $28,000, you receive a credit of only 20 percent of your qualified expenses (0.20 × $4,800 = $960). Of course, you can't get a credit for more than you owe in taxes.

There's also an **earned income credit** available to low-income taxpayers, which effectively serves as a negative income tax. With the child and dependent care credit, you couldn't get a credit for more than you owed in taxes, but with the earned income credit you could actually get a credit for more than you paid in taxes. In other words, you could pay no taxes and get money back from the IRS. Of all the credits, this one is perhaps the most complicated with respect to determining exactly what you qualify for. For those with no children, the maximum credit is $323, with the credit disappearing entirely when AGI or earned income exceeds $9,500.[6] The maximum credit is $2,152 for those with one qualifying child and is totally phased out when AGI or earned income rises above $25,078, and for those with more than one child, the maximum credit is $3,556 and is totally phased out once earned income or AGI reaches $28,495.[7]

Another important credit for some taxpayers is the **adoption credit**, which began in 1997. It allows for a tax credit of up to $5,000 for the qualifying cost of adopting a child under the age of 18, or someone who is physically or mentally incapable of self-care.[8] This credit is phased out for those with AGI (after certain adjustments) between $75,000 and $115,000.

There are other credits that are available to taxpayers, and they include

- Tax credits to totally disabled taxpayers and those over 65 with low incomes
- Tax credits to taxpayers who pay income tax to another country
- Tax credits for federal gasoline taxes to taxpayers who purchase gasoline for non-highway vehicles used in a business
- Tax credits to those who overpay their Social Security taxes because they work more than one job

Although there are not nearly the number of tax credits that there once were, it behooves you to be aware of what qualifies for a tax credit and take advantage of any credit that you qualify for. Once again, *tax credits are subtracted directly from taxes due on a dollar-for-dollar basis.* Thus, your total income tax becomes your base income tax less your tax credits.

> Base Income Tax (from tax tables or tax rate calculations)
>
> Less
>
> Tax Credits
>
> Equals
>
> Total Income Tax Due

Earned Income Credit

A tax credit available to low-income taxpayers, which effectively serves as a negative income tax.

Adoption Credit

A tax credit of up to $5,000 available for qualifying costs of adopting a child.

[6]Based on tax year 1996 laws.
[7]Based on tax year 1996 laws.
[8]This credit can even go up to $6,000 if the child has special needs.

Choose the tax form that's right for you.

Schedules
Attachments to Form 1040 on which you provide additional information.

CHOOSING A TAX FORM

A key to calculating your taxes is deciding which 1040 form to use: 1040EZ, 1040A, or 1040. If the IRS has sent you that material, it's already made a guess at what form you'll need and has included it. Still, you have the option of choosing a different form if you like.

Form 1040EZ is aimed at those with no dependents, and with taxable income less than $50,000 per year, who don't itemize. Presently, it's used by about 20 million taxpayers. As its name implies, it is an "easy" form to fill out. That's because if you have any complicating tax factors, you're disqualified from using it. As a result, Form 1040EZ consists of only 12 lines of information, and the instructions fit on the back of the form. In fact, it can even be filled out over the telephone. Table 4.6 provides some of the basic requirements you must meet in order to qualify to use form 1040EZ.

Slightly less "EZ" than Form 1040EZ, but still not too complicated, is Form 1040A, the original easy form. It loosens up the requirements for use quite a bit from those associated with Form 1040EZ, and, as a result, it is used by about 25 million taxpayers. Although it still limits total taxable income to $50,000, it allows for this income to come from interest, dividends, Social Security benefits, pensions and annuities, scholarships, IRA distributions, and unemployment compensation. In effect, it allows for a much broader range of income sources than is allowed on Form 1040EZ. Form 1040A also allows for dependents and deductible contributions to an IRA. Table 4.7 provides some of the basic requirements that must be met in order to qualify to use form 1040A.

Form 1040, which is also called the "1040 long form," is used by everyone else—about 75 million taxpayers—and throws "easy" right out the door. It's longer because it allows for the many complications that can make filing taxes a frustrating, if not fatal, experience. On the bright side, though, the 1040 long form allows for the opportunity to avoid paying more in the way of taxes than is legally required. That is, it allows for itemized deductions and adjustments to income that can result in lower taxes. Obviously, your choice of a tax form should not be based on what's easiest to fill out. It should be based upon what's most financially advantageous to you.

Along with Form 1040, you also get a number of **schedules**. A schedule is an attachment to Form 1040 on which you provide information regarding income and expenses that flow through to Form 1040. Some of the more common schedules are listed in Table 4.8.

The Facts of Life

Each year the IRS sends out about 8 billion pages of forms, requiring around 300,000 trees to make the paper. If you still need an IRS schedule or form, the easiest way of getting it is to call 800-TAX-FORM, and the IRS will send it directly to you just as soon as they're done chopping down more trees.

TABLE 4.6

You Might Be Able to Use Form 1040EZ if . . .

Your filing status is either single or married filing jointly.
You don't itemize deductions.
Your taxable income is less than $50,000.
Your taxable interest income is less than $400.
You have no dependents.
You aren't making a deductible contribution to an IRA.
You don't have alimony, taxable pension benefits, or social security benefits to report.

TABLE 4.7

MODEL TAXPAYERS: THE TAYLORS FILE THEIR 1996 RETURN

Let's take a look at how the various steps of calculating taxes are represented on Form 1040. We'll use the Taylors as an example. Chuck and Dianne Taylor have two children: Lindsey, who's 4, and Kathleen, who's 6. Chuck is a computer analyst for Burlington Industries, where he earned $31,450 in 1996, and Dianne works part-time at an art gallery, where she earned $6,250 in 1996. On Chuck and Dianne's wages and salary there was a total of $5,595 in federal tax withheld. In addition, Chuck has a consulting business where he does computer programming, and in 1996 this consulting business provided additional net income of $7,450. Because there were no taxes taken out of Chuck's consulting income, he made estimated tax payments of $1,200. In 1996 the Taylors also received interest income of $760, dividends of $580, $755 in capital gains (in 1996 the maximum capital gains tax rate was at 28 percent) on stock that they sold, and a gift of $10,000 from Chuck's parents. Chuck also contributed $1,000 to his **Keogh plan**, which is a tax-deferred retirement plan for self-employed individuals.

The Taylors had another, more interesting source of income: they were winners on *The Price Is Right*. That's right, Dianne won a 1996 Chevrolet Cavalier just by telling Bob Barker the third number in its price. A stunned Dianne Taylor stood on the stage of the CBS studio in Burbank, California, hearing the announcer say, "That's right, Dianne, this brand-new Chevrolet Cavalier comes fully equipped with air, AM/FM cassette, automatic windows, and California emission controls. You'll enjoy making heads turn as you drive down the street in this, *your new car!*" What she didn't hear is that she would have to pay taxes on her prize. What she's taxed on is the fair market price of the car, which is interpreted as what she could realize on an immediate resale of the car. In this case that amount is $12,500. This amount becomes part of their taxable income.

Because the Taylors have total taxable income greater than $50,000, they have no choice but to file using the 1040 long form. The first step in filing is to get organized, which means gathering together a copy of last year's return along with all of this year's tax-related information: salary, taxes withheld, mortgage payments, the market price of the car Dianne won, medical expenses, and so on. Fortunately, over the past year the Taylors set aside all their tax-related materials in a folder in Dianne's desk.

LEARNING OBJECTIVE #6

Calculate your income taxes.

Keogh Plan
A tax-deferred retirement plan for the self-employed.

TABLE 4.8

Schedules Included with Form 1040

Schedule A: Itemized Deductions
Schedule B: Interest and Dividend Income
Schedule C: Profit or Loss from Business
Schedule D: Capital Gains and Losses
Schedule E: Supplemental Income and Loss
Schedule EIC: Earned Income Credit
Schedule F: Profit or Loss from Farming
Schedule H: Household Employment Taxes
Schedule R: Credit for the Elderly or the Disabled
Schedule SE: Self-Employment Tax

One of the first questions asked on Form 1040 is your filing status. For the Taylors, filing a joint return makes the most sense. Remember, the rates are set up to encourage you to file a joint return if you are married. The total exemptions claimed by the Taylors were four—one each for Chuck, Dianne, Kathleen, and Lindsey. Figure 4.5 shows the Taylors' 1996 Form 1040. We'll use this figure as a reference as we now examine how the Taylors' calculated their taxes. All line references correspond to the numbered lines shown on the Taylors' Form 1040.

FIGURE 4.5

1996 Federal Income Tax Return for the Taylors, Using Form 1040

Take the time to set up a good tax record-keeping system. Once it's set up, use it!

Married people generally file as Married Filing Jointly (in general, it saves money over filing separately), but for those with widely divergent levels of income and deductions, it might be better to use the Married Filing Separately status.

If you work for yourself, your income gets reported on Schedule C.

If you put money into an IRA or tax-deferred retirement plan and you haven't yet paid taxes on that money, you will have to pay taxes on it when you withdraw it at retirement.

Form **1040** (M) **U.S. Individual Income Tax Return** **1996** | Department of the Treasury—Internal Revenue Service | IRS Use Only—Do not write or staple in this space.

For the year Jan. 1–Dec. 31, 1996, or other tax year beginning , 1996, ending , 19 | OMB No. 1545-0074

Label (See page 11.)

Your first name and initial: CHUCK B. | Last name: TAYLOR | Your social security number

If a joint return, spouse's first name and initial: DiANNE P. | Last name: TAYLOR | Spouse's social security number

Use the IRS label. Otherwise, please print or type.

Home address (number and street). If you have a P.O. box, see page 11.: 1970 JELLOWJACKET DR. | Apt. no.

For help finding line instructions, see pages 2 and 3 in the booklet.

City, town or post office, state, and ZIP code. If you have a foreign address, see page 11.: ROSS GA 12345 | Yes No | Note: Checking "Yes" will not change your tax or reduce your refund.

Presidential Election Campaign (See page 11.) Do you want $3 to go to this fund? . . . . If a joint return, does your spouse want $3 to go to this fund? . . . .

Filing Status
Check only one box.

1 Single
2 [X] Married filing joint return (even if only one had income)
3 Married filing separate return. Enter spouse's social security no. above and full name here. ▶
4 Head of household (with qualifying person). (See instructions.) If the qualifying person is a child but not your dependent, enter this child's name here. ▶
5 Qualifying widow(er) with dependent child (year spouse died ▶ 19). (See instructions.)

Exemptions

6a [✓] Yourself. If your parent (or someone else) can claim you as a dependent on his or her tax return, **do not** check box 6a . . . .

No. of boxes checked on lines 6a and 6b: 2

b [✓] Spouse

c Dependents:

(1) First name Last name	(2) Dependent's social security number. If born in Dec. 1996, see inst.	(3) Dependent's relationship to you	(4) No. of months lived in your home in 1996
KATHLEEN TAYLOR	— : — : —	daughter	12
LINDSEY TAYLOR	— : — : —	daughter	12

If more than six dependents, see the instructions for line 6c.

No. of your children on line 6c who:
• lived with you: 2
• did not live with you due to divorce or separation (see instructions)
Dependents on 6c not entered above
Add numbers entered on lines above ▶ 4

d Total number of exemptions claimed . . . .

Income

Attach Copy B of your Forms W-2, W-2G, and 1099-R here.

If you did not get a W-2, see the instructions for line 7.

Enclose, but do not attach, any payment. Also, please enclose Form 1040-V (see the instructions for line 62).

7	Wages, salaries, tips, etc. Attach Form(s) W-2	7	37,700 00
8a	**Taxable** interest. Attach Schedule B if over $400	8a	760 00
b	**Tax-exempt** interest. DO NOT include on line 8a	8b	
9	Dividend income. Attach Schedule B if over $400 . . .	9	580 00
10	Taxable refunds, credits, or offsets of state and local income taxes (see instructions) .	10	
11	Alimony received	11	
12	Business income or (loss). Attach Schedule C or C-EZ . . .	12	7,450 00
13	Capital gain or (loss). If required, attach Schedule D . . .	13	755 00
14	Other gains or (losses). Attach Form 4797	14	
15a	Total IRA distributions . . [15a] b Taxable amount (see inst.)	15b	
16a	Total pensions and annuities [16a] b Taxable amount (see inst.)	16b	
17	Rental real estate, royalties, partnerships, S corporations, trusts, etc. Attach Schedule E	17	
18	Farm income or (loss). Attach Schedule F	18	
19	Unemployment compensation	19	
20a	Social security benefits . [20a] b Taxable amount (see inst.)	20b	
21	Other income. List type and amount—see instructions .... Prize - Price is Right - 1996 Chevrolet Cavalier	21	12,500 00
22	Add the amounts in the far right column for lines 7 through 21. This is your **total income** ▶	22	59,745 00

Adjusted Gross Income

If line 31 is under $28,495 (under $9,500 if a child did not live with you), see the instructions for line 54.

23a	Your IRA deduction (see instructions) . . .	23a	
b	Spouse's IRA deduction (see instructions)	23b	
24	Moving expenses. Attach Form 3903 or 3903-F . . .	24	
25	One-half of self-employment tax. Attach Schedule SE . .	25	570 00
26	Self-employed health insurance deduction (see inst.) .	26	
27	Keogh & self-employed SEP plans. If SEP, check ▶ ☐	27	1,000 00
28	Penalty on early withdrawal of savings	28	
29	Alimony paid. Recipient's SSN ▶ :	29	
30	Add lines 23a through 29	30	1,570 00
31	Subtract line 30 from line 22. This is your **adjusted gross income** . . . . . . ▶	31	58,175 00

For Privacy Act and Paperwork Reduction Act Notice, see page 7. | Cat. No. 11320B | Form **1040** (1996)

63

(continued)

The Taylors: Determining Gross or Total Income (line 22)

Gross or total income is simply the sum of all your taxable income from all sources. For the Taylors it includes Chuck and Dianne's wages and salaries of $31,450 + $6,250 = $37,700 (line 7). It also includes taxable interest income of $760 (line 8a), $580 in dividends (line 9), and $755 in capital gains (line 13). In addition Chuck's consulting income of $7,450 appears on line 12 as business income. Line 21, other income, includes

FIGURE 4.5 *(continued)*

Before sitting down to do your taxes, gather up everything you will need including any tax-related business expenses from the previous year.

If you pay for child or dependent care while you are working, you may be entitled to a tax credit.

Form 1040 (1996) — Page 2

Tax Computation	32	Amount from line 31 (adjusted gross income)	**32** 58,175 00
	33a	Check if: ☐ You were 65 or older, ☐ Blind; ☐ Spouse was 65 or older, ☐ Blind. Add the number of boxes checked above and enter the total here ▶ 33a	
	b	If you are married filing separately and your spouse itemizes deductions or you were a dual-status alien, see instructions and check here ▶ 33b ☐	
	34	Enter the larger of your: Itemized deductions from Schedule A, line 28, OR Standard deduction shown below for your filing status. But see the instructions if you checked any box on line 33a or b or someone can claim you as a dependent. • Single—$4,000 • Married filing jointly or Qualifying widow(er)—$6,700 • Head of household—$5,900 • Married filing separately—$3,350	**34** 9,274 00
	35	Subtract line 34 from line 32	**35** 48,901 00
(If you want the IRS to figure your tax, see the instructions for line 37.)	36	If line 32 is $88,475 or less, multiply $2,550 by the total number of exemptions claimed on line 6d. If line 32 is over $88,475, see the worksheet in the inst. for the amount to enter	**36** 10,200 00
	37	**Taxable income.** Subtract line 36 from line 35. If line 36 is more than line 35, enter -0-	**37** 38,701 00
	38	**Tax.** See instructions. Check if total includes any tax from **a** ☐ Form(s) 8814 **b** ☐ Form 4972 ▶	**38** 5,809 00
Credits	39	Credit for child and dependent care expenses. Attach Form 2441	**39**
	40	Credit for the elderly or the disabled. Attach Schedule R	**40**
	41	Foreign tax credit. Attach Form 1116	**41**
	42	Other. Check if from **a** ☐ Form 3800 **b** ☐ Form 8396 **c** ☐ Form 8801 **d** ☐ Form (specify)	**42**
	43	Add lines 39 through 42	**43** 0 00
	44	Subtract line 43 from line 38. If line 43 is more than line 38, enter -0- ▶	**44** 5,809 00
Other Taxes	45	Self-employment tax. Attach Schedule SE	**45** 1,140 00
	46	Alternative minimum tax. Attach Form 6251	**46**
	47	Social security and Medicare tax on tip income not reported to employer. Attach Form 4137	**47**
	48	Tax on qualified retirement plans, including IRAs. If required, attach Form 5329	**48**
	49	Advance earned income credit payments from Form(s) W-2	**49**
	50	Household employment taxes. Attach Schedule H	**50**
	51	Add lines 44 through 50. This is your **total tax** ▶	**51** 6,949 00
Payments (Attach Forms W-2, W-2G, and 1099-R on the front.)	52	Federal income tax withheld from Forms W-2 and 1099	**52** 5,595 00
	53	1996 estimated tax payments and amount applied from 1995 return	**53** 1,200 00
	54	Earned income credit. Attach Schedule EIC if you have a qualifying child. Nontaxable earned income: amount ▶ and type ▶	**54**
	55	Amount paid with Form 4868 (request for extension)	**55**
	56	Excess social security and RRTA tax withheld (see inst.)	**56**
	57	Other payments. Check if from **a** ☐ Form 2439 **b** ☐ Form 4136	**57**
	58	Add lines 52 through 57. These are your **total payments** ▶	**58** 6,795 00
Refund (Have it sent directly to your bank account! See inst. and fill in 60b, c, and d.)	59	If line 58 is more than line 51, subtract line 51 from line 58. This is the amount you **OVERPAID**	**59**
	60a	Amount of line 59 you want **REFUNDED TO YOU** ▶	**60a**
	b	Routing number	
	c	Type: ☐ Checking ☐ Savings	
	d	Account number	
	61	Amount of line 59 you want **APPLIED TO YOUR 1997 ESTIMATED TAX** ▶ 61	
Amount You Owe	62	If line 51 is more than line 58, subtract line 58 from line 51. This is the **AMOUNT YOU OWE.** For details on how to pay and use Form 1040-V, see instructions ▶	**62** 154 00
	63	Estimated tax penalty. Also include on line 62 63	

Sign Here
Keep a copy of this return for your records.

Under penalties of perjury, I declare that I have examined this return and accompanying schedules and statements, and to the best of my knowledge and belief, they are true, correct, and complete. Declaration of preparer (other than taxpayer) is based on all information of which preparer has any knowledge.

Your signature	*Chuck B. Taylor*	Date 3/12/97	Your occupation Computer Analyst
Spouse's signature. If a joint return, BOTH must sign.	*Dianne P. Taylor*	Date 3/12/97	Spouse's occupation Part time Sales Person

Paid Preparer's Use Only

Preparer's signature		Date	Check if self-employed ☐	Preparer's social security no.
Firm's name (or yours if self-employed) and address			EIN	
			ZIP code	

✱ Printed on recycled paper
64

$12,500, the fair market value of the car Dianne won on *The Price Is Right*. Finally, all this taxable income is summed to make up total income (line 22).

Chuck and Dianne's salary and wages (line 7)	$37,700
Taxable interest income (line 8a)	760
Dividend income (line 9)	580
Business income (line 12)	7,450
Capital gains (line 13)	755
Other income (line 21)	12,500
Total income (line 22)	$59,745

You'll notice that the $10,000 gift that the Taylors received from Chuck's parents does not appear as income. This is because gifts are not considered taxable income. Other common sources of income that would not be taxed include interest on state and local debt.

Subtracting Out Adjustments to Gross or Total Income and Calculating Adjusted Gross Income (AGI) (line 31)

For the Taylors, the only adjustments to total income are the deduction of Chuck's contribution of $1,000 to his Keogh plan (line 27) and the deduction of half of the self-employment tax associated with Chuck's consulting. Recall that in addition to income tax, self-employment income is subject to Social Security tax at a rate of 15.3 percent until earned income from all sources reaches $62,700. Thus, Chuck's self-employment tax on his business income of $7,450 is $7,450 × 0.153 = $1,140 (line 45). Half of this amount ($570) is then tax-deductible as an adjustment to income on line 25. Thus, total adjustments are $1,000 + $570 = $1,570 (line 30). Subtracting these adjustments from total income gives the Taylors an adjusted gross income, or AGI, of $58,175 (line 31).

Subtracting Out Deductions (line 34)

The Taylors have their choice of either taking the standard deduction, which for 1996 was $6,700, or itemizing their deductions. The Taylors' itemized deductions amounted to $9,274, primarily as a result of the interest they paid on their home mortgage. Figure 4.6 shows the Taylor's deductions. In addition to home mortgage interest payments of $7,079, they paid $1,543 in state and local income taxes and real estate taxes, and made $652 in tax-deductible charitable contributions for a total of $9,274 in deductions. The Taylors were unable to deduct any medical or miscellaneous expenses because neither of these exceeded the AGI limitations set by the IRS. Because the level of the Taylors' itemized deductions exceeded the standard deduction, they chose to itemize. Their itemized deduction of $9,274 is entered in line 34 on Form 1040. Subtracting this amount from their AGI reduces their taxable income to $48,901 (line 35).

Claiming Their Exemptions (line 36)

The Taylors qualify for four exemptions, with the 1996 exemption amount being $2,550. Thus, the level of total exemptions entered on line 36 is 4 × $2,550 = $10,200. Subtracting this amount further reduces their taxable income to $48,901—$10,200 = $38,701 (line 37).

Calculating Their Total Tax (line 51)

For the Taylors, their base income tax can be calculated directly from the tax tables provided in the federal income tax instructions booklet. Their tax comes out to $5,809, which is shown in Figure 4.4 and is entered on line 38. The Taylors don't qualify for any tax credits, so the base income tax of $5,809 is carried down to line 44. Remember, the child tax credits don't begin until the 1998 tax year. The only additional taxes that the

FIGURE 4.6

Only those medical expenses that exceed 7.5% of your adjusted gross income are tax-deductible.

The state, local, personal property, real estate, and foreign income taxes you paid are tax-deductible.

Charitable contributions are deductible. However, if you make noncash contributions of clothing, goods, or property, they must be listed on Form 8283 if they exceed $500.

Only if total job-related and other expenses exceed 2% of your adjusted gross income are they tax-deductible.

SCHEDULES A&B (Form 1040)		Schedule A—Itemized Deductions (Schedule B is on back)			OMB No. 1545-0074
Department of the Treasury Internal Revenue Service (M)		▶ Attach to Form 1040. ▶ See Instructions for Schedules A and B (Form 1040).			1996 Attachment Sequence No. 07

Name(s) shown on Form 1040: Chuck and Dianne Taylor — Your social security number

Medical and Dental Expenses
Caution: Do not include expenses reimbursed or paid by others.
1 Medical and dental expenses (see page A-1) — 1 | 349 00
2 Enter amount from Form 1040, line 32. | 2 | 58,175 00
3 Multiply line 2 above by 7.5% (.075) — 3 | 4,363 00
4 Subtract line 3 from line 1. If line 3 is more than line 1, enter -0- — 4 | 0 00

Taxes You Paid (See page A-1.)
5 State and local income taxes — 5 | 1,217 00
6 Real estate taxes (see page A-2) — 6 | 326 00
7 Personal property taxes — 7
8 Other taxes. List type and amount ▶ — 8
9 Add lines 5 through 8 — 9 | 1,543 00

Interest You Paid (See page A-2.)
Note: Personal interest is not deductible.
10 Home mortgage interest and points reported to you on Form 1098 — 10 | 7,079 00
11 Home mortgage interest not reported to you on Form 1098. If paid to the person from whom you bought the home, see page A-2 and show that person's name, identifying no., and address ▶ — 11
12 Points not reported to you on Form 1098. See page A-3 for special rules. — 12
13 Investment interest. If required, attach Form 4952. (See page A-3.) — 13
14 Add lines 10 through 13 — 14 | 7,079 00

Gifts to Charity
If you made a gift and got a benefit for it, see page A-3.
15 Gifts by cash or check. If you made any gift of $250 or more, see page A-3 — 15 | 652 00
16 Other than by cash or check. If any gift of $250 or more, see page A-3. If over $500, you MUST attach Form 8283 — 16
17 Carryover from prior year — 17
18 Add lines 15 through 17 — 18 | 652 00

Casualty and Theft Losses
19 Casualty or theft loss(es). Attach Form 4684. (See page A-4.) — 19

Job Expenses and Most Other Miscellaneous Deductions (See page A-4 for expenses to deduct here.)
20 Unreimbursed employee expenses—job travel, union dues, job education, etc. If required, you MUST attach Form 2106 or 2106-EZ. (See page A-4.) ▶ — 20
21 Tax preparation fees — 21
22 Other expenses—investment, safe deposit box, etc. List type and amount ▶ Safe deposit box — 22 | 50 00
23 Add lines 20 through 22 — 23 | 50 00
24 Enter amount from Form 1040, line 32. | 24 | 58,175 00
25 Multiply line 24 above by 2% (.02) — 25 | 1,164 00
26 Subtract line 25 from line 23. If line 25 is more than line 23, enter -0- — 26 | 0 00

Other Miscellaneous Deductions
27 Other—from list on page A-4. List type and amount ▶ — 27 | 0 00

Total Itemized Deductions
28 Is Form 1040, line 32, over $117,950 (over $58,975 if married filing separately)?
NO. Your deduction is not limited. Add the amounts in the far right column for lines 4 through 27. Also, enter on Form 1040, line 34, the **larger** of this amount or your standard deduction. ▶
YES. Your deduction may be limited. See page A-5 for the amount to enter.
— 28 | 9,274 00

For Paperwork Reduction Act Notice, see Form 1040 instructions.   Cat. No. 11330X   Schedule A (Form 1040) 1996

149

Taylors owe is a self-employment tax on Chuck's consulting business. Once again, self-employment income is subject to Social Security tax at a rate of 15.3 percent until earned income from all sources reaches $62,700. Thus, Chuck's self-employment tax on his business income of $7,450 is $7,450 × 0.153 = $1,140 (line 45). This amount is added to the Taylors' base income tax of $5,809, resulting in total taxes due of $6,949 (line 51).

During 1996 the Taylors had $5,595 in federal income tax withheld and made estimated tax payments of $1,200 for total tax payments of $6,795 in line 58. Because they owed ($6,949) more than they paid ($6,795), they must pay the difference of $154 (line 62a). A check for this amount is included with their income tax return when it is filed.

> ### *The Facts of Life*
> The IRS has estimated that individuals are skipping out on $95 billion in income taxes. This estimate, which came out in a 1996 study based upon 1992 tax returns, also stated that collection efforts eventually bring in $15 billion of taxes due. The IRS attributes $73 billion of the $95 billion collection shortfall to individuals who file returns but don't report all income or take too many deductions or credits. The biggest offenders are small business owners, farmers, and workers paid in cash.

LEARNING OBJECTIVE #7

Explain the procedure for filing late and amended returns.

FILING LATE AND AMENDED RETURNS

Although most returns are filed by April 15, for whatever reason some taxpayers simply can't make the tax deadline. In addition, if you discover an error in a prior year's returns, you can file an amended return.

Filing Late

If you're unable to file your return by April 15, you can request a filing extension from the IRS. All you need to do is file Form 4868, Application for Automatic Extension of Time to File U.S. Individual Income Tax Return, and the extension is automatic—no questions asked. Although this is a relatively simple form, it does ask for an estimate of what you owe in taxes. This extension gives you an additional 4 months to file your return. As you might expect, a filing extension is a fairly popular request, with over 5 million taxpayers asking for one each year. However, the IRS isn't about to let you off the hook that easily. In addition to filling out the extension request form, you're asked to enclose a check for any estimated taxes that you owe. If you don't enclose a check for your estimated taxes, you'll be charged interest on them. Moreover, if the amount of taxes due is more than 10 percent of your tax bill, you'll also be charged a late penalty of ½ percent per month on your late taxes.

Amending Returns

It's not unusual for someone to make a mistake on a tax return or later to realize that a deduction was omitted that would have saved a good deal in taxes. To amend your return use Form 1040X, Amended U.S. Individual Income Tax Return. In fact, you can even amend an amended tax return. Occasionally, an amended return can be prompted by a retroactive change that the IRS may make. For example, in 1994 the IRS changed the deductibility of a fee associated with taking out a home mortgage and made this change retroactive to 3 years.

There are some limitations on the use of an amended return. For example, there is a limit on how far back you can go in amending a return. Specifically, you can't file an amended return more than 3 years after the original tax due date that you filed. Finally, if you file an amended return, make sure you also amend your state and local income tax returns. Amending a state return is also easy.

"DEAR I.R.S.: The Dog Ate My Form 1099. Honest."

Bob Devlin has fielded 400,000 tax-payer calls in his 19 years as an Internal Revenue Service worker in Dallas. But the story of the 30-ish husband who called to ask if he could amend his tax return for the third time in the same year is still one of his favorites.

The man had filed a joint return with his wife. Then the couple split. So he used form 1040X to amend his return to "married, filing separately" to get all the refund, rather than sharing it with his stay-at-home spouse. "Then, when they reconciled, he filed an amended joint return," Mr. Devlin recalled.

Finally, the frantic husband called Mr. Devlin. He'd broken up with his wife yet again on April 15 and couldn't get his third amendment—another "married, filing separately"—in the mail by that night's deadline.

The man was out of luck. "I had to quote him the 1040X instructions that related," Mr. Devlin said, referring to deadlines for filing the I.R.S. form used to amend returns. "He was disappointed. The refund check on a joint return is made out to both parties. So they had to decide between themselves how to split the proceeds."

Domestic turmoil is not the usual reason that taxpayers amend returns. The I.R.S. did not tally the justifications given for the more than 2.2 million amended individual returns it received last year, but based on Mr. Devlin's Ⓐ experience, the most common reason is "overlooking income."

That is not as suspicious as it sounds.

Most of the taxpayers who report revised income are elderly, Mr. Devlin said. And it is easy for taxpayers living off interest and dividend income to leave something out, said Robert Dawson, a certified public accountant in Dallas. At tax time, such people receive a flurry of 1099 forms from banks and investment houses, which are required to mail the forms by Jan. 31, telling both taxpayers and the I.R.S. how much each investor earned.

One of the most common deductions that taxpayers miss is for dependents, Mr. Devlin said. Ⓑ Not that parents forget how many children they have: "They might not have the child's Social Security number available at the time they file," he said. For 1996, the I.R.S. demands those numbers for any child born before Dec. 1. But taxpayers who are anxious for refunds, but don't yet have a child's Social Security number, can file returns now and amend them later. Also, taxpayers sometimes amend returns after learning they can claim an elderly relative they have supported.

Source: Carol Marie Cropper, "Dear I.R.S.: The Dog Ate My Form 1099. Honest." *The New York Times*, April 6, 1997, page F5. Copyright © 1997 by The New York Times Co. Reprinted by Permission.

Analysis and Implications …

A. If you've made a mistake, be sure to file an amended return. Obviously, with 2.2 million returns amended last year, it is not that uncommon—it's also the right thing to do and can save you some real headaches in the long run.

B. Some taxpayers also claim inappropriate deductions, and therefore need to file an amended return and pay more tax. Many times it is simply the result of bad advice. For example, during the O.J. Simpson trial, people at the I.R.S. were aghast at an article in a women's magazine that advised Marcia Clark, the prosecutor, that she could deduct the cost of her clothing because she needed to look good on television. Not so. Such clothing is considered "everyday wear" and is not deductible. It doesn't matter that you wear suits only to work.

BEING AUDITED

Each year the IRS audits the returns of more than 1 million taxpayers, which accounts for about 1 percent of all tax returns filed. What might bring on an **audit**? Unfortunately, you may just have bad luck—the IRS randomly selects a large number of returns each year. You may also be audited because you were audited in the past, particularly if the IRS found some error in your return. In this case, the IRS is merely checking to make sure that the error doesn't occur again. Another reason you may have been selected is that you earn a lot of money. You're over five times more likely to be audited if your income is over $100,000 than if your income is between $25,000 and $50,000. In the IRS's point of view, the more income you have, the more likely you are to fake a questionable deduction. In fact, if your itemized deductions are more than 44 percent of your income, your odds of being audited rise even further. In addition, your odds of being audited go up significantly if your return contains a Schedule C for self-employment income. Moreover, if your expenses on Schedule C amount to more than one-third of your Schedule C income, the odds of an audit rise even higher. In effect, there may be some randomness as to who is audited, but there are also signals that the IRS looks for, and those signals are based upon past IRS experience with respect to characteristics of taxpayers whose audits have turned up significant errors.

No one wants to be audited, but unless you've been cheating on your taxes, it's nothing to worry about. Audits come in different forms. Some only ask for additional information and can be handled through the mail, and others require you to meet face-to-face with an IRS representative. In either case, you're given several weeks to prepare your response.

The first step in preparing for an audit is to reexamine the areas in which the IRS has questions. You should gather all supporting data—canceled checks, receipts, records—you have, then try to anticipate any questions the IRS might have and formulate responses to them. If you need help, you can hire a tax accountant or attorney. In fact, this agent can go to the audit in your place, provided you sign a power of attorney form.

If you're not satisfied with the outcome of the audit, you have the right to appeal. The first step in an appeal is with the auditor. Present your argument and see if you can win the appeal with any additional information. If so, provide it. If you are still not satisfied with the results, you turn to your auditor's manager. If you are still not satisfied with the results, you can file a formal appeal and even go to tax court if necessary. Unfortunately, an appeal does not guarantee satisfaction, but you do have a right to appeal if you wish. The important point here is that you have the right to receive credit for any and all legal deductions, and you should not let fear of being audited interfere with your paying the minimum amount of income taxes, provided you do it legally. The key to winning an audit is good records.

HELP IN PREPARING YOUR TAXES

Sometimes preparing your taxes is more than you can handle by yourself. The first place to look for help is the IRS. While that may seem akin to consorting with the enemy, the IRS is a good place to start. Information from the IRS is knowledgeable and cheap—in fact, it's free. In addition to the instructions provided with your income tax form, the IRS also has a number of booklets, many of which are free, that can be extremely helpful. One of the more informative is IRS Publication 17, *Your Federal Income Tax*, which gives detailed step-by-step instructions to aid you in filing your taxes. The IRS also provides a phone service, a toll-free "hot line" for tax questions. Although the IRS won't accept any liability for incorrect advice that they give, they're generally correct with their advice. Moreover, using the IRS hot line as a reference can save you both time and money in getting that answer. The major problem with using the IRS hot

line is that it's often busy. The closer you get to April 15, the more difficult it is to connect with the IRS hot line. The IRS also provides a walk-in service in most areas, where you can meet directly with an IRS employee. Once again, the closer it is to April 15, the harder it is to make an appointment.

In addition to publications from the IRS, there are a number of excellent self-help tax publications, including J. K. Lasser's and Ernst & Young's income tax guides. Although these are somewhat similar to the tax guide published by the IRS, they differ in that they tend to point out areas in which legitimate deductions, which might otherwise be overlooked, can be found. There are also a number of tax planning guides including *J. K. Lasser's Year-Round Tax Strategies* and Jeff Schnepper's *How to Pay Zero Taxes* that go beyond merely filing taxes and instead provide tax planning strategies.

For those with access to a computer and some degree of computer literacy, there are a number of outstanding computer programs available for tax preparation, including Intuit's TurboTax and MacInTax, Parsons Technology's Personal Tax Edge, TaxCut by MECA, and Kiplinger's TaxCut. Intuit also has deluxe CD-ROM versions of Turbo-Tax and MacInTax, as does MECA for TaxCut and Kiplinger's Tax Cut. The Intuit CD-ROM versions, for example, contain an extensive tax library and tax center to aid in accessing tax reference material. They also contain 30 IRS publications and the *Money Income Tax Handbook,* along with Jeff Schnepper's *How to Pay Zero Taxes.* In addition, they contain a video library with nearly 100 tax help videos. Aside from the additional information contained in the CD-ROM versions, these programs all work essentially the same way, navigating you through a number of questions that help you construct your tax return. If you have access to a computer and are computer literate, these programs are generally both reliable and easy to use.

Your final option in preparing your taxes is to hire a tax specialist. Although going to a tax specialist sounds safe, you should realize that tax specialists are not licensed or tested—anyone can declare himself or herself to be a tax specialist. There are some rules governing tax specialists, but there's no penalty imposed on your advisor if you pay too much in the way of taxes. As such, you should take care in choosing a tax specialist.

Tax specialists can be divided into those with a national affiliation, such as H&R Block, and independent tax specialists. One advantage of the national affiliation is that the employees generally get standardized training, keeping them current with the latest IRS changes and rulings. With independent tax specialists, there's much more variability in terms of training and in the quality of work that they do.

If you decide to use a tax specialist, you should first of all make sure you avoid the April rush. Because of the volume of tax work that's done at the last minute, last-minute returns may not get the attention that they deserve. In addition, make sure you get references and inquire about the tax specialist's background and experience. If your tax specialist does not begin with an extensive interview in which your financial affairs are fully probed, you probably won't get your money's worth.

TAX PLANNING

So far we've looked only at preparing your taxes. We now turn to the very important topic of tax planning strategies. You should keep in mind that although a tax specialist can help you identify deductions that you might otherwise miss, once you begin to prepare your taxes it's probably too late to engage in any tax planning strategy that will result in reduced taxes. Tax planning, in general, must be done well ahead of time. Few people do their tax planning alone. Instead they consult a CPA or even a tax attorney. However, before you see a tax planning specialist, you should have a good understanding of how the tax code works. This understanding will allow you to work with the tax planning specialist in mapping out a strategy that suits you best.

LEARNING OBJECTIVE #10

Use the tools of tax planning.

The basic idea behind tax planning is to minimize unnecessary tax payments. If you can keep your tax payments down to a minimum, you'll have more money to use in meeting your financial goals. Unfortunately, the IRS has closed a number of tax loopholes in recent years, but there still are many tax strategies that make sense. Tax strategies should be methods of supplementing a sound investment strategy rather than the focal point of investing. Keep in mind that Congress and the IRS are continuously tinkering with the tax laws, and what may appear to be a wonderful loophole today may disappear tomorrow. As such, your strategy should not be to blindly seek out loopholes, but to supplement a solid investment strategy with tax considerations.

There are five general tax strategies that you can use. They include

- Maximize your deductions.
- Look to capital gains income.
- Shift income to family members in lower tax brackets.
- Receive tax-exempt income.
- Defer taxes to the future.

Each of these strategies is aimed at avoiding unnecessary taxes rather than at evading taxes, that is, overstating deductions or not claiming all your income on your tax return. It's certainly illegal and unwise to evade taxes, but it's foolish to pay more than your fair share.

Maximizing Your Deductions

Tax planning strategies for maximizing your deductions center on three different tactics: (1) using tax-deferred retirement programs to reduce taxes, (2) using your home as a tax shelter, and (3) shifting and bunching your deductions. Each of these three tactics has the same goal in mind: to reduce your taxable income to its minimum level.

Stop and Think

It's hard to overstress how valuable tax-deferred retirement plans actually are. Not only do they reduce your taxable income, but the contributions grow tax-deferred, and many companies match part of your contribution, putting in 50 cents for each dollar that you contribute.

Using Tax-Deferred Retirement Programs to Reduce Taxes.   To encourage retirement savings, the government allows several different types of tax-deferred retirement programs. The advantage of using tax-deferred retirement plans is that you (1) don't pay taxes on the money that you invest and (2) don't pay interest on the earnings from your retirement account. Let's look at the difference that results from putting your savings in a tax-deferred retirement plan instead of in a normal savings account, both earning a 10-percent return. Let's also assume that you are in the 28-percent marginal tax bracket. If you took $1,000 of your taxable earnings and decided to invest without using a tax-deferred retirement plan, you would first pay $280 in taxes, leaving you with only $720 to invest. During the first year you would earn $72 in interest and pay $20.16 in taxes, leaving you with $51.84 of interest after taxes. Thus, at the end of the year you would have $771.84 saved. If you let this amount grow at 10 percent before taxes for 25 years, it would accumulate to a total of $4,095. Now let's look at what would happen if you put your money in a tax-deferred account, also earning 10 percent. First, you wouldn't pay taxes on the $1,000, because taxes aren't assessed until you withdraw the money from this account. Thus, you would earn 10-percent interest on $1,000 for a total of $100 interest. In addition, because this is a tax-deferred account, you wouldn't pay taxes on any of this interest, giving you a total of $1,100 after the year. If you left this amount in the tax-deferred account for 25 years, you would have accumulated $10,834. Of course, you eventually would have to pay taxes on this amount, but even after taking 28-percent taxes on $10,834 you still have about $7,801. Why is the difference between the investments so great? Because you've been able to earn interest on money that would have otherwise already been collected by the IRS.

Use Your Home as a Tax Shelter.   The tax benefits associated with owning a home are twofold. First, mortgage interest payments are tax-deductible and, as such, reduce your taxes. Second, when you eventually sell your house, you are exempt from paying taxes on gains of up to $500,000 for couples filing jointly and $250,000 for those filing single on the sale of a principal residence.

> ### *Stop and Think*
> Your home is one of the last great tax shelters. As Congress works to cut loopholes and deductions, the home mortgage interest deduction stands out as a political death trap for anyone who suggests that it be cut. As a result, when you buy your first home, you can be assured that your taxes will be reduced. Why do you think the government does this?

Just how valuable is the deductibility of your home mortgage interest payments? That depends on several factors. For those in the highest tax brackets, the tax deductibility of mortgage interest payments is much more valuable than it is for those in the lowest tax bracket. In addition, if you do not itemize your deductions, the tax deductibility of mortgage interest payments is of no value to you. Moreover, if you would have taken the standard deduction without them, and now itemize with them, then they reduce your taxable income only by the difference between the standard deduction and your itemized deductions. The amount that this reduction in taxable income reduces your taxes is their value. In effect, the tax deductibility of mortgage interest payments reduces the cost of your mortgage by (1 – marginal tax rate). Thus, the after-tax cost of a home mortgage can be determined as follows:

$$\frac{\text{After-Tax Cost of}}{\text{Mortgage Interest}} = \frac{\text{Before-Tax Cost of}}{\text{Mortgage Interest}} \times (1 - \text{Marginal Tax Rate})$$

In short, the value of the tax deductibility of mortgage interest payments depends upon your marginal tax bracket and whether or not you itemize your deductions.

In addition, using your home as collateral, you can take out a home equity loan and deduct your interest payments. In effect, this deduction lowers the cost of borrowing. For example, you might consider a home equity loan to finance buying a car. In mid 1997 the average cost of a car loan was about 9.0 percent, and the average cost of a home equity loan was about 9.5 percent. However, the interest on the home equity is generally tax-deductible, whereas the interest on the car loan is not. Recalculating the cost of a home equity loan for an individual in the 28-percent tax bracket on an after-tax basis, it becomes 9.5(1 – marginal tax rate) or 9.5(1 – 0.28) = 6.84 percent. Thus, in many cases the cheapest way to borrow money is with a home equity loan.

Shifting and Bunching Your Deductions.   When we discussed itemizing versus taking the standard deduction, we presented the concept of shifting and bunching your deductions. As we noted, the decision between taking the standard deduction or itemizing becomes difficult when they are close in value. The concept of shifting and bunching your deductions involves trying to avoid incurring deductible expenses in years that you itemize. Instead, if possible, you postpone them to years when you do itemize and therefore get credit for them. For example, you may wish to make 13 mortgage payments and double up your charitable contributions during years that you itemize.

Look to Capital Gains Income in Particular if You Are in the Top Tax Brackets

Recall from our earlier discussion that capital gains refer to the amount by which the selling price of a capital asset—that is, an asset being kept for investment purposes such as stocks, bonds, or real estate—exceeds its purchase price. The example we used was the purchase of 100 shares of GM stock for $50 per share and the sale 2 years later of those same shares of GM stock for $70 per share. In this case, your capital gains would be 100 shares $\times$ ($70 – $50) = $2,000. If you hold an asset for a year and a half or more, the gain is taxed at a maximum rate of 20 percent if you are in the 28-percent bracket or above or 10 percent if you are in the 15-percent bracket. Thus, if you were in the 39.6-percent marginal tax bracket, you'd pay at half your ordinary tax rate. The other benefit from capital gains is the fact that you don't have to claim it—and therefore pay taxes on it—until you sell the asset. In effect, you can postpone paying taxes by not selling the asset. Without question, if you have to pay taxes, it's better to pay 10 years from now than today.

Shift Income to Family Members in Lower Tax Brackets

Income shifting involves transferring income from family members in high tax brackets to those in lower tax brackets. Although the concept is relatively simple, it can be a relatively complex process involving lawyers and the establishment of **trusts**. A less complicated facet of income shifting involves a relatively simple idea—gifts. You're allowed to give $10,000 per year tax-free to as many different people as you like. One of the nice things about annual gifts of under $10,000 is that the person receiving the gift doesn't pay any taxes on this gift. Thus, on annual gifts of $10,000 or less, neither the person who gives nor the person who receives pays any taxes. Best of all, every year you get another gift exclusion that allows you to give $10,000 tax-free to as many different people as you like.

If you're planning on passing your estate on to your children when you die, you might be wise to give some of it away now. That way you can pass on both income and taxes. For example, if Heshie Rothbaum is in the 36-percent tax bracket, he might be better off giving his son Izzy, who is in the 15-percent tax bracket, a $10,000 gift rather than keep the $10K for himself. If Heshie gives it as a gift, he doesn't pay taxes on it, and because Izzy is in a lower tax bracket, taxes paid on any future earning on this $10,000 are at a lower rate. As a result, the money grows more than it would otherwise.

Trust
A fiduciary agreement in which one individual holds property for the benefit of another person.

Receive Tax-Exempt Income

Interest paid on state and local government debt is tax-exempt for federal income tax purposes. That means if you buy a bond issued by a state or city (which is called a municipal bond), you can collect the interest and not have to pay any taxes on it. For example, in 1996, the North East Independent School District in Texas issued $80 million of bonds that were set to mature in 2016. The equivalent taxable yield on a municipal bond is calculated as follows:

$$\frac{\text{equivalent taxable}}{\text{yield}} = \frac{\text{tax-free yield on the municipal}}{(1 - \text{investor's marginal tax bracket})}$$

Thus, if you're in the 31-percent marginal tax bracket, the equivalent taxable yield on a 6-percent municipal bond would be $6\% / (1 - 0.31) = 8.70$ percent. In effect, that means that on an after-tax basis, a taxable bond yielding 8.70 percent and a municipal bond yielding 6 percent are equivalent. The higher your marginal tax bracket, the more beneficial tax-free income is.

Defer Taxes to the Future

As we've already seen, tax-deferred retirement programs such as traditional IRAs, Keogh plans, and **401(k) plans** allow you to defer taxes to the future rather than pay those taxes today. In addition Roth IRAs allow taxes to be paid on the contribution and never again. The idea is to allow you to earn interest on money that would have otherwise already been collected by the IRS. This concept also applies to capital gains, because you can postpone capital gains taxes until you sell the asset. If you don't recognize all these terms, don't worry. We'll discuss them in depth later in the book. For now, the important point is that saving on a tax-deferred basis has real benefits.

401(k) Plan
A tax-deferred retirement plan.

OTHER NONINCOME-BASED TAXES THAT YOU FACE

In addition to paying federal income taxes, Social Security taxes, and state and local taxes, you also face excise taxes, sales taxes, property taxes, and gift and estate taxes.

Excise taxes are taxes imposed on specific purchases, such as alcoholic beverages, cigarettes, gasoline, telephone service, jewelry, and air travel. These taxes many times are aimed at reducing consumption of the items being taxed. For example, liquor and tobacco taxes are referred to as "sin taxes."

In addition, most local taxes take the form of property taxes on real estate and personal property, such as automobiles and boats. The level of your property taxes is based upon the assessed value of your real estate or other property.

Some states and localities also impose sales taxes on purchases. These taxes can range up to around 8 percent (in New York) and in general cover most sales with the exception of food and drugs in some states. These taxes tend to be quite regressive in nature, with lower-income individuals having a higher percentage of their income going toward sales taxes. Unfortunately, these taxes are quite difficult to avoid.

Finally, gift and estate taxes are imposed when you transfer wealth to another person, either when you die, in the case of estates taxes, or while you're alive, in the case of gift taxes (remember, gifts of $10,000 or less aren't taxed). For 1997, the tax code allows for an estate valued at up to $600,000 to be transferred tax-free to any heir. This tax-free threshold is scheduled to begin rising in 1998 and eventually reach $1 million in 2006. Unfortunately, once this tax-free threshold has been reached, taxes begin at an effective rate of 37 percent, which quickly climbs to 55 percent. The U.S. tax code allows for an unlimited marital deduction for gift and estate tax purposes. This means that when a husband or wife dies, the estate, regardless of size, can be transferred to the survivor totally tax-free.

LEARNING OBJECTIVE #11

Describe other, nonincome-based taxes that you must pay.

SUMMARY

The U.S. tax code is a patchwork system that has grown in length to over 2,000 pages today, with its complexity, at times, overshadowing its logic. The rate structure for the U.S. tax code is progressive in nature, with five different marginal tax rates: 15 percent, 28 percent, 31 percent, 36 percent, and 39.6 percent. Of special importance is the marginal tax rate, because this is the rate that you'll pay on your next dollar of income.

A capital gain refers to the amount by which the selling price of a capital asset—that is, an asset being kept for investment purposes such as stocks or bonds—exceeds its purchase price. Net long-term capital gains less any net short-term capital losses are taxed at a lower maximum rate than ordinary income (short-term gains are treated as ordinary income).

To calculate your taxes, you must first determine your total income by summing up your income from all sources. From this amount, adjustments that center on tax-deductible expenses and retirement contributions are subtracted out, with the result being adjusted gross income, or AGI. From adjusted gross income, the deductions, the greater of either the itemized deductions or the standard deduction, and the exemptions are subtracted, with the end result being taxable income. We also looked at who must file tax returns, when they must file, what forms they use, and what information is needed to prepare a tax return.

If you're unable to file your return by April 15, you can request a filing extension from the IRS. In addition, if you discover an error in a prior year's returns, you can file an amended return.

Audits can happen to anyone, but are more likely to happen to those with higher incomes or those who are self-employed. The first step in preparing for an audit is to reexamine the areas in which the IRS has questions. In addition, if you are not satisfied with the outcome of the audit, you have the right to appeal.

If you need help in filing your return, the first place to look is the IRS. There are several good tax books you can use to help prepare your taxes. For those with access to a computer and some degree of computer literacy, there are a number of outstanding computer programs available for tax preparation. The final option in preparing your taxes is to hire a tax specialist.

There are five general tax strategies that can be used to keep your tax bill down to a minimum. They include

- Maximize your deductions.
- Look to capital gains income.
- Shift income to family members in lower tax brackets.
- Receive tax-exempt income.
- Defer taxes to the future.

In addition to paying federal income taxes, Social Security taxes, and state and local taxes, you also face excise taxes, sales taxes, property taxes, and gift and estate taxes.

Review Questions

1. What are the three figures that affect the amount of income tax paid? Which of these factors is determined by the federal government? (LO 2)
2. If someone's in the 28-percent marginal tax bracket, is that person's entire income taxed at 28 percent? Why or why not? (LO 2)
3. What is meant by the term "average tax rate"? (LO 2)
4. Describe the method used for collecting income tax and explain why it's done in this manner. (LO 3)
5. What are the three main types of income that are included in gross income? (LO 3)
6. List the five most common itemized deductions and describe the limits set on each. (LO 4)

7. What is the maximum allowable taxable income for someone filing a 1040A or 1040 EZ income tax form? (LO 5)
8. What is taxable income and what's the formula for determining taxable income? (LO 6)
9. What federal income tax form is used when filing a late return, and what's the procedure that must be followed? (LO 7)
10. What are the four most common "signals" that the IRS looks for when selecting people for audits? (LO 8)
11. What are the three main types of assistance available to the general public for completing their taxes? (LO 9)
12. What are the five general tax reduction strategies? Give a brief synopsis of each type. (LO 10)
13. List and describe the nonincome-based taxes. (LO 11)
14. Why are sales taxes considered regressive rather than progressive? (LO 11)

Problems and Activities

1. The Crosbys' 1996 gross annual income is $64,000 and their taxable income is $50,000. Determine their marginal and average tax rates assuming their filing status is married filing jointly. (LO 2)

WWW.
Take It to the Net

We invite you to visit the Keown Personal Finance page on the Prentice Hall Web site at:

http://www.prenhall.com/ persfin

for this chapter's World Wide Web exercise.

You might also want to visit the following Web sites:

IRS Digital Daily Report (the IRS, with a bit of humor): http://irs.ustreas.gov/prod/

An excellent tax and accounting site directory: http:// www.taxsites.com/

Another good commercial site (Blair Groates, CMA): http:// www.lis.ab.ca/goates/index.html

More income tax information: http://www.safari.net/taxes.html

J.K. Lasser's *Your Income Tax Online* (good information, but a subscription is needed for full access): http://www.mcp.com/ bookstore/jklasser/

2. A couple and four children have an annual adjusted gross income of $200,000. Calculate the total dollar amount of personal exemptions that can be claimed for the 1996 tax year. (LO 2)

3. Jack and Jill have $48,000 in gross income and enough allowable deductions to itemize. Determine the best income tax form for them to file, if filing jointly. Explain why they wouldn't use any of the other forms. (LO 5)

4. Calculate the total 1996 tax liability for a single parent of one child with gross income of $46,250, taking the standard deduction. (LO 2, 4, 6)

5. Using the married filing jointly status, calculate the 1996 tax liability for Betty and Billy Arnold. First use the standard deduction, then use the following itemized deductions.

Income

Earned income	$41,000
Interest income	2,100

Expenses

Home mortgage interest	$ 6,000
Unreimbursed medical bills	4,200
Job-related expenditures	800

Now write a paragraph explaining to the Arnolds which method they should use and why. (LO 6)

6. Using Figure 4.1, determine if a couple, ages 63 and 65, must file a return. Calculate their gross taxable income from the following information. (LO 4, 6)

Municipal bond interest	$ 1,750
Social Security benefit	9,200
Cash gift from children	8,000
Quilt sales income	12,500

If they don't have to file a return, should they anyway? Why or why not?

7. Calculate the 1996 total tax for Gordon Geist, a single taxpayer without dependents. He has active income of $36,000, investment income of $6,000 from the sale of stocks, and $4,000 of passive income. He doesn't itemize deductions. (LO 6)

8. Otto Marx is a self-employed mason with a 1996 gross income of $90,000. He reported a taxable annual income of $70,000 after adjustments, deductions, and his single exemption. Calculate his total tax liability, including federal, state income taxes (at 3.5 percent), and FICA. (LO 6, 11)

9. Mrs. Hubbard, a mother of two, has been selected for an audit. She has come to you to help her prepare for the process. Advise her on what to do to prepare for the audit and what to do if the audit doesn't turn out favorably (LO 8)

10. Harry and Harriet Porter are in their golden years. Discuss the best tax reduction method for them to use in reducing their estate taxes. (LO 10)

Suggested Projects

1. Research the marginal tax brackets from 1960 to present. Notice when and how the brackets changed. Make economic and political correlations and draw conclusions from your findings as to why the tax structure has changed. (LO 1, 2)

2. Write a one-page paper discussing why taxes are withheld as you're paid rather than collected on an annual basis. Also explain how the amount of taxes withheld is determined. (LO 3)

3. Calculate your income tax liability using two approaches. First, assume that your parents claim you as a dependent. What's your tax liability? Second, assume that

you're independent and claim yourself as a dependent. What's your tax liability? Explain the difference. (LO 2, 4)

4. Estimate your nonincome-based tax expenditures for the last 6 months. Consider sales tax, excise taxes, and personal property taxes.

   Hints: To estimate your *personal property tax,* consult your tax statements or talk with your parents about the taxes on your vehicle (if applicable).

   To estimate your *sales tax,* call the applicable state Department of Commerce to determine the tax rates and on which items the taxes apply, if necessary.

   To estimate your *excise taxes,* call the state Department of Commerce to establish the tax rates on items such as tobacco, gasoline, and alcohol. Excise taxes are also collected on phone usage. To get this figure consult your phone bill.

5. Prepare yourself for an audit by collecting all relevant tax records from the last year. Include all pay stubs that verify deductions, credit card bills and their matching receipts that verify tax-deductible expenditures, and all bank account statements. Now, grade yourself on how well you're prepared for an audit. (LO 8)

6. Call a certified public accountant (CPA) and explain that you're a student currently studying taxes. Ask the CPA to explain three of the most commonly recommended tax saving strategies and three of the most commonly audited tax return sections. Prepare a report on your findings. (LO 8, 9, 11)

7. Talk to your parents about their taxes. Do they follow any of the five tax reduction strategies presented in this chapter? Talk to them about the benefit of following one or more of these strategies. Summarize your discussion in a report. (LO 10)

Discussion Case 1

It's March 12th, and Deshawn Knapp, a 25-year-old single male without any dependents, is filing his own taxes for the first time for the 1996 tax year. He's collected all of the appropriate documents and is ready to begin filling out his federal tax form. He has the following documents, which detail all sources of his 1996 income:

Form	Income	Federal Tax Withheld
W-2, Wage and Tax Statement 1	$1,823	$199
W-2, Wage and Tax Statement 2	1,609	197
1099-INT, Interest Income Statement	120	0
1099-DIV, Ordinary Distribution	157	0
1099-DIV, Capital Gains	141	0

Knapp also knows he must use the standard deduction. He needs your help preparing his tax return.

QUESTIONS

1. What is his adjusted gross income? (LO 4)

2. Which is the most appropriate tax form for him to use? (LO 5)

3. What is his total tax liability? *Hint:* Remember the rules and rates for capital gains taxes. (LO 6)

4. What is the amount of his refund? (LO 6)

   One month later Knapp remembers that he cashed some Series EE savings bonds and needs to report the interest earned. He then calls the bank to have a supplementary 1099-INT sent. It shows interest income of $3,057. He now needs to know how to correct his mistake on the previously filed taxes.

5. Which form(s) does he need to file in order to correct his mistake? (LO 7)

6. Does this new information change the adjusted gross income, tax liability, and refund, if any? If so, recalculate the information. (LO 6)

7. Calculate Knapp's marginal and average tax rates using the revised information. (LO 6)

The year is 1996, and Philip and Claire Drummond are a middle-aged couple with two children, Rusty, age 11, and Sam, age 9. They also bought a new home in the area to give the children a larger yard. The Drummonds also have an extensive retirement portfolio invested primarily in growth-oriented mutual funds. Their annual investment income is only $500, none of which is attributable to capital gains. Philip works in the banking industry and receives an annual income of $32,500. Claire, who owns the only travel agency in town, makes about $40,000 a year.

The Drummonds give extensively to charities and make annual contributions to their IRAs. They also have tax deductions from their mortgage interest expense, business expenses, tax expenses, and medical expenses, as follows:

Health insurance (provided by Claire)	$2,200
Rusty's braces	1,500
Mortgage interest expense	7,200
Real estate taxes	900
Investment and tax planning expenses	1,450
Other medical expenses	3,600

IRA contributions	2,000 each parent
Charitable contributions	3,500
Moving expenses	3,000
Philip's business expenses	2,300
Qualified adoption expenses	6,700
State taxes withheld	4,000

Remember also that Claire has some special tax deductions because she's self-employed. Be sure to include them when calculating their taxable income and tax liability.

QUESTIONS

1. Calculate Claire's Social Security and Medicare taxes. Calculate how much of the taxes are deductible. (LO 2, 4)
2. Are the moving expenses deductible? Why or why not? (LO 4)
3. Will the Drummonds take the standard deduction, or will they itemize? What is the amount of their deduction? (LO 4)
4. Calculate their taxable income. (LO 2, 4)
5. Calculate their tax liability. (LO 2, 4)

Continuing Case: Don and Maria Chang

The objective of the continuing case study is to help you synthesize and integrate the many and varied financial planning concepts you have been learning. The case will help you apply your knowledge of constructing financial statements, assessing financial data and resources, calculating taxes, measuring risk exposures, creating specific financial plans for accumulating assets, and analyzing strengths and weaknesses in financial situations.

At the end of each part of this book, you will be asked to help Don and Maria Chang answer personal finance questions. By the end of the book you'll know more about Don and Maria than you ever thought you'd need to know.

BACKGROUND

Don and Maria Chang recently read an article on personal financial planning in *Good Housekeeping*. The article discussed common financial dilemmas that families face throughout their life cycle. After reading the article, Don and Maria realized that they needed to learn more about personal financial issues. They are considering enrolling in a personal finance course, but they think they need help now. Based on record-keeping suggestions in the *Good Housekeeping* article, Don and Maria have put together the following information for your use in helping them answer their personal finance questions.

(continued)

Family Background

Don and Maria have been married for 4 years. Don is 33 years old; Maria is 29. They have a son, Andy, who just turned 2 years old, and a cat named Freddie.

Employment

Don works as a bank teller and makes $26,000 a year. Maria works as an accountant and earns $33,000 a year.

Housing

The Changs currently rent a two-bedroom apartment for $700 per month, but they hope to eventually purchase a house. Maria indicated that she would like to purchase a home within the next 2 to 3 years. The Changs are well on their way to achieving their goal. When they were married they opted for a small wedding and applied all gifts and contributions to the Jimminy Jump-up Mutual Fund for a house. When they last checked, the account had a balance of $7,000.

Financial Concerns

1. *Taxes:* Don and Maria have been surprised at the amount of federal, state, Social Security, and Medicare taxes withheld from their pay. They aren't sure if the tax calculations are correct.

2. *Insurance:* They are also unsure about the amount of automobile, home, health, and life insurance they should have. Up until this point, they have always opted for the lowest premiums without much regard to coverage. They were a little amazed to learn recently that the cash value of Maria's life insurance policy is only $1,100 although they have paid annual premiums of $720 for several years.

3. *Credit:* Don and Maria are also curious about the use of credit. It seems they receive two to three offers per week for a new credit card that promises a low interest rate and lots of bonuses. They aren't sure if they should be taking these offers or keeping their current credit cards. They are often surprised by the amount charged on their monthly credit card statements, and although they pay $100 each month, the balance always seems to

hover around $1,300. They withdraw money from the ATM to cover daily expenses and usually carry about $100 in cash between them, but it still seems they often rely on their credit cards.

4. *Savings:* "Pay yourself first," recommended the *Good Housekeeping* article that prompted Don and Maria to undertake a review of their personal finances. They like the concept, but are unsure of how to go about implementing such a goal. They currently have a savings account that earns 3 percent in annual interest and has a balance of $2,500. Their checking account requires them to keep a minimum balance of $1,000 in order to earn interest of 1.75 percent. Their current balance is $1,800.

5. *College savings:* After talking with Don's mother about personal finances, it occurred to Don and Maria that they should start thinking about college expenses for Andy.

6. *Retirement savings:* Don and Maria both know that they participate in a "qualified retirement plan" at work, whatever that means. But they do not currently have an IRA or access to profit-sharing plans. A recent statement from Don's former employer indicated a value of $1,500 in pension funds he left with that company.

7. *Risk:* Don is quick to point out that he doesn't like financial surprises.

8. *Estate planning issues:* They do not have a will nor do they have any type of trust.

9. *Recreation and health:* Don and Maria enjoy hiking with Andy. They also enjoy playing tennis and have considered joining a tennis club that charges a $250 monthly fee. The Changs are in good health.

ADDITIONAL INFORMATION

Other Estimated Annual Expenditures

Food	$ 4,800
Clothing	2,200
Auto insurance	1,300
Transportation (use, maintenance, licensing)	1,750
Dental and health care	450

(continued)

Life insurance	720
Medical insurance	1,800
Renter's insurance	120
Utilities	1,800
Entertainment	2,500
Taxes (federal, state, Social Security, Medicare)	15,000
Property taxes (auto)	350
Charity donations	650
Day care	6,500
Savings	2,000
Miscellaneous	2,600

Other Assets

- Automobile 1
  3-year-old compact car with a fair market value (FMV) of $10,000
  Amount owed: $8,400 (30 months remaining on the loan)
  Monthly payment: $280
- Automobile 2
  5-year-old station wagon with an FMV of $4,100
  Amount owed: $0
- Household furniture and electronics worth approximately $10,000
- Antique jewelry that Maria received as an inheritance from her grandfather. The jewelry has an estimated value of $18,000; however, Maria has indicated that she would never part with the jewelry.
- Balance mutual fund currently worth $1,700. When Maria turned 21, her grandmother gave her $1,000 worth (100 shares) of the Great Guns Balanced Mutual Fund.

Current-Nonautomobile Debts

- Credit card debt (Visa, MasterCard, Discover, American Express, and several store cards) with a revolving outstanding balance of $1,300
  Minimum monthly payments: $32
  Actual monthly payment: $100
- Furniture company loan
  $3,750 balance
  $125 monthly payment (30 months remaining on the loan)

PART I: FINANCIAL PLANNING (Chapters 1, 2, 3, and 4)

Questions

1. Don and Maria are in what stage of the life cycle? What important financial planning issues characterize this stage?
2. Based on the issues identified above, help Don and Maria determine their short-term, intermediate-term, and long-term goals to guide their financial future. (*Hint:* Review Worksheet G.1, Personal Financial Goals Worksheet, for ideas.)
3. Using Worksheet G.7, A Simplified Income Statement, create an income and expense statement for the Changs.
4. Using Worksheet G.6, Balance Sheet—Calculating Your Net Worth, develop a balance sheet for the Changs.
5. Using information from the income and expense statement and the balance sheet, calculate the following ratios:
   a. Current ratio
   b. Months living expenses covered ratio
   c. Debt ratio
   d. Long-term debt coverage ratio
   e. Savings ratio
6. Use the information provided by the ratio analysis to assess the Changs' financial health. (*Hint:* Use the recommended ratio limits provided in the text as guidelines for measuring the Changs' financial flexibility and liquidity.) What recommendations would you make to improve their financial health? Do the Changs have an emergency fund? Should they? How much would you recommend that the Changs have in an emergency fund?
7. According to the *Good Housekeeping* article Don and Maria read, they can expect to pay as much as $100,000 in tuition and related college expenses when Andy enters college. The Changs think that Andy will receive academic scholarships which will reduce their total college costs to about $40,000. Assuming that the Changs started a college savings program today and managed to earn 9 percent a year, ignoring taxes, until Andy is 18, how much would they need to save at the end of each year? How much will the Changs need to save each year if Andy does not receive scholarships?

(continued)

8. How much will Maria's Great Guns Balanced Mutual Fund shares (currently valued at $1,700) be worth when Andy enters college, assuming the fund returns 9 percent after taxes on an annualized basis? How much will the fund be worth when Maria retires at age 67, assuming a 9-percent after-tax return?

9. How much will the Changs' house down payment fund be worth in 3, 5, and 7 years at the current rate of 8 percent they are receiving from the Jimminy Jump-up Mutual Fund? How much would the fund be worth in 3, 5, and 7 years if they could obtain a 12-percent rate of return?

10. Assuming an 8-percent return for the current year from the Jimminy Jump-up Mutual Fund, and a 28-percent federal marginal tax rate, how much will the Changs lose from their savings, or current income, to pay the income taxes due?

11. Calculate the amount of Social Security and Medicare taxes withheld from the Changs' pay based on their current income.

12. Using the income and expense estimates provided by Maria, calculate their taxable income using the 1996 tax information provided in the text. (*Hint:* See Figure 4.3.) Do the Changs have enough tax deductible expenses to itemize deductions?

13. Calculate the Changs' federal income tax liability using Table 4.2.

14. Calculate the child and dependent care credit. How much does this reduce the Changs' tax liability?

15. Assume the Changs' marginal state income tax rate is 5.75 percent calculated on the basis of the federal taxable income. Calculate their state tax liability.

16. Based on the total Social Security tax, Medicare tax, federal income tax, and state income tax liabilities calculated above, how close did Maria come in estimating their total tax liability for the year? How does the difference between Maria's estimated tax liability and their actual tax liability change their financial situation? What recommendations would you make?

Chapter 5

CASH OR LIQUID ASSET MANAGEMENT

What do Bob Dole and Daffy Duck have in common? Before you start commenting on the uncanny physical similarities, you should realize that Deion Sanders also has it in common with them. Sure, Daffy and Dole might have played a little football in their time, but that's not it. Give up? Well, they've all been hassled recently when trying to pay a bill with a check. At least, they have on commercials for Visa's new check card.

The commercials all happen just about the same way. Each "celebrity" is immediately recognized and fawned over by the store clerk or other store patrons, but when he goes to pay for a purchase with a check (Sanders is buying some posters of himself in a sports memorabilia store, Daffy's buying tons of merchandise at a Warner Brothers store—where his face is on about every other item, and Dole's just trying to buy a meal at a small diner in his hometown of Russell, Kansas), he's asked for a million different forms of ID, none of which he has. Dole, playing off his loss in the 1996 presidential election, claims he can't win; Daffy—as is his trademark—complains that the store clerk is ditttttth-picable, and poor Sanders is too shell-shocked to speak.

What saves the day for our beleaguered heroes? The Visa check card to the rescue! Instead of having to produce ID to pay with a check, our heroes could simply pay with the Visa check card, which works much like a credit card except that it takes the funds for the purchase right out of their checking account. It's better living through computers and little swipe cards!

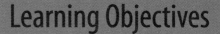

Learning Objectives

After reading this chapter you should be able to:

1. Manage your cash and understand why you need liquid assets.

2. Choose from among the different types of financial institutions that provide cash management services.

3. Compare the various available cash management alternatives and describe the advantages and disadvantages of each.

4. Compare rates on the different liquid investment alternatives.

5. Automate your savings.

6. Establish and use a checking account.

7. Transfer funds electronically using automated teller machines (ATMs), debit cards, and smart cards, and understand how these electronic funds transfers (EFTs) work.

Needless to say, Sanders's, Daffy's, and Dole's experiences weren't ideal—or so Visa would like us to believe. Hey, at least they actually had checking accounts with, we assume, enough funds to cover their purchases. What about people who don't have checking accounts? What about those people who are unfortunate enough to have major expenses just pop up out of nowhere—like the guy who didn't just run a red light but actually ran his Harley Davidson *into* the red light? As **Axiom 7** reminds us, **Stuff Happens**, so don't forget to expect the unexpected. Unless you're a psychic, you can't predict the unexpected (it wouldn't be unexpected then, would it?), but you can prepare for it. How? By keeping some liquid funds available. Or, in the case of Sanders, Daffy, and Dole, you could at least carry some ID.

Without liquid funds to cover the unexpected and even everyday expenses like that meal in Russell, you might have to compromise your long-term investments. For example, you might have to sell your stocks and incur unwanted taxes just to cover your bills. Why ruin your financial plan over some pocket change or an unforeseen expense? Liquid funds are a necessity of personal financial management, and in this chapter we'll discuss how to manage those liquid funds effectively.

AXIOM #7

Stuff Happens

Cash Management

The management of cash and near cash (liquid) assets.

Liquid Assets

Cash and investments that can easily be converted into cash, such as checking accounts, money market funds, and CDs.

AXIOM #1

The Risk-Return Trade-Off

THE NEED FOR LIQUIDITY

Thirty years ago, **cash management** meant depositing your cash in a checking or savings account at a local bank. You could shop around as much as you liked, but all banks pretty much looked the same and their services were limited. Cash management alternatives weren't exactly plentiful. Not today. Sparked by less regulation and increased competition, banks and other financial institutions offer what seems like an endless array of accounts and investments all vying for your cash savings. In fact, recent changes in the financial system have redefined what a bank is and what it can do. Banks are now providing services that don't look "banklike," and other financial institutions are competing directly with banks by looking more and more banklike. As a result, cash management is much more complex than it was in the past. To understand cash management you must also understand the institutions. The purpose here is not just to show you the underlying logic behind modern cash management, but to teach you how to manage your **liquid assets**.

Cash management begins and ends with liquid assets. It deals with choosing from all the alternatives out there in terms of different liquid assets and in terms of financial institutions, and it deals with maintaining and managing the results of those choices. In effect, cash management is deciding how much to keep in liquid assets and where to keep it. Why do you need to keep some of your money in liquid assets? So you can pay your bills and your other normal living expenses without having to dip into your long-term investments—that is, so you aren't forced to sell stocks or real estate when you don't want to. One way to think of liquid assets is as a reservoir, with money moving in as wages are received and moving out as living expenditures and savings aimed at long-term goals. In effect, money moves in and out, and keeping on hand an adequate level of liquid assets keeps this well from running dry. Hey, you don't want your liquid assets to evaporate!

Just as with everything else in personal finance, there are risk-return trade-offs associated with keeping money in the form of liquid assets—it's **Axiom 1: The Risk-Return Trade-Off** in action. Because liquid assets can be turned into cash quickly and with no loss, they have little risk associated with them. However, because they have little risk, they don't provide a high return. Simply put, liquid assets are characterized by low risk and low expected return. It's really the low risk that's important in cash management. The funds you keep in liquid assets are funds that you expect to use in the near future. For that reason, you want to make sure that you're not taking any chances with these funds, that they're invested in safe assets. Given the low return on liquid assets, though, you don't want to tie up too much of your money in them. You should keep in mind that it's the balancing of the risk of not having enough in the way of liquid assets against return that drives the logic behind cash management.

There's another type of risk associated with keeping liquid assets: The more cash you have, the more you're tempted to spend. Remember your cash budget from chapter 2? Well, the easiest way to blow your budget is by walking around a mall with your checkbook or a pocketful of cash. Don't worry, though—even if you have no self-restraint, cash management can help. You see, cash management doesn't just involve deciding where and in what to keep your cash, it involves managing your money and keeping on your budget.

FINANCIAL INSTITUTIONS

Before we examine the different types of liquid assets, let's take a look at the financial institutions that offer them. In recent years the difference between what you might think of as a bank and other types of financial institutions has blurred dramatically. The changes started with the passage of the Depositary Institutions Deregulation and Monetary Control Act of 1980, which allowed for increased competition between banks and other financial institutions. The result of the act has been increased competition and the introduction of a wide range of financial products for cash management available to the consumer. Let's now look at the various financial institutions that provide liquid assets.

Although it's become more and more difficult to differentiate between the different types of financial institutions, they can be categorized as either **deposit-type financial institutions**, which are commonly referred to as "banks," or **nondeposit-type financial institutions**, such as mutual funds and stockbrokerage firms. As you'll see, the distinction between these different financial institutions can seem a bit arbitrary.

"Banks" or Deposit-Type Financial Institutions

Financial institutions that provide traditional checking and savings accounts are commonly called "banks" or deposit-type financial institutions. Technically, many of these institutions aren't actually banks, but are, in fact, other types of financial institutions that act very similarly to banks.

Commercial Banks.
What most people think of when they hear the word "bank" is a commercial bank. Citibank, NationsBank, First Union—these are all commercial banks. Commercial banks dominate the financial services industry. They traditionally offer the widest variety of financial services, including checking and savings accounts, credit cards, safety deposit boxes, financial consulting, and all types of lending services.

They also have more branch offices or locations than any other type of financial institution, with approximately 15,000 commercial banks having around 65,000 main and branch locations. In addition, they dominate in terms of the dollar value of the assets that they hold. The neighborhood locations of commercial bank branches allow depositors to build personal relationships with their bankers, and the size of the overall banking organization ensures that each branch will offer most of the financial and cash management services that you might need. It is the convenience of their physical locations and comfort or security associated with knowing whom you are dealing with that draws many people to commercial banks.

Savings and Loan Associations.
Savings and loan associations (S&Ls), or "**thrifts**," were originally established to provide mortgage loans to their depositors. The depositors' money was pooled and then lent out to other depositors to use in paying for homes. There are two types of S&L ownership structures: *mutual* and *corporate*. In a mutual S&L the depositors are really the owners of the S&L. As such, they receive dividends rather than interest on their savings. With a corporate S&L the depositors aren't owners, so they receive interest rather than dividends, just like in a commercial bank. This is really a technical difference, with these dividends from mutual S&Ls treated as if they were really interest payments, and shouldn't play any major role in your personal finance decisions.

Since deregulation, the services offered by S&Ls and commercial banks have become very similar, with both offering almost identical savings alternatives. Interestingly, savings accounts at S&Ls many times earn one-quarter percent more than do savings accounts at competing commercial banks. However, the rates vary from location to location, so be sure to shop around. The other distinguishing feature of S&Ls is that they still play an important role in funding home mortgage loans, with laws requiring that at least 70 percent of the loans of federally chartered S&Ls go toward home mortgages. Commercial banks invest the money they gather from depositors in many different directions.

S&Ls also operate on a smaller scale than do commercial banks. There are approximately 5,000 S&Ls nationwide, with only around 25,000 main and branch offices. However, from the depositor's point of view, there's very little difference between a commercial bank and a savings and loan association.

Deposit-Type Financial Institutions
Financial institutions that provide traditional checking and savings accounts. Commonly referred to as "banks."

Nondeposit-Type Financial Institutions
Financial institutions such as mutual funds and stock brokerage firms, which don't provide checking and savings accounts.

Savings and Loan Associations (S&Ls), or "Thrifts"
Financial institutions similar to banks, which borrow money from depositors and primarily lend this money out in the form of home mortgages.

Mutual S&L
A savings and loan association in which the depositors are really the owners of the S&L and, thus, earn dividends, not interest, on their savings accounts.

Corporate S&L
A savings and loan association with an ownership setup similar to a commercial bank, and in which the depositors receive interest rather than dividends on their savings accounts.

Savings Banks. A savings bank is a close cousin to a savings and loan association, especially a mutual S&L, generally found in the Northeastern United States. Most savings banks are depositor owned, basically making them *mutual* savings banks. Like mutual S&Ls, then, they pay dividends rather than interest to their depositor/owners. Also like S&Ls, their primary purpose historically has been to provide mortgage funding to their depositors. In fact, in recent years many S&Ls have changed their charter and name and become savings banks. This change is purely cosmetic and is generally done just to allow the use of the word "bank" in their name. This name change by many S&Ls is a further sign of a continued blurring of the differences between the different deposit-type financial institutions.

Credit Unions. Credit unions are another type of depositor-owned financial institution. In this case, it's a not-for-profit cooperative made up of members with some type of common bond. For example, a member might be anything from a Baptist, to an employee at General Electric, to a student at a major college. Usually, it's this membership requirement that's the biggest drawback to credit unions. In fact, only about half of all Americans are eligible to join them. Aside from the organizational differences, credit unions are quite similar to commercial banks and S&Ls, and offer a wide range of competitive financial services. They do have one advantage over other financial institutions, and that's cost. Because of their tax-exempt status as not-for-profit organizations and their generally more efficient, smaller scale, they often pay depositors more than depositors would otherwise earn at a commercial bank. In addition, they tend to have lower fees and minimum balances associated with their accounts. Their loans also tend to be at favorable rates, again owing to their tax-exempt status. Another advantage of credit unions is their convenience—they're often located right at the members' place of "work." For example, a branch of the Virginia Tech credit union is located right in the student union.

Today, credit unions provide an array of services that tend to be competitive with other deposit-type financial institutions, but at lower costs. However, many smaller credit unions are reluctant to provide home mortgage loans. Because of their cost advantages, though, credit unions are well worth investigating.

Nondeposit-Type Financial Institutions

Willing to go almost anywhere to make money, mutual funds, stockbrokerage firms, insurance companies, and some other firms have moved into what used to be banking territory and have begun offering services that look an awful lot like those offered by banks. Today, it's possible to have a checking account with Merrill Lynch, a consumer loan with General Motors, and a home mortgage with General Electric. Actually, this banking competition from outside the normal banking industry is a relatively recent occurrence, with its roots in the deregulation of the 1980s. However, this competition has been a two-way street, with brokerage firms offering traditional banking services and banks offering stockbrokerage services.

Mutual Fund

An investment fund that raises funds from investors, pools the money, and invests it in stocks, bonds, and other investments. Investors own shares proportionate to the amount of their investment level.

Mutual Funds. With a **mutual fund**, investors pool their money, giving it to a professional investment manager hired by the investment company that operates the mutual fund, and the professional invests those funds for them. Although there are many different types of mutual funds, *money market mutual funds,* which invest in short-term (generally with an average maturity of less than 90 days or less) notes of very high denomination, provide effective competition for banks. Because these mutual funds are of such short maturity, they're generally regarded as practically risk-free, despite the fact that they're not insured.

Stockbrokerage Firms. Stockbrokerage firms have traditionally dealt only with investments, such as stocks (hence their name). To compete with traditional banks, though, many brokerage firms have recently introduced a wide variety of cash management tools, including financial counseling, credit cards, and their own money market mutual funds. In effect, they've entered into direct competition with traditional banks.

What to Look for in a Financial Institution

So how do you choose among all these alternatives? Well, there are three obvious questions you need to keep in mind. First, which financial institution offers the kind of services you want and need? Of course, this requires knowing what you need, but if you do and an institution won't give it to you, why deal with it? Second, is your investment safe? What guarantee do you have that money you deposit today won't vanish tomorrow? Third, what are all the costs and returns associated with the services you want? Are there minimum deposit requirements or hidden fees? Remember that costs and returns vary not only among different services but also between the same services at different financial institutions. Of course, you always want to have the lowest costs and highest returns.

Once you've answered these obvious questions, you should look to the personal service available. You want a financial institution that will work for you—one where you can talk to and get to know the manager. The more personal the relationship you have with your financial institution, the more you'll be able to adapt its services to your needs, and the better you'll feel about your investment. It's this personal relationship that welcomes questions, answers, and advice. Also consider convenience. You want an institution with a convenient location and convenient hours.

Finally, there's no reason why you should limit your financial activities to only one financial institution. In fact, financial institutions have different strengths and offer different services at different costs. Feel free to mix and match financial institutions to take advantage of their different strengths and rates, and to get the best and most appropriate services you can.

CASH MANAGEMENT ALTERNATIVES

Now that we know what kinds of financial institutions exist, let's take a look at the different cash management alternatives they all offer.

Checking Accounts

Many people use checking accounts as a convenient way of paying their bills. In choosing between the available checking accounts, it may seem as if there are countless choices, but there are really just two basic types: interest-bearing and noninterest-bearing. A noninterest-bearing checking account is actually a **demand deposit** and can be offered only by a commercial bank. The ability to offer demand deposit accounts is one thing that distinguishes commercial banks from other financial institutions. At one time, the ability to offer demand deposits provided commercial banks with a big competitive edge. Today, with other financial institutions offering interest-paying checking accounts, this distinction lacks real importance. Usually with a demand deposit account, the customer pays for the checking privilege by either maintaining a minimum balance or being charged per check.

As you can guess from the name, an interest-bearing checking account pays interest. Another name for an interest-bearing checking account is a **NOW (negotiable order of withdrawal) account**. These NOW accounts are simply checking accounts on which you earn interest on your balance. Although S&Ls can't offer demand deposits, they can offer checking accounts, but these accounts must pay interest. Everyone knows that an account that pays interest is more desirable from a financial standpoint than an account that doesn't pay interest, right? Not necessarily. Although you receive interest on your balance in a NOW account, you generally must maintain a high minimum balance in

addition to paying a monthly fee. The monthly fee, of course, represents a cost, but so does the minimum balance. The cost of a minimum balance is really an opportunity cost. Even though an interest-bearing checking account pays interest, it generally pays less than other cash management alternatives, which we'll discuss shortly. Because the minimum balance forces you to hold more money in your checking account than you otherwise would (this is called the forced balance), that checking account has an opportunity cost associated with it. Given these costs, an interest-bearing checking account is not always preferable to a noninterest-bearing account. To determine which type of account is better for you, compare the interest you earn on the interest-bearing checking account against any monthly fees that you incur plus any lost interest resulting from holding more money in your checking account than you otherwise would. Figure 5.1 provides a comparison between an interest-bearing and a noninterest-bearing checking account.

Because a checking account is one of the most important liquid assets you'll ever have, we'll take a much closer look at the mechanics of opening one later in this chapter.

FIGURE 5.1

Comparison Between an Interest-Bearing and a Noninterest-Bearing Checking Account

Savings & Loan

Statement – Noninterest Checking

Service Fee	$2.00 per month
1. Total Cost per Year	$24.00
Minimum Balance	$200.00
Interest Earned on	
2. Checking Account	$0.00
Forced Balance*	$0.00
3. Opportunity Cost of Forced Balance[†]	$0.00
Interest Minus Costs[‡]	-$24.00

Savings & Loan

Statement – Interest Checking (4% rate)

Service Fee	$3.00 per month
1. Total Cost per Year	$36.00
Minimum Balance	$1,000.00
Interest Earned on	
2. Checking Account	$40.00
Forced Balance*	$800.00
3. Opportunity Cost of Forced Balance[†]	$48.00
Interest Minus Costs[‡]	-$44.00

Assume that in the absence of minimum balances you would maintain a balance of $200 in your checking account. Thus, in this case it is less costly to maintain a noninterest-bearing checking account because of the relatively low return on the forced balance.

* The minimum balance forces you to hold more money in your checking account than you otherwise would. This additional money held in your checking account is called your forced balance. In this case, the interest checking account forces you to maintain $1,000 in your account, whereas the noninterest checking account only requires the desired balance of $200.

[†] Assume that your alternative investment for the forced balance is a money market mutual fund that earns 6%. Thus, the opportunity cost on the forced balance is $800.00 × 0.06 = $48.00.

[‡] Line 2 minus lines 1 and 3.

Savings Accounts

Although checking accounts are convenient, some don't pay any interest, and those that do generally pay a relatively low rate. A **savings account**, which is also called a time deposit, is one step removed from a checking account in terms of risk-return trade-off. With a savings account you deposit your money in the bank and are guaranteed a fixed return on your deposit. Then, when you want to withdraw your money, you must go to the bank to do so. A savings account is less liquid and therefore more risky than a checking account in that you must go to the bank to withdraw your funds, and, technically, the bank could require a grace period before relinquishing those funds to you. In the past, withdrawals and other transactions would have been registered in a passbook, which is why many savings accounts used to be called "passbook" accounts. Today, although passbook accounts still exist, statement accounts—where the customer receives a monthly statement of the balance—are replacing passbook accounts as the dominant type of savings account. Figure 5.2 provides a sample savings account statement.

Because savings accounts are extremely liquid, they don't have a high yield associated with them. In fact, up until 1982 the interest on savings accounts was limited by law to 5.25 percent for commercial banks and 5.5 percent for savings banks. The advantages of a savings account are really in the accessibility you have to your money and the ease with which you can set up and maintain the account. The disadvantages revolve around the low rate of interest relative to other liquid investments that a savings account provides. Keep in mind that your return on a savings account may be reduced even further by the requirement of a minimum balance or a service charge.

Money Market Deposit Account (MMDA)

A **money market deposit account (MMDA)** is an alternative to the savings account offered by commercial banks. It works about the same way a savings account works—you deposit your money in a bank and have to return to the bank when you want to withdraw it. But rather than receive a guaranteed fixed rate, with the MMDA you receive a rate of interest that varies with the current market rate of interest. The primary advantage of an MMDA over a savings account is that although this rate fluctuates on a weekly basis, it is, in general, higher than the fixed rate paid on savings accounts. In addition, some MMDAs also offer limited check-writing service of three checks per month, after which a substantial service fee of up to $10 per check is imposed.

The only disadvantage of an MMDA relative to a savings account is that it generally requires a high minimum balance, many times of up to $1,000, and imposes penalties if your balance drops below this level. The disadvantages relative to other investment alternatives stem from its relative return in addition to the minimum balance required. In general, MMDA pays less interest than do some of the other cash management alternatives we'll look at. Therefore, in making a decision as to whether to invest funds in an MMDA, you should determine whether this type of account meets your needs. You should then compare all the associated costs with the return. As with other investments, it's not simply what this investment returns, but what the alternative investments return that determines whether this is a desirable investment alternative.

> ### *Stop and Think*
> You shouldn't be enticed to put your savings in an MMDA just because it pays a bit more than a normal savings account. You must also look carefully at the minimum required balance. Many times this minimum balance forces you to keep more in the MMDA than you would otherwise.

Savings Account
A deposit account that pays interest.

Money Market Deposit Account (MMDA)
A bank account that provides a rate of interest that varies with the current market rate of interest.

FIGURE 5.2

A Savings Account Statement

Some savings accounts allow for withdrawals to be made with something that closely resembles a credit card.

This savings account allows for automatic transfers to be made to your checking account whenever your account doesn't contain enough cash to cover the checks that you've written against your account.

This savings account only provides statements on a quarterly basis. If you want to make telephone account inquiries, it provides for 5 free per month. After that a fee is charged.

1ˢᵗ National Bank

Personal Savings

Personal Savings		1/01/97 thru 3/31/97
Account number:	000000007	
Account holder(s):	Zachary Cohen	
	8142 Jerome St	
	Garcia, CA 41111	

Account Summary

Opening balance 1/01	$1,043.84
Deposits and other credits	100.00 +
Interest paid	6.45 +
Withdrawals	200.00 –
Closing balance 3/31	$950.29

Deposits and Other Credits

Date	Amount	Description
1/06	100.00	Deposit
1/31	2.19	Interest from 01/01/1997 through 01/31/1997
2/28	2.02	Interest from 02/01/1997 through 02/28/1997
3/31	2.24	Interest from 03/01/1997 through 03/31/1997
Total	**$106.45**	

Interest

Number of days this statement period	90
Annual percentage yield earned	2.32%
Interest earned this statement period	$6.45
Interest paid this statement period	$6.45
Interest paid this year	$6.45

This savings account earned only 2.32% interest.

Withdrawals

Date	Amount	Withdrawn
3/31	$200.00	Transfer to Checking
Total	**$200.00**	

RECEIVE 5 FREE ACCOUNT INQUIRIES/MONTH USING OUR AUTOMATED TOUCH-TONE SYSTEM. AFTER 5 FREE, THE CHARGE WILL BE $.50 PER INQUIRY. AFTER 2 FREE INQUIRIES/MONTH TO A CUSTOMER SERVICE REP, THE CHARGE WILL BE $2.00 PER INQUIRY. FEE IS NOT CHARGED ON CAP & EXPRESS ACCOUNTS OR ACCOUNTS MAINTAINING MINUMIM MONTHLY BALANCES

Certificates of Deposit (CDs)
Savings alternatives that pay a fixed rate of interest while keeping your funds on deposit for a set period of time that can range from 30 days to several years.

Certificates of Deposit (CDs)

A **certificate of deposit**, or **CD**, is a savings alternative that pays a fixed rate of interest while keeping your funds on deposit for a set period of time, which can range from 30 days to several years. The longer the time period for which the funds are tied up, the higher the interest rate paid on the CD. Because the interest rate is generally fixed, if interest rates drop you still receive the promised rate; however, if interest rates rise, the interest you receive on your CD stays fixed at its lower rate. In addition, the rate your CD earns depends upon its size. Generally, the higher the deposit on the CD, the higher the interest rates attached to it. One downside of investing in a CD is that if you need your money before the CD matures or comes due, you may face an early withdrawal penalty. With a CD, then, the trade-off is loss of liquidity versus higher return. CDs are for money that you have in hand now and want to keep safe, and are generally considered liquid assets because the time periods involved are fairly short. Maybe you have money now from your summer job with College Pro Painters that you'll want to use in a year for tuition or the down payment on a new car. A CD will hold that money out of temptation's way and return more than will a general savings account.

The rate you can earn on your CD varies from bank to bank and between banks and other institutions that offer them, such as brokerage firms. Interestingly, banks many times use CDs as a marketing tool to lure new customers by offering high interest rates. If you look around, you can usually find a great interest rate. Sometimes, though, you need to look a little further than just your neighborhood. The interest rate offered on CDs can vary dramatically from region to region—in fact, differences of 2 percent or more are possible. The bottom line here is that if you're considering investing in a CD, don't limit your search to your neighborhood—search nationally. The process of purchasing a CD from a bank in another geographic region merely involves wiring or mailing your funds to the target bank.

Money Market Mutual Funds (MMMFs)

Money market mutual funds (MMMFs) provide an interesting alternative to traditional liquid investments offered by financial institutions. Investors in MMMFs receive interest on a pool of investments less an administrative fee, which is, for most funds, less than 1 percent of the total investment. An MMMF draws together the savings of many individuals and invests those funds in very large, creditworthy notes issued by the government or by large corporations. The advantage of MMMFs is that by pooling investments, they can purchase higher-priced investments and thus earn a higher rate of return than investors could get individually. As a result, they almost always have a higher yield associated with them than do bank money market deposit accounts. The interest rate earned on an MMMF varies daily as interest rates change. In fact, the yield on these funds is extremely sensitive to changes in the short-term market interest rates, with MMMF rates varying between 2 percent and 17 percent. Exactly how much more than MMDAs they yield, of course, depends on the level of interest rates. When rates are low, the difference can drop to less than one-half percent. However, when rates are high, the difference can be several percentage points.

When you invest in an MMMF, you purchase shares at the price of $1 per share. You then earn interest, less administrative costs, on your shares on a daily basis, although it's posted to your account only on a monthly basis. For most MMMFs there's a minimum initial investment of between $500 and $2,000, after which there may be a minimum level for subsequent deposits. One nice feature of MMMFs is that they allow you limited check-writing privileges, although there's generally a minimum amount for which the check must be written. However, in an attempt to lure funds away from bank checking accounts, a number of MMMFs have lifted limits on both the number of checks written and check amounts. In fact, by 1997 there were more than 50 funds offering an unlimited checking feature. However, these funds generally don't provide canceled checks for record keeping. Thus, while MMMFs are not perfect substitutes for checking accounts, they do provide an attractive place to put excess funds awaiting more permanent investment. They also compare very favorably with savings accounts, the only difference being that money is deposited by mail and withdrawn by writing a check. They also generally pay more than traditional savings accounts.

Money Market Mutual Funds (MMMFs)
Mutual funds that invest in short-term (generally with a maturity of less than 90 days) notes of very high denomination.

Asset Management Account

Asset Management Accounts
Comprehensive financial services packages offered by a brokerage firm, which can include a checking account, credit and debit cards, a money market mutual fund, loans, automatic payment of any fixed payments such as mortgages or other debt, brokerage services (buying and selling stocks or bonds), and a system for the direct payment of interest, dividends, and proceeds from security sales into the money market mutual fund.

An **asset management account** is a comprehensive financial services package offered by a brokerage firm. It can include a checking account, a credit card, a money market mutual fund, loans, automatic payment on any fixed debt such as mortgages, brokerage services (buying and selling stock or bonds), and a system for the direct payment of interest, dividends, and proceeds from security sales into the money market mutual fund. The parent brokerage firm then provides the customer with a monthly statement summarizing all the customer's financial activities. These all-purpose accounts were established by brokerage firms primarily to bring new brokerage accounts to the firm, but as a result of their comprehensive nature they provide investors with a number of advantages over other cash management alternatives.

The major advantage of an asset management account is that it automatically coordinates the flow of funds into and out of your MMMF. The parent brokerage firm does this by means of a computer program that "sweeps" funds into and out of the MMMF. For example, interest and dividends received from securities owned are automatically "swept" into the MMMF. Also, if you write a check for an amount greater than what is held in your MMMF, securities from the investment portion of your asset management account are automatically sold with the proceeds "swept" into the money market fund to cover the check. Similarly, a deposit into the MMMF automatically first goes toward reducing any loans outstanding and thereafter automatically goes into the MMMF. For those with numerous security holdings and somewhat complicated financial dealings, an asset management account may be of value. One advantage it holds is that it provides the customer with a single consolidated monthly financial statement for tax purposes.

Although there are many different variations of the asset management account that are offered by different security brokers, they really don't involve any management of assets. The only automatic management of assets occurs when stocks are sold to cover checks that exceed the MMMF.

In addition to an annual service charge of from $50 to $125, there is generally a rather large minimum balance required, ranging upward of $5,000 in stocks and cash. Also, brokerage firms charge commissions on any stock transactions they perform. So, although the benefits of an asset management account may be great, they come with a fairly steep price. For example, the commissions paid on the sale of stocks associated with an asset management account may be much higher than the customer might have paid if there had been the opportunity to shop around and sell the stock through the least expensive broker. In short, although these accounts are an interesting alternative cash management tool, you must weigh the service charge, the high minimum balance, and the relatively high commissions on any stock sales made against their returns in making your decision.

U.S. Treasury Bills, or T-Bills

U.S. Treasury Bills, or **T-Bills**
Short-term notes of debt issued by the federal government, with maturities ranging from 3 months to 12 months.

Denomination
The face value or amount that's returned to the bondholder at maturity. It's also referred to as the bond's par value.

U.S Treasury bills, or **T-bills**, are short-term notes of debt issued by the federal government, with maturities ranging from 3 months to 12 months. The minimum **denomination** (face value) on T-bills is a whopping $10,000, which effectively puts them out of the range of most individuals. When you purchase a T-bill you don't receive any interest. Instead, you pay less than its face value, then when the T-bill matures you receive its full face value.

T-bills are extremely liquid investments. When you need cash, all you need do is sell the T-bill through a broker, which is quite easy. They are also extremely safe, having been issued by the federal government. In terms of returns, the interest rate carried on T-bills is similar to that on MMMFs. In addition, your return, although subject to federal taxes, isn't subject to state or local taxes. The big drawback to T-bills is the large investment they require.

TIRED OF BANKS? Try Checking Out an Alternative

Unlike many people, Charles Bamberger, a Fort Worth, Texas, physician is completely satisfied with his checking account—though, technically, he doesn't have one.

Dr. Bamberger "banks" at his brokerage firm, depositing cash in an asset-management account and writing checks on it to pay his bills. "I have never had a problem," he said.

For many people, old-fashioned checking accounts have much to be desired. They generally pay no interest and charge monthly fees of $5 or so to customers who fail to keep a minimum balance. Even those that do pay interest aren't much of a deal. They yield just 1.5% on average, less than one-third of the 5.4% paid by the average money-market fund.

But, for investors like Dr. Bamberger, there is an alternative. Asset-management accounts,  which combine stock and bond trading with access to money funds, pay market-related interest rates on cash balances and can be just as easy to use as checking accounts. Many come with staple checking-account features, such as direct deposit, unlimited check-writing and debit cards that can be used to withdraw cash from automated-teller machines. Some even offer such extras as home banking and bill-payment services.

"As long as someone is comfortable using direct deposit and ATMs, I can't see why he wouldn't want to use one of these accounts instead," said John Markese, president of the American Association of Individual Investors in Chicago, who has accounts at two brokerage firms.

Until recently, asset-management accounts were mainly available to customers of full-service brokerage firms with portfolios of at least $20,000 to $100,000. Today, investors can choose from scores of accounts at hundreds of brokerage firms, banks and insurance companies. Many are open to investors with as little as $5,000 to $10,000 in a combination of cash and securities.

Typically, asset-management accounts come with annual fees of $50 to $125. But, eager to attract business, a few discount brokerage firms offer no-fee accounts.

Even with fees, asset-management accounts can be attractive because yields on money funds typically whomp the rates available on other cash accounts. At today's rates, a cash balance of $3,000 in an asset-management account could earn $100 or so, even after taxes.

Source: Vanessa O'Connell, "Tired of Banks? Try Checking Out an Alternative," *The Wall Street Journal*, September 8, 1995, p. C1. Reprinted by permission of *The Wall Street Journal*, © 1995 Dow Jones & Company, Inc. All Rights Reserved Worldwide.

Analysis and Implications ...

A. What about deposit insurance? If the brokerage firm that holds your account fails, the Securities Investor Protection Corporation covers up to $500,000 in securities, including up to $100,000 in cash. Most brokerage firms also provide private insurance coverage through their clearing brokers, usually for as much as $10 million to $50 million an account.

B. Asset-management accounts may not be suitable for those who need canceled checks as proof of tax deductions. This is because many don't automatically return canceled checks.

Bond

A type of security that's actually a loan on which you receive interest, generally every 6 months for the life of the bond. When the bond matures, or comes due, you get back your investment, or "loan." What you get back at maturity is usually the face value of the loan, although the amount you get could be more or less than what you paid for the bond originally.

U.S. Series EE Bonds

In recent years government savings **bonds** have become attractive investment alternatives for short-term funds. U.S. Series EE bonds are issued by the Treasury with low denominations and variable interest rates. Their minimum denomination is low enough that they can be purchased for as little as $25 each. When a Series EE bond is purchased, its price is one-half its face value, with face values going from $50 to $10,000. Interest accrues on these bonds until they are worth their face value at the time of their maturity. In other words, you buy a bond, wait a specified amount of time, and get double your money back.

Series EE bonds are liquid in the sense that they can be cashed at any time, although cashing them before they mature may result in a reduced yield. In addition, they're safe because they're backed by the government. Making them more attractive is that they earn a minimum return of 4 percent. Although this minimum return can be changed at any time by the Treasury, the new minimum applies only to newly issued Series EE bonds, not to outstanding ones. The actual rate earned on Series EE bonds, which varies with the market interest rate, is currently quite competitive. If you'd like to get the current rate on Series EE bonds, you can call 800-US-BONDS.

One of the major advantages of Series EE bonds is that, because they're issued by the federal government, they aren't taxed at the state or local level. The taxes on their interest can either be reported annually or deferred until they are redeemed. Another tax advantage of Series EE bonds is associated with accumulating funds for college. Depending upon your tax level, they can be exempt from federal taxes if cashed to pay for college tuition and fees. Another advantage of Series EE bonds to some is their convenience—that is, they can be purchased through a payroll deduction plan or directly from a bank with no fees or commissions involved. How do they stack up against the competition—the other cash management alternatives? Returnwise, not bad; but in terms of liquidity, not that good. Remember, if you cash them before maturity, you may receive a reduced return. Moreover, if you're using them to save money for college, they really aren't liquid at all. After all, the money is for college, not for emergencies. Table 5.1 provides a summary comparison of these different types of cash management alternatives.

> ### *Stop and Think*
>
> One of the mistakes that many people make is keeping too much in very liquid assets. They view investments in CDs and money market mutual funds as "safe" investments. In reality, they're not "safe" in the sense that they'll have a difficult time keeping pace with inflation, let alone growing in terms of purchasing power. In short, too little in liquid assets is dangerous and can be costly when an emergency occurs, but too much in liquid assets is dangerous in that you may tie up too much of your savings in low-return investments. As a result, you may not be able to achieve your future spending goals.

LEARNING OBJECTIVE #4

Compare rates on the different liquid investment alternatives.

COMPARING CASH MANAGEMENT ALTERNATIVES

Now that you know what cash management alternatives are available to you, how do you compare them to determine what's best for you? We've already compared them in terms of their advantages and disadvantages, but how do you choose the best of what's available? Once we've examined their service and convenience, to decide between them we need to (1) examine their returns using comparable interest rates, (2) take into account their tax status, and (3) consider their safety or risk.

TABLE 5.1

Comparison of Different Cash Management Alternatives

Cash Management Technique	Advantages	Disadvantages
Checking or Demand Deposit Account	Convenience Easy to use Low minimum balance Insured	Either no interest or low relative interest Minimum requirements can be costly
Savings or Time Deposit Account	Higher return than on a checking account Insured	Low return relative to alternatives Not as liquid as a checking account
Money Market Deposit Account	Relatively attractive rate which varies with the current market rate of interest Limited checking privileges Insured	High minimum balance required Pays less than some other short-term investments such as CDs and money market mutual funds
Certificate of Deposit (CD)	High interest rate Fixed rate—if interest rates fall you still get your guaranteed return Insured Lends itself well to an automated payroll deduction plan	Limited liquidity—penalties for early withdrawal If interest rates rise, your rate is locked in Minimum deposit required
Money Market Mutual Fund	High interest rate Some checking privileges Limited risk due to short maturity of investments Lends itself well to an automated payroll deduction plan	Minimum initial balance required of between $500 and $1,000 Not federally insured Minimum check size
Asset Management Account	High return Automatic coordination of money management Lends itself well to an automated payroll deduction plan	Costly—monthly fees range from $25 to $200 Not insured Large minimum balance ranging upward of $5,000
U.S Treasury Bills, or T-Bills	Attractive interest rates Exempt from state and local taxes Guaranteed by the federal government Taxes vary with current rates	Low liquidity—can be sold; however, less convenient to liquidate than other cash management alternatives Very high denominations Redemption before 5 years
U.S. Series EE Bonds	Attractive interest rate which varies with current rates Low denominations Can be purchased through payroll deduction or at most banks Exempt from state and local taxes Can be redeemed at any bank Guaranteed by the federal government No sales commissions or fees Lends itself well to an automated payroll deduction plan Can be exempt from federal taxes if used for college	Low liquidity—penalty for redemption before 5 years Long maturity Must wait at least 6 months before redemption unless there is an emergency Interest only accrues twice per year

Using Comparable Interest Rates

To make intelligent decisions on where to invest your money, you need to compare interest rates. Unfortunately, the process of comparing interest rates is difficult because some rates are quoted as compounded annually, and others are quoted as compounded quarterly or even daily. As we already know from chapter 3, it's not fair to compare interest rates with different compounding periods to each other. Thus, the only way interest rates can logically be compared is to convert them to some common compounding period. That's what the **annual percentage yield (APY)** is all about.

The Truth in Savings Act of 1993 requires financial institutions to report the rate of interest using the APY so that it's easier for the consumer to make comparisons. The APY converts interest rates compounded for different periods into comparable annual rates, allowing you to compare interest rates easily. However, make sure that you're comparing APYs and not "quoted rates," which may assume different compounding periods.

Once you understand differences in rates, make sure you understand the method used to determine the account balance on which interest will be paid. Is it your actual balance, your lowest monthly balance, or what? The method that's the best for you, the saver, and is the most fair bases interest on your money from the day you deposit it until the day you withdraw it. Fortunately, this is the method most institutions use, but it's still good to make sure.

Tax Considerations

As we saw in chapter 4, taxes can affect the real rate of return on investments. In comparing the returns on cash management investment alternatives, you must also make sure that the rates that you compare are all on the same tax basis—that is, they are all either before- or after-tax calculations. The fact that some investments have both tax-exempt portions of their returns makes these calculations a bit tricky.

As you recall from chapter 4, the calculation of the after-tax return begins with a determination of your marginal tax bracket, that is, the tax rate at which any additional income you receive will be taxed. This marginal tax rate combines the federal and state tax rates that you pay on the investment that you're considering. The **after-tax return** can then be determined as follows:

$$\text{after-tax return} = \text{taxable return } (1 - \text{marginal tax rate}) + \text{nontaxable return}$$

Here's an example: Assume you're considering two money market mutual funds. Fund A is tax-exempt and pays 5 percent, and fund B is taxable and pays 6.5 percent. Further assume that your top tax bracket is 28 percent and that you live in a state that doesn't impose income taxes. Which of these two alternatives is better? To compare these MMMFs, you must put them both on an after-tax basis as follows:

$$\text{fund A's after-tax return} = 5\% \quad \begin{array}{l}\text{(Remember, it's a tax-exempt} \\ \text{fund, so it's all nontaxable.)}\end{array}$$

$$\text{fund B's after-tax return} = 6.5\% \times (1 - 0.28) = 4.68\%$$

Thus, given your marginal tax bracket, fund A, which provides a tax-exempt return of 5 percent, is the better of the two alternatives.

Keep in mind that although fund A may be the better alternative for you, it's not the best alternative for everyone. For example, the after-tax return on fund B for a person with a marginal tax rate of 15 percent is:

$$\begin{array}{l}\text{fund B's after-tax return given} \\ \text{a 15\% marginal tax bracket}\end{array} = 6.5\% \times (1 - 0.15) = 5.53\%$$

Thus, the higher your marginal tax bracket, the more you benefit from a tax-exempt investment.

Annual Percentage Yield (APY)
The simple annual percentage yield that converts interest rates compounded for different periods into comparable annual rates. It allows you to easily compare interest rates.

After-Tax Return
The actual return you earn on taxable investments once taxes have been paid. It is equal to the taxable return (1 − marginal tax rate) + the nontaxable return.

In calculating the after-tax return, you must keep in mind that you are interested in the return after *both* federal and state taxes. Thus, when calculating the after-tax return on a Treasury bond, which is taxed at the federal but not the state level, you must adjust for federal taxes. Likewise, when calculating the after-tax return on a municipal bond that is tax-exempt at the federal but not the state level, you must adjust for state taxes.

Safety

You might think that any deposit in any financial institution is safe. Not so. Some banks and S&Ls take more risk than they should. Sometimes that risk catches up with them, and it's your money that's lost. However, some deposits at different financial institutions are insured, and some cash management alternatives are safer than others. To understand how safe your investments are, it's necessary to understand how federal insurance works and how money market mutual funds operate.

Federal Deposit Insurance.
Although most liquid investments are quite safe, federal deposit insurance should eliminate any questions and worries you might have about safety. The **Federal Deposit Insurance Corporation (FDIC)** insures deposits at commercial banks and S&Ls, and the **National Credit Union Association** insures credit unions. These are federal agencies established to protect you against failures involving financial institutions.

Today if your account is with a federally insured institution, it's insured for up to $100,000 per depositor (not per account). For example, you may have $90,000 in a savings account and $80,000 in a checking account, both in your name at the same institution. Your combined money ($170,000) will be insured for only $100,000. However, if one of these accounts were held with one in your name and one in your spouse's name, they would both be fully insured. Moreover, if you would like more coverage, you can simply spread your accounts among different federally insured banks, and each account at each separate bank receives the $100,000 insurance. This insurance guarantees that you'll get back your money, up to the insured limit, if your financial institution goes bust.

Federal Deposit Insurance Corporation (FDIC)
The federal agency that insures deposits at commercial banks.

National Credit Union Association
The federal agency that insures accounts at credit unions.

Money Market Mutual Funds and Safety.
Although funds in money market mutual funds aren't insured, they're invested in a diversified portfolio of government bonds guaranteed by the government and short-term corporate bonds that are virtually risk-free. The safety of an investment in money market mutual funds comes from the fact that it is first of all well diversified, and second, investments are limited to very short-term government and corporate debt. It takes time for a corporation's problems to become so severe that it defaults on its debt. Thus, it's relatively easy to predict whether debt is risky if it has only a 90-day maturity. As such, money market mutual funds are essentially risk-free. The only risk they might have would be associated with possible criminal activity on the part of the fund managers. This risk is eliminated through effective monitoring of the fund's activities, which occurs in the larger funds. Investing in a large, high-quality money market mutual fund is pretty much risk-free.

> ### *Stop and Think*
> The idea behind cash management is to keep some money, but not too much, set aside in case there is an emergency. The more you keep set aside, the safer you are, but the money you set aside will be lucky to keep pace with inflation. For example, if you can earn 5 percent on a money market mutual fund, but you are in the 30 percent marginal tax bracket, your after-tax return would be 5%(1 − 0.30) = 3.5%. If inflation were 4 percent, your real return would be -0.5%. In short, it's difficult to do much better than keep up with inflation with cash management.

Automate your savings.

AXIOM #13

Pay Yourself First

AXIOM #15

Just Do It!

AXIOM #2

The Time Value of Money

**LEARNING
OBJECTIVE #6**

**Establish and use a
checking account.**

AUTOMATING SAVINGS: PAY YOURSELF FIRST—JUST DO IT!

You can easily use the cash management alternatives described earlier to automate your savings—it all boils down to **Axiom 13: Pay Yourself First**. The key here is to start saving early and to make saving a regimented part of your everyday life. As **Axiom 15: Just Do It!** points out, the earlier you start saving, the better off you are. Automating your savings is a great way to make saving less of a chore, and what you don't see you can't spend. That is, if you have some of your income automatically deducted from your paycheck and placed in savings, you learn to live at your take-home salary level. Therefore, it's a good idea to have some of your salary automatically deposited in savings. Moreover, as you know from **Axiom 2: The Time Value of Money**, the earlier you start, the easier it is to achieve your goals. Don't put off financial discipline until you're "making more money"—start it today.

Several of the various cash management alternatives described earlier lend themselves well to an automated deposit program. For example, money market mutual funds, asset management accounts, and Series EE savings bonds all work nicely with automated payroll deduction systems. The advantage of the automated payroll deduction plan is that not only is the money withdrawn from your pay before you get a chance to think about spending it, but it's immediately deposited in an account to earn interest. Thus, your money is immediately put to work at compounding.

ESTABLISHING AND USING A CHECKING ACCOUNT

We've seen that there are a lot of alternatives available with respect to cash management, but it would be almost impossible to function in today's economy without access to a checking account. It's how most people spend their money—writing checks to cover the purchase of groceries, textbooks, tuition, rent, and pizza. Carrying cash to cover these purchases would be too dangerous—checks are convenient and simple. In fact, each year somewhere around 60 billion checks are written. We'll now show you how to open and maintain a checking account. Keep in mind that checking accounts can be set up at all types of financial institutions, not just commercial banks.

Choosing a Financial Institution

The first step in opening a checking account is choosing a financial institution. In deciding where to open a checking account, you should consider the three C's—cost, convenience, and consideration—in addition to the safety of the financial institution. Figure 5.3 provides a summary of these concerns. Remember, in picking a checking account you're also picking a financial institution with which you'll have a financial relationship. Thus, you should consider not only the cost, but also the convenience of the financial institution and its "consideration," that is, how comfortable you are with the manager and employees.

The Cost Factor

The cost of the account is probably the most basic factor in determining what type of account to open and where to open it. If you meet a minimum balance level, some financial institutions provide you with free checking privileges. Unfortunately, this minimum balance is usually in the $500 to $1,000 range. If the minimum balance isn't met, one of a number of alternative fee structures will be imposed. Let's take a moment to examine the alternative fee arrangements for checking accounts.

Monthly Fee.　With a monthly fee arrangement, you pay a set fee regardless of your average balance and usage of your checking account.

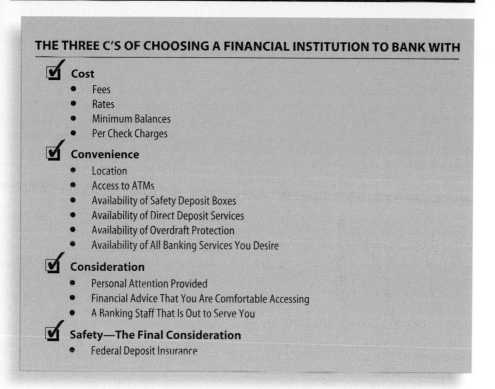

FIGURE 5.3

Choosing a Financial Institution

THE THREE C'S OF CHOOSING A FINANCIAL INSTITUTION TO BANK WITH

☑ **Cost**
- Fees
- Rates
- Minimum Balances
- Per Check Charges

☑ **Convenience**
- Location
- Access to ATMs
- Availability of Safety Deposit Boxes
- Availability of Direct Deposit Services
- Availability of Overdraft Protection
- Availability of All Banking Services You Desire

☑ **Consideration**
- Personal Attention Provided
- Financial Advice That You Are Comfortable Accessing
- A Banking Staff That Is Out to Serve You

☑ **Safety—The Final Consideration**
- Federal Deposit Insurance

Minimum Balance. Under a minimum balance arrangement, your monthly fee depends upon how much cash you maintain in your checking account. If your average balance exceeds a set level, the monthly fee is waived; if not, you pay the monthly fee. Even if the fee is waived, you still pay the opportunity cost of having your funds tied up in the minimum balance of your checking account, where they either do not earn interest or earn a very low rate.

Charge Per Check. At some financial institutions, in addition to paying a small fixed monthly fee, there's also a charge per check. The trade-off here is that if you don't use many checks, the total cost of this type of account may be considerably less than an account with a higher monthly fee and no per check charge.

Balance-Dependent Scaled Fees. Under balance-dependent scaled fees, the fee declines depending upon the average balance held. That is, for accounts with small average balances, there is a relatively high monthly fee. However, for accounts with larger average balances, the monthly fee declines, eventually being eliminated for accounts with very large average balances.

When opening a NOW account, which you will recall is simply a checking account on which you earn interest, remember that any interest you earn will help offset any fees and minimum balance requirements.

The Convenience Factor

In addition to low costs, your financial institution should offer services that make it easy to use and should be conveniently located. Obviously, you want a financial institution that's located near your home—the closer you are to the bank, the easier it is to

Direct Deposit

The depositing of payments—for example, payroll checks—directly into your checking account. This is done electronically.

Safety Deposit Box

A storage unit at a bank or other financial institution in which valuables and important documents are stored for safekeeping.

Overdraft Protection

Provision of an automatic loan to your checking account whenever sufficient funds are not available to cover checks that have been written against the account.

Stop Payment

An order you can give your financial institution to stop payment on a check you've written.

make financial transactions. However, there are other dimensions to convenience. For example, having access to a cash or automated teller machine not only at the financial institution's location but all across the nation makes it easier for you to access your account. In addition, having safety deposit boxes, **direct deposit** services, and overdraft protection are other conveniences.

Safety Deposit Boxes. **Safety deposit boxes** serve as important storage places for financial documents and valuables. Smaller safety deposit boxes can cost as little as $25 to $50 per year, with the costs varying by location and increasing as the size of the box increases. There are two keys to every safety deposit box. You're given one key, and the financial institution retains the second key. Both keys are needed to open the box. Given the importance of access to your stored items, it's worthwhile to have your safety deposit box located in a financial institution close to your home.

Overdraft Protection. **Overdraft protection** involves an automatic loan made to your checking account whenever your account doesn't contain enough cash to cover the checks that you've written against your account. As a result, checks drawn against a checking account with overdraft protection will not bounce. Given the charges made for bounced checks, and the hassle of dealing with them, overdraft protection is certainly a good feature. Overdraft loans generally come in $100 increments, so if your checking account is $5 overdrawn, you receive an automatic loan of $100 and now have a checking-account balance of $95. The downside of overdraft protection is that the interest rate charged on the overdraft loan may be quite high. Although overdraft protection is desirable, it's still a convenience that shouldn't be relied upon and should instead be viewed as a safety net against errors you may make in determining the balance of your checking account.

Another convenience is the ability to give a **stop payment** on a check. If you want to cancel a check that you've already written, you can call your financial institution and ask that payment on this check be stopped. You'll generally have to follow up with a written authorization to stop payment on the check, which generally involves a cost of between $5 and $20. This stop payment remains in effect for a limited time period, but can be extended at an additional cost. If the check slips through and gets paid while the stop payment is in effect, the financial institution will bear the responsibility for the payment.

The Consideration Factor

In choosing a financial institution, you want one that will give you personal attention. If you have a problem, you want to feel comfortable in approaching a manager or employee and have that person deal with it. If you need financial advice, is there a knowledgeable person who's easily approachable? Although automated teller machines are extremely convenient, they don't answer questions, correct whatever's wrong, or work with you when you need a loan. If you're not satisfied with the personal attention you get, move your account. A smaller financial institution and a small branch location are good places to look for the consideration characteristics you desire in a financial institution. Because of their smaller size, it's often easier for them to provide the personal attention that you need.

Balancing Your Checking Account

Anyone who's ever tried to build anything with blocks knows that unbalanced objects tend to fall over. Checking accounts can be the same way. If the records you keep in your check register produce the same numbers that appear in your statement, your checking account is balanced. If not, well, you'd better hope that you have overdraft protection. Although it's not essential that your checking account be perfectly balanced at all times, you're a lot less likely to accidentally bounce a check if your account is balanced. The basics of balancing your checkbook are relatively simple. First, you've got to keep track of every transaction on your account—every check you write, every deposit, every ATM transaction—and enter it in your check register. Obviously, if you don't keep track of the checks you've written and the ATM withdrawals you've made, you can't balance your checkbook. Then, when your monthly statement arrives, check it against your check register to make sure that no mistakes have been made. If you've received interest on your account or had any bad check charges, enter them. Then, try to reconcile what you think your balance is with what the bank says your balance is.

By reconciling your balance with the monthly statement you receive from your bank, you can locate any errors you or the bank might have made. Figures 5.4 and 5.5 show you how to balance an average checking account. Today, many banks provide a reconciliation form on the back of their monthly statements. To determine your account register balance, you begin with the ending statement balance shown on your monthly checking-account statement. To this you add any deposits or credits you've made since the statement date. You then subtract out any outstanding checks or debits issued by you but not yet paid as of the date of the monthly bank statement. The difference should be the ending balance on your current statement. If this number doesn't agree with the account register balance, then you should check your math and make sure that all transactions are correct and were entered into your register.

Other Types of Checks

Many times, if the purchase amount is very large or you are buying abroad, a personal check isn't an acceptable form of payment for sellers. After all, what guarantee do they have that you've got enough money in your account to cover the check? In that case, you can guarantee payment through the use of a cashier's check, a certified check, a money order, or a traveler's check.

Cashier's Check. A **cashier's check** is a check drawn on the bank or financial institution's account. These checks can be used by people with no checking account. Because it's really a check from a bank, it can bounce only if the bank doesn't have funds to cover it—which isn't too likely. A cashier's check will usually cost you a fee of around $10, as well as the amount of the check. The bank then writes a check from its own account to a specific payee.

Certified Check. A **certified check** is a personal check that has been certified as being good by the financial institution on which it's drawn. To certify a check, the bank first makes sure there are sufficient funds in the individual's account to cover the check. Funds equal to the amount of the check are then immediately frozen, and the check is certified. The cost for this service generally runs around $10 per certified check.

Money Order. A **money order** is a variation of the cashier's check, except that it's generally issued by the U.S. Postal Service or some other nonbanking institution. For example, money orders can be purchased at many 7-Eleven stores. The fee associated with a money order generally varies depending upon the size of the money order.

Traveler's Checks. **Traveler's checks** are similar to cashier's checks except that they don't specify a specific payee, and they come in specific denominations ($20, $50, and $100). They're issued by large financial institutions, such as Citibank, Visa, and American Express, and are sold through local banking institutions. The advantage of traveler's checks is that they're accepted almost anywhere in the world because they are viewed as riskless checks. Also, if lost or stolen, they're generally replaced quickly, without charge.

Cashier's Check
A check drawn on a bank or financial institution's account.

Certified Check
A personal check that's been certified as being good by the financial institution on which its drawn.

Money Order
A check similar to a cashier's check except that it is generally issued by the U.S. Postal Service or some other nonbanking institution.

Traveler's Checks
Checks issued by large financial institutions, such as Citibank, VISA, and American Express, which are sold through local banking institutions and which are similar to cashier's checks except that they don't specify a specific payee and come in specific denominations ($20, $50, and $100).

ELECTRONIC FUNDS TRANSFERS (EFTs)

Electronic Funds Transfer (EFT)
Any financial transaction that takes place electronically.

The area of cash management that's changing the fastest today centers on **electronic funds transfer (EFT)**, which refers to any financial transaction that takes place electronically. In effect, with an EFT, funds move between accounts instantly and without paper. Examples of EFTs are paying for your groceries with a debit card, withdrawing cash from an automated teller machine, or having your paycheck directly deposited at your bank. The advantages of electronic funds transfers are that the transactions take place immediately, and the consumer doesn't have to carry cash or write a check. They're great for things like paying bills without having to write checks—bills such as insurance premiums, mortgage payments, phone, and utilities. As a result, EFTs can tighten up your cash management habits by ensuring that you never carry cash. It's ironic that you might be better able to manage your cash by not using cash.

FIGURE 5.4

Worksheet for Balancing Your Checking Account

1. Record in your check register all items which appear on the monthly statement that you received from your bank that have not previously been entered, for example, cash withdrawals from an ATM, automatic transfers, service charges, and any other transactions.
2. In your checking-account register, check off any deposits or credits and checks or debits shown on the monthly statement from your bank.
3. In the Deposits and Credits section below (section A), list any deposits that have been made since the date of the statement.

Section A: Deposits and Credits

Date	Amount
1.	
2.	
3.	
4.	
5.	
6.	
Total Amount:	_____

4. In the Outstanding Checks and Debits section below (section B), list any checks and debits issued by you that have not yet been reported on your account statement.

Section B: Outstanding Checks and Debits

Check Number	Amount
1.	
2.	
3.	
4.	
5.	
6.	
7.	
Total Amount:	_____

(continued)

FIGURE 5.4

(continued)

5. Write in the Ending Statement Balance provided in the monthly statement that you received from your bank. . . . . _____

6. Write in the total amount of the Deposits and Credits you have made since the statement date (total of section A above). . . . . + _____

7. Total the amounts in lines 5 and 6. . . . . = _____

8. Write in the total amounts of outstanding Checks and Debits (total of section B above). . . . . − _____

9. Subtract the amount in line 8 from the amount in line 7. This is your **Adjusted Statement Balance**. . . . . = _____

If your Adjusted Statement Balance as calculated above does not agree with your Account Register Balance:

A. Review last month's statement to reconcilement to make sure any differences were corrected.

B. Check to make sure that all deposits, interest earned, and service charges shown on the monthly statement from your bank are included in your account register.

C. Check your addition and subtraction in both your account register and in this month's checking-account balance reconcilement above.

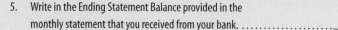

Balancing Your Checking Account

FIGURE 5.5

Ending Balance from Bank Statement

▼ Plus

Total Deposit and Credits Since the Bank Statement Date ▶ Less

Total Outstanding Checks and Debits
(for example, ATM charges)

▼ Equals

Adjusted Statement Balance

This should equal the balance on your checking-account register. If this doesn't equal your Account Register Balance:

● Check last month's statement to be sure it was balanced.

● Make sure all deposits and withdrawals, interest earned, and service charges are included on your account register.

● Check your math.

Transfer funds electronically using automated teller machines (ATMs), debit cards, and smart cards, and understand how these electronic funds transfers (EFTs) work.

Automated Teller Machine (ATM) or Cash Machine
Machines found at most financial institutions that can be used to make withdrawals, deposits, transfers, and account inquiries.

Personal Identification Number (PIN)
A four- to seven-digit personal identification number assigned to your credit account.

Debit Card
A card that allows you to access the money in your accounts electronically.

To give you a better understanding of EFT and how it affects you, we'll discuss automated teller machines, debit cards, and smart cards in the following sections. You'll notice that there's no mention of credit cards here. Why? Because credit cards don't involve the electronic transfer of money—they involve the electronic *borrowing* of money. Don't worry, we'll deal with them in detail in the next chapter.

Automated Teller Machines (ATMs)

An **automated teller machine (ATM)** or **cash machine** provides cash instantly and can be accessed through a credit or debit card. If you use a credit card to access the ATM, then the cash is "borrowed" from the line of credit you have with the financial institution that issued your credit card. Because these funds are borrowed, you begin paying usually very high interest on them immediately. It can also be used to access funds held in an account—for example, funds can be withdrawn from your checking account.

The obvious appeal of ATMs is their convenience. ATMs don't close and are available around the world. To use an ATM you must insert your card and punch in your **personal identification number**, or **PIN**, which is a four- to seven-digit personal identification number assigned to your account. However, as with everything else in finance, there's a cost to convenience. In the case of ATMs, most banks charge an access fee for any transaction. Moreover, if you're using an ATM not owned by the bank that issued your card, this charge can range up to $3 per transaction. The bank that owns the ATM can also charge you up to $2 for using its machine. At a grand total of up to $5 per transaction, using an ATM can be quite expensive.

Although costs can be a problem with an ATM transaction, the big problem is crime. Obviously, most people that walk away from an ATM machine have money on them. As a result, ATM machines tend to attract crime. This doesn't mean that you shouldn't use them, but you should be careful when using them. Don't use them late at night, don't use them in isolated areas, don't be the only person at the ATM, and don't drive up to an ATM in an unlocked car. In addition, take care to make sure that no one has access to your PIN. Although your liability for unauthorized transactions on an ATM is only $50 provided you notify the bank immediately (it jumps to $500 if a delay of 2 days in reporting occurs and becomes unlimited if the delay exceeds 60 days), you should choose a PIN different from your birthday, Social Security number, street address, or any other number that a criminal might logically guess. It simply isn't smart to be anything less than cautious. Figure 5.6 provides a number of steps to follow to ensure ATM security.

Debit Cards

A **debit card** is something of a cross between a credit card and a checking account. It's like a credit card in that it's a plastic card you can use instead of cash, but it works more like a checking account. When you write a check, you're spending money that you have in your checking account, and, unless you have overdraft protection, you can't write a check for more than what's in your account. Similarly, a debit card is linked to an account, and when you use it, you're spending the money in that account—kind of like writing an electronic check, only there's no paper involved, and the check gets "cashed" instantly. When the money in your account runs out, you can't use your debit card again until you make another deposit, which can be quite an advantage for those prone to overspending. Debit cards, like credit cards, allow you to avoid carrying cash, but, unlike credit cards, they also allow you to avoid carrying a big credit card balance. After all, with a debit card, you're spending your own money, as opposed to borrowing money when you use a credit card. You probably have a debit card now: Your ATM card is actually a type of debit card. Formal debit cards are gaining more popularity with financial institutions, and some predict that debit cards will soon replace checking accounts.

KEEP YOUR CARD SECURE

☑ **Treat your ATM card like cash.** Always keep your card in a safe place. It's a good idea to store your card in a card sleeve. The sleeve protects the card's magnetic strip and helps ensure that the card functions properly.

☑ **Keep your "secret code" a secret.** Your ATM card will only work with your personal identification number, or PIN. Memorize your code. Never write it on your card or store it with the card. Never tell your code to anyone. And never let someone else enter your code for you.

☑ **Do not give out any information over the telephone.** No one needs to know your secret code.

☑ **Report a lost or stolen card at once.** Even though your ATM card cannot be used without your secret code, promptly report a lost or stolen card.

☑ **Check your receipts against your monthly statement to guard against ATM fraud.**

SECURITY AT WALK-UP ATMs

☑ **Always observe your surroundings before conducting an ATM transaction.** If you are driving to an ATM, park as close as possible to the terminal. Observe the entire area from the safety of your car before getting out. If you see anyone or anything suspicious, leave the area at once.

☑ **If an ATM is obstructed from view or poorly lit, go to another ATM.**

☑ **Whenever possible, take a companion along when using an ATM—especially at night.**

☑ **Minimize time spent at the ATM by having your card out and ready to use.**

☑ **Stand between the ATM and anyone waiting to use the terminal so that others cannot see your secret code or transaction amount.**

☑ **If you see anyone or anything suspicious while conducting a transaction, cancel your transaction and leave.**

☑ **If you are followed after making an ATM transaction, go immediately to a heavily populated, well-lighted area and call the police.**

SECURITY AT DRIVE-UP ATMs

☑ **Keep your engine running, the doors locked, and the windows up at all times when waiting in line at a drive-up ATM.**

☑ **When possible, leave enough room between cars to allow for a quick exit should it become necessary.**

☑ **Before rolling down the windows to use the ATM, check the entire area for anything or anyone suspicious.**

☑ **Minimize time spent at the ATM by having your card out and ready to use.**

☑ **If you see anyone or anything suspicious while conducting a transaction, cancel your transaction and leave.**

☑ **If you are followed after making an ATM transaction, go immediately to a heavily populated, well-lighted area and call the police.**

There are actually two forms of debit cards. One is the basic debit card, which may have a somewhat limited usage. For example, a local bank may issue a debit card that electronically withdraws payment from the cardholder's account, and this card may be used in ATM machines. Debit cards are also issued in conjunction with Visa or Master-Card, called Visa Debit and MasterDebit cards, and are accepted almost anywhere.

Smart Cards

Smart cards, sometimes called memory cards or electronic wallets, are a variation on debit cards, but instead of withdrawing funds from a designated account with a bank, you withdraw them from an account that's actually stored magnetically in the smart card. The issuing bank or financial institution transfers funds into the smart card, which you can then use in much the same way you use a credit or debit card. When the funds allocated to your card run out, you have to put more funds into it before you can use it again. Smart cards perform the same service as credit or debit cards—they can be used at the grocery store to buy groceries, or at a restaurant to pay for food and such. In addition, there are smart cards with issuer-limited usage—they can be used only by the business that issues the cards. For example, Kinkos issues smart cards for copying. You receive a card and "buy" future usage at a Kinko's copying machine. In addition, many universities provide smart cards to their students. The student deposits funds in the smart card, and the card can then be used in vending machines throughout campus, for meals in dining halls, in copy machines in the library, and to buy tickets to university events. The advantages to the issuing agency are that they receive use of the funds in the smart cards before the transactions are completed and they can reduce paperwork considerably. The advantages to the user are that smart cards are convenient and they reduce the need to carry around cash.

Fixing Mistakes—Theirs, Not Yours

How can errors occur in EFTs? Sometimes they're human errors—not getting full credit for deposits—and sometimes they're computer errors. Unfortunately, electronic glitches can occur. The first step in dealing with errors is to avoid letting them occur. You may not have much control with computer errors, but you can help avoid human errors. Perhaps the most common human error involves deposits, with most problems stemming from cash deposits made directly in ATMs. To avoid this type of error, never deposit cash in an ATM. If an error occurs and you aren't credited for what you deposited, it's very difficult to prove that you're right. If an error occurs, report it immediately. Call the bank, and if it's closed, try to leave a message. By law you must write to the bank within 60 days of receiving your statement. If you can't settle the dispute with the bank, write to the Federal Reserve Board's Division of Consumer and Community Affairs, 20th and C Streets NW, Washington, DC 20551.

SUMMARY

Cash management refers to the management of your cash and liquid assets. Liquid assets allow you to invest your money while still keeping it available to pay bills or to cover an emergency. Although liquid asset investments are low risk and provide you with emergency funds, they don't provide you with a very good return. The basic idea behind cash management is balancing the risk of not having enough in the way of liquid assets with the potential for greater return on other investments.

In recent years there have been many changes in the field of cash management, and nowhere is this more evident than in financial institutions themselves. Industry changes and increased competition have resulted in a vast reshaping of many institutions. However, we can still divide them into deposit-type institutions (banks) and nondeposit-type institutions. Recently, nondeposit institutions have been offering traditional banking services, resulting in more choices than ever for managing your cash.

Given the number of different financial institutions vying for your liquid funds, it's no surprise that there are a variety of different cash management alternatives available. Table 5.1 provides a summary of these alternatives and their advantages and disadvantages.

When comparing the different liquid investment alternatives, you must look not only at their return, but also at how safe they are. In addition, you must remember that the only valid rate comparisons are ones that use similar compounding methods (annual, semiannual, and so on) and have similar tax treatment.

The key to meeting long-term goals is to start saving early and to make saving a regimented part of your everyday life. Remember, what you don't see you can't spend. As such, you should have some of your income automatically placed in savings, forcing you to learn to live at your take-home salary level.

Your checking account is your most essential cash management tool. When deciding where to open a checking account, you should give consideration to the three C's: cost, convenience, and consideration. You should also keep an eye out for safety—are your funds federally insured?

The term "electronic funds transfer" refers to any financial transaction that takes place electronically, for example, paying for dinner with a debit card or having your paycheck directly deposited at your bank. The advantages of electronic funds transfer is that the transaction takes place immediately and the consumer can make the transaction without having to carry cash or write a check.

Review Questions

1. What are liquid assets and why are they important in cash management? (LO 1)
2. What factors have affected the alternatives available to consumers for cash management? (LO 1)
3. Name three characteristics of liquid assets. (LO 1)
4. Give two examples of both deposit-type and nondeposit-type financial institutions. Describe their similarities. (LO 2)
5. Describe and compare the differences between commercial banks, S&Ls, and savings banks. (LO 3)
6. What is a credit union, and what are some of its distinguishing features? (LO 3, 4)
7. What factors should be considered in the selection of a financial institution? (LO 3)
8. What is a NOW account? What are its advantages and disadvantages? (LO 3, 4)
9. Describe and compare a money market deposit account (MMDA) and a money market mutual fund (MMMF). (LO 3, 4)
10. List three characteristics of certificates of deposit (CDs). (LO 3)
11. Describe how an asset management account works and what financial services are included. (LO 3)
12. Describe and compare two common federal government debt instruments: Treasury bills and U.S. Series EE savings bonds. (LO 3)
13. Explain how a person's marginal tax rate affects his or her real rate of return on investments. (LO 4)
14. What are electronic funds transfers (EFTs)? Describe and compare three different types of EFTs. (LO 7)

Problems and Activities

1. List five examples of financial emergencies that necessitate having liquid assets. (LO 1)
2. Brian and Cindy Duval together earn a $42,000 gross annual income, $36,000 after taxes. Their monthly expenses total $2,200. How much of an emergency fund should they have? (LO 1)

WWW.
Take It to the Net

We invite you to visit the Keown Personal Finance page on the Prentice Hall Web site at:

http://www.prenhall.com/ persfin

for this chapter's World Wide Web exercise.

You might also want to visit the following Web sites:

USA Today Saver's Scoreboard (with available rates listed): http:// web.usatoday.com/money/ savebox.htm

The Money Page: http:// www.moneypage.com

Banking Web site links: http:// www.occ.treas.gov/Sites.htm

Federal Reserve System: http:// www.stls.frb.org/fedsystm.html

Federal Deposit Insurance Corporation: http://www.irs.ustreas.gov/ prod/

Bank Rate Monitor: http:// www.bankrate.com

3. ABC Bank requires a minimum balance of $2,500 for an interest-bearing checking account. Your monthly expenses total $1,300. What is the annual opportunity cost of the forced balance if the checking account pays 2-percent interest and you could earn 5 percent elsewhere? (LO 3)

4. List three examples of short-term goals and expenses for which liquid assets would be an appropriate vehicle to place funds. (LO 1)

5. What is the amount of interest earned on a 3-month Treasury bill if you pay $9,812 to purchase it and receive its full face value at maturity? (LO 2)

6. Calculate the after-tax return of a 7-percent corporate bond for an investor in the 15-percent marginal tax bracket. Compare this yield to a 5.5-percent tax-exempt municipal bond and explain which is a better alternative. Repeat the calculations and comparison for a 28-percent tax bracket investor. (LO 4)

7. Jane Ryan has two accounts, one for $60,000 and the other for $75,000, at ABC Bank. What amount of savings is covered by FDIC insurance? If the two accounts were split between ABC Bank ($60,000) and XYZ Bank ($75,000), how much of Jane's savings would be FDIC insured? (LO 2)

8. Calculate the real rate of return to a taxpayer in the 28-percent marginal tax bracket on a $50,000 money market account, assuming a 4.5-percent yield and 3-percent inflation. What are the implications of this result for cash management decisions? (LO 1)

9. Describe the features you have used—or would use in the future—to select a checking account. (LO 3)

10. Ben James never seems to have enough change to make copies at the university library. What type of electronic funds transfer (EFT) instrument would help him do his copying with less hassle? (LO 7)

Suggested Projects

1. Pick a type of liquid asset (for example, money market mutual fund, checking account, CD) and compare the characteristics of at least three available products. Describe which is the best alternative for you. (LO 3)

2. Use the formula provided in Figure 5.5 to reconcile the balance in a bank or credit union checking account. (LO 6)

3. Based on your current income and expenses, calculate the amount of emergency funds you should have. Describe where you would place this money and why. (LO 1)

4. Interview a stockbroker about the characteristics of liquid assets sold by brokerage firms. Inquire about the fees charged for purchasing these products and the interest rates that can be earned. Request and read available product literature. (LO 3)

5. Compare your current bank or credit union checking account to at least two others according to the "three C's" criteria. Describe which is the best account for you and why. (LO 3)

6. Select and purchase a new liquid asset (for example, bank account, CD, Series EE bond). Describe the purchase process (for example, dollar cost, "paperwork") and your anticipated future use of this money. (LO 3)

7. Describe a past experience using electronic funds transfer (EFT) technology. What were the advantages and disadvantages? What additional ways do you plan to use EFTs in the future? (LO 7)

8. Review your latest savings account statement. Find the annual percentage yield (APY) paid on your account and compare it to the financial institution's "quoted rate." Also check the method used to determine the account balance on which interest is credited. (LO 4)

9. Calculate the after-tax return and real (after inflation) return of a liquid asset that you own. (LO 4)

Just Do It! *From the Desk of Marcy Furney, CFP*
Check It Out

☑ Balance your checkbook *immediately after receiving your statement every month*. You'll know where you stand and avoid possible charges for letting your balance get too low or bouncing checks. Follow the process of marking off each canceled check in your register and comparing your balance to the balance on the statement. Don't just take the bank's word for it.

☑ Subtract any automatic electronic fund transfers or bank drafts for next month when you do your checking-account reconciliation. This avoids forgetting them and the possibility of overdraft. EFTs are a great time and postage saver for such recurring bills as insurance payments, mortgages, and car payments, but you must keep up with them. A $20 insufficient funds fee for each returned check can cancel out a lot of benefit.

☑ If you have a computer, consider purchasing personal bookkeeping software. Most programs are very easy to use and are excellent sources of information for budgeting, cash flow analysis, and even tracking debt and investments.

☑ Include in your check register what each check was written for. Many registers provide a shaded line below each check entry for that purpose. If yours doesn't, just record checks on every other line and fill in the reason below each one. At the end of each month, take a few minutes to analyze your spending. *Caution:* Entries such as "misc." or "household item" aren't very useful.

☑ Examine your bank statement for any charges or maintenance fees and make sure they're actually due. Ideally you should find a bank that charges no monthly fees if the balance is kept at a reasonably low level. Be aware that minimum balances may be calculated in different ways. Some may charge a fee if your balance *ever* goes below a given amount, while others use an average daily balance calculation.

☑ Scan the inserts in your monthly bank statement. Even though they may appear to be "junk mail," they're your bank's means of notifying you regarding important procedural and charging changes.

☑ FYI—you don't have to use the bank's check-printing services in most cases. If you write many checks each year, you could have a sizable savings by ordering checks from other printing firms. Do ask your banker before ordering. Some claim their processing systems can't read "cheap checks."

Discussion Case 1

Sara Crane, 22, has just moved to Dallas to begin her first professional job. She's concerned about her finances and, specifically, wants to save for a "rainy day" and a down payment on a new car in 2 years. Sara's new job pays $28,500. She keeps $24,000 after taxes, and her monthly expenses total $1,600. Sara's new employer offers a 401(k) plan and matches employee contributions up to 6 percent of their salary. The employer also provides a credit union and a U.S. savings bond purchase program.

Sara's older brother, Todd, has urged Sara to start saving from "day one" on the job. Todd has lost a job twice in the last 5 years through company downsizing and now keeps $35,000 in a 4-percent money market mutual fund in case it happens again. Todd's annual take-home pay is $36,000.

Sara has started shopping around for accounts to hold her liquid assets. She'd like to earn the highest rate possible and avoid paying fees for falling below a specified minimum balance. She plans to open two accounts: one for paying monthly bills and another for short-term savings.

Questions

1. Name three ways that Sara could automate her savings.

2. What major factors should Sara consider when selecting a checking and/or savings account?

3. Why does Sara need an emergency fund? How much emergency savings should she try to set aside?

4. Comment on Todd's use of liquid assets.

5. Which liquid asset vehicle(s) would you recommend for paying Sara's monthly expenses and for her savings for the car down payment?

Discussion Case 2

Tony James recently received a $5,000 inheritance. He has an adequate emergency fund and is seeking a higher return than what's currently available on a bank savings account. Tony plans to use this money, plus the interest it earns, for the down payment on a car in 2 years. He recently talked to a car dealer who told him that, when he buys the car, he'll need to bring a cashier's check.

Tony recently learned that he's in the 28-percent marginal tax bracket. He has also narrowed his asset choices to the following: a 4-percent tax-free money market mutual fund, a 5.25-percent 2-year certificate of deposit (CD), a brokerage firm asset management account, and a stock mutual fund.

A frequent business traveler, Tony is out of town a lot or finds banks closed when he needs to cash his paycheck or make a cash withdrawal. He's looking for an easier way to manage his finances and pay his bills on time.

Questions

1. Why might the car dealer require a cashier's check for customer car down payments? Why do you think a cashier's check is preferable to a certified check?

2. Which investment will pay Tony the highest after-tax return, the 4-percent tax-free money market fund or the 5.5-percent CD?

3. Comment on the characteristics and appropriateness of Tony funding a brokerage asset management account or a stock mutual fund with his inheritance money instead of buying a car with it.

4. List at least three ways that Tony could simplify the management of his finances.

5. What are two major advantages for Tony of enrolling in an automated payroll savings program?

Chapter 6

USING CREDIT CARDS:
The Role of Open Credit in Personal Financial Management

As any parent knows, when you need Power Rangers "stuff," the place to go is Toys 'Я' Us, and, as any parent knows, you can spend a lot of money there. As a result, Toys 'Я' Us issues a lot of credit cards, but not to Lawrence B. Lindsey. Lindsey has a clean credit record, earns $123,100 a year, is a member of the Federal Reserve Board in Washington, DC, *and* was refused a Toys 'Я' Us, Inc., credit card from the Bank of New York.

Lindsey had two major strikes against him: eight companies had checked his credit history in the last 6 months and he doesn't have a savings account. These "strikes" usually indicate a bad credit risk, but not in Lindsey's case. The credit checks were due to refinancing a mortgage and a change in an equity line account. The lack of a savings account is actually considered by some as the sign of a wise investor. Not only is he a wise investor, but he's a member of the Federal Reserve Board, the agency that manages our economy, sets interest rates, and regulates banks. Hey, if a member of the Federal Reserve Board can't get a credit card, who can? Eventually, Lindsey was offered a Toys 'Я' Us credit card—and an apology. You might be wondering what happened to the poor bozo that turned down Lindsey's credit application. The answer is, not much. That "poor bozo" was a computer, and perhaps the same computer that's making credit decisions about you—not a comforting thought.

Learning Objectives

After reading this chapter you should be able to:

1. Know how credit cards work.
2. Understand the costs involved with credit cards.
3. Describe the different types of credit cards and their advantages and disadvantages.
4. Know what determines your credit card worthiness and how to secure a credit card.
5. Manage your credit cards and open credit.

If you've ever had to make hotel reservations or buy concert tickets over the phone, you understand the importance of having a credit card. To manage in today's economy, where so much is bought and sold over the phone or the Internet, you really need to have a credit card. And almost everyone has one. In fact, Americans hold more than 1.1 billion credit cards of all types, not to mention all the charge accounts they have. There's just no denying that having and using credit cards has become part of our financial culture. You can't beat them for convenience, but if you're not careful, you can't beat them for cost, either. Credit cards can be deceptively expensive, some even charging over 20-percent interest on unpaid balances. Most people don't consider these interest charges when they're buying whatever it is that they've just got to have at that moment. As a result, the total sum of outstanding balances on credit cards in the United States is estimated to be over $300 billion. If the interest rate on this sum were 20 percent, that would mean America is paying $60 billion each year in credit card charges. Unless you want to pay out your share of $60 billion, you'd better manage your credit cards wisely. How you manage them can either save you or cost you an awful lot of money.

Credit
Receiving cash, goods, or services with an obligation to pay later.

Open Credit or **Revolving Credit**
A line of credit that you can use and then pay back at whatever pace you like so long as you pay a minimum balance each month, paying interest on the unpaid balance.

Annual Percentage Rate (APR)
The true simple interest rate paid over the life of the loan. It's a reasonable approximation for the true cost of borrowing, and the Truth in Lending Act requires that all consumer loan agreements disclose the APR in bold print.

AN INTRODUCTION TO CREDIT CARDS AND OPEN CREDIT

Credit involves receiving cash, goods, or services with an obligation to pay later. In shopper's language, "Charge it," "Put it on my account," and "I'll pay for it with plastic," are all opening lines to the use of credit. Credit purchases made for personal, as opposed to business, needs other than for home mortgages are referred to collectively as consumer credit.

Open credit or **revolving credit** refers to a line of consumer credit that's extended before you make a purchase. Once you use open credit, you can pay back your debt at whatever pace you like so long as you pay a specified minimum balance each month. Today, most consumer credit comes in the form of credit card purchases, but consumer credit involves more than just credit cards. It's actually any type of charge or credit account, all the way from the charge account you have at a local hardware store, to an Exxon charge card, to a credit account you have with your broker, and back to your Rolling Stone Visa card. However, credit cards dominate, which isn't that surprising, given that there are around 7,000 different kinds of Visas, MasterCards, and other cards to choose from. Because of the dominance of credit cards, most of our discussion will focus on them, but the same basic principles also apply to all credit accounts.

When buying on credit, you can charge whatever you want, as long as you stay under the credit limit. Each month you'll receive a statement that shows both the outstanding balance on your account and the minimum payment due. You can then pay anywhere between the minimum payment and the balance. Any unpaid balance plus interest on that unpaid balance carries over and becomes part of next month's outstanding balance. As long as you pay the minimum balance every month, the credit issuer will continue to extend a line of credit to you.

As you probably already know, the higher the balance you maintain on your credit lines, the higher your costs will be. There are a number of factors that go toward determining exactly what your costs will be. Let's now take a look at the basic factors that affect the costs of credit cards and other forms of open credit: the interest rate, the balance calculation method, the grace period, the annual fee, and other additional or penalty fees.

Interest Rates

The main factor that determines the cost of a line of open credit is the **annual percentage rate (APR)**, which is the true simple interest rate paid over the life of the loan. It takes all costs into account, including interest on the balance, the cost of credit reports, the cost of all possible fees, and so forth. The importance of the APR is that it's calculated the same way by all lenders, and the Truth in Lending Act requires that all consumer loan agreements disclose the APR in bold print. As a result, it's a good place to start in comparing competing lines of credit. The APR can vary dramatically from one credit account to another. Looking at credit cards, in mid-1997 when the national average APR was 17.1 percent, one bank offered credit cards with rates as low as 7.99 percent. Rates can vary not only from one account to another, but also over time on the same card. Some rates stay fixed, but others can and will change based on market factors. Some credit cards also offer low introductory rates called "teaser rates." These initial rates, which last 3 months to a year, can run as low as 4.9 percent, but they typically jump to 17 to 18 percent after the introductory period is over. About two-thirds of the credit card offers that are sent out in the mail each year have some type of teaser rate.

Also keep in mind that most credit accounts compound interest—that is, you end up paying interest on interest. So, if your credit card compounds interest on a monthly basis and you carry a balance, you could end up effectively paying a rate of 21.7 percent on a credit card with a 19.8-percent APR.

Calculating the Balance Owed

Once you know your APR, it's easy to calculate the cost of your credit account. You simply multiply your APR by your outstanding balance. That's easy enough, right? Wrong. The **method of determining the balance** (or **balance calculation method**) can also vary from one credit account to another. The best way to keep the average balance calculation from confusing the process of selecting the best credit account is to pay off the outstanding balance each month. In that case there is no unpaid balance and therefore no interest charge.

The three primary methods used to determine interest charges on an unpaid credit balance are (1) the average daily balance method, (2) the previous balance method, and (3) the adjusted balance method.

The most commonly used method for calculating interest payments is the **average daily balance method**. This method adds up your daily balances for each day during the billing period and then divides this sum by the number of days in the billing period to calculate your average balance. Your interest payments are then based upon this balance.

An alternative to this method is the **previous balance method**, in which interest payments are charged against what you owed at the end of the previous billing period, with no credit given for this month's payments. This method is relatively simple, but it's also expensive.

A third method used by lenders is the **adjusted balance method**, which is a favorable variation of the previous balance method. Under this method interest is charged against the previous month's balance only after any payments have been subtracted out. Because interest isn't charged on payments, this method results in lower interest charges than does the previous balance method. An example of interest calculations using these three methods is given in Figure 6.1.

In addition, there are numerous variations to these three methods. For example, some lenders calculate the average daily balance *including* new purchases, while others *exclude* them. Also, there's been a recent trend toward using a two-cycle average daily balance. Under this approach, interest is calculated over the past two billing periods any time the entire balance isn't completely paid off. Actually, the interest payments are the same under the two-cycle and one-cycle average daily balance methods for anyone who pays off the balance each month or who carries a balance from month to month. The big losers under a two-cycle average daily balance method are those who periodically pay off their entire balance. In fact, a study by the Bankcard Holders of America showed that a cardholder with a 19.8-percent interest rate who charged $1,000 per month, paid only the minimum payment except for every third month when the entire balance was paid, and continued this pattern for the entire year, would pay only $132 in finance charges under the one-cycle method but would pay over $196 in finance charges under the two-cycle method. To say the least, calculating the charges on your balance is extremely confusing, but there's one surefire way around this problem: Pay off your balance every month.

> ### *The Facts of Life*
> In 1995, the number of credit card solicitations flooding mailboxes increased to approximately 2.7 billion. That's about 17 solicitations for every American aged 18 to 64.

Buying Money—The Cash Advance

Many credit cards allow you to receive cash advances at ATM machines. In effect, you're taking out a loan when you get a cash advance—and it's an extremely expensive

Method of Determining the Balance (or Balance Calculation Method)
The method by which a credit card balance is determined. The finance charges are then based upon the level of this balance.

Average Daily Balance Method
A method of calculating the balance upon which interest is paid by summing the outstanding balances owed each day during the billing period and dividing by the number of days in the period.

Previous Balance Method
A method of calculating interest payments on outstanding credit using the balance at the end of the previous billing period.

Adjusted Balance Method
A method of calculating interest payments on outstanding credit in which interest payments are charged against the balance at the end of the previous billing period less any payments and returns made.

FIGURE 6.1

Calculation of Interest on Outstanding Balances

Example: Your credit card interest rate is 18% and you begin the month with a previous balance of $1,000. In addition, your payments against your credit card balance this month are $900, which are made on the 15th of the month. You make no additional purchases during the month.

Calculate your average daily balance by summing the daily balances and dividing by the number of days in the period.

Average Daily Balance Method

Monthly Interest Rate	1.5%
Sum of All Daily Balances During the Billing Period	$16,500
Days in Billing Period	30 days
Average Daily Balance	$550
Interest Charged	$8.25
	($550 × 1.5%)

Under the previous balance method, interest payments are charged against the balance at the end of the previous billing period. In effect, interest is charged on the entire closing balance regardless of whether or not payments and returns are made. Thus, regardless of the size of any partial credit repayment during the month, you will still pay interest on the total unpaid balance you had at the end of the previous billing period.

Previous Balance Method

Monthly Interest Rate	1.5%
Previous Balance	$1,000
Payments	$900
Interest Charged	$15.00
	($1,000 × 1.5%)

The adjusted balance method is a favorable variation of the previous balance method in which interest payments are charged against the balance at the end of the previous billing period less any payments and returns made. Since interest is not charged on payments, this method results in lower interest charges than does the previous balance method.

Adjusted Balance Method

Monthly Interest Rate	1.5%
Previous Balance	$1,000
Payments	$900
Interest Charged	$1.50
	($100 × 1.5%)

way to borrow money. In addition, when you withdraw cash from an ATM machine using your credit card, you begin paying interest *immediately*. Not only do you begin paying interest immediately, but many credit cards charge a higher rate on cash advances than they do on normal purchases. Keep in mind that although you can give yourself a big, fat, immediate cash loan using your credit card, that loan comes with some big, fat immediate charges.

The Grace Period

Grace Period

The length of time given to make a payment before interest is charged against the outstanding balance on a credit card.

Typically, the lender allows you a **grace period** before charging you interest on your outstanding balance. For most credit cards, there's a 22- to 25-day grace period from the date of the bill. Once the grace period has passed, you're charged the APR on the balance as determined by the credit card issuer. As a result of the grace period, finance charges might not be assessed against credit card purchases for almost 2 months. For example, if the credit card issuer mails out bills on the first of the month, then a purchase made on the second of the month would not appear until the next month's bill and not have to be paid until the end of the grace period either—22 to 25 days after that—a total of almost 2 months. Although most credit cards allow a grace period on normal purchases, it's a general rule that with cash advances there is no grace period, meaning that finance charges are assessed against the cash advance from the date it is received.

About one-quarter of all credit cards don't have a grace period—that is, you start paying interest when you make the purchase. In effect, if your credit card doesn't provide for a grace period, then each month you not only pay for what you've charged against your credit card, but you also pay a finance charge on those purchases. Perhaps the greatest confusion with respect to grace periods comes from the fact that, with most credit cards, if you don't completely pay off all your previous month's borrowing, then the grace period doesn't apply. In fact, the size of your unpaid balance doesn't matter—it could be only one penny. The result is the same: On most credit cards the grace period is canceled if you carry an unpaid balance from the previous month.

> ## *Stop and Think*
> If you have credit card debt on a high-rate credit card that you can't pay off immediately, you might consider getting a lower rate card and transferring your debt to it (paying off the debt on your old card by charging it to your new card). *Money* magazine regularly carries a listing of low cost credit cards. There's no reason you should be paying 20 percent when you buy on credit.

The Annual Fee

Some credit card issuers also impose an **annual fee** for the privilege of using their card. The charge usually ranges from $10 to $100, but American Express charges $300 annually for its Platinum card. Although these fees can start to add up and seem like a lot to you if you have a lot of cards, rest assured that the credit card companies aren't getting rich off of your annual fee. In fact, over 70 percent of the 25 biggest credit card issuers don't charge a fee at all, and others don't charge one as long as you use their card at least once per year. How, then, do these card issuers make money? Well, there's the huge rate of interest they charge on outstanding balances. In addition, they charge a fee to the merchants that accept their card. Typically, when you charge a purchase against your credit card, the merchant pays a percentage of the sale, called the **merchant's discount fee**, to the credit card issuer. This fee typically ranges from 1.5 to 5 percent (and in some cases up to 10 percent) of the amount charged.

Additional Fees

If credit card issuers make money from merchant discount fees every time you use their cards, you'd think that paying your annual fee and the exorbitant interest on your balance would be enough to keep them happy. Of course, you'd be wrong. There are still plenty of additional and penalty fees you have to pay. First, there's a **cash advance fee**, which is either a fixed amount—for example, $2 per transaction—or a percentage—usually 2.5 percent—of the cash advance. Remember, that's on top of the interest you immediately start getting charged from the date of the advance. Actually some credit card issuers charge a higher interest rate on cash advances than they do on normal charges to the card. The bottom line here is that a small cash advance can wind up being a big financial setback.

The next fee you might get stuck paying is a **late fee**, which results from not paying your credit card bill on time. A late fee will usually cost you between $10 and $20. For example, the AT&T Universal card charges a late fee of $15 on its card. In addition,

Annual Fee
A fixed annual charge imposed by a credit card.

Merchant's Discount Fee
The percentage of the sale that the merchant pays to the credit card issuer.

Cash Advance Fee
A charge for making a cash advance, paid as either a fixed amount or a percentage of the cash advance.

Late Fee
A fee imposed as a result of not paying your credit card bill on time.

Over-the-Limit Fee
A fee imposed whenever you go over your credit limit.

AT&T informed its cardholders that if they pay late, their interest rate may be raised by two percentage points. Actually, the 2-percent rate increase imposed by AT&T on delinquent accounts pales relative to the increases of 10 percent or more imposed by some card issuers. Finally, you also might get hit with an **over-the-limit fee** for charging more than your credit limit allows. For example, the AT&T Universal card charges an over-the-limit fee of $15.

> ### *The Facts of Life*
> If you pay only your credit card's minimum balance, you might be paying for a long time. For example, if you have a balance of $3,900 on a card with an 18-percent APR, and you pay only the minimum amount required by some cards each month, paying off your bill would take 35 years. Moreover, you'd end up paying $10,096 in interest in addition to the principal of $3,900.

LEARNING OBJECTIVE #2

Understand the costs involved with credit cards.

YOUR CREDIT CARD: WHEN TO USE IT, WHEN TO AVOID IT

Now that you know how expensive credit can be, why would you ever want to use it? There are plenty of good answers to that question, both for and against credit use. As with any tool, there are plenty of pros and cons to using credit. Let's take a look at them.

The Pros of Credit Cards

Without question it would be difficult to function in society today without some kind of credit card or open credit. Simple tasks like making hotel reservations or purchasing an item through a mail-order catalog would be nearly impossible without them. Advantages of credit cards or open credit include the following.

Convenience or Ease of Shopping. It's often more convenient to purchase items with credit cards than with cash. Not only do you receive an itemized billing of exactly how much you spent and where you spent it, but you also reduce the risk of theft associated with carrying around large amounts of cash. Also, you can't make purchases over the phone or the Internet with cash. Using credit, then, extends your shopping opportunities.

AXIOM #7

Stuff Happens, or the Importance of Liquidity

Emergency Use. Open credit makes an easy source of temporary emergency funds. You know from **Axiom 7: Stuff Happens, or the Importance of Liquidity** just how important it is to have sufficient emergency funds. If you have enough open credit to cover emergency expenses, though, you don't need to keep as much in liquid emergency funds. Credit, then, frees you up from having to hold liquid assets so that you can put your money in higher-yielding investments.

Allows for Consumption Before the Purchase Is fully Paid For. By purchasing an item on credit, you get to use it before you actually pay for it. So, when you buy a new Ralph Lauren shirt or a new Blues Traveler CD and charge it, you can wear the shirt or play the CD as much as you like in spite of the fact that you won't really pay for it until you pay your credit card bill.

Allows for Consolidation of Bills. By using a single credit card to make purchases from a variety of sources, you can consolidate your bills. Having one bill to pay is a lot simpler than having 20 bills to pay. In fact, many individuals with numerous bills outstanding transfer all these debts to a single credit card in an effort to get better control over their borrowing. As a result, they have only one bill to deal with.

SAVOR CREDIT-CARD SAVINGS
Without Getting Snagged

Start carrying a balance on one or more of your credit cards, and suddenly, you're Mr. or Ms. Popular. Card issuers may raise your credit limits and congratulate you on the fine manner in which you have managed your account. Banks with which you don't currently do business will fall over themselves to convince you they are worthy of a spot in your wallet.

What makes you so irresistible? Your balance. To banks and other issuers, a cardholder with a balance is easy money. They figure you are careful enough to make payments on time, yet inattentive enough to inadvertently rack up finance costs by, say, taking an unduly long time to pay off your debts.

But savvy cardholders can turn the banks' marketing gambits to their own advantage. "If you're willing to put some effort into looking after your own interests, you can come out ahead with some of these deals," says Gerri Detweiler, author of the forthcoming second edition of "The Ultimate Credit Handbook: How to Double Your Credit, Cut Your Debt and Have a Lifetime of Great Credit."

To get the biggest savings from credit-card promotions, you have to sidestep the hidden costs. Here's a quick guide to the tricky art of transferring a balance with getting trapped.

- **Search Out the Best Prospects:** Gather several offers from your junk mail and line up their features. An offer-to-offer comparison can lay bare important subtleties you might otherwise overlook, Ms. Detweiler says.

- **Check Details Before You Commit:** Two niggling, relevant questions to ask any issuer who offers these deals: When does a transferred balance begin to incur interest? And, how long will the whole process take?

- **Preserve Your Perks:** Don't transfer your debts to cards on which you're already running a tab. Why not? Most banks have a little-known practice of reneging any "float" when you carry a balance. Thus, you'll miss out on the initial grace period some issuers offer.

- **Make Extra Payments:** To get the biggest benefit from these promotions, pay off as much of your balance as possible before the low interest rate expires.

- **Set a Deadline:** If you haven't gotten rid of a credit-card balance after several months, it's time to face reality and (gasp!) cut back on spending.

Source: Vanessa O'Connell, "Savor Credit-Card Savings Without Getting Snagged," *The Wall Street Journal,* October 6, 1995, p. C1. Reprinted by permission of *The Wall Street Journal,* © 1995 Dow Jones & Company, Inc. All Rights Reserved Worldwide.

Ⓐ Ⓑ Ⓒ

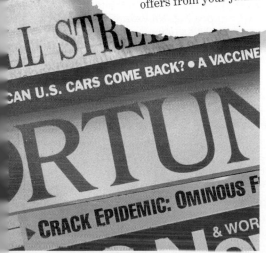

Analysis and Implications ...

A. Some programs give you an initial grace period during which time no finance charges are imposed on balances that have been transferred to their books.

B. Make sure that, once you move your debts to the new account, you cancel your old credit card. For most people, keeping more than three credit cards is unwise, even if you aren't using all of them.

C. You should keep one credit card on hand on which you only make purchases that you pay off at the end of the month, because most banks eliminate their grace period on new purchases when you carry a balance. If you carry a balance, you are charged on items you purchase on the date the charge is posted to your account.

Can Be Used in Anticipation of Price Increases.   If the price on an item that you intend to purchase is about to go up, buying the item on credit today lets you pay less than you'd have to pay tomorrow.

As a Source of Interest-Free Credit.   If you pay your full credit card balance each month, a credit card gives you the use of funds interest-free from the date of the purchase until the payment date.

For Making Reservations.   Credit cards can be used when making motel or hotel reservations almost anywhere in the world. They can be used not only to make the reservations, but also to guarantee late arrival.

For Use as Identification.   Credit cards can also be used as identification when cashing checks, for video rental memberships, and almost anywhere else multiple pieces of identification are needed.

As a Source of Free Benefits.   Today many credit cards provide you with "free benefits." For example, many products offer free extended product warranties and travel insurance. Also, there are credit cards that give you frequent flier miles on your favorite airline or credit toward the purchase of anything from Shell gasoline and GM cars to *Rolling Stone* magazine. These frequent flier and purchase benefits aren't actually free, because the cards that offer them are more likely to carry an annual fee. For example, the USAir Visa Gold card carries a $70 annual fee.

The Cons of Credit Cards

Although credit cards are indispensable in today's economy, they've also caused countless problems for many individuals. Listed below are a number of reasons why you should be wary of credit cards and open credit.

They Make It Easy to Lose Control of Spending.   It's simply too easy to spend money with a credit card, because it seems as if you haven't really spent money. Moreover, it's too easy to lose track of exactly how much you've spent. What you've charged doesn't appear until your monthly statement shows up, and, for many, it's too late at that point. Once you've overspent, your only recourse may be to pay off your purchases over time. As a result, you get stuck paying hefty amounts of interest and spending much more than you'd bargained for.

Credit Cards Are, in General, an *Expensive* Way to Borrow Money.   It's not just that you pay interest on your unpaid credit card balance, it's the high rate of interest that you pay that makes credit card borrowing so unappealing. For example, in mid 1997 the average 15-year fixed-rate home mortgage charged 7.54 percent, the average home equity line of credit charged 9.78 percent, and the average credit card charged 17.1 percent. At the same time, 1-year CDs paid only 5.22 percent. Banks are effectively borrowing money at 5.22 percent and lending it out at 17.1 percent. That's quite a tidy profit, and it explains why you keep getting all those credit card applications in the mail.

Credit Card Use Means You'll Have Less Spendable Income in the Future.   Any time you use a credit card, you're obligating future income. That is, in the future you'll have less budget flexibility because a portion of your take-home pay will have to be used to pay off your credit card expenditures plus any interest on your unpaid balance. In effect, when you use your credit card you're spending future income. If you don't control your spending, you can wind up with some heavy budgetary problems as a larger and larger portion of your income goes toward paying off past debt and interest owed. If this problem sounds familiar, look no further than our national debt. Figure 6.2 provides a summary of why to use and why to avoid credit cards.

FIGURE 6.2

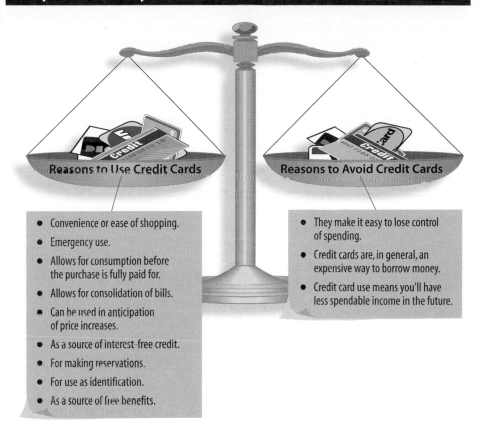

Why to Use and Why to Avoid Credit Cards

Reasons to Use Credit Cards

- Convenience or ease of shopping.
- Emergency use.
- Allows for consumption before the purchase is fully paid for.
- Allows for consolidation of bills.
- Can be used in anticipation of price increases.
- As a source of interest-free credit.
- For making reservations.
- For use as identification.
- As a source of free benefits.

Reasons to Avoid Credit Cards

- They make it easy to lose control of spending.
- Credit cards are, in general, an expensive way to borrow money.
- Credit card use means you'll have less spendable income in the future.

The Facts of Life

According to a 1996 credit card survey by the Bankcard Holders of America, more than half (53 percent) of consumers surveyed were in debt due to "overspending," while 11 percent cited medical bills as the major contributor to their indebtedness. Another 11 percent attributed their indebtedness to college expenses, and 9 percent cited a job layoff. Other reasons given were home repair, divorce, travel/vacations, and convenience. Interestingly, 89 percent of those surveyed said it was time to do something about the debt they had amassed.

CHOOSING A SOURCE OF OPEN CREDIT

There are several different types of open credit available to you today. However, almost all of these types of credit involve a card of some sort, and are remarkably similar to general credit cards. We'll now take a look at these credit options, after which we'll discuss how you choose which one is the best for your particular needs.

Bank Credit Cards

Most credit card purchases are made on bank credit cards. A **bank credit card** is simply a credit card issued by a bank or large corporation, generally as a Visa or MasterCard. Visa and MasterCard don't actually issue bank cards themselves. Rather, they act as

LEARNING OBJECTIVE #3

Describe the different types of credit cards and their advantages and disadvantages.

Bank Credit Card
A credit card issued by a bank or large corporation, generally as a Visa or MasterCard.

franchise organizations that provide credit authorization systems, accounting-statement record keeping, and advertising services, and allow banks and large corporations to issue the cards with the Visa or MasterCard name. Within certain broad limits, banks can then establish their own policies with respect to interest, grace periods, fees, and services. As a result, there are dramatic differences between bank credit cards.

It's the efficient system of credit authorization provided by Visa and MasterCard that has led to their popularity. Being able to easily check a customer's credit at the time of purchase provides merchants with an assurance that there is no problem with the credit card or line of credit, and has led to the wide acceptance of Visa and Master-Card bank credit cards as a means of payment both in the United States and abroad. As a result, there are over 7,000 cards to choose from.

Today, many bank cards also offer free benefits. These include such perks as rental-car damage coverage, extended warranties, and travel accident insurance, along with frequent flier miles and rebates of all kinds. Generally, when bank cards provide rebates, they're referred to as "co-branded" or "rebate cards" in that they have a "brand name" listed on the card and provide a rebate such as discounts on long-distance calls from AT&T or GE products, rebates on GM cars, or frequent flier miles from almost any airline. In general these cards also require an annual fee. For example the British Airways Visa has an annual fee of $50. Some, such as the GE Rewards MasterCard, also charge cardholders with a $25 annual penalty fee if they continue to pay off their balance every month. Still, if you pay off your balance each month and charge from $5,000 to $8,000 a year, you might want to look at these cards closely. Remember, you have to make sure that whatever benefits you receive are worth more than the card's annual fee.

The one card that is a bit different is the Discover card. Although Visa and Master-Card license their services to the banks that in turn issue the credit cards, the Discover card is issued by a single bank. Not only is the Discover bank card different in that it has a single issuer, but it also contains some unusual features in that it carries no annual fee and rebates to cardholders a small percentage of their annual purchases.

Bank Card Variations.   One popular variation of the traditional bank card is the **premium** or **prestige credit card**. Premium or prestige cards are simply bank credit cards that offer credit limits as high as $100,000 or more as well as numerous added perks, including emergency medical and legal services, travel insurance and services, rebates, and warranties on new purchases, In fact, MasterCard requires all issuers to provide valuable perks on all its premium cards. A Visa or MasterCard Gold card would be an example of a premium or prestige credit card. Many people carry these cards not for their added benefits, but for their "prestige." At one time credit cards were available only to a select few and were thus a status symbol. Today, even the lowly college student with no visible means of support can get a credit card. As a result, some people take pleasure in using a credit card that's issued only to those meeting rather high annual income requirements.

Another variation of the bank credit card is the **affinity card**, which is a credit card issued in conjunction with a specific charity or organization. For example, organizations such as the Sierra Club, MADD, the National Rifle Association, and most colleges and universities have affinity cards. The card bears the sponsoring group's name, logo, and/or picture. These cards send a portion of their annual fee or a percentage of the purchases back to the sponsoring organization. Typically, one-half percent of each purchase is sent back to the sponsoring group, although many affinity card issuers don't disclose how much the issuing bank actually donates back to the sponsoring group. Although the fees and annual interest rates on affinity cards vary from card to card, in general affinity cards are expensive, charging an annual fee of $20 or more and a high annual interest rate. Given the fact that, for the consumer, they work just like a traditional credit card and there are less expensive bank credit cards available, what accounts for the popularity of affinity cards? Many individuals see them as an easy,

Premium or **Prestige Card**
A bank or T&E credit card that offers credit limits as high as $100,000 or more in addition to numerous added perks, including emergency medical and legal services, travel services, rebates, and insurance on new purchases.

Affinity Card
A credit card issued in conjunction with a specific charity or organization. It carries the sponsoring group's name and/or picture on the actual credit card itself and sends a portion of the annual fee or a percentage of the purchases back to the sponsoring organization.

painless way to make donations to their favorite charity or organization. The fact is, it's generally an expensive way to make charitable donations, particularly if you ever maintain an unpaid balance on your credit card. Also, a large part of your charitable donation actually gets "donated" to the issuing bank, and you can't take a tax deduction for the donation!

The final variation of the bank credit card is the **secured credit card**. A secured credit card is a regular bank credit card that's backed by the pledge of some collateralized asset. That is, if you can't pay off what you've charged to your credit card, the issuing bank has a specific asset it can lay claim to. For example, your credit card may be linked to a CD you have held in the issuing bank. In this case, the issuing bank knows exactly where to go if you can't pay off your charges—so long, CD. For the bank, no customer is a bad risk if collateral can be put up. The question then becomes, If you also must hold a CD at the issuing bank, why would you ever want a secured credit card? If you're a bad credit risk, you may not have any alternative.

Travel and Entertainment (T&E) Cards

Travel and entertainment (T&E) cards, such as the American Express Corporate card, were initially aimed at providing business customers with a means of paying for travel, business entertainment, and other business expenses, while keeping these charges separate from cardholders' personal expenditures. Over time, however, T&E cards have come to be used like traditional bank credit cards. The major difference between T&E cards and bank credit cards is that T&E cards *do not* offer revolving credit and, therefore, require full payment of the balance each month. As such, aside from the prestige that they afford holders, their only advantage is the interest-free grace period that they provide holders. The issuer's only income from these cards is the annual fee, which can run as high as $300 per year, and the merchant's discount fee that they receive on each purchase. The three primary issuers of T&E cards are American Express, Diners Club, and Carte Blanche, with American Express dominating this market. It should also be noted that there are also T&E premium or prestige cards. For example, there is the American Express Platinum card, which allows for a higher credit limit than the normal American Express card and is issued by "invitation" only.

Single-Purpose Cards

A **single-purpose card** is a credit card that can be used only at a specific company. For example, a Texaco credit card can be used only to charge purchases at a Texaco service station, and an MCI credit card can be used only to make long-distance calls through MCI. These credit cards allow companies to issue their own credit cards and thereby avoid merchant's discount fees. The terms associated with single-purpose cards vary dramatically from card to card, with some allowing for revolving credit and others not, but in general, they don't require an annual fee. If you can also use your Visa card at the Texaco service station, why do you need a Texaco charge card? The answer is, you don't, and if you're trying to get enough miles for that free flight to San Francisco on your USAir Visa card, you might be better off using it instead. Why then might you want a single-purpose card? Many times these cards are used because they limit credit access to a single company. For example, a parent may want his or her 16-year-old daughter to have a Texaco credit card in case she needs to buy gas, but not really want her to have a Visa card.

Traditional Charge Account

A **traditional charge account** is simply a charge account offered by a business. For example, your phone and utility companies and perhaps even your doctor or dentist provide you with services and bill you later, usually giving you a grace period to pay up. In effect, this payment system is a type of open credit account—one in which no

Secured Credit Card
A credit card backed by the pledge of some collateralized asset.

Travel and Entertainment (T&E) Card
A credit card initially meant for business customers to allow them to pay for travel and entertainment expenses, keeping them separate from their other expenditures.

Single-Purpose Card
A credit card that can be used only at a specific company.

Traditional Charge Account
A charge account, as opposed to a credit card, that can be used to make purchases only at the issuing company.

cards are involved. After you receive your monthly bill, you're expected to pay it in full, and if payment is not received by the due date, an interest penalty is generally tacked on. The major advantage of a charge account is the convenience it affords the customer. Just think how tedious it would be to have to pay for each long-distance phone call as it is made, or to pay for your electricity usage on a daily basis. In addition to the advantage of convenience, there's the benefit of an interest-free grace period and enjoying services before having to pay for them. For the billing company, a traditional charge account is primarily a matter of convenience—it's just an easy and efficient way to collect bills.

The Facts of Life

There are more than 1.1 billion credit cards issued to Americans alone. To many, these cards are an extension of their personality. That probably explains the popularity of the Elvis Visa issued by Leader Federal Bank for Savings in Virginia, which has the King's picture right on it.

The Choice: It's a Matter of Your Credit Card Philosophy

In evaluating the many kinds of credit cards that are available, you'll find that different cards have different strong points. For example, some cards have low fees and extended grace periods but high interest rates. Although this may be the best combination for some, it may be the worst for others. You have to understand how you're going to use it before you can decide which credit card to choose. Most individuals tend to use credit cards for convenience, for credit, or for both convenience and credit.

A *credit user* generally carries an unpaid balance from month to month. Most credit users don't use the grace period, and the annual fee pales relative to the amount of interest that's paid annually. If you're a credit user, the most important decision factor is the card's APR or interest rate on the unpaid balance, because it will be the largest credit expense you face. Moreover, because interest rates on credit cards can vary dramatically, shopping around for the lowest-cost card is extremely important for a credit user. For example, in mid 1997 when the national average interest rate on credit cards was 17.1 percent, Pulaski B&T was offering a credit card with an interest rate of 7.99 percent. Pulaski B&T is located in Arkansas, but should the issuing bank's location be a concern in choosing a credit card? No. Wherever your credit card issuer is located, your card will work essentially the same. A credit user, then, should search as far and wide as necessary to get the card with the lowest possible rate attached to it.

The Facts of Life

Credit card interest charges for the typical baby boomer who is a credit user can amount to $1,200 annually. If these payments could be saved over 30 years in a tax-deferred account earning 10 percent, they would accumulate to $197,389.

For a *convenience user*—that is, someone who pays off the credit card balance each month—the interest rate is irrelevant. Convenience users should look for a credit card with a low annual fee and an interest-free grace period. The interest-free grace period is especially important because it allows convenience users to pay off their balance each month without incurring any interest payments. Beyond a low annual fee and an interest-free grace period, a convenience user might consider a card that carries free benefits, such as a GM credit card or one that gives frequent flier miles.

FIGURE 6.3

What Features Different Types of Credit Card Users Find Important

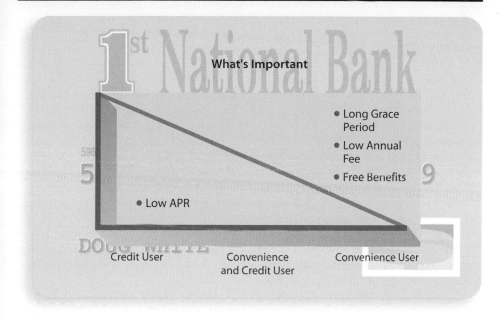

What's Important

- Long Grace Period
- Low Annual Fee
- Free Benefits

- Low APR

Credit User | Convenience and Credit User | Convenience User

A *convenience and credit user* is someone who generally, but not always, pays off all of the balance. For this type of credit user, the ideal card is one with no annual fee, an interest-free grace period, and a low interest rate on the unpaid balance. Unfortunately, finding all of this in one card is next to impossible. Convenience and credit users, therefore, must simply look for the combination of features they think will result in the lowest total cost considering both the interest rate and the annual fee. Figure 6.3 shows what features different types of credit card users find important.

GETTING A CREDIT CARD

For a college student today, getting a credit card is generally not a problem. Credit card issuers see college students as excellent prospects—although students may not be earning much now, their future earning prospects are bright. Also, lenders try to assure themselves of payment by either requiring parents to co-sign on the credit cards or simply assuming that the student's parents will step in if there are problems paying off any debt. Credit card issuers generally set up shop on large campuses by offering free gifts—anything from free or discount flights to free Frisbees—for those who apply. For a student, getting a credit card is an excellent idea. First, it can be used for emergency funds while away from home. Second, by using a credit card prudently, a student can build up a solid credit history. Is your credit history important? Well, yes, but only if you ever want to do such things as buy a house, rent an apartment, or get a job.

The first step in obtaining a credit card is applying. The application will focus on factors that determine your creditworthiness, or your ability and willingness to repay any charges incurred. Sometimes the lender may insist on an interview for further clarification. You've absolutely got to be honest and consistent in the application process. If your answers are inconsistent or don't conform to what the lender has independently found out, your application will likely be turned down. Let's now find out what makes you creditworthy.

LEARNING OBJECTIVE #4

Know what determines your credit card worthiness and how to secure a credit card.

Credit Evaluation: The Five C's of Credit

In determining what makes an individual creditworthy, most lenders refer to the "five C's" of credit: character, capacity, capital, collateral, and conditions. *Character* refers to your sense of responsibility with respect to debt payment. Have you established a record of timely repayment of past debts, such as your student loans? Keep in mind that exhibiting good character involves not overextending yourself with respect to credit—that is, not taking on too much debt given your income level. In assessing your character, lenders also look at how long you've lived at one address and how long you've held your current job. In effect, stability often passes for character.

Capacity and *capital* work together in determining your ability to repay any credit card charges you may incur. In assessing your *capacity*, lenders look to both your current income level and your current level of borrowing—that is, lenders are concerned with your level of nonobligated income. Most financial advisors suggest that your total debt payments, including mortgage payments, should account for less than 36 percent of your gross pay. *Capital* refers to the size of your financial holdings or investment portfolio. Obviously, the more you have in savings, the more creditworthy you are. The question answered by looking at your capital is, Given your financial holdings, is your income sufficient to provide for the debt you've already incurred? The larger your nonobligated annual income (capacity) and the value of your investment portfolio (capital), the more creditworthy you are.

Collateral refers to assets or property offered as security to obtain credit. Then, if you were to default, the property, perhaps a car or a piece of land, would be sold, and the proceeds from the sale would go to repay the outstanding debt. Obviously, the more the collateral is worth, the more creditworthy you are.

The last of the five C's is *conditions*. Conditions refer to the impact that the current economic environment may have on your ability to repay any borrowing. For example, you may appear to be strong in all other credit evaluation aspects, but if you're laid off due to a downswing in the economy, you might not be able to meet your debt obligations.

Credit Evaluation: The Credit Bureau

How does a credit card issuer verify the information you put down on your application, and how does it get information about your character and financial situation? Through your credit report supplied from a credit bureau. A **credit bureau** is a private organization that maintains credit information on individuals, which it allows subscribers to access for a fee. The credit bureau accumulates its credit information on individuals from information provided by subscribers, from public court records, and from information that the individual has forwarded to the credit bureau. Information is collected by local credit bureaus, which then share this information with one of the three national credit bureaus: Experian (formerly TRW), Trans Union, or Equifax Credit Information Services.

Your credit report contains only information regarding your financial situation and dealings. It doesn't contain any information regarding your personal lifestyle. Also, a credit bureau doesn't make credit decisions. It merely supplies data that a bank or S&L will in turn use in making a credit decision. Table 6.1 provides a listing of what's typically contained in a credit report, and Figure 6.4 shows a sample credit report.

Credit Bureau

A company that gathers information on consumers' financial history, including how quickly they have paid bills and whether they have been delinquent on bills in the past. The company then summarizes this information and sells it to customers.

The Facts of Life

Many credit cards have extremely low annual income requirements—running as low as $8,000. Although you may be able to qualify for a credit card at this level of income, if you get one, you should use it with the utmost discretion.

TABLE 6.1

Information Contained in Your Credit Report

Personal Information: Age, Social Security number, current address, previous address.
Employment Record: Current and past employers, and what you do for a living.
Your Credit History: The number of bank cards and charge cards you have and for how long you've had them, your payment history including the largest amount you've ever owed, the current amount owed, and the number of times payments have been past due.
Your Public Financial History: Bankruptcies (carried for 10 years), liens, criminal convictions, and court action including judgments awarded to creditors.
Past Inquiries Regarding Your Credit Report: A record of everyone who has seen your credit report over the past 2 years.

The Credit Bureau and Your Rights

Because your credit report is so important, Congress passed the Fair Credit Reporting Act (FCRA) in 1971 and subsequently amended it to help ensure consumers that their credit reports are accurate. Under the FCRA you have the right to view your credit report. It's a good idea to review your credit report every 2 to 3 years. Also, if you're turned down for credit, it's a good idea to review your report to make sure all the information contained in it is accurate. Your local bank or the institution that turned you down for credit should be able to supply you with the address and phone number of your local credit bureau. To get a copy of your credit report, you can contact either your local credit bureau or one of the three national credit bureaus listed in Table 6.2, and for a very minor fee of up to $15 you'll be sent a copy of your report. If you've been denied credit based on a credit report, the report will be free.

TABLE 6.2

National Credit Bureaus

Equifax Credit Information Services	Experian (formerly TRW)	Trans Union
Report fraud	**Report fraud**	**Report fraud**
800-525-6285	Experian Consumer Fraud Assistance P.O. Box 1017 Allen, Texas, 75013 800-301-7195 (fax)	800-916-8800
Get a copy of your report	**Get a copy of your report**	**Get a copy of your report**
P.O. Box 740241 Atlanta, GA 30374-0241 800-685-1111	P.O. Box 8030 Layton, Utah 84041 800-682-7654	P.O. Box 390 Springfield, PA 19064 800-851-2674
Dispute something in your report	**Dispute something in your report**	**Dispute something in your report**
P.O. Box 740256 Atlanta, GA 30374-0256 800-216-1035 800-685-5000	P.O. Box 2106 Allen, Texas 75013 800-422-4879	P.O. Box 34012 Fullerton, CA 92634 800-916-8800

FIGURE 6.4

A Sample Credit Report

Make sure you are not being confused with someone else with a similar name or Social Security number.

Make sure all information is accurate and let the credit bureau know if there are any errors.

Any adverse information in these accounts is listed >in brackets.<

Any time you dispute an item Trans Union will conduct an investigation and then inform you of their findings. In this case there were four disputed items reported upon.

Make sure all damaging information has been removed after a disputed issue has been resolved.

Whenever an inquiry is made concerning your creditworthiness, it appears. In this case two inquiries were made.

```
⊞ TRANS UNION                    YOUR TRANS UNION FILE NUMBER: 97ZZ0093-001
  PO BOX 123456                  PAGE  1 OF  2 (INTL USE: CC      0BIN 01)
  WICHITA, KS 12345-1234         DATE THIS REPORT PRINTED: 01/10/97

                                 SOCIAL SECURITY NUMBER: 123-12-1234
                                 BIRTH DATE:             09/61
                                 YOU HAVE BEEN IN OUR FILES SINCE: 07/83
CONSUMER REPORT FOR:

   *****
   ASTEB, JAMES, ROBERT
   2 RR 3 BOX 22
   GARY, IN 46162

FORMER ADDRESSES REPORTED:

   232 S EMERSON AV, GREENVILLE, IN 46143

                       INVESTIGATION RESULTS

WE HAVE COMPLETED OUR INVESTIGATION OF THE ITEM(S) YOU DISPUTED. OUR FINDINGS
ARE SUMMARIZED AS FOLLOWS:

ITEM                      DESCRIPTION           RESULTS

ATT UNIV CRD              # 432432432324329     VERIFIED AS ACCURATE
STAR BANK                 # 4897654020253144    DELETED
FIRST CARD                # 4321321321321       NEW INFORMATION BELOW
DISCOVER CRD              # 32132137281372819   VERIFIED AS ACCURATE

ANY CORRECTIONS TO YOUR IDENTIFICATION REQUESTED BY YOU HAVE BEEN MADE AS NOTED
ABOVE. IF OUR INVESTIGATION HAS NOT RESOLVED YOUR DISPUTE, YOU MAY ADD A 100
WORD CONSUMER STATEMENT TO YOUR REPORT. YOUR UPDATED CREDIT INFORMATION
FOLLOWS:

                     YOUR CREDIT INFORMATION

THE FOLLOWING ACCOUNTS CONTAIN INFORMATION WHICH SOME CREDITORS MAY CONSIDER TO
BE ADVERSE.  THE ADVERSE INFORMATION IN THESE ACCOUNTS HAS BEEN PRINTED IN
>BRACKETS< FOR YOUR CONVENIENCE, TO HELP YOU UNDERSTAND YOUR REPORT.  THEY ARE
NOT BRACKETED THIS WAY FOR CREDITORS. (NOTE: THE ACCOUNT # MAY BE SCRAMBLED BY
THE CREDITOR FOR YOUR PROTECTION).

ATT UNIV CRD - # 4324324324324329        REVOLVING ACCOUNT
>PROFIT AND LOSS WRITEOFF<               CREDIT CARD
    VERIF'D  12/96    BALANCE:      $556  INDIVIDUAL ACCOUNT
    OPENED   08/90    MOST OWED:   $2200  CREDIT LIMIT:    $2200
    CLOSED   10/93  >PAST DUE:      $556<
    >STATUS AS OF 10/93: CHARGED OFF AS BAD DEBT<


REPORT ON ASTEB, JAMES, ROBERT                            PAGE  2 OF  2
SOCIAL SECURITY NUMBER: 123-12-1234      TRANS UNION FILE NUMBER: 97ZZ0093-001

FIRST CARD   - # 4321321321321            REVOLVING ACCOUNT
>CANCELLED BY CREDIT GRANTOR<            CREDIT CARD
    VERIF'D  01/97    BALANCE:     $3721  INDIVIDUAL ACCOUNT
    OPENED   04/91    MOST OWED:   $4999  PAY TERMS: MONTHLY $77
    CLOSED   09/93                        CREDIT LIMIT:    $5000
    >IN PRIOR 14 MONTHS FROM DATE CLOSED  1 TIME 60 DAYS LATE<
    STATUS AS OF 09/93: PAID AS AGREED

DISCOVER CRD - # 32132137281372819        REVOLVING ACCOUNT
>CANCELLED BY CREDIT GRANTOR<            CREDIT CARD
    VERIF'D  12/96    BALANCE:     $1413  INDIVIDUAL ACCOUNT
    OPENED   10/89    MOST OWED:   $2065  PAY TERMS: MINIMUM $40
    CLOSED   09/92                        CREDIT LIMIT:    $2500
    >IN PRIOR 24 MONTHS FROM DATE CLOSED  2 TIMES 60 DAYS LATE<
    STATUS AS OF 09/92: PAID AS AGREED

THE FOLLOWING ACCOUNTS ARE REPORTED WITH NO ADVERSE INFORMATION

AMERICAN EXP - # 3213212121300            OPEN ACCOUNT
ACCOUNT CLOSED                          CREDIT CARD
    UPDATED  12/96    BALANCE:       $67  INDIVIDUAL ACCOUNT
    OPENED   03/91    MOST OWED:      $67
    CLOSED   03/95
    IN PRIOR 48 MONTHS FROM DATE CLOSED NEVER LATE
    STATUS AS OF 03/95: PAID AS AGREED

L S AYRES    - # 321321321                REVOLVING ACCOUNT
    UPDATED  04/92    BALANCE:        $0  JOINT ACCOUNT
    OPENED   07/83    MOST OWED:       $0
    IN PRIOR 25 MONTHS FROM LAST UPDATE NEVER LATE
    STATUS AS OF 04/92: NO RATING

THE FOLLOWING COMPANIES HAVE RECEIVED YOUR CREDIT REPORT.  THEIR INQUIRIES
REMAIN ON YOUR CREDIT REPORT FOR TWO YEARS.  (NOTE: "CONSUM DISCL" REFERS TO
TRANS UNION CONSUMER RELATIONS AND ARE NOT VIEWED BY CREDITORS).

                    INQUIRY TYPE                        INQUIRY TYPE
CONSUM DISCL 12/17/96  INDIVIDUAL    CONS ACPT   09/23/96  INDIVIDUAL
CONSUM DISCL 09/10/96  INDIVIDUAL    AM STAR FNCL 07/12/96  INDIVIDUAL

THE FOLLOWING COMPANIES DID NOT GET YOUR FULL REPORT, BUT INSTEAD RECEIVED ONLY
YOUR NAME AND ADDRESS INFORMATION FOR THE PURPOSE OF MAKING YOU A CREDIT OFFER,
OR TO REVIEW YOUR ACCOUNT. THEIR INQUIRIES ARE NOT SEEN BY CREDITORS.

CHASE NA     08/96    FIRST CARD   08/96    FIRST CARD   09/96

IF YOU BELIEVE ANY OF THE INFORMATION IN YOUR CREDIT REPORT IS INCORRECT,
PLEASE LET US KNOW.  PLEASE ADDRESS ALL CORRESPONDENCE REGARDING YOUR CREDIT
REPORT TO:

TRANS UNION CONSUMER RELATIONS
PO BOX 123456
WICHITA, KS 12345-1234
1-800-123-1234
```

Source: Trans Union Corporation, Chicago, Illinois, 1997. Used by permission.

If the information in your file isn't accurate or complete, under the FCRA the credit bureau must investigate any errors you point out and make any necessary corrections. For example, your file may inadvertently contain information about someone with a name very similar to yours, or it may contain incorrect or incomplete credit information, perhaps listing accounts that are closed or that you never had. If there are any mistakes, you should notify your credit bureau so it can investigate your charges and make the necessary corrections. If the credit bureau investigates your claim and determines that the information in your credit report is accurate, you have the right to have in your file a statement presenting your view of the disputed issue. This statement gives you the chance to dispute the accuracy of information in your file, not the chance to cough up lame excuses about why you really had credit problems. In any case, if you do find inaccuracies, they should be pointed out immediately.

The FCRA also limits the length of time over which damaging information can remain in your file. For example, bankruptcy information can remain in your file for only 10 years, and other negative information must be removed from your file after 7 years.

The FCRA also limits access to your credit file to those who have a legitimate right to view it, such as a financial institution considering extending you credit, an employer, or a company doing business with you. You also have the right to know who's seen your credit report, which is listed on the report.

The Facts of Life

Approximately 70 percent of all Americans have at least one negative remark in their credit reports. Moreover, almost half of all credit reports contain inaccurate, misleading, or obsolete material in them.

What to Do if Your Credit Card Application Is Rejected

If your credit card application is rejected, you have two choices. First, apply for a credit card with another financial institution. Because there's no set rule as to what type of credit risk a bank should take on, getting rejected at one bank doesn't necessarily mean you'll get rejected from another bank. Second, find out why you've been rejected. Set up an appointment with the credit card manager at the financial institution that rejected your application and find out what caused your rejection. Once you know why you've been rejected, correct the problem. You might have to correct inaccurate information on your credit report, or you might have to start doing some things differently to make yourself a better credit risk. In either case, the place to begin is by finding out why you've been rejected.

Stop and Think

For most people, a bad credit rating is a problem. However, if your inability to control your spending caused your credit-rating problem, then your lack of credit may actually keep you out of further trouble by helping to curb your spending habits. Lacking credit may not be enjoyable, but it may be the best thing for you.

Determining Your Creditworthiness—Credit Scoring

Once lenders have all your credit information, how do they evaluate it to determine your creditworthiness? Although a few look at each application individually, judge its creditworthiness, and make a judgment call, it's more common that your credit application

Credit Scoring
The numerical evaluation of credit applicants based on their answers to a simple set of questions.

will be evaluated using credit scoring. **Credit scoring** involves the numerical evaluation or "scoring" of applicants based on their answers to a simple set of questions. This score is then evaluated according to a predetermined standard. If your score is up to the acceptance standard, you get credit. The major advantage of credit scoring is that it's relatively inexpensive to perform. For example, once the standards are set, the evaluation can be done automatically by a computer.

The techniques used for constructing credit-scoring indexes range from the simple approach to the sophisticated. Figure 6.5 provides a sample credit "scorecard." This scorecard is somewhat simplified in that actual credit-scoring systems can involve evaluation of 20 or 30 different factors. The credit card issuer then assigns a minimum cutoff score; for example, this may be 57 points, with those scoring 57 points or more receiving a credit card and those scoring below 57 being rejected.

You'll notice in Figure 6.5 that age is used as a discriminating factor in credit scoring. Although the Equal Credit Opportunity Act prohibits lenders from discriminating against borrowers aged 62 or older, anyone younger can be penalized or rewarded

FIGURE 6.5

Sample Credit "Scorecard"

	POINTS
1. Annual Income	
Less than $15,000	2
$15,001–$25,000	5
$25,001–$35,000	10
$35,001–$45,000	16
$45,001–$60,000	21
Over $60,000	24
2. Length of Residence	
Less than 1 year	0
1–2 years	3
3–5 years	9
6–10 years	13
Over 10 years	17
3. Length of Time on Current Job	
Less than 6 months	0
6 months to 2 years	3
2–5 years	10
More than 5 years	18
4. Housing	
Rent	1
Home with mortgage	12
Own home	18
Other	0
5. Employment	
Self-employed	–5
Unskilled manual	0
Skilled manual	3
Clerical	6
Managerial	12
Professional	18

	POINTS
6. Age	
Under 20	–5
20–21	–1
22–24	3
25–30	7
31–40	10
41–50	14
Over 50	12
7. Bank Accounts	
None	–8
1	0
2	6
More than 2	8
8. Number of Credit Cards	
None	–4
1–4	10
Over 4	–4
9. Telephone	
Yes	5
No	–3
10. Credit History	
No history	–4
Bankruptcy	–15
Excellent	20

depending upon age. Also, bankruptcy remains a mark against you for a period of 10 years after it occurs. Credit scoring is efficient and relatively inexpensive to the lender, but it can also involve a lack of common sense and judgment that hurts the borrower. Remember the opening vignette to this chapter, when Lawrence B. Lindsey's application for a Toys 'Я' Us credit card was rejected. As we learned from that example, credit scoring doesn't always work perfectly.

Your creditworthiness determines not only whether you qualify for credit, but what interest rate you'll be offered. Many credit card issuers determine what rate to offer credit card holders depending upon their riskiness, with the more risky customers paying higher rates. In effect, there's a tiered pricing system present in credit cards, with less creditworthy, risky customers paying more.

> ## Stop and Think
>
> From the lender's point of view, creditworthiness deals with the probability that you'll pay off all that you charge. All the questions asked in credit scoring provide information that's historically been linked to individuals who were good credit risks. The more risk that the lender feels you have, the higher the rate charged on your borrowing, which is a direct application of **Axiom 1: The Risk-Return Trade-Off**.

AXIOM #1

The Risk-Return Trade-Off

STRATEGIES FOR CONTROLLING AND MANAGING YOUR CREDIT CARDS AND OPEN CREDIT

The first step in managing your credit is knowing what you have charged. It's far too easy to charge a pizza here, a gas fill-up there, and so forth until all control is lost. Remember, a lot of personal finance is about control. If you don't keep track of what you've spent, it's hard to know what kind of financial shape you're in.

Reducing Your Balance

In addition to knowing exactly what the interest charge is on your credit card, you should understand how long it takes to pay off your credit card debt if you don't make meaningful payments—that is, payments well above the minimum monthly payment required by the credit card. First, you should realize that most credit cards require that you pay only between 2 and 3 percent of your outstanding balance monthly. As a result, if you're paying 18-percent interest on that balance, you're getting almost nowhere. In other words, if you don't pay more than the minimum, you're almost assured of owing on your credit cards for life. To get an idea of how long it takes to get rid of credit card debt, let's look at how many months it would take to get rid of your credit card debt if you paid off a set percentage of your initial balance. For example, if your initial balance is $3,000 and you pay off 2 percent of it each month, you'd be paying off $60 each month. In addition to the amount you pay off each month, your credit card interest rate also plays a role in determining how long it takes to eliminate your debt. Table 6.3 shows you how to calculate how long it would take to pay off your balance. Simply find the intersection of the percentage of your initial balance that you are paying off and the interest rate on your credit card. Thus, if you pay off only 2 percent of your initial balance per month, and the credit card interest rate is 15 percent, it would take 79 months or over 6 and a half years before your credit card debt is exhausted. Keep in mind that this time frame assumes that you don't charge anything more on your card. If you have a substantial balance and keep charging, you may never get out of debt.

LEARNING OBJECTIVE #5

Manage your credit cards and open credit.

TABLE 6.3

How Many Months It Takes to Eliminate Your Credit Card Debt if You Pay a Constant Percentage of Your Initial Balance Each Month

Annual Credit Card Interest Rate

Each Month Pay This Percentage of the Initial Outstanding Balance	9%	12%	15%	18%
2%	63 months	70 months	79 months	93 months
3%	39 months	41 months	43 months	47 months
5%	22 months	22 months	23 months	24 months
10%	10 months	11 months	11 months	11 months
15%	7 months	7 months	7 months	7 months

Step 1: Find the row that corresponds to the percentage of your initial balance that you intend to pay off each month. If you have an initial outstanding balance of $5,000 and you intend to pay off $150 each month, you would be paying off $150/$5,000 = 3% each month. Thus, you should look in the 3% row.

Step 2: Find the column that corresponds to the annual percentage that you pay on your credit card. If your card charges 15%, look in the 15% column.

Step 3: The intersection of the payments row and the credit card interest column shows how many months it would take to pay off your initial balance. If you pay off 3% of your initial balance each month and the card charges 15%, it would take 43 months to pay off your initial balance.

Resolving Billing Errors

Unfortunately, bill errors do occur. Your statement may contain a math error, it may include billing for an item you never received, it may include double billing for an item you purchased—the possible errors are many. Fortunately, the Fair Credit Billing Act (FCBA) provides a procedure for correcting billing errors. Under the FCBA you're allowed to withhold payment for the billing item in question while you petition the card issuer to investigate the matter. Table 6.4 provides a summary of the major laws governing consumer credit.

To begin an investigation of a billing problem, the FCBA requires that you notify your card issuer *in writing within 60 days* of the statement date. In your inquiry you must include your name, address, and account number in addition to a description of the error, including its date, the dollar amount of the billing error, and the reason you feel it's in error. You should also note in your letter that you're making this billing inquiry under the FCBA. This letter should then be sent to the "billing inquiry" or "billing error" address given on your credit card bill. Because payments from most bills are handled automatically, including your complaint with your payment will likely ensure that it'll be lost forever. Moreover, the FCBA requires that an address to which billing questions should be directed be included on your statement. Make sure you keep a copy of your letter for future reference.

| Major Provisions of Consumer Credit Laws | TABLE 6.4 |

Truth in Lending Act of 1968: Requires lenders to disclose the true cost of consumer credit, explaining all charges, terms, and conditions involved. It requires that the consumer be provided with the total finance charge and annual percentage rate on the loan.

Truth in Lending Act (amended 1971): Prohibits lenders from sending unauthorized credit cards and limits cardholders' liability to $50 for unauthorized use.

Fair Credit Reporting Act of 1971: Requires that consumers be provided with the name of any credit agency supplying a credit report that leads to the denial of credit. It also gives consumers the right to know what is in their credit reports and challenge incorrect information.

Fair Credit Billing Act of 1975: Sets procedures for correcting billing errors on open credit accounts. It also allows consumers to withhold payment for defective goods purchased with a credit card. In addition, it sets limits on the time some information can be kept in your credit file.

Equal Credit Opportunity Act of 1975: Prohibits credit discrimination on the basis of sex and marital status. It also requires lenders to provide a written statement explaining any adverse action taken.

Equal Credit Opportunity Act (amended 1977): Prohibits credit discrimination based on race, national origin, religion, age, or receipt of public assistance.

Fair Debt Collection Practices Act of 1978: Prohibits unfair, abusive, and deceptive practices by debt collectors, and establishes procedures for debt collection.

Truth in Lending Act (amended 1982): Requires installment credit contracts to be written in plain English.

Within 30 days you should receive notice that an investigation of your complaint has been initiated, and the card issuer has 90 days or two billing cycles to complete the investigation. Upon completion of the investigation, either your account will be credited the disputed amount or you'll receive an explanation from the card issuer as to why it feels your complaint isn't legitimate. You can then continue to dispute your billing charges even if the investigation doesn't turn out in your favor by notifying the card issuer within your grace period, but the process of correcting it becomes more complicated. Unfortunately, if you don't pay, you can be reported delinquent to your credit agency, and, as such, you risk the chance of being sued by the card issuer and having your credit rating go down the tubes. Still, if you feel the bank isn't handling your inquiry in an appropriate manner, contact the regulatory agency that oversees the card. Alternatively, you could contact an attorney or consider filing a claim in small claims court.

Protecting Against Fraud

What happens if your credit card is stolen? That depends upon how quickly you report the loss. If you report the loss before any fraudulent charges occur, then you owe nothing. Even if your card has been used, your liability is limited to $50 per card, which makes the credit card insurance that's available unnecessary. Still, the inconvenience associated with the loss of your credit card makes it imperative that you take care to guard against fraud.

Most steps to guard against credit card fraud are obvious. First, save all your credit card receipts and compare them against your credit card bill. After you've compared them with your billings, you should destroy these credit card receipts, because they contain your credit card number. Use care in giving your credit card number over the phone unless you're purchasing an item and you initiated the sale. Even if you're initiating the sale, never give your credit card number out over a public phone—you never know who's listening. Finally, never leave a store without your card. One way of ensuring you never leave your card behind is to hold your wallet in your hand until you receive your credit card back.

Looking for Trouble Signs in Credit Card Spending

The next step in controlling credit card borrowing is to examine your credit card habits and determine whether you have a problem. Although there's no simple formula for highlighting problems, many financial planners use a credit card habits quiz that forces you to look at your credit card habits and recognize any weaknesses there might be.

The Credit Card Habits Quiz.   Figure 6.6 provides sample questions that might be used in a credit card habits quiz. The purpose of this quiz is to allow you to step away and view your credit card habits from a distance, focusing on the effect they have on your financial well-being. There's no cutoff for wrong answers. In fact, the questions are really intended to make you think and reevaluate your credit card habits, not to generate a right or wrong answer. However, if you answer yes to any question, you should know that you might have a problem.

Although the credit card habits quiz is not a quantitative method of evaluating the severity of your credit card habits, it does a good job of identifying problem credit card users. If you have problems with any of these questions you should seriously reevaluate your credit card usage habits.

Controlling Your Credit Card Spending

The first steps in controlling your credit card spending are to set your goals and develop a budget to achieve these goals—that is the point of **Axiom 8: Nothing Happens Without a Plan—Even (or Especially) a Simple Plan**. The next step in controlling credit card spending is to track it. The best way to control your credit card spending is to keep a running tab on how much you've charged. Every time you use your credit card, write down the date and amount charged. Your checkbook register is an ideal place to do this. In fact, Citibank will provide you with a free "Credit Minder" credit card register if you don't have a spare check register (800-669-2635). Subtract the amount of each charge from what you have in your checking account. When your credit card bill comes in, you'll have enough in your checking account to pay it off completely. Once you understand how your credit card has gotten you into trouble, it's much easier to control its use.

What to Do if You Can't Pay Your Credit Card Bills

Once you've gotten into trouble through the overuse of credit cards, getting out is a real hassle. The first step is, of course, putting in place a budget that brings in more money than you spend. This involves self-control in the use of your credit card—making sure you act your wage. Along with this remedy there are other options you might consider. First, you should make sure you have the least expensive credit card possible given your credit card use habits. As you saw earlier, the cost of cards differs dramatically, and you should have a credit card that fits your usage habits.

A second option to consider is using savings to pay off current credit card debt. Don't make dipping into your savings a habit. If it has to happen at all, it should happen only once—when you are reevaluating and changing your spending and credit

AXIOM #8

Nothing Happens Without a Plan—Even (or Especially) a Simple Plan

The Credit Card Habits Quiz

FIGURE 6.6

☐   Do you only make the minimum payment on your credit card each month?

☐   Have you reached your spending limit on one or more credit cards?

☐   When out to dinner with a group of friends, do you pay the entire bill with your credit card and have them reimburse you for their share with cash?

☐   Do you wait for your monthly bill to determine how much you have charged on your credit card rather than keep track of all your credit card spending as it occurs?

☐   Do you use your credit card to make impulse purchases or to purchase necessities like food or rent?

☐   Do you get cash advances because you do not have enough in your checking account?

☐   Have you been turned down for credit or had one of your credit cards canceled?

☐   Have you used some of your savings to pay off credit card bills?

☐   Do you know how much of your credit card bill is from interest?

☐   Does your stomach start churning when you get your credit card bill?

card use patterns in a permanent manner. Keep in mind that the interest rate on the unpaid balance on an average credit card is approximately 17.1 percent. If you're only earning 5 percent after taxes on your savings, then by using savings to pay off credit card borrowing, you'll save 12.1 percent. As Ben Franklin might have said, 12.1 percent saved is 12.1 percent earned. There may be no easier way of earning 12.1 percent risk-free than using savings that earn a low rate to pay off borrowing that costs a high rate. Again, your credit card use should be controlled in such a way that it doesn't get out of hand and doesn't warrant this remedy on a regular basis. There's a purpose to your savings, and to blow it in this way defeats the purpose of planning. In effect, using your savings is an emergency measure to be taken only in the extreme situation.

Another alternative that you might consider to lower the cost of your outstanding debt is to use a secured loan or a home equity loan to pay off your high-cost credit card debt. We'll look at consumer loans and debt of this type in the next chapter.

SUMMARY

Open credit is a running line of credit that you can use to make charges up to a certain point as long as you pay off a minimum amount of your debt each month. The main form of open credit is the credit card, which has become an essential part of our personal finances. Four basic factors that affect the cost of open credit are the interest rate, the balance calculation method, the grace period, the annual fee, and other additional or penalty fees. The advantages of the use of credit cards or open credit include the following: convenience or ease of shopping, emergency use, allowing you to consume before you pay, consolidation of bills, buying in anticipation of price increases, as a source of interest-free credit, to make reservations, as identification, and as a source of free benefits. The reasons why you should be wary of credit cards and open credit are that it's possible to lose control of spending, they are expensive, and you'll have less spendable income in the future.

There are many choices of open credit lines, including different types of credit cards, as well as charge accounts. Of the credit cards, there are three basic types, including bank credit cards, travel and entertainment cards, and single-purpose cards.

In determining what makes an individual creditworthy, most lenders refer to the "five C's" of credit—character, capacity, capital, collateral, and conditions—as the keys. How does a credit card issuer verify the information you put down on your application? Through your credit report from a credit bureau. A credit bureau is a private organization that maintains credit information on individuals. The three national credit bureaus are Experian, Trans Union, and Equifax Credit Information Services.

Different credit cards charge different APRs, and they also calculate the finance charges imposed in different ways. Of importance here is how the unpaid balance is calculated. How do you control credit card use? You focus attention on controlling credit card spending and looking for signs of trouble. Finally, you should know that under the Fair Credit Reporting Act (FCRA) passed by Congress in 1971 (and subsequently amended to help ensure consumers that their credit reports are accurate), you have the right to view your credit report. Although you'll be charged a small fee in the range of $8 to $15, you can generally obtain a copy of your credit report easily through the mail. If you're turned down for credit, it's a good idea to review your report to make sure all the information contained in it is accurate.

Review Questions

1. What is credit? What is open credit? What is revolving credit? (LO 1)
2. Although annual fees are paid only once a year, paying a $15 annual fee for the privilege of using a credit card could be thought of as adding $1.25 to your monthly bill. What other four factors directly affect a monthly credit card bill? (LO 1, 2)
3. Explain the differences in the commonly used balance calculation methods used by credit card issuers. Given similar account activity, which will result in the lowest monthly interest charge? The highest monthly interest charge? *Hint:* Review Figure 6.1, and don't forget the variation of including *or* excluding new purchases. (LO 1, 2)

Just Do It! *From the Desk of Marcy Furney, CFP*
Frozen Assets

One of my clients told me she finally got control of her impulse purchasing on credit by putting her cards in a zipper bag and freezing them in a bucket of water. That way she has some time to think things through while she waits for them to thaw. Recently, this method has been touted on morning shows throughout the nation. If it sounds too bizarre to you, or your freezer is too full of TV dinners and ice cream, here are some more ideas.

- ✓ Carry one credit card and use it only for convenience. That means you can use it only if there's money in the bank to cover the amount of the charge.

- ✓ Subtract the charge from your check register when you make it. Negative balance? Then no charging!

- ✓ Pay your entire balance each month.

- ✓ If you have large balances on high-interest cards, look for one with lower interest and transfer the debt. Don't use that card for any new charges. Set a date for clearing the balance, calculate how much you have to pay each month to meet the deadline, and pay it off. In 1996 one of my clients received an offer for 8-percent interest on the transferred balance until it was paid off, but the current charges incurred interest at 18 percent. Most cards offer the lower rate for only a year or so.

- ✓ Tear up and throw away all of those "you have already been approved" credit card applications. This applies also to the blank checks that are sent on your existing accounts. Be sure they are disposed of properly to avoid fraud.

- ✓ If you are in too deep but have an excellent payment record, call the credit card company to discuss lowering your interest rate. Some won't consider such a request if you have current charges on that card. If you own a home in any state but Texas, check into a home equity loan to pay off the debt. Be aware, though, that you must have your spending under control and be willing to pay off that loan quickly, or you jeopardize the roof over your head.

- ✓ Don't even consider investing money if you have consumer debt. No investment can guarantee you a return equal to the 18- to 21-percent cost of credit.

- ✓ If you're paying off a large balance, make that payment a fixed, rather than discretionary, expense in your budget. Never pay just the minimum amount on your statement. You may have to forgo entertainment or "brown bag" your lunch for a while.

- ✓ Take control. An excellent credit history is a true asset, and a large line of credit could be very important in case of emergency.

4. What is a grace period? Why would a grace period be canceled or eliminated? (LO 1, 2)

5. List five benefits, or advantages, associated with credit card or open credit use. In your opinion, what is the major disadvantage? (LO 2)

6. Explain the differences in a bank credit card, a premium or prestige credit card, an affinity credit card, and a secured credit card. (LO 3)
7. Although they're called "credit cards," T&E cards and single-purpose cards are uniquely different from bank credit cards. What are the differences? (LO 3)
8. What is (are) the most important decision factor(s) in choosing a credit card for a credit user, a convenience user, and convenience and credit user? (LO 3)
9. Explain the five C's of credit and how they relate to individual creditworthiness. (LO 4)
10. Define credit scoring. What is the role of the credit bureau in the calculation of your score? (LO 4)
11. List four ways to avoid credit card fraud. (LO 5)
12. Review Figure 6.6. Develop a list of five to eight warning signs of credit card abuse or spending trouble signs. (LO 5)
13. Based on **Axiom 8: Nothing Happens Without a Plan—Even (or Especially) a Simple Plan**, what plan might be necessary to control credit card spending and pay off large balances that have gotten out of hand? (LO 5)

Problems and Activities

1. Ricardo and his friends are going to the mall and then on to a favorite jazz club to hear a new band. Quickly totaling the anticipated cost of his purchases and his cash needs for the weekend, he stops by an ATM machine for a cash advance on his credit card. His friends laugh at his financial error, while Ricardo argues the convenience of "one-stop shopping for cash" when your bank account is low. Who's right? Thoroughly defend your answer to settle the argument. (LO 1, 2)
2. Based on the data in Figure 6.1, calculate the monthly interest charges for credit card accounts charging 14-, 16-, and 18-percent interest. Complete the chart below. Because average daily balance is the most commonly used balance calculation method, is shopping for a lower interest rate really that important? (LO 1)

	14%	16%	18%
Average daily balance			$ 8.25
Previous balance			15.00
Adjusted balance			1.50

3. A university professor and his wife, a public school teacher, in a recent month received 15 credit card offers in the mail, for credit limits totaling over $125,000. In light of this information, explain the three reasons that consumers should be wary of credit cards. Aside from the interest charges, annual fees, and other penalty fees, what is the "cost" of credit? (LO 2)
4. Credit card issuers use credit bureau data to "preselect" consumers who'll be sent application packets marketing their card. Name at least one unique characteristic of a consumer who might be sent an application for a bank credit card, a premium or prestige credit card, an affinity credit card, and a secured credit card. (LO 3)
5. Some merchants, such as gasoline stations, advertise two different prices. What is the rationale for charging one price to cash customers and another price to credit customers using bank credit cards or T&E cards? (LO 2, 3)
6. Using the sample credit score card in Figure 6.5, relate each question to one of the five C's of credit. Are all five considered? Why or why not? (LO 4)

7. It's commonly recommended that you should check your credit report every 2 to 3 years as well as before applying for credit, after being denied credit, and before applying for a job. Why? Should you add a statement to your report each time? Will you have to pay each time? (LO 4)

8. With only a part-time job and the need for a professional wardrobe, Mike quickly maxed out his credit card the summer after graduation. Upon receiving his first full-time paycheck in August, he vowed not to use the card and to pay $240 each month, or 3 percent of the $8,000 outstanding balance. The card has an annual interest rate of 18 percent. Using Table 6.3, how long will it take Mike to pay for his summer? (LO 5)

Suggested Projects

1. Working in a small group, collect credit card marketing information or the summary of account information sent to cardholders for three to five different cards. Using these materials, complete one or more of the following activities.
   a. Summarize the card information into a chart showing purchase balance calculation method, annual percentage rate of interest for purchases, grace period, annual fee, and minimum finance charge. Compare the results. (LO 1, 2)
   b. Summarize the card information pertaining to cash advances into a chart showing grace period, interest rate, and transaction fee for cash advances. Compare the results. (LO 1, 2)
   c. Summarize the card information pertaining to additional or penalty fees into a chart. Consider fees for late payment, exceeding the credit limit, or bounced checks. Compare the results. (LO 1, 2)
   d. Summarize the additional benefits, or "perks," that are available, such as insurance programs, car rental discounts, traveler assistance, and so on. Compare the results. (LO 1, 2)
   e. Select the card that'd be most appropriate for a credit user. Justify your choice. (LO 3)
   f. Select the card that'd be most appropriate for a convenience user. Justify your choice. (LO 3)
   g. Review the information requested on the application. Explain how the information relates to the five C's of credit. (LO 4)
2. Share the list of pros and cons of credit cards shown in Figure 6.2 with 15 to 20 other college students. From the list, ask each to identify the top three reasons they use credit cards *and* the primary reason they avoid, or limit, credit card use. Summarize your results in an oral or written report. In general, do the practices of these students suggest a sound financial plan or the potential for developing credit card problems? (LO 2, 5)
3. Interview individuals representing the three stages of the financial life cycle regarding their credit card usage. How many cards do they have? What kind of cards (rebate, premium, affinity, T&E, or single-purpose) do they have? How often are cards used, and typically for what purchases? What is their available line of credit? Classify them as convenience users, credit users, or convenience and credit users. Summarize your findings into an oral or written report noting differences in credit card use across the financial life cycle. *Hint:* Refer to chapter 1 to review the financial life cycle concept. (LO 3)
4. Contact the local credit bureau to determine how to check your credit report. Be sure to ask (a) what information should be included in the letter, (b) whether a copy of documentation showing your current address should be included, and (c) the charge and method of payment. For additional information, check the

Web site for Equifax at http://www.equifax.com or for Experian (formerly TRW) at http://www.experian.com. Report your findings. Request and review your credit report. (LO 4)

5. Consumer credit legislation offers consumers a variety of protection services when securing credit, using credit, or repaying credit. How are consumers educated about these laws? Identify as many sources as possible. Begin your search with (a) credit contracts and bills, (b) local, state, and federal offices of consumer affairs, (c) the extension service of a land grant university, or (d) the World Wide Web. Share your results in a report, including examples of brochures, bills, or other materials collected. (LO 5)

Discussion Case 1

Selena will be a college sophomore next year, and she's determined to have her own credit card. She's not employed during the school year, but is convinced she can qualify because of her summer earnings. Selena's parents have read a number of articles about the problems of credit cards and college students, including examples of students leaving school after a downward spiral of credit cards, overspending, working to pay bills, worrying about bills, working more hours to pay bills, and eventually flunking out of school. When Selena showed up with a handful of applications including Visa, a Gold MasterCard, Discover, a Visa sponsored by her university, an American Express, a secured MasterCard, and a gas station card, her parents were overwhelmed. Selena admitted she didn't want them *all*. "I'm not stupid," she declared. Because Selena obviously needed to learn about credit cards, her parents agreed to co-sign her application, on one condition. She had to approach her choice just like a class project and research the following questions.

Questions

1. Assuming Selena doesn't really care about her parents' approval and ignores their assignment, will she be able to apply for a credit card without their help? *Hint:* Consider the application process and the five C's of credit.

2. How can an unemployed college student possibly need a credit card? What are the advantages to having a credit card? What are the disadvantages?

3. Should Selena have more than one card? What's the recommended number of credit cards for the average consumer?

4. Shopping for credit can be compared to shopping for any other consumer product—consider the product cost, features, advantages, and disadvantages. In other words, does the product meet the user's needs? Help Selena compare her credit choices given the applications she has collected.

5. Based on the analysis in question 4, what credit card applications, if any, should Selena seriously consider? For what other "products," if any, might she consider applications?

6. Summarize the five basic factors that affect credit card costs and that should be compared by Selena when choosing a card.

7. To avoid problems, what might be considered the most important rule for Selena to follow when using a credit card?

Discussion Case 2

Good thing everyone paid his or her share for dinner last night, Bob thought as he looked at his checkbook balance. Because he charged the entire bill on his credit card, the cash would come in handy until he got paid again. However, this month's credit card bill had to be paid today. As he glanced over the bill, he couldn't believe the difference in interest charges for his purchases and that one cash advance. Just because he was a few days late last month, there was another $15 fee. Although they have a card from the same bank, Maria had said last night that her interest rate was lower than Bob's. That's it, Bob thought, I'm through with this card. Besides, he questioned all those charges, especially at the grocery store. Help him sort through his options.

Questions

1. Is it legal for Bob to be charged a higher rate than Maria by the same card issuer? Why?
2. Explain the differences in interest charges for purchases and cash advances. Be sure to explain grace periods as a part of your answer.
3. If Bob is truly "through with this card," how long will it take him to pay off the outstanding balance of $3,000 at an 18-percent APR? He can afford to pay approximately $150 each month.
4. What factors should Bob consider if he decides to transfer his current card balance to another card?
5. Based on a review of Figure 6.6, "The Credit Card Habits Quiz," help Bob review his credit use for trouble signs.

Chapter 7

USING CONSUMER LOANS:
The Role of Planned Borrowing in Personal Financial Management

A recent episode of *ER* found nurse Carol Hathaway and Dr. Carter wheeling a patient into Central Hospital. As they were about to enter the hospital, Dr. Doug Ross walked by, calling, "Carol, what happened to your car?"

"What do you mean?" she called back.

"A tow truck hauled it off."

A look of concern crossed Carol's face.

"Go, go, go, I'll take care of this," Dr. Carter said, as he grabbed the gurney.

Running out to the parking lot, Carol yelled, "Hey! Wait! Wait! Please wait! Hey, no, um, that's my car."

"Hey yourself, stop beating on my truck," the tow truck driver replied.

"Well, stop stealing my car."

"You Carol Hathaway?" the driver asked.

"Yeah."

"Repossessed," the driver responded.

"Wait, no, no, no, that can't be right."

"You missed three payments."

"So, I'm a little late, but I made the other seven on time," Carol shouted as the truck pulled away.

A bit later in the show Carol poured out her soul to her mother. "I feel good on my own, I'm enjoying it. I just can't afford it. The house, the car—somehow I've accumulated the debt of a fifty-year-old."

Sure, *ER* is only a TV show, but TV tends to reflect society. And this was one of those shows that left many viewers saying to themselves,

Learning Objectives

Learning Objectives

After reading this chapter you should be able to:

1. Understand and choose from the various consumer loans.
2. Calculate the cost of a consumer loan.
3. Pick an appropriate source for your loan.
4. Get the most favorable interest rate possible on a loan.
5. Know when to borrow.
6. Control your debt.

"That could happen to me." It's easy to think that going from the poor life as a student to the ranks of the employed is an automatic setup for the good life. It probably is, at least as long as you maintain control of your finances and don't use debt to live beyond your means. As Dr. Joyce Brothers once said, "Credit buying is much like being drunk. The buzz happens immediately and gives you a lift. . . . The hangover comes the day after."

Chapter 6 examined credit cards and other sources of open credit. We now turn our attention to **consumer loans**. You can think of consumer loans as the next step up in debt. They're stricter and more formal than credit cards and other open credit. Instead of giving you a limited borrow-when-you-want open line of credit, they involve formal contracts detailing exactly how much you're borrowing and exactly when and how you're going to pay it back. Open credit's used for making convenience purchases—tonight's dinner or a new pair of Reeboks. Consumer loans, however, are usually used for bigger purchases, such as Carol Hathaway's car. With consumer loans, you can borrow more and pay it back at a slower pace than you can with open credit, but you have to lock yourself into a set and prespecified repayment schedule. Because it forces you to plan your purchase and your repayment, consumer loans tend to be called "planned borrowing."

It would be ideal to be able to buy everything you need or want with your savings. Hey, no one likes owing someone else money. However, sometimes purchases are too big or the timing is such that you have to borrow money to finance a particular goal and pay for it later when you're in better financial shape or gradually over time. Consumer loans allow you to do just that. However, consumer loans are a double-edged sword. On one hand, they let you consume more now, but on the other hand, they create a financial obligation that can be a burden later. Remember, for Carol Hathaway, a consumer loan provided the funds for her car, and missing three payments on that consumer loan cost her that car.

Consumer Loan
A loan involving a formal contract detailing exactly how much you're borrowing and when and how you're going to pay it back.

**Understand and choose
from the various
consumer loans.**

Single-Payment or **Balloon Loan**
A loan that is paid back in a single lump-sum payment at maturity, or the due date of the loan, which is usually specified in the loan contract. At that date you pay back the amount you borrowed plus all interest charges.

Bridge or **Interim Loan**
A short-term loan that provides funding until a longer-term source can be secured or until additional financing is found.

Installment Loan
A loan that calls for repayment of both the interest and the principal at regular intervals, with the payment levels set in such a way that the loan expires at a preset date.

Loan Amortization
The repayment of a loan using equal monthly payments which cover a portion of the principal and the interest on the declining balance. The amount of the monthly payment going toward interest payment starts off large and steadily declines, while the amount going toward the principal starts off small and steadily increases.

Secured Loan
A loan that's guaranteed by a specific asset.

Unsecured Loan
A loan that's not guaranteed by a specific asset.

CHARACTERISTICS OF CONSUMER LOANS

Not all consumer loans look the same. They can range from single-payment, unsecured fixed-rate loans to secured, variable-rate installment loans. What does all that mean? Let's take a look at the characteristics and associated terminology of consumer loans.

Single-Payment versus Installment Loans

Consumer loans can be categorized as being either single-payment loans or installment loans. A **single-payment** or **balloon loan** is simply a loan that's paid back in a single lump-sum payment at maturity, or the due date of the loan, which is usually specified in the loan contract. At that date you pay back the amount you borrowed plus all interest charges. Single-payment loans generally have a relatively short maturity of less than 1 year associated with them. Needless to say, paying off a loan of this kind is generally quite difficult if you don't have access to a large source of money when it matures. As a result, they're generally used as **bridge** or **interim loans** to provide short-term funding until longer-term or additional financing is found. A bridge loan might be used in financing the building of a house, with the mortgage loan being used to pay off the bridge loan and provide more permanent funding for the house.

An **installment loan** calls for repayment of both the interest and the principal at regular intervals, with the payment levels set in such a way that the loan expires at a preset date. The amount of the monthly payment going toward interest payment starts off large and steadily decreases, while the amount going toward the principal starts off small and steadily increases. In effect, as you pay off more of the loan each month, your interest expenses decline; therefore, your principal payment increases. This process is commonly referred to as **loan amortization**. Installment loans are very common and are used to finance cars, appliances, and other big-ticket items.

Secured versus Unsecured Loans

Consumer loans are either secured or unsecured. A **secured loan** is guaranteed by a specific asset. If you can't meet the loan payments, then that asset can be seized and sold to cover the amount due. Many times the asset that's been purchased with the funds from the loan is used for security. For example, if you borrow money to buy a car, then that car is generally used as collateral for the loan. If you don't make your car payment, your car may be repossessed. Repossessed collateral, though, may or may not cover what you owe. That is, after the collateral is repossessed, you could still owe money. Other assets commonly used as security for a loan are CDs, stocks, jewelry, land, and bank accounts. Securities reduce lenders' risks, so lenders charge a lower rate on a secured loan than they would on a comparable unsecured loan.

An **unsecured loan** requires no collateral. In general, larger unsecured loans are given only to borrowers with excellent credit histories, because the only security that the lender has is the individual's promise to pay. The big disadvantage of unsecured loans is that they're quite expensive.

Variable-Rate versus Fixed-Rate Loans

The interest payments associated with a consumer loan can either be fixed or variable. A **fixed interest rate loan** isn't tied to market interest rates and maintains a single interest rate for the entire duration of the loan. Regardless of whether market interest rates swing up or down, the interest rate you pay remains fixed. While the vast majority of consumer loans have fixed rates, a few have variable rates.

A **variable** or **adjustable interest rate loan** is tied to a market interest rate, such as the prime rate or the 6-month Treasury bill rate, and the interest rate you pay varies as that market rate changes. As the market rate rises and falls, so does the interest rate you have to pay. The **prime rate** is the interest rate banks charge to their most creditworthy customers. Most consumer loans are set above the prime rate or the Treasury bill rate. For example, your loan might be set at 4 percent over prime. In this case, if the prime rate is 9 percent at the moment, the rate you pay on your variable-rate loan would be 13 percent. If the prime rate drops to 8 percent, your rate would change to 12 percent.

Not all variable-rate loans are the same. For example, their rates are adjusted at different, but fixed, intervals. For example, some loans adjust every month, while others every year. The less frequent the loan adjusts, the less you have to worry about rate changes. Another question that you should address before taking on a variable-rate loan is, How volatile is the interest rate to which the loan is pegged? In general, short-term market rates tend to change more than long-term market rates. Therefore, variable-rate loans tied to the 6-month Treasury bill rate expose you to more risk of rate changes than do loans tied to, say, the 20-year Treasury bond rate. Of course, variable-rate loans usually have rate caps that prevent their interest rates from varying too much. The periodic cap limits the maximum that the interest rate can jump during one adjustment. The lifetime cap limits the amount that the interest rate can jump over the life of the loan. The larger the fluctuations allowed by the caps, the greater the risk that you have to face. The bottom line on a variable interest rate loan is that if interest rates drop, you win, and if interest rates rise, you lose.

So which is better, a fixed-rate loan or a variable-rate loan? Neither one necessarily. The choice between a variable- or fixed-rate loan is another example of **Axiom 1: The Risk-Return Trade-Off**. With a variable-rate loan, you bear the risk that interest rates will go up and the payments will increase accordingly, and you might get stuck with interest payments you can no longer afford. With a fixed-rate loan, the lender bears the risk that rates will go up, causing a loss of potential interest income on an already fixed rate. Because the lender's bearing more risk, fixed-rate loans generally cost more than variable-rate loans.

An alternative to a fixed- or variable-rate loan is a convertible loan. A **convertible loan** is a variable-rate loan that can be converted into a fixed-rate loan at the borrower's option at specified dates in the future. Although convertible loans are much less common than variable- or fixed-rate loans, they do offer the advantage of enjoying the lower cost of a variable-rate loan while still being able to lock into the savings of a fixed-rate loan when a low interest rate comes along.

The Loan Contract

The loan contract simply spells out all the conditions and specifics of the loan in exhaustive detail. If the item being purchased is to be used as collateral for the loan, then the contract will contain a **security agreement** saying so. The security agreement identifies whether the lender or borrower retains control over the item being purchased. The formal agreement stating the payment schedule and the rights of both the lender and the borrower in the case of **default** are outlined in the **note**. The note is standard on all loans, and the security agreement is also standard on secured loans. In addition, there are other clauses that are sometimes included in a loan contract, including an insurance agreement clause, an acceleration clause, a deficiency payment clause, and a recourse clause. An example of an installment purchase contract is given in Figure 7.1.

Insurance Agreement Clause. With an **insurance agreement clause** you're required to purchase credit life insurance to pay off the loan in the event of your death. For you, credit life insurance adds nothing to the loan other than cost. It's really the lender who benefits from an insurance agreement clause. As such, if an insurance agreement clause is included, its cost should justifiably be included as a cost of the loan.

FIGURE 7.1

An Installment Purchase Contract

Keep in mind when taking out an installment purchase contract that, just as you have bought a product such as a television or an automobile, the loan that you are taking out is also a product. As such, you should make sure it's something you can afford and that you understand what you're signing.

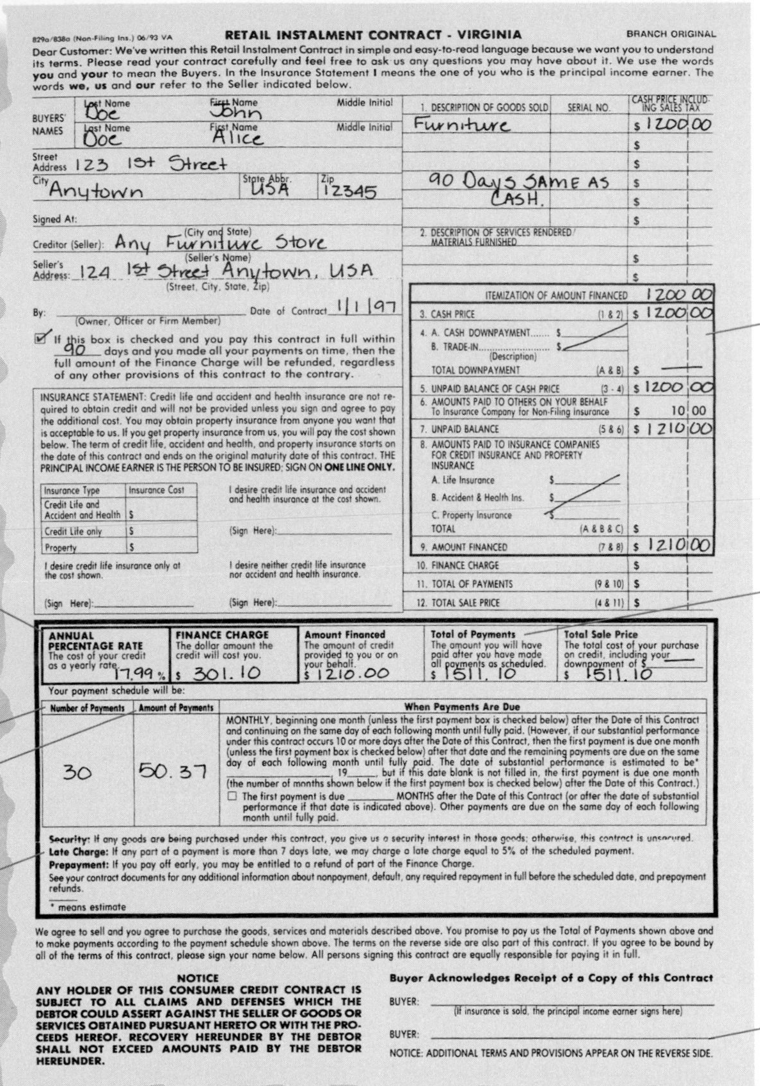

829a/838a (Non-Filing Ins.) 06/93 VA — **RETAIL INSTALMENT CONTRACT - VIRGINIA** — BRANCH ORIGINAL

Dear Customer: We've written this Retail Instalment Contract in simple and easy-to-read language because we want you to understand its terms. Please read your contract carefully and feel free to ask us any questions you may have about it. We use the words **you** and **your** to mean the Buyers. In the Insurance Statement **I** means the one of you who is the principal income earner. The words **we, us** and **our** refer to the Seller indicated below.

BUYERS' NAMES: Last Name Doe, First Name John, Middle Initial; Last Name Doe, First Name Alice, Middle Initial

Street Address 123 1st Street

City Anytown — State Abbr. USA — Zip 12345

Signed At: (City and State)

Creditor (Seller): Any Furniture Store (Seller's Name)

Seller's Address: 124 1st Street Anytown, USA (Street, City, State, Zip)

By: (Owner, Officer or Firm Member) — Date of Contract 1/1/97

☑ If this box is checked and you pay this contract in full within 90 days and you made all your payments on time, then the full amount of the Finance Charge will be refunded, regardless of any other provisions of this contract to the contrary.

INSURANCE STATEMENT: Credit life and accident and health insurance are not required to obtain credit and will not be provided unless you sign and agree to pay the additional cost. You may obtain property insurance from anyone you want that is acceptable to us. If you get property insurance from us, you will pay the cost shown below. The term of credit life, accident and health, and property insurance starts on the date of this contract and ends on the original maturity date of this contract. THE PRINCIPAL INCOME EARNER IS THE PERSON TO BE INSURED; SIGN ON **ONE LINE ONLY.**

Insurance Type	Insurance Cost
Credit Life and Accident and Health	$
Credit Life only	$
Property	$

I desire credit life insurance and accident and health insurance at the cost shown. (Sign Here):

I desire credit life insurance only at the cost shown. (Sign Here):

I desire neither credit life insurance nor accident and health insurance. (Sign Here):

1. DESCRIPTION OF GOODS SOLD	SERIAL NO.	CASH PRICE INCLUDING SALES TAX
Furniture		$ 1200.00
		$
		$
90 Days SAME AS CASH.		$
		$
		$
2. DESCRIPTION OF SERVICES RENDERED/MATERIALS FURNISHED		
		$
		$

ITEMIZATION OF AMOUNT FINANCED		1200.00
3. CASH PRICE	(1 & 2)	$ 1200.00
4. A. CASH DOWNPAYMENT $ B. TRADE-IN $ (Description)		
TOTAL DOWNPAYMENT	(A & B)	$ —
5. UNPAID BALANCE OF CASH PRICE	(3 - 4)	$ 1200.00
6. AMOUNTS PAID TO OTHERS ON YOUR BEHALF To Insurance Company for Non-Filing Insurance		$ 10.00
7. UNPAID BALANCE	(5 & 6)	$ 1210.00
8. AMOUNTS PAID TO INSURANCE COMPANIES FOR CREDIT INSURANCE AND PROPERTY INSURANCE A. Life Insurance $ B. Accident & Health Ins. $ C. Property Insurance $		
TOTAL	(A & B & C)	$
9. AMOUNT FINANCED	(7 & 8)	$ 1210.00
10. FINANCE CHARGE		$
11. TOTAL OF PAYMENTS	(9 & 10)	$
12. TOTAL SALE PRICE	(4 & 11)	$

ANNUAL PERCENTAGE RATE The cost of your credit as a yearly rate.	FINANCE CHARGE The dollar amount the credit will cost you.	Amount Financed The amount of credit provided to you or on your behalf.	Total of Payments The amount you will have paid after you have made all payments as scheduled.	Total Sale Price The total cost of your purchase on credit, including your downpayment of $ —
17.99 %	$ 301.10	$ 1210.00	$ 1511.10	$ 1511.10

Your payment schedule will be:

Number of Payments	Amount of Payments	When Payments Are Due
30	50.37	MONTHLY, beginning one month (unless the first payment box is checked below) after the Date of this Contract and continuing on the same day of each following month until fully paid. (However, if our substantial performance under this contract occurs 10 or more days after the Date of this Contract, then the first payment is due one month (unless the first payment box is checked below) after that date and the remaining payments are due on the same day of each following month until fully paid. The date of substantial performance is estimated to be* ______, 19____, but if this date blank is not filled in, the first payment is due one month (the number of months shown below if the first payment box is checked below) after the Date of this Contract.) ☐ The first payment is due ______ MONTHS after the Date of this Contract (or after the date of substantial performance if that date is indicated above). Other payments are due on the same day of each following month until fully paid.

Security: If any goods are being purchased under this contract, you give us a security interest in those goods; otherwise, this contract is unsecured.
Late Charge: If any part of a payment is more than 7 days late, we may charge a late charge equal to 5% of the scheduled payment.
Prepayment: If you pay off early, you may be entitled to a refund of part of the Finance Charge.
See your contract documents for any additional information about nonpayment, default, any required repayment in full before the scheduled date, and prepayment refunds.

* means estimate

We agree to sell and you agree to purchase the goods, services and materials described above. You promise to pay us the Total of Payments shown above and to make payments according to the payment schedule shown above. The terms on the reverse side are also part of this contract. If you agree to be bound by all of the terms of this contract, please sign your name below. All persons signing this contract are equally responsible for paying it in full.

NOTICE
ANY HOLDER OF THIS CONSUMER CREDIT CONTRACT IS SUBJECT TO ALL CLAIMS AND DEFENSES WHICH THE DEBTOR COULD ASSERT AGAINST THE SELLER OF GOODS OR SERVICES OBTAINED PURSUANT HERETO OR WITH THE PROCEEDS HEREOF. RECOVERY HEREUNDER BY THE DEBTOR SHALL NOT EXCEED AMOUNTS PAID BY THE DEBTOR HEREUNDER.

Buyer Acknowledges Receipt of a Copy of this Contract

BUYER: ______ (If insurance is sold, the principal income earner signs here)

BUYER: ______

NOTICE: ADDITIONAL TERMS AND PROVISIONS APPEAR ON THE REVERSE SIDE.

Annual Percentage Rate: The cost of the loan expressed as an annual percentage rate for easy comparison.

Number and Amount of Payments: The total number and amount of each monthly payment.

Late Charge: This defines what additional fee you would have to pay if you miss a payment.

Itemization of the Amount Financed: The contract shows any fees and insurance charges that are added to the unpaid balance in determining the total amount to be financed.

Total of Payments: The total amount you'll pay. This doesn't include your down payment.

Cosigner: If you have poor credit, you may be required to have someone cosign your loan. If you fail to repay the loan, the cosigner becomes liable for the amount you owe.

Acceleration Clause
A loan requirement stating that if the borrower misses one payment, the entire loan comes due immediately.

Acceleration Clause. An **acceleration clause** states that if you miss one payment, the entire loan comes due immediately. If at that time you can't pay off the entire loan, the collateral will be repossessed and sold to pay off the balance due. Acceleration clauses are standard in most loans. However, lenders usually won't immediately invoke the acceleration clause, but instead allow you a chance to make good on the overdue payments.

Deficiency Payments Clause. A **deficiency payments clause** states that if you default on a secured loan, not only can the lender repossess whatever is secured, but if when that asset is sold it doesn't cover what you owe, you can be billed for the difference. To make sense out of this clause, let's look back at Carol Hathaway, the nurse from *ER* who had her car repossessed. If Hathaway owed a balance on the car of $10,000, and when the car was sold at auction by the lender it brought only $9,000, she would still owe $1,000. In addition, under the deficiency payments clause she would also be responsible for collection costs, say $150, selling costs, perhaps another $150, and attorney fees of, say, $100. As a result, Carol would not only lose her car, but would also be billed for $1,400 ($1,000 + $150 + $150 + $100).

Recourse Clause. A **recourse clause** defines what actions a lender can take to claim money from you in case you default. For example, the recourse clause may allow the lender to attach your wages, which means that a certain portion of your salary would go directly to the lender to pay off your debt.

> ### *The Facts of Life*
> By 1996, the typical American household had total debts of around $40,000. Although mortgage debt is by far the biggest debt item for most households, the total level of personal loans is over $200 billion.

SPECIAL TYPES OF CONSUMER LOANS

Although consumer loans are used for almost anything, there are several special-purpose consumer loans that deserve close attention. It's important to look at these loans not only because they are extremely common, but because they also include unique advantages and disadvantages that you should be aware of.

Home Equity Loans

A **home equity loan** or **second mortgage** is a loan that uses your built-up equity in your home as collateral against the loan. In effect, a home equity loan is merely a special type of secured loan. Generally, you can borrow from 50 to 85 percent of your equity—that is, your home value minus your first mortgage balance. For example, if you own a home with a market value of $200,000 and have an outstanding balance on your first mortgage of $80,000 then your home equity would be $120,000. With this much equity, you would be able to get a home equity loan of between $60,000 and $102,000 (0.50 times $120,000, and 0.85 times $120,000, respectively). In this case, your home is used as security on a loan that can be used for any purpose (it needn't be home related). It should be noted that not all states allow home equity loans. For example, Texas, the Lone Star State, isn't the Loan Star State—it doesn't allow home equity loans.

Home Equity Loan or **Second Mortgage**

A loan that uses a borrower's built-up equity in his or her home as collateral against the loan.

Advantages of Home Equity Loans. The primary advantages of a home equity loan over an alternative loan center on costs. The first cost advantage arises because the interest paid on other consumer loans isn't tax-deductible. However, the interest on a home equity loan is generally tax-deductible up to a maximum of $100,000, provided the loan doesn't exceed your home's market value. So, for every dollar of interest you pay on your home equity loan, your taxable income is lowered by $1. Again, we're seeing the effect of the tax code on personal finance—another example of **Axiom 6: Taxes Bias Personal Finance Decisions**.

Thus, if you're in a 25-percent marginal tax bracket, paying $1 of interest on a home equity loan will save you 25¢ in taxes. The after-tax cost of paying $1 of interest on this home equity loan would be only 75¢, or $1(1 − 0.25). Hey, don't scoff at a 25¢ savings. Those quarters add up: If you're in a 25-percent marginal tax bracket and you borrow $33,333 at 12 percent, you'll save $1,000 a year if the interest is tax-deductible.

AXIOM #6

Taxes Bias Personal Finance Decisions

You can also calculate the after-tax cost of the home equity loan by taking the before-tax cost of the home equity loan and multiplying it by [1 − (marginal tax rate)]:

$$\text{after-tax cost of a home equity loan} = \text{before-tax cost } (1 - \text{marginal tax rate})$$

As you recall from chapter 4, you have to determine your marginal tax bracket before you can calculate the after-cost. This marginal tax rate is the rate at which any additional income you receive will be taxed, and it combines the federal and state tax rates that you pay on the investment that you're considering. If the before-tax interest rate on the home equity loan is 9 percent and you're in the 25-percent marginal tax bracket, then the after-tax cost of the loan would be 6.75 percent, calculated as follows:

$$6.75\% = 9\%(1 - 0.25)$$

Thus, you might pay 9 percent on this loan, but the cost to you, after taking into account the fact that paying interest on this loan lowers your taxes, is only 6.75 percent.

The second cost advantage of home equity loans comes from the fact that they generally carry a lower interest rate than do other consumer loans. Because home equity loans are secured loans, lenders consider them less risky than unsecured loans and subsequently charge a lower interest rate on them.

Disadvantages of a Home Equity Loan.
The major disadvantage of a home equity loan is that it puts your home at risk. Now, don't think that a home equity loan is by definition a bad idea. You should just use caution in taking out a home equity loan and make sure that you aren't taking on more debt that you can support.

The use of a home equity loan also limits future financing flexibility. Although it's an excellent source of emergency funding, you can have only one home equity loan outstanding at a time. Thus, with a home equity loan already out, you wouldn't have the financing flexibility you would otherwise have in any future financial emergency. Don't forget that any borrowing places an obligation on future earnings and as such reduces your future disposable income.

Student Loans

Student Loan

A loan with low, federally subsidized interest rates given to students based upon financial needs.

Student loans are simply loans with low, federally subsidized interest rates given, based upon financial need, to students making satisfactory progress in their degree program. This is a subject that many of you already know way more than you'd care to know about. There are a number of different student loans available, including Stafford loans, Perkins loans, Parents loans (PLUS), and Supplemental Loans for Students (SLS). The Stafford loan program is extremely popular. In fact, in 1995, approximately 18 percent of all undergraduates nationally received Stafford subsidized loans. This program allows for a borrowing limit of $17,250 over the length of your undergraduate program. As you may well know, the process of applying for one of these loans takes place in the financial aid office of your school. You merely fill out the financial aid form, and your school will submit it to a financial institution. Because these loans are intended to help you get an education and not a part-time job, you don't need to start repaying them until you've completed your studies and (hopefully) gotten a job. In addition, as was noted in chapter 4, with the passage of the Taxpayers Relief Act of 1997, you can now deduct interest on student loans regardless of whether you itemize or not. Obviously, an education is an excellent investment in your future, one worth going into some debt over. The student loan program offers a way to borrow at a below-market rate, regardless of your credit situation. Still, you must keep in mind that in taking out a student loan, you're sacrificing future financing flexibility. However, the increased income you get as a result of completing your education should more than offset this cost. Of course, nothing may offset the hassle of dealing with student loan officers, but that's just life.

Automobile Loan

An **automobile loan** is simply a secured loan made specifically for the purchase of an automobile, with the automobile being purchased used as the collateral for the loan. These loans are generally quite short in nature, often for only 24, 36, or 48 months, although they can be as long as 5 or 6 years. In recent years automobile loans have been used as a marketing tool to sell cars. In effect, very low cost loans of 3 percent or less are used to lure customers from GM to Ford or vice versa, or the low rates are used to sell slow-moving models. The loan rate on auto loans is also quite low because lenders know, if you don't pay, they'll repossess your car and sell it to someone else to pay off the loan—that's what happened to Carol Hathaway on *ER*. Auto companies also use low-cost auto loan rates to push cars when they produce more than they can sell or when they're trying to get rid of last year's models because new ones are coming out soon. As a result, in mid-1997, the national average auto loan rate at 9.00 percent was even below the average home equity loan rate of 9.78 percent.

THE COST AND EARLY PAYMENT OF CONSUMER LOANS

Before deciding whether to borrow money, you should know exactly what the loan costs and what flexibility you have in terms of paying it off early. Fortunately, this information should be readily available to you. In fact, under the Truth in Lending Act, you must be informed in writing of the total finance charges and the APR of the loan before you sign a loan agreement. The finance charges include all the costs associated with the loan—for example, interest payments, loan-processing fees, fees for a credit check, and any required insurance fees. The **APR**, or **annual percentage rate**, is the simple percentage cost of all finance charges over the life of the loan on an annual basis. Keep in mind that this includes noninterest finance charges.

As noted earlier, consumer loans fall into two categories: (1) single-payment or balloon loans, and (2) installment loans. We will first describe a single-payment loan and then examine its cost before moving on to look at installment loans.

Cost of Single-Payment Loans

The Truth in Lending Act requires lenders to provide you with the finance charges and APR associated with a loan, but it's a good idea to be familiar with the two different ways that loans are made—one that removes interest at the beginning (the discount method) and one that doesn't (the simple interest method). The APR and finance charges are disclosed to you in the form of a **loan disclosure statement** similar to the one provided in Figure 7.2.

The Simple Interest Method. The calculation of interest under the simple interest loan method is as follows:

$$\text{interest} = \text{principal} \times \text{interest rate} \times \text{time}$$

The principal is the amount borrowed, the interest rate is exactly what you think it is, and the time is the period over which the funds are borrowed. For example, if $10,000 were borrowed for 6 months at an annual rate of 12 percent, the interest charges would be calculated as $600, as follows:

$$\$600 = \$10,000 \times 0.12 \times \tfrac{1}{2}$$

Note that the value for time is ½ because the money is borrowed for half of a year. Recall that if we're talking about single-payment loans, then both the interest and the principal are due at maturity. Thus, in the loan we've just described, you'd receive $10,000 when you take out the loan, and 6 months later you'd repay $10,600.

Automobile Loan
A loan made specifically for the purchase of an automobile, which uses the automobile as collateral against the loan.

LEARNING OBJECTIVE #2

Calculate the cost of a consumer loan.

APR, or **Annual Percentage Rate**
The true simple interest rate paid over the life of a loan. It's a reasonable approximation for the true cost of borrowing, and the Truth in Lending Act requires that all consumer loan agreements disclose the APR in bold print.

Loan Disclosure Statement
A statement that provides the APR and interest charges associated with a loan.

FIGURE 7.2

A Loan Disclosure Statement

A loan disclosure statement is required by the Truth in Lending Act and provides the APR, the finance charge, and the total of payments associated with the loan.

Annual Percentage Rate: The APR, or annual percentage rate, is the true simple interest rate paid over the life of the loan. It is calculated by dividing the average annual finance charge by the average loan balance outstanding.

Finance Charge: The finance charge includes all the costs associated with the loan, for example, interest payments, loan processing fees, fees for a credit check, and any required insurance fees.

Amount Financed: This is the amount you are borrowing, or the principal.

Total of Payments: This is the sum of your finance charge and the amount that you are borrowing.

ANNUAL PERCENTAGE RATE The cost of my credit as a yearly rate.	FINANCE CHARGE The dollar amount the credit will cost me.	Amount Financed. The amount of credit provided to me or on my behalf.	Total of Payments. The amount I will have paid after I have made all payments as scheduled.

I have the right to receive at this time an itemization of the Amount Financed: (_____) I want an itemization. (_____) I do not want an itemization.
(Initials) (Initials)

My payment schedule will be:

No. of Payments	Payment Amount	Frequency	Due Date	No. of Payments	Payment Amount	Frequency	Due Date

Variable Rate.
If my loan, as indicated above, has a variable rate, my interest rate may increase during the term of my loan based on movement of the WSJ Prime Rate. My interest rate will not increase more than once each month. If my loan is secured by a principal dwelling for a term greater than one year, disclosures about the variable rate have been provided to me earlier.

____ If indicated, my loan has multiple payments for a term of more than 60 months. Any increase in my interest rate will increase the number of payments and may increase the payment amounts. If my loan were for $10,000 for 144 months at 12% and the interest rate increased to 12.50% in three months, my regular payment would increase by $7.30 beginning with my Sixty-First payment.

____ MAXIMUM RATE. If indicated, the maximum interest rate will not exceed:

____ If indicated, my loan has multiple payments for a term of 60 months or less. Any increase in my interest rate will increase the number of payments. If my loan were for $10,000 for 60 months at 12% and the interest rate increased to 12.50% in three months I would have to make one additional payment of $196.56.

____ If indicated, my loan has a single payment. Any increase in my interest rate will increase the amount due at maturity. If my loan were for $10,000 at 12% for 90 days, and my interest rate increased to 12.25% in 20 days, then my final payment would increase by $4.80.

Security. I am giving a security interest in:

____ the goods or property being purchased.   ____ other (describe):

Collateral securing other loans with you may also secure this loan, except my principal dwelling or household goods.

Filing Fees.   **Prepayment.** If I pay off early, I may have to pay a penalty and I will not be entitled to a refund of part of any prepaid finance charge.

Late charges. If you receive any payment 8 days or more after the due date, I agree to pay you a late charge of 5% of my payment.

____ If indicated, this loan is for the purchase of property used as my principal dwelling and someone buying my principal dwelling cannot assume the remainder of my loan on the original terms.

____ If indicated, the Annual Percentage Rate does not take into account my required deposit.

I may see my contract documents for any additional information about nonpayment, default, any required repayment in full before the scheduled due date, and prepayment refunds and penalties.

I understand that credit life and credit disability insurance are not required to get this loan. **You will not provide it unless I sign the NOTICE OF PROPOSED GROUP CREDIT INSURANCE form and agree to pay the cost.** If I want any of these insurance coverages, I must be sure that the insurance coverage I want is indicated, that the amount of the premium is filled in, and that I have signed below. If I request credit life insurance or credit disability insurance, I have the right to rescind the insurance policy or certificate of insurance by giving written notice to the insurance company within 15 days from the date I received the policy or certificate. The term of any insurance I request is for the stated term of this loan unless shown otherwise.

INSURED		TYPE	PREMIUM
#1	#2		
____	____	Credit Life	
____		Credit Disability	

If this loan is secured, I may obtain property insurance from any insurer I choose.

I request coverage(s) checked for the premiums shown above

_____
Signature of Insured #1 (Life only or Life and Disability)

I request coverage(s) checked for the premiums shown above

_____
Signature of Insured #2 (Life only)

For single-payment loans the stated interest rate and the APR are always the same if there are no noninterest finance charges. The APR, or annual percentage rate, can be calculated as follows:

$$APR = \frac{\text{average annual finance charges}}{\text{average loan balance outstanding}}$$

In this case, it's calculated as follows:

$$APR = \frac{(\$600/0.5)}{\$10,000} = \frac{\$1,200}{\$10,000} = 0.12, \text{ or } 12.0\%$$

Notice that the annual finance charges are equal to the total finance charges divided by the number of periods the loan continues. In this case, it's a 6-month loan, and because we paid $600 to have the loan for 6 months, we'd have had to pay $1,200 if the loan were outstanding for a full year. Therefore, $1,200 is the annual finance charge. Keep in mind that if there had been noninterest finance charges, they would be included as part of the finance charges.

The Discount Method. Under a discount method single-payment loan, the entire interest charge is subtracted from the loan principal before you receive the loan, and at maturity you repay the loan principal. For example, if you borrow $10,000 for 1 year and the interest rate is 11 percent, your finance charges would be $1,100 ($10,000 × 0.11). Under the discount method, you'd receive only $8,900 ($10,000 less the interest of $1,100), and in 1 year you'd have to repay the entire principal of $10,000. In effect, you'd really have a loan of only $8,900, because the interest is prepaid. Thus, the APR on this example is 12.36 percent, calculated as follows:

$$APR = \frac{\$1,100}{\$8,900} = 0.1236, \text{ or } 12.36\%$$

Again, you'll notice that we have assumed that there are no noninterest finance charges on this loan. If our earlier example of a $10,000 loan at 12 percent for 6 months had been lent using the discount method, the APR would be calculated to be 13.64 percent as follows:

$$APR = \frac{(\$600/0.5)}{\$8,800} = \frac{\$1,200}{\$8,800} = 0.1364, \text{ or } 13.64\%$$

Notice that the APR is larger when money is lent under the discounted method than when it's lent under the simple interest method. Why? Because under the discount method, with the interest taken out before you receive the loan, you actually receive a smaller principal than the stated principal of the loan.

Cost of Installment Loans

With an installment loan, repayment of both the interest and the principal occurs at regular intervals, with the payment levels set in such a way that the loan expires at a preset date. Installment loans use either the simple interest or the add-on method to determine what your payments will be.

The Simple Interest Method. The simple interest method is the most common method of calculating payments on an installment loan. Recall that the monthly payments on an installment loan remain the same each month, but the portion of your monthly payment that goes toward interest declines each month while the portion going toward the principal increases. In effect, you pay interest only on the unpaid balance of the loan, which declines as it's gradually paid off—that's the process of loan amortization we discussed earlier.

Thinking back to chapter 3, we can determine your monthly payment on an installment loan using either a financial calculator (using the present value of an annuity calculation to determine *PMT,* the payment) or we could use financial tables to determine the monthly payment. The trick here is to remember to set your calculator for 12 payments per year and that the payments occur at the end of each period. Let's look at the example of a 12-month installment loan for $5,000 at 14 percent. To determine the payments using a financial calculator you need only enter values of 12 for N, $5,000 for *PV*, and 14 for *I/Y*, then calculate *PMT*. If you do this with a Texas Instruments BAII Plus calculator, you get the answer of −$448.94. Remember, with a financial calculator, each problem will have two cash flows, and one will be a positive number and one a negative number. The idea is that you borrow money from the bank (a positive number, because "you receive the money"), and at some other point in time you pay the money back to the bank (a negative number, because "you pay it back"). Thus, a 12-month installment loan of $5,000 at 14 percent would result in monthly payments of $448.94.

We can also determine the monthly payment using installment loan tables, which appear in Appendix F in the back of the book and in an abbreviated form in Table 7.1. Looking in the interest rate = 14% row and the 12-month column, we find that the monthly payment on a similar $1,000 installment loan would be $89.79. Thus, to determine the monthly payment on a $5,000 loan, we need only multiply this amount by 5 because this loan is for $5,000, not $1,000. Thus, using the tables we find that the monthly payments would be $448.95 (the difference between this and what we

TABLE 7.1

Monthly Installment Loan Tables ($1,000 loan with interest payments compounded monthly)

Interest	Loan Maturity (in months)										
	6	12	18	24	30	36	48	60	72	84	96
11.50%	172.30	88.62	60.75	46.84	38.51	32.98	26.09	21.99	19.29	17.39	15.98
11.75%	172.42	88.73	60.87	46.96	38.63	33.10	26.21	22.12	19.42	17.52	16.12
12.00%	172.55	88.85	60.98	47.07	38.75	33.21	26.33	22.24	19.55	17.65	16.25
12.25%	172.67	88.97	61.10	47.19	38.87	33.33	26.46	22.37	19.68	17.79	16.39
12.50%	172.80	89.08	61.21	47.31	38.98	33.45	26.58	22.50	19.81	17.92	16.53
12.75%	172.92	89.20	61.33	47.42	39.10	33.57	26.70	22.63	19.94	18.06	16.67
13.00%	173.04	89.32	61.45	47.54	39.22	33.69	26.83	22.75	20.07	18.19	16.81
13.25%	173.17	89.43	61.56	47.66	39.34	33.81	26.95	22.88	20.21	18.33	16.95
13.50%	173.29	89.55	61.68	47.78	39.46	33.94	27.08	23.01	20.34	18.46	17.09
13.75%	173.41	89.67	61.80	47.89	39.58	34.06	27.20	23.14	20.47	18.60	17.23
14.00%	173.54	89.79	61.92	48.01	39.70	34.18	27.33	23.27	20.61	18.74	17.37
14.25%	173.66	89.90	62.03	48.13	39.82	34.30	27.45	23.40	20.74	18.88	17.51
14.50%	173.79	90.02	62.15	48.25	39.94	34.42	27.58	23.53	20.87	19.02	17.66
14.75%	173.91	90.14	62.27	48.37	40.06	34.54	27.70	23.66	21.01	19.16	17.80
15.00%	174.03	90.26	62.38	48.49	40.18	34.67	27.83	23.79	21.15	19.30	17.95

EXAMPLE: Determine the monthly payment on a 12-month, 14% installment loan for $5,000.

Step 1:   Looking at the intersection of the 14% row and the 12-month column, we find that the monthly payment on a similar $1,000 installment loan would be $89.79.

Step 2:   To determine the monthly payment on a $5,000 loan, we need only multiply $89.79 by 5 because this loan is for $5,000 rather than $1,000.

determined using a calculator, $448.94, is simply rounding error). Remember, under the amortization process your loan payments remain constant, and as you pay off more of the loan each month, your interest expenses decline. Therefore, your principal payment increases, as shown in Table 7.2.

Because you're paying interest only on the unpaid balance, if there are no nonfinance charges, the stated interest rate is equal to the APR. In effect, there's no trickery here, you just pay interest on what you owe.

The Add-On Method. With an add-on interest installment loan, interest charges are calculated using the original balance of the loan. These charges are then added to the loan, and this amount is paid off over the life of the loan. As you'll see, loans made using the add-on method can be quite costly and, in general, should be avoided. Looking back at our example of a 12-month, $5,000 loan at 14 percent, you'd first calculate the total interest payments to be $700, as follows:

$$interest = principal \times interest\ rate \times time$$
$$interest = \$5,000 \times 0.14 \times 1 = \$700$$

You'd then add this interest payment to the principal to determine your total repayment amount. To determine your monthly payments, just divide this figure by the number of months over which the loan is to be repaid. In this case, the loan is to be repaid over 12 months; thus, the monthly payments would be $475.

$$\frac{\$700 + \$5,000}{12} = \$475$$

These calculations result in an APR of close to 25 percent. As you can see, there's a very big difference between the stated interest rate and the APR for installment loans using the add-on method to determine interest payments. In fact, the add-on method generally results in an APR of close to twice the level of the stated interest rate, because

TABLE 7.2

Illustration of a 12-Month Installment Loan for $5,000 at 14%

Month	Starting Balance	Total Monthly Payment	Interest Monthly Payment	Principal Monthly Payment	Ending Balance
1	$5,000.00	$ 448.94	$ 58.33	$ 390.61	$4,609.39
2	4,609.39	448.84	53.78	395.16	4,214.23
3	4,214.23	448.94	49.17	399.77	3,814.46
4	3,814.46	448.94	44.50	404.44	3,410.02
5	3,410.02	448.94	39.78	409.16	3,000.86
6	3,000.86	448.94	35.01	413.93	2,586.93
7	2,586.93	448.94	30.18	418.76	2,168.17
8	2,168.17	448.94	25.30	423.64	1,744.53
9	1,744.53	448.94	20.35	428.59	1,315.94
10	1,315.94	448.94	15.35	433.59	882.35
11	882.35	448.94	10.29	438.65	443.70
12	443.70	448.94	5.18	443.76	0.00*
Total		$5,387.28	$387.22	$5,000.06	

*Actually, you've overpaid by 6¢.

you're paying interest on the original principal over the entire life of the loan. Even though the amount of outstanding principal keeps decreasing as you pay back the loan, you still pay interest on the entire amount you originally borrowed. That's why there was such a big difference between the advertised rate of 14 percent and the actual APR of close to 25 percent in the example we just looked at. Fortunately, the Truth in Lending Act requires lenders to disclose the loan's APR, thereby giving you a more accurate read on the cost of this loan regardless of the method used to calculate interest payments.

The calculation of the APR for add-on loans is extremely complicated. However, an approximation for the APR can be calculated using the **N-ratio method**. The N-ratio approximation for the APR is calculated as follows:

$$\text{N-ratio approximation for the APR} = \frac{M(95N+9)F}{12N(N+1)(4P+F)}$$

where

$M=$ the number of payments in a year

$N=$ the number of loan payments over the life of the loan

$F=$ the total finance charge

$P=$ the loan principal

In the example we just looked at, $M=12$, $N=12$, $F=\$700$, and $P=\$5,000$. Substituting these numbers into the N-ratio approximation formula, you get

$$\text{N-ratio approximation for the APR} = \frac{(12)[(95)(12)+9](\$700)}{(12)(12)(12+1)[(4)(\$5,000)+\$700]}$$

$$= \frac{(12)(1,149)(\$700)}{(12)(12)(13)(\$20,700)}$$

$$= \frac{\$9,651,600}{\$38,750,400}$$

$$= 24.91\%$$

Needless to say, these add-on loans are extremely expensive.

> ## Stop and Think
>
> The easiest way to avoid an add-on loan is to look closely at the fine print and the not-so-fine print. Remember, in our example, a 14-percent loan with an add-on interest rate actually works out to be a 25-percent loan. Remember, folks, check those APRs!

Early Payment

With an installment loan, if you decide to repay your loan before maturity you must first determine how much principal you still owe. Under the simple interest method, interest is paid only on the remaining principal, so it's relatively easy to determine how much principal remains to be repaid. Use of the add-on method makes life a little tougher, though. Just in case you want to repay an add-on interest installment loan early, some provision should be made in the loan contract for calculating the unpaid principal. The most common method of calculating the unpaid principal for an add-on installment loan is the **rule of 78s** or the **sum of the year's digits**.

N-Ratio Method
A method of approximating the APR.

Rule of 78s or **Sum of the Year's Digits**
A rule to determine what proportion of each loan payment goes toward paying the interest and what proportion goes toward paying the principal.

The rule of 78s is simply a rule to determine what proportion of each payment will go toward paying interest and what proportion will go toward paying the principal. Let's use our earlier example of a 12-month $5,000 loan at 14 percent to explain the rule. Under the rule of 78s, the monthly breakdown between interest and principal is determined by using a monthly interest factor. How do you determine the monthly interest factor? First, sum up all the digits for the number of months in the loan contract. In this case, we have a 12-month contract; thus, the sum of the digits becomes

$$1+2+3+4+5+6+7+8+9+10+11+12=78$$

As you can see, the name "rule of 78s" comes from the fact that the sum of the digits for a 12-month contract equals 78 (12-month contracts are extremely popular). As the loan duration increases, calculating the sum of the digits becomes more tedious. For longer loans we can save ourselves some hassles in calculating the sum of the digits by applying the following formula:

$$\text{sum of digits} = (N/2)(N+1)$$

where N is the number of months the loan will be outstanding. In our example, N equals 12. Thus:

$$\text{sum of digits} = \left(\frac{12}{2}\right)(12+1) = 6 \times 13 = 78$$

This sum-of-the-digits figure then becomes the denominator for the monthly interest factor. The numerator is simply the number of months remaining in the loan. Therefore, the first monthly factor is $^{12}\!/_{78}$, the second monthly factor is $^{11}\!/_{78}$, and the final monthly factor is $^{1}\!/_{78}$. You then multiply this monthly interest factor by the monthly payment to determine what proportion of each payment is considered an interest payment and what proportion is considered a principal payment. In effect, interest is divided into 78 portions, with 12 of those portions paid in the first month, 11 in the second month, and so forth.

If you repay your loan early, you have to pay interest on the loan only until the repayment occurs, and you get credit for all the payments you've already made. In effect, the amount needed to repay a loan early is the original principal plus the interest the lender is due over the length of time the loan was outstanding, less any payments that have been made. Let's assume you want to pay off a 12-month loan after only 6 months. To calculate the interest that's due over the first 6 months, you use the rule of 78. Thus, over the first 6 months you should be charged $^{57}\!/_{78}$ of a year's interest (remember $12+11+10+9+8+7=57$). In effect, you add the principal to the interest due and subtract out the payments made. For example, if you wanted to repay your loan after 6 months, you'd have to pay

Original loan principal	$5,000.00
Plus: interest due lender	
($^{57}\!/_{78} \times \$700 = 511.54$)	+ 511.54
Total amount due to the lender	$5,511.54
Less: payment made ($6 \times \$475 = \$2,850$)	−$2,850.00
Equals: amount necessary to repay the loan	$2,661.54

If you decide to pay the loan off early you can determine the amount of interest that would be avoided if the loan is paid off early using the steps outlined in Figure 7.3. The bottom line here is that add-on loans are very expensive and should be avoided.

FIGURE 7.3

Using the Rule of 78s

A.
To determine the portion of the interest that would be avoided if the loan is repaid early.

B.
To determine the dollar value of the total finance charges that would be avoided by repaying the loan early.

STEP 1

Sum up *all* the months' digits.

There are two ways this can be done. One way is to number each month in descending order down to 1. That is, if it is a 12-month loan, the first month would be assigned 12, the second month 11, and so forth, and then add up these numbers. Alternatively, you can calculate the sum of the months' digits by applying the following formula:
sum of digits = $(N/2)(N + 1)$ where N is the number of months the loan will be outstanding.

STEP 2

Sum the *remaining* months' digits.

Sum the digits from 1 to the number of payments remaining when the loan obligation is repaid. For example, if the loan will be repaid in 6 months, then, $1+2+3+4+5+6=21.$

STEP 3

Divide step 2 by step 1.

Divide the sum of the digits for the months remaining in the loan (step 2) by the sum of all the months' digits (step 1). This gives you the portion of the interest that would be avoided if the loan is repaid early.

STEP 4

Multiply step 3 by the total finance charges.

This gives you the dollar value of the total finance charges that would be avoided by repaying the loan early.

Understanding the Relationship Between Your Payment, Interest Rates, and the Term of the Loan

Thinking back to the time value of money, you know that a change in interest rate, i, or length of time, n, causes big changes in the amount of interest paid. Similarly, changes in the interest rate and the length of the loan cause big changes in the amount of interest you pay on an installment loan. Let's take a look at how the duration of your loan and your loan's interest rate affect the size of your loan payments.

The effect that a change in the interest rate has on an installment loan's payments can be best understood by examining a 5-year $2,500 loan whose interest rate varies between 6 percent and 36 percent, as shown in Figure 7.4. As you can see, as the interest rate increases, so do the monthly payments and the total finance charge over the life of the loan. For example, as we move from a 6-percent interest rate to a 36-percent interest rate, monthly charges increase from $48.33 to $90.33, and the total finance charge over the life of the loan climbs from $399.92 to $2,919.80. Keep in mind that in mid 1997, in states that didn't have interest rate limits, many small loan companies were charging high-risk customers up to 36 percent on debt consolidation loans.

The maturity of the loan can also have a major impact on both the monthly interest charge and the total finance charge. For example, Figure 7.5 shows an 18-percent $2,500 loan varying in maturity from 12 months or 1 year to 96 months or 8 years. As we change the term of the loan from 12 months to 96 months, the monthly charges decrease from $229.20 to $49.31, and the total finance charge over the life of the loan climbs from $250.40 to $2,233.76. Thus, the trade-offs involved in maturity are lower payments and higher total finance charges versus a quicker elimination of the loan and lower total finance charges. Moreover, lenders generally charge a lower interest rate on shorter-term loans because the shorter the term, the lower the probability that you will experience a financial disaster such as a loss of your job or a medical emergency.

SOURCES OF CONSUMER LOANS

You should approach applying for a consumer loan in the same way you'd approach any other consumer purchase. You should shop around for the best deal and be prepared to negotiate. Remember, you're the client or customer purchasing money and agreeing to pay for your purchase in the future.

The question then becomes, Where should you shop for a loan? Well, that depends. In short, there's no one perfect lender for everyone. Not everyone has family members with cash to lend, not everyone belongs to a credit union, and not everyone has a sufficient credit rating to qualify for a bank loan. Just about everyone has a few alternatives, though. Table 7.3 provides a listing of a number of possible credit sources along with the types of loans they make and the advantages and limitations of borrowing from those institutions. Let's take a look at some, starting with the least expensive sources and then moving to the more expensive sources.

LEARNING OBJECTIVE #3

Pick an appropriate source for your loan.

FIGURE 7.4

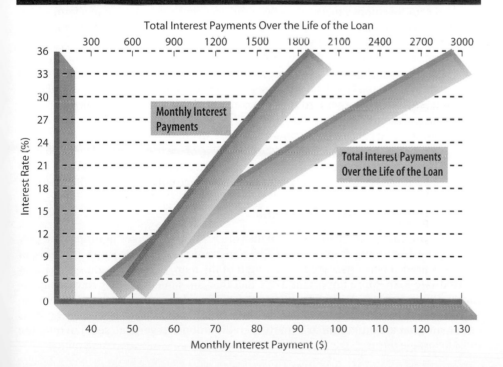

Changing Loan Interest Rate
The effect of a change in the interest rate on an installment loan's payments can be best understood by examining a 5-year $2,500 loan with interest rate varying between 6% and 36%.

FIGURE 7.5

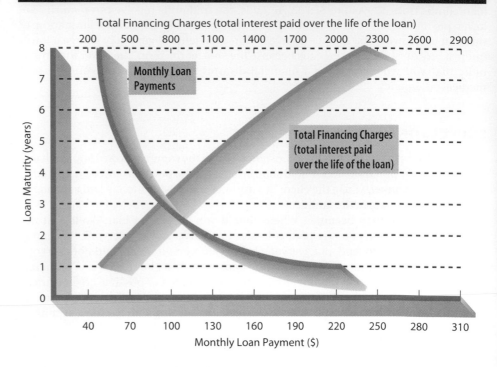

Changing Loan Maturity
The impact of a change in the maturity of a loan on both the monthly interest charge and the total finance charge. Looking at a $2,500 installment loan at 18% with maturities varying between 1 year and 8 years.

Inexpensive Sources for Loans

In general, the least expensive source of funds is your family. You don't usually pay the market rate on a family loan; instead you pay what your family would have earned if they had kept this money in a savings account. The obvious downside to a family loan is that if you can't repay it, it's your family that suffers. Also, many people simply feel uncomfortable borrowing money from their families.

Home equity loans and other types of secured loans are also relatively inexpensive because the lending agency has an asset to claim if you can't pay up. The downside of loans of this type is the fact that while assets are tied up as collateral, you can't take out additional first loans on them, so you lose some financing flexibility. Also, if you can't make your payments, you lose your assets. Where do you look for home equity loans? Almost any lending agency, such as banks, S&Ls, and credit unions, offer them.

Insurance companies that lend on the cash value of life insurance policies also offer relatively low rates. Their rates are low because they're really not taking on any risk—you're really just borrowing against the cash value of an insurance policy you have with them.

More Expensive Sources for Loans

Credit unions, S&Ls, and commercial banks are also good sources of funds. The precise cost of borrowing from each of these institutions depends upon the type of loan—secured versus unsecured—the length of the loan, and whether it's a variable- or fixed-rate loan. More important is the fact that the same loan may have a significantly different interest rate attached to it from one lender to another. Remember, you've got to shop around for your loan. Interestingly, although these three sources offer loans that are quite similar in nature, credit unions, in general, seem to offer the most favorable terms.

LAST YEAR, THEIR GOAL Was Zero Debt. Guess What?

They did it.

When *Your Money* visited Steve and Barbara Wells last fall, the Olney couple's immediate goal was to get out of debt by the end of the year. Hanging over them from their student and early working days were $15,000 in debts, and the payments were disposing of their disposable income.

So they were gritting their teeth, hanging on to their old cars, cutting out other expenses and paying off those debts as fast as they could.

They succeeded—and then some. Not only did they pay off the debt, but by continuing to scrimp and save and hold down expenses, they were able to buy a house this spring.

"We kept on schedule and paid it off by November," Steve said happily last week, adding that he was surprised at how quickly it went.

But that was not the only surprise. When the debts clicked off and the couple's savings started flowing into their own pockets instead of the lenders, they found themselves in a whole new world.

"That's when things took off. That's when we really got focused," he said.

By sticking to their regimen of living mostly on one salary and saving the other, they discovered they could make their own savings grow at almost unimaginable rates.

"It was amazing how much money we had after not having to pay off monthly loans," Steve said. They were able to put away more than $1,000 a month—many times closer to $1,500—which of course began to earn interest itself.

Source: Albert B. Crenshaw, "Last Year, Their Goal Was Zero Debt. Guess What?" *The Washington Post,* July 16, 1995, p. H4. © 1995, *The Washington Post.* Reprinted with permission.

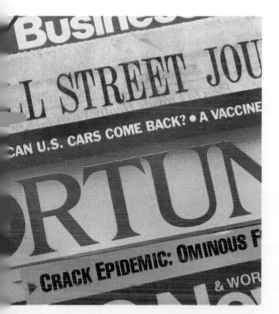

Analysis and Implications ...

A. Their approach to their debt problems was straightforward: Put their records on a computer and analyze cash flows as if they were a business. Income should always exceed expenses, and if it doesn't work, find out why. So far it's worked, so they plan to keep it up.

B. Many couples with good incomes still fail to get their heads above water because they sink too much of their cash into such start-up expenses as new cars and furniture in addition to entertainment.

TABLE 7.3

Possible Sources of Credit

Lenders	Types of Loans	Advantages	Limitations
Commercial Banks	Home improvement Education Personal Auto, mobile home	Widely available locations and funds Better rates for bank customers	Higher rates than some other sources Require good credit rating
Savings and Loans	Home improvement Education[a] Personal[a] Auto, mobile home[a]	Loans often cost less than at commercial banks	Require good credit rating
Savings Banks	Home improvement Personal	Some loans cost less than at commercial banks More personal service	Exist only in some states Require good credit rating
Credit Unions	Home improvement Education Personal Auto, mobile home	Easy to arrange for members in good standing Lowest rates Better service	Membership required in organization or group
Sales Financing Companies (Financing where you made the purchase)	Auto Appliance (major) Boat Mobile home	Convenience Good terms during special promotions	High rates Because loan is secured, defaulting can mean loss of item and payments already made
Small Loan Companies (personal finance companies)	Auto Personal	Easy to arrange Good credit rating not required	High rates Cosigner often required
Insurance Companies	General purpose	Easy to arrange low rates Can borrow up to 95% of policy's surrender value No obligation to repay	Outstanding loan and accumulated interest reduces payment to survivors Policy ownership is required
Brokerage Firms	Margin account General purpose loans, using investments as security	Easy to arrange Little delay in getting money Low rates (but subject to change) Flexible repayment	Changing value of investments can require payment of additional security Margin requirements can change

[a]In some states only.

SOURCE: From *The Wall Street Journal Guide to Understanding Personal Finance* by Kenneth Morris and Alan Siegel. Copyright © 1992. Reprinted with permission of Prentice Hall.

Most Expensive Sources for Loans

In general, financing from retail stores on purchases you make there is quite expensive. Borrowing from a finance company or small loan company is also extremely expensive. Unfortunately, to borrow from other sources, you generally need a solid credit rating. In effect, those who are in the most desperate financial shape generally have to pay the most for credit, which in turn keeps them in desperate financial shape.

> ### *The Facts of Life*
> Actually, when your borrowing isn't tax-deductible, which is the case when it's not your mortgage or a home equity loan, the cost of borrowing is actually higher than it appears. If you're in the 31-percent marginal tax bracket, in order to pay $69 of interest you must actually earn $100, with Uncle Sam taking the first $31 out for taxes and leaving you $69 for your interest payment.

HOW TO BORROW MOST INEXPENSIVELY

How do you get the most favorable interest rate on a loan? The key to getting a favorable rate on a loan, or even qualifying for a loan in the first place, is a strong credit rating. Unfortunately, those who need money the most generally have very weak credit ratings. As a result, they have the most difficult time getting credit and pay the highest rate. The other keys to securing a favorable rate all involve **Axiom 1: The Risk-Return Trade-Off**. To get a low rate, the loan must be relatively risk-free to the lender. There are four ways, other than improving your credit rating, that you can use to reduce the lender's risk: (1) use a variable-rate loan, (2) keep the term of the loan as short as possible, (3) provide collateral for the loan, and (4) put a large down payment toward anything being financed.

By accepting a variable-rate loan rather than a fixed-rate loan, you reduce the lender's interest rate risk. For example, you may be borrowing from a bank that's using money from savings deposits to fund your loan. If you had a fixed-rate loan and interest rates rose, the bank could actually end up paying more (in the form of interest on savings deposits) for the funds used to finance your loan than they receive from you in interest. A variable-rate loan allows a lender to charge you an interest rate that goes up and down with market interest rates, so the lender then gives you a lower interest rate. Of course, instead of the lender doing it, you're now taking on the interest rate risk, and if interest rates climb too high, you could end up paying more on the variable interest loan than you would have on a fixed-rate loan.

Interest rates decrease as the length of the loan decreases. As we mentioned earlier, the shorter the term, the lower the probability that you will experience a financial disaster, such as a loss of your job or a medical emergency, and the less risk of default.

Secured loans are less risky because the lender has an asset designated as collateral in the event of default by the borrower.

Finally, the larger your down payment, the less you have to borrow and the larger your ownership stake in the asset being financed. Having a large ownership stake in something is seen as increasing the borrower's desire to pay off the loan.

WHEN TO BORROW

Before looking at the financial aspects of borrowing, let's look at what you accomplish by borrowing. At the start of this chapter, when discussing consumer loans and a form of "planned borrowing," we stated that the decision to borrow should be based upon what the funds are to be used for and how the loan fits into your total personal financial planning program. That is, how much debt can you afford? We'll examine this question more closely in the next section, but for now let's assume you haven't borrowed as much or more than you can handle and must decide whether to use cash

LEARNING OBJECTIVE #4

Get the most favorable interest rate possible on a loan.

AXIOM #1

The Risk-Return Trade-Off

LEARNING OBJECTIVE #5

Know when to borrow.

instead of borrowing, or whether or not to borrow for investment purposes. In any debt decision, control and planning are the key words. Overriding all your personal finance decisions is the act of setting a budget, living within that budget, and understanding the consequences of your actions.

Unfortunately, debt is, in general, quite expensive. You should give pause before you borrow to spend. Actually, you shouldn't just pause, you should come to a complete stop. Not only do you pay more for what you purchase because of the interest on your loans, but making indebtedness a permanent feature in your financial portfolio tends to seriously impair your future financial flexibility. Don't borrow to spend if you can avoid it. Decide whether or not you really need to buy that new item. Does it fit into your personal financial planning program? If the answer is no, the process stops there. If the answer is yes, the question becomes whether or not to borrow. In deciding to use cash rather than credit, you must be sure that using cash doesn't materially affect your goal of having sufficient liquidity to carry you through a financial emergency. The answer to this question may leave you with no choice but to borrow. If not, you then have to ask whether the cost of borrowing to purchase the item is greater or less than the after-tax lost return from using savings to purchase the item. That is:

Borrow if:	after-tax cost of borrowing to purchase the asset	is less than	after-tax lost return from using savings to purchase the asset
Pay cash if:	after-tax cost of borrowing to purchase the asset	is greater than	after-tax lost return from using savings to purchase the asset

In essence, you're comparing the after-tax cost of borrowing with the lost income from taking money out of savings and using that money to purchase the item instead of earning income. You'll notice that we talk about the after-tax cost of both using cash and borrowing. Because you must pay taxes on any interest you earn, you must also look at lost income associated with using savings money to purchase the asset on an after-tax basis. Thus, the after-tax opportunity cost of taking money out of savings to purchase the asset would be equal to

$$\text{after-tax lost return from taking money out of savings to purchase the asset} = \text{before-tax interest on savings} \times (1 - \text{marginal tax rate})$$

For example, with your Super Bowl party coming up, it seems like you have no choice—TV City is running a sale on a 50-inch rear-projection TV, and is offering in-store financing at only 5 percent. Should you finance your new TV with a consumer loan at 5 percent from TV City, or should you take money out of your savings account, which is currently earning 6 percent before taxes? Let's assume your marginal state and federal tax rate is 28 percent. The after-tax lost return from taking money out of savings to purchase the TV would be

$$\text{after-tax lost return from taking money out of savings to purchase the asset} = 6\% \ (1 - 0.28) = 4.32\%$$

Thus, because the cost of borrowing from TV City to purchase the TV is greater than the after-tax lost return from using savings to purchase the item, you should tap your savings to purchase the TV.

Up to this point we've focused on borrowing to spend rather than on borrowing to invest. When you borrow to invest, you receive an income stream that may more than offset the costs of the borrowed funds. As such, borrowing to invest is much more in line with our goal of building wealth. When you borrow to invest, the benefits (in this case your earnings from the borrowed money) should be greater than the costs (the cost of the money you borrowed). Perhaps you're considering some investment land or a building to rent. If an investment will return 15 percent and a loan costs you 10 percent, then you'll still make 5-percent profit (15% − 10%), and you should take on this favorable investment. In short, if the benefits outweigh the costs, borrowing makes sense.

CONTROLLING YOUR USE OF DEBT

The first step in controlling debt is to determine how much debt you can comfortably handle. Unfortunately, there isn't an easy formula that you can use to determine this level of debt. In fact, as with much else in personal finance, your comfortable debt level changes as you pass through different stages of the financial life cycle. Early on, housing and family demands coupled with a relatively low income level make it natural for individuals to build up debt. In later years, as income rises, debt as a portion of income tends to decline. The bottom line is that you must use your common sense in analyzing your debt commitments. However, there are several measures that you can use to control your credit commitments. They include the debt limit ratio and the debt resolution rule.

Debt Limit Ratio. The debt limit ratio is simply a measure of the percentage of your take-home pay or income taken up by nonmortgage debt payments.

$$\text{debt limit ratio} = \frac{\text{total monthly nonmortgage debt payments}}{\text{total monthly take-home pay}}$$

An individual's total debt can be divided into consumer debt and mortgage debt. Mortgage payments aren't included in the debt limit ratio because this ratio takes aim at measuring your commitment to consumer credit, which tends to be a more expensive type of debt than mortgage debt. In order to maintain a reasonable degree of flexibility, ideally you should strive to keep this ratio below 15 percent. At that debt level, you still have a borrowing reserve for emergencies and the unexpected. That is, because of your low level of debt commitment, you should easily be able to secure additional borrowing without stretching your debt commitment to an uncomfortable level.

Once this ratio reaches 20 percent, most financial planners would advise you to limit the use of any additional consumer debt. One problem faced when consumer debt payments reach this level is the lack of access to additional consumer debt in the case of an emergency. The importance of maintaining an adequate degree of financial flexibility can't be overemphasized. Obviously, as this ratio increases, your future financial flexibility declines.

Interestingly, many lenders use what is called the $^{28}\!/_{36}$ rule in evaluating mortgage applicants. That is, if your total projected mortgage payments (including insurance and real estate taxes) fall below 28 percent of your gross monthly income, and your total debt payments including these mortgage payments plus any consumer credit payments fall below 36 percent, you're considered a good credit risk, and the mortgage application is approved. If you don't meet this minimum standard, you may be required to come up with an additional down payment, or you may simply be rejected for the loan.

Debt Resolution Rule. The debt resolution rule is used by financial planners to help control debt obligations, excluding borrowing associated with education and home financing, by forcing you to repay all your outstanding debt obligations every 4 years. The logic behind this rule is that consumer credit should be short-term in nature, and if it lasts over 4 years, it's not short-term. Unfortunately, it's all too easy to become reliant on consumer credit as a long-term source of funding. However, given its relative costs, this type of funding should be used sparingly. The debt resolution rule attempts to limit your reliance on it and its subsequent overuse.

LEARNING OBJECTIVE #6

Control your debt.

Controlling Your Consumer Debt

The key to controlling consumer debt is to make sure it fits with the goals you've set and the budget you've developed to achieve these goals. This was the process discussed in chapter 2. What we're talking about here is control. As you know, control is a major issue in personal finance. Unfortunately, it's easier to spend than it is to save. The inspiration for financial discipline must come with an understanding of how costly and potentially painful the alternative is. It's easy to walk out of college with a good deal of consumer debt. However, try not to live on too much of your future income, keeping in mind the costs of borrowing and how borrowing limits your future financial flexibility—that is, once you have borrowed up to your credit limit, financial emergencies become even more difficult to deal with.

WHAT TO DO IF YOU CAN'T PAY YOUR BILLS

Once you have gotten into trouble through the overuse of credit, getting out becomes a difficult and painful task. The first step is, of course, putting in place a budget that brings in more money than goes out. The second step involves self-control in the use of your credit.

What if your problems seem too overwhelming? The first place to go may be to the one to whom you owe the money. For example, if you owe money to a bank, go there first. The bank may be willing to accommodate you by restructuring the loan. If you're still lost, you might consider seeking help from a **credit counselor**, a trained professional specializing in developing personal budgets and debt repayment programs. However, as is always the case in personal finance, you must be careful in choosing a credit counselor. Just because someone advertises credit help doesn't mean his or her advice will be good or that he or she won't just take your money and do nothing. One good source for a credit counselor is the Consumer Credit Counseling Service (800-388-2227), which is a nonprofit agency affiliated with the National Foundation for Consumer Credit. This organization has offices across the nation, but if you can't find one in your town, simply phone or write the National Foundation for Consumer Credit, 8701 Georgia Avenue, Suite 507, Silver Spring, MD 20910. A credit counselor can be helpful in organizing your finances and developing a workable plan to pay off your debts.

Along with these remedies, there are other options you might consider. First, you should make sure you're borrowing as inexpensively as possible. Small loan companies sometimes charge as much as 40 percent on loans. Avoid them and see if there's a cheaper way to get money.

A second option to consider is using savings to pay off current debt. You shouldn't do so more than once—when you're reevaluating and changing your spending and credit use patterns in a permanent manner. If you are only earning 4 percent after taxes on your savings, then using savings to pay off consumer debt at 10 or 12 percent may be a good idea. However, your borrowing should be controlled in such a way that it doesn't get out of hand and doesn't warrant this remedy on a regular basis. There's a purpose to your savings, and to hijack it in this way defeats the purpose of planning. In effect, this is an emergency measure to be taken on only in the extreme situation.

Another alternative that might be considered to lower the cost of borrowing is to use a debt consolidation loan to stretch out your payments and possibly reduce your interest. A **debt consolidation loan** is simply a loan used to pay off all your current debts—in effect, substituting the debt consolidation loan for all your other debts. The purpose of a loan of this kind is to combine all your debts into a single loan and stretch out your payments over a longer period, thereby lowering your monthly

---

Credit Counselor

A trained professional specializing in developing personal budgets and debt repayment programs.

Debt Consolidation Loan

A loan used to pay off all your current debts.

payment. In effect, a debt consolidation loan doesn't eliminate your debt problems, it merely restructures the payments associated with paying off that debt. Again, this isn't the optimum solution. The best solution is to take control of your borrowing from the onset.

> ## *Stop and Think*
> Debt consolidation loans are very appealing because they offer hope to those who can't keep up with their current debt payment schedules. Before taking out a debt consolidation loan, however, keep in mind that you may be paying a higher interest rate on the consolidation loan than you are on your current debt. Moreover, if the problems that led you into this dilemma in the first place aren't solved, the solution will only be temporary.

A final alternative in the most extreme case of debt is personal **bankruptcy**. Personal bankruptcy is not a step to be taken lightly. However, if you do get into a situation in which the only solution is a fresh start, bankruptcy may be your best option. It doesn't wipe out all your obligations—for example, student loans, alimony, and tax liabilities remain—but it relieves some of the financial pressure. Bankruptcy probably happens more than you might think. In fact, in 1996, there were about 1.1 million bankruptcies nationwide. That's about 1 in every 100 U.S. households declaring bankruptcy. One contributing factor in the large number of bankruptcies is the easy availability of credit that's sinking so many consumers. In addition, divorce, job loss, and illness are also major contributors to bankruptcy. Bankruptcy also results from living beyond your means.

The two most commonly used types of personal bankruptcy available are Chapter 13, the wage earner plan, and Chapter 7, straight bankruptcy. Two other types of bankruptcy are also available, but are not commonly used: Chapter 11—which, although intended for business, accommodates those that exceed Chapter 13 debt limitations or lack regular income—and Chapter 12, a special purpose personal bankruptcy available only to family farmers. Because Chapter 11 and Chapter 12 bankruptcy are so specialized, we'll discuss only Chapter 13 and Chapter 7 bankruptcy in detail. Figure 7.6 provides a comparison of the two primary personal bankruptcy options.

Bankruptcy
The inability to pay off your debts.

Chapter 13 Personal Bankruptcy, the Wage Earner's Plan

To file for Chapter 13 bankruptcy, you must have a regular income, secured debts less than $350,000, and unsecured debts less than $100,000. Under Chapter 13 bankruptcy, you design a plan that will allow you to repay the majority of your debts. The repayment schedule is designed in such a way that you can continue to cover normal expenses while still meeting the repayment schedule. Under this type of bankruptcy, you maintain title and possession of your assets and, other than the new debt repayment schedule, continue on with life as before. For your creditors, it means a controlled repayment of debt obligations with the court's supervision. For the individual, it may mean relief from the harassment of bill collectors and the pressure of never knowing how your future obligations will be met.

Actually, if you exceed the debt limitations of Chapter 13 bankruptcy or don't have a regular source of income, you can file under Chapter 11 of the bankruptcy code. This is a relatively uncommon practice because Chapter 11 bankruptcy is really intended

FIGURE 7.6

Comparison of Personal Bankruptcy Options

CHAPTER 7

- **Who Can File:** Anyone. No minimum amount of debt is required. Most filers receive immediate forgiveness on all unsecured debt.

- **Repayment Requirements:** Varies from state to state. In most states, the home equity exemption is $7,500. Assets are liquidated to pay off creditors; however, filers generally are able to keep their car and some of their basic household possessions, and many times, their primary residence.

- **Long-Term Effect on Your Credit File:** Bankruptcy information remains in your credit file for 10 years.

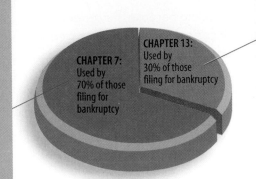

CHAPTER 7: Used by 70% of those filing for bankruptcy

CHAPTER 13: Used by 30% of those filing for bankruptcy

CHAPTER 13

- **Who Can File:** You must have a regular income, secured debts less than $350,000, and unsecured debts less than $100,000.

- **Repayment Requirements:** Under Chapter 13 bankruptcy, you design a repayment schedule in such a way that you can continue to cover normal expenses while still meeting the repayment schedule. Assets are not liquidated, and disposable income after living expenses is used to pay off debt over a 3- to 5-year period.

- **Long-Term Effect on Your Credit File:** Bankruptcy information remains in your credit file for 7 years from the end of repayment.

for businesses. However, for those who have piled up huge debts and want to restructure their debt, Chapter 11 is an option. The downside of Chapter 11 bankruptcy is that the creditors vote on the restructuring plan and can block it.

Bankruptcy happens to all kinds of good people, and it gives them some breathing room to start over when there's no hope. In fact, in December 1996, Burt Reynolds, Hollywood's number one box office draw from 1978 through 1982 and star of CBS's *Evening Shade*, filed for bankruptcy, having mounted $11.2 million in debts while having assets worth only $6.65 million. Because he exceeds the debt limits of Chapter 13 bankruptcy, he was forced to file under Chapter 11. Among his debts were a loan from CBS of $3.7 million plus interest and $121,797 to his custom wigmaker. Chapter 11 bankruptcy should give him the breathing room to begin again and regain control of his finances.

Chapter 7 Personal Bankruptcy, Straight Bankruptcy

Chapter 7 bankruptcy, or straight bankruptcy, is a more severe type of bankruptcy. Under Chapter 7, the individual who doesn't have any possibility of repaying all his or her debts is given the opportunity to eliminate them and begin again. Exactly what you can keep varies from state to state. For example, in Maryland none of your equity in your home is exempt, whereas in Florida your entire home equity is exempt in most cases. In most states, the home equity exemption is $7,500, but this varies considerably—in Minnesota, the home equity exemption is $250,000. The bottom line is that while you will not lose everything, you will have to sell a good portion of your assets in order to satisfy the Chapter 7 requirements. As a result, most of your debts will be wiped out. However, some will remain, for example, child support, alimony, student loans, and taxes. A trustee then arranges to collect and sell all of your nonexempt property with the proceeds divided among the creditors. In short, the courts confiscate and sell most of your assets to pay off creditors, and in return eliminate most of your debts. Needless to say, Chapter 7 bankruptcy is a drastic step to take and should be done only after consultation with a financial advisor and your lawyer.

SUMMARY

A single-payment loan is simply a loan that's paid back in a single lump-sum payment at maturity. In general, these loans have a stated maturity date. An installment loan calls for repayment of both the interest and the principal at regular intervals, with the payment levels set in such a way that the loan expires at a preset date. Consumer loans are either secured or unsecured. A secured loan is a loan that is guaranteed by a specific asset. With an unsecured loan, no collateral is required. With a fixed interest rate loan, the interest rate is fixed for the entire duration of the loan, but with a variable interest rate loan, the interest rate is tied to a market interest rate and periodically adjusts to reflect movements in that market interest rate. A home equity loan, or second mortgage, is a loan that uses a borrower's built-up equity in his or her home as collateral against the loan.

It's important to know exactly what a loan costs before you take one out. The finance charges include all the costs associated with the loan, for example, interest payments, loan processing fees, fees for a credit check, and any required insurance fees. The APR is the simple percentage cost of the credit paid over the life of the loan on an annual basis. In general, only the interest on mortgage debt on both your primary and secondary residences is tax-deductible. Thus, when comparing the cost of alternative loans, make sure you're comparing the after-tax costs. This adjustment can be made by taking the before-tax cost of the home equity loan and multiplying it by [1 − (marginal tax rate)].

There are numerous sources of consumer loans, which vary dramatically in terms of cost, including family, insurance companies, credit unions, savings and loan associations, commercial banks, small loan companies, retail stores, and credit cards.

The key to getting a favorable rate on a loan, or even qualifying for a loan in the first place, is a strong credit rating. In addition, there are four ways, other than improving your credit rating, that you can reduce the lender's risk and thereby secure a favorable rate: (1) use a variable-rate loan, (2) keep the term of the loan as short as possible, (3) provide collateral for the loan, and (4) put a large down payment toward the item being financed.

Before borrowing, you must make sure that borrowing fits within your financial plan, including living within your budget, and that you understand all the consequences of your actions. You must also determine how much debt can you afford. Not only should you use your common sense in analyzing your debt commitments, you should also measure the severity of your credit commitments using the ratio of the nonmortgage debt service to take-home pay and the debt resolution rule.

Review Questions

1. How does a single-payment or balloon loan differ from an installment contract with a balloon clause? (LO 1)
2. In the case of consumer default on a loan, credit contracts often include the acceleration clause, the deficiency payments clause, and the recourse clause to give the lender options for collecting the debt. Explain each clause. (LO 1)
3. Home equity credit loans and credit lines have become very popular sources of consumer credit. List the advantages and disadvantages. What is the security for this type of loan? (LO 1)

Just Do It! *From the Desk of Marcy Furney, CFP*

And Now, a Few Words from the "Loan Ranger"

When most people apply for a mortgage or other large loan, they often go in totally unprepared. This unpreparedness can result in delays, repeated trips, numerous phone calls, and possibly denial of credit if your situation is marginal. Make yourself as creditworthy as possible.

☑ If you have no credit history, obtain a credit card or a small loan and make payments on time. You may need a cosigner to obtain a large loan, even if you have an excellent income. Ability to pay isn't the same as demonstrated willingness to pay.

☑ Pay off all the debt you can before you apply. A relatively small credit card balance could cause your ratios to be too high to qualify.

☑ Order your own credit reports and examine them for any errors. Make sure they're in good order before you proceed. If there's been a payment problem, write out the reason for the problem and the resolution. Also document thoroughly any reports that are being contested.

☑ List all your investments and cash, show the name and address of the firm where they're being held, and include account numbers. Make copies of your current statement on each and attach them to the list. Do the same with all debt.

☑ If you're applying for a mortgage, take the lenders' names, their addresses, and your loan numbers for any previous home loans.

☑ Make copies of your last W-2 and most recent pay stub. If you're self-employed, take copies of your proof of income, for example, Schedule C and Form 1040 from your most recent tax return.

☑ Fill out applications neatly and concisely. Provide copies of all supporting documents. Don't try to hide anything and don't volunteer personal information that isn't requested and isn't directly related to your creditworthiness.

☑ The more complete and organized the information you provide, the less the loan processor will have to do. That could give you a slight edge.

☑ Once you've provided the lender with all the information needed to process the loan, take the initiative to check on progress periodically.

4. What is an APR? (LO 2)
5. What methods are used to calculate interest on a single-payment loan? Which method is preferable to the consumer? (LO 2)
6. What methods are used to calculate interest on an installment loan? Which method is preferable to the consumer? What is the most common method of calculating interest on an installment loan? (LO 2)
7. How does the interest rate charged and the term of the loan affect monthly payments? The overall cost of the loan? (LO 2)
8. Loan costs vary significantly with the lender. Identify at least two inexpensive loan sources, two more expensive loan sources, and the two most expensive loan sources. (LO 3)
9. Based on **Axiom 1: The Risk-Return Trade-Off**, "the higher the risk, the higher the return." Name five ways you can reduce the risk for the lender, thereby reducing the return for the lender and saving yourself money. (LO 4)
10. "Planned borrowing" is based on two key words: control and planning. Name five factors to consider when deciding to borrow. (LO 5)

11. Borrowing to spend provides immediate benefit from the good or service purchased on credit. What is the benefit when borrowing to invest? (LO 5)
12. What types of borrowing aren't considered in the debt resolution rule? According to this rule, what is the time frame for repayment of short-term debt? (LO 6)
13. Remedies for overcoming excessive credit use can impact your present and future financial situation. Name eight remedies to consider when you're having trouble paying your bills. (LO 6)
14. According to Figure 7.6, 70 percent of bankruptcy filers choose Chapter 7. What are the advantages of Chapter 7 compared to Chapter 13? What are the disadvantages? (LO 6)

Problems and Activities

1. A variable-rate mortgage is advertised with an initial rate of 6 percent, with a 2-percent annual cap and a lifetime cap of 6 percent. Assuming a period of rapidly rising interest rates, how much could the rate increase over the next 4 years? How would this affect the monthly payment, which would be recalculated at the annual anniversary of the loan? (LO 1)
2. Chris needs to buy a new computer costing approximately $2,500. A 2-year unsecured loan through the credit union is available for 14-percent interest. The current rate on her revolving home equity line is 9.75 percent, although she's reluctant to use it. Chris is in the 28-percent federal tax bracket and the 5.7-percent state tax bracket. Which loan should she choose? Why? (LO 1)
3. Regardless of the loan chosen, Chris wants to pay off the computer in 24 months. Calculate the payments for her, assuming both loans use the simple interest method. (LO 2)
4. Elizabeth, a recent college graduate, excitedly described the $1,200 sofa, chair, and tables she has found today. In a discussion with her parents, Elizabeth was surprised to hear that a few years earlier they had financed furniture with the add-on method of interest calculation. Elizabeth hadn't asked about the interest calculation method at the furniture store, but knew the bank personal, or unsecured, loan used the simple interest method. Calculate the monthly payments and total cost for the bank loan assuming a 1-year repayment period and 21-percent interest. Now, assume the store still uses the add-on method of interest calculation. Calculate the monthly payment and total cost with a 1-year repayment period of 21-percent interest. Which loan should Elizabeth choose? Why? (LO 2)
5. Which is a better deal, borrowing $1,000 to be repaid 12 months later as a single-payment loan or borrowing $1,000 to be paid monthly for 12 months? Assume a simple interest method of calculation at 6-percent interest. Defend your answer. (LO 2)
6. Consumers are encouraged to comparison shop for credit as for any other consumer good or service. How might one's stage of the financial life cycle or asset ownership affect the availability of loan sources and the associated cost of the loans offered? (LO 3)
7. Large down payments reduce loan costs. Provide this to yourself by calculating the monthly payments and total cost for a loan with a 9-percent interest rate to be repaid over 3 years. How will these costs vary if Bruce needs a total of $5,000 and is considering a down payment of $750 or $1,000? *Hint:* Ignore the potential interest earnings on the additional $250 that would remain in the bank. (LO 4)

8. Tony would like to replace his golf clubs, actually his father's old set, with a set of oversized clubs. A local sporting goods mega-store is advertising oversized clubs for $500, including a new bag. In-store financing is available at 5 percent, or Tony can choose not to renew his $500 certificate of deposit (CD) which just matured. The advertised CD renewal rate is 6.5 percent. Tony knows the in-store financing costs would not affect his taxes, but he knows he'll pay taxes (15 percent federal and 4 percent state) on the CD interest earnings. Should he cash the CD or use the in-store financing? (LO 5)

9. Noel and Herman know their finances are tight, but they want to replace her car. With the furniture and appliance payments, credit card bills that cover all sorts of expenses, and the other car payment, they just aren't sure they can afford another car payment. The auto financing representative had asked, "What size payments are you thinking of?" Current payments total $475 of their $2,800 combined monthly take-home pay. Calculate the debt limit ratio to help them decide about the car purchase and answer the question, "What size payments are you thinking of?" (LO 6)

Suggested Projects

1. Visit a bank, a credit union, a savings and loan, a consumer finance company, and a retail outlet that offer credit. Ask for a copy of the contract for a consumer installment loan. Compare the contracts for an explanation of the credit terms as well as the various contract clauses identified in this chapter. Prepare a report of your findings. (LO 1)

2. Visit the financial aid office at your school to learn about the different student loans available. What is the application process? Do qualification requirements and repayment plans vary with the different loan programs? What is the "average" monthly payment and repayment period? (LO 1)

3. Visit a bank, a credit union, a savings and loan, and a consumer finance company to learn about their consumer loan options. How do interest rates vary for secured and unsecured loans? Do they offer fixed and adjustable interest rate loans? What method(s) of interest calculation is used? Prepare a report of your findings. (LO 1, 2, 3)

4. Interview the financial manager at an auto dealership to learn about the financing options available. Because the auto purchased will serve as collateral, and the vehicle trade-in value can be the down payment, how do the interest rate and the term of the loan affect, or reduce, the lender's risk? How can the consumer get the best deal on auto financing? Discuss the debt resolution rule in light of the increasing number of 5-year auto loans. (LO 1, 4)

5. Using your anticipated entry-level take-home pay, calculate the maximum non-mortgage debt payment that you can safely handle. What are the implications given your actual or anticipated debt for credit cards, an auto loan, or school loans? Can you afford additional borrowing for furniture, appliances, travel, or other needs? (LO 6)

6. Check the local phone directory or call the National Foundation for Consumer Credit to locate a nearby office. Interview a counselor to determine the services offered to consumers as well as creditors. Ask the counselor to identify factors that commonly contribute to problems in repaying debt. What strategies are used to remedy the situation? (LO 6)

7. To learn more about personal bankruptcy, interview a lawyer who often handles bankruptcy proceedings. Question the lawyer about spending trends and household events that appear to contribute to bankruptcy, typical fees for filing bankruptcy, and the effect of filing on the consumer's financial future. Alternatively, if you know someone who has filed bankruptcy, ask him or her similar questions. Report your findings. (LO 6)

Discussion Case 1

Karou is considering different options for financing the $10,000 balance on her planned new-car purchase. The cheapest advertised rate among the local banks is 7.75 percent for a 48-month car loan. The current rate on her revolving home equity line is 9.75 percent. Karou is in the 28-percent federal tax bracket and the 5.75-percent state tax bracket.

Questions

1. Which loan should she choose? (LO 1, 3)
2. Regardless of the loan chosen, Karou wants to pay off the car in 48 months. Calculate the payments for her, assuming both loans use the simple interest method. (LO 2)
3. In a discussion with her father about financing her new car, Karou was surprised to hear that he had financed a car with the add-on method of interest calculation. He planned to repay the $2,000 loan within 1 year, but was able to do so after 9 months because of a bonus he earned at work. The interest rate was 5 percent. Calculate the monthly payments, as well as the final payment to pay off the loan. How much interest was "saved," or rebated, using this method of financing and the rule of 78s? (LO 2)
4. Assume Karou's father could finance $2,000 today at 5 percent using the simple interest method of calculation. How much would the payments be? If the loan is not paid off early, calculate the difference in the interest charges using the two methods. (LO 2)
5. Assuming Karou didn't have access to the home equity credit line, what factors might she consider to reduce the lender's risk and therefore "buy" herself a lower-cost loan? *Hint:* Consider **Axiom 1: The Risk-Return Trade-Off**. (LO 4)

Discussion Case 2

Your sister, Sue and, her husband, Steve, certainly appear to be living the good life. Since their marriage 5 years ago, they've bought a condominium, traded their "college" cars for two newer models, bought furniture and appliances, and gone on vacation every year. During a recent shopping trip, however, you noticed that Sue seemed reluctant to spend any money. When you jokingly suggested that she just "charge it," she made no reply. Over coffee, Sue admitted that she was getting worried about their financial situation, although Steve was anxious to start planning next summer's vacation.

Questions

1. Summarize for Steve and Sue factors to consider to ensure "planned borrowing" that doesn't negatively impact their financial plan. (LO 5)
2. Review with them how to shop for credit among different loan providers to find the most inexpensive source of credit. (LO 3)
3. Explain how to use the debt limit ratio and the debt resolution rule to determine whether they can responsibly handle additional borrowing. (LO 6)
4. If Steve and Sue are having difficulty paying their bills, what alternatives could you recommend? Categorize your suggestions as interventions for (a) minor, (b) moderate, and (c) extreme debt repayment problems. (LO 2, 6)

Chapter 8

MAJOR EXPENDITURES:
The Home and Automobile Decision

"Home, I have no home. Hunted, despised, living like an animal—the jungle is my home. But I shall show the world that I can be its master. I shall perfect my own race of people. A race of atomic supermen that will conquer the world." Those were the words of Martin Landau, playing the part of Bela Lugosi in the film *Ed Wood*—a role that won him an Oscar. He made this little speech as Ed Wood, the offbeat director of Lugosi's last movie, *Plan 9 from Outer Space,* watched on. In the movie, Ed Wood, who was played by Johnny Depp, adored Lugosi, and in real life Johnny Depp became pretty infatuated with Lugosi also. In fact, Depp was so fascinated by Lugosi that when Depp "had no home," he went after Lugosi's old house.

A beautiful and secluded house, Lugosi's former house and Depp's new one, is a gray, stone castle with 28 rooms, turrets, and iron trim. And it's big—7,430 square feet in all, with eight bedrooms, 10 bathrooms—and perhaps a secret vault for spare coffins in the basement. Even for a mega-star like Johnny Depp, the house was a major purchase, costing roughly $2 million. Hey, some people are willing to pay a lot for the perfect house. Of course, Johnny Depp's new place may be perfect for him, but you might cringe at the thought of 10 bathrooms to clean.

What you're looking for in a house generally reflects your lifestyle. For example, actor Anthony Edwards, who plays Dr. Mark Greene on *ER,* the prime-time hospital drama, calls an aluminum-skinned Airstream Excella 1000 trailer his home when shooting *ER.*

Learning Objectives

After reading this chapter you should be able to:

1. Make good buying decisions.
2. Choose a vehicle that suits your needs and budget.
3. Pay for your vehicle through leasing or financing.
4. Choose the type of house that meets your needs.
5. Decide whether to rent or buy housing.
6. Calculate the costs of buying a home.
7. Buy a house.
8. Get the most out of your mortgage.

He has his "silver love sub" parked on the backlot of *ER* and uses it as his office and retreat. Decorated in fifties motif, the trailer even sports a pink and silver dinette chair at the kitchen table, where he eats his oatmeal every morning before heading for the set. For him it's perfect. As Edwards proudly says, "The roundness, the curvature of the interior makes a really pleasing environment. It's very womblike."

Once again, this home's probably not right for you either. That's because buying a house isn't only a financial decision, it's also a personal and emotional one. You want a house, and you want the lifestyle that goes with it. That was certainly true for Johnny Depp and Anthony Edwards—and their picks were different, to say the least. What makes the decision to buy a home even more important is the fact that, for most people, buying a home is the single biggest investment that they'll ever make. Unfortunately, many first-time homebuyers simply don't understand all the complexities and financial implications of this purchase.

Actually, most people don't understand the financial implications and complexities of any major purchase, including the purchase of a car. Again, for most people, buying a car isn't only a financial decision, it's also a personal one. You don't just want transportation, you want to "look good in your car." However, although buying a car isn't considered a financial investment, it *is* an expenditure, and a huge one at that. In either case—buying a house or a car—you're probably going to need a loan and are thus committing a large portion of your future earnings over a long period of time. Because each purchase has a dramatic impact upon your personal finances, you need to look carefully at each one. You don't want to end up "hunted, despised, living like an animal"— on the run from bill collectors because you can't afford the house or car you just purchased.

**Make good buying
decisions.**

SMART BUYING

In this chapter we'll be dealing with spending money rather than saving it. Just as you work hard to save money, you should also make the effort when spending it. That means that you should get the most for it and make well thought-out spending decisions. Much of our focus will be on the automobile and housing purchase decisions, but the same basic decision process applies to all purchases. This decision-making process is outlined in Figure 8.1. As you can see, it's a controlled process, in which your final selection isn't only the best product for the best price, but a product that you need and a purchase that fits in with your monthly budget. One of the big benefits of this approach is that it eliminates impulse buying—the kind of buying that wreaks havoc on your monthly budget.

Step 1: Do Your Shopping Homework

The first step in smart buying is to separate your wants from your needs. This doesn't mean that you'll never buy anything that you simply want but don't need, such as that new stereo system. It does mean that you have to recognize that such a purchase is purely a "want" purchase, and that the cost has to fit within your monthly budget. Making a "want" purchase may mean that you'll be limited to eating macaroni and cheese for the next 6 months, but that's a trade-off that you have to face.

FIGURE 8.1

Smart Buying

STEP 1: Do Your Shopping Homework.

- The question of need versus want.
- Look at the alternatives.
- Examine the fit between purchase and your monthly budget.

STEP 2: Make Your Selection.

- Comparison shop: price, product attributes, and quality.

STEP 3: Make Your Purchase.

- Negotiate the price.
- Evaluate financing alternatives.
- Complete the purchase.

STEP 4: Maintain Your Purchase.

- Resolve complaints.

In buying that new stereo system, you'll want to make sure that your money isn't wasted. You want the best stereo system possible while considering the trade-offs between price, quality, and product attributes. Again, keep in mind that your purchase has to fit within your budget. You can't figure out what's best for your budget until you know what's actually out there, so go take a look at what your alternatives are.

Step 2: Make Your Selection

Once you've determined the alternatives, it's time to compare the different products, making trade-offs between quality, the different features of the products, and price. Of course, a lot of these trade-offs are based on personal choice, but it's personal choice while keeping within your budget. You want the best deal you can get for your money, and the only way to get it is through comparison shopping. One way to make this comparison a bit easier is to make a checklist of the different products, along with their price and features. Of course, you'll need to get all this information somehow. Fortunately, there are plenty of good sources of information dealing with product quality, starting at your local library with *Consumer Reports,* along with numerous specialty magazines that rate and compare computers, cameras, cars, and stereos.

The Facts of Life

There's also a good deal of on-line consumer information available on the Internet. One of the most complete listings of consumer information appears on Personal Finance Web Sites compiled by Ira Krakow at http://www.tiac.net/users/ikrakow/pagerefs.html. Also, perhaps the most informative guide on smart buying, the *Consumer's Resource Handbook,* is published by the U.S. Office of Consumer Affairs and is available free by calling 800-664-4435 or on the Internet at http://www.pueblo.gsa.gov/1997res.htm.

Step 3: Make Your Purchase

In making most purchases, it may simply be a matter of going to the cheapest source and buying the product. However, with other products, there may be some negotiations involved, especially if you're buying a big-ticket item such as a car, an appliance, or some furniture. In this case, you may have to do a good deal of haggling before you arrive at a final price. The key to successfully negotiating a good price is knowing as much as possible about the markup on the product (the price the dealer adds on above what he or she paid for the product), which gives you an idea about how much room there is for negotiation. Armed with this information, you then need to make sure you're dealing with someone with the authority to lower the price. You'll also want to look at the various financing alternatives, not only determining which is cheapest, but also which is best for you—that is, which fits best into your budget. Figure 8.2 gives some tips on smart buying.

Step 4: Maintain Your Purchase

The final step to smart buying is maintaining your purchase, which involves not only maintenance, but also resolving any complaints that might arise. If you have a complaint, the first thing to do is contact the seller (make sure you keep a record of your

FIGURE 8.2

☑ Take advantage of sales, but compare prices. Do not assume an item is a bargain just because it is advertised as one.

☑ Don't rush into a large purchase because the "price is only good today."

☑ Be aware of such extra charges as delivery fees, installation charges, service costs, and postage and handling fees. Add them into the total cost.

☑ Ask about the seller's refund or exchange policy.

☑ Don't sign a contract without reading it. Don't sign a contract if there are any blank spaces in it or if you don't understand it. In some states, it is possible to sign away your home to someone else.

☑ Before buying a product or service, contact your consumer protection office to see if there are automatic cancellation periods for the purchase you are making. In some states, there are cancellation periods for dating clubs, health clubs, and time-share and campground memberships. Federal law gives you cancellation rights for certain door-to-door sales.

☑ Walk out or hang up on high-pressure sales tactics. Don't be forced or pressured into buying something.

☑ Don't do business over the telephone with companies you do not know.

☑ Be suspicious of P.O. box addresses. They might be mail drops. If you have a complaint, you might have trouble locating the company.

☑ Do not respond to any prize or gift offer that requires you to pay even a small amount of money.

☑ Don't rely on a salesperson's promises. Get everything in writing.

Source: U.S. Office of Consumer Affairs, *Consumer's Resource Handbook,* 1997.

efforts to resolve the problem). If that doesn't resolve the problem, contact the headquarters of the company that made or sold the product. Most large companies have a toll-free 800 number. It's generally on the instructions; if not, you can probably get it through the directory of 800 telephone numbers at your local library or by calling 800–555–1212 (toll-free). Alternatively, you could write to the company. Make sure to address your letter to the consumer office or the company's president. In your correspondence you'll want to accurately describe the problem, what you've done so far to try to resolve it, and what action you'd like taken. For example, do you want your money back, or do you want the product exchanged? Keep in mind that your problem may not be resolved immediately—you have to allow time for the person you contacted to resolve your problem. When dealing with companies directly, you'll want to keep notes, including the name of the person you spoke with, the date, and what was done. Also, save copies of all letters to and from the company. If your problem still isn't resolved, it's time to work through such organizations as the Better Business Bureau, along with other local, state, and federal organizations that might provide help. Where do you look for help? Try the *Consumer's Resource Handbook*, published by the U.S. Office of Consumer Affairs. It provides an excellent outline of how to complain effectively, along with a listing of different organizations that will help if you have a complaint.

ADDRESSING YOUR TRANSPORTATION NEEDS

Although choosing a new stereo system is an important decision, it pales next to buying a car. In fact, next to buying a house, your car is probably your largest investment. It's also something that most people do every few years. There are major differences between buying a stereo and an automobile—the price, for one thing—but the process is essentially the same as that set out in Figure 8.1. Ten years ago the process of purchasing an automobile was relatively simple. It involved doing a bit of preshopping homework to determine what you needed and what you could afford, figuring out which cars were lemons and which were good, and negotiating with the dealer. Today, not only do you have to decide which car to purchase, but you also have to decide whether to lease or buy. Making this decision tougher is the fact that leasing has a language of its own.

What has brought on this revolution in automobile financing? Sticker shock. Today the cost of a new car is beyond the financial means of many Americans. As a result, leasing—which is in effect renting a car for an extended period—with a small or no down payment and low monthly payments has become increasingly popular. To understand the car-buying or -leasing process, we'll follow the basic smart-buying process outlined in Figure 8.1, adapting it to specifically fit the automobile decision.

Step 1: Preshopping Homework—Narrowing Down Your Car Choice

Although it's easy to look at purchasing a car as a financial decision, most people view it as a personal decision. Very few decisions pit needs versus wants as directly as the auto decision. For example, a new Dodge Caravan minivan costs about the same as and may satisfy your needs better than a Mazda Miata, but you still may want the Miata. Let's face it—for most people, picking a car is a lifestyle choice. In addition to having different "wants," different people also have different needs. The end result is, what's right for one person is a poor choice for someone else. In making this decision, as with any major purchase decision, you should do some preshopping research as to what the alternatives are that fit your needs, your lifestyle, and your budget.

Needs and Lifestyle Considerations. The first question to answer in making a car decision is, What features and qualities do you need and what features do you merely want? You'll find that your lifestyle will dictate many of these decisions. If you have young kids, you might want a minivan to haul them around in, but if you're single, that Miata may best fit your lifestyle. You may also decide that having a new car is just not that important to you, that saving money with a reliable used car is more important. You may also decide you're unwilling to pay extra for a sun roof or antitheft device. In making this list of styles and features you're looking for, you'll want to keep an eye to resale and safety. *Consumer Reports* regularly reports on desirable safety features and the cars and models that maintain strong resale value.

Fitting Your Car into Your Budget. What can you realistically afford? Cars are expensive. In fact, the typical family spends between 4 and 6 months' worth of its annual income when buying a new car. It makes no sense to purchase a car that will put such financial strain on you that either other goals or your lifestyle must be compromised. In short, your car, as with all purchases, must fit into your budget.

In looking at what will fit into your budget and meet your goals, you should first determine the size of the down payment you're willing to make. It's okay to tap into savings to pay for your car, as long as those savings dollars were earmarked for a new car. What you don't want to do is to raid savings that are set aside for your retirement or your children's college education to pay for your car. Once you know how large a down payment you can make, you can then determine how large the monthly payments on the car can be, and from that determine how much you can spend on a car.

How can you determine what the monthly payment will be? First, you'll want to call up your local bank and credit union and ask about auto loan rates. Using that rate, you can then determine what your monthly payment will be by using the same techniques you learned in chapter 3 and again in chapter 7 when you looked at installment loans. Basically, auto loans are simply installment loans for automobiles. Remember, you can determine your monthly payment on an installment or car loan using either a financial calculator (using the present value of an annuity calculation to determine *PMT,* the payment) or the installment loan tables that appear in Appendix F in the back of this book.

Because automobile loans require monthly payments, you must make sure your calculator is set for *12 payments per year* and that the payments occur at the end of each period. Let's look at an example of a 36-month installment loan for $15,000 at 10 percent. To determine the payments using a financial calculator, you need only enter the values of

$$N = 36,$$
$$PV = \$15,000,$$
$$I/Y = 10,$$

then calculate *PMT.*

The answer as shown in the margin is –$484.01. Thus, a 36-month installment loan of $15,000 at 10 percent would result in monthly payments of $484.01.

Using the installment loan tables that appear in Appendix F in the back of this book and in an abbreviated form in Table 7.1 is just as easy. Looking in the interest rate = 10% row and the 36-month column, we find that the monthly payment on a similar $1,000 installment loan would be $32.27. To determine the monthly payment on a $15,000 loan we need only multiply this amount by 15, because this loan is for $15,000, not $1,000. Thus, using the tables, we find that the monthly payments would be $484.05.

That means if you buy a car and finance $15,000 of its price over 36 months, you'll have to come up with $484.05 each month for your car payments. How can you come up with this much each month? There's no easy answer—perhaps you can cut down on some of your other expenditures, and perhaps you simply can't do it. It's at this point that you may want to rethink your decision, considering a less expensive car or perhaps a used car. In any case, you *must* make sure that your auto decision fits within your budget. Unfortunately, when it comes to fitting that new dream car into your budget, sometimes, as the movie title says, "reality bites."

Today, with all the formerly leased cars coming back to the market as used cars, a used car is a reasonable alternative to help you align what you want in a car with what you can afford. In general, a used car costs less and requires less in the way of a down payment. Moreover, a used car tends to decline in value much more slowly than a new car. The downside of purchasing a used car is that it is more likely to have mechanical problems and may not be under warranty. Figure 8.3 provides some tips on buying a used car. Buying a used car is a real money saver. In fact, the savings from buying a used car instead of a new car every 3 years have been estimated to be between $1,500 and $2,000 per year.

If you're trying to come up with a few more dollars to buy just what you want, you might consider selling your old car yourself rather than trade it in. The major advantage to trading in your old car is the convenience. However, if you can wait it out, and if you don't mind the hassle, selling your old car yourself will generally net you more money. The question is, do you have the time or the inclination to do it? Another alternative is not to replace your present car, but instead try to keep it running just a little longer.

Step 2: Selection Process—Picking Your Car

Deciding on which car is best for you centers on comparison shopping—looking at the final choices and trading off the price against product attributes and quality. In making this decision, once again, it's important to realize that buying a car is a personal

FIGURE 8.3

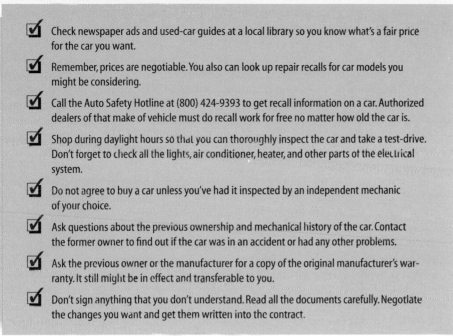

Buying a Used Car

☑ Check newspaper ads and used-car guides at a local library so you know what's a fair price for the car you want.

☑ Remember, prices are negotiable. You also can look up repair recalls for car models you might be considering.

☑ Call the Auto Safety Hotline at (800) 424-9393 to get recall information on a car. Authorized dealers of that make of vehicle must do recall work for free no matter how old the car is.

☑ Shop during daylight hours so that you can thoroughly inspect the car and take a test-drive. Don't forget to check all the lights, air conditioner, heater, and other parts of the electrical system.

☑ Do not agree to buy a car unless you've had it inspected by an independent mechanic of your choice.

☑ Ask questions about the previous ownership and mechanical history of the car. Contact the former owner to find out if the car was in an accident or had any other problems.

☑ Ask the previous owner or the manufacturer for a copy of the original manufacturer's warranty. It still might be in effect and transferable to you.

☑ Don't sign anything that you don't understand. Read all the documents carefully. Negotiate the changes you want and get them written into the contract.

Source: U.S. Office of Consumer Affairs, *Consumer's Resource Handbook*, 1997.

decision. Not all cars are right for everyone—which car is right for you is largely determined by your lifestyle. In addition, every car drives a bit differently, and your choice should fit you physically. As a result, a car should never be purchased without a serious test-drive. Try to answer the question, Do you feel comfortable driving it? Not everyone feels comfortable in the same car, and not all cars of the same model drive similarly. As such, you should never consider purchasing a car without test-driving it—not just a similar model, but the *exact* car under consideration.

In comparing different cars, make sure you consider differences in operating and insurance costs. Different cars can have dramatically different operating costs. For example, a used car will generally cost more to operate than a new car. You'll also want to consider the car's warranty—the better the warranty, the lower the future costs. In addition, insurance costs on different cars vary dramatically. That Miata is going to have much higher insurance costs than a Taurus station wagon.

Step 3: Making the Purchase

Once you've decided what's best for you, the next hurdle is getting it for a fair price. You should enter the buying phase only after you know exactly what you want and how much you're willing to spend. With this information in hand, you can avoid making a hasty decision or being pressured into something you don't want. Once you have a fair price, the next step is to determine how to finance the purchase.

Negotiating the Price. To determine how much you're willing to spend—that is, what's a fair price—you must first know what the dealer cost or invoice price is. This is a relatively easy number to come by. It can be found in *Edmund's Car Buying Guide*, which is available at most libraries and bookstores or on the Internet at AutoSite, at http://www.autosite.com/help/allabout.htm. AutoSite is a massive electronic buyer's guide, featuring the manufacturer's suggested retail price, the dealer's invoice, any rebates and financing incentives available, projected resale values, and insurance premium information, along with reviews and evaluations.

The factory invoice price is important in determining how much the dealer pays for the car, but it isn't the whole story, because when most cars are sold the dealer receives a **holdback** from the manufacturer. Generally, the holdback amounts to 2 to 3 percent of the price of the car. For example, in 1996 a new Ford Explorer had a sticker price of $24,600. The dealer cost or invoice price was $22,266. So, the markup appears to be 11 percent. However, when the dealer sold that Explorer, he or she would receive a 3-percent holdback amounting to $738. Including the holdback, the markup is 14 percent. Keep in mind that the average markup on a new car is approximately 6.7 percent.

In addition to the holdback, some cars also have rebates or additional dealer incentives. These holdbacks and dealer incentives are tracked by the Center for the Study of Services, 733 15th Street NW, Suite 820, Washington, DC, and are published semimonthly in *CarDeals*, which is available from the Center for a small fee.

With this information in hand, you're ready to approach several dealers and get quotes on the car you want. You want to be prepared when you're ready to negotiate. Figure 8.4 provides a list of buying tips that you might want to go over ahead of time.

In general, you shouldn't have to pay, after any rebates, more than $200 to $500 over the invoice price on the car if it's an American-made car, and a bit more over this price for a foreign-built car. However, what you'll pay depends on the demand for the

Holdback

In auto sales, an amount of money, generally in the 2- to 3-percent range, that the manufacturer gives the dealer upon the sale of an automobile.

FIGURE 8.4

Tips on Buying a New Car

☑ Evaluate your needs and financial situation. Read consumer magazines and test-drive several models before you make a final choice.

☑ Find out the dealer's invoice price for the car and options. This is what the manufacturer charged the dealer for the car. You can order this information for a small fee from consumer publications you can find at your local library.

☑ Find out if the manufacturer is offering rebates that will lower the cost.

☑ Get price quotes from several dealers. Find out if the amounts quoted are the prices before or after the rebates are deducted.

☑ Keep your trade-in negotiations separate from the main deal.

☑ Compare financing from different sources, for example, banks, credit unions, and other dealers, before you sign the contract.

☑ Read and understand every document you are asked to sign. Do not sign anything until you have made a final decision to buy.

☑ Think twice about adding expensive extras you probably don't need to your purchase, for example, credit insurance, service contracts, or rustproofing.

☑ Inspect and test-drive the vehicle you plan to buy, but do not take possession of the car until the whole deal, including financing, is finalized.

☑ Don't buy on impulse or because the salesperson is pressuring you to make a decision.

Source: U.S. Office of Consumer Affairs, *Consumer's Resource Handbook*, 1997.

car and the size of the holdbacks that the dealer receives from the manufacturer. Getting quotes is the best way to determine what a good price is. If you don't want to negotiate by yourself, Global Shopping Network (800-221-4001) will guide you through this process for just over $20, and for an additional $99 and up, depending upon the car, they will negotiate a deal on your behalf. The Center for the Study of Services' Car Bargains Service (800-475-7283) will also get you five competitive bids from dealers in your local area for $150.

If you're considering a used car, the negotiating process is a bit more complicated. Again, when you find the car you want, you must determine a fair price. Used-car prices can be found in the National Automobile Dealers Association (NADA) *Official Used Car Guide* and in *Edmund's Used Car Prices,* both of which are generally available at local libraries. In addition, you should have the car under consideration evaluated by an automobile mechanic. Most independent repair shops are willing to do an evaluation for a fee of between $50 and $80.

Evaluating Financing Alternatives.

Once you've established a price, the question of financing can be addressed. In general, the cheapest way to buy a car is with cash. Unfortunately, with the price of a new car many times going over $20,000, that's not always a realistic alternative for many people. Thus, the only alternatives are to borrow money or to lease the car. When you're negotiating a price, keep the question of financing out of the negotiations in order to keep the flexibility to borrow money where it's cheapest. You may find it cheaper to borrow from a bank than through the auto dealership, or you may want to consider a home equity loan with its tax advantages. In any case, you should investigate all options.

In chapter 7 when we introduced automobile loans, we noted that an automobile loan is simply a short-term (often for only 24, 36, or 48 months) secured loan made to finance the purchase of an automobile, with that auto serving as the collateral for the loan. Often, very low cost loans of 3 percent or less are offered by the automakers as a marketing tool, sometimes to sell slow-moving models.

As you might expect, the shorter the term you borrow for, the higher the monthly payments—and the difference can be dramatic. For example, if you were borrowing $15,000 at 9 percent for 24 months, your monthly payment would be $685.27, but if your payments were spread out over 48 months, they would drop to $373.28 per month.

Evaluating Financing Alternatives: The Lease versus Buy Decision.

Leasing appeals to those who are financially stable, like to get a new car every few years, drive less than 15,000 miles annually, and would rather not put up with the hassle of trade-in and maintenance. It's also popular with those who have good credit but don't have the up-front money needed to buy a new car. Figure 8.5 provides a brief profile of those who might want to give leasing serious consideration. That covers a lot of people. In fact, almost one-third of all new cars are leased instead of bought, and this figure rises to over 50 percent for the more expensive models. However, because leasing is so different from buying, many people don't fully understand the process.

Leasing a car is similar to renting a car for 2 or 3 years. The amount you pay for the lease is determined by how much the value of the car you're leasing is expected to decline while you're leasing it. For example, if you took out a 2-year lease on a car that was worth $25,000 new and was expected to drop in value to $16,000 after 2 years, you'd pay the difference ($25,000 − $16,000 = $9,000) plus finance charges. Thus, it's the amount that the car depreciates or drops in value during the lease that determines the cost of the lease.

There are two basic types of leases: closed-end leases and open-end leases. About 80 percent of all new car leases are **closed-end leases**, or **walk-away leases**, in which you return the car at the end of the lease and literally walk away from any further responsibilities. You need merely bring the car back in good condition with normal wear and tear, and the car dealer assumes the responsibility for reselling the car. Many

LEARNING OBJECTIVE #3

Pay for your vehicle through leasing or financing.

Closed-End Lease or **Walk-Away Lease**
An automobile lease in which you return the car at the end of the lease and literally walk away from any further responsibilities. You need merely bring the car back in good condition with normal wear and tear, and the car dealer assumes the responsibility for reselling the car.

FIGURE 8.5

Leasing May Make Sense If . . .

☑ The lease under consideration is a closed-end, not an open-end, lease.

☑ You are financially stable.

☑ It is important to you that you have a new car every two or four years.

☑ You do not drive over 15,000 miles annually.

☑ You take good care of your car and it ages with only normal wear and tear.

☑ You are not bothered by the thought of monthly payments that never end.

☑ You use your car for business travel.

☑ You do not modify your car (e.g., add superchargers or after-market suspension components).

☑ The manufacturer of the car you are interested in is offering very low financing charges.

Purchase Option
An automobile lease option that allows you to buy the car at the end of the lease for either its residual value or a fixed price that is specified in the lease.

Open-End Lease
An automobile lease stating that when the lease expires, the current market value of the car will be compared to the residual value of the car as specified in the lease. If the car's market value is equal to or greater than its residual value, then you owe nothing, or may even receive a refund.

closed-end leases also contain a **purchase option**, which allows you to buy the car at the end of the lease for either its residual value or a fixed price that is specified in the lease. With an **open-end lease**, when the lease expires, the current market value of the car is compared to what the value of the car was estimated to be as specified in the lease contract. If the vehicle is worth less at the end of the lease than was estimated originally, the open-end lease requires you to pay the difference. That difference can mean an awful lot of money to you; thus, the *Consumer's Resource Handbook* warns consumers to beware of open-end leases. Without question, you don't want an open-end lease.

Exactly how is your monthly lease payment determined? Actually, it's made up of two parts. First, there's a monthly depreciation charge that reflects how much the car will decline in value while you're leasing the car. For example, if you took out a 2-year lease on a car that was worth $25,000 new and was expected to drop in value to $16,000 after 2 years, you would pay the difference ($25,000 – $16,000 = $9,000) over the life of the lease. Thus, the amount that the car depreciates or drops in value during the lease plays a big part in determining the cost of the lease. Second, in addition to the monthly depreciation charge there's a rent charge, which is actually the finance charge that's built into the lease and is analogous to the total interest charged on a loan. Exactly what your monthly lease payment would be then depends on

- the agreed-upon price of the vehicle;
- any other up-front fees, such as taxes, insurance, or service contracts;
- your down payment plus any trade-in allowance or rebate;
- the value of the vehicle at the end of the lease;
- the rent or finance charges; and
- the length of the lease.

Because of all the difficulties consumers have had in evaluating automobile leases, in October 1997 the Federal Reserve Board began requiring dealers and other leasing companies to provide customers with a leasing worksheet explaining leasing charges. A copy of such a worksheet is provided in Figure 8.6.

One key to getting a good lease is to negotiate a fair agreed-upon value for the car. Just as with buying a car, you can negotiate the "agreed-upon value of the vehicle," which is analogous to the selling price, before you sign the lease. In fact, it's a good idea not to announce you're interested in leasing until you negotiate a price for the vehicle. You should also try to keep the down payment to a minimum. Also in choosing a car,

FIGURE 8.6

Federal Consumer Leasing Act Lease Disclosure Form

Be very wary of any "other charges." If there are any, ask about them and check with other dealers to see if they impose similar charges.

The gross capitalized cost is the negotiated "selling price." It should be less than the manufacturer's suggested retail price.

The residual value is the projected market value of the car at the end of the lease. This is negotiated. The difference between this value and the gross capitalized cost (less any down payment, trade-in rebate, or noncash credit) is what you're charged for over the lease period.

While it's difficult to define, normal wear and tear generally refers to normal dings, dents, small scratches, stone chips, and tire wear over the period of the lease. Excessive wear and tear would refer to missing parts, damaged body panels, cuts, tears, and burns in the upholstery, broken glass, and other damage beyond what might be expected. Because it's so difficult to define, you should insist that it be defined in the lease contract.

Date _____

Lessor(s) _____   Lessee(s) _____

Amount Due at Lease Signing	Monthly Payments	Other Charges (not part of your monthly payment)	Total of Payments (The amount you will have paid by the end of the lease)
(Itemized below)* $ _____	Your first monthly payment of $ _____ is due on _____, followed by ____ payments of $ _____ due on the ____ of each month. The total of your monthly payments is $ _____.	Disposition fee (if you do not purchase the vehicle) $ _____ [Annual tax] _____ _____ Total $ _____	$ _____

Itemization of Amount Due at Lease Signing

Amount Due At Lease Signing:		How the Amount Due at Lease Signing will be paid:	
Capitalized cost reduction	$ _____	Net trade-in allowance	$ _____
First monthly payment	_____	Rebates and noncash credits	_____
Refundable security deposit	_____	Amount to be paid in cash	_____
Title fees	_____		
Registration fees	_____		
_____	_____		
Total	$ _____	Total	$ _____

Your monthly payment is determined as shown below:

Gross capitalized cost. The agreed upon value of the vehicle ($ _____) and any items you pay over the lease term (such as service contracts, insurance, and any outstanding prior loan or lease balance) .... $ _____

If you want an itemization of this amount, please check this box. ☐

Capitalized cost reduction. The amount of any net trade-in allowance, rebate, noncash credit, or cash you pay that reduces the gross capitalized cost .... − _____

Adjusted capitalized cost. The amount used in calculating your base monthly payment .... = _____

Residual value. The value of the vehicle at the end of the lease used in calculating your base monthly payment .... − _____

Depreciation and any amortized amounts. The amount charged for the vehicle's decline in value through normal use and for other items paid over the lease term .... = _____

Rent charge. The amount charged in addition to the depreciation and any amortized amounts .... + _____

Total of base monthly payments. The depreciation and any amortized amounts plus the rent charge .... = _____

Lease term. The number of months in your lease .... ÷ _____

Base monthly payment .... = _____

Monthly sales/use tax .... + _____

.... + _____

Total monthly payment .... = $ _____

Early Termination. You may have to pay a substantial charge if you end this lease early. <u>The charge may be up to several thousand dollars.</u> The actual charge will depend on when the lease is terminated. The earlier you end the lease, the greater this charge is likely to be.

Excessive Wear and Use. You may be charged for excessive wear based on our standards for normal use [and for mileage in excess of ____ miles per year at the rate of ____ per mile].

Purchase Option at End of Lease Term. [You have an option to purchase the vehicle at the end of the lease term for $ _____ [and a purchase option fee of $ _____].] [You do not have an option to purchase the vehicle at the end of the lease term.]

Other Important Terms. See your lease documents for additional information on early termination, purchase options and maintenance responsibilities, warranties, late and default charges, insurance, and any security interest, if applicable.

make sure the warranty covers the entire lease period so that you don't have to pay for major repairs. In addition, make sure that "normal wear and tear" is defined in the contract, and that you understand exactly what the termination fees (fees for ending the lease early) are. Finally, make sure you have insurance protection that would cover any early termination penalty that might take place if the car were totaled in an accident.

A second important factor in getting a good lease is to find a car that doesn't depreciate quickly. Remember, the lease payment is based on what the vehicle is worth at the end of the lease. That means that you might pay less on a more expensive car that depreciates slowly than you would on a cheaper car that depreciates quickly.

Finally, the last key to getting a good lease is to find one with a low rent or finance charge. Periodically, carmakers will offer extremely low lease financing rates that result in very attractive leasing terms. For example, in 1995, Honda offered such a program on its Acura Legend, in which the rent charge translated into an APR of less than 1 percent.

To determine whether it's better to lease or to buy, you simply need to compare the costs of each over the *same* time horizon. That is, you need to compare a 2-year lease with buying and financing a car over 2 years. In addition, as the market for leasing previously leased, 2-year-old cars expands, there may be new leasing opportunities, provided you understand the mechanics of leasing. Figure 8.7 provides a comparative analysis for a lease versus purchase decision. In this figure the cost of purchasing is $13,504.32, whereas the cost of leasing is $14,328.42. Thus, it's cheaper to purchase the Lexus in this example than it is to lease it.

FIGURE 8.7

Worksheet for the Lease versus Purchase Decision

EXAMPLE Your decision has come down to either purchasing a new Lexus at an agreed-upon price of $34,000 or leasing it. If you purchase it, there is a required 20% down payment of $6,800, plus sales taxes, title, and registration.* The monthly payments over the 2 years if it is financed at 8% are $1,230.18. In addition, if you didn't buy that car, you could have earned 5% on the money you used for your down payment; thus, the opportunity cost of money is 5%. In negotiating the lease option, the residual value for the car at the end of 2 years was estimated to be $23,500. If the Lexus is leased with a capitalized cost of $34,000, there would be a down payment or capitalized cost reduction of $2,950. In addition to the down payment is a security deposit of $475, and at signing you must also make the first month's payment plus taxes, title, registration, and other fees similar to those incurred when buying a car outright. Finally, the monthly lease payment is $459.83.

COST OF PURCHASING

		Your Numbers
a. Agreed-upon purchase price	$34,000	
b. Down payment	$6,800	
c. Total loan payments (monthly loan payment of $1,230.18 × 24 months)	$29,524.32	
d. Opportunity cost on down payment (5% opportunity cost × 2 years × line b)	$680	
e. Less: Expected market value of the car at the end of the loan	− $23,500	
f. Total cost of purchasing (lines b + c + d − e)	**$13,504.32**	

COST OF LEASING

g. Down payment (capitalized cost reduction) of $2,950 plus security deposit of $475	$3,425	
h. Total lease payments (monthly lease payments of $459.83 × 24 months)	$11,035.92	
i. Opportunity cost of total initial payment (5% opportunity cost × 2 years × line g)	$342.50	
j. Any end-of-lease charges (perhaps for excess miles), if applicable	$0	
k. Less: Refund of security deposit	− $475.00	
l. Total cost of leasing (lines g + h + i + j − k)	**$14,328.42**	

*We ignore taxes, title, and registration in this example because they are generally the same whether you lease or purchase the car.

Step 4: Maintaining Your Purchase

Given the size of the investment you make when you buy a car, it only makes sense to keep the car in the best running order possible. The place to start is by reading the owner's manual and learning more about your car. You just can't ignore regular maintenance. For example, change your oil and oil filter as specified in your manual. Change the oil and oil filter every 3,000 miles if your driving is mostly stop-and-go or consists of frequent short trips. Also, flush and refill the cooling system about every 24 months, and keep your engine tuned up. A misfiring spark plug can reduce fuel efficiency as much as 30 percent. You'll want to make sure you keep a log of all repairs and service. If you think about it, you know your car better than anyone else does. You drive it every day and know how it feels and sounds when everything is right. So don't ignore its warning signals. Listen for unusual sounds, look for drips, leaks, smoke, warning lights, or gauge readings. Also, watch for any changes in acceleration, engine performance, gas mileage, or fluid levels. These all could be warning signs. When you take your car in for service, be prepared to describe the symptoms—the importance of accurate communication cannot be over-stressed.

You'll also want to start shopping for a repair facility before you need one; you generally make better decisions when you are not rushed or in a panic. Where should you start looking? Ask friends and associates for their recommendations. Even in this high-tech era, old-fashioned word-of-mouth reputation is still valuable. Keep in mind that the backbone of any shop is the competence of the technicians. Look for evidence of qualified technicians, such as trade school diplomas, certificates of advanced course work, and ASE certifications—a national standard of technician competence. Finally, if the service was not all you expected, don't rush to another shop. Discuss the problem with the service manager or owner. Give the business a chance to resolve the problem. Reputable shops value customer feedback and will make a sincere effort to keep your business.

ADDRESSING YOUR HOUSING NEEDS

Owning a home is perhaps the biggest part of the American Dream. In fact, home ownership is often people's primary goal in life. Why, though, is owning your home so important? Sure, your home is your castle, and somehow it just doesn't seem right for the king or queen to rent that castle. However, at least in the United States, home ownership means more. Many people equate owning your own home with financial success: You've made it, at least in part, if you own your own home. Also it's just kind of neat to own something large enough to walk around in.

Buying something that large, though, takes a lot of money. More precisely, for most people, housing costs take up over 26 percent of their after-tax income.[1] Yes, home ownership is the dream of many, but it's also an investment—the biggest investment you're likely to make. Just as you wouldn't normally approach buying another investment—say, a savings bond—as a dream, you shouldn't approach buying a house only as your big dream. If you don't approach it as an investment, your dream could easily become a nightmare. Lucky for you that this section shows you the ropes for making the biggest investment of your life—and making your dream come true.

How do you go about making a smart housing decision? Using the same smart-buying approach outlined in Figure 8.1—the one we just used for buying a car. In this case the decision at hand is housing, but the basic procedure works just as it does for buying a car or any other purchase. First, you must determine what you need, want, and can afford. Then you look at what alternatives fit into your budget, which may mean only renting. After all, buying a home and all the responsibilities that come

---

[1] In fact, according to the Tax Foundation, the typical American spends about an hour and 20 minutes of each day earning money to pay for housing.

with it isn't a dream for everyone. In fact, it may bring on insomnia for some. The next step is the selection process, where you trade off price against quality and product attributes. In the case of housing, those "product attributes" can be location and neighborhood, nearby schools, square footage, and so forth. After you've honed in on what you want, the process of negotiating price and, if you decide to buy, how best to finance your purchase begins. Finally, there are postpurchase activities, such as maintenance and possibly refinancing. Let's walk through the housing decision step by step.

HOUSING STEP 1: PRESHOPPING HOMEWORK

Just as with any other major smart-buying decision, the first step is to decide what you're looking for. Start by deciding what fits your housing needs best—are good schools the overriding concern, or is ease of moving, perhaps because of an impending transfer, most important?—and looking at the alternatives. You also need to examine your budget and determine how much you can spend on housing. The lists of housing can be very tricky, so you'll need to develop an understanding of the costs associated with owning a home. Finally, you must look at the alternatives of buying versus renting and decide which fits you best.

Needs versus Wants

Generally, although apartment and house shopping is exciting, it's also exhausting, with decision making often being both confusing and frustrating. The key to looking is to decide exactly what you're looking for before you begin your search. After all, how can you search if you don't even know what you're looking for? Before you can decide what to buy, you have to decide what you need and what you want in housing. How many bedrooms do you need? How many bathrooms? Do you need a basement? Do you want a guest room for Aunt Edna? Do you want a playroom? Do you want a walk-in humidor? Are schools a concern? How about closet space? How big should your property be? How about nice little extras such as a tennis court or a pool? These are the kinds of questions you have to answer before you can begin the selection process. In effect, you have to decide what housing qualities you're looking for before you can find housing with those qualities.

Before you search, you also need to consider location. Life in the country is a lot different from life in the suburbs or the city, so choose the location that's going to best suit your preferences. In addition, you should look to the safety of the neighborhood and whether it's conveniently located with respect to your job, shopping, and schools. A desirable location adds to the price of an apartment or home, so expect to pay more for some locations. Fortunately, you can also count on being able to sell for more, too.

In determining your housing needs, you should not only look to your present needs, but also allow for future needs, whether they be for additional space as your family grows, or for less space as your children leave home. Hopefully, the housing decision you make will be good enough to last for years.

> ### *The Facts of Life*
> Housing costs can vary dramatically across the nation. A 1994 survey showed that a 2,200-square-foot, eight-room home would cost $440,000 in San Francisco, but a comparable residence would cost $291,000 in New York, and only $127,800 in Phoenix.

What Are My Options?

For most people, lifestyle is a major player in their housing choice. Kids, schools, pets, privacy, sociability, ability to move around, and other lifestyle concerns tend to point people into one type of housing or another. The needs versus wants issue also plays a major role. Most people would prefer to live in a mansion, but that kind of housing just doesn't fit into many people's monthly budget. Together, your lifestyle, wants, and needs, constrained by your monthly budget, provide focus as to what's a realistic housing alternative for you.

You know what kind of lifestyle you have, but you might not know what type of housing will best suit it. In fact, you might not even know what the various types of housing are available to you. Let's take a minute to examine your basic choices.

A House. A house is the most popular choice for most individuals because it offers more space and privacy. It also offers you greater control over style, decoration, and home improvement. If you want your home to build equity or wealth, buying a house may be a good choice. However, home ownership carries with it more work than do other housing choices. If you own the house, you're responsible for maintenance, repair, and renovations.

Cooperatives and Condominiums. A **cooperative**, or **co-op**, is an apartment building or group of apartments owned by a corporation in which the residents of the building are the stockholders. The residents buy stock in the corporation, which in turn gives them the right to occupy a unit in the building. Although the residents don't own their units, they do have a right to occupy their units for as long as they own stock in the cooperative. Thus, when you "buy into" a co-op, you buy shares of the corporation that reflect the dollar value of your "space." The larger the size of your space and the more desirable its location, the more shares you have to buy. In addition to having to purchase stock in the corporation, tenants also have to pay a monthly **homeowner's fee** to the cooperative corporation, which in turn is responsible for paying taxes and maintaining the building and grounds.

Whether or not a co-op is for you depends on your lifestyle. If you're looking for an affordable, low-maintenance situation with a good helping of shared amenities such as swimming pools, tennis courts, health centers, and security guards, a co-op might be for you. However, if you're more interested in privacy and control over style and decoration, a co-op may be a poor choice. In addition, co-ops generally have less potential for capital appreciation than does a house, and they can be difficult to sell.

A **condominium (condo)** is a type of apartment or apartment complex that allows for individual ownership of the dwelling units but joint ownership of the land, common areas, and facilities, including swimming pools, tennis courts, health facilities, parking lots, and grounds. In effect, you pay for and own your apartment, and you have a proportionate share of the land and common areas. As with a co-op, you still have to pay a maintenance fee, which generally covers interest, taxes, groundskeeping, water, and utilities. The form that condos take can vary greatly—from apartment buildings or townhouses to office buildings or high-rises on the oceanfront. The advantages and disadvantages to living in a condo are similar to those of living in co-ops. However, condos allow for the direct ownership of a specific unit, not just shares in a corporation.

Apartments and Other Housing. Apartments and other rental housing appeal to those who are interested in an affordable, low-maintenance situation with little financial commitment, where it is possible to move with minimum inconvenience. This description often seems to fit the young, single person. As you start out, you simply

Cooperative or **Co-op**
An apartment building or group of apartments owned by a corporation in which the residents of the building are the stockholders.

Homeowner's Fee
A monthly fee paid by tenants to the cooperative corporation for paying property taxes and maintaining the building and grounds.

Condominium (Condo)
A type of apartment building or apartment complex that allows for the individual ownership of the apartment units but joint ownership of the apartment land, common areas, and facilities.

may not have the funds available to buy a home. Alternatively, changing rental housing may simply be a lifestyle decision. You may want limited upkeep and no long-term commitment, or you may be concerned that you might get transferred or change jobs. Regardless of the reason, at some point in time almost all of us live in rental housing. The downside of apartment life generally involves a lack of choice. For example, you may not be allowed to have a pet, or you may have limited ability to remodel the apartment to fit your taste.

The Cost of Housing: What's Involved

Of course, the biggest concern in choosing a type of housing and especially in choosing whether to buy or rent is money. Where you live is often a result of what you can afford. Do you have enough to buy, or do you have to rent? If you do have enough to buy, can you afford a house, or do you have to settle for a co-op? How do you even know what buying a home costs? Well, at least we can answer the last question.

The costs of home ownership can be divided into (1) one-time, or initial, costs, (2) recurring costs, and (3) maintenance and operating costs. The one-time costs involve the down payment, points, and closing costs that are paid when you first buy your house. The recurring costs involve mortgage payments, property taxes, and insurance on your home. Finally, the maintenance and operating costs will vary according to the age, size, and construction of your home. In fact, there may be some years in which the maintenance and operating costs are quite low. Of course, your roof might cave in, leaving a gaping hole through which many squirrels jump so they can gnaw through your carpeting, woodworking, and wiring. That'll be the year your maintenance costs go up through the roof.

To make a logical decision as to whether to rent or buy or to determine what you can afford, you need to understand the costs that come with home ownership.

One-Time, or Initial, Costs.

Houses cost a lot of money! As a result, almost no one can afford to pay for a house all at once. For anyone who can, the entire price of the house is a one-time cost. For the rest of us who can't, we take out loans called mortgages. However, mortgages don't cover all the costs associated with a house. Some of the money, which is referred to as the **down payment**, is the up-front money not included by a mortgage loan that you must pay at the time of the sale when buying a home. In effect, the down payment is the buyer's equity, or ownership share, in the house, and lenders like to see a large down payment. Why? Because if a borrower stops paying back a loan, he or she loses the title to the house as well as the equity. The more equity—that is, the larger the down payment—the more the borrower stands to lose by not paying, and thus the less likely the borrower is to not pay.

Your down payment will vary according to the type of financing that you receive. For traditional mortgage loans, the typical down payment is 20 percent. Thus, for a $150,000 home, a typical down payment is $30,000. Needless to say, that's an awful lot of money, and for those just starting out in the working world, it may simply be out of the question. Fortunately, for those who cannot come up with a 20 percent down payment, there are alternatives. For example, you can buy private mortgage insurance, which is insurance that covers the lender if you default. This will allow you to pay as little as 5 percent down.

Although the down payment is a major hurdle for most first-time homebuyers, it's not the only financial hurdle you'll face. You'll also have a one-time expense when the house's ownership title is transferred to your name. This one-time expense is referred to as **closing** or **settlement costs**. Although they vary quite a bit from house to house, depending upon the size of the loan, the local costs, and the

Down Payment
The amount of money outside of or not covered by mortgage funds that the home buyer puts down on a home at the time of sale.

Closing or **Settlement Costs**
Expenses associated with finalizing the transfer of ownership of the house.

loan arrangements made, they can easily range anywhere from 3 to 7 percent of the cost of the house. Several of the more important components of closing costs include the following:

- **Points** or **discount points:** Points are a one-time additional interest charge by the lender, due at closing—that is, when the sale is finalized. They are used to raise the effective cost of the loan. Each point is equal to 1 percent of the mortgage loan. Thus, if you get a $120,000 loan with two points, the two points would be $2,400, or $1,200 each. Lenders use these points to raise the effective cost of the loan, but points can also be used as a bargaining chip. Many times you'll see trade-offs between interest rates and points—you can get a lower rate with high points or a higher rate with no points. The longer you plan on staying in a home, the more important a low interest rate is. Remember, you pay points only once, at closing, but you pay interest over the life of the loan. If you're planning on staying in your home for a long time, you might be better off taking a few points to get a lower rate, but if you don't expect to be there too long, it's important to keep the points you pay down to a minimum. The only virtue of points is that they're tax-deductible when associated with the financing of the purchase of a home.
- **Loan origination fee:** A loan origination fee is generally one point, or 1 percent of the loan amount. Its purpose is to compensate the lender for the cost of reviewing and finalizing the loan. Unfortunately, because it's not considered an interest payment, it's not tax-deductible.
- **Loan application fee:** The loan application fee, also paid to the lender, is generally in the $200 to $300 range and covers some of the processing costs associated with the loan.
- **Appraisal fee:** An appraisal is an estimate of what your home and property are worth. Lenders require an appraisal before a mortgage loan is approved so they can be sure that they aren't lending you more money than the value of the property. Although the costs for an appraisal vary depending upon the size and location of the house, an appraisal fee can easily run between $200 and $300.
- **Other fees and costs:** There are countless other fees and charges you'll need to pay when buying a home. For example, a **title search** fee is paid to an attorney for searching ownership records to make sure the person selling you the property really owns it. Also, title insurance must be purchased to protect you against challenges to the title, perhaps from a forged deed sometime in the past. There's also an attorney's fee for work on the contract. In addition, there'll be a notary fee, along with a fee charged for recording the deed at the courthouse. Other charges include the cost of your credit report, along with the cost of termite and radon inspection to make sure the house is in good shape.

Figure 8.8 gives a summary of what typical initial costs might be on a $120,000 mortgage loan—buying a $150,000 house with 20 percent down. You'll notice in the example that initial costs amount to almost 24 percent of the cost of the house.

Points or **Discount Points**
Charges used to raise the effective cost of the mortgage loan, which must be paid in full at the time of the sale.

Loan Origination Fee
A fee of generally one point, or 1 percent of the loan amount. Its purpose is to compensate the lender for the cost of reviewing and finalizing the loan.

Loan Application Fee
A fee, generally in the $200 to $300 range, that is meant to defer some of the processing costs associated with the loan.

Appraisal Fee
A fee for an appraisal of the house, which is generally required before a mortgage loan is approved. Although the cost varies depending upon the size and location of the house, it can easily run between $200 and $300.

Title Search
An investigation of the public records to determine the legal ownership rights to property or a home.

The Facts of Life

The law requires that the annual percentage rate (APR) on a mortgage be disclosed to the borrower. Although points must be included in the calculations, fees for taking out the loan application, doing an appraisal, and the credit check aren't included. In addition, the lender can change the APR by as much as $\frac{1}{8}$ of a percent before settlement without notifying the buyer.

FIGURE 8.8

Estimated Initial Costs of Buying a Home: The Down Payment, Points, and Closing Costs on the Purchase of a $150,000 House, Borrowing $120,000, with 20% Down at a Rate of 8% with 2 Points

Down Payment	$30,000
Points	2,400
Loan Origination Fee	1,200
Loan Application Fee	300
Appraisal Fee	300
Title Search Fee	200
Title Insurance	500
Attorney's Fee	400
Recording Fee	20
Credit Report	50
Termite and Radon Inspection Fee	150
Notary Fee	50
Total Initial Costs	**$35,570**

Recurring Costs. The majority of recurring costs generally consists of monthly mortgage payments, the size of which depends on how much you borrow, at what interest rate, and for how long. Basically, the higher the interest rate on your loan, the higher your monthly payments. In addition, the shorter the maturity, or length, of the mortgage loan, the higher the monthly payments. Obviously, the more you pay each month, the less time it takes to pay off the loan. Table 8.1 shows the level of monthly payments that you'd need to make to repay a $10,000 loan at various combinations of interest rates and maturities. From Table 8.1 you can see that on a 15-year 6.0-percent, $10,000 mortgage, the monthly payments would be $84.39. If you increased the maturity to 30 years, though, the monthly payment at 6.0 percent drops to $59.96. Thus, if you are considering a $130,000, 15-year mortgage loan at 6.0 percent, the payments would be $1,097.07 ($130,000/$10,000 × $84.39 = 13 × $84.39 = $1,097.07). Similarly, the monthly payments on a $130,000, 30-year mortgage loan at 6.0 percent would be $779.48 ($130,000/$10,000 × $59.96 = 13 × $59.96 = $779.48).

Mortgage payments are the primary recurring cost, but they're actually made up of four costs, generally referred to as **PITI**, which stands for principal, interest, taxes, and insurance. In addition to paying off the loan principal and interest charges, you'll need to pay property taxes and insurance premiums. These monthly property taxes and insurance payments are generally made along with your loan principal and interest payments, and are held for you in a special reserve account, called an escrow account, where funds accumulate over time until they are drawn out to pay taxes and insurance. The logic behind an escrow account is that paying your insurance and taxes regularly, in small amounts, is less painful than paying them in one large, annual lump sum. Lenders often use the total PITI level to measure an individual's financial capacity to take on a loan. As a rule of thumb, your PITI costs shouldn't exceed 28 percent of your pretax monthly income.

Maintenance and Operating Costs. Whether you buy an old or new, big or small, country or city house, you'll have maintenance and operating costs. For example, you

PITI

An acronym standing for the total of your monthly principal, interest, taxes, and insurance.

WE NEVER MET A FEE
We Didn't Like

It's bad enough being nickel-and-dimed over a checking account. ("What? A $10 charge when *someone else's* check bounces?") But when banks make home loans, the extra fees can go through the roof—often to the point of being illegal.

Lenders are required by Respa, the Real Estate Settlement Procedures Act, to give you 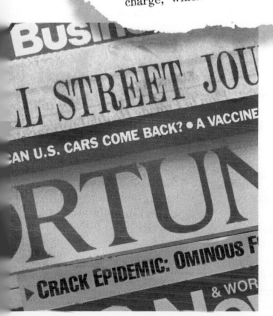a good-faith estimate of your closing costs when you hand in your application, and extra charges are a violation of the law. But some banks try to sneak them in anyway. "I've seen $150 messenger fees," says Charles Baird, a Florida lawyer who has represented a number of people who have sued their mortgage lenders. "I also see strange fees, like a 'jumbo warehousing' fee. Many don't refer to any real service, but I see them on settlement papers all the time. Lenders tend to be very creative when it comes to fees."

One of Baird's clients, Martha Rodash of Miami Beach, recently paid $7,670 in closing costs on her $102,000 loan, some of it incorrectly applied. Among the items for which she was wrongly charged: a $204 Florida intangible-tax charge, which her lender never notified her

about—and should have paid anyway—and a $22 Federal Express charge, considerably higher than FedEx's highest weekday rate of $15.50. To make matters worse, her lender, AIB Mortgage, included the charges in the amount she was financing with the loan—a violation of the federal Truth-in-Lending Act. She sued the company in U.S. District Court and got out of the loan, plus had her fees refunded.

Always ask for a detailed, itemized list of your estimated closing costs when you hand in your loan application. It's required by law. Then on closing day look carefully at the figure called "amount financed" on your settlement papers. If it does not equal the principal you are borrowing, minus any points or interest paid upfront, ask your loan officer why. It could mean he slipped some fees into the amount financed and you can guess what that means: You'll pay interest on those charges.

Source: Nellie S. Huang, "Ten Things Your Mortgage Lender Won't Tell You," *Smart Money,* April 1995, p. 124. Used by permission.

Analysis and Implications ...

A. The bottom line here is that you must always watch out for yourself. Again this gets back to
Axiom 9: The Best Protection Is Knowledge.

B. You should also be wary of recommendations provided by real estate agents as to where to get a loan. Although illegal, it's possible that the lender may be paying your agent for the referral. Your agent's recommendation might still be quite good, but you should make sure that you don't follow him or her blindly. Remember, you must watch out for your own financial interests.

TABLE 8.1

Monthly Mortgage Payments Required to Repay a $10,000 Loan with Different Interest Rates and Different Maturities

Rate of Interest	Loan Maturity					
	10 Years	15 Years	20 Years	25 Years	30 Years	40 Years
5.0%	$106.07	$ 79.08	$ 66.00	$ 58.46	$ 53.68	$ 48.22
5.5	108.53	81.71	68.79	61.41	56.79	51.58
6.0	111.02	84.39	71.64	64.43	59.96	50.22
6.5	113.55	87.11	74.56	67.52	63.21	58.55
7.0	116.11	89.88	77.53	70.68	66.53	62.14
7.5	118.71	92.71	80.56	73.90	69.93	65.81
8.0	121.33	95.57	83.65	77.19	73.38	69.53
8.5	123.99	98.48	86.79	80.53	76.90	73.31
9.0	126.68	101.43	89.98	83.92	80.47	77.14
9.5	129.40	104.43	93.22	87.37	84.09	81.01
10.0	132.16	107.47	96.51	90.88	87.76	84.91
10.5	134.94	110.54	99.84	94.42	91.48	88.86
11.0	137.76	113.66	103.22	98.02	95.24	92.83
11.5	140.60	116.82	106.65	101.65	99.03	96.83
12.0	143.48	120.02	110.11	105.33	102.86	100.85
12.5	146.38	123.26	113.62	109.04	106.73	104.89
13.0	149.32	126.53	117.16	112.79	110.62	108.95
13.5	152.27	129.83	120.74	116.56	114.54	113.03
14.0	155.27	133.17	124.35	120.38	118.49	117.11
14.5	158.29	136.55	128.00	124.22	122.46	121.21
15.0	161.33	139.96	131.68	128.08	126.44	125.32

Calculating monthly payments on a loan:

Step 1: Divide the amount borrowed by $10,000. For example, for a $100,000 loan, the step 1 value would be $100,000/$10,000 = 10.

Step 2: Find the monthly payment for a $10,000 loan at the appropriate interest rate and maturity in the table above. For a 15-year mortgage at 9%, the value would be $101.43.

Step 3: Multiply the step 1 value by the step 2 value. In the example, this is 10 × $101.43 = $1,014.30.

LEARNING OBJECTIVE #5

Decide whether to rent or buy housing.

might need to repair a roof, replace a refrigerator, or install a new heating system. Also, the landscaping surrounding your home usually needs some attention, even if it's well established. Don't forget to plan for these expenses when buying a home, or your first repair bill will come as a very rude shock.

Weighing the Alternatives: Renting versus Buying

For most people, the rent versus buy decision is not a financial decision, it's a personal one—you're making a lifestyle decision. Perhaps you want an apartment because you don't want the responsibilities and upkeep associated with a house, or you may want to buy a house because you want to live in a particular neighborhood. Still, buying a house is generally the largest single investment that most people ever make. It's also something that many people simply can't fit into their monthly budget without some serious cutting on other budget items. Thus, before making this decision, it's a good idea to understand its financial implications.

For many, the lifestyle choices and financial implications are intertwined—spending more or less on housing can have a big impact on your lifestyle. For example, the first factor you should consider in deciding whether to rent or to buy is how long you intend to live there. If it's for a short period—perhaps you expect to change jobs or get married and relocate in the next 2 or 3 years—then you're almost certainly better off renting as opposed to buying. Why? Simply because buying a house is a huge hassle, as is selling it—and as we just saw, these are expensive hassles.

Before examining the advantages of a rent versus buy decision from the financial perspective, let's examine Figure 8.9 which provides a listing of a number of advantages to both renting and buying. As you can see, many of the reasons for renting center on the flexibility—both in the form of financial flexibility, where renting generally involves lower monthly payments, and lifestyle flexibility, where you can avoid responsibilities associated with ownership while staying mobile. The advantages of buying seem to center on the financial benefits of owning a home and personal freedom to remodel and redecorate to suit your taste. The financial benefits come from the tax benefits, from building equity as your mortgage is paid off, and from the possibility of your home appreciating in value over time.

In looking at the rent versus buy decision from the financial perspective, we simply compare the costs associated with each alternative. Interestingly, the results that you get will many times depend mainly on how long you're planning to live in the house. Why? Well, when you buy a house, you experience a lot of up-front, one-time costs. However, the major financial advantages of buying—price appreciation of your home and the tax benefits—occur gradually over time. As a result, you generally must experience a number of years of price appreciation and tax benefits to offset those initial up-front costs. With renting, you don't have those large, one-time costs—in fact, you generally just have a security deposit that you get back when you move out.

Figure 8.10 presents the financial aspects of the rent versus buy decision. In the example, the alternatives being compared are renting an apartment for $900 per month versus buying a house for $100,000. The house would be financed by paying 20 percent down and taking a 30-year mortgage at 8 percent, which would include monthly payments of $587.01. (Calculated using a financial calculator. If calculated using Table 8.1 the monthly payment becomes $587.04, the difference is rounding error.) You'll notice in this example we've ignored the time value of money in order to simplify the analysis.

FIGURE 8.9

Renting versus Buying: The Advantages of Each

Advantages of Renting	vs.	Advantages of Buying

Advantages of Renting

- Very mobile, can relocate without incurring real estate selling costs.
- No down payment required.
- May involve a lower monthly cash flow—you only pay rent, while a homeowner pays the mortgage premium, taxes, insurance, and upkeep.
- Avoids the risk of falling housing prices.
- Many times extensive amenities like swimming pools, tennis courts, and health clubs are provided.
- No home repair and maintenance responsibilities.
- No groundskeeping responsibilities.
- No property taxes.

Advantages of Buying

- Allows you to build up equity over time as you pay off your mortgage.
- Possibility of home appreciation.
- Allows for a good deal of personal freedom to remodel, landscape, and redecorate to suit your taste.
- Significant tax advantages, including deduction of interest and property taxes.
- No chance of rent rising over time.
- Your home is a potential source of cash in the form of home equity loans.

FIGURE 8.10

Worksheet for the Rent versus Buy Decision

ASSUMPTIONS Buying option: $20,000 down and an $80,000, 30-year mortgage at 8%. Rental option: $900 per month. Time horizons: 1 year and 7 years, 28% marginal tax rate, after-tax rate of return = 5%, house appreciates in value at 3% per year, sales commission is 5% of the price of the house, closing costs = $5,000, which includes 2 points.

THE COST OF RENTING

	1 year	7 years	Your Numbers
a. Total monthly rent costs (monthly rent $900 × 12 months × no. years)	a. $10,800	a. $75,600	_____
b. Total renter's insurance (annual renters insurance $250 × no. years)	+ b. $250	+ b. $1,750	_____
c. After-tax opportunity cost of interest lost because of having to make a security deposit (security deposit of $1,800 × after-tax rate of return of 5% × no. years)	+ c. $90	+ c. $630	_____
d. **Total cost of renting (lines a + b + c)**	= d. $11,140	= d. $77,980	_____

THE COST OF BUYING

	1 year	7 years	Your Numbers
e. Total mortgage payments (monthly payments $587.01 × 12 months × no. years)	e. $7,044.12	e. $49,308.84	_____
f. Property taxes on the new house (property taxes of $2,200 × no. years)	+ f. $2,200	+ f. $15,400	_____
g. Homeowner's insurance (annual homeowner's insurance $600 × no. years)	+ g. $600	+ g. $4,200	_____
h. Additional operating costs beyond those of renting: Maintenance, repairs, and any additional utilities and heating costs (additional annual operating costs $500 × no. years)	+ h. $500	+ h. $3,500	_____
i. After-tax opportunity cost of interest lost because of having to make a down payment (down payment of $20,000 × after-tax rate of return of 5% × no. years)	+ i. $1,000	+ i. $7,000	_____
j. Closing costs, including points (closing costs of $5,000)	+ j. $5,000	+ j. $5,000	_____

(continued)

Looking first at the cost of renting, the primary cost is the rent itself. The total cost of renting for 7 years is simply seven times the cost of renting for 1 year, although rent will most probably increase over those 7 years. Other costs of renting include renter's insurance and the opportunity cost of lost interest due to having funds tied up in the security deposit.

As we've already seen, the costs of buying are more complex. Although we have discussed most of the costs associated with owning a home, one cost we didn't look at yet is the opportunity cost of having money tied up in a down payment. Because the money you used for your down payment is tied up and can no longer be invested to earn a

FIGURE 8.10 (continued)

k. Less savings: Total mortgage payments going toward the
   loan principal*   − k. $668.26   − k. $6,017.84   _____

l. Less savings: Estimated appreciation in the value of the home
   less sales commission at the end of the period (current
   market value of house $100,000 × annual growth in house
   value of 3% × no. years − sales commission at end of the
   period of 5% × future value of house)   − l. ($2,150)†   − l. $14,950   _____

m. Equals: Total cost of buying a home for those who do not
   itemize (lines e + f + g + h + i + j − k − l)   = m. $17,825.86   = m. $63,441.00   _____

Additional savings to home buyers who itemize

n. Less savings: Tax savings from the tax-deductibility of the
   interest portion of the mortgage payments (total amount
   of interest payments made × marginal tax rate of 28%)   − n. $1,785.24   − n. $12,121.48 _____

o. Less savings: Tax savings from the tax-deductibility of the
   property taxes on the new house (property taxes of
   $2,200 × marginal tax rate of 28% × no. years)   − o. $616   − o. $4,312   _____

p. Less savings: Tax savings from the tax-deductibility of the
   points portion of the closing costs (total points paid of
   $1,600 × marginal tax rate of 28%)   − p. $448   − p. $448   _____

q. Total cost of buying a home to homebuyers who itemize
   (line m minus lines n through p)   = q. $14,976.62 = q. $46,559.52   _____

**Advantage of buying to those who *do not itemize* = Total cost of
renting − Total cost of buying for those who *do not itemize*:
if negative, rent; if positive, buy**
   (line d − line m) . . . . −$6,685.86 $14,539.00   _____

**Advantage of buying to those who *itemize* = Total cost of
renting − Total cost of buying for those who *itemize*:
if negative, rent; if positive, buy**
   (line d − line q) . . . . −$3,836.62 $31,420.48   _____

*The total interest and principal payments can be calculated directly or approximated. To approximate the total annual interest payments, multiply the outstanding size of the loan by the interest rate, in this case $80,000 × 0.08 = $6,400, then multiply this by the number of years. In the case of the 1-year time horizon, the approximation method yields $6,400 of total interest while a direct calculation yields $6,375.86. While the approximation method works well for short time horizons, it is less accurate for longer time horizons.
†Note: If you only own the home for 1 year, the value here is negative, meaning the sales commission is greater than the appreciation in home value. Thus, this is an additional cost, not a savings, and we are subtracting a negative—in effect, adding the $2,150 to the cost of buying the house.

profit, you should consider the after-tax return that you'd have earned on this money as a cost of buying. Another cost of owning a home comes when you eventually sell it—that's the one-time selling cost resulting from the sales commission when the home-buyer moves and sells the house. You'll notice that the down payment itself isn't a cost; only the opportunity cost of money on the down payment represents a cost. That's because you still have that money; it's still yours. In fact, it's your equity in your house.

These costs are partially offset by the benefits of owning a home, which include the accumulation of equity resulting from a portion of the mortgage payment going toward the loan principal and the appreciation in the value of the home. There are further, substantial savings that are available only to those who itemize. These savings result from the tax deductibility of the interest portion of mortgage payments, property taxes, and any points paid in the closing costs. If you don't itemize your tax deductions, you don't reap the tax benefits from these deductions.

Looking at Figure 8.10, you should notice two major points. First, buying a home generally isn't financially desirable if you don't intend to stay in it for more than 2 or 3 years. The longer you stay in the house, the more it appreciates in value, and the more financially advantageous buying (and selling) is. Second, the benefits of buying instead of renting are substantially greater for those who itemize their taxes than for those who don't itemize. In fact, the advantage to buying over renting is more than twice as large for those who itemize ($31,420.48) than for those who don't itemize ($14,539.00) when looking at the 7-year time horizon.

Finally, for many people, a home is a good means of "forced savings." Because some of your mortgage payment goes toward paying off the loan principal, a mortgage forces you to save in a sense. Although you're really buying something rather than saving, you are buying something that not only doesn't get "used up," but rather, may appreciate in value over time. Moreover, by retirement you should own your house outright and be living "rent-free."

LEARNING OBJECTIVE #6

Calculate the costs of buying a home.

Determining What's Affordable: The Fit Between Your House and Your Budget

The final preshopping homework question to be answered is how much to spend? If you've decided to buy a house, there are three questions to be answered: (1) What is the maximum amount that a bank will lend me? (2) Should I borrow up to this maximum? and (3) How big a down payment can I afford? Although a bank may be willing to lend you $150,000, you might not want to borrow that much. You've got to decide just how much you're interested in borrowing. Don't let a bank tell you how much to borrow. Look at your own financial situation, monthly budget, goals, and lifestyle, and decide for yourself. Taking on a mortgage involves a large commitment of future earnings. Before you take it on, make sure that it jibes with your goals. Will it keep you from meeting your other goals—in particular, your retirement goals? Moreover, will it put such a strain on your monthly budget that you can no longer maintain the lifestyle that you want? You shouldn't let your mortgage payments, or any other debt payments, control your life.

Regardless of what you think you can afford, banks and other lenders will impose a maximum amount that they want to lend you based on your income and current debt levels. Specifically, they look at three things: (1) your financial history, (2) your ability to pay, and (3) the appraised value of the home.

Financial History. In evaluating your financial history, lenders generally focus on the steadiness of your income and your credit rating. If you're self-employed, you may have to provide proof that you've maintained steady income for the past several years. Lenders will also examine your credit report, so you may want to get a copy of your credit report several months before applying for a loan to allow for the correction of any errors that may appear on it. If a lender doesn't like the look of your financial history, you can forget about getting a mortgage.

Ability to Pay—PITI to Monthly Gross income. Lenders generally measure your ability to pay through the use of ratios. In particular, they look at the percentage of your income that housing costs make up. If the ratio's above a certain level, they won't make the loan. The ratio that lenders generally look at is that of your PITI, compared to your monthly gross income. In general, lenders would like to see this ratio at a maximum of 28 percent.

Ability to Pay—PITI Plus Other Debt Payments to Monthly Gross Income.
Lenders also look at the ratio of your PITI plus any other debt payments that will take over 10 months to pay off, compared to your monthly gross income. This ratio is used to account for the fact that many individuals have a sizable amount of outstanding debt, including student loans, car loans, and credit card debit. In general, lenders would like to see this ratio at a maximum of 36 percent. Note that different lenders may calculate these, or other ratios, a bit differently and have different acceptable maximums.

Appraised Home Value.
Regardless of your financial history and ability to pay ratios, most lenders limit mortgage loans to 80 percent of the appraised value of the house. This limitation protects lenders by forcing the borrower to put up a substantial down payment on the home. Lenders assume that the larger a borrower's down payment, the less likely he or she will default on the loan. If a borrower does default, the lender assumes possession of the home, and the 80-percent limitation protects the lender in another way. The lender will sell the home to recoup its losses on the loan, and with the 80-percent rule in effect, the asking price of the home could fall by a full 20 percent—the same amount the borrower initially had to pay out—and the lender would still be able to recover the full amount it loaned out.

Example of the Calculation of Your Mortgage Limit.
The maximum loan size you'll qualify for will be determined by the financial picture that develops as the lender reviews these three measures of your ability to pay. The lowest amount wins. Figure 8.11 shows the basic methods lenders use to determine how much they'll loan you.

As you can see using the information in Figure 8.11, if lenders limit your monthly housing costs as measured by PITI to 28 percent of your gross monthly income, your maximum mortgage payment will be $1,317 (as calculated in line d of Figure 8.11). This payment translates into a mortgage loan of $179,477, given a loan rate of 8 percent and a 30 year term (as calculated in line d, step 2 of Figure 8.11).

Alternatively, when lenders use the 36 percent of total current monthly fixed payments rule as a guide, the maximum monthly mortgage payment you qualify for, given the information in Figure 8.11, is $1,350 (line i of Figure 8.11). This monthly payment translates into a mortgage loan of $183,974, given a loan rate of 8 percent and a 30-year term (as calculated in line i, step 2 of Figure 8.11).

Using the rule of lending 80 percent of the appraised value of the house, your maximum mortgage level would be $184,000. In this example, you have $56,000 available for your down payment *and* closing costs. Because closing costs are estimated to be $10,000, you'll have only $46,000 available for a down payment. If your down payment must be at least 20 percent of the value of your home, then you can borrow four times your down payment, or $184,000.

The mortgage level that you qualify for is the lowest of these three figures. In this case, the lowest was the first mortgage limit of $179,477. Adding this amount to your down payment of $46,000, you see you can buy a house costing $226,477. However, you should keep in mind that whether these guideline ratios are applied more strictly or with some leniency will depend on your financial history.

Stop and Think
Although $179,477 is the likely limit that'll be imposed upon you by the bank, it isn't necessarily the limit that you'll want to impose upon yourself. The importance of not letting your mortgage payments, or any other debt payments, control your life and lifestyle can't be overstressed. Before taking on a mortgage, you should make sure that it squares with your goals, and that it won't prohibit you from meeting your other goals, especially your retirement goals.

FIGURE 8.11

Worksheet for Calculating the Maximum Monthly Mortgage Payment and Mortgage Size for Which You Can Qualify

ASSUMPTIONS: Annual gross income = $65,000

Estimated monthly real estate taxes and insurance = $200

Anticipated interest rate on the mortgage loan = 8%

Mortgage maturity = 30 years

Current nonmortgage debt payments on debt that will take over
   10 months to pay off = $400

Current monthly child support and alimony payments = $0

Funds available for down payment and closing costs = $56,000

Closing costs are estimated to be $10,000*

Minimum acceptable down payment = 20%

METHOD 1   Determine Your Maximum Monthly Mortgage Payment Using the Ability to Pay, PITI Ratio.

		Your Numbers
a. Monthly income (annual income divided by 12)	$5,417	
b. Times 0.28: Percent of PITI (principal, interest, taxes, and insurance) to your monthly gross income that lenders will lend in the form of a mortgage loan (multiply line a by 0.28)	× 0.28 = $1,517	
c. Less: Estimated monthly real estate tax and insurance payments (assumed to be $200 per month)	− $200	
d. Equals: Your maximum monthly mortgage payment using the 28 percent of PITI ratio	= $1,317	

To Determine the Maximum Mortgage Loan Level Using the Maximum Monthly Mortgage Payments as Determined Using the PITI Ratio (line d):

STEP 1: Monthly mortgage payment for a $10,000 mortgage with a <u>30-year</u> maturity and a <u>8%</u> interest rate (using Table 8.1)   = $73.38

STEP 2: Maximum mortgage level = maximum monthly mortgage payment (line d) divided by the monthly mortgage payment on a $10,000, 8%, 30-year mortgage (step 1 above) times $10,000 = ($1,317/$73.38) × $10,000   = $179,477

(continued)

*Closing costs generally vary as a percentage of the amount of the loan; however, to simplify calculations a bit, it is assumed they are estimated to be $10,000.

Coming Up with the Down Payment.   For many people, especially those buying their first home, their real challenge is getting together a down payment. The most obvious and best way of coming up with a down payment is to save. If owning a home is one of your financial goals, saving for it should have a place in your financial budget.

FIGURE 8.11 *(continued)*

METHOD 2 Determine Your Maximum Monthly Mortgage Payment Using the Ability to Pay, PITI Plus Other Fixed Monthly Payments, Ratio.

Your Numbers

e. Monthly income (annual income divided by 12) $5,417

f. Times 0.36: Percent of PITI + current monthly fixed payments to your monthly gross income that lenders will lend in the form of a mortgage loan (multiply line e by 0.36) $\times 0.36 =$ $1,950

g. Less: Current nonmortgage debt payments on debt that will take over 10 months to pay off and other monthly legal obligations like child support and alimony payments (assumed to be $400) $-$ $400

h. Less: Estimated monthly real estate tax and insurance payments (assumed to be $200 per month) $-$ $200

i. Equals: Your maximum monthly mortgage payment using the 36 percent of PITI + other fixed monthly payments ratio (line f - g - h) $=$ $1,350

  To Determine the Maximum Mortgage Loan Using the PITI Plus Other Fixed Monthly Payments Ratio (line i):
  STEP 1: Monthly mortgage payment for a $10,000 mortgage with a 30-year maturity and an 8% interest rate (using Table 8.1) $=$ $73.38

  STEP 2: Maximum mortgage level = maximum monthly mortgage payment (line i) divided by the monthly mortgage payment on a $10,000, 8%, 30-year mortgage (step 1 above) times $10,000 = ($1,350/$73.38) × $10,000 $=$ $183,974

METHOD 3 Determine Your Maximum Mortgage Level Using the "80% of the Appraised Value of the House" Rule.

Your Numbers

j. Funds available for down payment and closing costs $56,000

k. Less: Closing costs of $10,000 $-$ $10,000

l. Equals: Funds available for the down payment $=$ $46,000

m. Times 4: Maximum mortgage level using the "80% of the appraised value of the house" rule (the 20% down, line l, times 4 equals the 80% you can borrow) $\times 4 =$ $184,000

Conclusion: **Maximum Mortgage Level for Which You Will Qualify (the lower of the amounts using method 1, method 2, or method 3):** $=$ $179,477

In addition to saving, many first-time homebuyers also rely on gifts and funds from parents or relatives. In fact, approximately 30 percent of all first-time homebuyers receive some financial aid from their parents or relatives. But, for conventional—that is, nonfederally backed—loans, at least 5 percent of the closing costs have to come from the homebuyer rather than from gifts. Actually, most lenders require a "gift letter" stating that any funds contributed by relatives don't have to be repaid.

> ## Stop and Think
>
> The most common way of coming up with a down payment for a home purchase is saving. Saving for a down payment may mean that you'll have to cut down on or eliminate traveling or eating out. It may even mean that you need to take on an extra job. For most first-time homebuyers, saving enough for a down payment takes about $2\frac{1}{2}$ years.

If you're having trouble raising enough money for a down payment, you might consider trying to reduce the size of the down payment you need. Federally backed loans—Federal Housing Administration (FHA), the Department of Veteran Affairs (VA), and the Farmers Home Administration (FmHA) loans—don't require as large a down payment as conventional loans. In fact, the FHA allows a minimum down payment of as little as 5 percent on older homes and 10 percent on newly built homes.

If all else fails, consider **private mortgage insurance**. This type of insurance protects the lender in the event that the borrower is unable to make the mortgage payments. This insurance is paid for by the borrower and generally runs from 0.3 percent to 2.0 percent of the loan amount, depending on the down payment level. With private mortgage insurance, many lenders will allow you to borrow more than 80 percent of the appraised value of the home.

Knowing for Sure What's Affordable—Prequalifying. Although your ability to pay, in addition to the level of funds you have available for a down payment, should give you a realistic idea of how large a mortgage loan you'll qualify for, it's a good idea to have this amount confirmed by seeing a lender and prequalifying for a loan. The process of prequalifying for a mortgage loan simply involves having a lender determine how large a mortgage loan it'll lend you. While prequalification isn't a final loan, and the specifics will change as rates fluctuate, it does lessen the uncertainty surrounding what you can and can't spend.

HOUSING STEP 2: THE SELECTION PROCESS

Just as with any other major purchase, the selection process in buying a home involves comparison shopping with an eye on price, product attributes (in this case, location, schools, number of rooms, and so forth), and quality (in this case, the quality of the house or apartment). Finding the right house or apartment is both involved and important. In fact, few decisions you make will have as profound an impact on your life. Our discussion of the search process will focus primarily on buying a home, but the same search principles also apply to renting an apartment.

The Search Process

Once you know what you're looking for, it's time to start looking. In looking for a home, most buyers enlist the aid of a real estate agent. These agents can provide buyers with a lot of help in searching for homes and deciding on good neighborhoods, but you should

Private Mortgage Insurance
Insurance that protects the lender in the event that the borrower is unable to make the mortgage payments.

LEARNING OBJECTIVE #7

Buy a house.

note that the traditional real estate agent is really working for the seller. It's the seller who pays the real estate agent's commission; thus, it's the seller's interest that the real estate agent looks out for. As a result, your best interests and the agent's best interests may be in conflict. Thus, while the agent may be your friend, you should make your own decisions based upon a thorough understanding of the alternatives. Differentiating between advice and a sales pitch, and protecting yourself with knowledge, relate back to **Axiom 12: The Agency Problem in Personal Finance** and **Axiom 9: The Best Protection Is Knowledge**. In effect, the traditional real estate agent has a bit of a conflict of interest, and it's the buyer's interests that lose out. In addition, real estate agents can sell only listed property—that is, property on which a real estate firm has a contract to sell—which means the real estate agent will receive a commission. Although this conflict of interest doesn't negate the benefits of using a real estate agent, you should definitely take some precautions when dealing with one. For example, you should never let your agent know your top price. If you tell the agent your top price, you can rest assured that the seller will have that information by the end of the day and your negotiating power will go out the window. You should also say you intend on staying within your budget, and that if you don't get a particular house, that's OK, because there will be plenty of others around.

An alternative to the traditional real estate agent is the **independent** or **exclusive buyer-broker**. This type of broker is a real estate agent hired by the prospective homebuyer, who exclusively represents the homebuyer and is obligated to get the buyer the best possible deal. In general, the broker is paid by splitting the commission with the seller's agent. Buyer-brokers aren't limited in their search to properties that have been listed through real estate firms. They show both unlisted—that is, homes being sold directly by the homeowner—and listed homes. Moreover, because buyer-brokers work for the buyer, they tend to be more objective and critical in examining a house. In effect, they're not swayed by the fact that they may actually be the seller's agent. Although exclusive buyer-brokers have only recently gained popularity, they still aren't that common in many areas of the country. If you're interested in using a buyer-broker and can't find one, you can obtain a referral from either Buyers' Resources (800-359-4092) in Englewood, Colorado, or from Buyers' Agents (800-766-8728) in Memphis, Tennessee.

Independent or **Exclusive Buyer-Broker**
A real estate agent hired by the prospective homebuyer who exclusively represents the homebuyer. Such brokers are obligated to get the buyer the best possible deal and, in general, are paid by splitting the commission with the seller's agent.

The Facts of Life
A recent survey showed that individuals who used buyer-brokers saved an average of 9 percent off the home's asking price versus only 3 percent for all buyers.

When you find a house you like, you need to get it inspected. A given house might suit your needs and tastes, but it also might be falling apart from the inside out. Hey, it might even be haunted! A good home should be structurally sound, and its heating, air-conditioning, plumbing, and electrical systems should be free from problems. Unfortunately, very few homebuyers are truly qualified to inspect and judge these areas. If you're not one of the lucky few, you should enlist the aid of a professional building inspector to inspect your potential property. You should be able to get the name of an inspector from either your real estate agent or the local Chamber of Commerce.

HOUSING STEP 3: MAKING THE PURCHASE

Once you've decided which house or apartment you'd like to live in, the next step becomes making the purchase, or in the case of renting an apartment, signing the lease. Once again, the process followed here is essentially the same as with any other major purchase: Negotiate a price and evaluate the financing alternatives. Because this step of the process is so different for renting versus buying, we'll treat them separately.

LEARNING OBJECTIVE #7

Buy a house.

Guidelines for Renting

Lease

A contract between the renter and the owner of a property that defines the monthly rent, payment date, penalties for late payment, required deposits, length of the lease, and renewal options, in addition to restrictions—for example, no pets or children.

Let's assume you've weighed your options, considered your lifestyle concerns and the costs, and picked out a place to rent. What now? To begin with, when renting an apartment or a house, you're normally required to sign a **lease** or rental agreement. A lease is simply a contract between the renter and the owner of the property, which defines the amount of monthly rent, its payment date, penalties for late payment, required deposits, length of the lease, renewal options, and any restrictions—for example, no pets or children. Before signing a lease, you should do the following:

- Determine what you can realistically afford. In general, your monthly costs, including rent, utilities, and insurance, ideally shouldn't exceed 25 percent of your take-home pay.
- Make sure you like the location of the apartment. If quality schools or accessibility to transportation are important, make sure they're available. In addition, make sure you feel safe with the location of and access to your apartment.
- Make sure you understand your lease and are comfortable with it. Look closely at any restrictions and understand beforehand who's responsible for utilities. Remember, the terms of your lease can be negotiated, and if you want something specifically included, request that it be added to the lease. For example, if paying your rent on the fifth of the month rather than on the first of the month is more convenient for you, ask the landlord to write this change into your lease.
- Never agree to verbal promises. Make sure that any changes in the lease are written directly into it.
- Try to determine whether the landlord is reliable. Ask current tenants of the apartment building whether the landlord is responsive to complaints and repair requests.
- Make sure you have renter's personal property and liability insurance.

Making the Purchase—Negotiating a Price

Traditionally, negotiating a price for a house involves a good deal of bargaining. The house is "listed" at a certain selling price by the seller, meaning the seller would like to receive that price for the house. However, in the real estate market, all prices are open to negotiation. Many times the buyer will offer a price below what the house is listed at. In fact, the offer can also include conditions or contingencies to be met as part of the contract. For example, you may want certain furniture or draperies to remain in the house, or you may want the mobster who owns the house to remove any dead bodies from the foundation. The seller will either give the buyer a counteroffer or refuse to budge. The counteroffer is carried between the buyer and the seller by the real estate agent—in fact, you may never see the seller face to face. In some cases, the haggling can go for some time until a final price is set. In other cases, while the haggling is going on with one potential buyer, another person steps in, offers more, and buys the house.

Making the Purchase—The Contract

Once the price is agreed upon, an attorney can draw up a final contract to buy the house. Real estate contracts are relatively standardized, but you should make sure that your contract protects you and provides for your specific needs. Keep in mind that only what's specifically stated in the contract counts—don't rely on verbal agreements. If you want it done, get it in writing in the contract. In addition, the contract should provide for the following:

- The price, method of payment, buyer and seller, date on which the buyer will take possession, and a legal description of the property should all be stated clearly.

- The legal title to the house must be free and clear of all liens and encumbrances. Whether the buyer or the seller pays for the title search should be stated in the contract.
- The house must be certified to be found free of termite or radon problems.
- A contingent on suitable funding clause should be included, stating that if you're unable to secure suitable financing (where you specifically state the amount, rate, and terms), the contract will be voided and you'll receive your deposit back in full.
- Because the house will change ownership during, rather than at the end of, the year, the contract should state what portion of the utilities, insurance, taxes, and interest on mortgage payments will be paid by the buyer and what proportion will be paid by the seller.
- The condition that the house will be in at the date of transferal should be stated, and a final walk-through should be provided for to assure the buyer that the house is in the contracted condition.
- Any other contingencies that have been agreed upon should be included.

If the contract is accepted, the buyer will give the seller some **earnest money**, which is simply a deposit on the home purchase, assuring the seller that the buyer is serious about buying the house.

At **closing**, the title is transferred, the seller is paid in full, and the buyer takes possession of the house. At this point, the buyer must pay the balance of the down payment. For example, if you're buying a home for $150,000 with 20 percent down, at closing you must pay $30,000 less any earnest money you paid when the contract was signed. In addition to the remaining down payment, you'll also have to pay the closing costs with either a cashier's or certified check. You don't have to worry about figuring out exactly what you have to pay at closing. The lender will give you a **settlement** or **closing statement** at least one business day before closing for your review. Finally, the legal documents are examined and signed and the keys are passed. You now own a home!

Financing the Purchase—The Mortgage

Just as a home is the biggest purchase most people ever make, a mortgage is the biggest loan that they ever take on. To say the least, not all mortgages are the same. In fact, whether or not you can afford to buy a house doesn't just depend on how much the house costs, but also on the specifics of the mortgage, such as how long it lasts for, whether the interest rate changes over time, and whether it's insured by the government. Lets take a closer look at mortgages, where you get them, and how they work.

Sources of Mortgages

Savings and loan institutions and commercial banks are the primary source of mortgage loans, but they certainly aren't the only sources. Mortgage loans are also available from other traditional lenders, such as credit unions and mutual savings banks, in addition to specialized lenders, such as mortgage bankers and mortgage brokers.

Mortgage bankers originate mortgage loans, sell them to banks, pension funds, and insurance companies, and service or collect the monthly payments. In effect, their only business is making mortgage loans, and, in general, they deal only in fixed-rate mortgage loans. There's really no advantage or disadvantage to using a mortgage banker instead of a traditional source of mortgage loans, such as an S&L. Hey, if the mortgage banker's got the more favorable rate or the better deal, go for it.

Mortgage brokers are middlemen whose job is to place mortgage loans with lenders for a fee, but not originate those mortgage loans. The advantage of using mortgage brokers is that they do the comparison shopping for you. That is, they work with a number of lenders and choose the best terms and rates available.

Conventional and Government-Backed Mortgages

Conventional Mortgage Loan
A loan from a bank or savings and loan institution that is secured by the property being purchased.

Government-Backed Mortgage Loan
A mortgage loan made by a traditional lender, but insured by the government.

Once you find the right lender and get your mortgage, it can be categorized as being either **conventional** or **government-backed**. Conventional mortgage loans are simply loans from a bank or savings and loan institution that are secured by the property being purchased. If you default on a mortgage loan, the lender seizes the property, sells it, and recovers the funds owed. With government-backed loans, the traditional lender still makes the loan, but the government insures it.

VA (Veteran's Administration) and FHA (Federal Housing Administration) are the two primary types of government-backed loans, and together they account for approximately 20 percent of all mortgage loans. Both programs are quite similar, and they both share the same basic advantages and disadvantages. The primary advantages of VA and FHA loans are

- an interest rate one-half to 1 percent below that of conventional mortgage loans,
- a smaller down payment requirement, and
- less strict financial requirements for the loan.

The primary disadvantages of VA and FHA loans are

- increased paperwork required to qualify for the loan;
- higher closing costs, with FHA loans requiring a 3.8-percent mortgage default insurance fee and VA loans requiring a 1.25-percent VA funding fee; and
- limits on the amount of funding that can be obtained.

Although the FHA guarantees the entire loan, it doesn't assume all the costs for the required mortgage default insurance. In fact, with an FHA loan you're expected to pay for a portion of the cost, which generally runs 3.8 percent of the loan. However, because FHA loans are guaranteed, the interest rate charged on them is generally about one-half to 1 percent below the rate charged on conventional loans, so you can still wind up saving money.

VA mortgages are much more limited in access than are conventional or FHA mortgages in that only veterans and their unmarried surviving spouses are eligible for them. In addition, FHA loans allow for both fixed- and variable-rate loans, but VA loans must be fixed-rate loans with the rate generally being between one-half and one percentage point below that of conventional loans. However, VA loans don't require anything in the way of a down payment. They do, however, require a 1.25-percent VA funding fee payable at closing.

Fixed-Rate Mortgage Loan

While conventional and government-backed are broad classifications for mortgages, there are also more refined classifications, such as fixed versus variable rate. A fixed-rate mortgage loan is one on which the monthly payment doesn't change, regardless of what happens to market interest rates. That is, no matter how much interest rates fluctuate, your payment remains the same. As a result, you know with certainty what your mortgage payment will be and can plan accordingly. Thus, if mortgage interest rates are low, a fixed-rate mortgage allows you to lock in those low rates for the rest of the loan. The term or length of fixed-rate mortgages is generally set to be either 15 or 30 years, with 30-year fixed-rate mortgage loans being the most popular. Many mortgages also come with assumability and prepayment privileges.

Assumable Loan
A mortgage loan that can be transferred to a new buyer, who simply assumes or takes over the mortgage obligations. Such a mortgage saves the new buyer the costs of obtaining a new mortgage loan.

An **assumable loan** is one that can be transferred to a new buyer, who simply assumes or takes over the mortgage obligations. As a result, the new buyer doesn't incur the costs of obtaining a new mortgage loan. Moreover, if interest rates have gone up since the original assumable mortgage was taken out, the buyer can assume the mortgage at the lower rate. For example, if the mortgage was originally issued at 7.5 percent and rates have now gone up to 9 percent, the buyer could assume the mortgage at

7.5 percent. These advantages make it easier to sell a home with an assumable mortgage, particularly when interest rates have gone up since the mortgage was issued. The assumability privilege is common to all FHA loans and is also common to many conventional mortgage loans.

The **prepayment privilege** allows for the borrower to make early cash payments that are applied toward the principal, thus reducing the amount of interest due. Many mortgages restrict prepayment by either limiting the amount that can be prepaid or charging a penalty for prepayment. The prepayment privilege is also valuable, particularly if interest rates fall over the life of the mortgage. In that case, you can take out a loan at a lower rate and pay off your higher-rate mortgage loan early.

Adjustable-Rate Mortgage (ARM)

With an **adjustable-rate mortgage (ARM)** loan, the interest rate fluctuates up and down according to the level of current market interest rates within limits at specific intervals. From the lender's point of view, ARMs are wonderful because they allow for a matching between the rate that the lender pays on savings accounts to fund the loan and the income from the loan. Because lenders like ARMs so much, they generally charge a lower rate of interest on them—that's the appeal of ARMs to borrowers. Let's look at savings and loan institutions. During the 1980s, interest rates fluctuated wildly. When interest rates went up, S&Ls had to pay more on their savings accounts, but their income on fixed-rate mortgage loans stayed the same, squeezing profits. However, with ARMs, the income from interest payments on mortgage loans followed the interest rates up, thus allowing S&Ls to continue to make profits on their mortgage loans. From the borrower's perspective, you're better off with an ARM if interest rates drop, because your interest rate drops accordingly and you won't have to refinance, which costs money. On the other hand, if interest rates rise, you're better off with a fixed-rate loan, because you will have locked in at a low rate.

Adjustable-Rate Mortgage Loan Terminology

To understand ARMs you need to understand the terminology that surrounds them, including the initial rate, index, margin, adjustment interval, rate cap, payment cap, and negative amortization.

The Initial Rate. The **initial rate**, which is sometimes called the teaser rate, is the initial rate charged on the ARM. This rate holds only for a short period, generally between 3 and 24 months. Usually, the initial rate is set quite low, and in some cases, it's set deceptively low. Thus, once the rate is allowed to move up and down, or float, it generally rises. In evaluating the cost of the ARM, you should focus on the ARM's real rate, that is, what the rate would be today if it were not set by an initial rate.

The Interest Rate Index. The rate on ARMs is tied to an interest rate index that's not controlled by the lender. As that interest rate index rises and falls, so does the ARM rate. The following are some of the more common indexes used:

- The rate on 6- or 12-month U.S. Treasury securities
- The Federal Housing Finance Board's National Average Contract Mortgage rate, which is the national average mortgage loan rate
- The average cost of funds as measured by either the average rate paid on CDs or the 11th Federal Home Loan Bank District Cost of Funds

Which index is the best is debatable. However, stable indexes are better because they won't produce radical rate shifts. When shopping for an ARM, be sure to ask for some historical data on the index from your lender.

Prepayment Privilege

A clause in a mortgage allowing the borrower to make early cash payments that are applied toward the principal.

Adjustable-Rate Mortgage (ARM)

A mortgage loan in which the interest rate charged fluctuates with the level of current interest rates. The loan fluctuates, or is adjusted, at set intervals (say, every 5 years) and only within set limits.

Initial Rate

The initial rate charged on an ARM, sometimes called the teaser rate. This rate holds only for a short period, generally between 3 and 24 months, before being adjusted upward.

The Margin.

Depending on which index your ARM is tied to, your rate may be set higher than the index. If it's set higher than the index, it'll be set at a constant percentage above the index. For example, your ARM may be set at the 6-month U.S. Treasury bill rate plus 2 percent. The amount over the index rate that the rate on the ARM is set at is called the margin. Thus:

$$\text{ARM rate} = \text{index rate} + \text{margin}$$

Thus, if the index rate is 5.0 percent and the margin is 2.5 percent, then the ARM rate is 7.5 percent.

The Adjustment Interval.

The adjustment interval defines how frequently the rate on the ARM will be reset. One year is the most common adjustment period, although some ARMs have adjustment intervals as low as 3 months and some as long as 7 years. An adjustment interval of 1 year means that every year—generally on the anniversary of the loan—the rate on the ARM is reset to the index rate plus the margin. In general, it's better to have a longer adjustment interval, because the shorter the adjustment interval, the more volatile the mortgage payments.

The Rate Cap.

The rate cap limits how much the interest rate on an ARM can change. Most ARMs have both periodic caps and lifetime caps. A *periodic cap* limits the amount by which the interest rate can change during any adjustment. Normally, the ARM rate will go up 3 percent if the index goes up 3 percent. However, if the periodic cap is 2.0 percent and the index rate increases by 3.0 percent, the rate on the ARM would still only increase by 2.0 percent. Most conventional ARM loans have periodic caps of 2 percent, and FHA loans have 1 percent periodic caps. Obviously, smaller periodic caps are better for you than are bigger caps.

The *lifetime cap* limits the amount by which the interest rate can change during the life of the ARM. Thus, for an ARM with an initial rate of 6.0 percent and a lifetime cap of 5.0 percent, the highest and lowest this ARM could go would be down to 1.0 percent or up to 11.0 percent. Borrowers love lifetime caps because they limit the ARM rate to a specific range. In evaluating a lifetime cap, be sure that you know whether the cap is linked to the initial or the real rate.

The Payment Cap.

A payment cap sets a dollar limit on how much your monthly payment can increase during any adjustment period. However, a payment cap limits the change in the monthly mortgage payment, but it doesn't limit changes in the interest rate being charged on the borrowed money. If the payments are capped, and the interest rate isn't capped, when interest rates go up, more of your mortgage payment could end up going toward interest and not principal. In fact, if interest rates keep going up, it's possible that the monthly payment amount will be too small to even cover the interest due. In this case, **negative amortization** occurs. When this happens, the unpaid interest is added to the unpaid balance on the loan. In effect, the size of the mortgage balance can grow over time, and you can end up owing more on the loan than the original amount of the loan. You pay interest on your unpaid interest, and the term of the loan can drag out. Because negative amortization is something to avoid, and can only occur when there's a payment cap limit but not an interest rate cap, you should avoid mortgages with payment, but not interest rate, caps.

ARM Innovations.

Recently, several variations of the standard ARM have been introduced. They include the convertible ARM, the reduction-option ARM, the two-step ARM, and the price level adjusted mortgage. The convertible ARM is a traditional ARM that allows the borrower to convert the ARM loan to a fixed-rate loan, usually during the second through fifth year. A reduction-option ARM is an ARM with a one-time, optional interest rate adjustment. This allows the borrower to adjust the interest rate on the loan to market interest rates one time, generally limited to years 2 through 6.

Negative Amortization
A situation in which the monthly mortgage payments are less than the interest that's due on the loan. As a result, the unpaid interest is added to the principal, and you end up owing more at the end of the month than you did at the beginning of the month.

THIS ISN'T THE RIGHT LOAN FOR YOU

You've found your dream house and now all you need is a loan. Hold everything, even if you've been through this drill before. When interest rates are rising and lenders' business is slowing down, they often get desperate. The result: You may be pitched a loan that's totally inappropriate for your needs. "A loan is a product, and just as in any business where you make money by selling a product, [loan officers] overreach in their sales pitches," says Michael McCann, a California attorney specializing in banking law.

For the past year or so, lenders have been giving adjustable-rate mortgages an especially hard sell. Nearly 50 percent of all loans taken out from January through November 1994 were ARMs. Although ARMs' lower rates certainly make them attractive, North Carolina mortgage broker Christopher Cruise argues that "only 10 percent of all homeowners should get one."

Borrowers' most common mistake is taking a one-year ARM because of the "sucker rate," an artificially low rate that hops up quickly in the second year, Cruise says. "All they want is to get into the home." If you know you are going to be in your house for more than just two or three years, you ought to consider getting a delayed adjustable or two-step mortgage, which adjusts to a fixed rate after a set period. You'll pay a higher rate at first but won't get that immediate "bounce" that comes with most one-year ARMs.

Source: Nellie S. Huang, "Ten Things Your Mortgage Lender Won't Tell You," *Smart Money*, April 1995, p. 123. Used by permission.

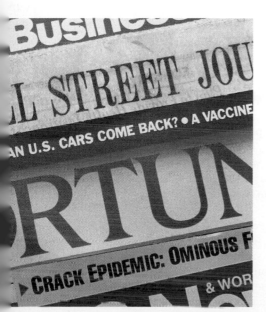

Analysis and Implications ...

A. You should be aware that it's not in your lender's best interests to get you the lowest rate. In fact, on top of your lender's normal commission, which generally runs at 1 percent of the loan, the lender can earn an "overage" of another 1 to 2 percent for selling you a more expensive loan. You should keep in mind at all times **Axiom 12: The Agency Problem in Personal Finance—Differentiating Between Advice and a Sales Pitch**, because you're the only one who bears the consequences of your bad financial decisions.

If interest rates fall, the borrower can exercise his or her option to lower the rates and set the adjustment into motion. If interest rates rise, then the borrower would just leave the rates as they are. With a two-step ARM, the interest rate is adjusted only once, generally at the end of the seventh year. After that, the interest rate remains constant for the remaining life of the loan. On a price level adjusted mortgage, the initial rate is set very low to make the mortgage more attractive. The monthly payments and interest rate then change with inflation. The idea here is that as inflation increases, so should your salary and ability to make higher and higher mortgage payments. Unfortunately, on a 30-year mortgage, your monthly payments could easily triple over this period.

Other Mortgage Loan Options

Most of the alternative mortgage loan options serve the same purpose: to keep the initial mortgage payments as low as possible to make buying a house more afford-able to first-time and cash-strapped buyers. Unfortunately, keeping the payments down in the early years generally means larger payments in later years, or some other concession.

The Balloon Payment Mortgage Loan. With a **balloon payment mortgage loan**, you make relatively small monthly payments for several years (generally 5 or 7 years), after which the loan comes due and you must pay it off in one large balloon payment. Exactly how large the initial payments are varies. In some cases, the initial mortgage payments are only large enough to cover the interest on the loan, and in other cases, the payments may be equivalent to the loan's amortized value over 30 years. However, what balloon payment mortgage loans all have in common is that the payments are constant for a few years and then the loan comes due and is paid off with a very large, final balloon payment.

Some traditional lenders don't offer balloon payment mortgages. In fact, most of these mortgages are offered by the actual sellers themselves, who are anxious to sell the house but don't need the funds from the sale immediately. Watch out for balloon mortgages, because they come with serious potential problems. For many individuals, coming up with the final balloon payment is difficult at best. It generally means they will have to take out a new mortgage just to pay off the old one. That means if interest rates have risen, then the homeowner will be forced to refinance at a higher rate. In ad-dition, when the balloon payment comes due, the homeowner may have very little in the way of equity in the home if the monthly payments have included only interest. In fact, if the market value of the home has declined, the balloon payment that's due could be greater than the house is worth.

Graduated Payment Mortgages. With a **graduated payment mortgage**, the payments are set in advance in such a way that they steadily rise for a specified period of time, generally 5 to 10 years, and then level off. The selling point behind graduated payment mortgages is that the initial payments are relatively low, so you'll be able to afford a house sooner than otherwise possible. The assumption is that then, as your earning power increases over time, you'll be able to afford the rising payments. In ef-fect, you're assuming that your income will grow into the level of future payments. Un-fortunately, you might be assuming incorrectly, and you might be putting an obliga-tion on your future income that you can't handle.

Growing Equity Mortgages. A **growing equity mortgage** is designed to let the homebuyer pay off the mortgage early, which is done by paying a little extra each year. As such, it doesn't really help the cash-strapped buyer. Payments on a growing equity mortgage begin at the same level as on a conventional 30-year fixed-rate mortgage. Then each year your payments increase, and this increase goes toward paying off the principal. With a growing equity mortgage, you know how your payments are going to

Balloon Payment Mortgage Loan

A mortgage with relatively small monthly payments for several years (generally 5 or 7 years), after which the loan must be paid off in one large balloon payment.

Graduated Payment Mortgage

A mortgage in which payments are arranged to steadily rise for a specified period of time, generally 5 to 10 years, and then level off.

Growing Equity Mortgage

A conventional 30-year mortgage in which prepayment is automatic and planned for. Payments begin at the same level as those for a 30-year fixed-rate mortgage and then rise annually—generally increasing at between 2 and 9 percent per year—allowing the mortgage to be paid off early.

increase ahead of time. Generally, they increase by between 2 and 9 percent each year. The end result is that a 30-year mortgage is paid off in less than 20 years. While a growing equity mortgage forces a disciplined prepayment of your mortgage, there is no advantage, and less flexibility, to a growing equity mortgage over a fixed-rate mortgage loan with a prepayment clause.

Shared Appreciation Mortgages. With a **shared appreciation mortgage**, the borrower receives a below-market interest rate, in return for which the lender receives a portion of the future appreciation (usually between 30 and 50 percent) in the value of the home. Thus, if you purchase a $100,000 home with a shared appreciation mortgage that promises the lender 50 percent of any price appreciation and 10 years later sell the home for $180,000, the lender would receive one-half of the $80,000 price appreciation. Generally, mortgages of this type are not issued by traditional mortgage lenders, but by family members or investors.

Adjustable-Rate versus Fixed-Rate Mortgages

For the homebuyer, the primary advantage of an adjustable-rate mortgage is that the initial rate charged on an ARM is lower than that on fixed-rate mortgage loans. Initial ARM rates are lower because the borrower assumes the risk that interest rates will rise. Thus, the rate gap between 1-year adjustable-rate mortgages and 30-year fixed-rate mortgages is generally above 1.5 to 2 percent. For example, in mid 1997, the rate gap was about 1.98 percent.

One commonly stated advantage of this low initial rate is that you may qualify for a larger loan because your monthly payment, PITI, is lower. However, if interest rates rise, pushing your monthly ARM payment upward, you may find yourself overcommitted to your mortgage payments.

Don't choose an ARM in hopes that interest rates will fall and your payments will be lower. You'll just be asking for trouble. Predicting future interest rates is next to impossible, and it certainly isn't something that you want to gamble your house and financial future on. You can be sure that interest rates will never fall below zero (which would mean that lenders would owe *you* money!), but you can never be sure just how high they'll rise. If you have a lifetime cap on your mortgage, you do know just how high your rates can rise, but this knowledge doesn't help if you're hoping never to have to pay that much. In short, if you can't afford the maximum payment you might have to make on an ARM should interest rates rise, you probably shouldn't take on the ARM.

In general, a fixed-rate mortgage is better than an adjustable-rate mortgage. With a fixed-rate mortgage, you know your payments, and, as a result, can plan for them in advance. Don't forget that the basis of personal financial management is control and planning, and a fixed-rate mortgage allows for both. ARMs allow for neither; thus, if you don't like taking on financial risk and have difficulty handling financial stress, ARMs are dangerous. Hey, you don't want to find yourself always looking to the financial pages for interest rate news and freaking out any time there's a small increase in those rates.

Still, if you intend to stay in the house only a few years, or if current interest rates are extremely high, you may want to consider an ARM. Remember, much of the advantage of an ARM comes in the early years when you're guaranteed a low rate. Consequently, if you're not planning on sticking around in your home for very long, an ARM may make sense.

Mortgage Decisions: A 15-Year Term versus a 30-Year Term

Another decision faced by homebuyers is whether to go for a 15- or 30-year maturity on their mortgage. If you can secure a 30-year mortgage with a prepayment privilege, you could easily pay it off in 15 years by making additional payments every month. Why not just take out a 15-year loan if you're planning on paying it off within 15 years anyway? Well, with a 30-year loan, you wouldn't be locked in to paying the higher

Shared Appreciation Mortgage
A mortgage in which the borrower receives a below-market interest rate in return for which the lender receives a portion of the future appreciation (generally between 30 and 50 percent) in the value of the home.

monthly rates of a 15-year loan, and you'd have the flexibility of being able to skip making your additional payments and paying a much lower amount per month if an emergency arose. Thus, at first glance, for those with financial discipline, the 30-year mortgage is preferable. However, there is one additional variable that needs to be added into the equation: interest.

In general, the interest rate on 15-year mortgages is lower than the rate on 30-year mortgages. For example, in late 1997 the average rate on a 30-year fixed-rate mortgage was 7.71 percent and the average rate on a 15-year fixed-rate mortgage was 7.31 percent. Thus, one good reason to go with a shorter-term mortgage is to get a lower interest rate on your mortgage. Interest also comes into play when you consider your overall payments. A longer term means you pay interest over a longer period. For example, let's look at a 30-year, 8-percent fixed-rate mortgage for $80,000. The monthly payments on such a mortgage are $587.01. Figure 8.12 graphically illustrates the portion of each payment that goes toward the principal on a 30-year, 8-percent fixed-rate mortgage. As you can see, initially less than 10 percent of the first monthly payment, only $53.68, goes toward paying off the loan balance. The result of this is that over the life of a longer-term mortgage, total interest payments are much larger. Table 8.2 shows the impact of the loan term on the total interest paid. Keep in mind that these calculations are for an 8-percent mortgage. If the mortgage rate were higher, the total interest payments for the longer-term loan would be proportionately greater than they are on the shorter-term loan. In effect, as interest rates increase, this relationship becomes even more dramatic. Also, keep in mind that this relationship is amplified by the fact that you would pay a lower interest rate on the shorter-term mortgage.

Unfortunately, the total level of interest paid doesn't tell the total story. There are two other complications: the time value of money and the effect of taxes. Remember, with a longer-term mortgage, your payments are lower but stretched out longer. As a result, you're paying back your loan with future dollars that are worth less because of inflation. In other words, when you make the smaller, 30-year payment, you can take the difference in payments and invest it until the end of the 30-year period. Of course, with a 15-year mortgage, when the 15-year period ends, you can invest the amount

FIGURE 8.12

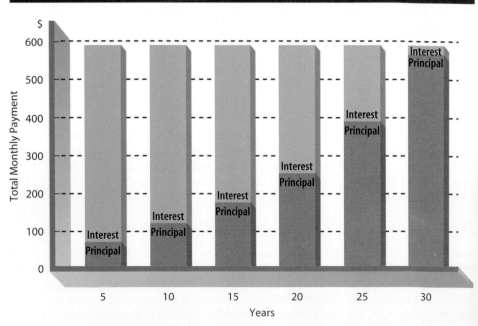

The Portion of Each Payment That Goes Toward the Principal and Interest on a 30-Year, 8% Fixed-Rate Mortgage for $80,000

TABLE 8.2

Impact of the Loan Term on the Total Interest Paid and Monthly Payment for an $80,000 Fixed-Rate Mortgage at 8%		
Length of Mortgage Loan	**Monthly Payment**	**Total Interest**
15 years	$764.52	$ 57,614.13
20 years	669.15	80,597.38
25 years	617.45	105,237.47
30 years	587.01	131,326.30

you were paying each month until the end of the 30-year period. Exactly what you have at the end of 30 years depends upon what assumptions you make about what you could earn on these investments. The more you assume you can earn on these investments, the better off the longer-term mortgage looks. Also, don't forget that interest on home mortgages is tax-deductible and, as such, lowers taxes. As a result, the tax effect favors the longer-term mortgage.

Figure 8.13 provides a listing of some of the advantages of different length mortgages. When deciding on a term length for your mortgage, make sure you weigh all these factors. You've also got to make sure that what you do fits into your grand financial planning scheme. You certainly don't want to be making extra payments to pay off an 8-percent mortgage while you're borrowing money on your credit card at 18 or 20 percent. Also, don't let repaying your mortgage get in the way of your other financial goals.

Step 4: Postpurchase Activities

Once you've purchased a home, you're then in charge of upkeep and maintenance. To say the least, owning a home can take up a good deal of time. In addition, you should always keep an eye out toward making sure that you have financed your home in the least expensive way possible. That leads us to a discussion of refinancing your mortgage.

Refinancing Your Mortgage

Refinancing your mortgage is simply taking out a new mortgage, usually at a lower rate, to pay off your old one. Whenever mortgage interest rates drop, people refinance in droves. No one wants to be paying 12 percent on a mortgage when the going rate is now down to 8 percent. The typical rule of thumb states that you should refinance when mortgage interest rates fall by 2 percent. However, there's more to refinancing than just interest rates. When you refinance, you again incur most of the closing costs we've already discussed, including points, the loan application fee, the termite and radon inspection fee, and so on. The refinancing decision really rides on whether or not the lower rate you could get will compensate for these additional costs in a reasonable amount of time.

Let's look at an example in which you currently have a 15-year-old, 30-year mortgage at 11 percent and are considering refinancing it with a 15-year mortgage at 8 percent. Originally when you bought your home, you took out a $100,000 mortgage with a monthly payment of $952.32. That means today, 15 years later, you still have a balance on your mortgage of $83,789.07. If you refinanced this loan over 15 years at 8 percent, your payments would drop to $800.73, which is $151.59 lower than the level of your present payments. If you estimate that your total after-tax closing costs would be $2,600, it would take you 23.8 months for the savings from the decrease in monthly payments to cover the closing costs incurred as a result of refinancing, as shown in Figure 8.14. Thus, if you expect to continue in your home for over 2 years, you should consider refinancing at the lower rate. Figure 8.15 provides a number of reasons why refinancing might be a good idea.

FIGURE 8.13

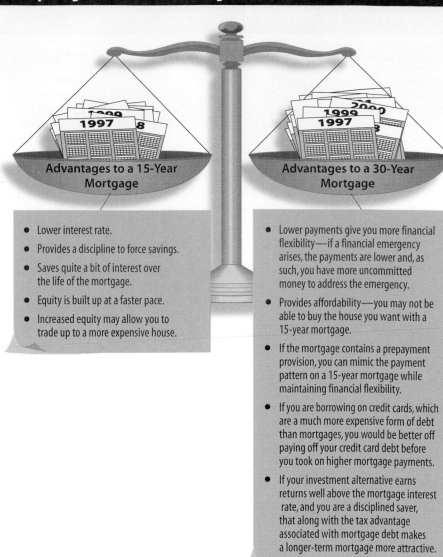

Comparing a Shorter- versus Longer-Term Loan

Advantages to a 15-Year Mortgage

- Lower interest rate.
- Provides a discipline to force savings.
- Saves quite a bit of interest over the life of the mortgage.
- Equity is built up at a faster pace.
- Increased equity may allow you to trade up to a more expensive house.

Advantages to a 30-Year Mortgage

- Lower payments give you more financial flexibility—if a financial emergency arises, the payments are lower and, as such, you have more uncommitted money to address the emergency.
- Provides affordability—you may not be able to buy the house you want with a 15-year mortgage.
- If the mortgage contains a prepayment provision, you can mimic the payment pattern on a 15-year mortgage while maintaining financial flexibility.
- If you are borrowing on credit cards, which are a much more expensive form of debt than mortgages, you would be better off paying off your credit card debt before you took on higher mortgage payments.
- If your investment alternative earns returns well above the mortgage interest rate, and you are a disciplined saver, that along with the tax advantage associated with mortgage debt makes a longer-term mortgage more attractive.

SUMMARY

The first step in smart buying is to separate your wants from your needs. Once you've determined the alternatives, it's time to compare the different products, making trade-offs between quality, the different features of the products, and price. The key to success in negotiating a good price is knowing as much as possible about the mark-up on the product—this gives you an idea about how much room there is for negotiation. The final step is the post-purchase process, involving maintenance and resolving any complaints that might arise. This process of "smart buying" works for just about any purchase decision you make.

While your home may be your largest investment, your automobile is your largest, frequent expense. Choose a car that fits both your personal and financial needs.

Once you have decided what is best for you, the next hurdle is getting it for a fair price. The place to start here is to find out what the dealer cost or invoice price is.

FIGURE 8.14

Worksheet for Refinancing Analysis

Monthly Benefits from Refinancing	Example	Your Numbers
a. Present monthly mortgage payments	$952.32	_____
b. Mortgage payments after refinancing	$800.73	_____
c. Monthly savings, pretax (line a — line b)	$151.59	_____
d. Additional tax on monthly savings (line c × 28% tax rate)	$42.45	_____
e. Monthly savings on an after-tax basis (line c — line d)	$109.14	_____

Cost of Refinancing

f. Total after-tax closing costs, including any prepayment penalty incurred	$2,600	_____

Number of Months Needed to Break Even

g. Months needed for interest saved to equal the refinancing costs incurred as a result of taking out a new mortgage loan (line f ÷ line e)	23.8 months	_____

FIGURE 8.15

Refinancing Can Be a Good Idea for Homeowners Who . . .

 Want to get out of a high-interest rate loan to take advantage of lower rates. This is a good idea only if they intend to stay in the house long enough to make the additional fees worthwhile.

 Have an adjustable-rate mortgage (ARM) and want a fixed-rate loan to have the certainty of knowing exactly what the mortgage payment will be for the life of the loan.

 Want to convert to an ARM with a lower interest rate or more protective features (such as a better rate and payment caps) than the ARM they currently have.

 Want to build up equity more quickly by converting to a loan with a shorter term.

 Want to draw on the equity built up in their home to get cash for a major purchase or for their children's education.

Source: *A Guide to Mortgage Refinancing* (Washington, DC: Federal Housing Administration, 1995).

In addition, you must address the financing decision. Should you buy or lease? Leasing a car is similar to renting. There are two basic types of leases: closed-end leases and open-end leases. About 80 percent of all new car leases are closed-end leases or walk-away leases. With this type of lease you return the car at the end of the lease and literally walk away from any further responsibilities. With an open-ended lease when the lease expires the current market value of the car is compared to the residual value of the car as specified in the lease. If the car's market value is equal to or greater than its residual value, then you owe nothing, and with some leases may, in fact, receive a refund. If, however, the car's market value is less than the residual value as stated in the lease, then you must pay the difference.

No single type of house is right for everyone. A single-family house is the traditional choice, and it is the most popular choice for most people because it offers more space, privacy, and owner control over its style and how it is decorated. A cooperative or co-op is an apartment building or group of apartments owned by a corporation where the residents of the building are the stockholders of the corporation.

There are a number of reasons why you might wish to rent as opposed to buy. As you start out, you simply may not have the funds available to buy a home. In order to make a logical decision as to whether to rent or buy or what is truly affordable, you need to have a basic understanding of the costs that come with home ownership. These include one-time or initial costs such as the down payment, points, and closing costs; recurring costs associated with financing including mortgage payments, property taxes, and insurance; and recurring costs associated with upkeep and maintenance of the house.

The first step in the housing decision involves pre-shopping, in which you focus on the rent versus buy decision and determine what is affordable. Just as with any other major purchase, the second step in the housing decision involves comparison shopping with an eye on price, product attributes such as location, schools, number of rooms, and so forth, and the quality of the house or apartment. Once you decide which house or apartment you'd like to live in, the next step is purchasing the house, or in the case of renting an apartment, signing the lease. Once again, the process followed here is essentially the same as with any other major purchase—negotiate a price and evaluate the financing alternatives. Once you've purchased a home you're then in charge of upkeep and maintenance.

Mortgages can be categorized as being either conventional or government-backed. Conventional mortgage loans are simply loans secured by the property being purchased from a bank or savings and loan institution. With governmental-backed loans, the bank or S&L still makes the loan, but the government insures the loan. Savings and loan institutions and commercial banks are the primary sources of mortgage loans, but they certainly are not the only sources. Mortgage loans are also available from other traditional lenders like credit unions and mutual savings banks as well as from specialized lenders: mortgage bankers and mortgage brokers. Mortgages also come with either fixed or adjustable rates. A fixed-rate mortgage loan is one on which the monthly payment does not change regardless of what happens to interest rates. With an adjustable-rate mortgage loan the interest rate fluctuates up and down with the level of current interest rates within limits at specific intervals. To the home buyer, the primary advantage of an adjustable-rate mortgage is that the initial rate charged is lower than that on fixed-rate mortgage loans. Another decision faced by home buyers is whether to go for a 15- or 30-year maturity on their mortgage.

Review Questions

1. What is the first question someone must answer before making a significant purchase? (LO 1)
2. Summarize the four-step process for smart buying. (LO 1)

Just Do It! *From the Desk of Marcy Furney, CFP*

Home Sweet Home

✓ A home isn't necessarily a money-making investment. Make sure your reasons for purchasing reach beyond making a few bucks. The real estate market is intricate, and many factors are at play in determining resale value.

✓ Beware of the "hidden costs" of homeownership. Decorating and landscaping can be major expenses in a new home. Utilities, maintenance, and repairs are ongoing budget items. If you're buying a pre-owned home, ask to see utility bills for different seasons.

✓ Whenever possible, prequalify for your loan so that you'll know approximately how much you can spend. You may want to stay below the maximum you could finance so that you will have some buffer for other expenses.

✓ Make sure the lender locks in the interest rate quoted you and find out how long it will be guaranteed. Be sure to get to closing before that period runs out or take the initiative to renegotiate the rate.

✓ Keep good records of any improvements, not repairs, you make on your home. Include the cost, what was done, and when. These improvements can be useful in boosting the market value of your home when you sell it. On high-dollar houses with potential capital gains tax, they will also serve to increase your cost basis.

✓ When you shop for your home, be sure to do detailed investigation of the neighborhood, schools, pending zoning issues, and so on. If you're considering an existing house, you may wish to hire an engineer to check it out.

✓ If you handle your money responsibly, you may want to get a loan without an escrow account. You'll be responsible for paying your own taxes and insurance, but you'll have the flexibility to make some interest on the money you set aside for those expenses. To some extent, you also time those payments to fit your cash flow and tax situation. Different states and lenders have varying requirements for such a loan.

✓ Remember that paying off your mortgage doesn't mean that you have free housing. Besides maintenance, you'll have tax and insurance expenses forever. People who are retiring now are finding that their housing costs from these items is almost equal to the original house payment 30 or so years ago.

3. Identify four sources of product/consumer information that might be needed when making a major purchase. Match the information source to the relevant steps in the smart-buying process. (LO 1)

4. What are some factors that help determine the vehicle someone should buy? (LO 2)

5. What three factors determine the monthly payment on an automobile loan? (LO 3)

6. What is the purpose of an auto lease? Identify the characteristics of a consumer who should seriously consider auto leasing. (LO 3)

7. What are the six factors that determine the monthly lease payment? (LO 3)

8. What are the two types of leases? What is the major difference between the two? (LO 3)

9. What is the difference between a condo and a co-op? What are the advantages and disadvantages of each compared to living in a single-family house? (LO 4)

10. From a financial point of view, over a 7-year period why is owning better than renting? Consider costs, return, and taxes in your answer. (LO 5)

11. Why is renting more financially advantageous for people who expect to move quite often? (LO 5)

12. What factors should be considered before signing a lease or rental agreement? (LO 5)

13. What are the advantages and disadvantages of buying versus renting a home? (LO 5)

14. What three major categories of expenses make up the cost of homeownership? (LO 6)

15. What are the initial costs associated with buying a home? (LO 6)

16. The mortgage payment consists of what four separate expenses? (LO 6)

17. What three factors determine the maximum amount a bank will finance for a home mortgage? (LO 6)

18. What is the difference between a traditional real estate agent and an independent buyer-broker? Is there an advantage to either for someone buying a home? (LO 7)

19. What provisions should be outlined in a real estate contract? (LO 7)

20. What are the advantages and disadvantages of government-backed loans, such as VA or FHA loans? (LO 8)

21. Explain how the interest rate index and the margin are used to determine the interest rate for an ARM. How might this differ from the initial rate? Why are the factors of rate caps and adjustment intervals important? (LO 8)

22. Balloon payment mortgages, graduated payment mortgages, and shared appreciation mortgages offer the advantage of reduced initial payments for first-time or cash-strapped homebuyers. What are the disadvantages of these mortgage options? (LO 8)

23. What are some factors that determine whether a homeowner should refinance? (LO 8)

Problems and Activities

1. Consider all the following costs of owning a vehicle valued and sold for $15,000. Now calculate the total annual cost of owning that vehicle during the first year. (LO 3)

   Auto loan: amount—$15,000, duration—4 years, APR—8.75%
   Property taxes: 2% of vehicle value per year
   Sales taxes: 3% of the sale price
   Title and tags: $40 per year
   Maintenance and usage costs: $1,500 per year
   Insurance: $2,000 per year

2. Calculate the monthly payments for a vehicle that costs $21,000 if you financed 80 percent of the price for 5 years at 7.5 percent. Also calculate the same loan for a 3-year payment schedule. Hint: Use Appendix F: Monthly Installment Loan Tables. (LO 3)

3. Calculate the monthly and total automobile loan payments for each of the following loans. (LO 3)

   a. $20,000, 60 months, 9%
   b. $18,000, 36 months, 8%
   c. $17,500, 48 months, 7.75%
   d. $14,000, 48 months, 10%

e. $16,000, 24 months, 9.5%

f. $24,000, 60 months, 7%

4. Calculate the monthly payments for a vehicle that costs $15,000 if you finance the entire purchase over 4 years at an annual interest rate of 7 percent. Also calculate the loan payments at rates of 8 and 9 percent. Compare the total amount spent on the vehicle under each assumption. (LO 3)

5. Connie's mortgage statement shows a total payment of $699.15 with $604.60 paid toward principal and interest and $94.52 paid for taxes and insurance. Taxes and insurance for three months had to be paid in advance at closing. Now after six months of payments, she's curious as to the total amount in her escrow account. Calculate the amount for her and explain the account. (LO 4)

6. Calculate the monthly payments of a 30-year fixed-rate mortgage at 8 percent if the amount financed is $100,000. How much interest is paid over the life of the loan? (LO 6)

7. Calculate how much money a perspective homeowner would need for closing costs on a house that costs $100,000. Calculate based on a 20-percent down payment, two discount points on the loan, a one-point origination fee, and $1,400 in miscellaneous other fees. (LO 6)

8. Calculate the monthly payments for a $100,000 mortgage loaned in each of the following ways.

   30-year fixed at 9%

   15-year fixed at 8%

   20-year fixed at 8.5%

   What are the total payments on each loan and which is the best option for a homeowner who can afford payments of $875 per month? Explain your answer. (LO 6, 8)

9. If someone has an annual salary of $40,000, what is the maximum 30-year fixed-rate mortgage a bank would allow if the annual interest rate is 8.5 percent. Assume that the homeowner will not need private mortgage insurance and the insurance and tax portion of the payment is $80. Hint: Refer to Table 8.1 to determine the mortgage amount. (LO 7)

10. Determine the maximum 30-year fixed-rate mortgage amount for which an individual could qualify if the rate is 10 percent. Assume there are other debt payments totaling $400 per month and an annual salary of $48,500. Monthly escrow payments for real estate taxes and homeowners insurance is estimated to be $125. (LO 7)

Suggested Projects

1. Research several automotive Web sites and write a one-page report on your findings. (LO 1)

2. List your needs (including budget) and your wants for a new automobile. Consult sources such as Web sites, magazines, and dealership literature, and make a financially and personally wise decision about which vehicle to buy. Write your lists and discuss your reasoning in a short report. (LO 2)

3. Go to a dealership and ask to see a copy of its lease agreement. Discuss your options and understanding of the agreement in a one-page report. *Note:* If asked, avoid giving your full name. This could lead to an unwanted and unauthorized check of your credit report. (LO 3)

4. List the pros and cons, from both a financial and a personal perspective, of leasing and financing a vehicle. (LO 3)

5. List as many house styles and room names as you can (*Hint:* A house-planning magazine may help.) Which style and combination of rooms suit you the best? Why? (LO 4)

6. List the pros and cons, from both a financial and a personal perspective, of renting and owning a home. Write a one-page summary on your choice, which can be verified by your list. (LO 5)

7. Talk with your parents or another homeowner, or consult your own records, to determine the amount of money that was paid in up-front closing costs for the most recent house closing. Write a report outlining the costs. (LO 6)

8. Obtain a copy of the real estate section in the local paper or real estate listings booklet. Choose a home, regardless of price, that you would like to own. Now choose a house with a price between $100,000 and $150,000 that you would like to own. (If the first house is between $100,000 and $150,000, choose another.) Finally, calculate the principal and interest portion of the mortgage payment on each home if you financed 80 percent of the cost over 30 years at a rate of 9 percent. Write a report outlining your calculations and the reasoning behind each of your choices. (LO 4, 6, 7)

9. Assume you are buying a new $130,000 home in the area. Find the mortgage rate information in the local paper and choose a loan from the ones listed. When considering your choice, consider rate, duration, type, monthly payment, closing costs, and points. Calculate the monthly payment based on financing 80 percent, and calculate the total amount paid over the life of the loan including up-front costs. (LO 8)

Discussion Case 1

Otto and Katarina Mikosinski are in the market for a new vehicle. Otto is a 41-year-old plumber with an income of $35,000 per year; Katarina, 37, is an executive with a local corporation and has an annual salary of $46,000. They already own two vehicles, but they need to replace the 1990 pickup Otto uses for work. The replacement needs to be a vehicle that fits his job.

Katarina is concerned about the depreciation expense with a new vehicle and is considering a lease. She also likes the idea of having a new car every few years without the hassle of resale. However, Otto knows that he drives a lot on the job and is worried about the high mileage penalty on many leases, as well as the fees for excessive wear and tear. Otto also doesn't like the fact that, if they lease, they would not own the vehicle he'll use for work.

They feel that they can afford to spend $450 per month over 4 years for a new vehicle, as long as their other associated expenses, such as insurance, gas, and maintenance, aren't too high. The Mikosinskis also don't know where to start looking for a vehicle without the hassle of negotiating with dealerships.

As their best friend, they have come to you with the following list of questions.

Questions

1. Make a list of seven sources of vehicle-buying information and the type of information available in each source. (LO 1)

2. For all the information available, specifically what information about the different makes and models is the most relevant to Otto and Katarina in making their vehicle buying decision? (LO 1)

3. What is the highest price they can pay if they can put a down payment of $4,000 on the new vehicle with financing at 8.75 percent for a 48-month loan? (LO 2)

4. According to the National Automotive Dealer Association guide, are the Mikosinskis better off selling their vehicle or using it as a trade-in? Consider both price and time in your answer. (LO 2)

5. Would you recommend leasing or financing? Why? (LO 3)

Discussion Case 2

With a raise from the investment firm, Seyed Abdallah, 28, is inspired to look for a new home. Buying a home will allow Abdallah, who is single and in the 31-percent marginal tax bracket, to itemize taxes. He has come to you for help.

Financially he is fairly secure but doesn't like to take risks. His salary is $61,500 a year, but he doesn't know how much he should spend on housing. He has lived debt-free since paying off his college and auto loans last year. His current housing expenditures include rent of $700 per month and renter's insurance premiums totaling $150 per year. He also paid a security deposit of 2 months' rent from which he could be earning 8 percent after taxes.

Abdallah has researched the recurring costs of homeownership. He has found that the real estate tax rate is $1.07 per $100 of assessed value. He is unsure of the maintenance costs but estimates them at $350 per year.

He likes the idea of owning his own home because as the real estate values increase, the value of his home will increase instead of his rent payment. Local property values have been increasing at 4 percent per year over the last 7 years, and real estate sales commissions equal 6 percent. One qualm about buying a home is the immediate cost of down payment and closing costs. These closing costs, he has found, include a 1 percent origination fee, two discount points on the mortgage, and 3 percent of the home cost in various other fees due at closing. He also knows that he would pay a 20-percent down payment. Another qualm is the lost investment income on this money that is currently earning an 8-percent after-tax return.

Questions

1. Write a short description of the four types of housing generally available for Abdallah. (LO 4)

2. List several sources of information applicable to any real estate purchase that might be helpful to Abdallah in making a decision. (LO 5)

3. Use the lending guidelines to determine the maximum dollar amount that he could spend per month on his home payment (PITI). (LO 6)

4. Calculate Abdallah's monthly PITI payment. To calculate principal and interest (PI), assume he has purchased a home for $140,000 and has a $112,000, 30-year, 7.5-percent fixed-rate mortgage. To calculate the local real estate taxes (T), use the real estate tax rate as given in the case, assuming the property has an assessed value of $128,000. Also, Abdallah's projected homeowner's insurance cost (I) is $280 per year. (LO 6)

5. Complete *Worksheet G.22, Worksheet for the Rent versus Buy Decision* to determine if Abdallah should buy or continue renting. To purchase the house considered in question 4, above, Abdallah would pay $7,000 in closing costs including $2,500 in interest discount points. Consider a 1- and 7-year time horizon. (LO 5)

6. Abdallah is considering a home selling for $180,000. Estimate the dollar amount Abdallah should be ready to pay on the day of closing. Assume that the closing costs are 5 percent of the sales price and Abdallah pays a 20-percent down payment on the house. (LO 7)

7. Given his risk tolerance, what type of mortgage would you recommend to Abdallah? (LO 8)

Continuing Case: Don and Maria Chang

PART II: MANAGING YOUR MONEY (CHAPTERS 5, 6, 7, AND 8)

Don and Maria are back asking for your help, only this time the topics are cash management and use of credit. Tempting credit card offers continue to come in the mail. Recall that they have Visa, MasterCard, Discover, and American Express credit cards as well as several store cards, with a combined average balance of $1,300. Minimum monthly payments equal approximately $32, although they typically pay $100 per month. Maria's sister and her husband just bought their first home, making Maria even more anxious to move from their rented apartment. Don wants to wait awhile longer before buying a home and has suggested that they should replace the old station wagon. Don and Maria realize that funds for another payment are limited, not to mention money for a house payment. Their options are to reduce payments on their credit cards or to reduce other expenses. At any rate, $200 a month seems to be the maximum amount available for an auto loan, not to mention any likely increase in their auto insurance premium associated with the new vehicle. Help them answer the following questions.

Questions

1. Maria recently found out that she is eligible to join her employer's credit union. What are the advantages and disadvantages of doing so? (*Hint:* Refer to Worksheet G.11, Choosing a Financial Institution, for ideas.)
2. The Changs' bank was recently taken over by a big out-of-state bank. Because required minimum balances and bank fees have increased, the Changs have decided to look for a new bank for their savings account. What factors should they consider?
3. Which provides the higher after-tax yield, the Changs' 3-percent bank savings account or a federal and state tax-free money market fund yielding 2.25 percent? The Changs are in the 28-percent federal marginal tax bracket.
4. Don recently attended a bank employee seminar about Treasury bills. Are Treasury bills an appropriate place to put the Changs' savings for a house?
5. Don also has easy access to Series EE bonds sold at the bank. How appropriate are EE bonds as a savings vehicle for one or more of the Changs' financial goals?
6. The *Good Housekeeping* article recommended "pay yourself first." Maria is not sure how to do this, but likes the idea of "saving money without having to think about it." Give her some advice about ways to "automate" her savings.
7. The Changs' take-home pay (after deductions for taxes and benefits) is approximately $3,500 monthly. Current nonmortgage debt payments equal $505 ($280 auto, $100 miscellaneous credit, and $125 furniture). Calculate and interpret their debt limit ratio. Assume they could purchase another auto with a $200 monthly payment. Calculate and interpret their revised debt limit ratio. What advice would you give the Changs?
8. Concerned that they might depend on credit too much, Maria and Don have asked you about typical warning signs of excessive credit use. List five to eight of those signs.
9. What is the maximum number of credit cards recommended? Given what you know about the typical characteristics of the cards Don and Maria carry, what recommendations would you make about holding the cards they have? Consider the advantages and disadvantages of each type of card. Also, what features are important to "credit users" as opposed to "convenience users"?
10. Doug, a friend of Maria's, suggests that they should "card surf" by frequently applying for new cards with low teaser rates and transferring the balances from their existing cards. They can then close the accounts from which they just transferred the balances so that they never pay high interest charges. Another friend suggests that a debt consolidation loan is the only way to pay off multiple creditors. Compare and contrast these alternatives. What factors should Don and Maria consider before utilizing either strategy?
11. Help Don and Maria apply the four steps of the smart-buying process to decide whether to replace their station wagon. What sources of consumer information might be useful to them?
12. A recent TV advertisement offered a lease option for $199 a month on a car that both Maria and Don like. It fits their budget, but they are

unsure of the contract obligations. What criteria should they consider to determine whether leasing is their best alternative? What cautions would you recommend about an open-end lease compared to a closed-end lease?

13. If Don and Maria decide to purchase instead of lease another car, what factors must they consider when comparing a new or used car purchase? What factors should they consider in determining whether to sell their car outright or trade it in toward their next purchase?

14. A used car that costs $12,000 can be financed through Don's bank for 7.75-percent interest for a maximum of 54 months. The rate for new-car financing is 7.25 percent for 48 months. If they could find a comparably priced new vehicle, how much would they save per month in interest charges on a 48-month loan? How much would they save over the life of the loan?

15. In reviewing the sample auto loan contract from Don's bank, Maria questioned him about the term "secured loan." She was also unsure of the terms "default," "repossession," and "deficiency payment clause." Explain these terms. What can they do to avoid repossession?

16. In a few years Maria and Don might want to consider a home equity loan to finance a car purchase or to help pay for Andy's college costs. What are the advantages and disadvantages of using this credit source as opposed to the typical auto or student loan?

17. Maria and Don often review the weekly mortgage rate column in their local paper. Last week the interest rate for a 30-year fixed-rate mortgage was 8.125 percent, while the rate for a 7-year balloon payment mortgage was 7.75 percent (payments calculated on the basis of 30-year amortization). A 1-year ARM was available for 6.125 percent (payments calculated on the basis of 30-year amortization). Assuming a loan amount of $100,000, calculate the payment for each mortgage. Aside from the significant differences in the mortgage payment amounts, what other factors should the Changs consider when choosing their mortgage?

18. Based on their gross monthly income of $4,917 and monthly debt repayments of $505, what is the maximum mortgage amount for which Don and Maria could currently qualify? Monthly real estate tax (T) and homeowner's insurance (I) are estimated at $150 per month. Calculate the mortgage amount using both the 28-percent qualification rule and the 36-percent qualification rule. (*Hint:* Refer to Figure 8.11). Use 8 percent as the current rate of interest and assume a 30-year fixed-rate mortgage.

19. Compare the Changs' monthly mortgage payment for PITI in question 18 with their current monthly rent and renter's insurance cost of $710. Should Don and Maria consider purchasing a house that would require their maximum mortgage qualification loan amount? Defend your answer.

20. Given the maximum mortgage qualification loan amount determined in question 18, calculate a 20-percent down payment. If closing costs average 5 percent of the cost of the house, how much will Don and Maria need on the day of closing? How does this compare with the $7,000 in the Jimminy Jump-up Mutual Fund account for their house down payment?

21. Using the monthly PI payment for the maximum mortgage qualification amount in question 18, calculate the total cost of the Changs' home if the mortgage is not paid off early. How much of this cost is interest?

22. Maria would like to consider a 15-year mortgage so that the house would be paid for before Andy enters college. Explain how the factors of monthly payment, total interest paid, the time value of money, and the effect of taxes impact this decision.

Chapter 9

THE ROLE OF LIFE INSURANCE

"So, you make movies, huh?" Those were the words of Chili Palmer, the Miami tough guy played by John Travolta in the movie *Get Shorty.*

"I produce feature motion pictures, not TV. You mentioned *Grotesque;* that happens to be *Grotesque Part 2* that Karen Flores was in. She also starred in two of my slime creature releases. You may have seen them," responded Harry Zimm, played by Gene Hackman.

"I got an idea for a movie," Palmer responded. "It's basically an idea about a guy who owes this shylock $15,000 and he's about three weeks over on the 'big,' that's the interest you've got to pay." From there, the plot unfolds like so many mystery novels, where life insurance inspires bumping someone off or faking a death—in this case, faking a death.

Not only does life insurance inspire this kind of action in fiction, but also real life. There are dozens of tragic real crime stores based on someone standing to inherit tons of money from insurance—just think of the Menendez brothers. However, novels, movies such as *Get Shorty,* and TV shows such as *Murder She Wrote* seem to do it best. The plot usually goes something like this. The murderer takes out a big policy on Aunt Ethel and then pushes her down the stairs, disguising it as an accident, or the murderer poisons her famous meatloaf, the one that always won first prize at the county fair, and gets arrested (many times with the help of Jessica Fletcher) as he or she is about to step on that plane (leaving Cabot Cove, Maine) bound for Tahiti. Now if you were going to kill poor Aunt Ethel and bilk the insurance company out of hundreds of thousands of dollars, would you know what kind of policy to take out on Aunt Ethel or how to buy it least expensively?

Learning Objectives

After reading this chapter you should be able to:

1. Reduce your financial risk through insurance.
2. Determine your life insurance needs and design a life insurance program.
3. Compare and contrast the various types of life insurance available.
4. Choose the contract clauses and policy riders that best meet your life insurance needs.
5. Purchase the life insurance policy that's best for you.

PROTECTING YOURSELF WITH INSURANCE

Would you make sure that there was a multiple indemnity rider if you're planning to make Aunt Ethel's death look like an accident?

These are some of the questions to be answered in this chapter. However, for those who aren't budding mystery writers (or intending to kill off their Aunt Ethel), the questions to be answered are equally important, because if you're like everyone else, you probably don't like thinking about death or life insurance. As a result, when it comes around to getting your first life insurance policy, you probably won't go out and buy it—instead someone will approach you and sell it to you. Because insurance seems to have a language known only to insurance salespeople, most people can't understand the differences between one policy and another, how much to buy, or what options to include. Basically, there probably isn't another topic in this book about which consumers, and mystery writers, are as ill-informed.

Life insurance is an odd thing to purchase—it's not meant to benefit you. Hey, you're dead—you no longer have any needs. When you consider your need for life insurance, you must keep in mind its role: to protect your dependents in the event of your death. Life insurance can be used to pay off your debts so that your dependents aren't burdened with that debt when you die. Life insurance can be used to provide the needed funds your income normally would have provided. In effect, life insurance is meant to give you peace of mind by ensuring that your dependents have the financial resources to pay off your debts, keep their home, send your children to college, and still have enough income to live comfortably. Most college students, as a rule, don't have a need for life insurance—they tend to be single and have no dependents. That doesn't mean they won't buy life insurance, especially if a persuasive insurance salesperson comes to call. The goal in this chapter is to give you a basic understanding of life insurance, the types of policies available, and the process of buying insurance so that you can buy the life insurance you need.

**Reduce your financial risk
through insurance.**

AXIOM #10

**Protect Yourself Against
Major Catastrophes—The Case
for Insurance**

Risk Pooling
Sharing the financial consequences
associated with risk.

AXIOM #3

Diversification Reduces Risk

Premium
A life insurance payment.

Actuaries
Statisticians who specialize in
estimating the probability of death
based upon personal characteristics.

Face Amount or **Face of Policy**
The amount of insurance provided
by the policy at death.

Insured
The person whose life is insured by
the life insurance policy.

Policy Owner or **Policyholder**
The individual or business that owns
the life insurance policy.

THE LOGIC BEHIND INSURANCE AND THE PROCESS OF RISK REDUCTION

The need for insurance rises from **Axiom 10: Protect Yourself Against Major Catastrophes—The Case for Insurance**. In the case of life insurance, it's not you that's being protected, but your family. The purpose of life insurance is to cushion the financial blow that'll hit your dependents when you die. If you haven't planned wisely, your death could be a financial catastrophe for your dependents—one that knocks them out of financial control. The key concepts here are *planning* and *control*. After all, this whole book, and all of personal finance, is based on controlling your financial situation through careful planning. Hey, if you plan carefully enough, you can control your finances even after your death. Planning now so that your loved ones won't have to worry in a time of loss is what life insurance is all about.

Of course, your life insurance planning involves deciding on what and how much insurance to buy. One problem you'll face in your life insurance decision is that the marketing of life insurance is unbelievably confusing. In fact, you're not likely to receive the same recommendation on your life insurance needs from any two life insurance salespeople. Moreover, not only won't you get the same recommendation, but you probably won't be able to compare the recommended policies because of the incomprehensible jargon that accompanies them. Keep in mind that an insurance policy is simply a contract with an insurance company that spells out what losses are covered, what the policy costs, and who receives payments if a loss occurs. Whether or not to take out an insurance policy is a matter of risk-return trade-offs. Are you willing to pay for an insurance policy to cover your risks? To start you on the road to understanding life insurance, let's take a look at some of the basic ideas behind it, starting with the relationship of insurance to risk.

Life Insurance and Risk Management—Pooling Risks

Unless medical science comes up with something mighty impressive in the next few years, we all have to die sometime. Life insurance allows you to effectively eliminate or at least substantially reduce the financial consequences of your death for your dependents.

Insurance is based upon the concept of **risk pooling**, which simply means that individuals share the financial risks that they face. The logic behind risk pooling is drawn from **Axiom 3: Diversification Reduces Risk**. In this case, life insurance allows individuals to pool the financial risks associated with death to eliminate the catastrophic loss associated with it. In effect, everyone pays something into the "pot," and the family of the unlucky loser receives the money, which offsets the lost income due to death. That way, the loser's dependents don't suffer financially from the loser's death. In the case of insurance, the small amount everyone pays is called a **premium**, and the size of the premium depends upon your chance of being the unlucky loser. Basically, the probability of your dying determines your premium. To determine your chance of death, insurance companies employ **actuaries**, who are statisticians that specialize in estimating the probability of death based upon personal characteristics. For example, smokers stand a much higher risk of dying than do nonsmokers. Because they're more likely to die, smokers get charged higher premiums by life insurance companies. In effect, insurance companies are able to predict with a good deal of accuracy the number of deaths that will occur from a given population of policyholders and charge each policyholder a fair premium.

The amount of insurance provided by the policy at death is called the **face amount** or **face of policy**, and the **insured** is the person whose life is insured by the life insurance policy. Sometime the policy is owned (or "held") by an individual, and other times it's held by a business. In either case, the owner is referred to as the **policyholder** or **policy owner**. The individual designated by the owner of the life insurance policy to receive the insurance policy's proceeds upon the death of the insured is called the **beneficiary**. What happens if you're terminally ill or very old? You might be uninsurable—that is, the chance of your death may be so high that insurers may not be willing to sell you life insurance.

DETERMINING YOUR LIFE INSURANCE NEEDS

Now that we know what life insurance is and how it works, we need to figure out whether we really need it. The purpose of life insurance is to provide for your dependents in the event of your death. If you're single and have no dependents, you generally don't need insurance. However, you still might want to buy life insurance if you're at a higher risk of contracting a terminal illness, such as cancer or AIDS, or an uninsurable condition that could prevent later purchases, such as diabetes or heart disease. Although insurance policies don't pay off until you are dead, if you're terminally ill it's possible to receive a discounted settlement, kind of like borrowing against your policy, or sell your insurance policy at a discount before you die. Thus, for those with a high risk of serious health problems, a life insurance policy can be viewed as a form of health insurance. For anyone else without a spouse or dependents, life insurance simply doesn't make sense.

However, if you do have a spouse or dependents, then life insurance can help make up for the wages lost as a result of your death. In addition to replacing lost income, it can cover burial expenses, medical and hospital expenses not covered by your health insurance, outstanding bills and loans, and attorney's fees related to estate settlement. Life insurance can also be used to provide funds for housing and for your children's education. In determining whether or not you need life insurance think back to what we said about the purpose of life insurance at the opening of this chapter—it's not meant to benefit the insured, but those left behind by him or her. Table 9.1 provides a listing of who might need life insurance.

Beneficiary
The individual designated to receive the insurance policy's proceeds upon the death of the insured.

LEARNING OBJECTIVE #2

Determine your life insurance needs and design a life insurance program.

TABLE 9.1

Should You Buy Life Insurance?

Life insurance is *not* necessary if:

You're single and don't have any dependents.

You're married, a double-income couple, with no children. Consider life insurance only if you're concerned that your surviving spouse's lifestyle will suffer if you die.

You're married, but aren't employed. Consider life insurance only if you have young children and your spouse would have financial problems with day care and housekeeping if you die.

You're retired. Consider life insurance only if your spouse couldn't live on your savings, including Social Security and your pension, if you die.

Consider life insurance if:

You have children. You should have coverage for raising and educating your children until they are financially self-sufficient.

You're married, a single-income couple, with no children. You should have insurance to allow your surviving spouse to maintain his or her lifestyle until he or she can become self-sufficient.

You own your own business. A life insurance policy can allow your family to pay off any business debt if you die.

The value of your estate is over the estate-tax-free transfer threshold, which was $600,000 per person in 1997 and rises annually to $1 million by year 2006. As you will see in chapter 18, life insurance can be an effective tool for passing on an estate without incurring taxes.

How Much Life Insurance Do You Need?

Let's say you need life insurance. The question then becomes *how much* you need. The first step in determining how much life insurance you need is deciding what your priorities and goals are for providing for your survivors. Do you want to provide enough money for your kids to go to college? Do you want enough money for your wife to buy her own home? Do you want to provide your husband with enough money to live on for the next few years while he takes care of the kids? Different people are going to have different philosophies about providing for their survivors, and none of those philosophies is necessarily right or wrong. Figure 9.1 provides a number of questions that are helpful to consider in determining your own life insurance philosophy.

Once you've developed your philosophy, the next step to figuring out how much insurance you need involves some numbers. Start with your net worth, because the larger your net worth, the more you have in the way of wealth to support your dependents, and consequently the less life insurance you need. Don't forget to throw in numbers to compensate for inflation and the earnings on possible future investments. Is the process starting to sound complicated? Luckily, there are two basic approaches you can use to crunch the numbers that will tell you how much life insurance you need: (1) the earnings multiple approach and (2) the needs approach.

Stop and Think

Your life insurance needs will change dramatically over the course of your life. If you're a single student right now, you probably don't need life insurance, but you'll need some when you get married or have kids. Once the kids are grown, you'll need less, and by the time you retire—if you've saved enough to provide for your spouse—you may not need any at all. In effect, one thing you may have in common with retirees is the absence of a need for life insurance.

FIGURE 9.1

Some Questions to Consider in Determining How Much Life Insurance You Need

☑ For how long after your death do you want to ensure your survivors' financial security?

☑ Will your surviving spouse be earning any income?

☑ Is a drop in your surviving spouse's lifestyle acceptable?

☑ Do you want to provide funding for your children's college education?

☑ What could your survivors reasonably expect to earn on their investments?

☑ Do you want to provide for the immediate repayment of your home mortgage? What about other debts?

☑ Do you want life insurance to pay for any estate taxes that might be due?

The Earnings Multiple Approach.   Some financial planners suggest that you purchase life insurance that covers from 5 to 15 times your annual gross income. The **earnings multiple approach** is used to figure out exactly how much insurance this actually amounts to. Although this approach is used often, it's still rather rough in that it doesn't take into account your individual level of savings or your financial well-being, but instead treats everyone the same.

The earnings multiple method is based upon the notion that you want to replace a stream of annual income that's lost due to the death of a breadwinner. That is, you want to replace one stream of annual income with another. What the earnings multiple approach does is tell you how big a lump-sum settlement you would need to replace that stream of annual income. Actually, a stream of annual income for a set number of years is just like the annuities we studied back when we looked at the time value of money in chapter 3. What that means is that the earnings multiple approach works the same way present value of annuity problems work. In effect, to determine the lump-sum settlement you need, simply multiply your present annual gross income by the appropriate earnings multiple, where the earnings multiple is simply the appropriate present value interest factor of an annuity ($PVIFA_{i\%,\ n\ yr}$). In this case, you use the $PVIFA_{i\%,\ n\ yr}$, where i is the percentage you assume you can earn both on an after-tax and after-inflation basis in the future on the insurance settlement, and n is the number of years for which you wish to replace the lost earnings. Table 9.2 uses these $PVIFA$ factors to provide an abbreviated table of earnings multiples. To simplify the presentation (and speed the sale), many insurance agents present the earnings multiple numbers without explaining the logic behind how those numbers were calculated. You need to keep in mind, then, that the earnings multiple that applies to your situation depends entirely on the number of years you need the lost income stream and the rate of return that you assume you can earn on the insurance settlement. As Table 9.2 shows, the longer you need to replace the income stream, the greater the multiple, and the higher the return you feel you can earn on the settlement, the lower the multiple.

Let's examine how this approach might be applied to Leonard and Nancy Cohen. Leonard's the breadwinner, making a cool $80,000 per year. The Cohens currently have two young children, aged 2 and 4, and they don't plan to have any more. The kids won't be self-supporting for another 20 years, and Leonard and Nancy want to make sure they're provided for, even if something happens to Leonard. Nancy's a good investor and is sure she could get a 5-percent return, after taxes and inflation,

Earnings Multiple Approach
A method of determining a rough estimate of how much life insurance you need by using a multiple of your yearly earnings.

TABLE 9.2

Earnings Multiples for Life Insurance

Number of Years You Wish the Lost Earnings Stream Replaced	After-Tax, After-Inflation Return Assumed on the Insurance Settlement		
	3%	4%	5%
3 years	2.83	2.76	2.73
5 years	4.58	4.45	4.33
7 years	6.23	6.00	5.79
10 years	8.53	8.11	7.72
15 years	11.94	11.12	10.38
20 years	14.88	13.59	12.46
25 years	17.41	15.62	14.09
30 years	19.06	17.29	15.37
40 years	23.12	19.79	17.16
50 years	25.73	21.48	18.26

on an invested insurance settlement. How much life insurance do the Cohens need? Rather than simply multiply Leonard's salary times the *PVIFA*, we need to first adjust his salary downward to compensate for the fact that the family's living expenses will drop slightly with Leonard's death. Generally, family living expenses fall by about 30 percent with the loss of an adult family member if there's only one surviving family member. The larger the size of the surviving family, the less the living expenses drop as a percentage of total family expenses. For example, expenses drop by only 26 percent for a surviving family of two, or 22 percent for a surviving family of three, and they continue to drop another 2 percent for each additional surviving family member. Thus, to calculate the Cohens' target replacement salary, we adjust Leonard's present salary downward by multiplying it by a factor of (1 − 0.22), or 0.78. The target replacement salary thus becomes $80,000 × 0.78 = $62,400.

Now we're ready to use the *PVIFA* value. In this case, $n = 20$ years and $i = 5\%$. Looking in the earnings multiples table, we find a *PVIFA* value of 12.46. Multiplying Leonard's adjusted salary by this factor, we get $777,504. That is, under the earnings multiple method, the level of life insurance needed becomes

$$\begin{array}{c}\text{life insurance} \\ \text{needs}\end{array} = \begin{array}{c}\text{income stream} \\ \text{to be replaced}\end{array} \times \begin{array}{c}(1 - \text{percentage of family income} \\ \text{spent on deceased's needs})\end{array} \times PVIFA_{i\%,\, n\,\text{yr}}$$

$$= \$80{,}000 \times (1 - 0.22) \times 12.46$$

$$= \$777{,}504$$

Because this method is relatively simple, it's used quite frequently. Keep in mind, though, that this method isn't very useful unless it considers the effects of taxes and inflation. Also, remember that this method is somewhat limited in that it considers only your income replacement needs, not your need to eliminate debt or save for specific goals. Most important, you've got to remember that your i and n factors are going to change over time. That means that your earnings multiple is going to change over time and that you're going to need to update your insurance coverage from time to time.

The Needs Approach.   The **needs approach** attempts to determine the amount of funds necessary to meet the needs of a family after the death of the primary breadwinner. Some of the more common family needs include the following:

- **Immediate needs at the time of death:**   Sometimes called the **cleanup funds**, these include final illness health costs, burial costs, inheritance taxes, estate taxes, and legal fees.
- **Debt elimination funds:**   Funds to cover outstanding debts, including credit card and consumer debt, car loans, and mortgage debt.
- **Immediate transitional funds:**   Funds needed to cover expenses such as new job training for the surviving spouse and child care. For spouses who are already employed, transition funds may be used to cover a leave of absence from their jobs.
- **Dependency expenses:**   These are family expenses while children are in school and dependent on family support.
- **Spousal life income:**   Income for the surviving spouse after the children have left home and are self-supporting.
- **Educational expenses for children.**
- **Retirement income:**   This includes retirement income less Social Security and pension income.

Once you've estimated your needs, you examine your survivors' anticipated income to determine the income shortfall that life insurance has to cover. Let's look at how this approach can be put into practice, using our old friends the Cohens, and using the worksheet shown in Figure 9.2.

Needs Approach

A method of determining how much life insurance you need based on funds your family would need to maintain its lifestyle after your death.

Cleanup Funds

Funds needed to cover immediate expenses at the time of your death.

TOTAL NEEDS

Step 1: Immediate Needs—Cleanup Funds

			Your Numbers
Final Illness Costs (assumed equal to your health insurance deductible)	a.	$750	___
Estate Administration Costs (assumed equal to 4% of your assets)	+ b.	$6,000	___
Burial Costs	+ c.	$6,000	___
Federal Estate Taxes (if any due)	+ d.	$0	___
State Estate Taxes	+ e.	$0	___
Additional Legal Fees	+ f.	$2,000	___
Other Immediate Needs	+ g.	$250	___
Total Immediate Needs (add lines a through g)	= h.	$15,000	___

Step 2: Debt Elimination Funds

Credit Card and Consumer/ Installment Debt	i.	$12,000	___
Auto Debt Outstanding	+ j.	$3,000	___
Desired Mortgage Reduction	+ k.	$60,000	___
Other Debt to Be Paid Off at Your Death	+ l.	$0	___
Total Debt Elimination Funds (add lines i through l)	= m.	$75,000	___

Step 3: Immediate Transitional Funds

Schooling Expenses for Surviving Spouse	n.	$15,000	___
Child Care and Housekeeping Expenses	+ o.	$4,000	___
Other Transitional Needs	+ p.	$1,000	___
Total Immediate Transitional Funds (add lines n through p)	= q.	$20,000	___

Step 4: Dependency Expenses (family needs while children are in school and dependent on family support)

Current Household Expenses (estimated as income less savings)	r.	$75,000	___
Less: Deceased's Expenses (estimated as 30% of line r if surviving family includes only one member, 26% for a surviving family of two, 22% for a surviving family of three, and dropping 2% more for each additional family member)	− s.	$16,500	___
Less: Spousal Income	− t.	$15,000	___
Less: Social Security Survivors' Benefits	− u.	$14,400	___
Less: Pension Benefits and Income	− v.	$9,000	___

(continued)

FIGURE 9.2

(continued)

Income to Be Replaced Until Children
Are Self-Supporting
(line r minus lines s through v) = w. $20,100 _____

Total Dependency Expenses or Money in Today's Dollars Needed
for Dependency Expenses (assuming the children have n years
until they become self-supporting and you can earn an i%
after-tax and after-inflation return on your investments)
(line w $\times$ $PVIFA_{i\%,\,n\text{ years}}$) = ($20,100 $\times$ $PVIFA_{5\%,\,20\text{ years}}$) =
($20,100 $\times$ 12.46) = x. $250,446 _____

Step 5: Spousal Life Income (spousal needs after children are self-supporting)

Desired Spousal Income y. $20,100 _____

Total Spousal Life Income or Money in Today's Dollars to Provide for
Desired Spousal Income (assuming n years until the children become
self-supporting and m years until the spouse qualifies for Social
Security or retirement income, and assuming you can earn an i%
after-tax and after-inflation return on your investments)
[line y $\times$ ($PVIFA_{i\%,\,m\text{ years}}$ − $PVIFA_{i\%,\,n\text{ years}}$)] =
[$20,100 $\times$ ($PVIFA_{5\%,\,40}$ − $PVIFA_{5\%,\,20\text{ years}}$)] =
[20,100 $\times$ (17.16 − 12.46)] = z. $94,470 _____

Step 6: Educational Expenses for Your Children

Total Educational Expenses (private school needs plus total
college needs) = aa. $100,000 _____

Step 7: Retirement Income

Additional Desired Annual Income
at Retirement bb. $20,100 _____

Total Retirement Income or Money in Today's Dollars to Provide
for Desired Retirement Income (assuming retirement in m years
and desiring the additional income for p additional years,
and assuming you can earn an i% after-tax and after-inflation return
on your investments)
[line bb $\times$ ($PVIFA_{i\%,\,m+p\text{ years}}$ − $PVIFA_{i\%,\,m\text{ years}}$)] =
[$20,100 $\times$ ($PVIFA_{5\%,\,60\text{ years}}$ − $PVIFA_{5\%,\,40\text{ years}}$)] =
[$20,100 $\times$ (18.93 − 17.16)] = cc. $35,577 _____

Step 8: Total Funds Needed in Today's Dollars to Cover Needs

Total (lines h + m + q + x + z + aa + cc) = dd. $590,493 _____

Step 9: Assets and Insurance Available to Cover Needs

Cash from Current Insurance Policies ee. $200,000 _____
Retirement Savings and Investments ff. $140,000 _____
Other Assets gg. $0 _____
Total Assets (add lines ee + ff + gg) = hh. $340,000 _____

Step 10: Additional Insurance Needs

Additional Insurance Needs (line dd minus line hh) = $250,493 _____

Step 1: Estimate immediate needs at the time of death. Let's estimate Leonard's final expenses to be $15,000. This figure includes all final medical, burial, tax, and other immediate expenses.

Step 2: Estimate debt elimination funds. Currently, the Cohens have $15,000 of credit card, consumer or installment debt, and auto debt outstanding. In addition, they owe $120,000 in principal on their mortgage. To reduce the financial burdens on Nancy, the Cohens would like to be able to pay off half of their outstanding mortgage principal and all the rest of their debts if Leonard dies. Therefore, the desired debt elimination funds total $75,000 ($60,000 worth of mortgage + $15,000 of additional debt).

Step 3: Estimate immediate transitional funds. For Nancy to reenter the workforce, she must complete her college degree. When Leonard and Nancy got married, Nancy still had 1 year of college remaining to complete her degree as a laboratory technician. To complete this degree, Nancy will need funds to cover child care, tuition, and books. The Cohens estimated that $20,000 would be needed.

Step 4: Estimate dependency expenses. Recall that the Cohen children will be dependents for the next 20 years. To a certain extent, Leonard's lost income will be offset if Nancy gets a job. One approach to determining the current total household expenses is to use the deceased's income less annual savings as an estimate. Presently, Leonard's earning $80,000 per year, and the Cohens are saving $5,000 per year, which leaves $75,000 in household expenses. From this $75,000 we have to subtract Leonard's expenses. Recall that the Cohens' expenses will drop an estimated 22 percent after Leonard's death. Thus, the Cohens would need to replace ($80,000 − $5,000) × (1 − 0.22) = $75,000 × 0.78 = $58,500 per year. Some of this amount will come from Nancy's income, and some will come from Social Security and Leonard's pension from his job. Nancy is sure that she'll earn $15,000 per year working part-time as a laboratory technician. She also estimates Social Security survivors' benefits to be $14,400 and pension income to be $9,000. The Cohens, then, need to replace $58,500 − $15,000 − $14,400 − $9,000 or $20,100 in annual income until the children are self-supporting. Where does that leave us? It leaves us calculating the present value of a $20,100 annuity for a 20-year period. We bring the annuity back to present by multiplying it by the $PVIFA_{i\%, \, 20 \text{ yr}}$, where the discount rate, $i\%$, is estimated on both an after-tax and after-inflation basis. Recall that Nancy thinks she can earn 5 percent, after taxes and inflation, on an invested insurance settlement, so the discount rate is 5 percent. Thus, the present value of the dependency expenses is $20,100 × $PVIFA_{5\%, \, 20 \text{ yr}}$, or $20,100 × 12.46 = $250,446.

Step 5: Estimate spousal life income. Assume that Nancy would like $20,100 per year in additional income for another 20 years after the children become self-supporting, which is when she'll retire. The present value of this 20-year annuity, beginning 20 years from now, can be calculated by first determining the value of a 40-year annuity and subtracting a 20-year annuity from that amount. The first 20 years of the 40-year annuity are canceled out, with only the last 20 years of the 40-year annuity remaining. Assuming an after-tax and after-inflation rate of 5 percent, the present value of this annuity is $94,470:

$$\$20,100 \times (PVIFA_{5\%, \, 40 \text{ yr}} - PVIFA_{5\%, \, 20 \text{ yr}})$$
$$= \$20,100 \times (17.16 - 12.46)$$
$$= \$20,100 \times (4.70)$$
$$= \$94,470$$

Step 6: Estimate educational expenses for your children. To estimate college expenses, you'll simply use the present cost of a college education and assume that if you invest this amount today, your college fund will be able to keep pace with increasing college costs. Under this assumption, the Cohens estimate college expenses for the two children will be $100,000 in today's dollars.

Step 7: Estimate retirement income. Given the uncertainty of the level of Social Security benefits that might be available in 40 years, the Cohens have chosen not to incorporate any adjustment for Social Security into their calculations. At retirement in 40 years, Nancy would like to have a supplemental stream of income of $20,100 for an additional 20-year period. To calculate this 20-year annuity, beginning 40 years from now, first determine the value of a 60-year annuity and then subtract the value of a 40-year annuity from that amount. The first 40 years of the 60-year annuity will then be canceled out, with only the last 20 years of the 60-year annuity remaining. Assuming an after-tax and after-inflation rate of 5 percent, the present value of this annuity is $35,577.

$$\$20,100 \times (PVIFA_{5\%,\ 60\ yr} - PVIFA_{5\%,\ 40\ yr})$$
$$= \$20,100 \times (18.93 - 17.16)$$
$$= \$20,100 \times (1.77)$$
$$= \$35,577$$

Thus, in today's dollars, Nancy needs $35,577 to provide her desired supplemental retirement income.

Step 8: Add all needs together. Summing the funds necessary to cover all the needs identified in steps 1 through 8 gives total needs of $590,493 in today's dollars.

Step 9: Examine assets and insurance available to cover needs. Fortunately, most people have assets or some existing insurance that will at least partially meet their life insurance needs. In this example, Leonard's employer provides him with $200,000 worth of life insurance. In addition, the Cohens also have $140,000 in retirement savings and investments. Thus, without any additional coverage, they have assets and insurance equal to $340,000 to cover their needs.

Step 10: Calculate additional life insurance needs (step 8 minus step 9). We calculate the level of life insurance the Cohens need by subtracting their current assets and insurance from the present value of the family's needs.

$$\begin{array}{ccc} \text{life insurance} \\ \text{needed} \end{array} = \begin{array}{c} \text{total funds needed} \\ \text{in today's dollars} \end{array} - \begin{array}{c} \text{available assets} \\ \text{and insurance} \end{array}$$

$$\$250,493 = \$590,493 \qquad - \$340,000$$

Once you know how much life insurance you need, it's time to figure out what kind of insurance is available.

> ### Stop and Think
> Many employers automatically provide life insurance to their employees. For many, this is the last thought they give to life insurance—after all, they have some. However, for those with dependents, the insurance provided may be far less than they need. Think about what protection you want from life insurance and then determine what your insurance needs actually are.

MAJOR TYPES OF LIFE INSURANCE AVAILABLE

There are two major types of life insurance available: term insurance and cash-value insurance. **Term insurance** is pure life insurance. You pay a set premium that's based upon the probability that you'll die—taking into account such factors as age, health, occupation, and whether or not you smoke. For that premium, you receive a set amount of coverage for a set number of years. In effect, term insurance isn't perpetual insurance. Instead, it covers only a very specific period, or "term." If you die, your beneficiary receives your death benefits. **Cash-value insurance**, however, is more than simple life insurance. It has two components: life insurance and a savings plan. Some of your premiums go toward life insurance and some go toward savings. With cash-value insurance, if you die, your beneficiary is paid those savings as part of your death benefit. There's an almost infinite number of variations of cash-value insurance, and there are several different categories of term insurance. Table 9.3 summarizes them all, and we'll now examine them in detail.

TABLE 9.3

What's What in Life Insurance

Type of Policy	Coverage Period	Annual Premium	Death Benefit	Cash Value
Term Life Insurance	Provides protection for a specified time period, typically 1 to 20 years.	Least expensive form of life insurance. Low initial premium, with the premium increasing as the insured gets older.	Fixed death benefit.	No cash value.
Whole Life Insurance	Provides permanent protection.	The premium is fixed.	Fixed death benefit.	The cash value is fixed. The investment portion of the policy grows on a tax-deferred basis while the policy is in force.
Universal Life Insurance	Provides permanent protection.	Allows for flexible premium payments so that policyholders can vary the amount and timing of their payments as their financial needs change.	Death benefits are flexible, although proof of insurability may be required if you want to raise them.	The cash value of the policy is dependent upon the level of payments made and the investment results of the insurance company. The investment portion of the policy grows on a tax-deferred basis while the policy is in force.
Variable Life Insurance	Provides permanent protection.	Allows for either fixed or flexible premium.	Death benefits are flexible, reflecting the performance of the mutual funds in the death benefits account.	The cash value of the policy is dependent upon the performance of the mutual funds in the cash value account. The policyholder controls the investment risk, choosing the investment strategy for the policy.

Term Insurance
A type of insurance that pays your beneficiary a specific amount of money if you die while covered by the policy.

Cash-Value Insurance
A type of insurance that has two components: life insurance and a savings plan.

Renewable Term Insurance
A type of term insurance that can be renewed for an agreed-upon period or up to a specified age (usually 65 or 70) regardless of the insured's health.

"Reentry" Term Insurance
Renewable term insurance that steeply increases your premium at each renewal unless you pass a medical exam.

Term Insurance and Its Features

As we mentioned earlier, term life insurance is pure life insurance that pays the beneficiary the death benefit of the policy if the insured dies during the coverage period. In effect, term insurance has no face value and only provides insurance protection. Its sole purpose is to provide death benefits to the policyholder's beneficiaries.

Renewable Term Insurance. The "term" of the term life insurance contract can be 1, 5, 10, or 20 years, and the coverage terminates at the end of this period unless it's renewed. In general, most term insurance is **renewable term insurance**, which allows it to be continually renewed for an agreed-upon period or up to a specified age, often 65 or 70 years of age, regardless of the insured's health. Thus, even if your health declines after you begin coverage, you're still able to renew your insurance coverage with renewable term insurance. The ability to renew term insurance is critical to your family's financial security. After all, if you're basing your family's security on a life insurance policy that you suddenly can't renew, you've got a big problem. You shouldn't consider taking on term insurance that isn't renewable. Each time your contract is renewed, the premium is increased to reflect your increased age and the accompanying increase in the chance of mortality. Once an individual reaches the age of 55, the premiums increase rather rapidly, as can be seen in Figure 9.3.

"Reentry" Term Insurance. Instead of renewable insurance, you might consider **"reentry" term insurance**, which is term insurance that's guaranteed renewable at one of two possible premium levels in the future. This insurance regularly evaluates your health—perhaps every 3 to 5 years—to determine which premium level you qualify for. If you pass a medical exam, you qualify for the lower rate. However, if you fail the exam, you're stuck with the higher—usually *much* higher—rate. The appeal of reentry insurance is that if you stay in good shape, you'll be rewarded with lower premiums. The downside of such policies is that it's often unclear exactly what requirements you must meet to pass the medical exam. Moreover, if you do

FIGURE 9.3

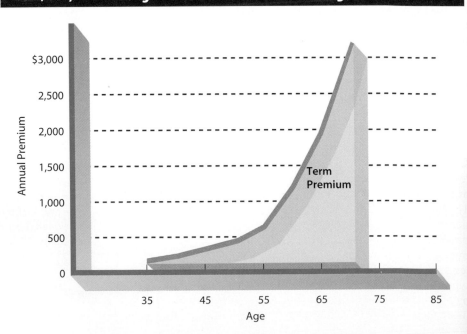

The Rising Cost of Yearly Renewable Term Insurance: Annual Premiums for $100,000 Coverage on a 35-Year-Old Nonsmoking Male

have medical problems, as your health breaks down, your premium will build up dramatically. In effect, reentry insurance is a gamble. Thus, when evaluating such insurance, you'll want to focus on the premium level under the assumption that you fail the physical exam.

Decreasing Term Insurance.
Each time renewable term insurance is renewed, the premium increases. With **decreasing term insurance**, the premiums remain constant, but the face amount of the policy declines. Thus, if you purchase decreasing term insurance, you decide on a premium level for your insurance, and the face amount—the amount of the death benefit to be paid—declines each year to reflect the increased probability that you'll die.

The logic behind decreasing term insurance is that your wealth should increase when your children leave home and become self-sufficient. As a result, you need less insurance. Term insurance provides the greatest insurance protection while your children are young and you need it the most. However, you must make certain that your insurance coverage is sufficient at all times. Just because most individuals' insurance needs tend to decline as they get older doesn't mean that'll happen in your case. Moreover, your need for insurance may be greatest as your children approach college age, just when the face value of the declining term insurance drops off. In addition, when considering declining term insurance, you must be aware that not all declining term insurance policies decline the same way. Some decline at a constant, steady rate, and others decline at accelerating rates. What's important here is that you choose a policy that's going to cover your future needs completely.

Decreasing Term Insurance
Term insurance in which the annual premium remains constant but the face amount of the policy declines each year.

Group Term Insurance.
Group term insurance refers to the way the insurance is sold rather than to any unusual traits of the policy itself. Group term insurance is term insurance provided, usually without a medical exam, to a specific group of individuals who are associated for some purpose other than to buy insurance. For example, the group may all be employees of the same company or members of a common association or professional group. If it's an association or professional group, the members might be required to take a medical exam; however, most employee term insurance doesn't require a medical exam. In addition, in some, but certainly not all, cases, an employer may pay all or a portion of the insurance premiums or perform much of the administrative work associated with the plan, thus lowering the cost of the insurance to the individuals. The rate that an individual pays is therefore based upon both the characteristics of the individuals that make up the group and the extent to which the employer or association contributes to the premiums. The advantage of group term insurance is that it's often less expensive than term insurance through an individual policy, but this isn't always the case, especially for individuals who are young and healthy. As such, the advantages of group term insurance many times flow to older or less healthy people. With group term insurance, because medical exams generally aren't required, uninsurable individuals are able to get relatively low-cost term insurance.

Group Term Insurance
Term insurance provided, usually without a medical exam, to a specific group of individuals, such as company employees, who are associated for some purpose other than to buy insurance.

Credit or Mortgage Group Life Insurance.
One variation of group life insurance that's promoted by lending agencies is **credit** or **mortgage group life insurance**, which is simply group life insurance that's provided by a lender for its debtors. The level of coverage is enough to cover the individual's outstanding debt. So, if the debtor dies while the policy is in effect, the life insurance proceeds would be used to pay off the debt. This type of term insurance is generally set up as a form of declining insurance in which the premiums are constant and the face amount of the policy declines, reflecting the declining balance in the debt due. Keep in mind that this type of insurance covers the lender as much as it covers you. After all, it's being sold by the financial institution to whom you owe money, and it, not your family, will be designated as the benefactor of your policy. It also may have a noncompetitive rate

Credit or **Mortgage Group Life Insurance**
Group life insurance that's provided by a lender for its debtors.

associated with it. On one hand, this insurance guarantees that your family won't be saddled with this particular debt if you die. On the other hand, such a policy also ensures the financial institution that it'll get its money back—not to mention the insurance premiums you'll pay!

Stop and Think

If, for example, you have a very low interest rate on your home mortgage, you may rather have your insurance proceeds go toward paying off some other more expensive debt. However, with mortgage group life insurance, you have no choice—it goes to pay off your mortgage.

Convertible Term Life Insurance.   **Convertible term life insurance** refers to term life insurance that you can convert into cash-value life insurance at your discretion regardless of your medical condition and without a medical exam. Many times this conversion feature is only offered during the first years of the policy. This conversion's accompanied by a corresponding increase in the size of the premium. One promoted advantage of convertible term insurance is that it allows an individual a smooth transition from term to cash-value insurance. The question, of course, is whether or not cash-value insurance is the best investment alternative. However, there are some real benefits to convertible term insurance. For instance, it can allow you to continue insurance coverage when your term insurance expires. For example, when you lose your job, you also tend to lose your group life insurance. To address this problem, most group term insurance plans are also convertible term plans. That is, they contain a conversion privilege that allows anyone leaving the group to convert the term insurance coverage to a cash-value life insurance policy over a short conversion period, many times 30 days.

The Facts of Life

The earliest life insurance dates back to the Babylonian Code of Hammurabi in 1800 B.C., which allows for the payment of "one mina of silver" to the deceased's family in the event of death. In the United States the first life insurance company was formed in 1759.

Cash-Value Insurance and Its Features

Cash-value insurance is any insurance policy that provides both a death benefit and an opportunity to accumulate cash value. It's a permanent type of insurance—if you make the premium payments, eventually you'll get paid. At some point, you'll have made all the required premium payments (which in the extreme case could last until you're 100), and your cash-value insurance will be completely paid up.

It'd be wrong to think that all cash-value insurance is the same. In fact, there are tons of different types of cash-value insurance. However, there are three *basic* types of cash-value insurance: whole life, universal life, and variable life insurance.

Whole Life Insurance and Its Features.   **Whole life insurance** provides a death benefit when the insured dies, turns 100, or reaches the maximum stated age. Thus, with whole life insurance, the face value of the policy will eventually be paid, provided the premiums have been paid. Another distinguishing feature of whole life insurance is that the premiums are known in advance and in many cases are fixed. Although

Convertible Term Life Insurance

Term life insurance that can be converted into cash-value life insurance at the insured's discretion regardless of his or her medical condition and without a medical exam.

Whole Life Insurance

Cash-value insurance that provides permanent coverage and a death benefit when the insured dies. If the insured turns 100, the policy pays off, even though the insured hasn't died.

premiums on term insurance tend to be small during your younger years and dizzyingly high during your latter years, whole life insurance premiums, because they are constant over your life, fall somewhere in between. Overall, the payments are higher than they are for term insurance, because the insurance company is guaranteed to eventually make a payout on the policy, which isn't the case with term insurance, because you may not die while the term policy is in place.

In the early years of the whole life policy, the insurance company deducts amounts for the commission, sales and administrative expenses, cost of death protection, and some profit from the premiums. What's left of the premiums goes into a savings account and is called the **cash value**. In effect, the premium charged is much larger than what's necessary to cover the death claims for a younger individual. This build-up continues over the initial years of the policy, eventually resulting in a large cash value. As time goes by and the policyholder ages, the premium, which remains constant, is no longer large enough to cover the death claim for an older individual. Thus, in the latter years the cash value is used to supplement the level premiums and provide the desired level of death coverage. In effect, there's a cash build-up in the younger years, resulting from the premium being greater than the death benefit cost or average policy payment for an individual of that age.

The cash value of the insurance policy is really the policyholder's savings. The policyholder can borrow against the policy's cash value, or, alternatively, the policyholder can gain access to the policy's cash value by terminating the policy. Access to the cash value is gained by exercising the policyholder's nonforfeiture right. The **nonforfeiture right** gives the policyholder the policy's cash value in exchange for the policyholder giving up his or her right to a death benefit. If the policyholder doesn't want cash, but instead wants insurance, the cash value can be used to purchase paid-up insurance—that is, insurance that doesn't have any additional payments due—or to buy extended term insurance. Many people see the nonforfeiture right as a major advantage to whole life—at least you get something back when you terminate the policy.

There are a number of different premium payment patterns available to whole life policyholders. *Continuous-, level-,* or *straight-premium whole life* requires the policyholder to pay a constant premium until the insured turns 100 or dies. With a *single-premium* or *-payment whole life* policy, the policyholder makes only one initial payment. Obviously, the payment is very large. The popularity of single-premium whole life was relatively shortlived, as it stemmed from a tax loophole in the Tax Reform Act of 1986 and was closed by a 1988 amendment. A hybrid of these two payment patterns is the *limited-premium whole life* policy, in which large premiums are required for a specified number of years, after which the policy is considered paid up. For example, you may pay until you are 65, after which the policy is paid up. As with all whole life insurance, it then provides insurance protection for the insured's entire life or until the policy is terminated and the policy's cash value is claimed. The size of the premiums depends, of course, on the number of premiums to be paid and the age of the insured. The popularity of the limited-payment plan stems from the fact that the payments will cease when retirement approaches, and at that point the policy has built up a significant cash value.

As with all else in the life insurance area, there are almost an unlimited number of variations on the whole life theme. One such variation worth noting is *modified whole life* insurance. With modified whole life, the premiums begin at a level below comparable whole life and gradually rise in steps until the final premiums are above those of comparable whole life. There are also *combination whole life* policies, which include elements of whole life and decreasing term insurance. The decreasing term coverage is offset by increasing whole life coverage, which is funded by the increasing cash value of the whole life policy. The change in coverage is done in such a way that the face amount of the policy remains constant, with the coverage gradually shifting from term to whole life.

Cash Value
The money that the policyholder is entitled to if the policy is terminated.

Nonforfeiture Right
The right of a policyholder to choose to receive the policy's cash value in exchange for the policyholder giving up his or her right to a death benefit.

What are the primary disadvantages of whole life insurance? First, it doesn't provide nearly the level of death protection that'd be secured with term insurance for the same price. Second, the yield earned on the cash value investment portion of the policy generally isn't competitive with the yields on alternative investments. However, whole life insurance does provide for both savings and permanent insurance needs. If you have a need for permanent insurance protection—perhaps you have a child or spouse who'll never be financially independent for whom you must provide—then you should seriously consider whole life insurance.

Universal Life Insurance and Its Features.

A **universal life** insurance policy is a type of cash-value insurance combining term insurance with a tax-deferred savings feature offered in a package in which both the premiums and benefits are flexible. These premiums can vary between the insurance company's minimum and the IRS's maximum.

You start out by paying an initial premium as dictated by the insurance company. After the company subtracts out company expenses and mortality charges to pay for the life insurance protection, the remainder of the premium plus interest is added to the cash value. The premium payments may then be increased or decreased by the policyholder, which will in effect speed up or decrease the cash value of the policy. You can also increase or decrease the death benefit, which may require a medical examination and would mean more of your premium would be considered a mortality charge—that is, more of your premium would go toward the cost of your insurance as opposed to building up the cash value. In effect, a universal life policy is much like a term insurance policy, with any additional premium going toward savings.

An important feature of universal life insurance is that the funds are unbundled, or broken down, into three separate parts: the mortality charge or term insurance, the cash value or savings, and the administrative expenses. This unbundling is what gives the policyholder the flexibility to vary the premium payments, because if you skip a payment or don't make one large enough to cover your mortality charge and the administrative expenses, the amount needed to cover this will simply be subtracted from the cash value. If the cash value on hand isn't enough to cover the premium, the policy will lapse! Although there are limits, if you make a huge payment, then the amount greater than that needed to cover the mortality charge and the administrative expenses is credited to your cash value or savings. The relationship that determines the cash value is shown in Figure 9.4.

One of the shortcomings of universal life is that the returns can, and do, fluctuate dramatically. Moreover, for many policyholders the flexibility to pass on premium payments is just too tempting, and as a result many policies simply lapse. Finally, given fluctuating returns and high expense charges, you may not end up with as much in the way of savings as you had anticipated.

The value of universal life comes from its flexibility. If you have uneven and fluctuating income and need the flexibility of being able to skip premium payments, this form of insurance might appeal to you. Still, universal life should be approached with caution. Insurance policies should be purchased mainly for their insurance protection. With universal life, the insurance and administrative portions of the policy are very expensive. In short, for most people universal life is not particularly attractive.

Variable Life Insurance and Its Features.

Variable life insurance is aimed at individuals who want to manage their own investments and are willing to take risks. It's a type of whole life insurance in which the cash value and death benefit are tied to and vary according to the performance of a set of investments that are chosen by the policyholder. Thus, the policyholder, rather than the insurance company, takes on the investment risk—that is, you decide how the cash value or savings portion of your policy is invested. If it does well, you benefit; if it bombs, you lose. There are two basic forms of variable life: (1) straight variable life, which has fixed premiums, and (2) variable universal life, on which the premiums are flexible. The array of

---

Universal Life

A type of cash value insurance that's much more flexible than whole life. It allows you to vary the premium payments and the level of protection.

Variable Life

Insurance that provides permanent insurance coverage as whole life does; however, the policyholder, rather than the insurance company, takes on the investment risk.

FIGURE 9.4

Determining the Cash Value on a Universal Life Insurance Policy

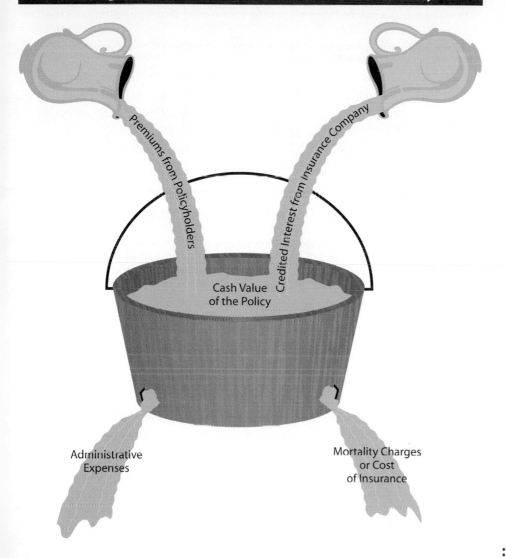

investment funds from which the policyholder chooses is quite large, including money market, bond, and stock funds. The returns are earned on a tax-deferred basis just as they are on other cash-value insurance forms. In fact, you can switch between different types of investment funds without suffering any tax consequences. The cash value of a variable life insurance policy results from fixed premiums minus company expenses and the mortality charges (the cost of the term insurance). This cash value is then invested according to the policyholder's wishes. Thus, the cash value of the policy is a function of the performance of the investment funds chosen by the policyholder. As a result, there is no guarantee of a minimum cash value. The cash buildup is a direct function of how well your investment funds perform—they can sink or soar! Thus, the policyholder, rather than the insurance company, takes on the investment risk—that is, what happens to the cash value doesn't affect the insurance company. In effect, variable life is similar to buying term insurance and investing money in mutual funds. Unfortunately, it's hard to produce outstanding results with variable life because of the high investment and administrative expenses that are levied against the accounts.

To be attracted to variable life insurance, you have to be a risk taker who wants to manage your own investments. However, if you're a risk taker who wants to manage your own investments, you'd be better off putting your money directly into the stock market.

> ## Stop and Think
> Seeing a computer printout that shows with precision exactly what your cash-value life insurance policy will be worth in the future is impressive, but it may be meaningless. As with any other financial analysis, the results are all based upon the assumptions—if it's "garbage in," it's also "garbage out." Make sure that any assumptions being made are conservative and realistic.

LEARNING OBJECTIVE #3

Compare and contrast the various types of life insurance available.

TERM VERSUS CASH-VALUE LIFE INSURANCE: WHICH IS RIGHT FOR YOU?

With all these different types of insurance, it can be pretty hard comparing policies and figuring out what you need. You could spend way too much of your waking hours—and even some of your sleeping hours if you're a vivid dreamer—trying to figure out what's best for you. We suggest starting off slowly. The most basic question you need to ask yourself when choosing a type of life insurance is whether you want term insurance or cash-value insurance.

It's easy to see why term insurance is popular: It provides basic, affordable insurance. So why would you want to attach a savings plan to your insurance—that is, why would you be interested in cash-value insurance? Let's take a look at some of the more common answers to that question, but let's see how valid those answers really are.

- **Term insurance may become prohibitively expensive for you in your latter years.** With term insurance, your premiums are based upon your probability of dying. As you renew your term insurance, the premiums increase to reflect your shorter life expectancy. As a result, the cost of term insurance gets steeper and steeper as you grow older. With cash-value insurance, the premiums generally stay constant. Is this a good reason to purchase cash-value insurance? No. First, as you approach retirement, life insurance becomes much less important. Hopefully, with the help of earlier personal financial planning, you've accumulated enough wealth to provide for your family's needs during retirement. Moreover, when you retire, that stream of income that you're protecting with life insurance is gone. Thus, although term life becomes sickeningly expensive in your latter years, it may also become irrelevant. Finally, you should note that if you wisely invest the savings from purchasing term as opposed to cash-value insurance, this savings could very well pay for any increases in term coverage.

- **Cash-value life insurance provides you with a simple means of forced savings.** The concept of forced savings isn't all too popular in personal financial planning. Financial control and flexibility is the name of the game. In effect the question becomes, Do you want to use your insurance policy as a piggy bank, or do you want to control where, when, and how much of your money goes to other investments?

- **With cash-value insurance you won't have life insurance premiums to pay for the rest of your life.** Cash-value insurance let's you build up savings that then are used to pay your premiums. In effect, by overpaying in the early years you're able to avoid payments in latter years. Is this a good reason to buy cash-value insurance? No! If you want to use cash-value insurance to save for the future, you should do so *only* after comparing it to the alternative investments.

- **Cash-value insurance presents a win-win situation—if you die you have insurance, if you live you have savings.** The situation is more pay-pay than it is win-win. Sure, you have insurance when you die and savings while you live, but you paid for them. In most cases, you paid a bundle for them. The question is whether or not you would've been better off putting your money into other insurance and savings vehicles. Although each plan deserves to be evaluated individually, cash savings plans generally involve high premiums, with the savings being invested at relatively low rates, making them generally unattractive as a means of saving.

- **If you buy cash-value insurance, look how much you'll have after 20 years.** You'd better take a good look, because estimated or promised rates of return on cash-value insurance tend to be overstated. Don't bet your life (literally) on unrealistic expectations. The bottom line here, **beware!** Overly optimistic assumptions regarding future returns will make for disappointing results.

- **The cash-value savings grow on a tax-deferred basis.** Yes, the money you put into a cash-value policy does grow on a tax-deferred basis until it's withdrawn, which presents an advantage over most other investment alternatives. However, there may be alternative tax-deferred investment plans, such as IRAs, 401(k)s, 403(b)s, or Keogh plans, available that allow for an immediate tax deduction of your contribution in addition to allowing your investment to grow on a tax-deferred basis. You should examine these alternatives before considering a cash-value insurance policy. You should also compare and contrast the accumulated savings earned from a cash-value policy with the accumulated savings earned from purchasing a lower-cost term insurance policy and investing the cost difference in the premiums. Historically, cash-value insurance policies have produced disappointing results. One of the difficulties encountered in evaluating their investment potential is that most insurance companies quote you an interest rate only for the first year of the policy. In effect, future rates aren't guaranteed and are free to fluctuate. Moreover, if you find future rates unsatisfactory and decide to terminate the policy, you may have to pay a penalty to get your money back.

- **Cash-value life insurance allows you to pass on wealth without paying estate taxes.** This is the most legitimate reason for purchasing cash-value life insurance; however, it's important only to those with estates valued at greater than the estate-tax-free transfer threshold. Unfortunately, for most individuals it's completely irrelevant. In 1997, an individual can pass on $600,000 free of inheritance taxes. This tax-free transfer threshold is scheduled to gradually rise to $1 million by 2006. If you have a large estate to pass on, you may want to consider cash-value life insurance as one alternative in your estate planning program.

Summing Up

For most individuals, term insurance is the better alternative. It provides for your life insurance needs at a relatively low cost, and that's the real purpose of insurance. Although it doesn't provide permanent coverage, it does allow for affordable coverage during the years in which you need life insurance most. Also, because the premiums on cash-value insurance are so high, you may be tempted to carry less insurance than you actually need.

The only true advantages of cash-value insurance are tax advantages—the growth of the cash value on a deferred tax basis and the fact that life insurance isn't considered part of your estate. These advantages generally don't make cash-value insurance a good investment in a relative sense—other tax-deferred investment plans are better; however, you should understand it and consider it as a possible investment alternative. Moreover, you should understand the shortcomings of cash-value insurance so that you can make an intelligent life insurance decision.

LEARNING OBJECTIVE #4

Choose the contract clauses and policy riders that best meet your life insurance needs.

FINE-TUNING YOUR INSURANCE POLICY: CONTRACT CLAUSES AND RIDERS

Although there are hundreds of variations on all the different types of insurance policies, there's still some standardization among policies. For example, a clause is actually a provision common to most life insurance contracts. In fact, there are 10 common features contained in almost all insurance contracts: (1) a beneficiary provision, (2) a grace period, (3) a loan clause, (4) a nonforfeiture clause, (5) a policy reinstatement clause, (6) a change of policy clause, (7) a suicide clause, (8) a payment premium clause, (9) an incontestability clause, and (10) settlement options.

The Beneficiary Provision

The beneficiary provision allows for the naming of a primary and contingent beneficiaries. The primary beneficiary is the person designated to receive the death benefits if the insured dies. This beneficiary can be a person, a business, or a trust. The contingent beneficiary receives the death benefits only if the primary beneficiary dies before the benefits have been distributed. For example, many individuals designate their spouse as the primary beneficiary and their children as contingent beneficiaries. This way, if the husband and wife die simultaneously, the benefits will be passed on to the children. The only caution here is that young children cannot be paid life insurance proceeds, with the age varying state by state. As such, if you have young children, you might want to set up an alternative plan to provide income to whoever will raise the children in the event of your death. An irrevocable beneficiary is a beneficiary who can be changed by the policyholder only with the permission of that beneficiary.

The Grace Period

The **grace period** is an automatic extension for premium payments, which is generally set to 30 or 31 days after the payment is due. During this period, payments can be made without penalty, and the policy remains in force. Thus, as a result of the grace period, slightly late payments don't result in a canceled policy. If you think about it, this type of grace period is similar to the grace period involved in credit card payments: They're both periods when payment is due, but no penalties occur.

The Loan Clause

Cash-value policies include a **loan clause** which allow for loans, generally at a guaranteed rate, against the cash value of the policy. Because these loans are secured by the cash value, the rate paid on the loan is usually quite favorable, generally being either fixed at 8 percent or variable and tied to a market interest rate. In addition to the relatively low rates, other advantages to a policy loan include paying no fees or carrying charges and not having a maturity date on the loan. In fact, policy loans don't have to be repaid at all, which makes them quite appealing. However, you should be careful about them. When you take out a policy loan, the death benefits are reduced by a corresponding amount. Thus, if the purpose of the insurance policy is to provide basic death protection, then the policy loan may conflict with this goal. As a result, before

Grace Period

The late-payment period for premiums during which time the policy stays in effect and no interest is charged. If payments still aren't made, the policy can be canceled after the grace period.

Loan Clause

A clause that provides the right to borrow against the cash value of the policy at a guaranteed interest rate.

you take on a policy loan, you need to examine the trade-off between the costs of the loan and the erosion of the death protection. It would also be prudent to consult a tax advisor before taking on a policy loan to make sure that the loan meets the IRS requirements to avoid tax penalties associated with policy withdrawals, because in some situations policy loans may be considered taxable withdrawals.

The Nonforfeiture Clause

As we discussed earlier, exercising the nonforfeiture clause or right gives the policyholder the policy's cash value in exchange for the policyholder giving up his or her right to a death benefit. The nonforfeiture clause defines the choices available to cash-value policyholders who terminate their policies prior to maturity. These options generally include

- receiving the policy's cash value,
- exchanging your policy's cash value for a paid-up policy with a reduced face value, and
- exchanging your policy's face value for a paid-up term policy.

The Policy Reinstatement Clause

The **reinstatement clause** deals with the conditions necessary to restore a lapsed policy to its full force and effect. Generally, the reinstatement clause allows you to restore your policy within 3 to 5 years after the policy has expired. Most insurance companies require that the insured pass a physical examination and pay all past-due premiums, any outstanding policy loans, and all accumulated interest before reinstatement is allowed.

The Change of Policy Clause

The **change of policy clause** allows the policyholder to change the form of the policy. For example, you may have a continuous-premium whole life policy and wish to change it to a limited-premium whole life so that the premiums cease. The change of policy clause will let you make this change, although you may have to pass a physical examination first.

The Suicide Clause

Virtually all insurance contracts include a suicide clause, which states that the insurance policy won't pay off for suicide deaths that occur within 2 years of the purchase of the contract. The 2-year limit is generally imposed on insurance companies by state law. The purpose of the suicide clause is both to protect the insurance company from suicide-motivated claims and to keep financial concerns from motivating suicide.

The Payment Premium Clause

The payment premium clause simply defines the alternatives available to the policyholder with respect to payment of premiums. These options typically include annual, semiannual, quarterly, or monthly premium payments. Because annual payments get all of your premium money to the insurance company faster and reduce administrative costs, they're generally the cheapest.

The Incontestability Clause

The incontestability clause states that the insurance company can't dispute the validity of the contract after it's been in place for a specified number of years, usually 2. In effect, it's like a short statute of limitations. This clause is crucial, and it protects the beneficiary against policy cancellations due to innocent misstatements made by the

Reinstatement Clause
A clause that provides the right to restore a policy that has lapsed after the grace period has expired. Generally, reinstatement is provided for within a specified period (usually 3 to 5 years after the policy has expired).

Change of Policy Clause
A clause that provides the right of the policyholder to change the form of the policy—for example, from a continuous-premium whole life policy to a limited-premium whole life policy.

insured on the original insurance application. Actually, this clause generally protects the beneficiary even if the insured made fraudulent statements when obtaining the insurance, as long as the fraud was not outrageous—for example, when a policy is taken out with the intent to murder the insured.

Settlement Options

Settlement Options

The alternative ways that a beneficiary can choose to receive the policy benefits upon the death of the insured.

Settlement options refer to the alternative ways that a beneficiary can choose to receive the policy benefits upon the death of the insured. The most common alternatives include (1) lump-sum settlement, (2) interest-only settlement, (3) installment-payments settlement, and (4) life-annuity settlement. However, before talking about these settlement options, let's discuss settlement and taxes.

Life Insurance Settlement and Taxes.

In general, life insurance death benefits are income tax-free. Thus, if there's a single lump-sum settlement, there are generally no taxes due on the full face value of the contract.

Still, there are situations in which taxes may be levied on a life insurance settlement, and these differences can vary dramatically depending upon whether the distribution is at death or during the insured's lifetime. For example, if a policy is surrendered for cash value, the excess of the cash value over the total premiums paid will be subject to taxes. However, all death benefit distributions are exempt from federal income tax and, in most cases, from state inheritance taxes. It's important to keep in mind that although you'll frequently hear that life insurance proceeds are tax-free, that isn't always the case. As such, you should make sure you know the tax status of your insurance.

Lump-Sum Settlement.

Although a lump-sum settlement may not, on the surface, seem to be an overly flexible option, it's actually extremely flexible. By receiving the settlement in a single lump-sum, the beneficiary then has the freedom to invest those funds in any investment alternative and to withdraw funds from that investment in any pattern desired. In effect, a single lump-sum settlement allows beneficiaries the ability to tailor the investment strategy and withdrawal pattern to suit their needs directly.

The only drawback to a single lump-sum settlement is that many people simply don't have the self-control to manage the settlement funds over a long time horizon. Forget about a long time horizon—many can't resist spending a huge hunk of such a big windfall as an insurance settlement. All of a sudden, the funds that were supposed to help put the kids through college are putting them through a trip to Disneyland. As a result, a single lump-sum settlement may be appropriate, but you may want to work out a long-run financial plan with a professional financial planner to manage the settlement.

Interest-Only Settlement.

Under the interest-only settlement, rather than receive the policy's death benefits immediately, you leave them on deposit with the insurance company for a specified length of time and receive interest on that deposit. Generally, the rate earned on this deposit is tied to the market interest rate, with a guaranteed minimum rate also provided. There are, of course, many variations associated with this settlement method, including the option of partial or complete withdrawal of the cash value if desired.

Installment-Payments Settlement.

Under the installment-payments settlement, the cash value, including both interest and principal, is completely distributed over either a fixed period or in fixed payments. If you choose the fixed-period option, then the size of the policy settlement, the number of periods for which payments are to be made, and the interest rate credited to the policy settlement work together to determine the size of the payments. Thinking back to the discussion of the time value of money, working out the payment size is simply a matter of solving for the payment size (PMT) in the present value of an annuity formula $PV = PMT(PVIFA_{i\%,\ n\ periods})$, where PV is the policy settlement, i is the interest rate credited to the policy settlement, and n is the number of periods over which the payments are to be made.

Instead of choosing a fixed period for the distribution of the settlement, you can actually choose the specific amount of the fixed payments. In this case, the size of the policy settlement, the interest rate credited to the policy settlement, and the desired size of the payments work together to determine the number of periods over which payments will be received. Again, thinking back to the discussion of the time value of money, we're now solving for n, the number of periods over which the payments are to be made, in the present value of an annuity formula $PV = PMT(PVIFA_{i\%,\ n\ periods})$, where PV is the policy settlement, PMT is the desired payment, and i is the interest rate credited to the policy settlement. Generally, if the beneficiary has a change in financial needs, it's possible to modify the size of the payments. However, modifications aren't as easily made if payments are being received for a stated period.

Life Annuity Settlement. Under a life annuity, the beneficiary receives income for life. There are several variations of the life annuity available that provide monthly income to the beneficiary for his or her entire life. Under a straight life annuity, beneficiaries receive monthly payments regardless of how long they live. If the beneficiary dies 1 month after the benefits begin, the insurance company's obligations are ended, and the insurance company keeps any remaining cash value. Thus, the size of the annuity payments depends entirely on the beneficiary's life expectancy, in addition to the size of the policy's death benefits and the interest rate credited to the policy settlement. As a result, a young beneficiary will receive much smaller monthly payments than would an older beneficiary. Why might people want a life annuity settlement? Because they're worried that they might outlive their available income. With a life annuity settlement, the payments just keep on coming.

An alternative to the straight life annuity is the life income with period certain annuity. Under this type of annuity, payments are guaranteed for the life of the beneficiary; however, if the beneficiary dies within a stated period (usually 5, 10, or 20 years), payments are then made to a secondary beneficiary until the stated period ends. This payment method, of course, guarantees that the insurance company will be making payments over at least the entire stated period. To the beneficiary, guaranteed payment is great, but it does come with costs—the payment size is smaller than payments received under the straight life annuity, because these payments continue even if the primary beneficiary dies.

A third annuity choice that's available is the refund annuity. This type of annuity provides the beneficiary with income for life in addition to returning any remaining death benefit to a secondary beneficiary if the primary beneficiary dies. This payment method allows beneficiaries to leave some of the death benefits to their heirs. Again, the insurance company will have to pay out more than it would with a straight annuity, because once the primary beneficiary dies, there still may be an additional payment. As a result, the monthly annuity payments from a refund annuity are less than they would be under a straight annuity.

The final annuity form is the joint life and survivorship annuity. Under this type of annuity, monthly payments continue as long as one of the two named beneficiaries remains alive. Generally, the two beneficiaries are husband and wife, with the annuity providing them with income as long as one survives. In effect, the surviving spouse is guaranteed income for life. Again, because the insurance company will have to pay out more than it would with a straight life annuity, the monthly annuity payments from a joint life and survivorship annuity are less than they would be under a straight life annuity.

Riders

Rider

A special provision that may be added to your policy, which either provides extra benefits to the beneficiary or limits the company's liability under certain conditions.

A **rider** is a special provision that may be added to your policy, which either provides extra benefits or limits the company's liability under certain conditions. Common riders include (1) waiver of premium for disability, (2) multiple indemnity or accidental death benefit, (3) guaranteed insurability, (4) cost-of-living adjustment (COLA), and (5) living benefits.

Waiver of Premium for Disability Rider.   A waiver of premium for disability rider allows your insurance protection to stay in place by paying your premiums if you become disabled before you reach a certain age, usually 65. Because your need for insurance certainly doesn't diminish if you become disabled, this is a pretty good rider to have—provided the cost isn't too high. Shop around, and if it's still higher than you'd like, see if you can cover your insurance expenses with a personal disability insurance plan.

Accidental Death Benefit Rider or Multiple Indemnity.   An accidental death benefit rider or multiple indemnity rider increases the death benefit—doubling it in the case of "double indemnity" and tripling it in the case of "triple indemnity"— if the insured dies in an accident rather than from natural causes. This is usually a relatively inexpensive rider because of the slim chance that the company will have to pay on it— most people die from natural causes.

Guaranteed Insurability Rider.   The guaranteed insurability rider gives you the right to increase your life insurance protection in the future without a medical examination. You can purchase additional coverage at specified times or after the birth of children. As with other riders, this rider comes with an additional fee.

One way to view the guaranteed insurability rider is to view it as insurance against uninsurability. If you anticipate increased insurance needs in the future, this rider is a relatively inexpensive way to insure the ability to get that insurance coverage.

Cost-of-Living Adjustment (COLA) Rider.   The cost-of-living rider increases your death benefits at the same rate as inflation without forcing you to pass a medical exam. You pay an annual fee for this protection, but it can be useful if your needs for life insurance change in the same proportion as the change in the cost of living.

Living Benefits Rider.   Some cash-value policies allow for "living benefits"; that is, they allow for the early payout of a percentage of the anticipated death benefits for the terminally ill. The purpose of this rider is to provide additional income to the terminally ill to allow them to pay their medical bills. A living benefits rider provides you with a portion of the face value of the life insurance policy if you contract a terminal disease such as Alzheimer's, cancer, AIDS, or kidney failure.

BUYING LIFE INSURANCE—CAVEAT EMPTOR

People don't buy insurance, it's sold to them. That is, most individuals don't have an insurance plan in mind when they talk to an insurance salesperson. The marketing of life insurance is about as confusing as it can be. In fact, you're not likely to receive the same recommendation on your life insurance needs from any two salespeople. Moreover, it's extremely difficult to compare policies because of their jargon and uniqueness—almost all policies are one-of-a-kind. As a result, most people rely on the insurance salesperson to tell them what to purchase.

Buyer Beware

Before you deal with an insurance agent, you should know a bit about the insurance industry and how it works. A little knowledge will give you a serious advantage over the clueless many who'll buy whatever an insurance agent throws their way. Also, you'll be able to show the salesperson that you mean business. First, you must keep in mind that most insurance is sold on a commission basis. In general, insurance agents make their living through commissions, so they're understandably eager to make a sale. Don't be shy about shopping around. Don't feel obligated to purchase your policy from an agent just because he or she did some research and put together a plan for you—that's the agent's job. If you don't do your homework, you could end up with the policy that pays the highest commission to the agent and provides you with the least protection. In addition, because most insurance companies try to produce a unique product, it's virtually impossible to compare one policy to another. Moreover, the legislation governing the insurance industry allows insurance companies to require their commission-based agents to sell specific policies at set prices. The result? Comparison shopping is almost impossible.

Given the fact that shopping for insurance is so difficult, how do you do it? The same way you should do everything else in personal finance—systematically. You've got to do your homework first. Earlier in this chapter you saw how to determine your life insurance needs. Use that information, and figure out your needs before you wind up letting insurance salespeople tell you what they think those needs are. Hopefully, you now know what basic life insurance products are available. Think about your needs in terms of those products, get a good picture of what kind of policy you need and want, and go get it.

If you don't do your homework, you're asking for trouble. Although the overwhelming majority of insurance salespeople are dedicated, responsible, and competent, there are still some out there who aren't. Keep in mind that the insurance salesperson has a lot to gain by selling you life insurance. This all relates back to **Axiom 12: The Agency Problem in Personal Finance—Differentiating Between Advice and a Sales Pitch**. In effect, an unscrupulous insurance salesperson, motivated by the commission, may try to sell you insurance that you don't need. As with everything else in personal finance, the best protection against this is understanding, bringing us back to **Axiom 9: The Best Protection Is Knowledge**.

Selecting a Quality Level for Your Insurance Company

You know what you want and need, now where do you find it? It's better to select several insurance companies that are of the highest quality level before you select an agent, because some agents carry insurance only from a limited number of companies. In effect some agents are "captive" and work for one specific company, while others are independent and deal with several different companies. Just as it's difficult to purchase a Ford from a GM dealership, it's difficult to purchase New York Life insurance from a Northwestern Mutual agent.

LEARNING OBJECTIVE #5

Purchase the life insurance policy that's best for you.

AXIOM #12

The Agency Problem in Personal Finance—Differentiating Between Advice and a Sales Pitch

AXIOM #9

The Best Protection Is Knowledge

In shopping for insurance, you must keep in mind that although your insurance premium is primarily based upon the chance that you'll die, that's not all it's based on. Your premium also reflects the expenses and profitability of the insurance company. The higher the insurance company's expenses, the higher your premiums. Comparison shop when selecting a company, and try to find one with lower expenses and premiums.

Without question, not all insurance companies are the same—some go under. When you put money in a bank, the government guarantees your account through the FDIC. There are no guarantees with life insurance. Although each state has a guarantee association that's set up to protect policyholders if an insurance company goes out of business, it is far from a government guarantee. Generally these state funds have no assets. As such, if an insurance company goes under, the other insurance companies doing business in that state are "taxed" and the funds are used to take care of any claims.[1] As you can imagine, delays and confusion are common. Don't get stuck dealing with those hassles; select a sound insurance company. If you're considering a cash-value policy, the selection process is even more critical. Keep in mind that cash-value policies generally specify only a minimum return; thus, the efficiency of the insurance company determines your actual return. Therefore, it's essential that you carefully choose an efficiently run life insurance company that'll be around when your policy "matures."

Fortunately, the selection process is made much easier by the existence of a number of insurance company rating services. A.M. Best (800-424-2378) evaluates an insurance company's financial strength, with A++ being the highest rating. In addition, Standard & Poor's (212-208-1527), Moody's (212-553-0377), and Duff & Phelps (312-368-3157) all rate the ability of insurance companies to pay off claims against them. Because you'll be charged a small fee for rating information if you call one of the rating agencies, the simplest way to get ratings and select a strong insurance company is to go to your local library. Most public libraries carry one or more of these companies' publications. Table 9.4 provides a listing of the highest and lowest ratings from each service. As you can see, a straight A grade is not necessarily the highest grade that a life insurance company can receive, and a C can be failing.

Selecting the Agent

Because it's difficult to know all you might like to know about insurance, selecting your agent is extremely important. Your agent should be willing to develop and fine-tune your insurance program rather than develop and fine-tune his or her commission. So

---

[1]In addition, most states impose a limit on the amount of coverage they'll honor. These limits are generally $100,000 for cash value for an individual life policy, and $300,000 in death benefits, or $300,000 for all claims combined for an individual or family. These limits may be well below what your desired coverage level is.

TABLE 9.4

Insurance Company Ratings

Rating Service	Top Four Ratings	Lowest Rating
A. M. Best	A++, A+, A, A−	F
Duff & Phelps	AAA, AA+, AA, AA−	CCC
Moody's Investors Service	Aaa, Aa1, Aa2, Aa3	Ca
Standard & Poor's	AAA, AA+, AA, AA−	CCC

OUR RIDERS Will Take You for a Ride

(A) When you've closed the sale on a $20,000 car and the salesman throws in extra rustproofing protection for a couple of hundred bucks, you don't think twice about it. Yet if you shop around for that separately, it would probably cost much less.

That's how Charles Ritzke, a consulting actuary in West Dundee, Ill., views the "riders" that are often tacked on to life insurance policies. Take the "waiver of premium" rider. For a little extra, your insurer will continue your coverage if you are disabled and unable to pay the annual premium. (B) But you are almost always better off getting disability insurance separately. Here's why: A typical rider for a 42-year-old man would cost 84 cents per $10 of coverage. An actual disability policy would be $1,593 for $48,000 of coverage, which translates into only 33 cents per $10. That's a 155 percent difference. Not just that, but the policy rider is far more restrictive, with a longer waiting period or more stringent definition of "disabled." (For instance, if you're a surgeon and lose a finger, the rider may not qualify you as disabled, since you could still do other jobs.) You are "paying for a Cadillac and getting a Chevy," says one Midwestern insurance executive.

(C) One of the few riders that might be worthwhile, for some at least, is the guaranteed-insurability rider. If you are young and healthy and want the option to continue buying more insurance in the future without another physical exam and lengthy questionnaire, this is for you. Unfortunately, less than half these options get exercised, according to the Midwestern insurance executive.

Source: Namita Devidayal, "Ten Things Your Life Insurer Won't Tell You," *Smart Money,* August 1996, pp. 115–121. Used by permission.

Analysis and Implications ...

A. The cost of different riders varies dramatically from policy to policy. Thus, if there is a rider that you are particularly interested in, make sure you price the policy with it included and shop around.

B. When considering various riders, ask yourself, Do I really need it? Does this rider make sense for me? And if so, is there another, cheaper policy that will give me the same coverage without having to purchase a rider?

C. The rider that's gained the most popularity in recent years is the living benefits rider. However, you should keep in mind your purpose in purchasing life insurance in the first place. You shouldn't use a living benefits rider on your life insurance policy as a substitute for disability insurance.

how do you find a good agent? Well, it helps to be aware of the agent's professional designation. Is the agent simply licensed to sell insurance, or is he or she a chartered life underwriter, or CLU, which is the most rigorous of all life insurance designations. To obtain this title, a life insurance salesperson must master both technical information on insurance and also show mastery in the related areas of finance, accounting, taxation, business law, and economics. Competence in these areas is tested in a series of examinations in addition to a requirement of at least 3 years of experience, with the professional designation conferred by the American College.

To begin the agent search process, make a list of prospective agents from good companies. This list can come from friends, colleagues, and relatives in addition to recommendations from bankers, accountants, and lawyers that specialize in personal financial planning. Next, interview the agents to find out which ones you feel comfortable with and whether they're full-time insurance agents with some degree of experience. Table 9.5 presents a list of possible questions to ask. Once you've selected several agents you feel comfortable with, have them give you a quote on your desired insurance plan.

The Facts of Life

It's not unusual for cash-value life insurance policies to have commissions of 80 to 100 percent of the first year's premium. The only way you can find out is to ask. Because this information may help you determine why one policy is being pushed instead of another, the size of the commission is good information to know—all you have to do is ask.

TABLE 9.5

Questions to Ask Potential Insurance Agents

Are you a full-time insurance agent? You shouldn't deal with someone who only works part-time as an insurance agent. Your insurance agent needs to be knowledgeable.

How long have you been a full-time insurance agent? You should only deal with someone with experience. While a new agent may be competent, a more established agent may have experience you can benefit from. Moreover, an established agent may not have the financial pressure to sell you a policy that doesn't precisely fit your needs.

What life insurance companies do you represent? You shouldn't consider an agent that doesn't represent at least one company with a top rating from A. M. Best for 10 consecutive years.

Are you a CLU? A CLU is preferred, particularly if you're considering something other than term insurance and if you're seeking advice.

Will I be allowed to keep the insurance proposal that you prepare for me? You shouldn't consider an agent that doesn't allow you to keep the proposal.

Would you be willing to inform me of the commission you'll receive on any policies you recommend? You want to make sure that your agent is working on your behalf. By knowing what the agent's interests are in selling various policies, you may be better able to avoid being sold a policy that is of more benefit to the agent than to you.

Do you have any clients who are willing to recommend you? Your agent should either supply you with a listing of satisfied customers, or testimonial letters from customers. In short, you shouldn't consider an agent without a recommendation.

Comparing Costs

Now that you've got a handful of quotes, it's time to compare the costs of the competing policies. There are several comparison methods you can use, the most common of which are the traditional net cost (TNC) method and the interest-adjusted net cost method (IANC), or surrender cost index.

The **traditional net cost (TNC) method** is calculated by summing the premiums over a stated period (usually 10 or 20 years) and from this subtracting the sum of all dividends over that same period. The policy's cash value at the end of the stated period is then subtracted from this amount. The final result is then divided by the number of years in the stated period and presented as total net cost per some level of coverage.

$$(\text{premiums} - \text{dividends} - \text{cash value}) / \text{number of years} = TNC$$

What's important here in this method isn't what's included in the calculations, but what's excluded. The traditional net cost method doesn't take into consideration the time value of money. As a result, it's virtually meaningless. Unfortunately, it's used quite often. If an agent presents it to you as a reasonable means of analyzing the costs of a policy, you might want to consider another insurance agent.

A more widely accepted means of comparing similar but competing policies is the **interest-adjusted net cost (IANC) method**, which is also called the **surrender cost index**. Although this method has its own shortcomings, it does incorporate the time value of money into its calculations and has gained a good deal of acceptance in the insurance industry. In fact, this method is just like the TNC method except that it recognizes the time value of money. Obviously, using the time value of money to compare cash flows that occur in different periods makes this method an improvement over the traditional method. However, this method depends on the choice of the appropriate discount rate and the estimate of the dividends and cash value from the policy. The agent's estimates may be high and might not be realistic. To be safe, take the results of every comparative analysis method with a hefty grain of salt. Note, though, that there are almost as many methods for comparing insurance costs as there are different types of policies, and they all involve making assumptions.

The Alternative Approach—Using an Advisor or Buying Direct

As you should realize by now, insurance shopping is extremely complicated, and the consequences associated with a poor decision can be extreme. As a result, you might want to approach the insurance decision with the help of a fee-only insurance advisor. The purpose of an advisor is to get an independent opinion on your insurance needs from an expert that doesn't have a vested interest in selling you something. Unfortunately, fee-only advisors aren't cheap, but when considering the magnitude of the decision at hand, they aren't outrageously expensive, with fees ranging from $100 to $200 per hour. Names of fee-only advisors are provided by the Life Insurance Advisors Association (800-521-4578) or Fee for Service (800-874-5662). An alternative to a fee-only advisor is to use a premium quote service, which, for a fee, will recommend a low-cost insurer. An example of a premium quote company is Insurance Information Inc. (800-472-5800), which covers more than 500 carriers and charges $50 for five or more quotes. Other premium quote services that receive a commission rather than charge a fee include SelectQuote (800-343-1985), QuoteSmith (800-431-1147), and LifeQuote (800-521-7873). You can also buy low-load life insurance directly through Charles Schwab & Co. (800-542-LIFE). With low-load life insurance, the insurance company doesn't pay any commission to the insurance agent, resulting in low marketing and overhead costs.

Another approach to saving money on insurance is to buy it directly from the insurance company and thereby eliminate commissions. Recall that an agent's commissions can run from 50 to 100 percent of the first year's premium, and from 2 to 10 percent of future premiums. When you purchase insurance directly from the company, these commissions don't exist, and therefore the premiums are lower. Two such companies that offer insurance directly to the consumer are USAA (800-531-8000) and Ameritas (800-552-3553).

SUMMARY

The purpose of insurance is to control the financial *effect* that your dependents experience when you die. Insurance is based upon the concept of risk pooling. With life insurance, everyone pays a premium, which is determined by the probability of your dying, and no one suffers a big loss.

Before designing a life insurance program, you must ask yourself whether you actually need life insurance. The main purpose of life insurance is to provide for your dependents in the event of your death. Thus, if you're single and have no dependents, you probably don't need insurance. However, if you do have a spouse or dependents to provide for, then life insurance can replace the lost income that would result from the death of the wage earner. The first step in determining how much life insurance you need is to review your net worth. The larger your net worth, the more you have in the way of wealth to support your family, and consequently the less life insurance you need. Some financial planners suggest that you purchase life insurance that covers from 5 to 15 times your annual gross income to meet your needs. This rule of thumb approach is called the earnings multiple approach. An alternative method of determining how much insurance you need is the needs approach, which involves an attempt to determine the funds necessary for a family unit to maintain its current lifestyle after the death of the primary breadwinner.

Once you've determined how much insurance you need, you must then decide between two very different categories of life insurance—term and cash-value. Term life insurance is pure life insurance that pays the beneficiary the face value of the policy if the insured individual dies during the coverage period. Cash-value insurance, however, is any insurance policy that provides both a death benefit and an opportunity to accumulate cash value. For most individuals, term insurance is the better alternative. It provides for the individual's life insurance needs at a relatively low cost, and that's the real purpose of insurance.

One way of fine-tuning your insurance policy is through riders. A rider is a special provision that may be added to your policy, which either provides extra benefits or limits the company's liability under certain conditions. Common riders include (1) waiver of premium for disability, (2) multiple indemnity or accidental death benefit, (3) guaranteed insurability, (4) cost-of-living adjustment (COLA), and (5) living benefits.

In general, life insurance death benefits are income tax-free. Thus, if there's a single lump-sum settlement, there are generally no taxes due on the full face value of the contract.

The first step in purchasing insurance is to develop your financial game plan—do you need life insurance, how much, and term or cash-value? Once you've determined your needs, the first order of business becomes selecting an insurance company. Because it's difficult to know all you might like to know about insurance, selecting your agent is also extremely important. Your agent should be willing to develop and fine-tune your insurance program. However, you should keep in mind that an agent makes a living from selling you insurance. The final step in securing insurance is to compare the costs of the competing policies.

PESTER US FOR A BETTER DEAL, and You'll Probably Get It

Try walking to a computer super-store and exchanging your 386 IBM-compatible for a newer model. Ridiculous, right? But with insurance, you can probably pull off an equivalent maneuver.

(A) Insurance actuaries regularly revise their mortality tables and pricing structures, which affect rates. Prices for term life insurance, for instance, are currently at historic lows. So if you bought a term life policy some years ago—or even if you're a smoker who's kicked the habit—you may be able to call your company and insist on changing over to a new, cheaper rate.

(B) It worked for Michael P. Grace of Baton Rouge, La. When he pressed his agent to get him a better deal on his New York Life policy and threatened to switch, she immediately bumped up his coverage to $500,000 from $300,000 at essentially no extra cost. Mel Feinberg, vice president and actuary at New York Life, concedes that this does happen from time to time: "there are situations where it can be to the client's benefit to cancel their existing insurance and buy a new one." That's especially true with term policies—the simplest, cheapest type of life insurance, which pays off a set amount when you die. It gets more complicated with cash-value policies, which have a savings component, because there may be surrender charges as well as tax issues when you replace your policy.

Source: Namita Devidayal, "Ten Things Your Life Insurer Won't Tell You," *Smart Money,* August 1996, pp 115–121. Used by permission.

Analysis and Implications ...

A. Also keep in mind that prices vary dramatically and, as such, it pays enormously to shop around. Try USAA (800-531-8000), Quotesmith (800-556-9393), and the Wholesale Insurance Network (800-808-5810) for quotes.

B. It's important to keep your insurance payments as low as possible while maintaining the level of insurance that's right for you. Keep in mind that every dollar you spend on insurance is a dollar that you can't put towards another one of your financial goals.

Just Do It! *From the Desk of Marcy Furney, CFP*

What They Never Told You about Life Insurance

Your primary concern should be sufficient death benefit to cover your dependents' needs. Accident coverage doesn't count in the calculation unless you're 100 percent sure you'll die by accident.

☑ Take your beneficiary designation seriously. If your beneficiary can't handle money, consider a periodic payment settlement option. Small children can't receive life insurance payments directly. To avoid red tape, you should use some type of guardian arrangement.

☑ Consider a common disaster clause in your beneficiary designation. It'll guarantee that your death benefit goes to your contingent beneficiary if the primary beneficiary dies within a stated number of days of your death. Otherwise, the proceeds could be tied up in the primary beneficiary's estate and go to someone you wouldn't have chosen.

☑ Never count on group life insurance as your total program. You could change jobs at a time when your medical condition would prevent obtaining replacement coverage. Some group policies are convertible to personal policies, but the rates can be 3 to 10 times higher than the group rate. Many group policies are owned by the employer, and proceeds are paid first to them and then forwarded to your beneficiary. Can your family wait several weeks or months for the money?

☑ Put some thought into ownership of your policies. Although death benefits are free of income tax, they are normally included in your estate. Certain ownership arrangements can avoid some or all estate taxes. Also, in cases of divorce, it seems best for spouses to own and control each other's policies. This is especially true if there are children relying on potential benefits.

☑ Investigate riders such as waiver of premium, waiver of charges (on universal policies), and living benefits. Know when they pay and under what conditions. Also evaluate the cost of riders versus their benefits.

☑ Good intentions without complete information could result in tremendous headaches for those you're trying to protect. A competent agent is valuable in assisting you to make important long-term decisions regarding your insurance.

Review Questions

1. What is the main purpose of life insurance? (LO 1)
2. What factors affect a person's need for life insurance? (LO 2)
3. Define the following life insurance terms: beneficiary, face amount, insured, policyholder. Describe how these terms are related. (LO 2)
4. Describe the types of households that need life insurance and those that don't. (LO 2)
5. Describe the two basic approaches to determining the amount of life insurance that a person needs. Compare and contrast each method. (LO 2)
6. Describe the major differences between term and cash-value life insurance. (LO 3)
7. Briefly describe six common types of term life insurance. (LO 3)

8. Briefly describe the three major categories of cash-value life insurance. (LO 3)
9. Define the following life insurance policy features: grace period, incontestability clause, loan clause, nonforfeiture clause, reinstatement clause, and suicide clause. (LO 4)
10. Describe four common life insurance policy settlement options. (LO 4)
11. Define an insurance policy rider and describe five common types. (LO 4)
12. What factors should be considered when selecting a life insurance policy? (LO 5)
13. Compare and contrast the two most common methods of comparing the cost of life insurance policies. (LO 5)

Problems and Activities

1. List three examples of situations in which the purchase of life insurance is unnecessary. (LO 2)
2. Sandra Hernandez is married with two children and earns $30,000 a year. She wants to purchase term life insurance for 15 years until her youngest child is self-supporting. Assuming she can receive a 5-percent after-tax, after-inflation return on insurance proceeds, use the earnings multiple method to calculate her insurance needs. Discuss the accuracy of the result. (LO 2)
3. John Huston has an employer group life insurance policy that pays two and a half times his $30,000 salary. He also has $15,000 saved in a 401(k) plan, $5,000 in mutual funds, and a $3,000 CD. His life insurance agent used the needs approach and recommended a total of $285,000 worth of life insurance. How much more insurance does John need to buy? (LO 2)
4. Give two examples of organizations through which individuals could qualify for group life insurance. (LO 3)
5. Joe Puska has a $100,000 whole life insurance policy with $30,000 of cash value. He decides to borrow $20,000 against the policy. If he dies before repaying $15,000 of the loan, how much would his beneficiary receive? (LO 4)
6. Nancy Liu purchased an insurance policy 5 years ago and mistakenly checked a box on her application that said she does not have high blood pressure. She does. Yesterday, she died of a heart attack. Will her beneficiary get paid? (LO 4)
7. Joe Torres wants to purchase a life insurance policy in which his coverage can be increased in the future without having to take another medical exam. Name two types of policy riders that he should consider. (LO 4)
8. Jayne Biel is in the 28-percent tax bracket and earned $42,000 last year. She also received the proceeds of her late mother's $50,000 life insurance policy. How much of the insurance settlement is taxable? (LO 1)
9. Roy Harris was recently diagnosed with AIDS and has been told he has less than 2 years to live. He is taking a number of experimental drugs to prolong his life. Which life insurance policy rider would benefit a terminally ill person like Roy? (LO 4)

Suggested Projects

1. Interview at least three people to determine if they own an insurance policy. If they do own a policy, ask them why. Also inquire about the amount of coverage, type of policy, and premium cost. Prepare a one-page report of your findings. (LO 3)
2. Contact an insurance agent or insurance quote service and obtain life insurance premium quotes for $100,000 of term, whole life, and universal life insurance. When making your request, assume a specific age, gender, and health characteristics (for example, nonsmoker). Prepare a one-page report of your findings. (LO 3)

3. Read your parents' life insurance policy, or that of a friend or relative, cover to cover. Prepare a one-page report of key policy features, including beneficiary designation, policy clauses, settlement options, and riders. (LO 4)
4. Visit the reference section of the library and look up the ratings for five different life insurance companies in a rating service publication, such as A.M. Best or Duff & Phelps. How do these ratings compare with those listed in Table 9.4? Write a one-page report of your findings. (LO 3)
5. Assume you're married with your first child on the way. You and your spouse depend on both of your paychecks to make ends meet. Should you purchase life insurance? Should your spouse purchase life insurance? What type of policy would you recommend? Defend your answers in a one-page report. (LO 5)
6. Make a list of life insurance policy riders that you would and wouldn't purchase. Compare your list with those of three classmates. Report on your findings. (LO 5)
7. Write to your state Department of Insurance to obtain information about the state guarantee association designed to protect policyholders if an insurance company goes out of business. (LO 1)

Discussion Case 1

Greg Hasti, 28, is divorced and has custody of two preschool-age children. He and the children presently live with his parents. Hasti has no life insurance and no will. He earns $27,000 a year as a construction worker and pays his parents $100 a week for room and board. This, plus his car loan, auto insurance, and $150 a week for child care, are his only fixed expenses.

Hasti's parents have urged him several times to buy life insurance. His 26-year-old ex-wife, Cathi, doesn't have any life insurance either. Hasti is concerned about the cost of premiums and says he can't afford it with all the other bills he has to pay. Even if he could, he's unsure about what type of policy to buy and continues to avoid the subject.

Questions

1. Does Greg need to purchase life insurance? Why or why not?
2. What could happen to Greg's children if he dies without buying a life insurance policy?
3. What type of insurance policy should Greg purchase?
4. Should Greg name his children as his life insurance beneficiaries?
5. Which life insurance riders should Greg select when purchasing a policy?

Discussion Case 2

Wendy and Frank Effron, 30 and 35, are considering the purchase of life insurance. Wendy doesn't have any coverage, but Frank has a $150,000 group policy at work. The Effrons have two young children, aged 3 and 5. Wendy earns $18,000 from a part-time, home-based business. Frank's annual salary is $55,000. From their income, they save $3,000 annually. The rest goes for expenses. The couple figure that the children will be financially dependent for another 20 years.

In preparation for a visit with their insurance agent, the Effrons have estimated the following expenses if Frank were to die:

• immediate needs at death	$ 20,000
• outstanding debt (including mortgage reduction)	90,000
• transitional funds for Wendy to increase job skills	15,000
• college expenses for their two children	120,000

They also anticipate receiving $20,000 a year in Social Security survivor's benefits and pension benefits.

Once the children are self-supporting, Wendy wants to plan a spousal life income for 10 more years, from ages 50 to 60, plus retirement income for another 20 years from ages 60 to 80. She anticipates receiving a 4-percent after-tax, after-inflation return.

To date, the Effrons have accumulated a total of $40,000 of assets. This amount includes $10,000 considered as an emergency fund and $30,000 in Frank's employer-sponsored 401(k) plan.

Questions

1. Using the needs approach as described in Figure 9.2, estimate the amount of additional life insurance, if any, that the Effrons should purchase to protect Wendy if Frank should die.

2. Should Wendy purchase an insurance policy? Why or why not?

3. What would happen to Frank's group life insurance if he were to leave his present job?

4. Should Frank purchase an additional life insurance policy? If so, what type?

Chapter 10

THE ROLE OF HEALTH INSURANCE

At 42, Christopher Reeve was in the prime of his life, and it was a good life. Most famous for starring as Superman in a series of movies, Reeve was the picture of good health and an ideal family man. Then on May 27, 1995, tragedy struck. While participating in an equestrian competition, Reeve was thrown off his horse and landed on his head, causing severe spinal cord damage and leaving him paralyzed from the neck down, unable to breathe without the aid of a respirator. At first, doctors gave him little hope of ever being off a respirator, but he continues to recover and is now able to breathe without a respirator for extended periods of time. However, as his long recovery continues, his medical bills have climbed.

Initially for Reeve, the costs of health care were assumed away—after all, he had an excellent health insurance policy. Unfortunately, Reeve later learned that his insurance policy had a lifetime cap of $1.2 million. Once it paid out that much money, it wouldn't pay any more. This was news to Reeve—and not good news at that. His ongoing treatment is costing about $400,000 per year, and at that rate of spending, he'll exhaust this cap within 3 years. As a result, in March 1996, Reeve began lobbying Congress to set a minimum insurance lifetime cap at $10 million. Although his insurance policy was better than most, and he certainly has better financial means than do most people, health costs will still have a major impact on his and his family's life. Fortunately for Reeve, his longtime friend Robin Williams has stepped in and pledged to pay his medical bills when his insurance runs out. Apparently, Williams and Reeve made a pact more than 20 years ago, when both were studying at Juilliard, that if

Learning Objectives

After reading this chapter you should be able to:

1. Understand the cost of not having health care coverage.
2. Describe the major types of coverage available and the typical provisions that are included in them.
3. Discuss the various health care providers, both private and public.
4. Control your health care costs.
5. Design a health care insurance program and understand what provisions are important to you.
6. Describe disability insurance and the choices available to you in a disability insurance policy.
7. Explain the purpose of long-term care insurance and the provisions that might be important to you.

either made it in show biz, he'd help the other out in time of crisis.

What about those of us not lucky enough to have a Robin Williams helping us out with our medical expenses? We'd better choose our health insurance carefully and wisely. Unfortunately, most people don't even want to think about illness or disability, let alone put a lot of effort into insuring against it. In fact, most people hate spending on health insurance. After all, you can't drive it, eat it, or live in it, so what good can it be? Ask that question to someone who's been hit by a bus, is racking up hundreds of thousands' worth of medical bills, and having them all paid for by insurance.

If you lose all your money on a bad investment, optimists will say, "At least you still have your health." Well, if you lose all your money because of sudden and unguarded medical problems, you're really in bad shape. That's where the need for health insurance rises—from **Axiom 10: Protect Yourself Against Major Catastrophes— The Case for Insurance**. In the case of health insurance, our philosophy will be to provide protection against major catastrophes while ignoring the small stuff. You don't really need protection against the small stuff. A $20 or $30 doctor's bill shouldn't cause any financial disruption—it's just part of life. In fact, minor medical expenses should be part of your monthly budget.

Today, approximately 85 percent of employed Americans have some form of health coverage, provided by an employer. As a result, we tend to assume our health worries are adequately taken care of. Unfortunately, they may not be. Christopher Reeve's certainly weren't, and his health care was being covered by what seemed like an excellent insurance policy. (Now his health care is being covered by a real joker— Robin Williams.) An hour before you're about to have life-saving surgery that costs upward of $200,000 isn't the time to find out that your insurance won't pay for the procedure. You've got to understand your health insurance before you buy it. If you buy good health insurance, it'll probably be the best investment you ever make. If you don't, you'd better be sure to look both ways before crossing the street, or at least make friends with a soon-to-be-famous-and-rich comedian. In this chapter, we'll tell you what you need to know to make the most of your health insurance.

AXIOM #10

Protect Yourself Against Major Catastrophes—The Case for Insurance

LEARNING OBJECTIVE #1

Understand the cost of not having health care coverage.

THE COST OF NOT HAVING HEALTH CARE

Health care costs continue to increase faster than inflation. Why is health care so costly? One of the major reasons is that there's a lack of incentives to economize. Presently, over 50 percent of Americans receive some government health care entitlements, such as Medicare or Medicaid, and 87 percent of all Americans have medical insurance. As a result, there simply isn't any incentive for the patients, doctors, or hospitals to exercise restraint in medical billing. If you aren't paying out of your own pocket, why should you care what your bills are? And if these bills are certain to be paid, why should doctors or hospitals care how much they charge? In addition, medical care has become extremely sophisticated and costly. For example, it now takes 12 years and costs over $231 million to develop, test, and certify a new drug. You'd better believe that the drug companies are passing these costs on to the patients. Finally, the cost of litigation from malpractice suits has skyrocketed. Today, it's not uncommon for doctors to pay malpractice insurance premiums of $150,000 or $250,000 per year. These costs are then passed directly on to their patients.

What do these high costs mean for you. First, the world of medical care and medical insurance must change. It has to become more efficient if we're to continue to be able to afford quality health care. This change may mean that your doctor joins an HMO, or your company's insurance policy no longer covers all your health care expenses. It also means that many companies will try to cut down on their health care costs by providing only limited insurance coverage or hiring only temporary workers who don't get a full benefits package. And what about those workers—and the unemployed—who have no health insurance? They have to pay the huge medical bills out of their own pockets. Ouch! It's just as bad to be underinsured, though. Imagine having your insurance policy give you a false sense of security and then leave you in the lurch when the bill arrives. Insurance is serious in the world of personal finance because as medical costs go up through the roof, so does your risk of having your financial roof cave in due to health-related problems. They say that one nuclear bomb can ruin your whole day. Well, one simple medical procedure can ruin your whole financial plan. Why risk your financial health when you can insure it instead?

HEALTH INSURANCE COVERAGE: DIFFERENT TYPES

LEARNING OBJECTIVE #2

Describe the major types of coverage available and the typical provisions that are included in them.

Basic Health Insurance
A term used to describe most health insurance, which includes a combination of hospital, surgical, and physician expense insurance.

We live in a world of choices, so of course there are several different types of health insurance coverage available. Hey, if you've got 31 choices when buying such a thing as ice cream, you should at least have a few choices when it comes to buying something as important as health insurance. As with buying ice cream, though, it's easy to get carried away with buying health insurance and want everything you can get. Remember, even though there are different types of insurance to cover just about everything down to a common sneeze (bless you), the purpose of insurance isn't to cover all the costs of health care. Face it, you're going to have to pay a doctor's bill every now and again, and you'll need to spring for that bottle of Tylenol when you get a headache. Of course, if you've got chronic headaches and go through a bottle of Tylenol every day, you're going to want someone to pick up that cost. Everyone's needs are different, and the key in picking insurance is choosing only the types of coverage you need. Let's see just what those types of coverage are.

Basic Health Insurance

Most health insurance includes a combination of hospital, surgical, and physician expense insurance. These three types of insurance are generally sold in a combination called **basic health insurance**. Many policies provide basic health insurance and then allow the policyholder to choose from a "cafeteria," or long list, of policy options. Although each additional option provides additional coverage, it also involves an additional premium. A premium is the fee that you pay for your insurance coverage.

Hospital Insurance.   **Hospital insurance** is generally part of any insurance plan. It covers the costs associated with a hospital stay, including room charges, nursing costs, operating room fees, and drugs supplied by the hospital. Depending upon the policy, hospital insurance may reimburse the policyholder for specific charges, give the policyholder a set amount of money for each day he or she is hospitalized, or pay the hospital directly for the policyholder's expenses. If the policyholder receives a set amount of money per day of hospitalization, the policyholder must make up the difference between what is charged and what is received from the insurance company. Almost all plans, regardless of their type, impose limits on both the daily hospital costs and the number of days covered.

Surgical Insurance.   **Surgical insurance**, as the name suggests, covers the cost of surgery. A surgical insurance policy generally lists the specific operations that it covers. It'll also cite either a maximum dollar amount that the insurance policy will pay for each operation, or it'll allow for reimbursement to the surgeon for what's considered reasonable and customary for each operation based upon typical charges in that geographic region. You'll have to cover any charges above what the insurance policy will cover, and you also might have to pay a deductible. Although surgical insurance may not completely cover surgery charges, it'll hopefully reduce them to a manageable level.

One complaint with surgical insurance policies is that many times they don't cover what might be considered "experimental" treatment. For example, insurance companies have refused to pay for bone marrow transplants to combat cancer and some experimental treatments for AIDS patients. Although the insurance companies look at these coverage limitations as an attempt to keep costs down (experimental surgery tends to be painfully expensive), if you're facing cancer or AIDS you're going to look at things differently. Remember, though, that surgical insurance has its limits. If you're considering a treatment not specified in your policy, you should see a lawyer to help you convince your insurance company ahead of time that this surgery should be covered.

Physician Expense Insurance.   **Physician expense insurance** covers physicians' fees outside of surgery, including such expenses as office or home visits, lab fees, and X-ray costs when they're not performed in a hospital.

Major Medical Expense Insurance

Major medical expense insurance is aimed at covering medical costs beyond those covered by basic health insurance. In effect, it's meant to offset all the financial effects of a catastrophic illness. Where basic health insurance leaves off, major medical expense insurance takes over. It generally doesn't provide complete coverage, but instead allows for deductibles and coinsurance payments in order to keep costs down. For example, the deductible may require the policyholder to pay for the first two office visits beyond what's covered by the policyholder's basic insurance policy. It may then cover only 80 percent of the costs, with the policyholder responsible for making up the difference. It's also not uncommon for such a policy to allow for **stop-loss provision**, which limits the total dollar amount that the policyholder is responsible for. For example, when deductibles and coinsurance payments by the policyholder reach a set limit, perhaps $4,000, the insurance company then takes full financial responsibility for any additional medical expenses incurred.

Most policies also have a lifetime cap associated with them. For example, most company-provided health care plans have a lifetime cap of $250,000. If that's the case, your health insurance doesn't do what it should—protect against major catastrophes. You should consider a major medical add-on policy that provides protection of up to at least $1 million. With a $25,000 or $50,000 deductible, such a policy isn't particularly expensive. Keep in mind the problems a lifetime cap has given Christopher Reeve.

Hospital Insurance
Insurance that covers the costs associated with a hospital stay, including room charges, nursing costs, operating room fees, and drugs supplied by the hospital.

Surgical Insurance
Insurance that covers the cost of surgery.

Physician Expense Insurance
Insurance that covers physicians' fees outside of surgery.

Major Medical Expense Insurance
Insurance that covers medical costs beyond those covered by basic health insurance.

Stop-Loss Provision
A medical insurance feature that limits the total dollar amount that the policyholder is responsible for paying.

Dental and Eye Insurance

As the names imply, dental insurance provides dental coverage and eye insurance provides coverage for eye examinations, glasses, and contact lenses. Although these are certainly nice to have, don't bother buying them if they're not provided by your employer. Remember that you can't afford to offset all the costs of health care, only the catastrophic ones. Dental and eye insurance pay for expenses that are relatively minor and regular—that is, they can be planned for. It would be nice to insure against every health-related cost, but that would probably exhaust your paycheck.

Dread Disease and Accident Insurance

Dread disease and accident insurance are sold to provide additional protection if you're struck by a specific disease or if you're in an accident. An example of dread disease insurance is cancer insurance, which is generally sold on television or through the mail. This insurance is aimed at providing additional coverage for the costs associated with this one specific disease. Accident insurance works about the same way. If you're in an accident, an accident insurance policy will provide a specific amount for every day you must stay in the hospital—for example, $100 per day—and a certain amount for the loss of any body parts or limbs—for example, it may pay $5,000 for the loss of an arm. Once again, the idea behind insurance is to provide protection against major catastrophes while ignoring the small stuff. Because you don't know ahead of time what might bring on this catastrophe, your health insurance must be comprehensive. Avoid the accident and dread disease insurance, and instead make sure your policy is comprehensive.

A LOOK AT THE BASIC HEALTH CARE CHOICES

Before you run out and get yourself some health insurance, you need to understand the basic health care choices that are available. First, who's providing the choices? In other words, where do we go to get health insurance? Well, we can turn to either a private insurance company or the government. In addition, there are two basic types of plans available: (1) traditional fee-for-service plans and (2) managed health care, or prepaid care. Under a **fee-for-service** or **traditional indemnity plan**, you are reimbursed for all or part of your medical expenditures, and, in general, you have a good deal of freedom to choose your doctor and hospital. Under **managed health care**, most of your expenses are already covered and don't need to be reimbursed, but you're limited to receiving the health care of a specified group of participating doctors, hospitals, and clinics.

Private Health Care Plans

There are more than 800 private insurance companies whose main business comes from selling health insurance policies both to individuals and to employers to be offered as part of a benefits package. These companies offer a variety of traditional fee-for-service as well as managed health care plans. Of note among the private insurance companies is Blue Cross and Blue Shield, which provides coverage to approximately 70 million individuals. Actually, Blue Cross and Blue Shield provides prepaid health care plans rather than insurance policies. The company contracts with hospitals and doctors to provide specified health care coverage to members for a contracted payment or fee. As such, Blue Cross and Blue Shield provides service benefits to members rather than cash benefits.

Health care insurance is also available from private commercial insurance companies. As you might expect, the benefits vary from plan to plan, with each contract spelling out exactly what is covered and to what extent.

LEARNING OBJECTIVE #3

Discuss the various health care providers, both private and public.

Fee-for-Service or **Traditional Indemnity Plan**
An insurance plan that provides reimbursement for all or part of your medical expenditures. In general, it gives you a good deal of freedom to choose your doctor and hospital.

Managed Health Care or **Prepaid Care Plan**
An insurance plan that entitles you to the health care of a specified group of participating doctors, hospitals, and clinics. These plans are generally offered by health maintenance organizations or variations of them.

Fee-for-Service or Traditional Indemnity Plans.   With a fee-for-service plan, the doctor or hospital bills you directly for the cost of services, and the insurance company simply reimburses you later. Although there may be some restrictions as to which doctors and hospitals you can use, these plans provide you with the greatest degree of health provider choice. Most fee-for-service plans include a coinsurance provision. A **coinsurance** or **percentage participation provision** defines the percentage of each claim that the insurance company will pay. For example, if there's an 80-percent participation premium on hospital claims up to $2,000 and 100-percent participation thereafter, then you'd pay 20 percent of the first $2,000 of your hospital insurance claim, and the insurance company would pay the remainder. Most fee-for-service plans also include a co-payment or deductible. A **co-payment** or **deductible** is the amount of your medical expenses that you must pay before the insurance company will reimburse you on a claim. A deductible can be set up in several different ways. For example, there may be a $10 deductible on all prescriptions. The insured pays the first $10 of the prescription, and the insurance company will cover the remainder. Alternatively, there might be an overall deductible of $250 or $500 on all health care. In this case, you'd pay the first $250 or $500 of any medical care costs you might have, and the insurance company will then cover any additional medical care costs up to a certain point.

Overall, fee-for-service plans are very desirable. Their big advantage is that you've got complete choice over your doctors, hospitals, and clinics. Unfortunately, these plans are relatively expensive and involve a good deal of paperwork. Many employers still provide fee-for-services plans for their workers. Figure 10.1 shows fewer employers are choosing to offer this kind of plan.

Managed Health Care.   Managed health care plans are offered by health maintenance organizations or variations of them and allow members access to needed health care services from specified doctors and hospitals. Unlike fee-for-service plans, managed health care plans both pay for and provide your health care services. For example, under a managed health care plan you may receive all your health services at one location, a local clinic. Under some managed care plans you may not be guaranteed that you'll see the same doctor each time, just that you'll get the health care you need at low or no cost. However, most managed care plans provide you with a primary care physician, and many plans allow that physician to be one of your own choosing (for a slight fee). Just as with the fee-for-service plans, it's quite common for there to be a visit fee or co-payment of around $10. There is also generally a co-payment on prescriptions. The purpose of these co-payments is to keep insurance costs down. Not only do they serve as a deductible, forcing the patient to pay the first portion of the health care bill, but they also serve as a disincentive to seek care—health care is no longer totally free. As a result, almost all employees have to kick in for their employer-sponsored health care coverage, as shown in Figure 10.2. Some of the costs shown in Figure 10.2 are for co-payments associated with visits to the doctor and prescriptions, and some of the costs are from monthly premiums.

The big advantage of a managed health care plan is its efficiency. Because managed health care plans offer you health care directly rather than reimburse you after you've received and paid for your care, there's considerably less in the way of paperwork and its associated costs. Moreover, because most managed health care plans involve a number of doctors, the entire facility can provide extended office hours, whereas each individual doctor is responsible only for staffing the facility over a limited period. In fact, in many managed health care facilities, doctors work at that facility in addition to carrying on a private practice. There are two basic types of managed health care forms: (1) health maintenance organizations, or HMOs, and (2) preferred provider organizations, or PPOs.

Coinsurance or **Percentage Participation Provision**

An insurance provision that defines the percentage of each claim that the insurance company will pay.

Co-payments or **Deductible**

The amount of expenses that the insured must pay before the insurance company will pay any insurance benefits.

FIGURE 10.1

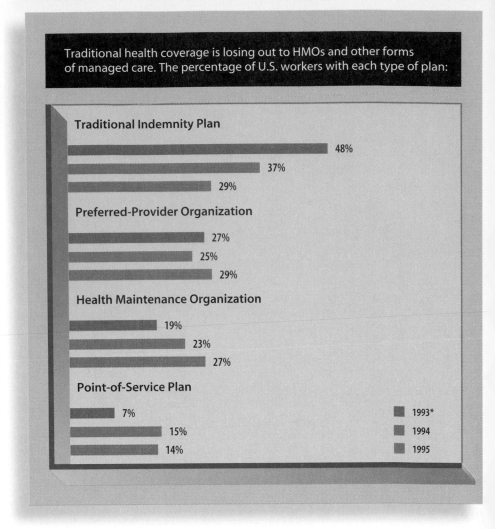

The Rise of Managed Health Care and the Fee-for-Service Coverage

Traditional health coverage is losing out to HMOs and other forms of managed care. The percentage of U.S. workers with each type of plan:

Traditional Indemnity Plan

48%
37%
29%

Preferred-Provider Organization

27%
25%
29%

Health Maintenance Organization

19%
23%
27%

Point-of-Service Plan

7%
15%
14%

■ 1993*
■ 1994
■ 1995

*Figures for each year may not total 100% due to rounding.

Source: Robert Langreth, "Picking a Plan," *The Wall Street Journal*, October 24, 1996, p. R4. Secondary source: A. Foster Higgins & Co. Reprinted by permission of *The Wall Street Journal*, © 1996 Dow Jones & Company, Inc. All Rights Reserved Worldwide.

Health Maintenance Organization (HMO)

A prepaid insurance plan that entitles members to the services of participating doctors, hospitals, and clinics.

Individual Practice Association Plan (IPA)

An HMO made up of independent doctors, in which the patients visit the doctors and receive their medical treatment in the doctors' regular offices.

Managed Health Care: HMOs.   The most popular form of managed health care is the **health maintenance organization**, or **HMO**, which is a prepaid insurance plan that entitles members to the services of participating doctors, hospitals, and clinics. Members pay a flat fee for this privilege and then can select an HMO managing physician who is responsible for the care of that member. There may also be an HMO co-payment required with each visit to the doctor or with each prescription filled. There are three basic types of HMOs: (1) individual practice association plans, (2) group practice plans, and (3) point-of-service plans.

An **individual practice association plan**, or **IPA**, is an HMO made up of independent doctors. The patients go to the doctors' regular offices and receive their medical

FIGURE 10.2

Employee Contributions to Employer-Sponsored Health Care

The price of overinsurance has risen as more employees have had to kick in for their employer-sponsored health coverage, and pay more for that coverage.

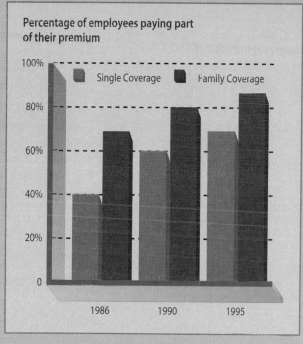

Percentage of employees paying part of their premium

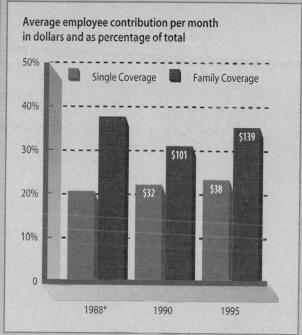

Average employee contribution per month in dollars and as percentage of total

*Percentages are estimated.

Source: Nancy Ann Jeffrey, "Enough Is Enough," *The Wall Street Journal*, October 24, 1996, p. R7 Secondary source: A. Foster Higgins & Co. Reprinted by permission of *The Wall Street Journal*, © 1996 Dow Jones & Company, Inc. All Rights Reserved Worldwide.

---

treatment there. In fact, many doctors working in IPAs also maintain a regular practice, seeing both IPA and regular patients interspersed throughout the day. With a **group practice plan**, doctors are generally employed directly by the HMO and work out of a central, shared facility. Members of the HMO can receive their medical treatment only from these doctors and only at these central facilities. A **point-of-service plan** allows its members to seek medical treatment from both HMO-affiliated doctors and non-HMO-affiliated doctors. Coverage by HMO-affiliated doctors tends to be free or at least covered at a very low co-payment rate. The co-payments for non-HMO-affiliated doctors tend to be much higher.

Although there are some individual differences, most HMOs have very broad coverage, with doctor, hospital, laboratory, and emergency costs covered. Prescription costs are often covered, too. Of course, this coverage also requires co-payments, and these co-payments vary greatly among HMOs.

Group Practice Plan
An insurance plan in which doctors are generally employed directly by an HMO, and members of the HMO must receive their medical treatment from these doctors at a central facility.

Point-of-Service Plan
An insurance plan that allows its members to seek medical treatment from both HMO-affiliated doctors and non-HMO-affiliated doctors.

Most HMOs are associated with an employer's group coverage. That is, the plans are offered through an employer as a part of the employee benefits package. Still, private individuals can join an HMO—and there are plenty to choose from. There are over 600 HMOs operating in the United States. Because each HMO has its own participating doctors and hospitals, each one serves a limited geographic area. In order to use health facilities elsewhere, you usually need a referral.

Because members receive comprehensive health care services, HMOs emphasize preventive medicine. No, despite claims by some HMOs, the preventive focus isn't evidence of true caring. It's a cost-effective measure: Preventing illnesses is an awful lot cheaper than curing them. As a result, many HMOs provide regular physical examinations. In contrast, most fee-for-service plans only cover illness-related health care claims.

Finally, HMOs are efficient, costing as little as 60 percent of what a comparable fee-for-service insurance plan would cost. The preventive care, coupled with minimized paperwork and efficient handling of patients, allows for the cost savings. It's no wonder then that employers prefer to offer HMO coverage. If HMOs are cheaper for you, they're also cheaper for your employer, which covers a good deal of your insurance premium each month.

There are, of course, some major drawbacks to HMOs. Service can be too quick or cursory and waits long as HMOs try to get the most out of their doctors' time. If you need a service not provided by your HMO, receiving a referral, especially one outside of the HMO's geographic area, can be an unbelievable hassle. Most commonly, many members feel their lack of choice is far too restricting. Having to choose from a small, fixed list of doctors, or not being able to choose at all, makes some people feel as if they're not being allowed to get the exact kind of care they want. They worry about not being able to build up trust or a personal relationship with a doctor, and they also worry that the available doctors might not be the best or most qualified. More questions about the quality of care stem from some of the incentive systems HMOs use for their doctors. Doctors often receive bonuses based on the number of patients seen or based on the amount of money they've saved, leading some to wonder if some doctors don't cut corners to earn bigger bonuses.

The Facts of Life

From 1981 to 1993, the cost of national health care tripled, from $290 billion to $884 billion. In 1997, about 15 percent of our gross national product went to pay for health care.

Managed Health Care: PPOs. A **preferred provider organization (PPO)** is a bit like a cross between a traditional fee-for-service plan and an HMO. Under a PPO, an employer or insurer negotiates with a group of doctors and hospitals to provide health care for its employees or members at reduced rates. Those doctors and hospitals that agree to the reduced pricing system become members of the PPO. In fact, a doctor or hospital can be a member of a number of different PPOs at the same time. To encourage use of member doctors, PPOs generally have an additional, or penalty, co-payment requirement for service from nonmember doctors. The big advantage of the PPO is that it allows for health care at a discount, with the negotiating power of the insurer or employer determining how great a discount is achieved.

Group versus Individual Health Insurance. **Group health insurance** refers to the way the health insurance is sold rather than to the characteristics of the insurance policy. Group health insurance is provided to a specific group of individuals who are associated for some purpose other than to buy insurance. Usually this group of individuals all work for the same employer or all belong to a common association or professional

Preferred Provider Organization (PPO)
An insurance plan under which an employer or insurer negotiates with a group of doctors and hospitals to provide health care for its employees or members at reduced rates.

Group Health Insurance
Health insurance that's sold, usually without a medical exam, to a specific group of individuals who are associated for some purpose other than to buy insurance.

A CLOSER LOOK at Plan English

A phone technician at Bell Atlantic Corp. thought his company's health policy through Prudential Health Care Plan Inc. would meet all of his prescription needs. The plan offered $4,000 worth of drug coverage a year with a $5 co-payment on each refill.

But the AIDS-stricken Baltimore man—who recently died and whose family requested that he not be identified—didn't grasp all the implications of his managed-care policy: After spending $4,000 on medication, he had no prescription coverage left.

According to executives at the Communications Workers of America, the union to which he belonged, he and his family appealed to Prudential for an extension of coverage because he needed expensive drugs to survive, but to no avail.

"We kept him alive by going to different doctors' offices and asking for free samples," said Charlie Gerhardt, an executive at the Communications Workers of America. "It was incredibly unfair."

Kevin Heine, a Prudential officer, said "the language [of the coverage], which clearly references a specific dollar figure per year, is extremely straightforward."

Yet the confusion created by the firm's summary of benefits is hardly unusual. Lured by low co-payments associated with HMO's, many consumers sign on the dotted line without understanding the limits of their coverage, and critics say the policies often disguise such limits in a morass of fine print.

With consumer complaints and lawsuits against HMOs on the rise, a number of states—including Maryland and Virginia—are considering legislation that would require insurers to spell out exactly what they cover, in a standardized format, in plain English.

HMO disclosure laws also would require carriers to answer a key question: Does the plan offer financial incentives to physicians that could encourage them to provide less care?

About 60 percent of managed-care plans limit the number of referrals to specialists by paying physicians a "capitated fee," a set sum per month, per patient. In effect, the fewer referrals to specialists that such doctors make, the more money they earn. Other plans withhold a percentage of a doctor's salary or offer bonuses for spending less on patients.

Source: David Segal, "A Closer Look at Plan English," *The Washington Post*, March 27, 1996, p. F1. © 1996, *The Washington Post*. Reprinted with permission.

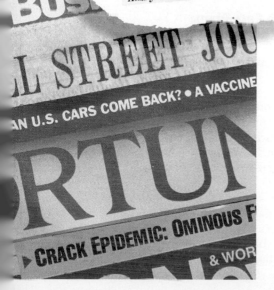

Analysis and Implications ...

A. What to ask your HMO:

1. Are any financial incentives provided to doctors that might discourage them from referring patients to specialists?
2. Are there any drugs that aren't covered?
3. Do I have a choice on where to buy my prescription drugs?
4. Are there limits on how much enrollees can spend on drugs each year, and do the drugs have to be generic, regardless of what the physician says?
5. If the plan charges a co-payment for drug refills, do members get a week's worth or a month's worth of drugs when they go to a pharmacy?
6. Does the plan cover durable medical goods, such as wheelchairs and braces?
7. Is oral surgery covered?
8. Is cosmetic surgery covered?
9. Under what conditions will the plan not pay for a visit to an emergency room?

group. Most employee health insurance doesn't require subscribers to pass a medical exam, but group insurance offered through an association or professional group does. In general, the cost of group health insurance is about 15 to 40 percent less than that of a comparable individual health insurance policy. Why? Because an individual simply doesn't have the bargaining power that a group has.

An **individual insurance policy** is one that is tailor-made for you reflecting your age, health (as determined by an examination), geographic location, and chosen deductible amount. Are there any advantages to individual health insurance policies? In general, other than the ability to tailor the policy to meet your specific and unique needs, there are none. Really, group and individual policies tend to offer the same coverage, so the only major difference between them is cost. Individual policies are expensive, so you should always try to get group insurance. If you can't possibly get in on group insurance, you'll need an individual policy. You may also need one as a supplement to your group policy if it doesn't provide adequate coverage.

> ## *Stop and Think*
> If you don't qualify for group coverage, you might want to consider joining a group that has such coverage. Trade groups, alumni, political, and religious organizations are logical places to check out. You'll probably end up saving much more in insurance than you pay in dues.

The Choice of Companies

You may have little choice with respect to your health insurance company. Your employer may have already chosen your insurance company for you. If, however, you don't have insurance through your employer, the choice of insurance companies is yours.

Just as with life insurance companies, it's important to get insurance from a company that's in sound financial condition, that is, one that could absorb higher-than-expected losses and continue to provide coverage. How do you go about selecting such a company? Your insurance company should receive either an A++ or an A+ rating from A. M. Best. Claim service provided by your company should be fast, fair, and courteous. Don't select a company that raises premiums based upon claims. Finally, select only a company that's prohibited from canceling policies. You should be able to determine how well a particular company fares in these areas from an interview with your insurance agent.

Government-Sponsored Health Care Plans

Government-sponsored plans fall into two categories: (1) state plans, which provide for work-related accidents and illness under state **workers' compensation laws**, and (2) federal plans, such as Medicare and Medicaid.

Workers' Compensation Laws

State laws that provide payment for work-related accidents and illness.

Workers' Compensation. The workers' compensation laws date from the early 1900s, when our economy changed from predominantly agricultural to industrial. At that time workers worked long hours in unsafe conditions, and, as a result, work-related accidents were all too common. Fueled by the public outcry to Upton Sinclair's 1906 book *The Jungle*, states passed a series of laws aimed at providing work-related accident and illness insurance to workers.

Because these are state laws, each state determines the benefits level for workers. Thus, some states provide broad coverage, and others exclude some workers. For example, some states exclude workers for small businesses from coverage. Given the variability in coverage from state to state, you shouldn't assume that you're covered or that the coverage is comprehensive. You should contact your benefits office to see exactly what workers' compensation coverage you have. For workers without enough workers' compensation coverage, or for those with no coverage at all, some private insurance companies offer a type of workers' compensation insurance to pick up the slack.

Interestingly, these laws were originally meant to be the final obligation of the employers to their employees. That is, the workers' compensation laws, while allowing for compensation regardless of whose fault the accident was, also initially took away the workers' right to sue. However, today it's common for an employee to sue his or her employer for any work-related accident.

Medicare.   The **Medicare** program was enacted in 1968 to provide medical benefits to the disabled and to persons 65 and older who qualify for Social Security benefits. The cost of this insurance is covered by Social Security, with the individual patient paying an annual deductible. To say the least, the Medicare program is way too complicated for us to explain here—but we'll try anyway.

Medicare coverage is divided into two parts: Part A, which provides hospital insurance benefits, and Part B, which allows for voluntary supplemental insurance. Participation in Part A of Medicare is compulsory and covers most hospital costs, including operating room costs, nursing care, a semiprivate room, and prescription drugs furnished by the hospital.

Part B of the Medicare plan is voluntary and provides coverage for doctors' fees and a wide range of medical services and supplies. The medically necessary services of a doctor are covered no matter where you receive them—at home, in the doctor's office, in a clinic, in a nursing home, or in a hospital.

With part B there's a monthly premium, which was $42.50 in 1996, rising to $43.80 in 1997, and a $100 annual deductible, after which Medicare pays 80 percent of the charges for covered medical services. Table 10.1 provides a listing of benefits available through Medicare. A more complete listing of Medicare benefits can be found in *Your Medicare Handbook*, which is available at any Social Security Administration office.

Although Medicare has proven to be a very important source of health insurance for many older Americans, there are limitations to its coverage. For example, out-of-hospital prescription drugs are not covered and care in skilled nursing facilities is limited to 100 days per benefit period. In addition, there are deductions and co-payments associated with Medicare. To bridge this gap in coverage, **Medigap insurance** is sold by private insurance companies. In order to make it easier for the customer to compare policies, the national Association of Insurance Commissioners limits the variations of Medigap insurance to 10 standardized contracts. The cost of the coverage, of course, depends upon how complete it is. Once you reach 65, you're automatically eligible to buy Medigap insurance, provided you apply within 6 months of enrolling in Medicare Part B. During this 6-month period, you can't be rejected because of illness. Although these policies are standard from company to company, the price of them tends to vary, so, it pays to shop around. Table 10.2 provides a listing of the benefits provided in these 10 Medigap plans.

In reviewing Medicare coverage, you must keep in mind that you must take responsibility for your own financial well-being. While counting on Medicare coverage may absolve you of some future financial responsibility, Medicare may not be around in its present form when you need it. Depending upon how fast medical costs rise and how long people live, Medicare could face severe financial problems, which would result in a government overhaul of the system. Be ready to take financial responsibility for your own health care costs in the future by getting some good coverage now.

Medicare
A government insurance program enacted in 1968 to provide medical benefits to the disabled and those over 65. It is divided into two parts: Part A, which provides hospital insurance benefits, and Part B, which allows for voluntary supplemental insurance.

Medigap Insurance
Insurance sold by private insurance companies aimed at bridging gaps in Medicare coverage.

The Facts of Life

In 1994, Medicare covered 36 million people—32 million elderly and 4 million disabled. In 1994, over 98 percent of older and 88 percent of disabled beneficiaries elected to have Part B coverage.

TABLE 10.1

Benefits and Services Available Through Medicare

Medicare Part A: 1997			
Services	**Benefit**	**Medicare Pays**	**You Pay**[a]
HOSPITALIZATION			
Semiprivate room and board, general nursing, and other hospital services and supplies. *(Medicare payments based on benefit periods.)*	First 60 days 61st to 90th day 91st to 150th day[b] Beyond 150 days	All but $760 All but $190 a day All but $368 a day Nothing	$760 $190 a day $368 a day All costs
SKILLED NURSING FACILITY CARE			
Semiprivate room and board, skilled nursing and rehabilitative services, and other services and supplies. *(Medicare payments based on benefit periods.)*	First 20 days Additional 80 days Beyond 100 days	100% of approved amount All but $92 a day Nothing	Nothing Up to $92 a day All costs
HOME HEALTH CARE			
Part-time or intermittent skilled care, home health aide services, durable medical equipment and supplies, and other services.	Unlimited as long as you meet Medicare conditions.	100% of approved amount; 80% of approved amount for durable medical equipment.	Nothing for services: 20% of approved amount for durable medical equipment.
HOSPICE CARE			
Pain relief, symptom management, and support services for the terminally ill.	For as long as doctor certifies need.	All but limited costs for outpatient drugs and inpatient respite care.	Limited costs for outpatient drugs and inpatient respite care.
BLOOD			
When furnished by a hospital or skilled nursing facility during a covered stay.	Unlimited if medically necessary.	All but first 3 pints per calendar year.	For first 3 pints.[c]

(continued)

[a]Either you or your insurance company are responsible for paying the amounts listed in the "You Pay" column.
[b]This 60-reserve-days benefit may be used only once in a lifetime.
[c]Blood paid for or replaced under Part B of Medicare during the calendar year does not have to be paid for or replaced under Part A.

Medicaid

A government medical insurance plan for the needy.

LEARNING OBJECTIVE #4

Control your health care costs.

Medicaid. Medicaid was enacted in 1965 and is a medical assistance program aimed at the needy. It's a joint program operated by the federal and state governments, with the benefits varying from state to state. The purpose of Medicaid is to provide medical care for the aged, blind, and disabled as well as to needy families with dependent children. Because some of those covered by Medicaid are also covered by Medicare, Medicaid payments go toward Medicare premiums, deductibles, and co-payments. Again, this program is very limited in scope, with no guarantee that it will be in its present form at a later point if and when you might need it.

CONTROLLING HEALTH CARE COSTS

Without question the first step in controlling health care costs is to stay healthy. Not only is health care insurance cheaper and more accessible if you're healthy, but your

TABLE 10.1 (continued)

Medicare Part B: 1997			
Services	**Benefit**	**Medicare Pays**	**You Pay**[a]
MEDICAL EXPENSES			
Doctors' services, inpatient and outpatient medical and surgical services and supplies, physical and speech therapy, diagnostic tests, durable medical equipment, and other services.	Unlimited if medically necessary.	80% of approved amount (after $100 deductible). Reduced to 50% for most outpatient mental health services.	$100 deductible, plus 20% of approved amount and limited charges above approved amount.
CLINICAL LABORATORY SERVICES			
Blood tests, urinalyses, and more.	Unlimited if medically necessary.	Generally 100% of approved amount.	Nothing for services.
HOME HEALTH CARE			
Part-time or intermittent skilled care, home health aide services, durable medical equipment and supplies, and other services.	Unlimited as long as you meet Medicare conditions.	100% of approved amount. 80% of approved amount for durable medical equipment.	Nothing for services; 20% of approved amount for durable medical equipment.
OUTPATIENT HOSPITAL TREATMENT			
Services for the diagnosis or treatment of illness or injury.	Unlimited if medically necessary.	Medicare payment to hospital based on hospital cost.	20% of whatever the hospital charges (after $100 deductible).
BLOOD			
	Unlimited if medically necessary.	80% of approved amount (after $100 deductible and starting with 4th pint).	First 3 pints plus 20% of approved amount for additional pints (after $100 deductible).[b]
AMBULATORY SURGICAL SERVICES			
	Unlimited if medically necessary.	80% of predetermined amount (after $100 deductible).	$100 deductible, plus 20% of predetermined amount.

[a]Either you or your insurance company are responsible for paying the amounts in the "You Pay" column.
[b]Blood paid for or replaced under Part A of Medicare during the calendar year does not have to be paid for or replaced under Part B.
SOURCE: Health Care Financing Administration, *Your Medicare Handbook 1997* (Baltimore, MD, 1997).

out-of-pocket health care expenditures decline, along with lost wages associated with missed work. In fact, a good part of staying healthy doesn't cost anything. Thus, maintaining a healthy lifestyle should be your first health care investment. Among those measures you should consider are the following:

• Have regular health care checkups.
• Quit smoking.

TABLE 10.2

Benefits Provided in the 10 Medigap Plans

A	B	C	D	E

Basic benefits	Basic benefits	Basic benefits
		Skilled nursing
		  coinsurance
			Basic benefits
			Skilled nursing
			  coinsurance
				Basic benefits
				Skilled nursing
				  coinsurance

	Part A deductible	Part A deductible
		Part B deductible
		Foreign travel
		  emergency
			Part A deductible
			
			Foreign travel
			  emergency
			At-home recovery
				Part A deductible
				
				Foreign travel
				  emergency
				
				Preventive care

F	G	H	I	J

Basic benefits
Skilled nursing
  coinsurance
Part A deductible
Part B deductible
Part B excess (100%)
Foreign travel
  emergency
	Basic benefits
	Skilled nursing
	  coinsurance
	Part A deductible
	
	Foreign travel
	  emergency
	At-home recovery
		Basic benefits
		Skilled nursing
		  coinsurance
		Part A deductible
		
		Foreign travel
		  emergency
		
		Basic drugs
		  ($1,250 limit)
			Basic benefits
			Skilled nursing
			  coinsurance
			Part A deductible
			
			Part B excess (100%)
			Foreign travel
			  emergency
			At-home recovery
			Basic drugs
			  ($1,250 limit)
				Basic benefits
				Skilled nursing
				  coinsurance
				Part A deductible
				Part B deductible
				Part B excess (100%)
				Foreign travel
				  emergency
				At-home recovery
				Extended drugs
				  ($3,000 limit)
				Preventive care

Basic Benefits: Included in all plans.
Hospitalization: Part A coinsurance plus coverage for 365 additional days after Medicare benefits end.
Medical Expenses: Part B coinsurance (20% of Medicare-approved expenses).
Blood: First 3 pints of blood each year.

SOURCE: Health Insurance Association of America, *Guide to Medicare Supplement Insurance* (Washington, DC, 1994).

- Exercise regularly.
- Eat healthy.
- Reduce stress.
- Get adequate rest.
- Eliminate excessive alcohol consumption.

    To gain an idea of the benefits of being healthy, let's just look at the savings experienced by a "two-pack-a-day" smoker who quits smoking. First, depending on how high your state's cigarette taxes are, the immediate savings could be up to $1,600. If you're in the 28-percent tax bracket, this figure translates to $2,222 of before-tax earnings. Now let's add on the savings from not getting lung cancer and not having a baby born with smoking-related illnesses. Of course, you'll have more expenses from living longer than you would if you kept on smoking.

    In addition to staying healthy, you can also help to control medical costs by using medical reimbursement accounts and, in some cases, opting out of your company's health care plan.

Medical Reimbursement Accounts

A **medical reimbursement** or **flexible spending account** is a savings plan established by an employer, which allows each employee to have pretax earnings deposited into a specially designated account for paying health care bills. Employees can withdraw funds from their accounts to offset unreimbursed medical or dental expenses or qualified child care. There's a cap set on the maximum that an employee can deposit into this account. In addition, there's a $5,000 ceiling set by the IRS for the child care portion of the account.

The biggest drawback to this plan is that any contributions to the flexible spending account not used by the end of the year are lost. In effect, it's a "use it or lose it" system. This means that care must be taken in estimating the amount of funds to be set aside in the account. Generally, it's a good idea to set aside only 80 percent of anticipated health care expenditures in order to avoid any forfeit of funds at year's end. The advantage of such a plan is that health care expenditures that are otherwise uncovered are made on a before-tax basis. For example, many people use their medical reimbursement accounts to cover the deductible from their insurance plan. Thus, for every $100 set aside into this account, taxable income is reduced by $100.

The advantages of a flexible spending plan are that it not only provides tax savings on unreimbursed health care expenditures, but also allows for pretax dollars to pay for other medical expenses that many health care plans do not cover, such as eyeglasses and orthodontia expenses. In fact, there is a good deal of flexibility with respect to how funds from a flexible spending plan can be used, as can be seen in Table 10.3.

Choosing No Coverage—Opting Out of Your Company Plan

As the cost of health care plans has rocketed, many firms have begun to look for ways to reduce health care costs as a means of increasing profitability. As a result more and more firms offer cash incentives to workers either to opt out of the firm's health care plan or to elect not to cover their families. In fact, presently about half of all companies allow for "opting out," and it's been estimated that up to 20 percent of those who can opt out do, receiving $300 and upward in cash or other benefits for opting out. For example, at Avon Products, Inc., about one-quarter of the 6,700 full-time workers opt out of the health care plan, freeing up $1,450 each in benefit credits. These workers can then either use these savings to buy other benefits or take the money in cash.

If your spouse also has health care coverage where he or she works, opting out may be reasonable. However, you must first consider what might happen if your spouse lost his or her job or if the company he or she works for discontinues health care coverage, perhaps in a downsizing move. The question becomes, Can you get back in your plan whenever you want? The answer depends upon your company. Some plans require a medical examination or only allow sign-up during an annual reenrollment period. If, however, opting out of your company's health care coverage means being left uncovered, then opting out probably doesn't make any sense at all. It's important not to get lured into trading your financial security for the "easy money" of opting out of health care coverage.

The Facts of Life

If you work for a company with 20 or more employees, you will, in general, be given the opportunity to continue your health care coverage for up to 18 months after you leave the company, regardless of whether you leave voluntarily. You are, of course, responsible for the cost of this insurance, but it will probably be less expensive than purchasing individual insurance.

TABLE 10.3

The Flexibility of Medical Reimbursement Accounts
A sampling of what medical reimbursement accounts generally can and can't be used for, based on Internal Revenue Service rules.

Can be used for:	Can't be used for:
Abortion	Baby-sitting and child care (may be reimbursed through flexible spending accounts for dependent care)
Acupuncture	
Artificial limb	
Braille books and magazines	
Cosmetic surgery (relating to congenital deformity or disfigurement from disease or injury)	Cosmetic surgery to improve appearance (face-lift, hair transplant, liposuction, etc.)
Removal of lead-based paint	Diapers
Nursing home care	Funeral expenses
Oxygen equipment	Health club dues
Psychoanalysis	Housekeeper
Special school for learning-disabled child	Maternity clothes
	Swimming lessons
Television equipment for the hearing impaired	Weight-loss program (for general health)

SOURCE: Nancy Ann Jeffrey, "Advance Planning," *Wall Street Journal*, October 24, 1996, p. R17. Reprinted by permission of *The Wall Street Journal*, © 1996 Dow Jones & Company, Inc. All Rights Reserved Worldwide.

LEARNING OBJECTIVE #5

Design a health care insurance program and understand what provisions are important to you.

FINDING THE PERFECT PLAN: THE PROVISIONS

What should you be looking for in a health insurance policy? First, it shouldn't allow for important exclusions and limitations, and it should include the full cost of basic services (minus your deductible). As Milton Berle once said, "The problem with a policy is that the big print giveth and the small print taketh away." Second, it should be noncancelable or guaranteed renewable. Don't understand what we just said? That's OK. You'll figure it out as we look at some of the important provisions provided in health insurance policies.

Who's Covered? Health insurance policies can cover individuals, families, or groups, for example, employees. If you have family coverage, you should have an understanding of (1) the age to which your children are covered and what happens if they're still dependents after this age, (2) what happens if you get divorced, and (3) whether stepchildren are covered. The point here is that you should have an understanding of exactly who's covered under your plan.

Stop and Think
Don't try to save money by buying less health insurance than you actually need—that only defeats the purpose of insurance, which is protection. You should also make sure your policy benefits keep up with inflation and your life circumstances. As such, you should review your policy every few years and whenever there's a major change, such as the birth of children, marriage, or divorce.

Terms of Payment. The terms of payment define what your financial obligation is on a health care claim, including any deductibles, coinsurance payments, limits on claims, and stop-loss provisions that are specified in your policy.

Deductibles or co-payments identify the amount of a claim that the policyholder pays on a claim. The higher the deductible, the lower the premium. It's a good idea to take the highest deductible that's available, because you get more coverage per dollar that way. High deductibles eliminate many smaller claims and also eliminate the administrative costs that go along with those claims. In this way, the insurance coverage is made more efficient and you accomplish your goal of providing protection against catastrophes due to the costs of health care.

There may also be limits set on specific claims. For example, there may be a maximum dollar amount that the policy will pay for specific operations. Alternatively, the limit may be set at what is customary in a particular geographic area.

In addition a stop-loss provision, which was discussed earlier and limits the total dollar amount that the policyholder is responsible for, may also be included in the policy. With stop-loss provision, when the policyholder reaches a set limit of spending, perhaps $4,000, the insurance company then takes full financial responsibility for any additional medical expenses incurred.

Preexisting Conditions. Most health insurance contains some type of preexisting condition provision, which excludes coverage for a specified length of time or forever for any preexisting illness that the policyholder may have. Obviously, this provision is meant to protect the insurance company and keep individuals from waiting until they identify health problems to sign up for health insurance.

Although it probably goes without saying, don't lie on your application—it could make the policy null and void. In addition, make sure you read your entire policy—don't assume the salesperson told you everything. Also, read all the updates that are sent to you—things can change.

Guaranteed Renewability. A **guaranteed renewability** provision allows you to renew your health insurance policy regardless of your health until you reach some preset age, generally 65. Although you can't be singled out for a rate increase, your premiums may rise if you are deemed more risky than before. Obviously, you want a health insurance plan you can always renew so that you don't get cut off if you get sick.

Noncancelable. A **noncancelable** provision ensures that your policy can't be canceled—that is, it guarantees renewability until you reach a preset age. It's similar to a guaranteed renewable policy, but it goes further in that it prevents premium rates from being raised. Because a noncancelable policy provides greater protection, it's more costly than a guaranteed renewable plan.

Exclusions. Some policies contain provisions that exclude certain injuries and illnesses. For example, costs associated with self-inflicted injuries, certain dental procedures, mental illness, injuries incurred when the covered individual commits a felony or misdemeanor, and cosmetic surgery are commonly excluded. Maternity expenses are also sometimes excluded, and coverage may not begin for children until they are 14 days old. Obviously, this last exclusion is amazingly unfair and shouldn't be accepted. The costs associated with having a child and the expenses that can occur during the first 14 days of a child's life are enormous. Without maternity coverage and immediate coverage for your children, you could easily wind up spending all your savings and more.

Emotional and Mental Disorders. As just mentioned, policies vary greatly with respect to the degree to which they allow for coverage of emotional and mental disorders. Today, stress-related disorders and depression, many times brought on by

Guaranteed Renewability
A health insurance provision that allows you to renew your policy regardless of your health until you reach some preset age, generally 65.

Noncancelable Provision
A health insurance provision that guarantees renewability, and guarantees that premium rates will not be raised.

chemical imbalances in the brain, are extremely common. Although some policies provide full coverage, others don't cover any of these costs, and still others provide only partial or limited coverage for a relatively short time period. In fact, costs from these disorders have risen so sharply in recent years that most policies require large co-payments or limit the number of annual visits to a psychiatrist or counselor. Given the very high costs that can be associated with emotional and mental disorders, it's a good idea to make sure your health insurance policy provides adequate coverage. Hey, you wouldn't want insurance worries to drive you crazy.

The Facts of Life

The best insurance is living a healthy, safe life. For young adults, this means driving safely. Auto accidents are the number one killer of teenagers. In fact, across the country teens make up 5 percent of the driving population, but account for 14 percent of the country's auto fatalities. Nearly half of all 16- to 19-year-old female deaths occur as a result of automobile accidents. Among boys of the same age, 36 percent of deaths are due to crashes. More than one-quarter of drivers under 21 killed on the roadways have blood alcohol content of 0.10 or higher. The likelihood of fatal crashes for teenagers is highest between 9 P.M. and 6 A.M.

Shopping for Health Insurance

If you don't have health insurance provided by your employer, you'll have to find it on your own. Unfortunately, an individual policy is expensive. That's why you'll want to see if you qualify for any group insurance, or if there are any groups you can join that would allow you to qualify for group insurance. The first rule in buying health care insurance is not to put the purchase off—you should buy health care insurance while you're healthy, because you may not be able to get it later. Figure 10.3 provides a number of suggestions on what you might look for.

It is extremely important that you buy health insurance while you are healthy if you don't have a policy through your place of employment. Once a health catastrophe occurs, it's unlikely that you'll be able to get affordable insurance to cover your health care costs. Health care insurance is too important to be without. Keep in mind that the bottom line is always with you. That is, your health care costs are your responsibility. After you have your health insurance, try to maintain a healthy lifestyle—its always better not to have the opportunity to use your insurance.

DISABILITY INSURANCE

Disability insurance is related to health insurance, but it's more like earning-power insurance. When a disability occurs, life, along with all its expenses, goes on. What stops is your income. Your house payments continue, your children's educational costs continue, food and utility costs continue, and your medical expenses generally rise—all while your income stops. Needless to say, that's a formula for financial disaster.

Who needs disability insurance? Anyone who relies on income from a job for financial support should have it. In fact, for individuals between the ages of 35 and 65, your chance of incurring a disability that'd cause you to miss 90 or more days of work is equal to your chance of dying. A 30-year-old has about a 47-percent chance of incurring a 90-day disability before the age of 65. Thus, you need disability insurance, even if you're single and without dependents. If you have dependents that rely on your

LEARNING OBJECTIVE #6

Describe disability insurance and the choices available to you in a disability insurance policy.

Disability Insurance
Health insurance that provides payments to the insured in the event that income is interrupted by illness, sickness, or accident.

FIGURE 10.3

Worksheet for Health Care Insurance Shopping

☑ The ideal plan is group health insurance through your employer.

☑ Don't put off buying health care insurance—buy it while you're healthy.

☑ Consider only a high-quality insurance company with either an A++ or an A+ rating from A. M. Best. Never consider TV-celebrity-advertised insurance.

☑ Look for group insurance—it's generally cheaper.

☑ Look for companies that provide fast, fair, and courteous claim service.

☑ Avoid policies with major exclusions and limitations.

☑ Get comprehensive health insurance; avoid single disease (like cancer) insurance and accident (as opposed to comprehensive health including illness) insurance.

☑ Only consider insurance that is noncancelable or guaranteed renewable.

☑ Consider Blue Cross and Blue Shield.

☑ Consider joining an HMO or PPO.

☑ Take as high a deductible and coinsurance payments as you can afford. This reduces your premiums greatly.

☑ Consider a policy that covers mental and emotional disorders.

earning power, this insurance is a must. Remember, disability insurance kicks in only if there's a financial catastrophe in the offing. Therefore, it fits in perfectly with our view of necessary insurance.

Given its importance, why are so many people without it? The answer is, the price. Although the price varies greatly depending upon your age, health, and occupation, in addition to the dollar amount of coverage and how long you're disabled before the policy kicks in, it's easy to spend over $1,000 per year on disability insurance. Your occupation may have the biggest impact on what your coverage costs. Insurers generally classify customers into one of five risk classes depending upon their occupation. For example, a college professor is generally classified as a class 5 risk, and a construction worker is classified as a class 1 risk. These ratings, in turn, are reflected in the rates that are charged, with the college professor being given a lower rate than a construction worker because the college professor has a lower probability of becoming disabled.

Sources of Disability Insurance

Many employers provide some level of disability insurance as part of their benefits package. Other employers, who don't include it in their benefits package, may make group disability insurance available to you at favorable prices. If you're self-employed, you'll have to find a group plan that's available to you or purchase an individual policy. Still, most individuals have some degree of coverage from Social Security or workers' compensation.

Disability Coverage Through Workers' Compensation. Although most workers are covered by some form of workers' compensation, these benefits apply only if the disability is work-related. As mentioned earlier, the degree of workers' compensation coverage is determined by the individual states and, as a result, there's a good deal of variability in coverage from state to state. Thus, you shouldn't assume that you're covered or that your coverage is comprehensive.

Disability Coverage Through Social Security. For those covered by Social Security, which includes most workers, there are some disability benefits available. These benefits vary according to the number of years you've been in the Social Security system and your salary. However, if you qualify, you don't receive any payments until you've been disabled for 5 months, and then you receive benefits only if your disability is expected to last for at least 1 year or until death. Moreover, in order to qualify for benefits, you must not be able to work at any job, not just what you were trained for. You can see that Social Security disability benefits, although available, are administered under very strict and narrow guidelines. To get an estimate of what these benefits might be, you can call the Social Security Administration at 800-772-1213 for a Personal Earnings and Benefits Estimate Statement.

How Much Disability Coverage Should You Have?

There's no standard rule as to how much disability insurance you should have. Basically, you should have enough disability insurance to maintain your living standard at an acceptable level if you were no longer able to work. Remember, your investment income won't stop with a disability, it's your income from working that'll stop, and it's the portion of your income from working that you rely on to maintain your current standard of living that must be replaced. Thus, if you've accumulated some investments and are earning more than you need to live on—that is, saving a good portion of your earnings—you may need to replace only 30 percent of your after-tax income. However, someone with little savings who's living hand-to-mouth may need disability insurance that covers 80 percent of his or her after-tax income. Interestingly, most insurance companies don't write disability insurance policies that cover over 67 to 80 percent of a person's after-tax salary. They figure that if too much of your income is covered, you won't have an incentive to go back to work. Notice that the discussion focuses on the replacement of after-tax income. Although the insurance premiums that you pay on disability income aren't tax-deductible, disability income is generally treated as tax-free income. Figure 10.4 provides a worksheet that you can use to get an estimate of how much disability insurance coverage you might want or need.

The Facts of Life

Finding affordable insurance is a tough task. In shopping around you should consider contacting USAA (800-531-8000), which sells directly to customers, bypassing insurance agents, and Quotesmith (800-556-9393), which will provide you with a listing of companies with low rates. Another good source of information is the National Insurance Consumer Helpline (800-942-4242).

Disability Insurance Features That Make Sense

Disability insurance policies vary more from insurance company to company than do health insurance policies. Therefore, you really need to have an idea of what's desirable in a disability plan. Here are a few key features to look out for.

The Definition of Disability. What exactly does your policy consider a disability? In general, most policies define people as disabled if they can't perform the duties of their "own occupation" or perform the duties of "any occupation for which reasonably suited." Unfortunately, deciding what occupation for which you are "reasonably suited" may be difficult at best. Thus, it's wise to stick with a policy that defines an individual as disabled if you can't perform your normal job.

FIGURE 10.4

Worksheet for Estimating How Much Disability Insurance Coverage You Need

1. Current monthly after-tax job related income* _____

2. Existing disability coverage on an *after-tax-basis*

   - Social Security benefits† _____

   - Disability insurance from employer + _____

   - Veterans' benefits and other federal and state disability insurance + _____

   - Other disability coverage in place + _____

   Total existing coverage = _____

3. Added disability coverage needed to maintain current level of after-tax job-related income in the event of a disability (subtract 2 from 1) _____

Note: We haven't included workers' compensation disability benefits because they accompany only work-related injuries.
*Keep in mind that your investment income won't stop with a disability. Only your income from working will stop. Thus, only the portion of your income from working that you rely upon to maintain your current standard of living must be replaced. This may also include savings for goals like your children's college education and other goals. However, you should keep in mind that your goals will generally change substantially if you are permanently disabled.
†To get an estimate of what these benefits might be, you can call the Social Security Administration at (800) 772-1213 for a Personal Earnings and Benefits Estimate Statement.

An alternative to these definitions involves a combination definition. Under the combination definition, you're covered if you can't perform your "own occupation" for the first 2 years of your disability. Thereafter, you're covered if you can't perform "any occupation for which you're reasonably suited." Defining "disability" in this way promotes retraining during the first 2 years of your disability. Policies using this definition tend to be less expensive than those that use only the "own occupation" definition. Given the cost trade-offs, you might want to give serious consideration to policies that use a combination definition.

Residual or Partial Payments When Returning to Work Part-Time. Some policies offer partial disability payments that allow workers to return to work on a part-time basis and still receive benefits. These payments make up the difference between what workers would make if working full-time and their part-time earnings. Partial disability payments are a desirable feature, especially for the self-employed whose earnings reflect the number of hours worked.

Benefit Duration. Disability policies generally provide benefits for either a maximum period, or until the disability ends (or the disabled person reaches 65 or 70 years of age). A **short-term disability (STD)** policy generally provides benefits on disabilities of from 6 months to 2 years after a short wait of 8 to 30 days. A **long-term disability (LTD)** policy generally provides benefits until the individual reaches an age specified in the contract, generally 65 or 70, or for the insured's lifetime. Only a long-term disability policy makes any sense, because only a long-term disability policy protects against the financial catastrophe that can accompany a disability.

Short-Term Disability (STD)
A disability policy that provides benefits over a given period, generally from 6 months to 2 years.

Long-Term Disability (LTD)
A disability policy that provides benefits until the individual reaches an age specified in the contract, generally 65 or 70, or for the insured's lifetime.

Waiting or **Elimination Period**
The period after the disability during which no benefits occur.

Waiver of Premium Provision
A disability insurance provision that allows your insurance to stay in force should you become unable to work due to disability or illness.

Rehabilitation Coverage
A disability insurance provision that allows payments for vocational rehabilitation, allowing the policyholder to be retrained for employment.

LEARNING OBJECTIVE #7

Explain the purpose of long-term care insurance and the provisions that might be important to you.

Long-Term Care Insurance
Insurance that's aimed at covering the costs associated with long-term nursing home care, commonly associated with victims of stroke, chronic illness, or Alzheimer's disease, or those who can simply no longer manage to live on their own.

Waiting (or Elimination) Period. The **waiting** or **elimination period** refers to the period after the disability during which no benefits occur. Another way of thinking about the waiting period is that it's equivalent to a deductible in a health care insurance policy—you must absorb the lost income during the waiting period. Most disability policies have waiting periods that range from 1 month to 6 months. Of course, the longer the waiting period, the less expensive the contract. In fact, a contract with a 3-month waiting period might lower costs by almost 30 percent from a contract with a 1-month waiting period. Moreover, keep in mind that the purpose of insurance is not to offset all of your medical costs, only the catastrophic ones. Thus, with sick pay and emergency savings, you may have already planned for a short period of disability. What disability insurance must protect you against is the loss of income associated with longer-term illnesses. Thus, in light of the cost differences, you should give serious consideration to a 3-month waiting period.

Waiver of Premium. In general, it's a good idea to have a **waiver of premium provision** in your contract, which waives premium payments if you become disabled, but be sure to look closely at the costs.

Noncancelable. You should also insist on a policy that's "noncancelable." This provision protects you against having your policy canceled if, for whatever reason, your risk of becoming disabled increases, and it guarantees that the policy is renewable. It also protects you against rate increases.

Rehabilitation Coverage. A **rehabilitation coverage** provision provides for vocational rehabilitation, allowing the policyholder to be retrained for employment. This coverage generally provides for employment-related educational or job-training programs so that the policyholder can become self-sufficient.

LONG-TERM CARE INSURANCE

Long-term care insurance pays for nursing home expenses as well as home health care. When first introduced some 20 years ago, it was marketed strictly as "nursing home insurance," but it has evolved to meet the needs of those individuals who need care but still can stay in their own home. The insurance is meant to cover the costs associated with long-term care commonly associated with those who have had strokes, chronic diseases, or Alzheimer's disease, as well as those who can simply no longer manage to live on their own. In effect, it's another form of disability insurance. Its downside is that it's expensive, and, as such, you should understand the benefits and alternatives that are available.

It would seem that long-term health care should either be a part of major medical insurance or covered under Medicare. It isn't. This is actually a relatively new area of coverage for insurance. It's been partially inspired by our increasing life expectancies and the resultant increase in the chance that you may eventually need some level of care. The interest in long-term health care coverage has also been inspired by the high cost of such care. For example, today, the cost of nursing home care averages around $40,000 per year, with some nursing homes charging far more.

Long-term health care insurance is meant to protect you against the financial consequences of these costs. These policies are generally set up to provide a daily dollar benefit over the time the policyholder requires nursing home care. These payments are generally sent directly to the nursing home to cover charges. They're generally not available to individuals under 40 years of age, with the premiums rising for older policyholders. In fact, the premiums that a 50-year-old would be charged are generally around one-third of what a 70-year-old policyholder is charged.

Unfortunately, many long-term care insurance policies come laden with exceptions and conditions. Moreover, this lack of understanding and uniformity associated with some policies allows them to be sold not as a part of a financial plan, but through the use of fear tactics.

Finally, if you're going to purchase long-term health care insurance, make sure you do so while you're healthy. As with other types of health care insurance, it's available only when you don't need it. It should also only be purchased from high-quality insurance companies. Table 10.4 provides a listing of some of the provisions that you might want to have included in a long-term health care policy.

Who Should Consider Long-Term Health Care Insurance?

- **It's intended only for those who have savings they want to protect.** If you don't have funds to cover nursing home care, Medicaid, which is aimed at the needy, will cover your costs.

- **If you have money but don't have dependents, you should consider passing on long-term health care insurance, and if you need nursing home care, pay for it out of your savings.** After all, you saved that money to provide for you in retirement.

- **If there's a history of long-term disabilities, Alzheimer's, or Parkinson's disease in your family, you should consider long-term health care.**

Most policies require the insured to be unable to perform one or more "activities of daily living" (ADLs) without assistance. These ADLs include such tasks as walking, dressing, and eating. Some plans also allow for cognitive impairment, such as the short-term memory loss suffered by Alzheimer's and Parkinson's disease patients, as sufficient for benefits. You should consider only policies that include coverage for Alzheimer's and Parkinson's disease.

TABLE 10.4

Long-Term Health Care Provisions

Necessary

Selection of Company. Consider only high-quality insurance companies with either an A++ or an A+ rating from A. M. Best. Never consider TV-celebrity-advertised insurance.
Qualifying for Benefits. The insured is unable to perform *at most* two "activities of daily living" (ADLs) without assistance.
Qualifying for Benefits. Policy includes coverage for Alzheimer's and Parkinson's disease.
Qualifying for Benefits. Hospital stay not required for benefits.
Benefit Period. A minimum 3- to 6-year benefit period.
Inflation Adjustment. The policy should give you the option of purchasing inflation coverage.
Noncancelability. The policy should not be cancelable.

Desirable, but Not Necessary—Cost-Benefit Trade-Offs Must Be Considered

Type of Care. Home care, adult day care, and hospice care for the terminally ill are all desirable provisions.
Benefit Period. Women should consider longer benefit periods.

Cost-Reducing Provision to Consider

Waiting Period. Consider a waiting period of 100 days or more—if affordable.

Provisions to Avoid—Not Worth the Cost

Waiver of Premium. While desirable, it may be too expensive to warrant serious consideration.
Nonforfeiture Provision. Simply too expensive.

Type of Care.
Policies also vary with respect to coverage of home care. Some policies only provide nursing home care, while others provide for adult day care and hospice care for the terminally ill. It's a good idea to seek out a policy with flexible coverage provisions and a home care option.

Benefit Period.
Benefit periods on long-term health care insurance can range all the way from 1 year to lifetime. Unfortunately, lifetime coverage provisions tend to be very expensive. However, because the average stay in a nursing home is under 2 years, you should make sure that your coverage has a minimum 3- to 6-year benefit period. In addition, because women tend to spend longer periods in nursing care than men, women should consider a longer benefit period.

Waiting Period.
Just as with disability insurance, the waiting period on long-term care insurance can be thought of as a deductible—you have to absorb the expense of nursing home care during the waiting period. This waiting period can run anywhere from 0 days up to a full year—but the most common is a waiting period of from 0 to 100 days. As you might expect, the longer the waiting period, the less the cost of the insurance. To keep costs down, you should consider taking as long a waiting period as you can afford.

Inflation Adjustment.
There's no telling how much the cost of nursing home care will be when you need it. If nursing home costs increase by 5 percent per year, they will double in only 15 years. Thus, without some inflation protection, your policy may not be of much help when you need it. To solve this problem, you should make sure to include an inflation protection provision if you buy long-term health care insurance.

Waiver of Premium.
A waiver of premium provision allows your insurance to stay in force while you are receiving benefits. The costs associated with this provision can vary dramatically from policy to policy and generally it is simply too expensive—be careful.

SUMMARY

Health insurance serves the same purpose as other forms of insurance—to protect you and your dependents from a financial catastrophe, in this case caused by health problems. Most health insurance includes a combination of hospital, surgical, and physician expense insurance, which are generally sold in a combination called basic health insurance. Major medical expense insurance is aimed at covering medical costs beyond those covered by basic health insurance. In effect, where basic health insurance leaves off, major medical expense insurance takes over.

The basic choices of health care providers are traditional fee-for-service plans and managed health care or prepaid care. Under a fee-for-service or traditional indemnity plan, you're reimbursed for all or part of your medical expenditures, and, in general, you have a good deal of freedom to choose your own doctor and hospital. Many times under a fee-for-service plan, there's a deductible or coinsurance fee charged. A deductible is the amount that the insured must pay before the insurance company will begin paying benefits, and a coinsurance or percentage participation provision defines the percentage of each claim that the insurance company will pay.

Under a managed health care or prepaid care plan, you're entitled to the health care of a specified group of participating doctors, hospitals, and clinics. The big advantage of a managed health care plan is its efficiency. The most popular form of managed health care is the health maintenance organization, or HMO, which is a prepaid insurance plan that entitles members to the services of participating doctors, hospitals, and clinics. There are three basic types of HMOs: individual practice association plans, group practice plans, and point-of-service plans.

Another alternative is a preferred provider organization (PPO), which is something of a cross between a traditional fee-for-service plan and an HMO. Under the PPO an employer or insurer negotiates with a group of doctors and hospitals to provide health care for its employees or members at reduced rates.

INSURANCE Won't Patch Hole in Medicaid Safety Net

Even with all of the caveats, some estate-planning attorneys and financial planners say long-term-care insurance can be a good idea for people who have assets they want to protect yet aren't wealthy enough that they could self-insure. If that is you—or maybe a parent you want to help—it is important to choose a policy very carefully.

Insurers have vigorously fought the type of rigorous federal standards that finally led to a consumer-friendly market for "Medigap" insurance, which picks up certain costs that aren't covered under Medicare. (Medicare, the federal health program for seniors, provides only a limited nursing-home benefit.) Also since many insurers have gotten into the long-term-care business as recently as the past decade, they don't have any real track record for paying claims.

As a general rule, consumer advocates say, people shouldn't spend more than 5% to 7% of their incomes on long-term-care premiums.

Here are some other tips to keep in mind:

(A)
- If you wait until you're sick or very old, it is too late. Folks who apply after they've been diagnosed with Alzheimer's disease or some other disabling condition will be rejected, while even healthy people in their mid-70s may face premiums that can run as high as $5,000 a year or more, says Daniel Fish, an elder-law attorney in New York.

(B)
- If you can't afford a good policy, forget it. While such features as home-care benefits and inflation indexing raise premium costs, it is essential to have inflation protection on a policy you may not use for a couple of decades. Moreover, many seniors are able to stay at home if they get help with such tasks as meal preparation, bathing or dressing.

- Check out employer-sponsored plans. More than 1,000 employers now offer long-term-care insurance, though only a handful pay any part of the premium.

(C)
- Choose your insurance agent carefully.

Source: Nancy Ann Jeffrey, "Insurance Won't Patch Hole in Medicaid Safety Net," *The Wall Street Journal,* November 16, 1995, p. C1. Reprinted by permission of *The Wall Street Journal,* © 1996 Dow Jones & Company, Inc. All Rights Reserved Worldwide.

Analysis and Implications ...

A. Premiums drop significantly if you're younger. Consider a policy that provides 4 years of nursing-home benefits with a reimbursement rate of $120 a day, home-care coverage at a $60 daily rate, and an inflation rider that increases benefits at a 5 percent annual compounded rate. That coverage would cost $1,616 a year for a 65-year-old, $862 for a 55-year-old, and $600 for a 45-year-old.

B. Just remember, the home care benefits in most long-term care policies are designed to supplement unpaid help provided by family and friends. Unless you have such a support network, the coverage will be of little or no use, says Priscilla Itscoitz, manager of the health insurance counseling program for the United Seniors Health Cooperative in Washington.

C. An independent agent who specializes in long-term care insurance—rather than an agent who works for one company—may be more likely to give you useful information comparing companies' underwriting procedures, claims-payment histories, and other vital information.

There are two basic types of insurance providers: private or government-sponsored, with private plans including both individual health insurance policies and group insurance policies. Government-sponsored plans fall into two categories: state plans, which provide for work-related accidents and illness under state workers' compensation laws, and federal plans, such as Medicare and Medicaid.

One way to reduce health care costs further is through a medical reimbursement or flexible spending account, which is a plan established by the employer allowing each employee to have pretax earnings deposited into a specially designated account for the purposes of paying health care bills. The employee can withdraw funds from this account to offset unreimbursed medical or dental expenses or qualified child care.

Finding the perfect plan should allow for coverage that reflects the needs of your family. Some of the important provisions provided in health insurance policies include the following:

- Who is covered
- Terms of payment
- Preexisting conditions
- Guaranteed renewability
- Exclusions
- Emotional and mental disorders

Disability insurance provides income in the event of a disability. Who needs disability insurance? Anyone who relies upon income from a job for financial support should have disability insurance. Many employers provide some level of disability insurance as part of the benefits package they provide to employees.

Long-term care insurance is another form of disability insurance that covers the cost of long-term nursing home care.

Review Questions

1. List three reasons why health care costs have increased faster than the rate of inflation. (LO 1)
2. What is the major risk of not having health insurance? (LO 1)
3. What is the difference between basic health insurance and major medical insurance? (LO 2)
4. Define the following insurance terms: coinsurance, deductible, lifetime cap, and stop-loss provision. (LO 2)
5. Why are dental and eye insurance, dread disease insurance, and accident insurance not recommended? (LO 2)
6. What is the difference between a fee-for-service health care plan and managed health care? (LO 2)
7. Describe the similarities and differences between an HMO and a PPO health plan. (LO 3)
8. Describe the major differences between group health insurance and individual health insurance. (LO 3)
9. Describe the following government-sponsored health care plans: workers' compensation, Medicare, and Medicaid. (LO 3)
10. List five steps that people can take to help control health care costs by maintaining a healthy lifestyle. (LO 4)
11. What are some factors to consider before opting out of an employer-sponsored health insurance plan? (LO 5)
12. Define the following health care policy terms: guaranteed renewable, noncancelable, and preexisting condition. (LO 2)
13. What is disability insurance? Why is it important, and how much coverage should consumers purchase? (LO 6)
14. Define the following disability insurance terms: benefit duration, definition of

Just Do It! *From the Desk of Marcy Furney, CFP*
Disability—The Secret Risk

Though health insurance has been considered an essential risk control for many years, few people recognize the potential devastation disability represents. How do you get past the "secrecy"?

☑ Face reality. The media report death in great detail, but give only current hospital status of the injured. We hear "guarded condition," not "severe brain damage and will never function as a normal human again." When was the last time you read in the paper that someone was diagnosed with multiple sclerosis? Statistically you are many times more likely to lose income from an extended illness than you are to die.

☑ Check immediately on disability benefits provided by your employer. If you're in the majority of American workers, you'll find you have none.

☑ If you do have coverage through work, check the definition of disability, benefit amount, length of time benefits are paid, when they start, and how they are reduced by Social Security or other public programs. Some group policies offer an option that will increase the benefit or improve the overall plan, but you usually have to pay for it yourself. It may be money well spent.

☑ Remember that disability insurance paid for by your employer yields benefits that are taxable to you. Can you live on 50 or 60 percent of your pay if you have to pay taxes on that amount? Examine your budget and cash flow to see what impact such a reduction would make.

☑ If you have no coverage, set a deadline to obtain a policy and get busy.

☑ Professionals may have access to insurance through an association. Beware that the association, not you, controls the benefits and the insuring company. Will the association decide to change carriers, or will the company drop the association and leave you unprotected?

☑ Look into personal policies to supplement any benefits you have. You must disclose existing coverage to the company that offers the supplement, and you probably won't be able to insure 100 percent of your income. Though group benefits are reduced by any Social Security payments, they normally aren't affected by payments from a personal policy.

☑ Business owners should investigate disability overhead coverage, which will pay operating expenses to keep the company afloat. Personal income policies for owners cover only a percentage of their actual salary or net income.

☑ If your spouse's income is necessary for survival, make sure he or she is covered, too. Share the secret.

---

disability, residual (partial) payments, and waiting (elimination) period. (LO 5)

15. Describe long-term care insurance. What policy features should a person considering a long-term care policy look for? (LO 7)

Problems and Activities

1. Jane Keno has a major medical policy with a $500 deductible, 80/20 coinsurance, and a $3,000 stop-loss limit. Recently, she had surgery and her bills totaled $5,250. How much of this amount will she have to pay out-of-pocket? How much will her insurance policy pay? (LO 2)

2. Mike and Tracie Martin have a 3-month-old son, Jake, who recently needed surgery to correct a number of birth defects. Their hospital bills totaled $120,000. Tracie works part-time and has no health benefits. Mike has a group major

WWW.
Take It to the Net

We invite you to visit the Keown Personal Finance page on the Prentice Hall Web site at:

http://www.prenhall.com/persfin

for this chapter's World Wide Web exercise.

You might also want to visit the following Web sites:

Health Care Financing Administration (Medicare and Medicaid information): http://www.hcfa.gov/

Health Insurance Resource Center (definitions, tips, questions and answers): http://www.membership.com/insurance.html

medical policy with a $250,000 lifetime cap. What steps, if any, should the Martins take to change their health insurance? (LO 4)

3. The Gibson family has a basic health insurance plan that pays 80 percent of out-of-hospital expenses up to $3,000 a year after a deductible of $250 per person. If three family members have doctor and prescription drug expenses of $480, $340, and $220, respectively, how much will the Gibsons and the insurance company each pay? (LO 2)

4. Ralph Thomas participates in a flexible spending account established by his employer. This year, he put $2,000 of pretax earnings into this account. What will happen to the money in this account if Ralph's medical expenses total only $1,000? How can he avoid future differences between planned and actual expenses? (LO 3)

5. Sam and Wendy Erwin each have group health insurance provided by their employers. Both health plans are adequate, with a $1 million lifetime limit. Recently, Sam's employer announced that it'll pay $150 a month in cash to those who "opt out" of the plan. Once an employee is "dropped," he or she can be reinstated only once a year at a designated time. Wendy's employer plan can cover Sam for an additional cost of $100 a month but, again, he can only sign up at a certain time. Discuss the pros and cons of "opting out." (LO 4)

6. Doris Lewis has a choice at work between a traditional health insurance plan that pays 80 percent of the cost of doctor visits after a $250 deductible and an HMO that charges a $10 co-payment per visit plus a $10 deduction once a month from her paycheck. Doris anticipates seeing a doctor once a month for her high blood pressure. The cost of each office visit is $50. Comment on the difference in costs between the two health care plans and the advantages and disadvantages of each. (LO 2)

7. Sandra Rios has a take-home pay of $2,000 per month and a disability policy that replaces 60 percent of earnings after a 90-day (3-month) waiting period. Assume she injures herself in an auto accident and is out of work for 4 months. How much income would she lose and how much would be replaced by her disability policy? How else could she replace her lost earnings? (LO 6)

8. Heather Avery has a disability insurance policy with a 1-month elimination period and residual benefits that pay the difference between full-time and part-time earnings. She was recently diagnosed with cancer and can only work 20 hours a week, instead of 40, as she receives various medical treatments. Heather's after-tax, full-time salary is $3,000 per month. She expects to work part-time for 6 months. How much will she receive in disability benefits? (LO 6)

9. Concetta Diaz is 62 and considering the purchase of a 3-year long-term care policy. If nursing home costs average $4,000 per month in her area, how much could she have to pay out-of-pocket for 3 years without long-term care insurance? What can Concetta do to reduce the cost of coverage? (LO 7)

Suggested Projects

1. Make a list of health care services that you or a family member received during the past year. Compute the percentage that was paid by the person receiving the care and by the health insurance carrier. (LO 1)

2. Read a health insurance policy or information about group health care benefits. Prepare a one-page report of the key features of the insurance. (LO 2)

3. Ask a friend or family member to discuss benefits that he or she receives as an employee (for example, health or disability insurance) and the dollar value, if known. Write a one-page report of your findings. (LO 3)

4. Interview an insurance agent about a particular type of health insurance (for example, disability or long-term care). Write a one-page report of your findings. (LO 2)

5. Find an article about health care costs or health insurance in a recent newspaper or magazine. Write a one-page summary. (LO 2)

6. Talk to one or more senior citizens about their experiences with Medicare and/or supplemental (Medigap) health insurance. Write a one-page report of your findings. (LO 4)
7. Begin or improve an activity associated with maintaining a healthy lifestyle (for example, diet or exercise). Maintain this activity for at least a week. Write a one-page report about your experience. (LO 4)
8. Interview your doctor about health insurance. What does he or she recommend? (LO 4)

Discussion Case 1

Ralph Corydon is thinking about switching jobs. His current job pays well, but it requires 60 hours of work and a 20-hour weekly commute. Ralph wants to have more free time. His job provides excellent health care benefits, which he hopes he can match at a job with a new employer. So far, however, Ralph hasn't found a job that he likes with a comparable health insurance plan.

Ralph's wife, Cassie, is self-employed and relies on Ralph's benefits package for her health insurance. She's been trying to get pregnant for the past year, but, so far, the couple has had no luck conceiving their first child. Cassie is concerned about possible gaps in the family's health coverage should Ralph change jobs.

Questions

1. What factors should Ralph consider as he compares the health benefits packages offered by potential employers?
2. What can Ralph and Cassie do to make sure that they have adequate health coverage if he changes jobs?
3. What health insurance policy features should the Corydons consider when they become parents?
4. What other type of health insurance coverage should Ralph and Cassie purchase?
5. What government-sponsored health benefits could the Corydons possibly qualify for?

Discussion Case 2

Joan Holly has recently learned about the importance of disability insurance and wants to buy a policy. She earns $2,800 per month after taxes, plus another $500 a month from earnings on her investments. Joan wants to replace 70 percent of her income from working with a disability insurance policy that pays benefits to age 65. She's accumulated 80 sick days at work and has no existing disability coverage.

Joan doesn't live in a state that provides short-term disability insurance. She'd rather not count on Social Security disability coverage either, because she knows it's difficult to qualify for. Joan is also looking for the most affordable policy possible. She wants to get the best policy features at the lowest cost.

Questions

1. How much disability insurance does Joan need to replace 70 percent of her monthly after-tax earnings?
2. What length of elimination period should Joan select?
3. What other disability insurance policy features should Joan purchase?
4. Will Joan have to pay federal income tax on any disability insurance benefits that are received? If yes, how much?

Chapter 11

THE ROLE OF PROPERTY AND LIABILITY INSURANCE

There are very few places as beautiful as Malibu, California. It's home to famous surf and even more famous stars, including Steven Spielberg, Bruce Willis, Demi Moore, Nick Nolte, Mel Brooks, Tom Hanks, and Sylvester Stallone. In 1993, however, it was home to fire. Fire fed by the seasonal Santa Ana winds roared through Malibu, destroying some homes yet miraculously leaving others untouched. Actress Ali McGraw lost her home, and the same was reported for Charles Bronson, Gary Busey, and Bruce Willis and Demi Moore. Those stories later proved to be untrue—their homes escaped damage thanks to the efforts of the firefighters who worked around the clock to control the blaze. So used to being applauded themselves, these stars gave credit where it was more than due and applauded the actions of some mighty brave and dedicated firefighters. In fact, the next day Charles Bronson and Mark Hamill (Luke Skywalker of *Star Wars* fame) spent the day personally thanking the firefighters. However, for the less fortunate—for those who lost their homes—it was their insurance agents who were thanked.

Living just a few hills away, Barbara and John Lane were some of the less fortunate, losing their entire house and all that was in it. However, before the ashes stopped smoldering, a State Farm representative was on the scene giving the Lanes a check for $5,000 temporary living expenses. Although the Lanes were still in shock, they certainly would have been in worse shape without some help from their insurance. State Farm agent Jim Lawler was on the scene at 5:45 in the morning, taking care of his clients and his friends. "These [clients] are my friends," said Lawler. "I've been an agent here since 1963, and I know these people. I raised four kids with them through parochial schools and high schools." For the Lanes, seeing Jim Lawler had special meaning. It was at his gentle prodding that they'd recently purchased a more expensive home insurance policy that allowed them to replace their home using materials that are up to today's stricter fire and earthquake codes. For others, the worth of their insurance policy was sorely tested. "I know our home was destroyed," were the words of Zari Shalchi upon seeing her burned-out

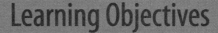

Learning Objectives

After reading this chapter you should be able to:

1. Understand, buy, and maintain home-owner's insurance in a cost-effective way.

2. Recover on a liability or a loss to your property.

3. Buy the automobile insurance policy that's right for you.

4. File a claim on your automobile insurance.

home for the first time. "I knew it, but I had to see it. . . . Insurance? I don't know the company's name. My husband does, I think."

People don't like to think about their homes burning down or being destroyed by an earthquake or hurricane, nor do they like to think about what might happen if they were in an automobile accident. It's like having a cavity filled—you don't want to think about it, you'd rather just deal with it if and when it happens. That was certainly the case with the Shalchis. Unfortunately, when it comes to your home burning or having an automobile accident, if you haven't prepared for it ahead of time with insurance, the experience becomes much worse.

Just as with health and life insurance, the logic behind property insurance is drawn from **Axiom 3: Diversification Reduces Risk**. In this case, property insurance allows individuals to pool the financial risks associated with property losses—such as a fire, burglary, or auto accident—to eliminate any catastrophic losses that might be associated with them. Everyone shares in everyone else's property losses by paying the average cost. As a result, no one experiences a catastrophic loss.

The purpose of homeowner's and automobile insurance and the other types of insurance is also the same: to guard against financial catastrophes. As with health and life insurance discussed in the previous two chapters, the need for property insurance rises from **Axiom 10: Protect Yourself Against Major Catastrophes—The Case for Insurance**. In the case of property insurance, our philosophy continues to be to provide protection against major catastrophes while ignoring the small stuff. It's not the $60 broken window that you should be concerned about—it's the $60,000 damage from a fire that could wipe out your entire savings if you don't have homeowner's insurance. Specifically, the insurance in this chapter protects you against the financial risks of loss of or damage to your home or automobile and the legal liabilities associated with injuries or property damage to others. Unfortunately, homeowner's and automobile insurance policies, just like life and health insurance policies, are filled with their own jargon. Also, deciding on how much and exactly what kind of insurance to buy is confusing and difficult. Don't worry, though. This chapter will teach you what you need to know to manage your homeowner's and automobile insurance like a pro.

AXIOM #3

Diversification Reduces Risk

AXIOM #10

Protect Yourself Against Major Catastrophes—The Case for Insurance

Peril

An event or happening, whether natural or man-made, that causes a financial loss.

HO's

The six standardized "homeowner's" insurance policies available to homeowners and renters.

Named Perils

A type of insurance that covers a specific set of named perils. If a peril isn't specifically named, it isn't covered.

Open Perils

A type of insurance that covers all perils except those specifically noted as excluded.

PROTECTING YOUR HOME

In the United States, the first type of homeowner's insurance was fire insurance, offered in 1735 by a small company in Charleston, South Carolina. However, it wasn't until 1958 that the first modern "homeowner's" policy was sold.

Before homeowner's insurance, separate insurance policies were needed for every **peril**—that is, an insurance policy to cover fire, theft, windstorm damage, and so forth. Homeowner's insurance simplified the process of buying home-related insurance by offering protection against multiple perils in one overarching policy. This new type of policy gave families peace of mind in knowing that they were covered against most major perils without having to run around and comparison shop for a million different insurance policies. It also helped families keep better track of their coverage by consolidating what would have previously been numerous different policies, probably with numerous different companies. Today's homeowner's insurance policies are standardized, sold in only six basic versions. Of course, you can add extra forms of coverage and individualize your insurance, but this standardization makes comparison shopping for homeowner's insurance easy—much easier than shopping for any other type of insurance. Unfortunately, standardization has actually stifled competition a bit. As a result, the homeowner's insurance industry is dominated by the five largest insurers, which insure about half of all homes. Let's take a look at these six standardized policies.

Packaged Policies: The HO's

Today's six basic homeowner's policies are known as **HO's**, which stands for homeowner's. Although they're called homeowner's insurance, they cover more than your home. They also provide liability insurance and cover renters. Three of them, HO-1, HO-2, and HO-3, provide basic, broad policies specifically for homeowners. Policy HO-4 is actually renter's insurance, HO-6 is for condominium owners, and HO-8 is for older homes. Here's a brief look at the typical HO policies currently offered.

- **HO-1: Basic form homeowner's insurance.** This form of homeowner's insurance provides very narrow coverage. As a result, it isn't available in most states.

- **HO-2: Broad form homeowner's insurance.** Although this form of homeowner's insurance provides broad coverage, it's a **named perils** form of insurance. That is, it specifically covers a set of named perils, such as fire, lightning, windstorm, hail, explosions, and so on. If a peril isn't specifically named in this policy, it isn't covered. Also, if that particular unnamed peril just so happens to turn your house into a pile of broken timber, you're stuck. This type of coverage generally costs 5 to 10 percent more than HO-1 coverage.

- **HO-3: Special form homeowner's insurance.** The only difference between HO-2 and HO-3 is the way they cover perils. This insurance is more comprehensive in its coverage because it covers all direct physical losses to your home. It offers **open perils** protection, meaning it covers all perils except those specifically noted as excluded. Excluding perils might include floods, earthquakes, wars, and nuclear accidents. Typically, this type of coverage costs 10 to 15 percent more than an HO-1 policy.

- **HO-4: Renter's or tenant's insurance.** This insurance is the same as HO-2, but is instead aimed at renters or tenants. Do you think you're covered by your landlord's insurance? You aren't! Let's say your neighbor's barbecue picnic gets out of hand and your apartment is destroyed by fire. Renter's insurance would allow you to replace your stereo equipment, TV, VCR, books, and whatever furnishings and personal stuff you lost. Renter's insurance covers your possessions but doesn't protect the actual dwelling. Your landlord's insurance policy should cover damages to the dwelling. After all, the building is the landlord's property, not yours. However, renter's insurance does provide liability coverage, so if you're the one who barbecued the building, you're covered.

- **HO-6: Condominium owner's insurance.**   This insurance covers the personal property of co-op or condominium owners much like HO-4 coverage for the property of renters. In addition, it covers any structural improvements or alterations you may have made on your unit.

- **HO-8: Modified coverage—older homes homeowner's insurance.**   This insurance is designed for older homes, insuring them for their repair costs or actual cash value rather than their replacement cost. Some older homes, because of their materials and details, have outrageously expensive replacement costs. In fact, with some older homes the replacement cost could easily be two or three times their market value.

Table 11.1 summarizes the basic coverage provided under each of these policies. Although each packaged policy provides a different type and level of insurance, all six HO's are divided into two sections. Section I addresses **property insurance**, which protects you against the loss of your property or possessions due to various perils. Section II provides for **personal liability insurance**, which protects you from the financial losses incurred if someone is injured on your property or as a result of your actions.

Section I: Property Coverage.

Property covered under homeowner's insurance is covered for a certain dollar amount. This amount signifies the maximum amount the insurance company will pay out for a given claim. So, if an item is insured for $100,000, the insurance company will pay out claims of up to $100,000. Of course, the insurer would much rather pay out claims well under the full insurance value.

Within Section I of all HO policies except HO-4, there are four basic coverages:

- Coverage A: Dwelling
- Coverage B: Other structures
- Coverage C: Personal property
- Coverage D: Loss of use

Coverage A protects the house and any attachments to it—for example, an attached garage. However, if the land surrounding the house is destroyed by an explosion, this coverage won't pay to repair or restore it.

Coverage B protects other structures on the premises that aren't attached to the house—for example, your landscaping, a detached garage, or an outhouse. The level of this coverage is limited to 10 percent of the home's coverage. For example, if the home carries $200,000 of insurance, the other structures would carry $20,000 insurance. Still, at $20,000, that's one valuable outhouse! Again, the land isn't covered, and if the additional structure is used for business purposes, it's not covered.

Coverage C protects any personal property that's owned or used by the policyholder, regardless of the location of this property. In other words, if you're on a vacation in Hawaii and someone hits you with a pineapple and steals your suitcase, your personal property is still covered. In addition, the personal property of your guests is covered while that property is in your home. So, if your home burns down during a party, any personal property losses of guests would be covered. The amount of this coverage is equal to 50 percent of the home's coverage. Thus, if the home carries $200,000 of insurance, the personal property insurance would be $100,000. Within this coverage there are limits on some types of losses. For example, there's a $200 limit on money, bank notes, gold, and silver. There's also a $1,000 limit on securities, valuable papers, manuscripts, tickets, and stamps, and a $2,500 limit on the theft of silverware, goldware, and pewterware. In addition, certain property is excluded from coverage. For example, animals, birds, and fish are excluded. These are just a few of the limits and exclusions in a homeowner's insurance policy. Before buying any policy, you should be aware of all of its limitations.

Property Insurance
Insurance that protects you against the loss of your property or possessions.

Personal Liability Insurance
Insurance covering all liabilities other than those resulting from the negligent operation of an automobile or those associated with business or professional causes.

TABLE 11.1

Comparing Homeowner's Insurance Policies

Coverage	HO-1 (Basic Form)	HO-2 (Broad Form)	HO-3 (Special Form)
Section I Coverages			
A. Dwelling	Based on structure's replacement value, minimum $15,000	Based on structure's replacement value, minimum $15,000	Based on structure's replacement value, minimum $20,000
B. Other structures	10% of insurance on house	10% of insurance on house	10% of insurance on house
C. Personal property	50% of insurance on house	50% of insurance on house	50% of insurance on house
D. Loss of use	10% of insurance on house	20% of insurance on house	20% of insurance on house
Covered perils	Fire or lightning Windstorm or hail Explosion Riot or civil commotion Aircraft Vehicles Smoke Vandalism or malicious mischief Theft Glass breakage Volcanic eruption	Fire or lightning Windstorm or hail Explosion Riot or civil commotion Aircraft Vehicles Smoke Vandalism or malicious mischief Theft Glass breakage Falling objects Weight of ice, snow, or sleet Accidental discharge or overflow of water or steam Sudden and accidental tearing apart, cracking, burning, or bulging of a steam, hot-water, air-conditioning, or automatic fire protective sprinkler system, or from within a household appliance Freezing of a plumbing, heating air-conditioning, or automatic fire sprinkler system, or of a household appliance Sudden and accidental damage from artificially generated electrical current Volcanic eruption	Dwelling and other structures are covered against risk of direct loss to property. All losses are covered except those losses specifically excluded. Personal property is covered for the same perils as HO-2.
Section II Coverages			
E. Personal liability	$100,000	$100,000	$100,000
F. Medical payments to others	$1,000 per person	$1,000 per person	$1,000 per person

(continued)

TABLE 11.1 *(continued)*

HO-4 (Contents Broad Form)	HO-6 (Joint Owner's Form)	HO-8 (Modified Coverage Form)
Section I Coverages		
Not applicable	$1,000 minimum on the unit	Based on structure's market value
Not applicable	Included in Coverage A	10% of insurance on house
Minimum varies by company	Minimum varies by company	50% of insurance on house
20% of insurance on personal property	40% of insurance on personal property	10% of insurance on house
Same perils as HO-2 for personal property	Same perils as HO-2 for personal property	Fire or lightning
		Windstorm or hail
		Explosion
		Riot or civil commotion
		Aircraft
		Vehicles
		Smoke
		Vandalism or malicious mischief
		Theft (applies only to loss on the residence premises or in a bank or public warehouse up to a maximum of $1,000)
		Glass breakage
		Volcanic eruption
Section II Coverages		
$100,000	$100,000	$100,000
$1,000 per person	$1,000 per person	$1,000 per person

Coverage D provides benefits if your home can't be used due to an insured loss. The amount of loss of use coverage is limited to 20 percent of the amount of insurance on the house. Under this coverage, three benefits are provided: additional living expenses, fair rental value, and prohibited use. The additional living expenses benefits reimburse you for the cost of living in a temporary location until your home is repaired. The fair rental value benefit covers any rental losses you might experience. For example, if you rent a room in your home for $300 per month, and because of a fire it's uninhabitable for 2 months, you'd receive $600 for the loss of rent. Prohibited use coverage provides living expenses for up to 2 weeks if a civil authority declares your home to be uninhabitable, perhaps due to a gas leak in a neighbor's home.

Stop and Think

When you consider buying a house, keep in mind how much the insurance will cost. The cost may affect your choice of an older versus a new home, because insurers may offer discounts of from 8 to 15 percent on a new house. Why? The electrical, heating, and plumbing systems, in addition to the overall structure, are likely in better shape in a newer home than in an older home, reducing the risk that a fire or some other peril might occur.

Section II: Personal Liability Coverage. Section II of a homeowner's insurance policy covers personal liability insurance, which protects the policyholder and his or her family members from the financial loss incurred if someone's injured on their property or as a result of their actions. The minimum level of liability coverage per accident is $100,000. In addition, the medical expenses of anyone injured by the policyholder or his or her family or by an animal that they might own are also covered in Section II. Although this portion of the homeowner's insurance policy is often overlooked, it's extremely important because of the protection that it provides against potentially catastrophic losses from liability suits. This protection covers liabilities from everything other than business and professional liability and liabilities resulting from the negligent operation of an automobile. These days, when everyone wants to sue everyone else for outrageous settlements, it's good to have your liabilities covered. You never know when your close friends or dear Aunt Edith might slip on your stairs, scrape a shin, and sue you for several million dollars in damages.

The portion of Section II that covers the actual medical insurance to others is really a small medical insurance policy. It covers payments up to $1,000 for medical expenses to those nonfamily members who are injured in your home. For example, if someone falls down your stairs and breaks a leg, this coverage would take care of up to $1,000 worth of medical expenses per person.

Supplemental Coverage

Coverage C of Section I of an HO provides protection for your personal property, but what if that protection isn't enough? Depending on the type and dollar value of your assets, or the perils that you face, you might want to consider supplemental coverage. There are dozens of types of supplemental coverage to choose from. Some of the more common types of added coverage include personal articles floaters, earthquake protection, flood protection, inflation guard, and replacement cost. In general, the additional coverage can be added through an **endorsement**, which is simply a written attachment to an insurance policy to add or subtract coverage.

Endorsement

A written attachment to an insurance policy to add or subtract coverage.

WE HAVE OUR OWN CASTE SYSTEM

When you buy a home-insurance policy, do you really know where it's coming from? Say you've chosen Allstate. Though you may think you're just getting a straight Allstate policy, you will in fact be handed off to one of two different carriers—Allstate Indemnity or Allstate Insurance. The choice could mean a difference of up to 50 percent on your premium. (The cheaper one for property insurance is Allstate Insurance.)

Almost all insurance firms slot their policies into different categories, such as preferred, standard and substandard. And even if your risk profile does not change in any substantial way, you can still be shifted from a company's preferred carrier to its more expensive counterpart, says Jim Davis, public-information director at the Texas Department of Insurance.

Sam Mayer, a physician in suburban Chicago, had insured his home, car and life with Metropolitan for 10 years without filing a single claim. But recently, a damaged roof and a burglary led to two legitimate claims totaling $3,000. Mayer promptly installed a new burglar-alarm system. But instead of giving him a discount, the company dropped Mayer from its preferred coverage, citing his "claims history," and instead offered him its standard carrier at a higher rate—even though his risk profile hadn't really changed.

"If you're not in the preferred carrier, ask why," urges Davis. Your agent—or even the insurance company itself—may be able to move you into a more favorable slot. Also, it's worth shopping around. A $200,000 home may be considered "high risk" for a small regional carrier, but the same home could actually be deemed preferred for a bigger outfit such as State Farm.

Source: Namita Devidayal, "Ten Things Your Home Insurer Won't Tell You," *Smart Money*, February 1996, p. 116. Used by permission.

Analysis and Implications ...

A. Not only aren't all policies the same, but not all agents are the same. Insurance companies treat their top sellers a bit differently than they do other agents. For example, State Farm has a President's Club, and Aetna has the Great Performers Club. Agents in these top categories are many times provided greater flexibility with respect to guidelines for writing policies and in accepting claims.

B. You'll also find that it is both more difficult and more expensive to get insurance on older homes—even homes only 30 or 40 years old. Moreover, many insurance companies won't sell policies that guarantee the replacement cost on homes in neighborhoods where property values are declining or where the property is old.

Personal Articles Floaters.

Personal articles floaters provide extended coverage for all personal property, regardless of where the property's located, for the policyholder and all household residents except children away at school. This coverage is generally sold as an extension to the homeowner's policy on an "all-risk" basis; thus, it covers losses of any kind other than specifically excluded perils, which generally include war, wear and tear, mechanical breakdown, vermin, and nuclear disaster.

There are a number of variations of the personal articles floater available, such as scheduled floaters or scheduled endorsements and blanket floaters, but they all perform the same task: They provide extended coverage to personal property. Recall the limit on personal property coverage is set at 50 percent of the dwelling coverage, but within this coverage there are also limits on some specific types of losses. For example, there's a $2,500 limit on the theft of silverware, goldware, and pewterware. Thus, if the value of your silverware is $25,000, you might want to take on a personal articles floater to extend the coverage on your silverware to its market value. If you tend to eat with plastic forks and knives, though, you've got nothing to worry about.

Earthquake Coverage.

Because damage from earthquakes is specifically excluded from coverage in the standardized packaged HO policies, supplemental earthquake coverage is an important addition to those in high-risk earthquake areas. In fact, in California, insurers are required to offer earthquake coverage as an add-on. Of course, not all Californians elect to buy such coverage, but they should be able to get it easily if they want it. Actually, only about 20 percent of those affected by the horrible 1989 San Francisco earthquake had earthquake coverage. The rates on earthquake coverage vary depending on a location's earthquake risk. Rates near the San Andreas fault cost up to $4 per $1,000 of coverage, which means coverage on a $200,000 home would run $800 per year.

Flood Protection.

Flood protection includes coverage from more than flood. It includes water damage from hurricanes, mudslides, and unusual erosion along the Great Lakes and the Great Salt Lake. It's also a bit different from other coverage in that it's generally administered and subsidized by the federal government through the Department of Housing and Urban Development (HUD). To be eligible for flood insurance, your community must comply with HUD requirements, which involve floodplain studies and planning. Once a community receives approval from HUD, you can purchase up to $185,000 of coverage on your dwelling and an additional $60,000 on its contents.

Inflation Guard.

An **inflation guard** endorsement automatically updates your level of property coverage based on an index of replacement costs that continually updates the cost of building a home. In effect, the coverage—along with the premiums—automatically increase each year. This endorsement makes sure that inflation doesn't silently eat away at the level of real coverage you have on your home and your property. For example, if the cost of building a home increases by 5 percent per year, in just over 14 years the cost of building a home will double. If your coverage stays the same over that time, you'd have enough insurance to buy only half a house. You should note that the adjustment generally reflects increases in the average cost nationally, not locally, of rebuilding. Because construction costs don't necessarily rise at an equal pace throughout the nation, it's a good idea to periodically review your level of coverage.

Personal Property Replacement Cost Coverage.

Homeowner's insurance is set up to pay the policyholder the actual cash value of the loss. Unfortunately, when you're talking about personal property, the **actual cash value**, which is the replacement cost minus estimated depreciation (wear-and-tear costs), can be well below the cost of replacing the asset. For example, if the property could be replaced for $500, and it's been used for half its expected life, it would have an actual cash value of $250. Moreover, under the actual cash value, you're responsible for maintaining detailed records of the date of purchase, purchase price, and estimated depreciation of all your property. As an alternative, most homeowner's policies come with optional **replacement cost coverage**, which provides for the actual replacement cost of a stolen or destroyed item as opposed to the actual cash value. Replacement cost coverage can generally be added for an additional 5 to 15 percent over the cost of the homeowner's insurance without this option. Although replacement cost coverage doesn't mean that you no longer have to keep track of your possessions, it does mean that you'll be able to replace them in the event of a loss.

Added Liability Insurance.

Basic packaged policies generally provide $100,000 of liability coverage. Although this figure may sound like a lot, it's no longer uncommon for court judgments to climb well above the $100,000 mark. Also, if you've accumulated a relatively sizable net worth, you need increased liability insurance to protect your assets. Fortunately, for a relatively small fee, most insurance companies will allow you to raise your level of liability coverage to $300,000 or $500,000.

Alternatively, you might want to buy a **personal umbrella policy**, which, for a reasonable cost, provides protection ranging from $1 million to $10 million against lawsuits and judgments. An umbrella policy provides excess liability insurance over basic underlying contracts. That is, it doesn't go into effect until you've exhausted your automobile or homeowner's liability coverage. It's also quite broad in coverage, generally covering most losses. However, it does exclude acts committed with the intent to cause injury, those activities associated with aircraft and some watercraft, and most business and professionally related activities. Business owner and professional policies must be purchased separately.

> ### *The Facts of Life*
> The average number of dog bites sustained by Americans each day is 12,877, and the average daily amount paid to cover those dog bites by U.S. insurers is $2,739,726. Maybe that little Chihuahua's more of a financial liability than you thought!

HOW MUCH INSURANCE DO YOU NEED?

Answering this question is easy. In fact, we've already started answering it. So far we've seen the need for inflation guard coverage to make sure inflation doesn't negate our insurance coverage. We've also seen the need for replacement cost coverage on our possessions. What about replacement cost coverage on our houses? This coverage actually provides us with the final answer to our question: You need enough insurance to allow for full replacement in the event of a loss—a total loss.

Coinsurance and the "80-Percent Rule"

Insurance companies have a way of encouraging you to be covered for a total loss. It's called a **coinsurance provision**, and it requires that you pay a portion of your own losses if you don't purchase what they consider an adequate level of insurance. Most companies follow the **80-percent rule** and require you to carry at least 80 percent of your home's full replacement cost. This 80-percent rule relates to losses on your dwelling only—not those on your personal property. There are some restrictions to this coverage, though. First, the amount paid is limited to the limits of the policy—that is, a $100,000 insurance policy will pay only up to its $100,000 limit. Second, you usually have to rebuild your home on the same location. Third, if you don't rebuild your home, the insurer is liable only for the actual cash-value loss, which is generally quite a

Replacement Cost Coverage
Additional homeowner's coverage that provides for the actual replacement cost of a stolen or destroyed item as opposed to the actual cash value.

Personal Umbrella Policy
A homeowner's policy that provides excess liability insurance with protection against lawsuits and judgments generally ranging from $1 million to $10 million.

LEARNING OBJECTIVE #1

Understand, buy, and maintain homeowner's insurance in a cost-effective way.

Coinsurance Provision
A provision or requirement of homeowner's insurance requiring the insured to pay a portion of the claim if he or she purchased an inadequate amount of insurance (in this case, less than 80 percent of the replacement cost).

"80-Percent Rule"
A homeowner's insurance rule stating that the replacement cost coverage is in effect only if the home is insured for at least 80 percent of its replacement cost. This rule is intended to discourage homeowners from insuring for less than the replacement cost of their homes.

bit less than the replacement cost. Finally, the replacement cost coverage is in effect only if your home is insured for at least 80 percent of its replacement cost. This "80-percent rule" makes insuring your home for less than at least 80 percent of its replacement cost seem unattractive. Thus, if your home currently has a replacement value of $100,000 and is insured for $80,000 and a fire causes damages of $50,000, you would be paid the full $50,000 with no deduction for depreciation (wear and tear). However, if the fire totally destroyed your home, you would only collect $80,000, the face value of your policy.

If the 80-percent rule isn't met, then the homeowner must pay for part of any losses. This is commonly referred to as the coinsurance provision. It requires that the insured pay a portion of the claim if an inadequate amount of insurance (in this case, less than 80 percent of replacement cost) was purchased. If your house is insured for less than 80 percent of its replacement value, in the event of a loss you'll receive the greater of the following:

- the actual cash value of the portion of your house that was destroyed (remember that the actual cash value is the replacement cost minus depreciation),

or

- $$\frac{\text{the amount of insurance purchased}}{80\% \text{ of replacement cost}} \times \frac{\text{the amount}}{\text{of loss}}$$

What does all this mean? It means that it would be a grave mistake not to insure your home for at least 80 percent of its replacement cost, because if you satisfy the 80-percent rule and your house is destroyed or damaged, your policy will pay to fully repair or replace your home up to the amount of insurance purchased. If you don't satisfy the 80-percent rule, you probably won't get enough to replace it. You may want more insurance, but certainly not less.

The Bottom Line

Unfortunately, there's no neat, tidy formula to quickly tell you exactly how much homeowner's insurance you need. Rather, determining the amount of coverage you need is a procedure that requires some thought and foresight on your part. Because the amount of assets and possessions you've managed to pick up is always changing, so are your insurance needs. As has been the case for just about every personal finance matter we've examined so far, you need to revisit your insurance needs from time to time, just to make sure those needs are being met. When determining how much homeowner's insurance you need, you should consider the following:

- You need enough insurance to cover the replacement of your home in the event of a complete loss. This coverage will need to reflect any changes in increased costs due to changing building codes.
- You should have protection against the effect of inflation eroding away your coverage.
- If you're in a flood or earthquake area, you'll also need special protection against these disasters.
- If you have detached structures or elaborate landscaping, you should determine whether or not they're adequately covered under a standard policy.
- If you have a home office, you should consider additional coverage. Remember, your homeowner's policy doesn't provide business liability coverage.
- You need adequate coverage for your personal property. For most people, replacement cost property insurance is a good idea.
- If you have possessions that need special protection—for example, a valuable coin collection or jewelry—you should consider a floater policy.

- If your assets are much greater than the liability limits on your homeowner's policy, you should consider additional liability coverage.
- If you're renting, you need adequate insurance for your personal property.

Appendix G presents Worksheet G.32 that can further help you determine your needs.

KEEPING YOUR HOMEOWNER'S INSURANCE COSTS DOWN

What determines the cost of your homeowner's policy? Three basic factors: (1) the location of your home, (2) its type of structure, and (3) your level of coverage and policy type. For example, the location affects coverage because of differences in crime levels and regional perils (such as earthquakes in California and tornadoes in the Midwest). Also, older and less sound structures cost more to insure because they're more likely to have problems. In addition, the greater the coverage and more comprehensive the policy, the more it costs. Still, there are some ways that the cost of homeowner's insurance can be kept down. Start by selecting a financially sound insurer with low comparative costs. Then take advantage of as many discounts as possible. The following are potential discounts and savings methods.

- **High deductible discounts.** **Deductibles**, which are what you agree to pay before insurance coverage kicks in, can be thought of as coinsurance. The larger the deductible you are willing to accept, the less you pay for insurance coverage. Typically, insurance companies require a $250 deductible and provide discounts if you're willing to accept a higher deductible. Keep in mind that the purpose of insurance is not to offset all the costs, only the catastrophic ones. To keep the costs of homeowner's insurance under control, you'll have to share some of the risks with the insurance company. In other words, you should be responsible for all minor expenses, and the insurance company should cover all large expenses. Thus, you should give serious consideration to taking as large a deductible as you can afford.

> ### The Facts of Life
> Typically the deductible on a homeowner's policy starts at $250. By increasing your deductible to $500, you could save up to 12 percent; $1,000, up to 24 percent; up to $2,500, up to 30 percent; and $5,000, up to 37 percent.

- **Security system/smoke detector discounts.** Many insurance companies also offer discounts of from 2 to 5 percent if you install security and smoke detector systems. Larger discounts are available if you install in-home sprinkler systems.
- **Multiple policy discounts.** Insurance companies often provide discounts to customers who have more than one policy—for example, their automobile *and* homeowner's coverage—with them.
- **Pay your insurance premiums annually.** If you pay your insurance premiums annually in one lump sum rather than quarterly, or extended over several months, most insurance companies will offer you a discount.
- **Other discounts.** Some, but not all, companies offer a homeowner's discount for homes that are made with fire-resistant materials, for homeowners over the age of 55, and for individuals who've had homeowner's insurance with a single company for an extended number of years.

LEARNING OBJECTIVE #1

Understand, buy, and maintain homeowner's insurance in a cost-effective way.

Deductible
The amount that you are responsible for paying before insurance coverage kicks in.

FIGURE 11.1

A Checklist for Homeowner's Insurance

☑ Determine the amount and type of homeowner's insurance you need.

☑ Put together a listing of top-quality (as listed in *A.M. Best's Key Rating Guide on Property and Casualty Insurers*) insurance agents with a good local reputation who carry these insurers.

☑ Consult with agents, letting them know what you are looking for. Give consideration to any recommendations or modifications they might suggest.

☑ Get several bids on the total package, including all modifications, floaters, and extensions.

☑ Conduct an annual review of your homeowner's insurance coverage.

Direct Writer

An insurance company that distributes its products directly to customers, without the use of agents.

- **Consider a direct writer.** A **direct writer** is an insurance company that distributes its products directly to customers, without the use of agents. Companies that don't use agents don't have to pay salaries or commissions, so they can afford to offer lower prices.

- **Shop around.** Compare the cost of homeowner's insurance among high-quality insurers. Premiums for similar coverage can vary by as much as 25 percent. Figure 11.1 provides a look at the process of shopping for homeowner's insurance.

- **Double-check your policy.** Make sure the policy that you receive is what you ordered. Check the type of coverage, the level of coverage, and any endorsements that you requested. It'll be too late to correct any errors once you file a claim.

The Facts of Life

One healthy way to reduce your insurance premiums is to quit smoking. Smoking accounts for about 23,000 residential fires a year. As a result, many insurance companies offer discounts to nonsmoking families.

LEARNING OBJECTIVE #2

Recover on a liability or a loss to your property.

MAKING YOUR COVERAGE WORK: THE INVENTORY

By now you should be able to go out and buy the insurance policy that's just right for you. However, is that policy enough to protect you from losing your possessions and assets? Nope. How can your insurance company make good on your policy and pay you back for a loss if it doesn't know what possessions you've lost or what they were worth? For your homeowner's insurance to provide effective protection against loss, you need to establish proof of ownership and value your assets using a detailed inventory of everything you own. Unfortunately, the tedious nature of putting together such a list stops many people from doing so. Still, if you can't prove that you owned a stereo worth $2,000, your insurance company isn't going to reimburse you for it if it gets stolen.

Fortunately, the inventory process isn't all that difficult. You should begin by putting together a list of your household items. To aid you in this process, most insurance agents should be able to provide you with an inventory worksheet. If not, you can get one from the Insurance Information Institute by calling 800-331-9146. Ideally, your inventory should be as detailed as possible and include the date of purchase, the cost, the model and serial number, and the brand name for each item. Unfortunately, most people simply never get around to compiling a complete written inventory. However, you should at least make sure you keep written documentation of any valuable items you own along with any appraisals that you may have had.

ANYTHING OUT OF "THE ORDINARY" Gives Us the Creeps

What do a couple going through a divorce and someone living in a shady part of town have in common? The answer: Insurance companies hate them.

Everyone knows that if your home is near the water or in an earthquake-prone area, insurers will shun you. Regulators can't do much about that. But some insurers use illegal guidelines to "red-line"—the industry term for discriminate against—certain groups or areas. Agents say they often get memos identifying undesirable zip codes or reminding them to stay away from couples who are having problems in their marriage. Bob Hunter, director of insurance for the Consumer Federation of America, describes his "favorite" memo from a company advising its agents: "Before writing a policy, drop by the house after work hours and see if the owner is sitting on his porch in a T-shirt and drinking beer."

If you think you've been discriminated against, raise a fuss. The Texas Public Insurance

Counsel, an industry watchdog, found in a 1994 study that 29 percent of all insurance companies use loose "lifestyle considerations"—including living arrangements and subjective moral judgments—that have very little to do with the actual risk profile of the customer.

In one such instance, an elderly woman who was purchasing a home with a companion was denied coverage due to "an additional nonrelative listed as the named insured," even though all other information was acceptable under company guidelines, according to the agent's report. The woman contacted an attorney as well as the American Civil Liberties Union. The response? The insurance company said it had made an error and immediately offered coverage.

Source: Namita Devidayal, "Ten Things Your Home Insurer Won't Tell You," *Smart Money*, February 1996, p. 115. Used by permission.

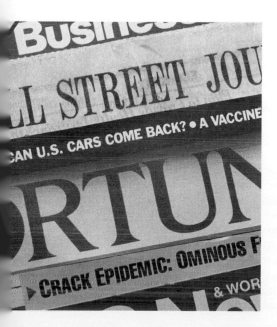

Analysis and Implications ...

A. Insurance companies are also very selective about whom they'll cover and whom they won't. Depending on the type of claim you file, it could result in your being dropped, and once you've been dropped, it becomes difficult to find a new carrier. If you're dropped and you don't feel it was deserved, contact your state insurance department and complain.

B. Insurance companies have their own version of credit scoring (remember, credit scoring is the numerical evaluation of credit applicants based on their answers to a simple set of questions), in which your potential risk is calculated. Just as with credit-scoring models, insurance companies tend to generalize and many times penalize people inappropriately.

As a time-saving measure, the Insurance Information Institute recommends that you also videotape your household inventory. Carefully walk through each room in your home and videotape the contents, giving a running dialogue of what you're taping as you go. Note the original cost and date of purchase of major items whenever possible. In addition, make sure that each room is taped from a number of different angles, with all closet doors open. Also, be sure to videotape the contents of drawers and cabinets. When taping valuables such as jewelry and silverware, take a careful shot of them. Try to make your recording as comprehensive as possible. For example, include your curtains, lamps, CDs, records, books, kitchenware, sporting equipment, and items in your attic and basement. You should also videotape the outside of your home, including your landscaping. If you don't have a video camera, many camera stores and independent claim services will tape your house for you. Once you've finished your video or your inventory, you should keep it in a safety deposit box, with a family member living elsewhere, or with your insurance agent. Why not keep it yourself? Well, if your house burns down, your video or inventory would burn, too, and all your efforts would quickly go up in smoke.

LEARNING OBJECTIVE #2

Recover on a liability or a loss to your property.

WHAT TO DO IN THE EVENT OF A LOSS

OK, now you've got a good insurance policy and a video inventory of your house. Now you're effectively covered, right? Not exactly. To effectively collect on a loss, you must follow a few basic steps.

- **Report your loss immediately.** In the case of a burglary or theft, report the incident immediately to the police. If a credit or ATM card has been stolen, you should also notify the issuing company. In addition, you should also notify your insurance agent.

- **Make temporary repairs to protect your property.** If your house has sustained damage and your insurance agent hasn't had time to inspect it, don't just let the damage sit untouched. Board up broken windows and holes in the roof or walls to prevent any further damage and to protect your home against burglary.

- **Make a detailed list of everything lost or damaged.** Using your inventory—now you'll be glad you made one—put together a detailed list describing the items that were lost or damaged and their value. Present this list to your insurance agent and the police.

- **Maintain records of the insurance settlement process.** Keep records of all your expenses.

- **Confirm the adjuster's estimate.** Your insurance company will send an adjuster to evaluate the claim and recommend to the insurance company a dollar amount for the settlement. Before settling, get an estimate from a local contractor as to how much the repairs will cost. Then you'll know if the settlement terms offered by your insurance company are realistic. Don't agree to anything less than a fair settlement. Work with your adjuster and your insurance company.

LEARNING OBJECTIVE #3

Buy the automobile insurance policy that's right for you.

AUTOMOBILE INSURANCE

At this point, you should be pretty safe at home, thanks to your homeowner's insurance and your newfound knowledge of how to manage it and file claims. You need to leave home at least every now and again, though. What happens when you get in your car? Are you safe there, too? Not unless you have automobile insurance. Of course, if you drive, you have to have some form of automobile insurance—it's the law in most states. Automobile insurance requirements are good to have as law, because there are an awful lot of car accidents each year. In fact, there are around 30 million car accidents each year in the United States alone. That works out to about one accident for every five licensed drivers. In reality, though, some drivers have at least one accident per year, and others never have any accidents in their lives.

Because you're going to need it if you drive, you're going to need to know how to buy automobile insurance. Let's start our discussion by taking a look at the standardized personal automobile policy.

The Personal Automobile Policy (PAP)

Fortunately, automobile insurance is relatively standard, with all policies following a similar package format called the **Personal Automobile Policy (PAP)**. Each policy contains both liability and property damage coverage, and each package of insurance will include four basic parts, which define the coverage as follows:

- **Part A: Liability coverage.**   This coverage provides protection for you if you're legally liable for bodily injury and property damage caused by your automobile. It includes payment for any judgment awarded, court costs, and legal defense fees.
- **Part B: Medical expense coverage.**   This coverage pays medical bills and funeral expenses, with limits per person for you and your passengers.
- **Part C: Uninsured motorist's protection coverage.**   This coverage is required in many states, and protects you by covering bodily injury (and property damage in a few states) caused by drivers without liability insurance.
- **Part D: Damage to your automobile coverage.**   This coverage is also known as collision or comprehensive insurance, and provides coverage for theft of your auto or for damage from almost any peril other than collision.

Figure 11.2 further illustrates the typical policy parts as they relate to the liability and property coverage. Now let's look at each coverage part in greater detail.

Personal Automobile Policy (PAP)

A standardized insurance policy for an individual or family.

FIGURE 11.2

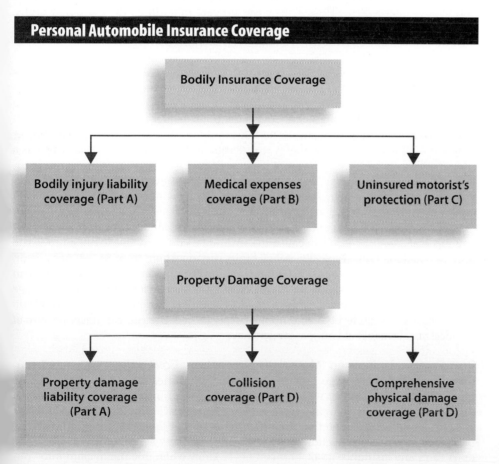

Personal Automobile Insurance Coverage

Bodily Insurance Coverage

- Bodily injury liability coverage (Part A)
- Medical expenses coverage (Part B)
- Uninsured motorist's protection (Part C)

Property Damage Coverage

- Property damage liability coverage (Part A)
- Collision coverage (Part D)
- Comprehensive physical damage coverage (Part D)

PAP Part A: Liability Coverage.

Part A of a personal automobile policy involves liability coverage, which provides protection from loss resulting from lawsuits that might arise due to an auto accident. Liability coverage can be presented as a **combined single limit**, meaning that the liability coverage applies to a combination of both bodily injury and property damage liability, without a separate limit for each person. For example, if you had total liability coverage of $100,000, then the total liability insurance—both bodily injury and property damage—in an accident, regardless of how many individuals were involved, would be $100,000. Some insurers also issue **split-limit coverage**, which allows for either separate coverage limits for bodily injury and property damage, split coverage limits per person, or both. For example, split-limit coverage limits of $200,000/$600,000/$100,000 would mean you have $200,000 of bodily injury liability coverage for each person and $600,000 for each accident, in addition to $100,000 of property damage liability coverage. Figure 11.3 shows these limits graphically.

Considering the absurd sums of money judges are handing out in settlements of lawsuits over automobile accidents, it's a good idea to carry adequate liability insurance. Although most states require minimum levels of liability coverage, this is generally well below what is needed by most people. In fact, most professional financial planners recommend that you carry at least $100,000 of bodily injury liability coverage per person and $300,000 of bodily injury liability coverage for all persons. Also, they recommend that you carry at least $50,000 of property damage liability insurance coverage. Of course, these are general recommendations and what you carry should reflect your net worth and annual income—the greater your assets, the more coverage you should carry.

In addition to paying the policy limits for the damages that you caused, the insurer also agrees under Part A to defend you in any civil cases arising from the accident and to pay all legal costs. These legal costs are paid *in addition* to your policy limits. However, the insurance company won't defend you against any criminal charges brought against you as a result of a charge such as drunk driving.

PAP Part B: Medical Expenses Coverage.

Your medical expenses coverage pays all reasonable medical and funeral expenses incurred within 3 years by the policyholder, his or her family members, and other persons injured in an accident involving your covered automobile. In fact, it covers the policyholder and his or her family regardless of whether they're in an automobile or walking along the street, just as long as they're not injured by a vehicle that wasn't designed for use on public roads, such as a snowmobile or farm tractor. However, if you're driving a car you don't own, your medical expenses will be covered, but not those of other passengers in the car or pedestrians who are injured—the owner of the car would be responsible for that insurance. In addition, your PAP medical expense coverage doesn't specify fault. That is, you're not insured based upon who is at fault in an accident. As a result, you receive payment for any medical expenses faster because the insurance company doesn't need to waste time establishing fault. Typically, policy limits run anywhere from $1,000 per person up to $10,000 or more per person, with no limit on the number of individuals that can be covered in an accident. Generally, you should maintain at least $50,000 of coverage per person. Even if you have adequate medical insurance of your own, you should still carry a relatively high level of automobile coverage, because you can never be sure of the level of coverage that your passengers have.

PAP Part C: Uninsured Motorist's Protection Coverage.

Uninsured motorist's protection coverage provides coverage for injuries caused by an uninsured motorist, a negligent driver whose insurance company is insolvent, or a hit-and-run driver. To collect on a claim, not only must the other driver not have available insurance, but it must be shown that the other driver was at fault. It's important to carry uninsured motorist's protection, because roughly as many as 15 percent of all drivers don't carry any insurance at all, and you never know when one might slam into your

FIGURE 11.3

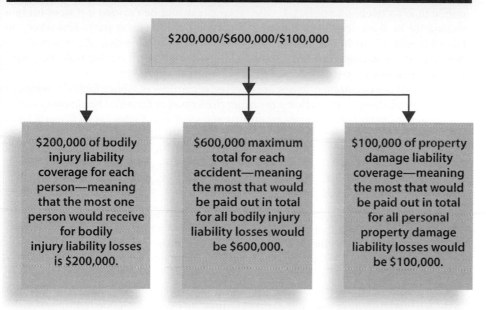

Reading Automobile Liability Split-Coverage Insurance Limits
Quoted as Split Coverage
Some insurers issue split-limit coverage policies, which allow for either separate coverage limits for bodily injury and property damage, split coverage limits per person, or both.

$200,000/$600,000/$100,000

$200,000 of bodily injury liability coverage for each person—meaning that the most one person would receive for bodily injury liability losses is $200,000.

$600,000 maximum total for each accident—meaning the most that would be paid out in total for all bodily injury liability losses would be $600,000.

$100,000 of property damage liability coverage—meaning the most that would be paid out in total for all personal property damage liability losses would be $100,000.

Quoted as a Combined Single Limit
A combined single limit covers both bodily injury and property damage liability. This means that the liability coverage applies to a combination of these two areas without a separate limit for each person.

$100,000

The total liability insurance—both bodily injury liability losses and property damage liability losses—in an accident, regardless of how many individuals were involved, would be $100,000.

car. Most financial planners recommend that you carry at least $250,000 of coverage per person and $500,000 of coverage per accident.

You can also add underinsured motorist's coverage to your policy to provide protection against negligent drivers who don't carry adequate liability insurance. If you purchase $150,000 of underinsured motorist's coverage, you'll be protected for up to $150,000 regardless of how much insurance the negligent driver carried. For example, if the negligent driver carried $50,000 of coverage and your injuries amounted to $125,000, you'd receive $50,000 from the negligent driver's insurance policy and $75,000 from your underinsured motorist's policy, for a total of $125,000.

Collision Loss

The portion of auto insurance coverage that provides benefits to cover damages resulting from an accident with another vehicle or object.

Other Than Collision Loss or Comprehensive Physical Damage Coverage

Auto insurance coverage for noncollision losses. For example, it would cover damage if the car were hit in a parking lot or if the door were damaged as a result of banging it into a parked car next to it.

PAP Part D: Coverage for Damage to Your Automobile.

Part D coverage includes both **collision loss** and **other than collision loss**, generally called **comprehensive physical damage coverage**. The collision loss portion of the coverage provides benefits to cover damages resulting from an accident with another vehicle or object. Thus, your automobile would be covered if it were in an accident with another automobile or hit a telephone pole. Likewise, your car would be covered if it were hit in a parking lot or if its door were damaged because the idiot who parked next to you dented it with his or her door and then drove off. Comprehensive physical damage coverage covers damage from fire, theft or larceny, windstorm, falling objects, earthquakes, and similar causes.

With collision insurance, losses are covered regardless of whose fault the accident was. You should keep in mind that if the other driver was at fault and has liability insurance, you should be able to recover your losses regardless of whether or not you have collision coverage. Thus, collision coverage assures you that you'll be able to pay for any damages to your car regardless of who was at fault. Interestingly, collision coverage used to also cover damages suffered to rental cars used for business purposes. Many insurers have stopped this practice, so if you commonly rent automobiles for business purposes, you might want to check your coverage.

The recommended limit on both collision and comprehensive physical damage coverage is the cash value of your automobile, and both coverages generally have deductibles associated with them. Usually, the deductible associated with collision coverage is larger than that for comprehensive physical damage coverage. Also, premiums decline sharply as deductibles are raised. For example, one major insurance company charges an annual premium of $412 on comprehensive insurance on a new Chrysler Cirrus for a youthful operator based on a deductible of $50. If the deductible is raised to $100, the premium drops to $346. Thus, by raising the deductible by $50, you can save $66 in annual premiums. In effect, a premium of $66 is being charged for $50 of additional coverage. In this case, the end result is that if you have less than one accident per year, you're better off with the $100 deductible. If you have more than one accident per year, you should probably pay some attention to improving your driving skills. Table 11.2 provides a summary of the different parts of the PAP.

Exclusions.

The PAP provides broad coverage, but there are a number of standard exceptions to this coverage. Although there may be others, standard exclusions generally include the following:

- You're not covered in the case of intentional injury or damage.
- You're not covered if you're using a vehicle without permission of the owner.
- You're not covered if you're using a vehicle with fewer than four wheels.
- You're not covered if you're driving another person's car that is provided for you on a regular basis.
- You're not covered if you own the automobile but don't have it listed on your insurance policy.
- You're not covered if you're carrying passengers for a fee.
- You're not covered while driving in a race or speed contest.

No-Fault Insurance

In an attempt to keep insurance costs down—in particular, those costs associated with settling claims—many states have turned to the concept of **no-fault insurance**. Today over half of all states have instituted some variation of a no-fault system. No-fault insurance is based on the idea that your insurance company should pay for your losses, regardless of who's at fault for the accident. All the legal expenses associated with attaching blame would then be lifted, and insurance coverage should prove to be less

No-Fault Insurance

A type of auto insurance in which your insurance company protects you in the case of an accident regardless of who is at fault.

TABLE 11.2

The Personal Automobile Policy (PAP)

Coverage Description	Individuals Covered	Recommended Policy Limits
Liability Coverage—Part A Part A of a personal automobile policy involves liability coverage and provides coverage against lawsuits that might arise from negligent ownership or operation of an automobile.	Nonexcluded relatives who live with the insured regardless of whether the automobile is owned or not.	$100,000 bodily injury liability coverage per person and $300,000 of bodily injury coverage for all persons. $50,000 of property damage liability coverage.
Medical Expenses Coverage—Part B Your medical expenses coverage covers all reasonable medical and funeral expenses incurred by the policyholder and family members in addition to other persons injured while occupying a covered automobile.	The policyholder and his or her family regardless of whether they are in an automobile or walking, as long as they are injured by a vehicle that was designed for use on public roads.	$50,000 of coverage per person.
Uninsured Motorist's Protection Coverage—Part C Uninsured motorist's protection coverage provides coverage for injuries caused by an uninsured motorist, a negligent driver whose insurance company is insolvent, or a hit-and-run driver.	Insured family members driving nonowned automobile with permission, and anyone driving an insured car with permission.	$250,000 of coverage per person and $500,000 of coverage per accident.
Coverage for Damage to Your Automobile—Part D Protection against damage to or theft of your automobile is provided in Part D coverage. This coverage includes both collision loss and loss resulting from other than collision loss, generally called comprehensive physical damage coverage.	Anyone driving an insured automobile with permission.	Actual cash value.

costly. Thus, under no-fault insurance, if you were in an accident, your insurance company would pay for your losses and the losses suffered by your passengers, and the other driver's insurance company would pay for his or her losses. Sounds like a good idea, right? Well, no-fault insurance has its problems. The biggest problem is that no-fault insurance imposes limits on medical expenses and other claims. In some states, the limited coverage simply may not be enough to cover all your legitimate medical expenses.

Although many states have instituted some form of no-fault insurance, many others haven't. It's a good idea to know what kind of insurance your state requires. If you live in a "fault" state and are in an accident that was the other driver's fault, you collect from his or her insurance company—that is, provided the other driver has insurance. If it's your fault it'll be tough to collect on your own injuries beyond your part B coverage and you can expect your premiums to rise. If it's not all your fault and not all the other driver's fault, then state law will determine what happens next. With no-fault insurance, you collect—up to a limit—regardless of who was at fault. You can still sue for "pain and suffering," but only if the other driver was at fault.

Buying Automobile Insurance

Now that you know about the basic types of coverage in automobile insurance, you can make an informed choice in buying some. How much will you need to spend? Well, that depends on how good a comparison shopper you are, but it also depends on some factors that are pretty much beyond your control. Let's take a look at these factors, and then let's take a look at what you can do to get the best possible deal.

Determinants of the Cost of Automobile Insurance.   The following are the major determinants of the cost of automobile insurance:

- **The type of automobile.**   The sportier and more high-powered your car is, the more your insurance will cost. In fact, in buying an automobile, the cost of insurance should be factored into the purchase decision.

- **The use of your automobile.**   The less you use your car, the less you'll have to pay in insurance premiums.

- **The driver's personal characteristics.**   Young unmarried males generally pay the most for their insurance, because they have a statistically greater chance of having an accident. Thus, your age, sex, and marital status all go into determining how much you'll pay for your insurance.

- **The driver's driving record.**   If you've received traffic tickets or had traffic accidents, you'll probably have to pay more for your insurance. Exactly how much your premiums go up depends on the nature of your violations. If you receive a driving-under-the-influence-of-alcohol citation, you can expect a hearty increase in your premiums.

- **Where you live.**   In general, because of a higher incidence of accidents and theft, insurance is more expensive for those who live in urban areas than it is for rural drivers. (Who says city-dwellers have all the advantages?)

- **Discounts that you qualify for.**   A wide variety of discounts are available for cars that have certain safety features and for individuals who have characteristics that are commonly identified with safe drivers. Figure 11.4 lists some of the most common automobile insurance discounts.

Keeping Your Costs Down.   In summary, there are several general ways you can keep your automobile insurance rates down while insuring complete coverage. They include the following:

- **Shop comparatively.**   Simply stated, different insurers don't charge identical prices for identical coverage. In fact, rates can vary by as much as 100 percent from carrier to carrier, and that's why you'll want to get a minimum of three different quotes on your automobile insurance. Figure 11.5 provides you with a comparative worksheet.

- **Consider only high-quality insurers.**   You should check both *A. M. Best Reports,* considering only insurers earning one of Best's two highest rankings, and *Consumer Reports* to assess the quality of the insurer before purchasing insurance.

- **Take advantage of discounts.**   You can lower your premiums considerably by taking available discounts. Those in driver's education courses, nonsmokers, graduates of defensive-driving courses, students with good grades, and car-pool participants are all some of the potentials for discounts. You'll want to check with your carrier for others.

- **Buy a car that's relatively inexpensive to insure.**   In making your purchase decision, factor in the cost of insurance on your new car.

- **Improve your driving record.**   You have control over your driving record, and it goes a long way toward determining what your premiums are.

FIGURE 11.4

Common Automobile Insurance Discounts

THE MOST COMMON DISCOUNTS

Shop for a low overall premium first. Then ask about these discounts to make certain you get the very lowest price you're entitled to. They're listed in roughly descending order of availability.

☑ **Defensive-driving course.** From 5 to 10 percent off most coverages for adults who have completed a state-approved course. Discount mandated in 29 states and Washington, D.C. Frequently applies only to people age 55 and over.

☑ **Auto/homeowners package.** From 5 to 15 percent off both policies, or just one, when both are with the same company.

☑ **Multicar.** Insurers say putting more than one vehicle on the same policy saves them processing costs, and they can then pass those savings on to consumers. If the policy covers more than one car, expect to pay from 10 to 25 percent less for liability, collision, medical payments, and personal injury protection (PIP) than you would have paid to insure each car on a separate policy.

☑ **Good driver/renewal.** From 5 to 10 percent off total premium as long as the driver maintains a good driving record.

☑ **Mature driver.** Usually 5 to 15 percent off most coverages. Often starts at age 50 and may apply only to retired drivers.

☑ **Automatic safety belts and air bags.** From 20 to 60 percent off the medical payments or PIP portion of the premium for one or two air bags. From 10 to 30 percent off the same coverages for automatic safety belts. (All 1991 and later cars have either automatic safety belts or at least one air bag.) Discounts for one or both safety features are mandated in Florida, New York, Pennsylvania, and Texas.

☑ **Antitheft devices.** From 5 to 50 percent off comprehensive for approved devices. Driver must provide proof of purchase and installation. Discount mandated in Florida, Illinois, Kentucky, Massachusetts, New Jersey, New York, Pennsylvania, and Rhode Island.

☑ **Antilock brakes.** Generally, from 5 to 10 percent off medical, liability, and collision coverages. Discount mandated in Florida and New York.

☑ **Student-driver training.** Typically, 10 percent off total premium.

☑ **Good student.** From 5 to 25 percent off most coverages. Generally a high-school or college student must show proof of a "B" average or better.

☑ **Student away at school.** From 10 to 40 percent off most portions of the premium. Student must live more than 100 miles from the family home.

Source: "The Most Common Discounts," *Consumer Reports,* August 1992, p. 500. Copyright 1992 by Consumers Union of U.S., Inc., Yonkers, NY 10703 1057. Reprinted by permission of *Consumer Reports,* August 1992.

- **Raise your deductibles.** As with homeowner's insurance, raising your deductibles can significantly lower your premiums.
- **Keep adequate liability insurance.** With increasing medical and hospital expenses, damage awards have dramatically increased in recent years. Therefore, it's a good idea to maintain adequate liability insurance.

FILING A CLAIM

There are a number of steps that you should take if you're involved in an automobile accident. Unfortunately, after an accident, you might be too shaken up to remember them. Therefore, it's a good idea to keep in your glove compartment a list of what to do in the case of an accident. Your "to do" list should include the following actions:

LEARNING OBJECTIVE #4

File a claim on your automobile insurance.

FIGURE 11.5

Insurance Shopper's Worksheet

INSURANCE SHOPPER'S WORKSHEET

	Write amount of coverage here	Write premiums from each company in these columns		
How much coverage do you want?		**COMPANY 1**	**COMPANY 2**	**COMPANY 3**
1. Bodily injury liability				
2. Property damage liability				
3. Uninsured motorist				
4. Underinsured motorist				
5. Medical payments				
6. Personal injury protection (no-fault states)				
7. Collision				
a. $100 deductible				
b. $250 deductible				
c. $500 deductible				
d. $1000 deductible				
8. Comprehensive				
a. No deductible				
b. $50 deductible				
c. $100 deductible				
d. $250 deductible				
e. $500 deductible				
	Subtotal A:			
Other charges or discounts:				
Membership fees				
Surcharges				
Discounts				
	Subtotal B:			
Subtotal A plus Subtotal B equals your **TOTAL PREMIUM**				

Source: "Insurance Shopper's Worksheet," *Consumer Reports,* August 1992, p. 500. Copyright 1992 by Consumers Union of U.S., Inc., Yonkers, NY 10703-1057. Reprinted by permission from *Consumer Reports,* August 1992.

1. Get help for anyone injured. Because it's a felony to leave the scene of an accident, you should have someone call the police and an ambulance.
2. Move your car to a safe place or put up flares to prevent further accidents.
3. Get the names and addresses of any witnesses. Get their license plate numbers if you can't get their names. Also get the names of those in the other car (or cars) involved in the accident.
4. Cooperate with the police.
5. If you think the other driver may have been driving under the influence, insist that you both take a test for alcohol.
6. Write down your recollection of what happened. If you have a camera, take pictures of the scene.
7. Don't sign anything, don't admit guilt, and don't comment on how much insurance you have.
8. Get a copy of the police report and make sure it's accurate.
9. Call your insurance agent as soon as possible.
10. Cooperate with your insurer. Remember, if there is a lawsuit, your insurer will defend you.
11. Keep records of all your expenditures associated with the accident.
12. In the case of a serious accident, meet with a lawyer so that you know what your rights are and what you can do to protect them.

SUMMARY

Today, there are six standardized packaged policies, each with a different type and level of insurance, available to homeowners and renters. All policies are identified as HO's. Three of them, HO-1, HO-2, and HO-3, are basic, broad policies specifically for homeowners. Policy HO-4 is renter's insurance, HO-6 is for condominium owners, and HO-8 is for older homes. Each of these HO policies is divided into two sections that provide (1) property insurance (in Section I), and (2) liability coverage (in Section II).

Because there are some gaps in coverage, many homeowners purchase supplemental coverage. Some of the more common types of added coverage include personal articles floaters, earthquake protection, flood protection, inflation guard, and replacement cost. In general, this supplemental coverage can be added through an endorsement, which is simply a written attachment to an insurance policy to add or subtract coverage.

You need enough insurance to cover the replacement of your home in the event of a complete loss. This coverage will need to reflect any changes in increased costs due to changing building codes. As your assets grow in value, it's important that you continuously review your homeowner's coverage to make sure that it properly reflects these changes.

How do you keep costs down? There are several ways of reducing your insurance costs, including taking a high deductible, installing a security system and smoke detector, having multiple policies with the same insurance company, paying your insurance premiums annually, not smoking, considering a direct writer, and shopping around. For your homeowner's insurance to provide effective protection, you must also be able to verify your loss by establishing proof of ownership and value of your assets with a detailed asset inventory. In the event of a loss, you should: report your loss immediately, make temporary repairs to protect your property, make a detailed list of everything lost or damaged, maintain records of the settlement process, and confirm the adjuster's estimate.

With automobile insurance, the various sections of the policy are divided up into "parts." There are two primary areas of automobile protection, which are detailed in the first four parts—labeled Parts A through D—of your automobile insurance policy.

Just Do It! *From the Desk of Marcy Furney, CFP*
Gotcha Covered

☑ Adopt the mind-set that insurance is to protect you from the *major* losses. It isn't a maintenance plan. Understand that the basis of insurance is pooling of risk. If all policyholders pay $100, and all make a $5,000 claim, the system won't work. Fraudulent and frivolous claims result in costs going up for everyone.

☑ If you must lower the bill for auto or home insurance, consider increasing the deductible, not decreasing the amount of coverage. Also, make sure you're taking advantage of any discounts.

☑ Keep the deductible on property insurance high enough to help avoid the temptation to file claims for small losses. A history of multiple claims may result in your policy being canceled or your coverage being moved to a higher-risk, higher-cost company. Claims experience may also prevent you from shopping around for lower rates.

☑ Check with your insurance company regarding requirements to insure valuables such as furs, jewelry, antiques, or collections. Most require fairly recent appraisals (2 years old or less). Appraisals can be expensive, so do it right the first time. Don't assume that all items you own are fully covered by your homeowner's or renter's policy.

☑ If you're a professional, be sure to obtain liability insurance to cover your particular activities. Doctors are not the only practitioners who need to protect their assets from malpractice claims. Businesses should also investigate general liability policies.

☑ When obtaining car insurance, disclose all information regarding the use of your auto. If you drive your vehicle in the course of doing business, you may need business-class coverage on your personal auto policy or a special commercial policy. Driving under the wrong class of coverage could subject you to denial of any claims.

☑ Many discounts are governed by the type of car you drive, how many cars you have, your age, or features of your home. In the states that allow defensive-driving course discounts without age restrictions, almost anyone can get a 5- to 10-percent reduction on many parts of a policy. Normally the discount will not apply to Parts C or D. One course can qualify you for up to 3 years of rate reduction and would probably pay for itself in 6 months to 1 year. Some states will allow you to take defensive driving for the insurance discount and then take it again in the same year to remove a ticket from your driving record.

First, there's protection against bodily injury, which includes bodily injury liability coverage (Part A), medical expenses coverage (Part B), and uninsured motorist's protection (Part C). Second, there's protection against property damage, which includes property damage liability coverage (Part A), collision coverage (Part D), and comprehensive physical damage coverage (Part D).

The four major determinants of the cost of automobile insurance are (1) the type of automobile and its use, (2) the drivers and their age, sex, marital status, and driving record characteristics, (3) where the policyholder lives, and (4) the discounts that the policyholder qualifies for. There are several general ways you can keep your automobile insurance rates down while insuring complete coverage. They include comparison shopping, considering only high-quality insurers, taking advantage of discounts, improving your driving record, raising your deductibles, and keeping adequate liability insurance. Because of the chaos following an accident, it's a good idea to keep an accident "to do" list in your glove compartment.

Review Questions

1. Describe the six basic types of standardized homeowner's (HO) policies. (LO 1)
2. Describe the four parts of Section I and the two parts of Section II of a homeowner's insurance policy. (LO 1)
3. Describe five common examples of supplemental coverage available as an addition to homeowner's policies. (LO 1)
4. Describe the "80-percent rule" as it applies to the purchase of homeowner's insurance. (LO 2)
5. List five factors that homeowners should consider when purchasing a homeowner's policy. (LO 1)
6. Describe five ways to reduce the cost of homeowner's insurance. (LO 1)
7. List steps a homeowner should take to establish proof of property ownership to substantiate a claim. (LO 1)
8. List the steps a homeowner should take to make an insurance claim in the event of a loss. (LO 2)
9. Describe the four parts of a standardized personal auto policy (PAP). (LO 3)
10. Describe the difference between split-limit auto liability coverage and single-limit liability coverage. (LO 3)
11. List five auto insurance discounts that are commonly available. (LO 3)
12. Describe the factors that are major determinants of the cost of auto insurance. (LO 4)
13. List five ways to reduce the cost of auto insurance premiums. (LO 3)
14. Describe the process of filing an auto insurance policy claim, starting with the moments immediately following an auto accident. (LO 4)

Problems and Activities

1. Ginny Dolan has $140,000 of dwelling (Coverage A) coverage on her home. What are the maximum dollar amounts for Coverages B, C, and D on her homeowner's policy? (LO 2)
2. Keith and Nancy Diem have personal property coverage with a $250 limit on currency, a $1,000 limit on jewelry, and a $2,500 limit on gold, silver, and pewter. They don't have a personal property floater. If $500 cash, $2,400 of jewelry, and $1,500 of pewterware were stolen from their home, what amount of loss would be covered by their homeowner's policy? (LO 2)
3. How much would a homeowner receive with actual cash-value coverage and replacement cost coverage for a 3-year-old sofa destroyed by a fire? The sofa would cost $1,000 to replace today, cost $850 three years ago, and has an estimated life of 6 years. (LO 2)
4. Carmella Estevez has a homeowner's insurance policy with $100,000 of liability insurance. She's concerned about the risk of lawsuits because her property borders a neighborhood park. What can she do to increase her liability coverage? (LO 1)
5. Ray Denton has a $170,000 home (replacement cost) that's insured for $140,000. If he has a $12,000 claim due to a kitchen fire, how much will his homeowner's insurance policy pay? How much would be paid if his home were totally destroyed? (LO 2)
6. Liz Gorman called her insurance agent to learn how to reduce her $700 annual homeowner's insurance premium. The agent suggested increasing the $250 deductible on her policy to $500 (10 percent savings), $1,000 (18 percent savings), or $2,500 (25 percent savings). Discuss the advantages and disadvantages of increasing her policy deductible. (LO 1)

7. Larry Simmons has 100/300/50 automobile liability insurance. Four passengers injured in a serious accident are awarded $100,000 each because Larry was found to be at fault. How much of this judgment will Larry's insurance policy cover? What amount will Larry have to pay? (LO 4)

8. Donna Greene has 25/50/10 auto insurance coverage. Driving home from work in a snowstorm, she hit a Mercedes Benz, slid into a guard rail, and knocked down a telephone pole. Damage to the Mercedes, the guard rail, and the telephone pole are $8,500, $2,000, and $4,500, respectively. How much will Donna and her insurance company each have to pay? (LO 4)

9. Lois Venitas is about to buy a condo and is shopping for an HO-6 policy. Her auto insurer quotes an annual rate of $550, with an 8-percent discount for purchasing two different policies with the same company. By how much will this reduce Lois's premium? In addition to the discount, what are other advantages of purchasing both auto and homeowner's insurance with the same company? (LO 3)

Suggested Projects

1. Prepare a detailed inventory of your personal property. Take photographs or make a videotape to provide additional evidence of property ownership. List the brand, model number, and serial number of valuable items, such as appliances, stereo equipment, and computers. (LO 2)

2. Read an auto or homeowner's insurance policy cover to cover. Write a one-page report of key policy features, including amount of coverage, deductibles, liability limits, and supplemental coverage. (LO 1)

3. Interview an insurance agent about differences in cost on a homeowners' or auto insurance policy based on changes in the amount of the deductible selected. Write a one-page report of your findings. (LO 1, 3)

4. Interview at least three people about their property inventory record-keeping method, if any (for example, written list, videotape). Write a one-page report about how your subjects would be able to prove ownership of specific personal property in the event of a loss. (LO 2)

5. Pick three different types of cars and compare the premiums for a given amount of coverage (for example, 100/300/50) for each vehicle. Write a one-page report of your findings. (LO 3)

6. Contact an insurance agent and compare the rates for a given amount of auto insurance for the following:

   - an unmarried male and an unmarried female of the same age
   - a driver under age 25 and a driver over 25
   - a city-dweller and a driver living in a suburban/rural area
   - a married driver and an unmarried driver of the same age

   Write a one-page report of your findings and discuss whether you think differences in premiums based on demographic and geographic factors are fair. (LO 3)

7. Interview a property and casualty insurance agent to find out what type of homeowner's and auto insurance policies are most commonly purchased and which policy features are recommended to clients. (LO 1, 3)

8. Visit the following Web sites on the Internet to obtain additional information about insurance-related topics. Then write a one-page report of your findings. (LO 1, 3)

   Insurance News Network   http://www.insure.com
   Independent Insurance Network   http://iiaa.iix.com/default.htm

Discussion Case 1

David and Sue Huxford are planning to buy a $185,000 home. The home is located 3 miles from a river that occasionally overflows its banks after a heavy rain. They estimate that their personal property is worth $75,000, but they really aren't sure. This estimate includes the office and computer equipment that Sue uses as a freelance writer and a $5,000 coin collection inherited from David's father. The Huxford's net worth, including their current $120,000 home, is $400,000.

The Huxfords have told their insurance agent to find them the best coverage possible, taking advantage of all possible cost-saving measures. They don't want a lot of out-of-pocket expenses if their home or personal property is destroyed. They want their insurance to keep pace with increasing building costs.

Questions

1. What type of homeowner's insurance policy is best for the Huxfords?
2. How much coverage should the Huxfords purchase on their new home?
3. Should the Huxfords buy flood insurance? How do they go about purchasing it?
4. How should the Huxfords insure their personal property?
5. What other advice would you give to the Huxfords regarding their homeowner's insurance?

Discussion Case 2

Lucy Chang was recently involved in a serious auto accident. A 21-year-old college student, she carried only the minimum state liability coverage of 15/30/5 and no collision and comprehensive. The accident, which started when Lucy slid on a slick road on a rainy night, caused $50,000 of bodily injury to two passengers in another car and $20,000 of property damage to the other driver's vehicle and a telephone pole. Lucy was admitted to a local hospital for observation and released. She credits an air bag with saving her life.

After exchanging information with the other driver and reviewing the police report, Lucy called her parents for a ride home. Her car was badly damaged and is considered totaled. A few days later, Lucy and her parents started arguing about what will happen if the other drives sues. "For a few more dollars, you could have had triple the liability coverage," said her father. "But I couldn't afford it," said Lucy, who works part-time and nets $85 a week. "Besides, I bought the amount the state requires . . . it's not like I broke the law."

Questions

1. Prepare an essay addressing the following questions: Should states require minimum auto insurance liability limits? If yes, how high? What should be done to drivers who fail to maintain adequate auto insurance?
2. Because Lucy has low liability limits, how will the others involved in the accident be compensated for their loss?
3. What could happen to Lucy as a result of having inadequate insurance?
4. Will Lucy receive any insurance money to replace her car?
5. What advice would you give Lucy to improve her auto insurance?

Continuing Case: Don and Maria Chang

PART III: PROTECTING YOURSELF WITH INSURANCE
(Chapters 9, 10, and 11)

Don and Maria read a recent newspaper article that stated that personal bankruptcy and other financial problems often result from uninsured losses. This made them curious about their own insurance coverage. Don and Maria have come back to you for assistance in reviewing their insurance coverage. Because they want to buy their home very soon, they are also interested in homeowner's insurance. They compiled the following information for you to review with them.

Life Insurance

	Don	Maria
Group life insurance	1.50 times gross income	1.50 times gross income
Whole life insurance	none	$50,000
Cash value		$1,100
Annual life insurance premiums	$0; employer paid	$0 for employer provided $720 for whole life (due next month)
Beneficiary	Maria	Don
Contingent beneficiary	Andy	Maria's parents

Health Insurance

Don's employer provides a comprehensive major medical insurance policy that covers all members of the Chang family to a lifetime cap of $500,000. The policy provides an 80/20 coinsurance provision with a $3,000 stop-loss provision. The Changs are subject to a $300 annual family deductible. Don is required to contribute $150 per month toward this insurance; his employer pays the remainder of the premium.

Automobile Insurance (both cars)

Type	Personal auto policy
Coverages	25/50/10 split-limit liability
Uninsured motorist	25/50/10 split-limit liability
Collision	$200 deductible
Comprehensive	$200 deductible
Annual premium, car 1	$750
Annual premium, car 2	$550
Annual premium total	$1,300

Homeowner's/Renter's Insurance

HO-4 renter's insurance policy with $20,000 of actual cash-value coverage on personal property, with an annual premium of $120.

Umbrella Liability Insurance

None

Disability Insurance

Maria	$800 per month up to 6 months, paid by employer
Don	None

Questions

1. After reviewing the earnings multiple approach and the needs approach, Don and Maria opt for the simpler earnings multiple approach to estimate their life insurance needs. Explains Don, "There are just too many unknowns in that needs approach formula. Years of income to be replaced I can understand. If I die tomorrow, I want to know that Maria can buy a home and Andy can finish college. Andy is 2. With 20 years of my income, they should be able to do that." Maria agrees, although she cautions that before purchasing insurance she would like to confirm their estimates by completing the needs formula. They agree that they could earn a 5-percent after-tax, after-inflation return on the insurance benefit. Do Maria and Don have adequate life insurance? If not, how much should each consider purchasing? (*Hint:* Remember that expenses drop by 26 percent for a surviving family of two. Be sure to consult Table 9.2, "Earnings Multiples for Life Insurance.")

2. All of Don's life insurance and half of Maria's are provided through their employers. Is this a good idea?

3. Don recently read an article about universal life and variable life insurance. He has asked your opinion about purchasing one of these policies to provide additional insurance coverage for Maria and Andy. What would you advise him to do? Defend your answer.

4. The Changs have asked you to review their life insurance policies and explain them "in plain English." What life insurance policy features would you look for?

5. The Changs' life insurance agent recently suggested purchasing a whole life policy for Andy. Is this a good idea?

6. Do Maria and Don have adequate health insurance? If not, what improvements would you suggest and why?

7. Assume Don is injured in a car accident and incurs $5,000 of medical bills. Assuming that no one else in his family has made a claim this year, how much of the bill would his insurance company pay?

8. Next month is the "annual open enrollment period" for health insurance benefits through Don's employer. It is the only time of the year when he can make changes to his policy. Don is considering switching to an HMO or PPO. What are the advantages and disadvantages of making a change?

9. Don works for a small community bank with 54 employees. He is concerned about a possible layoff due to bank mergers. Don is especially worried because the family's health insurance is provided by his employer. What are some health insurance options available to the Changs if Don voluntarily leaves his job or is laid off?

10. Both Maria and Don are considering the purchase of disability insurance, because Don has none and Maria's employer policy is very short-term. What policy features would you recommend that they look for?

11. Do Maria and Don have adequate renter's insurance? If not, what improvements would you suggest and why?

12. Do Maria and Don have adequate auto insurance? If not, what improvements would you suggest and why?

13. How much would the Changs' policy pay if Don or Maria were involved in an accident with an uninsured driver? Is this enough? If not, suggest a recommended amount.

14. What policy options could the Changs select to reduce the cost of their property insurance?

15. What type of homeowner's policy should the Changs select when they purchase their first home? Explain your answer.

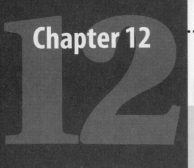
INVESTMENT BASICS:
Things You Should Know Before You Talk to a Broker or Financial Planner

A few years ago, Ki-Jana Carter didn't know anything about investing. How could he? Money had been tight in the two-bedroom apartment where he'd been raised outside of Columbus, Ohio. Carter's father had left when young Ki-Jana was just a baby, and his mom had to work 12- to 15-hour days just to make ends meet. Ki-Jana Carter didn't know about investing. He knew about football.

In 1995, Carter, a running back out of Penn State, became the first pick in the NFL draft. It was a dream come true for the 22-year-old—a career playing in the pros. During the preseason, Carter's mind wasn't on money or investments. It was on learning the playbook for the Cincinnati Bengals, his new team. However, a season-ending knee injury in his first preseason game served to teach him a more important lesson, one that many NFL players don't learn until too late: An NFL career—and the pay that comes with it—can vanish in an instant.

When Carter signed with the Bengals, he received a $19.2-million, 7-year contract, which included a $7.125-million signing bonus. Needless to say, he thought that the days of money being tight and living in a two-bedroom apartment were over. "I came out of college and felt invincible," says Carter. "After the injury it was like, 'Wow, I may not be making more money.'" Worried that he really might not make any more money, Carter decided to protect the money he already had. To help him handle his money, he interviewed 14 different financial planners and chose Mark Griege, a fee-only planner who's paid a percentage of Carter's investments. Griege and Carter agreed that it was time for Carter to learn

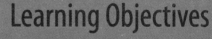

Learning Objectives

After reading this chapter you should be able to:

1. Set your goals and be ready to invest.
2. Differentiate between investing and speculating.
3. Understand how taxes impact your investments.
4. Calculate interest rates and real rates of return.
5. Manage risk in your investments.
6. Diversify your investments.
7. Allocate your assets in the manner that is best for you.

part four
MANAGING YOUR INVESTMENTS

about investing, so part of Griege's job is teaching Carter about investing. In other words, Griege not only tells Carter what to do with his money, but also tells him why.

Carter's investing goal is not only to protect his wealth and make money, but to understand investing from a commonsense perspective. "I see a lot of guys come into the league and want to go out and spend to show they have a lot of money," says Carter. "That's good now, but I'm trying to live like this when I'm 50, 60, 70." It's his new understanding of investing that'll allow him to achieve his financial goals.

An understanding of investing basics can go a long way toward helping you reach your financial goals, too. For example, understanding why interest rates fluctuate can mean the difference between getting in on an investment at the right time to make a nice profit and getting in at the wrong time to take a loss. Also, a wise investment may wind up providing you with that down payment on a house or new car.

Not only will an understanding of investments help you achieve your goals, but it'll also keep you from losing a bundle. Let's face it, the world of investments is littered with debt notices and red ink from all the people who went in unprepared—people losing their shirt, and the rest of their clothes, in a bad investment. Hey, it couldn't have all of its rewards without having a few challenges, too. Understanding investments means understanding how to get around the challenges while grabbing as many rewards as you can hold. Remember **Axiom 9: The Best Protection Is Knowledge**—an understanding of the basics and logic of investing will protect you from any potential pitfalls. That's Carter's approach, and it should also be yours.

AXIOM #9

The Best Protection Is Knowledge

AXIOM #8

Nothing Happens Without a Plan—Even (or Especially) a Simple Plan

AN INTRODUCTION TO INVESTMENT BASICS

Although it's important to understand the basic principles that guide investing, it's also important to keep in mind why you're investing in the first place. In personal financial planning, everything begins and ends with your goals, and investments are no exception. Before investing you must first decide what your goals are and how much you can set aside to meet those goals. Then you can develop an investment plan to reach those goals.

Setting Investment Goals

Without a plan and without goals, nothing happens. Let's face it, you won't make an A in this course if it isn't your goal. Things don't just happen without goals, planning, and the effort that's required. That's the point of **Axiom 8: Nothing Happens Without a Plan—Even (or Especially) a Simple Plan**.

You probably have goals, or at least dreams—there may be a house you'd like to buy, or maybe you'd like to retire early—but to reach those goals, you've got to formalize them. That means you've got to (1) write your goals down and prioritize them, (2) attach costs to them, (3) figure out when the money for those goals will be needed, and (4) periodically reevaluate your goals. Fortunately, it's not that difficult, but if you never set goals, you'll never reach them. In setting your goals it's important to be as specific as possible. Start with what you're saving for, then add in the cost and when you want to reach that goal. For example, rather than list "saving money" as a goal, state the purpose of your savings efforts, such as buying a car, and exactly how much you want saved by what time.

As we said in chapter 1, in formalizing your goals it's easiest to think about them in terms of short-term, intermediate-term, and long-term time horizons. Short-term goals are any financial goals that can be accomplished within a 1-year period, such as buying a television or taking a vacation. An intermediate-term goal is one that would take between 1 and 10 years to accomplish—perhaps paying for college for an older child or accumulating enough money for a down payment on a new house. A long-term goal is one for which it takes more than 10 years to accumulate the money—retirement, for example. In chapter 1 we also presented a worksheet, Figure 1.2, listing a number of possible short-, intermediate-, and long-term goals. In setting these goals the key is to be realistic, which means your goals should reflect your financial and life situation. The following questions might help you focus in on what goals are important to you:

- If I don't accomplish this goal, what are the consequences?
- Am I willing to make the financial sacrifices necessary to meet this goal?
- How much money do I need to accomplish this goal?
- When do I need this money?

If you don't formally set goals, you never have to think about what's going to happen 10, 20, or 30 years from now—you also don't have any control over what will happen in the future. Once you've set your goals, you then have to use the time value of money skills you've developed to translate them into action. For example, if you'd like to retire in 40 years with $500,000 and you feel you can earn 8 percent on your investments, you'd need to invest $1,930.11 at the end of each year.

$$FV = PMT(PVIFA)$$
$$\$500,000 = PMT(259.052)$$
$$\$1,930.11 = PMT$$

Financial Reality Check

Before you put your investment program into place, you should make sure you have a grip on your financial affairs. In other words, a financial reality check is in order. This reality check involves taking care of some very basic financial matters that serve as prerequisites to investing. We're talking about such things as making sure you're living within your means, having adequate insurance, keeping emergency funds—in effect, making sure your financial house is in order.

Balance Your Budget.
If you don't live within your means, you'll never be able to save, invest, or achieve any of your financial goals—it's that simple! There's no easier way to foil a financial plan than with a lack of control and a tendency toward impulse buying. Control is crucial. It means keeping your credit card under control, using restraint, and commonsense buying. It means acting your wage. If these are problems for you, consider trying the envelope system introduced in chapter 2. Under that system, you begin each month with the dollar amount allocated to each major expenditure category put into a separate envelope. Each time you spend in that area, you simply take the money out of the envelope, and when the envelope is empty, you're done spending in that area.

Put a Safety Net in Place.
Insurance seems awfully dull until you need it, but there's no question, you need it. The need for insurance rises from **Axiom 10: Protect Yourself Against Major Catastrophes—The Case for Insurance**. In the case of life insurance, it's not you that's being protected, but your family. The key concepts here are *planning* and *control*. After all, this whole book, and all of personal finance, is based on controlling your financial situation through careful planning. In the case of insurance, the last thing you want is to allow an unplanned event to destroy your financial future. Insurance provides you with some degree of control over the unexpected. As such, your insurance coverage—life, property and liability, and medical—should be in place before you begin an investment program.

AXIOM #10

Protect Yourself Against Major Catastrophes— The Case for Insurance

Maintain Adequate Emergency Funds.
It doesn't take much experience with a budget to realize that no budget is set in stone. As **Axiom 7** says, **Stuff Happens**. You never know when your car will have an unexpected meeting with a tree—you may walk away unharmed, but without some emergency funds, walking may be your only means of transportation for quite some time. You're a good driver—it won't happen to you, right? How about being a victim of downsizing or getting hit with a big medical bill? It can happen to anyone. Your emergency funds should be immediately available to you. Most financial planners recommend that you set aside an equivalent of 3 to 6 months' take-home pay. However, exactly what you need in the way of emergency funds depends upon whether you have access to other sources of emergency cash—for example, credit cards or lines of credit. In effect, access to other sources of emergency cash can reduce, but not eliminate, the level of emergency funds you need to maintain. These emergency or liquid funds are the income you may need in the event of an emergency. Saving up an emergency reserve can be painfully dull, especially if you see the stock market climbing or would like to buy a new car. If you don't have liquid funds to cover the unexpected, you might have to compromise your long-term investments. For example, you might need to sell your stock or real estate. Such actions might ruin your best-laid plans and cause you to miss opportunities.

AXIOM #7

Stuff Happens

Starting Your Investment Program

There's no easy way to start an investment program. In fact, the first step—making the commitment to get started—may be the most difficult step. As you start off, it's much easier to postpone your investment program "until I'm making more money." The longer you postpone investing, though, the longer you do without the help of your biggest investment ally. That investment ally is time. Because of **Axiom 2: The Time Value of Money**, the sooner you invest, the more you earn. As you should know by now, there's no substitute for time when it comes to investments—the earlier you begin

AXIOM #2

The Time Value of Money

AXIOM #15

Just Do It!

planning for the future, the easier it is to achieve your goals. That's why **Axiom 15: Just Do It!** is so important. Regardless of what your level of income is, there are an awful lot of people who are living on less than what you're earning—you can make room for investing. Keep in mind that time—your biggest investment ally—is stronger now than it ever will be.

> ### *Stop and Think*
> You can reach your financial goals! In fact, if you have time on your side, it may be easier to reach them than you think. In effect, a small change in your spending and investment habits could produce big returns later on. For example, if you're 20 now and you save $15 per month—that works out to about 50 cents per day, the cost of a package of M&M's—at 12 percent, 50 years later your savings will have grown to over $585,000. The key is to start early.

How do you go about starting an investment program? The first step is to revisit the first two questions you asked when setting up your goals: If I don't accomplish this goal, what are the consequences? and Am I willing to make the financial sacrifices necessary to meet this goal? Once you have the commitment, the next step is to come up with the money. There are several steps you can take to make this more effective and less painful.

AXIOM #13

Pay Yourself First—Making Your Financial Well-Being the Top Priority

Pay Yourself First.   This concept is so important that it became one of the axioms that we introduced in chapter 1—remember **Axiom 13: Pay Yourself First—Making Your Financial Well-Being the Top Priority**. There's no question that for most people, what they save is simply what they earn minus what they spend. However, when you pay yourself first, what you spend is what's left over. That is, you first set aside your savings, and what's left becomes the amount you can spend.

When you pay yourself first, you're acknowledging the fact that your long-term goals are of paramount importance. "Buying into" these goals first ensures the fact that your goals actually get funded. In effect, paying yourself first sets up a behavioral pattern in which saving for long-term goals becomes automatic, and excuses for why this month's savings can be passed up no longer work.

Make It Automatic.   When it comes to starting your investment program, the most important step is the first one, making a start, even if it's only $50 a month. Then when you can increase your monthly investments, do it—and make it automatic. If your employer allows for automatic withholding, take advantage of it. Your employer will automatically withhold money, which you can then direct to a bank, savings and loan, or credit union for investing. You can also have an amount automatically deducted from your checking account and sent to a brokerage firm or mutual fund for investing.

Take Advantage of Uncle Sam and Your Employer.   If your employer offers any matching investments, don't pass them by. Matching investments are about as close to getting something for nothing as you'll ever get. Also, keep an eye to any investments that are tax favored, such as traditional IRAs and Roth IRAs.

Windfalls.   Once in a while you're going to receive a bit of a windfall—perhaps an inheritance, a salary bonus, a gift, a tax refund, or maybe even something from the lottery. It would be easy to fritter away this windfall—don't. Instead, invest some or all of it. It's a painless way of building up your investments—take advantage of it.

Make Two Months a Year Your Investment Months. Some financial advisors suggest that if you're having trouble starting up your investment program, pick 2 months per year to cut back on your spending and make those your investment months. If you know that your "life of poverty" is over at the end of the month, it may be easier to stick to your savings.

Investing versus Speculating. As the title says, this chapter's about investing, not about speculating. What's the difference? Well, both involve risk. When you buy an **investment**, you put your money in an asset that *generates* a return. That is, part of its return comes in the form of an **income return**. For example, real estate pays rent, stocks pay dividends, and bonds pay interest—even if the stock (such as Microsoft) or bond isn't paying interest now, it will sometime—so buying these assets is considered investing. It's the return that the asset generates now and will generate in the future that determines its value. However, some assets don't generate a return. Gold coins and baseball cards, for example, are worth more in the future only if someone's willing to pay more for them. Their value depends *entirely* on supply and demand, not on the return that they generate. As a result, an asset of this type is considered a **speculation**. Other examples of speculation would include comic books, autographs, rare books and coins, nonincome-producing real estate, and gems. Of course, you can make a pretty penny speculating. The first issue of the X-Men appeared in September 1963 and cost 12¢. About 34 years later it was worth around $5,200—that's an appreciation rate of over 37 percent per year. Why has it grown so in value? The answer is simple: Supply and demand—someone's willing to pay $5,200 for it, so that's its value. It could have just as easily gone down in value and be worth nothing today. That's the case with many baseball cards and "collector's POGs" purchased in the early 1990s. As the baseball card market crashed in the early 1990s, many speculators who'd put their entire savings into this market after witnessing the spectacular increase in the value of these cards during the 1970s and 1980s took on heavy losses. Why did the value of baseball cards drop so in value? No one wanted to buy them, so their price dropped.

People have speculated for centuries. In fact, in the sixteenth century, tulip bulb speculation was the equivalent of the recent comic book and baseball card speculation, with the prices of a single tulip bulb reaching outrageous levels. In fact, shortly before the tulip bulb market crashed, one recorded trade had a single bulb being exchanged for the following total: 17 bushels of wheat, 34 bushels of rye, 4 fat oxen, 8 fat swine, 12 fat sheep, 2 goat's-heads of wine, 4 kegs of beer, 2 tons of butter, 1,000 pounds of cheese, a complete bed, a suit of clothes, and a silver drinking cup!

Today, there's a new variation of speculative securities available—derivatives, such as futures and options. Derivative securities are those whose value is derived from the value of other assets. These securities are extremely risky and, for the beginning investor, should be considered speculative in nature. They allow you to invest with a small amount of cash in such commodities as gold, orange juice futures, and stock indices. Granted, they have appeal to those with nerves of steel and to those who don't realize the risks they're taking. However, they're extremely dangerous. In effect, you're betting on short-term movements in these underlying assets. In short, they're not something to rely on to achieve your financial goals.

With *investing*, as opposed to speculating, the value of your asset is determined by what return it earns, not merely by whether that asset is a fashionable asset to own. In other words, investments have intrinsic value because they produce income, and although in the short-term their price may wander a bit from their intrinsic value, in the long-run the price approaches the intrinsic value. As a result, investments are less risky, and their value is simply an extension of how much income they're producing now along with what they're expected to produce in the future. Certainly, investment is quite a bit duller than speculation, but when you're dealing with your future financial security, dull and certain aren't bad things.

Investment
An asset that generates a return. For example, stocks pay dividends and bonds pay interest, so they're considered investments.

Income Return
Investment return received directly from the company or organization in which you've invested, usually in the form of dividends or interest payments.

Speculation
An asset whose value depends solely on supply and demand, as opposed to being based upon the return that it generates. For example, gold coins and baseball cards are worth more in the future only if someone is willing to pay more for them.

Investment Choices

Today there are more investment alternatives than ever. As a result, the process of deciding on the right investment seems so bewildering that some people give up responsibility for their own investments and blindly pass that duty on to an advisor. That doesn't mean the help of a financial advisor isn't right for some people, but just like Ki-Jana Carter, you should have an understanding of what you're doing with your money. Fortunately, investments aren't as confusing as they seem from the outside. Actually, there are only two basic categories of investments:

- **Lending investments.** Savings accounts and bonds, which are debt instruments issued by corporations and by the government, are examples of lending investments.

- **Ownership investments.** Preferred stocks and common stocks, which represent an ownership position in the corporation, along with income-producing real estate, are examples of ownership investments.

Let's take a closer look at these two types of investments.

Lending Investments. Whenever you put money in a savings account or buy a bond, you're actually lending someone your money. The amount that you've lent them is your investment. A savings account pays you interest on the balance you hold in your savings account. With a bond, your return is generally fixed and known ahead of time. It has a set **maturity date,** at which time the bond is terminated and the investor is returned the money that has been lent. The face value of the bond, which is the amount you receive when the bond matures, is referred to as the **par value** or **principal.** Most bonds issued by corporations trade in units of $1,000, although bonds issued by federal, state, or local governments may trade in units of $5,000 or $10,000. Then, over the life of the bond, you receive interest payments, which are set when the bond is issued. The **coupon interest rate** refers to the actual rate of interest the bond pays, with these payments generally being made on a semiannual basis. Most bonds have fixed interest rates, but some have variable or floating rates, meaning that the bond's interest rate changes periodically to reflect the current level of interest rates.[1] Let's assume, for example, that you've bought a 20-year bond issued by the government, with a par value of $1,000 and an interest rate of 8 percent. You'll receive $80 per year in interest payments ($0.08 \times \$1,000$). Then, at maturity, which in this case is in 20 years, you'll be returned the par value, which is $1,000.

Maturity Date
The date at which the borrower must repay the loan or borrowed funds.

Par Value or **Principal**
The stated amount on the face of a bond, which the firm is to repay at the maturity date.

Coupon Interest Rate
The interest to be paid annually on a bond as a percentage of par value, which is specified in the contractual agreement.

[1] There are also zero-coupon bonds, which make no interest payments to the bondholder. We will talk about these in chapter 15.

BEFORE RISKING THE MONEY,
Invest in Financial Literacy

A little knowledge may be a dangerous thing, but when it comes to investing, no knowledge is even worse.

And little or no knowledge about money and investing is what all too many Americans have these days, even those who are active investors and whose future economic well-being depends upon it.

Like voters who are content to choose their candidate on the basis of a few sound bites, rather than find out what the candidate really stands for, many of us prefer to invest on the basis of a friend's advice rather than hard-earned fundamental market knowledge.

Investor attitudes probably have been like this since markets began, but as Americans become more and more dependent on their own decisions for retirement and other forms of saving, regulators and even some corporate personnel executives are becoming alarmed over the potential consequences.

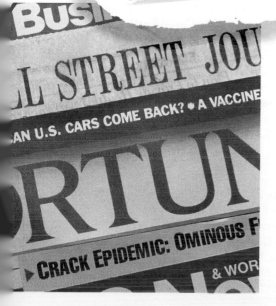

Ⓐ A recent survey by the Investor Protection Trust, an Arlington nonprofit organization that works to educate investors and assist in prosecuting securities fraud, found that fewer than one in five investors is "financially literate"—meaning that they could answer basic questions on such topics as bond prices and interest rates, blue-chip stocks, and financial adviser background and credentials.

"These are not encouraging findings for a society that is moving increasingly to a self-serve approach to personal finance," said Mark Griffin, the chief securities regulator in Utah and a trustee of the Investor Protection Trust.

Two out of three investors—and the survey covered only people who actively invest, either on their own or through an employer-sponsored retirement program—do not have a financial plan, "a basic cornerstone of responsible money management," Griffin said.

And of those who use a financial professional, either a broker or a planner, only about one in 10 bothered to check the adviser's background.

The figures "suggest that millions of investors, particularly women and older investors, are sitting ducks for investment fraud and abuse," he said. Ⓑ

Source: Albert B. Crenshaw, "Before Risking the Money, Invest in Financial Literacy," *The Washington Post*, May 19, 1996, p. H1. © 1996, *The Washington Post*. Reprinted with permission.

Analysis and Implications ...

A. This course and this text should go a long way toward making you financially literate. However, with the ever-changing world investment scene, it's important that you continuously keep updating your understanding of investments. One good way of keeping up-to-date is reading any one of the several magazines directed at personal investing, such as *Money*, *Smart Money*, and *Kiplinger's Personal Finance*. Just keep in mind that you're reading them for background, not "hot investment tips."

B. From **Axiom 9: The Best Protection Is Knowledge** we know that the only way you can protect yourself is with an understanding of the investment world. You also know from **Axiom 12: The Agency Problem** that the investment advice you receive may be motivated by commissions.

With lending investments, you usually know ahead of time exactly what your return will be, which isn't always a good thing. For example, because you've locked in on an 8-percent return on your bond, if inflation suddenly climbs to 16 percent, your return won't even keep up with inflation. However, if inflation instead drops, your 8-percent return may look even better than it did when you purchased the bond. The biggest potential problem with lending investments arises when the lender experiences financial difficulties and can't pay the interest on the bond, or can't pay off the bond at maturity. For example, if the firm that issued the bond goes bankrupt, the bondholders would most likely lose their entire investment. In other words, if the company whose bonds you bought goes broke, you go broke, too. Unfortunately, even though lending investments let you share a lender's financial pain, they don't let you share any of the pleasure. Basically, if the lender suddenly makes a ton of money, you don't. With lending investments, the best-case scenario is that the issuer pays you all the interest that's owed and at maturity gives you back your principal. Actually, this best-case scenario is much better than it at first seems. If you carefully choose whom you lend money to, whose bonds you buy, or where you open a savings account, there can be much less risk with lending investments than with ownership investments. In addition, as we'll see later, the returns can be quite respectable.

The Facts of Life

Bonds aren't always the best investment over a very long period of time. Over the 10-year period from 1987 through 1996, the average annual return on long-term corporate bonds was 9.5 percent, and the average inflation rate was 3.7 percent. However, over the 30-year period from 1967 through 1996, the average annual return on long-term corporate bonds was 8.2 percent, and the average inflation rate was 5.4 percent.

Ownership Investments. The two major forms of ownership investment are real estate and stocks. Real estate investments include such things as rental apartments and investments in income-producing property, such as shopping malls and office buildings. In each case, you're investing in something that generates a return: rent. Your home could also be considered a real estate investment. In a sense it generates income because it eliminates rent payments that you would otherwise have to make. The major disadvantage of real estate investments is that they tend to be quite illiquid. That is, when it comes time to sell off your investment, you may have a hard time getting a fair price for it or even finding someone interested in buying it.

The most popular ownership investment is stocks, but the actual "ownership" isn't of an asset you can hold in your hand or live in. When you purchase 50 shares of General Electric's common or preferred stock, you've purchased a small portion of the General Electric corporation. Although you own only a tiny fraction of GE, buying stock does make you an owner or equity holder, with "equity" being another term for ownership. What do you get as an owner of GE? Don't count on any free lightbulbs. In the case of common stock ownership, you get a chance to vote for the board of directors, which oversees GE's operations. In addition, if GE earns a profit, you'll most likely receive a portion of those profits in the form of **dividends**, which are generally paid out on a quarterly basis. As profits and dividends continue to increase, investors see the stock as more valuable and are thus willing to pay more to purchase it. Thus, the price goes up, and there's no limit as to how high a stock's price can rise. Look at 1995 and 1996, when the average U.S. stock went up by over 30 percent and 20 percent, respectively. In 1996, one winner was Rational Software, a company that makes business

Dividend

A payment by a corporation to its shareholders.

software. Its stock price went up 253 percent. Stock prices can also fall, and the fall can be huge. For example, on the downside in 1996, Acclaim Entertainment, the maker of the video games NBA Jam and Mortal Kombat saw its stock price drop by 73.7 percent. Of course, there's a limit as to how far a stock's price can fall: to $0.00.

In the case of preferred stock, the dividend is generally fixed, with the preferred stockholder receiving a constant annual dividend as long as the firm has the cash to pay that dividend. However, whereas you get a chance to vote for the board of directors if you own GE common stock, you don't get to if you own GE preferred stock, unless GE has suffered some financial problems and omitted some preferred stock dividends. Of course, companies must pay the interest to their debt holders before they can distribute dividends to their stockholders. Thus, if debt, such as bonds, eat up a company's profits, stockholders get no dividends. Moreover, preferred stockholders take a "preferred" position to common stockholders—that is, they receive their dividends first, and common stockholders receive their dividends from whatever's left over.

The Returns from Investing

When you invest your money, you can receive your return in one of two ways. First, an investment can go up or down in value—in the language of investments, this is referred to as a **capital gain** or **loss**. Although most people associate capital gains and losses with real estate and common stock, these gains and losses also come with bonds. In fact, most of the time when you buy a bond, you buy it for something other than its par value. That means if you hold it to maturity, you'll experience some capital gains or losses on your bond. In effect, capital gains or losses come from any price movements in the investment.

The second component of the return on your investment is the income return that you receive from the investment. Income return consists of any payments you receive directly from the company or organization in which you've invested. In the case of bonds, your income return is the interest you receive, and, in the case of common and preferred stocks, your income return comes in the form of dividends. Thus, the rate of return can be calculated as follows:

$$\text{rate of return} = \frac{(\text{ending value} - \text{beginning value}) + \text{income return}}{\text{beginning value}}$$

Thus, if a stock climbs from a price of $45 to $55 per share over 1 year while paying $3 in dividends, its rate of return over that year would be

$$\text{rate of return} = \frac{(\$55 - \$45) + \$3}{\$45} = \frac{\$10 + \$3}{\$45} = \frac{\$13}{\$45} = 28.89\%$$

If you're calculating the rate of return over a number of years, you may want to break this rate down into the annual rate of return. To annualize the rate of return, you need only multiply the rate of return times $1/N$, where N is the number of years for which the investment is held. Thus, the annualized rate of return can be calculated as follows:

$$\frac{\text{annualized}}{\text{rate of return}} = \frac{(\text{ending value} - \text{beginning value}) + \text{income return}}{\text{beginning value}} \times \frac{1}{N}$$

Thus, if over a 3-year period a stock climbs from $45 to $68 per share and pays a total of $7 in dividends over that period, its annualized rate of return would be

$$\frac{\text{annualized}}{\text{rate of return}} = \frac{(\$68 - \$45) + \$7}{\$45} \times \frac{1}{3} = \frac{\$23 + \$7}{\$45} \times \frac{1}{3} =$$

$$= \frac{\$30}{\$45} \times \frac{1}{3} = 0.667 \times 0.333 = 0.222, \text{ or } 22.2\%$$

Capital Gain or **Loss**
The gain (or loss) on the sale of a capital asset. For example, any return (or loss) from the appreciation (or drop in value) in value of a share of stock would be considered a capital gain (or loss).

**Understand how taxes
impact your investments.**

AXIOM #6

**Taxes Bias Personal
Finance Decisions**

Leverage

Using borrowed funds to increase
your purchasing power.

FITTING TAXES INTO INVESTING

Certainly, when we compare investment returns we'll want to make our comparison on an after-tax basis—that is, what we pay to Uncle Sam doesn't count. As we examine the different investment alternatives, we'll look closer at taxes, but several points hold true regardless of what we invest in.

- You should keep in mind that the tax rate you're concerned with is your marginal tax rate, because that's the rate you pay on the next dollar of earnings.

- There are a number of tax-free investment alternatives, and they should be compared only on an after-tax basis. Of course, the higher your marginal tax bracket, the more attractive tax-free investments become.

- There are a number of ways in which you can make your investments on a *tax-deferred* basis, which means that not only does your investment grow free of taxes, but the money you invest isn't taxed until you liquidate your investment.

- When it comes to taxes, capital gains are better than income return. Recall from chapter 4 that under the Taxpayer Relief Act of 1997, the maximum tax rate paid on long-term capital gains dropped from 28 to 20 percent. And, for those in the 15-percent tax bracket, it dropped to 10 percent. Then, beginning in the year 2001, these rates drop to 18 and 8 percent on long-term capital gains on assets purchased beginning in the year 2001 and held for at least 5 years. For example, if you were in the 39.6-percent marginal tax bracket and had $50,000 of additional ordinary income, your tax bill would come to ($50,000 × 36.9%) = $18,450. If this $50,000 of additional income came in the form of long-term capital gains, your taxes would be only ($50,000 × 20%) = $10,000, saving you ($18,450 − $10,000) = $8,450. Just as valuable as the tax break on capital gains income is the fact that you don't have to claim it—and therefore pay taxes on it—until you sell the asset. That is, you can time when you want to claim your capital gains.

As a result, we'll have to keep an eye to taxes as we evaluate the different investment alternatives. Taxes make some investments better than they would otherwise be, and others worse—it all gets back to **Axiom 6: Taxes Bias Personal Finance Decisions**.

UNDERSTANDING THE CONCEPT OF LEVERAGE

Another factor, in addition to taxes, that can affect your investment return is borrowing some of the money you invest. Is this a common practice? Yes. In fact, although some investors borrow some of the money they invest in stocks and bonds, most investors in real estate borrow a large portion of the money they invest. To understand the potential risks and returns from this investment strategy, you must first understand the principle of leverage. **Leverage** refers to the use of borrowed funds to increase your purchasing power. If the value of your investment increases, the use of leverage will increase your return. However, if the value of your investment declines, the use of leverage will magnify your losses. In effect, leverage is a double-edged sword.

When you borrow money to pay for your investments, you're leveraging yourself. You've increased your purchasing power because borrowing allows you to invest more than you would otherwise be able to. Let's look at a case in which you invest $100,000 with 20 percent down, borrowing the remaining $80,000 at 10 percent. That means you would pay $8,000 per year in interest to finance your investment. If your investment went up by 20 percent, to $120,000, and you paid off your loan, you would be left with $32,000 or ($120,000 − $80,000 − $8,000), which is a 60-percent return (you started out with $20,000 and now have $32,000). What leverage does is allow you to put down a small amount (in this case, $20,000) and benefit from the capital gains on a much larger amount (in this case, $100,000 made up of your $20,000 and $80,000 of borrowed money).

Although the concept of leverage allows you to magnify the effect of any capital appreciation that your investment may experience, it also magnifies any losses. For example, if your investment drops by 20 percent, you'd not only lose the $20,000 you invested, but also be out the $8,000 interest you paid—in effect, you'd lose even more than you invested. Thus, leverage is a two-edged sword—it magnifies both the good and the bad.

A BRIEF INTRODUCTION TO MARKET INTEREST RATES

As you will see, interest rates play an extremely important role in determining the value of a share of stock, a bond, or a real estate investment. Interest rates also determine what we earn on our savings and are closely tied to the rate of inflation. Therefore, you need to understand interest rates—how they're determined and what affects them—before making any investments. Let's start off by taking a look at what a real interest rate is.

Nominal and Real Rates of Return and Interest Rates

The **nominal** (or **quoted**) **rate of return** is the rate of return earned on an investment without any adjustment for inflation. It's the rate that's quoted in the *Wall Street Journal* for specific bonds or the rate your bank advertises for its savings accounts, and it determines how much interest you earn when you lend money to someone. How much have you *really* earned? The **real rate of return**, which is simply the nominal rate of return minus the inflation rate, tells you how much you've really earned after adjusting for inflation. Thus, if you earn 12 percent on an investment while the inflation rate is 4 percent, the nominal rate of return is 12 percent, and the real rate of return is 8 percent (12% − 4%). In effect, the real rate is just the nominal rate adjusted for inflation.

Historical Interest Rates

The nominal interest rates for high-quality bonds issued by corporations (corporate Aaa bonds), bonds with 30-year maturities issued by the federal government (30-year Treasury bonds), and bonds with 3-month maturities issued by the federal government (3-month Treasury bonds) over the recent past are shown in Figure 12.1. In looking at these historical interest rates, you should notice that nominal interest rates have dropped considerably over the past 15 years. Today, the high rates experienced in 1981 seem almost too high to believe. In effect, as inflation slowed down, investors demanded a lower return on money they lent, which resulted in a drop in the nominal interest rates. This link between inflation and nominal interest rates has its roots in **Axiom 1: The Risk-Return Trade-Off**.

Although it's not shown in Figure 12.1, the real rate of interest can be calculated by simply subtracting the inflation rate from the nominal interest rate. Thus, for 1996, the real rate of interest on 3-month Treasury bills was only 1.89 percent (the nominal rate of 5.19 percent minus the inflation rate of 3.3 percent). You'll notice that the real rate of interest is different for long-term corporate bonds from the rate for 3-month Treasury bills. Why? The real rate of interest includes a compensation for risk, and corporate bonds have more risk than Treasury bills. Once again, that's **Axiom 1: The Risk-Return Trade-Off—Investors Don't Take on Additional Risk Unless They Expect to Be Compensated with Additional Return** at work.

What Makes Up Interest Rate Risk?

From Axiom 1 we know that investors receive a return for delaying consumption. We call this return for delaying consumption k^*, the **real risk-free rate of interest**. You can think of it as the interest rate on a bond with no risk in a world with no inflation. Because very short-term Treasury bills are virtually risk-free, the interest rate on them

Nominal (or **Quoted**) **Rate of Return**
The rate of return earned on an investment, unadjusted for lost purchasing power.

Real Rate of Return
The current or nominal rate of return minus the inflation rate.

The Risk-Return Trade-Off—Investors Don't Take on Additional Risk Unless They Expect to Be Compensated with Additional Return

Real Risk-Free Rate of Interest k^*
The hypothetical interest rate existing on a security with no risk in a world with no inflation. It's generally thought of as the interest rate that would exist on very short-term Treasury bills in a world of no inflation.

FIGURE 12.1

Interest and Inflation Rates, 1981–1996

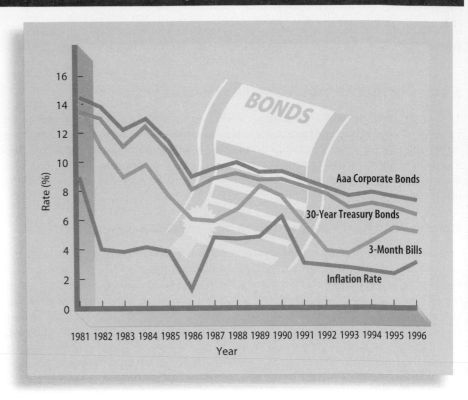

Inflation Risk Premium *IRP*

The premium rate above the real rate of return that investors demand to compensate for anticipated inflation over the life of a security. The size of this premium goes up and down as the level of anticipated inflation rises and falls.

Default

The failure of a debtor to make interest or principal payments when they are due.

Default Risk Premium *DRP*

An additional investment return to compensate investors for taking on the risk that the issuer may not pay the interest or principal on a security. The default risk premium should reflect the riskiness of the issuer and should be zero for government securities, because the government can print more money if need be.

can be thought of as the real risk-free rate. We also know from Axiom 1 that bond investors receive an additional return for taking on risk. The question we want to answer now is, What makes up interest rate risk?

Interest rate risk has many components. One risk investors face is the possibility of changes in inflation. Increased inflation snatches up a portion of return on investments. As Axiom 1 points out, investors will demand a return above the real rate of return to compensate for the anticipated inflation over the life of the investment. This additional return is referred to as the **inflation risk premium** *IRP*. The size of this premium goes up and down based on changes in the level of anticipated inflation.

In looking back at Figure 12.1, it's interesting to note that these three debt instruments all carry different interest rate levels. Much of the difference between the high rates on long-term corporate bonds and the lower rates on 30-year Treasury bonds can be explained by the fact that corporate bonds may someday fail to make, or **default** on, their interest payments, whereas Treasury bonds won't—remember, the government can just print more money if need be. In effect, corporate bonds, regardless of how highly rated they are, carry more risk than do Treasury bonds—the risk of defaulting. As a result, they also have a higher return attached to them to compensate investors for taking on the risk of default. This additional return is referred to as the **default risk premium** *DRP*.

The default risk premium explains the difference between the interest rate levels on Treasury bonds and long-term corporate bonds, but it doesn't explain the rate differences between 3-month Treasury bills and 30-year Treasury bonds. After all, neither has any default risk, because they're both issued by the government, which can print more money to make its interest and principal payments if need be. Instead, this difference is a result of the **maturity risk premium** *MRP*. This premium▶

is an additional return demanded by investors on longer-term bonds to compensate for the fact that the value of bonds with longer maturities tends to fluctuate more when interest rates change. The longer the time to maturity, the greater the bond's price will fluctuate when interest rates change. Also, if you think about savings accounts, there's no maturity risk associated with them, because they don't really have a maturity date associated with them—you can withdraw your money at any time. This lack of a maturity risk premium explains why they have a lower interest rate than bonds.

Although it's not evident from the information presented in Table 12.1 and Figure 12.1, there's one final risk factor affecting interest rates—the **liquidity risk premium LRP**. This premium reflects the risk that some bonds can't be converted into cash quickly at a fair market price. Some bonds, particularly bonds issued by small municipalities, are very infrequently traded. As a result, if you're forced to sell one of these bonds in a hurry due to an emergency, you may not find any buyers. To attract a buyer, you might have to sell it for less than it's actually worth, or you might get stuck holding on to it. Investors will therefore tack on a liquidity risk premium if they think a bond won't be able to be converted to cash quickly and at a fair market value.

Determinants of the Quoted, or Nominal, Interest Rate

What do we get when we put all of these premiums and required returns together? Quite simply, we get the quoted or nominal interest rate.

$$\text{Nominal (or Quoted) Interest Rate} = k^* + IRP + DRP + MRP + LRP$$

where

$$k^* = \text{the real risk-free rate of interest}$$
$$IRP = \text{the inflation risk premium}$$
$$DRP = \text{the default risk premium}$$
$$MRP = \text{the maturity risk premium}$$
$$LRP = \text{the liquidity risk premium}$$

This equation (12.1) is simply an in-depth explanation of **Axiom 1: The Risk-Return Trade-Off** as applied to bonds. The return that bondholders demand for delaying consumption is $k^* + IRP$, and the return that they demand for taking on added risk is $DRP + MRP + LRP$. As long as you keep thinking back to Axiom 1, this equation will make more sense.

How Interest Rates Affect Returns on Other Investments

The relationship between returns on all the different investment alternatives is extremely tangled. For example, common stocks tend to be riskier than bonds, so you won't invest in common stocks unless they have a higher expected return. That means that if bonds are returning 6 percent, you may be satisfied with a 9-percent return on stocks. However, if bonds were returning 12 percent, you wouldn't invest in stocks if the expected return were only 9 percent. You might demand a 15-percent return on your common stock investment.

In effect, the expected returns on all the investments are related—what you can earn on one investment determines what you demand on another. Interest rates can be thought of as a kind of a "base" return. When interest rates go up, investors demand a higher return on all other investments, and when interest rates go down, the return investors demand on other investments goes down. In effect, all the different investments compete for your investment dollars, and when interest rates go up, the other investments have to match that increase.

Maturity Risk Premium MRP

An additional return demanded by investors in longer-term securities to compensate for the fact that the value of securities with longer maturities tends to fluctuate more when interest rates change.

Liquidity Risk Premium LRP

An additional return for compensation for the risk that a security cannot be converted into cash quickly at a fair market price. It's close to zero for Treasury securities, which are easy to sell, and larger for securities issued by very small firms.

AXIOM #1

The Risk-Return Trade-Off

TABLE 12.1

Interest and Inflation Rates, 1981–1996

Year	3-Month Treasury Bills	30-Year Treasury Bonds	Aaa Rated Corporate Bonds	Inflation Rate
1981	14.08%	13.44%	14.17%	8.9%
1982	10.69	12.76	13.79	3.9
1983	8.63	11.18	12.04	3.8
1984	9.52	12.39	12.71	4.0
1985	7.49	10.79	11.37	3.8
1986	5.98	7.80	9.02	1.1
1987	5.82	8.58	9.38	4.4
1988	6.68	8.96	9.71	4.4
1989	8.12	8.45	9.26	4.6
1990	7.51	8.61	9.32	6.1
1991	5.42	8.14	8.77	3.1
1992	3.45	7.67	8.14	2.9
1993	3.02	6.59	7.22	2.7
1994	4.41	7.23	7.96	2.7
1995	5.56	6.96	7.59	2.5
1996	5.19	6.41	7.36	3.3
Mean	6.98	9.12	9.87	3.89

SOURCE: *Federal Reserve Bulletin*, various issues, and *Federal Reserve Release* H. 15 (519), various issues.

LEARNING OBJECTIVE #5

Manage risk in your investments.

A LOOK AT THE RISK-RETURN TRADE-OFFS

From Axiom 1 you know that risk goes hand in hand with potential return. The more risk you are willing to take on, the greater the potential return—but also, the greater the possibility that you will lose money. What does all this mean to investors? It means you must take steps to eliminate risk without affecting your potential return. Also, there's no question that you must accept some risk to meet your long-term financial goals, so you must balance the amount of risk you're willing to take on with the amount of return you need from your investments. Before we examine the sources of risk in investments, let's take a look at the historical levels of risk and return in the investment markets.

Historical Levels of Risk and Return

Because a historical perspective in investments is a healthy thing to acquire, let's look at the historical levels of risk and return. We'll look at these levels for the past 71 years.[2] If you look at these returns graphically, plotting average annual return against risk, or variability of returns as our measure of risk, you get the graph in Figure 12.2. As you can see, it bears a strong resemblance to the risk-return trade-off graph first presented in chapter 1 (Figure 1.4). Remember, when we presented the risk-return relationship described in Axiom 1, we talked about expected return. Here you see that what was predicted by Axiom 1 in fact holds. Investments that produce higher returns have higher levels of risk associated with them.

[2]Roger G. Ibbotson and Rex A. Sinquefield, *Stocks, Bonds, Bills, & Inflation 1997 Yearbook* (Chicago: Ibbotson Associates, 1997).

FIGURE 12.2

Risk-Return Relationship

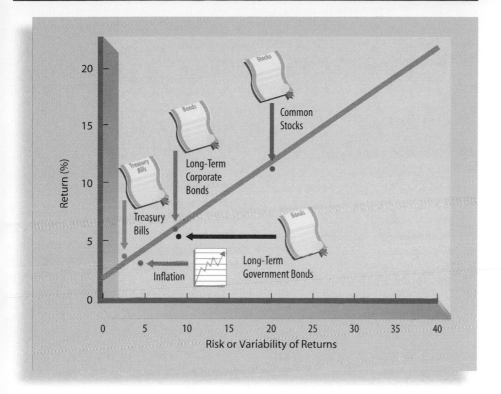

Sources of Risk in the Risk-Return Trade-Off

The compensation that investors demand for taking on added risk differs for every investment because every investment has a different level of risk. Here we described a number of different sources of investment risk. The purpose behind presenting these "sources of risk" is to give you an intuitive understanding of what causes fluctuations in the prices and values of different investments. Keep in mind that these sources are not mutually exclusive—that is, there's a good deal of overlap between some of them. In effect, it's very difficult to look at price fluctuation in an investment and try to attribute it solely to one or another "source" of risk. However, some investments are more vulnerable to one source of risk, while some are to another, so understanding these sources can tell you a lot about many investments.

Interest Rate Risk.   One source of risk to investors finds its roots in changes in interest rates. These interest rate changes may be a result of economic factors or of the intervention of the government in trying to simulate or control the economy. Regardless of their source, interest rate changes can be bad news for investors. For example, when market interest rates rise, the price of outstanding bonds declines, because new bonds with higher interest rates are now available, making the older bonds with a lower interest rate less attractive. No one will want to buy your $1,000, 6.5-percent, 10-year bond when $1,000, 8-percent, 10-year bonds are now available. The higher the interest rate climbs, the less your bond will be worth. The same basic relationship holds for common stock. When market interest rates rise, the price of common stock drops. This fluctuation in security prices due to changes in the market interest rate is a result of **interest rate risk**. Unfortunately, because increases in interest rates affect all securities in the same way, it's impossible to completely eliminate interest rate risk.

Interest Rate Risk
The risk of fluctuations in security prices due to changes in the market interest rate.

Inflation Risk

The risk that rising prices will eat away the purchasing power of your money, and that changes in the anticipated level of inflation will result in interest rate changes, which will in turn cause security price fluctuations.

Business Risk

The risk of fluctuations in security prices resulting from good or bad management decisions, or how well or poorly the firm's products are doing in the marketplace.

Financial Risk

The risk associated with a company's use of debt. As a firm takes on more debt, it also takes on interest and principal payments that must be made regardless of how well the firm does. If a company takes on too much debt and can't meet its obligations, investors risk the company defaulting or dropping in stock value.

Liquidity Risk

Risk associated with the inability to liquidate a security quickly and at a fair market price. For securities that are thinly traded—that is, there's relatively little trading in them—liquidity risk can be substantial.

Market Risk

Risk associated with overall market movements. There tend to be periods of bull markets, when all stocks seem to move upward, and times of bear markets, when all stocks tend to decline in price.

Inflation Risk.   **Inflation risk** reflects the likelihood that rising prices will eat away the purchasing power of your money, and that changes in the anticipated level of inflation will result in interest rate changes, which will in turn cause security price fluctuations. Inflation risk is thus closely linked to interest rate risk. Inflation risk is important enough in the valuation and investment processes that it's generally treated as a totally separate source of risk. Unexpected increases in inflation may cause a financial plan that appears to be solid to fall short in achieving its goals. As a result, you need to reevaluate your financial plan periodically to make sure it is adequate to meet your goals. Fortunately for those of you with stocks, over long periods of time common stocks have produced a return well above the rate of inflation, thereby preserving the purchasing power of your money.

Business Risk.   Most stocks and bonds are influenced by how well or poorly the company that issued them is performing. **Business risk** deals with fluctuations in investment value that are caused by good or bad management decisions, or how well or poorly the firm's products are doing in the marketplace. Businesses can go bankrupt, and management does make some poor decisions. Look at Smith Corona, the typewriter company. They decided to stand firm and continue to make typewriters in the face of the onslaught by personal computers. Bad decision! In 1995 the company's common stock fell in value by 98.6 percent. Interestingly, business risk is different for different companies. Some companies seem to post even profits year in and year out, regardless of what's happening in the economy, while the profits levels of other firms tend to swing wildly.

Financial Risk.   **Financial risk** is risk associated with the use of debt by the firm. As a firm takes on more debt, it also takes on interest and principal payments that must be made regardless of how well the firm does. Thus, when the firm does poorly, it still must make these payments. If the firm can't make the payments, it could go bankrupt. Thus, how the firm raises money affects its level of risk.

Liquidity Risk.   **Liquidity risk** deals with the inability to liquidate a security quickly and at a fair market price. For investments that are infrequently traded, it can be hard to find a buyer. Many times this is the case for collectibles, art, real estate, and common stocks of very small firms. With these investments you may be able to realize a fair market value when you liquidate them, but it may take weeks or even months before they are sold. Sometimes it's impossible to find a buyer at a fair market price, and you wind up having to sell for less than an asset's worth—sometimes even for a loss. Buying a piece of your favorite sports team has long been a popular investment for the super-rich, but there's a good deal of liquidity risk in such a venture. Harvey Lighton, owner of 3.1237 percent of the New York Yankees, learned this lesson in 1995 when he took out a newspaper ad offering a 1-percent stake in the Yankees for $2.95 million. There were no takers. He then considered a plan to take a 2-percent stake in the Yankees and divide it into 20,000 pieces, each representing one millionth of the team, and sell them for $500 each. That didn't work either. For investors that need money fast, liquidity risk is an important consideration. Not all your investments need to be liquid, but you certainly need some liquid investments.

Market Risk.   **Market risk** is risk associated with overall market movements. There tend to be periods of bull markets—that is, times when all stocks seem to move upward—and times of bear markets, when all stocks tend to decline in price. The same tends to be true in the bond markets, where bond prices tend to move together. These periods may be a result of changes in the economy, changes in the mood of investors, or changes in interest rates. Thus, market risk and interest rate risk are examples of overlap in "sources" of risk.

Political and Regulatory Risk. **Political** and **regulatory risk** comes from our nation's and states' capitals. This source of risk results from unanticipated changes in the tax or legal environment that have been imposed by the government. Changes in the capital gains tax rate, or in the tax-deductibility of interest on municipal bonds, or the passage of any new regulatory reform laws would affect investment values and are thus examples of political and regulatory risk.

Exchange Rate Risk. **Exchange rate risk** refers to the variability in earnings resulting from changes in exchange rates. For example, if you invest in a German bond, you first convert your dollars into German marks. When you liquidate that investment, you sell your bond for German marks and convert those marks into dollars. What you earn on your investment depends on how well the investment performed and what happened to the exchange rate. For the international investor, exchange rate risk is simply another layer of risk that must be faced.

> ### *The Facts of Life*
> Much of exchange rate risk comes from fluctuations in inflation rates in other countries. For example, in 1993 the inflation rate in Argentina was 4,924 percent, and by 1995 it had fallen to 3.9 percent. At the extreme in terms of inflation rates was Serbia, which in 1993 experienced an inflation rate of 363 quadrillion (363,000,000,000,000,000) percent.

Call Risk. **Call risk** is the risk to bondholders that a bond may be called away from them before maturity. **Calling a bond** refers to redeeming the bond early, and many bonds are callable. When a bond is called, the bondholder generally receives the face value of the bond plus 1 year of interest payments. This is a risk that applies only to investments in callable bonds.

Understanding Your Tolerance for Risk

Not everyone has the same tolerance for risk. Some individuals are continuously checking their investments' results—elated by their successes and depressed by their losses. Others can take on risk without breaking a sweat or looking at a financial page in the newspaper. Which is better? That's a judgment call we don't really need to make. It doesn't matter whether you freak out at the slightest sign of risk or you act like a complete daredevil. What's important is recognizing your tolerance for risk, and acting—and investing—accordingly.

One way of developing an understanding of your tolerance for risk is to take one of the many risk-tolerance tests offered in many magazines and personal finance self-help books. The answers are weighted with points, and according to the number of points you accumulate you're labeled "more conservative," "less conservative," and so on. Generally, the questions go something like this: You have a lottery ticket that has a one-in-five chance of winning a $100,000 prize. The minimum you would sell that lottery ticket for before the drawing is

1. $10,000
2. $15,000
3. $20,000
4. $30,000
5. $40,000

Political and Regulatory Risk
Risk resulting from unanticipated changes in the tax or legal environment.

Exchange Rate Risk
The risk of fluctuations in security prices from the variability in earnings resulting from changes in exchange rates.

Call Risk
The risk to bondholders that a bond may be called away from them before maturity.

Calling a Bond
The redeeming of a bond before its scheduled maturity. Many bonds are callable.

These tests can be helpful, but only if you answer honestly. When used by a financial planner, it's the discussions that they spawn with the client that tend to reveal the most about risk tolerance.

Another way of determining your level of risk tolerance is to review your past actions and see what your willingness to take on risk has been. Are you willing to switch to a less secure job if it has opportunities that your present job doesn't have? Do you worry about losing your job even if it's secure? Are you conservative or aggressive with your investments? Do you keep a very large emergency fund in liquid assets? If you're willing to take on risks elsewhere but not in your investments, your aversion to this type of risk might be caused by a lack of knowledge. That is, your present investment strategy may be decidedly conservative simply because you do not understand investments and risk.

Finally, as you learn more about risk-return trade-offs and the effect of diversification on risk and the time dimension of risk, you'll better realize the investment challenges that you actually face. You'll also better understand how important it is not to let your aversion to risk stop you from making lucrative investments to meet your goals.

DIVERSIFICATION AND INVESTMENTS

Axiom 3: Diversification Reduces Risk introduced the concept of diversification. It's a simple concept that most investors understand: Don't put all your eggs in one basket. **Diversification** works by allowing the extreme good and bad returns to cancel each other out, resulting in a reduction of the total variability or risk without affecting expected return.

It's important to understand the process of diversification. It not only eliminates a lot of risk, but also helps us understand what risk is relevant to us as investors. It's also important that you understand that diversification reduces risk without affecting the expected return. That's what we saw when we introduced Axiom 3 in chapter 1. It works by allowing the good and bad observations to cancel each other out, and, as a result, variability, or risk, is reduced.

Systematic and Unsystematic Risk

Axiom 4: Diversification and Risk—All Risk Is Not Equal, Because Some Risk Can Be Diversified Away and Some Cannot takes the concept of diversification and carries it further. As you diversify your investments, the variability or risk of the combined holdings of your investments, which is called your **portfolio**, should decline. This reduction, as we've seen, occurs because the stock returns in your portfolio don't fluctuate in the same way over time. For example, if you increase the number of stocks in your investment portfolio, the amount of variability in your portfolio declines, as shown in Figure 12.3. However, you'll also notice in Figure 12.3 that not all risk is eliminated through diversification. The variability in returns that's common to all stocks, perhaps associated with movements in interest rates or in the economy, isn't eliminated through diversification. It affects all stocks in the same way and thus isn't canceled out by buying diverse stocks. However, variability in one stock's returns that's unique to that stock tends to be countered and canceled out by the unique variability of another stock in the portfolio. For example, maybe in 1996 one of the stocks in your portfolio was Best Products (a retail discounter that went bankrupt, with its stock price dropping 99.7 percent), but another stock in your portfolio was Noble Drilling Corporation (which had a great year, with its stock price climbing by 120.8 percent). The end result of holding these two stocks is that the bad year for Best Products was canceled out by the really good year that Noble Drilling had. Thus, in a diversified portfolio the variability that's unique to individual stocks is canceled out or diversified away, but variability that's common to all stocks remains.

LEARNING OBJECTIVE #6

Diversify your investments.

AXIOM #3

Diversification Reduces Risk

Diversification

The elimination of risk by investing in different assets. It works by allowing the extreme good and bad returns to cancel each other out. The result is that total variability or risk is reduced without affecting expected return.

AXIOM #4

Diversification and Risk— All Risk Is Not Equal, Because Some Risk Can Be Diversified Away and Some Cannot

Portfolio

A group of investments held by an individual.

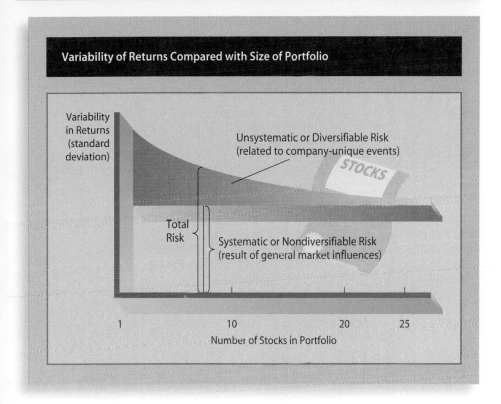

FIGURE 12.3

The Reduction of Risk as the Number of Stocks in the Portfolio Increases

Variability of Returns Compared with Size of Portfolio

Variability in Returns (standard deviation)

Unsystematic or Diversifiable Risk (related to company-unique events)

STOCKS

Total Risk

Systematic or Nondiversifiable Risk (result of general market influences)

1   10   20   25

Number of Stocks in Portfolio

What does the ability of diversification to eliminate only certain types of risk mean to us? It basically means that there are two types of risk: systematic risk and unsystematic risk. **Systematic risk**, which is sometimes called **market-related** or **nondiversifiable risk**, is that portion of a stock's risk or variability that *can't be eliminated* through investor diversification. This type of variability or risk results from factors that affect all stocks. In fact, the term "systematic" comes from the fact that this type of risk systematically affects all stocks. **Unsystematic risk**, which is also called **firm-specific** or **company-unique risk** or **diversifiable risk**, is risk or variability that *can be eliminated* through investor diversification. Unsystematic risk results from factors unique to a particular stock. All risk has to be either systematic or unsystematic. Keep in mind that these are *types* of risk, which is different from the *sources* of risk or variability that we examined earlier. Figure 12.4 shows the relationship between these two types of risk graphically.

As an example of unsystematic risk, think of what might happen to stocks of an oil producer and to those of a chemical firm as a result of an increase in oil prices. The oil producer would benefit from the increase in oil prices, which would in turn push its stock price up. The chemical firm may rely on oil as a primary factor in production and, as a result of the increase in oil prices, face increased costs. These increased costs would in turn push the price of the chemical firm's stock downward. If these two stocks were in the same portfolio, the price of the oil producer's stock would have risen while the chemical firm's stock declined, and these price changes would've canceled each other out.

Relating this back to **Axiom 1: The Risk-Return Trade-Off**, we find that the only risk we're compensated for taking on is systematic risk because unsystematic risk can be eliminated through investor diversification. In effect, unsystematic risk doesn't exist for diversified investors and, as such, the market doesn't compensate investors for taking on risk that they can eliminate for free. Looking back at Axiom 1, we can now

Systematic or **Market-Related** or **Nondiversifiable Risk**

That portion of a security's risk or variability that *can't be eliminated* through investor diversification. This type of variability or risk results from factors that affect all securities.

Unsystematic or **Firm-Specific** or **Company-Unique Risk** or **Diversifiable Risk**

Risk or variability that *can be eliminated* through investor diversification. Unsystematic risk results from factors that are unique to a particular firm.

AXIOM #1

The Risk-Return Trade-Off

FIGURE 12.4

The Relationship Between Total Risk, Systematic Risk, and Unsystematic Risk

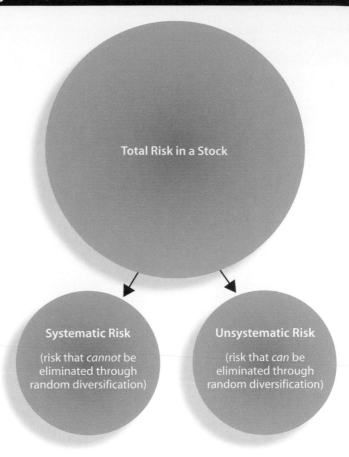

Total Risk in a Stock

Systematic Risk

(risk that *cannot* be eliminated through random diversification)

Unsystematic Risk

(risk that *can* be eliminated through random diversification)

LEARNING OBJECTIVE #7

Allocate your risk assets in the manner that is best for you.

AXIOM #11

The Time Dimension of Risk

see that investors demand a return for delaying consumption, and a return for taking on added *systematic* risk.

THE TIME DIMENSION OF RISK

In chapter 1 we introduced **Axiom 11: The Time Dimension of Risk**. The essence of this axiom is that much of the risk of any investment—stocks, bonds, or real estate—appears to disappear as the length of the investment horizon increases. In effect, the longer you hold an investment, the less risky it becomes. Take stocks, for example, although the same principle holds for all investments. Without question, common stocks have provided the greatest return over the past 71 years, with large-company stocks earning on average 10.7 percent per year over this period. However, it hasn't been a smooth ride. Common stocks have also had the greatest risk, or volatility, over that same period. In fact, on October 19, 1987, the stock market dropped by 23 percent and on October 27, 1997, it dropped by 7.2 percent. Thus, the problem with stocks is that "on average" may not be what you actually get. You may, for whatever reason, put your money in the stock market on the wrong day.

Fortunately, the volatility of any investment declines as the holding period increases. In fact, with any investment, you can almost guarantee that there'll be some bad years along with the good years. As a result, when you invest for a longer period, the exceptionally good and exceptionally bad years cancel each other out; thus, your investment

DIVERSIFICATION Works Best in Small Doses

How many different stocks should you own? If you have total confidence in your ability as a stock-picker, then the answer is simple: One is all you need.

(A) Of course, only a fool or a genius has such confidence. For the rest of us, diversification is the answer. That way, if you do have a big loser, there's a good chance you'll have enough winners to balance it.

But don't go overboard. I see diversification as a necessary evil; use as little of it as you can afford. How little? According to economists who have studied the subject, about eight to 10 stocks are all you need.

If you own 10 stocks, the risk in your portfolio—that is, the severity of annual ups and downs, as measured by "standard deviation"—is nearly the same as if you owned 100 stocks.

(B) In fact, owning just four stocks is about 40 percent less risky than owning one stock, according to what economists call "modern portfolio theory." But owning 500 stocks is only 60 percent less risky.

I'm using "risk" here in its dry, mathematical sense. But there's another kind of risk that awaits investors who put their eggs in too many baskets.

James Gipson, who manages the Clipper Fund, based in Beverly Hills, Calif., explains: "If you are intellectually honest with yourself, you'll admit that you don't have that many good ideas. So you serve your clients better by concentrating on your best ideas."

As an individual, you serve yourself better with the same strategy. Keep it simple. Keep it manageable. If you buy too many different stocks, you won't be able to keep track of what you own—or what you should buy or sell next.

Source: James K. Glassman, "Diversification Works Best in Small Doses," *The Washington Post*, May 14, 1995, p. H1. Copyright James K. Glassman. Used by permission.

Analysis and Implications ...

A. The benefits of diversification generally come fast. The only time they don't is when you invest in assets that move together. For example, if you invested in 10 high-tech computer chip manufacturers, you'd eliminate only a small amount of risk, because these stocks all move together. Diversification works by having a bad year in one investment offset by a good year in another investment. Thus, if the investments move up and down together—that is, they have their bad years all at the same time—there's little gained from diversification.

B. Keep in mind that some mutual funds with holdings of several hundred common stocks aren't well diversified, because they tend to concentrate all their holdings in one industry.

FIGURE 12.5

The Reduction of Risk Over Time

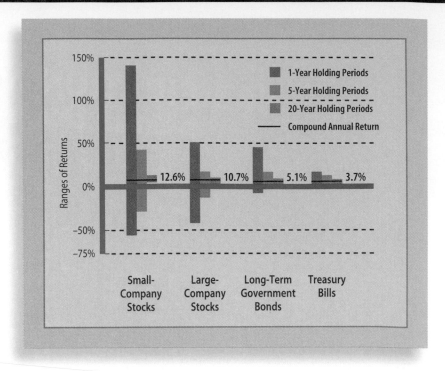

Each bar shows the range of compound annual total returns for each asset class over the period 1926–1996.

Source: © Computed using data from *Stocks, Bonds, Bills & Inflation 1997 Yearbook*™, Ibbotson Associates, Chicago (annually updates work by Roger G. Ibbotson and Rex A. Sinquefield). Used with permission. All rights reserved.

has less risk. For common stocks, this is shown in Figure 12.5. Although the worst single year for large-company stocks, 1931, resulted in a 43.3-percent loss, the worst 5-year period involved an average loss of 12.5 percent annually—this covered the period from December 31, 1927, through December 31, 1932. As we increase the investment horizon, this amount of loss declines further. In fact, looking at the range of returns for 20-year investment horizons, we find that the best average return was 16.9 percent, and the worst was a positive 3.1 percent. Clearly, stocks are extremely volatile in the short run, and clearly this isn't the case in the long run. The same holds true for other investments. This is an extremely important concept, because it means that our investment horizon plays an important role in determining how we should invest our savings.

Asset Allocation: Its Meaning and Role

Asset Allocation

An attempt to ensure that the investor's strategy reflects his or her investment time horizon and is well diversified, generally with investments in several different classes of investments, such as domestic common stocks, international common stocks, and bonds.

Asset allocation is an investments term that deals with how your investment money should be divided between stocks, bonds, and other investments. Asset allocation attempts to ensure that the investor is well diversified, generally with holdings in several different classes of investments, such as domestic common stocks, international common stocks, and bonds, with the objective being to increase your return on those investments while decreasing your risk. Therefore, it also incorporates the concept of the time dimension of risk into the allocation process. Asset allocation does so by recognizing that investing in common stocks is much less risky the longer the investment horizon. As such, investors with more time to reach their goals should have a larger proportion of common stocks in their portfolios than should those with very short investment horizons. In effect, the closer you get to retirement, the smaller the proportion of your retirement funds that should be invested in common stocks.

The logic behind the asset allocation process is surprisingly simple, and finds its roots in the concepts of three axioms: **Axiom 3: Diversification Reduces Risk; Axiom 4: Diversification and Risk—All Risk Is Not Equal, Because Some Risk Can Be Diversified Away and Some Cannot;** and **Axiom 11: The Time Dimension of Risk, or Why Investments Become Less Risky When You Plan to Hold Them Longer**. First, you should diversify to reduce your risk. In addition, your ideal mix of stocks and other investments changes as your investment horizon changes. This is because much of the risk associated with investing in common stocks is diversified away over time. As a result, the longer your investment horizon, the more money you should invest in common stocks.

Keep in mind that no two investors should allocate in the same way. You don't want to do what your Uncle Bill does, nor will you want to follow your neighbor's plan, because your age, income, family situation, personal financial goals, and tolerance for risk will certainly vary. It'll be these factors that'll lead you in your own direction. The idea behind asset allocation is very simple and straightforward, but it's clearly the most important task you'll undertake in your investing career. How you go about your asset allocation will have far greater impact on your return than will choosing each individual stock or bond that you hold.

Let's look at what asset allocation might mean for a typical investor when that investor is saving for retirement. Keep in mind that saving for different goals implies different investment horizons. To simplify the presentation somewhat, let's also divide the investor's retirement savings life into the three financial life cycle stages: (1) the early years—a time of wealth accumulation (through age 54), (2) approaching retirement—the golden years (ages 55 to 64), and (3) the retirement years (over age 65).

Asset Allocation and the Early Years—A Time of Wealth Accumulation (Through Age 54)

Because the investment horizon is quite long, investors in this investment stage should be placing the majority of their savings into common stocks, because these have the highest return associated with them. They also have the highest risk associated with them. However, because of the time dimension of risk and the long investment horizon, investing in common stocks doesn't involve nearly as much volatility as it would if the investment horizon were short. In fact, for investors who are just beginning this investment stage, an investment strategy of only investing in common stocks can be justified. However, most financial planners recommend that a portion of the investment funds be maintained in bonds, with a mix of 80-percent common stocks and 20-percent bonds being relatively common. Although this can be used as a benchmark asset allocation breakdown, remember that your personal life picture will ultimately affect what the appropriate breakdown is for you.

Looking at the performance of such an asset allocation breakdown since 1926, we find that the average annual total return would have been 11.23 percent (see Figure 12.6). The risk associated with such an asset allocation can be seen by examining the fact that in 19 out of 71 years since 1926, such an asset allocation would have earned losses, with the average loss being –9.77 percent. Moreover, the worst annual loss over this period would've occurred in 1931, when such an asset allocation would've resulted in a 35.73-percent loss. In addition, over the 1973–1974 bear market there would've been a 32.25-percent loss.

Asset Allocation and Approaching Retirement— The Golden Years (Ages 55 to 64)

For an individual approaching retirement, the goal becomes to preserve the level of wealth that has already been accumulated and to allow this wealth to continue to grow. Reflecting on the logic behind asset allocation, as the investment horizon shortens and common stocks take on more risk, the investor should move some of his or her retirement portfolio into bonds. In addition, the investor should maintain a diversified

AXIOM #3
Diversification Reduces Risk

AXIOM #4
Diversification and Risk— All Risk Is Not Equal, Because Some Risk Can Be Diversified Away and Some Cannot

AXIOM #11
The Time Dimension of Risk, or Why Investments Become Less Risky When You Plan to Hold Them Longer

FIGURE 12.6

Return and Risk to Benchmark Asset Allocation Breakdown During the Early Years

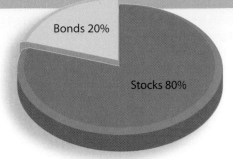

1926–1996	
Stock/bond mix	80/20
Average annual return	11.23%
Years with losses (out of 71)	19
Average loss	−9.77%
Worst annual loss (1931)	−35.73%
Bear market (1973–1974)	−32.25%

1962–1996	
Stock/bond mix	80/20
Average annual return	11.21%
Years with losses (out of 35)	9
Average loss	−7.14%
Worst annual loss (1974)	−20.30%

Bonds 20%

Stocks 80%

Source: © Computed using data from *Stocks, Bonds, Bills & Inflation 1997 Yearbook*™, Ibbotson Associates, Chicago (annually updates work by Roger G. Ibbotson and Rex A. Sinquefield). Used with permission. All rights reserved.

portfolio. For individuals approaching retirement, a mix of 60-percent common stocks and 40-percent bonds is a relatively common recommendation from financial planners. Again, depending upon the investor's degree of risk tolerance, the proportion invested in common stocks may either increase or decrease.

Looking at the performance of a 60/40 asset allocation between stocks and bonds since 1926, we find that the average annual total return would've been 9.78 percent (see Figure 12.7). For this asset allocation, losses were experienced in only 16 out of 71 years since 1926, with the average loss being −8.18 percent. Moreover, the worst annual loss over this period would've occurred in 1931, when such an asset allocation would've resulted in a 28.13-percent loss. In addition, over the 1973–1974 bear market, there would've been a 23.38-percent loss.

Asset Allocation and the Retirement Years (Over Age 65)

During your retirement years, you're no longer saving, you're spending. However, it's still necessary to allow for some growth in your savings simply to keep inflation from eating it away. As such, income is now of importance, with capital appreciation a secondary goal. Safety is provided by diversification among various investment categories and movement out of common stocks. As we saw in Figure 12.5, the volatility of common stocks increases as the holding period declines, making common stocks riskier for the investor with a short investment horizon. For individuals in their retirement years, a mix of 40-percent common stocks, 40-percent bonds, and 20-percent short-term Treasury bills is a relatively common recommendation from financial planners.

Looking at the performance of a 40/40/20 asset allocation between stocks, bonds, and Treasury bills since 1926, we find that the average annual total return would've been 8.01 percent (see Figure 12.8). For this asset allocation, losses were experienced in

FIGURE 12.7

Return and Risk to Benchmark Asset Allocation Breakdown Approaching Retirement—The Golden Years

1926–1996		1962–1996	
Stock/bond mix	60/40	Stock/bond mix	60/40
Average annual return	9.78%	Average annual return	10.32%
Years with losses (out of 71)	16	Years with losses (out of 35)	8
Average loss	−8.18%	Average loss	−5.84%
Worst annual loss (1931)	−28.13%	Worst annual loss (1974)	−14.14%
Bear market (1973–1974)	−23.38%		

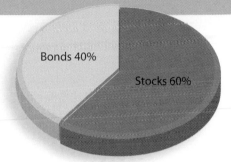

only 15 out of 71 years since 1931, with the average loss being only −4.89 percent. Moreover, the worst annual loss over this period would've been a 19.24-percent loss in 1931, and over the 1973–1974 bear market there would've been only a 12.17-percent loss.

In the late retirement years, safety and income are of utmost importance. For this reason the portion of your portfolio invested in common stocks declines further. For individuals in their late retirement years, a mix of 20-percent common stocks, 60-percent bonds, and 20-percent short-term Treasury bills is a relatively common recommendation from financial planners.

Looking at the performance of a 20/60/20 asset allocation between stocks, bonds, and Treasury bills since 1926, we find that the average annual total return would've been 6.56 percent (see Figure 12.9). Here, only 12 out of 71 years since 1926 experienced losses, with the average loss being only 3.05 percent and the worst annual loss being an 11.64-percent loss in 1931. Over the 1973–1974 bear market, there would've been only a 3.29-percent loss.

It should be obvious by now that asset allocation is not a one-time decision. Adjustments will need to be made as your life circumstances change. As you keep an eye on your portfolio you may occasionally need to rebalance your mix to keep the percentage of each investment category in line with your current personal financial goals.

WHAT YOU SHOULD KNOW ABOUT EFFICIENT MARKETS

Efficient markets concern the speed at which new information is reflected in security prices. The more efficient the market is, the faster prices react to new information. Thus, in a perfectly efficient market, security prices always equal their true value at all

Efficient Market
A market in which all relevant information about the stock is reflected in the stock price.

FIGURE 12.8

Return and Risk to Benchmark Asset Allocation Breakdown During the Retirement Years

1926–1996		1962–1996	
Stock/bond/Treasury Bill mix	40/40/20	Stock/bond/Treasury Bill mix	40/40/20
Average annual return	8.01%	Average annual return	9.17%
Years with losses (out of 71)	15	Years with losses (out of 35)	7
Average loss	−4.89%	Average loss	−3.15%
Worst annual loss (1931)	−19.24%	Worst annual loss (1974)	−7.25%
Bear market (1973–1974)	−12.17%		

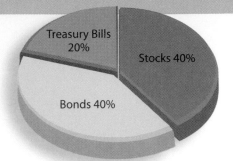

FIGURE 12.9

Return and Risk to Benchmark Asset Allocation Breakdown During the Late Retirement Years

1926–1996		1962–1996	
Stock/bond/Treasury Bill mix	20/60/20	Stock/bond/Treasury Bill mix	20/60/20
Average annual return	6.56%	Average annual return	8.28%
Years with losses (out of 71)	12	Years with losses (out of 35)	5
Average loss	−3.05%	Average loss	−2.23%
Worst annual loss (1931)	−11.64%	Worst annual loss (1994)	−3.62%
Bear market (1973–1974)	−3.29%		

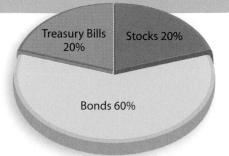

times—in other words, you can't systematically "beat the market." In effect, with efficient markets you're just as likely to pick winners as losers.

Is the Stock Market Efficient?

As you can well imagine, the question of whether the stock market is efficient is a very emotional one for many investment advisors and analysts on Wall Street. If the stock market is truly efficient, then there are costs without benefits to much of what's done by stock analysts. Before dealing with the question of how efficient the stock market is, it's important to understand why there can't be a definitive answer to this question. First of all, there's a question of the degree of efficiency. That is, although historical information may not help small investors earn abnormal profits, it has value to large investors. In effect, improving your performance by 0.01 percent may be irrelevant for you, but for a portfolio manager with a $4-billion portfolio, it means an increase in profits of $400,000 (0.0001 × $4 billion = $400,000). In addition, if someone uncovers a new technique for predicting prices, he or she would be much better off using it rather than publishing it. As a result, we may only see results that indicate that the market is efficient. However, reports of beating the market don't indicate that the market is inefficient. On average we would expect, just by chance, that half the investors will outperform the market and half will underperform the market. In general, you usually hear about those who beat the market, and, not surprisingly, those who underperform the market tend not to publicize their results. The bottom line here is that while we can't present a definite answer as to whether you can beat the market, we can give you enough understanding of the difficulties in beating the market to help you define an investment strategy that makes sense.

How Tough Is It to Consistently Beat the Market?

The answer is, Very tough! On average, half the time you should outperform the market, and half the time you should underperform the market. It's very difficult to consistently outperform the market. Let's look at the performance of the "superstars" of investing. Every year *Barron's* offers a roundtable of Wall Street superstars giving their predictions for the upcoming year. Looking at their predictions from 1967 through 1991, an investor who bought each one of the "picks" the day after the publication and held it for 1 year would have earned 0.021 percent above what was expected. If these picks were held for 2 or 3 years, they actually would have done worse than average. Actually, the "superstar" picks were not as bleak as appears. If the stocks were purchased on the day that the picks were made, not on the day they were published in *Barron's*, investors could have earned a return of just over 2 percent above the norm. What does this mean for the average investor? It means it's very difficult to pick underpriced stocks.

If it's so difficult to pick underpriced stocks, should we focus our attention on timing the market—that is, buying stocks before the market rises? To get some perspective on how difficult it is to time the market, let's look at what the experts said about 1995—a great year, one in which the stock market went up by over 30 percent. The weekly Standard and Poor's advisory publication, *Outlook*, predicted the market would go up by 8.5 percent. Prudential Securities predicted no change in the stock market in 1995, saying that it was "fully valued."

The *Wall Street Journal* didn't get it right either. Its first-quarter prediction was for "A Grim First Quarter"—the market rose by 8 percent. More of the same was predicted for the second quarter—the market rose by 9.6 percent. The third quarter opened with the headline "Wall Street Still Has Jitters Despite First Half's Surge"—the market rose by 5 percent more. In the last quarter the *Wall Street Journal* cautioned that analysts "Expect Decline"—the market continued to climb, rising 6.8 percent in the final quarter.

The bottom line here is that you should keep to your plan and invest for the long term and ride out the ups and downs. If you try to time the market, you're just as likely to miss an upswing as you are to avoid a downswing.

The Bottom Line—What to Do

What does our understanding of efficient markets tell us about investing? It tells us several things.

- **Systems don't beat the market. It's long-term investing that works.** There simply is no easy foolproof method for beating the market. Beware of "hot tips" and cold calls from stockbrokers. Remember the lessons of **Axiom 12: The Agency Problem in Personal Finance—Differentiating Between Advice and a Sales Pitch**. There's an old saying on Wall Street: "Those that know don't tell, and those that tell don't know." If it sounds too good to be true, it probably is. The good news in all this is that if you can do as well as the market, you have done quite well indeed.

- **Keep to the plan.** Don't try to time the market. Keep in mind that stock prices and interest rates go up and they go down, but it's almost impossible to only buy when stock prices are low and sell when they are high. As such, you should invest regularly and view stocks in accordance with your investment horizon. That is, if you're investing for retirement in 30 years, ignore the market's ups and downs.

- **Focus on the asset allocation process.** It's very difficult to beat the market on a consistent basis. As such, you should spend your energy focusing on the appropriate asset allocation given your goals, your plan, and where you are in your financial life cycle. Recognize the time dimension of risk. Your asset allocation strategy should reflect your investment horizon, and over long time horizons, stocks are less risky.

- **Keep the commissions down.** Because it's difficult to beat the market, make sure you don't give away too much of your return in the way of commissions. Be aware of what the commissions are and shop around.

- **Diversify, diversify, diversify.** The benefits of diversification are still unchallenged.

- **If you don't feel comfortable, seek help!** Don't let the fear of investing keep you out of the game. If you feel uncomfortable, seek the help of a qualified financial advisor.

SUMMARY

In personal financial planning, everything begins and ends with your goals. You must first decide what your goals are and how much you can set aside to meet those goals. Once you've done this, you can develop an investment plan to reach those goals.

AXIOM #12

The Agency Problem in Personal Finance— Differentiating Between Advice and a Sales Pitch

It's important to know the difference between investments and speculation. Investing involves buying an asset that generates a return. Speculation occurs when an asset's value depends solely on supply and demand, as opposed to being based upon the return that it generates. For example, buying gold coins and baseball cards is considered speculation because they're worth more in the future only if someone is willing to pay more for them.

There are two basic categories of investments:

- lending investments—for example, bonds, which are debt instruments issued by corporations and by the government; and
- ownership investments—for example, preferred stock and common stock, which represent an ownership position in a corporation.

When you invest your money, you can receive your return either as a capital gain or in the form of interest or dividends.

Interest rates play an extremely important role in determining the value of an investment. They are also closely tied to the rate of inflation. The nominal rate of return is the rate of return earned on an investment without any adjustment for lost purchasing power. The real rate of return is simply the current or nominal rate of return minus the inflation rate. It tells you how much you have earned after you've adjusted for inflation.

There are a number of different sources of risk associated with investments, including interest rate risk, inflation risk, business risk, liquidity risk, market risk, political and regulatory risk, exchange rate risk, and call risk.

The volatility of an investment declines as the holding period increases. By investing for a longer period, the exceptionally good and exceptionally bad years cancel each other out and therefore your investment has less risk.

Diversification works by allowing the extreme good and bad returns to cancel each other out. The ability to eliminate a portion of a portfolio's risk through diversification has led to the segmentation of risk into two types: systematic risk and unsystematic risk. Systematic risk is that portion of a stock's risk or variability that *can't be eliminated* through investor diversification. This type of variability or risk results from factors that affect all stocks. Unsystematic risk is risk or variability that *can be eliminated* through investor diversification. Unsystematic risk results from factors unique to a particular firm. Asset allocation attempts to ensure that the investor is well diversified, generally with investments in several different classes of investments, such as domestic common stocks, international common stocks, and bonds. It also incorporates the concept of the time dimension of risk into the allocation process.

Efficient markets concern the speed in which information is reflected in security prices. The more efficient the market is, the faster prices react to new information. Our understanding of efficient markets tells us several things:

- Systems don't beat the market. It's long-term investing that works best.
- Keep to your plan. Don't try to time the market.
- Focus on the asset allocation process.
- Keep the commissions down.
- Diversify!
- If you need help, turn to a financial advisor.

Review Questions

1. To turn your goals from dreams to reality, you need to first formalize them. List the four steps in formalizing goals. (LO 1)
2. Briefly distinguish between short-, intermediate-, and long-term goals. Provide an example of each type of goal. (LO 1)
3. Distinguish between investing and speculating. Give an example of each. (LO 2)
4. Derivative securities have grown in importance in the past 10 years. What is a derivative security? Give an example. (LO 2)

WWW.
Take It to the Net

We invite you to visit the Keown Personal Finance page on the Prentice Hall Web site at:

http://www.prenhall.com/ persfin

for this chapter's World Wide Web exercise.

You might also want to visit the following Web sites:

The Advisor (by American Express): http:// www.americanexpress.com/ advisors

CNNfn The Financial Network: http://www.cnnfn.com/

Microsoft Investor: http://investor.msn.com

The Wall Street Research Net: http://wsrn.com

Bloomberg Personal (interactive investment news):http:// www.bloomberg.com

American Association of Individual Investors:http://www.aaii.org

Money Magazine Online (all kinds of great investment information): http://money.com

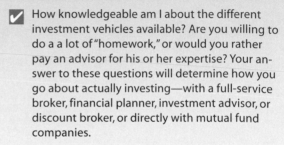

The typical question at every social gathering is, "So, what's good to invest in these days?" My answer is, "It all depends!" The best advice I can give anyone is to invest based on your own personal profile, not on a hot tip from the media, a party, or coffee break conversation. To establish your profile, ask yourself the following questions:

☑ What am I investing for? Is it retirement, a new home, college for children, and so forth? For some lucky people, the goal may just be to make some extra money grow.

☑ When will I need the money? In other words, what is your time horizon? Will you need all the funds at some definite date, or will it be used to provide an income? For example, many people think they must have all their money accessible on the day they retire. In reality, they need to continue to have their "nest egg" invested so that it will provide for them over many years. Short time limits (a year or two) normally do not allow you to work around the inherent volatility of the market.

☑ How much will I be investing? If you have a large sum, the options are quite different from those open to you with a small monthly amount. In the latter case, you may need to choose from mutual funds, which allow purchases as little as $50 monthly, rather than attempt to buy one or two shares of stock each time. The dollar amount will also control the level of diversification you can achieve in individual stocks and bonds versus mutual funds.

☑ What is my volatility or risk tolerance? If you anticipate a panic attack the first time your account statement shows a current balance much lower than what you contributed, you have some decisions to make. Can you learn to cope with it? Will you settle for small returns from "safe" investments? Or do you need an advisor to help you over the humps?

☑ How knowledgeable am I about the different investment vehicles available? Are you willing to do a a lot of "homework," or would you rather pay an advisor for his or her expertise? Your answer to these questions will determine how you go about actually investing—with a full-service broker, financial planner, investment advisor, or discount broker, or directly with mutual fund companies.

So now that you know yourself, "just do it." If fear, lack of time, or inadequate information is holding you up, "Get thee to an advisor!"

5. From an investor's standpoint there are only two basic categories of investments. What are they? Provide two examples of each. (LO 2)

6. Bond investors often sleep well knowing that they're receiving a guaranteed rate of interest. After reading this chapter, you now know that bonds aren't as safe as people once thought. What are two serious threats that all bond investors face? How can these threats work against bond investors? (LO 2)

7. Real estate has long been touted as a great investment, because "they don't make land anymore." What is the single greatest problem associated with a real estate investment that many investors fail to recognize? (LO 2)

8. When it comes to taxes, why are capital gains better than dividends or interest? (LO 3)

9. Investors in both government and corporate bonds require compensation for what type of risk? (LO 4)

10. Investors require compensation for increased levels of risk. Name four types of risk that corporate bond investors pay close attention to. Do investors require more or fewer interest rate premiums as compensation for these risks? (LO 4)

11. Investors must be aware of nine sources of risk when calculating the risk-return trade-off. List and briefly describe these nine sources of risk. (LO 6)
12. The calculation of risk-return trade-offs is undertaken by both buyers and sellers. Using this insight, explain why a company would call a bond. Which party benefits when a bond is called? (LO 6)
13. Differentiate between systematic risk and unsystematic risk. Which of these two risks is more important to the average investor? (LO 7)
14. Explain, in your own words, the trade-off between risk and time. (LO 7)
15. When should an investor change his or her asset allocation mix? (LO 7)
16. Explain market efficiency. (LO 7)
17. Define market timing. Does market timing work consistently? What is a better recommended investing strategy? (LO 7)

Problems and Activities

1. Using the table in Appendix D, calculate how much you will need to save at the end of each year assuming the following: (LO 4)
     You have 30 years until retirement.
     You'll need $1 million in savings.
     You feel you can earn a 9-percent annualized return on your investment.
2. Everyone needs an emergency fund. Assume your best friend asks you to rank a list of investments, based on liquidity, for an emergency savings fund. Using 1 as the most liquid and 5 as the least liquid, rank the following investments and make a recommendation to your friend: (LO 1)
   a. insured bank account earning some interest
   b. real estate
   c. certificate of deposit
   d. portfolio of technology stocks
   e. basketball signed by Michael Jordan
3. Corporate bonds and bank accounts are both considered lending investments, but they differ in terms of maturity dates. Define "maturity date," and describe why a bond and a bank account differ in terms of maturity dates. (LO 2)
4. As a savvy student of personal finance, you've just learned that a high-technology company in your hometown made so much money last year that they're going to distribute a huge cash distribution to owners of the company. In order to get in on the deal, you've got to make a quick decision. Which security should you buy in order to receive the cash payment—stock in the company or a bond offered by the company? (LO 2)
5. After reading this chapter it isn't surprising that you've become an investment wizard. Last year you purchased 100 shares of BIG for $37 per share. Over the past 12 months, BIG's price has gone up to $45 per share, and you received a dividend of $1 per share. What was your total rate of return on your investment in BIG? (LO 2)
6. Your investment in BIG was so successful that you decided to hold it for 5 more years. Remember, you purchased 100 shares for $37 per share. Unfortunately, the price of BIG hasn't done much. It's back to where it was when you purchased it. The good news is that you earned $1 per share for 5 years. Calculate your annualized total rate of return. Compared to a savings account earning 2-percent interest, how did BIG do? (LO 2)
7. You just learned the Disney Company will issue a bond with a maturity of 100 years. The bond appears to be a good deal because it yields 8.50 percent. Assuming today's inflation rate is 4 percent, what's the bond's real rate of return today? Assuming you were looking for a bond to purchase and hold for several years, would you buy this bond? Explain your answer in terms of future inflation projections and the length of the bond's maturity. (LO 5)
8. Suppose a stockbroker called you one afternoon asking you to purchase a corporate bond with a 15-year maturity. You know that T-bills currently yield 5 percent,

and that inflation is anticipated to be 3 percent this year. The bond will mature in 30 years, but the stockbroker indicates that the company has a high level of debt and that the risk of default is high. The broker tells you that long-term government bonds yield 8.50 percent. You quickly calculate that you should be compensated an additional 4 percent to cover potential default and liquidity risk. What is the minimum interest rate that this bond should yield? (LO 5)

9. Use the following date to determine the average return for the two securities. Plot each security's annual return and the average return. What does your figure indicate about diversification? (LO 6)

Year	Return Stock A	Return Stock B	Average Return A & B
1	20%	−10%	
2	0%	10%	
3	8%	2%	
4	−20%	30%	
5	13%	− 3%	

10. Outline the typical investment goals associated with each of the following life cycle events. Provide a recommended asset allocation for each stage. (LO 7)
    a. Early years
    b. The golden years
    c. Retirement years
    d. Late retirement years

Suggested Projects

1. Before you can develop an investment plan, you must know what your investment goals are. List five short-term and five long-term investment goals for yourself. Ask your spouse or other members of your family what investment goals they have for themselves. (LO 1)

2. This chapter pointed out that control is crucial in establishing, maintaining, and meeting financial goals. Briefly explain, in your own words, what is meant by control, and provide two or three examples of "out-of-control" behaviors that might lead investors to fail in meeting their financial objectives. (LO 1)

3. College students often think they don't need an emergency fund. Take an informal poll of students you know and find out how many have emergency savings. Find out the reasons why or why not. Think of three reasons a college student should have an emergency fund. (LO 1)

4. A derivative security obtains its value from another security. Many people buy and sell options, which are speculative devices that move up and down in value almost in tandem with a stock or other security. Are derivatives based only on security prices? Can you think of a derivative that you and your classmates could create? *Hint:* Think about the presidential elections. (LO 2)

5. You've learned that interest rates can be used as a base return to compare all investments. Using a current edition of either the *Wall Street Journal, USA Today,* or your local newspaper, find the current yield on a long-term U.S. government bond (10- or 30-year maturity). What is the minimal return that you'd require before purchasing the following investments: a) a Aaa rated corporate bond, b) a speculative technology stock, and c) a baseball card collectible? (LO 5)

6. It's commonly accepted by financial planners, researchers, and investors alike that the older people get, the less risk-tolerant they become. Do you believe this assumption? Interview several senior citizens about their risk tolerance. What do your results tell you? (LO 5)

7. Academics proclaim that the stock market is efficient. Explain market efficiency and provide an example of a contradiction. Explain why the average investor often has a hard time taking advantage of "market inefficiencies." (LO 7)

Discussion Case 1

Roger, aged 28, and Sarah, aged 27, have just had their first child, Diane. They have a combined income of $45,000 and rent a two-bedroom apartment. For the past several years, Roger and Sarah have taken financial responsibilities one day at a time, but it's finally dawned on them that they now must start thinking about the future of their family. For several months Roger has seen the stock market move higher, and he's convinced that they should be investing in stocks. Sarah is more interested in investing in collectibles, such as sports memorabilia, because she's been reading reports of baseball trading card speculators making huge profits. When asked what their goals are, Roger replies that he'd like to save for retirement, and Sarah mentions her top priority as saving for Diane's college expenses. They both agree that they'd like to buy a house and pay off their credit card bills, which amount to $4,000. When asked to list their current savings, all they come up with is a savings account worth $650.

Questions

1. What should be Roger and Sarah's first priority before investing or making any plans?

2. Before investing in stocks, bonds, or collectibles, what type of account should Roger and Sarah establish? What would be an appropriate "investment" for this type of account? How much should they accumulate before investing in other assets?

3. If Roger and Sarah were to ask you to prioritize their goals, how would you rank their investment objectives?

4. Match investment alternatives to the goals ranked in question 3.

5. Should Roger and Sarah invest all their money in one investment strategy (stocks or collectibles)? Explain your answer in terms of diversification and the asset allocation process.

Discussion Case 2

Linda just inherited $25,000 from her favorite uncle. In his will, Linda's uncle specified that she should invest the money in either stocks or bonds, but at no time was she to speculate with the money. Linda is in her mid-30s and has no experience in investing. She's come to you because she's heard that you're an expert in basic investment planning. You've agreed to meet with Linda, and before your meeting you've discovered that she has a relatively low personal risk tolerance. On the day of your meeting you notice that U.S. T-bills are yielding 5.50 percent, and that longer-term bonds are yielding anywhere from 6.50 percent to 7.25 percent, indicating the possibility of increasing inflation in the future. The stock market has been very volatile during the past 6 months, with most investors anticipating an increase in interest rates and continued market fluctuations. Linda has indicated that although she wants to make a long-term investment, she also might need the money within the next few years to purchase a house.

Questions

1. Based on this chapter's learning objectives, develop a short outline of five or six concepts that Linda needs to consider before making any investment decisions.

2. Prepare a short discussion concerning the risk-return trade-offs of bonds with different maturities. Also discuss risk-return trade-offs of stocks in relation to Linda's objectives.

3. Taking into account the current interest rates on the day of your meeting with Linda, and the market's anticipation of future increases in interest rates, briefly sketch an asset allocation plan for Linda. The plan should include allowances for her objectives, risk tolerance, and time horizons. Given this analysis, would you be comfortable recommending a 100-percent allocation to stocks?

Chapter 13

AN INTRODUCTION TO THE SECURITIES MARKETS

Most parents don't buy stocks on the recommendation of their children, but that's what Linda and Ron Knutson did. In March 1986, their 15-year-old son, Eric, a self-proclaimed "computer geek," convinced them to invest $10,000, which was about 15 percent of their total savings, into a stock that was going public at the time—Microsoft. In fact, Eric also invested his entire savings (paper route money, along with some money from his grandparents) of $750.

Back then Microsoft was far from a sure thing. It was a small firm in Seattle with an unknown future run by a young, untested computer genius, Bill Gates. In fact, Microsoft was so small and unknown that for Linda and Ron, it was difficult finding a stockbroker who had access to Microsoft shares at its initial price of $21 per share. They did, though, and they're glad of it. They even convinced Linda's brother Jim to invest $5,000 in Microsoft. He wasn't fortunate enough to be able to buy in at $21, but he was able to buy the stock later that month at $26. By early 1997, the Knutsons' $10,000 investment has grown to over $1 million, and Linda's brother Jim's investment of $5,000 has grown to over $400,000, and it may well be worth considerably more today. As for Eric, his $750 would have been worth about $75,000, but instead it took the form of a new Mazda Miata, along with about $50,000 in savings.

It wasn't until about 10 years later that Eric made another recommendation. Eric was then working for a consulting firm as a computer programmer and spending most of his time "surfing the Net." Through

Learning Objectives

After reading this chapter you should be able to:

1. Identify and describe the primary and secondary securities markets.
2. Trade securities using a broker.
3. Locate and use several different sources of investment information to trade securities.

his work, he came across another small computer firm that had developed a product that Eric thought "no one could live without"—an affordable and removable storage disk with much greater capacity than conventional floppies. The company was Iomega, maker of the Zip drive. On Eric's recommendation, both Eric and his parents invested $50,000 each. When they bought their Iomega stock in January 1995, it was selling at 75¢ per share. Seventeen months later, in May 1996, when they sold their Iomega stock, again on Eric's recommendation, its price was $52 per share. Both Eric and his parents took home a tidy profit of about $3.4 million. Needless to say, Eric is now known as an "investment wizard" rather than as a "computer geek."

Not everyone does as well with their investments as the Knutsons did. However, there's one way you can greatly improve your chances at successful investing. That's through an understanding of the rules of the investment game—in this case, how the securities markets work. Very few people feel comfortable, or should feel comfortable, playing the game without knowing the rules. That's the purpose of this introduction to the securities markets—to introduce you to the rules. In effect, this chapter is actually a continuation of the previous chapter. This chapter will look at how the investments markets operate and prepare you to go out and make your own investments.

It would be nice if we all have the same success as the Knutsons when it comes to investing. Unfortunately, that kind of success can't be guaranteed. However, one thing is certain: The first step to becoming rich through a great investment is learning how to make that investment, because you can't win the investments game if you don't even know how to get to the arena.

Primary Market
A market in which newly issued, as opposed to previously issued, securities are traded.

Initial Public Offering (IPO)
The first time a company's stock is traded publicly.

AXIOM #5

The Curse of Competitive Investment Markets—Why It's Hard to Find Exceptionally Profitable Investments

SECURITY MARKETS

Securities, both stocks and bonds, are first bought when they are issued by corporations as a means of raising money. After they are initially issued, stocks and bonds are traded—bought and sold—countless times between investors. These trades occur in the securities markets. Just as retail goods are bought and sold at markets, such as Kmart or Sears, securities are also bought and sold at appropriate markets. Of course, these markets aren't necessarily the kind you walk into or find at the mall (don't go looking for Securities "Я" Us at a shopping center near you). A securities market is simply a place where you can buy or sell securities, and these markets can take the form of anything from an actual building on Wall Street in New York to an electronic hookup between security dealers all over the world. Basically, securities markets are divided into primary and secondary markets. Let's take a look at what these terms mean.

The Primary Markets

A **primary market** is a market in which new, as opposed to previously issued, securities are traded. For example, if Nike issues a new batch of stock, this issue would be considered a primary market transaction. Actually, there are two different types of offerings in the primary markets: initial public offerings (IPOs) and seasoned new issues. An **initial public offering**, or **IPO**, is the first time the company's stock is traded publicly. For example, the initial offering of Microsoft stock we mentioned at the beginning of the chapter was an IPO. IPOs draw a good deal of attention in the press because they show how much a company is worth in the public's eye, and they tend to be great opportunities for huge financial gains or losses. It's hard to determine how much people will be willing to pay for a share of a newly traded company's stock. As a result, some IPO prices are set way too low, resulting in huge profits for anyone lucky enough to buy shares at the IPO price. A good example of a company whose low IPO price resulted in huge profits is Netscape, which first went public in August 1995. Within a year, the company's stock had risen to a full five times what the IPO price had been. Of course, some IPO prices are set too high, resulting in horrible losses for those few unlucky enough to buy. For example, PST Vans "went public" (the term used when companies make their initial public offering) in March 1995. By the end of that year, the company's stock had lost almost 70 percent of its value.

IPOs are quite enticing as an investment, because they give the investor the chance to get in on the ground floor of a company. It's always nice when you then wind up riding the investment elevator all the way to the penthouse, but, of course, you do run the risk that the ground floor will cave in and your investment will wind up in the basement, buried under rubble. Figure 13.1 provides a listing of the big winners and losers in the IPO market for 1995. However, IPOs are particularly tough on the small investor, because the most promising IPOs tend to be "bought up" by large investors before the smaller investor has a chance to buy in. In effect, there may not be enough stock to go around. This brings us back to **Axiom 5: The Curse of Competitive Investment Markets—Why It's Hard to Find Exceptionally Profitable Investments**. The end result with IPOs is that bigger accounts and more-favored clients might get first pick on exciting IPOs—certainly that was the case when Netscape went public—and the smaller investor may be left out.

> ### *The Facts of Life*
> The most attractive IPOs are many times snatched up by big accounts and favored clients, including politicians and celebrities, before the general public has a chance to invest in them. A case in point involves the former Speaker of the House Thomas Foley, who over a 4-year period invested in 42 IPOs and lost money only twice.

FIGURE 13.1

The Best and Worst IPOs of 1995

The Five Best

	IPO Date	Initial Offering Price	Year-End Share Price	% Gain
*Premisys Communications	April 6	8	56	+600
*Spyglass	June 27	$8^1/2$	57	+570.6
Netscape Communication	August 9	28	139	+396.4
*PDT	April 13	$10^{11}/16$	$50^1/4$	+371.1
UUNET	May 25	14	63	+350

*Prices adjusted for stock splits.

The Five Worst

	IPO Date	Initial Offering Price	Year-End Share Price	% Loss
PST Vans	March 7	15	$4^5/8$	−69.2
Electronics Communications	May 12	5	2	−60
AHI Healthcare	Sept. 28	14	$5^3/4$	−58.9
Integrated Communications Network	June 29	5	$2^1/8$	−57.5
Pace Health Management	April 21	5	$2^5/8$	−47.5

Source. Standard & Poor's.

Seasoned new issues refer to stock offerings by companies that already have common stock traded in the marketplace. For example, a sale by Reebok of new shares of stock would be considered a seasoned new issue.

Stocks and bonds are generally sold in the primary markets with the help of an **investment banker** serving as the **underwriter**. An underwriter is simply a middleman who buys the entire stock or bond issue from the issuing company and then resells it to the general public in individual shares. Such firms as Merrill Lynch, Goldman Sachs, Lehman Brothers, and Kidder Peabody all specialize in investment banking. Actually, we use the term "investment banker" to refer to both the overall firm and the individuals who work for it. Single investment banking companies rarely underwrite securities

Seasoned New Issue

A stock offering by companies that already have common stocks traded in the marketplace.

Investment Banker

The "middleman" between the firm issuing securities and the buying public. This term is used to describe both the firms that specialize in selling securities to the public and the individuals who work for investment banking firms.

Underwriter

An investment banker who purchases and subsequently resells a new security issue. The issuing company sells its securities directly to the underwriter, who then sells the issue to the public. The risk of selling the new issue at a satisfactory price is thus assumed by the underwriter.

Tombstone Advertisement

An advertisement that provides a listing of the underwriting syndicate involved in the new offering in addition to basic information on the offering.

Prospectus

A legal document that describes a securities issue. The prospectus for the company is made available to potential investors.

Secondary Markets

The markets in which previously issued securities are traded.

Organized Exchange

An exchange that occupies a physical location where trading occurs, such as the New York Stock Exchange.

Over-the-Counter Market

A market in which transactions are conducted over the telephone or via a computer hookup rather than in an organized exchange.

Regional Stock Exchanges

Organized stock exchanges located outside New York City and registered with the Securities and Exchange Commission.

issues by themselves. Usually, there will be one managing investment banking company handling the issue—advising and working with the issuing company on pricing and timing concerns—that then forms a syndicate of other investment banking companies. Together, this syndicate will underwrite the IPO or seasoned new issue. Most security issues are announced using **tombstone advertisements**, which are merely ads placed in a newspaper, magazine, or on-line service, providing details on the offering and the names of the underwriting syndicate. Figure 13.2 shows a tombstone advertisement for a new issue of New York Bagel Enterprises common stock. If a tombstone ad interests investors, they should simply contact a member of the underwriting syndicate to request a **prospectus**, which describes the issue and the issuing company's financial prospects.

Secondary Markets—Stocks

Securities that have previously been issued and bought are traded in the **secondary markets**. In other words, if you bought 100 shares of stock in an IPO and then wanted to resell them because the stock price had risen considerably and you wanted to make a profit, you'd have to sell the shares in the secondary market. Only issuing companies (and their underwriters) can sell securities in the primary markets. In effect, the proceeds from the sale of a share of IBM stock on the secondary market goes to the previous owner of the stock, not to IBM. In fact, the only time IBM ever receives money from the sale of one of its securities is on the primary market.

The secondary markets can take the form of either an organized exchange or an over-the-counter market. An **organized exchange** occupies a physical location where trading occurs. In other words, an organized exchange is actually a building in which stocks are traded. In an **over-the-counter market**, transactions are conducted over the telephone or via a computer hookup rather than on an exchange. How is it determined where a security will trade? Larger, more frequently traded securities, such as GM, IBM, General Electric, and Exxon, are traded on organized exchanges, whereas those that are less frequently traded are relegated to the over-the-counter markets. In either case, the secondary markets make it much easier for sellers to find buyers and vice versa.

Secondary Markets: The Organized Exchanges.   There are nine major organized exchanges in the United States: (1) the New York Stock Exchange (NYSE), (2) the American Stock Exchange (AMEX), (3) the Pacific Stock Exchange (Los Angeles and San Francisco), (4) the Chicago Stock Exchange, (5) the Philadelphia Exchange (Philadelphia and Miami), (6) the Cincinnati Stock Exchange, (7) Intermountain Stock Exchange (Salt Lake City), (8) Spokane Stock Exchange, and (9) the Boston Stock Exchange. The New York Stock Exchange and the American Stock Exchange are considered national stock exchanges, and the others are generally termed **regional stock exchanges**. If a firm's stock trades on a particular exchange, it is said to be listed on that exchange. Interestingly, securities can be listed on more than one exchange. Without question, the NYSE is the big player, with over 80 percent of the typical trading volume occurring on the NYSE.

The New York Stock Exchange (NYSE).   The New York Stock Exchange, also called the "Big Board," is the oldest of all the organized exchanges, dating back over 200 years. It began in 1792 when 24 traders signed the Buttonwood Agreement, a pact named after the tree under which traders gathered in New York, obligating them to "give preference" to each other in security trading. When winter came, those 24 traders moved to the back room of Wall Street's Tontine Coffee House, leaving the other traders out in the cold.

The members of the Exchange occupy "seats." In effect, a seat is a membership card, and the number of seats on the New York Stock Exchange is limited to 1,366, a number that hasn't increased since 1953. The only way to acquire a seat is to buy one

FIGURE 13.2

A Tombstone Advertisement for a New Issue of Stock by New York Bagel Enterprises

*This announcement is neither an offer to sell nor a solicitation of an offer to buy any of these securities.
The offer is made only by the Prospectus.*

New Issue

August 26, 1996

2,000,000 Shares

 **NEW YORK BAGEL ENTERPRISES, INC.**

Common Stock

Price $9 Per Share

*Copies of the Prospectus may be obtained in any State in which this announcement
is circulated only from such of the underwriters as are qualified
to act as dealers in securities in such State.*

RAUSCHER PIERCE REFSNES, INC.   J.C. BRADFORD & CO.

ADAMS, HARKNESS & HILL, INC.	ADVEST, INC.	ALLEN & COMPANY INCORPORATED
ROBERT W. BAIRD & CO. INCORPORATED	CROWELL, WEEDON & CO.	DAIN BOSWORTH INCORPORATED
EQUITABLE SECURITIES CORPORATION		GERARD KLAUER MATTISON & CO., LLC
JANNEY MONTGOMERY SCOTT INC.		JEFFERIES & COMPANY, INC.
LADENBURG, THALMANN & CO. INC.		MCDONALD & COMPANY SECURITIES, INC.
MORGAN KEEGAN & COMPANY, INC.		PIPER JAFFRAY INC.
PRINCIPAL FINANCIAL SECURITIES, INC.		THE ROBINSON-HUMPHREY COMPANY, INC.
RODMAN & RENSHAW, INC.	STEPHENS INC.	SUTRO & CO. INCORPORATED
UNTERBERG HARRIS	VECTOR SECURITIES INTERNATIONAL, INC.	WHEAT FIRST BUTCHER SINGER
GEORGE K. BAUM & COMPANY	HANIFEN, IMHOFF INC.	SOUTHWEST SECURITIES
STARR SECURITIES, INC.	STIFEL, NICOLAUS & COMPANY INCORPORATED	VAN KASPER & COMPANY

Source: New York Bagel Enterprises, Inc., 1996. Used by permission.

from a present owner for whatever the market price is. Interestingly, the highest a seat has ever sold for was $1.15 million, and that transaction took place less than a month before the great market crash of October 1987. Large brokerage firms such as Merrill Lynch might own over 20 seats.

To be listed on the NYSE, a firm must meet strict profitability, size, market value, and public ownership requirements. Figure 13.3 lists the present requirements for the NYSE and demonstrates how restrictive those requirements really are. If a firm fails to maintain the minimum requirements, it's delisted and no longer traded on the NYSE. In mid-1997 there were over 2,900 NYSE-listed companies from all over the world, with more than 154 billion shares worth $6 trillion available for trading, making the NYSE the largest organized securities exchange in the world. Included among NYSE-listed stocks are companies such as PespiCo, AT&T, Wal-Mart, Coca-Cola, and Circuit City.

The American Stock Exchange (AMEX). The American Stock Exchange is the second most important of the organized exchanges and generally lists stocks of firms that are somewhat smaller than those listed on the NYSE. Although the AMEX operates in a manner similar to the NYSE, it has only 660 seats and lists just over 1,000 firms, with its trading volume being only 3 percent of that on the NYSE. It may rank as number two in terms of the number of companies it lists, but when it comes to the dollar volume of daily trades, it's actually smaller than some regional exchanges.

Regional Stock Exchanges. Regional exchanges trade in securities of local or regional firms, specializing in small companies with strong management. Requirements for listing are much more relaxed (for example, net assets of $1 million as compared to $40 million for the NYSE). Many regional exchanges also list stocks found on the NYSE and AMEX to encourage more trading. In effect, some stocks trade on both the NYSE or AMEX and also on a regional exchange. Actually, the West Coast exchanges have the advantage of operating in a different time zone, allowing customers to trade well after the NYSE closes.

FIGURE 13.3

Initial Listing Requirements for the NYSE, 1996

Profitability

Earnings before taxes (EBT) for the most recent year must be at least $2.5 million.
For the 2 years preceding that, EBT must be at least $2.0 million.

Size

Net tangible must be at least $40.0 million.

Market Value*

The market value of publicly held stock must be at least $40.0 million.

Public Ownership

There must be at least 1.1 million publicly held common shares.
There must be at least 2,000 holders of 100 shares or more.

*The market value is tied to the level of common stock prices prevailing in the marketplace at the time of the listing application. From time to time the $40.0 million requirement noted above may be lessened. Under current regulations of the NYSE, the requirement can never be less than $9.0 million.

Secondary Markets: The Over-the-Counter (OTC) Market.

The over-the-counter market is simply a linkup of dealers for trading, with no listing or membership requirements. For the most part, the over-the-counter market is highly automated, with a nationwide computer network allowing brokers to see up-to-the-minute price quotes on roughly 35,000 securities. OTC shares are often made up of companies that are too new or too small to be listed on a major exchange. These companies will also often have fewer shares available, and as a result, in some cases, small amounts of buying or selling may have a significant impact on the price of these companies' stocks.

Depending upon the frequency of trading activity, trading information will be passed among dealers in one of several ways. Information on stocks that trade very infrequently will be mailed daily to member dealers on what are called "pink sheets," which are named for the color of paper on which they're printed. For example, if you wanted to buy or sell shares of a local Blacksburg, Virginia, bank, information for that bank would most likely be mailed to dealers by the National Quote Bureau. Unfortunately, the quote on the "pink sheet" may not be current, making trading in these thinly traded securities a bit more difficult.

An OTC stock that's more frequently traded would be handled by the NASDAQ. In 1971 the National Association of Securities Dealers Automated Quotations system, or NASDAQ, was set up to allow dealers to post bid and ask prices for OTC stocks over a computer linkup. A **bid price** is the price at which an individual is willing to purchase a security, and an **ask price** is the price at which an individual is willing to sell a security. If a security is traded more frequently, it might be listed on the National Market System (NMS), which is just a sophisticated version of the NASDAQ. In total, about 5,500 of the 35,000 OTC securities are listed on the NASDAQ/NMS. Although there are approximately twice as many securities listed on the NASDAQ/NMS as there are listed on the NYSE, the dollar volume of trading on the NASDAQ/NMS is substantially less than it is on the NYSE. Still, the NASDAQ/NMS has grown to the point where it's the second largest secondary securities market in the United States, as measured by dollar trading volume. Interestingly, many large high-tech companies have chosen not to seek listing on the NYSE, but instead remain traded on the NASDAQ/NMS. As a result, you see firms such as Intel and Microsoft traded on the NASDAQ/NMS alongside smaller companies, such as Noodle Kid.

Secondary Markets—Bonds

Most of the buying and selling of bonds doesn't occur on the organized exchanges (although some bonds are actually traded at the New York Stock Exchange). Instead, at the center of the secondary market for bonds are bond dealers, who buy and sell bonds out of their holdings. Generally, bond dealers deal directly only with large financial institutions; thus, the smaller investor can gain access to them only through a broker acting as an intermediary. Your broker will buy or sell the bond from the bond dealer and then, in turn, pass it on to you, charging you a commission for the service.

There really isn't too much demand for corporate bonds in the secondary market. Secondary markets tend to be for smaller, individual investors, and there just aren't all that many small, individual investors interested in corporate bonds. However, volume of trading in the secondary market for government bonds is enormous. In fact, trading volume in government bonds runs in the billions of dollars each month. Government bond trading is dominated by the Federal Reserve, commercial banks, and other financial institutions.

International Markets

International security markets have been around for centuries. In fact, around 2000 B.C. the Babylonians introduced debt financing, and by 400 B.C. the Greeks had developed a security market of sorts. Today, it's possible to allow your investment funds to cross borders and invest internationally, with huge investment markets across the globe. For

Bid Price

The price at which an individual is willing to purchase a security.

Ask Price

The price at which an individual is willing to sell a security.

example, the world bond market is valued at over $11 trillion. In terms of this market, the United States dominates. However, Japan, Germany, the United Kingdom, and France are all major players.

How do you buy a Japanese stock? There are two ways. First, some foreign shares are traded on exchanges in the United States. For example, just over 50 foreign companies are traded on the NYSE and over 60 are traded on the AMEX. In addition, over 200 are traded on the NASDAQ. However, many of these companies are Canadian, and as such, are quite similar to domestic stocks. Another way international stocks can be traded is through **American Depository Receipts (ADRs)**. With ADRs, shares of stock aren't traded directly. Instead, the foreign firm's stock is held on deposit in a bank in the foreign firm's country. The foreign bank issues an ADR, which represents direct ownership over those shares. The ADR then trades internationally just like a normal share of stock. Examples of foreign firms with ADRs include Sony, Toyota, and Volvo.

Today, many investment advisors are recommending that their clients increase their international investments. In pointing to investments abroad, they cite relatively low-priced stocks coupled with strong economies. Certainly, there are real opportunities abroad. However, there are also risks. For example, the Japanese stock market started plummeting in January 1990 and didn't stop until it lost 63 percent of its value by August 1992. From then until early 1997, it pretty much stood still—missing the great stock market surges that took place in the United States in 1995 and 1996.

Regulation of the Securities Markets

Securities market regulation is aimed at protecting the investor and providing a level playing field so that all investors have a fair chance of making money. There are actually two levels of regulation of the securities markets: general regulation by the Securities and Exchange Commission (SEC, a federal agency) and self-regulation directly by the exchanges (or, in the case of the OTC market, by the National Association of Securities Dealers, NASD).

SEC Regulation.   The great stock market crash of 1929 inspired much of the legislation that governs the securities markets today. In the period following the crash, the Securities Act of 1933 and the Securities Exchange Act of 1934 both were enacted. The Securities Act of 1933 required disclosure of relevant information on initial public offerings and registration with the Federal Trade Commission. Firms issuing securities must provide a registration statement with detailed financial information to the SEC at least 20 days prior to the offering date so that the SEC can determine whether the information is factual. If found to be factual, this information must then be provided to all potential investors in the form of a prospectus. The Securities Exchange Act of 1934 spoke directly to the secondary market and created the Securities and Exchange Commission to enforce the trading laws. Keeping with the principle of disclosure, publicly traded companies were required to provide periodic financial statements to the SEC and to provide shareholders with annual reports. This act also required all exchanges to register with the SEC, bringing them further under the SEC's control.

The cornerstone of both of these pieces of legislation is disclosure of relevant information relating to the offering of the security. Many other acts and laws have been passed to regulate the securities markets. For example, the Investment Advisers Act of 1940 provides investor protection against unethical investment advisors and requires advisors to register with the SEC and provide the SEC with semiannual reports. Also, under the Investor Protection Act of 1970 the Securities Investor Protection Corporation (SIPC) was established to provide up to $500,000 of insurance to cover investors' account balances in the event that their brokerage firm goes bankrupt.

FORGOING FUNDS

Thirty years ago, when Indiana accounting professor Dan Edwards placed an order to buy some shares of Sony Corp., his broker tried to talk him out of it, saying "nobody's ever heard of that company." Mr. Edwards persisted, however, and his broker made the purchase.

But right from the start, the stock was something of a trial. To begin with, it took two days for the order to go through, and once it did, Mr. Edwards couldn't find price quotes without calling his broker. When annual reports came, they were in Japanese.

How times have changed. Thanks largely to the rise of American Depository Receipts or ADRs, buying many foreign shares is a snap these days. With no more difficulty than it takes to buy domestic stock, U.S. investors can trade the shares in hundreds of companies from around the world. Prices are quoted in dollars, and the companies provide financial data in English, adjusted to reflect U.S. accounting standards.

Fueled by Americans' interest in foreign markets—and some relentless cheerleading on Wall Street—ADRs now account for more than 5% of all trading volume on the major U.S. exchanges. Three of the 10 most-active Big Board

stocks last year were ADRs: Telefonos de Mexico SA, Hanson PLC and Glaxo Wellcome PLC.

But for all the newfound convenience, investing abroad through ADRs still amounts to a walk on the wild side. Many of the old warnings still apply: Your investment could be gutted by foreign-currency fluctuations or volatile international markets. Information is still sometimes spotty. And, despite all the publicity, ADRs remain misunderstood—even controversial in some quarters—with some historical baggage you should know about before you take out your wallet.

"The ADR market has grown like a jerrybuilt house, especially over the last 15 years," says Eric Fry, president of Holl International, a San Francisco money-management firm. "It started at 2,500 square feet, and now it's 14,000 square feet. It's not your typical glossy investment-banking product."

Source: Michael Allen, "Forgoing Funds," *The Wall Street Journal,* June 27, 1996, p. R5. Reprinted by permission of *The Wall Street Journal,* © 1996 Dow Jones & Company, Inc. All Rights Reserved Worldwide.

Analysis and Implications …

A. There are two ways in which a foreign firm can have its shares traded on an exchange in another country. The first is to arrange for the stock to be listed directly on an exchange or on the NASDAQ, which is becoming increasingly common, with over 200 foreign companies traded on the NASDAQ alone. The other is via American Depository Receipts, or ADRs. ADRs represent indirect ownership of stocks and are actually tradeable receipts for shares held on deposit in a bank in the foreign company's home country. In effect, the shares are held in a bank in the home country, and you buy and sell receipts for those shares. Companies such as Sony, Volvo, Toyota, and DeBeers all trade via ADRs.

B. An alternative way of investing internationally is via a mutual fund that holds shares of stock of foreign companies. Some of these international funds specialize in one region, one country, or one type of country—for example, emerging nations.

Self-Regulation.   Much of the day-to-day regulation of the markets is left to the securities industry and is performed by the exchanges and, for the OTC market, the NASD. The willingness and zeal with which the exchanges approach self-regulation is inspired by the fear that if self-regulation doesn't work, government regulation, over which the exchange has no control, will be imposed. For example, after the October 1987 market crash, the NYSE self-regulated like mad and imposed a number of "circuit breakers" to head off or slow potential future market crashes. The idea behind these "circuit breakers" is that by closing the market in the event of sharp declines, investors will be given a chance to step back and assess the rationality of the price decline rather than react on instinct.

Insider Trading and Market Abuses.   Much of the logic behind regulation of the market stems from the desire to level the playing field with respect to the securities markets. As such, the Insider Trading Sanctions Act of 1984 and the Insider Trading and Securities Fraud Enforcement Act of 1988 served to make it illegal to trade while in the possession of inside information, or "material" nonpublic information held by officers, directors, major stockholders, or anyone with special insider knowledge.

Has insider trading disappeared? Certainly not. In fact, *Business Week,* after analyzing the largest 100 mergers and takeovers of 1994, came to the conclusion that one out of three of those deals was preceded by stock price run-ups or abnormal volume that could not be explained by the publicly available information at the time.

Another potential abuse involves **churning**, or excessive trading on a client's account. Although churning is illegal, it's also practically impossible to prove. Churning can easily take place if the client has relinquished trading control to the broker, but it also takes place on traditional accounts. That's why it's so important to select an honest broker whom you can trust.

Churning

Excessive trading in a security account that is inappropriate for the customer and serves only to generate commissions.

HOW SECURITIES ARE TRADED

Trading securities is like so many other important things in life: You can't really do it unless you know how. Luckily for you, this section will teach you how to do it and explain the different types of trades and trading mechanisms. You'll notice that when we discuss the different trading mechanisms, we refer to all securities as stocks. We're not favoring stocks or saying that these trading mechanisms apply only to stocks. We're just being lazy, and stocks are the most frequently traded of the different securities.

The Role of the Specialist in an Organized Exchange

The NYSE and the AMEX both are considered **continuous markets**, which means that trading can occur on them at any time the exchanges are open. Unfortunately, buyers and sellers don't necessarily come to the market at the same time. For example, a large order to buy stock in Guidant, a producer of medical products, may arrive at the market at 11:07 A.M. If there isn't much in the way of Guidant stock for sale at that time, the price of that stock might rise considerably. Then, at 11:10 A.M. a large order to sell Guidant stock may reach the market. This time, if there isn't much demand for the stock, its price may drop by quite a bit. This bouncing up and down of stock prices is caused when supply and demand don't meet in the market at the same time. It's the role of the specialist to take care of this potential problem and to "maintain a fair and orderly market."

Exchanges assign specialists to each stock. These specialists act as both broker and dealer. If you'd like to buy a stock at a particular price or better, the specialist handles your order. The specialist keeps track of your order, and when the stock price drops to the level you specified, the specialist executes your order. In effect, the specialist acts as a facilitator, keeping track of all the buy and sell offers and matching trades when appropriate.

The specialist also buys and sells stock from inventory to relieve the price changes that result when buy and sell orders randomly reach the market at different times. Specialists not only maintain an inventory of stock but also are required to maintain bid and ask prices at which they're willing to buy or sell additional inventory. Thus, when someone wants to sell a bunch of stock and there's no one to buy, the specialist will buy it. Likewise, if someone wants to buy some stock and there's no one to buy it from, the specialist is there to supply the stock. In effect, at times the specialists absorb excess supply and at other times they provide stock out of their inventory for excess demand. In that way they keep the market from fluctuating more than it would otherwise. Don't think that specialists can always prevent market problems. They can't. They certainly didn't manage to prevent the big market crash on October 17, 1987, when stock prices fell by about 25 percent. On that day, specialists, in a desperate attempt to stabilize the market, bought $486 million of stock. Still, the market fell dramatically. In attempting to keep prices from bouncing around too much, NYSE specialists generally act as either the buyer or the seller in almost 20 percent of the share volume traded. The remaining shares traded involve individuals' orders meeting directly in the NYSE market without the help of the specialist.

Order Characteristics

When you place an order to buy or sell stock, you need to be clear on the size of the order and the length of time the order is to be outstanding.

Order Sizes.
Common stock is sold in lots or groups of 100 shares on the New York Stock Exchange. These lots are referred to as **round lots**. Orders involving between 1 and 99 shares of stock are referred to as **odd lots** and are processed by "odd lot dealers" who buy and sell out of their inventory.

LEARNING OBJECTIVE #2

Trade securities using a broker.

Continuous Markets
Markets in which trading can occur at any time, with prices free to fluctuate as trading occurs.

Round Lot
A group or lot of 100 shares of common stock. Stocks are traded in round lots on the New York Stock Exchange.

Odd Lot
An order involving between 1 and 99 shares of stock.

Day Order
A trading order that expires at the end of the trading day during which it was made.

Open or Good-Till-Canceled (GTC) Order
A trading order that remains effective until filled or canceled.

Discretionary Account
An account that gives your broker the power to make trades for you.

Market Order
An order to buy or sell a set number of securities immediately at the best price available.

Limit Order
An order that specifies that a securities trade is to be made only at a certain price or better. Thus, if a limit order to sell stock is made, the stock will be sold only at a certain price or above.

Stop or Stop-Loss Order
An order to sell a security if the price drops below a specified level or to buy if the price climbs above a specified level.

Time Period for Which the Order Will Remain Outstanding. When you order a hamburger at Burger King, you want your order filled right away, not in a week. Well, when you order stock, you better specify when you want your order filled, or you just might have to wait a week and pay more than you bargained for. Ordering alternatives include **day orders**, which expire at the end of the trading day during which they were made; **open orders**, also called **good-till-canceled (GTC) orders**, which remain effective until filled or canceled; and fill-or-kill orders, which, if not filled immediately, expire. Finally, your broker can be given the power to make trades for you if you open a **discretionary account**. Because a discretionary account gives your broker power over your money, it should be considered only if you've worked with your broker for years, and only under unusual circumstances at that. There's no question that problems do occur with discretionary accounts, and the easiest way to avoid such problems is to avoid discretionary accounts.

"Types of Orders"

Market Orders. A **market order** is simply an order to buy or sell a set number of securities immediately at the best price available. These orders can generally be executed within minutes of being placed. Once your order is placed with your broker, it's then teletyped to the floor of the NYSE, where it's either executed electronically or received by a floor broker. The floor broker takes the order to the location on the exchange floor where that stock trades and executes the trade. As a result, when you place a market order, you can be relatively certain that the order will be executed quickly. However, you can't be certain of the price at which it'll be executed.

Limit Orders. A **limit order** specifies that the trade is to be made only at a certain price or better. In other words, if a limit order to sell stock is made, the stock will be sold only at a certain price or above, and if a limit order to buy is made, the stock is bought only at a certain price or below. In effect, limit orders allow you to limit your bid or ask price to what you feel is an acceptable level. If the specified price isn't available, your trade isn't made, and your order is given to the specialist, who'll in turn execute the limit order if the price moves to your acceptable level.

Stop Orders. A **stop** or **stop-loss order** is an order to sell if the price drops *below* a specified level or to buy if the price climbs *above* a specified level. Stop-loss orders are used to protect your profits. They allow you to bail out of the stock if the market starts to tumble, or to buy in if the price starts to rise. For example, say you'd purchased Netscape in August 1995 at $27 per share and 4 months later it was selling at $147—a gain of $120 per share. Of course, you never know when Netscape might have some problems, or when the market might fall and Netscape's price could dive, killing part or all of your $120 per share gain. If you wanted to lock in some of the gains you'd already made, you could do so by using a stop-loss order to sell Netscape at $127. You wouldn't want to use a stop-loss order for the full $147 current price, because your stock would then be immediately sold while the price remained $147. You also wouldn't want to use a stop-loss order for an amount very close to $147, say $145 or so, because market prices commonly fluctuate up and down, and you wouldn't want your stop-loss order to be executed on a routine fluctuation just before an uncommon rise up to, say, $160 per share. You want to set the stop loss order price just right so that you're safeguarding against only a major, not a minor, fluctuation. Thus, if the price of Netscape tumbled to $127 your stop-loss order would activate and sell your Netscape stock at the best price possible, which may end up being less than $127. In this way you can "lock in" some of the paper profits.

Short Selling—Sell High, Then Buy Low

Although it's obvious that you can make money in the stock market when stocks rise in price, you can also make money in the stock market when stock prices decline. With **short selling** you're wishing for bad news: The more the stock drops in price, the more money you make. Short selling involves borrowing stock from your broker, selling it, and replacing the stock later. Then, if the stock price goes down, you buy it back and return it to your broker. You made a profit by buying it for less than you sold it. However, if the price of the stock goes up, you have to buy it back at a higher price. You lose! In effect, selling short lets you reverse the order of buying and selling. That is, when you invest in stock, the goal is to buy low and later to sell high. With short selling the goal is to sell high and later to buy low.

Short selling isn't necessarily free, or even cheap. Because you've borrowed someone's stock and sold it, you not only have to replace it later, but also have to repay any dividends that were paid during the period for which the broker was without the stock. Also, to protect itself from stupid short sellers who might lose the money, the broker keeps the proceeds from the short sale until it gets its stock back. To provide the brokerage firm with further protection that the short seller will be able to repurchase the stock in the future, the short seller must put up some collateral—referred to as a margin requirement—during the period of the short sale.

Let's suppose that you feel strongly that McDonald's stock price is about to fall from its present level of $70 per share, and you want to make money off McDonald's misfortune. First, you laugh wickedly. Then, you call your broker and sell 1,000 shares of McDonald's short. The proceeds of $70,000 are credited to your account, although you can't withdraw those funds. Your broker also has a 50-percent margin requirement, which means you must have an additional $35,000 in cash or securities in your account to serve as collateral. Most short sellers keep Treasury bills or notes in their account to serve this purpose. Now let's assume that McDonald's drops in price to $50 per share, and you decide it's time to buy. You call your broker to purchase 1,000 shares of McDonald's for a total cost of $50,000. Thus, you've made $20,000 on your short sale by selling high ($70 per share) and later buying low ($50 per share). Remember, though, that when you sell short, you also have to cover any dividends that occurred during the period the broker was without the stock. Thus, your profits are actually equal to the initial price less the total of the ending price and the dividends, as shown in Figure 13.4.

Of course, if McDonald's price went up, you'd lose money, because at some time you'd have to buy back the stock. Thus, if McDonald's stock went up to $90 per share instead of down, you'd lose $20,000 on your short sale, in addition to having to cover any dividends that occurred during the period the stock was sold short. You'd also have to

Short Selling
Borrowing stock from your broker and selling it with an obligation to replace the stock later.

FIGURE 13.4

Profit from Purchasing Stock and Later Selling It

Profit = (Ending Price + Dividends) − Initial Price − Total Commissions Paid

▼ Versus

Profit from Selling Stock Short

Profit = Initial Price − (Ending Price + Dividends) − Total Commissions Paid

listen to your broker laugh at you when you gave back the more expensive stock. In this case, you'd have sold low ($70 per share) and later bought high ($90 per share). Given the fact that the long-term trend of the stock market is upward, selling short is extremely risky and isn't something you should become involved in.

LEARNING OBJECTIVE #2

Trade securities using a broker.

DEALING WITH BROKERS

Although you can purchase securities through most financial planners, the most common means of directly purchasing common stock is through a stockbroker. A stockbroker is simply someone licensed to buy or sell stocks for others. In fact, most financial planners are, among other things, stockbrokers. There are three general categories of brokers: full-service brokers, discount brokers, and deep discount brokers. The differences between them center on advice and cost. As we'll see later when we examine the cost of trading, the difference in cost between these different types of brokers can be substantial.

Brokerage Accounts

Just as a bank account represents the money you have on deposit at a bank, a brokerage account represents the money or investments you have at a brokerage firm. For most investors this account includes securities and possibly some cash. However, it can also include other investments, and if there are enough different investments, combining these different accounts into an all-in-one account, called an asset management account, might be best. When we first introduced asset management accounts in chapter 5, we defined such an account as a comprehensive financial services package offered by a brokerage firm that can include a checking account, a credit card, a money market mutual fund, loans, automatic payment on any fixed debt (such as mortgages), brokerage services (buying and selling stocks or bonds), and a system for the direct payment of interest, dividends, and proceeds from security sales into the money market mutual fund. The major advantage of an asset management account is that it automatically coordinates the flow of funds into and out of your money market mutual fund. For example, interest and dividends received from securities owned are automatically "swept" into the money market mutual fund. Also, if you write a check for an amount greater than what is held in your money market mutual fund, securities from the investment portion of your asset management account are automatically sold with the proceeds "swept" into the money market fund to cover the check.

Full-Service Brokers

A **full service broker**, or **account executive** as they're frequently called, is paid on a commission that's based upon the sales volume generated. With a full-service broker, each investor is assigned a broker who oversees his or her account. That broker gives advice and direction to the client, and then executes the trades. The more frequently trades are made, the more the broker earns.

Discount Service Brokers

A **discount service broker** simply executes trades without giving any advice. Because discount brokerage firms don't provide advice, they're able to operate more efficiently, and as a result their commissions generally run between 50 and 70 percent lower than commissions charged by full-service brokers.

Deep Discount Brokers

In 1994, some of the discount brokers cut prices even further, undercutting the dominant discount brokers, such as Charles Schwab and Fidelity Investments. These **deep discount brokers** will execute some trades for up to 90 percent off the price of what a full-service broker might charge.

Services

In deciding which broker to use, regardless of whether you're considering a full-service, discount, or deep discount broker, you need to answer several questions.

- Are you willing to pay a higher commission for investment advice? If so, a full-service broker may be for you.
- Does the brokerage firm provide both safekeeping and record-keeping services?
- Are the accounts insured up to $500,000 by the Securities Investor Protection Corporation (SIPC) against the event that the brokerage firm faces financial difficulties?
- Does the brokerage firm provide an 800 number for transactions and quotes?
- Do you receive interest on idle cash in your account?

Not all brokerage firms provide the same services at the same cost, so it's a good idea to investigate the alternatives before choosing one to work with.

Cash versus Margin Accounts

Investors with **cash accounts** pay in full for their security purchases, with the payment due within 3 business days of the transaction. Investors with **margin accounts**, however, borrow a portion of the purchase price from their broker. In other words, with a margin account, both you and your broker put in $500 to purchase $1,000 worth of stock. The broker comes up with this money by borrowing the funds from a bank and paying what's referred to as the "broker's call money rate," which is generally the prime rate. The broker then charges you this rate plus a 1 to 2 percent service fee. There's a limit on the percentage of the purchase price that you must initially pay, called the **margin** or **initial margin**, which is set by the Federal Reserve. For the past 20 years it's been 50 percent. Keep in mind that 50 percent is the minimum margin required by the Federal Reserve and that the broker you work with may require a higher margin.

The only time that purchasing on margin is to the advantage of the investor is when the return on the stocks is greater than the cost of the borrowing. To demonstrate, let's assume that the margin is 50 percent and that you purchase 200 shares of Chrysler stock at $50 per share. In this case, the stock would cost a total of $10,000 (200 × $50), and you'd pay $5,000 and borrow the remaining $5,000 from your broker.

Full-Service Broker or **Account Executive**
A broker who gives advice and is paid on commission, where that commission is based upon the sales volume generated.

Discount Service Broker
A "no-frills" broker who executes trades without giving any advice and thus charges much lower commission than a full-service broker.

Deep Discount Service Broker
A very low cost, no-frills discount broker with prices that undercut traditional discount brokers.

Cash Accounts
Securities trading accounts in which the traders pay in full for their security purchases, with the payment due within 3 business days of the transaction.

Margin Accounts
Securities trading accounts in which the traders borrow a portion of the purchase price from their broker.

Margin or **Initial Margin**
A maximum limit set on the percentage of the purchase price of a security that must initially be paid for by the investor, which is set by the Federal Reserve.

Total cost: 200 shares at $50 per share	$10,000
Amount borrowed: total cost (1 – margin %)	−5,000
Margin: investor's contribution	$ 5,000

When you purchase securities on margin, they remain in the brokerage firm's name rather than in your name because the shares are used as collateral for the margin loan. What drives investors to make margin purchases is their desire to leverage their profits as those securities go up in price. For example, let's look at what'd happen to your investment if the price of Chrysler's stock rose 40 percent to $70 per share.

Total value of 200 shares at $70 per share	$14,000
Margin loan	−5,000
Margin (the net value of your investment)	$ 9,000

Your initial contribution of $5,000 is now worth $9,000, meaning you made $4,000 on an investment of $5,000—an 80-percent gain on your investment despite a stock price increase of only 40 percent. Actually, your return would be a bit less because you'd also have been paying interest on the portion of the purchase that was financed with borrowed funds, not to mention the commissions that you pay when you buy and sell the stock.

Don't get too excited about margin purchases just yet. Although the leverage that margin purchases provide can amplify stock price gains in a positive way, it can also amplify stock price losses in a negative way. For example, let's assume that the value of the Chrysler stock drops to $30 per share.

Total value of 200 shares at $30 per share	$6,000
Margin loan	−5,000
Margin (the net value of your investment)	$1,000

Your initial investment of $5,000 is now worth $1,000, meaning you lost $4,000—an 80 percent loss despite only a 40-percent drop in Chrysler's stock price. Thus, the leverage that margin purchases produce is often referred to as a "double-edged sword," as it amplifies both gains and losses. Table 13.1 summarizes the impact on profits and losses of buying on margin, including the payment of interest on the borrowed portion of the purchase.

Margin accounts are set up in such a way that when stock prices fall, only the amount you've put in suffers the loss in value. To protect your broker, a maintenance margin is in place. The maintenance margin specifies a minimum percentage margin of collateral that you must maintain—which is often the same as the initial margin. If the margin falls below this percentage, the broker issues a margin call. A margin call requires you to replenish the margin account by adding additional cash or securities to bring the margin back up to a minimum level. Otherwise, the broker can sell securities from your margin account to bring the margin percentage up to an acceptable level. Again, you take the loss.

As you should be able to see, margin accounts aren't for the novice investor. To protect yourself from the increased risk of margin accounts, you should use only a cash account when you purchase securities. As the name implies, with a cash account, you pay for your stock purchases in cash. The biggest hurdle with a cash account is the short settlement period—3 days—which often isn't enough time to mail a check to your broker. Of course, overnight mail will solve this problem, but it'll cost you. A less expensive alternative is to electronically link your bank with your brokerage firm, which you can do through the **Automated Clearing House (ACH) Network**. The ACH Network is an electronic payment system that links 14,000 banks, credit unions, and savings and loan institutions. In fact, you may already rely on it if you have your paycheck directly deposited or if you have your checking account automatically debited for your utility or cable TV payments. The big advantage to using

Automated Clearing House (ACH) Network
An electronic payments system that links 14,000 banks, credit unions, and savings and loan institutions.

TABLE 13.1

The Impact on Profits of Buying on Margin, Allowing for Interest and Commissions

For margin purchases, it's assumed that the investor purchases 200 shares of Chrysler common stock at $50 per share, borrowing $5,000 at an annual interest rate of 10% and paying the rest in cash, and sells the stock 1 year later. Note that this doesn't include commissions that'd be paid regardless of whether the stock was purchased on margin or not.

Date, Transaction, and Price Movement	Normal Purchase (not on margin)	Margin Purchase
Today: Purchase 200 shares of Chrysler Stock at $50 per share		
Amount borrowed (if purchased on margin)	$ 0	$ 5,000
Investor's contribution	$10,000	+ 5,000
Total cost: 200 shares at $50 per share (ignoring commissions)	$10,000	$10,000
The Stock Rises by 40%		
One year later: Sell the Chrysler Stock (assuming a stock price of $70 per share)		
Proceeds from sale (ignoring commissions)	$14,000	$14,000
Less interest on borrowed funds (10%)	− 0	− 500
Net proceeds from sale	$14,000	$13,500
Less initial cost	−10,000	−10,000
Net profits	$ 4,000	$ 3,500
Return on investment (net profit/amount invested)	$4,000/$10,000 = 40%	$3,500/$5,000 = 70%
The Stock Falls by 40%		
One year later: sell the Chrysler Stock (assuming a stock price of $30 per share)		
Proceeds from sale (ignoring commissions)	$ 6,000	$ 6,000
Less interest on borrowed funds (10%)	− 0	− 500
Net proceeds from sale	$ 6,000	$ 5,500
Less initial cost	−10,000	−10,000
Net loss	−$ 4,000	−$ 4,500
Return on investment (net profit/amount invested)	−$4,000/$10,000 − −40%	−$4,500/$5,000 = −90%

the ACH Network is the speed and cost. To set up such a payment system, you generally need only sign a form authorizing your brokerage firm to access your bank account. After the agreement goes into effect, which generally takes about 2 weeks, all you need do to transfer funds is dial an automated service or call your brokerage firm directly.

Registered in the Street Name or in Your Name. Another choice you have when buying securities is whether you'd like the securities registered in the street name or in your name. Securities registered in the "street name" remain in the broker's custody and appear in the broker's computers as a computer entry in your name. You still own the securities and you'll receive any dividends or interest payments just as if the securities were registered in your name, but these securities are, in fact, more convenient to sell because the actual stock certificates or bonds don't have to be delivered to your broker. The only disadvantage to leaving your securities in the broker's "street name" comes with brokerage firms that impose a charge called a "maintenance fee" against accounts that don't trade within a certain time frame. In this case, you may accrue charges if you don't make additional trades within a set time period. Before opening an account with a broker, you should ask if maintenance charges are imposed against dormant accounts. If so, try another broker.

Joint Accounts.   If you're buying securities along with your spouse, there are several alternative forms of joint accounts, each with different estate planning implications. As such, you should have a strong understanding of how they work or confer with your lawyer before setting up your account. Under an account with **joint tenancy with the right of survivorship**, when one of the individual owners dies, the other receives full ownership of the assets in the account. Under such an account, the assets bypass the lengthy court process called probate where the assets are transferred according to the instructions left in the deceased's will. However, they may be subject to estate taxes. With a **tenancy-in-common account**, the deceased's portion of the account goes to the heirs of the deceased rather than to the surviving account holder.

Brokers and the Individual Investor

To understand the advice you typically receive from a broker, you need to understand that although you may consider your broker a friend, when talking investments, he or she is a salesperson. Moreover, your broker isn't a security analyst and most likely lacks the time or background to evaluate the recommendations he or she receives from analysts. Thus, when you get advice to buy or sell a security, you should realize that this may simply be someone else's recommendation that your broker is passing on, and the only way your broker makes money is by having you trade as often as possible. In fact, the dialogue your broker uses in convincing you to invest may have been carefully scripted by the marketing wizards back at the brokerage firm's main office. Keep in mind that a typical broker with 3 years or more of experience is expected to bring in between $40,000 and $120,000 in trades every working day. That doesn't mean you shouldn't take advice. Rather, you should take that advice and investigate it. This relates back to **Axiom 12: The Agency Problem in Personal Finance—Differentiating Between Advice and a Sales Pitch**. As has been said often throughout this text, you bear all the consequences of bad decisions, and, as a result, you *must* take responsibility for your own financial affairs. This is also why it's so important to do your homework when selecting a broker and pick a good one— one you can trust.

You must also realize where you fit into the scheme of things at a brokerage firm: at the bottom of the totem pole. Brokerage firms make a lot less money from helping you than they do from helping institutional investors, such as managers of pension funds or mutual funds. As a result, it's the institutional investors that talk directly with the analysts, and it's the institutional investors that are first in line to receive the analysts' reports. Although you'll get phone calls and you'll get research reports from your broker, you must remember that they're coming from a salesperson, and that, although convincingly written, they may not be overly valuable. Again, you must take responsibility for your own financial affairs.

There's one thing that you *can* do to increase the performance of your investments, and that's to keep the transaction costs—that is, the commissions and fees— down to a minimum. Unfortunately, that's becoming more and more difficult with a full-service broker, because over the past decade institutional investors have placed increasing pressure on brokerage firms to cut costs. To please institutional investors, many brokerage firms have transferred costs down to the individual investor—you—by

Joint Tenancy with the Right of Survivorship
A type of joint ownership in which the surviving owner receives full ownership of the assets in the account when the joint owner dies.

Tenancy-in-Common Account
A type of joint ownership in which the deceased's portion of the account goes to the heirs of the deceased rather than to the surviving account holder.

AXIOM #12

The Agency Problem in Personal Finance— Differentiating Between Advice and a Sales Pitch

DOUBLE TROUBLE

How buying on margin works, and how it amplifies losses when things go wrong.

(A) 1. An investor opens a margin account with a broker. The investor can now buy stocks with both his money and money borrowed from the broker.

2. The investor thinks that Coram Healthcare (stock symbol: CRH), which provides intravenous therapy for homebound patients, is a winner. He buys 1,000 shares on March 31, 1995, at $26 a share, putting up $13,000 himself and borrowing the other $13,000 from the broker. If the stock rises, the investor reasons, the loan will enable him to profit from twice as many shares.

3. The best-laid plans: On May 31, Coram's stock closes at $17.75, a decline of more than 30 percent. Under the broker's rules, the investor must put more money into his account to further secure the loan. This is known as a margin call.

4. On June 30, Coram's stock closes at $14.125. The investor decides to cut his losses and sell the stock.

(B) 5. If the person had invested his own $13,000 in Coram and had borrowed nothing, he would have suffered only a 46 percent loss on that sum, exclusive of commissions. But because he borrowed an additional $13,000, his loss, with loan interest included and commissions excluded, amounted to 94 percent of his personal outlay.

Source: Bill Alpert, "Double Trouble," *The New York Times*, August 27, 1995, p. F3. Copyright © 1995 by The New York Times Co. Reprinted by Permission.

Analysis and Implications . . .

A. The total amount of money that's borrowed by investors buying on margin is huge—in fact, it can run between $60 billion and $70 billion. It's not unusual for margin purchases to account for over 1 percent of the value of all listed stock.

B. The lure of buying on margin comes from both the chance for large gains and the low cost of borrowing. Because the stockbroker has the stocks as collateral for the loan, the interest rate charged is relatively low—8 to 11 percent. These rates vary from broker to broker and also are lower the more you borrow. Regardless of the cost, buying on margin is dangerous, and no stock is safe. IBM looks like a solid stock today, but think of those who bought it on margin in 1987 for $175 per share and watched it drop to $40 per share.

charging for such services as initiating accounts, maintaining dormant accounts, and closing them down. So much for being low man on the totem pole. If you have a portfolio worth over $100,000, you should probably use a discount broker. Although you might not have an account executive to hold your "investments hand," you'll have a greater return on your investments. However, you should keep in mind that not all discount brokers are the same—services and costs can vary dramatically from one to another. If you're a smaller investor, you might not want to deal with a broker at all and instead put your money directly in a mutual fund.

When purchasing bonds, there's no advantage to using a discount broker. In general, the commissions charged by a full-service versus a discount broker when purchasing bonds will pretty much be the same, especially for larger purchases. If you're going to be buying bonds through a broker, you might as well use a full-service broker, because it doesn't cost more. However, if you're buying Treasury bonds, there's no reason to go through a broker at all. Treasury bonds can be purchased directly through the Treasury Department or through any of the Federal Reserve Banks, and no commissions will be charged.

Choosing a Broker

As with choosing a financial advisor, choosing a broker should be done with great care. It's a serious decision, one that can have a major impact on your financial future. First, you must decide whether you want a full-service, discount, or deep discount broker, recognizing that a full-service broker will be more costly. If you decide on a discount broker, you should look for one with a reputation for honesty and efficiency in servicing clients. If you do decide on a full-service broker, you should look for the following:

- A broker with a reputation for integrity, intelligence, and efficiency in servicing clients. Ask business colleagues, your banker, and your friends who are successful investors for recommendations.

- A broker with experience over both up markets and down markets, and with a record of proven advice. Avoid the overeager newcomer who may end up learning the hard way—on your money. If you work with someone who's been in the business since 1987, that broker will have experienced at least one market downturn.

- A broker who understands your investment philosophy and is willing to work within your investment boundaries to achieve your financial goals. Interview prospective brokers to find out about their background, training, and experience. Be upfront about your financial circumstances and how much you could invest. Ask for their general recommendation for a person in your situation, and listen. Ask for a sample portfolio. Do you feel comfortable with them? Be sure to interview several candidates and compare notes to find a good fit.

- A broker who has a reputation for allowing customers to say no without undue pressure. Ask for names of clients whose financial situation is similar to yours whose accounts he or she has handled for at least 3 years. Call them and ask what the broker has done for them.

- A broker who is upfront with you regarding costs—both maintenance costs on your account and commissions—and what research their recommendations are based on.

THE COST OF TRADING—AND THE IMPLICATIONS

We've already touched briefly on the cost of trading in our discussion of full-service, discount, and deep discount brokers. We'll now look at what the costs are. Interestingly, the savings can be dramatic, with the commissions associated with the purchase of 500 shares of stock at $20 per share—a total purchase of $10,000 of common

LEARNING OBJECTIVE #2

Trade securities using a broker.

stock—ranging from a high of $253 with a full-service broker to $25 with a deep discount broker. In percentage terms, that's 2.53 percent versus 0.25 percent. Keep in mind that this sales commission is to buy the stock. The broker would charge a similar commission to sell the stock. Thus, your stock would have to rise by 5.06 percent before you'd break even and cover your commissions if the stock were purchased from the more expensive full-service broker. Many brokers also charge a transaction fee, which in general is quite small. What's not quite small is the inactive account annual fee, which is imposed by most full-service brokers at a rate of $50 per year. In effect, if you don't make a security transaction during the year, your account's debited $50, which can be a sizable cost for smaller accounts. Moreover, this fee has the effect of encouraging trading when the trading may not be in your best interest. Needless to say, you should try to avoid firms that charge annual fees on inactive accounts.

With smaller transactions, the savings from using a discount broker are less noticeable. For a $3,000 purchase (100 shares of stock at $30 per share) the costs might range from a high of $91 with a full-service broker to $25 with a discount broker. In percentage form, that's a cost of 3.03 percent versus 0.83 percent. Again, you should keep in mind that these costs are doubled with a "round trip"—that is, buying the stock and later selling it.

With respect to the purchase of Treasury bills, there's no cost advantage to using a discount broker. In fact, when the amounts purchased go above $10,000, the cost advantage many times swings to the full-service broker.

So what's the bottom line on the cost of trading? In a nutshell, discount brokers are less expensive than full-service brokers. For larger purchases, this cost difference is even more dramatic. Thus, if you make large purchases, you should definitely consider a discount broker. If you're a smaller investor, you should and can avoid the potentially costly inactive account fee regardless of whether you choose a full-service, discount, or deep discount broker. Finally, if you're purchasing Treasury securities through a broker, you should do so with a full-service broker that doesn't charge an inactive account fee. However, if you're buying Treasury securities, you can totally avoid any fee by purchasing them directly from the Treasury or a Federal Reserve Bank.

SOURCES OF INVESTMENT INFORMATION

LEARNING OBJECTIVE #3

Locate and use several different sources of investment information to trade securities.

To say the least, there's a wealth of investment information available to you. Before presenting a brief overview of these sources, let's look at some decisions you have to make before you invest. First, it's more important that you decide on the general types of investment (common stock, bonds, CDs) you'll put your savings into than it is to choose the individual securities. It's also extremely important that you diversify your investments. Finally, your choice of individual securities can't make up for a lack of savings. In effect, an awful lot of planning and many decisions have to be made before you're at the point of selecting specific securities in which to invest. Once you're ready to invest, you'll want to gather up as much information as you can.

However, if you're going to make informed investment decisions, you do have to seek out that information, read it, and interpret it. Fortunately, you don't have to do your own research. That's already done for you, and it's available from the companies themselves, from brokerage firms, and from the press—magazines, newspapers, and investment advisory services.

Corporate Sources of Information

Annual reports are a great source of investment information. In reading an annual report, the first thing to keep in mind is that although the report is factual, those facts are interpreted in as favorable a light as possible. For example, annual reports generally begin with a letter from the president to the stockholders. This letter generally highlights the year and gives prospects for the upcoming year. It does so with real attention to public relations. That means that if the president says, "It was a challenging and troublesome year," he or she may really be trying to say, "We lost a lot of money last year."

In looking at an annual report, you should concern yourself with the trends in sales, profits, and dividends, looking for upward movement in all three. You should also pay attention to the company's explanation of how well the firm performed during the year and what management projects for the future. Finally, give close attention to the positives and negatives outlined in the annual report. Are profits up or down? Are new products being introduced? How are the sales on those new products? Are sales climbing or falling? Are new plants being opened or closed? You're looking at these items because most changes a firm experiences are gradual. Things tend to get worse or better over time, and by looking at an annual report you may be able to judge the direction of the changes that are taking place today and that will affect the company's stock price tomorrow. Most annual reports are available for free directly from the company itself.

Brokerage Firm Reports

Most full-service and some discount brokers provide their customers with access to research reports prepared by the brokerage firm's security analysts. These reports cover the direction of the economy as a whole—suggesting a general strategy of where you should invest your money. They also look directly at individual companies, analyzing the companies' prospects and concluding with recommendations of buy, hold, or sell, with "buy" indicating a positive recommendation, "sell" a negative recommendation, and "hold" a neutral recommendation.

These reports do most of the work for you and provide you with the logic behind the recommendation. Even if you don't buy the recommended stocks, the reports are of value to read because they show you the logic that leads an analyst to recommend that a stock be bought or sold. If you're interested in a research report on a specific company, simply call up your broker and request it—it's as simple as that.

The Press

To begin with, every investor should read the *Wall Street Journal.* It contains insights, data, and financial news that are essential for any investor. There are also a number of other excellent financial magazines that are worth a look, including *Forbes, Fortune,* and *Barron's,* along with a number of personal finance magazines, such as *Money, Smart Money, Kiplinger's Personal Finance,* and *Worth,* that contain excellent articles on investing. The best place to start looking into financial periodicals is the public library. If you're just starting out, what you're likely to find is that some of the personal finance magazines are the easiest to digest. At whatever level you're comfortable with, dig in right there, because the only way to really learn about investments is to jump in. The more you read, the more sense it'll all make, and, more important, the more comfortable you'll feel entering the investments arena.

Once you're ready to move beyond the magazines and the *Wall Street Journal,* the major sources of information on the market and individual stocks are Moody's Investors Service, Standard & Poor's, and Value Line. These are all investment advisory services and are available at many libraries.

Moody's, which is published by Dun and Bradstreet, puts out a number of different investment publications, including their weekly *Bond Survey,* which highlights the week's activity in the bond market, and *Moody's Handbook of Common*

Stock, which is published quarterly and includes background and a brief description of over 1,000 companies. They also publish the *Moody's Manuals,* which present historical financial data in addition to management information on both listed and OTC firms.

Standard & Poor's also provides comprehensive financial information on large listed and OTC firms in *Standard & Poor's Corporate Records.* Equally interesting is their publication *Corporation Reports,* which contains a brief summary of the firm's current outlook, any important developments, and a business summary. To keep the information current, it's updated quarterly.

Of the investment advisory services, the *Value Line Investment Survey* is perhaps the most useful for investors. This publication follows approximately 1,700 companies and provides a one-page summary of each firm's outlook, updating the forecast four times a year. What makes Value Line unique is that it rates every stock on a scale of 1 to 5, with 1 being the most favorable rating on their timeliness and safety. Figure 13.5 provides an example of a Value Line company summary for Disney.

In addition to evaluating individual stocks, Value Line also examines and ranks different industries, picking out those they feel have the highest investment potential. Value Line also gives weekly evaluations of the economy, as well as the stock and bond markets, advising investors where they should put money, which direction interest rates are headed, and whether or not the stock and bond markets are headed up or down.

Other Sources of Information

In addition to all these paper publications, there's also a wealth of information available on the Internet, with new investment sites being added almost daily. One of the problems with these sites is that there are no controls on who can post information on the Internet. As a result, you may end up with a market analysis written by a 12-year-old. A listing of some interesting World Wide Web sites is given at the end of the chapter in Taking It to the Net, and Table 13.2 gives some of the pros and cons of tapping into the Internet for investment information.

Another excellent source of information can come from "investment clubs." In recent years, investment clubs have become increasingly popular for their social, educational, and investment value. Every club works a bit differently, but most clubs have required dues (of, say, $10 per month), with the dues then being pooled and invested in the club's name. The real value of these clubs is not from what you might earn on your investment, but on the knowledge and experience you gain from going through the investment process. With a club, you're often able to gain access to financial planners and investment advisors that you wouldn't be able to access as an individual. Once again, the more you know, the better off you are.

SUMMARY

The primary securities market is where new, as opposed to previously issued, securities are sold. For example, a new issue of IBM stock would be considered a primary market transaction. Actually, the primary markets can be divided into two other markets: those for initial public offerings (IPOs) and those for seasoned new issues. An initial public offering, or IPO, is the first time the company's stock is traded publicly. Seasoned new issues refer to stock offerings by companies that already have common stock traded in the marketplace.

Securities that have previously been issued are traded in the secondary markets. Many securities in secondary markets are traded on organized exchanges, which actually occupy a physical location where trading occurs. The New York Stock Exchange is the oldest of all the organized exchanges, dating back over 200 years. The American

FIGURE 13.5

The Value Line Investment Survey

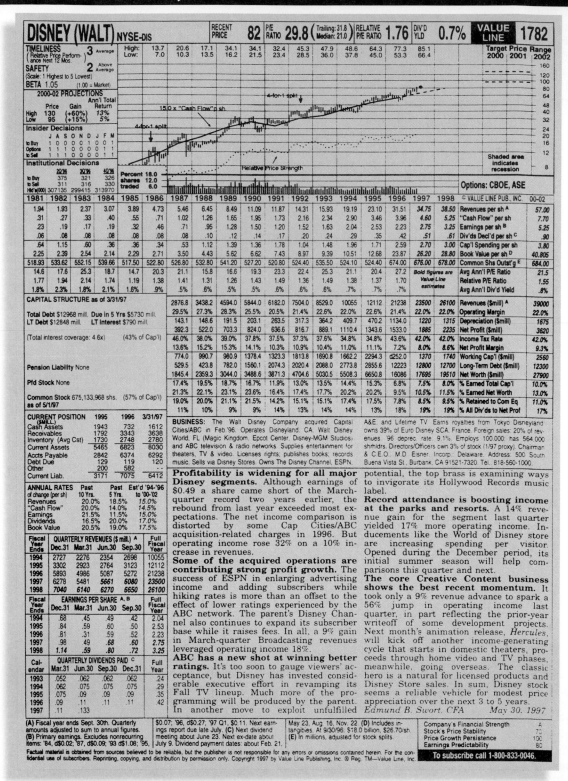

TABLE 13.2

On-line Investment Information—Pros and Cons

The Pros	The Cons
A Wealth of Investment Information There is an incredible amount of information, including news groups, mailing lists, free software, and the commercial discussion groups. Some are self-promoting and others are objective.	**Garbage In, Garbage Out** Because anyone can access Internet news groups, the hot tip you're considering may actually come from a precocious 12-year-old, or it may be a self-promotion.
Corporate Information Securities and Exchange Commission filings for companies and mutual funds that file electronically can be accessed via the Edgar project at no charge. Corporate information is also available from investment companies and commercial on-line services.	**The Agency Problem Abounds on the Internet** Much of what appears on the Internet is self-serving in nature. It is either placed there by stockbrokers trying to push stocks on their own Web home pages or by companies trying to improve their stock prices.
Data, Data, Data Economic, monetary, and stock data are available from the Federal Reserve, the University of Michigan Web server, and other data providers on the World Wide Web.	**Beware of Get-Rich-Quick Schemes** The Internet is loaded with outright scams.
You Have the Same Opportunities as Any Other Investor Regardless of how small an investor you are, you have immediate access to the same information as the larger investors.	

Stock Exchange is the second most important of the organized exchanges and generally lists stocks of firms that are somewhat smaller than those listed on the NYSE. The OTC market, in which transactions are conducted over telephone or via a computer hookup rather than on an exchange, is a highly automated nationwide computer network that allows brokers to see up-to-the-minute price quotes on roughly 35,000 securities and execute trades on those securities.

Securities market regulation is aimed at protecting the investor and providing a level playing field so that all investors have a fair chance of making money. There are actually two levels of regulation of the securities markets: the Securities and Exchange Commission, and self-regulation directly by the exchanges or, in the case of the OTC, by the National Association of Securities Dealers (NASD).

Common stocks are sold in lots or groups of 100 shares on the New York Stock Exchange—this is referred to as a round lot. Orders involving between 1 and 99 shares of stock are referred to as odd lots, and are processed by "odd lot dealers," who buy and sell out of their inventory. An investor must specify a time period for which the order will remain outstanding. Alternatives include day orders, which expire at the end of the trading day during which they were made; open orders, also called good-till-canceled (GTC) orders, which remain effective until filled; and fill-or-kill orders, which, if not filled immediately, expire. Other types of orders can specify the price you want to trade on. For example, a market order is simply an order to buy or sell a set number of securities immediately at the best price available. A limit order specifies that the trade is to be made only at a certain price or better. A stop loss order is an order to sell if the price drops below a specified level or to buy if the price climbs above a specified level.

Just Do It! *From the Desk of Marcy Furney, CFP*

Terms of Enrichment

Some studies estimate that up to 95 percent of individual investors lose money or just break even on stock trades. Primarily this is true because they didn't enter into the process armed to make logical, informed decisions. Be prepared to avoid some of the pitfalls, such as these:

☑ *"Falling in love" with a stock.* Just because you inherited a stock from your favorite grandmother doesn't mean it'll always be a viable part of your portfolio. One that's made money for you for several years may become a loser over time. Emotion doesn't belong in the decision-making process, and there's no "rate of return" for loyalty to a particular investment. Know when to let go.

☑ *Investing too heavily in your employer.* Many people purchase large amounts of their employer's stock because they feel that they work for a good company. If the company goes away, not only have they lost their job, but they may have lost a fair amount of their assets. The value of stock in the secondary market may have little to do with how good an employer the company is. (This isn't to say that you shouldn't take advantage of some of the excellent company-sponsored stock purchase plans.)

☑ *Selling low and buying high.* Stock is the one thing in America that people don't seem to want when it's "on sale" (when prices are down). Professional money managers normally don't sell just because the price falls or buy because everyone else does. In fact, they more often do the opposite. Their decisions are based on detailed analysis of the stock and how it fits with their portfolio objectives. The key is to be able to evaluate what may be driving the movement of the price and avoid making decisions based on panic or fear of loss.

☑ *The hog factor.* Don't be "a hog" and hold on to your investments when they're way up in the hopes they'll go up even further. The saying is, "Bears make money, bulls make money, and hogs get slaughtered," or something like that. Not "selling high" in hopes of "selling higher" can have disappointing results. You may want to sell part of the holdings and keep the rest for potential continued rise. Alternatively, you could buy the same stock again later and "ride another wave."

☑ *Failing to realize the commitment involved.* If you aren't willing or able to invest the time necessary to do good research and actively tend to your portfolio, perhaps you should seek professional assistance via a mutual fund or other managed account.

☑ *Excessive trading costs.* The phrase "playing the market" is sadly appropriate for the actions of some people. They think that success in investing lies in moving things around a lot. Consequently, even if they're lucky enough to make some good choices, trading costs and taxes on short-term gains eat up most of what they made.

Investors have a choice on whether to pay cash or borrow from their broker. Investors with cash accounts pay in full for their security purchases, with the payment due within 3 business days of the transaction. Investors with margin accounts borrow a portion of the purchase price from their broker. Short selling involves borrowing stocks from your broker and selling them with an obligation to replace the stocks later.

Then, if the price goes down, you buy them back, make a profit, and return the stocks to your broker.

A full-service broker gives investment advice and is paid on commission, where that commission is based upon the sales volume generated. A discount service broker simply executes trades without giving any advice and charges less for transactions. What is the cost difference? In general, discount brokers are less expensive than full-service brokers, and for larger purchases, this cost difference is quite dramatic. Thus, if you make large purchases, you should definitely consider a discount broker.

If you're going to make informed investment decisions, you have to seek out investment information, read it, and interpret it. Fortunately, you don't have to do your own research. That's already done for you, and it's available from the companies themselves, from brokerage firms, and from the press—magazines, newspapers, and investment advisory services. In addition, joining an "investments club" can also be a real learning experience and can provide you with access to investment research that you might not otherwise find.

Review Questions

1. What is a securities market? Does a market have to take the form of an actual building? Give an example to support your response. (LO 1)
2. Differentiate between an IPO and a seasoned new issue. (LO 1)
3. What is a "seat" on the New York Stock Exchange? Why is it important? (LO 1)
4. The OTC market is significantly different from organized exchanges. Briefly explain listing and membership requirements in the OTC market and how the market is determined. (LO 1)
5. Differentiate between the bid price and the ask price. (LO 1)
6. International investments are recommended by brokers because they help diversify one's portfolio. Name another advantage and risk associated with international investments. (LO 1)
7. Name three ways that a U.S. investor can purchase international equities. (LO 1)
8. Name the two securities regulation organizations. (LO 1)
9. What is the primary purpose for securities market regulation? (LO 1)
10. Much has been written about insider trading abuses. What exactly is insider trading? What two pieces of legislation have been enacted to curb insider trading abuses? (LO 1)
11. What is meant by the term "churning"? Why should individual investors be concerned about this issue? (LO 1, 2)
12. What is a continuous market? What is the primary reason stock prices move up and down in a continuous market? (LO 1)
13. What is a discretionary account? Who can make buy and sell decisions in such an account? Should individual investors open discretionary accounts? (LO 2)
14. The timing of a securities transaction is very important. Differentiate between day orders and open orders. In addition to timing of orders, pricing instructions are also important. Differentiate between the following: (a) market order, (b) limit order, and (c) stop-loss order. Why would someone consider using a limit or a stop-loss order? (LO 2)
15. Should the average investor consider using short selling techniques? Why or why not? (LO 2)
16. If an investor receives a margin call, what has just happened? (LO 2)
17. The typical broker is required to bring in between $40,000 and $120,000 in trades every working day. Does this cause an agency problem? (LO 2)
18. In looking at an annual report, what three trends should investors look for? (LO 3)

Problems and Activities

1. After studying the fundamental trends from CDX Company's annual report, you've decided to purchase a round lot of the firm's stock on the open market. On Monday morning you call a stockbroker and ask for the price of CDX stock. The broker indicates that CDX is bid at 45⅛ with an ask of 45⅝. Assuming you wanted to place a market order to purchase shares, how much would you pay? (LO 1)

2. Sung Ho, an active investor, recently recorded the following transactions in her brokerage account:

June 10	Bought 300 shares of BTU
June 17	Bought 50 shares of CDR
June 22	Sold 150 shares of BTU
June 28	Bought 100 shares of TXBI
June 30	Sold 100 shares of BTU

   Which of the transactions would be considered a round lot? Which were odd lot transactions? (LO 1)

3. You've just made another fantastic investment. Based on your analysis, you purchased 300 shares in SBBI Corporation for $26.50 per share. Yesterday the stock closed at $53.25 per share. To lock in on your gains, you've decided to employ a stop-loss order. Assuming you set the order at $53, what is likely to happen? At what price would you recommend setting the stop-loss order? Why? (LO 2)

4. You've just heard that your uncle Joe has been selling short shares in IA Associates Corporation. The stock had been selling as high as $92 per share, but over the past 6 months the stock's price has fallen to $45 per share. Your uncle thought the price would continue to fall, so he short sold 100 shares of IA Associates at $45. In actuality, the price of IA Associates zoomed to $90 per share. Your uncle is worried, and he asks you to calculate his profit or loss excluding commissions or interest rates. How did your uncle do? (LO 2)

5. Assume that the margin rate is 50 percent and that you just purchased 300 shares of Apple Computer at $20 per share. Fill in the blanks to determine your contribution to this transaction:

Total cost	$
Amount borrowed	– _____
Contribution	_____

   What would happen to your investment if the price of Apple Computer rose to $40 per share?

Total value	$
Loan	– _____
Margin	_____

   What was your profit?

   What would happen to your investment if the price of Apple Computer fell to $15 per share?

Total value	$
Loan	– _____
Margin	_____

   What was your loss? (LO 2)

6. The cost of trading may be the single most important factor in increasing your investment returns. Assume that you want to buy 100 shares of MNC Corporation at $45 per share. You've found two brokerages that are willing to make the trade for you. Calculate, in percentage terms, the cost of each brokerage. Which is a better deal?

	Firm 1	Firm 2
Total cost	$4,500	$4,500
Commission	253	35

Would your answer change if Firm 1 indicated that its commission was for a round-trip transaction? (LO 2)

7. Determine which of the following two companies would be eligible for listing on the NYSE: (LO 2)

	Firm 1	Firm 2
Earnings before taxes for the year	$5 million	$2.7 million
Value of publicly held stock	$45 million	$40 million
Number of common shares	3 million	1 million
Number of holders of 100 shares	3,000	2,100

8. Last year you sold short 100 shares of stock, selling at $60 per share. Six months later the stock had fallen to $20 per share. Over the 6-month period, the company paid out two dividends of $1 per share. Your total commission cost for buying and selling the shares came to $125. Determine your profit or loss from this transaction. (LO 2)

Suggested Projects

1. Make a list of 10 products and services that you use on a daily basis. Examples might include soft drinks, detergents, utilities, and textbooks. Next to the list of products and services, make a note of which company produced the good or service. Take the list to a library that has either Moody's, Standard & Poor's, or Value Line and use these sources to determine on which stock exchange the companies are traded, a recent closing stock price, and any relevant trends that might lead to the recommended purchase or sale of the company's stock. (LO 1)

2. Go to your library's business reference section and obtain a list of companies listed on the "pink sheets." Why are these companies listed here rather than on the NASDAQ or the NYSE? Using the information presented in this chapter, would you consider investing in a security listed in the pink sheets? Would you recommend a pink sheet listed company to a close friend or relative? (LO 1)

3. Obtain one week's worth of the *Wall Street Journal*. Read through each issue and either photocopy or clip as many examples of tombstone advertising as you can find. Which firms consistently show up as underwriters and syndicate participants? Based on your sample of tombstone advertisements, what types of security issues are being circulated? As an investor, do you find tombstone advertisements very useful? (LO 1)

4. Using your local phone book, obtain a listing of stockbrokers, financial planners, and investment advisors in your area (check the yellow pages using the above categories). Call three different investment firms and ask them how they are compensated for their services. Also ask them to send this information to you via mail. Do you think that there'll be a difference in how the three are compensated? Do you see any potential agency problems in the way these firms or individuals are compensated? (LO 2)

5. Obtain the phone number of a deep discount broker. You can usually obtain phone numbers of firms in personal finance magazines or through an Internet search. Using the five questions presented on page 427 as a basis for questioning, ask the discount brokerage firm's representative these questions. Based on this information, does the firm appeal to you? Why or why not? (LO 2)

6. This chapter has pointed out that small investors fit very "low on the totem pole" within the scheme of things at most brokerage firms. Why do you think this is? In terms of receiving timely and unique investment advice, what do you think being low man on the totem pole means for you? (LO 2)

7. Some investors continue to hold stock certificates as proof of ownership, but most investors hold their securities in a street name. Ask relatives or friends who own stocks if they hold the certificates directly or if the certificates are held in a "street name," and determine why your friends or relatives made this choice. This chapter describes one possible disadvantage of leaving securities in a street name. Do you think this was a consideration in the choice? (LO 2)

8. Did you know that every publicly owned and traded company in the United States is required by law to provide quarterly and annual reports to anyone who asks for one? Based on this knowledge, obtain the phone number for a company that you purchase goods or services from (use Moody's, Value Line, Standard & Poor's, or phone numbers from a product's packaging). Call the company and request an annual report. In looking at the annual report, do you see any noticeable trends in sales, profits, and dividends? (LO 3)

Discussion Case 1

Wayne and May have just heard that you're enrolled in a personal finance course. They need your help. It turns out that Wayne has heard about a fantastic restaurant that's going to go public in an initial public offering. Last night Wayne took May to eat at one of the company's restaurants, and, to say the least, they loved it. The restaurant specializes in Middle Eastern food and Turkish coffee, and according to the tombstone advertisement, the underwriting syndicate appears very reputable. Wayne thinks that this opportunity may be the next "Microsoft," and he thinks that buying stock in the IPO is almost a sure thing. May isn't quite convinced, because she reasons that if the investment was such a sure thing, why would she and Wayne get a shot at the deal? Wayne and May have an investment account at a brokerage worth $20,000. They're thinking of investing at least $5,000 in the IPO. Wayne and May have put together a list of questions that they'd like your help answering. What advice would you give Wayne and May to these questions?

Questions

1. Is Wayne correct in thinking that an IPO can increase in value dramatically?

2. What might Wayne be overlooking when he envisions huge profits?

3. How easy is it for small investors to invest in an IPO?

4. Using data from Figure 13.1, how much could Wayne and May lose if this deal does not work out?

5. Based on your perception of risk and return in relation to IPOs, what would you recommend to Wayne and May?

Discussion Case 2

Wally and Bonnie are in their early 40s and until now they have always kept their savings in the bank. They liked the idea that a deposit in a bank was insured and guaranteed, and that regardless of what happened in the economy or to the bank, they could always get their money. Wally and Bonnie recently talked with a stockbroker about funding their retirement. The stockbroker pointed out that in terms of reaching their retirement goals, a bank account did not pay enough interest. The broker recommended that Wally and Bonnie invest in a combination of stocks, bonds, mutual funds, and money market accounts. Wally and Bonnie are skeptical about the ultimate safety of their investments. Specifically, Wally is worried about what would happen to their securities and cash if the brokerage firm went bankrupt, and Bonnie is concerned that the markets are rigged and that only those with inside information ever make any money. Both are equally concerned that the markets are unregulated gambles, and that there is no way to regulate the ethics of brokers. They've come to you for some advice on what to do.

Questions

1. Does Wally need to be concerned about the lack of insurance in his brokerage account? Is there a specific Securities Act you could sight to back up your answer?

2. Bonnie is concerned about insider trading. Do you agree with Bonnie? Why or why not?

3. Name two securities acts that protect investors in terms of regulation. Also name two organizations that oversee the securities markets and the actions of investors.

4. In working with a broker, what should Wally and Bonnie watch for that might lead them to conclude that the broker is not working for their best interest?

5. Provide Wally and Bonnie a list of questions to ask potential brokers to assure them of receiving the best service at the lowest cost.

14

INVESTING IN STOCKS

While Anne Scheiber was alive, no one paid much attention to her. After all, she was just a frugal spinster living alone in a studio apartment in Manhattan. Her life seemed uneventful: She never took vacations or traveled, she never bought furniture, she never ate out, she didn't spend money on new clothes. In fact, neighbors claimed that when they saw her outside her apartment, which was rare, she always wore the same inexpensive black coat and hat. It wasn't until her death in 1995 at 101 that she received much notice. In her will, Anne Scheiber revealed that she had a $22 million fortune, almost all of which she bequeathed to Yeshiva University, a small New York University. This gift came as a huge surprise, not only because Scheiber had seemed poor for most of her life, but also because she hadn't attended Yeshiva and, in fact, was totally unknown at the university.

Although the idea of a seemingly poor spinster leaving a fortune to an institution she'd never even visited is fascinating, how Anne Scheiber amassed her fortune is even more interesting. She started out plainly enough, working as an auditor for the IRS, earning $3,150 per year. As an auditor, though, she had the opportunity to scrutinize the investment habits of many of the wealthy people she audited—much to their chagrin. Over time, Scheiber noticed that most of the fortunes of the wealthy were based on common stock investments. She decided that if it worked for the wealthy, it could work for her, too. When she retired in 1943, Scheiber invested her $5,000 nest egg entirely in common stocks. At first she stuck to

Learning Objectives

After reading this chapter you should be able to:

1. Invest in stocks.
2. Read stock quotes in the newspaper or in financial periodicals.
3. Classify common stock according to basic market terminology.
4. Value stocks.
5. Understand the risks associated with investing in common stock.

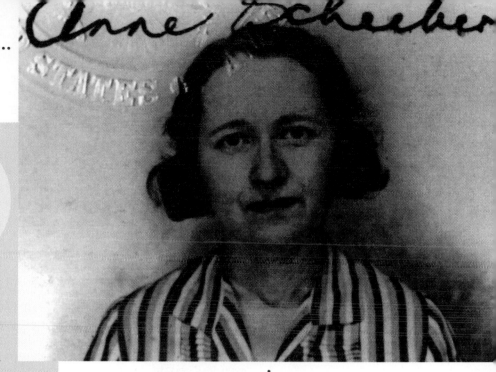

companies she knew, beginning with the popular movie studios Universal and Paramount. She also went in for the then small soft drink companies Coca-Cola and PepsiCo, as well as a number of drug companies, including Bristol-Myers Squibb and Schering-Plough, both small companies at the time. Her stock dabblings continued throughout her life. On the rare occasions when Scheiber ventured out of her apartment in her later years, she usually went to see her stockbroker or to read the *Wall Street Journal* at the local library (in keeping with what appeared to be a miserly existence, she never actually bought the paper). In the 42 years up to her death in early 1995, Anne Scheiber's stock holdings increased in value over 4,000-fold, making her a multimillionaire, even though she never lived like one. One of her best investments was the 1,000 shares of Schering-Plough she bought for $10,000 in 1950 and sold in 1994 for over $4 million.

Anne Scheiber may not have lived like one, but she certainly invested like a millionaire. Even if you didn't have her investing prowess, it would've been hard not to make money in the stock market any time over the past 70 years. In fact, even with the ups and downs and all the risks of investing in the stock market (such as the crash on October 19, 1987, when the value of a typical stock fell by over 20 percent in one day), if you'd invested a dollar in the common stock of a typical large company on the last day of 1925, it would've grown to $1,370.95 by the end of 1996. Moreover, if you'd invested your dollar in a typical small-company stock, it would've grown to $4,495.99 over the period 1926–1996. Now you're probably thinking that you don't want to wait 71 years to see some serious returns on your stock investments. That's fine—you don't have to. The cumulative return on the stock of a typical small company from 1991 through 1996 was a cool 234 percent. Five years isn't that long to wait to more than double your money, now is it? Unfortunately, you never know when another 1987 will come along to gut your profits. Thus, when we talk about common stock, we're talking about risk and return. It's an investment that fits with a longer investment horizon. We're also talking about the place where fortunes—such as Anne Scheiber's—are made.

Invest in stocks.

Dividends

A company's distribution of its profits in the form of cash or stock to its shareholders.

WHY CONSIDER STOCKS?

Now you know that the possible returns on stock investments are high and that the accompanying risks are also high, but you may be wondering just how stocks generate returns. Simply, they generate returns the same way owning your own business does. When you buy common stock, you purchase a small part of the company. When the company does well, you do well and receive a small part of the profits. If the company does poorly, so do you, and you either get diddly or even lose money. Returns from common stocks come in the form of dividends and capital appreciation. A **dividend** is simply a company's distribution of profits to its stockholders. It can be in the form of either cash or more company stock, but it's always a liquid asset you can use right away. Capital appreciation isn't exactly an asset. Instead, the term refers to an increase in the selling price of your shares of stock, perhaps as the company's earning prospects improve. You can't really appreciate or benefit from capital appreciation until you actually sell your stock.

Unfortunately, neither dividends nor capital appreciation is guaranteed with common stocks. You never know when a seemingly healthy company's going to have a lousy year and not have any profits to distribute—Apple Computer is a good example of this. Even when companies do have good years and plenty of profits, they're not required to distribute dividends. For example, in early 1997 Microsoft still hadn't issued any dividends. Of course, capital appreciation on stock prices is even less certain. Look, for example, at what happened to the common stock of Marvel Entertainment (publisher of Spider-Man, X-Men, and Silver Surfer comic books) in 1996—it fell by 86.5 percent. At the same time, the common stock of Tyco Toys, the makers of Matchbox cars, Tickle-Me-Elmo, and the View-Master and Magna Doodle brands, rose by 161.1 percent. Stock prices can jump up and down for the strangest reasons or for no reason at all. Now you're probably wondering why you should bother investing in stocks if they don't guarantee you any return. Here's why:

- **Over time, common stocks outperform all other investments.** Although stocks aren't guaranteed to give you any return at all, they usually give you a great return anyway. Figure 14.1 compares the returns on various investments over the period 1926–1996. Common stock clearly blows away the alternatives and exceeds the inflation rate by a wide margin.

- **Stocks reduce risk through diversification.** When you include different types of investments that don't move (experience changes in returns) perfectly together over time in your portfolio, you're able to reduce the risk in your portfolio. Stocks move differently than other investments—such as bonds—and different stocks move in different ways. Holding several types of stock can greatly reduce your risk.

- **Stocks are liquid.** You can't be assured of what you'll get when you want to sell your stock, but you won't have a difficult time selling it. The secondary markets for common stock are extremely well developed, and, as such, you will be able to sell your stock whenever you want with minimum transaction costs.

- **The growth in your investment is determined by more than just interest rates.** With some investments, the potential for price appreciation is largely a function of interest rates going down. With common stock, you're not a slave to interest rates. Sure, a change in interest rates can and often will affect your stock prices. However, the earning prospects and performance of the firm will also affect stock prices. If you hitch your star on a company that performs well, you can make money even when interest rates jump.

Now that you know why common stocks make good investments, you should know a thing or two about them in general. Let's take a look at some stock basics.

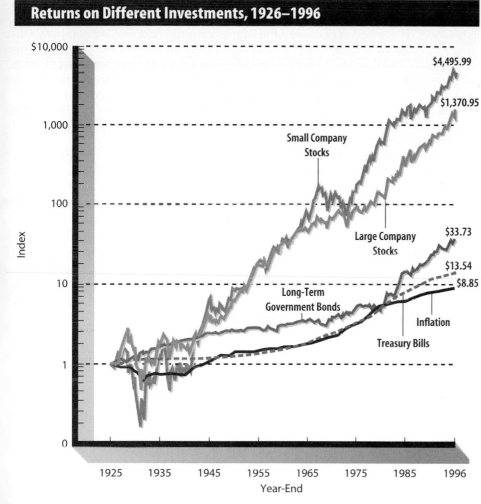

Returns on Different Investments, 1926–1996

FIGURE 14.1

Index

$4,495.99

$1,370.95

Small Company Stocks

Large Company Stocks

$33.73

$13.54

$8.85

Long-Term Government Bonds

Inflation

Treasury Bills

$10,000

1,000

100

10

1

0

1925   1935   1945   1955   1965   1975   1985   1996

Year-End

BASIC COMMON STOCK TERMINOLOGY AND FEATURES

If you're going to be investing in common stock, you certainly ought to know a bit about common stock and what your rights are as a common stockholder. In effect, you shouldn't invest in common stock if you can't talk the language of common stock. This section should get you fairly proficient in the language of common stock.

Limited Liability

Although as a common shareholder you're considered one of the many actual owners of the corporation, your liability in the case of bankruptcy is limited to the amount of your investment. In effect, the most you can lose, if the company goes broke, is what you invest.

Claim on Income

As owners of the corporation, the common stockholders have the right to any earnings that are left after all debt and other obligations have been paid. The dividend is the

LEARNING OBJECTIVE #1

Invest in stocks.

typical way to distribute these earnings, but the corporation isn't obligated to pay any dividends to its shareholders. Instead, the board of directors gets to decide whether to pay dividends or whether to reinvest the leftover earnings back into the company. Obviously, the common stockholders benefit from the distribution of income in the form of dividends, but they also benefit from the reinvestment of earnings. How? Plowing earnings back into the firm results in an increase in the value of the firm, in its earning power, and in its future dividends. These increases in turn cause the price of the common stock to rise. In effect, leftover earnings are distributed either directly to the common stockholder in the form of dividends, or indirectly in the form of capital appreciation on the common stock.

Common stockholders' claim on leftover earnings is a double-edged sword. On the one side, there's no limit to the amount of earnings stockholders can get. If the company has a banner year and takes in millions in extra earnings, the stockholders are entitled to the whole kaboodle. On the other side, if after paying off debt and other monetary obligations the company has no leftover earnings, the stockholders get zilch.

Paying Dividends.   Although most corporations pay dividends on a quarterly basis, common stock dividends aren't automatic. They must be declared by the corporation's board of directors. On the **declaration date**, the board of directors announces the size of the dividend, which is expressed as the dividend per share, the ex-dividend date, and the payment date. Because companies need to know who actually owns their stock before they can pay a dividend, they set a cutoff date known as the **ex-dividend date**. On the ex-dividend date, the stock begins trading "without dividend"—that is, if you buy it after the ex-dividend date, you don't get the dividend for that year. Of course, if you buy the stock prior to the ex-dividend date, you get the dividend. Finally, on the payment date the corporation sends out the dividend checks to the shareholders.

Claims on Assets

We've seen that when a company does well and has a lot of earnings to distribute, common stockholders receive their share only after creditors are paid. What happens when a company does so poorly that it goes bankrupt? Well, common stockholders are stuck waiting in line again. The creditors have the right to sell off the remaining company assets to regain their money. Only after the claims of the creditors have been paid off do stockholders get to sort through the rubble and try to extract the money they'd invested. Unfortunately, when companies do go bankrupt, the stockholders are usually plain out of luck.

Voting Rights

Common stockholders are entitled to elect the company's board of directors. Usually, one share of stock equals one vote, although some, but not many, companies issue different "classes" of stock with greater or less voting power. Common stockholders not only have the right to elect the board, but also must approve any changes in the rules that govern the corporation. Voting for directors and charter changes occurs at the corporation's annual meeting. Stockholders may attend the meeting and vote in person, but most vote by proxy. A **proxy** is a legal agreement to allow a designated party to vote for a stockholder at the corporation's annual meeting. A proxy vote isn't the same as asking your buddy to hand in something for you that's already filled out. It gives your "buddy" the right to make decisions for you. Usually the firm's management goes after and gets most of the proxy votes. However, in times of financial distress or when management takeovers are threatened, *proxy fights*—battles for proxy votes between rival groups of shareholders who want to take control of the company or aim it in a new direction—occur.

Declaration Date
The date on which the board of directors announces the size of the dividend, the ex-dividend date, and the payment date.

Ex-Dividend Date
The date on which the stock "goes ex," meaning it begins trading in the secondary market "without dividend." In other words, if you buy the stock after its ex-dividend date, you don't get the dividend.

Proxy
A legal agreement a stockholder signs to allow someone else to vote for him or her at the corporation's annual meeting.

Stock Splits

Occasionally a firm will feel that its stock price is getting too high for the smaller investor to consider purchasing the stock. To keep the price down to a desired level and thereby encourage more investors to buy, the company "splits the stock." A **stock split** involves substituting more shares for the existing shares of stock. In effect, the number of shares of stock outstanding increases without there being any increase in the market value of the firm. As a result, each share of stock is worth less. For example, let's assume that you own 100 shares of Coca-Cola common stock and that it's just reached $120 per share. Thus, your investment is worth $12,000. The management of Coca-Cola feels that $120 per share is more than the normal small investor can afford and wants the price lowered. To bring the price of the stock down, Coca-Cola's managers decide to split the stock three for one. Thus, investors would receive three shares of new Coca-Cola stock for every share of "old" Coca-Cola common stock that they owned. There's no gain in wealth to the stockholder, so each new share of stock would be worth $40 ($120/3). Thus, you now own 300 shares of Coca-Cola stock, which is selling at $40 per share, but your total investment is still worth $12,000.

Stock Repurchases

Sometimes companies buy back their own issued shares of common stock in what's called a **stock repurchase**. As a result of the repurchase, there are fewer shares outstanding, so each remaining stockholder owns a larger proportion of the firm. Interestingly, stock repurchases are extremely common, with well over 1,000 of these plans announced during most years.

Book Value

The book value of a company is calculated by subtracting the value of all the firm's liabilities from the value of its assets, as given on the balance sheet. To relate book value more easily to the price of the stock, we divide the company's book value by the number of shares it has outstanding to get the book value per share. Book value is a historical number. That is, it will reflect the value of the firm's assets when they were purchased, which may be vastly different from their value today. Thus, for a firm whose assets were purchased a number of years ago, book value has little or no meaning.

Earnings Per Share

Earnings per share reflects the level of earnings achieved for every share of stock. Because it focuses on the return earned by the common stockholder, it looks at earnings after preferred stock dividends have been paid. It is calculated as follows:

$$\text{earnings per share} = \frac{\text{net income} - \text{preferred stock dividends}}{\text{number of shares of common stock outstanding}}$$

Preferred stock dividends are subtracted from net income because, as we will see in the next chapter, they're paid before common stock dividends are paid. As such, it's net income less preferred stock dividends that are available to the common shareholders. In effect, this figure tells investors how much they've earned on each share of stock that they own—but not necessarily how much the company will pass along in dividends. This figure is available in the daily stock price listings in most newspapers and can be used to compare the financial performance of different companies.

Dividend Yield

The **dividend yield** on a share of common stock is the annual dividends divided by the market price of the stock. The dividend yield tells investors how much in the way of a return they would receive if the stock price and dividend level remained constant. For

Stock Split
Increasing the number of stock shares outstanding by replacing the existing shares of stock with a given number of shares. For example, in a two-for-one split for every share of existing stock you hold, you would receive two shares of new stock.

Stock Repurchase
A company's repurchasing, or buying back, of its own common stock.

Dividend Yield
The ratio of the annual dividends to the market price of the stock.

example, if the price of the stock is $50 and it pays $4 per share in dividends, the dividend yield would be 8 percent ($4/$50 = 8%). Many companies that have tremendous growth possibilities choose to reinvest their earnings rather than pay them out in dividends. As a result, many growth companies simply don't pay dividends. For example, Microsoft has never paid a dividend.

Market-to-Book or Price-to-Book Ratio

The market-to-book or price-to-book ratio is a measure of how highly valued the firm is. When interpreting this ratio, remember that book value reflects historical costs and, as such, may not be overly meaningful. This ratio is calculated as follows:

$$\text{market-to-book ratio} = \frac{\text{stock price}}{\text{book value per share}}$$

Most stocks have market-to-book ratios above 1.0, and they commonly range up to about 2.5.

The Facts of Life

According to a 1997 survey by the NASDAQ, the number of adult Americans owning stocks doubled between 1990 and 1997, to 43 percent of the adult population. Of those investors, 47 percent are women, of whom 45 percent say they are primarily responsible for making family investment decisions. Also, 55 percent of the investors are under the age of 50, with 19 percent being between the ages of 18 and 34—members of so-called Generation X. In addition, the study found that 9 percent are black, Hispanic, or other minorities. Clearly, the investors in the stock market reflect our population.

STOCK INDEXES: MEASURING THE MOVEMENTS IN THE MARKET

Did you ever hear a financial report on television or the radio in which someone claimed, "The market was up today as the Dow rose 27 points"? Did you ever wonder just what the heck that person was talking about? "The Dow" is simply a stock market index that measures the performance—rise and fall—of various stock prices. A stock index won't tell you exactly how each one of your investments performed. Instead, indexes provide us with a simple way of measuring stock performance in general. To understand stock listings and stock performance, you need to be familiar with the Dow and other market indexes.

The oldest and most widely quoted of the stock indexes is the **Dow Jones Industrial Average (DJIA)**, or **Dow**. The DJIA's original purpose when it was started by Charles Dow in 1896 was to gauge the sense or well-being of the market based on the performance of 12 major companies. The Dow is currently comprised from the prices of 30 large industrial firms, only one of which—General Electric—was in the original group of 12. Because the DJIA is based on the movement of only 30 large, well-established stocks, many investors feel it reflects price movements for large firms rather than for the general market. Actually, these 30 stocks represent over 25 percent of the market value of the NYSE, making this average more representative than one might think at first glance. Another criticism of the DJIA is that it weights stocks based upon their relative prices. As a result, when a high-priced stock moves a small amount, it has an inordinately large impact on the index. Still, with all its faults, the DJIA does a relatively good job of reflecting market movements. As you can see in Figure 14.2, the DJIA has had its share of ups and down since 1960.

LEARNING OBJECTIVE #2

Read stock quotes in the newspaper or in financial periodicals.

Dow Jones Industrial Average (DJIA), or Dow
A commonly used stock index or indicator of how well stocks have done. This index is comprised of the stock prices of 30 large industrial firms.

FIGURE 14.2

The Dow Jones Industrials Average (DJIA), Since 1960

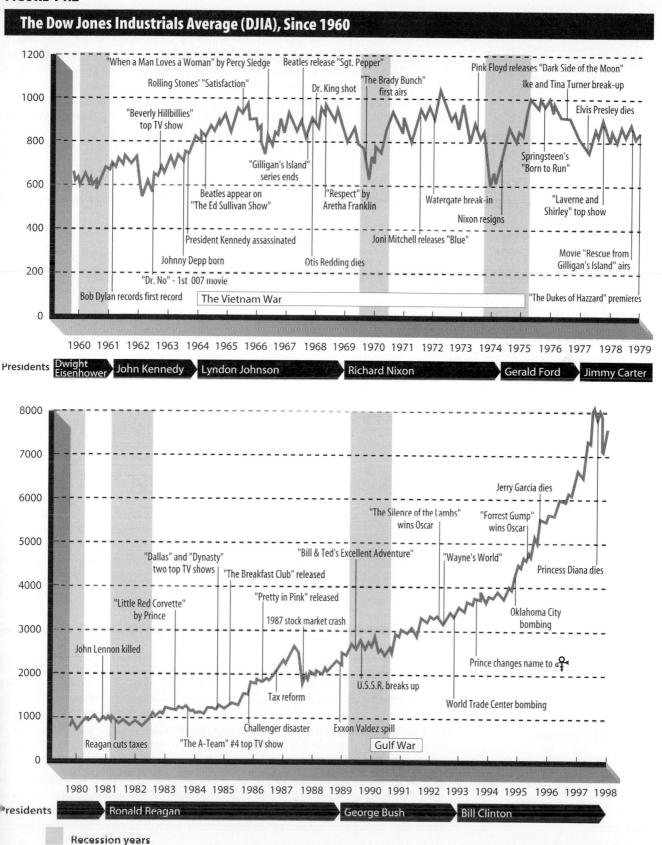

Presidents: Dwight Eisenhower, John Kennedy, Lyndon Johnson, Richard Nixon, Gerald Ford, Jimmy Carter

Presidents: Ronald Reagan, George Bush, Bill Clinton

Recession years

Standard & Poor's 500 Stock Index or S&P 500

Another commonly used stock index or indicator of how well stocks have done based on the movements of 500 stocks, primarily from the NYSE.

Bear Market

A stock market characterized by falling prices.

Bull Market

A stock market characterized by rising prices.

LEARNING OBJECTIVE #3

Classify common stock according to basic market terminology.

Blue-Chip Stocks

Common stocks issued by large, nationally known companies with sound financial histories of solid dividend and growth records.

Growth Stocks

Common stocks issued by companies that have exhibited sales and earnings growth well above their industry average. Generally, these are smaller stocks, and many times they are newly formed.

Income Stocks

Common stocks issued by mature firms that pay relatively high dividends, with little increase in earnings.

In addition to the Dow, there are a number of other stock indexes. The most well known of these is the **Standard & Poor's 500 Stock Index** or **S&P 500**. The S&P 500 is a much broader index than the DJIA, because it's based on the movements of 500 stocks, primarily from the NYSE, but also including some stocks from the AMEX and the OTC market. Because the S&P 500 is a broader index, it probably better represents movements in the overall market than does the Dow. Broader still are such indexes as the Russell 2000 and the Wilshire 5000, which try to measure the movements of all stocks. Also, the NYSE, the AMEX, and the NASDAQ all have indexes that chronicle the movements of their listed stocks, and Standard & Poor's calculates six other general indexes. Still, when investors talk about the movements in the market, they generally refer to the Dow.

So what do all these indexes tell us? Basically they tell us whether stock prices in general are rising or falling. A **bear market** is simply a stock market characterized by falling prices. The term "bear" comes from the fact that bears swipe downward when they attack. A **bull market** is one characterized by rising prices. The term "bull" comes from the fact that bulls fling their horns upward when they attack.

Reading Stock Quotes in the Newspaper

Figure 14.3 provides a visual summary of how to read New York Stock Exchange listings. Actually, most newspapers use the same basic format for stocks listed on the NYSE, the AMEX, and the OTC market. The price and volume listings for stocks traded on the NYSE are actually a combination of all trades of NYSE-listed firms, regardless of where the trade occurred—whether on the NYSE or on one of the regional exchanges. By looking at the stock quote in the paper, investors can see how much a stock's price jumped up or down by examining the stock's highest and lowest prices during the previous day, which are listed along with the stock's closing price. Finally, the change from the previous day's closing price is listed, which, along with the stock's high and low over the past 52 weeks, gives you a sense of the direction that the stock price is taking. You'll notice that, in most cases, trades are given in fractions of dollars, ranging from $1/16$ to $15/16$. Thus, if a stock is listed as trading at $26 5/8$, it's actually trading at $26.625. In late 1997 the trading fractions were in sixteenths of a dollar and headed for decimal-based trading.

GENERAL CLASSIFICATIONS OF COMMON STOCK

Analysts just love to use such terms as "blue-chip," "speculative," and "growth" to describe common stocks. These aren't formal classifications, but they're frequently used terms that you should be familiar with. As such, we'll introduce several of the most prevalent "classifications" of common stock, noting that different analysts may view the same stock as falling into different classifications.

- **Blue-chip stocks.** **Blue-chip stocks** are common stocks issued by large, nationally known companies with sound financial histories of solid dividend and growth records. Some examples of companies whose common stock is considered blue-chip are: General Electric, Texaco, and Procter & Gamble.

- **Growth stocks.** **Growth stocks** are those issued by companies that have exhibited sales and earnings growth well above their industry average. Generally, these are smaller companies, and many times they are newly formed. In general, these companies pay very low or no dividends, instead retaining earnings and plowing those funds back into the company. An example of a company whose common stock is considered a growth stock is Microsoft, which has posted huge increases in earnings while not paying dividends.

- **Income stocks.** **Income stocks** are generally associated with more mature firms that pay relatively high dividends, with little increase in earnings. The stocks of most utilities are considered income stocks, because utilities generally pay relatively high dividends and don't experience much growth in earnings.

FIGURE 14.3

52 Weeks Hi and Lo: The highest price and lowest price paid for the stock over the past 52 weeks excluding the latest day's trading. As you can see, Disney's stock has traded between 53¼ and 85⅛ over the past 52 weeks.

Sym: Each stock's ticker symbol appears to the right of the stock's name. For example, the symbol DIS identifies the Disney Corporation. A *pf* next to the stock's name indicates that it is preferred stock.

Div: The stock's annual cash dividend, if any, is given in dollars and cents. For example, Donnelly's annual dividend is estimated to be $0.40.

PE: The P/E ratio is used as a measure of relative stock performance. It is calculated by dividing the stock's closing price by its earnings per share for the most recent four quarters. A high P/E ratio suggests that investors are optimistic about the stock's prospects. Some of the reasons for high and low P/E ratios include the firm's growth prospects, the riskiness of the firm, its industry, and the accounting procedures that the firm uses.

Yld%: The percentage yield is calculated by dividing the cash dividend by the closing price of the stock.

Vol 100s: The number of shares traded during the previous day is given under Vol 100s. This is expressed in 100s since shares are generally traded in units of 100 shares. Thus, the number 21165 under Disney indicates that 2,116,500 shares traded during the previous day.

Net Chg: Net change refers to the change from the previous day's close. For example, Disney's stock closed up 5/16 point, or $0.3125, higher than it did the previous day. Keep in mind that in mid-1997 stocks generally traded in increments of 1/16, or 6.25 cents. The NYSE plans to move to decimal trading in the future.

Hi Lo Close: The highest, lowest, and price at which the last trade of the day took place are given in these three columns. Stocks that go up or down 5% from the previous day's close are printed in bold.

NEW YORK STOCK EXCHANGE COMPOSITE TRANSACTIONS

Quotations as of 5 p.m. Eastern Time
Wednesday, July 23, 1997

52 Weeks Hi	Lo	Stock	Sym	Div	Yld %	PE	Vol 100s	Hi	Lo	Close	Net Chg
s↓ 44⅞	28	Diebold	DBD	.50	1.1	28	2440	45½	44⅝	45³⁄₁₆	+ ⁹⁄₁₆
42⅞	25	DigitalEqp	DEC	...	dd	22466	40¹⁄₁₆	38	39¼	+ 1⅛
25⅞	22¾	DigitalEqp pfA		2.22	8.7	...	149	25½	25¾	25⁷⁄₁₆	– ⁷⁄₁₆
▲ 35⅞	28	Dillards	DDS	.16	.4	17	4410	36	35¼	36	+ ⅝
19	11⅝	DimeBcp	DME	.04p	...	18	8888	18⅝	18¾	18⁹⁄₁₆	+ ⅛
26¾	17¹⁄₁₆ ♣ Dimon	DMN	.60	2.5	17	821	24⅜	23⅞	24³⁄₈	+ ½
3¾	1⅝	CG Dina	DIN	...	...	...	482	3¹⁄₁₆	3⁵⁄₁₆	3⅜	...
2⅞	1⅜	CG Dina L	DINL	...	...	...	7	2⁷⁄₁₆	2⅜	2⅜	...
46⅛	18⅛	Disco	DXO	...	...	...	546	42	41¹¹⁄₁₆	42	+ ⅜
26½	12⅞	DiscountAuto	DAP	...	...	12	93	19¼	19	19	...
85⅛	53¼	Disney	DIS	.53	.7	28	21165	79⅝	77¾	77¹⁵⁄₁₆	+ ⁵⁄₁₆
44½	30⅞	DeleFood	DOL	.40	1.0	23	3301	41⅞	41⅜	41⅝	– ¼
s42¹¹⁄₁₆	20³⁄₃₂ ♣ DlrGen	DG	.20	.5	39	3291	42	41³⁄₁₆	42	+ ¹³⁄₁₆
n 15¼	13½	DomainEngy	DXD	...	...	...	220	14¹³⁄₁₆	14⅝	14⅝	– ¼
n30¹⁵⁄₁₆	17¾	DomSprmkt	DFF	...	...	...	183	30⅛	29⅝	29⅝	– ⅜
24⅝	18½	DominRes ubi	DOM	3.28e	13.7	...	160	24⅝	24	24	– ¼
41¾	33¼ ♣ DominRes	D	2.58	7.2	14	2332	36½	35¾	36	– ⁷⁄₁₆
10	6⅞ ♣ Domtar g	DTC	.14	...	...	175	9⅜	9³⁄₁₆	9³⁄₁₆	...
▲ 40⅜	24	Donaldson	DCI	.36	.9	21	261	40⁵⁄₁₆	40	40⅛	...
▲ 65	27⅝	DonLufJen	DLJ	.50	.8	14	1604	66⅜	64¼	66⁵⁄₁₆	+ 2⁷⁄₁₆
nl 25⅞	24⅝	DLJ CapTr pf		2.11	8.1	...	732b	¹¹⁄₁₆ 25 ¹³⁄₁₆	25 ¹⁵⁄₁₆	1 ¹⁄₁₆
n 25	17	Doncasters	DCS	...	...	...	236	24⅜	23⁷⁄₁₆	23⁷⁄₁₆	– ¹³⁄₁₆
27¼	8⅞	DonnaKrn	DK	...	...	21	447	10¹¹⁄₁₆	10⁷⁄₁₆	10⁹⁄₁₆	+ ¼
41¾	29⅜	Donelley	DNY	.76	1.9	24	3526	40¼	39¹⁵⁄₁₆	40¼	+ ¹⁄₁₆
s 20	11¾	Donnelly	DON	.40	2.1	14	120	19½	19¼	19⅜	...
▲ 70	41	Dover	DOV	.68	1.0	18	2047	70⅜	69¾	70⅛	+ ⅜
n 26⅞	16⅛ ♣ DoverDowns	DVD	.16e	.9	16	155	17⅝	17	17¹⁄₁₆	– ⁹⁄₁₆
93	69¾	DowChem	DOW	3.48	3.8	12	3742	91	90³⁄₁₆	90¹¹⁄₁₆	– ³⁄₁₆
46⅛	31⅞ ♣ DowJones	DJ	.96	2.3	25	2118	41¹⁵⁄₁₆	41⁹⁄₁₆	41¾	+ ¼
s 24	12¹³⁄₁₆	DowneyFnl	DSL	.32b	1.4	27	2039	22¾	22⅜	22⁹⁄₁₆	+ ⁷⁄₁₆
15¾	8¾	Drew	DRV	...	...	15	232	10¼	10²¼	10³⁄₄	– ¾

- **Speculative stocks.** **Speculative stocks** carry considerably more risk and variability than do typical stocks. Moreover, with speculative stocks it's generally difficult to forecast with precision the direction of the issuing company's future profits. These stocks are usually traded on the OTC market. Borland, a company that posted huge increases in profits in 1991 before its stock price dropped in price by over 70 percent in 1992, is an example of a company whose stock is considered speculative.

- **Cyclical stocks.** **Cyclical stocks** are those issued by companies whose earnings tend to move with the economy. When the economy slumps, its earnings drop. When the economy recovers, so do its earnings. Stocks issued by firms in the auto, steel, and housing industries are generally considered cyclical.

Speculative Stocks
Common stocks that carry considerably more risk and variability than a typical stock. A stock's classification can change over time.

Cyclical Stocks
Common stocks issued by companies whose earnings tend to move with the economy. A stock's classification can change over time.

Defensive Stocks

Common stocks issued by companies whose earnings tend not to be affected by swings in the economy and in some cases actually perform better during downturns. A stock's classification can change over time.

Large Caps, Mid Caps, and **Small Caps**

Classifications of common stock that refer to the size of the issuing firm—more specifically, to the level of the firm's capitalization, or its market value. A stock's classification can change over time.

- **Defensive stocks.** Whereas cyclical stocks tend to move with the economy, **defensive stocks** aren't nearly as affected by swings in the economy, and in some cases, they actually perform better during downturns. Why? Because companies behind defensive stocks tend not to be hurt by downturns in the economy. The insurance industry, for example, is largely unaffected by swings in the economy, and some auto parts suppliers, such as Midas and Monroe, actually see increased sales during downturns as consumers avoid purchasing new cars and instead repair their present cars.

- **Large caps, mid caps, and small caps.** **Large-**, **mid-**, and **small-cap stocks** refer to the size of the firm issuing the stock—more specifically, to the level of its capitalization, or market value. Over the period 1926–1996, small-cap stocks outperformed large-cap stocks.

> ## The Facts of Life
>
> Historically, the stocks of small companies have outperformed those of large companies. In fact, the average return on small-company stocks between 1926 and 1996 was 12.58 percent, while the compound return on large-company stocks over the same period was 10.71 percent. However, over the 10-year period 1987–1996, large-company stocks outperformed small-company stocks by an annual rate of 15.3 percent to 13.0 percent.

LEARNING OBJECTIVE #4

Value stocks.

Technical Analysis

A method of stock analysis that focuses on supply and demand, using charts and computer programs to identify and project price trends for a stock or for the market as a whole.

VALUATION OF COMMON STOCK

What's the value of any investment? There are a number of different methods used to determine what an investment is worth, all of which can be more than a bit tricky. These methods can also help us understand why an investment's price moves one way or the other. Let's take a look at three of the most popular valuation methods.

The Technical Analysis Approach

Technical analysis focuses on supply and demand, using charts and computer programs to identify and project price trends for a stock or for the market as a whole. The logic behind technical analysis is that although economic factors are of great importance in determining stock prices, so are psychological factors, such as *greed* and *fear.* Technical analysts feel that these two factors, greed and fear, reinforce trends in the market. Greed pushes investors to put their money in the market when the market is rising, and fear has them pull their money out if a downturn appears. In effect, no one wants to be the last aboard a market upturn, and no one wants to be the last out if the market is falling.

Technical analysis takes a number of forms, including the interpretation of charts and graphs and mathematical calculations of trading patterns, all aimed at spotting some trend or direction for stocks. For example, with charts, technical analysts might look into the past for trends or patterns that give some clue as to where investors might be heading. In addition, they might look for price levels where stock prices might get stuck. These price levels are referred to as resistance or support levels.

Unfortunately, technical analysis may appeal to the novice investor, but it's been found to be of little value. Although there appear to be distinct trends in past movements of the market, the problem comes in identifying these trends before they appear. Moreover, some of these patterns may have been useful in the past, but without any economic logic behind them, what's to say they'll continue to act as good predictors?

In short, technical analysis should be viewed as something to avoid because it encourages moving in and out of the market, which is dangerous, as opposed to simply buying and holding your stocks. So what method should we use to value stocks?

The Price/Earnings Ratio Approach

The price/earnings ratio is used regularly by security analysts as a measure of a stock's relative value. This price-earnings ratio (P/E ratio), or earnings multiplier, is simply the price per share divided by the earnings per share. In effect, it's an indication of how much investors are willing to pay for a dollar of the company's earnings. The more positive investors feel about a stock's future prospects, or the less risk they feel the stock has, the higher the stock's P/E ratio.

For example, a stock with estimated earnings per share next year of $6.50, which is currently selling for $104, would have a P/E ratio of 16 ($104/$6.50). If the prospects for this stock improved—perhaps the company introduces a new product that in a few years should greatly increase profits—the stock price might rise to $130, which would be a new P/E ratio of 20 ($130/$6.50). A stock with a P/E ratio of 20 would likely be referred to as "selling at 20 times earnings." How do we use P/E ratios to value stocks? By deciding whether or not the stock's P/E ratio is too high or too low.

How do you determine what's an appropriate P/E ratio for a specific stock? First, you begin by determining a justified P/E ratio for the market as a whole by looking at past market P/E ratios, taking into consideration the strength of the economy, interest rates, the deficit, and the inflation rate, and then simply making a judgment call. In effect, it's a bit arbitrary. Second, this overall market P/E ratio is then adjusted depending upon the specific prospects for the individual stock. For example, if the growth potential is above average, it is adjusted upward—but how much higher is the real question. Although determining an appropriate or justified P/E ratio for a given stock is difficult, we can at least point to some of the factors that drive P/E ratios up and down.

- **The higher the firm's earnings growth rate, the higher the firm's P/E ratio.** In effect, the market values a dollar of earnings more if those earnings are expected to grow more in the future.

- **The higher the investor's required rate of return, the lower the P/E ratio.** Thus, if interest rates rise, or if the firm becomes more risky, the P/E ratio will fall. Likewise, if interest rates drop, or the firm becomes less risky, the P/E ratio should rise.

Figure 14.4 shows the average P/E ratio since 1958, which should give you an idea of what a typical P/E ratio is. These ratios seem to vary from 7 on up, with a postwar average of 13.5, whereas in recent years the average has been in the 15 to 20 range. The P/E ratio for growth stocks is much higher—generally beginning at 30 or 40 and going on up. As you can see, since 1980 the average P/E ratio has risen. One reason for this rise is the drop in inflation over this period. Because this valuation method focuses on such fundamental determinants as future earnings, expected levels of interest rates, and the firm's risk, it's considered to be a type of **fundamental analysis**.

Fundamental Analysis
Determining the value of a share of stock by focusing on such determinants as future earnings and dividends, expected levels of interest rates, and the firm's risk.

FIGURE 14.4

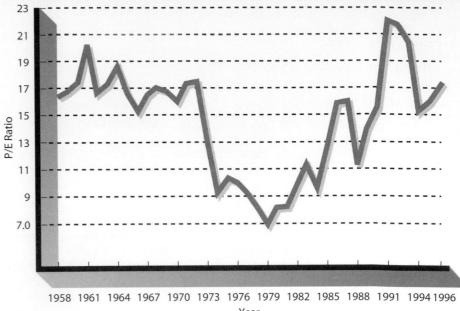

The Average Price-Earnings Ratio on the S&P 500, Since 1958

Stop and Think

Many analysts and investors use the market's P/E ratio as a measure of whether the market is over- or under-priced. In recent years they've viewed the average market P/E ratio as being in the 15 to 20 range. If the market's P/E ratio is much above this level, the market is overpriced, and if it's much below this level, the market is underpriced. However, you should keep in mind that anticipated inflation and the health of the economy and future corporate earnings play a major role in determining the market's P/E ratio.

The Discounted Dividends Valuation Model

If we take the returns that result from owning an investment and bring them back to present, all we need do is add them up to determine the value of that investment. In effect, *the value of any investment is the present value of the benefits or returns that you receive from that investment.* We're simply taking what we learned in chapter 3, in which we moved money through time, and applying it. This simple valuation principle—bring the returns back to the present and add them up—will serve as the foundation for valuing all securities and assets.

When you purchase a share of common stock, you get dividend payments whenever they're declared, and then at some future point in time you generally sell the stock. Hopefully, you'll sell it for more than you purchased it for, thus receiving capital gains (the difference between what you purchased the stock for and what you sold it for). Where does that price you're going to get when you sell your common stock come from? Well, it's based on the future dividend payments the buyer expects while the stock is held plus some capital gains, and what that buyer eventually gets for the stock when it's sold is again based on future dividend payments plus capital gains. This little exercise can be carried on ad nauseam. And what it illustrates is that the value of a share of stock should be the present value of its future dividends. That's all that the firm pays out, and that's what the value of a share of stock should be based on. Moreover, companies can pay out those dividends forever, because common stock has no termination date. Of course, you'll be hoping for capital gains, but how much the stock rises in price will be based on what investors feel is going to happen to dividends in the future. This is an important concept, but it's also one that's difficult for many students to understand, especially when you have stock in a firm such as Microsoft, which has yet to pay any dividends at all. However, as Microsoft earns more and more, the level of its future dividends grows larger and larger, and its price should rise. The point to keep in mind is that earnings eventually turn into dividends, the company pays its shareholders in dividends, and those dividends go on forever.

Thus, the value of a share of common stock is simply the present value of the infinite stream of dividend payments. As such, the value of a share of common stock can be written as follows:

$$\text{value of a share of common stock} = \text{present value of the infinite stream of future dividends}$$

Determining the value of a share of common stock then becomes a three-step process. First, we must estimate the future dividends, then we must estimate our required rate of return, and finally, we must discount the dividends back to present values at the required rate of return. Because this process focuses on future earnings and dividends, expected levels of interest rates, and the firm's risk, it's considered fundamental analysis.

Unfortunately, although this process sounds quite simple, estimating future dividends is an almost unmanageable task. Remember, dividends aren't known until they're declared. If the company does poorly, it won't pay dividends. If the company does well, it'll usually pay nice fat dividends. In effect, we know how stocks *should* be valued, but we have a very difficult time implementing this valuation process.

To use this valuation method, we must assume what will happen to dividends in the future. Unfortunately, this assumption means that the answers that we get from our valuation formula won't be overly reliable. That is, because the assumption we make might not be accurate, our conclusions using this valuation method also might not be accurate. However, this method is still valuable for the insights and implications it yields as to what determines and affects stock prices.

To simplify the calculations, we must assume that *dividends will grow at a constant rate forever.* Making this assumption, the value of a share of stock can be written as follows:

$$\text{value of common stock} = \frac{\text{dividend next year}}{\text{required rate of return} - \text{growth rate}}$$

Rewriting this using the notation from chapter 3, we get

$$\text{value of common stock} = \frac{D_1}{k - g}$$

where

D_1 = the dividend next year

k = the appropriate required rate of return given the risk level of the common stock

g = the constant annual growth rate in dividends

Let's look at an example of a share of common stock that's expected to pay $5 in dividends next year (D_1 = $5). In addition, let's assume that dividends are expected to grow at a rate of 4 percent per year forever ($g = 0.04$), and that given the risk level of this common stock, the investor's required rate of return is 12 percent ($k = 0.12$). Plugging this information into our stock valuation formula, we can calculate the value of the common stock as follows:

$$\text{value of common stock} = \frac{D_1}{k - g}$$

$$= \frac{\$5}{0.12 - 0.05}$$

$$= \frac{\$5}{0.07} = \$71.43$$

Thus, the value of this stock is $71.43. If the stock's selling for less than its value, we should buy it. If it's selling for more than its value, we shouldn't buy it. Although we now have a value for the share of stock, the formula we used to get it was very limited. In fact, if we try to take this formula and apply it to a company such as Microsoft, which hasn't paid any dividends in the past, it simply doesn't make sense. Of course, we used a very simple and basic assumption about dividend values. In the real world, this "discounted dividends valuation model" is used by most major brokerage firms to estimate the value of common stock. However, when analysts use this approach, they don't use such simple assumptions about future dividends. As a result, the analysts' calculations are much more complicated than ours, but both calculations are based on the same principles. For our purposes, though, even more important than the exact calculations are this model's principles and implications about stock valuation.

Understanding Why Stocks Fluctuate in Value

Although the assumptions we made with our discounted dividend valuation model limit its use as an accurate tool for valuing stocks, the model does help us understand the underlying factors that affect the price of a share of common stock. Let's examine these factors now.

Interest Rates and Stock Valuation. There's an inverse relationship between interest rates and the value of a share of common stock. As interest rates rise, investors demand a higher return on their common stock, and, as the required return rises, the present value of the future dividends declines. If you look at the common stock valuation equation, you can easily see that when k increases, the value of the stock decreases, and when k decreases, the value of the stock increases.

For example, in 1995 declining inflation resulting in a 2-percent drop in interest rates. Keep in mind, as anticipated inflation declines, investors demand less in the way of a return for delaying consumption (remember, that's what **Axiom 1: The Risk-Return Trade-Off** states), and as a result, interest rates also drop. The bottom line here was that declining inflation caused interest rates to drop by 2 percent in 1995 and the result of this was that stocks surged by 37! In effect, there's an inverse relationship between interest rates and stock prices.

Risk and Stock Valuation. As the stock's risk increases, so does the investor's required rate of return. Again, we have to remember **Axiom 1: The Risk-Return Trade-Off**. Investors demand additional return for taking on added risk. Looking at Apple Computer in early 1996, as the prospects for Apple became more uncertain, investors began to view Apple as a more risky investment than they had previously. To compensate for this added risk, investors increased their required rate of return on Apple's stock, resulting in a decline in its market value.

Earnings (and Dividend) Growth and Stock Valuation. Although the stock valuation equation uses dividend growth to determine value, most analysts think about value in terms of earnings. As earnings grow, so does the company's capacity to

AXIOM #1

The Risk-Return Trade-Off

pay dividends. In effect, the more earnings a company has, the more it can give out in the way of dividends. As a result, earnings growth is generally viewed as the *cause* of any increase in dividends. As such, we generally talk about a positive relationship between the expected growth rate for earnings and stock prices, which makes sense. As the firm earns more and is able to return more to its shareholders, the stock price should rise. Looking at our valuation equation, you can see that as *g* increases, the denominator decreases, and thus, the value of the stock should increase.

> ## *Stop and Think*
> It's a bit intimidating to think about all the analysis that you can do in selecting a stock. Fortunately, much of it's already done for you and is available in most libraries. Go to your school or local library and ask the librarian for the investments section. It's likely that you'll find a publication by Value Line. Look your stock up in the *Value Line Investment Survey*—it's guaranteed you'll find it quite interesting.

STOCK INVESTMENT STRATEGIES

There are several investment strategies you can follow when purchasing stock. As we take a look at a few of them, keep in mind that you can use more than one of these approaches at once.

Dollar Cost Averaging

Dollar cost averaging is the practice of purchasing a fixed dollar amount of stock at specified intervals, for example, quarterly. The logic behind dollar cost averaging is that by investing the same dollar amount each period instead of buying in one lump sum, you'll be averaging out price fluctuations by buying more shares of the common stock when the price is lowest, and fewer shares when the price is highest. Table 14.1 presents an example of dollar cost averaging, where the investor buys $500 worth of stock each quarter for 2 years instead of investing everything all at once. The reason the investor in this example did better with dollar cost averaging is that the market price bounced from $40 to $55, allowing the investor to buy more shares for the same amount of money when prices dipped.

Lucky people buy stocks when the price is low, and unlucky people buy when the price is high. The problem is that no one knows if a given price is going to be a high or a low, because you never know what stocks will do in the future. Dollar cost averaging's intent is to even out your luck by letting the highs and lows cancel each other out.

Recently, dollar cost averaging has come under some criticism as an inefficient way to invest a lump sum in the market. This criticism centers on the fact that over time, stocks generally tend to rise in price. As such, if you have a lump sum of money to invest, it's better to get it into the market as soon as possible to get in on those rising prices. For example, looking at the year 1995, during the first two quarters stocks went up by over 9 percent, in the third quarter stocks rose by over 7 percent, and in the final quarter they rose by over 5 percent. The sooner investors put money into the market, the more they made. In fact, history shows that over all the 12-month periods from 1926 through 1991, you would be better off investing in a lump sum 64.5 percent of the time.

However, in spite of all this, dollar cost averaging has merit. First, it's good if you want to avoid being killed rather than make a killing in the market. That is, if you buy stock over an extended period, it's less likely that all your money will be invested right before a market crash. Second, dollar cost averaging keeps you from trying to time the market. "Timing the market" is attempting to wait for the lowest possible price before

TABLE 14.1

Dollar Cost Averaging

| Date | Dollar Cost Averaging, Investing $500 per Quarter | | | | | Lump Sum Investment Buying 80 Shares at $50/Share |
	Money Invested	Price	Shares Purchased	Total Shares Owned	Market Value	Market Value
Year 1, quarter 1	$ 500	$50	10.0	10.0	$ 500	$4,000
Year 1, quarter 2	500	46	10.9	20.9	961	
Year 1, quarter 3	500	40	12.5	33.4	1,336	
Year 1, quarter 4	500	50	10.0	43.4	2,170	
Year 2, quarter 1	500	55	9.1	52.5	2,888	
Year 2, quarter 2	500	45	11.1	63.6	2,862	
Year 2, quarter 3	500	50	10.0	73.6	3,680	
Year 2, quarter 4	500	52	9.6	83.2	4,327	
Total	$4,000	$48.50	83.2	83.2	$4,327	$4,160

buying. It's virtually impossible to do. Unfortunately, it's awfully tempting to try. Moreover, in timing the market, an investor can wait and wait for the market to come down and miss a major market upturn. This certainly would have been the case in 1995—if you were looking for a low point in the 1995 market to invest, you never would have entered the market. Third and most important, dollar cost averaging forces investing discipline. With dollar cost averaging, you are investing in stocks regularly, and investing becomes part of your budgeting and planning process.

Buy-and-Hold Strategy

Buy-and-Hold

An investment strategy that involves simply buying stock and holding it for a period of years.

As you might guess, a **buy-and-hold** investment strategy involves buying stock and holding it for a period of years. There are four reasons why a buy-and-hold strategy is worth considering. First, it aims at avoiding attempts at timing the market. By buying and holding the stock, the ups and downs that occur over shorter periods become irrelevant. Second, the buy-and-hold strategy minimizes brokerage fees and other transaction costs. Constant buying and selling really racks up the charges, but buying and holding has only the charge of buying. By keeping these costs down, the investor retains more of the stock's returns. Third, holding and not selling the stock postpones any capital gains taxes. The longer you can go without paying taxes, the longer you hold your money, and the longer you have to reinvest and earn returns on your returns. Finally, a buy-and-hold strategy means your gains will be taxed as long-term capital gains.

Stop and Think

If you employ a buy-and-hold strategy while buying stock using the dollar cost averaging method, a downturn in the market isn't necessarily bad. It simply means that when you're buying, you're getting more shares of stock. Dollar cost averaging is best served by a market that doesn't climb steadily, but bounces up and down.

DOLLAR-COST AVERAGING, Mocked by Some, Is Still a Way to Profit Steadily in Stocks

Ⓐ

Dollar-cost averaging is for wimps. You would be amazed at how many rich wimps there are.

Sure, gradually moving money into stocks isn't necessarily the smartest or bravest strategy. As many academics and investment experts point out, if you want the highest possible return, you should shovel every spare dime into the market as quickly as possible. After all, share prices go up over time. The sooner you buy, the more you're likely to make.

Yet many folks defy the experts and persist in spooning their money into stocks. I think they're right to do so. No, it isn't simply that stocks have risen sharply in recent years and could be ripe for a fall. Even in less exuberant times, dollar-cost averaging makes a lot of sense, given the temperament of most investors. Here's why:

- Investing gradually helps folks get off the sidelines. "Before you make fun of dollar-cost averaging, you have to think what the alternative is," says Richard Thaler, an economics professor at the University of Chicago and an expert in behavioral finance.

- "If the alternative is to leave money in guaranteed investment contracts and savings accounts, then dollar-cost averaging looks pretty smart to me," Mr. Thaler continues. "It seems people have more courage if they invest their money gradually and regularly."

- Dollar-cost averaging reduces the risk of losing money. Most of the time, we invest gradually because that's how we get paid. We take a little bit of our weekly or monthly paycheck and toss it into the market.

- Santa Clara University finance professor Meir Statman, who specializes in behavioral finance, says dollar-cost averaging isn't only about reducing risk, but also about avoiding regret. If we throw everything into stocks and the market tanks, we don't just lose money. We also feel like idiots.

- Investing gradually makes us more disciplined. "Dollar-cost averaging gives you a rigid plan," Mr. Statman says. "Once set in motion, it gives you self-control. To the extent that you are tempted to use that money for consumption, you have made a pledge to yourself, so you keep at it."

- By investing regularly, we become less emotional about the market. Many investors put their dollar-cost averaging on autopilot, by signing up for an automatic investment plan. With these plans, money is yanked out of your bank account or paycheck every month and stuffed straight into a mutual fund.

- Dollar-cost averaging forces us to invest in falling markets. We tend to extrapolate the recent past, so that when stocks tumble, we presume that the market will keep on falling. That prompts us to avoid further investments and maybe even to bail out.

Source: Jonathan Clements, "Dollar-Cost Averaging, Mocked by Some, Is Still a Way to Profit Steadily in Stocks," *The Wall Street Journal,* January 14, 1997, p. C1. Reprinted by permission of *The Wall Street Journal,* © 1997 Dow Jones & Company, Inc. All Rights Reserved Worldwide.

Analysis and Implications …

A. Many investors also use dollar cost averaging when they are getting out of stocks. That is, rather than sell out all on one day, they spread out their selling over a longer period of time to make sure they don't sell at a low point in the market.

Dividend Reinvestment Plans (DRIPs)

Dividend Reinvestment Plan (DRIP)

An investment plan that allows the investor to automatically reinvest stock dividends in the same company's stock without paying any brokerage fees.

If you want to use common stock to accumulate wealth, you must reinvest rather than spend your dividends. Without reinvesting the dividends, your accumulation of wealth will be limited to the stock's capital gains. Unfortunately, many dividends may be small enough that you figure you might as well spend them on a pack of Juicy Fruit rather than reinvest them. Hey, you don't need to pay a brokerage fee to buy Juicy Fruit.

One way to avoid buying too much gum and not enough stock is through a **dividend reinvestment plan**, or **DRIP**. Under a dividend reinvestment plan, you're allowed to reinvest the dividend in the company's stock automatically without paying any brokerage fees. Most large companies offer such plans, and many stockholders take advantage of them. For example, nearly 40 percent of all PepsiCo stockholders participate in dividend reinvestment plans. In addition, by late 1995, 55,000 out of 190,000 stockholders in Mobil Oil participated in a dividend reinvestment plan.

A dividend reinvestment plan is a great way to let your savings grow, but it's not without drawbacks. The major drawback is that when you sell your stock, you'll have to figure out your income taxes—and that can be overwhelming. Each time you reinvest dividends, you're effectively buying additional shares of stock at a different price. Moreover, even though you don't receive any cash when your dividends are reinvested, you still have to pay income tax as if you actually received those dividends. A final drawback of dividend reinvestment plans is the fact that you can't choose what to do with your own dividend. What if the company you've invested in is performing moderately well, and you just heard about another company whose stock price is rising faster than the blood pressure of a fat man with a love of salt? You're stuck reinvesting instead of trying something new.

Despite these drawbacks, dividend reinvestment plans appeal to many investors. Two sources of companies offering DRIPs are Standard & Poor's *Directory of Dividend Reinvestment Plans* and Evergreen Enterprises' *Directory of Companies Offering Dividend Reinvestment Plans,* both of which may be available at your library. However, before entering into a DRIP, make sure you understand the drawbacks, in particular those associated with tax calculations.

The Facts of Life

Trying to time the market and move in and out rather than employ a buy-and-hold strategy can be dangerous. The danger lies in missing upturns. One study that looked at the cost of being "out of the market" during the bull market of 1982 through August 27, 1987, estimated that the average annual return over the entire trading period was 26.7 percent. If you were out of the market during the 10 days when the biggest daily gains occurred, your average annual return would have dropped to 18.3 percent. Taking out the top 20 biggest gain days, the average annual return would have been only 13.1 percent—about half of the total return over the entire period.

RISKS ASSOCIATED WITH COMMON STOCKS

LEARNING OBJECTIVE #5

Understand the risks associated with investing in common stock.

In chapter 12 we examined several different sources of risk associated with investing in all securities. How do stocks compare with other investments in terms of risk? Stocks have more risk than other investments, but they also have more potential return associated with them. You should already know quite a bit about risk and return from our list of axioms. Let's use some of those axioms to explore the relationship between stocks and risk, and to see if we can't lower our risk while still maintaining our return.

TO BUY AND TO HOLD,
for Richer, Not Poorer

Although 1996 has had some wild ups and downs, that boring mantra —buy-and-hold, buy-and-hold, buy-and-hold—has served investors well. Look at International Business Machines Corp. In March, IBM peaked at $125 a share, then skidded all the way down to $90 by July. If you had bailed out in mid-summer (as many did), you would have missed the rebound last week to $122.

Or consider Gillette Co. A friend said his broker called in April to warn that because the stock had "broken its support level"—that is, dipped below the supposed magic number of $50 a share—it was time to sell, quickly (thus generating a nice commission). My friend, a buy-and hold type who wants to own Gillette until Chelsea Clinton's first term as president, resisted. A week later Gillette had bounced back to $55, and last week it topped $68.

These are mere anecdotes, but the scientific research is even more convincing. It shows that a policy of buying stocks and hanging on to them through good markets and bad produces returns that are four times greater than the typical buy-and-sell, in-and-out behavior of actual investors. Four times!

That figure is hard to believe, but it comes from a study by a respected Boston firm that conducts surveys and compiles information for the financial services industry.

Since 1984, the firm, DALBAR Inc., (617-723 6400) has been comparing the performance of individual investors with the performance of the market averages. Last week I asked for an update. The new numbers are startling. From Jan. 1, 1984, to March 31, 1996, the Standard & Poor's 500-stock index, which reflects the performance of the largest stocks and is a good proxy for the broad market, has returned 491 percent, with dividends reinvested.

But the return over the same period for an investor who invested directly was only 97 percent. The return for an investor buying funds through a sales agent (such as a bank or broker) was 113 percent.

"The difference," says a special report that DALBAR issued in June, "is attributable to poor market-timing attempts by investors and the fact that investor cash does not remain invested [in stocks] for the entire period."

In its report, DALBAR summed up the findings this way: "Investment return is far more dependent on investor behavior than on fund performance." You'll never read a more important sentence on investing.

Source: James K. Glassman, "To Buy and to Hold, for Richer, Not Poorer," *The Washington Post,* September 15, 1996, p. H1. Copyright James K. Glassman. Used by permission.

(A)

(B)

Analysis and Implications ...

A. You must keep in mind that your broker makes money only when you trade. Although most brokers don't "churn" accounts—that is, encourage trading just for commissions—they're still eager to point out any recommended selling or buying "opportunity." Keep in mind **Axiom 12: The Agency Problem in Personal Finance—Differentiating Between Advice and a Sales Pitch**.

B. In effect, if you're investing over some long time horizon to meet long-term goals, what you buy is less important than whether you have the discipline to keep it. For example, between 1986 and 1995, growth funds earned 12.0 percent annually; small-company funds, 12.3 percent; aggressive growth funds, 12.3 percent; and foreign stock funds, 10.5 percent. Not much difference, despite the variety of investment styles. However, investors who stayed out of the market from 1995 through mid-1997 because they thought it was overvalued missed some serious returns.

AXIOM #1

The Risk-Return
Trade-Off—Investors Don't
Take on Additional Risk Unless
They Expect to Be Compensated
with Additional Return

AXIOM #3

Diversification Reduces Risk

AXIOM #4

Diversification Reduces
Risk—All Risk Is Not Equal,
Because Some Risk Can Be
Diversified Away and
Some Cannot

FIGURE 14.5

Axiom 1: The Risk-Return Trade-Off—Investors Don't Take on Additional Risk Unless They Expect to Be Compensated with Additional Return

Thinking back to the idea of a risk-return trade-off as described in Axiom 1, we can view stocks as being at the upper end of the risk-return line as shown in Figure 14.5. Watching the stock market drop by 7.2 percent on October 27, 1997, serves to remind us of the risk associated with common stock. Without those risks, you wouldn't expect the high returns that common stocks provide. Thus, there's a great deal of potential risk, if the firm does poorly, and a great deal of potential return, if the firm does well, associated with stocks.

Axiom 3: Diversification Reduces Risk

Fortunately, you can eliminate much of the risk associated with common stock simply by diversifying your investments. In this way, when one of your stocks goes bust, another investment soars, making up for the loss. Basically, diversification lets you iron out the ups and downs of investing. You don't experience the great returns, but you don't experience great losses either. What you're looking for to help diversification along is investments that don't move in like patterns. For example, you might invest in stocks from a wide variety of industries and also include international stocks. In addition, you might make sure that you invest in more than just stocks, diversifying to include other types of investments. Remember, diversification works to smooth out the ups and downs and in so doing, eliminates risk.

Axiom 4: Diversification and Risk—All Risk Is Not Equal, Because Some Risk Can Be Diversified Away and Some Cannot

As you saw in chapter 12, the ability to eliminate a portion of a portfolio's risk through diversification has led to the segmentation of risk into two types: systematic or non-diversifiable risk, and unsystematic or diversifiable risk. Axiom 4 deals with the fact that in a well-diversified portfolio, only systematic risk remains. In fact, as your stock portfolio increases in size to 10 or 20 stocks, approximately 60 percent of the total risk

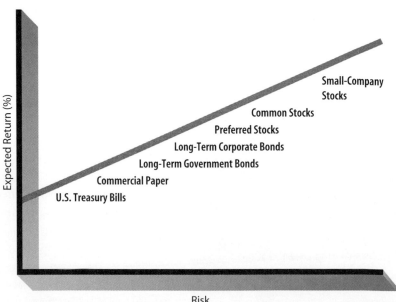

The Risk-Return Relationship

Small-Company Stocks
Common Stocks
Preferred Stocks
Long-Term Corporate Bonds
Long-Term Government Bonds
Commercial Paper
U.S. Treasury Bills

Expected Return (%)

Risk

is eliminated, and almost all of the remaining risk is systematic risk. As a result, we're very concerned with how much systematic risk an investment has.

To measure systematic risk, we use **beta** which can be found in Value Line and other investment publications. The beta for the market is 1.0—that's the benchmark against which specific stock betas are measured. A stock with above average systematic risk would have a beta greater than 1.0, and a stock with below average systematic risk would have a beta less than 1.0. The vast majority of betas are positive because most stocks move with the market. The easiest way to interpret beta is to think of it as a measure of relative responsiveness of a stock. For example, if the market goes up by 20 percent and a stock has a beta of 1.5, then that stock would go up by 30 percent (20% × 1.5 = 30%). Conversely, if the market went down by 20 percent, that same stock would go down by 30 percent (−20% × 1.5 = −30%). In other words, a stock with a beta greater than 1.0 tends to amplify both the up and the down movements in the market. By the same token, a stock with a beta of less than 1.0 tends to mute the movements in the market. Thus, beta is a measure of the relative responsiveness of stock to market movements, with a stock that's 30 percent more volatile than the market having a beta of 1.3, and one that's 50 percent more volatile than the market having a beta of 1.5.

What does all this mean to you as an investor? First, once your stock portfolio is diversified, it tends to move closely with all the other stocks in the marketplace. That is to say, the returns to a diversified portfolio are more a function of major changes in anticipated inflation, interest rates, or the general economy rather than from events that are unique to any specific company in the portfolio. Second, it means that the only way to fully diversify is to make sure that you invest in more than one type of investment—include domestic and international stocks along with bonds in your portfolio. Finally, if your portfolio is well diversified, you should keep an eye on its beta.

Axiom 11: The Time Dimension of Risk, or Why Investments Become Less Risky When You Plan to Hold Them Longer

We know how to reduce or even eliminate unsystematic risk, but wouldn't it be nice if we could also reduce systematic risk? We can, or at least we can make it less important—as long as we're patient. In the short run, systematic market fluctuations are a killer. Nothing heaps on the risk or generates a stock loss like a big fat market downturn. However, over the long run, much of the risk of short-term investing disappears. As **Axiom 11** tells us, the longer we keep our stocks, the less risky they become.

When you invest in stocks, you're almost certain to experience a bad year or two. Holding on to stock for only a year is very risky, because the year you choose to hold it just might be one of those bad years. Figure 14.6 lists the average yearly return for large- and small-cap stocks and shows how bad a bad year can really be. For example, if you'd chosen to make a 1-year investment in small company stocks in 1973, you'd have been one unhappy camper by year's end. Of course, if you'd made that same investment a mere 2 or 3 years later, you'd have made a hefty return—more than enough to go out and buy a new pair of bell-bottoms and the latest disco records. As you can see, 1-year returns are amazingly variable, making short-term investments in stocks very risky.

The longer you hold on to stocks, the more likely you are to hit a very good year, such as 1995 or 1996. Of course, you're also more likely to hit a bad year, but the very good will cancel out the very bad, thereby reducing your risk of losing money. It follows that the longer you hold on to stocks, the more good years you'll experience to even out the bad years, and the less risk you'll have. Does this reduction of risk mean an equivalent reduction of profits? Not at all. Figure 14.7 shows how holding stocks for longer periods reduces the variability—and thus the risk—of your return but not the amount of your return. The truth is, it's hard to beat the long-term returns from common stock investments. For example, take a look at Figure 14.8 and you'll see that common stocks far outperformed corporate bonds and Treasury bills over the 10-year period 1987–1996. Now you can see why so many investors favor the buy-and-hold strategy for investing in stocks.

Beta
The measure of systematic risk. It is a measure of how responsive a stock or portfolio is to changes in the *market portfolio,* such as the S&P 500 Index or the New York Stock Exchange index.

AXIOM #11

The Time Dimension of Risk, or Why Investments Become Less Risky When You Plan to Hold Them Longer

FIGURE 14.6

A Histogram of Annual Percentage Returns, 1960–1996

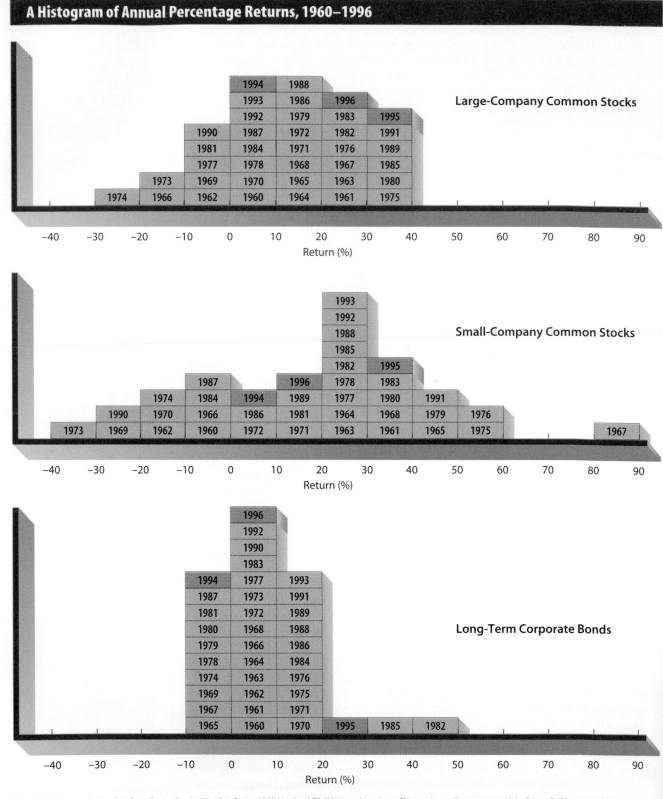

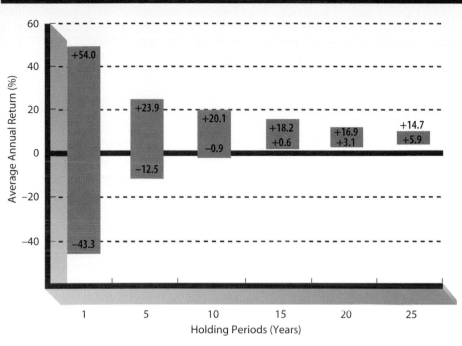

FIGURE 14.7

The Range of Returns on Common Stocks, 1926–1996

Holding Periods (Years)

Average Annual Return (%)

+54.0
+23.9
+20.1
+18.2
+0.6
+16.9
+3.1
+14.7
+5.9
−0.9
−12.5
−43.3

Source: © Computed using data from *Stocks, Bonds, Bills, & Inflation 1997 Yearbook* ™, Ibbotson Associates, Chicago (annually updates work by Roger G. Ibbotson and Rex A. Sinquefield). Used with permission. All rights reserved.

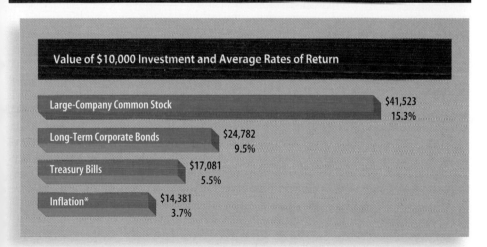

FIGURE 14.8

A Comparison of Investment Performance Over the 10-Year Period Ending December 31, 1996

Value of $10,000 Investment and Average Rates of Return

Large-Company Common Stock — $41,523 — 15.3%

Long-Term Corporate Bonds — $24,782 — 9.5%

Treasury Bills — $17,081 — 5.5%

Inflation* — $14,381 — 3.7%

*This means that, given the 3.7% average inflation over this 10-year period, the purchasing power of $10,000 at the beginning of 1987 would be equivalent to that of $14,381 at the end of 1996.

Source: © Computed using data from *Stocks, Bonds, Bills, & Inflation 1997 Yearbook* ™, Ibbotson Associates, Chicago (annually updates work by Roger G. Ibbotson and Rex A. Sinquefield). Used with permission. All rights reserved.

If you can understand Axiom 11, you can understand the concepts behind all the "asset allocation" talk of brokers and financial planners. Understanding Axiom 11 can also provide you with an understanding of why you can't answer the question, Which investment is the best one for me? until you first answer another question, How long is my investment time horizon? That is, when do I need my money back? In short, stocks are, without question, extremely volatile in the short run, but they're pretty solid in the long run. If you're investing for the long run, it's hard to beat stocks.

SUMMARY

Stock is a solid investment because over time common stocks outperform all other investments, stocks reduce risk through diversification, stocks are liquid, and the growth in your investment is determined by more than just interest rates.

The health of the stock market is measured by stock indexes. The oldest and most widely quoted of the stock indexes is the Dow Jones Industrial Average (DJIA) or Dow. Other useful indexes include the Standard & Poor's 500, the Russell 2000, and the Wilshire 5000.

Stocks can be classified according to the traits of the company issuing the stock. Common classifications include blue-chip, growth, income, speculative, cyclical, defensive, and large-, mid-, and small-cap stocks.

There are a number of methods used to determine what a share of stock is worth. One approach is technical analysis. However, the usefulness of technical analysis is very questionable.

An alternative approach to technical analysis is the price/earnings ratio approach. Under this approach, a justified price-earnings ratio is estimated for each stock. This price-earnings ratio (P/E ratio), or earnings multiplier, is simply the price per share divided by the earnings per share.

A final approach is the discounted dividend model. We know that the value of any investment is simply the present value of all the returns that we receive from that investment. Thus, the value of a share of common stock is simply the present value of the infinite stream of dividend payments. We'll find that three factors—interest rates, risk, and expected future growth—combine to determine the value of common stock.

When purchasing stock there are several investment strategies that you can follow including dollar cost averaging, buy-and-hold, and dividend reinvestment plans. Dollar cost averaging involves investing over time rather than jumping into the market all at once. Buy-and-hold simply involves investing and leaving your money invested for a number of years. Dividend reinvestment plans involve having your dividends automatically reinvested in the stock so that you don't spend the dividends.

Four of our axioms play an important role when we invest in stocks. Using the idea of a risk-return trade-off as described in Axiom 1, we can view stocks as being at the upper end of the risk-return line. Axiom 3 describes how diversification works to smooth out the ups and downs in stock returns and in so doing, eliminates risk. Axiom 4 leads us to a distinction between systematic and unsystematic risk, using the beta to measure systematic risk. Finally, Axiom 11 shows that although stocks are extremely volatile in the short run, they aren't in the long run. This concept is very important because it means that our investment horizon plays a large role in determining how we should invest our savings. If we're investing for the long run, it's hard to beat stocks.

Review Questions

1. How do common stockholders expect their stocks to generate returns? (LO 1)
2. List and describe four reasons why someone should consider investing in stocks. (LO 1)
3. What is meant by the term "limited liability," and why is this concept important to common stock investors? (LO 1)

4. Distinguish between the following dates: declaration, ex-dividend, and payment. If investors purchase shares in a company after the ex-dividend date, will they receive a dividend? (LO 1)
5. In terms of a common shareholder's claim on assets, when will a stockholder receive payment if a company declares bankruptcy? (LO 1)
6. What is a stock split? Why might a company split its stock? (LO 1)
7. How are stocks weighted in the Dow Jones Industrial Average? How does this differ from the Standard & Poor's 500 Stock Index? Which of these two better represents movements in the overall market? Why? (LO 2)
8. What do people mean when they say the market is "bearish"? What is meant by the term "bullish"? (LO 3)
9. Define the following terms: (a) blue-chip stock, (b) growth stock, (c) income stock, and (d) speculative stock. Give an example of each. (LO 3)

10. Define P/E ratio. Describe two factors that help drive P/E ratios up and down. (LO 4)

11. All stock prices are based on what investors expect to happen to dividends in the future. Explain why this rule applies even when a company isn't currently paying dividends. (LO 4)

12. In terms of the risk-return trade-off (Axiom 1), why is there an inverse relationship between interest rates and the value of a share of common stock? (LO 4)

13. Name and define three investment strategies that someone can follow when purchasing stock. What factors should investors consider before employing one of these strategies? (LO 4)

14. How can common stock investors reduce unsystematic risk (see Axiom 4)? If an investor wants to eliminate approximately 60 percent of the total risk in a portfolio, how many stocks should be included in the portfolio? (LO 5)

Problems and Activities

1. Assume you own 200 shares of Intel, which just reached $130 per share. In order to make the stock a bit more affordable for the average investor, Intel's management has decided to split the stock. (LO 1)
   a. How much was your investment worth prior to the split?
   b. Assuming Intel's management decides to split the stock three for one, how many shares would you own after the split?
   c. How much would a share of Intel sell for immediately after the split?
   d. How much would your investment be worth after the three-for-one split?

2. JEG Corporation has just announced year-end results as follows: (LO 1)

Value of company assets	$5,000,000
Net income	$1,200,000
Common stock dividends	$ 500,000
Preferred stock dividends	$ 100,000
Number of shares of common stock outstanding	1,000,000
Closing price of JEG stock	$50 per share

   a. Calculate the book value per share.
   b. Calculate earnings per share.
   c. Calculate JEG's dividend yield.
   d. Calculate the market-to-book ratio.

3. The LEG Corporation recently announced that its year-end estimated earnings per share next year will be $3.25. LEG stock is currently selling for $43 per share. (LO 4)
   a. What is the P/E ratio for LEG?
   b. Assume prospects for the LEG Corporation deteriorate and the company now estimates next year's earnings to be $1.50 per share. What would be the new P/E ratio?

4. You've just learned that Graham Records has purchased the lifetime distribution rights to the music of Big Daddy and the French Fries. Based on this good news, you've estimated that Graham Records should pay $4 in dividends next year. You also think that the dividends paid out should increase by 5 percent a year forever. As a knowledgeable investor, you've determined that the required rate of return is 10 percent. (LO 4)
   a. What is your estimate of the value of Graham Records common stock?
   b. What would the value of the stock be if you didn't anticipate any increase in the dividend over time?

5. Use the following data to answer the questions below. (LO 5)

Company	Beta
JEG Corp.	0.85
LEG Corp.	1.25
Graham Records	2.20

GOLD Corp.	−0.45
S&P 500	1.00

a. If the S&P 500 goes up by 35 percent, how much will JEG, LEG, Graham Records, and GOLD change in value?

b. If the stock market drops by 10 percent, which of the above stocks should outperform the others? Why?

6. Use the following information to answer the questions below. (LO 2)

52 Weeks					Div Yld			Vol				Net
Hi	Lo	Stock	Sym	Div	%	PE	100s	Hi	Lo	Close	Chg
76½	35⅛	Digital	DEC	2.00		10	1000	40	39⅝	40	½

a. What is the current dividend yield for Digital Equipment Corporation based on the stock's recent closing price?

b. What is your estimate of Digital's earnings for the year based on the recent closing price?

c. Based on the net change list above, at what price did Digital close at yesterday?

7. Assume an investor made the following purchases on the first day of every quarter for a year. Use the information provided to fill in the missing blanks. (LO 4)

Quarter	Price	Money Invested	Shares Purchased	Total Shares Owned	Market Values
1	$30	$100	___		___
2	$50	$100	___	___	___
3	$60	$100	___	7	___
4	$35	$100	2.86	___	$345.10
Ave. ___		Totals $400	___	___	___

8. Using the calculations from question 7, answer the following question. (LO 1)

a. Assume that instead of investing $100 every quarter, the investor decided to make a lump-sum purchase on the first day of the year with $400. If at year's end the price of the stock closed at $35 per share, which investment strategy, dollar cost averaging or lump-sum investing, produced the greater return?

Suggested Projects

1. Visit your local library and find a recent copy of the *Value Line Investment Survey,* Moody's, or Standard & Poor's. Use one of these sources to obtain the book value, earnings per share, dividend yield, price-to-book ratio, and P/E ratio on a company of your choice. (LO 1)

2. Some of the stocks that make up the Dow Jones Industrial Average were changed in early 1997. Using either the *Wall Street Journal, Barron's,* or another source, such as your local newspaper, make a list of the firms that currently make up the DJIA and record the dividend yields of each stock. Considering that each of these stocks is considered a blue-chip firm, why would the dividend yields be so different? (LO 2)

3. Using the Internet, visit the NASDAQ home page (www.nasdaq.com) each day for a week. Track the performance of the NASDAQ composite index for the week. Did you notice any significant trend during that time? Do you think that investors were bullish or bearish for the week? (LO 2)

4. Review the general classifications of common stock presented in the chapter. Based on your personal comfort level (risk aversion), which type of stock would most interest you? Why? (LO 5)

5. Either working with members of your class or by yourself, make a list of industries that you'd consider defensive. For each industry, provide two or three stocks that fit the category of defensive stocks. Do the same for industries and stocks you would consider cyclical. (LO 3)

WWW. Take It to the Net

We invite you to visit the Keown Personal Finance page on the Prentice Hall Web site at:

http://www.prenhall.com/ persfin

for this chapter's World Wide Web exercise.

You might also want to visit the following Web sites:

Corporate Financials Online (information on publicly traded companies): http://www.cfonews.com/

GSI (Global Securities Information, with a database of information on companies): http://www.gsionline.com/websites.htm

SEC EDGAR Database (with SEC filings): http://edgar.stern.nyu.edu/tools.shtml

Investor Guide (a strong investing section): http://www.investorguide.com

CheckFree Investment Services (stock quotes delayed 15 minutes and more): http://www.secapl.com/cgi-bin/qs

CNNfn The Financial Network: http://www.cnnfn.com/

Microsoft Investor: http://investor.msn.com

The Wall Street Research Net: http://wsrn.com

(continued)

Zacks Investment Research
(earnings estimates on lots of
stocks): http://www.zacks.com

Bloomberg Personal (interactive
investment news): http://
www.bloomberg.com

New York Stock Exchange:
http://www.nyse.com/

NASDAQ: http://www.nasdaq.com/

American Stock Exchange: http://
www.amex.com/

6. As you'll recall from the chapter, technical analysis focuses on the supply and demand of a stock, using charts and computer programs to identify and project trends for a stock or for the market as a whole. Besides economic factors, what is the logic behind technical analysis? What is your feeling regarding the effectiveness of technical analysis? (LO 4)

7. On your next visit to the library, spend some time looking through a copy of the *Value Line Investment Survey*. This publication provides investors information on most major U.S. industries. Using this information, choose an industry that interests you (for example, technology or transportation), and find the average P/E ratio for the industry. Next, choose a stock from your chosen industry and compare the stock's P/E ratio against the industry average. Are the ratios different? What factors do you think influence the stock's P/E ratio? Based on your findings, would you consider the stock to be over- or undervalued compared to other stocks in its industry? (LO 4)

8. Which investment strategy do you personally favor, dollar cost averaging or lump-sum investing? If you chose dollar cost averaging, would you agree with Professor Statman of Santa Clara University that part of the reason is to avoid regret? Explain your answer in terms of the discipline dollar cost averaging provides. If you chose lump-sum investing, explain why the fear of regret might prompt someone to choose lump-sum investing. *Hint:* In which type of market, bull or bear, does lump-sum investing outperform dollar cost averaging? (LO 4)

Discussion Case 1

After working as a customer service representative for the past 4 years, Rosa, 27 years old, has decided to quit her job and relocate across the country to be closer to her parents. Because she wasn't employed for at least 5 years with the company, she's been informed that her accrued pension benefits will be distributed to her in a lump-sum distribution when she leaves. Rosa is expecting to receive approximately $10,000. She hopes to invest this money for her retirement, but she knows very little about stocks or investing strategies. After discussing financial planning topics with Rosa, the following concepts became clear. First, the $10,000 is all the money Rosa has saved for her retirement, and, second, Rosa's very cautious financially and is fearful of investing her money all at once, because she thinks stocks are overvalued. Use your knowledge of common stock classifications and investing strategies to answer the following questions.

Questions

1. Which type of stock or combination of stocks would be appropriate for Rosa? Develop your answer in terms of Rosa's risk tolerance, time frame, and goal.

2. What role should cyclical and defensive stocks play in Rosa's portfolio?

3. Would you recommend small-cap stocks to Rosa? Why or why not?

4. Given Rosa's fear that stocks may be overpriced, what investment strategy would you recommend for her? Why?

5. Why might Rosa consider enrolling in an automatic investment plan?

6. Provide Rosa with four reasons she should consider using a buy-and-hold strategy.

7. Explain to Rosa what a dividend reinvestment plan is. Would you recommend that she participate in such DRIPs with a portion of her portfolio?

Discussion Case 2

Onslo and Daisy have recently emigrated from Ireland to the United States. After selling their potato farm in Ireland, they decided to begin investing in stocks. Unfortunately, neither Onslo nor Daisy has any experience or knowledge of common stock terminology or features. They recently met with a stockbroker. However, once the stockbroker started talking about limited liabilities, claims on income, dividends, claims on assets, voting rights, proxies, stock splits, and stock repurchases, Onslo and Daisy became confused and left the broker's office without making a single investment decision. Onslo and Daisy have come to you for help in understanding common stock investing.

Questions

1. Provide Onslo and Daisy with four reasons why they should consider investing in common stocks for a long-term investment portfolio.

2. Briefly define each of the terminology points and features of common stocks that caused Onslo and Daisy so much confusion in the broker's office. Of these, which should they be most concerned about?

3. Explain why corporate earnings are so important in the valuation of common stocks.

4. Should Onslo and Daisy consider investing in international common stocks? Why? Provide two ways in which they can purchase stocks in foreign firms.

Chapter 15

BONDS AND OTHER INVESTMENTS

For Marvin Lee Aday, the road to riches has been a strange and bumpy one. After graduating from high school, he started his career as the lead vocalist for the rock group Popcorn Blizzard. Unfortunately, the Popcorn Blizzard wasn't much of a money maker, so Aday took a job as a parking-lot attendant at the Aquarius Theatre in Los Angeles. It was there that he met an actor appearing in the musical *Hair*, who suggested he try out for a part in the play. And so began his career in theater, cast in the role of Ulysses S. Grant, in which he continued when *Hair* moved to Broadway. For the next several years, Aday was a Broadway regular, even appearing as Buddha in the musical *Rainbow*, but his big break came when he was cast in the dual role of Eddie and Dr. Scott in one of the strangest musicals ever to hit New York—*The Rocky Horror Show*. He also played Eddie in the film version, *The Rocky Horror Picture Show*. Finally, in 1977, Aday, who was by now going by his nickname, Meatloaf, hit the big time financially when he released his first album, *Bat Out of Hell*, with the hit songs "Paradise By the Dashboard Lights" and "Two Out of Three Ain't Bad."

From there, however, his career just seemed to take a wrong turn. Bad management, bad lawyers, bad advice, contract problems with his record company, and problems with the IRS all seemed to hit at once. He lost his condo and house in Connecticut, his Mercedes-Benz, and his grand piano, and he was forced to scrimp and save just to make ends meet. Faced with financial ruin, Meatloaf regrouped and began touring small clubs, with his wife serving as the tour manager

Learning Objectives

After reading this chapter you should be able to:

1. Invest in the bond market.
2. Understand basic bond terminology and compare the various types of bonds available.
3. Calculate the value of a bond and understand the factors that cause bond value to change.
4. Weigh the risks associated with bond investments.
5. Compare preferred stock to bonds as an investment option.
6. Understand the risks associated with investing in real estate.
7. Know why you shouldn't *invest* in gold, silver, gems, or collectibles.

just to cut costs. Finally, in 1989, he took on Bernie Gilhuly as his business manager. After straightening out Meatloaf's tax problems, Gilhuly set up an investment strategy aimed at insuring Meatloaf's financial future. However, given Meatloaf's rocky road to riches, he was a bit shy when it came to taking risks. As a result, Gilhuly put most of Meatloaf's investment money into bonds. For Meatloaf, things kept getting better in the nineties. He staged one of the biggest rock music comebacks of all time, releasing the album *Bat Out of Hell II: Back Into Hell* in 1993, which featured the song "I'll Do Anything for Love (But I Won't Do That)." Today, the money keeps pouring in as his rock career continues to flourish, and he keeps about half his investment portfolio in bonds. "I don't need to take big risks with my investments," says Meatloaf. "I take a risk with what I do as a performer, where the odds of success are ridiculously low."

Like a lot of investors, Meatloaf chose to invest in bonds because they carry less risk than stocks do. Many investors, though, are drawn to bonds because of the steady income that they provide. However, merely because they offer a steady income doesn't mean that you can't earn spectacular returns from bonds. This is something Meatloaf certainly knows. In fact, in 1995, long-term Treasury bonds went up in value by almost 32 percent! Bonds are a great source of income and a great source of diversity for your investment portfolio; now let's jump ("to the left, and a step to the") right in and explore the world of bonds.

WHY CONSIDER BONDS?

To begin with, a bond is simply a loan or an IOU. In effect, when you buy a bond, you become a lender. The bond issuer—generally a corporation, the federal government and its agencies, a city, or a state—gets the use of your money and in return pays you interest, generally every 6 months, for the life of the bond. At maturity, the issuer returns your money, or actually returns the face value of the bond, which may be more or less than what you originally paid for the bond.

How exactly do bonds fit into your investment portfolio?

- **Bonds reduce risk through diversification.**   As you learned earlier, when you put together investments whose returns don't move together over time, you're able to reduce the risk in your portfolio. Remember October 27, 1997, when the stock market went down by 7.2 percent in one day, that same day bond prices rose.

- **Bonds produce steady current income.**   For those needing some income from their investment portfolio to achieve their financial goals, bonds are a good choice. For example, you may be retired and desire additional income from your investment portfolio to supplement your pension income. With bonds, provided they don't fail to make, or default on, their interest payments, you'll receive steady interest income annually.

- **Bonds can be a safe investment if held to maturity.**   Interest on bonds must be paid, or the firm can be forced into bankruptcy. Thus, bond interest payments will be made at all costs—unlike dividend payments, on common stocks. As a result, bonds are a relatively safe investment. In addition, bond rating services provide reliable information on the riskiness of bonds, allowing you to avoid risky bonds. Thus, if the bond doesn't default and you hold it to maturity, you know exactly what your return will be. In the world of personal finance, it's unusual to find an investment that's so low in risk that it actually returns exactly what it promises, making bonds very appealing.

Now that you know why bonds make good investments, you should know a thing or two about bonds in general. Let's take a look at bond basics.

Understand basic bond
terminology and compare
the various types of
bonds available.

Par Value
The face value of a bond, or the amount that's returned to the bondholder at maturity. It's also referred to as the bond's denomination.

Maturity
The length of time until the bond issuer returns the par value to the bondholder and terminates the bond.

Coupon Interest Rate
The annual rate of interest to be paid out on a bond, calculated as a percentage of the par value.

BASIC BOND TERMINOLOGY AND FEATURES

Bonds are like just about everything else we've seen so far in this book in that if you can't talk the talk, you're going to fall flat on your face when you try to walk the walk. This section should get you fairly conversant in the language of bonds.

Par Value

The **par value** of a bond is its face value, or the amount that's returned to the bondholder at **maturity**, the date when the bond comes due. For bonds issued by corporations, the par value is generally $1,000. A bond's market price, which is its selling price, is generally expressed as a percentage of the bond's par value. For example, a bond that matures or comes due in the year 2010 that has a $1,000 par value may be quoted in the *Wall Street Journal* as selling for 95⅛. That doesn't mean you can buy the bond for $95.125. It means that the bond is selling in the secondary market for 95⅛ percent of its par value, which is actually $951.25 ($1,000 × 95⅛%). At maturity in the year 2010, the bondholder will receive the par value of $1,000 and the bond will be terminated (but not by Arnold Schwarzenegger).

Coupon Interest Rate

The **coupon interest rate** on a bond indicates what percentage of the par value of the bond will be paid out annually in the form of interest. Thus, an 8 percent coupon interest rate and a $1,000 par value will pay out $80 ($8\% \times \$1,000$) annually in interest until maturity, generally in semiannual installments.

Keep in mind that when you purchase a bond and hold it to maturity, your entire return is based upon the return of the par value or principal and the payment of interest at the coupon interest rate. The only real risk involved is that the bond issuer won't have the funds to make these payments and will default.

Indenture

An **indenture** is the legal document that provides the specific terms of the loan agreement, including a description of the bond, the rights of the bondholders, the rights of the issuing firm, and the responsibilities of the bond trustees. A bond trustee, usually a banking institution or trust company, is assigned the task of overseeing the relationship between the bondholder and the issuing firm, protecting the bondholder, and seeing that the terms of the indenture are carried out. A bond indenture may run 100 pages or more in length, with the majority of it devoted to defining protective provisions for the bondholder.

Call Provision

A **call provision** entitles the bond issuer to repurchase, or "call," the bonds from their holders at stated prices over specified periods. In effect, if interest rates go down, the issuer will call the bonds and replace them with lower-cost debt. The terms of the call provision are provided in the indenture and generally set the call provision at approximately the par value plus 1 year's worth of interest. Obviously, a call provision works to the disadvantage of the investor. However, bonds with call provisions generally pay higher returns as compensation for buying a bond that might be called away if interest rates drop. Still, if you own high-paying long-term bonds and you're counting on receiving those semiannual interest payments for the next 10 years or so, having them called away from you could rain on your parade.

To make callable bonds more attractive, the issuer many times includes in the indenture some protection against calls. Generally, that call protection comes in the form of a **deferred call**. With a deferred call, the bond can't be called until a set number of years have passed since the bond was issued. Although not as safe as a noncallable bond, a bond with a deferred call at least provides protection against an immediate call.

Sinking Fund

No one likes to have to pay off debts all at once, and that goes for bond issuers, too. Most bond issuers set up a **sinking fund** to set aside money on a regular basis to pay off the bonds at maturity. With a sinking fund, the firm either calls, using the bond's call provision, or repurchases in the open market a fraction of the outstanding bonds annually. In this way, the issuer spreads out the large payment that would have otherwise occurred at maturity. The advantage of a sinking fund for the investor is that the probability that the debt will be successfully paid off at maturity increases, thereby reducing risk. Without a sinking fund, the issuer faces a major payment at maturity. If the issuer were to experience temporary financial problems when the debt matures, the repayment of the debt could be jeopardized. Using a sinking fund reduces this danger. The big disadvantage of a sinking fund for investors comes from the fact that it may result in your bond being called away from you.

DIFFERENT TYPES OF BONDS

There's an old science joke saying that there are four different types of bonds: ionic, covalent, metallic, and James. Well, in the world of finance there are a bunch more types

Indenture
A legal agreement between the firm issuing a bond and the bond trustee who represents the bondholders.

Call Provision
A bond provision that gives the issuer the right to repurchase, or "call," the bonds from their holders at stated prices over specified periods.

Deferred Call
A bond provision stating that the bond can't be called until a set number of years have passed since it was issued.

Sinking Fund
A fund to which the bond issuer deposits money to pay off a bond issue.

LEARNING OBJECTIVE #2

Understand basic bond terminology and compare the various types of bonds available.

of bonds than that (but James is the only one with a license to kill). There are thousands of outstanding bonds floating around the securities markets, and more are probably on the way as you read this. Without question, it's a vast understatement to say that these bonds aren't all alike. The easiest way to explain their differences is to break them down into bonds issued by corporations, by the U.S. government and its agencies, and by states and localities, and examine each group separately. As you'll see, each type of bond has unique advantages and disadvantages to the investor.

> ### *The Facts of Life*
> It's hard to imagine how many bonds there are actually in existence and how unusual some can be. One of the most unusual ones was issued in early 1997 by David Bowie. The stylish rock star, who morphed his way from Ziggy Stardust to a financial pioneer, issued $55 million worth of bonds, which pay 7.9 percent and come due in 10 years. These bonds are funded with royalties on sales of his past music.

Corporate Bonds

Corporate Bonds
Bonds issued by corporations.

Borrowing money by issuing bonds is a major source of funding for corporations. In fact, **corporate bonds** account for about half of the bonds outstanding today. Generally these bonds are issued in denominations of $1,000 in order to appeal to smaller investors. Of course, life's just not simple enough that there's only one type of corporate bond. There are several different types of corporate bonds from which you can choose, with one major differentiation being whether or not the bond is secured.

Secured Bond
Any bond that is backed by the pledge of collateral.

Mortgage Bond
A bond secured by a lien or real property.

Secured Corporate Debt.   A **secured bond** is one that's backed by collateral, which, as you should remember, is a real asset that can be seized and sold if a debtor doesn't pay off his or her debt. A **mortgage bond** is secured by a lien on real property. Typically, the value of the real property is greater than that of the mortgage bonds issued, providing the investor with a margin of safety in case the market value of the secured property declines. In the event of bankruptcy, the bond trustees have the power to sell the secured property and use the proceeds to pay the bondholders. If the proceeds from this sale don't cover the bonds, the bondholders fall in line with the others who are owed money and may well be out of luck and out of some money.

Debenture
Any unsecured long-term bond.

Unsecured Corporate Debt.   The term **debenture** applies to any unsecured long-term bond. When bonds are unsecured, the earning ability of the issuing corporation is of great concern to the investor. Debentures are also viewed as being more risky than secured bonds and, as a result, have a higher yield associated with them than do secured bonds.

Firms with more than one issue of debentures outstanding often specify a hierarchy by which some debentures get paid back before others if the firm goes bankrupt. The claims of the subordinated debentures—bonds lower down in the hierarchy—are honored only after the claims of secured bonds and unsubordinated debentures have been satisfied. As you might imagine, subordinated debentures are riskier than "normal" or unsubordinated debentures and, as such, have a higher return associated with them to compensate for their added risk.

Treasury and Agency Bonds

Without question, the biggest single player—and payer—in the bond market is the U.S. government. Given the constant talk on the news about our national debt and the balanced budget flap, it should come as no surprise that our government spends more than it takes in. The alternatives to financing this unbalanced budget are to either sell some assets (anybody want to buy Nebraska?), raise taxes, or borrow more money. The latter choice has been found to be the most acceptable approach and has led to the issuance of huge sums of debt by our government. Given the enormous amount of debt financing that goes on, it's not surprising that there are a number of different types of government debt to choose from.

These securities are generally viewed as being risk-free, given the government's ability to tax and print more money. When corporations run out of money, they can't just print more, but the government can. Hey, it owns the mints! In addition to there being no default risk on Treasury bonds, there's no risk that government bonds will be called, because the government no longer issues callable bonds. Just as you might expect, because there's no default or call risk associated with government bonds, they generally pay a lower rate of interest than other bonds. In addition, most interest payments received on federal debt is exempt from state and local taxation.[1]

Treasury-issued debt can have maturities that range from 3 months all the way to 30 years. Although in recent years approximately 70 percent of that debt has had a maturity of 5 years or less, the Treasury has a good deal of latitude in its choice of maturities. When investors speak of Treasury debt with different maturities, they speak of *bills*, *notes*, and *bonds*. The only difference between these is the maturity and the denomination. If the Treasury debt has a maturity of 3, 6, or 12 months, it's referred to as Treasury *bills*. If, when issued, it has a maturity of 2, 3, 5, or 10 years, it's referred to as Treasury *notes*. Treasury *bonds* have maturities of more than 10 years and are issued today with 30-year maturities. In terms of denomination, Treasury bills have a minimum denomination of $10,000, Treasury notes with maturities of less than 5 years have a minimum denomination of $5,000, and securities that mature in 5 or more years have denominations of $1,000, just like corporate bonds.

The Facts of Life

One advantage of purchasing Treasury securities is that you can do it yourself through a program called Treasury Direct, thereby avoiding brokerage fees, which range upward from $49 per transaction. You need only set up an account with the Federal Reserve and Treasury Direct, then you can make trades and keep track of all your transactions electronically. Since late 1997, you can also sell your security before maturity through the Fed for a $34 fee. For instructions, contact the Bureau of Public Debt at http://www.publicdebt.treas.gov.

In addition to the Treasury, a number of other government agencies, such as the Federal National Mortgage Association (FNMA) and the Federal Home Loan Banks (FHLB), issue debt called **agency bonds**. Although these aren't directly issued by our government through the Treasury, they're issued by federal agencies and authorized by Congress. As such, they're still viewed as being virtually risk-free and carry an interest rate slightly higher than that carried on Treasury securities. In general their minimum denomination is $5,000, with maturities that vary from 1 to 40 years, although the average maturity is approximately 15 years.

Agency Bonds

Bonds issued by government agencies other than the Treasury.

Pass-Through Certificates. Of the agency securities, the most interesting to investors are those issued by the Government National Mortgage Association (GNMA),

---

[1] Federal debt issued by FNMA, the Federal National Mortgage Association, is not exempt from state and local taxation.

or "Ginnie Mae," called **pass-through certificates**. A GNMA pass-through certificate represents an interest in a pool of federally insured mortgages. What GNMA has done is packaged a group of mortgages worth $1 million or more, guaranteed those mortgages, and sold "certificates" with minimum denominations of $25,000, called pass-through certificates, to finance the mortgages. In effect, pass-through certificates can put an average homeowner with $25,000 to invest on the other side—the lending side—of a mortgage. Because all the payments from the mortgages financed by the pass-through certificates (less a processing fee and a GNMA insurance fee) go to the certificate holders, the size of the monthly check varies depending on how fast the mortgages are paid off. In addition, the monthly check that the investor receives represents both the principal and the interest. As such, at maturity there's no return of principal as there is with a bond. With the last payment, the pass-through security is completely paid off, just as your home mortgage would be.

Treasury Inflation-Indexed Bonds.   The newest and most exciting Treasury bond for investors is the inflation-indexed bond. In early 1997, the Treasury began selling **inflation-indexed bonds**. These bonds have a maturity of 10 years and a minimum par value of $1,000, and they initially carried a coupon interest rate of 3.375 percent, meaning they paid $33.75 interest a year. When there are changes in the consumer price index (the government's measure of the effect of inflation on prices), there's a corresponding change in the par value of the bond. For example, if there's a 1 percent increase in the consumer price index, the par value of these bonds will go up by 3 percent, from $1,000 to $1,030. That means you get a little more interest each year, and at maturity you also get a little more. That's because, interest payments are then determined using this new par value. So if the par value of the bond rises to $1,030, the bondholder now gets 3.375 percent of $1,030, or $34.76 ($3.375\% \times \$1,030$) per year, and at maturity this bond now pays $1,030. The big headache with respect to these bonds comes in determining taxes. The IRS considers the upward adjustment in the par value of the bonds as interest income, and you have to pay taxes on it during the year the adjustment was made, even though you don't receive this money until the bond matures.

The advantage of these bonds to investors is that investors will be guaranteed a real return—that is, a return above inflation—on their investment. In addition, the effects of inflation on interest rates will be equalized as the interest payments and the bond's par value rise to reflect inflation. In effect, you win if there's inflation.

U.S. Series EE Bonds.   The government also issues savings bonds directly aimed at the small investor. As we saw in chapter 5, U.S. Series EE bonds are issued by the Treasury with variable interest rates and denominations so low that they can be purchased for as little as $25 each. When a Series EE bond is purchased, its price is one-half its face value, with face values going from $50 to $10,000. In other words, you buy a bond, wait a specified amount of time, and get double your money back.

Series EE bonds are liquid in the sense that they can be cashed at any time, although cashing them before they mature may result in a reduced yield. Making them

> ### *The Facts of Life*
> After a certain number of years, savings bonds don't earn any more interest. On newly issued savings bonds the date when interest stops being earned is listed on the face of the bond, on older bonds it's generally 30 or 40 years after the date of issue. Unfortunately, many people don't realize this. The result is that currently there are over $4 billion of savings bonds outstanding that aren't earning interest.

more attractive is that they earn a minimum return of 4 percent. Although this minimum return can be changed at any time by the Treasury, the new minimum applies only to newly issued Series EE bonds, not to outstanding ones. The actual rate earned on Series EE bonds varies with the market interest rate, but it's currently quite competitive.

Municipal Bonds

Municipal bonds, or "**muni's**," are bonds issued by states, counties, and cities, in addition to other public agencies, such as school districts and highway authorities, to fund public projects. To say the least, there are thousands of different issues of municipal bonds with over 1 trillion in outstanding value. Their popularity stems from the fact that they're tax-exempt—interest payments aren't taxed by the federal government or, in general, by the state as long as you live in the state in which the bonds were issued. In fact, if you live in a city and buy a municipal bond issued by that city, your income from that bond would be exempt from city, state, and federal taxes. For example, if you live in New York, which has an income tax, and purchase a municipal bond issued by that city, you'll be exempt from paying taxes on the interest you receive at the federal, state, and city levels. Capital gains made from selling municipal bonds before maturity, though, are taxed.

There are two basic types of municipal bonds: general obligation bonds and revenue bonds. A **general obligation bond** is backed by the full faith and credit—that is, the taxing power—of the issuer. **Revenue bonds**, however, derive the funds to pay interest and repay the bonds from a designated project or specific tax and can pay only if a sufficient amount of revenue is generated. For example, the revenue bond may derive its funding from a toll road, and if traffic isn't very heavy, the bond might go unpaid.

Municipal bonds also come with many different maturities. In fact, most municipal bond offerings have **serial maturities**. That is, a portion of the debt comes due, or matures, each year until the issue is exhausted. In effect, it works like a sinking fund. It's important that you choose the maturity date that you want so you get the bond's principal back when you need and expect it.

Although municipal bonds are issued by a "government," they're not risk-free. In fact, in the past there have been several cases in which local governments have failed to pay on municipal bonds. For example, Cleveland defaulted on some debt in the late 1970s, and then in the mid-1990s, Orange County, California, defaulted on $800 million of its short-term debt. The primary revenue source for most municipal bonds is real estate taxes. If local governments overestimate future tax intakes—say, the government thinks more people will move in when instead a bunch of people move out— they get stuck holding a lot of debt they can't handle. Remember, unlike the federal government, state and local governments can't print more money when they run short. As you might expect, it's very difficult for an investor to judge the quality of a municipal bond offering. Fortunately, the rating agencies that we will discuss shortly in conjunction with corporate bonds also rate municipal bonds.

One of the disadvantages of municipal bonds is that if you have to sell them before they mature, it can be difficult to find a buyer. This is especially true for many smaller issues for which there simply is not a secondary market.

Special Situation Bonds

We've already seen the main classification of bonds, but before moving on there are two special types of bonds that deserve mention. They are zero coupon bonds and junk bonds.

Zero Coupon Bonds.
Zero coupon bonds are simply bonds that don't pay interest. Instead, these bonds are sold at a discount from their face or par value, and at maturity they return the entire par value. As a result, the entire return is made up by the bond's appreciating in value from its discount purchase price to its price at maturity. In effect,

Municipal Bonds, or "**Muni's**"
Bonds issued by states, counties, and cities, as well as other public agencies, such as school districts and highway authorities, to fund public projects.

General Obligation Bond
A state or municipal bond backed by the full faith and credit—that is, the taxing power—of the issuer.

Revenue Bonds
State or municipal bonds that have interest and par value paid for with funds from a designated project or specific tax.

Serial Maturities
Bonds, generally municipals, with various maturity dates, usually at set intervals.

Zero Coupon Bonds
Bonds that don't pay interest and are sold at a deep discount from their par value.

a zero coupon bond can be thought of as something like a savings bond. The obvious appeal of zero coupon bonds is to those investors who need a lump sum of money at some future date but don't want to be concerned about reinvesting interest payments. There are zero coupon bonds issued by corporations and municipals, and there are even mortgage-backed zeros, but without question the dominant player in this market is the U.S. government. The government's zero coupon bonds are called STRIPS.

The major disadvantage of zero coupon bonds is that while you don't receive any income annually, you're taxed as though you do. The IRS considers any annual appreciation in value (or as the IRS calls it, the undistributed interest) as subject to tax. Another disadvantage of zero coupon bonds is that they tend to fluctuate in value with changes in the interest rate more than traditional bonds do. For example, in 1994, 30-year zero coupon Treasury bonds dropped 18.7 percent, then in 1995 they rose in price by 63.1 percent. As such, zero coupon bonds aren't a good investment alternative if you may have to sell the bond before it matures. Zero coupon bonds are best suited for tax-deferred retirement accounts such as IRAs or Keogh plans. With tax-deferred accounts, the tax disadvantage of zero coupon bonds disappears.

Junk Bonds

Junk Bonds

Very risky, low-rated bonds, also called high-yield bonds. These bonds are rated BB or below.

Junk Bonds.   **Junk bonds**, or low-rated bonds, also called high-yield bonds, are bonds rated BB or below. (We'll fully explain bond ratings in the next section.) Originally, the term applied to bonds issued by firms with previously sound financial histories, which were currently facing severe financial problems and suffering from poor credit ratings. Today, junk bonds refer to any bond with a low rating. The major issuers of junk bonds are new firms that haven't yet established a record of performance.

Because junk bonds carry a much greater risk of default than high-grade bonds, they also carry a higher interest rate 3 to 5 percent above AAA grade long-term bonds. The problem with junk bonds is that they haven't been around long enough for us to really know what will happen to them if we face a major recession. In investing, it's never a good idea to volunteer to be a guinea pig. With junk bonds that's what you'd be doing. Moreover, most junk bonds are callable. That means that if the firm does do well and recovers from its financial difficulties, then the bond will be called. If the firm doesn't do well, the bond could default. Neither of these alternatives is a good one. Thus, junk bonds are probably something that the prudent investor should avoid. Hey, they're not called junk for nothing!

EVALUATING BONDS

Not only do you need to know bond terms and what kind of bonds there are, you also need to know how to evaluate them. That means understanding what a bond yield and a rating are, and knowing how to read a bond quote in the newspaper.

Bond Yield

The bond's yield is simply the return on investment in a bond. Note that a bond's yield isn't the same as the bond's coupon interest rate. Although the coupon interest rate tells you what your interest payments are as a percentage of the bond's par value, the bond's yield tells you what your return is as a percentage of the price of the bond. There are two ways of measuring a bond's yield. The first, called the current yield, simply looks at the return from interest payments from the bond. The second, called the yield to maturity, takes into account your total return, including interest and allowing for the fact that you may have purchased the bond for either more or less than it returns at maturity.

Current Yield.   The **current yield** on a bond refers to the ratio of the annual interest payment to the bond's market price. If, for example, you're considering a bond with an 8-percent coupon interest rate, a par value of $1,000, and a market price of $700, it

LEARNING OBJECTIVE #3

Calculate the value of a bond and understand the factors that cause bond value to change.

Current Yield

The ratio of the annual interest payment to the bond's market price.

would have a current yield of

$$\text{current yield} = \frac{\text{annual interest payments}}{\text{market price of the bond}}$$

$$= \frac{0.08 \times \$1,000}{\$700} = \frac{\$80}{\$700} = 11.4 \text{ percent}$$

Yield to Maturity.

The **yield to maturity** is the true yield or return that you receive if you hold a bond to maturity. Basically, it's the measure of expected return for a bond. In effect, calculating the yield to maturity is the same concept as that of solving for the annual interest rate, i, in chapter 3, where we discussed the time value of money. This measure of return considers the annual interest payments that the bondholder receives as well as the difference between the bond's current market price and its value at maturity. Remember, regardless of whether you bought your bond at a price above or below its par value, at maturity you get exactly its par value. Thus, if you paid less than $1,000 for your bond, the bond will appreciate over its lifetime, climbing up to $1,000 at maturity. Conversely, if you paid more than $1,000 for your bond, it'll slowly drop in value over its lifetime, falling to $1,000 at maturity when it's redeemed. As we saw when we discussed the time value of money, if you have a financial calculator, solving for the yield to maturity, or i, is quite easy. However, if you don't have a financial calculator at hand, you can use a formula to calculate the approximate yield to maturity (you need a calculator to calculate the actual yield to maturity). This formula first determines the average annual return by adding the annual interest payments to the average amount that the bond increases or decreases in price each year. The annual change in bond price is based on the notion that at maturity the bond will be worth its par value—because it'll be redeemed at this price—and simply calculates the amount that the bond must increase or decrease to get to its par value and divides this by the number of years left to maturity. This average annual return is then divided by the average value of the bond—the average of its par value and current market price. Thus, the *approximate yield to maturity* is calculated as follows:

$$\text{approximate yield to maturity} = \frac{\text{annual interest payments} + \dfrac{\text{par value} - \text{current price}}{\text{number of years to maturity}}}{\dfrac{\text{par value} + \text{current price}}{2}}$$

Let's look at an example of a bond that has 10 years left to maturity, has a par value of $1,000, a current price of $880, and a coupon interest rate of 10 percent, meaning that it pays $100 annually in interest to the bondholder (coupon interest rate × par value = annual interest payment, or $0.10 \times \$1,000 = \$100$). Plugging these numbers into the approximate yield to maturity formula, you get

$$\text{approximate yield to maturity} = \frac{\$100 + \dfrac{\$1,000 - \$880}{10}}{\dfrac{\$1,000 + \$880}{2}}$$

$$\text{approximate yield to maturity} = \frac{\$100 + \dfrac{\$120}{10}}{\$1,880/2}$$

$$= \$112/\$940 = 11.91 \text{ percent}$$

As we mentioned earlier, you'd need a financial calculator to get the true yield to maturity. If you did calculate the true yield to maturity, you would find it to be 12.14 percent, a difference of only 0.23 percent.

Yield to Maturity

The true yield or return that the bondholder receives if a bond is held to maturity. It's the measure of expected return for a bond.

The approximate yield to maturity formula also works for bonds that are selling above their par or maturity value. Thus, looking back at our example and changing the current market price to $1,100, we can recalculate the approximate yield to maturity as follows:

$$\text{approximate yield to maturity} = \frac{\$100 + \dfrac{\$1,000 - \$1,100}{10}}{\dfrac{\$1,000 + \$1,100}{2}}$$

$$\text{approximate yield to maturity} = \frac{\$100 - \dfrac{\$100}{10}}{\$2,100/2}$$

$$= \$90 / \$1,050 = 8.57 \text{ percent}$$

Equivalent Taxable Yield on Municipal Bonds. Obviously the appeal of municipal bonds (Munis) is their tax-exempt status. Thus, in comparing municipal bonds to other, taxable bonds, the comparison must be between equivalent taxable yield—that is, the yield a taxable bond must offer to match the equivalent taxable yield on the municipal bond. The equivalent taxable yield on a municipal bond is calculated as follows:

$$\frac{\text{equivalent}}{\text{taxable yield}} = \frac{\text{tax-free yield on the municipal bond}}{(1 - \text{investor's marginal tax bracket})}$$

Keep in mind that the tax bracket that's referred to includes all taxes that are avoided by the muni. In effect, this bracket could include federal, state, and local taxes. Thus, if the municipal bond were yielding 7 percent and the investor were in the 38 percent marginal tax bracket, the equivalent taxable yield on a municipal bond would be

$$\frac{\text{equivalent}}{\text{taxable yield}} = \frac{0.07}{(1 - 0.38)} = \frac{0.07}{0.62} = 0.1129, \text{ or } 11.29\%$$

The higher the individual's tax bracket, the more attractive municipal bonds are.

Bond Ratings—A Measure of a Bond's Riskiness

John Moody first began to rate bonds in 1909. Since that time, two major rating agencies—Moody's and Standard & Poor's—have provided ratings on thousands of corporate, city, and state bonds. These ratings involve a judgment about the future risk potential of a bond—specifically its default risk or the chance that it may not be able to meet its obligations of interest or repayment of principal sometime in the future. The poorer the bond rating, the higher the rate of return demanded by investors. That's exactly what you'd expect, given **Axiom 1: The Risk-Return Trade-Off—Investors Don't Take on Additional Risk Unless They Expect to Be Compensated with Additional Return**. Generally, these bond ratings run from AAA for the safest bonds to D for extremely risky bonds. Interestingly, a bond with an A rating is considered only a medium-grade bond rather than a high-grade bond. Table 15.1 provides a description of the different bond ratings.

As an investor, you should be aware of a bond's rating and its risk. Unfortunately, because bonds are so expensive—selling for around $1,000 each, diversification can be difficult unless you have a great deal of money invested in bonds. So if you buy bonds, avoid the risky ones. Check out their ratings, which are available at most local libraries, or ask your broker.

AXIOM #1

The Risk-Return Trade-Off—Investors Don't Take on Additional Risk Unless They Expect to Be Compensated with Additional Return

TABLE 15.1

Interpreting Bond Ratings

Bond Rating Category	Standard & Poor's	Moody's	Description
Prime	AAA	Aaa	Highest quality, extremely strong
Very strong	AA	Aa	Very strong capacity to pay
Strong	A	A	Strong capacity to pay
Medium	BBB	Baa	Changing circumstances could impact the firm's ability to pay
Speculative	BB, B	Ba, B	Has speculative elements
Very speculative	CCC, CC	Caa, Ca	Extremely speculative
Default	C	C	An income bond that doesn't pay interest
Default	D	D	Has not been paying interest or repaying principal

Reading Corporate Bond Quotes in the *Wall Street Journal*

Figure 15.1 provides a visual summary of how to read corporate bond listings. Recall that although corporate bonds generally have a par or face value of $1,000, their selling price is quoted as a percentage of par. Even though a bond may appear to be selling at 101, it's actually selling at 101 percent of its par value, which is $1,000. Thus, a bond listed as selling at 101 is actually selling for $1,010.

Actually, what's listed in the paper isn't exactly what you'd pay if you purchased the bond. You're also expected to pay for any **accrued interest** on the bond. Remember, interest is generally paid only every 6 months. Thus, if it's been 5 months since interest was last paid, the bond has accrued 5 months' worth of interest. This accrued interest isn't reflected in the listed price of the bond, but you still need to pay the seller for the 5 months' of accrued interest that's already been earned. If this bond pays $48 in interest every 6 months, then 5 months' worth of accrued interest would be ⅚ × $48 = $40. That means that although the bond is listed as selling for $1,010, if you purchased it you'd actually pay $1,010 + $40 = $1,050. This sum of both the quoted or stated price and the accrued interest is often referred to as the **invoice price**.

Accrued Interest
Interest that has been earned on the bond but has not yet been paid out to the bondholder.

Reading Treasury Quotes in the *Wall Street Journal*

Figure 15.2 provides a visual summary of how to read Treasury securities listings. When reading Treasury and agency securities listings, you'll notice quotes for both a bid price and an ask price, with the bid price representing what another investor was willing to pay for the security and the ask price representing what another investor was willing to sell the security for. In addition, Treasury and agency securities trade in thirty-seconds (1/32). Thus, if a security is listed at 102:31, that translates to $102\frac{31}{32}$ percent of the security's par value. If the par value of this bond is $10,000, then it would sell for $10,296.88 ($10,000 × $102\frac{31}{32}$%).

Invoice Price
The sum of both the quoted or stated price of a bond and the bond's accrued interest. It's the price you pay if you buy the bond in the secondary market.

FIGURE 15.1

A Visual Summary of How to Read Corporate Bond Listings in the *Wall Street Journal*

The Money and Investing Section of the Wall Street Journal *contains daily trading details for corporate bonds traded on the New York Stock Exchange. This actually represents only a small portion of bond trading, with most bond trading taking place in the over-the-counter market among securities dealers.*

Bonds: The name of the issuer is given in the first column, followed by the original interest rate, and the year the bond matures in, with an occasional *s* added as a break between numbers. For example, the 6s00 is referred to as a "six of oh-oh," meaning it is a 6% bond due in 2000.

Vol: Volume provides the volume of trading during the previous day in thousands of dollars. For example, 23 ATT 5⅛01 bonds traded during the previous day.

Net Chg.: Net change refers to the change in the closing price from the prior day's close. Again, a ⅛ change reflects a change of $1.25. That is, ⅛% of the bond's par value which is $1,000.

THE WALL STREET JOURNAL WEDNESDAY, JULY 23, 1997

NEW YORK EXCHANGE BONDS

Quotations as of 4 p.m. Eastern Time
Tuesday, July 22, 1997

CORPORATION BONDS
Volume, $25,201,000

Bonds	Cur Yld.	Vol.	Close	Net Chg.
AMR 8.10s98	8.0	10	101¾	...
AMR 9s16	8.0	13	112½	...
ATT 4⅜99	4.5	50	97¼	+ ¼
ATT 6s00	6.0	1	99¼	+ ¾
ATT 5⅛01	5.4	23	95⅝	− ⅛
ATT 7⅛02	6.9	74	102⅞	+ ¼
ATT 6¾04	6.7	40	101	+ ⅜
ATT 7s05	6.8	60	102⅞	+ ⅝
ATT 7¾07	7.2	28	107¼	− ¼
ATT 8⅛22	7.8	121	104⅞	− ⅛
ATT 8⅛24	7.8	7	104¾	+ ½
ATT 8.35s25	7.8	72	107½	+ ⅝
ATT 8⅝31	8.0	8	108⅛	...
AirbF 6¾01	cv	41	128	...
AlaPw 9¼21	8.8	26	105	− ⅛
AlskAr 6⅞14	cv	103	101½	+ ¾
AlldC zr2000	...	18	82	+ ⅝
Allwst 7¼14	cv	5	100	+ 1
Alza 5s06	cv	42	105	..

Bonds	Cur Yld.	Vol.	Close	Net Chg.
KaufB 9⅜03	9.1	50	102⅞	− ⅛
Kolmrg 8¾09	cv	12	102	...
Koppers 8½04	8.6	67	99	− ½
LehmnBr 8¾02	8.1	10	107½	+ 1⅛
Lilly 8⅛01	7.7	7	105⅝	+ ⅛
LglsLt 7.05s03	7.1	124	100	+ ½
LslsLt 7s04	7.1	37	99	+ ⅜
LglsLt 8½06	8.3	10	102	− ¾
LglsLt 7½07	7.5	5	100¼	+ ⅛
LglsLt 8.9s19	8.5	24	105¼	...
LglsLt 9¾21	9.5	133	103	− ¼
LglsLt 9s22	8.1	20	110½	...
LglsLt 8.2s23	7.9	205	104	− ⅝
LglsLt 9⅝24	9.3	52	103⅛	+ ⅛
MacNS 7⅞04	cv	24	102¼	− ½
MarO 7s02	7.0	1	100½	...
Masco 5¼12	cv	14	105¾	+ ⅝
Mascotch 03	cv	24	91¼	− ½
Mattel 10⅛cld	...	5	103¾	...
McDnl 7⅜02	7.3	5	101	− ¼
McDnlDg 9¾12	7.8	20	125	+ ⅞

Cur Yld: The current yield gives the annual interest divided by the most recent price. In effect it tells you how much you would earn on this bond over the next year if the bond's price remained the same. If it is a zero coupon bond, there will be no current yield. That is the case for the AlldC, or Allied Chemical, bonds. A *cv* indicates a convertible bond.

Close: The closing price from the prior day is shown in this column. You must keep in mind that bond prices are traditionally quoted as a percent of par, with the typical par value of a corporate bond being $1,000. Thus, the closing price on the ATT 5⅛01 bond of 95⅝ means that this bond's last trade during the prior day was at $956.25. In effect, each ⅛ reflects $1.25. Thus, a bond quoted at 101⅝ would be selling for $1,016.25.

Source: Reprinted by permission of *The Wall Street Journal*, ©1997 Dow Jones & Company, Inc. All Rights Reserved Worldwide.

FIGURE 15.2

A Visual Summary of How to Read Treasury and Agency Securities Listings in the *Wall Street Journal*

The Money and Investing section of the Wall Street Journal *contains daily trading details for U.S. Treasury offerings. Treasury bills are issued with maturities of 3 or 6 months every Monday in minimum denominations of $10,000, and with 1-year maturities on a monthly basis. Treasury issues maturing in between 1 and 10 years are referred to as notes, while those with maturities greater than 10 years are called bonds.*

Maturity Mo/Yr: The year and month of maturity are given in this column. An *n* to the right of the year of maturity denotes a note. A *p* identifies bonds that are exempt from withholding tax if held by nonresident aliens.

Rate: Rate refers to the original interest rate on the bond.

Ask Yld.: This refers to the yield or effective return on the investment. If you bought the bond today and held it to maturity, this would be your return.

Days to Maturity: Because of their short maturity, Treasury Bills also list the number of days to maturity.

TREASURY BONDS, NOTES & BILLS

Tuesday, July 22, 1997
Representative and indicative Over-the-Counter quotations based on $1 million or more.

GOVT. BONDS & NOTES

Rate	Maturity Mo/Yr	Bid	Asked	Chg.	Ask Yld.
5^1/2	Jul 97n	99:30	100:00	....	5.36
5^7/8	Jul 97n	99:30	100:00	....	5.71
6^1/2	Aug 97n	100:00	100:02	....	5.36
8^5/8	Aug 97n	100:05	100:07	....	4.98
5^5/8	Aug 97n	99:31	100:01	....	5.21
6	Aug 97n	100:00	100:02	....	5.28
5^1/2	Sep 97n	99:31	100:01	....	5.24
5^3/4	Sep 97n	100:00	100:02	....	5.32
8^3/4	Oct 97n	100:22	100:24	....	5.32
5^5/8	Oct 97n	100:00	100:02	+ 1	5.32
5^3/4	Oct 97n	100:01	100:03	+ 1	5.33
7^3/8	Nov 97n	100:16	100:18	....	5.47
8^7/8	Nov 97n	100:31	101:01	....	5.43
5^3/8	Nov 97n	99:29	99:31	....	5.42
6	Nov 97n	100:04	100:06	....	5.42
5^1/4	Dec 97n	99:27	99:29	....	5.45
6	Dec 97n	100:06	100:08	+ 1	5.39
7^7/8	Jan 98n	101:02	101:04	....	5.45
5	Jan 90n	99:21	99:23	+ 1	5.55
5^5/8	Jan 98n	99:31	100:01	....	5.56
7^1/4	Feb 98n	100:27	100:29		5.59

Rate	Maturity Mo/Yr	Bid	Asked	Chg.	Ask Yld.
9^7/8	Nov 15	135:26	136:00	+41	6.49
9^1/4	Feb 16	129:11	129:17	+41	6.49
7^1/4	May 16	108:04	108:06	+35	6.49
7^1/2	Nov 16	110:23	110:27	+36	6.50
8^3/4	May 17	124:18	124:24	+40	6.51
8^7/8	Aug 17	126:03	126:09	+41	6.51
9^1/8	May 18	129:10	129:16	+42	6.51
9	Nov 18	128:05	128:11	+42	6.52
8^7/8	Feb 19	126:28	127:02	+43	6.52
8^1/8	Aug 19	118:13	118:17	+40	6.53
8^1/2	Feb 20	122:30	123:04	+42	6.53
8^3/4	May 20	125:31	126:05	+43	6.53
8^3/4	Aug 20	126:03	126:09	+43	6.53
7^7/8	Feb 21	115:28	116:00	+41	6.53
8^1/8	May 21	118:30	119:02	+42	6.53
8^1/8	Aug 21	119:01	119:05	+42	6.53
8	Nov 21	117:19	117:23	+41	6.53
7^1/4	Aug 22	108:24	108:26	+39	6.53
7^5/8	Nov 22	113:12	113:16	+41	6.53
7^1/8	Feb 23	107:11	107:13	+39	6.53
6^1/4	Aug 23	96:20	96:22	+27	6.51

U.S. TREASURY STRIPS

Mat.	Type	Bid	Asked	Chg.	Ask Yld.
Aug 97	ci	99:22	99:22	....	5.30
Aug 97	np	99:22	99:22	....	5.30
Nov 97	ci	98:10	98:10	+ 1	5.53
Nov 97	np	98:10	98:10	+ 1	5.58
Feb 98	ci	97:00	97:00	+ 2	5.50
Feb 98	np	96:31	97:00	+ 2	5.53
May 98	ci	95:21	95:21	+ 2	5.55
May 98	np	95:21	95:21	+ 2	5.54
Aug 98	ci	94:08	94:08	+ 3	5.65
Aug 98	np	94:07	94:08	+ 3	5.68
Nov 98	ci	92:28	92:28	+ 4	5.71
Nov 98	np	92:27	92:27	+ 4	5.74
Feb 99	ci	91:16	91:16	+ 4	5.76
Feb 99	np	91:16	91:17	+ 4	5.76
Aug 99	ci	90:04	90:05	+ 5	5.81
May 99	np	90:04	90:05	+ 5	5.81
Aug 99	ci	88:26	88:27	+ 5	5.82
Aug 99	np	88:24	88:25	+ 5	5.86
Nov 99	ci	87:14	87:15	+ 6	5.88
Nov 99	np	87:13	87:14	+ 6	5.89
Feb 00	ci	86:04	86:05	+ 7	5.99

TREASURY BILLS

Maturity	Days to Mat.	Bid	Asked	Chg.	Ask Yld.
Jul 24 '97	1	5.27	5.23	+ 0.11	5.30
Jul 31 '97	8	4.69	4.65	− 0.02	4.72
Aug 07 '97	15	4.99	4.95	− 0.04	5.03
Aug 14 '97	22	5.02	4.98	− 0.01	5.07
Aug 21 '97	29	5.08	5.04	− 0.01	5.13
Aug 28 '97	36	4.85	4.81	− 0.02	4.90
Sep 04 '97	43	5.06	5.02	+ 0.11	5.12
Sep 11 '97	50	5.09	5.05	+ 0.01	5.16
Sep 18 '97	57	5.11	5.07	− 0.01	5.18
Sep 25 '97	64	4.99	4.97	− 0.03	5.08
Oct 02 '97	71	5.09	5.00	− 0.05	5.12
Oct 09 '97	78	5.06	5.04	− 0.02	5.17
Oct 16 '97	85	5.10	5.08	− 0.05	5.21
Oct 23 '97	92	5.09	5.08	− 0.04	5.22
Oct 30 '97	99	5.01	4.99	− 0.02	5.13
Oct 30 '97	99	5.13	5.11	....	5.25
Nov 06 '97	106	5.10	5.08	− 0.02	5.23
Nov 13 '97	113	5.15	5.13	− 0.02	5.29
Nov 20 '97	120	5.12	5.09	− 0.04	5.25
Nov 28 '97	128	5.15	5.10	+ 0.05	5.25
Dec 04 '97	134	5.12	5.10	− 0.03	5.27

Bid: Bid refers to the previous day's mid-afternoon bid price that Treasury dealers were willing to buy the issue for. In the bond market, prices are quoted at a percent of par and each one-hundredth of par is referred to as a point. Treasury bond prices generally trade in 32nds of a point. To keep things simple and avoid repeating the figure 32 all the time, all numbers after a colon in a price represent 32nds. Thus, the price of 126:03 means 126^3/32 of the bond's par value. If the bond's par is $10,000, you could sell it for $12,609.38

Chg.: Change reflects the change in the bid price from the previous day.

Asked: Asked refers to the asking or selling price dealers were willing to sell the issue for at midafternoon during the previous day.

U.S. Treasury STRIPS: This is a zero coupon bond issued by the Treasury; that is, it does not pay any interest. At maturity you receive the par value of the bond. You will notice that STRIPS that mature in the more distant future are sold at a deeper discount. That is because the only return the investor receives is in appreciation of the bond's value.

Treasury Bills: Bid and Asked: You will also note that Treasury Bills are quoted in hundredths. Thus, a yield of 5.08 is 5.08%.

AXIOM #2

The Time Value of Money—A Dollar Received Today Is Worth More Than a Dollar Received in the Future

AXIOM #1

The Risk-Return Trade-Off—Investors Don"t Take on Additional Risk Unless They Expect to Be Compensated with Additional Return

VALUATION PRINCIPLES

The valuation of bonds has its roots in Axioms 1 and 2. **Axiom 2: The Time Value of Money—A Dollar Received Today Is Worth More Than a Dollar Received in the Future** allows us to bring the investment returns back to present, while **Axiom 1: The Risk-Return Trade-Off—Investors Don't Take on Additional Risk Unless They Expect to Be Compensated with Additional Return** tells us what discount rate to use in bringing those returns back to present.

From the previous chapter, you already know that the value of any investment is simply the present value of all the returns that you receive from that investment. This is how you valued stocks, and it's also how you'll value bonds. In effect, we'll simply bring the returns or benefits back to the present and add them up. With bonds, the process is quite simple—you merely find out the value in today's dollars of the interest and principal payments, and add them together.

Bond Valuation

When you purchase a bond, you get interest payments for a number of years, and then at maturity the bond is redeemed and you receive the par value of the bond back. Thus, *the value of a bond is simply the present value of the interest payments plus the present value of the repayment of the bond's par value at maturity*. In general, the value of a bond should be approximately the same as its price, because that's what you and other investors would be willing to pay for the bond. Thus, by understanding how bonds are valued, we can also understand what causes bond prices to rise and fall.

Now, let's bring the interest payments and the repayment of the bond's par value at maturity back to present. The interest payments come in the form of an annuity—that is, the investor receives the same dollar amount each year—and the repayment of par comes in the form of a single cash flow.[2] Thus, the value of the bond can be written as

$$\text{value of the bond} = \text{present value of the interest payments} + \text{present value of repayment of par at maturity}$$

Rewriting this using the notation from chapter 3, we get

$$\text{value of the bond} = \$I(PVIFA_{k\%,\, n\,\text{yr}}) + \$\text{par}(PVIF_{k\%,\, n\,\text{yr}})$$

where

$\$I$ = the annual interest payments

$\$\text{par}$ = the par value, or what the bond will be redeemed for at maturity

n = the number of years to maturity

k = the appropriate discount rate or required rate of return given the risk level of the bond

Let's look at an example. We're considering buying a bond that matures in 20 years with a coupon interest rate of 10 percent and a par value of $1,000. How much should we pay for it? Well, first we need to decide what return we require on that bond. Let's assume that given the current interest rates and risk level of this bond, our required rate of return is also 10 percent per year. To determine the value of the bond, we need only bring the interest payments and repayment of par back to present using our required

---

[2] Actually, the calculation of the value of a bond is slightly more complicated owing to the fact that most bonds pay interest semiannually rather than annually. Although accommodating this complication is relatively simple, the principles behind bond valuation don't change. Moreover, the effect on the value of the bond is only slight. As such, because our presentation is meant to illustrate how the value of a bond is determined in the marketplace and how changes in interest rates are reflected in bond prices, we won't deal with semiannual interest payments.

rate of return as the discount rate to do this. The annual interest payments we'll receive if we buy this bond are equal to the bond's coupon interest rate of 10 percent times the par value of the bond, which is $1,000. Thus, the annual interest payments are $100. Recall that the *PVIFA* can be determined using a financial calculator or looked up directly in Appendix E, and the *PVIF* can also be determined using a financial calculator or looked up in Appendix C. The value of the bond can now be calculated as follows:

$$\text{value of the bond} = \frac{\text{present value of the}}{\text{interest payments}} + \frac{\text{present value of repayment}}{\text{of par at maturity}}$$

$$= \$100(PVIFA_{10\%, \ 20 \ yr}) + \$1,000(PVIF_{10\%, \ 20 \ yr})$$

$$= \$100(8.514) + \$1,000(0.1486)$$

$$= \$851.40 + \$148.60$$

$$= \$1,000$$

Thus, the value of this bond would be $1,000. If we purchased it for $1,000, we'd be paying exactly its par value. The reason we'd buy at par is that we'd be earning our entire required rate of return from the interest payments—we required a 10 percent return and we receive a 10 percent return in the form of interest. As a result, there's no need for any additional return from appreciation.

Now let's look at the same bond and assume that the current level of interest rates has gone up and, as a result, so has our required rate of return—to 12 percent. How much should we pay for this bond now? In this case, the only change is in the value of k, the discount rate or required rate of return. Recalculating the value of the bond, we find it to be

$$\text{value of the bond} = \frac{\text{present value of the}}{\text{interest payments}} + \frac{\text{present value of repayment}}{\text{of par at maturity}}$$

$$= \$100(PVIFA_{12\%, \ 20 \ yr}) + \$1,000(PVIF_{12\%, \ 20 \ yr})$$

$$= \$100(7.469) + \$1,000(0.104)$$

$$= \$746.90 + \$104.00$$

$$= \$850.90$$

Thus, when we raise our required rate of return to 12 percent, the value of the bond falls to $850.90. As a result, we would want to buy this bond *at a discount,* that is, below its par value. We're requiring a 12 percent return on this bond, but its interest rate is only 10 percent. We'd get only a portion of our required return from interest payments, and we'd need to receive the remaining return from the appreciation of the bond in value. As a result, we'd buy it for $850.90 and at maturity receive $1,000 for it.

Let's see what happens to the value of this bond when our required rate of return goes down. Assume that the current level of interest rates has gone down and, as a result, so has our required rate of return, this time to 8 percent. Again, the only change is in the value of k, the discount rate or required rate of return. Recalculating the value of the bond, we find it to be

$$\text{value of the bond} = \frac{\text{present value of the}}{\text{interest payments}} + \frac{\text{present value of repayment}}{\text{of par at maturity}}$$

$$= \$100(PVIFA_{8\%, \ 20 \ yr}) + \$1,000(PVIF_{8\%, \ 20 \ yr})$$

$$= \$100(9.818) + \$1,000(0.215)$$

$$= \$981.80 + \$215.00$$

$$= \$1,196.80$$

Thus, when the required rate of return drops to 8 percent, the value of the bond climbs to $1,196.80. As a result, we would be willing to buy this bond *at a premium,* that is, above its par value. Again, this makes sense, because if the bond pays 10 percent in interest and we only require an 8-percent return, we'd be willing to pay more than $1,000 for it.

In reflecting upon this example, you'll notice that as your required rate of return goes up, the value of the bond drops, and when your required rate of return goes down, the value of the bond increases. What can cause your required rate of return to change? First, if the firm that issued the bond becomes riskier, your required rate of return should rise. The result of this would be a drop in the value of the bond—that certainly makes intuitive sense. A second factor that can cause you to alter your required rate of return on a bond is a change in general interest rates in the market. Perhaps there is an increase in expected inflation and, as a result, you demand a higher return for delaying consumption, pushing interest rates up—remember, that's part of Axiom 1. That means that you can now earn a higher return on alternative investments. As a result, you won't buy this bond unless its return is adjusted upward to meet the competition. Thus, when interest rates in general rise, the value of outstanding bonds falls. Since, the value of these bonds falls, so does their price. Alternatively, when interest rates fall, the value and price of outstanding bonds rise. As we'll see, this inverse relationship between bond values or prices and interest rates is extremely important.

Understanding Why Bonds Fluctuate in Value

Obviously, if you invest in bonds, it's important to know what makes them move up and down in value, and therefore in price. Let's begin by summarizing the key relationship that underlies bond valuation. *There's an inverse relationship between interest rates and bond values in the secondary market: When interest rates rise, bond values drop, and when interest rates drop, bond values rise.*

As interest rates rise, investors demand a higher return on bonds. If a bond has a coupon interest rate that's already fixed, the only way the bond can increase its return to investors is to drop in value and sell for less. Thus, we have an inverse relationship between interest rates and bond values (and prices).

AXIOM #5

The Curse of Competitive Investment Markets—Why It's Hard to Find Exceptionally Profitable Investments

Stop and Think

Your immediate reaction to learning of this inverse relationship between interest rates and bond prices may be to try to use it to make money. Before you forecast interest rates and invest in bonds, let's think back to **Axiom 5: The Curse of Competitive Investment Markets—Why It's Hard to Find Exceptionally Profitable Investments**. From this axiom we learned that beating the market is extremely difficult. To use this inverse relationship between interest rates and bond prices, you not only have to forecast interest rates, but you have to outforecast the experts. Knowing which way interest rates are going will not be enough if other investors know the same thing—in that case, the interest rate changes will already be built into the bond prices. You need to know which way interest rates are going when no one else knows. Unfortunately, beating the experts is a tough job. It's like trying to beat Grant Hill at a game of one-on-one basketball. The purpose in presenting this bond valuation relationship isn't to set you on the path to extraordinary profits through bond trading, but to help you understand why bond prices fluctuate and the risks associated with them.

FIGURE 15.3

The Relationship Between Bond Prices and Changes in Interest Rates
When yields (interest rates) increase, bond prices decrease.

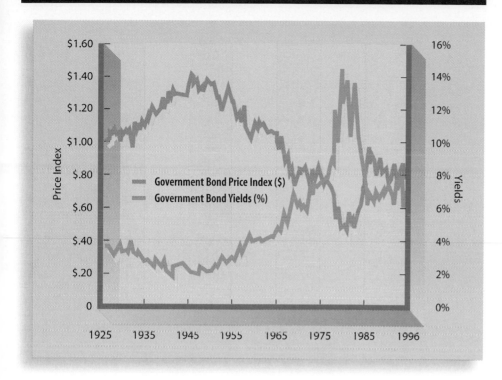

Source: © *The Asset Allocation Decision* Presentation 1990–1997. Ibbotson Associates, Chicago. Used with permission. All rights reserved.

The importance of this relationship can't be overstated. Bond prices fluctuate dramatically, and this relationship explains much of the fluctuation. For example, in 1994 interest rates went up, and as a result long-term Treasury bonds posted average losses of 7.8 percent. Then, in 1995, interest rates dropped, with those same bonds returning 31.7 percent. Interest rates turned the other way in 1996, and as a result, Treasury bonds returned –0.9 percent in 1996. Figure 15.3 shows the relationship between bond prices and interest rates since the end of 1925 and illustrates the inverse relationship that exists between them.

Not only do bond values change when interest rates change, but *longer-term bonds fluctuate in price more than shorter-term bonds.* Remember from chapter 3 that the further in the future a cash flow is, the more its present value will fluctuate as a result of a change in the interest or discount rate. Thus, when interest rates change, longer-term bonds fluctuate in price more than shorter-term bonds. Figure 15.4 shows how between 1970 and 1996, long-term bonds bounced up and down much more dramatically in response to interest rate changes than did short-term bonds. In addition, *as a bond approaches its maturity date, its market value approaches its par or maturity value.* Without question, a bond will sell for its par or maturity value at maturity when the bond's terminated. We know this because at maturity the bondholder receives the par value from the issuer, and the bond is terminated. As a result, as the bond approaches maturity, the market price of the bond approaches its par value. Figure 15.5 illustrates this point. Finally, *when interest rates go down, bond prices go up, but the upward price movement on bonds with a call provision is limited by the call price.* In effect,

FIGURE 15.4

The Relationship Between the Length of a Bond's Maturity and the Amount of Price Fluctuation That Occurs When Interest Rates Change

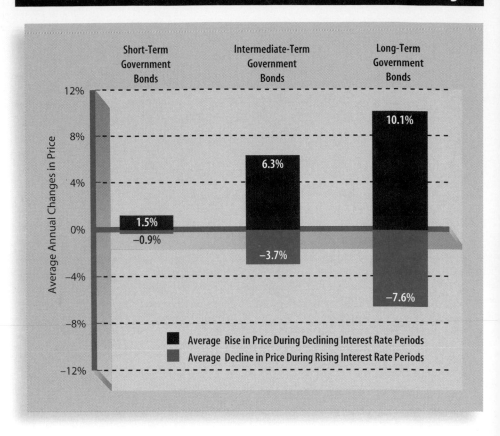

Source: © *The Asset Allocation Decision* Presentation 1990–1997. Ibbotson Associates, Chicago. Used with permission. All rights reserved.

investors simply won't pay more than the call price for a bond, because they know that it could be called away from them for that price at any time.

Bond Valuation Relationships: What They Mean to the Investor

Several important points can be gleaned from the discussion of bond valuation relationships. You know that bond prices can fluctuate dramatically and that interest rates drive these changes. In addition, you know that there's an inverse relationship between interest rates and bond prices: When interest rates go up, bond prices go down. Conversely, when interest rates go down, bond prices go up. Given this inverse relationship between interest rates and bond prices:

- If you expect interest rates to go up (and therefore bond prices to fall), you'd want to mute the inverse relationship between interest rates and bond prices by purchasing very short-term bonds. Although there still may be some price fluctuation, it'll be quite minor.

- If you expect interest rates to go down, and therefore bond prices to rise, you'd want to amplify this relationship as much as possible by purchasing bonds with very long maturities that aren't callable. In this case, the bonds will fluctuate as much as possible, and if interest rates go down, the price of the bonds will rise.

FIGURE 15.5

The Price Path of a 12% Coupon Bond Over Its Life

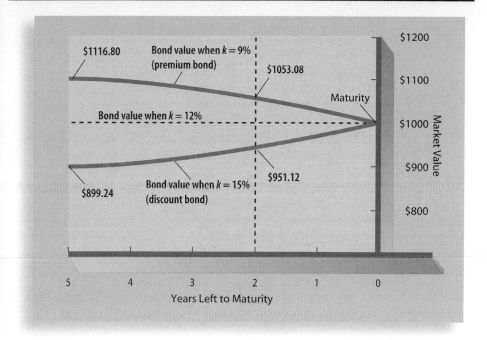

- $1116.80
- Bond value when $k = 9\%$ (premium bond)
- $1053.08
- Bond value when $k = 12\%$
- Maturity
- $899.24
- Bond value when $k = 15\%$ (discount bond)
- $951.12
- $1200
- $1100
- $1000
- $900
- $800
- Market Value
- Years Left to Maturity
- 5 4 3 2 1 0

THE PROS AND CONS OF INVESTING IN BONDS

Before moving on, let's make sure you understand the pros and cons of bonds. The following are some of the benefits of bonds:

- **If interest rates drop, bond prices will rise.**   If interest rates drop, that inverse relationship between interest rates and bond prices will work out in your favor. In that case, you'll want a long-term, noncallable bond.

- **Bonds reduce risk through diversification.**   Any time you add a new investment to your portfolio that doesn't move in tandem with the other investments in your portfolio, you reduce your portfolio's risk.

- **Bonds produce steady current income.**   What more need we say?

- **Bonds can be a safe investment if held to maturity.**   If you hold the bond to maturity and it doesn't default, it'll return exactly what it promises.

The dangers of investing in bonds include the following:

- **If interest rates rise, bond prices will fall.**   The longer the maturity, the more the bond will fluctuate.

- **If the issuer experiences financial problems, the bondholder may pay.**   If an issuer is broke and can't make interest or principal payments, the bond will plummet in value. However, simply experiencing minor financial problems can also cause the bond to drop in value. Of course, any time the bond rating drops—due to financial distress or a bond rater's bad mood—bond values drop like a stone. Thus, not just bankruptcy, but any movement toward bankruptcy or anything that would lower bond ratings can cause a drop in the value of a bond.

LEARNING OBJECTIVE #4

Weigh the risks associated with bond investments.

- **If interest rates drop, rather than experience price appreciation, the bond may be called.** Most corporate bonds are callable. In theory, when interest rates drop, the value of a bond should rise. However, if interest rates drop, the issuer may decide to refinance the bond offering with bonds that have a lower interest rate. As a result, these bonds may be called away from investors, leaving investors to reinvest the proceeds from the called bonds at lower interest rates.
- **If you need to sell your bonds early, you may have a problem selling them at a reasonable price, particularly if they're bonds issued by a smaller corporation.** There simply isn't a strong secondary market for the bonds of smaller corporations. In short, bonds aren't a very liquid investment.
- **Finding a good investment outlet for the interest you receive may be difficult.** If you're using bonds to accumulate wealth, it may be difficult to find a good investment outlet for the interest that you receive from your bond. Without reinvesting the interest payments, there'll be no accumulation of wealth from investing in bonds unless you're investing in zero or very low coupon bonds—that's the whole idea of compounding and the time value of money.

LEARNING OBJECTIVE #4

Weigh the risks associated with bond investments.

PICKING A GOOD BOND

Now that you know something about bonds, let's put it all together with some things to look for in picking out a good bond to invest in.

- **Think about taxes.** Make sure you consider the effect of taxes. Consider municipals, particularly if you're in a high tax bracket.
- **Keep that inverse relationship between interest rates and bond prices in mind.** If interest rates are very low, the only way they can go is up (which would cause bond prices to drop), so you might want to invest in shorter-term bonds.
- **Avoid losers and don't worry about picking winners.** This advice applies if you're buying a corporate bond rather than a government bond. First, you must keep in mind that with corporate bonds you get the same return unless the firm defaults. That is, whether the firm does exceedingly well or poorly, you still receive the same returns if you hold the bond to maturity. It's only when the firm does horribly and as a result can't make interest or principal payments that the bondholder is affected. When it comes to picking corporate bond issues, look for and avoid firms that might experience major financial problems. All other firms are pretty much the same.
- **Consider only high-quality bonds.** Limit yourself to bonds rated AA or above. In this way you minimize any worry regarding a possible default by the issuer.
- **Buy your bond when it's first issued, rather than in the secondary market.** The price is generally fair, and the sales commission on newly issued bonds is paid by the issuer.
- **Avoid bonds that might get called.** Before you buy a bond, ask your broker or financial planner if the bond is likely to be called. If so, pick another one.
- **Match your bond's maturity to your investment time horizon.** Try to pick a bond with a maturity that matches your investment time horizon. In this way you can hold the bond to maturity and avoid having to sell your bond in the secondary market, where you don't always get a fair price.
- **Stick to large issues.** If you think you might have to sell before maturity and are buying a corporate bond, make sure you buy a bond issued by a large corporation—the secondary market is generally more active for them.
- **When in doubt, go Treasury!** If you're still unsure, it's better to be safe than sorry—buy a Treasury bond.

CLIMBING THE LADDER
to Safer Investing

Even if you have no interest in having Brian McMahon manage your investments, you might find something interesting in his management style.

(A) McMahon, managing director at Thornburg Management Co. in Santa Fe, N.M., runs a group of specialized bond funds with "laddered" portfolios. This strategy, which can be used by individual investors as well as the pros, is one practical alternative to trying to outguess the ups and downs of interest rates as you manage your money.

"We practice it carefully, but we certainly didn't invent it," McMahon said. "It's been around for a long time."

A laddered portfolio is made up of a series of bonds or other similar investments that are scheduled to mature at different times. For instance, a simple ladder might be constructed by dividing your nest egg in five parts and buying Treasury securities with remaining lives of one, two, three, four and five years.

Then, as one-fifth of the portfolio matures each year, the proceeds are rolled over into new five-year Treasury notes.

(B) Because some of the securities you own are approaching maturity and others are not, you have diversified the risks that come with interest rate fluctuations.

In effect, you have your portfolio on automatic pilot, and do not need to try to steer around every cloud you encounter as the economy strengthens and weakens and the Federal Reserve adjusts its credit policy.

Source: Chet Currier, "Climbing the Ladder to Safer Investing," *The Washington Post*, April 7, 1996, p. H3. Copyright © The Associated Press. Used by permission.

Analysis and Implications...

A. With a laddered portfolio, you always have bonds coming due, and you in turn invest that money in longer-term bonds. As a result, if you need funds, you don't have to sell your bonds, because a good portion of them should mature in the coming year.

B. As you know, longer-term bonds not only generally return more, but they also fluctuate more. A laddered portfolio allows you to diversify among different bond maturities, thereby reducing risk.

LEARNING OBJECTIVE #5

Compare preferred stock to bonds as an investment option.

Preferred Stock

Stock that offers no ownership or voting rights and generally pays fixed dividends. The dividends on preferred stock are paid out before dividends on common stock can be issued.

Cumulative Feature

A feature of preferred stock that requires all past unpaid preferred stock dividends to have been paid before any common stock dividends can be declared.

Adjustable-Rate Preferred Stock

Preferred stock on which the quarterly dividends fluctuate with the market interest rate.

Convertible Preferred Stock

Preferred stock that the holder can exchange for a predetermined number of shares of common stock.

PREFERRED STOCK—AN ALTERNATIVE TO INVESTING IN BONDS

Preferred stock is often referred to as a hybrid security because it has many of the characteristics of both common stock and bonds, but from the investor's point of view, preferred stock is probably closer to bonds. On the one hand, preferred stock is similar to common stock in that it has no fixed maturity date and not paying its dividends won't bring on bankruptcy. On the other hand, preferred stock is similar to bonds in that its dividends are of a fixed size and are paid before common stock dividends are paid. A share of preferred stock is also similar to a bond in that it doesn't carry voting rights.

The size of the preferred stock dividend is generally fixed either as a dollar amount or as a percentage of the preferred stock's par value. Because these dividends are fixed, preferred stockholders don't share in any profits of the firm but are limited to their stated annual dividend. Thus, just as with a bond, if the firm has a great year and earns lots of money, your preferred stock dividend doesn't change.

Features and Characteristics of Preferred Stock

To gain a better understanding of preferred stock, let's take a moment to look at some of its features and characteristics.

Multiple Issues of Preferred Stock. A firm can issue more than one issue of preferred stock, each with a different set dividend. In fact, some firms have well over 10 different issues of preferred stock outstanding.

Cumulative Feature. Most preferred stock carries a **cumulative feature**, which requires that all past unpaid preferred stock dividends be paid before any common stock dividends are declared. This feature provides the preferred stock investor with some degree of protection, because without such a feature, there'd be no reason why preferred stock dividends wouldn't be omitted or passed when common stock dividends are passed.

Adjustable Rate. In the early 1980s, **adjustable-rate preferred stock** was first introduced to provide investors with some protection against wide swings in the value of preferred stock that resulted from interest rate swings. With adjustable-rate preferred stock, the amount of quarterly dividends fluctuates with interest rates under a formula that ties the dividend payment to a market interest rate. As a result, when interest rates rise, rather than the value of the preferred stock dropping, the preferred stock's dividend rises and the value of the preferred stock stays relatively constant.

Convertibility. Some preferred stock is also **convertible preferred stock**, which means that its holder can, at any time, exchange it for a predetermined number of shares of common stock. The trade-off associated with convertible preferred stock is that the convertibility feature may allow the preferred stockholder to participate in the company's capital gains, but the preferred stock has a lower dividend associated with it than does regular preferred stock.

Callability. Much of the preferred stock outstanding is callable. Just as with bonds, if interest rates drop, there's a good chance that the preferred stock will be called away from the investor by the issuing firm.

The Valuation of Preferred Stock

When you buy a share of preferred stock, you get a steady stream of preferred stock dividends that go on forever, because preferred stock never matures. Thus, *the value of a share of preferred stock is simply the present value of the perpetual stream of constant dividends that the preferred stockholder receives.* As such, the value of a share of preferred stock can be written as follows:

$$\frac{\text{value of}}{\text{preferred stock}} = \frac{\text{present value of the perpetual}}{\text{stream of constant dividends}}$$

Because the preferred stock dividends go on forever, they constitute a perpetuity (remember this term from chapter 3). The calculation of their present value can be reduced to

$$\frac{\text{value of}}{\text{preferred stock}} = \frac{\text{annual preferred stock dividend}}{\text{required rate of return}}$$

When interest rates rise (causing your required rate of return to rise), the value of a share of preferred stock declines. Conversely, when interest rates decline (causing your required rate of return to drop), the value of a share of preferred stock rises. This is the primary valuation relationship in valuing preferred stock and, as we just saw, in valuing bonds.

Let's look at an example. If the Gap has an issue of preferred stock outstanding with an annual dividend of $4, and given the level of risk on this issue, investors demand a required rate of return of 10 percent on this preferred stock, its value would be

$$\frac{\text{value of}}{\text{preferred stock}} = \frac{\$4}{0.10} = \$40$$

As you can see, if the required rate of return on this preferred stock dropped to 8 percent, its value would climb to $4/0.08, or $50. Thus, as market interest rates rise and fall (causing investors' required rates of return to rise and fall), the value of preferred stock moves in an opposite manner.

The Risks Associated with Investing in Preferred Stock

We've said that preferred stock is a hybrid between bonds and common stock. Unfortunately, when it comes to advantages and disadvantages for the investor, it's also a hybrid, taking disadvantages from both common stock and bonds but taking advantages from neither. The problems with preferred stock for the individual investor include the following:

- If interest rates rise, the value of the preferred stock drops.
- If interest rates drop, the value of the preferred stock rises and the preferred stock is called away from the investor (remember, most preferred stock is callable).
- The investor doesn't participate in the capital gains that common stockholders receive.
- The investor doesn't have the safety of bond interest payments, because preferred stock dividends can be passed without the risk of bankruptcy.

Given all these drawbacks and very few advantages, you may be wondering who buys preferred stock. The answer is, other corporations, because corporations receive a tax break on the dividend income from preferred stock.

> ### *Stop and Think*
> Preferred stock just doesn't compete well with the alternatives. Common stock offers better growth potential, bonds are safer if you're interested in income, and if all goes well, they will probably be called. Given this, who buys preferred stock? Actually, corporations buy it. That's because they get a tax break on any dividend income they receive from preferred stock.

LEARNING OBJECTIVE #6

Understand the risks associated with investing in real estate.

INVESTING IN REAL ESTATE

Since the end of World War II, real estate investments have served to create more fortunes than almost any other investment. Unfortunately, since the late 1980s, those same real estate investments have also destroyed quite a few fortunes. Still, real estate remains a popular investment, particularly for the very wealthy.

Most American households—in fact, about two-thirds of them—own their own homes, and for them, it's the biggest investment they're likely to make. In fact, as we saw in chapter 8, housing costs take up over 26 percent of their after-tax income. The question now becomes, Do you want to go beyond this personal investment and make an additional investment in real estate? First, let's discuss what types of investments in real estate you might consider. Real estate investments can be categorized as either direct or indirect. With a direct investment, you directly own the property. This type of investment might include a vacation home or commercial property—for example, an apartment building or undeveloped land. With an indirect investment, you're an investor in a group that owns the property and has hired a professional to manage the property. Indirect investments include partnerships that buy and manage property, called real estate syndicates, and investment companies that pool the money of many investors and invest in real estate, called real estate investment trusts, or REITs.

Direct Investments

Vacation homes are the most popular of all the direct real estate investments. However, since 1987 their investment appeal has suffered severely because of a change in the tax laws that now views your vacation home as a second home only if you don't rent it out for more than 14 days per year. The significance of this change is that only if your vacation home is viewed as a second home can you deduct your mortgage interest and taxes when you compute your income taxes. If you rent your vacation home for more than 14 days per year, which many investors do, it's considered rental property, and your deductions are determined by how the property is managed and your income. In the best case, your income will cover your expenses, providing you with a home rent-free during vacations, but this generally isn't the case. Because of the complexity surrounding the tax benefits of a vacation home, you really need the help of a tax accountant or financial planner to adequately analyze a vacation home before you invest. Even then, you should realize that much of your return is likely to depend on the future price appreciation of your vacation home. The bottom line is that if you buy a vacation home, it should be bought for pleasure, not investment purposes. As rental property, vacation homes are best left to professionals.

Commercial property, such as apartment buildings, duplexes, and office buildings, are also best left to the professional—those who specialize in the management of such investments. It's simply too active an investment for most individuals. Not only does management of such property take a good deal of sophistication, but evaluating a price for commercial property is complicated beyond the ability of most nonprofessionals. As such, this is another area that the individual investor should avoid. Fortunately, there are enough good investment opportunities in stocks and bonds to make passing on real estate relatively painless.

Investing in undeveloped land, although popular among very rich and sophisticated investors, is risky, and because the land is undeveloped, it doesn't produce any cash flow. In fact, because you have to pay taxes on the undeveloped land, it produces a cash outflow while you're holding it. Obviously, the purpose of buying undeveloped land is to have it rise in value and then sell it later. However, developing the land to the point where it climbs in price can cost a lot of money. Moreover, there's no guarantee that the land will rise in price. As a result, this, too, is better left to the experts.

Indirect Investments

Indirect investments in real estate, because you're working directly with professional managers, are better suited for the individual investor. Unfortunately, the appeal of real estate syndicates was severely dampened as a result of tax reform in the late 1980s. Again, evaluating how attractive an investment a real estate syndicate actually is can be quite difficult. As a result, this is another investment alternative that should be left to the experts.

The most attractive real estate alternative is the real estate investment trust, or REIT. Because this type of investment is akin to a mutual fund that specializes in real estate investments, we'll hold off discussion of this investment alternative until mutual funds are presented in chapter 16.

Investing in Real Estate: The Bottom Line

Without question, the major draw for investing in real estate is the income that the property can generate coupled with the opportunity for capital gains as the property rises in value over time. Unfortunately, the tax advantages that helped produce real estate fortunes in the past are largely gone or are on the way out. In addition, direct investments in real estate are very active forms of investing, in which time, energy, and knowledge are all important ingredients. Why work that hard when you don't have to?

Other drawbacks to investing in real estate include illiquidity. That is, if you do have to sell your property holdings, it may take months to find a buyer, and there's no guarantee that you'll actually get what you feel is a fair price. In addition, overbuilding in some areas has actually resulted in a decline of property prices. For example, Southern California has seen dramatic drops in property values in recent years. The bottom line here is that real estate investment is not well suited to the novice investor.

INVESTING (SPECULATING) IN GOLD, SILVER, GEMS, AND COLLECTIBLES

Don't do it! Putting your money in gold, silver, platinum, precious stones, and the like is speculation. When we differentiated between investing and speculating in chapter 12, we said that with investing, as opposed to speculating, the value of your asset is determined by what return it earns, not merely by whether that asset is a fashionable asset to own or not. If an asset doesn't generate a return, its value is determined by supply and demand, and putting money in it is speculating.

LEARNING OBJECTIVE #7

Know why you shouldn't *invest* in gold, silver, gems, or collectibles.

Gold, silver, platinum, diamonds, rubies, and collectibles are perfect examples of speculation. Look at gold. Since 1982 it's been selling for between $320 and $500—most recently (mid-1997) at the low end of this price range. Still, on late-night infomercials across the nation you'll still see hucksters proclaiming gold as "the place for your savings." Don't buy into their sales pitch—it's simply another form of speculation. The bottom line is, "Invest," don't speculate.

Collectibles deserve a bit more discussion because as entertainment, they're a perfectly fine purchase, but they shouldn't be confused with investments. Again, they involve speculation, not investment. Stamps, coins, comic books, and baseball cards, for example, are worth more in the future only if someone's willing to pay more for them. Their value depends entirely on supply and demand, and it doesn't always go up, as the baseball card "crash" in the early 1990s demonstrates. Does this mean you should avoid collectibles? Yes, if you're looking to them as an investment. Remember, as we learned in chapter 12, investment is quite a bit duller and more certain than speculation, but when you're dealing with your future financial security, dull and certain aren't bad things. However, if you want to spend your money on collectibles for entertainment purposes, go ahead. They can be fun, but don't expect them to provide for your financial future. I (the author), for example, collect old *Mad* magazines, not for investment purposes, but for fun. There's no question that their price may go down, but to me, that's not a concern ("What, me worry?"), because they aren't an investment and aren't intended to be sold. Thus, when it comes to buying collectibles, you should consider purchasing them only if you aren't concerned about what might happen to their price in the future, because they aren't an investment.

The Facts of Life

Some people make fortunes dealing in collectibles. Look at Mike Gidwitz, for example, a collector and investment adviser from Chicago. In 1997 he paid a record $640,500 for the hobby's most famous and valuable card, the T206 Honus Wagner. Mike is a very interesting person who also owns the original paintings for the covers of 44 *Mad Magazines*. But as Mike says, "I look at baseball cards like gambling—if you can't afford to lose the money then you shouldn't buy them. I don't buy baseball cards for investment, I buy them for the pleasure I get out of them." That's a good philosophy—keep your investment money out of collectibles.

SUMMARY

Why might you consider investing in bonds? There are several reasons. Bonds reduce risk through diversification, produce steady current income, and if held to maturity, can be a safe investment.

When you invest in a bond and hold it until it matures, your return is based upon two things: (1) semiannual or annual interest payments and (2) the return of the par value or principal. The danger is that the bond issuer will not have the funds to make these payments. There are two measures of return on a bond: current yield and yield to maturity. The current yield on a bond refers to the ratio of the annual interest payment to the bond's market price. The yield to maturity is the true yield or return that the bondholder receives if the bond is held to maturity.

There are thousands of bonds outstanding that have been issued by corporations, the U.S. government and its agencies, states, and localities. There are also a number of special situation bonds, including zero coupon bonds, which are simply bonds that

Just Do It! *From the Desk of Marcy Furney, CFP*

A Bonding Experience

☑ Because you don't have to pay tax on the earnings of Series EE savings bonds until you cash them, they can serve as a tax-deferred account for any funds that you need to keep liquid. Consider them an alternative to bank savings accounts for money you don't wish to expose to any risk of loss of principal.

☑ Be aware of the potential downside of pass-through certificates. Because they're a pool of mortgages, homeowners' reactions to interest rates determine their outcome. If interest rates fall, a number of mortgagees will refinance, and you'll start getting your principal back in large chunks. Normally, the older the mortgage pool, the greater the principal return. This means you must deal with some reinvestment risk throughout the life of the pool rather than just at a future maturity date. In other words, where will you put the return of principal in a falling interest rate environment?

☑ The tax-free nature of municipal bonds may not be truly beneficial to everyone. Compute the equivalent taxable return for your tax bracket before you choose them. If you're in a low bracket, you may find that you can make enough with taxable alternatives to pay the taxes and still come out ahead. If you are attempting to avoid state income tax, buy municipals for your state of residence. Keep in mind that, while dividends are income tax-free, capital gains are not.

☑ If you're relying on a steady income flow from bonds, make sure they're not callable and that you hold them to maturity. Laddering the maturity of bonds will help stabilize income and reduce the amount of funds exposed to reinvestment risk at any one time. Liquid funds are available at each maturity, so selling a bond to get money for other needs is seldom necessary.

☑ Even if you're an aggressive investor, don't discount the value of holding some bonds for diversification. They may be boring when the market is riding high, but you'll appreciate them when they slow the downward spiral of your portfolio.

☑ Owning a bond mutual fund is not the same as holding individual bonds. In a fund, the average maturity and manager's trading activity will determine the impact of price volatility when interest rates change. If you hold individual bonds to maturity, price volatility is not a factor you must deal with.

don't pay interest, and junk bonds, or low-rated bonds, also called high-yield bonds, which are bonds rated BB or below.

The value of a bond is simply the present value of the stream of interest payments plus the present value of the repayment of the bond's par value at maturity. There's an inverse relationship between the value of a bond and the investors' required rate of return. Thus, when the required rate of return goes up, the value of the bond drops, and when the investor's required rate of return goes down, the value of the bond increases.

Preferred stock is a security with no fixed maturity date and with dividends that are generally set in amount and don't fluctuate. Just as with bonds, a firm can issue more than one series or class of preferred stock, each with unique characteristics. In addition, most preferred stock carries a cumulative feature, which requires that all past unpaid preferred stock dividends be paid before any common stock dividends are declared.

Real estate investments can be categorized as either direct or indirect investments. With a direct investment, you directly own the property, but with an indirect investment, you're an investor in a group that owns the property and has hired a professional to manage the property. These are probably investments best left to the professional.

Gold, silver, platinum, diamonds, rubies, and collectibles are perfect examples of speculation, and should be avoided. As such, you should only consider purchasing them if you aren't concerned about what might happen to their price in the future, because they aren't an investment.

Review Questions

1. Briefly describe the difference between owning equity in a firm and owning a bond issued by a firm. (LO 1)
2. Name three reasons investors might wish to add bonds to their portfolios. (LO 1)
3. As a bond investor, would you prefer to invest in a bond with or without a call provision? (LO 2)
4. What is an indenture, and why is it an important document for bond investors? (LO 2)
5. Why are government bonds considered risk-free? Describe the possibility of default risk associated with Treasury bonds. (LO 2)
6. Differentiate between Treasury bills, notes, and bonds in terms of maturity and yield. (LO 2)
7. What type of entities issue municipal bonds? What significant feature of municipal bonds attracts investors? Given this feature, are municipal bonds more attractive to some investors than to others? (LO 2)
8. What is a zero coupon bond? Give an example of when the use of zero coupon bonds might be appropriate in an investment portfolio. Do you think this type of bond should be owned in taxable or tax-deferred accounts? (LO 2)
9. What is a junk bond? Using published ratings, how would an investor know if a given bond is a junk bond? Compared to AAA long-term bonds, how much more, at a minimum, should investors expect to receive in interest if they purchase junk bonds? Why? (LO 2)
10. Which yield should long-term investors be interested in calculating, current yield or yield to maturity? Why? (LO 2)
11. An investor's required rate of return is important when valuing a bond. What two factors can cause an investor's required rate of return to change? (LO 3)
12. What three features should investors look for when examining preferred stock? What feature, similar to bonds, should cause investors to demand a higher dividend yield? (LO 5)
13. Provide three examples of direct real estate investments. (LO 6)
14. Provide five examples of speculation. What distinguishes these "investments" from such investments as stocks, bonds, and real estate? (LO 7)

Problems and Activities

1. Suppose that you're interested in purchasing a bond from TYU Corporation. The bond is quoted in the *Wall Street Journal* as selling for 78⅝. How much will you pay for the bond if you purchase it at the quoted price? Assuming you hold the bond until maturity, how much will you receive at that time? (LO 1)
2. Rank the following bonds in the following two ways: (a) safest, A, to riskiest, E, and (b) highest yield, 1, to lowest yield, 2. (LO 1)
   - U.S. Treasury 5-year note
   - AAA 5-year corporate bond
   - Ginnie Mae pass-through certificate with 5 years remaining until maturity
   - BBB 5-year corporate bond
   - 5-year revenue municipal bond

3. You own a Treasury inflation-indexed bond with a par value of $1,000 that will increase 4 percent for every 1 percent increase in the consumer price index. You're currently receiving 3.25 percent interest. (LO 2)
   a. How much annual interest do you currently receive?
   b. Assuming interest rates increase 1 percent, how much (in dollars) will the par value of the bond increase?
   c. Assuming interest rates increase 1 percent, how much annual interest will you now receive?
4. If you want to purchase a $100 Series EE savings bond, how much will you initially need to purchase the bond? Assuming the bond earns 4 percent annually, approximately how long will it take for the bond to reach its stated face value? (LO 2)
5. An investor is considering purchasing a bond with a 6.50 percent coupon interest rate, a par value of $1,000, and a market price of $850. The bond will mature in 9 years. Based on this information, answer the following questions: (LO 3)
   a. What is the bond's current yield?
   b. What is the bond's approximate yield to maturity using the formula on page 483?
   c. What is the bond's yield to maturity using a financial calculator?
6. Three friends, Bob, Mary, and Kai, have asked you to determine the equivalent taxable yield on a municipal bond. The bond's current yield is 3.30 percent, with 8 years left until maturity. Bob is in the 15-percent tax bracket, Mary is in the 28-percent bracket, and Kai is in the 38-percent bracket. Calculate the equivalent taxable yield for your three friends. Assuming a similar AAA corporate bond yields 4 percent, which of your friends should purchase the municipal bond? (LO 3)
7. A highly rated corporate bond with 5 years left until maturity was recently quoted as selling for 105½. The bond's par value is $1,000, and its initial interest rate was 6 percent. If this bond pays interest every 6 months, and it has been 4 months since interest was last paid, how much will you be required to pay for the bond? (LO 3)
8. If the par value of a Treasury bond you're interested in purchasing is $10,000, how much would you pay if the bond were "asked" at 99:32? (LO 2)
9. Using Appendices E and C, calculate the value of the following bonds: (LO 3)

Par Value	Interest Rate	Required Rate of Return	Years to Maturity Value
$1,000	8%	8%	10
$1,000	8%	12%	10
$1,000	8%	7%	10

10. What is the value of preferred stock that pays an annual dividend of $4.75 when the required rate of return is 10 percent? What is the value when the required rate of return changes to 8 percent and 13 percent, respectively? (LO 5)

Suggested Projects

1. Using the World Wide Web, connect to the Federal Reserve Bank Web page (www.frb.gov) to determine your nearest regional Federal Reserve Bank. Using the home page to either link to your regional bank site or obtain the bank's mailing address, request information on the Treasury Direct program. What do you think is the single greatest advantage involved in purchasing U.S. government securities directly versus through a broker? According to the text, if you need to sell bonds held in the Treasury Direct program, what must you do? (LO 2)
2. Think about the advantages offered by municipal bonds. In terms of marginal tax rates, what type of investor should consider investing in municipal bonds? Is there an advantage to purchasing municipal bonds issued by the state in which you live? If yes, what is that advantage? (LO 2)

WWW.
Take It to the Net

We invite you to visit the Keown Personal Finance page on the Prentice Hall Web site at:

http://www.prenhall.com/persfin

for this chapter's World Wide Web exercise.

You might also want to visit the following Web sites:

Fixed Income Home Page (prices on bonds): http://www.fixedincome.com

MMR Software (find out what your Series EE savings bonds are worth): http://www.mmrsoft.com/

Investor Guide (a strong investing section): http://www.investorguide.com

CNNfn The Financial Network: http://www.cnnfn.com/

Microsoft Investor: http://investor.msn.com

3. Do you think a college student who lives in New York and is in the 15 percent federal marginal tax bracket should consider buying a municipal bond or bond fund if she needs an interest-earning investment? Why or why not? Would your answer differ if the student lived in a tax-free state, such as Nevada, Texas, or Washington? (LO 2)

4. Cities, towns, counties, and states issue municipal bonds that are traded in the open market. Such firms as Moody's and Standard & Poor's provide ratings on thousands of these bonds. Using your library's subscription to these ranking publications, record either Moody's or Standard & Poor's ratings for bonds issued by the city, county, and state where you currently reside. Were the bonds you found general obligation or revenue bonds? Was there a significant difference in ratings between different bonds offered by different agencies? How do you think different ratings will impact interest rates between bonds? (LO 2)

5. A wealthy uncle has asked you to help him value a potential bond portfolio. Unfortunately, your uncle doesn't understand why some bonds sell well below or well above stated par values. He has asked your assistance in clarifying how to value a bond. How would you explain the concept of present value both in technical and layman's terms? What does your uncle need to provide you with before you can begin to value a bond using the formula given in the text? (LO 3)

6. After reading this chapter, a classmate has come to you confidentially after class to discuss making some money trading bonds based on an interest rate projection formula she learned in economics class. She tells you that it's easy to make money whenever interest rates fall, because bond prices always move in the opposite direction of interest rates. Do you think that your classmate is correct in her thinking? Using Axiom 5, discuss why it's hard to find exceptionally profitable trading opportunities. (LO 5)

7. Until recently, investors purchased bonds almost entirely for income. Over the past 20 years, investors have witnessed increased bond price volatility and the advent of junk bonds. Assume that you were going to advise a favorite relative on picking a good bond. Using as many of this chapter's concepts as possible, put together a discussion list to share with your relative. (List at least five points.) (LO 5)

8. Provide three or four examples of collectibles and whether you agree with the rule that "collectibles are a form of speculation and should be avoided." Explain your answer. Under what circumstances should someone consider purchasing speculative investments? (LO 7)

Discussion Case 1

Jan and Karen are just beginning their lives together, and since graduating from college 3 years ago, they've been able to save about $10,000. Most of their money is in the bank, but they've recently started working on a financial plan with a stockbroker. The broker has recommended that they invest 70 percent of their savings in stocks, 20 percent in bonds, and 10 percent in a money market account. Jan and Karen have come to you because they're concerned about making a decision regarding the purchase of a bond. They aren't sure whether they should buy a government, a corporate, or a municipal bond. Based on your readings from this chapter, you are able to find out that their marginal tax bracket is 28 percent. You know that their risk level is relatively low, and that interest rates have been very volatile over the past year. You're also able to determine that the broker offered the following bond options for Jan and Karen: (a) a 15-year revenue municipal bond from an adjacent state yielding 5.50 percent, (b) a 10-year U.S. Treasury bond yielding 6.80 percent, (c) a BBB-rated corporate bond yielding 8.50 percent, and (d) an AAA-rated corporate bond yielding 7.75 percent.

(continued)

Questions

1. Based on an analysis of equivalent after-tax yields, which bond offers the best yield?
2. Based on your knowledge of the bond markets, rank the bonds in terms of default risk.
3. If interest rates were to increase, would the value of the bonds increase or decrease? Which bond would be impacted the most?
4. Assume that Jan and Karen have a required rate of return of 12 percent. Calculate the current value of each bond (assuming a $1,000 par value for each bond).
5. Before picking a bond fund, what factors should Jan and Karen take into account?
6. Assuming Jan and Karen are interested in purchasing only one bond, which bond would you recommend? Provide a brief overview of the factors you took into consideration before making your recommendation.

Discussion Case 2

Your landlord has learned that you're taking a course in personal finance. She's very interested in talking with you about certain bond investments that she has just inherited, and since she knows nothing about investing, she hopes that you can help her evaluate a chart that she received from her broker. Apparently, your landlord owns seven corporate bonds, ranging in maturity from 3 to 20 years. The chart below indicates the bond, its Standard & Poor's rating, its maturity, and its current yield.

Bond	Standard & Poor's Rating	Years to Maturity	Current Yield
ABC Corporation	AAA	3	9.00%
XYX Industries	AA	5	8.25%
INTL Limited	A	7	7.00%
MED Corporation	BBB	10	9.00%
SPEC Incorporated	BBB	12	7.00%
LAM Corporation	CCC, CC	15	10.00%
BAD Incorporated	C	20	11.00%

Your landlord senses that something may be wrong in the bond portfolio. Use what you've learned in this chapter to answer the following questions.

Questions

1. Using an eyeball review of the yields, does anything stand out that would warrant your landlord's sense of worry?
2. In terms of bond maturity dates, what should an investor expect? What is happening in this example?
3. In terms of Standard & Poor's ratings, are the differences in yields reasonable?
4. Using your responses from questions b and c, is your landlord being adequately compensated for the risk she is taking?
5. What is the minimum interest rate differential that your landlord should expect between an AAA-rated bond and a BBB-rated bond? Is this the case in the example?
6. If interest rates were to increase by 1 percent or 2 percent, which of the bonds would be least affected? Why?
7. If your landlord asked for a recommendation on which bonds to sell and which to buy more of, what would be your recommendation?

Chapter 16

MUTUAL FUNDS:
An Easy Way to Diversify

It's been a long, and unusual, road to the top for Scott Adams. He worked at Crocker Bank in San Francisco from 1979 to 1986 before moving on to Pacific Bell. At Pacific Bell he was earning about $70,000 and working in cubicle 4S700R when he was fired on June 30, 1995—"budget constraints" was the reason given. For most people, getting laid off from a high-paying job would have been devastating, but for Adams, the creator of the Dilbert comic strip, his job had become a social release and more of a source of material than of income. He began drawing his comic strip about Dilbert, a mouthless engineer with a perpetually bent necktie, and company back in 1989. Today, *Dilbert* appears in more than 1,200 newspapers in 29 countries. Adams's Dilbert books ride the top of the best-sellers list, and his speaking fee is now up to $10,000 a speech (he gives about 35 per year). In short, he's doing a lot better than he was at Pacific Bell, although he won't reveal his actual earnings because, as he says, "my family might expect better gifts from me."

What does Adams do with all his money? He invests it in mutual funds. That might not be what you'd expect from a guy who's used his cartoon to make fun of mutual funds. In one comic strip, he had Dilbert consulting with a financial advisor who was pushing his firm's "churn 'n' burn" family of mutual funds. "We'll turn your worth-

less equity into valuable brokerage fees in just three days!" the advisor raved. In another strip, he had Dogbert, Dilbert's potato-shaped dog and companion, set himself up as a financial consultant and announce that "I'll tell all my clients to invest in the 'Dogbert Deferred Earnings Fund.'" "Isn't that a conflict of interests?" Dilbert asks. "Only if I show interest in the client," replies Dogbert.

Adams tried picking his own stocks for a while, but decided to hand his money over to the professionals. "My

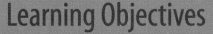

Learning Objectives

After reading this chapter you should be able to:

1. Weigh the advantages and disadvantages of investing in mutual funds.
2. Differentiate between open- and closed-end mutual funds, unit investment trusts, and real estate investment trusts.
3. Classify mutual funds according to their objectives.
4. Use those mutual fund services that best meet your needs.
5. Select a mutual fund that's right for you.
6. Calculate mutual fund returns.

years of dabbling versus the experts just showed me that they were better than me." Today he primarily relies on the Morningstar fund rankings he picks up off America Online, not to pick stocks, but to pick which mutual funds to invest in.

Scott Adams, like so many small or novice investors, has found mutual funds to be an ideal way of entering and maintaining a presence in the market. There's an awful lot of comfort in first entering the market by letting a professional manager do all the work for you. As more and more investors have taken advantage of this comfort, mutual funds have seen a dramatic surge in popularity in recent years. In fact, there are approximately 6,000 mutual funds to choose from today—up from a mere 161 mutual funds in 1960. Not only has the number of mutual funds skyrocketed, but the total assets of mutual funds have also—to over $3.5 trillion by year-end 1996. As Figure 16.1 shows, this is an annual growth rate of 22 percent over the past 20 years.

Mutual funds aren't another category of investments. Instead, they're simply a way of holding such investments as stocks and bonds. They pool your money with that of other investors and invest it in stocks, bonds, and various short-term securities. Professional managers then tend this investment, making sure it grows nicely. Mutual funds let you diversify even with smaller investment amounts. In fact, your investment may be only $1,000 or even less, and with that investment you may own a fraction (a very small fraction at that) of up to 1,000 different stocks. It's this instant diversification that makes mutual funds so popular with many investors. Remember, as **Axiom 3** tells us, **Diversification Reduces Risk**, and mutual funds give smaller investors the same ability to diversify and reduce risk as big investors with lots of money have. Still, not all mutual funds are created equally—at least from the investor's perspective. This chapter will help you to be careful in choosing the right mutual fund and avoiding the "churn 'n' burn" family of funds.

Mutual Fund
An investment fund that raises funds from investors, pools the money, and invests it in stocks, bonds, and other investments. Each investor owns a share of the fund proportionate to the amount of his or her investment.

AXIOM #3

Diversification Reduces Risk

FIGURE 16.1

Mutual Fund Growth

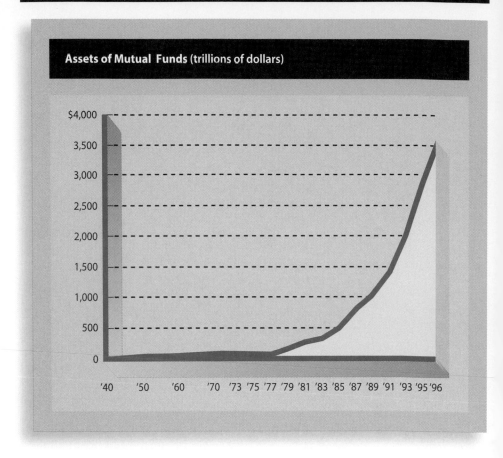

Assets of Mutual Funds (trillions of dollars)

Source: Investment Company Institute, *1997 Fact Book*, 37th ed. (Washington, DC, 1997).

WHY INVEST IN MUTUAL FUNDS?

Investing in mutual funds provides you with a bevy of benefits, especially if you're a small investor. In effect, mutual funds serve to level the investments playing field between large and small investors. Unfortunately, there are also drawbacks to investing in mutual funds. These disadvantages don't offset the advantages of mutual funds, particularly for small investors, but it's good to know what they are. After all, forewarned is forearmed. Let's take a look at first the advantages and then the disadvantages of investing in mutual funds.

Advantages of Mutual Fund Investing

- **Diversification.**   Mutual funds are an inexpensive way to instantly diversify. For the small investor, this is an extremely important benefit. If you have only $10,000 to invest, it'd be difficult to diversify your security holding without paying exorbitant commissions. But, when you invest in a mutual fund, you're purchasing a small fraction of the mutual fund's already diversified holdings. Table 16.1 provides a listing of just a portion of the securities held by Fidelity's Low-Priced Fund. As you can see, that degree of diversification simply couldn't be obtained by an individual investor with limited funds.

TABLE 16.1

A Listing of a Portion of the Stocks Held by Fidelity's Low-Priced Fund Investments August 31, 1996
Showing Percentage of Total Value of Investment in Securities

Common Stocks—92.8%

	Shares	Value (000s)
AEROSPACE AND DEFENSE—1.7%		
Aerospace and Defense—1.4%		
Boeing Co.	306,106	$ 27,703
Lockheed Martin Corp.	177,566	14,938
McDonnell Douglas Corp.	199,910	10,020
Northrop Grumman Corp.	50,369	3,614
Rockwell International Corp.	193,848	10,080
		66,355
Defense Electronics—0.2%		
Raytheon Co.	216,252	11,137
Ship Building and Repair—0.1%		
General Dynamics Corp.	56,079	3,596
TOTAL AEROSPACE AND DEFENSE		81,088
BASIC INDUSTRIES—5.8%		
Chemicals and Plastics—3.0%		
Air Products & Chemicals, Inc.	99,743	5,461
Avery Dennison Corp.	47,501	2,428
Dow Chemical Co.	233,580	18,628
du Pont (E.I.) de Nemours & Co.	495,390	40,684
Eastman Chemical Co.	71,571	3,999
Engelhard Corp.	128,549	2,619
FMC Corp. (a)	32,670	2,091
Goodrich (B.F.) Co.	47,090	1,766
Grace (W.R.) & Co.	86,880	5,702
Great Lakes Chemical Corp.	57,804	3,324
Hercules, Inc.	98,137	4,882
Monsanto Co.	518,610	16,660
Morton International, Inc.	131,070	4,866
Nalco Chemical Co.	60,057	1,929
PPG Industries, Inc.	172,007	8,493
Praxair, Inc.	134,481	5,531
Raychem Corp.	39,668	2,722
Rohm & Haas Co.	59,931	3,746
Union Carbide Corp.	122,329	5,291
		$140,822

SOURCE: *Fidelity's Low-Priced Fund* Annual Report, 1996.

- **Professional management.** A mutual fund is an inexpensive way to gain access to professional management. The manager continuously monitors the fund's holdings and reacts to market changes. Because fund managers control millions and sometimes even billions of dollars in assets and make huge securities transactions, they have access to all the best research from several brokerage houses. As a result, professional managers are in a much better position to evaluate investments, especially alternative investments. For example, if you're interested in investing in Asian stocks, as an individual investor it'd be extremely difficult to evaluate prices and opportunities in that market. For a professional fund manager, it's a piece of cake. For the small or novice investor, having a professional to lead the way may be essential in taking that first step into the market.

- **Minimal transaction costs.**   Because mutual funds trade in such large quantities, they pay far less in terms of commissions. For example, if you were trading stocks valued at less than $1,000, the brokerage fees might run up to 50 cents per share. For a mutual fund, those fees might be only 2 cents per share, because volume traders (investors who make a ton of trades) often have the power to negotiate lower fees. Over the long run, these lower transaction costs should translate into higher returns.

- **Liquidity.**   Mutual funds are easy to buy and sell—just pick up the phone. Although many securities can be hard to trade, mutual funds never keep your money tied up while you're waiting for a transaction to take place. In effect, mutual funds are liquid enough to provide easy access to your money.

- **Flexibility.**   Given that there are over 6,000 different mutual funds to choose from, it should come as no surprise that they cover many varied objectives and risk levels. As an individual investor, you should be able to spell out your desired objectives and risk level, and from that find a fund that fits your needs.

- **Service.**   Mutual funds provide you with a number of services that just wouldn't be available if you invested individually. For example, they provide bookkeeping services, checking accounts, automatic systems to add to or withdraw from your account, and the ability to buy or sell with a single phone call. With a mutual fund, you can also automatically reinvest your dividends and capital gains.

- **Avoidance of bad brokers.**   With a mutual fund you avoid the potentially bad advice, high sales commissions, and churning that can come with a bad broker. Remember, a broker's job is trading—brokers don't make money unless you trade. A mutual fund manager's job is to make you money.

Disadvantages of Mutual Fund Investing

- **Lower-than-market performance.**   Not only is there no guarantee that mutual funds will outperform the market, but on average they underperform the market. In fact, only 15 percent of the mutual funds beat or tied the S&P 500 in 1995. Why don't mutual funds beat or at least match the market? Simply because they have some expenses to pay—administrative and brokerage costs—whereas "the market" has no transaction costs at all—it's just a measure of how much stocks go up or down. Still, if your goal in investing is to make money, not beat a standard, mutual funds do quite well.

- **Costs.**   The costs associated with investing in mutual funds can vary dramatically from fund to fund; therefore, you should investigate their costs before investing. Some funds charge a sales fee that can run as high as 8.5 percent, in addition to an annual expense fee that can run up to 3 percent. You have to pick your funds wisely, or you might wind up spending your money foolishly.

- **Risks.**   Not all mutual funds are truly safe. In an attempt to beat the competition, many mutual funds have become very specialized or segmented. When mutual funds focus on small sectors of the market, such as "health/biotechnology stocks" or "Latin America," they tend not to be very well diversified. As a result, their returns are subject to unsystematic risk. For example, in 1995 funds in the "Latin America" category returned on average –20.56 percent, because of problems unique to that market sector. A more diversified fund would have been able to smooth out these losses with gains in other industries. Remember, diversification is a huge advantage of mutual funds, but choosing a nondiversified, segmented fund turns that advantage into a disadvantage.

- **Systematic risk.** Many investors view the diversification of mutual funds as eliminating all risk. You should know better. Remember, as **Axiom 4: Diversification and Risk** says, you can't diversify away systematic or market risk (risk resulting from factors that affect all stocks). Thus, if there's a market crash, investing in mutual funds isn't going to protect you.

- **Taxes.** When you invest using a buy-and-hold strategy, you can assure yourself of long-term capital gains, and you don't pay taxes on your capital gains until you sell your stock. Mutual funds, though, tend to trade relatively frequently, and when they sell a security for a profit, you have to pay taxes on your capital gains. Thus, mutual funds don't let you defer your taxes—they make you pay as you go.

MUTUAL FUND-AMENTALS

A mutual fund pools money from investors with similar financial goals. Thus, when you invest in a mutual fund, you receive shares in that fund. You're really investing in a diversified portfolio that's professionally managed according to set goals or financial objectives—for example, investing only in international stocks or only in high-yield bonds. These investment objectives are clearly stated by the mutual fund and then used by the fund investment advisor in deciding where to invest. Your shares in the mutual fund give you an ownership claim to a proportion of the mutual fund's portfolio. In effect, individual investors buy mutual fund shares, the mutual fund managers take this money and buy securities, and the mutual fund shareholders then own a portion of this portfolio. This concept is illustrated in Figure 16.2. It's important to note that mutual fund shareholders don't directly own the fund's securities. Rather, they own a proportion of the overall value of the fund itself.

AXIOM #4

Diversification and Risk

LEARNING OBJECTIVE #2

Differentiate between open- and closed-end mutual funds, unit investment trusts, and real estate investment trusts.

FIGURE 16.2

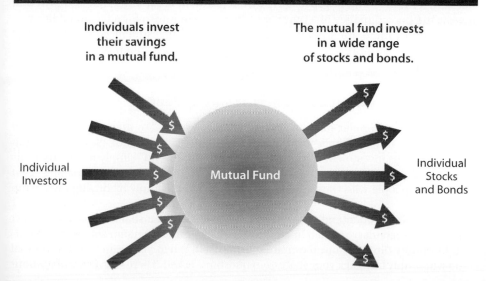

Pooled Investments

Investors pool their funds, give them to a professional investment manager, and the professional invests those funds in a diversified portfolio.

Individuals invest their savings in a mutual fund.

The mutual fund invests in a wide range of stocks and bonds.

Individual Investors

Mutual Fund

Individual Stocks and Bonds

When you own shares in a mutual fund, you make money in three ways. First, as the value of all the securities held by the mutual fund increases, the value of each mutual fund share also goes up. Second, most mutual funds pay dividends to the shareholders. If a fund receives interest or dividends from its holdings, this income is passed on to the shareholders in the form of dividends. Finally, if the fund sells a security for more than it originally paid for it, the shareholders will receive this gain in the form of a capital gains distribution, which is generally paid annually. The shareholder, of course, can elect to have these dividends and capital gains reinvested back into the fund or receive these earnings in the form of a check from the fund.

Before looking at the different types of mutual funds that are available, let's look at how a mutual fund is organized. The fund itself is generally set up as a corporation or trust and is owned by the fund shareholders, who elect a board of directors. The fund is then run by a management company, generally the group that initially organized the mutual fund. Often a management company will run many different mutual funds. In fact, Fidelity and Vanguard, two of the largest management companies, each have a mutual fund for almost every goal, with Fidelity operating over 100 different funds.

Each individual fund then hires an investment advisor, generally from the management company, to directly oversee that particular fund. The investment advisor then supervises the management of the portfolio—the buying and selling of securities. For this service, the investment advisor is generally paid a percentage of the total value of the fund on an annual basis. This management fee usually runs about one-half of 1 percent, although it can vary considerably from fund to fund. In addition to the management fee, there are other operating expenses that bring the average total cost of operations to about 1 percent of the fund's total assets per year.

In addition to the investment advisor, the fund generally contracts with a custodian, a transfer agent, and an underwriter. The custodian acts as a third party safeguarding the fund's assets, in addition to making payments for the fund's securities and receiving money when securities are sold. Generally, the custodian is a bank not affiliated with the fund's management company. In this way the fund shareholders get an independent watchdog to safeguard their investment. The transfer agent is really a record keeper, keeping track of purchases and redemptions, and distributing dividends and capital gains. Finally, the underwriter is responsible for selling new shares in the mutual fund.

INVESTMENT COMPANIES

Actually, a mutual fund is a special type of investment company—that is, a firm that invests the pooled money of a number of investors in return for a fee. In addition to mutual funds, there are a number of other types of investment companies, all of which closely resemble mutual funds. Let's look at several different types of investment companies.

Open-End Investment Companies or Mutual Funds

By far the most popular form of investment companies are **open-end investment companies** or **mutual funds**. These account for over 95 percent of all the money put into the various investment companies. The term "open-end" simply means that this type of investment company can issue an unlimited number of ownership shares. That is, as many people who want to invest in the fund can, simply by buying ownership shares.

A share in an open-end mutual fund is not really like a share of stock. It doesn't trade in the secondary market. In addition, you can buy ownership shares in the mutual fund only directly from the mutual fund itself. When you want out, the mutual fund will simply buy back your shares. No questions asked. There's never a worry about

Open-End Investment Company or **Mutual Fund**
A mutual fund that has the ability to issue as many shares as investors want. As investors buy more shares, the fund grows, and when they sell shares, the fund shrinks. The value of all the investments that the fund holds determines how much each share in the mutual fund is worth.

finding a buyer. The price that you pay when you buy your ownership shares and the price you receive when you sell your shares is based on the **net asset value** of the mutual fund. The net asset value is determined by taking the total market value of all securities held by the mutual fund, subtracting out any liabilities, and dividing this result by the number of shares outstanding.

$$\text{net asset value (NAV)} = \frac{\text{total market value of all securities} - \text{liabilities}}{\text{total shares outstanding}}$$

For example, if the value of all the fund's holdings is determined to be $850 million, the liabilities are $50 million, and there are 40 million shares outstanding, the net asset value would be

$$\text{net asset value (NAV)} = \frac{\$850 \text{ million} - \$50 \text{ million}}{40 \text{ million shares}} = \$20 \text{ per share}$$

In effect, one share, which represents a one-forty-millionth ownership of the fund, can be bought or sold for $20. Thus, the value of the portfolio that the mutual fund holds determines the value of each share in the mutual fund.

Closed-End Investment Companies or Mutual Funds

A **closed-end investment company** or **mutual fund** can't issue new shares in response to investor demand. In fact, a closed-end fund has a fixed number of shares. Those shares are initially sold by the investment company at its inception, and after that they trade between investors at whatever price supply and demand dictate. In effect, a closed-end fund trades more like common stock than like a mutual fund. Just as with common stock, there are a limited number of closed-end fund shares outstanding, and when you want to buy (or sell) ownership shares in a closed-end fund that's already in operation, you have to buy (or sell) them from (to) another investor in the secondary market. Unlike open-end mutual funds, closed-end funds don't sell directly to you and certainly won't buy back your shares when you want to sell them. Finally, because the price of ownership shares in a closed-end fund is determined by supply and demand for those shares, not by their net asset value, shares in some closed-end funds actually sell above, while others sell below, their net asset value.

In recent years closed-end funds have enjoyed a good deal of popularity, because closed-end funds are the only means by which investors can participate in some markets. For example, the South Korean government holds a tight reign on the common stock of Korean companies. As a result, the only means of investing in South Korean companies is through a closed-end fund such as the Korea Fund.

Unit Investment Trusts

A **unit investment trust** is simply a fixed pool of securities, generally municipal bonds, with each unit representing a proportionate ownership in that pool. Although very similar to a mutual fund, a unit investment trust is actually an entirely different beast. For example, unit investment trusts aren't managed. Also, instead of actively trading securities (as mutual funds), unit investment trusts have passive investments. That is, the trust purchases a fixed amount of bonds and then holds those bonds until maturity, at which time the trust is dissolved.

A unit investment trust generally works something like this: First, the investment company announces the formation of the trust, advertises, and sells the ownership shares through brokers. Generally, there's a minimum required investment of around $1,000, from which a sales commission of 3.5 to 4.9 percent is subtracted. The remaining funds are then invested in municipal bonds. The investment company's role is then reduced to collecting and passing on the interest and principal payments accruing from the bond portfolio to the investors.

Net Asset Value
The dollar value of a share in a mutual fund. It's the value of the fund's holdings (minus any debt) divided by the number of shares outstanding.

Closed-End Investment Company or **Mutual Fund**
A mutual fund that can't issue new shares. Those funds raise money only once, issuing a fixed number of shares, and thereafter the shares can be traded between investors. The value of each share is determined both by the value of the investments that the fund holds and investor demand for the shares in the fund.

Unit Investment Trust
A fixed pool of securities, generally municipal bonds, in which each share represents a proportionate ownership interest in that pool. The primary difference between a unit investment trust and a mutual fund is that with a unit investment trust the investments are passive. That is, the bonds are purchased and then held until maturity, at which time the trust is dissolved.

The advantage of unit investment trusts comes from the diversification that they offer. Many municipal bonds are relatively risky, and as a result, diversification holds real value. Unfortunately, because most municipal bonds sell with a minimum price of $1,000, many smaller investors simply don't have the funds to allow for sufficient diversification. A unit investment trust solves this problem handily. Although most investors hold unit investment trusts until maturity, there's a secondary market for some of the larger units. In addition, most brokers stand ready to repurchase and then resell units, although when units are sold to brokers, they generally are sold at a discount. Unit investment trusts are really aimed at the long-term investor. If your time horizon is less than 10 years, you should avoid unit investment trusts and stick with mutual funds.

Real Estate Investment Trusts (REITs)

A **real estate investment trust**, or **REIT**, is similar to a mutual fund in that a professional manager uses the pooled funds of a number of investors to buy and sell a diversified portfolio. In this case, though, all the holdings in the portfolio deal with real estate. Shares in REITs are traded on the major exchanges, and most REITs have no predetermined life span. In effect, from the investor's perspective, a REIT looks just like a mutual fund that specializes in real estate rather than securities. There are some technical differences, though. For example, a REIT must collect at least 75 percent of its income from real estate and must distribute at least 95 percent of that income in the form of dividends. In addition, most REITs also are actively involved in the management of the real estate that they own.

You should note that not all REITs are the same. There are actually three different types of REITs: equity, mortgage, and a hybrid of the two. An equity REIT is one that buys property directly and, in general, also manages that property. When investors buy into an equity REIT, they're hoping that the real estate will appreciate in value. With a mortgage REIT, the investment is limited to mortgages. Thus, investors receive interest payments only, with little chance for capital appreciation. A hybrid REIT invests in both property and mortgages, resulting in some interest and capital appreciation.

Do REITs make sense? They certainly have some diversification value in that they don't move closely with the general stock market. They're also reasonable alternatives for investors who want to invest in real estate, but don't know enough to do it alone. Moreover, although some REITs aren't that liquid, they do tend to be much more liquid than direct investments in real estate. Thus, if you're serious about investing in a REIT, you should make sure that it's actively traded. (The more heavily traded a security is, the more liquid it is.) However, you should keep in mind that there are real risks in real estate. As you probably already know, the real estate market is highly volatile, as the crash in housing prices in California in the late 1980s and early 1990s demonstrates.

THE COSTS OF MUTUAL FUNDS

Although some mutual funds have no sales commission, others impose a sales commission when you buy into the mutual fund or when you liquidate your holdings; some require a hefty annual management fee, and still others pass on their marketing expenses to the fund shareholders. To say the least, the costs associated with mutual funds are complicated at best. Let's take a look at some of those costs.

Load versus No-Load Funds

Mutual funds are classified as either being load or no-load funds. A **load** is simply a sales commission on your ownership shares; thus, a **load fund** is one that charges a sales commission. Load funds are actually mutual funds that are sold through brokers

---

Real Estate Investment Trust or REIT

An investment vehicle similar to a mutual fund that specializes in real estate investments, such as shopping centers or rental property, or makes real estate loans.

Load

A sales commission charged on a mutual fund.

Load Fund

A mutual fund on which a load or sales commission is charged.

financial advisors, and financial planners, who tack on the sales commissions/loads for themselves. These commissions can be quite large, typically in the 4-percent to 6-percent range, but in some cases they can run all the way up to 8.5 percent. In general, the commission is charged when you purchase ownership shares in the fund. However, some funds charge the commission when you liquidate your holdings and sell your ownership shares back to the fund. This type of liquidation charge is referred to as a **back-end load**. With a back-end load, the up-front sales commission is eliminated and replaced with an annual charge of 1 percent, in addition to a liquidation fee of up to about 5 percent of your initial investment or the market value of your investments, whichever is smaller. This liquidation fee is generally set up on a sliding scale, though. For example, you might pay 5 percent if you sell the fund in the first year, 4 percent if you sell the fund in the second year, 3 percent if you sell the fund in the third year, and so forth until the fee just disappears.

A mutual fund that doesn't charge a commission on your ownership shares is referred to as a **no-load fund**. When you purchase a no-load mutual fund, you generally don't deal with a broker or advisor. Instead you deal directly with the mutual fund investment company via direct mail or through an 800 telephone number. There's no salesperson to pay, and as a result, no load. Keeping costs down is always an excellent idea, which makes no-load funds seem the obvious choice. It's a fact that no-load funds perform just as well as load funds—they just don't have salespeople on commission. Without question, you're better off with a no-load fund.

Management Fees and Expenses

Managing a mutual fund costs money—a lot of it. Funds run up big expenses paying the investment advisor, the custodian, the transfer agent, and the underwriter, in addition to the sales commissions on securities trades, operating expenses, legal fees, and so on. You'd be wise to keep an eye on these expenses. Be sure to check out a fund's **expense ratio**, which compares the fund's expenses to its total assets (expense ratio = expenses/assets). Typically, this ratio ranges from 0.25 to 2.0 percent, although some funds have expense ratios that run in excess of 4 percent. You want to be sure to invest in a fund with a nice, low expense ratio. Why? Because the funds themselves don't pay the cost of their expenses—you do. Mutual funds are quick to pass their expenses on to you, with these expenses being paid for by selling some of the fund's securities and thereby lowering the fund's net asset value. The trading costs make up a good sized portion of a typical fund's expenses and are closely related to the fund's **turnover rate**, which provides a measure of the level of the fund's trading activity. In general, the higher the turnover rate, the higher the fund's expenses.

12b-1 Fees

Mutual funds have to make themselves known to investors, thus they tend to run up some marketing expenses. Marketing expenses, including advertising and promotional fees, are passed on to the fund shareholders through **12b-1 fees**. These fees can run up to 1 percent annually, and they don't benefit the shareholders in the least. Really, they serve only to allow the fund manager to pass on some of the fund's expenses. In fact, in studies that have looked at funds that charge 12b-1 fees and those that don't, it's been found that funds that charge these fees have higher expense ratios but don't exhibit better performance. In effect, a 12b-1 fee is a hidden (you have to read through the fund's literature or ask to find it) and continuous load, as every year you pay out a portion of your investment to cover the fund's marketing costs. Is there any value to you from the 12b-1 fee? No, no, and no. If your fund earns 10 percent before a 1 percent 12b-1 fee, after the fee it earns only 9 percent. If you invested $10,000 in this fund and left it in for 20 years, earning 10 percent you'd end up with $67,275, but earning 9 percent you'd end up with only $56,044. The 12b-1 fee just cost you $11,231. Where's the advantage to that?

Back-End Load
A commission that's charged only when the investor liquidates his or her holdings.

No-Load Fund
A mutual fund that doesn't charge a commission.

Expense Ratio
The ratio of a mutual fund's expenses to its total assets.

Turnover Rate
A measure of the level of a fund's trading activity, indicating what percentage of the fund's investments are turned over during the year.

12b-1 Fee
An annual fee, generally ranging from 0.25 to 1.00 percent of a fund's assets, that the mutual fund charges its shareholders for marketing costs.

> ## Stop and Think
>
> It's impossible to overemphasize how important a fund's expenses ratio is in determining a fund's eventual return. Of course, you shouldn't pick your fund based upon the expense ratio alone, but you should eliminate all load funds and those with above-average expense ratios from consideration. Let's face it, there are enough funds to pick from so that you can be choosy.

TYPES AND OBJECTIVES OF MUTUAL FUNDS

To make choosing from the approximately 6,000 mutual funds available a little easier, funds are categorized according to their objective. However, you should note that these classifications aren't always completely reliable. Fund managers get to classify their own funds, and they've been known to be fairly inaccurate. For example, a fund manager might classify a fund as a stock fund, only to have major holdings in bonds. Hey, you don't have to believe everything you read. When choosing a mutual fund, you'll need to first figure out what your objectives are. What do you want a mutual fund to do for you? Once you've figured that out, you have but to look, and chances are one of the many mutual funds will suit your needs perfectly—or at least claim to. Before investing, be sure that a given mutual fund actually lives up to its classification. Let's now take a look at some various mutual fund classifications and the objectives they serve.

Money Market Mutual Funds

Money market mutual funds invest in Treasury bills and other very short-term notes, usually those with maturities of under 30 days. Because these investments are of such short maturity, they're generally regarded as practically risk-free. Most of these investments require massive investments—ranging from $10,000 upward, making these investments out of the reach of the common investor. Thus, money market mutual funds use the pooling principle to make these short-term investments available to the smaller investor. You may have even seen money market funds offered at your local bank, and, in fact, many of these funds work much like interest-bearing checking accounts. For a minimum investment of usually $1,000, you tend to get interest rates that are tied to short-term interest rates and are thus higher than you can earn on a basic savings account, as well as limited check-writing privileges. One of the limits on this privilege is that you can't write checks for less than anywhere between $250 and $500. Money market mutual funds have proved immensely popular because they carry no loads, trade at a constant NAV of $1, and charge very minimal annual maintenance fees.

The extreme popularity of money market mutual funds has spawned several specialized variations of them. One variation is the **tax-exempt money market mutual fund**, which invests only in very short-term municipal debt. The returns on the funds are exempt from federal taxes, making them popular investments among people in higher tax brackets. There are also money market mutual funds that invest solely in U.S. government securities in order to avoid any risk whatsoever. These funds are commonly called **government securities money market mutual funds**. They pay a rate slightly lower than traditional money market mutual funds, but in theory are safer. However, because of the very short maturities of their holdings and the extreme diversification associated with money market mutual funds, there's virtually no risk in them anyway. Thus, you don't really need to bother with government securities money market mutual funds.

INCREASE YOUR RETURNS
by Cutting Fund Expenses

The only sure-fire way to raise your investment returns is to lower your expenses. "If you pay 1% less in fees, you earn an additional 1% risk-free on your portfolio each year," says Don Phillips, president of Morningstar Inc., a Chicago mutual-fund tracking service.

But keeping costs down is getting harder and harder. Mutual-fund expenses have soared in recent years. Investors today pay $99 for each $10,000 invested in funds, up from $71 in 1980, according to Morningstar data.

Figuring out how much you really pay for your funds is more difficult. Many funds have dropped or lowered conspicuous upfront commissions in recent years and are recouping the cost by charging higher annual fees, which are less obvious. So while it always makes sense for cost-conscious investors to avoid paying commissions, they need to zero in on a fund's annual expenses, too.

With all of the higher costs, many investors are getting soaked. Fund expenses will take an even bigger toll should the markets settle down. Someone who earns, say, 7% a year before expenses could end up losing 30% of that return to fund fees. If he hired a broker or planner to manage his funds, he might fork over 40% or more of his potential return.

But don't throw in the towel. There are several ways to lower fund cost—and increase returns:

- **AIM LOW:** One way to get a handle on a fund's expenses is to look at its so-called annual expense ratio, listed in The Wall Street Journal's mutual-fund tables on Fridays. **(A)**

- **LOOK OUT FOR HIDDEN COSTS:** A few of the fees that fund investors pay aren't reflected in the annual expenses. **(B)**

- **DON'T OVERPAY FOR CONVENIENCES:** The small but growing number of "no-fee" fund supermarkets have attracted thousands of bargain-shoppers during the past few years, in part because they are so convenient. The supermarkets offered by discount brokerage firms like Charles Schwab Corp. and Fidelity, for instance, allow investors to choose from hundreds of mutual funds without having to pay a load or transaction fee. That sounds like a steal—however Morningstar has reported that funds at the three biggest no-fee supermarkets charge at least 50% more than do other funds.

- **OWN BONDS INSTEAD OF BOND FUNDS:** The continuing fees you pay for bond funds can really add up over the years. **(C)**

Source: Vanessa O'Connell, "Increase Your Returns by Cutting Fund Expenses," *The Wall Street Journal,* December 1, 1995, p. C1. Reprinted by permission of *The Wall Street Journal,* © 1995 Dow Jones & Company, Inc. All Rights Reserved Worldwide.

Analysis and Implications ...

A. The annual expense ratio tells you how much of your potential returns will go toward covering the fund's fees based on the previous year's experience. For example, if your stock fund gained 10 percent over the past year but has an expense ratio of 2 percent, it earned about 12 percent before expenses.

B. Unfortunately, most investors simply don't know what they pay to cover the commissions and trading costs their funds incur. That's because these costs are deducted from the fund's assets before the fund's expenses are calculated.

C. Rather than incur expenses annually, you should consider buying individual bonds if your total bond holdings are in excess of $200,000.

Stock Mutual Funds

Of the different types of mutual funds, **stock funds** are by far the most popular. In fact, as Figure 16.3 shows, stock funds now account for close to half of all the approximately 6,000 different mutual funds. There is a mutual fund for almost every need. This is not surprising, given the fact that there are approximately 6,000 mutual funds in existence today. Don't think that these funds hold *nothing* but stocks, though. They do have some limited holdings in cash, bonds, and short-term investments (such as those in money market mutual funds), but their main emphasis is indeed firmly on stock. Because the stock market is so varied and wide-ranging, as we've seen in earlier chapters, there are of course many different types of stock funds to choose from. When reading the following discussion of some of the more popular types of stock funds, think about which ones might be best suited for your investment needs.

Aggressive Growth Funds.
An aggressive growth fund is one that tries to maximize capital appreciation while ignoring income. In other words, these funds tend to go for stocks whose prices could rise dramatically, even though these stocks tend to pay very small dividends. Thus, the dividend yield on stocks in funds of this type tends to be quite low. Stocks with high P/E ratios and those of young companies that primarily trade on the OTC market are perfect for aggressive growth funds. Unfortunately, these stocks can not only gain big, but can lose big, too. As a result, the ownership shares of aggressive growth funds tend to experience wider price swings, both up and down, than do the share prices on other funds.

Small-Company Growth Funds.
Small-company growth funds are similar to aggressive growth funds except they limit their investments to small companies that trade on the OTC market. The purpose of small-company growth funds is to uncover and invest in undiscovered companies with unlimited future growth. Again, these are very risky funds with a good deal of price volatility.

FIGURE 16.3

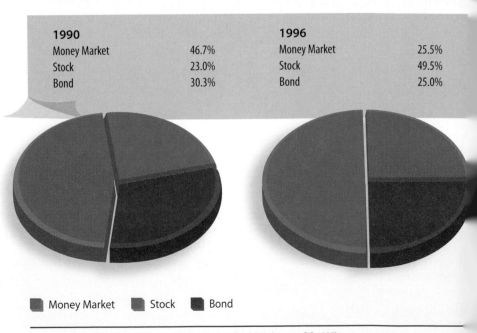

Distribution of Total Net Assets by Type of Fund

1990		1996	
Money Market	46.7%	Money Market	25.5%
Stock	23.0%	Stock	49.5%
Bond	30.3%	Bond	25.0%

■ Money Market   ■ Stock   ■ Bond

Source: Investment Company Institute, *1997 Fact Book*, 37th ed. (Washington, DC, 1997).

Growth Funds.   The differences between aggressive growth funds and growth funds are pretty small, but growth funds generally pay more attention to strong firms that pay dividends. Still, these funds are looking for the potential big gainers. Growth funds are less risky than their aggressive growth cousins, though. Because of the stable dividends, their shares tend to bounce around less in price.

Growth-and-Income Funds.   This general category of funds tries to invest in a portfolio that will provide the investor with a steady stream of income in addition to having the potential for increasing value. These funds focus on everything from well-established blue-chip companies with strong stable dividends and growth opportunities to stocks with low price-earnings ratios and above-average dividends. Because of the steady income these mutual funds provide, the shares in a growth-and-income mutual fund tend to fluctuate in price less than the market as a whole.

Sector Funds.   A sector fund is a specialized mutual fund that generally invests at least 65 percent of its assets in securities from specific industries. For example, there are sector funds dealing with the chemicals, computer, financial services, health/biotechnology, automobile, environmental, utilities, and natural resources industries, to name just a few. In effect, these are growth funds that limit their investments to a specific industry. Although investing in these funds is much less risky than investing in a single stock, sector funds are riskier than traditional mutual funds because they're less diversified. In fact, the idea behind a sector fund is to *limit* the degree of diversification by limiting investment to a specific industry. If that industry does well, the sector fund does well. If that industry has a rough year, so does the sector fund. For example, in 1995 Fidelity's Select Electronics sector fund earned 69.40 percent, while their Precious Metals sector fund went down by 3.3 percent. What's this mean for you? Well, if you're going to invest in a sector fund, you should make sure that you diversify your holdings, perhaps among a number of different mutual funds. In effect, investing in a single sector fund isn't going to provide you with the diversity that makes mutual funds so advantageous.

> ### *Stop and Think*
> When you see a listing of which mutual funds did best last year, invariably a sector fund will appear at the top of the list. Of course, a sector fund will also appear at the bottom of the list. Their lack of diversity makes sector funds highly volatile and not for the weak of heart. If you'd rather not risk putting all your marbles—and dollars—on a single industry, sector funds aren't for you.

Index Funds.   An index fund is one that simply tries to track a market index, such as the S&P 500. It does so by buying the stocks that make up the S&P 500. Much of the value of an index fund comes from its low expense ratio, which can be anywhere from 0.25 to 1.25 percent lower than those of other funds. These funds are great for those who don't want to try to "beat the market"—they just want to mimic the market—and want the diversification of a mutual fund with costs as low as possible.

International Funds.   An international fund, as the name suggests, is one that concentrates its investments in securities from another country. In fact, two-thirds of the fund's assets must be invested outside the United States. There are international funds that focus on general world regions—the Pacific Basin, Latin America, or emerging nations—and funds that focus on specific countries—Japan or Canada—in an attempt to capture abnormal growth in that specific area of the world. Other international funds look for companies outside the United States that have the potential for abnormal growth, and invest directly in them regardless of their location. As with sector funds, international funds don't offer the level of diversification that traditional mutual funds offer, so putting all your money in an international fund wouldn't be wise. However, these funds are good in small doses, because they tend not to move with the U.S. stock market and thus can serve to reduce the variability of returns for all your holdings combined. Unfortunately, these funds open you up to political and currency risks that you'd never have to consider with domestic stocks. As a result, you need to understand the political and economic climate of all the countries represented in an international fund. Otherwise, you won't know what kind of risky situation you could be getting into.

Balanced Mutual Funds

A **balanced mutual fund** is one that holds both common stock and bonds, and in many cases, it also holds preferred stock. The objective of these funds is to earn steady income plus some capital gains. In general, these funds are aimed at those who need steady income to live on, moderate growth in capital, and moderate stability in their investment. As you might expect, the ratio of bonds to stocks can vary dramatically between balanced funds. Thus, not all balanced funds are equally balanced. In fact, some balanced mutual funds specialize in international securities, hoping to cash in on high returns elsewhere around the world. Still, on the whole, balanced funds tend to be less volatile than stock mutual funds.

Asset Allocation Funds

An **asset allocation fund** is quite similar to a balanced fund in that it invests in a mix of stocks, bonds, and money market securities. In fact, these funds have been described as balanced funds with an attitude. Asset allocation funds differ from balanced funds in that they move money between stocks and bonds in an attempt to outperform the market. That is, when the fund manager feels stocks are on the rise, a higher proportion of the fund's assets are allocated to stocks. In effect, asset allocation funds can be viewed as balanced funds that practice market timing. Unfortunately, the track record for market timers is less than impressive. In fact, market-timing attempts are more likely to produce additional transaction costs rather than additional returns. Thus, you should think carefully before investing in such a fund.

Life Cycle Funds

Life cycle funds are the newest "type" of mutual fund to hit the market. They're basically asset allocation funds that try to tailor their holdings to the investor's individual characteristics, such as age and risk tolerance. Life cycle funds go beyond the traditional strategies of growth and income and instead focus on where you are in your financial life cycle. For example, in early 1996, Vanguard had four LifeStrategy funds, each one aimed at satisfying the objectives of the four different stages of the financial life cycle we discussed in chapter 1.

Bond Funds

Bond funds appeal to investors who want to invest in bonds but don't have enough money to adequately diversify. In general, bond funds emphasize income over growth. Although they tend to be less volatile than stock funds, bond funds fluctuate in value as market interest rates move up and down.

Bond funds involve a number of differences from individual bond purchases. Let's take a look at these differences.

Balanced Mutual Fund

A mutual fund that tries to "balance" the objectives of long-term growth, income, and stability. To do this, these funds invest in a mix of common stock and bonds, as well as preferred stock in some cases.

Asset Allocation Fund

A mutual fund that invests in a mix of stocks, bonds, and money market securities. Asset allocation funds differ from balanced funds in that they aggressively move money between stocks and bonds in an attempt to outperform the market. That is, when the fund manager feels stocks are on the rise, a higher proportion of the fund's assets are allocated to stocks.

Life Cycle Funds

Mutual funds that try to tailor their holdings to the investor's individual characteristics, such as age and risk tolerance.

Bond Funds

Mutual funds that invest primarily in bonds.

- With an investment of as little as $1,000 you can buy into a diversified bond portfolio. Then you can add to your investment with smaller amounts whenever you wish.

- Bond funds offer more liquidity than individual bonds. As we noted in chapter 15, one of the disadvantages of investing in bonds is that they can be difficult to sell before their maturity. With a bond fund, you can both buy and sell at whatever the fund's NAV is, and you don't have to worry about getting a bad price when forced to sell an individual bond at the "wrong time."

- With a bond fund, you're getting professional management.

- Like an individual bond, a bond fund produces regular income. However, with a bond fund, you can choose to receive a monthly check to help your cash flow, or you can have your money automatically reinvested in the fund to buy more bonds.

- If you buy bonds directly rather than through a bond fund, you won't have any mutual fund expenses to deal with.

- The bond fund doesn't mature, whereas individual bonds do. When bonds within the bond fund mature, they're replaced with new bonds as the funds constantly reinvest. As a result, you're never guaranteed to receive a lump-sum payment.

If you're looking for income, a logical place to look is either to bonds or to a bond fund. Whether to buy a bond or a bond fund will depend on your individual goals and needs. You'll probably look closer at a bond fund if you want to invest small amounts of money, you need to keep your investments liquid, and you'll sleep better at night knowing a professional's choosing the securities and keeping them well diversified. Conversely, if you need to know with certainty that in a specific number of years you'll get the principal back, you have a large amount to invest, and you're disciplined enough to reinvest your interest payments, then you might want to stick with individual bonds.

Bond funds can be differentiated both by the type of bond that they invest in—U.S. government, municipal, or corporate—and by maturity—short-term, intermediate-term, or long-term.

The Facts of Life

The expense ratios on bond mutual funds can vary dramatically. The average expense ratio in 1995 for bond funds was 1.01 percent. However, this ratio ranged between approximately 0.28 and 2.06 percent. Given the fact that long-term bonds averaged a return of only about 6.0 percent from 1926 to 1996, it's extremely important to keep expenses low if you're investing in bonds. If your expenses are 2 percent and your return is only 6 percent, one-third of your return is already gone.

U.S. Government Bond Funds or GNMA Bond Funds.   U.S. government bond funds invest in securities issued by the federal government or its agencies. For example, U.S. Treasury bond funds specialize in Treasury securities. Obviously, there's no default risk associated with these funds. However, they do fluctuate in value as interest rates move up and down. There are also a number of funds that specialize in mortgage-backed securities issued primarily by the Government National Mortgage Association, or GNMA. These funds hold pools of individual residential mortgages that have been packaged by GNMA and resold to the bond fund. This type of fund also carries interest rate risk in addition to prepayment risk—that is, the risk that as interest rates drop, the mortgages will be refinanced and prepaid. As with other bond funds, a government bond fund is aimed at those who need steady current income.

Municipal Bond Funds.   The advantage of municipal bond funds is that the interest is generally exempt from federal taxes. Moreover, if you invest in a municipal bond fund that invests only in bonds from your state, the income may also be exempt from state taxes. In fact, if you live in New York City and invest in a fund that limits its investments to municipal bonds issued by New York City, you avoid federal, state, and local income taxes on the interest payments. Obviously, for investors in higher tax brackets, avoiding taxes is a big deal.

Corporate Bond Funds.   Unless you haven't been paying any attention at all, you've probably guessed that corporate bond funds invest in various corporate bonds. Some corporate bond funds focus mainly on high-quality, highly rated bonds, but others, usually called high-yield corporate bond funds, focus on the much lower rated and much riskier junk bonds. As you know from **Axiom 1: The Risk-Return Trade-Off**, when you take on more risk, as you do when you invest in junk bonds, your expected return is higher. Because corporate bonds have the potential for defaulting, it's essential that you diversify if you're going to invest in them. That's where a corporate bond mutual fund comes in—it does the diversifying for you. Of course, you'll also want to carry this diversification a bit further by investing in more than just bonds. When selecting a corporate bond fund, be sure to remember that approximately two-thirds of them carry loads in the 4 to 5 percent range. Although the loads are pretty constant, the returns aren't. As interest rates go up, corporate bond funds and their NAV go down in value. As interest rates drop, corporate bond fund values rise, along with their NAV.

Bond Funds and Their Maturities.   Different bond funds also specialize in different length maturities, with short-term (1 to 5 years in maturity), intermediate-term (5 to 10 years in maturity), and long-term (10 to 30 years in maturity) funds. We know from bond valuation relationships presented in chapter 15 that there's an inverse relationship between interest rates and bond prices. That is, when interest rates rise, bond prices drop, and when interest rates drop, bond prices rise. We also know that when interest rates change, longer-term bonds fluctuate in price more than shorter-term bonds. As a result, the longer the bond fund's maturity, the higher its expected return, but also the greater the fluctuation in its NAV if interest rates change.

SERVICES OFFERED BY MUTUAL FUNDS

Aside from the fact that you can most probably find a mutual fund with objectives that almost perfectly match your investment goals, what's so special about mutual funds? A lot, actually. Diversification is probably the biggest advantage of mutual funds, but convenience may well be a close second. As you've already seen, mutual funds offer the convenience of being able to buy and sell securities at will, with reduced commissions and professional advice. That's really just the tip of the convenience iceberg, though. Mutual funds offer myriad services for investors small and large alike— services that make investing easy and even fun. Let's take a look at a few of the more popular services. As we do, think about which services would be most helpful and appealing to you.

Automatic Investment and Withdrawal Plans.   An automatic investment plan allows you to make regular deposits directly from your bank account. For example, if you want to invest $100 on the fifteenth of each month, an automatic investment plan lets you do so without lifting a finger. Basically, all you need do is check a box on the mutual fund's account registration form and *voilà*—your $100 will find its way from

AXIOM #1

The Risk-Return Trade-Off

LEARNING OBJECTIVE #4

Use those mutual fund services that best meet your needs.

(UN)TRUTH IN PACKAGING

You decide you want a fund that invests in the stocks of large, established companies. How about the Fidelity Blue Chip Growth Fund? Oops! The fund has a fourth of its assets in stocks of small companies with market values below $500 million. Among them: tiny Hawaiian home builder Schuler Homes, and newly public software vendor Firefox Communications. Truth in packaging?

(A) You would never have guessed from the name Fidelity Asset Manager that this tame-sounding fund that cycles between stocks, bonds and cash had 25% of its assets in emerging markets when they collapsed in 1994.

The problem is widespread. Suppose you want the stocks of small, growing companies. Target Small Capitalization Growth sounds like a good bet. Sorry, it has 21% of its assets in large companies, those with market values over $4 billion.

(B) Have you carefully apportioned your portfolio between domestic and overseas stocks? Take another look. Your domestic fund may be a global fund in disguise. The Fidelity Capital Appreciation, Mutual Discovery, Oak Hall Equity and Analysts Stock funds all have more than 30% of assets invested in foreign companies (see table).

Bond funds lead investors down the garden path, too. To a naive investor, "government" in the name connotes safety. But Investors Trust Government B fund lost 9% in 1994, when its stake in mortgage derivatives blew up. The fund sponsor recently set up a fund to reimburse investors up to $7.3 million.

What's in a name?

Fund	% foreign stocks
Fidelity Capital Appreciation	36.7
Mutual Discovery	35.9
Oak Hall Equity	33.8
Analysts Stock	33.3
Putnam Diversified Equity B	28.9
T Rowe Price Spectrum Growth	28.7
Capital Income Builder	27.8
Target Small Cap Value	27.7
Robertson Stephens Partners	27.5
Fairmont	26.5
Fidelity Retirement Growth	24.9

Source: *Morningstar Inc.*

Source: Mary Beth Grover, "(Un)Truth in Packaging," *Forbes,* May 6, 1996, p. 134. Reprinted by Permission of FORBES Magazine © Forbes, Inc., 1996.

Analysis and Implications ...

A. You must keep in mind that the manager names the fund and picks its classification. Hopefully, what's picked reflects the fund's investment philosophy, but that's not necessarily the case.

B. What's the moral? Don't judge a fund by the cover of the prospectus. Look at what's inside. The latest financial statement will list the portfolio holdings. If it doesn't spell out what percentage of assets is in each type of holding, call the sponsor and ask.

your savings account to your fund account each and every month. In effect, an automatic investment plan is a way of dollar cost averaging when investing in a mutual fund. You should recall from chapter 14 that the logic behind dollar cost averaging is that by investing the same dollar amount on a regular basis, you'll be buying more common stock when the price is lowest and less when the price is highest. The automatic investment plan is also a good way of moving excess funds from a money market account into the stock market. For example, if you have more money than you feel you need invested in a money market account but are worried about transferring it all at once into the stock market, an automatic investment plan will let you move the funds into the market smoothly over a longer period of time.

Conversely, an automatic or systematic withdrawal plan allows you to withdraw a dollar amount or a percentage of your mutual fund account on a monthly basis. For example, if you were retired and wanted to supplement your income, you might elect to have $250 paid out to you automatically on a monthly basis. Many funds require a minimum fund balance of between $5,000 and $10,000 to participate in an automatic withdrawal plan, with a minimum withdrawal of $50 per month.

Automatic Reinvestment of Interest, Dividends, and Capital Gains. With a mutual fund, you have your choice of receiving interest, dividends, and capital gains payments or having them reinvested by purchasing more shares in the fund. If you're using the mutual fund as a long-term investment, you should have the distributions automatically reinvested. Reinvestment in the securities markets produces the same growth effect as compound interest—that is, you'll start earning money on your past earnings. If you're investing in a bond and income fund, you'll get little or no capital appreciation on your holdings. Instead, most of your return will be from dividends, which are distributed back to you each year. If you don't reinvest these distributions, you won't accumulate much wealth. You'll be spending your earnings instead. Over 70 percent of all mutual fund shareholders choose to reinvest their dividends and capital gains.

Wiring and Funds Express Options. If you anticipate needing your funds or your returns fast, you can choose a wiring and funds express option. This option allows you to have your returns/money wired directly to your bank account. It also works the other way and allows you to invest money in the fund immediately by wiring money directly to the fund. In this way you can have your money sent and invested in the fund all in the same day. This option is a bit like the automatic investment and withdrawal plan, except the transactions don't happen automatically/monthly.

Phone Switching. Phone switching allows you to move money from one fund to another simply by making a phone request. Thus, if you want to move some of your money from your domestic stock fund to an international stock fund, you can do it easily and, generally, cost-free with just one phone call.

Easy Establishment of Retirement Plans. Most mutual funds provide for the easy establishment of IRS-approved tax-deferred retirement accounts, including IRA, 401(k), and Keogh plans. The fund will provide you with everything you need to establish such a plan, and then the fund will handle the administrative duties. In addition, most funds have representatives available to answer any questions that you might have when setting the plan up. Retirement plans are a key part of any sound personal financial plan, and getting someone else to set one up and manage it for you is a huge advantage.

Check Writing.   Check-writing privileges associated with money market mutual funds can prove very handy when you need to use money from your investments directly for making purchases or in an emergency. As we mentioned before, there are minimum levels, generally in the $250 to $500 range, for which the checks can be written.

Bookkeeping and Help with Taxes.   Some of the larger investment companies provide a "tax cost" service that actually calculates your taxable gains or losses when you sell shares in your mutual fund. Because the calculation of taxes associated with buying and selling shares in a mutual fund can be enough to drive you crazy, this is a service well worth having. Unfortunately, it's also a service not offered by all mutual funds.

BUYING A MUTUAL FUND

Now that you know a bunch about mutual funds, you may well be wondering how you go out and buy one. If you're wondering something else, you're out of luck, because now we're going to talk about buying mutual funds. The process of buying a mutual fund involves determining your investment goals, identifying funds that meet your objectives, and evaluating those funds. Your local library should hold a wealth of information to help your evaluation. Brush up on your math, though, because much of the evaluation process is going to focus on cost considerations. As you'll see, mutual fund expenses can vary dramatically from one fund to another.

Step 1: Determining Your Investment Goals

The first step in buying a mutual fund involves determining exactly what your investment goals are and the time horizon associated with meeting those goals. In chapters 1 and 2 we discussed identifying your goals and putting together an investment plan. We described the budgeting and planning procedure as a five-step process, as shown in Figure 1.1. Investing in mutual funds conforms to step 4 in this process. However, before you make it to step 4, you need to proceed through the first three steps. In other words, you must have a clear understanding of why you're investing. Is it to provide additional income to supplement your retirement income, or is it to save for your children's education or for your own retirement 30 years from now? Do you want your investments to be tax-deferred? How much risk are you comfortable with? Once you've answered these questions, you're ready to go out and find a fund with objectives that match your own.

Step 2: Identifying Funds That Meet Your Objectives

To identify a fund's objectives, the first place to look is in one of the mutual fund advisory publications. For example, *Morningstar Mutual Funds,* a publication that provides fund analysis, classifies funds by both their objective and their management style. The objective classification uses the categories of funds we examined earlier and is based on the wording the fund uses in its prospectus. Figure 16.4 presents an example of a Morningstar fund analysis for the Fidelity Low-Priced Stock Fund. As you can see, the objective here is "small company." Note that it's not always safe to assume that the fund's name reflects its investment strategy or objectives. What's in a name, right? In truth, the fund's name may imply an objective, but that objective may not bear much resemblance to that fund's actual investment strategy. Morningstar will usually adjust its objective classifications to reflect the fund's actual investment practices, not just its name.

LEARNING OBJECTIVE #5

Select a mutual fund that's right for you.

FIGURE 16.4

Morningstar Analysis for Fidelity's Low-Priced Stock Fund

Investment Objective: This section contains a brief description of the fund's objective. The objective assigned to this fund by Morningstar is given in the upper right-hand corner of the report.

Manager's History: Identifies who is running the fund and for how long. If the manager is new at the job, you should be wary of putting too much weight on past performance.

Historical Performance: Here you find historical performance for a number of periods in addition to how different indexes performed over those same periods.

Analyst's Review: This section presents Morningstar's analysis of the fund's prospects and performance.

Category Rating: The category rating is based on the fund's relative performance in one of 44 categories according to investment styles, for example, big-company growth funds, utility funds, Europe funds, and so on.

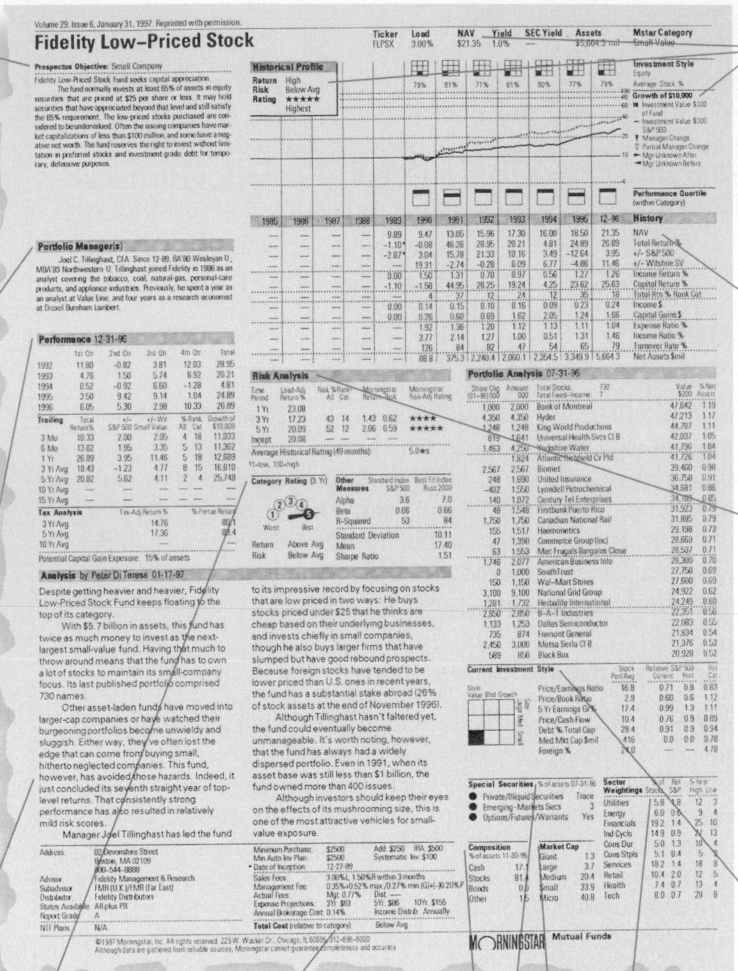

Expenses and Fees: The fund's expenses and fees are listed here. The sales fee, or lack of one, tells you if this is a load or no-load fund.

Composition, Market Cap, Special Securities, and Sector Weightings: These sections tell you what percentage of the fund's holdings consist of different types of investments. These sections give you a good deal of insight into the fund manager's true investment philosophy.

Summary Data: Information on fund objectives, NAV, fund size, and any load imposed. The graph shows the growth of a $10,000 investment in this fund.

Calendar-Year Returns: The fund's returns for the past 11 years or inception and the year to date.

Risk Analysis: The Morningstar ranking of the fund's risk relative to other funds with the same very broad investment style, ranging from 1 (lowest) to 100 (highest). Also, the Morningstar Risk-Adjusted Ranking ranging up to 5 stars is given.

Investment Style: The explanation of Morningstar's nine-section style boxes is given in Figure 16.5.

Source: *Morningstar Mutual Funds*, Vol. 29, Issue 6, January 31, 1997. Morningstar, Inc., Chicago, IL 1997. Used by permission.

Unfortunately, just knowing the fund's stated objective isn't always very helpful. As the mutual fund industry has grown, so have the number of different objectives, and with growth comes confusion. For example, three funds, all investing in identical portfolios made up of high-technology, small-cap firms could end up with three different objective categories—small company, aggressive growth, and specialty or sector (technology), depending on how they marketed themselves. Moreover, the different objective categories are open to misinterpretation. For example, the term "growth" can be interpreted to mean growth in capital, growth in earnings, or an investment style. To help out with this problem, Morningstar provides an investment style box, which serves as a visual tool for better understanding the fund's true investment style. Figure 16.5 shows the setup for Morningstar's investment style boxes for stock and bond funds. For stock funds, the horizontal axis of the investment style box covers a value-oriented style to a growth-oriented style. A value-oriented style would reflect investments in stocks that are currently undervalued in terms of price, while a growth-oriented style would indicate investments in stocks that have the potential to grow at an above average rate. A blend investment style is somewhere between those two styles. The vertical axis categorizes funds by the size of the companies in which the fund invests, from small to large. For bond funds, the investment style categorization used by Morningstar groups funds by maturity—short, intermediate, and long—and by credit quality or risk—high, medium, and low. With this information you don't need to be concerned about what a fund's objective actually means. The investment style classification should be more helpful.

Of course, you should also go directly to the source and examine the **mutual fund prospectus** which you can get simply by calling the mutual fund and asking. Let's look at the prospectus for Fidelity's Low-Priced Stock Fund, portions of which are

Mutual Fund Prospectus
A description of the mutual fund, including the fund's objectives and risks, its historical performance, its expenses, the manager's history, and other information.

FIGURE 16.5

Morningstar's Investment Style Boxes

Equity Style Box

Risk	Investment Style			Median Market Capitalization
	Value	Blend	Growth	
Low ●	Large-Cap Value	Large-Cap Blend	Large-Cap Growth	Large
Moderate ●	Mid-Cap Value	Mid-Cap Blend	Mid-Cap Growth	Medium
High ●	Small-Cap Value	Small-Cap Blend	Small-Cap Growth	Small

Fixed-Income Style Box

Risk	Investment Style			Quality
	Value	Blend	Growth	
Low ●	Short-Term High Quality	Interm-Term High Quality	Long-Term High Quality	High
Moderate ●	Short-Term Medium Quality	Interm-Term Medium Quality	Long-Term Medium Quality	Medium
High ●	Short-Term Low Quality	Interm-Term Low Quality	Long-Term Low Quality	Low

Within the equity style box grid, nine possible combinations exist, ranging from large-cap value for the safest funds to small-cap growth for the riskiest.

Within the equity style box grid, nine possible combinations exist, ranging from short maturity, high quality for the safest funds to long maturity, low quality for the riskiest.

Source: *Morningstar Mutual Funds*, 1997. Morningstar, Inc., Chicago, IL 1997. Used with permission.

highlighted in the Morningstar analysis in Figure 16.4. Investment companies are required by law to offer a prospectus, which contains the following information:

- **The fund's goal and investment strategy.** For example, Fidelity's Low-Priced Stock Fund prospectus states that the fund seeks "capital appreciation by investing primarily in low-priced common and preferred stocks" and that it "normally invest[s] at least 65% of the fund's total assets in these securities." It also says say that this investment strategy will most likely lead to investments in "smaller, less well-known, or overlooked companies." The prospectus goes on to state that this is a fund for investors "who are willing to ride out stock market fluctuations," meaning that only the strong of stomach should consider this fund.

- **The fund manager's past experience.** For example, Fidelity's Low-Priced Stock Fund is managed by Joel Tillinghast, who has managed the fund since 1989.

- **Any investment's limitation that the fund may have.** For example, Fidelity's Low-Priced Stock Fund prospectus states that "the fund currently intends to limit its investments in lower than Baa-quality debt securities to 5% of its assets."

- **Any tax considerations of importance to the investors.** For example, Fidelity's Low-Priced Stock Fund's prospectus states that "distributions are subject to federal income tax, and may also be subject to state or local taxes. Your distributions are taxable when they are paid, whether you take them in cash or reinvest them."

- **The redemption and investment process for buying and selling shares in the fund.** Fidelity's Low-Priced Stock Fund has four distribution options: (1) you can reinvest the entire distribution, (2) you can reinvest only the capital gains portion and receive a check for the dividend distribution, (3) you can receive a check for both the dividend and capital gains distribution, or (4) you can direct them into a different Fidelity fund.

- **Services provided investors.** The prospectus should explain the investor services provided. For example, Fidelity's Low-Priced Stock Fund provides telephone representatives 24 hours a day, 365 days a year.

- **Performance over the past 10 years or since the fund has been in existence.** Most funds generally show this by demonstrating what would've happened if you had put $10,000 in the fund 10 years earlier or when the fund was formed.

- **Fund fees and expenses.** Information on the fund's sales and redemption charges is given. In addition, information on the management fee and fees for marketing expenses, called 12b-1 fees, are included.

- **The fund's annual turnover ratio.** Information is provided on how frequently the fund's investment portfolio changes or turns over. For 1996, Fidelity's Low-Priced Stock Fund turnover ratio was 79 percent.

There's also a part B to the prospectus, which can be obtained separately and contains a listing of the fund's holdings, as well as additional information on the fund management.

In assessing a fund's objective, you should pay close attention to the fund's past performance. If it's intended as a long-term investment, how has it done over the past 10 years? If it's intended to produce current income, what's it paying out in terms of its current yield?

Step 3: Evaluating the Fund

Once you've found some funds with objectives that match your own, it's time to get picky and start evaluating them. Evaluation centers on looking closely at past performance and scrutinizing the costs associated with the funds. Although past performance doesn't necessarily predict future results, it can give you further insights as to the investment philosophy and style of the fund.

In evaluating performance, be sure not to compare apples to oranges. Just as it'd be inappropriate to compare a fund that has an objective of income with one that has an objective of growth, it's also inappropriate to compare any single fund to an average for all mutual funds of all categories combined. Be sure to limit your comparisons to those between funds with the same investment objectives.

It's also important to look at longer periods of performance to see how the fund does in both market upturns and downturns. Looking at only short-term performance won't help you gauge whether the fund's overall performance is improving or deteriorating.

The Facts of Life

It's not necessarily true that funds that do well in one year will do well in the following year. For example, in 1991 the Oppenheimer Bio-Tech Fund rose 121 percent. However, in 1992 it fell by 23 percent. In picking a mutual fund, you should first focus on objectives, diversification, and keeping expenses to a minimum. After that, look at what the fund has done in the past. A fund's past volatility and investment approach tend to continue into the future. There's even some (weak) evidence of consistency in performance—winners stay winners and losers stay losers—but as Oppenheimer Bio-Tech Fund shows, that's not always the case.

Sources of Information

"So," you may be thinking, "I have a hard time finding my socks. How am I supposed to find all this stuff about mutual funds?" Start by trucking over to the library. There's a wealth of information available to aid you in evaluating mutual funds, and just about all of it can be found in the average library. The *Wall Street Journal* provides daily mutual fund listings and quotes. In addition, on Friday, the *Wall Street Journal* expands its coverage of mutual funds and presents data prepared by Lipper Analytical Services. These data include the fund's objective, its year-to-date return, and its return over the past 4 weeks, 12 months, 3 years, and 5 years. These returns are also ranked relative to other funds with similar objectives. In addition, the data include the maximum initial sales commission for the fund and the annual expenses for each fund. Figure 16.6 provides an example of the fund listings from the *Wall Street Journal*, along with an explanation of how to read the tables.

Another good source of information on mutual funds is *Forbes*, which publishes an annual mutual fund survey each August. In this survey, funds are ranked for their performance in both up and down markets, and on the average P/E ratios and the average size of the stocks that the funds invest in. *Forbes* also provides mailing addresses and telephone numbers for all the major funds. Other special issues on mutual funds are offered by such magazines as *Consumer Reports, Business Week, Kiplinger's, Personal Finance,* and *Smart Money.*

Two other excellent sources of information that are available at many libraries are *Wiesenberger Investment Companies Service* and *Morningstar Mutual Funds.* An example of the Morningstar listing for a stock fund was presented earlier in Figure 16.4 when we discussed investment style. You'll note that there's a ton of information contained in the Morningstar listing. Among other things, it provides information on the fund's potential capital gains exposure, which gives the investor an idea of the

FIGURE 16.6

A Listing of Mutual Fund Quotes from a Friday Edition of _The Wall Street Journal,_ Along with an Explanation of How to Read the Tables

How to Read These Tables

Data come from two sources. The daily Net Asset Value (NAV) and Net Change calculations are supplied by the National Association of Securities Dealers (NASD). The NASD requires a mutual fund to have at least 1,000 shareholders or net assets of $25 million before being listed. Performance and cost data come from **Lipper Analytical Services Inc.**

Though verified, the data cannot be guaranteed by Lipper or its data sources. Double-check with funds before investing.

Performance calculations assume reinvestment of all distributions, and are after subtracting annual expenses. But figures don't reflect sales charges ("loads") or redemption fees.

These expanded tables appear Fridays. Other days, you'll find net asset value and the daily change and year-to-date performance.

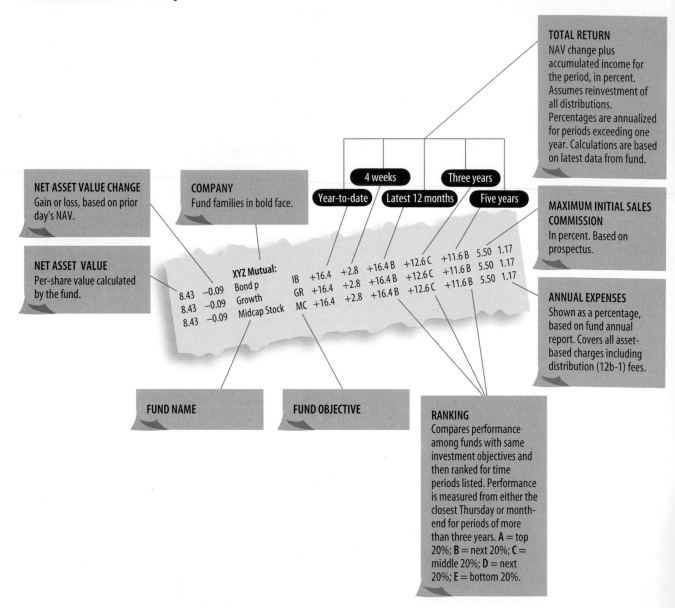

TOTAL RETURN
NAV change plus accumulated income for the period, in percent. Assumes reinvestment of all distributions. Percentages are annualized for periods exceeding one year. Calculations are based on latest data from fund.

NET ASSET VALUE CHANGE
Gain or loss, based on prior day's NAV.

NET ASSET VALUE
Per-share value calculated by the fund.

COMPANY
Fund families in bold face.

MAXIMUM INITIAL SALES COMMISSION
In percent. Based on prospectus.

ANNUAL EXPENSES
Shown as a percentage, based on fund annual report. Covers all asset-based charges including distribution (12b-1) fees.

FUND NAME

FUND OBJECTIVE

RANKING
Compares performance among funds with same investment objectives and then ranked for time periods listed. Performance is measured from either the closest Thursday or month-end for periods of more than three years. **A** = top 20%; **B** = next 20%; **C** = middle 20%; **D** = next 20%; **E** = bottom 20%.

4 weeks | Three years
Year-to-date | Latest 12 months | Five years

XYZ Mutual:

			IB	+16.4	+2.8	+16.4 B	+12.6 C	+11.6 B	5.50	1.17
8.43	−0.09	Bond p	GR	+16.4	+2.8	+16.4 B	+12.6 C	+11.6 B	5.50	1.17
8.43	−0.09	Growth	MC	+16.4	+2.8	+16.4 B	+12.6 C	+11.6 B	5.50	1.17
8.43	−0.09	Midcap Stock								

fund's vulnerability to taxation. It also provides information on the fund's expense ratio, turnover ratio, and performance relative to the S&P 500 and the Russell 2000, a broader-based stock index. You'll also find a historical profile of the fund's performance, including an evaluation of its return, risk, and ranking. Morningstar awards stars to the best performers in four large fund groups—U.S. equity, international equity, taxable bond, and municipal bond—as well as a "category rating" to the top performers in 44 categories according to investment style—for example, big-company growth funds, utility funds, Europe funds, and so on. A fund can be awarded as many as five stars or a category rating of up to five, but only the top 10 percent of the funds in each group receive a top rating. For example, Fidelity's Low-Priced Stock Fund presented in Figure 16.4 received a historical rating of all five stars and a category rating of five out of five.

LEARNING OBJECTIVE #6

Calculate mutual fund returns.

Calculating Fund Returns

You've set your goals, found some mutual funds that share those goals, and narrowed down your list of funds by reading through several helpful sources of information. Now what do you do? Well, as when making any investment, you want to pick the one that's going to cost the least and return the most. In terms of costs, we've already seen the various loads, management, and other fees that can be charged to mutual funds. All we need to say is, avoid as many as you can. Morningstar and the other sources of information we've discussed will help you figure out which funds charge which expenses and thus which funds to skip. Let's now take a look at returns and how you can figure out how much a mutual fund will make for you.

The return from investing in a mutual fund can be in the form of distributions of dividends, capital gains, or a change in net asset value (NAV) of the shares held. To qualify as an investment company and avoid being taxed on the fund's earnings, a fund must distribute a minimum of 97 percent of the interest and dividends earned and at least 90 percent of capital gains income. (Capital gains result from selling securities for more than what they were originally bought for.) Thus, the total return from a mutual fund can be calculated as follows:

$$\text{total return} = \frac{\text{dividends distributed} + \text{capital gains distributed} + (\text{ending NAV} - \text{beginning NAV})}{\text{beginning NAV}}$$

For example, let's assume we have a fund with

beginning NAV	= $19.45
ending NAV	= $23.59
dividends distributed	= $ 0.60
capital gains distributed	= $ 0.47

Our return can be calculated as follows:

$$\text{total return} = \frac{\$0.60 + \$0.47 + (\$23.59 - \$19.45)}{\$19.45}$$

$$= \frac{\$0.60 + \$0.47 + \$4.14}{\$19.45}$$

$$= \frac{\$5.21}{\$19.45} = 26.79\%$$

Thus, the return was 26.79 percent.

If you automatically reinvest any distributions that are made, your return results from both the increase in the NAV of the shares and the increased number of shares that you hold. In effect, as you automatically reinvest any distributions, the number of shares that you hold increases. As a result, your return can be calculated by taking the value of your ending holdings minus your initial investment and dividing this by the value of your initial investment.

$$\text{total return} = \frac{(\text{number of ending shares} \times \text{ending price}) - (\text{number of beginning shares} \times \text{beginning price})}{(\text{number of beginning shares} \times \text{beginning price})}$$

Thus, if you initially purchase 500 shares at an NAV of \$19.45 and, as a result of automatically reinvesting any distributions, you end up with 585 shares with an NAV of \$23.59, your return would be

$$\text{total return} = \frac{(585 \times \$23.59) - (500 \times \$19.45)}{(500 \times \$19.45)}$$

$$= \frac{\$13,800.15 - \$9,725.00}{\$9,725.00}$$

$$= \frac{\$4,075.15}{\$9,725.00}$$

$$= 41.90\%$$

Thus, the return would be 41.9 percent. Keep in mind, though, that these formulas don't take taxes into account.

You now can calculate a fund's return. This information should help you in spotting those funds that have been consistent winners over time and avoiding those that have performed poorly. Once you've found a fund that fits your objectives and keeps expenses to a minimum, you might as well go for past winners and avoid losers. That's the message from Yale's Roger Ibbotson, who's found some evidence of strong performers over the past 3 years remaining strong performers for the following 3 years. It's also the message of New York University's Edwin Elton and Martin Gruber, who find that poor performers tend to continue to lag for the following 3 years.

The Facts of Life

It's hard to beat the market, but you can avoid expenses. Mutual fund expenses account for the fact that in 1995, according to Lipper Analytical Services, only 15 percent of the mutual funds beat or tied the S&P 500. Moreover, over the 12-year period 1984–1995, mutual funds outperformed the S&P 500 in only 4 years. The bottom line here is that you should be very aware of any and all mutual fund expenses and try to avoid them if at all possible. You're better off avoiding load funds and seeking out those funds with minimal expenses.

Making the Purchase

After all of your figuring, matching, picking, evaluating, and calculating, you should know exactly what fund you want. Now it's time to do some buying. Load funds are generally sold through salespeople—perhaps a broker or a financial advisor. No-load funds, though, tend to be sold directly by the investment company. If you decide to keep costs down and go for a no-load fund, you have two choices. You can either deal directly with the investment company that runs the fund, or you can purchase the no-load fund through a "mutual fund supermarket."

Buying Direct: Dialing 1-800 . . .

The easiest way to buy a mutual fund is to just pick up the phone. For example, Vanguard and Fidelity, the two largest mutual fund families, both have 800 numbers you can use to set up an account, to move money into and out of your funds, to switch funds, and to request educational material. However, unless you want to transfer money electronically, you'll still have to send your money to Vanguard or Fidelity through the mail, and when you sell your holdings, you'll generally receive a check in the mail. Otherwise, most everything can be done over the phone. Again, it's not having salespeople that allows these families of funds to keep their costs down.

Buying Through a "Mutual Fund Supermarket."

The downside of buying directly from the mutual fund is that if you have money in eight different mutual fund families, you'll have eight different statements to deal with. If you decide you want to move money from one family to another, you're in for a real headache. Luckily, in 1992 Charles Schwab & Co. introduced the concept of the "mutual fund supermarket," where you could pick from among 600 mutual funds that make up 70 different mutual fund families and buy them through Schwab. The question most people ask is, Why does Schwab do it? If they make a commission, don't these no-load funds now become load funds? The answer is that Schwab convinced the mutual fund companies to give up a portion of their management fees—initially about $2.50 per year for every $1,000 in assets invested—for any mutual funds purchased through Schwab. Both parties seemed to benefit—Schwab got some commissions they wouldn't otherwise have received, and the mutual funds got some new investors.

Today there are eight major players in the "mutual funds supermarket" arena. How do you go about choosing from them? You should begin by looking at the lineup of no-transaction-fee funds that are available. The biggest three, Fidelity Funds Network, Schwab, and Jack White, have all signed up key mutual fund families. However, not all funds are available on a no-transaction-fee basis from each "supermarket." For example, mutual funds from the Lindner mutual fund family are available only from Jack White, and funds from the Twentieth Century mutual fund family are only available from Charles Schwab. You should also be aware of differences in minimum balances necessary to open an account. For example, Fidelity requires a minimum balance of $5,000, but Jack White requires only $1,000. Fidelity, Schwab, and Jack White also have different transaction fees for funds not available on a no-fee basis. For example, each of these three "supermarkets" charges a relatively small transaction fee when purchasing any no-load mutual funds from the T. Rowe Price, USAA, or Vanguard mutual fund families. You can avoid these transaction fees altogether by simply purchasing these funds directly from their mutual fund families. Table 16.2 presents a comparison of the different "mutual fund supermarkets."

The Facts of Life

Many banks also sell mutual funds. Unfortunately, many investors don't realize that mutual funds sold by banks aren't insured by the federal government, as are most bank accounts. Moreover, most mutual funds sold by banks are also load funds.

TABLE 16.2

Mutual Fund Supermarkets

	Fidelity Funds Network	Charles Schwab	Jack White
Number of No-Transaction-Fee Funds Available			
	443	600	747
Number of Fund Families Available			
	48	70	126
Minimum Investment to Open Account			
	$5,000	$1,000 and up	$1,000 and up
Some Key Fund Families Not Available in No-Transaction-Fee Program			
	Lindner, Scudder, Twentieth Century	Fidelity, Lindner	Fidelity, Janus, Scudder, Twentieth Century
Transaction Fees for Funds That Are Not Available on No-Fee Basis			
$2,500 transaction	$35	$39	$27
$10,000 transaction	$35	$70	$35
$50,000 transaction	$35	$175	$50
Number of Walk-In Offices			
	82	220	1
800 Number for Information			
	544-9697	435-4000	323-3263

SUMMARY

When you invest in a mutual fund, you're buying a fraction of a very large portfolio. This portfolio may include stocks, bonds, short-term securities, and even cash. Your money is pooled with that of other investors to purchase the fund's holdings. The shareholders then own a proportionate share of the overall portfolio. The value of mutual fund shares goes up and down as the value of the mutual fund's investments goes up and down.

Investment companies invest the pooled money of a number of investors in return for a fee. An open-end investment company is actually an open-end mutual fund. It has the ability to issue and redeem shares on a daily basis, and the value of the portfolio that it holds determines the value of each ownership share in the mutual fund. The price that's paid for an open-end mutual fund share or received when the share is sold is the net asset value.

A closed-end fund has a fixed number of shares. Those shares are initially sold by the fund at its inception, and after that they trade between investors at whatever price supply and demand dictate. A unit investment trust is a pool of securities, generally municipal bonds, with each share representing a proportionate ownership in that pool. A real estate investment trust, or REIT, is similar to a mutual fund, with the funds going either directly into real estate or for real estate loans.

Although some mutual funds have no sales commission, others impose a sales commission, and still others require a hefty annual management fee. A load is simply a sales commission; thus, a load fund is one that charges a sales commission. A mutual fund that doesn't charge a commission is referred to as a no-load fund.

The Feeling Is Mutual

When deciding how and where to invest, many people fail to take into account their particular tax situation. Consequently, income taxes eat up a large part of their return. Understanding some of the tax implications may allow more of the earnings to end up in your pocket.

☑ Mutual funds pass along to shareholders the taxable income from their investments in the form of dividends and capital gains. Even if all distributions are automatically reinvested, the tax liability is your responsibility. The percentage of total return that these taxable elements comprise could be of great concern to anyone attempting to lower his or her income taxes.

☑ When funds pay out capital gains (normally at the end of the year), the price per share decreases by the amount paid out. If you buy just before a capital gains distribution is made, you pay the higher share price, and part of your original investment is immediately returned to you in the form of a taxable capital gain. In other words, don't buy a tax liability by investing right before a distribution date.

☑ Consider tax implications when moving money from one fund to another. Even if you "transfer" within the same fund family, the IRS deems the transaction a sale and purchase, and you are taxed on any gain from the sale.

☑ Unlike individual stocks on which you control when gains will be taken, mutual funds have capital gains when the manager decides to sell appreciated assets. Morningstar and other analyses give an estimate of the percentage of the fund's assets with such exposure. This information may sway your choice when selecting from a group of similar funds. Some have extremely large unrealized capital gains which could become the shareholders' tax liability at any time.

☑ Fund companies may not provide you with information regarding the cost basis of your shares if you make several partial redemptions. It is important to keep records of all purchases, distributions, and withdrawals so that you can determine the gain or loss from any sale. When selling part of your shares, you may be able to choose an average cost per share figure or designate specific shares to sell. It all depends on whether you are trying to reduce or increase your taxable gain at that time. Beware, once you choose a method of determining cost basis, you normally cannot change it for the life of that particular fund.

☑ You may wish to consult your financial planner or tax advisor before any purchases or redemptions are made. Ownership of the fund (for example, parent versus child), taxability of the income, and use of gains and losses are important aspects of your overall financial picture.

To allow you to more easily choose from the approximately 6,000 mutual funds available, funds are categorized according to their objective. The process of selecting a mutual fund involves determining your investment goals, identifying funds that meet your objectives, and evaluating those funds. There's a wealth of information available to aid you in evaluating mutual funds. The *Wall Street Journal* provides daily mutual fund listings and quotes. Two other excellent sources of information that are available at many libraries are *Wiesenberger Investment Companies Service* and *Morningstar Mutual Funds*.

You should be very aware of any and all mutual fund expenses and try to avoid them if at all possible. The return from investing in a mutual fund can be in the form of dividends or capital gains distributions, or a change in the net asset value (NAV) of the shares held. Capital gains result from selling securities for more than what they were originally bought for.

Review Questions

1. What makes investing in a mutual fund different from owning a stock or bond directly? How does a mutual fund work? (LO 1)
2. If a small investor wants to implement Axiom 3, why is a mutual fund a good investment choice? (LO 1)
3. Name and briefly describe the seven advantages associated with owning a mutual fund. (LO 1)
4. In addition to offering advantages, mutual funds also have five disadvantages. Name and briefly describe these five disadvantages. (LO 1)
5. Why can't a mutual fund diversify away systematic risk? (LO 1)
6. What is meant by the term "pooling money from investors" in relation to mutual fund investing? Is this an advantage or a disadvantage? Why? (LO 2)
7. Mutual fund investors make money in three ways. Name and briefly describe these three methods. (LO 2)
8. How are mutual funds organized? How are investment managers typically compensated for their services? (LO 2)
9. Identify and describe the four most common types of investment companies. (LO 2)
10. Balanced funds are very similar to asset allocation funds. Describe how these two types of funds differ from each other. (LO 2)
11. What is a REIT, and how is one similar to and different from a mutual fund? (LO 2)
12. What's the primary difference between a load fund and a no-load fund? (LO 2)
13. Why are money market mutual funds considered practically risk-free? (LO 3)
14. List six ways in which bond funds are different from individual bonds. What type of investor would be interested in investing in a bond fund? (LO 3)
15. Before purchasing a mutual fund, you should undertake a specific evaluation process. What are the three steps involved in this process? (LO 5)
16. What is an index fund and why should most investors consider purchasing shares in an index fund versus another type of stock fund? (LO 3)
17. How does Morningstar classify equity mutual funds into boxes? Briefly describe the differences associated with each box (see Figure 16.5). (LO 5,6)

Problems and Activities

1. Calculate the net asset value for a mutual fund with the following values: (LO 2)

    Market value of securities held in the portfolio = $650 million
    Liabilities of the fund = $25 million
    Shares outstanding = 80 million

2. The following information pertains to The Big Returns Fund: (LO 2)

    Front-end load: 4.50 percent
    Back-end load: 3 percent if sold within 3 years
    Management fee: 1.25 percent
    12b-1 fee: 0.25 percent

    Assume that you wanted to purchase $1,000 worth of shares in this fund. How much would you pay in initial commissions? If you sold your shares 2 years after your initial purchase, how much would you pay in commissions? How much in annual expenses would you pay to own this fund?

3. Match the following types of stock funds to the appropriate stocks that would typically be found in each portfolio: (LO 3)

Growth funds   a. foreign stocks

Growth-and-income funds   b. market basket that represents the S&P 500

Sector fund   c. 65 percent of stocks from the technology industry

Index fund   d. dividend-paying blue-chip stocks

International fund   e. high growth and high P/E companies

Small-company fund   f. companies with strong earnings and some dividends

Aggressive growth fund   g. small companies that trade on the OTC market

4. Assume that you're invested in the WOW Fund. Calculate your total return based on the following information: (LO 6)

Capital gains distribution = $0.68
Dividends distributed = $1.12
Beginning NAV = $43.00
Ending NAV = $44.56

5. At the beginning of last year, Mike purchased 200 shares of The Super Duper Fund at an NAV of $23.75 and automatically reinvested all distributions. As a result of reinvesting, Mike ended the year with 265 shares of the fund with an NAV of $20.50. What was Mike's total return for the year on this investment? (LO 6)

6. Which of the following funds, in terms of costs, would be the better investment for someone who initially invests $5,000 and knows the fund will be sold at the end of 5 years? (Assume that each fund's total return is 12 percent a year before expenses. (LO 2)

	Fund 1	Fund 2	Fund 3
Front-end load	8.50%	4.50%	0.00%
Back-end load	0.00%	2.00% within 3 years	0.00%
Management fee	0.85%	1.00%	1.35%
12b-1 fee	0.00%	0.25%	0.50%

7. Use the following information to answer the questions: (LO 5)

Fund Name	NAV	YTD % Ret	Max Init Chrg	Exp Ratio
Invest Small	$18.47	−0.4	5.50	1.33
JEG Bold	$12.24	+16.3	0.00	0.95
Zippy Growth	$ 4.56	+1.2	0.00	2.25

a. How much would you pay for one share of each fund listed above?
b. Calculate tomorrow's NAV for each fund, assuming each fund loses 5 percent.

8. Melanie is considering purchasing shares in an international bond fund. She's limited her search to one open-end and one closed-end fund. Information of the funds follows: (LO 2)

	Open-End	Closed-End
NAV	$15.50	$27.25
Sales price	no-load	$29.00
Annual expenses	1.45%	1.40%
YTD return	12.00%	12.50%

a. How much would Melanie pay for the open-end fund? How much would she pay for the closed-end fund?

b. Is the closed-end fund selling at a discount or a premium to its NAV?

c. Given both funds' similar returns and expense ratios, would you recommend that Melanie purchase the closed-end fund? Why or why not?

Suggested Projects

1. Take a survey of classmates, friends, and relatives to find out what they think accounts for the popularity of mutual funds among investors. Why do you think mutual funds are so popular? (LO 1)

2. Go to the library and browse through the most recent copy of *Morningstar Mutual Funds* or *Wiesenberger Investment Companies Service.* Which service seems to offer the most useful information in the easiest to read and understand format? Compare the ratings from each service for a single mutual fund. Were the ratings significantly different from each other? Why might this happen? (LO 2)

3. Using your newly attained knowledge of the differences between equity, mortgage, and hybrid REITs, use a recent copy of *Value Line* to obtain phone numbers for REITs representing each sector. Call each firm and request an annual report. When you receive the annual reports, read through them and determine if the REIT's focus is clear. (LO 2)

4. Check out the Web site offered by the Mutual Fund Education Alliance at www.mfea.com. Use this Web site to sort the funds listed according to their expense ratios. Do you see any correlation between low expense ratios and better performance? Make a list of why it's always a good recommendation to invest in mutual funds with low expense ratios. (LO 2)

5. Refer to the different types of stock and bond funds listed in the chapter. Which type of fund would you recommend to a close family member? What information might you need to make an informed selection? (LO 4)

6. Obtain a mutual fund's toll-free number from a source such as Morningstar or a magazine such as *Kiplinger's Personal Finance* or *Money.* Call the fund and request a prospectus. When you receive the prospectus, look for the key pieces of information as outlined in this chapter. In general, did you find the information provided easy to read and understand? Was the mutual fund's purpose and investment strategy stated in a clear and concise manner? (LO 5)

7. Call one of the three largest brokerage firms that offer a "mutual fund supermarket" (Charles Schwab at 800-435-4000; Fidelity at 800-544-9697; Jack White at 800-323-3263). Obtain a list of funds available through the supermarket. What are some of the advantages given for purchasing funds through a supermarket, according to the information you received? Does the information describe how the brokerage firms selling the funds get paid? How do you think they get compensated for offering this service? (LO 5)

8. Pick a mutual fund (either using your own research or randomly from the newspaper) and track the fund's price change for 2 to 3 weeks. If you owned 100 shares of the fund, how much would you have made or lost (in dollars and percentage) during the tracking period? Find historical data on the fund from a source such as Morningstar. Did the fund perform as predicted over the time you tracked it? Prepare a short report, including a graph of the fund's daily price changes, detailing the fund's performance and what type of investor the fund might appeal to. (LO 6)

9. Use the three-step process offered in the text to pick an actual mutual fund for yourself based on your current circumstances. Look ahead a bit and use the same process to pick a mutual fund for yourself after graduation. Prepare a short report indicating the differences or similarities in the types of funds you would choose for yourself before and after graduation. (LO 5, 6)

Discussion Case 1

Ken Mercer recently inherited $5,000. He's always been interested in investing, but until he received the inheritance he lacked sufficient resources to even think about investing. Ken just got off the phone with a stockbroker who recommended that he invest in the stock of a small company that makes computer components and is traded over-the-counter. Over the past year the stock has fluctuated in value dramatically, but Ken is definitely interested in this type of stock because Ken feels that high-tech companies offer good returns. When asked about the risk associated with such an investment, Ken indicated that he was willing to take high risks if superior returns could be obtained.

Questions

1. Given the fact that Ken has only $5,000 to invest, explain why he should consider investing in mutual funds rather than in individual stocks.

2. What type(s) of stock mutual fund(s) would you recommend Ken invest in? Why?

3. In helping Ken make an investment choice, what factor would you tell him is most important when choosing a mutual fund?

4. Although most mutual funds will provide Ken with diversification, what type of risk will Ken still be exposed to if he purchases a mutual fund?

5. In order to assure Ken of the liquidity and marketability of his investment, would you recommend that he invest in an open-end or a closed-end mutual fund? Why?

6. In terms of costs, which would you recommend to Ken, load or no-load funds? Why?

Discussion Case 2

Naomi has decided that she needs to invest her savings somewhere besides her bank account, where she's earning only about 3 percent annually. She's heard that money market mutual funds and bond funds may provide higher yields than bank accounts and offer safety equal to the bank. Naomi's primary investment goal is to keep her savings (about $11,000 when she last checked) secure and accessible so that she can make a down payment on a house within the next 3 years. Naomi has several questions regarding investing in mutual funds, and she's come to you for help.

Questions

1. Identify the types of mutual funds that would be appropriate in meeting Naomi's objective.

2. What sources could Naomi use to obtain specific information and ratings on different funds?

3. When reviewing a fund's prospectus or an analysis provided by Morningstar, what specific type of information should Naomi look for?

4. When evaluating a fund, how much importance should Naomi place in a fund's past performance?

5. Given Naomi's goal and your response to question 1, how important are loads, fees, and expenses in her search for a good mutual fund?

6. Provide Naomi with six reasons she should consider purchasing shares in a bond fund.

7. What type of bond fund would you recommend? Why?

8. In terms of the risk-return trade-off, what length of maturity for a bond fund would be appropriate for Naomi?

9. Name and describe at least four services provided by mutual funds that should appeal to Naomi.

Continuing Case: Don and Maria Chang

PART IV: MANAGING YOUR INVESTMENTS
(Chapters 12, 13, 14, 15, and 16)

The bank where Don works is expanding customer services to include the sale of mutual funds. Don has always preferred the safety of a bank account, but now that the bank is starting to sell mutual funds, he's curious about the investment risk and return from other investments such as stocks and bonds. Again, they have come to you with a list of questions, only their investments have not changed. They still have the Jimminy Jump-up Mutual Fund account for the house down payment, the Great Guns Balanced Mutual Fund, and the collection of antique jewelry. They did, however, on your recommendation reduce some expenses and have accumulated $1,500 for an emergency fund.

Questions

1. What type of investment risk should be of most concern to Don and Maria when they choose an investment for their emergency fund? What investment risk is most important when thinking about investments for a college fund and retirement?

2. Based on the Changs' stage in the life cycle, what type of investment asset allocation would be appropriate, assuming they want to establish a retirement savings fund? What types of stocks would be appropriate for the Changs to include in the equity portion of their asset allocation plan? Should they consider international common stocks? Why or why not? Would you recommend that they consider investing in a stock index mutual fund? Why or why not? What type of bond would be appropriate for the fixed-income portion of their asset allocation plan? (*Hint:* Be sure to list the bond maturity, rating, and issuer.)

3. Under which circumstances should Don and Maria change their initial asset allocation plan?

4. Assume that the Changs decided to begin investing in stocks for their retirement at the onset of a bear market. What recommendation would you give to them?

5. What sources of investment information could Don and Maria use to obtain additional information on potential stock, bond, and mutual fund investments?

6. Would you recommend that Don and Maria work with a financial planner in creating, implementing, and monitoring a plan to meet their goals? When choosing a financial planner or broker, what type of agency problems should they consider?

7. If Don and Maria wanted to create a portfolio of common stocks, approximately how many stocks would they need to include in their portfolio to achieve adequate diversification? What type of investment would provide the same type of diversification in one step?

8. The Changs are concerned about the federal taxes paid on various investment alternatives. They are in the 28-percent marginal tax bracket. Show the calculations necessary to answer the following questions.
   a. A tax-free money market mutual fund is currently yielding 2.40 percent. Should Don and Maria move their savings into this fund or keep their money in the bank earning 3.00 percent?
   b. If a U.S. Treasury note is currently yielding 8 percent, what is the minimum interest rate that the Changs must receive in order to purchase an equivalent municipal bond?

9. A stockbroker has recommended that Don and Maria purchase a 20-year corporate bond to help meet Andy's college savings goal. The bond currently yields 8 percent and sells for $1,000. If interest rates increase two percentage points and the bond is sold, how much will the bond sell for at that time? Calculate the bond price if the rates were to fall by 1 percent. What investing rule has this proven?

10. Why should Don and Maria consider investing in mutual funds to meet their goals? What specific types of mutual funds would be appropriate for meeting their investment objectives? (*Hint:* Feel free to combine funds into an asset allocation strategy by providing percentages to invest in each type of fund.)
    a. emergency fund
    b. house down payment savings
    c. college fund
    d. retirement fund

11. In order to help the Changs systematically save for their goals, what mutual fund services would you recommend that they use? Why?

12. Would you recommend no-load or load funds to the Changs? Why?

Chapter 17

RETIREMENT PLANNING

Most people assume that if you make it big early in life, retirement planning should be a breeze. You live off your plenty and put a little away and let time and compounding work their magic. For Tina Turner, though, making it big early in life didn't make anything a breeze. Born in 1939 to cotton plantation workers in Brownsville, Tennessee, Turner moved to St. Louis to live with relatives when she was in her teens. It was there she met Ike Turner, her future husband and singing partner. Together they hit the big time, becoming huge stars by the time the seventies arrived, with such hits as *River Deep, Mountain Wide,* and an R&B-style version of Creedence Clearwater Revival's *Proud Mary.* Unfortunately, the big time isn't all that Ike hit. After being beaten bloody in July 1976, Tina Turner finally walked out of her 20-year abusive marriage to Ike. When she left, she had no recording contract, no savings, no fancy cars or homes—just 36 cents and a Mobil gas card.

For a while, Turner and her four children lived on food stamps. Although facing poverty, she couldn't bring herself to take any money whatsoever when she finally divorced Ike in 1978. Instead, she managed to support herself and her family by playing Holiday Inns and any other minor clubs that would book her. By 1979, she found herself $500,000 in debt, with no prospects and no one to lend a helping hand. It looked as if Tina Turner had retired to a life of poverty and obscurity. Fortunately, along came Roger Davies, a young Australian promoter, who signed on as her manager. With his

Learning Objectives

After reading this chapter you should be able to:

1. Understand the changing nature of retirement planning.
2. Plan for your retirement.
3. Set up a retirement plan.
4. Contribute to a tax-favored retirement plan to help fund your retirement.
5. Choose how your retirement benefits are paid out to you.
6. Put together a retirement plan and effectively monitor it.

part five
RETIREMENT AND ESTATE PLANNING

help, Turner paid off her bills, put together a new backup band, and got a fresh start in 1980. Despite record company skepticism, she managed to get a new recording contract, and by 1984 she had a number one hit with *What's Love Got to Do With It*. Today Turner continues to be a major star, and you'd better believe that she's planned for her next retirement to be a life of comfort and ease.

You may think you're too young or not wealthy enough to worry about retirement. Think again. Regardless of your age, you need to start thinking about retirement. Actually, you need to do more than think—you need to start saving for retirement. By saving for retirement, you're really focusing on a specific financial goal. Of course, as you learned in chapters 1 and 2, you're going to have a lot of financial goals in your life. Retirement, though, is a biggie. After all, how well you do in achieving your retirement goal is probably going to determine how much you enjoy the last 20 or more years of your life.

Unfortunately, for most people, today looms larger than tomorrow. That car loan or mortgage you're trying to pay off this year will no doubt seem to be far more important than your financial situation 30 to 40 years from now. It's hard to worry about retiring when you're young, but just think how worried you'll be when you're 65 and you don't have a dime to retire on. Big money in a second career may have worked for Tina Turner, but it probably won't work for you. Fortunately, you never need to really worry about retirement. With a sound plan and a little savings discipline, you can retire to a life of relative ease without ever having to fret or fear. Let's take a look at how to do it.

RETIREMENT IN THE PAST: SOCIAL SECURITY AND EMPLOYER-FUNDED PENSIONS

Time was when retirement planning wasn't necessary—retirement meant taking a pension from your longtime employer and letting Social Security pick up any slack. Not anymore. Thanks to the recent drive to cut spending, employers tend not to pay pensions, and those that still do have reduced them to as little as possible. That leaves a lot of slack for Social Security, but thanks to the government's drive to cut its own spending, there might not be such a thing as Social Security by the time you retire. Nowadays, you've got to come up with the funds for your retirement all by yourself. Sound scary? Well, it's actually not. All you need is a good retirement plan. We'll explain exactly how to make a good retirement plan, but first we should explain how Social Security and employer-funded pensions work. No, we're not trying to rub it in and show you what you're missing. You simply need to know about past retirement plans before you can dive into the present ones.

SOCIAL SECURITY

For many senior citizens, Social Security is their primary source of retirement income. However, for younger workers who won't face retirement until 40 years down the road, the Social Security system may seem more like a mirage—they can see it now, but when they get there it may disappear. Still, for many of the 40 million individuals receiving benefits, Social Security is the difference between living in poverty and modest comfort. Let's take a look at how the Social Security system currently functions.

> ### The Facts of Life
> A recent survey by Third Millennium of 500 people between the ages of 18 and 34 found that while 46 percent thought UFOs existed, only 28 percent believed that Social Security would be there when they retired.

Financing Social Security

To begin with, Social Security isn't an investment. When you pay money into Social Security, you aren't investing for retirement, you're purchasing mandatory insurance that provides for you and your family in the event of death, disability, health problems, or retirement. Moreover, the benefits paid by Social Security aren't intended to allow you to live in comfort after you retire. They're intended to provide a base level of protection.

Whether you want to or not, you fund Social Security during your working years by paying taxes directly to the Social Security system. If you're not self-employed, both you and your employer pay into the system—each paying 7.65 percent of your gross salary up to $62,700 in 1996. This deduction appears on your pay slip as "FICA," which stands for the Federal Insurance Contributions Act. These funds actually go to both Social Security and to Medicare (the government's health insurance program for the elderly, which we discussed in chapter 10). Medicare also keeps on taxing after the Social Security cap has been reached, taking an additional 1.45 percent from both you and your employer. Thus, if your salary were $62,700 in 1996, your FICA contribution would be $4,796.55. If you're self-employed, you have to pay both the employer and employee portions of FICA, at a rate of 15.3 percent up to the $62,700 limit, paying a total of $9,593.10. In addition, you pay Medicare 2.9 percent on all net earnings above $62,700.

These funds cover the payments currently being made to retirees by Social Security, while allowing for a "built-in surplus" aimed at handling payouts in the future. In other words, the FICA taxes currently being paid by today's workers are providing the money for benefit payments for today's retirees. The money you pay to FICA isn't saved up and invested just for you. Instead it gets pooled with the money all other current workers are paying to FICA and goes into a senior citizen's Social Security benefits check. The idea is that when you get old and retire, the FICA taxes paid by people working then will go into your benefits check. Unfortunately, the proportion of current workers to current Social Security recipients is shrinking rapidly. Whereas 40 years ago there were 16 workers contributing for every Social Security recipient, today the ratio is down to 3 workers to every recipient. Even worse, the problem won't go away. In fact, it will only get worse when in 40 years the ratio of working contributors to recipients will be down to a 2-to-1 ratio.

The Facts of Life

Perhaps the best way to live well during retirement is to win the lottery when you turn 65. That's pretty much what happened to Ida May Fuller, a legal secretary from Ludlow, Vermont, when she turned 65. She "invested" just $20.33 and walked away with $20,884.52 in "benefits." Granted, she received those benefits over the next 35 years as she lived to be 100, but still, that's about a 1,000-to-1 return. Even more, she didn't need to buy a ticket or stay up late and catch the drawing results on TV. How did she do it? She was the first recipient of Social Security benefits. When it's your turn, will you do as well? The answer is, not from Social Security. Fuller was at the right place at the right time. Unfortunately, you probably won't be that lucky.

Who's Eligible for Social Security?

Roughly 95 percent of all Americans are covered by Social Security. The major groups outside the system include police officers, and workers who've been continuously employed by the government since 1984, both of whom are covered by alternative retirement systems.

To become eligible for Social Security, all you have to do is pay money into the system. As you pay into the system, you receive Social Security credits. In 1996, you earned one credit for each $640 in earnings, up to a maximum of four credits per year. To qualify for benefits, you need 40 credits. Once you've met this requirement, you then become eligible for retirement, disability, and survivor benefits. Earning beyond 40 credits won't increase your benefits. If you die, some of your family members may also be eligible for Social Security benefits, even if they never paid into the system.

Retirement Benefits

The size of your Social Security benefits is determined by (1) your number of years of earnings, (2) your average level of earning, and (3) an adjustment for inflation. The formula used by Social Security attempts to provide benefits that would replace 42 percent of your average earnings over your working years, adjusted upward somewhat for those in lower income brackets and downward for those in higher income brackets. Thus, the benefits are slightly weighted toward individuals in lower income brackets because they, in general, have less savings to rely upon at retirement.

To be eligible for full retirement benefits, you need to be at least 65 years old and this age is scheduled to rise. Reduced benefits can be received by those who retire before the full retirement age as early as age 62. However, those benefits are *permanently* reduced by five-ninths of 1 percent for each month of early retirement. That means people who retire at age 62 will receive only 80 percent of their full retirement benefits, and that this reduced level of benefits is permanent.

If instead of retiring early you delay retirement, you can increase your Social Security benefits. The longer you work, the higher the average earnings base on which your benefits are calculated. In addition, those who delay retirement also have a percentage added to their Social Security benefits. In 1996, this percentage was 4.5 percent per year. Table 17.1 provides an estimate of the size of the Social Security benefits at retirement for someone who was 45 in 1996 and retired at the Social Security retirement age.

Keep in mind that, depending upon the level of your income and how you file your tax return, your Social Security benefits may be taxed. The amount of your benefits that can be taxed is based on your "combined income," which is determined by combining these factors: the sum of you and your spouse's adjusted gross income as reported to the IRS on your 1040 tax form, plus nontaxable interest, plus one-half of your Social Security benefits. In 1996, for those retirees filing joint returns with "combined income" between $32,000 and $44,000, 50 percent of their benefits was taxable. For those retirees with "combined income" greater than $44,000, 85 percent of their benefits was taxable. If you're retired, file an individual return, and have a "combined income" between $25,000 and $34,000, you'd have to pay taxes on 50 percent of your Social Security benefits. If your "combined income" is above $34,000, you'd pay taxes on 85 percent of your benefits.

You can continue to work after you officially retire, but there are earnings limits placed on those who wish to receive Social Security benefits. This limit covers those under the age of 70 who receive either retirement, dependent, or survivor benefits. In 1996, if you're under 65 and collecting Social Security, you can earn up to $8,280 without affecting your benefits. Then, for every $2 over $8,280 that you earn, your Social Security benefits are reduced by $1. If you're between 65 and 69, you can earn up to $11,520 without affecting your benefits. Above that level your benefits are reduced by $1 for every $3 that you earn. This income doesn't include pensions, annuities, investment income, Social Security, or other government benefits.

You should also be aware of the fact that the government won't automatically start sending you your Social Security check just because you're officially retired. You must notify your Social Security office and file an application 3 months before you want your first check to arrive. You'll then have the option of receiving the check in the mail or having it direct deposited in your checking or savings account at your bank. Although effective January 1, 1999, all Social Security checks must be direct deposited.

TABLE 17.1

Approximate Monthly Benefits If You Retire at Full Retirement Age and Had Steady Lifetime Earnings

Your Age in 1996	Your Family	Your Earnings in 1995				
		$20,000	$30,000	$40,000	$50,000	$61,200 or More[a]
		Your Monthly Social Security Benefits				
45	You	$ 786	$1,053	$1,201	$1,326	$1,457
	You and your spouse[b]	1,179	1,579	1,801	1,989	2,185

[a]Earnings equal to or greater than the OASDI wage base from age 22 through the year before retirement.
[b]Your spouse is assumed to be the same age as you. Your spouse may qualify for a higher retirement benefit based on his or her own work record.
Note: The accuracy of these estimates depends on the pattern of your actual past earnings and on your earnings in the future.
SOURCE: Social Security Administration, *Social Security, Understanding the Benefits,* January 1996.

Disability and Survivor Benefits

Although retirement benefits are the focus of our attention in this chapter, Social Security, as we mentioned at the onset, is actually a mandatory insurance program with insurance against poverty at retirement being only one portion of its coverage. Social Security also provides disability and survivor benefits.

Disability benefits provide protection for those who experience a physical or mental impairment that is expected to result in death or keep them from doing any substantial work for at least a year. "Substantial work" is generally defined as anything that generates monthly earnings of $500 or more.

Social Security also provides survivor benefits to families when the breadwinner dies. These payments include a small, automatic one-time payment at the time of death to help defray funeral costs, as well as continued monthly payments to your spouse if he or she is over 60, over 50 if disabled, or any age and caring for a child either under 16 or disabled and receiving Social Security benefits. Continued monthly payments are also available to your children if they're under 18 or under 19 but still in elementary or secondary school, or if they're disabled. Finally, your parents can also qualify for survivor benefits if you die and they're dependent upon you for at least half of their support.

EMPLOYER-FUNDED PENSIONS

Twenty years ago a "guaranteed" pension provided by your employer was the norm. You'd work for one company for most or all of your working life, and that company would reward your loyalty and hard work by taking care of you during your retirement. In today's job scene, where companies aren't quite so generous anymore and where employees change jobs as often as they change clothes, pension plans are rare. However, some companies do still offer pensions, but instead of calling them "pensions," most companies call them "defined-benefit plans."

Under a **defined-benefit plan**, you receive a promised or "defined" pension payout at retirement. These plans are generally **noncontributory retirement plans**, which means you don't have to pay anything into them. (With a **contributory retirement plan**, you, and usually your employer, do pay into the plan.) The payout, which you receive as taxable income, is generally based upon a formula that takes into account your age at retirement, salary level, and years of service. The formulas used can vary dramatically from company to company. Some focus only on your salary during your final few years of service, which is better for you, while others use an average of all your years' salary as a base to calculate your pension benefits. One commonly used formula is to pay out 1.5 percent of the average of your final 3 to 5 years' worth of salary times your number of years of service.

$$\text{monthly benefit} = \frac{\text{average salary}}{\text{over "final years"}} \times \text{years of service} \times 0.015$$

Defined-Benefit Plan

A traditional pension plan in which you receive a promised or "defined" pension payout at retirement. The payout is based upon a formula that takes into account your age at retirement, salary level, and years of service.

Noncontributory Retirement Plan

A retirement plan in which the employer provides all the funds and the employee need not contribute.

Contributory Retirement Plan

A retirement plan in which the employee, possibly with the help of the employer, provides the funds for the plan.

Portability

A pension fund provision that allows employees to retain and transfer any pension benefits already earned to another pension plan if they leave the company.

Vest

To gain the right to the retirement contributions made by your employer in your name. In the case of a pension plan, employees become vested when they've worked for a specified period of time and thus gained the right to pension benefits.

Funded Pension Plan

A pension plan in which the employer makes pension contributions directly to a trustee who holds and invests the employees' retirement funds.

Unfunded Pension Plan

A pension fund in which the benefits are paid out of current earnings on a pay-as-you-go basis.

LEARNING OBJECTIVE #2

Plan for your retirement.

AXIOM #8

Nothing Happens Without a Plan—Even (or Especially) a Simple Plan

Thus, if you retired after 25 years of service with an average salary of $70,000 over the final years, you'd receive $26,250 ($70,000 × 25 × 0.015 = $26,250), which would be 37.5 percent of your final average salary. In general, the most that employees, even those who've spent their entire careers with the same company, ever receive from a defined-benefit pension is only 40 to 45 percent of their before-retirement income.

One nice thing about a defined-benefit plan is that the employer bears the investment risk associated with the plan. That is, regardless of what the stock and bond markets do, you're still promised the same amount. You also have the option of extending pension coverage to your spouse. Thus, when you die, your spouse will continue to receive pension payments.

Unfortunately, companies can change their pension policies with little notice. For example, in 1995 Kmart froze its pension obligations for 290,000 workers and closed its defined benefits plan to new employees. One additional problem with defined-benefits programs is that they lack **portability**—that is, if you leave the company, your pension doesn't go with you. If you're **vested**, meaning you've worked long enough for the company to have the right to receive pension benefits, you'll eventually get a pension. However, it'll likely be small owing to the fact that pensions are generally based on years of service and salary levels. If you're not yet vested and you leave, you can kiss your pension good-bye.

Another problem with defined-benefit plans is that few of them—in fact only 1 in 10—adjust for inflation once the benefits begin. Thus, the benefit level stays constant over your retirement while inflation reduces the spending power of each dollar.

A final problem with defined-benefit plans is that they're not all **funded pension plans**, in which the employer makes regular pension contributions to a trustee who collects and invests the employees' retirement funds. In other words, the employer sets up a separate account to guarantee the payment of pension benefits. In an **unfunded pension plan**, the pension expenses are paid out of current company earnings. In effect, these are pay-as-you-go pension plans. Needless to say, a funded plan is much safer than an unfunded plan, which would disappear if the company went under. Fortunately, the law requires employers to notify employees if their pension fund is less than 90 percent funded.

PLAN NOW, RETIRE LATER

It's incredibly easy to avoid thinking about retirement—retirement is simply too far away. This brings us back to **Axiom 8: Nothing Happens Without a Plan—Even (or Especially) a Simple Plan**. If you're like most people, you can probably spend money without thinking about it, but you can't save money without thinking about it. That's the problem. Saving isn't a natural event—it must be planned. Unfortunately, by the same token, planning isn't natural either. For that reason, although an elaborate, complicated plan might be ideal, in general, it never comes to fruition. Thus, you might be better off starting with a modest, uncomplicated retirement plan. Once the plan becomes part of your financial routine, then you can modify and expand your plan. The bottom line is that a retirement plan can't be postponed. The longer it's put off, the more difficult accomplishing your goals becomes. Figure 17.1 shows the steps of the retirement planning process. Let's take a look at each step in depth.

Step 1: Set Goals

The first step in planning for your retirement is figuring out just what you want to do when you retire. Naturally, you'll want to be able to support yourself and pay any possible medical bills you might have, but that could cost a little or it could cost a whole lot. Therefore, you need to start by asking yourself some basic questions: How costly a lifestyle do you want to lead? Do you want to live like a king or live more economically, perhaps like a minor duke or nobleman? Do you currently have any medical conditions that you know are going to be costly later in life? Once you've answered these questions,

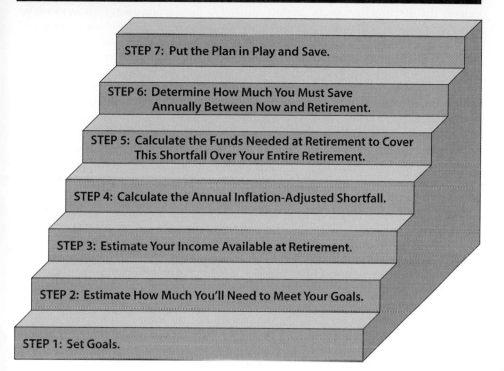

The Seven Steps to Funding Your Retirement Needs

FIGURE 17.1

STEP 7: Put the Plan in Play and Save.

STEP 6: Determine How Much You Must Save Annually Between Now and Retirement.

STEP 5: Calculate the Funds Needed at Retirement to Cover This Shortfall Over Your Entire Retirement.

STEP 4: Calculate the Annual Inflation-Adjusted Shortfall.

STEP 3: Estimate Your Income Available at Retirement.

STEP 2: Estimate How Much You'll Need to Meet Your Goals.

STEP 1: Set Goals.

you can pretty much set your most basic goal of being able to support yourself and pay your medical expenses. Then it's time to think about other goals you might have. Do you want to stay in your current house, or will you want to move to Florida and eat early-bird specials? Do you want to live in a retirement community or your own residence? Do you want to travel? Do you want to be able to buy that Dodge Viper and hit the open road? Do you want to have money set aside for your family? It might be hard to sit down and consider everything you might want to do when you retire, but you'll need to be as exhaustive as possible when thinking about and setting your goals.

As you learned back in chapter 1, goals aren't entirely useful unless you include the element of time and decide when you hope to achieve those goals. In the case of retirement, you need to figure out exactly when you'd like to retire. Typical retirement age is 65, but more and more people are putting off retirement until 70 or even later. The time frame for achieving your retirement goals is more important than you might think. For example, if you want to retire at age 60, you'll need to save up a lot of money to be able to pay for a lengthy period of retirement. If you really love your job and don't want to retire until you're 70, though, you won't need to save as much because your period of retirement should be shorter, and you'll be giving yourself an extra 10 years to prepare for it.

Step 2: Estimate How Much You'll Need to Meet Your Goals

Once you've got your retirement goals in place, it's time to start thinking about how to achieve them and turn them into a secure retirement. The second step of retirement planning helps you do so by turning your goals into estimated dollar figures. These figures will be estimates of how much money you're going to need to achieve your goals once you reach retirement. Of course, estimates aren't always accurate or reliable, but, hey, it's the best we can do. It'd be nice if we could all see into the future—that way we wouldn't have to rely on estimates of our needs. We'd just know them. Unfortunately, we're stuck guessing about the future. If you're smart, though, you can make some pretty good educated guesses. All you need do is start with your current living expenses.

Why do your future needs start with your current living expenses? Well, as we've already seen, your main goal is going to be supporting yourself. You'll need to use the amount that it currently takes to support yourself as the starting point for how much it's going to cost to support yourself in retirement. Because elderly people have usually paid off their houses and consume less than younger people, most financial planners estimate that supporting yourself in retirement will cost only 70 to 80 percent of what it costs to support yourself before retirement. Back in chapter 2, you examined "living expenditures" or what it costs to support yourself when you calculated your personal income statement. Let's say the number you came up with was $35,000. Well, your basic retirement living expenses would then be somewhere around $28,000 ($35,000 × 0.8).

Of course, this $28,000 amount is just the tip of the iceberg. Remember, you have other goals that are going to cost money. You'll need to estimate—in today's dollars—how much each goal is going to cost you annually. Adding up the estimated costs of achieving all your goals, including the base amount for your living expenses, will give you, in today's dollars, the income amount you'll need each year to fund your retirement. However, you're not done yet. Don't forget the government. Yes, you need to factor in the effect of taxes, too. Table 17.2 will give you a rough idea of the average tax rate you'll pay on your required retirement income. All you need do is divide the amount of retirement income you'll need by (1 – your tax rate). This figure will tell you exactly how much pretax income, in today's dollars, you'll need each year to fund your retirement.

Take a look at Mary and Lou Grant, introduced in chapter 2. They calculated their annual living expenditures to be $52,234. To obtain an estimate of their annual living expenses at retirement in today's dollars, they'd multiply this amount by 0.8, which would come to $41,787. They'd then need to adjust this amount for any additional expenditures to meet their other goals. For example, the Grants may wish to move to a more expensive area of the country, or they may wish to travel more after retirement. Let's assume that the Grants wish to take two additional vacation trips annually at $2,000 per trip, measured in today's dollars, for an increase of $4,000 per year. They would thus need a total of $45,787 for their annual living expenditures at retirement in today's dollars, as calculated on line D of Figure 17.2. The Grants now must adjust this number for taxes. Using Table 17.2, we see that the average tax rate for retirement income between $40,000 and $50,000 is approximately 12 percent. However, since the Grants intend to retire in a state with a relatively high state income tax, they have decided to use 14 percent rather than 12 percent as

TABLE 17.2

The Average Tax Rate
To estimate your anticipated average tax rate at retirement, you can use the following tables based upon current tax rates. If you anticipate a change in future tax rates—for example, a flat tax—use that number.

Retirement Income	Average Tax Rate	
	Couples Filing Jointly	Individuals
$ 20,000	7%	10%
30,000	10	14
40,000	12	17
50,000	14	20
60,000	17	22
70,000	19	23
80,000	21	24
90,000	22	25
100,000	23	26
150,000	28	30

FIGURE 17.2

Worksheet for Funding Your Retirement Needs

	The Grant's Example	Your Numbers
STEP 1: Estimate Your Annual Needs at Retirement.		
A. Present level of your living expenditures on an after-tax basis	$52,234	
B. Times 0.80 equals: Base retirement expenditure level in today's dollars	× 0.80 = $41,787	
C. Plus or minus: Anticipated increases or decreases in living expenditures after retirement	+ $4,000	
D. Equals: Annual living expenditures at retirement in today's dollars on an after-tax basis	= $45,787	
E. Before-tax adjustment factor, based on an average tax rate of 14 % (If the average tax rate is not known, it can be estimated using Table 17.2, "The Average Tax Rate.") This is used to calculate the before-tax income necessary to cover the annual living expenses in line D. In this case, assume an average tax rate of 14%. Thus, line F, the before tax income = line D/line E, where line E = (1 − Average Tax Rate)	÷ 0.86	
F. Equals: The before-tax income necessary to cover the annual living expenses in line D line D divided by line E =	$53,241	
STEP 2: Estimate Your Income Available at Retirement.		
G. Income from Social Security in today's dollars	$18,000	
H. Plus: Projected pension benefits in today's dollars	+ $25,000	
I. Plus: Other income in today's dollars	+ $0	
J. Equals (lines G + H + I): Anticipated retirement income, in today's dollars	= $43,000	
STEP 3: Calculate the (Annual) Inflation-Adjusted Shortfall.		
K. Anticipated shortfall in today's dollars (line F minus line J)	= $10,241	
L. Inflation adjustment factor, based on an anticipated inflation rate of 4% between now and retirement with 30 years to retirement (FVIFs are found in Appendix B): $FVIF_{\text{inflation rate \%, no. years to retirement}}$	× 3.243	
M. Equals: Inflation-adjusted shortfall (line K × line L)	= $33,212	
STEP 4: Calculate the Total Funds Needed at Retirement to Cover This Shortfall Over the Number of Years You Expect to Be Retired (assuming an inflation-adjusted return of 5% [return (9%) minus the inflation rate (4%)] during your retirement period, with retirement anticipated to last for 30 years).		
N. Calculate the funds needed at retirement to cover the inflation-adjusted shortfall over the entire retirement period, assuming that these funds can be invested at 9% and that the inflation rate over this period is 4%. Thus, determining the present value of a 30-year annuity assuming a 5% inflation-adjusted return (PVIFAs are found in Appendix E). $PVIFA_{\text{inflation-adjusted return, no. years in retirement}}$	= 15.373	
O. Equals: Funds needed at retirement to finance the shortfall (line M × line N) × line M =	$510,568	
STEP 5: Determine How Much You Must Save Annually Between Now and Retirement (30 years until retirement and earning a 9% return) to Cover the Shortfall.		
P. Future value interest factor for an annuity for 30 years, given a 9% expected annual return: $FVIFA_{\text{expected rate of return, no. years to retirement}}$ (FVIFA's are found in Appendix D)	= 136.305	
Q. Equals: PMT, or the amount that must be saved annually for 30 years and invested at 9% in order to accumulate the line O amount at the end of 30 years line O divided by line P =	$3,746	

their estimated tax rate. The Grants must simply divide their annual living expenditures by $(1 - 0.14)$, or 0.86, resulting in $53,241. In effect, of this $53,241, 14 percent, or $7,454 will go to pay taxes, leaving $45,787 to cover the Grants' living expenditures.

Step 3: Estimate Your Income Available at Retirement

As you've probably guessed, once you know how much income you're going to need when you retire, the logical next step is figuring out just how much income you're going to have. First, estimate your Social Security benefits. The easiest way of doing this is to contact the Social Security Administration directly—they'll provide you with an estimate. Just call Social Security (800-772-1213) and request a Personal Earnings and Benefits Estimate Statement. To the Social Security benefits, you add any projected pension benefits in today's dollars plus any other retirement income available.

To determine how much your pension will pay, you should stop at your company's employee benefits office. Get a copy of your individual benefit statement, which describes your pension plan and estimates how much your plan is worth today and the level of benefits you'll receive when you retire. There are a number of basic questions included in Figure 17.3 that you should be able to answer about your company's pension fund. If you can't answer any of these questions, you should contact your employee benefits office and ask them directly.

Returning to our example of the Grants, they estimate their Social Security income to be $18,000 and their pension benefits to be $25,000, giving them a total level of retirement income of $43,000 in today's dollars.

AXIOM #15

Just Do It!

> ### *Stop and Think*
> Much of retirement planning deals simply with facing reality and forcing yourself to recognize what your financial needs for retirement actually are. Once you know what your needs are, and how difficult it will become to achieve those goals if you postpone the saving process, it becomes easier to bite the bullet and, as **Axiom 15** says, **Just Do It!**

Step 4: Calculate the Inflation-Adjusted Shortfall

Now it's time to compare the amounts from steps 2 and 3. For most people, there's a big difference between the retirement income they need and the retirement income they'll have available. As pensions are phased out and Social Security becomes less certain, that difference is going to get bigger and bigger. For the Grants, the before-tax income level they need is $53,241 (line F of Figure 17.2), whereas their available income is only $43,000 (line J), leaving a shortfall of $10,241 (line K). Of course, this shortfall is in today's dollars, as have been all of our calculations so far. To determine what the shortfall will be in retirement dollars, 30 years from now, the Grants must project $10,241 into the future, which is simply a problem involving the future value of a single cash flow. As you should recall, we need an inflation rate to work a future value problem. Let's assume that the inflation rate over the next 30 years will be 4 percent annually. Thus, to move money forward in time 30 years, assuming a 4-percent rate of inflation, multiply it by the $FVIF_{4\%,\,30\,\text{yr}}$, which is 3.243 (as found in Appendix B), yielding an inflation-adjusted shortfall of $33,212.

$$FV = PV(FVIF_{i\%,\,n\,\text{yr}})$$
$$FV = \$10,241(FVIF_{4\%,\,30\,\text{yr}})$$
$$FV = \$10,241(3.243)$$
$$FV = \$33,212$$

FIGURE 17.3

Questions You Should Be Able to Answer about Your Company's Pension Plan

☑ Is this a noncontributory or contributory plan?

☑ What are the pension requirements in terms of age and years of service?

☑ Is there an early retirement age, and if so, what are the benefits?

☑ What is the full benefits retirement age?

☑ How does the vesting process work?

☑ If I retire at age 65, how much will I receive in the way of pension payments?

☑ If I die, what benefits will my spouse and family receive?

☑ What is the present size of my pension credit today?

☑ If I am disabled, will I receive pension benefits?

☑ Can I withdraw money from my retirement fund before retirement?

☑ Can I borrow on my retirement fund, and if so, what are the terms?

☑ If my company is taken over or goes bankrupt, what happens to the pension fund?

☑ Is the plan funded? If not, what portion of the benefits could the company pay today?

☑ Is my pension plan a defined contribution plan or a defined benefit plan?

☑ What are the choices available to me regarding ways that the pension might be paid out?

Step 5: Calculate the Funds Needed at Retirement to Cover This Shortfall

By now you should know how much of an annual shortfall you'll have in your retirement funding. That is, you'll know how much additional money you'll need to come up with each year to support yourself in retirement. The question then becomes, How much must you have saved by retirement to fund this annual shortfall? Let's return to our example of the Grants. We know they have an annual shortfall of $33,212 in retirement (future) dollars. They don't want inflation, which we assumed to continue at 4 percent, to erode the value of their retirement savings. That means they'll want their retirement savings to grow by 4 percent each year just to cover inflation. In addition, assume they can earn a 9-percent return on their retirement funds. That is to say, whereas the shortfall payout will increase by 4 percent per year to compensate for inflation, they earn 9 percent per year on their investment. In effect, they earn an inflation-adjusted rate of 5 percent (that is, 9% − 4%) per year. Thus, in determining how much the Grants need to have saved if they wish to withdraw $33,212 per year while earning a 5-percent inflation-adjusted return, you're really determining the present value of an annuity. In this case, it's a 30-year annuity, because the Grants want this retirement supplement to continue for 30 years, and it's discounted back to present at 5 percent as follows:

$$PV = PMT(PVIFA_{i\%,\ n\ yr})$$
$$PV = \$33{,}212(PVIFA_{5\%,\ 30\ yr})$$
$$PV = \$33{,}212(15.373)$$
$$PV = \$510{,}568$$

Thus, we multiply the inflation-adjusted shortfall of $33,212 by the $PVIFA_{5\%,\ 30\ yr}$ of 15.373 (found in Appendix E), which shows that $510,568 is the amount that the Grants need to accumulate by retirement.

Step 6: Determine How Much You Must Save Annually Between Now and Retirement

Now you know the total amount you'll need to have saved up by the time you retire, but you're not about to put it all away at once. Instead, you'll need to put money away little by little, year by year. The question you'll need to answer in this step is, How much do you need to put away each year? The Grants know they need to accumulate $510,568 by the time they retire in 30 years. To determine how much they need to put away each year to achieve this amount, they need to know how much they can earn on their investments between now and when they retire. Let's assume they can earn 9 percent. This then becomes a simple future value of an annuity problem, solving for PMT in the formula.

$$FV = PMT(FVIFA_{i\%,\ n\ yr})$$
$$\$510,568 = PMT(FVIFA_{9\%,\ 30\ yr})$$
$$\$510,568 = PMT(136.305)$$
$$PMT = \$3,746$$

Therefore, the Grants must save $3,746 each year for the next 30 years at 9 percent to meet their retirement goals.

Step 7: Put the Plan in Play and Save

OK, you've finally figured out exactly how much you need to save each year to achieve all of your retirement goals. Now all you need do is save. This last step should be the easiest, right? Wrong. It's actually one of the hardest. There are countless ways to save for retirement, and choosing the one that's best for you requires knowing something about what's available out there. In the next few sections, we'll walk you through the various types of retirement savings plans, and we'll give you plenty of good advice to get you on your way. Whatever you decide to do, be sure not to take saving too lightly in the retirement planning process. Hey, watch out for that last step—it's a doozie!

RETIREMENT SAVINGS PLANS

LEARNING OBJECTIVE #3

Set up a retirement plan.

AXIOM #6

Taxes Bias Personal Finance Decisions

What's the best way to save for retirement? Well, that really depends on your circumstances. There are so many options available, some of them very job- or occupation-specific, that it's hard to make general statements about what plans are right for everyone. However, it's safe to say that you should most certainly try to use a tax-favored retirement plan. The IRS makes tax-favored plans available to encourage you to save for your own retirement.

Most of these plans are tax-deferred and work by allowing investment earnings to go untaxed until you remove these earnings at retirement. In essence, they allow you to put off paying taxes so that money that would have gone to the IRS can be invested by you. In addition, some plans allow for the contributions to be made on either a fully or partially tax-deductible basis. In retirement planning, **Axiom 6: Taxes Bias Personal Finance Decisions** can't be overstressed.

There are several advantages to tax-deferred retirement plans. First, because the contributions may not be taxed, you can contribute more. In essence, you can contribute funds that would otherwise go to the IRS. Second, because the investment earnings aren't taxed until they're withdrawn at retirement, you can earn money on earnings that also would have otherwise gone to the IRS. In other words, you can earn compound interest on money that would normally have gone to the IRS. Figure 17.4 shows just how dramatic this compounding can be. Let's assume that you wish to invest $2,000 of before-tax income on an annual basis in a retirement account. Let's also assume that you can earn 9 percent compounded annually on this investment and that your marginal tax rate is 31 percent. If you invest in a tax-deferred retirement account to which the contributions are fully tax-deductible, you'll start off and end up with more money. You'll start with more money because, after taxes, you'll still have your full $2,000 to invest. You'll end up with more money because you'll be able to compound more of your earnings instead of paying them to the IRS. Investing in a fully taxable retirement account is a different story. To begin with, you won't be able to invest your entire $2,000 because 31 percent of this amount will go toward taxes, leaving you with only $1,380 to invest after taxes. In addition, the investment earnings will also be taxed annually, at a rate of 31 percent. Figure 17.4 compares these retirement plans with your annual investments of $2,000 of your before-tax income continuing for 30 years. After 10 years you'd have accumulated $33,121 in the tax-deferred account but only $19,511 in the taxable account. After 20 years the tax-deferred account would have grown to $111,529, whereas the taxable account would be at $55,150. Finally, after 30 years the tax-deferred account would have grown to $297,150, whereas the taxable account would have accumulated only $120,250. Of course, Uncle Sam does catch up eventually. When you withdraw your retirement funds, the interest earned on them over the years is taxed, but at least you had the chance to earn plenty of extra interest.

Obviously, there are major advantages to saving on a tax-deferred basis. It's pure and simple, smart investing. Before you look into any other types of retirement investments, check out the ones that are tax-favored. There are plenty of these plans currently available. Some are employer-sponsored, and others are aimed at the self-employed. Let's now look at the different types of tax-deferred employer-sponsored retirement plans: defined-contribution plans and 401(k) plans.

FIGURE 17.4

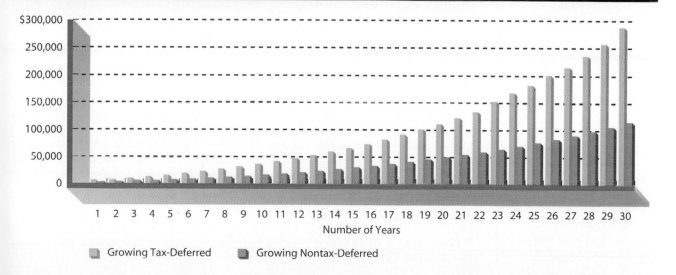

Saving in a Tax-Deferred Retirement Account versus Saving on a Nontax-Deferred Basis
Assuming an investment of $2,000 of before-tax income on an annual basis in a retirement account where those contributions are fully tax-deductible versus investing $2,000 of before-tax income on a nontax-deferred basis. A 9% annual return is assumed on these investments, with investment earnings in the tax-deferred account being tax-deferred, and earnings in the other account being taxed annually. A marginal tax rate of 31% is also assumed.

EMPLOYER-SPONSORED RETIREMENT PLANS

Defined-Contributions Plans

Defined-Contribution Plan

A pension plan in which you and your employer or your employer alone contributes directly to a retirement account set aside specifically for you. In effect, a defined-contribution plan can be thought of as a savings account for retirement.

Under a **defined-contribution plan**, your employer alone or you and your employer together contribute directly to an individual account set aside specifically for you. In effect, a defined contribution plan can be thought of as a personal savings account for retirement. Your eventual payments aren't guaranteed. Instead, what you eventually receive depends upon how well your retirement account performs. In fact, many defined-contribution plans allow for you to choose how your account is invested.

In recent years the popularity of such programs has skyrocketed for the simple fact that they involve no risk for the employer. The employer's job with a defined-contribution plan involves a bit of bookkeeping and making a financial contribution. Thus, employers don't really care what you eventually receive, as their responsibility ends with their contribution. In effect, defined-contribution plans pass the responsibility for retirement from the employer to the employee. They also pass the risk, because they aren't insured and payments aren't guaranteed.

Defined-contribution plans generally take one of several basic forms, including profit-sharing plans, money purchase plans, thrift and savings plans, or employee stock ownership plans.

Profit-Sharing Plan

A pension plan in which the company's contributions vary from year to year depending upon the firm's performance. The amount of money contributed to each employee depends upon the employee's salary level.

Profit-Sharing Plans. Under a **profit-sharing plan**, employer contributions can vary from year to year depending upon the firm's performance. The exact size of the company's contribution to each employee depends upon the employee's salary level. Although many firms set a minimum and a maximum contribution to be made—for example, between 2 and 12 percent of each employee's salary annually—not all firms do, and, as such, a contribution is not necessarily guaranteed under this type of plan. If the firm has a poor year, it may pass on making a contribution to the plan.

Money Purchase Plan

A pension plan in which the employer contributes a set percentage of employees' salaries to their retirement plans annually.

Money Purchase Plans. Under a **money purchase plan**, the employer contributes a set percentage of employees' salaries to their retirement plans annually. For the employer, such a plan offers less flexibility, because contributions are required regardless of how well the firm does. For the employee, these plans are preferable to profit-sharing plans because of the guaranteed contribution.

Thrift-and-Savings Plan

A pension plan in which the employer matches a percentage of the employees' contributions to their retirement accounts.

Thrift-and-Savings Plans. Under a **thrift and savings plan**, the employer matches a percentage of employees' contributions to their retirement accounts. For example, Viacom (the company that owns MTV, Blockbuster, VH1, Showtime, and Nickelodeon, among others) matches employee contributions to their retirement plans at a rate of 50 cents for every dollar contributed, up to 6 percent of their salary for employees earning under $65,000. For those employees making more than $65,000 Viacom matches at the same rate, but only up to 5 percent of their salary. Above this amount, contributions aren't matched, but employees can continue to contribute up to 15 percent of their salary.

Employee Stock Ownership Plan or ESOP

A retirement plan in which the retirement funds are invested directly in the company's stock.

Employee Stock Ownership Plan (ESOP). Under an **employee stock ownership plan**, or **ESOP**, the company's contribution is made in the form of the company's stock. Of all the retirement plans, this is the riskiest, because your return at retirement is dependent upon how well the company does. If your company goes bankrupt, you might lose not only your job, but also all your retirement benefits. Of course, if your company's stock price soars, you could do extremely well. However, an ESOP doesn't allow for the degree of diversification that you need with your retirement savings. In short, an ESOP isn't something you can safely rely on.

401(k) Plans

401(k) Plan

A retirement plan in which both the employee's contributions to the plan and the earnings on those contributions are tax-deductible, with all taxes being deferred until retirement withdrawals are made.

A **401(k) plan** is really a do-it-yourself variation of a profit-sharing/thrift plan. These can be set up as part of an employer-sponsored defined-contribution plan, with both the employer and the employee contributing to the plan, or with only the employee making a contribution. Over the past 20 years these plans have exploded in terms of popularity. In fact, about 9 out of 10 large employers—that is, companies employing over 500 workers—provide 401(k) plans for their workers. Corporations love them because they allow the retirement program to be handed over entirely to the employee.

A 401(k) plan is simply a tax-deferred retirement plan in which both the employee's contributions to the plan and the earnings on those contributions are tax-deductible, with all taxes being deferred until retirement withdrawals are made.[1] In essence, a 401(k) is equivalent to the tax-deferred retirement plan presented earlier in Figure 17.4. As you recall, the advantages to such an account are twofold. First, you don't pay taxes on money contributed to 401(k) plans, which means that you can contribute into your retirement account money that would have otherwise been paid out as taxes. Second, your earnings on your retirement account are tax-deferred. Thus, you can earn a return on money that would otherwise have been paid out in taxes. The end result, as was shown in Figure 17.4, is that you can accumulate a much larger retirement nest egg using a 401(k) account than you otherwise could. As a result, you should invest the maximum allowable amount in your 401(k) account. You should do this before you consider any other taxed investment alternatives. Moreover, this should be automatic—that is, *your 401(k) should be paid first* before you receive anything. Only after you have maxed out on your 401(k) contributions should you consider other investments.

Many 401(k) plans are set up as thrift-and-savings plans, in which the employer matches a percentage of the employee's contribution. For example, Coca-Cola matches dollar for dollar the first 3 percent of their employees' earnings contributed to the 401(k) plan. This matching program has resulted in an 87-percent participation rate in the plan, and an average savings balance per worker of $108,400. At rival PepsiCo, the 401(k) benefits aren't nearly as attractive. PepsiCo doesn't match any employee contributions. As a result, only 45 percent of PepsiCo's employees participate in their 401(k) plan, and their average savings balance per worker is only $13,700. So much for the choice of a new generation. Needless to say, a matching 401(k) program increases participation. In addition, a matching plan is an offer too good to refuse. It's free money, and you should take advantage of any matching the company is willing to do.

Also, 401(k) plans offer employees a wide variety of investment options. In fact, over half of all 401(k) plans offer five or more investment choices. These options range from conservative guaranteed investment contracts (GICs) to aggressive stock funds. **Guaranteed investment contracts**, or **GICs**, are just relatively conservative investments that look much like certificates of deposit. They're issued by insurance companies and generally pay a fixed rate of interest one-half to 1 percent above the Treasury rates. In spite of their name, GICs aren't guaranteed. As such, you should be aware of the issuer's rating—they could be quite risky. In most cases, you're much better off with the aggressive stock funds, especially if you have a long time to go before you retire. Keep in mind what we learned in **Axiom 11: The Time Dimension of Risk, or Why Investments Become Less Risky When You Plan To Hold Them Longer**. If you're going to be retiring shortly, perhaps you're better off avoiding the risk of stocks by investing in a solid GIC. However, if you have a while before retirement, holding on to stocks will reduce their risk while not reducing their return. A conservative investment such as a GIC will allow you to keep pace with inflation but not much more. Stocks will have more ups and downs, but over time your results will be better. Despite this fact, almost half of all participants choose GICs when they're available. Unfortunately, most people simply don't have the knowledge about investments or personal finance to protect themselves financially.

---

[1] A **403(b) plan** is essentially the same as a 401(k) plan except that it's aimed at employees of schools and charitable organizations. Although our discussion will focus on 401(k) plans, it also holds true for 403(b) plans.

Guaranteed Investment Contracts or **GICs**
A contract with an insurance company that guarantees a specified return on all investments in the pension plan. These are similar to CDs.

AXIOM #11

The Time Dimension of Risk, or Why Investments Become Less Risky When You Plan to Hold Them Longer

403(b) Plan
A tax-deferred retirement plan that's essentially the same as a 401(k) plan except that it's aimed at employees of schools and charitable organizations.

What a Good Plan Looks Like: AT&T's Retirement Package

AT&T provides both a pension plan and access to a 401(k) for its workers. The pension plan aims to replace approximately 37 percent of employees' salary if they retire at 55 with 30 years of service. In addition, AT&T provides workers with a 401(k) savings plan to which AT&T contributes 67¢ for every $1 that the employee contributes, up to 6 percent of the employee's salary. Employees are allowed to contribute up to 16 percent of their pretax salary to the plan. Thus, an employee earning $40,000 could contribute $6,400 and have AT&T throw in an additional $1,600 for a total contribution of $8,000 per year. Keep in mind that this contribution is tax-deductible and also grows on a tax-deferred basis.

TAX-FAVORED RETIREMENT PLANS FOR THE SELF-EMPLOYED AND SMALL BUSINESS EMPLOYEES

Fully tax-deductible retirement plans for the self-employed or small business employee—which includes anyone who has his or her own business, works for a small business, or does freelance work on a part-time basis—hold the same basic advantages as employer-sponsored plans available in large corporations. You qualify for such a plan if you do any work for yourself (even if you work full-time for an employer and are covered by another retirement plan there). It's surprising how many individuals qualify for these plans and either don't realize it or do nothing to take advantage of another tax-deferred retirement tool. Examples of those who are eligible are lawyers, doctors, dentists, carpenters, plumbers, artists, freelance writers, and consultants. Basically, if you're at all self-employed, either full-time or part-time, or work for a small business, you can contribute to a Keogh plan, a simplified employee pension plan (SEP-IRA), or the new savings incentive match plan for employees (SIMPLE) plan.

Keogh Plan

The **Keogh plan** was introduced in 1962 in an effort to provide self-employed individuals and employees of unincorporated businesses an opportunity to make large tax-deductible payments to a retirement plan. Today, Keogh plans are quite similar to corporate pension or profit-sharing plans. The establishment of a Keogh plan is relatively easy. You need simply select a bank, mutual fund, or other financial institution and approach them. In general, they'll have the paperwork that's needed to establish the plan already completed. They'll provide you with a prototype plan, and you need simply fill in the blanks.

When you set up the Keogh plan, you'll be asked to choose a defined-contribution and/or a defined-benefit Keogh plan. Bear in mind that these two options are not mutually exclusive—your Keogh plan can contain both. Under a defined-contribution plan, you choose the level of your contribution to the plan. There's no guarantee of the retirement payout, because the benefit will depend solely on the income earned on what went in. If you don't put anything in, you can't get anything out. There are a number of ways to set up defined-contribution Keogh plans. With some you must annually contribute a fixed percentage of profits. Others give you a good deal of flexibility in terms of varying your level of annual contributions and may even let you skip a year with no penalty. In general, the limit on contributions can run as high as 25 percent for an employee, 20 percent for the employer, with the maximum for either the employee or employer set at $30,000.

Under a defined-benefit Keogh plan, rather than contribute a percentage of your earnings, you're allowed to contribute whatever amount you deem necessary to meet your retirement payout schedule, which is determined by an IRS formula along with some actuarial assumptions. In the extreme case, you could actually contribute 100 percent of your self-employed earnings, up to almost $120,000, in your Keogh plan. The big

LEARNING OBJECTIVE #4

Contribute to a tax-favored retirement plan to help fund your retirement.

Keogh Plan
A tax-sheltered retirement plan for the self-employed.

EARLY RETIREMENT FORMULA:
Save Plenty, Invest It Aggressively and Live Frugally

If you're dreaming about early retirement, it's time for a wake-up call.

The brutal reality is, most folks won't retire early, because they spend too much, save too little and steer clear of stocks. Here is what it takes to quit the work force at age 55:

- You have to save like crazy

"Go and talk to all those guys who took the early-retirement packages," says Deena Katz, a financial planner in Coral Gables, Fla. "These people got $300,000, more money than they thought they'd ever see. What are they doing today? They had to go back to work. It takes a lot of dollars to retire."

Unfortunately, saving a few thousand a year isn't going to cut it. Ross Levin, a Minneapolis financial planner, took a look at how much you would have to sock away each year if you wanted to retire at age 55 and you expected to live past age 90.

His findings? If you saved an amount equal to 20% of your pretax salary every year for 25 years, you would be able to retire early and still maintain your pre-retirement standard of living. Maybe.

"If you plan for Social Security, saving 20% for 25 years looks great," Mr. Levin figures.

"But if you don't have Social Security, saving 20% for 25 years may not be enough."

- You have to invest aggressively

Sure, it seems like everybody is in love with stock these days. But if you want to retire early, a fleeting passion isn't enough. You have to marry your fortunes to the stock market early, and stick with it for the rest of your days. Ⓐ

- You have to live frugally

Most folks aren't going to shovel every penny into stocks, and they aren't going to save 20% of their pre-tax salary every year for 25 years. Which leaves them with one option. Spend less in retirement. Ⓑ

Indeed, that's the key to early retirement, argues Kenneth Klegon, a financial planner in Lansing, Mich. "Retiring early is achievable, but only if you're willing to spend less," he says.

Source: "Early Retirement Formula: Save Plenty, Invest It Aggressively and Live Frugally," by Jonathan Clements, *The Wall Street Journal,* October 29, 1996, p. C1. Reprinted by permission of *The Wall Street Journal,* © 1996 Dow Jones & Company, Inc. All Rights Reserved Worldwide.

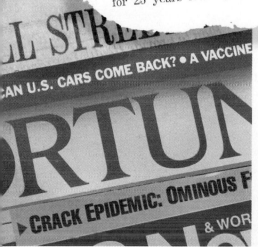

Analysis and Implications ...

A. Why is this so? Compounding is what makes your retirement savings grow, and how much it grows is a function of the amount of time it compounds for and the rate that it compounds at. When you retire early, you lose time, and that means your investment won't grow nearly as large. In addition, your Social Security benefits will be lower and you will have longer to live off your savings because your retirement will be longer.

B. It's much easier to talk about cutting spending than it is to actually do it. It becomes even more difficult if you have large financial obligations you can't get out of, like a large mortgage or dependent children. In fact, possibly the biggest hurdle to early retirement is your children's college education. In general, it's pretty tough for those helping with tuition costs to retire before their kids graduate.

drawback with the defined-benefit Keogh plan is that it's both costly and complicated to administer, requiring a professional actuary to oversee the plan. As a result, it's generally used as a catch-up plan by those who've neglected to set up a pension plan in the past.

Regardless of which type of Keogh plan you end up with, they're all self-directed, meaning you decide what securities to buy and sell and when. As with 401(k)s, the payment to the plan comes out before you determine your taxes, so any contributions reduce your bill to Uncle Sam. With respect to withdrawals, they can begin as early as age 59½ and must begin by age 70½. If you need your money early, you'll have to pay a 10-percent penalty except in cases of serious illness, disability, or death.

Simplified Employee Pension Plan (SEP-IRA)

A **simplified employee pension plan**, or **SEP-IRA**, works like a defined-contribution Keogh plan, where your contributions go in on a before-tax basis and grow tax-free until withdrawn. Although SEP-IRAs are aimed at the self-employed, employers can also establish SEP-IRAs for their workers. The contribution limits are set at 15 percent for an employee and 12.98 percent for the employer, up to a maximum of $22,500. In addition, there's flexibility in making contributions. For example, they can be made one year and not the next, and when they are made, they're immediately vested. The advantage of a SEP-IRA program is that it works about the same as a Keogh plan but is easier to set up. It involves simply filling out a one-page form. In addition, a SEP-IRA doesn't have the reporting requirements of a Keogh plan. However, the big disadvantage is that you can't contribute as much to a SEP-IRA as you can to a Keogh plan, with your contributions to a SEP-IRA limited to 15 percent.

Savings Incentive Match Plan for Employees (SIMPLE) Plans

As of 1997, small employers can establish a **savings incentive match plan for employees** or **SIMPLE plan**—SIMPLE IRAs and SIMPLE 401(k)s—but can no longer establish SEPs. These new SIMPLE plans may be set up by employers with fewer than 100 employees earning $5,000 or more, covering all their employees, including themselves, as part of a 401(k). Employee contributions are excluded from income, and the earnings in the retirement plan are tax-deferred. In addition to employee contributions, there are some matching funds provided by the employer—although the employer does have some flexibility in determining how much to contribute. Why did Congress decide to establish one more type of retirement plan? Because many smaller businesses were put off by complex and expensive alternative plans and thus didn't provide retirement plans for their employees. That's where the SIMPLE plans fit in, because the rules governing them are, as the name implies, simple.

INDIVIDUAL RETIREMENT ACCOUNTS, OR IRAS

With the passage of the Taxpayer Relief Act of 1997, there are now three types of IRAs to choose from: the traditional IRA, the Roth IRA, and the Education IRA.

Traditional IRAs

Individual retirement accounts, or **IRAs**, were established in 1981, and for the first five years were relatively simple. They let you deposit up to $2,000 of before-tax income in your IRA. With the Tax Reform Act of 1986, simplicity was stripped from the program. Today, this $2,000 IRA contribution can be fully tax-deductible, partially tax-deductible, or not tax-deductible, depending upon the level of your earnings and whether you or your spouse have a company retirement plan.

If both you and your spouse are employed and aren't covered by a company retirement plan, you can contribute up to $2,000 annually on a tax-deferred basis to your IRA.

Self-Employed Pension Plan or **SEP-IRA**
A tax-sheltered (you don't pay taxes on any earnings while they remain in the plan) retirement plan aimed at small businesses or at the self-employed. It works like a 401(k) plan, allowing employers to contribute up to 15 percent of the employee's earnings in the SEP, up to a total of $30,000 annually, with the employer contribution going directly into the employee's IRA.

Savings Incentive Match Plan for Employees or **SIMPLE Plan**
A tax-sheltered retirement plan aimed at small businesses or the self-employed that provides for some matching funds by the employer to be deposited in your retirement account.

LEARNING OBJECTIVE #4

Contribute to a tax-favored retirement plan to help fund your retirement.

Individual Retirement Account or **IRA**
A retirement account to which an individual can contribute up to $2,000 annually. This contribution may or may not be tax-deductible depending on the individual's income level and whether he or she or his or her spouse is covered by a company retirement plan.

Since 1997, a married couple with only one spouse working outside the home may contribute a total of $4,000 to an IRA, provided the "working spouse" has at least $4,000 in earned income. If neither of you is an "active participant" in a retirement plan at work, or if your joint adjusted gross income is below the IRS cutoff (which recently changed with the passage of the Taxpayer Relief Act of 1997), your IRA contributions are entirely tax-deductible. What's an "active participant"? If you have a defined-benefit retirement plan, you're considered an "active participant." In addition, if you have a defined-contribution plan and either you or your employer contributed to it during the year, you're considered an "active participant." However, if neither you nor your employer contributed to your defined-contribution plan during the year or your income is below the cutoff level, you can make a fully deductible contribution to your IRA.

Partial tax deductions are also available for IRA contributions, again, depending upon your income level. Above those dollar limits, IRA contributions are still allowed, but they're nondeductible for tax purposes if your spouse is in a qualified plan. However, even if you don't qualify for a tax deduction, an IRA may be a smart move. Nondeductible IRAs have the advantage that your investment grows free of income taxes until you withdraw money from the account. If you do contribute to a nondeductible IRA, you must file IRS Form 8606 with your income taxes. You'll want to keep a copy of this form showing that your contribution was made on an after-tax basis to avoid paying taxes a second time on your contribution when you finally withdraw your money. Also, don't mix deductible and nondeductible IRA contributions together; it will be hard to prove down the road what is not taxable.

If all your contributions to your IRA are tax-deductible, then all your withdrawals from your IRA will be taxed, unless you're just moving your money into another IRA. There are also restrictions on the timing and amount of your IRA withdrawals as follows:

- Distributions prior to age 59½ are subject to a 10-percent tax penalty with few exceptions, for example, if you are disabled, educational use, or buying a first home (with a limit of a $10,000 withdrawal).
- After you turn 70½ you must start receiving annual distributions under a life expectancy calculation.

Stop and Think

Saving for retirement using an IRA can reap big benefits. If you're in the 31-percent tax bracket, putting $2,000 a year into an IRA equates to less than $5.50 per day, and only $3.78 per day of spendable, after-tax income. If you start your IRA when you're 22—putting it in an IRA that pays 10 percent at the beginning of each year—and continue that practice for 45 years, you'll end up with over $1.58 million in your IRA. If you tried to do this without an IRA, paying taxes on your $2,000 and then investing it at a before-tax rate of 10 percent, you'd end up with only $409,151. Granted the money in your IRA would be taxable income when you withdrew it, but it's still a pretty sizable sum.

In addition to annual contributions to your IRA, you can also roll over a distribution from a qualified employer plan or from another IRA into a new IRA. Why would you ever do this? If you get a new job or if you retire early, you may be faced with that 10 percent early distribution penalty on retirement fund distributions before the age of 59½. To get around this penalty, you can instead have your distributions "rolled over" into a new IRA.

What are your investment choices with an IRA? You can go with stocks, bonds, mutual funds, real estate, CDs—almost anything. It's your call because IRAs are self-directed, and you can change your IRA funds from one investment to another at any time without paying taxes. The only things you can't invest in are life insurance or collectibles, other than gold or silver U.S. coins. You also can't borrow from your IRA, and you can't use it as collateral for a loan.

The Taxpayer Relief Act of 1997 and Traditional IRAs. How did the new tax law affect traditional IRAs? One major change was that while contributions to the traditional IRA remained at $2,000 per person, the eligibility to make tax-deductible contributions was greatly expanded. Under the old law, there were strict rules on what income level you had to be at in order to make a tax-deductible contribution to an IRA if you were an active participant in an employer sponsored retirement plan. The new tax law gradually doubles those income limits. Under the old law, IRAs were totally deductible only for single individuals with incomes of less than $25,000 and were phased out entirely for those with incomes greater than $35,000. Under the new law, this limit for total deductibility gradually rises to a level of $50,000 in the year 2004 with the phaseout level climbing to $60,000. For couples, this income level limit on total deductibility for IRA contributions rises from the current level of $40,000 to $80,000, while the phaseout level rises from $50,000 to $100,000, again, being slowly phased in by the year 2004.

Another change deals with who can contribute. Under the new law, a nonworking spouse can make a fully deductible contribution of $2,000 to an IRA even if the other spouse participates in a qualified retirement plan at work at incomes up to $150,000.

The final change deals with withdrawals. You can make penalty-free withdrawals provided you (a) are making them to buy your first home, (b) are using them for college expenses, or (c) are at least 59½ years old. There is, however, a limit of $10,000 on penalty-free withdrawals used to buy a first home.

The Taxpayer Relief Act of 1997: Two New IRAs to Choose From

With the passage of the Taxpayer Relief Act of 1997, effective January 1, 1998, there are three IRAs to choose from—the old familiar IRA, the "Roth IRA" and the "Education IRA." The reason Congress passed this legislation was to encourage saving—both for retirement and for education. Also under the new law, more people quality for the tax breaks from an IRA—particularly nonworking spouses and middle income taxpayers who are covered by pension plans.

Under the **Roth IRA**, contributions would not be tax deductible. That is, you'd make your contribution to your Roth IRA out of after-tax income. But once the money is in there, it grows tax-free and when it is withdrawn, the withdrawals are tax-free. Remember, with a traditional IRA, your contributions are made with before-tax income, but withdrawals are taxed. With the Roth IRA the taxation process is inverted: You put after-tax income into the IRA, but you don't pay taxes when the money is withdrawn. One similarity between the traditional IRA and the Roth IRA is that with both, you don't pay any taxes while your money is in the IRA.

Obviously, the big advantage of the Roth IRA is that you can avoid those taxes when you finally withdraw your money from your IRA. Of course, as with everything else in the tax code, there are some exceptions. First, to avoid taxes, you must keep your money in your Roth IRA for at least five years.

Who's eligible to put money into a Roth IRA? A lot of people! The income limits don't begin until $95,000 for single taxpayers and $150,000 for couples, and are totally phased out at $110,000 for individuals and $160,000 for couples. Keep in mind that even if you have a 401(k) account, you can also contribute to an IRA. You can also have both a traditional IRA and a Roth IRA; however, your total contributions to both are limited to $2,000 per year.

Roth IRA

An IRA in which contributions are not tax deductible. That is, you'd make your contribution to this IRA out of after-tax income. But once the money is in there, it grows tax-free and when it is withdrawn, the withdrawals are tax-free.

Another great feature of the Roth IRA is that, at any time, you can pull out an amount up to your original contribution without getting hit with a tax penalty. Also new with the Roth IRA, there isn't a requirement that distributions begin by age 70½.

In addition to your annual contribution, if your income is less than $100,000 (either on a joint or individual return) you can also roll money from your existing IRA into your Roth IRA without incurring a 10-percent penalty. Granted, it would trigger taxes on your withdrawal, but these taxes can be spread over four years if the switch is made before 1999. Then, when you make your future withdrawals at retirement, there would be no taxes to pay. According to a study by T. Price Rowe, a major mutual fund company, this switch is probably a good idea if you have enough money outside your IRA to pay taxes and you are under 55. However, this study was based on the assumption that you stay in the same tax bracket after retirement. If you expect to drop to a lower tax bracket after retirement, the decision becomes more difficult.

What about the **Education IRA**, how does it work? The Education IRA works just like the Roth IRA, except with respect to contributions. Contributions are limited to $500 annually per child for each child younger than 18, with the income limits beginning at $95,000 for single taxpayers and $150,000 for couples. Again, the earnings are tax-free and there is no tax on withdrawals made to pay for education. Savings must be withdrawn by the time the child reaches 30, although any leftover amounts can be rolled over into accounts for younger siblings. If the money in the education IRA isn't used for college you may have to pay taxes plus a 10-percent penalty on its withdrawal.

How much can you save using an education IRA? If you contribute $500 when your child is born, and $500 on each birthday in an education IRA that earns 10 percent, you'd have $28,138 by the time your child is 18 years old. The only downside to all this is that you can't take a Hope Credit during the same year you withdraw money from an education IRA.

Traditional IRA versus the Roth IRA: Which Is Best for You?

Mathematically, you end up with the same amount to spend at retirement if you use a traditional IRA or a Roth IRA, provided both are taxed at the same tax rate. So which one should you choose? If you can afford it, the answer is the new Roth IRA. That's because you can take care of taxes ahead of time and end up with more money to spend at retirement. In effect, you're actually putting more money into the Roth IRA because the Roth IRA includes a $2,000 contribution *plus* the taxes you'd pay on that $2,000 contribution. In terms of after-tax contributions, if you are in the 31-percent tax bracket a $2,000 contribution to a Roth IRA would cost you $2,899 of before-tax income—$2,000 for the contribution and $899 for taxes ($2,899 × 0.31 = $899). If you put $2,000 in a traditional IRA and let it grow at 10 percent for 40 years, you end up with $90,519 before you paid any taxes—after taxes, at 31 percent, you'd have $62,458. If you'd put $2,000 in a Roth IRA, you'd need a bit more money on the front end (as we just showed, $2,899), because you'd have to pay taxes, but you'd end up with $90,519 after 40 years and no taxes!

FACING RETIREMENT—THE PAYOUT

You might think that once you've saved enough for retirement, coming up with a plan for distributing those savings would be simple. Think again. Your distribution or payout decision affects how much you receive, how it's taxed, whether you're protected against inflation, whether you might outlive your retirement funds, and a host of other important concerns. Some plans have more flexibility than others—for example, IRAs allow for withdrawals to begin at age 59½, and at age 70½ withdrawals become compulsory. Still, there are also several basic distribution choices that include receiving your payout as a lump sum, receiving it in the form of an annuity either for a set number of years or for your lifetime, or some combination. Unfortunately, there isn't one best way to receive your retirement distribution. However, there are a number of important points to keep in mind when making this decision.

LEARNING OBJECTIVE #5

Choose how your retirement benefits are paid out to you.

- Make sure you plan ahead before you decide how a payout is to be received. Make sure you understand the tax consequences of any move.
- In deciding how a payout is to be received, make sure you look at all your retirement plan payouts together. You may want to take some plan distributions in a lump sum and others as an annuity.
- Once you receive your retirement plan payout, make sure you use your understanding of investing, including diversification and the time dimension of risk, when deciding what to do with those funds.

Let's now take a look at some of the specifics behind these distribution options.

An Annuity, or Lifetime Payments

An annuity provides you with an annual payout. This payout can go for a set number of years, it can be in the form of lifetime payments for either you or you and your spouse, or it can be in the form of lifetime payments with a minimum number of payments guaranteed. In short, just deciding on an annuity isn't enough—you must also decide among several variations of an annuity.

Single Life Annuity
An annuity in which you receive a set monthly payment for your entire life.

Single Life Annuity. Under a **single life annuity**, you receive a set monthly payment for your entire life. Think of this type of annuity as the Energizer bunny—it just keeps going and going, at least as long as you do. If you die after 1 year, the payments cease. Alternatively, if you live to be 100, so do your payments.

Annuity for Life or a **"Certain Period"**
A single life annuity that allows you to receive your payments for a fixed period of time. Payments will be made to you for the remainder of your life, but if you die before the end of the time period (generally either 10 or 20 years), payments will continue to be made to your beneficiary until the end of the period.

An Annuity for Life or a "Certain Period." Under an **annuity for life or a "certain period,"** you receive annuity payments for life. However, if you die before the end of the "certain period," which is generally either 10 or 20 years, payments will continue to your beneficiary until the end of that period. Because there's a minimum number of payments that must be made (payments must continue until the end of the certain period), an annuity for life or a "certain period" pays a smaller annuity than does a single life annuity. In addition, the longer the "certain period," the smaller the monthly annuity.

Joint and Survivor Annuity
An annuity that provides payments over the life of both you and your spouse.

Joint and Survivor Annuity. A **joint and survivor annuity** provides payments over the life of both you and your spouse. Under this choice, the two most common options are: (1) a 50-percent survivor benefit, which pays your spouse 50 percent of the original annuity after you die, or (2) a 100-percent survivor benefit, which continues benefits to your spouse at the same level after you die. Of course, the higher the survivor benefit, the lower the size of the annuity. Also, many firms provide medical benefits to pensioners and their spouses over their entire life when this type of annuity is chosen as the payout method. Most individuals who are married choose this option. In fact, if you're married and you choose another option, your spouse must sign a waiver giving you permission to accept that alternative annuity payout.

The advantages of an annuity include the fact that it can be set up in such a way that you or you and your spouse will continue to receive benefits regardless of how long you live. In addition, many firms allow for medical benefits to continue while an annuity pension payout is being received. The disadvantages include the fact that there's no inflation protection. Although you know for certain how much you'll receive each month, the spending power of this amount will be continuously eroded by inflation. In addition, such an annuity payout method doesn't allow for flexibility in payout patterns. For example, if there's a financial emergency, the pattern can't be altered to deal with it. In addition, under the annuity there is little flexibility to leave money to heirs.

Annuities are usually available with employer-sponsored retirement plans, but insurance companies also sell them. Depending upon how attractive your employer's annuity options are, you may be better off taking a lump-sum distribution and purchasing an insurance company annuity on your own. The point here is that you aren't restricted to the annuity options offered by your employer. You should compare them with the other options available from the highest-rated insurance companies before making a decision.

A Lump-Sum Payment

Under a **lump-sum option**, you receive your benefits in one single payment. If you're concerned about inflation protection, or if you're concerned about having access to emergency funds, a lump-sum distribution, or taking part of your money in a lump sum and putting the rest toward an annuity, may be best. However, if you do take your benefits in a lump sum, you'll then be faced with the job of making your money last for your lifetime and for your loved ones after you're gone. That's not all bad—you get to invest the money wherever you choose, and you may end up earning a high return. The big advantage to a lump-sum payout is the flexibility that it provides. Unfortunately, you'll run the risk of making a bad investment and losing the money you so carefully saved up. As a result, you might outlive your retirement fund. Table 17.3 provides a listing of some of the advantages and disadvantages of an annuity versus a lump-sum payout.

Lump-Sum Option
A payout arrangement in which you receive all your benefits in one single payment.

Tax Treatment of Distributions

If you receive your payout in the form of an annuity, those payments will generally be taxed as normal income. If you receive a lump-sum payout, you'll generally be allowed to use a 5- or 10-year averaging technique, which allows taxes to be calculated as if the payout were received in smaller amounts over a 5-year period.[2] In this way you can ease your tax burden slightly. But you must pay the taxes all at once—not over 5 or 10 years.

As mentioned earlier, an alternative to paying taxes on a lump-sum payout is to have the distribution "rolled over" into an IRA or qualified plan. This rollover makes a lot of sense if you've taken a new job or retired early and don't need the money now. In this way you avoid paying taxes on the distribution while the funds continue to grow on a tax-deferred basis.

[2] The 10-year averaging technique is allowed only for individuals born before 1936.

TABLE 17.3

An Annuity or Lifetime Payments versus a Lump-Sum Payout

Advantages of an Annuity or Lifetime Payments	**Advantages of a Lump-Sum Payout**
Payments continue as long as you live.	Flexibility to allow for emergency withdrawals.
Employer health benefits may continue with the annuity.	Allows for big-ticket purchases—for example, a retirement home if desired.
Disadvantages of an Annuity or Lifetime Payments	Potential for inflation protection.
	Allows for money to be passed on to heirs.
In general, no inflation protection.	Control over how the money is invested.
No flexibility to make withdrawals in the event of a financial emergency.	**Disadvantages of a Lump-Sum Payout**
Doesn't allow for money to be passed on to heirs—payments stop when you die.	You could run out of money.
	You might not have the discipline to keep from spending the money.
	Complicates the financial planning process because you're responsible for your own retirement funding.

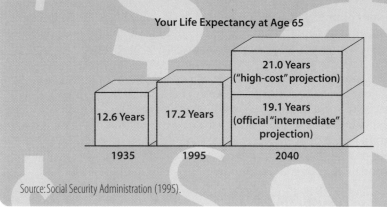
LEARNING OBJECTIVE #6

Put together a retirement plan and effectively monitor it.

AXIOM #11

The Time Dimension of Risk

AXIOM #14

Money Isn't Everything

PUTTING A PLAN TOGETHER AND MONITORING IT

It's important to realize that for most individuals, there won't be a single source of retirement income. Most people rely on retirement savings from a combination of different plans. What works best for you depends upon where you work and what your retirement benefits are. However, the place to start is with the seven steps outlined at the beginning of this chapter. In addition, you should make sure you invest the maximum allowable amount in tax-sheltered retirement plans, as they both reduce your taxes and allow your retirement funds to grow on a tax-deferred basis. Also, your investment strategy should reflect your investment time horizon until retirement. Thinking back to **Axiom 11: The Time Dimension of Risk**, early on you should be willing to take on more risk—going with a strong dose of stocks in your retirement portfolio—and as retirement draws near, you should gradually switch over to less risky investments. If you're uncertain about putting together your plan, or if you'd like another opinion, don't hesitate to see a professional financial planner. Figure 17.5 illustrates the typical sources of retirement income for a retired couple earning approximately $21,000.

FOR RETIREMENT SAVINGS,
Modest Boosts in Annual Returns Make Big Difference

When saving for retirement, little things can mean a lot.

Robert Bingham, a San Francisco investment adviser, looked at a 40-year-old investor with $80,000 in retirement savings who socked away $6,000 a year until age 65 and then used those savings to pay for a retirement that lasts 25 years. Mr. Bingham assumed that inflation ran at 3% throughout the period and that our hypothetical investor boosted the amount he or she saved each year along with inflation.

(A) Result? If our investor earned 7% a year, annual retirement income would be $27,665, figures in today's dollars. You want more? Suppose our investor earned 7½% instead. That would produce $31,719 a year, or 15% more. What about 8%? That raises retirement income to $36,347, an extra 31%. How about 8½%? That gets the investor up to $41,626, or more than 50% more.

Not bad. You earn an extra 1.5 percentage points a year and you get 50% more retirement income. But how? Here are a few simple steps that should crank up your returns:

(B) • Boost Your Stock Holdings
 • Snatch the Match

In pursuit of higher returns, make full use of your employer's 401(k) or 403(b) retirement-savings plan. Your employer may match your contribution, throwing in maybe 50 cents for every $1 you contribute. Thanks to a combination of tax savings, investment gains and the employer match, your contributions could garner a first-year return of 80% or 90%.

• Flee the Bank

When buying cash investments, steer clear of bank products, such as savings accounts, short-term certificates of deposit and money-market accounts.

• Trim Investment Costs **(C)**

If you skimp on brokerage commissions, trade infrequently and stick with low-expense mutual funds, you should bolster your annual returns.

• Act Your Tax Bracket

If you are in the 28% tax bracket or above and you want to buy high-quality U.S. bonds for your taxable account, go to tax-exempt municipals.

• Stay the Course

Source: Jonathan Clements, "For Retirement Savings, Modest Boosts in Annual Returns Make Big Difference," *The Wall Street Journal,* December 17, 1996, p. C1. Reprinted by permission of *The Wall Street Journal,* © 1996 Dow Jones & Company, Inc. All Rights Reserved Worldwide.

Analysis and Implications ...

A. The importance of earning a higher rate of return becomes especially dramatic when your investment horizon increases. For example, if you saved $6,000 per year at 7 percent for 40 years you'd end up with $1.198 million and $2.656 million if you earned 10 percent.

B. Remember, since 1950 the average return on stocks as measured by the S&P 500 stock index has been 12.8 percent, while long-term corporate bonds averaged 6.0 percent.

C. Fees and brokerage charges eat right into your returns. This becomes more important since the Taxpayer Relief Act of 1997 lowered the capital gains tax rates. If you trade a lot, your broker makes money off you, and you realize your gains quickly and thus trigger a tax bill.

FIGURE 17.5

Where Your Retirement Income Comes From

Source: Social Security Administration, 1996.

Monitoring your retirement planning, both before and after you retire, is an ongoing process in which adjustments are constantly made for new and unexpected changes that occur in your financial and personal life. Although it's impossible to point out all the complications and changes that might occur, there are a number of things that should be kept in mind.

- **Changes in inflation can have a drastic effect on your retirement planning.** Not only do changes in anticipated inflation affect the value of any stocks and bonds that you own, but they also affect the amount of money that you'll need for a comfortable retirement. Thus, you should keep an eye out for changes in inflation.

- **Once you retire, you still may live for a long time.** Your investment strategy should include a dose of stocks that reflect your investment time horizon. The strategy of investing in bonds and CDs after retirement, while widely advised, probably doesn't match most retirees' investment time horizons. Simply stated, the traditional, ultraconservative investment strategy for retirees has been invalidated by longer life spans and inflation. Remember, you want to earn enough on your retirement savings to cover inflation and allow your money to grow conservatively, but grow just the same.

- **Monitor your progress and monitor your company.** When changes occur, build them into your plan. Don't be afraid to adjust your goals along with what's necessary to meet those goals. Make sure you track the performance of your retirement investments. In addition, monitor your company's health, especially if you participate in an ESOP. If your company's financial future is questionable, try to move your investments into something other than your company's stock.

- **Don't neglect your insurance coverage.** There's no quicker way to get in financial trouble than to experience a disaster that should have been covered by insurance but wasn't. Make sure your coverage is both up to date and at an adequate level.

- **An investment planning program may make things easier.** There are a number of very good and inexpensive retirement planning software programs. The advantage to them is that they allow you to make different assumptions regarding the rate of return that you earn on your investments and how much you save annually. In this way you can get a better idea of the role these factors play in determining how much you will have at retirement. Three good software programs include T. Rowe Price Retirement Planning Analyzer ($20, 800-541-1472); Vanguard's Retirement Planner (due out mid-1998, 800-876-1840); and Fidelity's Retirement Planning Thinkware (downloadable free at http://www.fidelity.com). These programs are extremely easy to use and do a good job of allowing you to see into the future.

SUMMARY

For many individuals, Social Security is the primary source of retirement income. About 95 percent of all Americans are covered by Social Security. The size of your Social Security benefits is determined by (1) the number of years of earnings, (2) the average level of earning, and (3) an adjustment for inflation.

Funding your retirement needs can be thought of as a seven-step process:

Step 1: Set goals.

Step 2: Estimate how much you'll need to meet your goals.

Step 3: Estimate your income available at retirement.

Step 4: Calculate the inflation-adjusted shortfall.

Step 5: Calculate the funds needed at retirement to cover this shortfall.

Step 6: Determine how much you must save annually between now and retirement.

Step 7: Put the plan in play and save.

One way in which you can earn more on your investments is through the use of tax-deferred retirement plans. Some of these plans are employer-sponsored plans, whereas others are aimed at the self-employed individual. In either case, the advantages are essentially the same. First, because the contributions may not be taxed, you can contribute more. In essence, you can contribute funds that would otherwise go to the IRS. Second, because the investment earnings aren't taxed, you can earn money on earnings that also would have otherwise gone to the IRS.

A 401(k) plan is really a do-it-yourself tax-deferred retirement plan. Over the past 20 years 401(k)s have exploded in terms of popularity. A 403(b) plan is essentially the same as a 401(k) plan except that it is aimed at employees of schools and charitable organizations. These are excellent investment vehicles.

The three basic types of plans for the self-employed are SEP-IRAs, SIMPLE plans, and Keogh plans. Another method to fund retirement is via an individual retirement account, or IRA. There are three types of IRAs: traditional IRAs, Roth IRAs, and Education IRAs.

Another important retirement decision is your distribution or payout decision, which affects how much you receive, how it is taxed, whether you are protected against inflation, whether you might outlive your retirement funds, and a host of other important concerns. Your basic distribution choices are either to receive your payout as a lump sum, to receive it in the form of an annuity or lifetime payments, or some combination of the two.

Finally, you must realize that you must monitor your progress toward your retirement goal, both before and after you retire, constantly allowing for new and unexpected changes that occur in your financial and personal life. In this regard, you should keep the following in mind:

* Changes in inflation can have a drastic effect on your retirement planning.
* Once you retire, you still may live for a long time.
* Monitor your progress and monitor your company.
* Do not neglect your insurance coverage.
* An investment planning program may make the planning process easier.

Review Questions

1. What are you purchasing with your payroll deduction to Social Security? (LO 1)
2. How is Social Security funded? (LO 1)
3. To qualify for Social Security benefits, how many credits does one need? How is a credit determined? (LO 1)

WWW.
Take It to the Net

We invite you to visit the Keown Personal Finance page on the Prentice Hall Web site at:

http://www.prenhall.com/ persfin

for this chapter's World Wide Web exercise.

You might also want to visit the following Web sites:

AARP WebPlace (lots of good retirement planning information): http://www.aarp.org

Retirement Calculator (to help in your retirement planning): http://www.awa.com/softlock/ tturner/401k/401k.html

The Vanguard Group (visit their retirement planning center— it's excellent): http:// www.vanguard.com/

Retirement Planning by Nerd World Media™ (links to retirement planning sites): http:// www.nerdworld.com/ nw767.html

Life's Financial Concerns— Retirement (Prudential's site): http://www.prusec.com/ retr1.htm

Just Do It! *From the Desk of Marcy Furney, CFP*
Retiring Right

☑ Don't consider your retirement funds a source of money for emergencies. Withdrawal from qualified retirement accounts can result in taxes, penalties, and even investment company charges. Money in employer-sponsored plans is normally not even accessible as long as you're employed by the company, unless the plan allows for loans or special IRS-defined hardship withdrawals.

☑ Include medical insurance costs in your calculation of retirement needs, especially if you're planning to retire before you're eligible for Medicare. Many employers are paring down or eliminating postretirement medical coverage. Even with Medicare, you may need a supplemental plan, which could cost several hundred dollars a month for you and your spouse.

☑ Get information on the shortfalls of Medicare coverage for nursing home and custodial care and on the eligibility requirements for Medicaid. You may find that you need to obtain long-term care insurance prior to retirement and include its cost in your calculation of annual financial needs. If you anticipate having to care for elderly family members, assisting them in purchasing such coverage could be advantageous.

☑ If you plan to "roll over" money from a company retirement plan to an IRA, get assistance from your financial advisor or IRA investment company in executing a "trustee to trustee transfer." Through this process the money flows directly to the IRA account or comes to you via check made payable to the IRA. If you take possession of the funds at any time, you're subject to 20 percent withholding.

☑ If you are in a low income tax bracket and meet the requirements to do a Roth IRA or a regular deductible IRA, give the potential outcome great consideration when deciding which to use. Foregoing a small tax deduction now (i.e., doing the Roth IRA) could result in a sizable source of tax-free money at retirement.

☑ Investigate joint and survivor annuity options carefully. Once you make a decision, it's usually irrevocable. You'll receive a lower monthly payment while you're living so that income can go to your spouse when you die. If your spouse dies before you do, your monthly amount won't go up. You may find that you can take a single life annuity, use some of the money to pay for life insurance to provide your spouse an income, and still net more money than the joint and survivor annuity would provide.

4. How is the size of someone's Social Security benefit determined? What percentage of income does Social Security typically replace? (LO 1)
5. Define what is meant by the term "disability and survivor benefits." How is "substantial work" defined by the Social Security Administration? (LO 1)
6. Why is a defined-benefit plan considered noncontributory? (LO 1)
7. When someone becomes vested, what right does he or she receive? (LO 1)
8. Name and briefly describe the seven steps involved in retirement planning. (LO 2)
9. How does a tax-deferred retirement plan work? Discuss two advantages associated with these types of plans. (LO 3)

10. What is a defined-contribution plan? How are benefits determined? From an employer's perspective, why are these plans advantageous? (LO 3)
11. What is a 401(k) plan and how does it differ from a 403(b) plan? Describe two advantages associated with contributing to such plans. (LO 3)
12. What is a guaranteed investment contract (GIC)? What type of investor would a GIC appeal to? (LO 3)
13. What type of occupations qualify for tax-favored retirement plans designed for the self-employed? (LO 4)
14. What are the three types of IRA? How does the Roth IRA differ from the traditional IRA? (LO 4)
15. What is an annuity? Describe the different variations of annuities that someone could use to receive a retirement distribution. (LO 5)
16. What is meant by the term "rollover"? Why is this important? (LO 5)
17. When putting together a retirement plan, what two factors should be paramount in your thinking? (*Hint:* Review Axioms 6 and 11.) Why? (LO 6)

Problems and Activities

1. Todd earned $47,855 last year. Calculate his total FICA contribution for the year. How much did his employer pay toward FICA? (LO 1)
2. Last year Ruth earned $9,400 in Social Security benefits. For the entire year, she had a combined income of $27,500. How much, if any, of her Social Security benefit is taxable? (LO 1)
3. Van is 66 years old. He has a full-time job working as a gardener on a large estate in Newport, Rhode Island. This year he anticipates earning $17,500 from his job. How much, in dollars, will Van's Social Security benefits be reduced? How much will his benefits be reduced when Van turns 70 years old? (LO 1)
4. Use the formula provided on page 547 to answer the following question: What will be Sandra's monthly pension benefit if she retires after 30 years of service with an average salary of $45,000 over the final 5 years of her employment? What percentage of her final average salary would this represent? (LO 1)
5. Timur and Tasha have current living expenses equal to $67,000 a year. Based on the percentage figures provided in this chapter, estimate the amount of income Timur and Tasha need in retirement. Assuming that when they retire their average tax rate will be 15 percent, how much pretax income will Timur and Tasha need? (LO 2)
6. Anne-Marie and Yancy calculate their living expenditures to be $47,000 a year. During retirement they plan on taking one cruise a year, which will cost $3,000 in today's dollars. Anne-Marie estimates that their average tax rate in retirement will be 12 percent. Yancy estimates their Social Security income to be about $17,000 and their pension benefits approximately $20,000. Use this information to answer the following questions: (LO 2)
   a. How much income will Anne-Marie and Yancy need in retirement?
   b. Calculate their projected earnings shortfall.
   c. Determine, in dollars, the future value of the shortfall 20 years from now, assuming an inflation rate of 5 percent.
7. Peter and Jessica recently reviewed their future retirement income and expense projections. They hope to retire in 15 years. They have determined that they'll have a retirement income equal to $57,000 in today's dollars. They also calculate that they'll actually need $73,000 in retirement income to meet all of their objectives. Calculate the total amount that Peter and Jessica must save if they wish to meet their income projection (assuming a 4-percent inflation rate). (LO 2)
8. Claude Messier has determined that he needs to have $1 million in savings in order to retire comfortably in 30 years. He's estimated that he can earn 9 percent a year over the 30-year period. How much must Claude save per year in order to meet his goal? (LO 2)

9. Over the years, Boris (aged 57) has accumulated a total of $400,000 in his IRA. Three months ago he took a distribution from his IRA in the amount of $175,000 for a once-in-a-lifetime vacation around the world. Calculate the penalties Boris must pay when he files his next tax return. (LO 4)

Suggested Projects

1. Take a survey of friends, relatives, and classmates using the following question: "How are Social Security benefits paid to retirees—from money previously paid in and invested, or directly from current employee contributions?" Were you surprised at the responses? Do your respondents consider Social Security a part of their retirement plan? Prepare a report of your results. (LO 1)

2. Call the Social Security Administration (800-772-1213) and request an estimate of what your benefits might be, using your current and past earnings or projected future earnings. When you receive the estimate, be sure to confirm that the recorded annual salary figures match your records. Use the estimated benefits statement to calculate how much other income you need in order to retire comfortably. (LO 1)

3. Ask your employer or the benefits administrator at your school or other business for a defined-benefit pension plan summary. Use this document to calculate your own retirement income. Does the summary document indicate whether the plan is funded or unfunded? From an employee's perspective, which type of plan, funded or unfunded, is preferable? Why? (LO 1)

4. Make a list of factors that you'd want to consider before establishing your own retirement goals. How would these factors change if you were assisting a close older relative in setting retirement goals? (LO 2)

5. There are several types of defined-contribution plans offered by employers. Contact your current employer, or an employer you'd like to work for, and request a pension benefits package summary. Specifically, what types of defined-contribution plans does the organization offer? Using the list of available plans offered in this chapter, what types of plans do you think the employer should offer? Why? (LO 3, 5)

6. Some people argue that you should never invest in an IRA if the contribution is nondeductible. Ask a benefits administrator, a human resource specialist, or someone currently employed whether he or she agrees with this assertion. Make a list of the reasons why someone should consider making nondeductible IRA contributions. Would your answer change if either a 401(k) or 403(b) plan was available in addition to an IRA? Why or why not? (LO 4)

7. Ask relatives or friends who are thinking about retirement if you can talk with them about their retirement planning. Generally speaking, do you think your relatives or friends have taken Axioms 11 and 14 into account when establishing their plans? Do you sense that they are putting enough effort into monitoring the plan? *Hint:* Be sure to think about the factors that someone should keep in mind with monitoring a retirement plan. (LO 6)

8. Talk with someone who is currently retired about his or her sources of retirement income. Is the person's current income sufficient to meet needs? Find out what planning was done to prepare for retirement. What recommendations does he or she have for people currently planning for retirement? (LO 6)

9. Talk with an employee assistance professional or benefits administrator about common mistakes employees make when planning for their retirement. Find out what type of pension plan distribution option is the most popular, and whether the person you talk with thinks this is the best option for most employees. Ask what percentage of current income retirees should plan to earn in order to live comfortably, and whether, in general, retirees will be able to reach this percentage using retirement plans and Social Security. What recommendations, based on this interview, would you make to someone considering retiring? (LO 5, 6)

Richard and Eustacia, both aged 35, need your help in establishing a retirement plan. During retirement their goal is to move to the country, purchase some land and a small house, and enjoy each other's company while gardening, reading, and relaxing. Both are in good health, and they expect to live very economically during their retirement years. They would, however, like to retire by age 55. Use the information below to answer the questions that follow:

Current expenditures	$39,000
Retirement income ratio	0.80
Average retirement tax rate	0.10
Yearly retirement vacations	$2,000
Social Security benefits	$16,000
Pension benefits	$13,000
IRA savings	$10,000
Projected inflation rate	4.50 percent

Questions

1. What is Richard and Eustacia's retirement goal?
2. Calculate Richard and Eustacia's retirement living expenses.
3. Determine their income shortfall in today's dollars.
4. Calculate their inflation-adjusted shortfall.
5. Calculate the funds needed at retirement to cover their shortfall.
6. Determine how much Richard and Eustacia must save annually between now and retirement.
7. What type of retirement plans would you recommend Richard and Eustacia use to meet their goal and to meet Axioms 6 and 15? Why?

Maurice and Maurguerite are facing retirement. Maurice will turn 67 in 2 months, and Maurguerite, a self-employed artist, will be 62 in 6 months. They have met with the benefits administrator at Maurice's employer to establish a retirement date and to discuss payout options for his pension. The benefits administrator was helpful in outlining potential sources of income that Maurice and Maurguerite can expect in retirement. Estimates are as follows:

Social Security	$9,000
Defined benefit	$12,000 (single life annuity)
Maurguerite's work	$5,000
Defined contribution	$10,000 (single life annuity)
Other	$4,000

The defined-contribution payout was calculated based on a 401(k) balance of $250,000 earning approximately 4 percent. The benefits administrator indicated that a 100-percent joint and survivor annuity would decrease yearly benefits by about $2,000 in the defined-benefit plan and $1,500 in the defined-contribution plan. Maurice's company doesn't offer an annuity for life option.

Questions

1. To receive a single life annuity, what would Maurice need from Maurguerite?
2. What are the advantages associated with taking the pension payouts in the form of an annuity? What are the disadvantages?
3. Based on the information provided, which type of annuity would you recommend that Maurice and Maurguerite choose?
4. Concerning the defined-contribution plan, would you recommend that Maurice and Maurguerite take the annuity offered, or would you counsel them to take a lump-sum payment? Why? What are the disadvantages associated with your recommendation?
5. Assuming they decided to take the 401(k) in a lump-sum payment, what two methods could they employ to reduce the impact of taxes?

ESTATE PLANNING:
Saving Your Heirs Money and Headaches

It's amazing that a favorite hippie band from the sixties could have such a following in the nineties, but the Grateful Dead managed it. For 30 years the Grateful Dead had fans—the deadheads—like no other band, and the group remained one of rock's biggest concert draws. However, on August 9, 1995, all that ended with the death of their vocalist and lead guitarist, Jerry Garcia. Garcia's death marked the end of the "long strange trip" for the band, but it was just the beginning of a "long strange trip" for Garcia's estate. Although Garcia prided himself on never selling out to commercialism, he and the Grateful Dead did make a lot of money. In fact, between 1990 and his death in 1995, the band grossed $226.4 million in ticket sales, and their corporation had annual revenues in excess of $50 million. Upon his death, Garcia's estate was estimated to be worth somewhere in the range of $10 million.

Fortunately, Jerry Garcia did something that might seem strange for someone who used to sing, "I will get by, I will survive"—he planned for his death. He was smart enough to do a bit of estate planning, including writing a will to ensure that his assets went exactly where he wanted them to. As a result, his wife and four daughters, aged 7 to 31, along with his brother and Sunshine Kesey, daughter of his friend Ken Kesey, author of *One Flew Over the Cuckoo's Nest*, were taken care of. He even found a home for some of his guitars, stating, "I give all my guitars made by Douglas Erwin, to Douglas Erwin." Unfortunately, his will was fairly unsophisticated and

Learning Objectives

After reading this chapter you should be able to:

1. Understand the importance and the process of estate planning.
2. Calculate and avoid your estate taxes.
3. Draft a will and understand its purpose in estate planning.
4. Avoid probate.

did nothing to avoid estate taxes. In addition, it didn't seem to dictate an incontrovertible last word. Since his death, demands for a piece of the estate have come from Carolyn "Mountain Girl" Adams Garcia, Garcia's former wife and mother of two of his children (who won her suit for $5 million in 1997), his personal manager, a publishing company, his personal trainer, his acupuncturist, and others. Moreover, his will also did nothing to avoid probate. As a result, the long, strange trip of Garcia's estate could wind up being so long and expensive that there'll be considerably less left for his heirs.

Most people cringe at the thought of estate planning, mostly because it involves death. As a result, many individuals avoid it, ignoring the inevitable or assuming that only the rich need to deal with it. However, there's value in estate planning for practically everyone. Once you're dead, there might not be anyone to provide or look out for your spouse or kids. With estate planning you're ensuring that you preserve as much as possible of your wealth—no matter how little that may be—for your heirs. It also ensures that the guardianship of your children will fall to whomever you wish. Basically, estate planning finds much of its logic in **Axiom 10: Protect Yourself Against Major Catastrophes**—in this case, the catastrophe is your death. You'll also find that much of what happens in estate planning is done to keep taxes to a minimum, which brings us back to **Axiom 6: Taxes Bias Personal Finance Decisions**. As you'll see, the basic choices available to you with respect to minimizing taxes and passing on your estate are the use of a will, gifts, and trusts. You'll also see that estate planning can be an extremely complicated process. Thus, our purpose here isn't to make you an expert in estate planning, but to alert you to its benefits and challenges. Hopefully, after carefully studying this chapter you'll have a better understanding of the concepts, terminology, process, techniques, and tools of estate planning.

AXIOM #10

Protect Yourself Against Major Catastrophes

AXIOM #6

Taxes Bias Personal Finance Decisions

LEARNING
OBJECTIVE #1

**Understand the
importance and the
process of estate planning.**

Estate Planning
The process of planning for what
happens to your accumulated wealth
and your dependents after you die.

ESTATE PLANNING

Estate planning is simply planning for what happens to your accumulated wealth and your dependents after you die. Regardless of how large your estate is, the basic objectives of estate planning remain the same. First, you want to make sure that your property is distributed according to your wishes and that your dependents are provided for. Providing for your dependents will, among other things, involve selecting a guardian for your children if they're under 18. Second, you want to pass on as much of your estate as possible, which means you'll want to minimize estate and inheritance taxes. Finally, you'll want to keep settlement costs, including legal and accounting fees, down to a minimum, thereby leaving more for your heirs. In essence, you'll be developing a strategy to give away and distribute your assets while paying the minimum in taxes and fees. Estate planning may seem a bit gloomy because it forces you to think about your own demise. Fortunately, there's one aspect of estate planning that doesn't deal with your own death. Unfortunately, it deals with your incapacitation. Yes, the final objective of estate planning is determining who is to have decision-making authority in the event that you become unable to care for yourself as a result of physical or mental impairment.

The Estate Planning Process

Once you recognize these basic objectives, you'll want to fine-tune them to meet your specific needs and goals. For example, you might want to protect your current spouse from claims on your assets by your ex-spouse. You might also want to induce your kids to go to college by leaving all of your money to them in a fund that they can access only after they graduate. No matter how you choose to fine-tune the basic objectives of estate planning, the financial planning process remains the same for everyone. Let's take a look at that process.

The estate planning process has four steps.

Step 1: Determine What Your Estate Is Worth. Estate planning starts with determining the value of your assets. After all, you can't really think about distributing what you've got until you *know* what you've got. The easiest way to figure out what you've got and what it's worth is by looking at your personal balance sheet, which was introduced and discussed in chapter 2. It should list all of your assets and their respective values, as well as your net worth. As you recall, your net worth was calculated by determining what you own and subtracting from that what you owe.

$$\frac{\text{your estate's}}{\text{net worth}} = \frac{\text{value of your}}{\text{estate's assets}} - \frac{\text{level of estate's}}{\text{liabilities}}$$

In this case, your estate's net worth should be recalculated with several changes. First, you must keep in mind that when you die, your life insurance will pay off. Thus, in calculating the value of your life insurance in your estate's assets, you should use the death benefit as its value rather than its cash or surrender value. In addition, you should include any death benefits associated with your employer-sponsored retirement plan. It's important to get a sense of your wealth, not only because you'll need to know what you have to distribute, but also because its level will determine how much tax planning you'll need. For example, in 1997 the first $600,000 of your estate can be passed on tax-free with this limit climbing gradually to a level of $1 million in 2006. Thus, you'd approach estate planning differently if your estate were worth $500,000 than you would if it were worth $3 million.

Step 2: Choose Your Heirs, Determine Their Needs, and Decide What They Receive.

Once you know just what you've got, you can then go about figuring out who's going to get it when you go. Most married people will just leave everything to their spouse, and others might just get a little silly and leave everything to their faithful pet horse. If all you own is a bunch of oats, maybe leaving your assets to a horse isn't such a bad idea. However, most of us have more complicated estates, and we thus need to put a great deal of thought into dividing them up among our heirs. You'll want to consider the relationships you have with various people and the relationships those people have with your assets. For example, if you've been collecting Grateful Dead concert tapes (you didn't think we'd forget about Jerry Garcia, did you?) with a friend for the last 10 years, you might want to leave your tapes to that friend. You also have to consider the various needs of your dependents and potential heirs. If you have a child with special needs, such as a handicapped child needing special schooling or a child who's an exceptionally talented artist in need of a special art program, you may want to make sure that those needs are taken care of before you consider passing on any of your estate to others. Alternatively, some of your children may have already completed college, and you may want to earmark college funds to those children who haven't yet finished or even started college.

Step 3: Determine the Cash Needs of the Estate.

Once you know what you've got and who's going to get it, your estate planning is done, right? Nope. Before your property can be distributed to your heirs, all legal fees, outstanding debt, and estate and inheritance taxes must be paid. It's a good idea to have enough funds in the form of liquid assets—Treasury bills, stocks, and bonds—to cover your estate tax needs, or to provide tax-free income to your heirs from a life insurance policy that will cover your estate taxes.

Step 4: Select and Implement Your Estate Planning Techniques.

The final step in estate planning is determining which estate planning tools are most appropriate to achieve your goals. In general, you'll need a combination of several estate planning techniques. Some of the most commonly used techniques or tools include a will, a durable power of attorney, joint ownership, trusts, life insurance, and gifts. These tools can be a little tricky to use, and once you've figured out how to use them, implementing your estate plan can be amazingly complex. As a result, you should consult a legal specialist in estate planning to help you with the tools and to handle the details of implementing your plan. Just because you'll need a professional to help you use them doesn't mean you don't need to understand the tools of estate planning. After all, you'll need to be able to speak the same language as the professional so you can fully understand his or her advice. Remember **Axiom 9: The Best Protection Is Knowledge**. In the following sections, we'll examine and explain all the major tools of estate planning that you'll need to understand. First, however, we'll need to discuss taxes, because the use of most estate planning tools is based on tax implications.

AXIOM #9

The Best Protection Is Knowledge

Unified Tax Credit
An estate and gift tax credit in 1997 of $192,800, which equates to allowing the first $600,000 of your estate and lifetime gifts (beyond the $10,000 annual gift exclusion) to be passed on tax-free. This is scheduled to increase gradually and allow $1 million to be passed on tax-free by 2006.

UNDERSTANDING AND AVOIDING ESTATE TAXES

Estate taxes should be central to your estate planning because of the high tax rate imposed on estates. Earlier we mentioned that in 1997 the first $600,000 of your estate can be passed on tax-free. The Taxpayer Relief Act of 1997 provides that this $600,000 tax-free transfer be raised gradually until it reaches $1 million in 2006. Of course, the IRS likes to make everything as complicated as possible, so we'd better explain how this tax-free transfer works. In 1997, instead of simply charging no taxes at all on the first $600,000 of an estate, the IRS actually charges a hefty 18-percent tax rate on the first $10,000 of an estate and keeps raising this rate all the way up to 37 percent by the time this estate hits $600,000. The IRS then issues an estate tax credit, called a **unified tax credit**, to everyone which in 1997 was $192,800, which effectively nullifies the taxes on the first $600,000 of an estate. Unfortunately, above this tax-free threshold of $600,000, rates kick in at an effective rate of 37 percent, which then quickly climbs to 55 percent. Table 18.1 presents the 1997 rate schedule.

Estate Taxes and the Taxpayer Relief Act of 1997

Prior to the Taxpayer Relief Act of 1997, the unified gift and estate tax individual exemption was set at $600,000. This exemption, or tax-free transfer threshold, was increased, with the increase to be phased in gradually, beginning in 1998, climbing to $1,000,000 by the year 2006. The increase is phased in as follows:

1998	$ 625,000
1999	$ 650,000
2000	$ 675,000
2001	$ 675,000
2002	$ 700,000
2003	$ 700,000
2004	$ 850,000
2005	$ 950,000
2006	$1,000,000

This means that an awful lot of wills have to be re-written to make sure that full advantage of the new exemption is taken. It also means there's a moving target as to how big

TABLE 18.1

Federal Estate and Gift Tax Rates for Tax Year 1997	
Value of Taxable Estate Plus Taxable Gifts	**Your Tax Liability Is**
Less than $600,000	$0
$600,000 to $750,000	37% of amount over $600,000
$750,000 to $1,000,000	$55,500 plus 39% of amount over $750,000
$1,000,000 to $1,250,000	$153,000 plus 41% of amount over $1,000,000
$1,250,000 to $1,500,000	$255,500 plus 43% of amount over $1,250,000
$1,500,000 to $2,000,000	$363,000 plus 45% of amount over $1,500,000
$2,000,000 to $2,500,000	$588,000 plus 49% of amount over $2,000,000
$2,500,000 to $3,000,000	$833,000 plus 53% of amount over $2,500,000
over $3,000,000*	$1,098,000 plus 55% of amount over $3,000,00

*Taxable estates/gifts transfers in excess of $10,000,000 and $21,040 are subject to an additional 5% surtax that effectively eliminates the benefit of the unified gift and estate tax credit.

an estate can be passed on tax-free. As a result, sometimes we'll refer to this amount as the "estate-tax-free transfer threshold" and not even mention the dollar amount since it changes each year. Under the Taxpayer Relief Act of 1997, small business owners and those owning family farms also get special treatment. For them the exemption jumps to $1.3 million and takes effect beginning in 1998. There are, as you might expect, some limitations on what types of small businesses qualify for this $1.3 million exemption. Among others, the business must account for at least half of the owner's estate, and the tax comes due unless family members materially participate in the running of the business for the next 10 years. The purpose of this tax break is to allow small businesses and farms to remain with their families.

Given the high estate tax rates imposed, your personal tax strategy should shift toward estate tax planning once your net worth climbs above the tax-free transfer threshold. Individuals with a net worth below the tax-free transfer threshold should focus on income tax strategies and on nontax estate planning concerns. To deal with your estate taxes properly, you'll need to calculate what those taxes will be. However, before you can calculate these taxes, there are a couple other taxes—gift and generation skipping—as well as a deduction that we need to consider.

Gift Taxes

Gifts are an excellent way of transferring wealth before you die. They reduce the taxable value of your estate and allow you to help out your heirs while you're still alive, *and the recipient of the gift isn't taxed on the gift.* Under the present law, you're permitted to give $10,000 per year tax-free to as many different people as you like. Let's look at a couple with two children and an estate valued at $2.4 million. Over a 10-year period, the couple could transfer to *each* of their children a total of $20,000 per year tax-free—$10,000 from the husband and $10,000 from the wife—for a total of $200,000 to each child. These gifts would reduce the couple's taxable estate from $2.4 million to $2.0 million and result in significantly lower estate taxes. It's important to keep in mind that the exclusion for annual gifts applies to each spouse. That is, a husband and wife can give up to $20,000 jointly to each of their children or to whomever they wish without paying any taxes.

> ## *Stop and Think*
> Keep in mind that because gift giving is an annual exclusion, it's renewable. That means every year you get another gift exclusion that allows you to give $10,000 tax-free to as many different people as you like.

If you'd like to give more than that, you can. However, the gift tax and the estate tax *work together with a total lifetime tax-exempt limit (which was $600,000 in 1997) on gifts over and above the yearly tax-free limit of $10,000 per recipient.* Therefore, in 1997 the first $600,000 of your estate *minus* total lifetime nontax-exempt gifts (that portion of gifts in excess of $10,000 per year per person) can be transferred tax-free. Thus, if your lifetime nontax-exempt gifts total $100,000, in 1997 the first $500,000 rather than the first $600,000 of your estate would not be taxed.

The reason gifts and estates are taxed together at the same rates is to avoid presenting an incentive, beyond the annual $10,000 gift exclusion, for individuals to give away as gifts the assets in their estates before they die, instead of as bequests after they die. Thus, once you get beyond the annual $10,000 exclusion, you'll pay exactly the same amount in taxes whether you pass on your estate as a gift while you are alive or pass it on at death.

$10,000-Per-Year Tax-Free Gift and the Taxpayer Relief Act of 1997. Another change put into play by the Taxpayer Relief Act of 1997 is that the $10,000-per-year tax-free gift will be indexed to inflation in $1,000 increments. Thus, if the consumer price index rises by 11 percent over the next 4 years, the tax-free exclusion would rise by $1,000 to $11,000. While 11 percent of $10,000 is actually $1,100, the tax-free gift exemption only increases by $1,000, because changes have to be in $1,000 increments. However, that extra $100 or 1 percent wouldn't be lost, it would carry over and count toward the next $1,000 adjustment.

Unlimited Marital Deduction

The U.S. tax code allows for an unlimited marital deduction for gift and estate tax purposes, which means that there's no limit to the size of transfers between spouses that can be made on a tax-free basis. In other words, when a husband or wife dies, the estate, regardless of size, can be transferred to the survivor totally tax-free. Thus, whereas an estate valued at up to the tax-free transfer threshold (which was $600,000 in 1997) can be transferred tax-free to any beneficiary, there's no limit on the value of an estate that can be transferred to a spouse. As a result, all federal estate taxes can be avoided through the use of the unlimited marital deduction.

Unfortunately for some, the unlimited marital deduction doesn't apply to spouses who aren't U.S. citizens. The logic behind this law is to prevent non-U.S. spouses from returning to their home countries with an untaxed estate. Once they left the United States, Uncle Sam would never get any more tax dollars from the estate, and the IRS isn't about to let that happen. For tax year 1997, if you're married to a non-U.S. citizen and your estate is less then $600,000, there's no need to be concerned, because you can pass on $600,000 tax-free to anyone, regardless of their citizenship. However, to offset the limited marital deduction for noncitizens, the annual gift tax exclusion of $10,000 is raised to $100,000 per year for non-U.S. citizen spouses. That is, if you are married to a non-U.S. citizen, you can make an annual $100,000 tax-free gift to your spouse.

The Generation-Skipping Transfer Tax

There's an additional tax imposed on gifts and bequests that skip a generation—for example, gifts or bequests that pass assets from a grandparent to a grandchild. The purpose of such a tax is to wring potentially lost tax dollars from the intervening generation, in effect, taxing the assets as if they moved from the grandparents to their own children, and then from their children to the grandchildren. The **generation-skipping tax** is a flat 55-percent tax and is imposed *in addition to* any estate and gift taxes.

Obviously, this is a tax you want to avoid. Fortunately, there are two ways around it. First, if you have the resources, you should make effective use of the $10,000 gift tax exclusion in addition to the education and medical expense gift tax exclusions provided in the law. Second, there is a $1 million exemption from the generation-skipping transfer tax for lifetime gifts and bequests at death. For a couple, this would mean a total of $2 million can be passed on to grandchildren without triggering the generation-skipping tax. Thus, unless you're amazingly rich, you don't need to worry about the generation-skipping tax. If you are amazingly rich, you can afford to hire a professional to help you attempt to work around the nasty old generation-skipping tax.

Generation-Skipping Tax
A tax on wealth and property transfers to a person two or more generations younger than the donor.

Calculating Your Estate Taxes

The calculation of estate taxes can be viewed as a four-step process as outlined in Figure 18.1. To walk you through this process, we'll use the example using the 1997 tax-free transfer threshold of $600,000 presented in Figure 18.2. The process of

FIGURE 18.1

Calculation of Estate Taxes

STEP 1	STEP 2	STEP 3	STEP 4
Calculate the Value of the *Gross Estate*.	**Calculate Your *Taxable Estate*.**	**Calculate Your *Gift-Adjusted Taxable Estate*.**	**Calculate Your *Estate Taxes*.**
The gross estate is the value of all the deceased's assets and property. This includes proceeds of life insurance and pension plans, collectibles, and investments, in addition to the value of other assets you own at the time of your death.	Your taxable estate is equal to your gross estate less funeral and administrative expenses; any debt, liabilities, or mortgages; certain taxes; and any marital or charitable deductions.	Before calculating your estate taxes, your cumulative taxable lifetime gifts must be added to your taxable estate as calculated in step 2.	Estate taxes are then calculated on the tentative estate tax base allowing for both the unified gift and estate tax credit which was $192,800 in 1997 along with any state death tax credit. For 1997 this resulted in a tax-free transfer threshold of $600,000 and is scheduled to rise to $1 million by 2006.

calculating your estate taxes starts by calculating the value of the gross estate, which is simply the value of all your assets and property at the time of your death. Remember, you'll have to include the death benefits of any insurance policy or retirement plan you have. The example in Figure 18.2 assumes you have a gross estate of $1.4 million. In step 2, you calculate your taxable estate by subtracting the funeral and estate administrative expenses, along with any debts and taxes you owe, from the gross estate calculated in step 1. Table 18.2 provides a listing of typical funeral and administrative expenses. Keep in mind that in step 2 you need to subtract out any and all liabilities or mortgages you'll have existing at the time of death. In addition, you also subtract any allowable deductions, such as the unlimited marriage deduction and any charitable deductions you have coming. Remember, gifts to charity are tax-deductible, and there's no limit on the size of charitable gifts. Our example in Figure 18.2 assumes that your expenses, debt, and income and other taxes owed totaled $100,000. To calculate the gift-adjusted taxable estate in step 3, the step 2 value must be adjusted for any taxable lifetime gifts that you've made. Remember that the annual gift tax exclusion allows for only one $10,000 gift per year per individual. Let's assume over your life you have given heavily to your children, and one of your gifts exceeded the $10,000 allowable gift tax exclusion by $200,000. Thus, the gift-adjusted taxable estate is $1.5 million, on which results in taxes of $363,000 (calculated from Table 18.1).

How about state death taxes? The federal government provides a maximum credit for state estate taxes that are paid, allowing you to receive credit toward your federal estate taxes for the amount you pay in state estate taxes. About half of the states use this maximum credit level as their state estate tax rate. As a result, you may have to pay state estate taxes, but in general, these taxes have no impact on the total amount of estate taxes, both state and federal, that you pay. The only difference is to whom the money is paid.

FIGURE 18.2

Worksheet for the Calculation of Estate Taxes for the 1997 Tax Year

	Amount	Total Amount
STEP 1: Calculate the value of the *gross estate*.		
A. Value of gross estate		$1,400,000
STEP 2: Calculate your *taxable estate*.		
Less:		
Funeral expenses	$ 10,000	
Estate administrative expenses	40,000	
Debt	0	
Taxes	0	
Marital deduction	0	
Charitable deduction	50,000	
Total		− $ 100,000
Equals:		
B. Taxable estate		= $1,300,000
STEP 3: Calculate your *gift-adjusted taxable estate*.		
Plus:		
Cumulative taxable lifetime gifts (in excess of $10,000 per person per year)		+ $ 200,000
Equals:		
C. Gift-adjusted taxable estate		= $1,500,000
STEP 4: Calculate your *estate taxes*.		
Calculation of taxes on the value in line C (from Table 18.1):		$ 363,000

TABLE 18.2

Typical Funeral and Administrative Expenses

Typical Funeral Expenses

Burial costs
The cost of a burial plot
Costs of future care of the burial plot

Typical Estate Administrative Expenses

Court costs
Executor's fees
Attorney's fees
Accountant's fees
Appraiser's fees

WILLS AND WHAT THEY DO

A **will** is a legal document that describes how you want your property to be transferred to others. Within your will you designate **beneficiaries**, or individuals who are willed your property; an **executor**, sometimes called a **personal representative**, who'll be responsible for carrying out the provisions of your will; and a **guardian**, who'll care for any of your children under the age of 18 and manage their property. Wills are the cornerstone of solid estate planning, so let's examine them more closely.

Wills and the Probate Process

Probate is the legal process of distributing an estate's assets. The first step in the probate process is the validation of the will. Once the court is satisfied that the will is valid, the process of distributing the assets begins. First, the probate court appoints the executor, generally selecting whoever was designated in the will. The executor usually receives a fee ranging from 2 to 5 percent or more of the value of the estate for overseeing the distribution of the estate's assets and managing those assets during the probate process. Once the assets have been distributed and the taxes have been paid, a report is filed with the court and the estate is closed.

The advantage, and really the only purpose, of going through the probate process is to allow for a validation of the will—allowing for challenges and making sure that this is in fact the last will and testament of the deceased. In the case of a challenge to the will, probate allows for the challenge or dispute to be settled. Probate also allows for an orderly distribution of the assets of an individual who dies intestate, or without a valid will.

The disadvantages associated with probate center on its cost and speed. There are numerous expenses—legal fees, executor fees, court costs—that make the probate process expensive. In fact, probate can run from 1 to 8 percent of the value of the estate, depending upon the laws of the state in which the deceased lived. In addition, the probate process can also be quite slow, especially if there are challenges to the will or tax problems.

The Role of Wills in Estate Planning

Because all wills must go through the potentially slow and costly probate process, wills aren't the preferred way to pass on your property. However, wills still play an extremely important role in the estate planning process. There are a number of reasons why you need to have a will, including the following:

- If you don't have a will, the court will likely choose a relative as the guardian to your children under the age of 18 and their property. This relative may be your choice for guardian anyway, but you may feel more comfortable naming a friend as their legal guardian. Through a will, you call the shots.

- In the case of children with special needs, a will may be the most appropriate way of seeing that those needs are taken care of.

- Property that isn't co-owned or in trusts is transferred according to your wishes as expressed in your will.

- If you wish to make special gifts or bequests, they can be easily made through a will. Even the future care of your pets can be easily handled though a will.

- If you don't have a will, the court will appoint an administrator to distribute your assets. Not only might this distribution conflict with your desires, but the costs of an administrator to your estate will be more than the cost of having a will drawn up, leaving less for your heirs.

In short, if you don't have a will, your assets will be distributed according to state law, which may very well be different from your wishes.

Draft a will and understand its purpose in estate planning.

Will
A legal document that describes how you want your property to be transferred to others after your death.

Beneficiary
An individual who is willed your property.

Executor or **Personal Representative**
An individual who is responsible for carrying out the provisions of your will and managing your property until the estate is passed on to your heirs.

Guardian
An individual who'll care for any children under the age of 18 and manage their property.

Probate
The legal procedure that establishes the validity of a will and then distributes the estate's assets.

If you die without a valid will, the state laws dictate the distribution of your assets. These laws will determine who gains custody of your children and how your property is dispersed. Thus, regardless of the size of your estate, a will is a good idea, especially if you have kids.

The Facts of Life

Howard Hughes died in 1976, seemingly without a will and with an estate valued at $42 billion. Within 5 months, over 30 different wills appeared, all of which were eventually declared invalid. Eventually, after 11 years, the estate was finally settled, with lawyers claiming about $8 million, Uncle Sam taking half, and the rest going to his 22 cousins.

The Basics of Writing a Will

Although it's possible to write your own will, it's not a particularly good idea. Handwritten wills, and even oral wills, are accepted in some states, but they're a lot riskier than a formally prepared legal will. Without a formal will, you're taking the chance that the probate court might disallow your will on the grounds of some overlooked technicality. As such, you should have a lawyer either draw up or review your will. Fortunately, a simple will should cost only around $250. Of course, the more complicated the will is, the more expensive its preparation will be.

Once your will has been drawn up, it needs to be signed, and the signing needs to be witnessed by two or more people. It then must be stored in a safe place and periodically reviewed and updated. The most common storage place is with your lawyer. If you change lawyers, though, you need to remember to retrieve and relocate your will. An alternative is to store it at home in a safe fireproof place. Of course, you should make sure that others know exactly where it can be found. Many people store their wills in safety deposit boxes. However, after you die your safety deposit box may be sealed until it can be examined and inventoried for tax purposes. Thus, storing your will in your safety deposit box isn't a particularly good idea. Finally, in some states your will can be stored with the clerk of probate court. Hey, if probate's going to take up a lot of your heirs' time and money, you can at least make the court do a little work for you.

The Basic Organization of a Will

A will should contain several basic features or clauses, including the following:

- **Introductory statement.** The introductory statement identifies whose will it is and revokes any prior wills. Revoking prior wills is important so that there aren't conflicting wills circulating. Multiple wills can really make a mess out of the probate process and slow things down terribly (to the point that your heirs might drop dead from old age before your estate is settled).

- **Payment of debt and taxes clause.** This clause directs the payment of any debts, dying and funeral expenses, and taxes.

- **Disposition of property clause.** This clause allows for the distribution of money and property. It states who is to receive what, and what happens to the remainder of the estate after all the bequests have been honored.

- **Appointment clause.** This clause names the executor of the estate and the guardian if there are children under 18.

- **Common disaster clause.** This clause identifies which spouse is assumed to have died first in the event that both die simultaneously.

- **Attestation and witness clause.** This clause dates and validates the will with a signing before two or more witnesses.

Approximately one in three wills is challenged. For that reason, it's important that you understand what the requirements are for a will to be considered valid. First, you must be mentally competent when the will is written. Second, you can't be under undue influence of anyone at the time the will is made. For example, if you're physically threatened or forced to sign the will, it will be invalidated. Finally, the will must conform to the laws of the state. For example, some states recognize wills that are entirely handwritten, while other states don't.

Updating or Changing Your Will—The Codicil

You should periodically review your will to make sure that it conforms to your present situation. For example, if your family expands or if you get married or divorced, you should alter your will appropriately. If the changes are substantial, it's best to write a new will and expressly revoke all prior wills. If the changes are minor, though, they can be effected through the use of an attachment called a **codicil**. A codicil is simply a document that alters or amends a portion of the will. A codicil should be drawn up by a lawyer, witnessed, and attached to the will.

Letter of Last Instructions

A **letter of last instructions** isn't a legally binding document, but rather a letter, generally to the surviving spouse, that provides information and directions with respect to the execution of the will. Much of what's contained in the letter of last instructions is simply information—information on the location of the will, who should be notified of your death, and the location of legal documents such as birth certificates, Social Security numbers, and tax returns. It also has information as to the location of financial assets, including insurance policies, bank accounts, safety deposit boxes, stocks, and bonds. A letter of last instructions often includes a listing of personal property and valuables as well. Finally, the letter contains funeral and burial instructions, along with your wishes regarding organ donation. The purpose of such a listing is simply to make dealing with your estate easier on your survivors. Generally, if you have an attorney prepare your will, he or she will also prepare a letter of last instructions for you to sign. Although it doesn't carry the same legal weight as a will, it's honored in most states.

Selecting an Executor

An executor takes on the dual role of (1) making sure that your wishes are carried out and (2) managing your property until the estate is passed on to your heirs. To say the least, this is both an important and a time-consuming task. As such, you should take care in naming your executor. For smaller estates it may be a family member, but for larger estates, it should be either a lawyer or a bank trust officer with experience as an executor. Generally, executors are paid for their services, but on smaller estates, family members many times accept money only to cover expenses. Not only does the executor deal with personal matters such as sending copies of the will to all the beneficiaries and publishing death notices, but he or she is also responsible for paying any necessary taxes, paying off the debts of the estate, managing the financial matters of the estate, distributing the assets remaining after bequests have been honored as specified in the will, and reporting a final accounting of the distribution to the court.

Other Estate Planning Documents: Durable Power of Attorney and the Living Will

A **durable power of attorney** provides for someone to act in your place in the event that you become mentally incapacitated. In effect, it empowers someone to act as your

---

Codicil
An attachment to a will that alters or amends a portion of the will.

Letter of Last Instructions
A letter, generally to your surviving spouse, that provides information and directions with respect to the execution of the will.

Durable Power of Attorney
A document that provides for someone to act in your place in the event that you become mentally incapacitated.

legal representative. The durable power of attorney is, of course, a document separate from your will, and it goes into effect while you're alive but unable to act on your own. You can set up the power of attorney so that any degree of legal power is transferred. It should be very specific as to which aspects of your affairs it covers and does not cover, and should mention specific accounts.

A **living will** allows you to state your wishes regarding medical treatment in the event of a terminal illness or injury. Included with the living will should be a health care proxy, which designates someone to make health care decisions should you become unable to make those decisions for yourself. For example, a health care proxy would allow you to designate a trusted friend to make life support decisions for you if you lose the capacity to decide.

AVOIDING PROBATE

Unless you really want to tie up the time and money of your heirs, it's a good idea to avoid probate. Think of probate as a necessary evil. It's essential to validate your will and ensure that the provisions therein are carried out, but it can be a time- and money-eating hassle of enormous proportions. The three simplest ways of avoiding probate are through joint ownership, gifts, and trusts. Let's now look at these ways.

Avoiding Probate Through Joint Ownership

When assets are owned jointly, they're transferred to the surviving owner(s) without going through probate. In effect, the surviving owner(s) immediately assumes your ownership share of the property. There are three different forms of joint ownership: tenancy by the entirety, joint tenancy, and tenancy in common. **Tenancy by the entirety** ownership exists only between married couples. Property held by a married couple under tenancy by the entirety can be transferred only if both the husband and wife agree. In addition, upon the death of one, the property automatically passes directly to the survivor. Under **joint tenancy with the right of survivorship**, two or more individuals share the ownership of assets, which many times are held in a joint account at a bank or a brokerage firm. When one joint owner dies, the ownership passes directly on to the surviving owner or owners, bypassing the will. With **tenancy in common**, two or more individuals share ownership of the assets. However, when one of the owners dies, that owner's share becomes part of the deceased's estate and is distributed according to the deceased's will. The other joint owner or owners don't receive the deceased's ownership shares unless the deceased's will states so expressly.

Although joint ownership—particularly tenancy by the entirety and joint tenancy—is probably the simplest way of avoiding probate, it does have some drawbacks. If a husband and wife have an estate valued at $1.2 million that they would like to pass on to their children and own it jointly, when one dies, the estate is left in total to the surviving spouse. In 1997 that spouse would then only be able to pass on $600,000 of the $1.2 million estate

---

Living Will

A directive to a physician that allows you to state your wishes regarding medical treatment in the event of an illness or injury that renders you unable to make decisions regarding life support or other measures to extend your life.

LEARNING OBJECTIVE #4

Avoid probate.

Tenancy by the Entirety

A type of ownership limited to married couples. Property held this way can be transferred only if both the husband and wife agree. In addition, upon the death of one, the property automatically passes directly to the survivor.

Joint Tenancy with the Right of Survivorship

A type of ownership in which two or more individuals share the ownership of assets, usually in a joint account at a bank or a brokerage firm. When one joint owner dies, the ownership passes directly on to the surviving owners, bypassing the will.

before estate taxes kick in. Of course, as was pointed out earlier, this estate tax-free threshold climbs to $1 million by the year 2006. If the property weren't owned jointly, the first spouse could pass on $600,000 tax-free to his or her children, and then, when the surviving spouse dies, the remaining $600,000 could be passed on tax-free. Another disadvantage of joint ownership is that all owners have the right to use the jointly owned asset, and if the relationship between those involved deteriorates, one of the joint owners could use the asset up. For example, if a bank account is jointly owned, one of the joint owners could "take the money and run." This nasty kind of rip-off is illegal, but it's also difficult to stop. In addition, because joint ownership takes mutual agreement or a divorce settlement to dissolve, there can be problems if the relationship between the parties deteriorates. For example, one individual may wish to sell some jointly owned property for a great profit, but another joint owner might block the sale just out of spite. Without cooperation between the parties, joint ownership can seem like a prison.

Still, there are situations in which joint ownership is an excellent idea. For example, a jointly owned bank account allows survivors to access funds immediately, which can help pay for funeral expenses. In addition, joint property is also valuable in a divorce because it gives both parties some bargaining power, thereby forcing compromises that might not otherwise occur.

The concept of **community property** represents another form of joint ownership. Community property is simply any property acquired during a marriage, assuming both the husband and the wife share equally in the ownership of any assets acquired during the marriage. It doesn't include assets each spouse owned individually before the marriage or gifts and inheritances acquired during marriage that have been kept separate. Upon the death of either the husband or the wife, the surviving spouse automatically receives one-half of the community property. The remaining portion of the property is disposed of according to the will, or in the absence of a will, according to the state laws. Currently only nine states, located primarily in the West, recognize community property.

Avoiding Probate Through Gifts

Not only can you give away $10,000 per year tax-free to as many people as you want, but anything you have given away is no longer yours and, as such, doesn't go through probate. Gifts avoid probate, reduce the taxable value of your estate, and allow you to help out your heirs while you're still alive, and the recipient doesn't pay taxes on the gift.

Gifts are also a good way of transferring property that grows in value, such as stocks or real estate. If, for example, you hold on to a stock investment that continues to grow in value, your estate will continue to grow in value, and the more your estate is worth over the estate tax-free transfer threshold, the more your heirs will lose to estate taxes. If you can afford to part with the stock investment and you know you want to pass it on to someone else anyway, you might consider giving it as a gift. One major exception to the annual gift exclusion rule deals with life insurance policies. If a life insurance policy is given away within 3 years of the owner's death, it is included in the estate for tax purposes. Here's how it works. Let's assume that you gave to your daughter a $500,000 policy that had a cash value of $10,000. First, there'd be no gift tax on the gift because its cash value would fall into the $10,000 or less tax-free gift category. Then let's assume that 3 years and 1 day later you die. In this case, the $500,000 insurance policy payout wouldn't be included in your estate for tax purposes. If, however, you'd died one day before 3 years was up since you gave the policy to your daughter, the entire $500,000 would be included in your estate for tax purposes. The bottom line here is that if you're intending to give away a life insurance policy, it's much better to do it sooner rather than later.

In addition to the $10,000 gift tax exclusion, there is an *unlimited gift tax exclusion on payments made for medical or educational expenses*. You can make this type of gift to anyone regardless of whether the person is related to you or not. The only requirement on these gifts is that you make the payment directly to the school, in the case of education expenses, or to the institution providing the service, in the case of medical

Tenancy in Common
A type of ownership in which two or more individuals share ownership of assets. When one of the owners dies, that owner's share isn't passed on to the other owners. It becomes part of the deceased's estate and is distributed according to the deceased's will.

Community Property
Property acquired during marriage (depends on state law).

expenses. In fact, the unlimited gift tax exclusion for medical expenses can even cover health insurance payments. In effect, you can give someone $10,000 and then pay for his or her health insurance, medical, and educational expenses!

The primary disadvantage to gifts is that once you've given your assets away, you might find that you need them. In addition, because you no longer have control over the assets you give, they may be squandered. Wouldn't it just stink to give your son $10,000 to go buy a car and watch him squander it on a full-body tattoo? Still, a lifetime gift-giving program should be given serious consideration.

Up to this point we've been talking about avoiding probate by giving gifts to your family and other individuals. You can also avoid probate by giving gifts to charity, in which case you don't have to worry about any limits on what can be given tax-free, because there aren't any. If you have a specific charity in mind, or if you're just an incredibly nice person, you can give an unlimited amount of your estate away to federally recognized charities on a tax-free basis. In fact, your charitable gifts are even tax-deductible, so you not only reduce your estate taxes by giving to charity, you also reduce your yearly income tax. See, it pays to be charitable!

Avoiding Probate Through Naming Beneficiaries in Contracts

Insurance contracts and employee retirement plans can also be used to transfer wealth while avoiding probate. Insurance policies, either term or cash-value, can be set up so that someone other than the insured owns the policy. For example, a wife could own an insurance policy on the life of her husband, or a child could own an insurance policy on the life of a parent. One of the major advantages of life insurance is that the proceeds don't go through probate.

Many employee retirement plans pay benefits to spouses upon the death of the employee. These benefits don't go through probate and begin immediately upon the death of the worker. As such, they provide an alternative method for passing on wealth outside of probate. In addition, Social Security benefits go directly to the surviving spouse and dependent children, avoiding probate and federal estate taxes.

The Facts of Life

Estate taxes can take a big chunk out of an estate. Estate taxes reduced Walt Disney's estate by about 30 percent (almost $7 million) when he died. They also took a 64-percent bite (over $17 million in taxes) out of John D. Rockefeller, Sr.'s estate.

Avoiding Probate Through Trusts

Trust
A legal entity in which some of your property is held for the benefit of another person.

A **trust** is a legal entity that holds and manages an asset for another person. A trust is created when an individual, called a grantor, transfers property to a trustee—which can be an individual, an investments firm, or a bank—for the benefit of one or more people, the beneficiaries. Virtually any asset can be put in a trust—money, securities, life insurance policies, and property.

Why do people use trusts? The following are some of the more common reasons:

- **Trusts avoid probate.** Trusts bypass the costly and time-consuming process of probate.

- **Trusts are much more difficult to challenge in court than are wills.** If there are concerns that a will may be challenged, placing the property in a trust can minimize the problem. Challenges to the will don't affect a trust unless the challenge is that the deceased was incompetent or was under undue influence when the trust was formed.

CHECKS AND BALANCES
Are a Must with Trusts

It's tough to find somebody you can trust.

Many wealthier Americans want to make absolutely sure that their money is managed properly after their death, so they ask a bank trust department, trust company or brokerage firm to oversee their estate.

What should you do? Finding an institution with a top-notch reputation is a good start. But if you really want to stack the odds in your favor, take the time to check out the corporate trustee thoroughly, including its investment record and the qualifications of key employees.

(A) In wooing an account, some institutions may subtly suggest that family members aren't the best choice. "The implication certainly is there that lives change and that your wife's wishes 10 years after you die might not be the same as your wishes when you die," says Evan Bell, a certified public accountant in New York who frequently has been a trustee.

(B) But if you decide to use an institutional trustee, rather than an individual, there are some key issues to keep in mind.

For starters, consider the costs.

Look for a corporate trustee who has a record of experience and stability. If it is a relatively new player, ask about the background of its staff. If your trust will include a family business, real estate or other nonfinancial assets, find out about the company's experience in those areas.

(C) Request a meeting with some of the trust department staff.

Catherine Henderson of Colorado Springs, Colo., says the local bank trust officers overseeing her late husband's estate used to meet with her over lunch and ask about her grandchildren. The bank, taken over about two years ago, recently made some changes in its trust staff.

Since then, Mrs. Henderson says she hasn't heard from anyone at the bank. "I'm used to knowing the people I'm dealing with," says Mrs. Henderson, 77. "I don't know them now."

Source: Nancy Ann Jeffrey, "Checks and Balances Are a Must with Trusts," *The Wall Street Journal,* June 16, 1995, p. C1. Reprinted by permission of *The Wall Street Journal* © 1995, Dow Jones & Co., Inc. All Rights Reserved Worldwide.

Analysis and Implications ...

A. To get your wishes carried out, of course, you don't have to use an institutional trustee. Indeed, many people prefer to name as trustee a relative, friend, financial advisor, or other individual close to the family. If you do name an individual, make sure the person you choose has the honesty and basic financial smarts to serve competently. Keep in mind that a trustee must know both what to do and how to get the proper advice.

B. Bank trust departments charge an annual fee that often is in the neighborhood of 1 percent of the assets under management, depending on the size of the estate. This fee is sometimes negotiable. For your money, you should get a full array of services from the institution, including investment management, tax filing, record keeping, and overseeing distributions.

C. Although you may not get to meet the officer who ultimately will handle your trust, you can get a sense of the institution's attitude toward your specific concerns. Also ask about employee turnover and any pending mergers that might affect the institution's trust business.

- **Trusts can reduce estate taxes.** Trusts can be used to shelter assets from estate taxes.
- **Trusts allow for professional management.** If a spouse doesn't have the understanding or desire to manage money effectively, a trust can provide the desired professional management.
- **Trusts provide for confidentiality.** Whereas a will becomes a matter of public record, a trust does not. Thus, if you want privacy, perhaps to keep from offending a relative who doesn't receive all he or she may expect, a trust may be just the thing for you.
- **Trusts can be used to provide for a child with special needs.** A trust can be set up to provide the necessary funds for a child with special needs. For example, if you have a handicapped child in need of special care or schooling, or a gifted child who may benefit from summer enrichment programs, trusts can be set up to provide the necessary funding. A special needs trust can provide funds for disabled children of majority age without eliminating government benefit programs like Medicaid.
- **Trusts can be used to hold money until a child reaches maturity.** Because most children don't have the maturity or understanding necessary to handle large sums of money, a trust can be used to hold those funds until the children reach a designated age. The funds don't have to be immediately dispersed. Instead, they can be distributed over any period of time that is desired.
- **Trusts can assure that children from a previous marriage will receive some inheritance.** If you leave your estate to a second spouse, children from your previous marriage may never receive any inheritance. A trust can ensure that they receive what you wish.

Because there are so many different types of trusts, many people find them confusing. However, all trusts can be classified as being either living trusts or testamentary trusts.

Living Trust

A **living trust** is one in which you place your assets while you're living. There are two types of living trusts, revocable and irrevocable. Let's take a look at these trusts.

Revocable Living Trusts. With a **revocable living trust** you place the assets into the trust while you're alive, and you can withdraw the funds from the trust later if you wish. In effect, it's simply an alternative way of holding your assets. While your assets—for example, your house—are in a revocable living trust, you have access to them, can receive income from them, and can use them. In addition, you pay taxes on whatever income your assets earn. In other words, there doesn't appear to be much difference between assets in a revocable living trust and assets owned outright until you die or become incompetent, at which point the trust beneficiary takes control of the assets in the trust. It's important to remember that there are no tax advantages to a revocable living trust—they don't reduce your estate taxes. However, when you die, assets held in a living trust don't go through probate, but instead go directly to your beneficiary. It is the high costs of probate and the privacy attained by avoiding probate that explain much of the use of revocable living trusts. Table 18.3 summarizes the advantages and disadvantages of a revocable living trust.

Irrevocable Living Trusts. An **irrevocable living trust**, as the name suggests, is permanent. It can't be changed or altered once it's been established, because you no longer hold title to the assets in the trust. In effect, the trust becomes a separate legal entity. It pays taxes on the income and capital gains that its assets produce. This fact takes on major importance when you die, because assets in an irrevocable living trust aren't considered part of your estate, and therefore, any appreciation of assets would not be subject to estate tax. This type of trust also bypasses probate, and because the assets in the trust are no longer yours, they're not subject to estate taxes.

Living Trust
A trust created during your life.

Revocable Living Trust
A trust in which you control the assets in the trust and can receive income from the trust without removing assets from the estate.

Irrevocable Living Trust
A trust in which you relinquish title and control of the assets when they are placed in the trust.

TABLE 18.3

Advantages and Disadvantages of Revocable Living Trusts

Advantages of Revocable Living Trusts

The assets in the trust avoid probate upon your death.
You maintain the power to alter or cancel the trust before your death.
If you become incompetent, your assets will continue to be professionally managed by the trustee.
You can observe the ability of the trustee and replace the trustee if you do not have confidence in his or her skills.

Disadvantages of Revocable Living Trusts

There are no tax advantages—you pay taxes on any income and capital gains on the assets in the trust
The assets in the revocable living trust are considered part of your estate for estate tax purposes.
The assets in the revocable living trust cannot be used as collateral for a loan.

Obviously, the major difference between a revocable and an irrevocable living trust centers on the fact that with a revocable trust, you retain title to and have control of the assets in the trust. Table 18.4 summarizes the advantages and disadvantages of an irrevocable living trust.

Testamentary Trusts

A **testamentary trust** is one that's created by a will. Therefore, it doesn't exist until probate has been completed. There are a number of different purposes for testamentary trusts, including reducing estate taxes, providing professional investment management, and making sure your estate ends up in the right hands. Let's look at some of the more common types of testamentary trusts.

Standard Family Trusts (also known as A-B trusts, credit-shelter trusts, and Unified Credit trusts).
Standard **family trusts** can be used to reduce estate taxes when one spouse dies before the other. Look, for example, at a husband whose estate is valued at $600,000 with a wife whose estate is valued at $600,000 in 1997. Eventually, the couple would like their estate to pass on to their children rather than to the government in the form of taxes. Figure 18.3 shows how this couple would pass their estates on to their

Testamentary Trust
A trust created by your will, which becomes active after you die.

Family Trust
A trust established to transfer assets to your children, while allowing the surviving spouse access to funds in the trust if necessary. Upon the death of the surviving spouse, the remaining funds in the trust are distributed to the children tax-free.

TABLE 18.4

Advantages and Disadvantages of Irrevocable Living Trusts

Advantages of Irrevocable Living Trusts

The assets in the trust avoid probate upon your death.
Any price appreciation on assets in the trust are not considered part of your estate, and as such, there are no estate taxes imposed on them when you die.
Income earned on assets in the trust can be directed to the beneficiary, which can result in tax savings if the beneficiary is in a lower tax bracket.

Disadvantages of Irrevocable Living Trusts

You no longer maintain control over the assets in the trust.
The assets in the trust cannot be used as collateral for a loan.
It may be more expensive to set up than the probate costs you are trying to avoid.
Setting up the trust can involve a lot of paperwork.

FIGURE 18.3

Using Trusts to Reduce Estate Taxes: A Simple Will and a $1.2 Million Estate in 1997

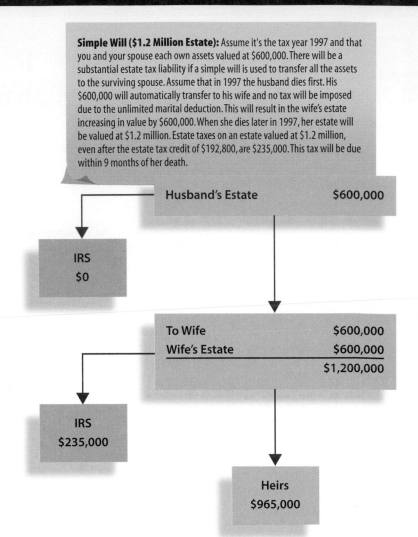

Simple Will ($1.2 Million Estate): Assume it's the tax year 1997 and that you and your spouse each own assets valued at $600,000. There will be a substantial estate tax liability if a simple will is used to transfer all the assets to the surviving spouse. Assume that in 1997 the husband dies first. His $600,000 will automatically transfer to his wife and no tax will be imposed due to the unlimited marital deduction. This will result in the wife's estate increasing in value by $600,000. When she dies later in 1997, her estate will be valued at $1.2 million. Estate taxes on an estate valued at $1.2 million, even after the estate tax credit of $192,800, are $235,000. This tax will be due within 9 months of her death.

| Husband's Estate | $600,000 |

| IRS | $0 |

To Wife	$600,000
Wife's Estate	$600,000
	$1,200,000

| IRS | $235,000 |

| Heirs | $965,000 |

children using a simple will, and Figure 18.4 shows how they do it using a trust instead. Using a simple will, the husband would pass his estate to his wife tax-free (remember, in 1997 there was no estate tax on estates of $600,000 and less). His wife's estate, though, then becomes worth $1.2 million. If his wife uses a simple will to leave her estate to the children, the government will impose estate taxes of $235,000. However, using a standard family trust, when the husband dies his assets go directly into the trust for their children. There are no taxes imposed on this transfer, because the estate would not be valued at more than $600,000. Such a trust allows the wife to get income from the children's trust for as long as she lives, and even to take funds directly from the trust's principal if necessary. Although the trustee must agree to allow her access to the funds in the trust, the selection of an understanding trustee by the husband at the onset of the trust can assure her all the access she needs. However, because she doesn't technically own the funds in the trust, her estate is still valued at $600,000, which she can leave to the children tax-free. Upon the death of the wife, the funds in the trust are automatically distributed to the children as well, all tax-free. Thus, using a trust saved the family in our example $235,000.

LIFE INSURANCE TRUSTS Can Help Your Heirs

On his deathbed, Oscar Wilde was offered a sip of champagne. He accepted, saying, "I am dying beyond my means."

Ⓐ Make no mistake: death can be an expensive proposition, even if you have the means to go out in style. You can blame estate taxes for that. But one way to ease the cost—to your survivors, at any rate—is with a life insurance trust.

"Since a life insurance payout isn't subject to income taxes, many people assume it's equally immune to estate taxes," said Kevin Flatley, director of estate planning at the Bank of Boston. That's not so. For tax purposes, the proceeds are part of your estate, along with your home, car, savings and investments. But with a life insurance trust, proceeds from a policy can be shielded from the Internal Revenue Service.

Many people do not worry much about estate taxes because the I.R.S. lets you leave $600,000 in assets tax free and places no ceiling on what you can leave your spouse.

Ⓑ But even a seemingly modest estate can suddenly swell to $600,000, especially with the stock market spiraling higher. Add the proceeds of a life insurance policy, and plenty of estates would go over the limit. To paraphrase Everett Dirksen, a hundred thousand here, a hundred thousand there and soon you're talking about real money.

A life insurance trust can save at least part of your estate from those taxes. Stripped down to its essentials, the trust works like this: You hire a lawyer to create an irrevocable trust. Next, you buy a life insurance policy and make the trust its sole owner. (You can also transfer an existing policy into the trust, but there is a risk: If you die within three years, the proceeds go into your estate and are fully taxed.) You then contribute annually to the trust so that it can pay the premiums. If you follow the rules, the proceeds of your policy will stay out of the clutches of the I.R.S.

Source: Bruce Felton, "Life Insurance Trusts Can Help Your Heirs," *The New York Times*, April 7, 1996, p. F7. Copyright © 1996 by The New York Times Co. Reprinted by Permission.

Analysis and Implications ...

A. Most people never give serious thought to creating a life insurance trust. Promoted by private banks as the last of the great estate tax shelters, life insurance trusts are often regarded as the exclusive province of the rich and the superrich. If you think that rules you out, consider this: You could be a prime candidate for a life insurance trust for the simple reason that your estate may be worth a lot more than you think.

B. It doesn't take as long as you might expect to hit the estate tax-free transfer threshold. While it's scheduled to rise to $1 million by 2006, that too may be reachable for many people. Once estate taxes kick in, they take a real toll—with Uncle Sam getting as much as $55 out of every $100. Given the tax bite, it only makes sense to take a close inventory of your assets to see what you're really worth.

FIGURE 18.4

Using Trusts to Reduce Estate Taxes: A Family Trust and a $1.2 Million Estate in 1997

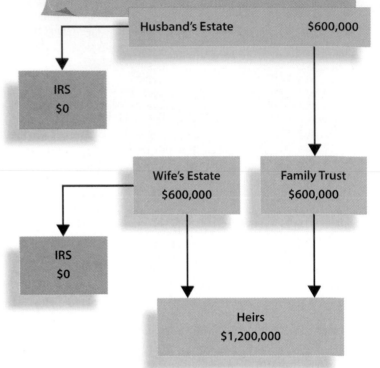

Optimum Marital Will Plan ($1.2 Million Estate): Assume it's the tax year 1997 and that you and your spouse each own assets valued at $600,000. At death, your assets can be directed into a trust rather than have them passed directly to the surviving spouse. Assume that in 1997 the husband dies first. Up to $600,000 can automatically pass into a trust—known as a standard family trust. This trust allows his estate to shelter his unified credit equivalent (his $600,000 tax-free transfer), plus appreciation, from estate taxes when his wife eventually dies. At her death, her $600,000 will pass tax-free to family members or heirs.

| Husband's Estate | $600,000 |

IRS $0

| Wife's Estate $600,000 | Family Trust $600,000 |

IRS $0

Heirs $1,200,000

Qualified Terminable Interest Property Trust (Q-TIP)

A trust that gives the individual establishing the trust the ability to direct income from the trust to his or her spouse over the spouse's life, and then, at the spouse's death, to choose to whom the assets go.

Sprinkling Trusts

A trust that distributes income according to need rather than to some preset formula. The trustee is given discretion to determine who needs what among the designated beneficiaries and then "sprinkles" the income among them according to need.

Qualified Terminable Interest Property Trust (Q-TIP). A **qualified terminable interest property trust**, or **Q-TIP**, gives the individual establishing the trust the ability to direct income from the trust to his or her spouse over the spouse's life, and then, at the spouse's death, to choose to whom the assets go. The primary reason for using a Q-TIP trust is to keep your estate from ending up in the hands of your spouse's future husband or wife rather than your children after you die. As such, Q-TIP trusts are generally set up so that your spouse receives the income on your estate while he or she is alive, and after your spouse's death, the assets in the trust are passed on to your children.

Sprinkling Trusts. A **sprinkling trust** is simply a trust that distributes income according to need rather than to some preset formula or your whims. The trustee is given discretion to determine who needs what among a designated group of beneficiaries, and then "sprinkles" the income among them according to need.

A LAST WORD ON ESTATE PLANNING

After viewing the complexities associated with estate planning, it is a natural reaction to say to yourself, "It's a great idea to look at some day." Today should be that some day, and estate planning begins with a will. From there, what happens next depends upon the value of your estate and whether or not you have loved ones with special needs. Once you have a basic understanding of the process, objectives, and tools of estate planning, you should approach a professional. By no means should you attempt your own estate planning. Finally, you should make sure that your family knows where your estate planning documents are. Figure 18.5 provides an estate planning checklist that will help you organize your affairs.

FIGURE 18.5

Estate Planning Worksheet

Do you and the members of your family know the location of ...

- ☑ Your will, durable power of attorney, and living will (with the name of the attorney who drafted them)?
- ☑ The name of your attorney?
- ☑ Your letter of last instructions, including burial requests and organ donor information?
- ☑ Your Social Security number?
- ☑ Your safety deposit box and the key to it?
- ☑ A record of what is in your safety deposit box?
- ☑ Your birth certificate?
- ☑ Your marriage certificate?
- ☑ Any military discharge papers?
- ☑ Insurance policies (life, health, and property/liability) along with the name of your insurance agent?
- ☑ Deeds and titles to property (both real estate and real, for example, automobiles)?
- ☑ Your stocks, bonds, and other securities, and who your broker is?
- ☑ Any business agreements, including any debts owed you?
- ☑ All checking, savings, and brokerage account numbers, along with the location of those accounts?
- ☑ The name of your accountant?
- ☑ Your last year's income tax return?
- ☑ The name of past employers, along with any pension or retirement benefits information?

You should also:

1. Calculate the size of your estate.
2. Estimate how much of your estate would be lost to taxes if you died.
3. Know who the executor of your will is and who your beneficiaries are.
4. Select a guardian for your children if they are under 18.

SUMMARY

Estate planning involves planning for what happens to your accumulated wealth and your dependents after you die. The estate planning process can be viewed as a four-step process.

Step 1: Determine what your estate is worth.

Step 2: Choose your heirs, determine their needs, and decide what they receive.

Step 3: Determine the cash needs of the estate.

Step 4: Select and implement your estate planning techniques.

The purpose of going through the probate process is to allow for a validation of the will—allowing for challenges and making sure that this is in fact the last will and testament of the deceased. A will is a legal document that describes how you want your property to be transferred to others. Within your will, you designate beneficiaries or individuals who are willed your property. You also designate an executor who'll be responsible for carrying out the provisions of your will. In addition, you can also designate a guardian who'll care for any children under the age of 18 and manage their property. You should periodically review your will to make sure that it conforms to your present situation.

Trusts are legal entities that hold money or assets. Some of the more common reasons for trusts are (1) trusts avoid probate, (2) trusts are much more difficult to challenge in court than are wills, (3) trusts can reduce estate taxes, (4) trusts allow for professional management, (5) trusts provide for confidentiality, (6) trusts can be used to provide for a child with special needs, (7) trusts can be used to hold money until a child reaches maturity, and (8) trusts can assure that children from a previous marriage will receive some inheritance. With a revocable living trust, you place the assets into the trust while you are alive, and you can withdraw the funds from the trust later if you wish. An irrevocable living trust, as the name suggests, is permanent. A testamentary trust is one that is created by a will. Because these trusts are established by a will, they aren't created until probate has been completed. Here are some guidelines based upon the 1997 estate tax-free transfer threshold of $600,000. Keep in mind that this threshold will gradually rise to $1 million in the year 2006.

If your estate's valued at less than $600,000 (in 1997): Other than a will, which is especially important if you have children, there's no need for estate planning because you can pass on up to $600,000 free of taxes. The only exception is if you have children with special needs that require a trust set up to manage their investments.

If you're married and have an estate valued between $600,000 and $1.2 million (in 1997): With an estate valued above $600,000 but below $1.2 million, you should make sure that the $600,000 tax-free estate transfer for both you and your spouse is taken advantage of. If your estate is valued at $1.2 million and your assets are owned jointly, when either one of you dies, the entire estate is passed on to the survivor, leaving an estate valued at $1.2 million and tax problems when your spouse dies. These problems could be avoided with a standard family trust.

If you're single and have an estate valued at over $600,000 or are married and have an estate valued at over $1.2 million (in 1997): For estates valued at more than $600,000 for individuals or $1.2 million for couples, the only way to avoid taxes is to reduce the value of the estate. Three effective ways of reducing your estate are by spending, giving money away, and giving away your life insurance policy. Take advantage of the $10,000 annual gift exclusion—give the money directly or have it build up in a trust. (A married couple can give a child up to $20,000 annually tax-free, in addition to unlimited payments made directly to schools for tuition or for medical expenses.)

Review Questions

1. What is estate planning and why is it important? (LO 1)
2. Describe the four steps in the estate planning process. (LO 1)

✓ If you have any assets, a spouse, and/or children—*get a will!* If you die without one, your state will "write one for you" based on its inheritance laws. Often those laws are directly opposed to your intent. For example, part of your estate may go to your parents when you would've wanted your spouse to inherit everything, or your children may be appointed to a guardian you always detested.

✓ Beware of do-it-yourself will packages or computer software. Although many are good, some leave out very important sections of a viable will or aren't valid in your state. Also, such tools may not provide any coaching on how bequests should be worded to avoid confusion at probate. One error could run your beneficiaries more in probate costs than the attorney's fee to do it right the first time.

✓ Living trusts are excellent tools for certain people, but do your homework before deciding if one is right for you. Unfortunately, they're being "sold" by persons quoting highly exaggerated probate costs and using other scare tactics. Be sure your situation warrants the time and expense. Probate costs vary greatly from state to state, and you may find the expense of such a trust is much more than your estate would pay for probate. If you do choose a living trust, use a qualified attorney to set it up.

✓ One of the biggest erosions of large estates with business or real estate holdings is forced sale of assets at "fire sale" prices to pay taxes. If your assets are primarily illiquid, you may want life insurance to provide the funds necessary to preserve those valuable holdings.

✓ Consider using an irrevocable life insurance trust as a source of money for estate taxes. If structured properly, the trust may use $10,000 annual exclusion gifts to beneficiaries to pay insurance premiums. Proceeds from the policy are not your assets, and you're able to reduce the size of your estate further each year with the exclusions. By purchasing the life insurance initially through the trust, you avoid the chance that proceeds will revert to your estate if you die within 3 years.

✓ Business owners who don't wish to burden their beneficiaries with trying to run a company after their death should investigate a "buy-sell agreement." There are several types of such plans that provide for another shareholder, partner, or key employee to purchase the business from the estate. Funding is often provided through life insurance. In such a win-win situation, forced sale of the company is avoided, and the deceased owner's family receives the liquidity they may need.

3. Describe the unified credit. How much federal estate tax does it offset? How is this set to change in the future? (LO 2)
4. Describe the annual gift tax exclusion and how it can be used as an estate planning tool. (LO 2)
5. Describe the unlimited marital deduction. When is it not a good idea to make use of it? (LO 2)
6. What is the generation-skipping tax and how can it be avoided? (LO 2)
7. Describe the four-step process of calculating estate tax. (LO 2)

WWW.
Take It to the Net

We invite you to visit the Keown Personal Finance page on the Prentice Hall Web site at:

http://www.prenhall.com/persfin

for this chapter's World Wide Web exercise.

You might also want to visit the following Web sites:

SeniorLaw Home Page (estate planning links and articles): http://www.seniorlaw.com/index.htm

Wills on the Web (famous wills on the Web, including those of Elvis Presley, John Lennon, Babe Ruth, and more): http://www.ca-probate.com/wills.htm

LifeNet Estate Planning (along with a calculator to help determine your estate value): http://lifenet.com/abestate.html#AboutEstate

WebTrust.com (basic estate planning information): http://www.webtrust.com

Estate Planning sites (a good listing of sites): http://www.ca-probate.com/links.htm

8. Define the following estate planning terms: beneficiary, codicil, executor, guardian, probate, and will. (LO 2)
9. List five reasons why having a will is important. (LO 3)
10. Describe the basic clauses in a will. (LO 3)
11. List three characteristics of a valid will. (LO 3)
12. Describe the following estate planning documents: durable power of attorney, letter of last instructions, and living will. (LO 1)
13. Describe four different ways of owning property with other people. (LO 4)
14. Define a trust and list five possible advantages of creating one. (LO 4)
15. Describe each of the following types of trusts: irrevocable trust, living trust, qualified terminable interest property (Q-TIP) trust, revocable trust, sprinkling trust, standard family trust, and testamentary trust. (LO 4)

Problems and Activities

1. Earlier this year, Mae and Joe Phillips gave $20,000 to their son, Paul, for a down-payment on a house.
   a. How much gift tax will be owed by Mae and Joe?
   b. How much income tax will be owed by Paul?
   c. List three advantages of making this gift. (LO 1)
2. Evelyn Ayers is a widow with a taxable estate of $1,250,000. She has made no taxable lifetime gifts. If she dies in 1997:
   a. What is the federal estate tax due before the unified credit?
   b. What is the amount of the unified credit?
   c. What is the estate tax due? (LO 2)
3. What can Evelyn Ayers do to reduce the estate tax that would be due upon her death? (LO 2)
4. Zane Wulster has a taxable estate of $800,000. He has made $200,000 of gifts that exceeded the annual $10,000 gift tax exclusion. If he dies in 1997:
   a. What is federal estate tax due before the unified credit?
   b. What is the amount of the unified credit?
   c. What is the estate tax due? (LO 2)
5. Raul Carera, 65, recently gave $50,000 to his 2-month old granddaughter, Selena. How much generation-skipping transfer tax (GSTT) is due on this gift? (LO 2)
6. Chi-kok Ting has a $300,000 net worth. In addition, he has a $250,000 whole life policy with $40,000 of accumulated cash value and a $50,000 pension plan benefit. If he dies in 1997:
   a. What is the value of Chi-kok's gross estate?
   b. How much of his estate is taxable?
   c. How much estate tax will he be required to pay? (LO 2)
7. Jeff Lennon is a generous soul. During each of the past 20 years, he has given $15,000 to each of his eight grandchildren, plus $50,000 in 1992 to his son and two daughters.
   a. What portion of Jeff's gifts can be transferred tax-free?
   b. What is the total amount of gifts over the years that are taxable?
   c. How much gift tax is due? (LO 2)
8. Maria and Harold Jolly have $1.4 million of assets: $400,000 in Harold's name, $400,000 in Maria's, and $600,000 of jointly owned property. They own their jointly owned property under joint tenancy with right of survivorship. Maria also co-owns a $300,000 beach house with her sister, Julia, as tenants in common.
   a. In 1997, what is the maximum amount of estate value that can be transferred by the Jollys free of estate tax?
   b. What do the Jollys need to do to reduce their expected estate tax liability?
   c. Who would receive Maria's half-share in the beach house if she were to die? (LO 4)

9. Martha and Steve Kaye are the parents of two pre-school children. Neither of them has a will. They carpool to work together and die in an unfortunate head-on crash. Who will be selected to raise their children? (LO 3)

Suggested Projects

1. Locate a recent article about problems experienced by individuals or families who failed to do proper estate planning. Write a one-page summary. (LO 1)
2. Prepare a list of information about yourself that would be helpful for others to know in the event of your death or incapacitation. (LO 1)
3. Using Figure 18.2, calculate the value of your taxable estate and the amount of estate tax due, if any, upon your death. (LO 2)
4. Make a list of criteria that you would use in selecting the executor of your estate and heirs named to inherit your assets. (LO 3)
5. Contact three law firms to determine the cost of preparing a simple will and what information, if any, needs to be provided for an attorney. Write a one-page report of your findings. (LO 3)
6. Prepare a letter of last instructions. Share and discuss it with one or more family members. (LO 3)
7. Write a one-page report describing your feelings regarding medical treatment in the event of a terminal illness. Make a list of criteria that you would use in selecting a health care proxy. (LO 3)
8. Discuss with a close adult friend or relative their estate plans including the use of a will, trusts, lifetime gifting, a living will, and/or a durable power of attorney. Write a one-page report of your findings. (LO 1)

Discussion Case 1

Lois and Jim Aaronson are both in their early seventies and are very concerned about avoiding probate. Together, in 1997, they have a net worth of $780,000. This includes a $200,000 home and $400,000 in Jim's 401(k) plan and various other investments. They also have $100,000 of life insurance each. The Aaronsons would like to help their daughter Julia, a single parent, purchase a condo. They are also concerned about Lois's lack of investment experience should Jim predecease her.

Sometime in the next few months, Lois will receive an inheritance from the estate of her recently deceased 104-year-old mother. She expects to receive about $400,000 and wants to see Julia and their son, Rob, receive as much as possible after her death. The Aaronsons have wills, which were last reviewed 10 years ago, that leave everything to each other with the children as contingent beneficiaries. They have not used any other estate planning tools.

Questions

1. Discuss the appropriateness for the Aaronsons of the four methods for avoiding probate listed in this chapter.
2. Assume the Aaronsons give Julia $100,000 next month to help purchase a condo. How much tax must Julia pay on this gift?
3. Will the Aaronsons have to pay gift tax on their $100,000 gift to Julia? If yes, how much?
4. Discuss the appropriateness of the Aaronsons using the unlimited marital deduction upon the death of the first spouse to die.
5. What changes would you advise the Aaronsons to make to their wills and other estate documents?

Discussion Case 2

Cindy and Ned Lipman are in their early 50s and were recently married, each for the second time. Both are very concerned about leaving assets to the adult children from their previous marriages. Together, they have an estate valued in 1997 at $1 million, of which $750,000 is in Cindy's name and $250,000 of assets is in Ned's name. Due to financial difficulties experienced in their first marriages, both Cindy and Ned are leery about co-mingling their individual assets. The house that they live in is Cindy's $200,000 home, which she received in her divorce settlement.

Another estate planning concern of the Lipmans is planning for incapacitation. Cindy's 86-year-old mother and 84-year-old uncle both have Alzheimers disease and she is concerned that it may be hereditary and affect her. Ned recently lost his father to a long-term illness and has vowed never to become a "vegetable" lying in a hospital bed like his father was. Cindy, on the other hand, believes all steps should be taken to try to prolong a person's life in case a cure is found. Neither Cindy nor Ned have revised their wills since their marriage. The wills still name their previous spouses as executor and beneficiary of their respective estates.

Questions

1. What type of trust is appropriate for remarried couples such as the Lipmans?

2. How much estate tax would Cindy and Ned owe on their respective estates?

3. What can Cindy and Ned do to address their concerns about estate planning in the event of incapacitation?

4. Would Cindy and Ned make good health care proxies for one another? Why or why not?

5. Should Cindy and Ned revise their wills? If so, what changes should be made?

Continuing Case: Don and Maria Chang

PART V: RETIREMENT AND ESTATE PLANNING (Chapters 17 and 18)

Although Don and Maria don't plan to retire or to transfer their estate until sometime far in the future, they have once again compiled a list of questions for you. With your assistance they have reviewed their spending, credit usage, insurance needs, and investment plans. In short, through sound financial planning and changing a few spending habits, they're building an estate for the future. They also are concerned about being financially independent during their "golden years" and want to make the most of their retirement options.

Questions

1. At what age can Don retire and receive full Social Security benefits? If he delays retirement, his benefit will increase by what percentage? What is the earliest age that Don can retire and receive Social Security? Will Don receive more or less than his regular benefit if he retires early?

2. Assuming Don and Maria were old enough to retire today and receive Social Security, what percentage of their Social Security benefit would be taxable?

3. If Don were to die tomorrow, Maria would be eligible for what Social Security benefits? Would Andy be eligible for benefits? What kind and for how long?

4. Both Don and Maria have indicated that they're eligible for a qualified retirement plan at work, but they don't know what that means.
   a. Briefly describe what the term "qualified retirement plan" means.
   b. Are the Changs considered "active participants"?
   c. Why are these concepts important in retirement planning? (*Hint:* Think about qualified plans in relation to IRAs.)

d. What is the maximum amount Don and Maria can contribute to an IRA this year? If they decide to contribute to an IRA, would they receive a full or partial tax deduction? Why?

5. What type of questions should Don and Maria ask about their company's pension plans?

6. Use the Changs' original current living expenses as the basis for answering the following questions. (*Hint:* Refer to Worksheet G.37, *Worksheet for Funding Your Retirement Needs.*)

   a. How much income, before and after taxes, will they need to retire? (*Hint:* Assume an average tax rate of 10 percent during retirement.)

   b. Assume that through a combination of savings, Social Security, and pension plan distributions Don and Maria are able to earn $42,000 annually in retirement. Determine their retirement income shortfall. Assuming a 4-percent inflation rate and 30 years until retirement, calculate their inflation-adjusted shortfall.

   c. If Don and Maria can earn a 5-percent inflation-adjusted return, determine how much they must accumulate in savings by retirement (in 30 years) to fund the annual inflation-adjusted shortfall as calculated above.

   d. How much do the Changs need to start saving each year for the next 30 years at 10 percent to meet their savings accumulation goal as calculated in part c?

7. If, for 30 years, Don and Maria were to invest $2,000 at the end of every year in a tax-free account, what would be the future value of the account if they could earn 9 percent annually? If instead they first paid taxes (marginal tax rate of 28 percent), then made the investment, how much would the account be worth at the end of 30 years? Based on these calculations, what advice would you give to Don and Maria regarding their retirement savings?

8. Assuming Maria's employer decided to offer a profit-sharing plan, what would be the advantages and disadvantages of this type of plan?

9. During the upcoming tax year, Maria is considering working as an independent tax preparer. She has obtained a business license and is planning to work out of her home. Would she qualify for a small business/self-employed retirement

plan? What retirement plan options would be appropriate for her situation?

10. Maria has indicated that she thinks a single life annuity will be her choice when she begins to receive pension benefits at retirement. She has concluded that this is the best payout structure because (a) she has earned the entire benefit, and (b) Don will be covered by his own pension. Will Maria automatically be able to choose a single life annuity payout option? If not, what will be received from Don? Assuming that Don does not want Maria to have a single life annuity, what type of joint and survivor annuity will provide the greatest immediate payout while providing Don a guaranteed income?

11. Besides monitoring finances related to retirement planning, what advice would you give the Changs as they consider the retirement process?

12. If Don or Maria were to die this year, how much federal estate tax would need to be paid by their estate?

13. Andy's grandparents (Don's mother and father) were concerned about his college funding and recently gave Andy a $20,000 gift to be invested for college. How much federal income tax and gift tax is due on this transfer? Will there be any generation-skipping transfer tax due?

14. Many experts recommend that young families like the Changs prepare wills. What are the advantages of doing so? What would happen if Don or Maria were to die without a will?

15. Maria's shares in the Great Guns Balanced Mutual Fund are held individually in her name alone. If Maria were to die without preparing a will, who would receive her shares?

16. In addition to wills, what other estate planning techniques should the Changs consider?

17. What steps can the Changs take to avoid probate?

18. Don's older sister, Cindy, recently drafted a will and asked him to serve as executor of her estate. Don said yes, reluctantly, but he really isn't sure what he would need to do. What are the duties that Don would be expected to perform as an executor?

19. The Changs recently read their bank statement and noticed that their $7,000 savings account is owned jointly with right of survivorship. They've asked you to explain this term. Provide a simple explanation.

Appendix A:
Using a Financial Calculator

Much of personal finance involves either determining how much you need to save to meet a future financial goal, or determining how big your payments will be on money you borrowed today. All this finds its roots in **Axiom 2: The Time Value of Money**. In fact, there's very little in personal finance that doesn't have some thread of the time value of money woven through it. With an understanding of the time value of money, we can compare dollar values from different periods.

With just a little time and effort, you'll be surprised how much you can do with a calculator, such as stripping away the effects of inflation and seeing what future cash flows are worth in today's dollars or what rate of return you are earning on an investment or paying on a loan. The role of the time value of money in personal finance is almost endless.

In demonstrating how calculators make your work easier, you must first decide which calculator to use. The options are numerous and largely depend upon personal preference. We have chosen the Texas Instruments BA-II Plus.

I. INTRODUCTORY COMMENTS

In the examples that follow, you are told (1) which keystrokes to use, (2) the resulting appearance of the calculator display, and (3) a supporting explanation.

The keystrokes column tells you which keys to press. The keystrokes shown in an unshaded box tell you to use one of the calculator's dedicated, or "hard," keys. For example, if +/− is shown in the keystrokes instruction column, press that key on the keyboard of the calculator. To use a function printed in gray lettering above a dedicated key, always press the gray **2nd** key first, then the function key.

II. AN IMPORTANT STARTING POINT

Example: You want to display four numbers to the right of the decimal.

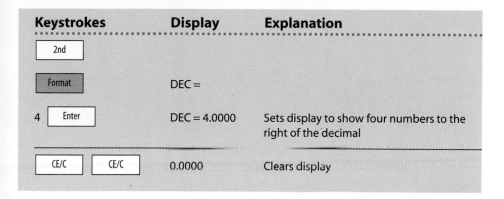

Keystrokes	Display	Explanation
2nd		
Format	DEC =	
4 Enter	DEC = 4.0000	Sets display to show four numbers to the right of the decimal
CE/C CE/C	0.0000	Clears display

Example: You want to set two payments per year to be paid at the end of the period.

Keystrokes	Display	Explanation
2nd		
P/Y	P/Y =	
2 Enter	P/Y = 2.0000	Sets number of payments per year at 2
2nd		
BGN	END	Sets timing of payment at the end of each period
CE/C CE/C	0.0000	Clears display

III. BASIC TIME VALUE OF MONEY CALCULATIONS

A. The future value (Appendix B)

Example: Calculate the future value of $100 invested for 5 years at 12% interest rate.

Keystrokes	Display	Explanation
2nd		
P/Y	P/Y =	
1 Enter	P/Y = 1.0000	Sets number of payments per year at 1
2nd		
BGN	END	Sets timing of payments at the end of each period
CE/C CE/C	0.0000	Clears display
2nd		
CLR TVM	0.0000	Clears *TVM* variables
100 + / −	PV = −100.0000	Stores initial $100 as a negative present value.
PV		Otherwise the answer will appear as a negative.
5 N	N = 5.0000	Stores number of periods
12 I/Y	I/Y = 12.0000	Stores interest rate
CPT FV	FV = 176.2342	Calculates the future value

III. BASIC TIME VALUE OF MONEY CALCULATIONS *(continued)*

B. The present value (Appendix C)

Example: How much would you have to deposit in the bank today if you wanted it to grow to $8,000 in 8 years, earning 10% compounded annually?

Keystrokes	Display	Explanation
2nd		
P/Y	P/Y =	
1 Enter	P/Y = 1.0000	Sets number of payments per year at 1
2nd		
BGN	END	Sets timing of payments at the end of each period
CE/C CE/C	0.0000	Clears display
2nd		
CLR TVM	0.0000	Clears *TVM* variables
8000 FV	FV = 8000.0000	Stores future amount to be received
8 N	N = 8.0000	Stores number of periods
10 I/Y	I/Y = 10.0000	Stores interest rate
CPT PV	PV = −3,732.0590	Calculates the present value, which will be negative indicating a cash outflow

III. BASIC TIME VALUE OF MONEY CALCULATIONS *(continued)*

C. The future value of an annuity (Appendix D)

Example: What is the future value of $1,000 deposited at the end of each year for 15 years in an account earning 8% compounded annually?

Keystrokes	Display	Explanation
2nd P/Y	P/Y =	
1 Enter	P/Y = 1.0000	Sets number of payments per year at 1
2nd BGN	END	Sets timing of payments at the end of each period
CE/C CE/C	0.0000	Clears display
2nd CLR TVM	0.0000	Clears *TVM* variables
1000 +/− PMT	PMT = −1000.0000	Stores annual payment (annuity) as a negative number. Otherwise the answer will appear as a negative.
15 N	N = 15.0000	Stores number of periods
8 I/Y	I/Y = 8.0000	Stores interest rate
CPT FV	FV = 27,152.1139	Calculates the future value

III. BASIC TIME VALUE OF MONEY CALCULATIONS *(continued)*

D. The present value of an annuity (Appendix E)

Example: What is the present value of an annuity of $500 per year for 12 years at 9% annual interest rate?

Keystrokes	Display	Explanation
2nd		
P/Y	P/Y =	
1 Enter	P/Y = 1.0000	Sets number of payments per year at 1
2nd		
BGN	END	Sets timing of payments at the end of each period
CE/C CE/C	0.0000	Clears display
2nd		
CLR TVM	0.0000	Clears *TVM* variables
500 +/− PMT	PMT = −500.0000	Stores annual payment (annuity) as a negative number. Otherwise the answer will appear as a negative.
12 N	N = 12.0000	Stores number of periods
9 I/Y	I/Y = 9.0000	Stores interest rate
CPT PV	PV = 3,580.3626	Calculates the present value

IV. LOANS

A. Calculating the APR

Example: Determine the annual percentage rate (APR) on a $6,000, 4-year (48-month) loan with monthly payments of $188.

Keystrokes	Display	Explanation
2nd		
BGN	END	Sets timing of payments at the end of each period
2nd		
P/Y	P/Y =	
12 Enter	P/Y = 12.0000	Sets 12 payments per year
CE/C CE/C	0.0000	Clears display
2nd		
CLR TVM	0.0000	Clears *TVM* variables
48 N	N = 48.0000	Sets *n*, the number of months for the investment
6000 PV	PV = 6,000.0000	Stores *PV*, the present value, which is the amount of the loan
188 +/− PMT	PMT = −188.0000	Stores *PMT*, the monthly payment (with a minus sign for cash paid out)
CPT I/Y	I/Y = 21.6813	Calculates *i*, which is the loan's APR

IV. LOANS (continued)

B. Calculating the monthly payment on a fixed-rate loan and the loan amortization (the amount going toward principal and interest)

1. Example: What would be the monthly payment on a 15-year, $110,000 loan at a fixed rate of 8.5%?

Keystrokes	Display	Explanation
2nd		
BGN	END	Sets timing of payment at the end of each period
2nd		
P/Y	P/Y =	
12 Enter	P/Y = 12.0000	Sets 12 payments per year
CE/C CE/C	0.0000	Clears display
2nd		
CLR TVM	0.0000	Clears *TVM* variables
180 N	N = 180.0000	Sets *n*, the number of months for the investment (15 years × 12 months/year = 180 months)
110000 PV	PV = 110,000.0000	Stores *PV*, the present value, which is the amount of the loan
8.5 I/Y	I/Y = 8.5000	Stores *i*, the annual interest rate
CPT PMT	PMT = −1,083.2135	Calculates *PMT*, the monthly payment on the loan (with a minus sign for cash paid out)

IV. LOANS *(continued)*

B. Calculating the monthly payment on a fixed-rate loan and the loan amortization (the amount going toward principal and interest)

Continuing with this example:

2. Example: On the sixtieth payment, what amount of the monthly payment goes toward interest and principal, and what is the unpaid balance on the loan?

Keystrokes	Display	Explanation
2nd		
Amort		
60 Enter	P1 = 60.0000	Sets beginning payment at 60
↓		
60 Enter	P2 = 60.0000	Sets ending payment at 60
↓	BAL = 87,366.0124	Calculates the unpaid balance when payment 60 is made
↓	PRN = −461.1048	Calculates the portion of payment 60 that goes toward the principal
↓	INT = −622.1087	Calculates the portion of payment 60 that goes toward interest

IV. LOANS *(continued)*

B. Calculating the monthly payment on a fixed-rate loan and the loan amortization (the amount going toward principal and interest)

Continuing further with this example:

3. Example: Now you want to determine what portion of the total of your first 60 payments went toward interest and what portion went toward principal.

Keystrokes	Display	Explanation
2nd		
Amort		
1 Enter	P1 = 1.0000	Sets beginning payment at 1
↓		
60 Enter	P2 = 60.0000	Sets ending payment at 60
↓	BAL = 87,366.0124	Calculates the unpaid balance when payment 60 is made
↓	PRN = −22,633.9876	Calculates the portion of the first 60 payments that went toward the principal
↓	INT = −42,358.8224	Calculates the portion of the first 60 payments that went toward the interest

V. CALCULATING FUTURE VALUES WITH MONTHLY PAYMENTS (COMPOUND SUM)

Example: If you deposit $300 a month (at the beginning of each month) into a new account that pays 6.25% annual interest, compounded monthly, how much will you have in the account after 5 years?

Keystrokes	Display	Explanation
2nd BGN	END	Sets timing of payment at the end of each period
2nd SET	BGN	Sets timing of payments to beginning of each period
2nd P/Y	P/Y =	
12 Enter	P/Y = 12.0000	Sets 12 payments per year
CE/C CE/C	0.0000	Clears display
2nd CLR TVM	0.0000	Clears *TVM* variables
60 N	N = 60.0000	Stores *n*, the number of months for the investment
6.25 I/Y	I/Y = 6.2500	Stores *i*, the annual interest rate
300 +/− PMT	PMT = −300.0000	Stores *PMT*, the monthly amount invested (with a minus sign for cash paid out)
CPT FV	FV = 21,175.7613	Calculates the future value after 5 years

VI. CALCULATING THE NUMBER OF PAYMENTS OR RECEIPTS

Example: If you wish to retire with $500,000 saved, and can only afford payments of $500 each month, how long will you have to contribute toward your retirement if you can earn a 10% return on your contribution?

Keystrokes	Display	Explanation
2nd		
BGN	BGN	Verifies timing of payment at the beginning of each period
2nd		
P/Y	P/Y = 12.0000	
12 Enter	P/Y = 12.0000	Sets 12 payments per year
CE/C CE/C	0.0000	Clears display
2nd		
CLR TVM	0.0000	Clears *TVM* variables
10 I/Y	I/Y = 10.0000	Stores *i*, the interest rate
500 +/− PMT	PMT = −500.0000	Stores *PMT*, the monthly amount invested (with a minus sign for cash paid out)
500,000 FV	FV = 500,000.0000	Stores *FV*, the value we want to achieve
CPT N	N = 268.2539	Calculates the number of months (because we considered monthly payments) required to achieve our goal

VII. CALCULATING THE PAYMENT AMOUNT

Example: Suppose your retirement needs were $750,000. If you are currently 25 years old and plan to retire at age 65, how much will you have to contribute each month for retirement if you can earn 12.5% on your savings?

Keystrokes	Display	Explanation
2nd BGN	BGN	Verifies timing of payment at the beginning of each period
2nd P/Y	P/Y = 12.0000	
12 Enter	P/Y = 12.0000	Sets 12 payments per year
CE/C CE/C	0.0000	Clears display
2nd CLR TVM	0.0000	Clears *TVM* variables
12.5 I/Y	I/Y = 12.5000	Stores *i*, the interest rate
480 N	N = 480.0000	Stores *n*, the number of periods until we stop contributing (40 years × 12 months/year = 480 months)
750,000 FV	FV = 750,000.0000	Stores the value we want to achieve
CPT PMT	PMT = −53.8347	Calculates the monthly contribution required to achieve our ultimate goal (shown as a negative because it represents cash paid out)

VIII. CALCULATING THE INTEREST RATE

Example: If you invest $300 at the end of each month for 6 years (72 months) for a promised $30,000 return at the end, what interest rate are you earning on your investment?

Keystrokes	Display	Explanation
2nd		
BGN	BGN	Sets timing of payment to beginning of each period
2nd		
SET	END	Sets timing of payment to end of each period
2nd		
P/Y	P/Y = 12.0000	
12 Enter	P/Y = 12.0000	Sets 12 payments per year
CE/C CE/C	0.0000	Clears display
2nd		
CLR TVM	0.0000	Clears *TVM* variables
72 N	N = 72.0000	Stores *n*, the number of deposits (investments)
300 +/− PMT	PMT = −300.0000	Stores *PMT,* the monthly amount invested (with a minus sign for cash paid out)
30,000 FV	FV − 30,0000.0000	Stores the future value to be received in 6 years
CPT I/Y	I/Y = 10.5892	Calculates the annual interest rate earned on the investment

IX. BOND VALUATION

A. Computing the value of a bond

Example: What is the value of a bond that matures in 10 years and has a coupon rate of 9% (4.5% semiannually)? Your required rate of return is 12%.

Keystrokes	Display	Explanation
2nd BGN	END	Verifies timing of payments to end of each period
2nd P/Y	P/Y = 12.0000	
2 Enter	P/Y = 2.0000	Sets 2 payments per year and mode (END) assumes cash flows are at the end of each 6-month period
CE/C CE/C	0.0000	Clears display
2nd CLR TVM	0.0000	Clears *TVM* variables
20 N	N = 20.0000	Stores the number of semiannual periods (10 years × 2)
12 I/Y	I/Y = 12.0000	Stores annual rate of return
45 PMT	PMT = 45.0000	Stores the semiannual interest payment
1,000 FV	FV = 1,000.0000	Stores the bond's maturity or par value
CPT PV	PV = −827.9512	Calculates the value of the bond, expressed as a negative number

IX. BOND VALUATION *(continued)*

B. Computing the yield to maturity of a bond

Example: What is the yield to maturity on a bond that matures in 8 years and has a coupon rate of 12% (6% semiannually)? The bond is selling for $1,100.

Keystrokes	Display	Explanation
2nd		
BGN	END	Verifies timing of payment to end of each period
2nd		
P/Y	P/Y = 12.0000	
2 Enter	P/Y = 2.0000	Sets 2 payments per year and mode (END) assumes cash flows are at the end of each 6-month period
CE/C CE/C	0.0000	Clears display
2nd		
CLR TVM	0.0000	Clears *TVM* variables
16 N	N – 16.0000	Stores the number of semiannual periods (8 years × 2)
1100 +/− PV	PV = −1,100.0000	Stores the value of the bond, expressed as a negative number
60 PMT	PMT = 60.0000	Stores the semiannual interest payment
1,000 FV	FV = 1,000.0000	Stores the bond's maturity or par value
CPT I/Y	I/Y = 10.1451	Calculates the yield to maturity, expressed on an annual basis

Appendix B:
Compound Sum of $1

n	1%	2%	3%	4%	5%	6%	7%	8%	9%	10%
1	1.010	1.020	1.030	1.040	1.050	1.060	1.070	1.080	1.090	1.100
2	1.020	1.040	1.061	1.082	1.102	1.124	1.145	1.166	1.188	1.210
3	1.030	1.061	1.093	1.125	1.158	1.191	1.225	1.260	1.295	1.331
4	1.041	1.082	1.126	1.170	1.216	1.262	1.311	1.360	1.412	1.464
5	1.051	1.104	1.159	1.217	1.276	1.338	1.403	1.469	1.539	1.611
6	1.062	1.126	1.194	1.265	1.340	1.419	1.501	1.587	1.677	1.772
7	1.072	1.149	1.230	1.316	1.407	1.504	1.606	1.714	1.828	1.949
8	1.083	1.172	1.267	1.369	1.477	1.594	1.718	1.851	1.993	2.144
9	1.094	1.195	1.305	1.423	1.551	1.689	1.838	1.999	2.172	2.358
10	1.105	1.219	1.344	1.480	1.629	1.791	1.967	2.159	2.367	2.594
11	1.116	1.243	1.384	1.539	1.710	1.898	2.105	2.332	2.580	2.853
12	1.127	1.268	1.426	1.601	1.796	2.012	2.252	2.518	2.813	3.138
13	1.138	1.294	1.469	1.665	1.886	2.133	2.410	2.720	3.066	3.452
14	1.149	1.319	1.513	1.732	1.980	2.261	2.579	2.937	3.342	3.797
15	1.161	1.346	1.558	1.801	2.079	2.397	2.759	3.172	3.642	4.177
16	1.173	1.373	1.605	1.873	2.183	2.540	2.952	3.426	3.970	4.595
17	1.184	1.400	1.653	1.948	2.292	2.693	3.159	3.700	4.328	5.054
18	1.196	1.428	1.702	2.026	2.407	2.854	3.380	3.996	4.717	5.560
19	1.208	1.457	1.753	2.107	2.527	3.026	3.616	4.316	5.142	6.116
20	1.220	1.486	1.806	2.191	2.653	3.207	3.870	4.661	5.604	6.727
21	1.232	1.516	1.860	2.279	2.786	3.399	4.140	5.034	6.109	7.400
22	1.245	1.546	1.916	2.370	2.925	3.603	4.430	5.436	6.658	8.140
23	1.257	1.577	1.974	2.465	3.071	3.820	4.740	5.871	7.258	8.954
24	1.270	1.608	2.033	2.563	3.225	4.049	5.072	6.341	7.911	9.850
25	1.282	1.641	2.094	2.666	3.386	4.292	5.427	6.848	8.623	10.834
30	1.348	1.811	2.427	3.243	4.322	5.743	7.612	10.062	13.267	17.449
40	1.489	2.208	3.262	4.801	7.040	10.285	14.974	21.724	31.408	45.258
50	1.645	2.691	4.384	7.106	11.467	18.419	29.456	46.900	74.354	117.386

n	11%	12%	13%	14%	15%	16%	17%	18%	19%	20%
1	1.110	1.120	1.130	1.140	1.150	1.160	1.170	1.180	1.190	1.200
2	1.232	1.254	1.277	1.300	1.322	1.346	1.369	1.392	1.416	1.440
3	1.368	1.405	1.443	1.482	1.521	1.561	1.602	1.643	1.685	1.728
4	1.518	1.574	1.630	1.689	1.749	1.811	1.874	1.939	2.005	2.074
5	1.685	1.762	1.842	1.925	2.011	2.100	2.192	2.288	2.386	2.488
6	1.870	1.974	2.082	2.195	2.313	2.436	2.565	2.700	2.840	2.986
7	2.076	2.211	2.353	2.502	2.660	2.826	3.001	3.185	3.379	3.583
8	2.305	2.476	2.658	2.853	3.059	3.278	3.511	3.759	4.021	4.300
9	2.558	2.773	3.004	3.252	3.518	3.803	4.108	4.435	4.785	5.160
10	2.839	3.106	3.395	3.707	4.046	4.411	4.807	5.234	5.695	6.192
11	3.152	3.479	3.836	4.226	4.652	5.117	5.624	6.176	6.777	7.430
12	3.498	3.896	4.334	4.818	5.350	5.936	6.580	7.288	8.064	8.916
13	3.883	4.363	4.898	5.492	6.153	6.886	7.699	8.599	9.596	10.699
14	4.310	4.887	5.535	6.261	7.076	7.987	9.007	10.147	11.420	12.839
15	4.785	5.474	6.254	7.138	8.137	9.265	10.539	11.974	13.589	15.407
16	5.311	6.130	7.067	8.137	9.358	10.748	12.330	14.129	16.171	18.488
17	5.895	6.866	7.986	9.276	10.761	12.468	14.426	16.672	19.244	22.186
18	6.543	7.690	9.024	10.575	12.375	14.462	16.879	19.673	22.900	26.623
19	7.263	8.613	10.197	12.055	14.232	16.776	19.748	23.214	27.251	31.948
20	8.062	9.646	11.523	13.743	16.366	19.461	23.105	27.393	32.429	38.337
21	8.949	10.804	13.021	15.667	18.821	22.574	27.033	32.323	38.591	46.005
22	9.933	12.100	14.713	17.861	21.644	26.186	31.629	38.141	45.923	55.205
23	11.026	13.552	16.626	20.361	24.891	30.376	37.005	45.007	54.648	66.247
24	12.239	15.178	18.788	23.212	28.625	35.236	43.296	53.108	65.031	79.496
25	13.585	17.000	21.230	26.461	32.918	40.874	50.656	62.667	77.387	95.395
30	22.892	29.960	39.115	50.949	66.210	85.849	111.061	143.367	184.672	237.373
40	64.999	93.049	132.776	188.876	267.856	378.715	533.846	750.353	1051.642	1469.740
50	184.559	288.996	450.711	700.197	1083.619	1670.669	2566.080	3927.189	5988.730	9100.191

n	21%	22%	23%	24%	25%	26%	27%	28%	29%	30%
1	1.210	1.220	1.230	1.240	1.250	1.260	1.270	1.280	1.290	1.300
2	1.464	1.488	1.513	1.538	1.562	1.588	1.613	1.638	1.664	1.690
3	1.772	1.816	1.861	1.907	1.953	2.000	2.048	2.097	2.147	2.197
4	2.144	2.215	2.289	2.364	2.441	2.520	2.601	2.684	2.769	2.856
5	2.594	2.703	2.815	2.932	3.052	3.176	3.304	3.436	3.572	3.713
6	3.138	3.297	3.463	3.635	3.815	4.001	4.196	4.398	4.608	4.827
7	3.797	4.023	4.259	4.508	4.768	5.042	5.329	5.629	5.945	6.275
8	4.595	4.908	5.239	5.589	5.960	6.353	6.767	7.206	7.669	8.157
9	5.560	5.987	6.444	6.931	7.451	8.004	8.595	9.223	9.893	10.604
10	6.727	7.305	7.926	8.594	9.313	10.086	10.915	11.806	12.761	13.786
11	8.140	8.912	9.749	10.657	11.642	12.708	13.862	15.112	16.462	17.921
12	9.850	10.872	11.991	13.215	14.552	16.012	17.605	19.343	21.236	23.298
13	11.918	13.264	14.749	16.386	18.190	20.175	22.359	24.759	27.395	30.287
14	14.421	16.182	18.141	20.319	22.737	25.420	28.395	31.691	35.339	39.373
15	17.449	19.742	22.314	25.195	28.422	32.030	36.062	40.565	45.587	51.185
16	21.113	24.085	27.446	31.242	35.527	40.357	45.799	51.923	58.808	66.541
17	25.547	29.384	33.758	38.740	44.409	50.850	58.165	66.461	75.862	86.503
18	30.912	35.848	41.523	48.038	55.511	64.071	73.869	85.070	97.862	112.454
19	37.404	43.735	51.073	59.567	69.389	80.730	93.813	108.890	126.242	146.190
20	45.258	53.357	62.820	73.863	86.736	101.720	119.143	139.379	162.852	190.047
21	54.762	65.095	77.268	91.591	108.420	128.167	151.312	178.405	210.079	247.061
22	66.262	79.416	95.040	113.572	135.525	161.490	192.165	228.358	271.002	321.178
23	80.178	96.887	116.899	140.829	169.407	203.477	244.050	292.298	349.592	417.531
24	97.015	118.203	143.786	174.628	211.758	256.381	309.943	374.141	450.974	542.791
25	117.388	144.207	176.857	216.539	264.698	323.040	393.628	478.901	581.756	705.627
30	304.471	389.748	497.904	634.810	807.793	1025.904	1300.477	1645.488	2078.208	2619.936
40	2048.309	2846.941	3946.340	5455.797	7523.156	10346.879	14195.051	19426.418	26520.723	36117.754
50	13779.844	20795.680	31278.301	46889.207	70064.812	104354.562	154942.687	229345.875	338440.000	497910.125

n	31%	32%	33%	34%	35%	36%	37%	38%	39%	40%
1	1.310	1.320	1.330	1.340	1.350	1.360	1.370	1.380	1.390	1.400
2	1.716	1.742	1.769	1.796	1.822	1.850	1.877	1.904	1.932	1.960
3	2.248	2.300	2.353	2.406	2.460	2.515	2.571	2.628	2.606	2.744
4	2.945	3.036	3.129	3.224	3.321	3.421	3.523	3.627	3.733	3.842
5	3.858	4.007	4.162	4.320	4.484	4.653	4.826	5.005	5.189	5.378
6	5.054	5.290	5.535	5.789	6.053	6.328	6.612	6.907	7.213	7.530
7	6.621	6.983	7.361	7.758	8.172	8.605	9.058	9.531	10.025	10.541
8	8.673	9.217	9.791	10.395	11.032	11.703	12.410	13.153	13.935	14.758
9	11.362	12.166	13.022	13.930	14.894	15.917	17.001	18.151	19.370	20.661
10	14.884	16.060	17.319	18.666	20.106	21.646	23.292	25.049	26.924	28.925
11	19.498	21.199	23.034	25.012	27.144	29.439	31.910	34.567	37.425	40.495
12	25.542	27.982	30.635	33.516	36.644	40.037	43.716	47.703	52.020	56.694
13	33.460	36.937	40.745	44.912	49.469	54.451	59.892	65.830	72.308	79.371
14	43.832	49.756	54.190	60.181	66.784	74.053	82.051	90.845	100.509	111.120
15	57.420	64.358	72.073	80.643	90.158	100.712	112.410	125.366	139.707	155.567
16	75.220	84.953	95.857	108.061	121.713	136.968	154.002	173.005	194.192	217.793
17	98.539	112.138	127.490	144.802	164.312	186.277	210.983	238.747	269.927	304.911
18	129.086	148.022	169.561	194.035	221.822	253.337	289.046	329.471	375.198	426.875
19	169.102	195.389	225.517	260.006	299.459	344.537	395.993	454.669	521.525	597.625
20	221.523	257.913	299.937	348.408	404.270	468.571	542.511	627.443	724.919	836.674
21	290.196	340.446	398.916	466.867	545.764	637.256	743.240	865.871	1007.637	1171.343
22	380.156	449.388	530.558	625.601	736.781	865.668	1018.238	1194.900	1400.615	1639.878
23	498.004	593.192	705.642	838.305	994.653	1178.668	1394.986	1648.961	1946.854	2295.829
24	652.385	783.013	938.504	1123.328	1342.781	1602.988	1911.129	2275.564	2706.125	3214.158
25	854.623	1033.577	1248.210	1505.258	1812.754	2180.063	2618.245	3140.275	3761.511	4499.816
30	3297.081	4142.008	5194.516	6503.285	8128.426	10142.914	12636.086	15716.703	19517.969	24201.043
40	49072.621	66519.313	89962.188	121388.437	163433.875	219558.625	294317.937	393684.687	525508.312	700022.688

Appendix C:
Present Value of $1

n	1%	2%	3%	4%	5%	6%	7%	8%	9%	10%
1	.990	.980	.971	.962	.952	.943	.935	.926	.917	.909
2	.980	.961	.943	.925	.907	.890	.873	.857	.842	.826
3	.971	.942	.915	.889	.864	.840	.816	.794	.772	.751
4	.961	.924	.888	.855	.823	.792	.763	.735	.708	.683
5	.951	.906	.863	.822	.784	.747	.713	.681	.650	.621
6	.942	.888	.837	.790	.746	.705	.666	.630	.596	.564
7	.933	.871	.813	.760	.711	.665	.623	.583	.547	.513
8	.923	.853	.789	.731	.677	.627	.582	.540	.502	.467
9	.914	.837	.766	.703	.645	.592	.544	.500	.460	.424
10	.905	.820	.744	.676	.614	.558	.508	.463	.422	.386
11	.896	.804	.722	.650	.585	.527	.475	.429	.388	.350
12	.887	.789	.701	.625	.557	.497	.444	.397	.356	.319
13	.879	.773	.681	.601	.530	.469	.415	.368	.326	.290
14	.870	.758	.661	.577	.505	.442	.388	.340	.299	.263
15	.861	.743	.642	.555	.481	.417	.362	.315	.275	.239
16	.853	.728	.623	.534	.458	.394	.339	.292	.252	.218
17	.844	.714	.605	.513	.436	.371	.317	.270	.231	.198
18	.836	.700	.587	.494	.416	.350	.296	.250	.212	.180
19	.828	.686	.570	.475	.396	.331	.277	.232	.194	.164
20	.820	.673	.554	.456	.377	.312	.258	.215	.178	.149
21	.811	.660	.538	.439	359	.294	.242	.199	.164	.135
22	.803	.647	.522	.422	.342	.278	.226	.184	.150	.123
23	.795	.634	.507	.406	.326	.262	.211	.170	.138	.112
24	.788	.622	.492	.390	.310	.247	.197	.158	.126	.102
25	.780	.610	.478	.375	.295	.233	.184	.146	.116	.092
30	.742	.552	.412	.308	.231	.174	.131	.099	.075	.057
40	.672	.453	.307	.208	.142	.097	.067	.046	.032	.022
50	.608	.372	.228	.141	.087	.054	.034	.021	.013	.009

n	11%	12%	13%	14%	15%	16%	17%	18%	19%	20%
1	.901	.893	.885	.877	.870	.862	.855	.847	.840	.833
2	.812	.797	.783	.769	.756	.743	.731	.718	.706	.694
3	.731	.712	.693	.675	.658	.641	.624	.609	.593	.579
4	.659	.636	.613	.592	.572	.552	.534	.516	.499	.482
5	.593	.567	.543	.519	.497	.476	.456	.437	.419	.402
6	.535	.507	.480	.456	.432	.410	.390	.370	.352	.335
7	.482	.452	.425	.400	.376	.354	.333	.314	.296	.279
8	.434	.404	.376	.351	.327	.305	.285	.266	.249	.233
9	.391	.361	.333	.308	.284	.263	.243	.225	.209	.194
10	.352	.322	.295	.270	.247	.227	.208	.191	.176	.162
11	.317	.287	.261	.237	.215	.195	.178	.162	.148	.135
12	.286	.257	.231	.208	.187	.168	.152	.137	.124	.112
13	.258	.229	.204	.182	.163	.145	.130	.116	.104	.093
14	.232	.205	.181	.160	.141	.125	.111	.099	.088	.078
15	.209	.183	.160	.140	.123	.108	.095	.084	.074	.065
16	.188	.163	.141	.123	.107	.093	.081	.071	.062	.054
17	.170	.146	.125	.108	.093	.080	.069	.060	.052	.045
18	.153	.130	.111	.095	.081	.069	.059	.051	.044	.038
19	.138	.116	.098	.083	.070	.060	.051	.043	.037	.031
20	.124	.104	.087	.073	.061	.051	.043	.037	.031	.026
21	.112	.093	.077	.064	.053	.044	.037	.031	.026	.022
22	.101	.083	.068	.056	.046	.038	.032	.026	.022	.018
23	.091	.074	.060	.049	.040	.033	.027	.022	.018	.015
24	.082	.066	.053	.043	.035	.028	.023	.019	.015	.013
25	.074	.059	.047	.038	.030	.024	.020	.016	.013	.010
30	.044	.033	.026	.020	.015	.012	.009	.007	.005	.004
40	.015	.011	.008	.005	.004	.003	.002	.001	.001	.001
50	.005	.003	.002	.001	.001	.001	.000	.000	.000	.000

n	21%	22%	23%	24%	25%	26%	27%	28%	29%	30%
1	.826	.820	.813	.806	.800	.794	.787	.781	.775	.769
2	.683	.672	.661	.650	.640	.630	.620	.610	.601	.592
3	.564	.551	.537	.524	.512	.500	.488	.477	.466	.455
4	.467	.451	.437	.423	.410	.397	.384	.373	.361	.350
5	.386	.370	.355	.341	.328	.315	.303	.291	.280	.269
6	.319	.303	.289	.275	.262	.250	.238	.227	.217	.207
7	.263	.249	.235	.222	.210	.198	.188	.178	.168	.159
8	.218	.204	.191	.179	.168	.157	.148	.139	.130	.123
9	.180	.167	.155	.144	.134	.125	.116	.108	.101	.094
10	.149	.137	.126	.116	.107	.099	.092	.085	.078	.073
11	.123	.112	.103	.094	.086	.079	.072	.066	.061	.056
12	.102	.092	.083	.076	.069	.062	.057	.052	.047	.043
13	.084	.075	.068	.061	.055	.050	.045	.040	.037	.033
14	.069	.062	.055	.049	.044	.039	.035	.032	.028	.025
15	.057	.051	.045	.040	.035	.031	.028	.025	.022	.020
16	.047	.042	.036	.032	.028	.025	.022	.019	.017	.015
17	.039	.034	.030	.026	.023	.020	.017	.015	.013	.012
18	.032	.028	.024	.021	.018	.016	.014	.012	.010	.009
19	.027	.023	.020	.017	.014	.012	.011	.009	.008	.007
20	.022	.019	.016	.014	.012	.010	.008	.007	.006	.005
21	.018	.015	.013	.011	.009	.008	.007	.006	.005	.004
22	.015	.013	.011	.009	.007	.006	.005	.004	.004	.003
23	.012	.010	.009	.007	.006	.005	.004	.003	.003	.002
24	.010	.008	.007	.006	.005	.004	.003	.003	.002	.002
25	.009	.007	.006	.005	.004	.003	.003	.002	.002	.001
30	.003	.003	.002	.002	.001	.001	.001	.001	.000	.000
40	.000	.000	.000	.000	.000	.000	.000	.000	.000	.000
50	.000	.000	.000	.000	.000	.000	.000	.000	.000	.000

n	31%	32%	33%	34%	35%	36%	37%	38%	39%	40%
1	.763	.758	.752	.746	.741	.735	.730	.725	.719	.714
2	.583	.574	.565	.557	.549	.541	.533	.525	.518	.510
3	.445	.435	.425	.416	.406	.398	.389	.381	.372	.364
4	.340	.329	.320	.310	.301	.292	.284	.276	.268	.260
5	.259	.250	.240	.231	.223	.215	.207	.200	.193	.186
6	.198	.189	.181	.173	.165	.158	.151	.145	.139	.133
7	.151	.143	.136	.129	.122	.116	.110	.105	.100	.095
8	.115	.108	.102	.096	.091	.085	.081	.076	.072	.068
9	.088	.082	.077	.072	.067	.063	.059	.055	.052	.048
10	.067	.062	.058	.054	.050	.046	.043	.040	.037	.035
11	.051	.047	.043	.040	.037	.034	.031	.029	.027	.025
12	.039	.036	.033	.030	.027	.025	.023	.021	.019	.018
13	.030	.027	.025	.022	.020	.018	.017	.015	.014	.013
14	.023	.021	.018	.017	.015	.014	.012	.011	.010	.009
15	.017	.016	.014	.012	.011	.010	.009	.008	.007	.006
16	.013	.012	.010	.009	.008	.007	.006	.006	.005	.005
17	.010	.009	.008	.007	.006	.005	.005	.004	.004	.003
18	.008	.007	.006	.005	.005	.004	.003	.003	.003	.002
19	.006	.005	.004	.004	.003	.003	.003	.002	.002	.002
20	.005	.004	.003	.003	.002	.002	.002	.002	.001	.001
21	.003	.003	.003	.002	.002	.002	.001	.001	.001	.001
22	.003	.002	.002	.002	.001	.001	.001	.001	.001	.001
23	.002	.002	.001	.001	.001	.001	.001	.001	.001	.000
24	.002	.001	.001	.001	.001	.001	.001	.001	.000	.000
25	.001	.001	.001	.001	.001	.001	.000	.000	.000	.000
30	.000	.000	.000	.000	.000	.000	.000	.000	.000	.000
40	.000	.000	.000	.000	.000	.000	.000	.000	.000	.000

Compound Sum of an Annuity of $1 for *n* Periods

n	1%	2%	3%	4%	5%	6%	7%	8%	9%	10%
1	1.000	1.000	1.000	1.000	1.000	1.000	1.000	1.000	1.000	1.000
2	2.010	2.020	2.030	2.040	2.050	2.060	2.070	2.080	2.090	2.100
3	3.030	3.060	3.091	3.122	3.152	3.184	3.215	3.246	3.278	3.310
4	4.060	4.122	4.184	4.246	4.310	4.375	4.440	4.506	4.573	4.641
5	5.101	5.204	5.309	5.416	5.526	5.637	5.751	5.867	5.985	6.105
6	6.152	6.308	6.468	6.633	6.802	6.975	7.153	7.336	7.523	7.716
7	7.214	7.434	7.662	7.898	8.142	8.394	8.654	8.923	9.200	9.487
8	8.286	8.583	8.892	9.214	9.549	9.897	10.260	10.637	11.028	11.436
9	9.368	9.755	10.159	10.583	11.027	11.491	11.978	12.488	13.021	13.579
10	10.462	10.950	11.464	12.006	12.578	13.181	13.816	14.487	15.193	15.937
11	11.567	12.169	12.808	13.486	14.207	14.972	15.784	16.645	17.560	18.531
12	12.682	13.412	14.192	15.026	15.917	16.870	17.888	18.977	20.141	21.384
13	13.809	14.680	15.618	16.627	17.713	18.882	20.141	21.495	22.953	24.523
14	14.947	15.974	17.086	18.292	19.598	21.015	22.550	24.215	26.019	27.975
15	16.097	17.293	18.599	20.023	21.578	23.276	25.129	27.152	29.361	31.772
16	17.258	18.639	20.157	21.824	23.657	25.672	27.888	30.324	33.003	35.949
17	18.430	20.012	21.761	23.697	25.840	28.213	30.840	33.750	36.973	40.544
18	19.614	21.412	23.414	25.645	28.132	30.905	33.999	37.450	41.301	45.599
19	20.811	22.840	25.117	27.671	30.539	33.760	37.379	41.446	46.018	51.158
20	22.019	24.297	26.870	29.778	33.066	36.785	40.995	45.762	51.159	57.274
21	23.239	25.783	28.676	31.969	35.719	39.992	44.865	50.422	56.764	64.002
22	24.471	27.299	30.536	34.248	38.505	43.392	49.005	55.456	62.872	71.402
23	25.716	28.845	32.452	36.618	41.430	46.995	53.435	60.893	69.531	79.542
24	26.973	30.421	34.426	39.082	44.501	50.815	58.176	66.764	76.789	88.496
25	28.243	32.030	36.459	41.645	47.726	54.864	63.248	73.105	84.699	98.346
30	34.784	40.567	47.575	56.084	66.438	79.057	94.459	113.282	136.305	164.491
40	48.885	60.401	75.400	95.024	120.797	154.758	199.630	295.052	337.872	442.580
50	64.461	84.577	112.794	152.664	209.341	290.325	406.516	573.756	815.051	1163.865

n	11%	12%	13%	14%	15%	16%	17%	18%	19%	20%
1	1.000	1.000	1.000	1.000	1.000	1.000	1.000	1.000	1.000	1.000
2	2.110	2.120	2.130	2.140	2.150	2.160	2.170	2.180	2.190	2.200
3	3.342	3.374	3.407	3.440	3.472	3.506	3.539	3.572	3.606	3.640
4	4.710	4.779	4.850	4.921	4.993	5.066	5.141	5.215	5.291	5.368
5	6.228	6.353	6.480	6.610	6.742	6.877	7.014	7.154	7.297	7.442
6	7.913	8.115	8.323	8.535	8.754	8.977	9.207	9.442	9.683	9.930
7	9.783	10.089	10.405	10.730	11.067	11.414	11.772	12.141	12.523	12.916
8	11.859	12.300	12.757	13.233	13.727	14.240	14.773	15.327	15.902	16.499
9	14.164	14.776	15.416	16.085	16.786	17.518	18.285	19.086	19.923	20.799
10	16.722	17.549	18.420	19.337	20.304	21.321	22.393	23.521	24.709	25.959
11	19.561	20.655	21.814	23.044	24.349	25.733	27.200	28.755	30.403	32.150
12	22.713	24.133	25.650	27.271	29.001	30.850	32.824	34.931	37.180	39.580
13	26.211	28.029	29.984	32.088	34.352	36.786	39.404	42.218	45.244	48.496
14	30.095	32.392	34.882	37.581	40.504	43.672	47.102	50.818	54.841	59.196
15	34.405	37.280	40.417	43.842	47.580	51.659	56.109	60.965	66.260	72.035
16	39.190	42.753	46.671	50.980	55.717	60.925	66.648	72.938	79.850	87.442
17	44.500	48.883	53.738	59.117	65.075	71.673	78.978	87.067	96.021	105.930
18	50.396	55.749	61.724	68.393	75.836	84.140	93.404	103.739	115.265	128.116
19	56.939	63.439	70.748	78.968	88.211	98.603	110.283	123.412	138.165	154.739
20	64.202	72.052	80.946	91.024	102.443	115.379	130.031	146.626	165.417	186.687
21	72.264	81.698	92.468	104.767	118.809	134.840	153.136	174.019	197.846	225.024
22	81.213	92.502	105.489	120.434	137.630	157.414	180.169	206.342	236.436	271.028
23	91.147	104.602	120.203	138.295	159.274	183.600	211.798	244.483	282.359	326.234
24	102.173	118.154	136.829	158.656	184.166	213.976	248.803	289.490	337.007	392.480
25	114.412	133.333	155.616	181.867	212.790	249.212	292.099	342.598	402.038	471.976
30	199.018	241.330	293.192	356.778	434.738	530.306	647.423	790.932	966.698	1181.865
40	581.812	767.080	1013.667	1341.979	1779.048	2360.724	3134.412	4163.094	5529.711	7343.715
50	1668.723	2399.975	3459.344	4994.301	7217.488	10435.449	15088.805	21812.273	31514.492	45496.094

n	21%	22%	23%	24%	25%	26%	27%	28%	29%	30%
1	1.000	1.000	1.000	1.000	1.000	1.000	1.000	1.000	1.000	1.000
2	2.210	2.220	2.230	2.240	2.250	2.260	2.270	2.280	2.290	2.300
3	3.674	3.708	3.743	3.778	3.813	3.848	3.883	3.918	3.954	3.990
4	5.446	5.524	5.604	5.684	5.766	5.848	5.931	6.016	6.101	6.187
5	7.589	7.740	7.893	8.048	8.207	8.368	8.533	8.700	8.870	9.043
6	10.183	10.442	10.708	10.980	11.259	11.544	11.837	12.136	12.442	12.756
7	13.321	13.740	14.171	14.615	15.073	15.546	16.032	16.534	17.051	17.583
8	17.119	17.762	18.430	19.123	19.842	20.588	21.361	22.163	22.995	23.858
9	21.714	22.670	23.669	24.712	25.802	26.940	28.129	29.369	30.664	32.015
10	27.274	28.657	20.113	31.643	33.253	34.945	36.723	38.592	40.556	42.619
11	34.001	35.962	38.039	40.238	42.566	45.030	47.639	50.398	53.318	56.405
12	42.141	44.873	47.787	50.895	54.208	57.738	61.501	65.510	69.780	74.326
13	51.991	55.745	59.778	64.109	68.760	73.750	79.106	84.853	91.016	97.624
14	63.909	69.009	74.528	80.496	86.949	93.925	101.465	109.611	118.411	127.912
15	78.330	85.191	92.669	100.815	109.687	119.346	129.860	141.302	153.750	167.285
16	95.779	104.933	114.983	126.010	138.109	151.375	165.922	181.867	199.337	218.470
17	116.892	129.019	142.428	157.252	173.636	191.733	211.721	233.790	258.145	285.011
18	142.439	158.403	176.187	195.993	218.045	242.583	269.885	300.250	334.006	371.514
19	173.351	194.251	217.710	244.031	273.556	306.654	343.754	385.321	431.868	483.968
20	210.755	237.986	268.783	303.598	342.945	387.384	437.568	494.210	558.110	630.157
21	256.013	291.343	331.603	377.461	429.681	489.104	556.710	633.589	720.962	820.204
22	310.775	356.438	408.871	469.052	538.101	617.270	708.022	811.993	931.040	1067.265
23	377.038	435.854	503.911	582.624	673.626	778.760	900.187	1040.351	1202.042	1388.443
24	457.215	532.741	620.810	723.453	843.032	982.237	1144.237	1332.649	1551.634	1805.975
25	554.230	650.944	764.596	898.082	1054.791	1238.617	1454.180	1706.790	2002.608	2348.765
30	1445.111	1767.044	2160.459	2640.881	3227.172	3941.953	4812.891	5873.172	7162.785	8729.805
40	9749.141	12936.141	17153.691	22728.367	30088.621	39791.957	52570.707	69376.562	91447.375	120389.375

n	31%	32%	33%	34%	35%	36%	37%	38%	39%	40%
1	1.000	1.000	1.000	1.000	1.000	1.000	1.000	1.000	1.000	1.000
2	2.310	2.320	2.330	2.340	2.350	2.360	2.370	2.380	2.390	2.400
3	4.026	4.062	4.099	4.136	4.172	4.210	4.247	4.284	4.322	4.360
4	6.274	6.362	6.452	6.542	6.633	6.725	6.818	6.912	7.008	7.104
5	9.219	9.398	9.581	9.766	9.954	10.146	10.341	10.539	10.741	10.946
6	13.077	13.406	13.742	14.086	14.438	14.799	15.167	15.544	15.930	16.324
7	18.131	18.696	19.277	19.876	20.492	21.126	21.779	22.451	23.142	23.853
8	24.752	25.678	26.638	27.633	28.664	29.732	30.837	31.982	33.167	34.395
9	33.425	34.895	36.429	38.028	39.696	41.435	43.247	45.135	47.103	49.152
10	44.786	47.062	49.451	51.958	54.590	57.351	60.248	63.287	66.473	69.813
11	59.670	63.121	66.769	70.624	74.696	78.998	83.540	88.335	93.397	98.739
12	79.167	84.320	89.803	95.636	101.840	108.437	115.450	122.903	130.822	139.234
13	104.709	112.302	120.438	129.152	138.484	148.474	159.166	170.606	182.842	195.928
14	138.169	149.239	161.183	174.063	187.953	202.925	219.058	236.435	255.151	275.299
15	182.001	197.996	215.373	234.245	254.737	276.978	301.109	327.281	355.659	386.418
16	239.421	262.354	287.446	314.888	344.895	377.690	413.520	452.647	495.366	541.985
17	314.642	347.307	383.303	422.949	466.608	514.658	567.521	625.652	689.558	759.778
18	413.180	459.445	510.792	567.751	630.920	700.935	778.504	864.399	959.485	1064.689
19	542.266	607.467	680.354	761.786	852.741	954.271	1067.551	1193.870	1334.683	1491.563
20	711.368	802.856	905.870	1021.792	1152.200	1298.809	1463.544	1648.539	1856.208	2089.188
21	932.891	1060.769	1205.807	1370.201	1556.470	1767.380	2006.055	2275.982	2581.128	2925.862
22	1223.087	1401.215	1604.724	1837.068	2102.234	2404.636	2749.294	3141.852	3588.765	4097.203
23	1603.243	1850.603	2135.282	2462.669	2839.014	3271.304	3767.532	4336.750	4989.379	5737.078
24	2101.247	2443.795	2840.924	3300.974	3833.667	4449.969	5162.516	5985.711	6936.230	8032.906
25	2753.631	3226.808	3779.428	4424.301	5176.445	6052.957	7073.645	8261.273	9642.352	11247.062
30	10632.543	12940.672	15737.945	19124.434	23221.258	28172.016	34148.906	41357.227	50043.625	60500.207

Present Value of an Annuity of $1 for *n* Periods

n	1%	2%	3%	4%	5%	6%	7%	8%	9%	10%
1	.990	.980	.971	.962	.952	.943	.935	.926	.917	.909
2	1.970	1.942	1.913	1.886	1.859	1.833	1.808	1.783	1.759	1.736
3	2.941	2.884	2.829	2.775	2.723	2.673	2.624	2.577	2.531	2.487
4	3.902	3.808	3.717	3.630	3.546	3.465	3.387	3.312	3.240	3.170
5	4.853	4.713	4.580	4.452	4.329	4.212	4.100	3.993	3.890	3.791
6	5.795	5.601	5.417	5.242	5.076	4.917	4.767	4.623	4.486	4.355
7	6.728	6.472	6.230	6.002	5.786	5.582	5.389	5.206	5.033	4.868
8	7.652	7.326	7.020	6.733	6.463	6.210	5.971	5.747	5.535	5.335
9	8.566	8.162	7.786	7.435	7.108	6.802	6.515	6.247	5.995	5.759
10	9.471	8.983	8.530	8.111	7.722	7.360	7.024	6.710	6.418	6.145
11	10.368	9.787	9.253	8.760	8.306	7.887	7.499	7.139	6.805	6.495
12	11.255	10.575	9.954	9.385	8.863	8.384	7.943	7.536	7.161	6.814
13	12.134	11.348	10.635	9.986	9.394	8.853	8.358	7.904	7.487	7.103
14	13.004	12.106	11.296	10.563	9.899	9.295	8.746	8.244	7.786	7.367
15	13.865	12.849	11.938	11.118	10.380	9.712	9.108	8.560	8.061	7.606
16	14.718	13.578	12.561	11.652	10.838	10.106	9.447	8.851	8.313	7.824
17	15.562	14.292	13.166	12.166	11.274	10.477	9.763	9.122	8.544	8.022
18	16.398	14.992	13.754	12.659	11.690	10.828	10.059	9.372	8.756	8.201
19	17.226	15.679	14.324	13.134	12.085	11.158	10.336	9.604	8.950	8.365
20	18.046	16.352	14.878	13.590	12.462	11.470	10.594	9.818	9.129	8.514
21	18.857	17.011	15.415	14.029	12.821	11.764	10.836	10.017	9.292	8.649
22	19.661	17.658	15.937	14.451	13.163	12.042	11.061	10.201	9.442	8.772
23	20.456	18.292	16.444	14.857	13.489	12.303	11.272	10.371	9.580	8.883
24	21.244	18.914	16.936	15.247	13.799	12.550	11.469	10.529	9.707	8.985
25	22.023	19.524	17.413	15.622	14.094	12.783	11.654	10.675	9.823	9.077
30	25.808	22.397	19.601	17.292	15.373	13.765	12.409	11.258	10.274	9.427
40	32.835	27.356	23.115	19.793	17.159	15.046	13.332	11.925	10.757	9.779
50	39.197	31.424	25.730	21.482	18.256	15.762	13.801	12.234	10.962	9.915

n	11%	12%	13%	14%	15%	16%	17%	18%	19%	20%
1	.901	.893	.885	.877	.870	.862	.855	.847	.840	.833
2	1.713	1.690	1.668	1.647	1.626	1.605	1.585	1.566	1.547	1.528
3	2.444	2.402	2.361	2.322	2.283	2.246	2.210	2.174	2.140	2.106
4	3.102	3.037	2.974	2.914	2.855	2.798	2.743	2.690	2.639	2.589
5	3.696	3.605	3.517	3.433	3.352	3.274	3.199	3.127	3.058	2.991
6	4.231	4.111	3.998	3.889	3.784	3.685	3.589	3.498	3.410	3.326
7	4.712	4.564	4.423	4.288	4.160	4.039	3.922	3.812	3.706	3.605
8	5.146	4.968	4.799	4.639	4.487	4.344	4.207	4.078	3.954	3.837
9	5.537	5.328	5.132	4.946	4.772	4.607	4.451	4.303	4.163	4.031
10	5.889	5.650	5.426	5.216	5.019	4.833	4.659	4.494	4.339	4.192
11	6.207	5.938	5.687	5.453	5.234	5.029	4.836	4.656	4.487	4.327
12	6.492	6.194	5.918	5.660	5.421	5.197	4.988	4.793	4.611	4.439
13	6.750	6.424	6.122	5.842	5.583	5.342	5.118	4.910	4.715	4.533
14	6.982	6.628	6.303	6.002	5.724	5.468	5.229	5.008	4.802	4.611
15	7.191	6.811	6.462	6.142	5.847	5.575	5.324	5.092	4.876	4.675
16	7.379	6.974	6.604	6.265	5.954	5.669	5.405	5.162	4.938	4.730
17	7.549	7.120	6.729	6.373	6.047	5.749	5.475	5.222	4.990	4.775
18	7.702	7.250	6.840	6.467	6.128	5.818	5.534	5.273	5.033	4.812
19	7.839	7.366	6.938	6.550	6.198	5.877	5.585	5.316	5.070	4.843
20	7.963	7.469	7.025	6.623	6.259	5.929	5.628	5.353	5.101	4.870
21	8.075	7.562	7.102	6.687	6.312	5.973	5.665	5.384	5.127	4.891
22	8.176	7.645	7.170	6.743	6.359	6.011	5.696	5.410	5.149	4.909
23	8.266	7.718	7.230	6.792	6.399	6.044	5.723	5.432	5.167	4.925
24	8.348	7.784	7.283	6.835	6.434	6.073	5.747	5.451	5.182	4.937
25	8.442	7.843	7.330	6.873	6.464	6.097	5.766	5.467	5.195	4.948
30	8.694	8.055	7.496	7.003	6.566	6.177	5.829	5.517	5.235	4.979
40	8.951	8.244	7.634	7.105	6.642	6.233	5.871	5.548	5.258	4.997
50	9.042	8.305	7.675	7.133	6.661	6.246	5.880	5.554	5.262	4.999

n	21%	22%	23%	24%	25%	26%	27%	28%	29%	30%
1	.826	.820	.813	.806	.800	.794	.787	.781	.775	.769
2	1.509	1.492	1.474	1.457	1.440	1.424	1.407	1.392	1.376	1.361
3	2.074	2.042	2.011	1.981	1.952	1.923	1.896	1.868	1.842	1.816
4	2.540	2.494	2.448	2.404	2.362	2.320	2.280	2.241	2.203	2.166
5	2.926	2.864	2.803	2.745	2.689	2.635	2.583	2.532	2.483	2.436
6	3.245	3.167	3.092	3.020	2.951	2.885	2.821	2.759	2.700	2.643
7	3.508	3.416	3.327	3.242	3.161	3.083	3.009	2.937	2.868	2.802
8	3.726	3.619	3.518	3.421	3.329	3.241	3.156	3.076	2.999	2.925
9	3.905	3.786	3.673	3.566	3.463	3.366	3.273	3.184	3.100	3.019
10	4.054	3.923	3.799	3.682	3.570	3.465	3.364	3.269	3.178	3.092
11	4.177	4.035	3.902	3.776	3.656	3.544	3.437	3.335	3.239	3.147
12	4.278	4.127	3.985	3.851	3.725	3.606	3.493	3.387	3.286	3.190
13	4.362	4.203	4.053	3.912	3.780	3.656	3.538	3.427	3.322	3.223
14	4.432	4.265	4.108	3.962	3.824	3.695	3.573	3.459	3.351	3.249
15	4.489	4.315	4.153	4.001	3.859	3.726	3.601	3.483	3.373	3.268
16	4.536	4.357	4.189	4.033	3.887	3.751	3.623	3.503	3.390	3.283
17	4.576	4.391	4.219	4.059	3.910	3.771	3.640	3.518	3.403	3.295
18	4.608	4.419	4.243	4.080	3.928	3.786	3.654	3.529	3.413	3.304
19	4.635	4.442	4.263	4.097	3.942	3.799	3.664	3.539	3.421	3.311
20	4.657	4.460	4.279	4.110	3.954	3.808	3.673	3.546	3.427	3.316
21	4.675	4.476	4.292	4.121	3.963	3.816	3.679	3.551	3.432	3.320
22	4.690	4.488	4.302	4.130	3.970	3.822	3.684	3.556	3.436	3.323
23	4.703	4.499	4.311	4.137	3.976	3.827	3.689	3.559	3.438	3.325
24	4.713	4.507	4.318	4.143	3.981	3.831	3.692	3.562	3.441	3.327
25	4.721	4.514	4.323	4.147	3.985	3.834	3.694	3.564	3.442	3.329
30	4.746	4.534	4.339	4.160	3.995	3.842	3.701	3.569	3.447	3.332
40	4.760	4.544	4.347	4.166	3.999	3.846	3.703	3.571	3.448	3.333
50	4.762	4.545	4.348	4.167	4.000	3.846	3.704	3.571	3.448	3.333

n	31%	32%	33%	34%	35%	36%	37%	38%	39%	40%
1	.763	.758	.752	.746	.741	.735	.730	.725	.719	.714
2	1.346	1.331	1.317	1.303	1.289	1.276	1.263	1.250	1.237	1.224
3	1.791	1.766	1.742	1.719	1.696	1.673	1.652	1.630	1.609	1.589
4	2.130	2.096	2.062	2.029	1.997	1.966	1.935	1.906	1.877	1.849
5	2.390	2.345	2.302	2.260	2.220	2.181	2.143	2.106	2.070	2.035
6	2.588	2.534	2.483	2.433	2.385	2.339	2.294	2.251	2.209	2.168
7	2.739	2.677	2.619	2.562	2.508	2.455	2.404	2.355	2.308	2.263
8	2.854	2.786	2.721	2.658	2.598	2.540	2.485	2.432	2.380	2.331
9	2.942	2.868	2.798	2.730	2.665	2.603	2.544	2.487	2.432	2.379
10	3.009	2.930	2.855	2.784	2.715	2.649	2.587	2.527	2.469	2.414
11	3.060	2.978	2.899	2.824	2.752	2.683	2.618	2.555	2.496	2.438
12	3.100	3.013	2.931	2.853	2.779	2.708	2.641	2.576	2.515	2.456
13	3.129	3.040	2.956	2.876	2.799	2.727	2.658	2.592	2.529	2.469
14	3.152	3.061	2.974	2.892	2.814	2.740	2.670	2.603	2.539	2.477
15	3.170	3.076	2.988	2.905	2.825	2.750	2.679	2.611	2.546	2.484
16	3.183	3.088	2.999	2.914	2.834	2.757	2.685	2.616	2.551	2.489
17	3.193	3.097	3.007	2.921	2.840	2.763	2.690	2.621	2.555	2.492
18	3.201	3.104	3.012	2.926	2.844	2.767	2.693	2.624	2.557	2.494
19	3.207	3.109	3.017	2.930	2.848	2.770	2.696	2.626	2.559	2.496
20	3.211	3.113	3.020	2.933	2.850	2.772	2.698	2.627	2.561	2.497
21	3.215	3.116	3.023	2.935	2.852	2.773	2.699	2.629	2.562	2.498
22	3.217	3.118	3.025	2.936	2.853	2.775	2.700	2.629	2.562	2.498
23	3.219	3.120	3.026	2.938	2.854	2.775	2.701	2.630	2.563	2.499
24	3.221	3.121	3.027	2.939	2.855	2.776	2.701	2.630	2.563	2.499
25	3.222	3.122	3.028	2.939	2.856	2.776	2.702	2.631	2.563	2.499
30	3.225	3.124	3.030	2.941	2.857	2.777	2.702	2.631	2.564	2.500
40	3.226	3.125	3.030	2.941	2.857	2.778	2.703	2.632	2.564	2.500
50	3.226	3.125	3.030	2.941	2.857	2.778	2.703	2.632	2.564	2.500

Monthly Installment Loan Tables ($1,000 loan with interest payments compounded monthly)

Interest	6	12	18	24	Loan Maturity (in months) 30	36	48	60	72	84	96
4.00%	168.62	85.15	57.33	43.42	35.08	29.52	22.58	18.42	15.65	13.67	12.19
4.25%	168.74	85.26	57.44	43.54	35.19	29.64	22.69	18.53	15.76	13.78	12.31
4.50%	168.86	85.38	57.56	43.65	35.31	29.75	22.80	18.64	15.87	13.90	12.42
4.75%	168.98	85.49	57.67	43.76	35.42	29.86	22.92	18.76	15.99	14.02	12.54
5.00%	169.11	85.61	57.78	43.87	35.53	29.97	23.03	18.87	16.10	14.13	12.66
5.25%	169.23	85.72	57.89	43.98	35.64	30.08	23.14	18.99	16.22	14.25	12.78
5.50%	169.35	85.84	58.01	44.10	35.75	30.20	23.26	19.10	16.34	14.37	12.90
5.75%	169.47	85.95	58.12	44.21	35.87	30.31	23.37	19.22	16.46	14.49	13.02
6.00%	169.60	86.07	58.23	44.32	35.98	30.42	23.49	19.33	16.57	14.61	13.14
6.25%	169.72	86.18	58.34	44.43	36.09	30.54	23.60	19.45	16.69	14.73	13.26
6.50%	169.84	86.30	58.46	44.55	36.20	30.65	23.71	19.57	16.81	14.85	13.39
6.75%	169.96	86.41	58.57	44.66	36.32	30.76	23.83	19.68	16.93	14.97	13.51
7.00%	170.09	86.53	58.68	44.77	36.43	30.88	23.95	19.80	17.05	15.09	13.63
7.25%	170.21	86.64	58.80	44.89	36.55	30.99	24.06	19.92	17.17	15.22	13.76
7.50%	170.33	86.76	58.91	45.00	36.66	31.11	24.18	20.04	17.29	15.34	13.88
7.75%	170.45	86.87	59.03	45.11	36.77	31.22	24.30	20.16	17.41	15.46	14.01
8.00%	170.58	86.99	59.14	45.23	36.89	31.34	24.41	20.28	17.53	15.59	14.14
8.25%	170.70	87.10	59.25	45.34	37.00	31.45	24.53	20.40	17.66	15.71	14.26
8.50%	170.82	87.22	59.37	45.46	37.12	31.57	24.65	20.52	17.78	15.84	14.39
8.75%	170.95	87.34	59.48	45.57	37.23	31.68	24.77	20.64	17.90	15.96	14.52
9.00%	171.07	87.45	59.60	45.68	37.35	31.80	24.89	20.76	18.03	16.09	14.65
9.25%	171.19	87.57	59.71	45.80	37.46	31.92	25.00	20.88	18.15	16.22	14.78
9.50%	171.32	87.68	59.83	45.91	37.58	32.03	25.12	21.00	18.27	16.34	14.91
9.75%	171.44	87.80	59.94	46.03	37.70	32.15	25.24	21.12	18.40	16.47	15.04
10.00%	171.56	87.92	60.06	46.14	37.81	32.27	25.36	21.25	18.53	16.60	15.17
10.25%	171.68	88.03	60.17	46.26	37.93	32.38	25.48	21.37	18.65	16.73	15.31
10.50%	171.81	88.15	60.29	46.38	38.04	32.50	25.60	21.49	18.78	16.86	15.44
10.75%	171.93	88.27	60.40	46.49	38.16	32.62	25.72	21.62	18.91	16.99	15.57
11.00%	172.05	88.38	60.52	46.61	38.28	32.74	25.85	21.74	19.03	17.12	15.71
11.25%	172.18	88.50	60.63	46.72	38.40	32.86	25.97	21.87	19.16	17.25	15.84
11.50%	172.30	88.62	60.75	46.84	38.51	32.98	26.09	21.99	19.29	17.39	15.98
11.75%	172.42	88.73	60.87	46.96	38.63	33.10	26.21	22.12	19.42	17.52	16.12
12.00%	172.55	88.85	60.98	47.07	38.75	33.21	26.33	22.24	19.55	17.65	16.25
12.25%	172.67	88.97	61.10	47.19	38.87	33.33	26.46	22.37	19.68	17.79	16.39
12.50%	172.80	89.08	61.21	47.31	38.98	33.45	26.58	22.50	19.81	17.92	16.53
12.75%	172.92	89.20	61.33	47.42	39.10	33.57	26.70	22.63	19.94	18.06	16.67
13.00%	173.04	89.32	61.45	47.54	39.22	33.69	26.83	22.75	20.07	18.19	16.81
13.25%	173.17	89.43	61.56	47.66	39.34	33.81	26.95	22.88	20.21	18.33	16.95
13.50%	173.29	89.55	61.68	47.78	39.46	33.94	27.08	23.01	20.34	18.46	17.09
13.75%	173.41	89.67	61.80	47.89	39.58	34.06	27.20	23.14	20.47	18.60	17.23
14.00%	173.54	89.79	61.92	48.01	39.70	34.18	27.33	23.27	20.61	18.74	17.37
14.25%	173.66	89.90	62.03	48.13	39.82	34.30	27.45	23.40	20.74	18.88	17.51
14.50%	173.79	90.02	62.15	48.25	39.94	34.42	27.58	23.53	20.87	19.02	17.66

Interest	6	12	18	24	30	36	48	60	72	84	96
14.75%	173.91	90.14	62.27	48.37	40.06	34.54	27.70	23.66	21.01	19.16	17.80
15.00%	174.03	90.26	62.38	48.49	40.18	34.67	27.83	23.79	21.15	19.30	17.95
15.25%	174.16	90.38	62.50	48.61	40.30	34.79	27.96	23.92	21.28	19.44	18.09
15.50%	174.28	90.49	62.62	48.72	40.42	34.91	28.08	24.05	21.42	19.58	18.24
15.75%	174.41	90.61	62.74	48.84	40.54	35.03	28.21	24.19	21.55	19.72	18.38
16.00%	174.53	90.73	62.86	48.96	40.66	35.16	28.34	24.32	21.69	19.86	18.53
16.25%	174.65	90.85	62.97	49.08	40.78	35.28	28.47	24.45	21.83	20.00	18.68
16.50%	174.78	90.97	63.09	49.20	40.91	35.40	28.60	24.58	21.97	20.15	18.82
16.75%	174.90	91.09	63.21	49.32	41.03	35.53	28.73	24.72	22.11	20.29	18.97
17.00%	175.03	91.20	63.33	49.44	41.15	35.65	28.86	24.85	22.25	20.44	19.12
17.25%	175.15	91.32	63.45	49.56	41.27	35.78	28.98	24.99	22.39	20.58	19.27
17.50%	175.28	91.44	63.57	49.68	41.39	35.90	29.11	25.12	22.53	20.73	19.42
17.75%	175.40	91.56	63.69	49.80	41.52	36.03	29.24	25.26	22.67	20.87	19.57
18.00%	175.53	91.68	63.81	49.92	41.64	36.15	29.37	25.39	22.81	21.02	19.72
18.25%	175.65	91.80	63.93	50.04	41.76	36.28	29.51	25.53	22.95	21.16	19.88
18.50%	175.77	91.92	64.04	50.17	41.89	36.40	29.64	25.67	23.09	21.31	20.03
18.75%	175.90	92.04	64.16	50.29	42.01	36.53	29.77	25.80	23.23	21.46	20.18
19.00%	176.02	92.16	64.28	50.41	42.13	36.66	29.90	25.94	23.38	21.61	20.33
19.25%	176.15	92.28	64.40	50.53	42.26	36.78	30.03	26.08	23.52	21.76	20.49
19.50%	176.27	92.40	64.52	50.65	42.38	36.91	30.16	26.22	23.66	21.91	20.64
19.75%	176.40	92.51	64.64	50.77	42.51	37.04	30.30	26.35	23.81	22.06	20.80
20.00%	176.52	92.63	64.76	50.90	42.63	37.16	30.43	26.49	23.95	22.21	20.95
20.25%	176.65	92.75	64.88	51.02	42.75	37.29	30.56	26.63	24.10	22.36	21.11
20.50%	176.77	92.87	65.00	51.14	42.88	37.42	30.70	26.77	24.24	22.51	21.27
20.75%	176.90	92.99	65.12	51.26	43.00	37.55	30.83	26.91	24.39	22.66	21.42
21.00%	177.02	93.11	65.24	51.39	43.13	37.68	30.97	27.05	24.54	22.81	21.58
21.25%	177.15	93.23	65.37	51.51	43.26	37.80	31.10	27.19	24.68	22.96	21.74
21.50%	177.27	93.35	65.49	51.63	43.38	37.93	31.24	27.34	24.83	23.12	21.90
21.75%	177.40	93.47	65.61	51.75	43.51	38.06	31.37	27.48	24.98	23.27	22.06
22.00%	177.52	93.59	65.73	51.88	43.63	38.19	31.51	27.62	25.13	23.43	22.22
22.25%	177.65	93.71	65.85	52.00	43.76	38.32	31.64	27.76	25.27	23.58	22.38
22.50%	177.77	93.84	65.97	52.13	43.89	38.45	31.78	27.90	25.42	23.74	22.54
22.75%	177.90	93.96	66.09	52.25	44.01	38.58	31.91	28.05	25.57	23.89	22.70
23.00%	178.02	94.08	66.21	52.37	44.14	38.71	32.05	28.19	25.72	24.05	22.86
23.25%	178.15	94.20	66.34	52.50	44.27	38.84	32.19	28.33	25.87	24.20	23.02
23.50%	178.27	94.32	66.46	52.62	44.39	38.97	32.33	28.48	26.02	24.36	23.19
23.75%	178.40	94.44	66.58	52.75	44.52	39.10	32.46	28.62	26.18	24.52	23.35
24.00%	178.53	94.56	66.70	52.87	44.65	39.23	32.60	28.77	26.33	24.68	23.51
24.25%	178.65	94.68	66.82	53.00	44.78	39.36	32.74	28.91	26.48	24.83	23.68
24.50%	178.78	94.80	66.95	53.12	44.91	39.50	32.88	29.06	26.63	24.99	23.84
24.75%	178.90	94.92	67.07	53.25	45.03	39.63	33.02	29.20	26.78	25.15	24.01
25.00%	179.03	95.04	67.19	53.37	45.16	39.76	33.16	29.35	26.94	25.31	24.17

These financial planning worksheets provide you with the opportunity to develop and implement your own financial plan. Many of them are taken directly from figures within the text; others provide checklists or worksheets not provided within the text. They should make the financial planning process a bit easier for you. As you learned early on in this text, as you experience personal and financial changes in your life, you've got to revise your financial plan. That means that you'll be reworking these worksheets many times over throughout your life. In effect, financial planning is an ongoing process, and a good plan is always changing.

Unfortunately, financial planning isn't something that comes naturally to most people, and as a result many people work themselves into a financial corner that is much easier to avoid than it is to get out of. These worksheets provide some guidance so you can avoid the financial pitfalls that are lurking in your future. The worksheets can help you to achieve all your financial goals.

Once you've developed a plan, keep in mind that it's even more important to implement and actually stick to that plan. That means using common sense and moderation—you don't want to become a slave to your financial plan. Instead, keep in mind that your financial plan is not the goal, it is the tool you use to achieve your goals. In effect, think of your financial plan as a financial road map to guide you through life. Your destination may change, and you may get lost or even go down a few dead ends, but if your road map is good enough, you'll always find your way again. Remember to add in new roads as they are built, and be prepared to pave a few yourself to get to where you want to go. Always keep your goals in mind and keep driving toward them.

WORKSHEET G.1 (from Figure 1.2)

Personal Financial Goals Worksheet

Make sure your goals are realistic and stated in specific, measurable terms. In addition, prioritize your goals and identify a specific time frame within which you would like to accomplish them. The listing below is not meant to be all-inclusive, but merely to provide a framework within which goals can be formalized.

SHORT-TERM GOALS (less than 1 year)

Goal	Priority Level	Desired Achievement Date	Anticipated Cost
Accumulate Emergency Funds Equal to 3 Months' Living Expenses			
Pay Off Outstanding Bills	_____	_____	_____
Pay Off Outstanding Credit Cards	_____	_____	_____
Purchase Adequate Property, Health, Disability, and Liability Insurance	_____	_____	_____
Purchase a Major Item	_____	_____	_____
Finance a Vacation or Some Other Entertainment Item	_____	_____	_____
Other Short-Term Goals (Specify)	_____	_____	_____

INTERMEDIATE-TERM GOALS (1 to 10 years)

Goal	Priority Level	Desired Achievement Date	Anticipated Cost
Save Funds for College for an Older Child	_____	_____	_____
Save for a Major Home Improvement	_____	_____	_____
Save for a Down Payment on a House	_____	_____	_____
Pay Off Outstanding Major Debt	_____	_____	_____
Finance Very Large Items (Weddings)	_____	_____	_____
Purchase a Vacation Home or Time-Share Unit	_____	_____	_____
Finance a Major Vacation (Overseas)	_____	_____	_____
Other Intermediate-Term Goals (Specify)	_____	_____	_____

LONG-TERM GOALS (greater than 10 years)

Goal	Priority Level	Desired Achievement Date	Anticipated Cost
Save Funds for College for a Young Child	_____	_____	_____
Purchase a Second Home for Retirement	_____	_____	_____
Create a Retirement Fund Large Enough to Supplement Your Pension So That You Can Live at Your Current Standard	_____	_____	_____
Take Care of Your Parents After They Retire	_____	_____	_____
Start Your Own Business	_____	_____	_____
Other Long-Term Goals (Specify)	_____	_____	_____

Job Search Worksheet

Notes

The Search (Complete items 1 to 3 on this checklist before starting your job search.)

1. Identify Occupations
- Make a background and experience list.
- Review information on jobs.
- Identify jobs that use your talents.

2. Identify Employers
- Ask relatives and friends to help you look for job openings.
- Go to your State Employment Service Office for assistance.
- Contact employers to get company and job information.
- Utilize other sources to get job leads.
- Obtain job announcements and descriptions.

3. Prepare Materials
- Write résumés (if needed). Use job announcements to "fit" your skills with job requirements.
- Write cover letters or letters of application.
- Assemble a job search kit: pens, writing tablet, maps, public transportation guides, clean copies of résumés and applications, background and experience list, Social Security card, and picture ID.

The Daily Effort (Complete items 4 to 5 every day of your job search.)

4. Plan Your Time
- Wake up early to start looking for work.
- Make a "to-do" list of everything you'll do to look for a job.
- Work hard all day to find a job.
- Reward yourself (do a hobby or sport, visit friends)!

5. Contact Employers
- Call employers directly (even if they're not advertising openings). Talk to the person who would supervise you if you were hired. Make note of names.
- Go to companies to fill out applications.
- Contact your friends and relatives to see if they know about any openings.

The Interview (Complete items 6 to 9 when you have interviews.)

6. Prepare for Interviews
- Learn about the company you're interviewing with.
- Review job announcements to determine how your skills will help you do the job.
- Assemble résumés, application forms, etc. (make sure everything is neat).
- Arrange for baby-sitters, transportation, etc.
- Give yourself plenty of time.

(continued)

7. **Go to Interviews**
   - Dress right for the interview.
   - Go alone.
   - Be clean, concise, and positive.
   - Thank the interviewer.

   _____

8. **Evaluate Interviews**
   - Send a handwritten thank-you note to the interviewer within 24 hours of the interview.
   - Think about how you could improve the interview.

   _____

9. **Take Tests**
   - Find out about the test(s) you're taking.
   - Brush up on job skills.
   - Relax and be confident.

   _____

10. **Accept the Job!**
    - Get an understanding of job duties and expectations, work hours, salary, benefits, and so on.
    - Be flexible when discussing salary (but don't sell yourself short).
    - *Congratulations!*

    _____

Balance Sheet—Calculating Your Net Worth

Assets		Value
Cash		_____
Checking	+	_____
Savings/CDs	+	_____
Money Market Funds	+	_____
Other Monetary Assets	+	_____
A. Monetary Assets	A. =	_____
Mutual Funds		_____
Stocks	+	_____
Bonds	+	_____
Life Insurance (cash-value)	+	_____
Cash Value of Annuities	+	_____
Investment Real Estate (REITs, partnerships)	+	_____
Other Investments	+	_____
B. Investments	B. =	_____
401(k) and 403(b)		_____
Company Pension	+	_____
Keogh	+	_____
IRA	+	_____
Other Retirement Plans	+	_____
C. Retirement Plans	C. =	_____
Primary Residence		_____
2nd Home	+	_____
Time-Shares/Condominiums	+	_____
Other Housing	+	_____
D. Housing (market value)	D. =	_____
Automobile 1		_____
Automobile 2	+	_____
Other Automobiles	+	_____
E. Automobiles	E. =	_____
Collectibles		_____
Boats	+	_____
Furniture	+	_____
Other Personal Property	+	_____
F. Personal Property	F. =	_____
Money Owed You		_____
Market Value of Your Business	+	_____
Other	+	_____
G. Other Assets	G. =	_____
H. Total Assets (add lines A–G)	H. =	_____

(continued)

Liabilities or Debts	Value	
I. Current Bills (unpaid balance)	I.=	_____
Visa		_____
MasterCard	+	_____
Other Credit Cards	+	_____
J. Credit Card Debt	J.=	_____
First Mortgage		_____
2nd Home Mortgage	+	_____
Home Equity Loan	+	_____
Other Housing Debt	+	_____
K. Housing	K.=	_____
Automobile 1		_____
Automobile 2	+	_____
Other Automobile Loans	+	_____
L. Automobile Loans	L.=	_____
College Loans		_____
Loans on Life Insurance Policies	+	_____
Bank Loans	+	_____
Installment Loans	+	_____
Other	+	_____
M. Other Debts	M.=	_____
N. Total Debt (add lines I–M)	N.=	_____

Net Worth

H. Total Assets	H.+	_____
N. Less: Total Debt	N.−	_____
O. Equals: Net Worth	O.=	_____

The Budget Tracker: Personal Income Statement Worksheet

	Month _____			Month _____			
	Budget Income	Actual Income	Difference	Budget Income	Actual Income	Difference	Total Difference
INCOME							
Wages and Salaries							
Wage earner 1							
+ Wage earner 2							
= Total Wages and Salaries							
+ Interest and Dividends							
+ Royalties, Commissions, and Rents							
+ Other Income							
= **A. TOTAL INCOME**							
TAXES							
Federal Income and Social Security							
+ State Income							
= **B. TOTAL INCOME TAXES**							
C. AFTER-TAX INCOME AVAILABLE FOR LIVING EXPENDITURES OR TAKE-HOME PAY (LINE A MINUS LINE B)							

	Budget Amount	Actual Spending	Difference	Budget Amount	Actual Spending	Difference	Total Difference
LIVING EXPENSES							
HOUSING							
Rent							
+ Mortgage Payments							
+ Utilities							
+ Maintenance							
+ Real Estate and Property Taxes							
+ Fixed Assets—Furniture, Appliances, Televisions, etc.							
+ Other Living Expenses							
= **D. TOTAL HOUSING EXPENDITURES**							
FOOD							
Food and Supplies							
+ Restaurant Expenses							
= **E. TOTAL FOOD EXPENDITURES**							
CLOTHING AND PERSONAL CARE							
New Clothes							
+ Cleaning							
+ Tailoring							
+ Personal Care—hair care							
+ Other Clothing and Personal Care Expenses							
= **F. TOTAL CLOTHING AND PERSONAL CARE EXPENDITURES**							

(continued)

	Month _____			Month _____			
	Budget Amount	Actual Spending	Difference	Budget Amount	Actual Spending	Difference	Total Difference
TRANSPORTATION							
Automobile Purchase	_____	_____	_____	_____	_____	_____	_____
+ Payments	_____	_____	_____	_____	_____	_____	_____
+ Gas, Tolls, Parking	_____	_____	_____	_____	_____	_____	_____
+ Automobile Registration/Tags/Stickers	_____	_____	_____	_____	_____	_____	_____
+ Repairs	_____	_____	_____	_____	_____	_____	_____
+ Other Transportation Expenses	_____	_____	_____	_____	_____	_____	_____
= **G. TOTAL TRANSPORTATION EXPENDITURES**	_____	_____	_____	_____	_____	_____	_____
RECREATION							
Movies, Theater, Sporting Events	_____	_____	_____	_____	_____	_____	_____
+ Club Memberships	_____	_____	_____	_____	_____	_____	_____
+ Vacations	_____	_____	_____	_____	_____	_____	_____
+ Hobbies	_____	_____	_____	_____	_____	_____	_____
+ Sporting Goods	_____	_____	_____	_____	_____	_____	_____
+ Gifts	_____	_____	_____	_____	_____	_____	_____
+ Reading Materials (books, newspapers, magazines)	_____	_____	_____	_____	_____	_____	_____
+ Other Recreation Expenses	_____	_____	_____	_____	_____	_____	_____
= **H. TOTAL RECREATION EXPENDITURES**	_____	_____	_____	_____	_____	_____	_____
MEDICAL EXPENDITURES							
Doctor	_____	_____	_____	_____	_____	_____	_____
+ Dental	_____	_____	_____	_____	_____	_____	_____
+ Prescription Drugs and Medicines	_____	_____	_____	_____	_____	_____	_____
= **I. TOTAL MEDICAL EXPENDITURES**	_____	_____	_____	_____	_____	_____	_____
INSURANCE EXPENDITURES							
Health	_____	_____	_____	_____	_____	_____	_____
+ Life	_____	_____	_____	_____	_____	_____	_____
+ Automobile	_____	_____	_____	_____	_____	_____	_____
+ Disability	_____	_____	_____	_____	_____	_____	_____
+ Liability	_____	_____	_____	_____	_____	_____	_____
+ Other Insurance Expenses	_____	_____	_____	_____	_____	_____	_____
= **J. TOTAL INSURANCE EXPENDITURES**	_____	_____	_____	_____	_____	_____	_____
OTHER EXPENDITURES							
Educational Expenditures	_____	_____	_____	_____	_____	_____	_____
+ Child care	_____	_____	_____	_____	_____	_____	_____
+ Other	_____	_____	_____	_____	_____	_____	_____
= **K. TOTAL OTHER EXPENDITURES**	_____	_____	_____	_____	_____	_____	_____
L. TOTAL LIVING EXPENDITURES (ADD LINES D–K)	_____	_____	_____	_____	_____	_____	_____
M. INCOME AVAILABLE FOR SAVINGS AND INVESTMENT (LINE C MINUS LINE L)	_____	_____	_____	_____	_____	_____	_____

WORKSHEET G.5 (from Table 2.2)

Storing Financial Files

If you're still stuck on what to store and where, consider buying a kit to help you. Two such products to consider are Homefile (800-695-3453) and FileSolutions (214-488-0100).

Long-term or Permanent Storage (keep at home in a file cabinet or safe spot):

TAX RECORDS (may be discarded after 6 years)   **LOCATION**

- [ ] Tax returns _____
- [ ] Paychecks _____
- [ ] W-2 forms _____
- [ ] 1099 forms _____
- [ ] Charitable contributions _____
- [ ] Alimony payments _____
- [ ] Medical bills _____
- [ ] Property taxes _____
- [ ] Any other documentation _____

INVESTMENT RECORDS

- [ ] Bank records and nontax-related checks less than a year old _____
- [ ] Safety deposit box information _____
- [ ] Stock, bond, and mutual fund transactions _____
- [ ] Brokerage statements _____
- [ ] Dividend records _____
- [ ] Any additional investment documentation _____

RETIREMENT AND ESTATE PLANNING

- [ ] Copy of will _____
- [ ] Pension plan documentation _____
- [ ] IRA documentation _____
- [ ] Keogh plan transactions _____
- [ ] Social Security information _____
- [ ] Any additional retirement documentation _____

PERSONAL PLANNING

- [ ] Personal balance sheet _____
- [ ] Personal income statement _____
- [ ] Personal budget _____
- [ ] Insurance policies and documentation _____
- [ ] Warranties _____
- [ ] Receipts for major purchases _____
- [ ] Credit card information (account numbers and telephone numbers) _____

(continued)

- ☐ Birth certificates _____
- ☐ Rental agreement, if renting a dwelling _____
- ☐ Automobile registration _____
- ☐ Powers of attorney _____
- ☐ Any additional personal planning documentation _____

Safety Deposit Box Storage

INVESTMENT RECORDS

- ☐ Certificates of deposit _____
- ☐ Listing of bank accounts _____
- ☐ Stock and bond certificates _____
- ☐ Collectibles _____

RETIREMENT AND ESTATE PLANNING

- ☐ Copy of will _____
- ☐ Nondeductible IRA records _____

PERSONAL PLANNING

- ☐ Copy of will _____
- ☐ Deed for home _____
- ☐ Mortgage _____
- ☐ Title insurance policy _____
- ☐ Personal papers (birth and death certificates, alimony, adoption/custody, divorce, military, immigration, etc.) _____
- ☐ Documentation of valuables (videotape or photos) _____
- ☐ Home repair/improvement receipts _____
- ☐ Auto title _____
- ☐ Listing of insurance policies _____
- ☐ Credit card information (account numbers and telephone numbers) _____

Throw out

- ☐ Nontax-related checks over a year old
- ☐ Records from cars and boats you no longer own
- ☐ Expired insurance policies on which there will be no future claims
- ☐ Expired warranties
- ☐ Nontax-related credit card slips over a year old

**WORKSHEET G.6
(from Figure 2.2)**

Personal Balance Sheet—Determining Your Net Worth

Assets (What You Own)

Your Numbers

A.	Monetary Assets (bank account, etc.)		_____
B.	Investments	+	_____
C.	Retirement Plans	+	_____
D.	Housing (market value)	+	_____
E.	Automobiles	+	_____
F.	Personal Property	+	_____
G.	Other Assets	+	_____
H.	Your Total Assets (add lines A–G)	=	_____

Liabilities or Debt (What You Owe)

Current Debt

I.	Current Bills		_____
J.	Credit Card Debt	+	_____

Long-Term Debt

K.	Housing	+	_____
L.	Automobile Loans	+	_____
M.	Other Debt	+	_____
N.	Your Total Debt (add lines I–M)	=	_____

Your Net Worth

H.	Total Assets		_____
N.	Less: Total Debt	–	_____
O.	Equals: Your Net Worth	=	_____

A Simplified Income Statement

Your Take-Home Pay

A. Total Income   A. _____

B. Total Income Taxes   − B. _____

C. After-Tax Income Available for Living Expenditures
or Take-Home Pay (line A minus line B)   = C. _____

Your Living Expenses

D. Total Housing Expenditures   D. _____

E. Total Food Expenditures   + E. _____

F. Total Clothing and Personal Care Expenditures   + F. _____

G. Total Transportation Expenditures   + G. _____

H. Total Recreation Expenditures   + H. _____

I. Total Medical Expenditures   + I. _____

J. Total Insurance Expenditures   + J. _____

K. Total Other Expenditures   + K. _____

L. Total Living Expenditures
(add lines D–K)   = L. _____

M. Income Available for Savings and Investment
(line C minus line L)   = M. _____

1996 Tax Rates

Taxable Income	Tax
Single	
Up to $24,000	15% of taxable income
$24,001 to $58,150	$3,600 plus 28% of amount over $24,000
$58,151 to $121,300	$13,162 plus 31% of amount over $58,150
$121,301 to $263,750	$32,738.50 plus 36% of amount over $121,300
Over $263,750	$84,020.50 plus 39.6% of amount over $263,750
Married Filing Jointly and Surviving Spouses	
Up to $40,100	15% of taxable income
$40,101 to $96,900	$6,015 plus 28% of amount over $40,100
$96,901 to $147,700	$21,919 plus 31% of amount over $96,900
$147,701 to $263,750	$37,667 plus 36% of amount over $147,700
Over $263,750	$79,445 plus 39.6% of amount over $263,750
Heads of Household	
Up to $32,150	15% of taxable income
$32,151 to $83,050	$4,822.50 plus 28% of amount over $32,150
$83,051 to $134,500	$19,074.50 plus 31% of amount over $83,050
$134,501 to $263,750	$35,024 plus 36% of amount over $134,500
Over $263,750	$81,554 plus 39.6% of amount over $263,750
Married Filing Separately	
Up to $20,050	15% of taxable income
$20,051 to $48,450	$3,007.50 plus 28% of amount over $20,050
$48,451 to $73,850	$10,959.50 plus 31% of amount over $48,450
$73,851 to $131,875	$18,833.50 plus 36% of amount over $73,850
Over $131,875	$39,722.50 plus 39.6% of amount over $131,875

YOU MIGHT BE ABLE TO USE FORM 1040Z IF ...

- ☐ Your Filing Status is Either Single or Married Filing Jointly
- ☐ You Do Not Itemize Deductions
- ☐ Your Taxable Income is Less Than $50,000
- ☐ Your Taxable Interest Income is Less Than $400
- ☐ You Have No Dependents
- ☐ You Are Not Making a Deductible Contribution to an IRA
- ☐ You Do Not Have Alimony, Taxable Pension Benefits, or Social Security Benefits to Report

YOU MIGHT BE ABLE TO USE FORM 1040A IF ...

- ☐ You Do Not Itemize Deductions
- ☐ Your Taxable Income is Less Than $50,000
- ☐ The Only Adjustment You Make to Income is an IRA Contribution
- ☐ You Do Not Have Alimony or Capital Gains to Report

WORKSHEET G.10

1996 Tax Year—Calculating Your Federal Income Tax: Assuming You Are Single with No Dependents

Income Range	A Tax Rate (%)	×	B Amount of Your Adjusted Gross Income Within This Range	=	C Tax
$0–$6,550[a]	0%		_____		_____
$6,551–$30,550[b]	15		_____		_____
$30,551–$64,700	28		_____		_____
$64,701–$127,850	31		_____		_____
$127,851–$270,300	36		_____		_____
Over $270,300	39.6		_____		_____
Totals					_____

[a]Because of the standard deduction of $4,000 and the exemption of $2,550 (tax year 1996), the first $6,550 of income is not taxed (keep in mind, this assumes you are single with no dependents and that no one else can claim you as a dependent on their tax return).

[b]The federal income tax brackets are based upon taxable income, not upon your adjusted gross income. Taxable income, equals your adjusted gross income less your deduction and exemption amount. Thus, if your deduction and exemption amount is $6,550, then the 15 percent marginal tax bracket would go from $6,550 to $30,550 (that is, $6,550 + $24,000) of adjusted gross income.

Note: Based on 1996 tax rates.

WORKSHEET G.11 (from Figure 5.3)

Choosing a Financial Institution

THE THREE C'S OF CHOOSING A FINANCIAL INSTITUTION TO BANK WITH

	Financial Institution 1	Financial Institution 2	Financial Institution 3
COST			
• Fees	_____	_____	_____
• Rates	_____	_____	_____
• Minimum Balances	_____	_____	_____
• Per-Check Charges	_____	_____	_____
CONVENIENCE			
• Location	_____	_____	_____
• Access to ATMs	_____	_____	_____
• Availability of Safety Deposit Boxes	_____	_____	_____
• Availability of Direct Deposit Services	_____	_____	_____
• Availability of Overdraft Protection	_____	_____	_____
• Availability of All Banking Services You Desire	_____	_____	_____
CONSIDERATION			
• Personal Attention Provided	_____	_____	_____
• Financial Advice That You Are Comfortable Accessing	_____	_____	_____
• A Banking Staff That Is Out to Serve You	_____	_____	_____
SAFETY—THE FINAL CONSIDERATION			
• Federal Deposit Insurance	_____	_____	_____

Worksheet for Balancing Your Checking Account

1. Record in your check register all items that appear on the monthly statement you received from your bank that have not previously been entered, for example, cash withdrawals from an ATM, automatic transfers, service charges, and any other transactions.
2. In your checking-account register, check off any deposits or credits and checks or debits shown on the monthly statement from your bank.
3. In the Deposits and Credits section below (section A), list any deposits that have been made since the date of the statement.

Section A: Deposits and Credits

Date	Amount
1.	
2.	
3.	
4.	
5.	
6.	

Total Amount: _____

4. In the Outstanding Checks and Debits section below (section B), list any checks and debits issued by you that have not yet been reported on your account statement.

Section B: Outstanding Checks and Debits

Check Number	Amount
1.	
2.	
3.	
4.	
5.	
6.	
7.	

Total Amount: _____

5. Write in the Ending Statement Balance provided in the monthly statement that you received from your bank. . . . . ._____
6. Write in the total amount of the Deposits and Credits you have made since the statement date (total of section A above). . . . .+ _____
7. Total the amounts in lines 5 and 6. . . . . = _____
8. Write in the total amounts of outstanding Checks and Debits (total of section B above). . . . . − _____
9. Subtract the amount in line 8 from the amount in line 7. This is your **Adjusted Statement Balance**. . . . . = _____

If your Adjusted Statement Balance as calculated above does not agree with your Account Register Balance:

A. Review last month's statement to reconcilement to make sure any differences were corrected.
B. Check to make sure that all deposits, interest earned, and service charges shown on the monthly statement from your bank are included in your account register.
C. Check your addition and subtraction in both your account register and in this month's checking-account balance reconcilement above.

How Many Months It Takes to Eliminate Your Credit Card Debt if You Pay a Constant Percentage of Your Initial Balance Each Month

STEP 1

Find the row that corresponds to the percentage of your initial balance that you intend to pay off each month. If you have an initial outstanding balance of $5,000 and you intend to pay off $150 each month, you would be paying off $150/$5,000 = 3% each month. Thus, you should look in the 3% row.

STEP 2

Find the column that corresponds to the annual percentage that you pay on your credit card. If your card charges 15%, look in the 15% column.

STEP 3

The intersection of the payments row and the credit card interest column shows how many months it would take to pay off your initial balance. If you pay off 3% of your initial balance each month and the card charges 15%, it would take 43 months to pay off your initial balance.

ANNUAL CREDIT CARD INTEREST RATE

Each Month Pay This Percentage of the Initial Outstanding Balance	9%	12%	15%	18%
2%	63 months	70 months	79 months	93 months
3%	39 months	41 months	43 months	47 months
5%	22 months	22 months	23 months	24 months
10%	10 months	11 months	11 months	11 months
15%	7 months	7 months	7 months	7 months

Using the Rule of 78s

A.
To determine the portion of the interest that would be avoided if the loan is repaid early.

B.
To determine the dollar value of the total finance charges that would be avoided by repaying the loan early.

STEP 1
Sum up *all* the months' digits.

There are two ways this can be done. One way is to number each month in descending order down to 1. That is, if it is a 12-month loan, the first month would be assigned 12, the second month 11, and so forth, and then add up these numbers. Alternatively, you can calculate the sum of the months' digits by applying the following formula:
sum of digits = $(N/2)(N+1)$ where N is the number of months the loan will be outstanding.

Step 1 = $(N/2)(N+1)$ = _____

STEP 2
Sum the *remaining* months' digits.

Sum the digits from 1 to the number of payments remaining when the loan obligation is repaid. For example, if the loan will be repaid in 6 months, then, $1+2+3+4+5+6=21$.

Step 2 = _____

STEP 3
Divide step 2 by step 1.

Divide the sum of the digits for the months remaining in the loan (step 2) by the sum of all the months' digits (step 1). This gives you the portion of the interest that would be avoided if the loan is repaid early.

$\dfrac{\text{Step 2}}{\text{Step 1}} = $ _____
= _____ = **Step 3**

STEP 4
Multiply step 3 by the total finance charges.

This gives you the dollar value of the total finance charges [which is all payments (number of months times the dollar amount of the monthly payments) minus the amount financed (that is, what you borrowed)] that would be avoided by repaying the loan early.

(Step 3) _____
× (total finance charges) _____
= _____

Credit Evaluation Worksheet

Kind of Debt	Interest Rate (APR)	Annual Fee	Last Finance Charge	Minimum Payment	Balance Outstanding
CREDIT CARDS					
CONSUMER LOANS					
AUTO LOANS					
MORTGAGE LOANS					
OTHER LOANS					

Before You Buy

- [ ] Take advantage of sales, but compare prices. Don't assume an item is a bargain just because it's advertised as one.

- [ ] Don't rush into a large purchase because the "price is only good today."

- [ ] Be aware of such extra charges as delivery fees, installation charges, service costs, and postage and handling fees. Add them into the total cost.

- [ ] Ask about the seller's refund or exchange policy.

- [ ] Don't sign a contract without reading it. Don't sign a contract if there are any blank spaces in it or if you don't understand it. In some states, it is possible to sign away your home to someone else.

- [ ] Before buying a product or service, contact your consumer protection office to see if there are automatic cancellation periods for the purchase you are making. In some states, there are cancellation periods for dating clubs, health clubs, and time-share and campground memberships. Federal law gives you cancellation rights for certain door-to-door sales.

- [ ] Walk out or hang up on high-pressure sales tactics. Don't be forced or pressured into buying something.

- [ ] Don't do business over the telephone with companies you don't know.

- [ ] Be suspicious of P.O. box addresses. They might be mail drops. If you have a complaint, you might have trouble locating the company.

- [ ] Don't respond to any prize or gift offer that requires you to pay even a small amount of money.

- [ ] Don't rely on a salesperson's promises. Get everything in writing.

SOURCE: U.S. Office of Consumer Affairs, *Consumer's Resource Handbook*, 1997.

Buying a Used Car

- ☐ Check newspaper ads and used-car guides at a local library so you know what's a fair price for the car you want.

- ☐ Remember, prices are negotiable. You also can look up repair recalls for car models you might be considering.

- ☐ Call the Auto Safety Hotline at 800-424-9393 to get recall information on a car. Authorized dealers of that make of vehicle must do recall work for free no matter how old the car is.

- ☐ Shop during daylight hours so that you can thoroughly inspect the car and take a test-drive. Don't forget to check all the lights, air conditioner, heater, and other parts of the electrical system.

- ☐ Don't agree to buy a car unless you've had it inspected by an independent mechanic of your choice.

- ☐ Ask questions about the previous ownership and mechanical history of the car. Contact the former owner to find out if the car was in an accident or had any other problems.

- ☐ Ask the previous owner or the manufacturer for a copy of the original manufacturer's warranty. It still might be in effect and transferable to you.

- ☐ Don't sign anything that you don't understand. Read all documents carefully. Negotiate the changes you want and get them written into the contract.

SOURCE: U.S. Office of Consumer Affairs, *Consumer's Resource Handbook*, 1997.

WORKSHEET G.18
(from Figure 8.4)

Tips on Buying a New Car

❏ Evaluate your needs and financial situation. Read consumer magazines and test-drive several models before you make a final choice.

❏ Find out the dealer's invoice price for the car and options. This is what the manufacturer charged the dealer for the car. You can order this information for a small fee from consumer publications you can find at your local library.

❏ Find out if the manufacturer is offering rebates that will lower the cost.

❏ Get price quotes from several dealers. Find out if the amounts quoted are the prices before or after the rebates are deducted.

❏ Keep your trade-in negotiations separate from the main deal.

❏ Compare financing from different sources—for example, banks, credit unions, and other dealers—before you sign the contract.

❏ Read and understand every document you are asked to sign. Don't sign anything until you have made a final decision to buy.

❏ Think twice about adding expensive extras you probably don't need to your purchase, for example, credit insurance, service contracts, or rustproofing.

❏ Inspect and test-drive the vehicle you plan to buy, but don't take possession of the car until the whole deal, including financing, is finalized.

❏ Don't buy on impulse or because the salesperson is pressuring you to make a decision.

SOURCE: U.S. Office of Consumer Affairs, *Consumer's Resource Handbook,* 1997.

Leasing May Make Sense if . . .

- [ ] The lease under consideration is a closed-end, not an open-end, lease.
- [ ] You are financially stable.
- [ ] It is important to you that you have a new car every 2 to 4 years.
- [ ] You do not drive over 15,000 miles annually.
- [ ] You take good care of your car and it ages with only normal wear and tear.
- [ ] You are not bothered by the thought of monthly payments that never end.
- [ ] You use your car for business travel.
- [ ] You do not modify your car (e.g., add superchargers or after-market suspension components).
- [ ] The manufacturer of the car you are interested in is offering subvented leases.

Worksheet for the Lease versus Purchase Decision

COST OF PURCHASING

Your Numbers

a. Agreed-upon purchase price

b. Down payment

c. Total loan payments (monthly loan payment of _____ × ___ months)

d. Opportunity cost on down payment (_% opportunity cost × _ years × line b)

e. Less: Expected market value of the car at the end of the loan

f. **Total cost of purchasing (lines b + c + d − e)**

COST OF LEASING

g. Down payment (capitalized cost reduction) of _____ plus security deposit of _____

h. Total lease payments (monthly lease payments of _____ × ___ months)

i. Opportunity cost of total initial payment (_% opportunity cost × _ years × line g)

j. Any end-of-lease charges (perhaps for excess miles), if applicable

k. Less: Refund of security deposit

l. **Total cost of leasing (lines g + h + i + j − k)**

WORKSHEET G.21

Monthly Mortgage Payments Required to Repay a $10,000 Loan with Different Interest Rates and Different Maturities

Rate of Interest	Loan Maturity					
	10 Years	15 Years	20 Years	25 Years	30 Years	40 Years
5.0%	$106.07	$ 79.08	$ 66.00	$ 58.46	$ 53.68	$ 48.22
5.5	108.53	81.71	68.79	61.41	56.79	51.58
6.0	111.02	84.39	71.64	64.43	59.96	50.22
6.5	113.55	87.11	74.56	67.52	63.21	58.55
7.0	116.11	89.88	77.53	70.68	66.53	62.14
7.5	118.71	92.71	80.56	73.90	69.93	65.81
8.0	121.33	95.57	83.65	77.19	73.38	69.53
8.5	123.99	98.48	86.79	80.53	76.90	73.31
9.0	126.68	101.43	89.98	83.92	80.47	77.14
9.5	129.40	104.43	93.22	87.37	84.09	81.01
10.0	132.16	107.47	96.51	90.88	87.76	84.91
10.5	134.94	110.54	99.84	94.42	91.48	88.86
11.0	137.76	113.66	103.22	98.02	95.24	92.83
11.5	140.60	116.82	106.65	101.65	99.03	96.83
12.0	143.48	120.02	110.11	105.33	102.86	100.85
12.5	146.38	123.26	113.62	109.04	106.73	104.89
13.0	149.32	126.53	117.16	112.79	110.62	108.95
13.5	152.27	129.83	120.74	116.56	114.54	113.03
14.0	155.27	133.17	124.35	120.38	118.49	117.11
14.5	158.29	136.55	128.00	124.22	122.46	121.21
15.0	161.33	139.96	131.68	128.08	126.44	125.32

Calculating monthly payments on a loan:

STEP 1: Divide the amount borrowed by $10,000. For example, for a $100,000 loan, the step 1 value would be $100,000/$10,000 = 10.

Step 1 = _____

STEP 2: Find the monthly payment for a $10,000 loan at the appropriate interest rate and maturity in the table above. For a 15-year mortgage at 9%, the value would be $101.43.

Step 2 = _____

STEP 3: Multiply the step 1 value by the step 2 value. In the example, this is 10 × $101.43 = $1,014.30.

Step 3 = _____

WORKSHEET G.22 (from Figure 8.10)

Worksheet for the Rent versus Buy Decision

THE COST OF RENTING

	1 year	7 years
a. Total monthly rent costs (monthly rent \$_____ × 12 months × no. years)	a. _____	a. _____
b. Total renter's insurance (annual renter's insurance \$_____ × no. years)	+ b. _____	+ b. _____
c. After-tax opportunity cost of interest lost because of having to make a security deposit (security deposit of \$_____ × after-tax rate of return of _____% × no. years)	+ c. _____	+ c. _____
d. **Total cost of renting (lines a + b + c)**	= d. _____	= d. _____

THE COST OF BUYING

	1 year	7 years
e. Total mortgage payments (monthly payments \$_____ × 12 months × no. years)	e. _____	e. _____
f. Property taxes on the new house (property taxes of \$_____ × no. years)	+ f. _____	+ f. _____
g. Homeowner's insurance (annual homeowner's insurance \$_____ × no. years)	+ g. _____	+ g. _____
h. Additional operating costs beyond those of renting: Maintenance, repairs, and any additional utilities and heating costs (additional annual operating costs \$_____ × no. years)	+ h. _____	+ h. _____
i. After-tax opportunity cost of interest lost because of having to make a down payment (down payment of \$_____ × after-tax rate of return of _____% × no. years)	+ i. _____	+ i. _____
j. Closing costs, including points (closing costs of \$_____)	+ j. _____	+ j. _____
k. Less savings: Total mortgage payments going toward the loan principal*	− k. _____	− k. _____
l. Less savings: Estimated appreciation in the value of the home *less* sales commission at the end of the period (current market value of house \$_____ × annual growth in house value of _____% × no. years − sales commission at end of the period of _____% × future value of house)	− l. _____ [†]	− l. _____
m. **Equals: Total cost of buying a home for those who do not itemize (lines e + f + g + h + i + j − k − l)**	= m. _____	= m. _____

Additional *savings* to homebuyers who itemize

	1 year	7 years
n. Less savings: Tax savings from the tax-deductibility of the interest portion of the mortgage payments (total amount of interest payments made × marginal tax rate _____%)	− n. _____	− n. _____
o. Less savings: Tax savings from the tax-deductibility of the property taxes on the new house [(property taxes of \$_____ × marginal tax rate of _____%) × no. years]	− o. _____	− o. _____
p. Less savings: Tax savings from the tax-deductibility of the points portion of the closing costs (total points paid of \$_____ × marginal tax rate of _____%)	− p. _____	− p. _____
q. **Total cost of buying a home to homebuyers who itemize (line m minus lines n through p)**	= q. _____	= q. _____

Advantage of buying to those who *do not itemize* = Total cost of renting − Total cost of buying for those who *do not itemize*: if negative, rent; if positive, buy
(line d − line m) .... ═════ ═════

Advantage of buying to those who *itemize* = Total cost of renting − Total cost of buying for those who *itemize*: if negative, rent; if positive, buy
(line d − line q) .... ═════ ═════

*The total interest and principal payments can be calculated directly or approximated. To approximate the total annual interest payments, multiply the outstanding size of the loan by the interest rate, then multiply this by the number of years. While the approximation method works well for short time horizons, it is less accurate for longer time horizons.
†Note: If you only own the home for 1 year, the value here may be negative, meaning the sales commission is greater than the appreciation in home value. If this is the case, this is an additional cost, not a savings, and we are subtracting a negative—in effect, adding in the cost of buying the house.

WORKSHEET G.23 (from Figure 8.11)

Worksheet for Calculating the Maximum Monthly Mortgage Payment and Mortgage Size for Which You Can Qualify

METHOD 1 Determine Your Maximum Monthly Mortgage Payment Using the Ability to Pay, PITI Ratio.

a. Monthly income (annual income divided by 12) _____

b. Times 0.28: Percentage of PITI (principal, interest, taxes, and insurance) to your monthly gross income that lenders will lend in the form of a mortgage loan (multiply line a by 0.28) $\times 0.28 =$ _____

c. Less: Estimated monthly real estate tax and insurance payments $-$ _____

d. Equals: Your maximum monthly mortgage payment using the 28% of PITI ratio $=$ _____

To Determine the Maximum Mortgage Loan Level Using the Maximum Monthly Mortgage Payments as Determined Using the PITI Ratio (line d):

STEP 1: Monthly mortgage payment for a $10,000 mortgage with a _____ year maturity and a _____ % interest rate (using Table 8.1) $=$ _____

STEP 2: Maximum mortgage level = maximum monthly mortgage payment (line d) divided by the monthly mortgage payment on a $10,000, _____ %, _____ year mortgage (step 1 above) times $10,000 = (line d/step 1) $\times$ $10,000 $=$ _____

METHOD 2 Determine Your Maximum Monthly Mortgage Payment Using the Ability to Pay, PITI Plus Other Fixed Monthly Payments, Ratio.

e. Monthly income (annual income divided by 12) _____

f. Times 0.36: Percentage of PITI + current monthly fixed payments to your monthly gross income that lenders will lend in the form of a mortgage loan (multiply line e by 0.36) $\times 0.36 =$ _____

g. Less: Current nonmortgage debt payments on debt that will take over 10 months to pay off and other monthly legal obligations such as child support and alimony payments $-$ _____

h. Less: Estimated monthly real estate tax and insurance payments $-$ _____

i. Equals: Your maximum monthly mortgage payment using the 36% of PITI + other fixed monthly payments ratio (line f - g- h) $=$ _____

To Determine the Maximum Mortgage Loan Using the PITI Plus Other Fixed Monthly Payments Ratio (line i):

STEP 1: Monthly mortgage payment for a $10,000 mortgage with a _____ year maturity and a _____ % interest rate (using Table 8.1) $=$ _____

STEP 2: Maximum mortgage level = maximum monthly mortgage payment (line i) divided by the monthly mortgage payment on a $10,000, _____ %, _____ year mortgage (step 1 above) times $10,000 = (line i/step 1) $\times$ $10,000 $=$ _____

METHOD 3 Determine Your Maximum Mortgage Level Using the "80% of the Appraised Value of the House" Rule.

j. Funds available for down payment and closing costs _____

k. Less: Closing costs $-$ _____

l. Equals: Funds available for the down payment $=$ _____

m. Times 4: Maximum mortgage level using the "80% of the appraised value of the house" rule (the 20% down, line l, times 4 equals the 80% you can borrow) $\times 4 =$ _____

Conclusion: Maximum Mortgage Level for Which You Will Qualify
(the lower of the amounts using method 1, method 2, or method 3) $=$ _____

WORKSHEET G.24
(from Figure 8.15)

❑ Want to get out of a high-interest-rate loan to take advantage of lower rates. This is a good idea only if they intend to stay in the house long enough to make the additional fees worthwhile.

❑ Have an adjustable-rate mortgage (ARM) and want a fixed-rate loan to have the certainty of knowing exactly what the mortgage payment will be for the life of the loan.

❑ Want to convert to an ARM with a lower interest rate or more protective features (such as a better rate and payment caps) than the ARM they currently have.

❑ Want to build up equity more quickly by converting to a loan with a shorter term.

❑ Want to draw on the equity built up in their home to get cash for a major purchase or for their children's education.

SOURCE: *A Guide to Mortgage Refinancing* (Washington, DC: Federal Housing Administration, 1995).

Worksheet for Refinancing Analysis

Monthly Benefits from Refinancing	**Your Numbers**
a. Present monthly mortgage payments	_____
b. Mortgage payments after refinancing	_____
c. Monthly savings, pretax (line a — line b)	_____
d. Additional tax on monthly savings (line c × __% tax rate)	_____
e. Monthly savings on an after-tax basis (line c — line d)	_____

Cost of Refinancing

f. Total after-tax closing costs, including any prepayment penalty incurred	_____

Number of Months Needed to Break Even

g. Months needed for interest saved to equal the refinancing costs incurred as a result of taking out a new mortgage loan (line f ÷ line e)	_____

**WORKSHEET G.26
(from Figure 9.2)**

Worksheet for Estimating Life Insurance Needs

TOTAL NEEDS

**Step 1: Immediate
Needs—Cleanup Funds**

Final Illness Costs (assumed equal to your health insurance deductible)	a. _____	
Estate Administration Costs (assumed equal to 4% of your assets)	+ b. _____	
Burial Costs	+ c. _____	
Federal Estate Taxes (if any due)	+ d. _____	
State Estate Taxes	+ e. _____	
Additional Legal Fees	+ f. _____	
Other Immediate Needs	+ g. _____	
Total Immediate Needs (add lines a through g)		= h. _____

Step 2: Debt Elimination Funds

Credit Card and Consumer/Installment Debt	i. _____	
Auto Debt Outstanding	+ j. _____	
Desired Mortgage Reduction	+ k. _____	
Other Debt to Be Paid Off at Your Death	+ l. _____	
Total Debt Elimination Funds (add lines i through l)		= m. _____

Step 3: Immediate Transitional Funds

Schooling Expenses for Surviving Spouse	n. _____	
Child Care and Housekeeping Expenses	+ o. _____	
Other Transitional Needs	+ p. _____	
Total Immediate Transitional Funds (add lines n through p)		= q. _____

Step 4: Dependency Expenses (family needs while children are in school and dependent on family support)

Current Household Expenses (estimated as income less savings)	r. _____	
Less: Deceased's Expenses (estimated as 30% of line r if surviving family includes only one member, 26% for a surviving family of two, 22% for a surviving family of three, and dropping 2% more for each additional family member)	− s. _____	
Less: Spousal Income	− t. _____	
Less: Social Security Survivors' Benefits	− u. _____	
Less: Pension Benefits and Income	− v. _____	
Income to Be Replaced Until Children Are Self-Supporting (line r − lines s through v)	= w. _____	

(continued)

Total Dependency Expenses or Money in Today's Dollars Needed
for Dependency Expenses (assuming the children have n years
until they become self-supporting and you can earn an $i\%$
after-tax and after-inflation return on your investments)
(line w $\times PVIFA_{i\%,\,n\,yr}$) = (_____ $\times PVIFA$___%,___ yr) =
(_____ $\times$_____)   = x. _____

Step 5: Spousal Life Income (spousal needs after children are self-supporting)

Desired Spousal Income   y. _____

Total Spousal Life Income or Money in Today's Dollars to Provide for
Desired Spousal Income (assuming n years until the children become
self-supporting and m years until the spouse qualifies for Social
Security or retirement income, and assuming you can earn an $i\%$
after-tax and after-inflation return on your investments)
[line y $\times (PVIFA_{i\%,\,m\,yr} - PVIFA_{i\%,\,n\,yr})$] =
[_____ $\times (PVIFA$___%,___ yr $- PVIFA$___%,___ yr)] =
[_____ $\times$(_____ $-$ _____)]   = z. _____

Step 6: Educational Expenses for Your Children

Total Educational Expenses (private school needs plus total
college needs)   aa. _____

Step 7: Retirement Income

Additional Desired Annual Income
at Retirement   bb. _____

Total Retirement Income or Money in Today's Dollars to Provide for
Desired Retirement Income (assuming retirement in m years and
desiring the additional income for p additional years, and
assuming you can earn an $i\%$ after-tax and after-inflation return
on your investments)
[line bb $\times (PVIFA_{i\%,\,m+p\,yr} - PVIFA_{i\%,\,m\,yr})$] =
[_____ $\times (PVIFA$___%,___ yr $- PVIFA$___%,___ yr)] =
[_____ $\times$(_____ $-$ _____)]   = cc. _____

Step 8: Total Funds Needed in Today's Dollars to Cover Needs

Total   (lines h $+$ m $+$ q $+$ x $+$ z $+$ aa $+$ cc)   = dd. _____

Step 9: Assets and Insurance Available to Cover Needs

Cash from Current Insurance Policies   ee. _____
Retirement Savings and Investments   ff. _____
Other Assets   gg. _____
Total Assets (add lines ee $+$ ff $+$ gg)   = hh. _____

Step 10: Additional Insurance Needs

Additional Insurance Needs (line dd $-$ line hh)   = _____

WORKSHEET G.27
(from Table 9.5)

❑ **Are you a full-time insurance agent?** Agent's Answer:

_____

_____

Preferred Answer: You shouldn't deal with someone who only works part-time as an insurance agent. Your insurance agent needs to be knowledgeable.

❑ **How long have you been a full-time insurance agent?** Agent's Answer:

_____

_____

Preferred Answer: You should only deal with someone with experience. While a new agent may be competent, a more established agent may have experience you can benefit from. Moreover, an established agent may not have the financial pressure to sell you a policy that doesn't precisely fit your needs.

❑ **What life insurance companies do you represent?** Agent's Answer:

_____

_____

Preferred Answer: You shouldn't consider an agent that doesn't represent at least one company with a top rating from A. M. Best for 10 consecutive years.

❑ **Are you a CLU?** Agent's Answer:

_____

_____

Preferred Answer: A CLU is preferred, particularly if you're considering something other than term insurance and if you're seeking advice.

❑ **Will I be allowed to keep the insurance proposal that you prepare for me?** Agent's Answer:

_____

_____

Preferred Answer: You shouldn't consider an agent that doesn't allow you to keep the proposal.

❑ **Would you be willing to inform me of the commission you'll receive on any policies you recommend?** Agent's Answer:

_____

_____

Preferred Answer: You want to make sure that your agent is working on your behalf. By knowing what the agent's interests are in selling various policies, you may be better able to avoid being sold a policy that is of more benefit to the agent than to you.

❑ **Do you have any clients who are willing to recommend you?** Agent's Answer:

_____

_____

Preferred Answer: Your agent should either supply you with a listing of satisfied customers, or testimonial letters from customers. In short, you shouldn't consider an agent without a recommendation.

Should You Buy Life Insurance?

LIFE INSURANCE IS <u>NOT</u> NECESSARY IF:

❑ **You're single and don't have any dependents.**

❑ **You're married, a double-income couple, with no children.** Consider life insurance only if you're concerned that your surviving spouse's lifestyle will suffer if you die.

❑ **You're married, but don't work.** Consider life insurance only if you have young children and your spouse would have financial problems with day care and housekeeping if you die.

❑ **You're retired.** Consider life insurance only if your spouse couldn't live on your savings, including Social Security and your pension, if you die.

CONSIDER LIFE INSURANCE IF:

❑ **You have children.** You should have coverage for raising and educating your children until they are financially self-sufficient.

❑ **You're married, a single-income couple, with no children.** You should have insurance to allow your surviving spouse to maintain his or her lifestyle until he or she can become self-sufficient.

❑ **You own your own business.** A life insurance policy can allow your family to pay off any business debt if you die.

❑ **The value of your estate is over the tax-free estate transfer threshold which, for the tax year 1997, was $600,000 if you're single, or $1,200,000 if you're married.** As you will see in chapter 18, life insurance can be an effective tool for passing on an estate without incurring taxes.

WORKSHEET G.29
(from Figure 10.3)

Worksheet for Health Care Insurance Shopping

☐ 1. The ideal plan is group health insurance through your employer.

☐ 2. Don't put off buying health care insurance—buy it while you're healthy.

☐ 3. Consider only a high-quality insurance company with either an A++ or an A+ rating from A. M. Best. Never consider TV-celebrity-advertised insurance.

☐ 4. Look for group insurance—it's generally cheaper.

☐ 5. Look for companies that provide fast, fair, and courteous claim service.

☐ 6. Avoid policies with major exclusions and limitations.

☐ 7. Get comprehensive health insurance; avoid single-disease (for example, cancer) insurance and accident (as opposed to comprehensive health including illness) insurance.

☐ 8. Only consider insurance that is noncancelable or guaranteed renewable.

☐ 9. Consider Blue Cross and Blue Shield.

☐ 10. Consider joining an HMO or a PPO.

☐ 11. Take as high a deductible and coinsurance payments as you can afford. This reduces your premiums greatly.

☐ 12. Consider a policy that covers mental and emotional disorders.

Worksheet for Estimating How Much Disability Insurance Coverage You Need

1. Current monthly after-tax job-related income* _____

2. Existing disability coverage on an *after-tax-basis*

   - Social Security benefits† _____

   - Disability insurance from employer + _____

   - Veterans' benefits and other federal and state disability insurance + _____

   - Other disability coverage in place + _____

   Total existing coverage = _____

3. Added disability coverage needed to maintain current level of after-tax job-related income in the event of a disability (subtract 2 from 1) _____

Note: We haven't included workers' compensation disability benefits because they accompany only work-related injuries.
*Keep in mind that your investment income won't stop with a disability. Only your income from working will stop. Thus, only the portion of your income from working that you rely upon to maintain your current standard of living must be replaced. This may also include savings for such goals as your children's college education and other goals. However, you should keep in mind that your goals will generally change substantially if you are permanently disabled.
†To get an estimate of what these benefits might be, you can call the Social Security Administration at 800-772-1213 for a Personal Earnings and Benefits Estimate Statement.

Long-Term Health Care Provisions

NECESSARY

☐ **Selection of Company.** Consider only high-quality insurance companies with either an A++ or an A+ rating from A. M. Best. Never consider TV-celebrity-advertised insurance.

☐ **Qualifying for Benefits.** The insured is unable to perform *at most* two "activities of daily living" (ADLs) without assistance.

☐ **Qualifying for Benefits.** Policy includes coverage for Alzheimer's and Parkinson's disease.

☐ **Qualifying for Benefits.** Hospital stay not required for benefits.

☐ **Benefit Period.** A minimum 3- to 6-year benefit period.

☐ **Inflation Adjustment.** The policy should give you the option of purchasing inflation coverage.

☐ **Noncancelability.** The policy should not be cancelable.

DESIRABLE, BUT NOT NECESSARY— COST-BENEFIT TRADE-OFFS MUST BE CONSIDERED

☐ **Type of Care.** Home care, adult day care, and hospice care for the terminally ill are all desirable provisions.

☐ **Benefit Period.** Women should consider longer benefit periods.

COST-REDUCING PROVISION TO CONSIDER

☐ **Waiting Period.** Consider a waiting period of 100 days or more—if affordable.

PROVISIONS TO AVOID—NOT WORTH THE COST

☐ **Waiver of Premium.** While desirable, it is generally too expensive to warrant serious consideration.

☐ **Nonforfeiture Provision.** Simply too expensive.

WORKSHEET G.32

How Much Coverage Do You Need?

If you haven't reviewed your homeowners policy in the last few years, your home may be underinsured. The house you insured for $115,000 five years ago could cost $150,000 to rebuild today. Any additions, renovations, or major purchases could also have boosted your coverage needs. And if your other assets have grown substantially, your personal liability limits should be adjusted to keep up with them. This worksheet can help you determine how much insurance you need.

HOW MUCH FOR THE HOUSE?

Buy enough insurance to cover the cost of rebuilding your home. That may bear little relation to its market value. A finely crafted 19th-century house in a run-down 20th-century neighborhood could cost far more to rebuild than it cost to buy. But a modest home on a prime piece of real estate might be rebuilt for a fraction of its purchase price. If the limit of your homeowners coverage is based on your mortgage, make sure that's enough to cover the current cost of rebuilding.

To determine the rebuilding cost, ask an insurance agent to calculate the current cost of construction for a house like yours or hire a professional appraiser to do it. You can make your own ball-park estimate by multiplying the square footage of your house by the current building cost per square foot for similar homes in your area. An insurance agent, real-estate agent, or county builders association should be able to give you the rough square-foot cost for your type of home.

Most insurance companies recommend that you insure your home for 100 percent of the rebuilding cost, including the foundation. Though very few homes are totally destroyed, it does happen—as victims of the 1991 fire in Oakland, Calif., can attest. There, foundations melted in the 2000-degree heat. If your home isn't covered for 100 percent of its replacement cost, in the event of total loss you might not receive enough insurance money to replace it with a house of similar size or quality.

In any case, you should buy insurance for at least 80 percent of your home's replacement value. If you buy less, you forfeit the right to collect the full replacement value of insured property, even for a partial loss. For example, if the replacement cost of your house is $100,000 and you have a fire in the kitchen that causes $10,000 in damage, you'll collect $10,000 as long as you have at least $80,000 in insurance.

If you're insured for less, the company will make two estimates and pay whichever is larger. The first estimate is the actual cash value—the replacement cost minus depreciation. (If your $10,000 kitchen had depreciated 50 percent, its cash value would be only $5000.) The second estimate is based on the amount of insurance you carry. If your $100,000 house is insured for only $60,000, you have only 75 percent as much insurance as you should ($60,000 is 75 percent of $80,000). So the company would pay only 75 percent of your $10,000 claim, or $7500.

Your safest bet is to buy a guaranteed-replacement-cost policy, which will generally pay up to 20 or 50 percent more than the face value of the policy to rebuild your home. (A few companies offer unlimited coverage.) With such a policy, the insurer automatically adjusts the amount of insurance each year to keep up with rising construction costs in your area. The policy also protects you against the unexpected, such as a sudden increase in construction costs due to a shortage of building supplies (a problem for Hurricane Andrew victims). Companies that offer this option usually require that you insure your house for 100 percent of its replacement cost to begin with. Owners of high-risk or older homes may not be eligible for this type of policy.

The replacement cost of your home is .... $_____ .

ARE YOU PROTECTED AGAINST INFLATION?

If you don't have a policy that automatically adjusts the amount of your coverage to reflect rising construction costs in your area, you can add an inflation-guard clause to your regular policy. Some insurers offer this protection free, others charge $2 to $5 a year.

You (❑do/❑don't) need an inflation-guard clause.

HAVE BUILDING CODES CHANGED SINCE YOUR HOME WAS BUILT?

Local building codes require that structures be built to certain minimum standards, which can change over time. If your home is severely damaged, you might be required to rebuild it to current codes. That could mean a costly change in design or building materials. Even guaranteed replacement cost policies

(continued)

do not generally cover the expense. However, many insurers offer an endorsement that will pay for some or all of the upgrading cost. Ask your insurance agent or local building inspector's office about any change in building codes that might affect your home.

You (❑do/❑don't) need an endorsement for building-code upgrading.

IS YOUR HOME IN AN AREA PRONE TO FLOODS OR EARTHQUAKES?

Those two risks are not covered by standard home-owners policies. Most insurers, however, will write earthquake coverage as an endorsement. (California insurers are required to offer it to homeowners-insurance policyholders.) The Federal Government sells a separate policy for flood insurance through the National Flood Insurance Program.

You (❑do/❑don't) need coverage for floods or earthquakes.

HOW MUCH FOR PERSONAL PROPERTY?

You'll have a much easier time collecting on a claim if you can establish the value of your property. So take an inventory of your personal possessions. Go room to room and list the valuable items you own, any serial numbers (usually found on the bottom or back of appliances), the approximate purchase dates, and prices paid. Your insurance agent can probably give you an inventory form. It's a good idea to photograph or videotape your possessions as well. Store the inventory, any appraisals, and pictures or videotapes in a safe place away from your home, such as in a safe-deposit box or where you work.

Once you know what you have, estimate what it would all cost to replace. Most policies cover personal possessions for 50 percent of the insured value of the house. If, for instance, the house is covered for $100,000, the insurer will pay up to $50,000 for loss or damage of its contents. For a higher premium, you can increase that coverage to 75 percent.

Most policies do not cover damage to, or loss of, cars, aircraft, or pets. For some items, there are limits to coverage for theft. Those vary somewhat from company to company, but the following limits are typical: $200 on coin collections, gold, silver, and currency; $1000 on securities, deeds, manuscripts, and other valuable papers; $1000 on boats; $1000 to $2000 on jewelry, watches, and furs; $2500 on silver-ware; $2500 on firearms; $3000 on computers; and $2500 for business property kept at home. Those limits apply to each category of item, not each item. (You can buy additional insurance to raise the limits on any of these categories or to protect specific valu-ables, as we explain below.)

The value of your belongings is .....$_____.

DO YOU NEED REPLACEMENT-COST COVERAGE ON CONTENTS?

There are two ways to insure your personal property. An actual-cash-value policy pays the amount needed to replace the item, minus depreciation. If, for instance, a fire destroyed a sofa you paid $1000 for five years ago, you would receive only $750 for it, assuming it had a 10-year life and would cost $1500 to replace at today's prices. A replacement-cost policy would pay you $1500. For most people, replacement-cost coverage on property is worth the extra 10 to 15 percent that companies typically charge for it.

DO YOU NEED TO PROTECT SPECIFIC ITEMS?

You can protect a particularly valuable item with a floater. That's an endorsement tailored to a specific item; the coverage "floats" with the property wher-ever it goes.

Floaters can be used to cover jewelry, furs, cam-eras, computer equipment, musical instruments, sil-verware, stamps, coins, antiques, paintings, or other valuables. They can be written either as separate policies or as endorsements to standard policies. The property insured by a floater must be "scheduled"—described in terms of quantity, quality, style, manu-facturer, value, and so forth. In most cases, a profes-sional appraiser's report or a bill of sale is required. Floaters can cost from a few cents to a few dollars per $100 of coverage, depending on the item and the crime rate in your area. Floaters typically exclude such risks as war, nuclear accident, wear and tear, and confiscation by the Government.

You can also buy additional "blanket" coverage for a specific category of protection. For example, instead of buying a floater for an expensive wrist-watch, you might want to raise your coverage in the jewelry category from $1000 to $5000. Most blanket policies, however, limit the amount you can collect for any single item. The ceiling is usually between $500 and $5000.

You (❑do/❑don't) need a floater or blanket policy.

(continued)

HOW MUCH ARE OTHER STRUCTURES AND LANDSCAPING WORTH?

Most policies cover a structure that's detached from your house, such as a gazebo or freestanding garage, for up to 10 percent of the total insured value of your home. To qualify as "separate," a structure must be separated from the main house by a clear space, connected at most by a fence or utility line. Any structure that is connected by something more substantial, such as a shared roof, is not considered separate and should be figured into the total value of the house.

Trees, plants, and shrubs are generally covered for no more than 5 percent of the insurance on the house. They also aren't covered for as many perils. Wind damage, for instance, is usually excluded. If that's inadequate, ask about buying more coverage.

You (❏do/❏don't) need additional coverage for other structures or landscaping.

HOW MUCH LIABILITY COVERAGE DO YOU NEED?

Your homeowners policy offers liability protection for bodily injury and property damage. That covers injuries or damage caused by you, a member of your family, or a pet. Your insurance covers the injured person's claim and the cost of defending you if you are sued. The protection applies not only at home but elsewhere in the U.S. and Canada.

Most policies provide $100,000 in liability insurance, but some companies offer $200,000 or $300,000 in coverage as part of their basic policy. If yours provides only $100,000 in liability protection, you can raise it to $300,000 for about $10 a year. If your assets are much greater than the liability limits of your homeowners policy, you may want to purchase an additional "umbrella" policy that will extend your liability coverage to $1-million or more. It starts paying after your regular policy has reached its limit. Umbrella policies also extend the liability coverage of your auto insurance.

Umbrella policies provide broader coverage than typical homeowners policies. In addition to bodily injury and property damage, they cover false arrest, wrongful eviction, libel, slander, defamation of character, and invasion of privacy. Such policies usually cost about $150 to $200 a year for $1-million in coverage.

Your liability coverage should be....$_____

DO YOU HAVE A HOME OFFICE?

Most homeowners policies cover business equipment and furniture in your home for up to $2500. But they provide no coverage for business liability, which you might need if, for instance, a messenger slipped on your steps while delivering a business package. If you have a home office, you should consider buying additional business coverage. For about $20 to $30 a year, you can buy $5000 in coverage for business equipment and furniture, plus $100,000 in liability coverage.

You (❏do/❏don't) need additional home-office coverage.

WHAT SIZE DEDUCTIBLE SHOULD YOU GET?

Homeowners policies are sold with deductibles, the part of the loss you must pay on each claim before your insurance company kicks in. If you have a policy with a $250 deductible and you suffer a $700 loss, you pay $250 and your insurer pays $450.

The higher your deductible, the lower your premium. If you raise the deductible from $250 to $500, you may be able to trim more than 10 percent off your premium. Raise it to $1000 and you could save more than 25 percent. For example, if you buy $250,000 in guaranteed-replacement-cost coverage for a standard, wood-frame home in Atlanta, and opt for a $250 deductible, *State Farm* will charge approximately $850 a year. Raise that deductible to $1000 and the annual premium drops to $613, a reduction of nearly 28 percent. Even if you make a claim once every four years and have to pay the $1000 deductible, you'll come out ahead. (*State Farm* says the average policyholder makes a claim about once every 12 years.)

We recommend taking the highest deductible you could comfortably handle in the event of a claim.

You want a policy with a......$_____ deductible.

WORKSHEET G.33
(from Figure 11.1)

☐   1.   Determine the amount and type of homeowner's insurance you need.

_____

_____

☐   2.   Put together a listing of top-quality insurers (as listed in *A. M. Best's Key Rating Guide on Property and Casualty Insurers*) and insurance agents with a good local reputation who carry these insurers.

_____

_____

☐   3.   Consult with agents, letting them know what you're looking for. Give consideration to any recommendations or modifications they might suggest.

_____

_____

☐   4.   Get several bids on the total package, including all modifications, floaters, and extensions.

_____

_____

☐   5.   Conduct an annual review of your homeowner's insurance coverage.

_____

_____

WORKSHEET G.34 (from Figure 11.5)

Insurance Shopper's Worksheet

INSURANCE SHOPPER'S WORKSHEET

How much coverage do you want?	Write amount of coverage here	Write premiums from each company in these columns		
		COMPANY 1	COMPANY 2	COMPANY 3
1. Bodily injury liability				
2. Property damage liability				
3. Uninsured motorist				
4. Underinsured motorist				
5. Medical payments				
6. Personal injury protection (no-fault states)				
7. Collision				
a. $100 deductible				
b. $250 deductible				
c. $500 deductible				
d. $1000 deductible				
8. Comprehensive				
a. No deductible				
b. $50 deductible				
c. $100 deductible				
d. $250 deductible				
e. $500 deductible				
Subtotal A:				

Other charges or discounts:

		COMPANY 1	COMPANY 2	COMPANY 3
Membership fees				
Surcharges				
Discounts				
Subtotal B:				
Subtotal A plus Subtotal B equals your **TOTAL PREMIUM**				

Source: "Insurance Shopper's Worksheet," *Consumer Reports,* August 1992, p. 500. Copyright 1992 by Consumers Union of U.S., Inc., Yonkers, NY 10703–1057. Reprinted by permission from *Consumer Reports,* August 1992.

Insurance Tracker

Type of Coverage (Insurer and Policy Number)	Amount of Coverage, Deductibles, and Cost	Policy Location	Agent (Name, Phone Number)	Is This Coverage Adequate?
Life _____	_____	_____	_____	_____
Health Care _____	_____	_____	_____	_____
Disability _____	_____	_____	_____	_____
Long-Term Care _____	_____	_____	_____	_____
Homeowner's _____	_____	_____	_____	_____
Auto _____	_____	_____	_____	_____
Personal Umbrella Liability _____	_____	_____	_____	_____

WORKSHEET G.36

Investments and Property Inventory

INVESTMENTS

	Institution and Phone Number	Account Number	Purchase Date and Price	Location of Key Records
Mutual Funds	_____	_____	_____	_____
Brokerage Accounts (and location)	_____	_____	_____	_____
Other Investments (and location)	_____	_____	_____	_____

PROPERTY OWNED

Description	Purchase Date and Price	Outstanding Mortgages and Home Equity Loans (Lender and Account No.)	Location of Deed
Houses/Land (and location) _____	_____	_____	_____
Automobiles _____	_____	_____	_____
Other Property (and location) _____	_____	_____	_____

WORKSHEET G.37 (from Figure 17.2)

Worksheet for Funding Your Retirement Needs

Your Numbers

STEP 1: Estimate Your Annual Needs at Retirement.

A. Present level of your living expenditures on an after-tax basis

B. Times 0.80 equals: Base retirement expenditure level in today's dollars $\times 0.80$ = _____

C. Plus or minus: Anticipated increases or decreases in living expenditures after retirement   + or − _____

D. Equals: Annual living expenditures at retirement in today's dollars on an after-tax basis   = _____

E. Before-tax adjustment factor, based on an average tax rate of _____ % : (If the average tax rate is not known, it can be estimated using Table 17.2, The Average Tax Rate.) This is used to calculate the before-tax income necessary to cover the annual living expenses in line D. Thus, line F, the before-tax income = line D/line E where line E = (1 − Average Tax Rate)   = _____

F. Equals: The before-tax income necessary to cover the annual living expenses in line D   Line D divided by Line E = _____

STEP 2: Estimate Your Income Available at Retirement.

G. Income from Social Security in today's dollars   _____

H. Plus: Projected pension benefits in today's dollars   + _____

I. Plus: Other income in today's dollars   + _____

J. Equals (lines G + H + I): Anticipated retirement income, in today's dollars   = _____

STEP 3: Calculate the (Annual) Inflation-Adjusted Shortfall.

K. Anticipated shortfall in today's dollars (line F minus line J)   = _____

L. Inflation adjustment factor, based on an anticipated inflation rate of _____ % between now and retirement with _____ years to retirement (FVIFs are found in Appendix B):

$FVIF_{\text{inflation rate \%, no. years to retirement}}$ $\times$ _____

M. Equals: Inflation-adjusted shortfall (line K × line L)   = _____

STEP 4: Calculate the Total Funds Needed at Retirement to Cover This Shortfall Over the Number of Years You Expect to Be Retired (assuming an inflation-adjusted return of _____ % [return (_____ %) minus the inflation rate (_____ %)] during your retirement period, with retirement anticipated to last for _____ years).

N. Calculate the funds needed at retirement to cover the inflation-adjusted shortfall over the entire retirement period, assuming that these funds can be invested at _____ % and that the inflation rate over this period is _____ %. Thus, determining the present value of a _____-year annuity assuming a _____ % inflation-adjusted return: $PVIFA_{\text{inflation-adjusted return, no. years in retirement}}$ (PVIFA's are found in Appendix E).   _____

O. Equals: Funds needed at retirement to finance the shortfall (line M × line N) $\times$ line M = _____

STEP 5: Determine How Much You Must Save Annually Between Now and Retirement (_____ years until retirement and earning _____ %) to Cover the Shortfall.

P. Future value interest factor for an annuity for _____ years, given a _____ % expected annual return:

$FVIFA_{\text{expected rate of return, no. years to retirement}}$ (FVIFA's are found in Appendix D).   = _____

Q. Equals: PMT, or the amount that must be saved annually for _____ years and invested at _____ % in order to accumulate the line O amount at the end of _____ years   line O divided by line P = _____

Questions You Should Be Able to Answer about Your Company's Pension Plan

☐ Is this a noncontributory or a contributory plan?

_____

_____

☐ What are the pension requirements in terms of age and years of service?

_____

_____

☐ Is there an early retirement age, and if so, what are the benefits?

_____

_____

☐ What is the full-benefits retirement age?

_____

_____

☐ How does the vesting process work?

_____

_____

☐ If I retire at age 65, how much will I receive in the way of pension payments?

_____

_____

☐ If I die, what benefits will my spouse and family receive?

_____

_____

☐ What is the present size of my pension credit today?

_____

_____

☐ If I am disabled, will I receive pension benefits?

_____

_____

☐ Can I withdraw money from my retirement fund before retirement?

_____

_____

(continued)

Questions You Should Be Able to Answer about Your Company's Pension Plan

☐ Can I borrow on my retirement fund, and if so, what are the terms?

_____

_____

☐ If my company is taken over, or goes bankrupt, what happens to the pension fund?

_____

_____

☐ Is the plan funded? If not, what portion of the benefits could the company pay today?

_____

_____

☐ Is my pension plan a defined-contribution plan or a defined-benefit plan?

_____

_____

☐ What are the choices available to me regarding ways that the pension might be paid out?

_____

_____

Worksheet for the Calculation of Estate Taxes for the 1997 Tax Year

	Amount	Total Amount
STEP 1: Calculate the value of the *gross estate*.		
A. Value of gross estate		_____
STEP 2: Calculate your *taxable estate*.		
Less:		
Funeral expenses	_____	
Estate administration expenses	_____	
Debt	_____	
Taxes	_____	
Marital deduction	_____	
Charitable deduction	_____	
Total		− _____
Equals:		
B. Taxable estate		= _____
STEP 3: Calculate your *gift-adjusted taxable estate*.		
Plus:		
Cumulative taxable lifetime gifts		+ _____
Equals:		
C. Gift-adjusted taxable estate		= _____
STEP 4: Calculate your estate taxes.		
Calculation of taxes on the value in line C (from Table 18.1):		_____

Estate Planning Worksheet

Do you and the members of your family know the location of ...

☐ Your will, durable power of attorney, and living will (with the name of the attorney who drafted them)?

_____

_____

☐ The name of your attorney?

_____

_____

☐ Your letter of last instructions, including burial requests and organ donor information?

_____

_____

☐ Your Social Security number?

_____

_____

☐ Your safety deposit box and the key to it?

_____

_____

☐ A record of what is in your safety deposit box?

_____

_____

☐ Your birth certificate?

_____

_____

☐ Your marriage certificate?

_____

_____

☐ Any military discharge papers?

_____

_____

☐ Insurance policies (life, health, and property/liability), along with the name of your insurance agent?

_____

_____

(continued)

☐ Deeds and titles to property (both real estate and real, for example, automobiles)?

_____

_____

☐ Your stocks, bonds, and other securities, and who your broker is?

_____

_____

☐ Any business agreements, including any debts owed you?

_____

_____

☐ All checking, savings, and brokerage account numbers, along with the location of those accounts?

_____

_____

☐ The name of your accountant?

_____

_____

☐ Your last year's income tax return?

_____

_____

☐ The name of past employers, along with any pension or retirement benefits information?

_____

_____

You should also

1. Calculate the size of your estate.

2. Estimate how much of your estate would be lost to taxes if you died.

3. Know who the executor of your will is and who your beneficiaries are.

4. Select a guardian for your children if they are under 18.

Safety Deposit Box Information

	Box 1	Box 2
Name of Bank Where Located		
Address of Bank		
Box Number		
Location of Keys		
Inventory of Contents and Description		

INDEX

Note: Boldface page numbers indicate first use of key terms.

Mid-cap stocks, **454**

Million dollars, calculating value of, 91

Minuit, Peter, 73, 75

Modified whole life insurance, 297

Money, 434

Money, time value of, 20, 23, 67

Money market deposit account (MMDA), **149**

Money market mutual funds (MMMFs), 146, **151**, **516**
and safety, 157

Money order, **161**

Money purchase plan, **556**

Months living expenses covered ratio, 49

Moody's, 434, 484
Handbook of Common Stock, 434–35
Manuals, 435

Moore, Demi, 348

Morningstar Mutual Funds, 525, 529, 531

Mortgage bankers, 263, **263**

Mortgage bond, **478**

Mortgage brokers, **263**

Mortgage group life insurance, **295**–96

Mortgage insurance, private, **260**

Mortgages, 263–64
15-year term versus 30-year term, 269–71, 272
adjustable-rate, 265–66, 268
adjustable-rate versus fixed-rate, 269
balloon payment, 268
fixed-rate, 264
graduated payment, 268
growing equity, 268–69
obtaining, 275
refinancing, 271, 272
shared appreciation, 269
sources of, 263

Multiple indemnity, 306

Multiple policy discounts, 359

Municipal bond funds, 522

Municipal bonds, **481**
equivalent taxable yield on, 484

Mutual fund prospectus, **527**–28

Mutual funds, 103, 146, 507, 535
advantages of investing in, 508–10

basics of, 511–12
buying, 525–33
calculating returns, 531–32
costs of, 514–15
disadvantages of investing in, 510–11
evaluating, 528–29
reasons for investing in, 508–11
services offered by, 522, 524–25
sources of information, 529–31
supermarket for, 533
types and objectives of, 516, 518–22

Mutual Savings & Loans, **145**

N

Named perils, **350**, 352

National Association of Securities Dealers Automated Quotations system, 419

National Association of Securities Dealers (NASD), 420

National Credit Union Association, **157**

National Market System (NMS), 419

National Quote Bureau, 419

Needs approach in determining life insurance needs, **288**, 291–92

Negative amortization, **266**

Nelson, Willie, 96–97

Net asset value, **513**

Net worth, **34**, 38, 41

Newspaper, reading stock quotes in, 452

New York Stock Exchange (NYSE), 416, 418

No-fault insurance, **366**–67

No-load fund, **515**

Nolte, Nick, 348

Nominal interest rate, determinants of, 391

Nominal rate of return, **389**

Noncancelable provision, **335**, 340

Noncontributory retirement plans, **547**

Nondiversifiable risk, **397**

Nonforfeiture clause, 303

Nonforfeiture right, **297**

Nonincome-based taxes, 133

Note, **205**

NOW (negotiable order of withdrawal) account, **147**–48

O

Odd lots, **423**

Open credit, **174**
strategies for controlling and managing, 191–96

Open-end investment companies, **512**–13

Open-end lease, **242**

Open orders, **424**

Open perils, **350**

Options, 469

Order sizes, 423

Organized exchange, **416**, 418
role of specialist in, 423

Overdraft protection, **160**

Over-the-counter (OTC) market, **416**, 419

Over-the-limit fee, **178**

Ownership investments, 386–87

P

Pacific Stock Exchange, 416

Par value, **384**, 476

Passive income, **107**

Pass-through certificates, 479–**80**

Paying dividends, 448

Payment cap, 266

Payment premium clause, 303

Payment whole life policy, 297

Percentage participation provision, **323**

Perils, **350**
named, 350, 352
open, 350

Perpetuities, 89–90

Personal articles floaters, **356**

Personal Automobile Policy (PAP), **363**–66

Personal balance sheet, **34**

Personal bankruptcy, **225**

Personal exemptions, **99**

Personal finance
agency problem in, 25
axioms forming foundations of, 19–26
tax bias in decisions, 23

Personal Finance, 529

TEXAS INSTRUMENTS

BAII PLUS Rebate Terms and Conditions

This offer is valid only for BAII PLUS purchases between July 1, 1997 and March 31, 1999. All claims must be postmarked by April 30, 1999. Allow 8 to 10 weeks for processing. All purchases must be made in the U.S. or Canada. Rebates will be sent only to addresses in the U.S. and Canada and paid in U.S. dollars. Not redeemable at any store. Send this completed form along with the cash register receipt (original or copy) and the UPC bar code to the address indicated. This original mail-in certificate must accompany your request and may not be duplicated or reproduced. Offer valid only as stated on this form. Offer void where prohibited, taxed, licensed, or restricted. Limit one rebate per household or address. Texas Instruments reserves the right to discontinue this program at any time and without notice.

Yes! I Want $5 Back On My Purchase of the BAII PLUS.